Microsoft

PROGRAMMING MICROSOFT® ASP.NET

Microsoft® .net

Dino Esposito

Wintellect® Know how.

PUBLISHED BY
Microsoft Press
A Division of Microsoft Corporation
One Microsoft Way
Redmond, Washington 98052-6399

Library of Congress Cataloging-in-Publication Data
Esposito, Dino, 1965-
Programming Microsoft ASP.NET / Dino Esposito.
p. cm.
ISBN 0-7356-1903-4
1. Active server pages. 2. Web sites--Design. 3. Web site development. I. Internet programming. I. Title.

TK5105.8885.A26E88 2003
005.2'76--dc21 2003046492

Printed and bound in the United States of America.

1 2 3 4 5 6 7 8 9 QWT 8 7 6 5 4 3

Distributed in Canada by H.B. Fenn and Company Ltd.

A CIP catalogue record for this book is available from the British Library.

Microsoft Press books are available through booksellers and distributors worldwide. For further information about international editions, contact your local Microsoft Corporation office or contact Microsoft Press International directly at fax (425) 936-7329. Visit our Web site at www.microsoft.com/mspress. Send comments to *mspinput@microsoft.com.*

Acquisitions Editor: Anne Hamilton
Project Editor: Devon Musgrave
Technical Editor: Robert Lyon
Copyeditor: Roger LeBlanc
Principal Desktop Publisher: Kerri DeVault
Interior Artist: Andrea Houston
Interior Graphic Designer: James D. Kramer
Cover Designer: Methodologie, Inc.

Body Part No. X09-39053

To Silvia, Francesco, and Michela
To my mom and dad

"I know nothing except the fact of my ignorance."
—Socrates

Contents at a Glance

Table of Contents

Acknowledgments

My name is the only one to appear on the cover, but my two kids, Francesco and Michela, contributed a lot. Instead of watching movies or playing with cars and dolls, many nights they sat close to me (often too close, actually) with the precise intention of helping out. Francesco, five years old, asked for an Internet connection and a shortcut to the FBI's Web site on the desktop of my secondary laptop. The official explanation is that he has a particular interest in the fate of the FBI's ten most-wanted fugitives. A former hot fan of New York firefighters, Francesco is now considering joining the New York Police Department. (Thanks to Josh Trupin who quite timely got him a football with the NYPD logo just the day before Christmas.) Francesco has chosen to work with Word 2000 because he doesn't feel particularly comfortable with Office XP.

Michela, two years old, at first contented herself with a toy laptop that plays music as one clicks buttons—yep, much like real ones! Soon after, though, as expected, she applied for an upgrade, and my working laptop was the dangerously nearest one. Michela is a great fan of Winnie the Pooh and can be still well over 15 minutes watching a movie. She's learning about honey and bees and gets a little bit confused when she hears me speaking about API. In Italian, "bees" and the acronym "API" (application programming interface) are pronounced the same way. It's hard to explain context to a two-year-old child!

So, many nights, after dinner, we started working together, everyone on a separate machine. Sounds like the perfect family, in which all members unite efforts to reach a goal and each one gives his best contribution? Well, it normally lasts five, maybe ten, minutes. Then Francesco wants to try the newest—dad's—laptop, and Michela is fascinated by the colorful screen. After the third cry in the night, Silvia, mom and wife, gets involved and fixes things. The really great news is that a day has 24 hours. (But I wouldn't mind an upgrade to at least 32, like the bits of the operating system!)

Anne Hamilton, acquisitions editor, firmly believed in this project and quickly arranged it. I still remember her first suggested deadline, dreadfully close to the start date! Thanks, Anne, for your confidence in me.

Erik Olson from the ASP.NET team played an important role. I don't even recall how I got in contact with him, but I do remember that I said, "I'm looking for someone to pester with questions at all hours." And his quiet reply was "OK, what's your first one?" Thanks, Erik, you did a great job, in all ways.

Other people also did an excellent job with this book—Devon Musgrave, project editor, coordinated, and Roger LeBlanc, copyeditor, edited text, smoothing humps, and shedding light on twisted and intricate periods (:-)). Robert Lyon, technical editor, worked patiently and effectively on all chapters and the code of the book and provided invaluable help by catching errors and omissions. Laura Barsan, Susan Chory, Joseph Croney, Luca Passani, Chris Riccio, Andres Sanabria, David Sceppa, and Kenn Scribner all shared their hands-on experience and added many insights on various topics. Definitely, they added incalculable value to the book.

Next are the 24x7 people, available at all times, who in a way or the other, directly or indirectly, contributed tips, tricks, suggestions, advice, gotchas, or simply their own work that I used as a resource. They are, in no particular order, Jeff Prosise, Jason Clark, John Lam, Francesco Balena, Jeffrey Richter, Peter Debetta, Berni McCoy, John Robbins, Don Kiely, and Paul Wilson.

A special thanks goes to Jay Freeman, the author of Anakrino, a .NET decompiler that proved to be the perfect tool for me to discover the hidden wonders of ASP.NET and explore its largely untangled underwood.

My final thought is for Silvia, my wife. Without you, the world looks like sand. Maybe warm, maybe rich, maybe concrete, maybe beautiful and palpable, but with no substance to build anything on. You're my essence and my strength.

Thanks you to all.

—Dino

Introduction

Some years ago, on a rainy Italian morning in November, I was sitting in front of a top manager of a top consulting firm for a job interview. To the developer/consultant/solution builder I was then, the Internet meant very little. I was still making a living with my Win32 and C++ skills. Yes, I had heard about something named HTTP that was widely used to browse Web pages, but I'd never considered writing such applications. At that time, I would have seriously hesitated before associating the words "Web" and "application"! To me, an application was too far serious a thing to reduce to a handful of script and markup code.

To somehow justify my salary request, I came up with a throwaway remark about the growing importance of the Internet to the industry. Much more serious than I was, the manager cast a glance at me and, nodding, pronounced the words that, well, changed my career and even my whole professional life. He said, "The Internet is a real breakthrough; it allows you to achieve outcomes impossible with traditional means." You can easily imagine the rest of the story. I was hired and soon began working on my first Web project. A few weeks later, my project manager came to see me looking rather worried. He asked, "How much C++ do you do?" "C++?" I replied, "I was born—instantiated, actually—in C++." What sort of a question was that? With the Internet, a new world of business opportunities opened up in the industry. Web specialists soon became a valuable resource, but only in a few cases could they solve tough system or network issues. In a certain way, while the Internet was getting more and more popular, its back-end programming model was still a distinct, stand-alone API bolted onto the operating system and following a different API and scheme.

Microsoft first attempted to solve this system issue with COM, and ASP was the perfect tool to use COM over the Web. But it's only with the Microsoft .NET Framework and Microsoft ASP.NET that the circle—which for me opened that rainy November morning—is finally closed. With ASP.NET, you have a rich Web development platform perfectly integrated with the operating system's programming framework. Like icing on the cake, this programming framework—the .NET Framework—is also language-neutral. I quit that consulting firm a few years ago, but I'm sure that with ASP.NET, my work there would have been easier and my productivity much higher.

So, you want to write Web applications by using Microsoft technologies. Welcome, you've come to just the right place! The ultimate goal of this book is to take you to a more advanced level of knowledge of ASP.NET so that you can shave precious hours off your development time. No matter what your starting point is, this book should make you a smarter programmer or simply—and who isn't interested in this?—a more productive developer. Plato used to say that nobody who continually makes progress, no matter how slowly, should be discouraged.

This book contains several layers—much like an onion—and several perspectives, too. You don't need to know ASP to use this book, but if you're a former ASP programmer you'll more fully catch the gist of the new Web platform. Also, you don't need knowledge of ASP.NET 1.0, but if you're an experienced developer you can enjoy the changes in the newest version more deeply, ASP.NET 1.1, and in Microsoft Internet Information Services 6.0 (IIS). Finally, if you're a skilled programmer, this book has several sections where the internals of ASP.NET components are thoroughly discussed, making the book an ideal complement to the public MSDN documentation.

What Does This Book Cover?

This book is divided into six parts that outline a relatively common learning path. In Part I, "Building an ASP.NET Page," you'll build a page and understand the basics of the ASP.NET model and its controls. In Part II, "Adding Data in an ASP.NET Site," you'll add some data support and meet the ADO.NET object model. After that, in Part III, "ASP.NET Controls," we'll return to server controls—a central element in ASP.NET's architecture—to cover the richest controls, including mobile controls. At this point, you'll have learned enough to work on real-world projects and be reasonably productive. If you want to do more, you'll need to go a level or two deeper and understand other essential aspects of ASP.NET applications, which are covered in Part IV, "ASP.NET Application Essentials." These essentials include configuration, security, and state management, as well as file I/O and Web services—a system component and an application model that are often used within ASP.NET projects. Once you appreciate server controls, can you do without custom controls? Part V, "Custom ASP.NET Controls," is an entire section devoted to custom controls. And Part VI, "Advanced Topics," covers image processing, HTTP handlers and modules, and hosting ASP.NET outside IIS.

In this book, I'll answer, among others, the following common questions:

- How does ASP.NET compile a page?
- Where are dynamic assemblies created and stored?
- What is the HTTP pipeline?
- What is the exact sequence of events in the page life cycle?

- What's the difference between HTML and Web controls?
- Why is a single form always used?
- How can I more effectively work with a *DataSet* object?
- What's the best way to page through a data set?
- Can I achieve *that* effect with the *DataGrid* control? (Yes, you typically can.)
- Are the *DataList* and the *Repeater* controls more flexible than the *DataGrid* control?
- How can I leverage my ASP.NET skills to write applications for mobile devices?
- Web user controls? What are those?
- What's the difference between the various Session modes?
- How can I take advantage of the Cache object?
- Is the ViewState encrypted or encoded? Is it really safe to use?
- What's the most flexible way to authenticate users?
- What's the ASPNET user?
- Can I share session state between Web services and ASP.NET applications?
- How can I configure my custom controls to look great at design time?
- Can I generate images dynamically?
- How can I use HTTP handlers and HTTP modules?
- Is there a way to run ASP.NET without IIS?

Some of the most interesting examples you can find in this book are:

- A *LinkLabel* Web control that uses regular expressions to transforms Web site names and e-mail addresses into hyperlinks
- A *DataGrid* control whose pager bar is rendered as a tab strip
- A *Form* control that allows to set the action URL explicitly
- Data-bound tooltip and subtotals in the *DataGrid* control
- An HTML-based control to generate bar charts
- A demonstration of response output filters
- Multirow *DataGrid* controls

System Requirements

This book is designed to be used with the following software:

- Microsoft Windows with IIS installed (one of the following)
  - Windows 2000
  - Windows XP Professional
  - Windows Server 2003
- Microsoft Visual Studio .NET 2003 (one of the following)
  - Visual C# .NET Standard 2003
  - Visual Basic .NET Standard 2003
  - Visual Studio .NET Professional 2003
  - Visual Studio .NET Enterprise Developer 2003
  - Visual Studio .NET Enterprise Architect 2003
- Microsoft SQL Server (one of the following)
  - SQL Server 2000
  - SQL Server 2000 Desktop Engine (available for download)

This book is written for the .NET Framework 1.1 and Visual Studio .NET 2003. Most of the code will work with version 1.0 of the .NET Framework, but all the code samples were tested using the .NET Framework 1.1 and Visual Studio .NET 2003. Some code samples require that you have Microsoft SQL Server 2000 or Microsoft SQL Server 2000 Desktop Engine (MSDE 2000) installed. The code samples that use SQL Server assume a blank *sa* password, although the use of a blank password is strongly discouraged in any serious development environment. If you don't use a blank *sa* password in your SQL Server installation, you'll need to add your own password to the connection strings. For example, if your password is "Hello", you should change the connection strings to the following:

```
string nwind = "SERVER=localhost;UID=sa;PWD=Hello;DATABASE=northwind;";
```

Code Samples

The book doesn't have a companion CD, but all the code samples discussed in the book are available on the Web at the following address. Click the Companion Content link in the More Information box on the right side of the page.

- *http://www.microsoft.com/mspress/books/6667.asp*

The language used in the book is C#, but all the code samples are written in both C# and Visual Basic .NET.

How to Touch Base

Please feel free to send any question about the book directly to the author. Dino Esposito can be reached via e-mail at one of the following addresses:

- dinoe@wintellect.com
- desposito@vb2themax.com

For additional information and resources, check out the following Web sites: Wintellect at *http://www.wintellect.com* and VB2-The-Max at *http://www.vb2themax.com*.

Microsoft Press Support

Every effort has been made to ensure the accuracy of the book and the companion content. Microsoft Press provides corrections for books through the World Wide Web at:

http://www.microsoft.com/mspress/support/

If you have comments, questions, or ideas regarding the book or the companion content, or questions that are not answered by querying the Knowledge Base, send them to Microsoft Press via e-mail to

mspinput@microsoft.com

or via postal mail to

Microsoft Press
Attn: Programming Microsoft ASP.NET Editor
One Microsoft Way
Redmond, WA 98052-6399

Please note that product support is not offered through the above addresses.

Part I

Building an ASP.NET Page

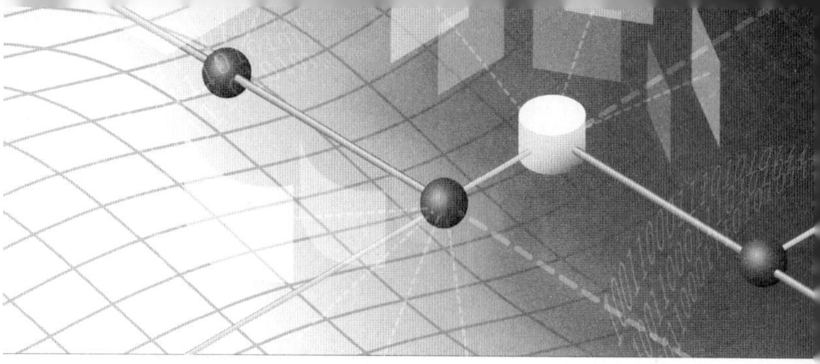

1

The Web Forms Model

A journey of a thousand miles begins with a single step.

—Lao Tzu

ASP.NET is a Web development platform that provides the programming model and software infrastructure necessary to build enterprise-class applications. Although largely syntax compatible with its popular predecessor—Active Server Pages (ASP)—ASP.NET is a revolutionary new programming framework designed to enable the rapid development of Web applications and Web services. As part of the Microsoft .NET platform, ASP.NET provides a component-based, extensible, and easy-to-use way to build, deploy, and run Web applications that target any browser or mobile device.

ASP.NET is supported on a variety of platforms, including Microsoft Windows 2000 with at least Service Pack 2, Windows XP Professional, and Windows Server 2003. To develop ASP.NET server applications, Internet Information Services (IIS) version 5.0 or later is also required. Other software you need—for example, Microsoft Data Access Components (MDAC) 2.7—is automatically installed when you set up the .NET Framework.

ASP.NET fits perfectly in the trend that has shifted the focus of development from client/server applications to Web-based architectures and Internet-deployed applications. It is the next step in the evolution and a giant step indeed. ASP.NET is the summation of Web development technologies that rapidly followed one after another in the past five years—one building over another, and each filling the gaps of its predecessor. As a result, ASP.NET is currently the most technologically advanced, feature-rich, and powerful platform for building distributed applications transported by the HTTP protocol. The

Web Forms model is simply a blanket term that figuratively describes the abstraction model ASP.NET constructs atop the evergreen, old, and faithful HTTP protocol.

What's ASP.NET, Anyway?

Prior to the advent of ASP.NET, three main technologies and platforms were available to develop Web applications: ASP, Java Server Pages (JSP), and the open source Web platform commonly referred to as LAMP (Linux plus Apache plus MySQL plus either Perl, Python, or PHP as the programming language).

> **Note** For completeness, we should also mention a couple of platform-specific, lower-level technologies that ASP and JSP rely on. ASP is actually an Internet Server Application Programming Interface (ISAPI) extension, whereas JSP is implemented as a special *servlet* application. ISAPI extensions on IIS-based platforms and servlets on Java-based systems let you create server-side, Web-deployed applications using a more classic approach. You write a module that builds and renders the page rather than declaratively design the page using a mix of markup text and embedded code.

Although each has language-specific and architecture-specific features, all these Web development platforms are designed to create interactive pages as part of a Web-based application. To some extent, all enable developers to separate programming logic from the page layout through the use of components that the page itself is responsible to call and render. Aside from this common ultimate goal, significant differences exist among those platforms, most of which relate to the programming model and languages they promote and support. For example, JSP exploits the Java framework of classes and, with JavaBeans, provides an effective extensibility model for reusing components. In addition, JSP supports tag customization and lets developers associate code with a custom tag definition. Finally, because it's a key element of the Java 2 Enterprise Edition (J2EE) platform, JSP relies on the Java language, a first-class language as opposed to the scripting languages used by both ASP and LAMP platforms. So how does ASP.NET fit in exactly?

Like ASP and other Web development environments, ASP.NET also works on top of the HTTP protocol and takes advantage of HTTP commands and policies to set up two-way, browser-to-server communication and cooperation.

What really differentiates ASP.NET from the plethora of other Web development technologies—and what makes it especially *revolutionary*—is the abstract programming model it propounds, the Web Forms model. In addition, the whole ASP.NET platform comes as a native part of the Microsoft .NET Framework. To be sure you grasp the importance of this last point, let me explain. ASP.NET applications are now compiled pieces of code, are made of reusable and extensible components, can be authored with first-class languages (including C#, Microsoft Visual Basic .NET, JScript .NET, and J#), and can access the entire hierarchy of classes in the .NET Framework.

In short, ASP.NET combines the best of all worlds. It is syntax compatible (and to a large extent, also language compatible) with ASP. It provides the same object-oriented features as JSP applications (tag customization, first-class compiled languages, components, extensibility, and reusability). And as icing on the cake, ASP.NET delivers a wealth of goodies, tools, and powerful system features that can be effectively grouped within the blanket expression *tools for abstracting the HTTP programming model.* Lots of programmer-friendly classes let you develop pages using typical desktop methods. The Web Forms model promotes an overall event-driven approach, but it's deployed over the Web and has the potential to target any vendor's platform through the support of XML.

> **Note** From a technical point of view, ASP.NET adopts the best of the ASP and JSP programming models. Conversely, it doesn't inherit much from the LAMP platform in terms of technical aspects. The appeal of LAMP is that it excels as a robust and extensible (because it is open-source) platform with flourishing and proactive grassroots community sites and Web boards.

Whichever way you look at ASP.NET, it's a quantum leap beyond any other Web programming style you might have experienced in the past. In this chapter, we'll present an overview of the ASP.NET platform, introducing topics such as the Web Forms model, structure of Web pages, and tasks involved when building ASP.NET applications. In Chapter 2, "Web Forms Internals," we'll drill down into the architectural elements of the Web Forms model, and then bear off into the sea of ASP.NET features and widgets. So get ready, and let the show begin.

Programming in the Age of Web Forms

A key point I need to explain so that you understand the rationale behind the ASP.NET Web Forms model is that there is a need to provide a better strategy to deal with the strong and growing demand for cheap Web interaction. As a matter of fact, the HTTP protocol, especially its stateless nature, creates a sort of bottleneck for the development of Web applications. On the other hand, the inherent simplicity of HTTP is the key to its worldwide adoption and effectiveness—in short, we probably couldn't have the Internet as we know it without a protocol like HTTP. Yet, as demand increases, programmers have to devise better ways of setting up easy and effective communication from the client to the server and vice versa.

Various techniques have been experimented with over time to smooth the communication across different pages and across multiple invocations of the same page. Programmers are used to thinking in terms of a client-generated action that results in a server-side reaction. Such a basic and fundamental pattern simply cannot be accomplished, at least not literally, over the Web. A certain degree of abstraction and some system-provided services are needed to make smooth communication happen. Although they aren't perfect, JSP and ASP let programmers target any browser while coding against a relatively familiar and understandable model. ASP, much more than JSP, thinks declaratively and has quite a slim and scanty object model. Overall, programmers who become Web programmers are forced to adopt a different mindset and toss the familiar action/reaction paradigm out the door.

Event-Driven Programming over HTTP

With Web Forms, the event-driven model of interaction finally comes to the Web. Implementing an event model over the Web requires any data related to the client-side user's activity to be forwarded to the server for corresponding and *stateful* processing. For the model to work, the server needs to process the output of client actions and trigger reactions while being aware of the overall state of the application. The state of the application contains two types of information: the state of the client and the state of the session. The state of the client is easily accessible through the syntax and the implementation of the *<form>* HTML element. But what about the overall state of the session?

As mentioned, HTTP is a stateless protocol, which means two successive requests across the same session are resolved by newly instantiated environments in which no session-specific information is maintained, except all the information the application itself might have stored in global objects. In ASP, reentrant forms are a common way to work around such a system limitation. A reentrant form is an HTML <*form*> element that posts to the same page that contains it. Reentrant forms alone do not fully solve the issue. However, by combining them with code blocks and hidden fields storing state information that is critical for the page, many developers elegantly overcame the obstacle.

What was once an ASP best-practice has been standardized and integrated in the ASP.NET runtime to become the key feature that endows ASP.NET applications with automatic state maintenance. The ASP.NET runtime carries the page state back and forth across page requests. When generating HTML code for a given page, ASP.NET encodes and stuffs the state of server-side objects into a few hidden, and transparently created, fields. When the page is requested, the same ASP.NET runtime engine checks for embedded state information—the hidden fields—and utilizes any decoded information to set up newly created instances of server-side objects. The net effect of such a mechanism is not unlike the Windows Forms model on the desktop and is summarized in Figure 1-1.

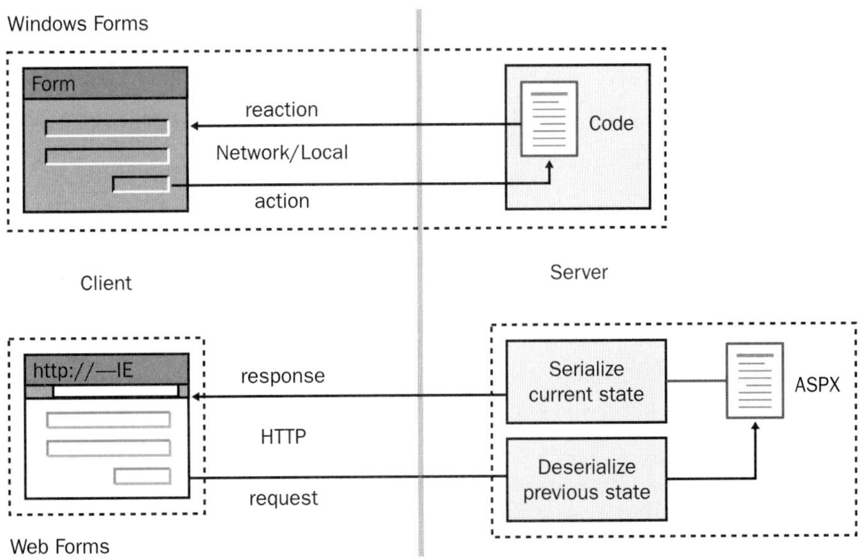

Figure 1-1 Comparing the Windows Forms and Web Forms models in the .NET Framework.

The Windows Forms model stems from the typical event-driven desktop programming style. No matter what connectivity exists between the client and server components, the server always works in reaction to the client's input. The server is aware of the overall application state and operates in a two-tier, connected manner. The Web Forms model needs some machinery to support the same event-driven programming model. In Figure 1-1, the needed machinery is represented by the state deserialization that occurs when the page is requested and the state serialization performed when the HTML response is being generated.

In charge of this filtering work is the ASP.NET HTTP runtime—a piece of code that extends and specializes the overall capabilities of the hosting Web server. Reentrant forms and hidden fields are the low-level tools used to perform the trick. Such a model wouldn't be as effective without a back-end, rich object model spanning the whole content of the server page. Crucial to the building and effective working of the ASP.NET development platform is the component model. The ASP.NET component model is shared with all other types of .NET applications—Windows Forms, console applications, and Web services.

The ASP.NET object model is a branch of the .NET Framework and is designed to provide a server-side counterpart to virtually any HTML page elements, such as HTML tags like *<form>* and *<input>* and page-wide tags like *<link>* and *<script>*. In addition, the ASP.NET object model includes numerous components (called server controls or Web controls) that represent more complex elements of the user interface (UI). Some of these controls have no direct mapping with individual HTML elements but are implemented by combining multiple HTML tags. Typical examples of complex UI elements are the *Calendar* control and the *DataGrid* control. An ASP.NET page is made of any number of server controls mixed with verbatim text, markup, and images. Sensitive data excerpted from the state of each constituent control is silently stored in hidden fields, and it forms the context of that page request. The association between an instance of the page and its state is unambiguous, not programmatically modifiable, and controlled by the ASP.NET HTTP runtime. We'll delve more deeply into this topic in Chapter 2, which also covers the Web Forms architecture in detail.

In the meantime, let's briefly review the basics of the HTTP protocol—which remains at the foundation of Web interaction. After that, we'll move on to describe the structure of an ASP.NET page and how to write and deploy ASP.NET applications.

The HTTP Protocol

This section provides a relatively quick overview of the way in which Web applications operate. If you already have a good knowledge of the Web underpinnings, feel free to jump ahead directly to the section "The Structure of ASP.NET Pages."

The acronym HTTP became so familiar to us developers that we sometimes don't remember exactly what it stands for. Actually, HTTP stands for Hypertext Transfer Protocol. HTTP is a text-based protocol and defines how Web browsers and Web servers communicate. The format of HTTP packets is fully described in RFC 2068 and is available for download from *http://www.w3.org/Protocols/rfc2068/rfc2068.txt*. HTTP packets travel over a TCP connection directed toward default port 80 at the target Internet Protocol (IP) address.

The HTTP Request

When you point the browser to a URL, it utilizes the available Domain Name System (DNS) to translate the server name you provided with the URL into an IP address. Next, the browser opens a socket and connects to port 80 at that address. The packet with the download request for *http://expo-one/page.aspx* can take the following simple form:

```
GET /page.aspx HTTP/1.1
Host: expo-one
```

An HTTP request can contain, and usually does contain, a number of headers. These include: *User-Agent*, to identify the type of browser that originated the request; *Connection*, to close a connection or keep a connection alive; and *If-Modified-Since*, to provide client-side cache validation. An HTTP header is a line of text that provides additional information about the request. The first line of text represents the *start line* of the request. It must contain the name of the HTTP command to execute (GET, in this case), the URL of the resource, plus the version of the HTTP protocol you want to target.

The HTTP Response

The server's response includes a *status line* made from the message's protocol version and an exit code (indicating success or error). The status line is followed by a bunch of headers—typically the page content type and length—and the body content. A blank line separates the body content from the rest of the message, as shown in the following response:

```
HTTP/1.1 200 OK
Server: Microsoft-IIS/5.0
Content-Type: text/html
Content-Length: 51

<html><body><h1>ASP.NET is cool!</h1></body></html>
```

The preceding code illustrates the simple HTML output returned by the Web server. Requests and responses are strings formatted according to the HTTP schema, and they travel over a TCP connection. The code *200* means that all went OK with the request. The specified Web server processes the request and returns some content expressed in the given Multipurpose Internet Mail Extensions (MIME) type (*text/html*) and of a certain length.

What happens next mostly depends on the MIME type and the browser's capabilities. As long as the MIME type is *text/html*, the browser displays the content as HTML. If the MIME type is, say, *text/xml* some browsers will render the content as plain text, while others (for example, Internet Explorer 6.0) will apply a built-in style sheet.

Building a Server-Side Abstraction Layer

Every conversation between browsers and Web servers consists of the exchange of packets similar to the ones we have just examined. If the requested URL is an HTML page, the Web server typically reads the contents of the .html file and flushes it into the body of the response packet. If the URL is an ASP.NET page, a special IIS module gets involved. The module is an IIS plug-in known as an ISAPI extension. An ISAPI extension is a dynamic-link library (DLL) registered on a per-file extension basis. An ISAPI extension registered to handle .aspx files will get involved whenever a request comes in for this type of resource.

The ISAPI extension analyzes the request and uses any contained information to configure the server-side environment that will actually process the source of the page.

> **Note** As we'll see in more detail in Chapter 2, the ISAPI extension that processes .aspx pages first deserializes the session state carried back and forth through hidden fields—the call context. The information is used to configure newly instantiated controls that create the page output. The persisted call context is then merged with any fresh information that comes from client-side controls such as text boxes and check boxes. When the state has been restored completely, the page is allowed to run and produce the HTML output.

Submitting Forms

The HTML *<form>* tag is the only element authorized to transmit client-side data to the server. When the user clicks a button of type *submit*, by design the browser stuffs the current content of all the controls that belong to the form into a string. The string is then passed to the server as part of the GET or POST command.

The following HTML snippet illustrates a simple form containing a text box and submit button. As you can see, the form is associated with the POST command and the page.aspx URL:

```
<form method="post" action="page.aspx">
    <input type="text" name="EmpCode" />
    <input type="submit" value="Send" />
</form>
```

The following request shows the POST command that hits the Web server when the user clicks the submit button:

```
POST /page.aspx HTTP/1.1
Host: expo-one
Content-Type: application/x-www-form-urlencoded
Content-Length: 12

EmpCode=1001
```

While processing the page request, the ISAPI extension parses the body of the request and exposes any information found through a more programmer-friendly object model. For example, instead of remaining a simple name/value string, the *EmpCode* variable is moved within an application-wide collection—the *Request.Form* collection. This represents a first level of abstraction built over the raw HTTP programming model. Objects such as *Request*, *Response*, and *Server* form the HTTP context for the call and, as such, represent the minimum set of objects you find in all Web development platforms, including JSP, ASP and, of course, ASP.NET. In ASP.NET, though, you find much more.

The Structure of ASP.NET Pages

An ASP.NET page is a server-side text file saved with the .aspx extension. The internal structure of the page is extremely modular and comprises three distinct sections—page directives, code, and page layout:

- **Page directives** Page directives set up the environment in which the page will run, specify how the HTTP runtime should process the page, and determine which assumptions about the page are safe to make. Directives also let you import namespaces to simplify coding, load assemblies not currently in the global assembly cache (GAC), and register new controls with custom tag names and namespace prefixes.
- **Code section** The code section, with the misleading tag name of *<script>*, includes any source code pertinent to the page. (The name *<script>* has been chosen for backward-compatibility reasons.) You

typically place event handlers and helper routines here. Code in this section is always compiled before execution.

- **Page layout** The page layout represents the skeleton of the page. It includes server controls, literal text, and HTML tags. The user interface of the server controls can be fleshed out a bit using either inline or declared code.

For the page to work, you don't need to specify all sections. Although real-world pages include all the sections mentioned, perfectly valid and functional pages can include only the code section or page layout. In some very special cases, you can even have an ASP.NET page made of a single directive.

A Sample ASP.NET Page

Let's consider our first ASP.NET page. To start off, a simple text editor will suffice; let's open Notepad and let the sleeping giant (Microsoft Visual Studio .NET) lie. The following code implements a simple ASP.NET page that lets you enter a string and then makes it uppercase:

```
<% @Page Language="C#" %>

<script runat="server">
private void MakeUpper(object sender, EventArgs e)
{
    string buf = TheString.Value;
    TheResult.InnerText = buf.ToUpper();
}
</script>

<html>
<title>Pro ASP.NET (Ch 01)</title>
<body>
<h1>String Converter</h1>
<form runat="server">
    <input runat="server" type="text" id="TheString" />
    <input runat="server" type="submit" value="Convert..."
        OnServerClick="MakeUpper" />
    <hr><span runat="server" id="TheResult" />
</form>
</body>
</html>
```

Blank lines in the preceding listing separate the three sections—directives, code, and page layout. Notice the unsparing use of the *runat* attribute—it's one of the most important pieces of the whole ASP.NET jigsaw puzzle. Later in this chapter, we'll discuss *runat* in more detail. For now, it suffices to say that the *runat* attribute promotes an otherwise lifeless server-side tag to the rank of a component instance. Let's quickly review the code.

Thanks to the *runat* attribute, the input text box becomes an instance of the *HtmlInputControl* class when the page is processed on the server. The *Value* property of the class returns the current content of the control. This value is converted to uppercase and then assigned to the *InnerText* property of the server-side control used to render an HTML *<span>* tag. When the user clicks the Submit button, the page automatically posts back to itself. This time, the magic is performed by the *runat* attribute set for the *<form>* tag. Once on the server, the current value of the text box is read and automatically assigned to a newly created instance of the *HtmlInputControl*. Next, the code associated with the *OnServerClick* event runs. The code works on controls whose state has been restored and updated with client information. When the *MakeUpper* event handler completes, the page is ready for rendering. At this point, updated HTML code is sent to the browser.

To test the page, copy the .aspx file to your Web server's root directory. Normally, this is c:\inetpub\wwwroot. If you want, create an ad hoc virtual directory. Next, point the browser to the page. Figure 1-2 shows what you get.

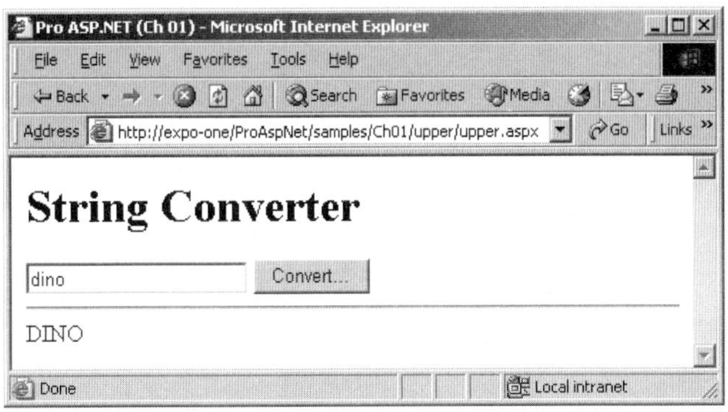

Figure 1-2 Our first ASP.NET page in action.

No matter how simple you keep a test ASP.NET page, a lot of complex features and techniques are always involved. This page is no exception. In the following chapters, you'll learn more about server-side controls and the difference between HTML and Web controls. You'll also see how to deploy real applications and not just individual pages. Now that we've dirtied our hands with some ASP.NET code, let's step back and review the layers that actually make an ASP.NET page.

The Processing Directives of a Page

Directives configure the run-time environment that will execute the page. In ASP, only one directive was supported—*@Language*—and you had to place it on the very first line of the page. The following code shows an ASP directive:

```
<% @Language="VBScript" CodePage="1232" %>
```

Several new directives have been added to ASP.NET and, at the same time, their usage has been made easier and dependent on less strict conditions. In ASP.NET, directives can be located anywhere in the page, although it's a good and common practice to place them at the beginning of the file. In addition, the name of a directive is case-insensitive and the values of directive attributes don't need to be quoted.

> **Tip** The ASP *@Language* directive is no longer officially supported in ASP.NET. The same goal is accomplished by the *Language* attribute within the *@Page* directive. However, for migration purposes, ASP.NET treats the old-style *@Language* directive block as an *@Page* directive with the *Language* attribute set. As a result, the ASP-style syntax shown below is still accepted:
>
> ```
> <% @Language="VBScript" CodePage="1232" %>
> ```
>
> It gets silently translated into the following code:
>
> ```
> <% @Page Language="VBScript" CodePage="1232" %>
> ```
>
> The ASP.NET *@Page* directive supports the same set of processing directives as ASP—*CodePage*, *EnableSessionState*, *LCID*, *Transaction*—plus a few more.

The most important and most frequently used directive in ASP.NET is *@Page*. The complete list of ASP.NET directives is shown in Table 1-1.

Table 1-1 Directives Supported by ASP.NET Pages

Directive	Description
@ Assembly	Links an assembly to the current page or user control
@ Control	Defines control-specific attributes that guide the behavior of the control compiler
@ Implements	Indicates that the page, or the user control, implements a specified .NET Framework interface
@ Import	Indicates a namespace to import into a page or user control
@ OutputCache	Controls the output caching policies of a page or user control
@ Page	Defines page-specific attributes that guide the behavior of the page compiler and the language parser that will preprocess the page

Table 1-1 Directives Supported by ASP.NET Pages

Directive	Description
@ Reference	Links a page or user control to the current page or user control
@ Register	Creates a custom tag in the page or the control. The new tag (prefix and name) is associated with the namespace and the code of a user-defined control

With the exception of *@Page* and *@Control*, all directives can be used both within a page and a control declaration. *@Page* and *@Control* are mutually exclusive. *@Page* can be used only in .aspx files, while the *@Control* directive can be used only in .ascx files.

> **Note** As we'll see in more detail in Chapter 10 and Chapter 18, ASP.NET features two types of user-defined controls. Custom controls are controls that derive from existing .NET Framework classes. User controls (also known as pagelets) are smaller and simpler ASP.NET pages that can be embedded in host pages and programmatically driven through methods and properties. Custom controls are created as assemblies and have a .dll extension. User controls are source files, similar to ASP.NET pages, but they have the .ascx extension.

We'll cover the *@Control*, *@OutputCache*, and *@Register* directives in detail in Chapter 10. In the meantime, let's learn more about the other, more page-specific, directives.

The syntax of a processing directive is unique and common to all supported types of directives. Multiple attributes must be separated with blanks, and no blank can be placed around the equals sign (=) that assigns a value to an attribute, as the following line of code demonstrates:

```
<%@ Directive_Name attribute="value" [attribute="value"...] %>
```

Each directive has its own closed set of typed attributes. Assigning a value of the wrong type to an attribute, or using a wrong attribute with a directive, results in a compilation error.

> **Important** The content of directive attributes is always rendered as plain text. However, attributes are expected to contain values that can be rendered to a particular type. When the ASP.NET page is parsed, all the directive attributes are extracted and stored in a dictionary. The names and number of attributes must match the expected schema for the directive. The string that express the value of an attribute is valid as long as it can be converted into the expected type. For example, if the attribute is designed to take a Boolean value, "*true*" or "*false*" are its only acceptable values.

The *@Page* Directive

The *@Page* directive can be used only in .aspx pages and generates a compile error if used with other types of ASP.NET pages such as controls and Web services. Each .aspx file is allowed to include at most one *@Page* directive. Although not strictly necessary from the syntax point of view, the directive is realistically required by all pages of some complexity.

@Page features about 30 attributes that can be logically grouped in three categories: compilation (Table 1-2), overall page behavior (Table 1-3), and page output (Table 1-4). Each ASP.NET page is compiled upon first request, and the HTML actually served to the browser is generated by the methods of the dynamically generated class. Attributes in Table 1-2 let you fine-tune parameters for the compiler and choose the language to use.

Table 1-2 *@Page* Attributes for Page Compilation

Attribute	Description
ClassName	Specifies the name of the class that will be dynamically compiled when the page is requested. Must be a class name without namespace information.
CompilerOptions	A sequence of compiler command-line switches used to compile the page.
Debug	A Boolean value that indicates whether the page should be compiled with debug symbols.
Explicit	A Boolean value that determines whether the page is compiled with the Visual Basic *Option Explicit* mode set to *On*. *Option Explicit* forces the programmer to explicitly declare all variables. The attribute is ignored if the page language is not Visual Basic .NET.

Table 1-2 *@Page* Attributes for Page Compilation

Attribute	Description
Inherits	Defines the base class for the page to inherit. It can be any class derived from the *Page* class. (I'll cover this in Chapter 2.)
Language	Indicates the language to use when compiling inline code blocks (<% … %>) and all the code that appears in the page <*script*> section. Supported languages include Visual Basic .NET, C#, JScript .NET, and J#. *(J# is not allowed with version 1.0 of the .NET Framework and Visual Studio .NET 2002.)* If not otherwise specified, the language defaults to Visual Basic .NET.
Src	Indicates the source file that contains the implementation of the base class specified with *Inherits*. The attribute is not used by Visual Studio .NET and other RAD designers. They, in fact, precompile the class and make the assembly available in the application's virtual directory.
Strict	A Boolean value that determines whether the page is compiled with the Visual Basic *Option Strict* mode set to *On*. When enabled, *Option Strict* permits only type-safe conversions and prohibits implicit conversions in which loss of data is possible. (In this case, the behavior is identical to that of C#.) The attribute is ignored if the page language is not Visual Basic .NET.
Trace	A Boolean value that indicates whether tracing is enabled. If tracing is enabled, extra information is appended to the page's output. The default is *false*.
TraceMode	Indicates how trace messages are to be displayed for the page when tracing is enabled. Acceptable values are *SortByTime* and *SortByCategory*. The default, when tracing is enabled, is *SortByTime*.
WarningLevel	Indicates the compiler warning level at which you want the compiler to abort compilation for the page. Possible values are 0 through 4.

Notice that the default values of the *Explicit* and *Strict* attributes are read from the application's configuration settings. As we'll see in greater detail in Chapter 12, the configuration settings of an ASP.NET application are obtained by merging all machine-wide settings with application-wide and even folder-wide settings. This means you can also control what the default values for the *Explicit* and *Strict* attributes are. Unless you change the default configuration settings—the .config files are created when the .NET Framework is installed—both *Explicit* and *Strict* default to *True*. Should the related settings be removed from the configuration files, both attributes would default to *False* instead.

ASP.NET Languages

As of version 1.0 of the .NET Framework, ASP.NET supports three programming languages—Visual Basic .NET, C#, and JScript .NET. To choose Visual Basic .NET, set the *Language* attribute to any of the following strings: *VB*, *VBS*, *VisualBasic*, or *VBScript*. Valid shortcuts to select C# are *C#*, *CS*, or *CSharp*. Finally, if your language of choice is JScript .NET, use *JS*, *JScript*, or *JavaScript*.

Support for a fourth language—J#—has been added in version 1.1 of the .NET Framework. To choose J#, set the *Language* attribute to *VJ#*. Generally, though, you can make ASP.NET support any language for which you hold a .NET-compatible compiler and a companion class implementing the compiler's object model. To extend ASP.NET with new languages, add a new row to the machine.config file (or the application's web.config file) that looks like the following:

```
<compiler language="Pascal;Delphi" extension=".pas;"
   type="MyCompany.PascalCodeProvider,MyAssembly" />
```

The new line would add support for the Pascal language, whose files are expected to have a .pas extension. Pascal and Delphi are both valid words to use with the *@Page Language* attribute. In the *type* attribute, *MyCompany.PascalCodeProvider* identifies the class that implements the compiler's object model. *MyAssembly* is the name of the assembly in which the class is contained.

Attributes listed in Table 1-3 allow you to control to some extent the overall behavior of the page and the supported range of features. For example, you can set a custom error page, disable session state, and control the transactional behavior of the page.

Table 1-3 *@Page* Attributes for Page Behavior

Attribute	Description
AspCompat	A Boolean attribute that, when set to *true*, allows the page to be executed on a single-threaded apartment (STA) thread. The setting allows the page to call COM+ 1.0 components and components developed with Microsoft Visual Basic 6.0 that require access to the unmanaged ASP built-in objects. (I'll cover this in Chapter 13.)

Table 1-3 *@Page* Attributes for Page Behavior

Attribute	Description
AutoEventWireup	A Boolean attribute that indicates whether or not page events are automatically enabled. Set to *true* by default. Pages developed with Visual Studio .NET have this attribute set to *false*, and page events are individually tied to handlers. (I'll cover this in Chapter 2.)
Buffer	A Boolean attribute that determines whether HTTP response buffering is enabled. Set to *true* by default.
Description	Provides a text description of the page. The ASP.NET page parser ignores the attribute, which subsequently has only a documentation purpose.
EnableSessionState	Defines how the page should treat session data. If set to *true*, the session state can read and be written. If set to *false*, session data is not available to the application. Finally, if set to *ReadOnly*, the session state can be read but not changed.
EnableViewState	A Boolean value that indicates whether the page *view state* is maintained across page requests. The view state is the page call context—a collection of values that retain the state of the page and are carried back and forth. View state is enabled by default. (I'll cover this in Chapter 14.)
EnableViewStateMac	A Boolean value that indicates ASP.NET should calculate a machine-specific authentication code and append it to the view state of the page (in addition to Base64 encoding). The Mac in the attribute name stands for *machine authentication check*. When the attribute is *true*, upon postbacks ASP.NET will check the authentication code of the view state to make sure that it hasn't been tampered with on the client.
ErrorPage	Defines the target URL to which users will be automatically redirected in case of unhandled page exceptions.
SmartNavigation	A Boolean value that indicates whether the page supports the Internet Explorer 5 or later smart navigation feature. Smart navigation allows a page to be refreshed without losing scroll position and element focus.
Transaction	Indicates whether the page supports or requires transactions. Acceptable values are: *Disabled*, *NotSupported*, *Supported*, *Required*, and *RequiresNew*. Transaction support is disabled by default.
ValidateRequest	A Boolean value that indicates whether request validation should occur. If *true*, ASP.NET checks all input data against a hard-coded list of potentially dangerous values. This functionality helps reduce the risk of cross-site scripting attacks for pages. *True* by default. (This feature is not supported in ASP.NET 1.0.)

Attributes listed in Table 1-4 allow you to control the format of the output being generated for the page. For example, you can set the content type of the page or localize the output to the extent possible.

Table 1-4 *@Page* Directives for Page Output

Attribute	Description
ClientTarget	Indicates the target browser for which ASP.NET server controls should render content.
CodePage	Indicates the code page value for the response. Set this attribute only if you created the page using a code page other than the default code page of the Web server on which the page will run. In this case, set the attribute to the code page of your development machine. A code page is a character set that includes numbers, punctuation marks, and other glyphs. Code pages differ on a per-language basis.
ContentType	Defines the content type of the response as a standard MIME type. Supports any valid HTTP content type string.
Culture	Indicates the culture setting for the page. Culture information includes the writing and sorting system, calendar, and date and currency formats. The attribute must be set to a non-neutral culture name, which means it must contain both language and country information. For example, *en-US* is a valid value unlike *en* alone, which is considered country neutral.
LCID	A 32-bit value that defines the locale identifier for the page. By default, ASP.NET uses the locale of the Web server.
ResponseEncoding	Indicates the character encoding of the page. The value is used to set the *CharSet* attribute on the content type HTTP header. Internally, ASP.NET handles all strings as Unicode.
UICulture	Specifies the default culture name used by the Resource Manager to look up culture-specific resources at run time.

As you can see, many attributes discussed in Table 1-4 concern the issue of page localization. Building multilanguage and international applications is a task that ASP.NET, and the .NET Framework in general, greatly simplify. In Chapter 5, we'll delve into the topic.

The *@Assembly* Directive

The *@Assembly* directive links an assembly to the current page so that its classes and interfaces are available for use on the page. When ASP.NET compiles the page, a few assemblies are linked by default. So you should resort to the directive only if you need linkage to a nondefault assembly. Table 1-5 lists the .NET assemblies that are automatically provided to the compiler.

Table 1-5 Assemblies Linked by Default

Assembly File Name	Description
Mscorlib.dll	Provides the core functionality of the .NET Framework, including types, *AppDomains*, and run-time services.
System.dll	Provides another bunch of system services, including regular expressions, compilation, native methods, file I/O, and networking.
System.Data.dll	Defines data-container and data-access classes, including the whole ADO.NET framework.
System.Drawing.dll	Implements the GDI+ features.
System.EnterpriseServices.dll	Provides the classes that allow for serviced components and COM+ interaction.
System.Web.dll	The assembly implements the core ASP.NET services, controls, and classes.
System.Web.Mobile.dll	The assembly implements the core ASP.NET mobile services, controls, and classes. *Not included if version 1.0 of the .NET Framework is installed.*
System.Web.Services.dll	Contains the core code that makes Web services run.
System.Xml.dll	Implements the .NET Framework XML features.

In addition to these assemblies, the ASP.NET runtime automatically links to the page all the assemblies that reside in the Web application *Bin* subdirectory. Note that you can modify, extend, or restrict the list of default assemblies by editing the machinewide configuration settings set in the machine.config file. In this case, changes apply to all ASP.NET applications run on that Web server. Alternately, you can modify the assembly list on a per-application basis by editing the application's specific web.config file. (I'll cover configuration settings in Chapter 12.) To prevent all assemblies found in the *Bin* directory from being linked to the page, remove the following line from the machine.config file:

```
<add assembly="*" />
```

To link a needed assembly to the page, use the following syntax:

```
<%@ Assembly Name="AssemblyName" %>
<%@ Assembly Src="assembly_code.cs" %>
```

The *@Assembly* directive supports two mutually exclusive attributes: *Name* and *Src*. *Name* indicates the name of the assembly to link to the page. The name cannot include the path or the extension. *Src* indicates the path to a source file to dynamically compile and link against the page. The *@Assembly* directive can appear multiple times in the body of the page. In fact, you need a new directive for each assembly to link. *Name* and *Src* cannot be used in the same *@Assembly* directive, but multiple directives defined in the same page can use either.

Note In terms of performance, the difference between *Name* and *Src* is minimal, although *Name* points to an existing and ready-to-load assembly. The source file referenced by *Src* is compiled only the first time it is requested. As we'll see in more detail in Chapter 2, the ASP.NET runtime maps a source file with a dynamically compiled assembly and keeps using the compiled code until the original file undergoes changes. This means that after the first application-level call, the impact on the page performance is identical whether you use *Name* or *Src*.

The *@Import* Directive

The *@Import* directive links the specified namespace to the page so that all the types defined can be accessed from the page without specifying the fully qualified name. For example, to create a new instance of the ADO.NET *DataSet* class, you either import the *System.Data* namespace or resort to the following code:

```
System.Data.DataSet ds = new System.Data.DataSet();
```

Once you've imported the *System.Data* namespace into the page, you can use more natural coding, as shown here:

```
DataSet ds = new DataSet();
```

The syntax of the *@Import* directive is rather self-explanatory:

```
<%@ Import namespace="value" %>
```

As with *@Assembly*, *@Import* can be used as many times as needed in the body of the page. The *@Import* directive is the ASP.NET counterpart of the C#

using statement and the Visual Basic .NET *Imports* statement. Looking back at unmanaged C/C++, we could say the directive plays a role nearly identical to the *#include* directive.

For example, to be able to connect to a Microsoft SQL Server database and grab some disconnected data, you need to import the following two namespaces:

```
<%@ Import namespace="System.Data" %>
<%@ Import namespace=" System.Data.SqlClient" %>
```

> **Caution** *@Import* helps the compiler only to resolve class names; it doesn't automatically link required assemblies. Using the *@Import* directive allows you to use shorter class names, but as long as the assembly that contains the class code is not properly linked, you have a type error. In this case, using the fully qualified class name is of no help because the compiler lacks the type definition.
>
> You might have noticed that, more often than not, assembly and namespace names coincide. Bear in mind this happens only by chance and assemblies and namespaces are radically different entities, each requiring the proper directive.

You need the *System.Data* namespace to work with the *DataSet* and *DataTable* classes, and you need the *System.Data.SqlClient* namespace to prepare and issue the command. In this case, you don't need to link against additional assemblies because the System.Data.dll assembly is linked by default. The namespaces listed in Table 1-6 are automatically imported into all pages.

Table 1-6 Namespaces Imported by Default

Namespace	Description
System	Contains the definition of the basic types.
System.Collections	Contains base collections classes, arrays, and lists.
System.Collections.Specialized	Contains more advanced collection classes, including strings and name/values collection.
System.Configuration	Contains classes to read configuration settings.
System.IO	Contains classes to perform file I/O.
System.Text	Contains classes to manage string builders and character sets.
System.Text.RegularExpressions	Contains classes to process regular expressions.

Table 1-6 Namespaces Imported by Default *(continued)*

Namespace	Description
System.Web	Contains classes that implement the ASP.NET runtime underpinnings.
System.Web.Caching	Contains classes to implement caching.
System.Web.Security	Provides the definition of classes for ASP.NET security.
System.Web.SessionState	Provides the definition of classes for ASP.NET session state.
System.Web.UI	Contains classes for ASP.NET data-binding, page compilation, and user controls.
System.Web.UI.HtmlControls	Contains HTML control classes.
System.Web.UI.WebControls	Contains Web control classes.

The *@Implements* Directive

The directive indicates that the current page implements the specified .NET Framework interface. An interface is a set of signatures for a logically related group of functions. An interface is a sort of contract that shows the component's commitment to expose that group of functions. Unlike abstract classes, an interface doesn't provide code or executable functionality. When you implement an interface in an ASP.NET page, you declare any required methods and properties within the *<script>* section. The syntax of the *@Implements* directive is as follows:

```
<%@ Implements interface="InterfaceName" %>
```

The *@Implements* directive can appear multiple times in the page if the page has to implement multiple interfaces. Note that if you decide to put all the page logic in a separate class file (code-behind), you can't use the directive to implement interfaces. Instead, you implement the interface in the code-behind class. We'll cover code-behind in Chapter 2.

The *@Reference* Directive

The *@Reference* directive is used to establish a dynamic link between the current page and the specified page or user control. This feature has significant relapses in the way in which you set up cross-page communication. It also lets you create strongly typed instances of user controls. Let's review the syntax.

The directive can appear multiple times in the page, and it features two mutually exclusive attributes—*Page* and *Control*. Both attributes are expected to contain a path to a source file:

```
<%@ Reference page="source_page" %>
<%@ Reference control="source_user_control" %>
```

The *Page* attribute points to a .aspx source file, whereas the *Control* attribute contains the path of a .ascx user control. In both cases, the referenced source file will be dynamically compiled into an assembly, thus making the classes defined in the source programmatically available to the referencing page. When running, an ASP.NET page is an instance of a .NET Framework class with a specific interface made of methods and properties. When the referencing page executes, a referenced page becomes a class that represents the .aspx source file and can be instantiated and programmed at will. Note that for the directive to work the referenced page must belong to the same domain as the calling page. Cross-site calls are not allowed, and both the *Page* and *Control* attributes expect to receive a relative virtual path. We'll return to this topic, with practical examples, in Chapter 4, "Working with the Page."

The *<script>* Section

The *<script>* section of an ASP.NET page contains all the declared code that makes up the page. If the page implements an interface, the code for the interface methods is placed here. If the page handles some system events, the needed code belongs here. Likewise, the *<script>* section contains all the code to execute when the controls in the page are clicked or change their state. The *<script>* tag supports the following syntax:

```
<script runat="server" language="..." src="...">
   Code goes here...
</script>
```

When the *runat* attribute is set to *server*, all the code comprised between the opening and closing tags is given special meaning. In this case, the code is extracted from the .aspx source file, compiled into an assembly, and then executed when the page runs. No line of this code will ever be output to the client.

When the *runat* attribute is not included, the content of the *<script>* block is considered as client-side script code and emitted verbatim in the resulting HTML page. ASP.NET pages can have both server-side and client-side *<script>* blocks.

> **Note** The .NET Framework documentation uses the name *code declaration block* to refer to the content of a *<script>* block in which the *runat* attribute equals *server*. The name code render block refers to an ASP-style code block, which is defined as inline code (*<%...%>*) or inline expression (*<%=...%>*). Declared code becomes part of the page's programming interface once the page is compiled into an assembly. Rendered code is embedded in the class logic and executes only when the page is rendered.

The *Language* Attribute

The *Language* attribute defines the language used within the block. Of course, the range of acceptable values is slightly different according to the value of the *runat* attribute. If the *runat* attribute is set to *server*, you can use C#, Visual Basic .NET, JScript .NET, or maybe J# (if version 1.1 of the .NET Framework is used). If the *runat* attribute is not included, the code will run on the client, which allows you to use JavaScript or maybe VBScript (if the Web browser supports VBScript).

Generally, valid languages for the server-side script block are those for which you have a .NET assembly that implements the interfaces defined in the .NET compilers object model. Similarly, valid languages for the client-side script block are those languages that are supported by the client Web browser. For example, Netscape browsers support JavaScript and Internet Explorer supports JavaScript and VBScript.

The behavior of the *<script>* tag changes considerably according to the value of the *runat* attribute. The presence of the *runat* attribute marks an important difference regarding the use of the *Language* attribute. While you can have multiple client-side scripts each using a different language, you can't have more than one language in use within an ASP.NET page. If you have multiple server-side *<script>* blocks, make sure all of them use the same language. Although this seems to violate the much-hyped language neutrality of .NET, the reason will be made clear in Chapter 2.

If the *<script>* block doesn't contain a *Language* attribute, the language set in the *@Page* directive is used. You could also set the language both in the directive and script block, but in this case the settings must match. In no way, in fact, does ASP.NET make one of them win. When settings conflict, you simply get a compile error on the *<script>* line stating that another language has been specified earlier in the page.

The *Src* Attribute

The *Src* attribute denotes the URL of the source file to load. When this attribute is used, any other code specified in the *<script>* block is ignored:

```
<script runat="server" language="c#" src="content.cs" />
```

If you plan to use the *Src* attribute, you might want to be more elegant and use an empty *<script>* tag, as in the code just shown.

ASP-Style Code Blocks in ASP.NET

As mentioned earlier, ASP.NET supports two types of code blocks—those declared in a server-side *<script>* block, and those defined as inline code or inline expressions in the body of the page. Obviously, there's nothing you can do with inline code that can't be done even more elegantly and more effectively with declared code. ASP.NET supports inline code blocks simply to ease the migration of ASP applications.

ASP.NET inline code and inline expressions follow this quite familiar syntax:

```
<% inline code %>
<%=inline expression %>
```

Just as in ASP, inline expressions are simply shortcuts for the *Response.Write* method. Inline code, on the other hand, is a sequence of statements and variable declarations that are executed in a top-down fashion, as in ASP. However, unlike ASP, ASP.NET won't allow you to declare a function between <% and %> tags. The following ASP-style code is no longer supported and, if used, generates a compile error:

```
<% Sub DeclareLove() %>
    <h1>ASP.NET Is Love!</h1>
<% End Sub %>
```

The code can be rewritten as follows:

```
<script language="VB" runat="server">
    Sub DeclareLove()
        Response.Write("<h1>ASP.NET Is Love!</h1>")
    End Sub
</script>
```

You can use the method *DeclareLove* from within a <% … %> block. Another difference with ASP concerns variable declarations. In ASP.NET, the variables declared in <% … %> blocks are no longer globally available to other functions and methods in the page; they can be accessed only by code defined in other render blocks on the page.

In ASP, you were used to putting all initialization code at the beginning of the first code block. In ASP.NET, initialization code must be included within the *Page_Load* method. You can still use ASP-style programming, but keep in mind that all the code in <% … %> blocks will be executed only when the page is rendered, and therefore, after the page is loaded.

Aside from the few but important differences we just mentioned, ASP.NET can run a significant portion of the existing old-style ASP code. For example, the following typical loop produces the same results as in ASP:

```
<% for (int i=0; i<8; i++) { %>
    <font size="<%=i %>"> ASP.NET is Love! </font><br>
<% } %>
```

Figure 1-3 shows the output when you run this code.

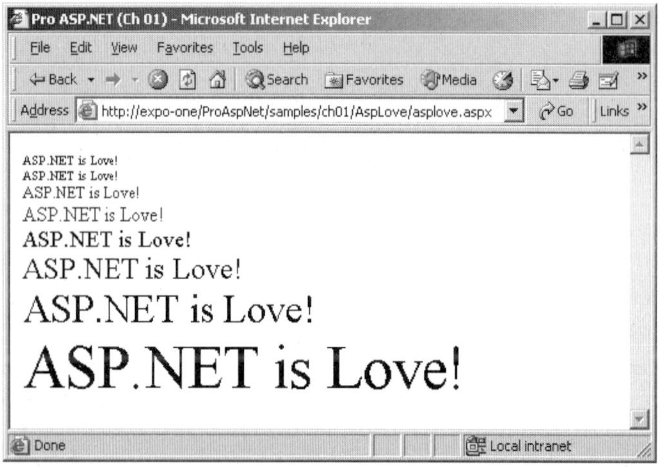

Figure 1-3 Programmers' love for ASP.NET grows constantly.

> **Note** Some ASP.NET pages can lack the *<script>* section completely. These pages exploit a unique ASP.NET feature called *code-behind*. With code-behind, you isolate the code for the page in a distinct class, thus obtaining a physical separation between code and page layout. We'll learn more about code-behind in Chapter 2.

The Layout Section

The layout section of an ASP.NET page contains the literals and markup text that provides the graphical infrastructure of the page. The layout can also contain ASP-style code blocks, although their use is discouraged. Simply put, the layout is an HTML page with some *placeholders* that are expanded on the server and generate the HTML that is sent to the browser.

All the literal text in the layout section is emitted verbatim in the target HTML page. What will become of markup text depends on the *runat* attribute. If the *runat* attribute is present, the ASP.NET runtime attempts to map that tag with an instance of a server control. If a match is found, an instance of that control is created. Otherwise, a type-not-defined exception is thrown. Markup text without the *runat* attribute is treated like literal text and emitted verbatim.

ASP.NET comes with a full complement of server-side controls—that is, .NET classes that implement ad hoc interfaces and render their content as HTML. Classic HTML tags automatically map to a particular family of ASP.NET server controls known as *HTML server controls*. Their programming interface mirrors the set of attributes of the native HTML tag. Another family of ASP.NET server controls are known as *Web server controls*. Web server controls are prefixed by the <*asp*> namespace and represent more complex user-interface elements. Custom controls can be mapped to custom tags using the *@Register* directive.

User controls are an effective way to simplify and componentize the page layout. HTML is quite verbose as a language. Especially in cases where you need to structure the contents with tables, the final markup can be quite complex and hard to read and maintain. User controls are to Web pages as classes or subroutines are to applications. They provide a way to encapsulate logical blocks of the user interface (such as the toolbar, menu, grids, and headers) into more manageable and object-oriented components.

Finally, the layout of an ASP.NET page must group all interactive controls under a single <*form*> tag marked with the *runat* attribute. Only the controls that belong to this server-side form can persist their state across page requests and actually be an active part of the page. Place only decorative controls and static user-interface elements such as images, headers, and footers outside of the <*form*> tag. We'll return to this point in Chapter 2 and in Chapter 4.

The ASP.NET Component Model

A key aspect of ASP.NET is that it represents the Web branch of the .NET Framework. The .NET Framework is made entirely of an object-oriented hierarchy of classes (about 9,000 classes) that span all programming topics for Windows operating systems. A Web application is made of pages the user requests from a server and that the server processes and returns as HTML code. How the requested resource is processed is server-specific. In particular, when the resource happens to have a .aspx extension, IIS delegates any elaboration to the ASP.NET runtime system.

The ASP.NET runtime transforms the source code of the requested .aspx page into the living instance of a .NET Framework class that inherits from the base *Page* class. (How such a transformation takes place is the subject of Chapter 2.) At the end of the day, a running ASP.NET page is an object, and so it is for some of its components—the server-side controls.

A large number of new ASP.NET features are just a direct or an indirect propagation of the .NET infrastructure. ASP.NET benefits from cross-language integration and exception handling, garbage collection and code access security, deployment and configuration, and an incredibly rich class library. All these features aren't the products of a self-contained engine, they are available to you because ASP.NET applications are a special breed of a .NET application.

A Model for Component Interaction

A close metaphor for client-side scripting is found in ASP.NET—the Dynamic HTML object model (DHTML). Any element can be identified through an ID, and you can write code against it. While this is a natural approach on the client, it represents a brand new scheme for server applications. Two factors make this revolutionary approach possible:

- The component-based architecture of the .NET platform and the fact that ASP.NET is a constituent part of it
- The ASP.NET built-in mechanism for the application's state management

The component-based design of .NET makes component interaction easy and effective in all environments including ASP.NET applications. On the other hand, the availability of an automatic mechanism for state persistence overcomes all the hurdles represented by the stateless nature of the HTTP protocol. ASP.NET components access page features and interact by calling one another's methods and setting properties.

The fact that all elements in the page are true components, and not simply parsable text, provides a flexible and powerful extensibility model. Creating new controls is as easy as deriving a new class; creating master pages is as easy as specifying a code-behind page more complex than the base *Page* class.

The *runat* Attribute

The *runat* attribute is what determines whether a piece of markup text is to be emitted verbatim at render time or transformed into a stateful instance of a particular .NET class. In an ASP.NET page, all markup elements that have the *runat* attribute set to *server* are considered server-side controls. The control class exposes methods and properties that let you configure the state of the component. The control is responsible for emitting HTML code when the page is rendered to the browser. Let's consider the following simple code that creates an anchor element in the page:

```
Response.Write("<A id=myAnchor href=www.asp.net>Click me</A>")
```

The anchor element is created programmatically and is not defined in the page layout. In ASP, code blocks and the *Response.Write* method are the only ways you have to create or configure controls dynamically. In some development environments, such as Microsoft Visual InterDev, *design-time controls* provided an object-based way to output dynamically generated HTML. Design-time controls, though, are just what the name indicates—that is, controls you can use at design time to generate markup and script code. In ASP.NET, you have a new breed of controls that we could call *run-time controls* to mark the contrast with design-time controls.

Working with Server-Side Controls

Within an ASP page, there's no way for you to code against the *myAnchor* element. It's just frozen, lifeless text, only good for sending to the browser. Once on a client, the *myAnchor* element gets back to life and can accept script instructions. Suppose now that you need to set the *href* attribute of the anchor based on run-time conditions. In ASP, you could first obtain the value for the *href* attribute and then call *Response.Write*:

```
strHref = "www.asp.net"
strHtml = "<A id=myAnchor "
strHtml = strHtml + "href=" + strHref
strHtml = strHtml + ">Click me</A>"
Response.Write(strHtml)
```

This code will work unchanged in an ASP.NET page, but it's certainly not the best you can do. By declaring the *<A>* tag with the *runat* attribute, you can give life to the anchor element on the server too:

```
<A runat="server" id="myAnchor">Click me</A>
```

When the page is loaded, the ASP.NET runtime parses the source code and creates instances of all controls marked with the *runat* attribute. Throughout the page, the *myAnchor* ID identifies an instance of the server-side control mapped to the *<A>* tag. The following code can be used to set the *href* attribute programmatically:

```
<script runat="server" language="C#">
void Page_Load(object sender, EventArgs e)
{
    myAnchor.HRef = "http://www.asp.net";
}
</script>
```

The markup elements found in the body of the page whose name matches an HTML element are mapped to the corresponding HTML server control. Elements that belong to the *<asp>* namespace are mapped to Web server controls. Other markup elements are mapped to the assembly and class name declared by using an *@Register* directive.

Pagewide Tags

The *runat* attribute can be used also with pagewide tags such as *<title>*, *<link>*, and *<body>*. These tags are represented through an instance of the *HtmlGenericControl* class. *HtmlGenericControl* is the .NET class used to represent an HTML server-side tag not directly represented by a .NET Framework class. The list of such tags also includes *<span>*, *<div>*, *<font>*, and *<iframe>*.

In the following page, the page title and page background are set programmatically using a server-side object instance:

```
<%@ Page Language="C#" %>
<script runat="server">
void Page_Load(object sender, EventArgs e) {
    TheTitle.InnerText = "Pro ASP.NET (Ch 01)";
    TheBody.Attributes["bgcolor"] = "yellow";
}
</script>
<html>
<title id="TheTitle" runat="server" />
<body id="TheBody" runat="server" >
Click the <b>View|Source</b> menu item...
</body>
</html>
```

The resulting HTML code is as follows:

```
<html>
<title id="TheTitle">Pro ASP.NET (Ch 01)</title>
<body id="TheBody" bgcolor="yellow">
Click the <b>View|Source</b> menu item...
</body>
</html>
```

Likewise, you can set any of the properties of the *<link>* tag, thus deciding programmatically, say, which style sheet to use for the page. You use the *HtmlGenericControl*'s *Attributes* collection to create attributes on the tag and the *InnerText* property to set the text. We'll discuss the programming interface of the *HtmlGenericControl* class in Chapter 3.

Meta Tags

The *runat* attribute can be applied also to the *<meta>* tag, but a little trick is needed this time. In HTML, you normally add the *<meta>* tag without a closing tag. This is not permitted by ASP.NET when the *runat* attribute is added. The ASP.NET parser scans the whole file looking for *</meta>* tag; if the tag is not found, a compile error is generated.

The following code shows how to programmatically set meta content that instructs the browser to wait four seconds and then to go to the specified URL:

```
<%@ Page Language="C#" %>
<script runat="server">
void Page_Load(object sender, EventArgs e) {
    meta1.Attributes["content"] = "4;URL=http://www.asp.net";
}
</script>
<html>
<meta id="meta1" runat="server" http-equiv="refresh" />
<title>Pro ASP.NET (Ch 01)</title>
<body>
```

```
Click the <b>View|Source</b> menu item in the next few seconds...
</body>
</html>
```

The resulting HTML meta tag is shown below. Notice the fundamental presence of the closing tag:

```
<meta id="meta1" http-equiv="refresh"
content="4;URL=http://www.asp.net"></meta>
```

> **Note** You can also use the *Response.AppendHeader* method to add an HTTP header to the output stream. The programming interface of the *Response* object also features an *AddHeader* method. *AddHeader* is the same as *AppendHeader* and is provided only for compatibility with previous versions of ASP. With ASP.NET, you should always use *AppendHeader*.

Unknown Tags

In case of unknown tags, namely tags that are neither predefined nor user-defined, the ASP.NET runtime can behave in two different ways. If the tag doesn't contain namespace information, ASP.NET treats it like a generic HTML control. The empty namespace, in fact, evaluates to the HTML namespace, thereby leading the ASP.NET runtime to believe the tag is really an HTML element. No exception is raised, and markup text is generated on the server. For example, let's consider the following ASP.NET page:

```
<%@ Page Language="C#" %>
<script runat="server">
void Page_Load(object sender, EventArgs e) {
    dinoe.Attributes["FavoriteFood"] = "T-bone steak";
}
</script>
<html><body>
<Person id="dinoe" runat="server" />
Click the <b>View|Source</b> menu item...
</body></html>
```

The *<Person>* tag is still processed as if it was a regular HTML tag, and the *FavoriteFood* attribute is added. Figure 1-4 shows what the HTML code for this page actually is. In the preceding sample, the type of the *dinoe* object is *HtmlGenericControl.*

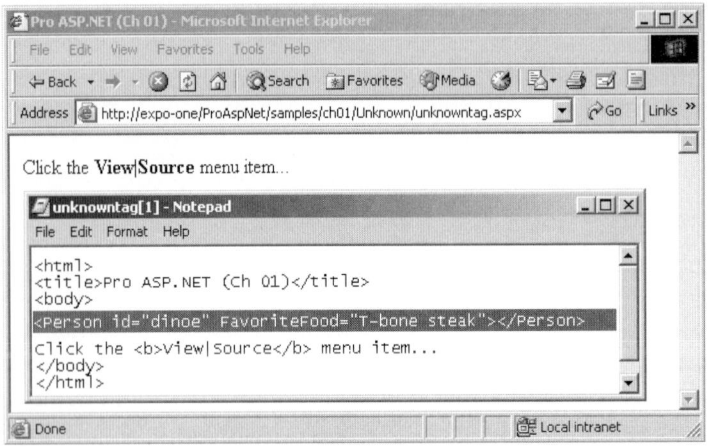

Figure 1-4 ASP.NET also processes namespace-less custom tags, mapping them to the *HtmlGenericControl* class.

If the tag does contain namespace information, it is acceptable as long as the namespace is *<asp>* or a namespace explicitly associated with the tag name using an *@Register* directive. If the namespace is unknown, a compile error occurs.

ASP.NET Server Controls

There are basically two families of ASP.NET server controls. They are HTML server controls and Web server controls. *System.Web.UI.HtmlControls* is the namespace of HTML server controls. *System.Web.UI.WebControls* groups all the Web server controls.

HTML server controls are classes that represent a standard HTML tag supported by most browsers. The set of properties of an HTML server control matches exactly the set of attributes of the corresponding tag. The control features properties such as *InnerText*, *InnerHtml*, *Style*, and *Value* and collections such as *Attributes*. Instances of HTML server controls are automatically created by the ASP.NET runtime each time the corresponding HTML tag marked with *runat="server"* is found in the page source.

Web server controls are controls with more features than HTML server controls. Web server controls include not only input controls such as buttons and textboxes, but also special-purpose controls such as a calendar, an ad-rotator, a drop-down list, and a data grid. Web server controls also include components that closely resemble some HTML server controls. Web server controls, though, are more abstract than the corresponding HTML server controls in that their object model doesn't necessarily reflect the HTML syntax. For example, let's compare the HTML server text control and the Web server *TextBox* control. The HTML server text control has the following markup:

```
<input runat="server" id="FirstName" type="text" value="Dino" />
```

The Web server *TextBox* control has the following markup:

```
<asp:textbox runat="server" id="FirstName" text="Dino" />
```

Both controls generate the same HTML code. However, the programming interface of the HTML server text control matches closely that of the HTML *<input>* tag, while methods and properties of the Web server *TextBox* control are named in a more abstract way. For example, to set the content of an HTML server text control, you must use the *Value* property because *Value* is the corresponding HTML attribute name. If you work with the Web server *TextBox* control, you must resort to *Text*. With very few exceptions (which I'll discuss in Chapter 3), using HTML server controls or Web server controls to represent HTML elements is only a matter of preference.

Migrating from ASP to ASP.NET

In the past five years, one million developers all over the world have chosen ASP as the development platform of choice to build Web applications. You can bet that with such a huge base of installed applications, the problem of ensuring backward compatibility between ASP and ASP.NET has been taken very seriously. The result is that ASP and ASP.NET applications can run side by side on an IIS Web server without any form of interference occurring. In addition, and in spite of the radical changes in the underlying architecture and implementation, a significant portion of existing ASP pages can just be renamed as .aspx files and will continue working (even a bit faster) and be managed by a different IIS module. Does this really mean you can migrate ASP applications to ASP.NET simply by renaming files? Well, not exactly. As always, code migration is a delicate art that becomes impracticable when huge architectural differences exist between the starting and ending points. ASP.NET is designed to make migration easier, but a migration plan is still needed and a 100 percent pure ASP.NET solution is needed to be really effective.

Side-by-Side Execution

IIS makes use of the file extension to determine which module has to process a requested resource. As a result, only files with a .aspx extension are served by ASP.NET. All the files with a .asp extension will continue to be served by the existing (and unchanged) ASP engine. Because completely different and independent modules serve ASP and ASP.NET requests, existing ASP applications cannot be corrupted simply by installing and running ASP.NET applications on the same Web server.

Not only can you make ASP and ASP.NET applications live side by side on the same Web server, but—more importantly—you can also manage to create applications that use both ASP and ASP.NET pages. After all, from the perspective of an ASP application, what's a .aspx resource if not a simple URL on the same domain?

> **Important** Obviously, mixed applications—applications in which ASP and ASP.NET pages run side-by-side—are recommended only if you take an existing, complex ASP application and enhance it with new ASP.NET pages. The opposite approach, although possible, doesn't make sense. If you're engaged on a new ASP.NET project, by all means forget about ASP.

Note, though, that when ASP and ASP.NET pages live within the context of the same application, some restrictions apply. For example, session state and application state are not shared between ASP and ASP.NET pages. In particular, the problem of sharing session state between ASP and ASP.NET applications is fully dissected in an article available at *http://msdn.microsoft.com/library/en-us/dnaspp/html/converttoaspnet.asp*.

Rewriting ASP Pages as ASP.NET Pages

Although far richer and created with different design centers, the new ASP.NET programming model has been kept as close as possible to the old ASP model. As a result, ASP.NET programming might seem familiar to developers with good ASP skills. However, although still available in ASP.NET, the ASP-intrinsic objects have been redesigned to make them more structured and object-oriented, and new objects have been provided.

The net effect is that existing ASP code, albeit accepted and functional, is not necessarily the best way of accomplishing a given task. For example, you can still build a list of check-box items by merging plain HTML text and data-bound information in a string buffer. Nevertheless, using the new *CheckBoxList* control would result in more compact, safe, readable, and maintainable code. Likewise, using ActiveX Data Objects (ADO) to access a back-end database server is supported, but it might require some changes to the code and would penalize the performance because data destined to COM objects must be marshaled in and out of the .NET Common Language Runtime (CLR). Global data that you stored in the *Application* object sometimes can be more efficiently stored in the new *Cache* object, which manages perishable data and automatically garbage-collects it when needed.

These are a few examples of the performance hitches you can unwittingly generate in your ASP.NET pages if you create them to resemble existing ASP pages. But there's another key issue to consider when you plan to rewrite ASP pages as ASP.NET pages—the language. Many existing ASP pages are written with VBScript, but only a small portion of the VBScript syntax is acceptable to the Visual Basic .NET compiler. Those pages will not port directly to ASP.NET and will require changes. The necessary changes will probably be limited to only a few lines of code, but those changes must be applied to all pages in the application.

All in all, adapting existing pages as ASP.NET pages is possible but comes at a cost; and such adaptations will not give you highly optimized code. So what should you do with existing ASP applications?

Suggested Migration Plans

Before continuing with this topic, I need to issue a disclaimer of sorts and mention situations in which migrating to ASP.NET might not be ideal. Understand that ASP.NET—and the subsequent installation of the ASP.NET runtime and the .NET Framework on the Web server—does not affect or compromise existing ASP applications. Existing applications will continue working in the same way and with the same performance as before. Additionally, new and ad hoc designed ASP.NET applications feature far better performance and an improved scalability and programming model. If I had to choose a single word to explain what ASP.NET is all about, that word would be productivity.

ASP.NET-enhanced productivity applies at all levels. You have less code to write (and that code is easier to understand and maintain); a relatively flat learning curve; significant cuts in the cost of the deployment; and a greatly simplified model for localization and customization. ASP.NET is also language-independent and performs much better than ASP. And in my humble opinion, even all that pales in comparison to the gains you experience in productivity.

With that said, I can issue my disclaimer. You probably know better than I do that in this little imperfect world, new projects require new budgets. Upgrading a huge and complex Web site, such as a portal, can be expensive even with the productivity advantages of ASP.NET. If budget is not a concern, then by all means redesign and rewrite the application from scratch. Period. If the budget is a severe concern, you should seriously consider holding off and waiting for better times—the old ASP application will still work. At the very least, the current version of ASP.NET increases your productivity and the application's overall performance, but as of now it can't fit more cheaply into a project's budget! For that to happen, we have to wait for the next version at the earliest.

In between upgrading and not upgrading, I see a few options to move ASP applications towards ASP.NET even when working with relatively small budgets.

Same Application, New Pages

My first suggestion is that you keep the existing ASP application as is and use ASP.NET only if you're required to add new features and new pages. While extremely cost-effective, the plan poses a few development issues because ASP and ASP.NET pages running together can't share the internal state. Aside from this, no other interoperability issues or interference exist between old and new pages.

New Application, Same Framework, New Pages

In this case, you develop a new ASP.NET application but without revisiting and redesigning the application's framework. The skeleton and the functions of the application remain the same. The migration roughly consists of translating the constituent pages from ASP to ASP.NET. Basically, you rename each .asp page to .aspx and adapt it to work.

We already discussed the nature of this approach in the "Rewriting ASP Pages as ASP.NET Pages" section. Here, we provide a more detailed list of the issues you must be ready to face:

- **Page directives** ASP has a rough model for setting up the environment in which the page will run. ASP.NET directives have been designed to be fully compatible with ASP directives. However, in an ASP.NET page you might want to exploit some extra *@Page* attributes for a more effective compilation (for example, *AspCompat*, *Explicit*, and *Strict*) and certainly for tracing or debugging purposes. Finally, bear in mind that you also need to link extra assemblies if you import .NET wrappers of COM components.

- **Programming languages** ASP pages are normally written with VBScript, but VBScript is scarcely compatible with Visual Basic .NET. You must carefully review the code of all pages and probably replace *On Error* statements with the more effective .NET exception handling. You must replace the VBScript *CreateObject* with *Server.CreateObject* to preserve the syntax to some extent, or choose a different approach and import the COM object through a .NET wrapper class. Pay attention to turn the *@Page*'s *AspCompat* attribute on if you're using COM and COM+ objects within an ASP.NET page. If the page was written with JScript, things are a bit simpler, as JScript is highly compatible with JScript .NET. However, a careful code review is nevertheless in order.

- **Code blocks** ASP.NET pages support ASP-style code blocks but with some limitation, as explained previously in the "The *<script>* Section" section. The suggestion is to remove all ASP code blocks and rewrite the page, taking advantage of ASP.NET declared code.
- **Security** In ASP.NET, impersonation is disabled by default and you must explicitly enable it to preserve ASP compatibility. A simple line of text in the web.config file would do the job. (I'll cover this in Chapter 12.) Unlike ASP, ASP.NET does not run applications within the context of the System account. ASP.NET applications execute under the ASPNET account and by default have no writing permissions. Subsequently, pages accessing the Web server's file system will explicitly need to be granted write permissions on files and folders to operate successfully.
- **Data Access and XML** ASP pages normally use ADO for any data access need and Microsoft XML Core Services (MSXML) to parse XML documents. Both are COM components and can be used in ASP.NET pages, although you'll pay a bit in performance. The .NET Framework provides an effective data access model (ADO.NET) and a bunch of powerful XML classes you might want to use instead. However, consider that ADO.NET does not support server cursors (a feature that will come with a future version) and the XML API does not support the Simple API for XML (SAX) parsing model. For server cursors, you can only stick to ADO or redesign the feature; for SAX parsing, you can even more effectively use the XML reader component to obtain the same feature.
- **COM compatibility** ASP.NET pages can use COM objects in two ways: directly as a COM object or through a .NET wrapper class. In the former case, the object is referenced in the page using the *<object runat=server …>* tag or dynamically created using the *Server.CreateObject* method. Alternatively, you can create a .NET wrapper for the COM object and use it as you would any other assembly. In both cases, remember to set the *AspCompat* attribute of the *@Page* directive to *true* to prevent excessive overhead, if not deadlock.

Same Application, New Presentation Layer

The idea behind this approach is that you completely rewrite the presentation layer of the application—that is, the server pages–based front end of the system. On the other hand, you leave intact any business objects you might have and, to the extent possible, you don't touch the entire middle and data tiers. In the new, ASP.NET-driven presentation layer, you make use of Web server controls, data-binding, configuration, and all the features that make ASP.NET so cool and effective.

The connection between the COM-based middle tier and the managed presentation tier is ensured by the ADO.NET OLE DB data adapter class. (I'll cover ADO.NET in Chapter 5.) Methods on the OLE DB data adapter class are able to import an ADO *Recordset* into ADO.NET objects. In this way, you call your middle-tier objects from ASP.NET pages, get their output in the form of ADO *Recordset* objects, transform them into managed data containers, and link to the page's data-bound controls. Of course, this approach is recommended (and works) only if your middle-tier objects communicate with the rest of the system by exchanging ADO *Recordset* objects. You should also note that the OLE DB data adapter component provides a one-way data-binding mechanism. You should figure out a way to send an updated ADO *Recordset* back to the middle tier.

So much for ASP compatibility and migration. Let's see how to create full-blown ASP.NET applications using the king of all .NET programming tools—Visual Studio .NET.

Setting Up ASP.NET Applications

To create an ASP.NET application, you need very few ingredients—pages, assemblies, a virtual directory, and maybe some ancillary files to provide for initialization and configuration. Once everything is in place and the virtual directory is properly set up, to test the application you simply point the browser to the URL of the application's main page. What you need to do to build a Web application is quite different from what you need to do to build, say, a Windows Forms application. In spite of these structural differences, Visual Studio .NET manages to unify the working model and successfully brings the familiar rapid application development (RAD) approach to the Web.

Much better than its Web predecessor—Visual InterDev—Visual Studio .NET lets you create ASP.NET pages as Web-based visual forms. You work on an empty surface that mimics the body of an HTML page and populate it with server controls picked from a palette of components. Once dropped on the Web form, the control can be configured using the Properties browser and moved around as appropriate. To handle the events fired by the control, you just select the event from a list or double-click the control in the designer area. If you find that all this eerily resembles the Visual Basic way of working, well, it's not coincidental!

Creating a Visual Studio Project

When you create a new ASP.NET application with Visual Studio .NET, you specify a virtual path, not a physical directory. You pass Visual Studio .NET the URL of the virtual directory in which the project files are to be created. As shown in Figure 1-5, you also select the language for the project. Visual Studio .NET lets you create ASP.NET applications only in Visual Basic .NET and C#. (You can use J# only if you have installed the version 1.1 of the .NET Framework along with Visual Studio .NET 2003.)

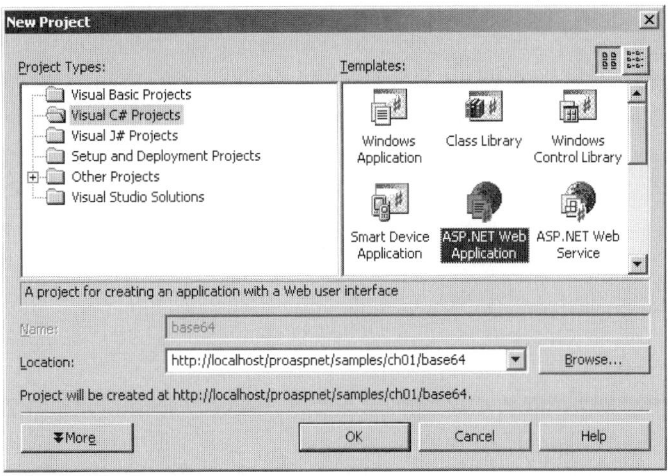

Figure 1-5 Starting a new ASP.NET project with Visual Studio .NET 2003.

All the classes that the Visual Studio .NET wizard generates belong to a namespace named after the project. The classes will be compiled into an assembly that will be given the same name as the project. The assembly is created when you build the solution and put it in the *Bin* subdirectory of the virtual directory. The namespace name, as well as the name of the project's assembly, can be changed by right-clicking the project node in Solution Explorer, and choosing Properties. Figure 1-6 shows the project Property Pages dialog box for a project in Visual Studio .NET 2003.

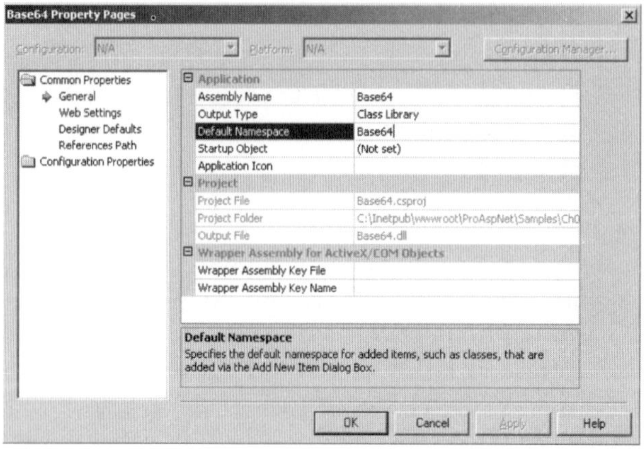

Figure 1-6 Renaming assembly and default namespaces in Visual Studio .NET 2003.

Upon creation, the project includes an empty page named WebForm1.aspx. The page supports code-behind, meaning that all the code for the page resides in a separate class—the code-behind class. The name of the code-behind class matches the name of the .aspx file. (In Chapter 2, you'll learn more about code-behind classes.) As shown in the References node of Solution Explorer, an ASP.NET project references a few assemblies by default. They are: *System*, *System.Data*, *System.Drawing*, *System.Web*, and *System.Xml*.

> **Caution** The Visual Studio default procedure for naming newly created pages and related code-behind classes causes a little hassle when you have multiple pages with the same name, even though they might be located in different folders. Visual Studio .NET doesn't consider that, say, the new default.aspx page you're adding to the project actually resides in a different folder and indeed has a unique path. Visual Studio .NET correctly detects that a *Default* class already exists in the namespace and automatically renames the class adding a trailing index (for example, *Default1*). If you don't like this approach—and you'd be wise not to—either give the class a new name or, better yet, call it *Default*, but define the class in a child namespace to reflect the fact that the file belongs to a different directory.

The Project Files

Aside from the pages, classes, and resources that actually comprise the application, a number of additional files form a Visual Studio .NET ASP.NET project. In a C# project named MyProject, they would be:

- **MyProject.csproj** This XML file contains build and file information for the project. The *<Build>* section contains the application settings (root namespace, output type, and default client script) and the assemblies to link. The *<Files>* section contains the list of the files in the project. A file is identified by a relative path, a build action, a type, and optionally a dependency. To view the content of this file, use a text editor or make a copy and change the extension to .xml.
- **MyProject.csproj.webinfo** This XML file contains the path of the .csproj file expressed as a URL. The information in this file complements the content of the previous file in that the .csproj file doesn't contain absolute path information.
- **MyProject.vsdisco** This Web service dynamic discovery file is used to track the project's Web references—that is, project references that point to Web services.
- **AssemblyInfo.cs** This codeless C# file is filled only with attributes. It contains information to sign the assembly being generated as well as general assembly information such as the build number, copyright text, and the company and product name.
- **Global.asax** This optional file contains code for responding to application-level events raised by ASP.NET. Visual Studio .NET always adds such a file to its ASP.NET projects. Just as with Web pages, the global.asax file can be constructed using code-behind, thus delegating a background class to implement all needed event handlers. All global.asax files created by Visual Studio .NET are code-behind.
- **Global.asax.cs** This is the code-behind class for global.asax. The class is named *Global* by default and inherits from *HttpApplication*. We'll cover global.asax in Chapter 13.
- **Global.asax.resx** This is the XML resource file for the global.asax.cs file, and it's marked as being dependent on the global.asax.cs file. By default, the file contains a standard block of information that specifies the schema of the contained resources. You can fill a .resx file with name/value pairs of application-specific data.

- **Web.config** This XML file contains configuration information for the Web application. Multiple configuration files, all named web.config, can appear in multiple directories on an ASP.NET Web application. We'll discuss the web.config file in detail in Chapter 12.

Each ASP.NET page included in the project features three files: .aspx, .cs, and .resx. The .aspx file contains the layout of the page; the .cs contains the code-behind class; the .resx file contains resources associated with the page. You should note, however, that having three files per page is simply the Visual Studio way of working. In no way is this a strict syntactical or architectural requirement.

> **Note** A Visual Basic .NET ASP.NET project contains an extra file—styles.css. This file contains the default cascading style sheet (CSS) definitions for the HTML tags you can use throughout the project.

Creating the Web Forms Page

Creating a Web Forms page is as easy as picking controls from the Visual Studio toolbox and dropping them onto the surface that represents the page. If you're like me and feel more comfortable when you can see some HTML code every now and then, you'll consider it good news that you can switch between HTML and design view at any time with a simple click. The following code snippet is the HTML code being generated for an empty ASP.NET page belonging to a project named Base64:

```
<%@ Page language="c#" Codebehind="WebForm1.aspx.cs"
    AutoEventWireup="false" Inherits="Base64.WebForm1" %>
<!DOCTYPE HTML PUBLIC "-//W3C//DTD HTML 4.0 Transitional//EN" >
<HTML>
    <HEAD>
        <title>WebForm</title>
        <meta name="GENERATOR" Content="Microsoft Visual Studio 7.1">
        <meta name="CODE_LANGUAGE" Content="C#">
        <meta name="vs_defaultClientScript" content="JavaScript">
        <meta name="vs_targetSchema"
            content="http://schemas.microsoft.com/intellisense/ie5">
    </HEAD>
    <body MS_POSITIONING="GridLayout">
        <form id="Form1" method="post" runat="server">
             
        </form>
    </body>
</HTML>
```

The page has a code-behind class in the file webform1.aspx.cs that explicitly wires up to all the page events it needs to handle. (*AutoEventWireup* is purposefully set to *false*.) The name of the class that implements the page behavior is *Base64.WebForm1*.

The *vs_defaultClientScript* meta tag indicates that the page will use JavaScript for client-side scripting. More interesting is the role of the *vs_targetSchema* tag. It contains a Uniform Resource Identifier (URI) that uniquely identifies the HTML schema being supported. By default, Visual Studio .NET generates HTML code targeted to Internet Explorer 5.0. You can change meta tag settings using the project Property Pages dialog box shown in Figure 1-7. You display the dialog box by right-clicking the project in Solution Explorer and choosing Properties.

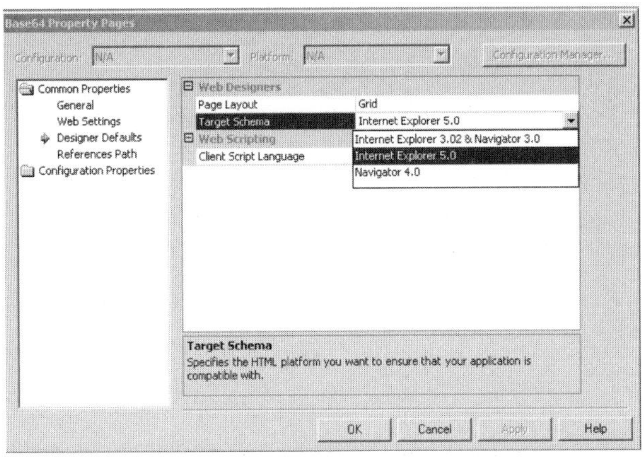

Figure 1-7 Choosing a target HTML schema for the application.

In the HTML code examined a moment ago, you might have noticed the MS_POSITIONING attribute within the *<body>* tag. The *GridLayout* value lets you place HTML controls on the form at absolute positions, similar to the procedure you'd follow with a Windows Forms application. The *GridLayout* mode leverages the underlying browser support for CSS absolute positioning. However, not all browsers support this feature, so this will probably be a setting you want to change to safely reach a wider audience. From the project Property Pages dialog box shown in Figure 1-7, set the page layout attribute of the Web designer to *Flow*.

> **Tip** You can also set the page layout attribute from the Properties browser window. Select the DOCUMENT view from the top drop-down list in the Properties window, and scroll the list to the *pageLayout* property. The property list also lets you declaratively set graphical settings for the page, including margins, colors, and styles.

After you change the page layout from *Grid* to *Flow*, the *<body>* tag is rendered without the MS_POSITIONING attribute. Note, though, that if you change the page layout attribute on a nonempty page, existing controls maintain their absolute positions and the new settings are applied only to new controls. Let's rename the page and add a label and a text box (both Web server controls) to the page as shown in Figure 1-8.

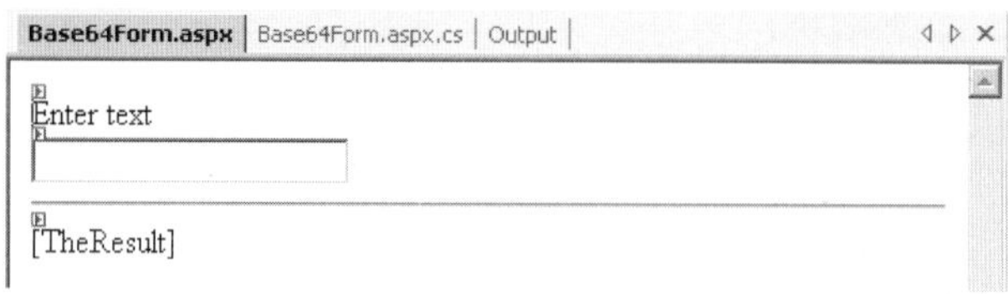

Figure 1-8 The visual designer completed with a few server controls.

On the Web Forms tab of the Toolbox, add a *Label* control and a *TextBox* control. Set the *Text* property of the *Label* control to "Enter text", and the *ID* property of the *TextBox* control to "TheText". Here's the HTML code that's added:

```
<form id="Form1" method="post" runat="server">
    <asp:Label id="Label1" runat="server">Enter text</asp:Label>
    <br>
    <asp:TextBox id="TheText" runat="server"></asp:TextBox>
</form>
```

Only a few HTML elements such as the inline frame (*<iframe>*) and page-break (*
*) can't be added visually. However, as shown in Figure 1-9, the Visual Studio IntelliSense feature intercepts your typing and prompts suggestions.

Figure 1-9 IntelliSense at work trying to make your programming life easier.

To top off the Web Forms, let's add a button and connect it to some concrete code. The *ID* property is set to "DoIt" and the *Text* property is set to "Encode…". The output generated by the code behind the button will be displayed through a new *Label* control named "TheResult". Figure 1-10 shows the form.

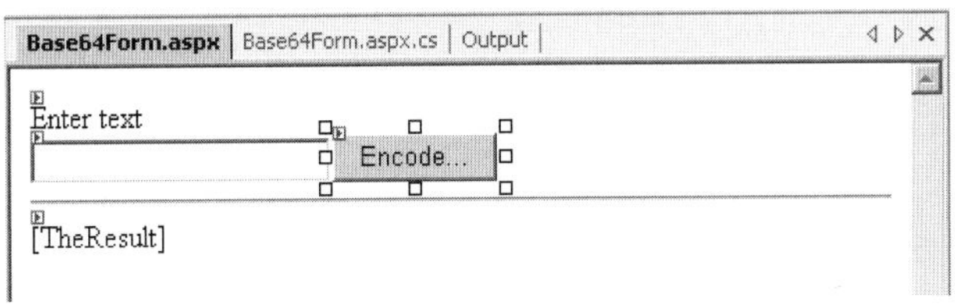

Figure 1-10 A submit button has been added to the page.

```
<form id="Form1" method="post" runat="server">
    <asp:Label id="Label1" runat="server">Enter text</asp:Label><br>
    <asp:TextBox id="TheText" runat="server"></asp:TextBox>
    <asp:Button id="DoIt" runat="server" Text="Encode..." />
    <hr>
    <asp:Label id="TheResult" runat="server" />
</form>
```

The simplest way to add some code to the button's click event is by double-clicking the button in the Web Forms editor. Visual Studio changes the view and then prompts you with some C# code—the code-behind class:

```
public class WebForm1 : System.Web.UI.Page
{
    protected System.Web.UI.WebControls.Label Label1;
    protected System.Web.UI.WebControls.Button DoIt;
    protected System.Web.UI.WebControls.Label TheResult;
    protected System.Web.UI.WebControls.TextBox TheText;

    private void Page_Load(object sender, EventArgs e)
    {
        // Put user code to initialize the page here
```

```
    }

    override protected void OnInit(EventArgs e)
    {
        InitializeComponent();
        base.OnInit(e);
    }

    private void InitializeComponent()
    {
        this.DoIt.Click += new System.EventHandler(this.DoIt_Click);
        this.Load += new System.EventHandler(this.Page_Load);
    }
    private void DoIt_Click(object sender, System.EventArgs e)
    {
        // Execute when the button is clicked...
    }
}
```

Interestingly, the link between the button-click event and the code is established directly in the code-behind class. The class method *DoIt_Click* runs when the user clicks the button. The same link can be established in the .aspx code through the *OnClick* attribute of the *<asp:Button>* element.

```
<asp:Button id="DoIt" runat="server" Text="Encode..."
    onclick="DoIt_Click" />
```

As you can see, though, this approach is much less neat and elegant because it violates the principle of separation between the code and the layout of the page.

At this point, let's complete the example by adding some significant code to the button handler. The idea is to take the text written in the text box, encode it as a Base64 string, and display it. The following code shows how we fill the *DoIt_Click* method:

```
private void DoIt_Click(object sender, EventArgs e)
{
    string buf = TheText.Text;
    TheResult.Text = ConvertToBase64String(buf);
}

private string ConvertToBase64String(string input)
{
    byte[] info = Encoding.Unicode.GetBytes(input);

    // Convert the binary input into Base64 UUEncoded output.
    // Each 3 byte sequence in the source data becomes a 4 byte
    // sequence in the character array.
    long dataLength = (long) ((4.0d/3.0d) * info.Length);

    // If length is not divisible by 4, go up to the next multiple of 4.
```

```
    if(dataLength % 4 != 0)
        dataLength += 4 - dataLength % 4;

    // Allocate the output buffer
    char[] base64CharArray = new char[dataLength];

    // Converting...
    Convert.ToBase64CharArray(info, 0, info.Length, base64CharArray, 0);

    // Display the converted data
    return new string(base64CharArray);
}
```

The core code of the *ConvertToBase64String* method has been borrowed from the MSDN documentation. To use the *Encoding* class, you must import the *System.Text* namespace. Figure 1-11 shows the page in action.

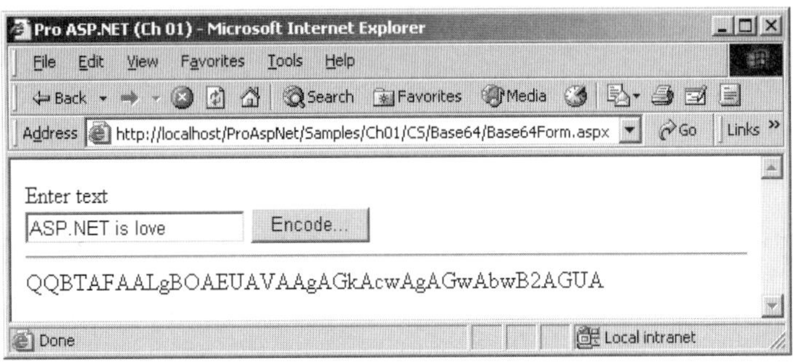

Figure 1-11 ASP.NET is love...even if encoded as Base64.

Building and Debugging

To build and run the ASP.NET application, you simply click the Start button and wait for something—typically an Internet Explorer window—to pop up. Visual Studio .NET compiles all the classes in the project into an assembly and gives it the name of the project. The assembly is created in the Bin subdirectory of the source virtual directory. The Bin subdirectory is specifically created during the setup of the project. The Bin directory of a virtual directory is the principal location in which ASP.NET attempts to locate the assemblies needed to run a page.

> **Note** If you run a manually created page from within the root of your Web server—typically the \inetpub\wwwroot directory—you should put any needed assemblies in the \inetpub\wwwroot\bin subdirectory. In most cases, this directory does not exist and will have to be created manually.

Once the project assembly has been successfully built, Visual Studio .NET auto-attaches to the ASP.NET run-time process—aspnet_wp.exe—for debugging purposes. Next, it opens the start page of the application, causing the browser to issue a page request to the ASP.NET runtime. Once the runtime has loaded all the assemblies and processed the page source, the browser appears with the final HTML output. As long as you compiled the project in debug mode (the default), you can set a few breakpoints in the page class source and step into the code, as shown in Figure 1-12.

```
// ********************************************************************
// Execute the actual Base64 string encoding
private string ConvertToBase64String(string input)
{
    byte[] info = Encoding.Unicode.GetBytes(input);

    // Convert the binary input into Base64 UUEncoded output.
    // Each 3 byte sequence in the source data becomes a 4 byte
    // sequence in the character array.
    long dataLength = (long) ((4.0d/3.0d) * info.Length);

    // If length is not divisible by 4, go up to the next multiple of 4.
    if(dataLength % 4 != 0)
        dataLength += 4 - dataLength % 4;
```

Figure 1-12 Stepping into the code of the page using the Visual Studio .NET integrated debugger.

> **Note** Many practical reasons justify the Visual Studio .NET choice of implementing a full object-oriented approach to Web Forms application development. Even more than design considerations about code and layout separation was the need to support step-by-step debugging, syntax-coloring, and RAD features while maintaining a uniform, consistent, and cross-project approach to development. In this context, having a class behind each page is a wise and timely choice.
>
> This said, if you've been a former brave-heart Win32 SDK programmer, bear in mind that a Visual Studio–generated ASP.NET page is to an ordinary ASP.NET page roughly what an MFC application is to an SDK-based Win32 application.

Deploying the Application

Of all the files that form a Visual Studio .NET project, only a few are actually needed to run the application on a production server. For example, you don't need any of the .cs files. For the sample project, only the following files need to be deployed: base64form.aspx, global.asax, web.config, and base64.vsdisco, as well as the project's assembly. Consider also that global.asax, web.config, and base64.vsdisco are optional files, which means that by using them you can better configure the application. However, choosing not to use them does not affect the functionality of the application.

Deploying a Web application is a two-step operation: create and configure the virtual directory, and copy the needed files. Visual Studio .NET makes creating a Web setup application a snap. You just create a new type of project—Web Setup Project—select the files to copy, and build the project. Figure 1-13 shows the user interface of the setup project.

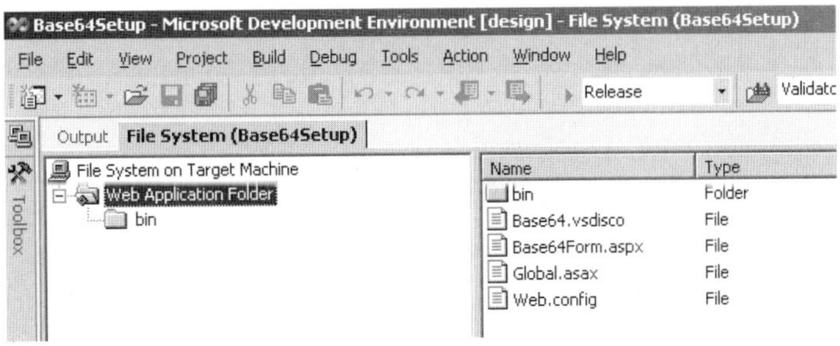

Figure 1-13 Creating a Web setup project.

The Web Application Folder node represents the virtual directory of the new application on the target machine. The property box lets you configure the settings of the new virtual directory. For example, the *AllowDirectoryBrowsing* property lets you assign browsing permission to the IIS virtual directory you will create. You can also control the virtual directory name, application execute permissions, level of isolation, and default page. The Bin subfolder is automatically created, but you can ask the setup to create and populate as many subfolders as you need.

When you build the project, you obtain a Windows Installer .msi file that constitutes the setup to ship to your clients. The default installer supports repairing and uninstalling the application. The setup you obtain in this way—which is the simplest you can get—does not contain the .NET Framework, which must be installed on the target machine or explicitly included in the setup project itself. I'll make more real-world considerations about deployment of ASP.NET applications in Chapter 12.

Multilanguage Projects with Visual Studio .NET

ASP.NET projects created with Visual Studio .NET don't allow you to use multiple languages. In other words, you can't have in the same application .aspx pages that use Visual Basic .NET and .aspx pages that use C#. Note, though, that this is a Visual Studio .NET limitation, not an ASP.NET limitation. To work around the issue, you can write your pages (in any language) without the code-behind feature and import them in the project using the Add Existing Item menu. In this case, though, you have all the page-specific code concentrated in the *<script>* section. In addition, no IntelliSense and syntax-coloring facilities will be provided to edit the *<script>* section.

The *CodeBehind* Attribute in Visual Studio .NET

When you try to add an existing page to a project, Visual Studio .NET proves a bit choosy: it first complains, asks for confirmation, and then looks for a code-behind class for the page. The code-behind class, though, cannot be any source or compiled class that inherits from *Page*. To meet the requirements of Visual Studio .NET, a code-behind class must fulfill a special naming convention and be written in the same language used throughout the project. For example, a page named MyPage.aspx can only have a code-behind class named MyPage.aspx.cs if C# is the project language.

Visual Studio .NET tracks the relationship between the page and the code-behind class through an undocumented *CodeBehind* attribute in the *@Page* directive. The content of the *CodeBehind* attribute cannot be edited from within Visual Studio .NET and, if you edit it with another text editor, you get an error as soon as you reload the page within Visual Studio .NET.

Visual Studio *CodeBehind* vs. ASP.NET *Src*

Visual Studio utilizes the *CodeBehind* attribute only for internal editing purposes. This probably explains why the attribute is not even mentioned in the MSDN documentation. *CodeBehind* is not intended to be used at the application level and, in fact, the ASP.NET runtime just ignores it. Let's consider the following header, typical of an ASP.NET page developed with Visual Studio .NET:

```
<%@ Page Language="c#" Inherits="ProAspNet.MyBasePage"
    CodeBehind="MyBasePage.cs" %>
```

The ASP.NET runtime expects to find the code for the page in a class named *ProAspNet.MyBasePage* located in one of the reachable assemblies. There's no need to have in the page folder the C# file referenced in the *CodeBehind* attribute—that piece of information is used only by the Visual Studio .NET project.

If you want the .aspx page to inherit from a local .cs or .vb file, use the *Src* attribute of the *@Page* directive instead. You should note that, in turn, Visual Studio .NET ignores the *Src* attribute. Using both *Src* and *CodeBehind* in a page does not result in an error, but it's a programming practice I strongly discourage because of the side-effects and confusion it could generate.

> **Tip** If you need to develop the ASP.NET application using different languages, group the various pages in multiple language-homogeneous projects. Next, make all projects share the same virtual directory. To keep all projects within reach all the time, group them in the same Visual Studio .NET solution.

The Web Matrix Editor

Developing code for ASP applications has never been particularly easy in spite of the availability of third-party products and Visual InterDev. A much better lot is reserved for ASP.NET applications, which have a comprehensive and easily usable integrated development environment (IDE) in Visual Studio .NET. Visual Studio .NET, though, is certainly not the only tool available for quickly and effectively building ASP.NET applications. Furthermore, Visual Studio .NET is a full-blown IDE designed to build multiple types of applications, including Windows applications, console applications, Web services, and setup programs. Other commercial products focus more on the building of ASP.NET-specific solutions. One of the most complete products is Macromedia Dreamweaver MX.

ASP.NET Web Matrix is another story. Web Matrix is a community-supported, totally free tool and has been specifically designed for ASP.NET applications. To get it, you simply need a 1.2 MB download from the ASP.NET community Web site. The URL is *http://www.asp.net/webmatrix/download.aspx*. Web Matrix provides most of the features of cutting-edge code editors (such as syntax-coloring, WYSIWYG designers, and different views of the code), and although it has different goals than Visual Studio .NET, in some ways Web Matrix complements it.

Visual Studio .NET vs. Web Matrix

Let's say it up front: Visual Studio .NET is much more powerful than Web Matrix. While Visual Studio .NET is the must-have tool for building complex, professional ASP.NET Web applications, Web Matrix is a more compact, efficient, and made-to-measure tool for those frequent situations in which Visual Studio .NET would be overkill. For example, in a previous comment, I noted that Visual Studio .NET forces you to always use the code-behind approach to develop ASP.NET pages. Visual Studio .NET insists on a project-based approach, which certainly makes a lot of sense for many real-world projects. In contrast, Web Matrix is designed around the standalone ASP.NET page. It supports only pages with inline code and lets you develop applications as a set of standalone pages and resources.

> **Note** Web Matrix was created entirely using .NET technologies! In particular, the team used Windows Forms to set up the user interface and Web services to communicate with the back-end system on *http://www.asp.net*. The code was written in C# and spans about 150,000 lines of code, resulting in an installed base of about 2.5 MB.

What Web Matrix Doesn't Provide

By design, Web Matrix lacks a number of user-interface features that are available in Visual Studio .NET. A short list includes primarily IntelliSense support, statement completion and code tips, debugging support, version source control for multideveloper projects, and almost all class and code designers you find in Visual Studio .NET.

Note also that Web Matrix can be used only to create ASP.NET and mobile applications and Web services. No support is provided for building Windows Forms and Windows NT services and languages other than Visual Basic .NET and C#.

> **Caution** If you make use of classes in your Web Matrix project, bear in mind that, unlike Visual Studio .NET, Web Matrix does not compile your classes in assemblies. To accomplish this, you must resort to the command-line compiler. The following code shows a typical command line for compiling a C# and Visual Basic .NET class:
>
> ```
> csc.exe /r:system.dll myclass.c
> vbc.exe /r:system.dll myclass.vb
> ```
>
> The */r* switch is used to link a needed assembly. You get the above compilers with the .NET Framework installation. They are located in the \Microsoft.NET\Framework\v1.1.4322 directory under the Windows folder. Note that for ASP.NET 1.0, the final directory of the path changes to v1.0.3705.

What Web Matrix Does Provide

As a community-supported product, Web Matrix is rigorously built around the feedback users provide through the *http://www.asp.net/webmatrix* Web site. Given this, it comes as no surprise that the overall user interface presents handy features and facilities you won't find even in Visual Studio .NET.

The page you're editing provides four views—a graphical view of the page, HTML markup, code (the *<script>* section), and the full .aspx file. The

Web Matrix toolbox (shown in Figure 1-14) separates custom controls from standard HTML and Web server controls and provides a couple of extra tabs for code snippets and code builders.

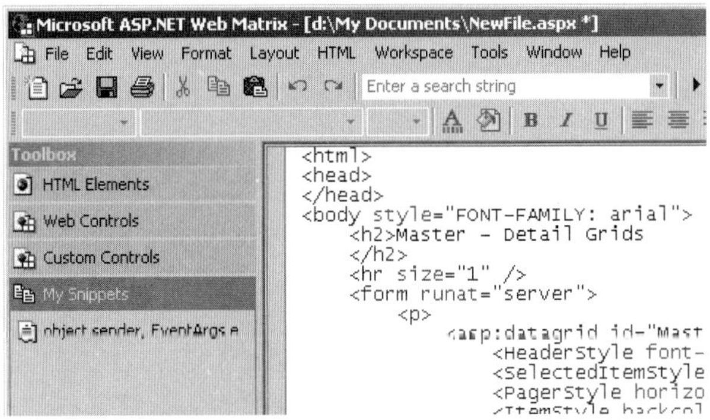

Figure 1-14 The My Snippets tab shows off the toolbox of Web Matrix.

My Snippets is a tab similar to the Visual Studio Clipboard Ring but with a couple of key differences: you can drag and drop text onto it and the snippets are persisted to disk, allowing you to retrieve them the next time Web Matrix starts up. The Code Builders tab appears only when you're in code view mode and provides a list of wizards to build commonplace pieces of code such as database commands or code to send an e-mail.

Another interesting aspect of the Web Matrix user interface is that it provides a lot of predefined templates for commonly used types of pages. Figure 1-15 shows some of them.

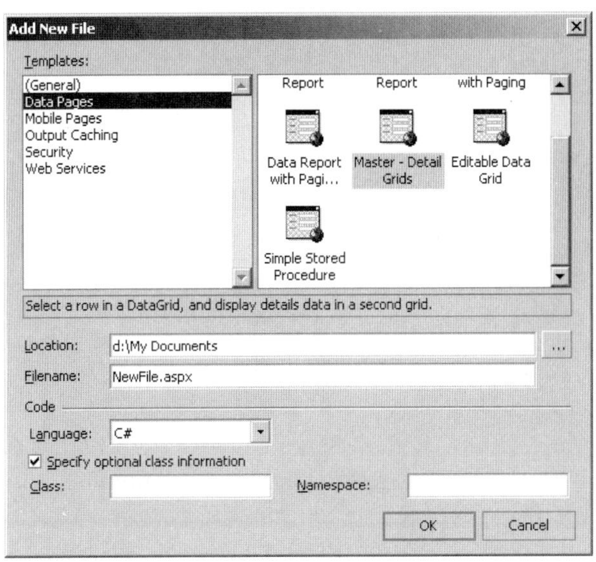

Figure 1-15 Some of the Web Matrix page templates.

As you can see, Web Matrix provides standard pieces of code to implement editable grids, master/detail views, and pageable reports. Other templates provide for login and logout pages, cacheable pages, Web services, SOAP headers, and pages for mobile controls.

As a final note, consider that Web Matrix ships with FTP client support, which means you can develop ASP.NET applications remotely and host them at any provider that offers both ASP.NET and FTP support.

> **Note** Web Matrix does not require IIS on a machine used for development purposes. Web Matrix, in fact, includes its own mini-Web server capable of hosting the ASP.NET runtime locally. (I'll cover this ASP.NET feature in Chapter 24.) This mini-Web server—codenamed Cassini—handles only local requests and does not allow remote connections. Of course, you need IIS running on the production server to deploy ASP.NET applications developed using Web Matrix or any other product.

Help and Community

Web Matrix comes with no compiled help files. All the support you get from the Help menu and Community page comes from the ASP.NET Web site and is gathered through Web services calls. Figure 1-16 shows the page with all the links to documentation, Web sites, forums, and other online resources.

Figure 1-16 The Community tab with links to online resources.

Web Matrix also distributes a class browser with direct links to the Web or local documentation. In terms of information retrieval, the class browser can be as useful as the official .NET Framework documentation, but it provides a class-based view of the information. To display the class browser, double-click a class in the Classes window. Figure 1-17 shows the class browser.

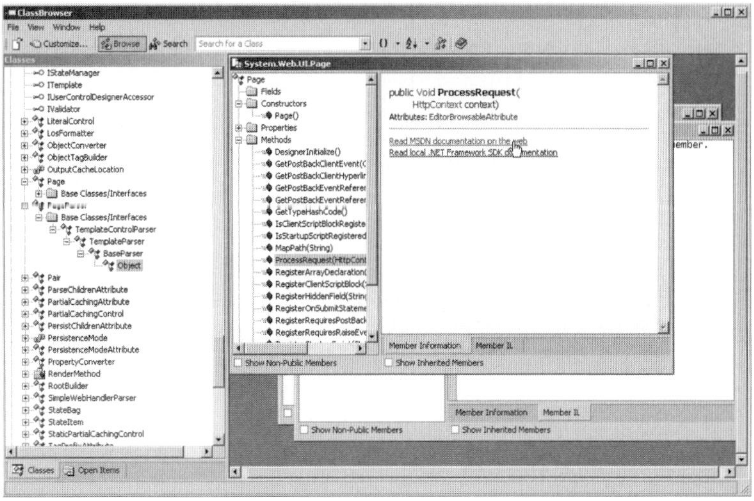

Figure 1-17 The Web Matrix class browser in action.

Conclusion

In this chapter, we discussed the Web Forms model of ASP.NET as a new and, in many aspects, revolutionary approach to Web programming. As part of the .NET Framework and therefore designed completely from scratch, ASP.NET is perceived as the inevitable successor to ASP. It is a Web development platform that more than one million developers have chosen over the past few years.

The programmer affinity for ASP and ASP.NET and compatibility between the two platforms is only part of the success of the approach. The key aspect of ASP.NET is that it is part of the .NET Framework. As such, it allows you to take full advantage of features of the common-language runtime, such as type safety, inheritance, language interoperability, and versioning. We analyzed the component model of ASP.NET and reviewed the main differences between ASP and ASP.NET you should take into account if you have an existing ASP application to upgrade or maintain. Visual Studio .NET is probably the most feature-rich and professional tool to employ for building ASP.NET applications. Web Matrix is a free ASP.NET-specific development tool with unique and handy features.

ASP.NET promotes a programming model that, although built on top of the stateless HTTP protocol, appears to be stateful and event-driven to programmers. The abstraction layer that performs the magic is the Web Forms model, whose underpinnings will be tackled and unveiled in the next chapter.

Resources

- ASP.NET: Web Forms Let You Drag and Drop Your Way to Powerful Web Apps (*http://msdn.microsoft.com/msdnmag/issues/01/05/webforms*)
- How to Share Session State Between Classic ASP and ASP.NET (*http://msdn.microsoft.com/library/en-us/dnaspp/html/converttoaspnet.asp*)
- NET Migration Case Study: Using ASP.NET to Build the beta.visualstudio.net Web Site (*http://msdn.microsoft.com/msdnmag/issues/01/09/migration*)
- Migrating to ASP.NET: Key Considerations (*http://msdn.microsoft.com/library/en-us/dnaspp/html/aspnetmigrissues.asp*)
- *Debugging Applications for Microsoft .NET and Microsoft Windows*, by John Robbins (Microsoft Press, 2003)

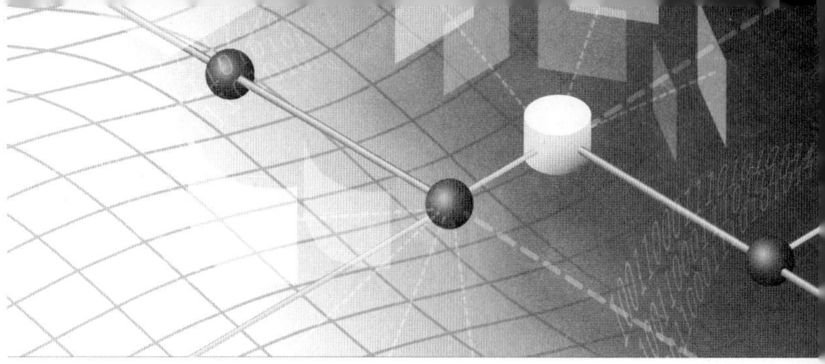

2

Web Forms Internals

Few things are harder to put up with than the annoyance of a good example.
—Mark Twain

ASP.NET pages are dynamically compiled on demand when first required in the context of a Web application. Dynamic compilation is not specific to ASP.NET pages (.aspx files); it also occurs with Web Services (.asmx files), Web user controls (.ascx files), HTTP handlers (.ashx files), and ASP.NET application files such as the global.asax file. But what does it mean exactly that an ASP.NET page is compiled? How does the ASP.NET runtime turn the source code of an .aspx file into a .NET Framework compilable class? And what becomes of the dynamically created assembly when the associated source file gets updated? And finally, what happens once a compiled assembly has been associated with the requested .aspx URL?

Don't be too surprised to find all these questions crowding your mind at this time. Their presence indicates you're on the right track and ready to learn more about the underpinnings of the Web Forms programming model.

Executing ASP.NET Pages

The expression *compiled page* is at once precise as well as vague and generic. It is *precise* because it tells you exactly what happens when a URL with an .aspx extension is requested. It is *vague* because it doesn't specify which module launches and controls the compiler and what actual input the compiler receives on the command line. Finally, it is *generic* because it omits a fair number of details.

In this chapter, we simply aim to unveil all the mysteries fluttering around the dynamic compilation of ASP.NET pages. We'll do this by considering the actions performed on the Web server, and which modules perform them, when a request arrives for an .aspx page.

> **Note** Much of the content of this chapter is based on the behavior of the ASP.NET runtime version 1.0 and version 1.1 with Internet Information Services (IIS) 5.0 serving as the Web server. Some key differences apply when using Windows Server 2003 and IIS 6.0. Any significant differences that affect the ASP.NET way of working are noted. Throughout this chapter, IIS is always IIS 5.0 unless another version is explicitly mentioned.
>
> The first part of this chapter discusses under-the-hood details that might not interest you, as they aren't strictly concerned with the development of ASP.NET applications. Reading this chapter in its entirety is not essential to understanding fundamental techniques of ASP.NET programming. So, if you want, you can jump directly to the "The Event Model" section, which is the section in which we discuss what happens once an ASP.NET page has been requested and starts being processed.

The IIS Resource Mappings

All resources you can access on an IIS-based Web server are grouped by their file extension. Any incoming request is then assigned to a particular run-time module for actual processing. Modules that can handle Web resources within the context of IIS are ISAPI extensions—that is, plain-old Win32 DLLs that expose, much like an interface, a bunch of API functions with predefined names and prototypes. IIS and ISAPI extensions use these DLL entries as a sort of private communication protocol. When IIS needs an ISAPI extension to accomplish a certain task, it simply loads the DLL and calls the appropriate function with valid arguments. Although the ISAPI documentation doesn't mention an ISAPI extension as an interface, it is just that—a module that implements a well-known programming interface.

When the request for a resource arrives, IIS first verifies the type of the resource. Static resources such as images, text files, HTML pages, and scriptless ASP pages are resolved directly by IIS without the involvement of external modules. IIS accesses the file on the local Web server and flushes its contents to the output console so that the requesting browser can get it. Resources that require server-side elaboration are passed on to the registered module. For example, ASP pages are processed by an ISAPI extension named asp.dll. In general, when the resource is associated with executable code, IIS hands the request to that executable for further processing. Files with an .aspx extension are assigned to an ISAPI extension named aspnet_isapi.dll, as shown in Figure 2-1.

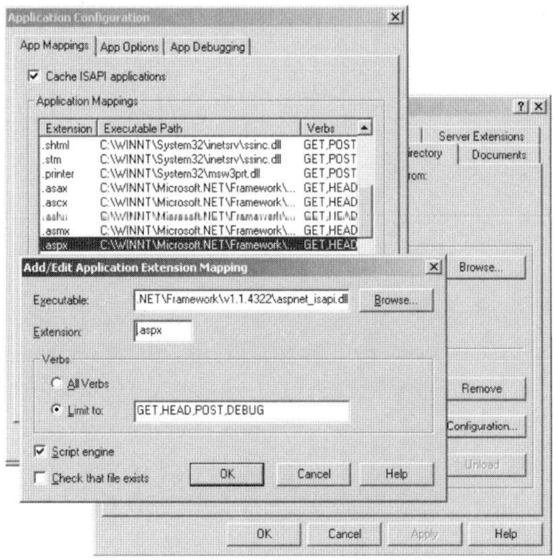

Figure 2-1 The IIS application mappings for resources with an .aspx extension.

Just like any other ISAPI extension, aspnet_isapi.dll is hosted by the IIS 5.0 process—the executable named inetinfo.exe. Resource mappings are stored in the IIS metabase. Upon installation, ASP.NET modifies the IIS metabase to make sure that aspnet_isapi.dll can handle all the resources identified by the extensions listed in Table 2-1.

Table 2-1 IIS Application Mappings for aspnet_isapi.dll

Extension	Resource Type
.asax	ASP.NET application files. The typical example is global.asax.
.ascx	Web user control files used to embed pagelets in ASP.NET pages.
.ashx	HTTP handlers, namely managed modules that interact with the low-level request and response services of IIS. (See Chapter 23.)
.asmx	Files that implement XML Web services.
.aspx	Files that represent ASP.NET pages.

(continued)

Table 2-1 IIS Application Mappings for aspnet_isapi.dll *(continued)*

Extension	Resource Type
.axd	Extension that identifies the ASP.NET trace-viewer application (trace.axd). When invoked in a virtual folder, the trace viewer displays trace information for every page in the application. (See Chapter 4.)
.rem	Fake resource used to qualify the Uniform Resource Identifier (URI) of a .NET Remoting object hosted by IIS.
.soap	Same as .rem.

In addition, the aspnet_isapi.dll extension handles other typical Microsoft Visual Studio .NET extensions such as .cs, .csproj, .vb, .vbproj, .licx, .config, .resx, .webinfo, and .vsdisco. Other extensions added with Visual Studio .NET 2003 for J# projects are .java, .jsl, .resources, .vjsproj.

The ASP.NET ISAPI extension doesn't process the .aspx file but acts as a dispatcher. It collects all the information available about the invoked URL and the underlying resource, and it routes the request toward another distinct process—the ASP.NET worker process.

The ASP.NET Worker Process

The ASP.NET worker process represents the ASP.NET runtime environment. It consists of a Win32 unmanaged executable named aspnet_wp.exe, which hosts the .NET common language runtime (CLR). This process is the executable you need to attach to in order to debug ASP.NET applications. The ASP.NET worker process activates the HTTP pipeline that will actually process the page request. The HTTP pipeline is a collection of .NET Framework classes that take care of compiling the page assembly and instantiating the related page class.

The connection between aspnet_isapi.dll and aspnet_wp.exe is established through a *named pipe*—a Win32 mechanism for transferring data over process boundaries. As the name suggests, a named pipe works like a pipe: you enter data in one end, and the same data comes out the other end. Pipes can be established both to connect local processes and processes running on remote machines. Figure 2-2 illustrates the ASP.NET layer built on top of IIS.

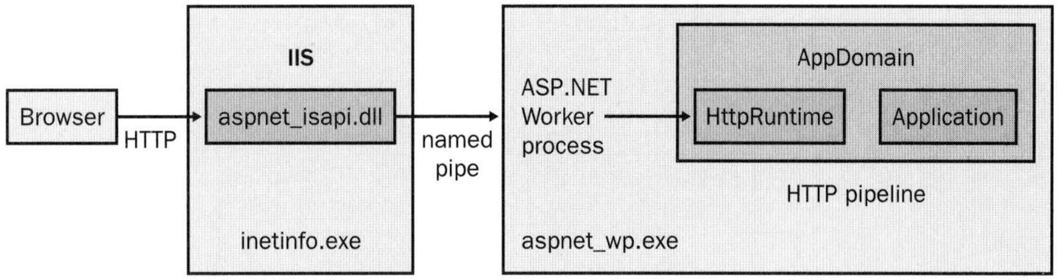

Figure 2-2 IIS receives page requests and forwards them to the ASP.NET runtime.

How the ASP.NET Runtime Works

A single copy of the worker process runs all the time and hosts all the active Web applications. The only exception to this situation is when you have a Web server with multiple CPUs. In this case, you can configure the ASP.NET runtime so that multiple worker processes run, one for each available CPU. A model in which multiple processes run on multiple CPUs in a single server machine is known as a *Web garden* and is controlled by attributes on the *<processModel>* section in the machine.config file. (I'll cover ASP.NET configuration files in Chapter 12.)

When a single worker process is used by all CPUs and controls all Web applications, it doesn't necessarily mean that no process isolation is achieved. Each Web application is, in fact, identified with its virtual directory and belongs to a distinct application domain, commonly referred to as an AppDomain. A new AppDomain is created within the ASP.NET worker process whenever a client addresses a virtual directory for the first time. After creating the new AppDomain, the ASP.NET runtime loads all the needed assemblies and passes control to the HTTP pipeline to actually service the request.

If a client requests a page from an already running Web application, the ASP.NET runtime simply forwards the request to the existing AppDomain associated with that virtual directory. All the assemblies needed to process the page are now ready to use because they were compiled upon the first call. Figure 2-3 provides a more general view of the ASP.NET runtime.

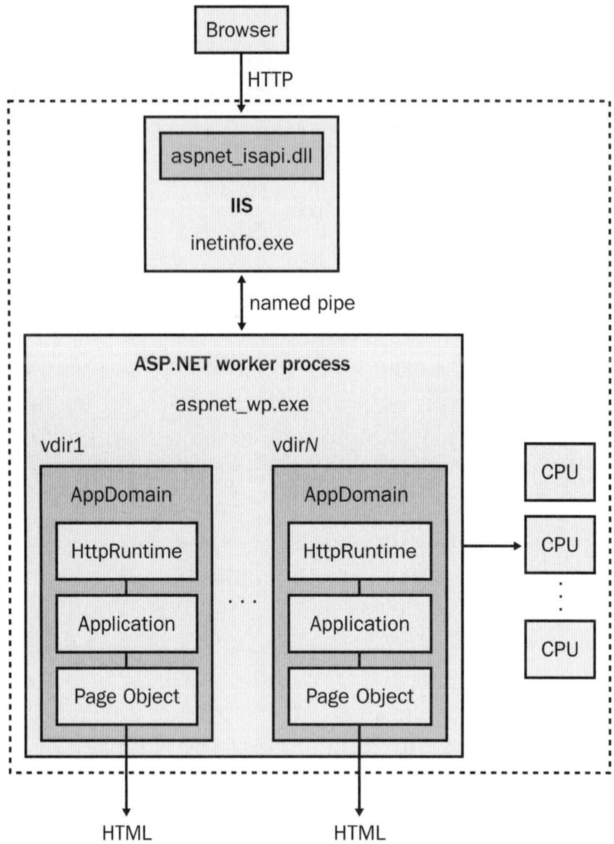

Figure 2-3 The ASP.NET runtime and the various AppDomains.

> **Tip** To configure the ASP.NET runtime to work as a Web garden—that is, to have more worker processes running on multiple CPUs in the same physical server—open the machine.config file and locate the *<processModel>* section. Next, you set the *webGarden* attribute to *true* (because it is *false* by default) and the *cpuMask* attribute to a bit mask in which each 1 identifies an available and affined CPU. If ASP.NET is running with IIS 6.0, you must use the IIS Manager to configure Web gardens. In this case, the settings in machine.config are ignored. If *webGarden* is *false*, the *cpuMask* setting is ignored and only one process is scheduled regardless of how many CPUs you have.
>
> *Note that the documentation available with version 1.0 of the .NET Framework is a bit confusing on this point. Documentation in version 1.1 is clear and correct.*

Processes, AppDomains, and Threads

In .NET, executable code must be loaded into the CLR to be *managed* while running. To manage the application's code, the CLR must first obtain a pointer to an AppDomain. AppDomains are separate units of processing that the CLR recognizes in a running process. All .NET processes run at least one AppDomain—known as the default AppDomain—that gets created during the CLR initialization. An application can have additional AppDomains. Each AppDomain is independently configured and given personal settings, such as security settings, reference paths, and configuration files.

AppDomains are separated and isolated from one another in a way that resembles process separation in Win32. The CLR enforces isolation by preventing direct calls between objects living in different AppDomains. From the CPU perspective, AppDomains are much more lightweight than Win32 processes. The certainty that AppDomains run type-safe code allows the CLR to provide a level of isolation that's as strong as the process boundaries but more cost effective. Type-safe code cannot cause memory faults, which in Win32 were one of the reasons to have a physical separation between process-memory contexts. An AppDomain is a logical process and, as such, is more lightweight than a true process.

Managed code running in an AppDomain is carried out by a particular thread. However, threads and AppDomains are orthogonal entities in the sense that you can have several threads active during the execution of the AppDomain code, but a single thread is in no way tied to run only within the context of a given AppDomain.

The .NET Remoting API is as a tailor-made set of system services for accessing an object in an external AppDomain.

Process Recycling

The behavior and performance of the ASP.NET worker process is constantly monitored to catch any form of decay as soon as possible. Parameters used to evaluate the performance include the number of requests served and queued, the total life of the process, and the percentage of physical memory (60% by default) it can use.

The *<processModel>* element of the machine.config file defines threshold values for all these parameters. The aspnet_isapi.dll checks the overall state of the current worker process before forwarding any request to it. If the process breaks one of these measures of good performance, a new worker process is started to serve the next request. The old process continues running as long as there are requests pending in its own queue. After that, when it ceases to be invoked, it goes into idle mode and is then shut down.

This automatic scavenging mechanism is known as *process recycling* and is one of the aspects that improve the overall robustness and efficiency of the ASP.NET platform. In this way, in fact, memory leaks and run-time anomalies are promptly detected and overcome.

Process Recycling in IIS 6.0

Process recycling is also a built-in feature of IIS 6.0 that all types of Web applications, including ASP.NET and ASP applications, automatically take advantage of. More often than not and in spite of the best efforts to properly build them, Web applications leak memory, are poorly coded, or have other run-time problems. For this reason, administrators will periodically encounter situations that necessitate rebooting or restarting a Web server.

Up to the release of IIS 6.0, restarting a Web site required interrupting the entire Web server. In IIS 6.0, all user code is handled by worker processes, which are completely isolated from the core Web server. Worker processes are periodically recycled according to the number of requests they served, the memory occupied, and the time elapsed since activation. Worker processes are also automatically shut down if they appear to hang or respond too slowly. An ad hoc module in IIS 6.0 takes care of replacing faulty processes with fresh new ones.

> **Note** In IIS 6.0, you'll find many design and implementation features of ASP.NET that are enhanced and extended to all resources. Historically, Microsoft was originally developing IIS 6.0 and ASP.NET together. Microsoft split them into separate projects when a decision was made to ship an initial version of ASP.NET prior to shipping IIS with a new version of Windows. ASP.NET clearly needed to support older versions of IIS, so a parallel IIS 5.0 model for ASP.NET was also built. In that sense, the ASP.NET model for IIS 5.0 matured much more quickly and inspired a lot of features in the newest IIS 6.0 model. As a significantly different product, IIS 6.0 takes the essence of the ASP.NET innovations and re-architects them in a wider and more general context. As a result, specific features of ASP.NET (for example, output caching and process recycling) become features of the whole Web server infrastructure with IIS 6.0. Those features are available to all Web applications hosted by IIS 6.0, including ASP.NET applications. ASP.NET is designed to detect the version of IIS and adjust its way of working.

Configuring the ASP.NET Worker Process

The aspnet_isapi module controls the behavior of the ASP.NET worker process through a few parameters. Table 2-2 details the information that gets passed between the ASP.NET ISAPI extension and the ASP.NET worker process.

Table 2-2 Parameters of the ASP.NET Process

Parameter	Description
IIS-Process-ID	The process ID number of the parent IIS process.
This-Process-Unique-ID	A unique process ID used to identify the worker process in a Web garden configuration.
Number-of-Sync-Pipes	Number of pipes to listen to for information.
RPC_C_AUTHN_LEVEL_XXX	Indicates the required level of authentication for DCOM security. Default is *Connect*.
RPC_C_IMP_LEVEL_XXX	Indicates the authentication level required for COM security. Default is *Impersonate*.
CPU-Mask	Bit mask indicating which CPUs are available for ASP.NET processes if the run time is configured to work as a Web garden.
Max-Worker-Threads	Maximum number of worker threads per CPU in the thread pool.
Max-IO-Threads	Maximum number of IO threads per CPU in the thread pool.

Default values for the arguments in Table 2-2 can be set by editing the attributes of the *<processModel>* section in the machine.config file. (I'll cover the machine.config file in more detail in Chapter 12.)

These parameters instruct the process how to perform tasks that need to happen before the CLR is loaded. Setting COM security is just one such task, and that's why authentication-level values need to be passed to the ASP.NET worker process. What does ASP.NET have to do with COM security? Well, the CLR is actually exposed as a COM object. (Note that the CLR itself is not made of COM code, but the interface to the CLR is a COM object.)

Other parameters are the information needed to hook up the named pipes between the ISAPI extension and the worker process. The names for the pipes are generated randomly and have to be communicated. The worker process retrieves the names of the pipes by using the parent process ID (that is, the IIS process) and the number of pipes created.

> **Note** All the system information needed to set up the ASP.NET worker process (that is, the contents of the machine.config file) is read by the aspnet_isapi.dll unmanaged code prior to spawning any instance of the worker process.

About the Web Garden Model

The *This-Process-Unique-ID* parameter is associated with Web garden support. When multiple worker processes are used in a Web garden scenario, the aspnet_isapi.dll needs to know which process it's dealing with. Any HTTP request posted to the pipe must address a precise target process, and this information must be written into the packet sent through the pipe. The typical way of identifying a process is by means of its process ID.

Unfortunately, though, aspnet_isapi.dll can't know the actual ID of the worker process being spawned because the ID won't be determined until the kernel is done with the *CreateProcess* API function. The following pseudocode demonstrates that the *[process_id]* argument of aspnet_wp.exe can't be the process ID of the same process being created!

```
// aspnet_isapi.dll uses this code to create a worker process
CreateProcess("aspnet_wp.exe", "[iis_id] [process_id] ...", ...);
```

For this reason, aspnet_isapi.dll generates a unique but fake process ID and uses that ID to uniquely identify each worker process running on a multiprocessor machine configured as a Web garden. In this way, the call we just saw is rewritten as follows:

```
// [This-Process-Unique-ID] is a unique GUID
// generated by aspnet_isapi.dll
CreateProcess("aspnet_wp.exe", "[iis_id] [This-Process-Unique-ID] ...", ...);
```

The worker process caches the *This-Process-Unique-ID* argument and uses it to recognize which named-pipe messages it has to serve.

ASP.NET and the IIS 6.0 Process Model

IIS 6.0, which ships as a part of Windows Server 2003, implements its HTTP listener as a kernel-level module. As a result, all incoming requests are first managed by such a driver—http.sys—and in kernel mode. No third-party code ever interacts with the listener, and no user-mode crashes will ever affect the stability of IIS. The http.sys driver listens for requests and posts them to the request queue of the appropriate *application pool*. An application pool is a blanket term that identifies a worker process and a virtual directory. A module, known as the Web Administration Service (WAS), reads from the IIS metabase and instructs the http.sys driver to create as many request queues as there are application pools registered in the metabase.

So when a request arrives, the driver looks at the URL and queues the request to the corresponding application pool. The WAS is responsible for creating and administering the worker processes for the various pools. The IIS worker process is an executable named w3wp.exe, whose main purpose is extracting HTTP requests from the kernel-mode queue. The worker process hosts a core application handler DLL to actually process the request and load ISAPI extensions and filters as appropriate.

Looking at the diagram of ASP.NET applications in Figure 2-4, you can see the IIS 6.0 process model eliminates the need for aspnet_wp.exe. The w3wp.exe loads the aspnet_isapi.dll, and in turn, the ISAPI extension loads the CLR in the worker process and launches the pipeline. With IIS 6.0, ASP.NET is managed by IIS and no longer concerns itself with things like process recycling, Web gardening, and isolation from the Web server.

(continued)

ASP.NET and the IIS 6.0 Process Model (continued)

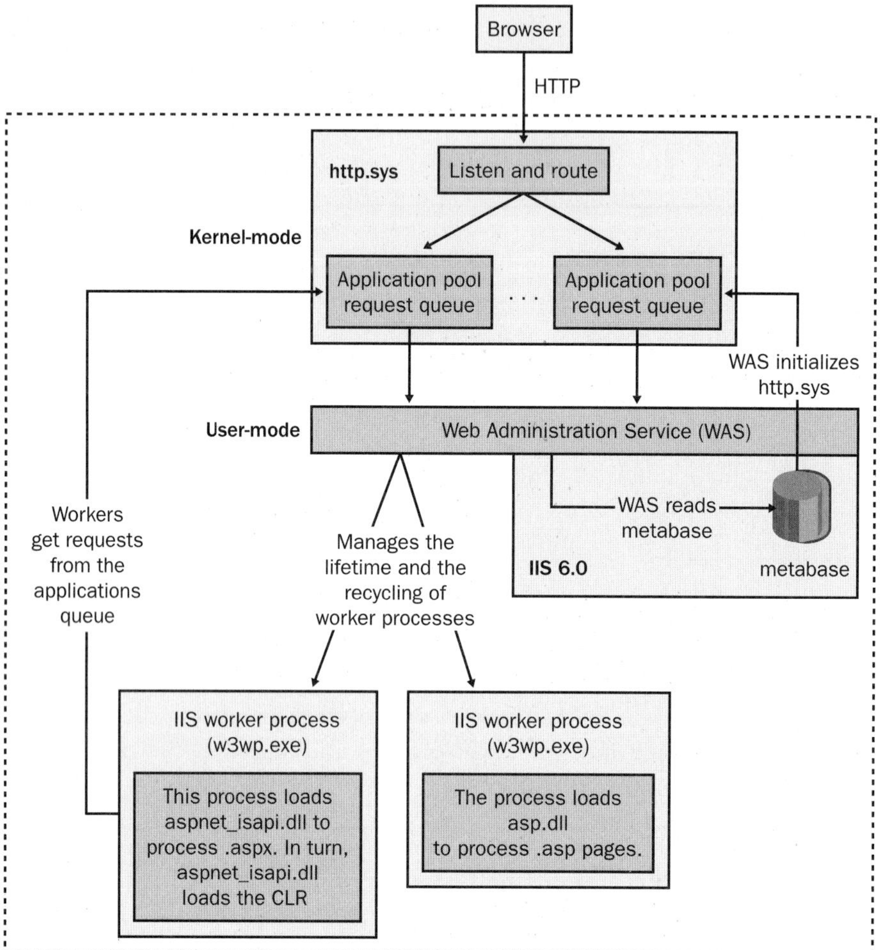

Figure 2-4 How Web applications are processed in IIS 6.0.

In summary, in the IIS 6.0 process model, ASP.NET runs even faster because no interprocess communication between inetinfo.exe (the IIS executable) and aspnet_wp.exe is required. The HTTP request arrives directly at the worker process that hosts the CLR. Furthermore, the ASP.NET worker process is not a special process but simply a copy of the IIS worker process. This fact shifts to IIS the burden of process recycling and health checks.

ASP.NET and the IIS 6.0 Process Model

In IIS 6.0, ASP.NET ignores the contents of the *<processModel>* section from the machine.config file. Only thread and deadlock settings are read from that section of the machine.config. Everything else goes through the metabase and can be configured only by using the IIS Manager. (Other configuration information continues being read from .config files.)

The ASP.NET HTTP Pipeline

The ASP.NET worker process is responsible for running the Web application that lives behind the requested URL. It passes any incoming HTTP requests to the so-called HTTP pipeline—that is, the fully extensible chain of managed objects that works according to the classic concept of a pipeline. Unlike ASP pages, ASP.NET pages are not simply parsed and served to the user. While serving pages is the ultimate goal of ASP.NET, the way in which the resultant HTML code is generated is much more sophisticated than in ASP and involves many more objects.

A page request passes through a pipeline of objects that process the HTTP content and, at the end of the chain, produce some HTML code for the browser. The entry point in this pipeline is the *HttpRuntime* class. The ASP.NET runtime activates the HTTP pipeline by creating a new instance of the *HttpRuntime* class and then calling the method *ProcessRequest*.

The *HttpRuntime* Object

Upon creation, the *HttpRuntime* object initializes a number of internal objects that will help carry out the page request. Helper objects include the cache manager and the file system monitor used to detect changes in the files that form the application.

When the *ProcessRequest* method is called, the *HttpRuntime* object starts working to serve a page to the browser. It creates a new context for the request and initializes a specialized text writer object in which the HTML code will be accumulated. A context is given by an instance of the *HttpContext* class, which encapsulates all HTTP-specific information about the request. The text writer is an instance of the *HttpWriter* class and is the object that actually buffers text sent out through the *Response* object.

After that, the *HttpRuntime* object uses the context information to either locate or create a Web application object capable of handling the request. A Web application is searched using the virtual directory information contained in the URL. The object used to find or create a new Web application is *HttpApplicationFactory*—an internal-use object responsible for returning a valid object capable of handling the request.

The Application Factory

During the lifetime of the application, the *HttpApplicationFactory* object maintains a pool of *HttpApplication* objects to serve incoming HTTP requests. When invoked, the application factory object verifies that an AppDomain exists for the virtual folder the request targets. If the application is already running, the factory picks an *HttpApplication* out of the pool of available objects and passes it the request. A new *HttpApplication* object is created if an existing object is not available.

If the virtual folder has not yet been called, a new *HttpApplication* object for the virtual folder is created in a new AppDomain. In this case, the creation of an *HttpApplication* object entails the compilation of the global.asax application file, if any is present, and the creation of the assembly that represents the actual page requested. An *HttpApplication* object is used to process a single page request at a time; multiple objects are used to serve simultaneous requests for the same page.

> **Note** ASP.NET global.asax files are dynamically compiled the first time any page or Web service is requested in the virtual directory. This happens even before the target page or Web service is compiled. ASP.NET pages and Web services within that Web application are subsequently linked to the resulting global.asax compiled class when they are in turn compiled.

The *HttpApplication* Object

HttpApplication is a global.asax-derived object that the ASP.NET worker process uses to handle HTTP requests that hit a particular virtual directory. A particular *HttpApplication* instance is responsible for managing the entire lifetime of the request it is assigned to, and the instance of *HttpApplication* can be reused only after the request has been completed. The *HttpApplication* class defines the methods, properties, and events common to all application objects—.aspx pages, user controls, Web services, and HTTP handlers—within an ASP.NET application.

The *HttpApplication* maintains a list of HTTP module objects that can filter and even modify the content of the request. Registered modules are called during various moments of the elaboration as the request passes through the pipeline.

HTTP modules represent the managed counterpart of ISAPI filters and will be covered in greater detail in Chapter 23.

The *HttpApplication* object determines the type of object that represents the resource being requested—typically, an ASP.NET page. It then uses a handler factory object to either instantiate the type from an existing assembly or dynamically create the assembly and then an instance of the type. A handler factory object is a class that implements the *IHttpHandlerFactory* interface and is responsible for returning an instance of a managed class that can handle the HTTP request—an HTTP handler. An ASP.NET page is simply a handler object—that is, an instance of a class that implements the *IHttpHandler* interface.

> **Caution** Although the name sounds vaguely evocative of the intrinsic ASP *Application* object, the ASP.NET *HttpApplication* has nothing to do with it. The ASP *Application* object is fully supported in ASP.NET, but it maps to an object of type *HttpApplicationState*. However, the *HttpApplication* object has a property named *Application*, which returns just the ASP.NET counterpart of the ASP intrinsic application-state object.

The Handler Factory

The *HttpApplication* determines the type of object that must handle the request, and it delegates the type-specific handler factory to create an instance of that type. Let's see what happens when the resource requested is a page.

Once the *HttpApplication* object in charge of the request has figured out the proper handler, it creates an instance of the handler factory object. For a request that targets a page, the factory is an undocumented class named *PageHandlerFactory*.

> **Note** The *HttpApplication* object determines the proper handler for the request and creates an instance of that class. To find the appropriate handler, it uses the information in the *<httpHandlers>* section of the machine.config file. The section lists all the currently registered handlers for the application.

The page handler factory is responsible for either finding the assembly that contains the page class or dynamically creating an ad hoc assembly. The *System.Web* namespace defines a few handler factory classes. These are listed in Table 2-3.

Table 2-3 Handler Factory Classes in the .NET Framework

Handler Factory	Type	Description
HttpRemotingHandlerFactory	*.rem; *.soap	Instantiates the object that will take care of a .NET Remoting request routed through IIS. Instantiates an object of type *HttpRemotingHandler*.
PageHandlerFactory	*.aspx	Compiles and instantiates the type that represents the page. The source code for the class is built while parsing the source code of the .aspx file. Instantiates an object of a type that derives from *Page*.
SimpleHandlerFactory	*.ashx	Compiles and instantiates the specified HTTP handler from the source code of the .ashx file. Instantiates an object that implements the *IHttpHandler* interface.
WebServiceHandlerFactory	*.asmx	Compiles the source code of a Web service, and translates the SOAP payload into a method invocation. Instantiates an object of the type specified in the Web service file.

Bear in mind that handler factory objects do not compile the requested resource each time it is invoked. The compiled code is stored in a directory on the Web server and used until the corresponding resource file is modified.

So the page handler factory creates an instance of an object that represents the particular page requested. This object inherits from the *System.Web.UI.Page* class, which in turn implements the *IHttpHandler* interface. The page object is built as an instance of a dynamically generated class based on the source code embedded in the .aspx file. The page object is returned to the application factory, which passes that back to the *HttpRuntime* object. The final step accomplished by the ASP.NET runtime is calling the *ProcessRequest* method on the page object. This call causes the page to execute the user-defined code and generate the HTML text for the browser.

Figure 2-5 illustrates the overall HTTP pipeline architecture.

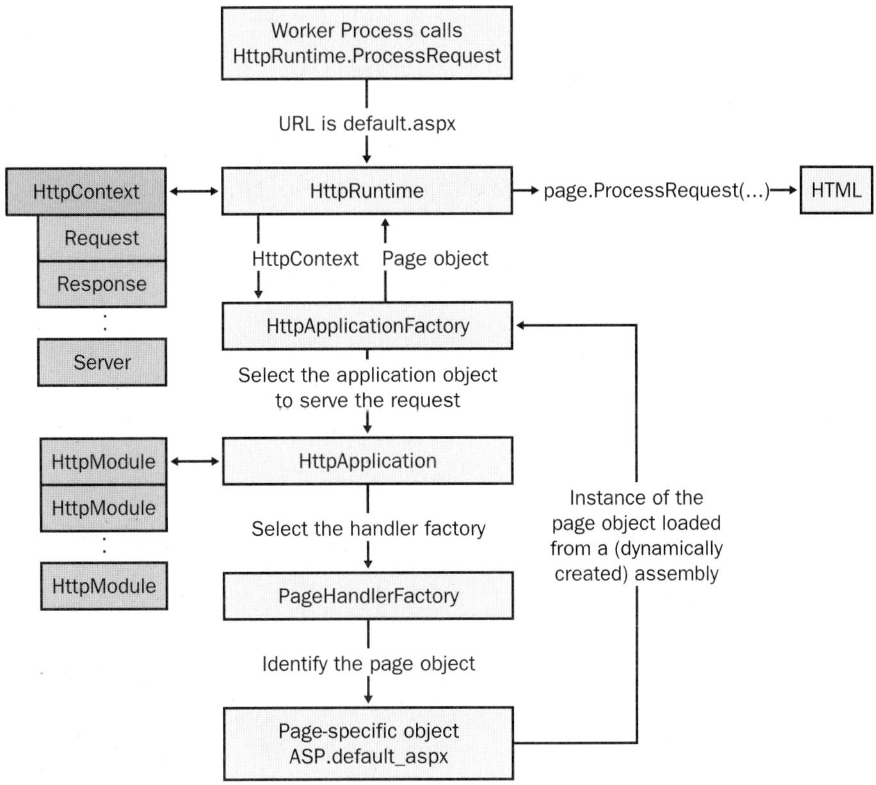

Figure 2-5 The HTTP pipeline processing for a page.

The ASP.NET Page Factory Object

Let's examine in detail how the .aspx page is converted into a class and compiled into an assembly. Generating an assembly for a particular .aspx resource is a two-step process. First, the source code for the class is created by merging the content of the <*script*> section with the code-behind file, if any. Second, the dynamically generated class is compiled into an assembly and cached in a well-known directory.

Locating the Assembly for the Page

Assemblies generated for ASP.NET pages are cached in the Temporary ASP.NET Files folder. The path for version 1.1 of the .NET Framework is as follows.

```
%SystemRoot%\Microsoft.NET\Framework\v1.1.4322\Temporary ASP.NET Files
```

Of course, the directory depends on the version of the .NET Framework you installed. The directory path for version 1.0 of the .NET Framework includes a subdirectory named v1.0.3705. The Temporary ASP.NET Files folder has one child directory for each application ever executed. The name of the subfolder matches the name of the virtual directory of the application. Pages that run from the Web server's root folder are grouped under the Root subfolder.

Page-specific assemblies are cached in a subdirectory placed a couple levels down the virtual directory folder. The names of these child directories are fairly hard to make sense of. Names are the result of a hash algorithm based on some randomized factor along with the application name. A typical path is shown in the following listing. The last two directories (in boldface) have fake but realistic names.

```
\Framework
    \v1.1.4322
        \Temporary ASP.NET Files
            \MyWebApp
                \3678b103
                    \e60405c7
```

Regardless of the actual algorithm implemented to determine the folder names, from within an ASP.NET application the full folder path is retrieved using the following, pretty simple, code:

```
string tempAspNetDir = HttpRuntime.CodegenDir;
```

So much for the location of the dynamic assembly. So how does the ASP.NET runtime determine the assembly name for a particular .aspx page? The assembly folder contains a few XML files with a particular naming convention:

```
[filename].[hashcode].xml
```

If the page is named, say, default.aspx, the corresponding XML file can be named like this:

```
default.aspx.2cf84ad4.xml
```

The XML file is created when the page is compiled. This is the typical content of this XML file:

```
<preserve assem="c5gaxkyh" type="ASP.Default_aspx"
    hash="fffffeda266fd5f7">
    <filedep name="C:\Inetpub\wwwroot\MyWebApp\Default.aspx" />
</preserve>
```

I'll say more about the schema of the file in a moment. For now, it will suffice to look at the *assem* attribute. The attribute value is just the name of the assembly (without extension) created to execute the default.aspx page. Figure 2-6 provides a view of the folder.

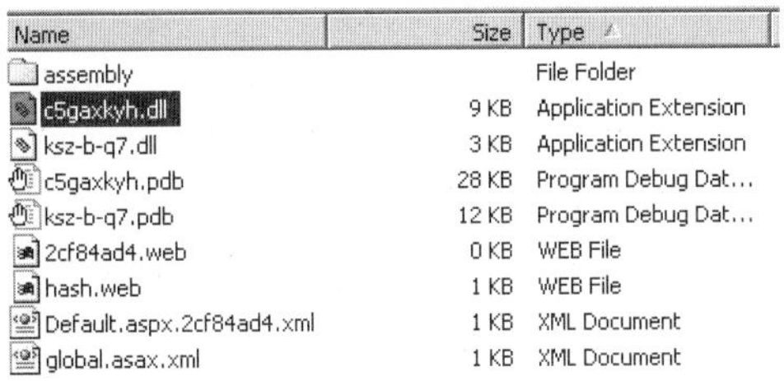

Figure 2-6 Temporary ASP.NET Files: a view of interiors.

The file c5gaxkyh.dll is the assembly that represents the default.aspx page. The other assembly is the compiled version of the global.asax file. (If not specified, a standard global.asax file is used.) The objects defined in these assemblies can be viewed with any class browser tool, including Microsoft IL Disassembler, ILDASM.exe.

> **Important** If the *Debug* attribute of the *@Page* directive is set to *true*, in the same folder as the assembly, you'll also find the source code of the page class. The source code is a Microsoft Visual Basic .NET or C# file according to the value of the *Language* attribute. The name of the source file is *assembly_name.0.ext*, where *assembly_name* denotes the name (without extension) of the assembly and *ext* denotes the language extension. For example, c5gaxkyh.0.cs is the C# source file for default.aspx.

Detecting Page Changes

As mentioned earlier, the dynamically compiled assembly is cached and used to serve any future request for the page. However, changes made to an .aspx file will automatically invalidate the assembly, which will be recompiled to serve the next request. The link between the assembly and the source .aspx file is kept in the XML file we mentioned a bit earlier. Let's recall it:

```
<preserve assem="c5gaxkyh" type="ASP.Default_aspx" hash="fffffeda266fd5f7">
    <filedep name="C:\Inetpub\wwwroot\MyWebApp\Default.aspx" />
</preserve>
```

The *name* attribute of the *<filedep>* node contains just the full path of the file associated with the assembly whose name is stored in the *assem* attribute of the *<preserve>* node. The *type* attribute, on the other hand, contains the name of the class that renders the .aspx file in the assembly. The actual object running when, say, default.aspx is served is an instance of a class named *ASP.Default_aspx*.

Based on the Win32 file notification change system, this ASP.NET feature enables developers to quickly build applications with a minimum of process overhead. Users, in fact, can "just hit Save" to cause code changes to immediately take effect within the application. In addition to this development-oriented benefit, deployment of applications is greatly enhanced by this feature, as you can simply deploy a new version of the page that overwrites the old one.

When a page is changed, it's recompiled as a single assembly, or as part of an existing assembly, and reloaded. ASP.NET ensures that the next user will be served the new page outfit by the new assembly. Current users, on the other hand, will continue viewing the old page served by the old assembly. The two assemblies are given different (because they are randomly generated) names and therefore can happily live side by side in the same folder as well as be loaded in the same AppDomain. Because that was so much fun, let's drill down a little more into this topic.

How ASP.NET Replaces Page Assemblies

When a new assembly is created for a page as the effect of an update, ASP.NET verifies whether the old assembly can be deleted. If the assembly contains only that page class, ASP.NET attempts to delete the assembly. Often, though, it finds the file loaded and locked, and the deletion fails. In this case, the old assembly is renamed by adding a .DELETE extension. (All executables loaded in Windows can be renamed at any time, but they cannot be deleted until they are released.) Renaming an assembly in use is no big deal in this case because the image of the executable is already loaded in memory and there will be no need to reload it later. The file, in fact, is destined for deletion. Note that .DELETE files are cleaned up when the directory is next accessed in *sweep* mode, so to speak. The directory, in fact, is not scavenged each time it is accessed but only when the application is restarted or an application file (global.asax or web.config) changes.

Each ASP.NET application is allowed a maximum number of recompiles (with 15 as the default) before the whole application is restarted. The threshold value is set in the machine.config file. If the latest compilation exceeds the threshold, the AppDomain is unloaded and the application is restarted. Bear in mind that the atomic unit of code you can unload in the CLR is the AppDomain, not the assembly. Put another way, you can't unload a single assembly without unloading the whole AppDomain. As a result, when a page is recompiled, the old version stays in memory until the AppDomain is unloaded because either the Web application exceeded its limit of recompiles or the ASP.NET worker process is taking up too much memory.

Getting ASP.NET Runtime Information

The page runtimeinfo.aspx in the book samples displays some run-time information about the running application and AppDomains. Obtained from properties of the *HttpRuntime* class, the information includes the ID, path, and virtual path of the current AppDomain, plus useful paths such as the directory in which ASP.NET generates dynamic assemblies (*CodegenDir*), the machine.config path, and the Bin directory of the application (*BinDirectory*).

The runtimeinfo.aspx page also lists all the assemblies currently loaded in the AppDomain. The sample page needs 12 system assemblies, including those specific to the application—global.asax and the page class. This number increases each time you save the .aspx file because after a page update, a new assembly is loaded but the old one is not unloaded until the whole AppDomain is unloaded. If you save the .aspx file several times (by just opening the file and hitting Ctrl+S), you see that after 15 recompiles the AppDomain ID changes and the number of loaded assemblies reverts back to 12 (or whatever it was). Figure 2-7 shows the result of this exercise.

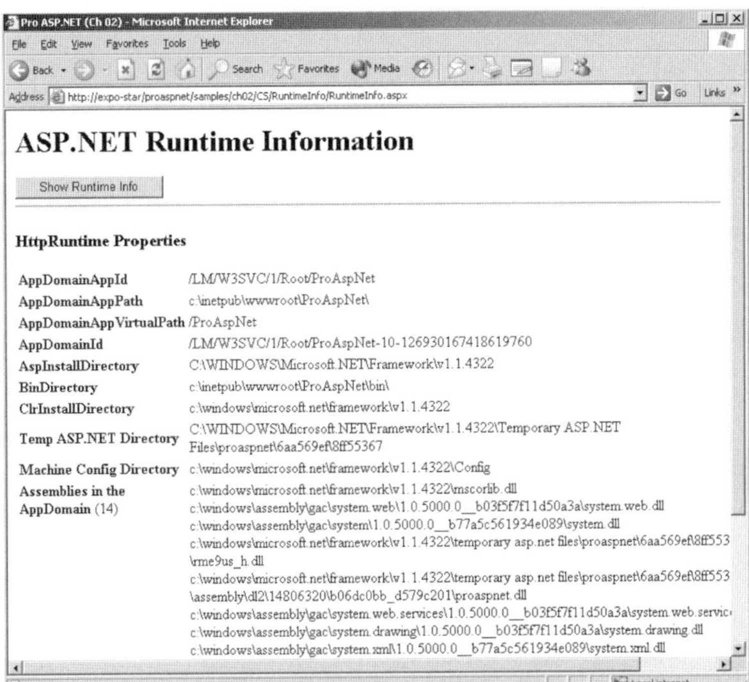

Figure 2-7 Runtimeinfo.aspx shows ASP.NET runtime information.

Batch Compilation

Compiling an ASP.NET page takes a while. So even though you pay this price only once, you might encounter situations in which you decide it's best to happily avoid that. Unfortunately, as of version 1.1, ASP.NET lacks a tool (or a built-in mechanism) to scan the entire tree of a Web application and do a precompilation of all pages. However, you can always request each page of a site before the site goes live or, better yet, have an ad hoc application do it.

In effect, since version 1.0, ASP.NET has supported batch compilation, but this support takes place only at run time. ASP.NET attempts to batch into a single compiled assembly as many pages as possible without exceeding the configured maximum batch size. Furthermore, batch compilation groups pages by language, and it doesn't group in the same assembly pages that reside in different directories.

Just as with many other aspects of ASP.NET, batch compilation is highly configurable and is a critical factor for overall site performance. Fine-tuning the related parameters in the *<compilation>* section of the machine.config file is important and should save you from having and loading 1000 different assemblies for as many pages or from having a single huge assembly with 1000 classes inside. Notice, though, that the problem here is not only with the size and the number of the assemblies but also with the time needed to recompile the assemblies in case of updates.

> **Note** The next version of ASP.NET should fully support precompilation of Web sites and provide an offline tool to precompile an entire Web site as well as build manager classes to programmatically control the process. In addition, ASP.NET 2.0 will extend dynamic compilation to class files (typically, code-behind .cs or .vb files) that currently must be compiled either manually or through Visual Studio.

How ASP.NET Creates a Class for the Page

An ASP.NET page executes as an instance of a type that, by default, inherits from *System.Web.UI.Page*. The page handler factory creates the source code for this class by putting a parser to work on the content of the physical .aspx file. The parser produces a class written with the language the developer specified. The class belongs to the *ASP* namespace and is given a file-specific name. Typically, it is the name and the extension of the file with the dot (.) replaced by an underscore (_). If the page is default.aspx, the class name will be *ASP.Default_aspx*. You can check the truthfulness of this statement with the following simple code:

```
void Page_Load(object sender, EventArgs e)
{
    Response.Write(sender.ToString());
}
```

As mentioned earlier, when the page runs with the *Debug* attribute set to *true*, the ASP.NET runtime does not delete the source code used to create the assembly. Let's have a quick look at the key parts of the source code generated. (Complete sources are included in this book's sample code.)

> **Important** As hinted earlier, the base page class is *System.Web.UI.Page* only by default. In either machine.config or web.config, you can change the base class by using the *pageBaseType* attribute of the *<pages>* element. The same thing can be done for user controls. We'll return to this point later in this chapter and in Chapter 12.

Reviewing the Class Source Code

For a better understanding of the code generated by ASP.NET, let's first quickly review the starting point—the .aspx source code:

```
<%@ Page Language="C#" Debug="true" %>
<%@ Import Namespace="System.IO" %>

<script runat="server">
private void Page_Load(object sender, EventArgs e)  {
    TheSourceFile.Text = HttpRuntime.CodegenDir;
}
private void MakeUpper(object sender, EventArgs e)  {
        string buf = TheString.Value;
        TheResult.InnerText = buf.ToUpper();
}
</script>

<html>
<head><title>Pro ASP.NET (Ch 02)</title></head>
<body>
    <h1>Sample Page</h1>
    <form runat="server">
        <asp:Label runat="server" id="TheSourceFile" /><hr>
        <input runat="server" type="text" id="TheString" />
        <input runat="server" type="submit" id="TheButton"
            value="Uppercase..." onserverclick="MakeUpper" /><br>
        <span id="TheResult" runat="server"></span>
    </form>
</body>
</html>
```

The following listing shows the source code that ASP.NET generates to process the preceding page. The text in boldface type indicates code extracted from the .aspx file:

```
namespace ASP
{
    using System;
    ⋮
    using ASP;
    using System.IO;

    public class Default_aspx : Page, IRequiresSessionState
    {
        private static int __autoHandlers;
        protected Label TheSourceFile;
        protected HtmlInputText TheString;
        protected HtmlInputButton TheButton;
        protected HtmlGenericControl TheResult;
        protected HtmlForm TheAppForm;
        private static bool __initialized = false;
        private static ArrayList __fileDependencies;

        private void Page_Load(object sender, EventArgs e)
        {
            TheSourceFile.Text = HttpRuntime.CodegenDir;
        }
        private void MakeUpper(object sender, EventArgs e)
        {
            string buf = TheString.Value;
            TheResult.InnerText = buf.ToUpper();
        }

        public Default_aspx()
        {
            ArrayList dependencies;
            if (__initialized == false)
            {
                dependencies = new ArrayList();
                dependencies.Add(
                  "c:\\inetpub\\wwwroot\\vdir\\Default.aspx");
                __fileDependencies = dependencies;
                __initialized = true;
            }
            this.Server.ScriptTimeout = 30000000;
        }

        protected override int AutoHandlers {
            get {return __autoHandlers;}
            set {__autoHandlers = value;}
        }

        protected Global_asax ApplicationInstance {
```

```
    get {return (Global_asax)(this.Context.ApplicationInstance);}
}

public override string TemplateSourceDirectory {
    get {return "/vdir";}
}

private Control __BuildControlTheSourceFile() {
    Label __ctrl = new Label();
    this.TheSourceFile = __ctrl;
    __ctrl.ID = "TheSourceFile";
    return __ctrl;
}

private Control __BuildControlTheString() {
    // initialize the TheString control
}

private Control __BuildControlTheButton() {
    // initialize the TheButton control
}

private Control __BuildControlTheResult() {
    // initialize the TheResult control
}

private Control __BuildControlTheAppForm() {
    HtmlForm __ctrl = new HtmlForm();
    this.TheAppForm = __ctrl;
    __ctrl.ID = "TheAppForm";
    IParserAccessor __parser = (IParserAccessor) __ctrl;
    this.__BuildControlTheSourceFile();
    __parser.AddParsedSubObject(this.TheSourceFile);
    __parser.AddParsedSubObject(new LiteralControl("<hr>"));
    this.__BuildControlTheString();
    __parser.AddParsedSubObject(this.TheString);
    this.__BuildControlTheButton();
    __parser.AddParsedSubObject(this.TheButton);
    __parser.AddParsedSubObject(new LiteralControl("<br>"));
    this.__BuildControlTheResult();
    __parser.AddParsedSubObject(this.TheResult);
    return __ctrl;
}

private void __BuildControlTree(Control __ctrl)
{
    IParserAccessor __parser = (IParserAccessor)__ctrl;
    __parser.AddParsedSubObject(
        new LiteralControl("<html>…</h1>"));
    this.__BuildControlTheAppForm();
    __parser.AddParsedSubObject(this.TheAppForm);
    __parser.AddParsedSubObject(new LiteralControl("…</html>"));
}
```

```
        protected override void FrameworkInitialize() {
            this.__BuildControlTree(this);
            this.FileDependencies = __fileDependencies;
            this.EnableViewStateMac = true;
this.Request.ValidateInput();
        }

        public override int GetTypeHashCode() {
            return 2003216705;
        }
    }
}
```

Important As you can see, portions of the source code in the .aspx file are used to generate a new class in the specified language. Just because the inline code in a page will be glued together in a class doesn't mean you can use multiple languages to develop an ASP.NET page. The .NET platform is language-neutral but, unfortunately, .NET compilers are not capable of cross-language compilation!

In addition, for ASP.NET pages, the language declared in the *@Page* directive must match the language of the inline code. The *Language* attribute, in fact, is used to determine the language in which the class is to be created. Finally, the source code is generated using the classes of the language's Code Document Object Model (CodeDOM). CodeDOM can be used to create and retrieve instances of code generators and code compilers. Code generators can be used to generate code in a particular language, and code compilers can be used to compile code into assemblies. Not all .NET languages provide such classes, and this is why not all languages can be used to develop ASP.NET applications. For example, the CodeDOM for J# has been added only in version 1.1 of the .NET Framework, but there is a J# redistributable that adds this functionality to version 1.0.

All the controls in the page marked with the *runat* attribute are rendered as protected properties of the type that corresponds to the tag. Those controls are instantiated and initialized in the various *__BuildControlXXX* methods. The initialization is done using the attributes specified in the .aspx page. The build method for the form adds child-parsed objects to the *HtmlForm* instance. This means that all the parent-child relationships between the controls within the form are registered. The *__BuildControlTree* method ensures that all controls in the whole page are correctly registered with the page object.

All the members defined in the *<script>* block are copied verbatim as members of the new class with the same level of visibility you declared. The base class for the dynamically generated source is *Page* unless the code-behind approach is used. In that case, the base class is just the code-behind class. We'll return to this later in "The Code-Behind Technique" section.

Processing the Page Request

The *HttpRuntime* object governs the HTTP pipeline in which a page request is transformed into a living instance of a *Page*-derived class. The *HttpRuntime* object causes the page to generate its HTML output by calling the *ProcessRequest* method on the *Page*-derived class that comes out of the pipeline. *ProcessRequest* is a method defined on the *IHttpHandler* interface that the *Page* class implements.

The Page Life Cycle

Within the base implementation of *ProcessRequest*, the *Page* class first calls the *FrameworkInitialize* method, which, as seen in the source code examined a moment ago, builds the controls tree for the page. Next, *ProcessRequest* makes the page go through various phases: initialization, loading of view-state information and postback data, loading of the page's user code, and execution of postback server-side events. After that, the page enters rendering mode: the updated view state is collected, and the HTML code is generated and sent to the output console. Finally, the page is unloaded and the request is considered completely served.

During the various phases, the page fires a few events that Web controls and user-defined code can intercept and handle. Some of these events are specific to controls and can't be handled at the level of the .aspx code. In theory, a page that wants to handle a certain event should explicitly register an appropriate handler. However, for backward compatibility with the Visual Basic programming style, ASP.NET also supports a form of implicit event hooking. By default, the page tries to match method names and events and considers the method a handler for the event. For example, a method named *Page_Load* is the handler for the page's *Load* event. This behavior is controlled by the *AutoEventWireup* attribute on the *@Page* directive. If the attribute is set to *false*, any applications that want to handle an event need to connect explicitly to the page event. The following code shows how to proceed from within a page class:

```
// C# code
this.Load += new EventHandler(this.MyPageLoad);
' VB code
AddHandler Load, AddressOf Me.MyPageLoad
```

By proceeding this way, you will enable the page to get a slight performance boost by not having to do the extra work of matching names and events. Visual Studio .NET disables the *AutoEventWireup* attribute.

Page-Related Events

To handle a page-related event, an ASP.NET page can either hook up the event (for example, *Load*) or, in a derived class, override the corresponding method—for example, *OnLoad*. The second approach provides for greater flexibility because you can decide whether and when to call the base method, which, in the end, fires the event to the user-code. Let's review in detail the various phases in the page life cycle:

- **Page initialization** At this stage, the page is called to initialize all the settings needed during the lifetime of the incoming page request. The event you need to hook up from an ASP.NET page is *Init*. The method to use to override in a derived class (for example, code-behind) is *OnInit*.
- **Loading the view state** During this phase, the previously saved state of the page—the *ViewState* property—is restored. The restored value for *ViewState* comes from a hidden field that ASP.NET spookily inserts in the HTML code (more on this later). There is no event associated with this phase. You can override the default implementation of the *LoadViewState* method of the *Page* only by deriving a new class.
- **Loading postback data** The page loads all incoming *<form>* data cached in *Request* and updates page and control properties accordingly. For example, suppose a page contained a list of check boxes. In *ViewState*, the page stores the selected items when the page is generated. Next, the user works with check boxes on the client, selects a different set of items, and posts back. In the previous phase, the server-side list of check boxes has been restored to the state it was in the last time it was processed on the server. In this stage, the list of check boxes is updated to reflect client-side changes. No user event is associated with this stage.
- **Loading the user code** At this point, server controls in the page tree are created and initialized, the state is restored, and form controls reflect client-side data. The page is ready to execute any initialization code that has to do with the logic and behavior of the page. The event you need to hook up from an ASP.NET page is *Load*. The method to use to override in a derived class (for example, code-behind) is *OnLoad*.

- **Send postback change notifications** Raise change events in response to state changes between the current and previous postbacks. Any further change entered by the *Load* event handler is also taken into account to determine any difference. This notification is sent if, for example, the aforementioned list of check boxes is changed on the client.
- **Handle postback events** Execute the .aspx code associated with the client-side event that caused the postback. For example, if you click a Submit button, the page posts back and, at this stage, executes the code bound to the *onclick* event of the button. This phase represents the core of the event model of ASP.NET.
- **Prerendering** Perform any updates before the output is rendered. Any changes made to the state of the control in the prerender phase can be saved, while changes made in the rendering phase are lost. The event you need to hook up from an ASP.NET page is *PreRender*. The method to use to override in a derived class (for example, code-behind) is *OnPreRender*.
- **Saving the view state** During this phase, the page serializes the content of the *ViewState* property to a string, which will then be appended to the HTML page as a hidden field. No user event is associated with this phase. You can override the default implementation of the *SaveViewState* method of the *Page* only by deriving a new class.
- **Page rendering** Generate the HTML output to be rendered to the client. The default implementation can be customized by overriding the *Render* method. No user event is associated with this phase.
- **Page unload** Perform any final cleanup before the *Page* object is released. Typical operations are closing files and database connections. The event you need to hook up from an ASP.NET page is *Unload*. The method to use to override in a derived class (for example, code-behind) is *OnUnload*. The page unload notification arrives when the page is unloaded. The *Dispose* method of the *Page* provides the last possibility for the page to perform final clean up before it is released from memory. To customize the behavior of *Dispose*, you need to derive a new class. *Dispose* is called immediately after the *OnUnload* method returns.

The Event Model

When a page is requested, its class and the server controls it contains are responsible for executing the request and rendering HTML back to the client. The communication between the client and the server is stateless and disconnected because of the HTTP protocol. Real-world applications, though, need some state to be maintained between successive calls made to the same page. With ASP, and with other server-side development platforms such as Java Server Pages (JSP) and LAMP (Linux plus Apache plus MySQL plus either Perl, Python, or PHP as the programming language), the programmer is entirely responsible for persisting the state. In contrast, ASP.NET provides a built-in infrastructure that saves and restores the state of a page in a transparent manner. In this way, and in spite of the underlying stateless protocol, the client experience appears to be that of a continuously executing process. It's just an illusion, though.

The illusion of continuity is created by the view-state feature of ASP.NET pages and is based on some assumptions on how the page is designed and works. Also server-side Web controls play a remarkable role. In brief, before rendering its contents to HTML, the page encodes and stuffs into a hidden field all the state information that the page itself and its constituent controls want to save. When the page posts back, the state information is deserialized from the hidden field and used to initialize instances of the server controls declared in the page layout.

The view state is specific to each instance of the page because it is embedded in the HTML. The net effect of this is that controls are initialized with the same values they had the last time the view state was created—that is, the last time the page was rendered to the client. Furthermore, an additional step in the page life cycle merges the persisted state with any updates introduced by client-side actions. When the page executes after a postback, it finds a stateful and up-to-date context just as it is working over a continuous point-to-point connection.

Two basic assumptions are made. The first assumption is that the page always posts to itself and carries its state back and forth. The second assumption is that the server-side controls have to be declared with the *runat* attribute.

The Single Form Model

Admittedly, for programmers whose experience is with ASP, the single form model of ASP.NET can be difficult to understand. Where's the *Action* property of the form? Why can't I redirect to a particular page when a form is submitted? These are common questions, frequently asked on forums and newsgroups.

ASP.NET pages are built to support exactly one server-side *<form>* tag. The form must include all the controls you want to interact with on the server.

Both the form and the controls must be marked with the *runat* attribute; otherwise, they will be considered as plain text to be output verbatim. A server-side form is an instance of the *HtmlForm* class. The *HtmlForm* class does not expose any property equivalent to the *Action* property of the HTML *<form>* tag. The reason is that an ASP.NET page always posts to itself. Unlike the *Action* property, other common form properties such as *Method* and *Target* are fully supported.

> **Note** Valid ASP.NET pages are also those that have no server-side forms and those that run HTML forms—a *<form>* tag without the *runat* attribute. In an ASP.NET page, you can also have both HTML and server forms. In no case, though, can you have more than one *<form>* tag with the *runat* attribute set to *server*. HTML forms work as usual and let you post to any page in the application. The drawback is that in this case, no state will be automatically restored. In other words, the ASP.NET Web Forms model works only if you use exactly one server *<form>* element.

Auto-Reentrant Web Pages

Let's consider a simple ASP.NET page and see the HTML code that ASP.NET generates for it:

```
<% @Page Language="C#" %>
<script runat="server">
private void MakeUpper(object sender, EventArgs e)
{
    string buf = TheString.Text;
    TheResult.Text = buf.ToUpper();
}
</script>

<html>
<body>
<form runat="server" id="TheForm">
    <asp:textbox runat="server" id="TheString" />
    <asp:button runat="server" text="Convert..." onclick="MakeUpper" /><hr>
    <asp:label runat="server" id="TheResult" />
</form>
</body>
</html>
```

As shown in Figure 2-8, the page lets the user type some text in an input field and then posts all the data to the server for further processing. If you point your browser to this page, the actual HTML code being displayed is the following. The text in boldface is the page's view state:

```
<html>
<body>
<form name="TheForm" method="post" action="MyForm.aspx" id="TheForm">
    <input type="hidden"
        name="__VIEWSTATE"
        value="dDwtMTM3NjQ2NjY2NTs7PrH3U/xuqPTNI63I1Lw5THHvPFUf" />
    <input name="TheString" type="text" id="TheString" />
    <input type="submit" name="_ctl0" value="Convert..." /><hr>
    <span id="TheResult"></span>
</form>
</body>
</html>
```

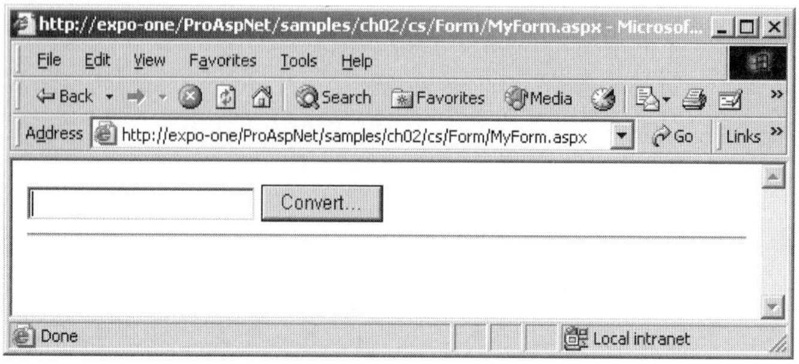

Figure 2-8 The sample ASP.NET page in action.

> **Note** A question I often get at conferences and classes (but rarely a publicly asked question) concerns the use of hidden fields in ASP.NET. The question is typically, "Should I really use hidden fields also in ASP.NET?" Hidden fields have a bad reputation among ASP developers because they appear to be a quick fix and a sort of dirty trick. In some way, developers tend to think that they use hidden fields because they're unable to find a better solution. A similar feeling was common among Windows SDK programmers regarding the use of global variables or temporary files.
>
> Developers seem to fear using hidden fields in the dazzling new object-oriented world of ASP.NET. Well, nothing really prohibits the use of hidden fields in ASP.NET applications and using them is in no way shameful, as long as HTTP remains the underlying protocol. The real point is even more positive.
>
> Using hidden fields in ASP.NET allows you to create more useful Web pages—for example, the view-state mechanism. In light of this, hidden fields are especially recommended when you need to pass information to be consumed through client-side scripts.

The server-side *<form>* tag is rendered as a plain old HTML form in which the *Name* attribute matches the ID property of the *HtmlForm* control, the *Method* attribute defaults to POST and *Action* is automatically set with the URL of the same page. The form contains as many HTML elements as there are server controls in the .aspx source. The form also includes any static text or HTML tags declared in the page layout. The view state is rendered as a hidden field named __VIEWSTATE and filled with Base64-encoded text.

The View State of the Page

The contents of the view state are determined by the contents of the *ViewState* property of the page and its controls. The *ViewState* property is a collection of name/value pairs that both pages and controls fill with data they determine should be preserved across page requests. The various collections are merged together to form a unique object graph, which is then encoded as a Base64 string. Seen from the client side, the __VIEWSTATE hidden field is just a more or less overwhelming sequence of characters. The more state information you save in the *ViewState* property, the bigger your page becomes. Other security and performance concerns apply to the page view state, but we'll cover them in greater detail in Chapter 14. Note that for a real-world page, the size of the view state can easily be more than 10 KB of data, which is an extra burden of 10 KB transmitted over the network and simply ignored on the client.

> **Note** The implementation of the view state in ASP.NET raises hidden fields from the rank of a dirty trick to the higher and more noble role of an internal system feature. Today, lots of ASP developers use hidden fields to persist small pieces of page-specific information. This information is, in most cases, written as plain text and serialized with home-made schemes. The view state implementation revamps that old trick and, more, exposes persisted information in an extremely handy, object-based fashion.
>
> Some developers are afraid of having their own state information at the mercy of the client. That this is the actual situation cannot be denied; but that this automatically qualifies as a security hole has yet to be proven. However, if you were among the many who used to cache plain text in hidden fields, the ASP.NET view state represents a quantum leap! In addition, there are some extra security enforcements that can be applied to the view state. We'll review those in Chapter 14.

Postback Events

A postback event is a page request that results from a client action. Typically, when the user clicks on a submit button, like the Convert button in Figure 2-8, a postback event occurs. In this case, the HTML form posts to the same .aspx page and, as normally happens with HTTP POST commands, the contents of the various input fields in the form are packed in the body of the request.

On the server, the code in charge of processing the request first gets an instance of the class that represents the .aspx page and then goes through the steps described earlier in the "Page-Related Events" section.

State Restoration

As the first step of the page processing, the HTTP runtime builds the tree of controls for the page and sets the *IsPostBack* property. *IsPostBack* is a Boolean property that equals *true* if the page is being processed after a post from the same page—a postback event.

After initialization, the HTTP runtime instructs the page to deserialize the view-state string and transform it into an instance of the *StateBag* class. *State-Bag* implements a dictionary that is populated with the name/value pairs stored and encoded in the view-state string. Once the *StateBag* object has been completely set up, user code can start playing with its contents. From a user-code perspective, however, this timing means it can't do anything before the *OnLoad* event fires. Before *OnLoad* is fired, though, another step needs to be accomplished.

At this point, the various controls active on the page have been restored to the state stored in the view state. Unless the view state has been sapiently and maliciously corrupted on the client (an extremely remote possibility, if not completely impossible), the state of the objects is the state that existed when that page was rendered to the client. It is not yet the state the user set with client-side input actions such as checking radio buttons or typing text. The next step updates the state of the various controls to reflect any client action. This final step ends the state restoration phase, and the page is now ready to process user code. Fire the *OnLoad* event.

Handling the Server-Side Event

The goal of a postback event is executing some server-side code to respond to user input. How can the page know what method it has to execute? The post is always the result of a form submission. However, the submit action can be accomplished in two ways: if the user clicks a control or if the user takes some action that causes some script to run. Let's examine the first case.

The HTML syntax dictates that the ID of the button clicked be inserted in the post data. On the server, the ASP.NET page digs out this information in its attempt to locate an element whose name matches one of its server controls. If a match is found, ASP.NET verifies that the control implements *IPostBackEventHandler*. This is enough to guarantee that the button clicked on the server was a submit button. Generally, it means the control has some code to execute upon postback. At this point, the page raises the postback event on the control and has the control execute some code. To raise the postback event on the control, the ASP.NET page invokes the control's *RaisePostBackEvent* method—one of the members of the *IPostBackEventHandler* interface. For a submit button, this causes the invocation of the method associated with the *onclick* property.

If some script code can post the page back to the server, the author of the script is responsible for letting ASP.NET know about the sender of the event. To understand how to accomplish this, let's see what happens when you use a Web control such as the *LinkButton*—a button rendered as a hyperlink:

```
<asp:linkbutton runat="server" id="TheLink"
    text="Convert..." onclick="MakeUpper" />
```

The HTML code for the page changes slightly. A JavaScript function and a couple of extra hidden fields are added. The two hidden fields are __EVENTTARGET and __EVENTARGUMENT. They are empty when the page is rendered to the browser and contain event data when the page is posted back. In particular, __EVENTTARGET contains the name of the control that caused the postback. The __EVENTARGUMENT field contains any argument that might be useful to carry out the call. A short piece of JavaScript code sets the two fields and submits the form:

```
<!--
<script language="javascript">
function __doPostBack(eventTarget, eventArgument) {
var theform;
if (window.navigator.appName.toLowerCase().indexOf("netscape") > -1) {
theform = document.forms["TheForm"];
}
else {
theform = document.TheForm;
}
theform.__EVENTTARGET.value = eventTarget.split("$").join(":");
theform.__EVENTARGUMENT.value = eventArgument;
theform.submit();
}
// -->
</script>
```

But what's the link between the *__doPostBack* function and the *LinkButton* object? Let's look at the HTML generated for the *LinkButton*:

```
<a href="javascript:__doPostBack('TheLink','')">Convert...</a>
```

Quite simply, any click on the anchor is resolved by executing the *__doPostBack* function.

If you want to provide a completely custom mechanism to post the page back, just borrow the preceding code and make sure the form is submitted with the __EVENTTARGET field set to the name of the sender of the event. (For example, you could have the page post back when the mouse hovers over a certain image.)

To find the sender control that will handle the server-side event, ASP.NET looks at the __EVENTTARGET hidden field if no match is found between its controls and the content of the *Request.Form* collection—that is, if the previous case (the submit button) does not apply.

Rendering Back the Page

After executing the server-side code, the page begins its rendering phase. At first, the page fires the *PreRender* event; it then serializes the content of the *ViewState* object—that is, the current state of the various controls active on the page—to a Base64 string. Next, the HTML code is generated and that Base64 string becomes the value of the __VIEWSTATE hidden field. And so on for the next round-trip.

The *Page* Class

In the .NET Framework, the *Page* class provides the basic behavior for all objects that an ASP.NET application builds starting from .aspx files. Defined in the *System.Web.UI* namespace, the class derives from *TemplateControl* and implements the *IHttpHandler* interface:

```
public class Page : TemplateControl, IHttpHandler
```

In particular, *TemplateControl* is the abstract class that provides both ASP.NET pages and user controls with a base set of functionality. At the upper level of the hierarchy, we find the *Control* class. It defines the properties, methods, and events shared by all ASP.NET server-side elements—pages, controls, and user controls. It's useful to also look at the functionalities of the *Page* class from an interface perspective, as in Figure 2-9.

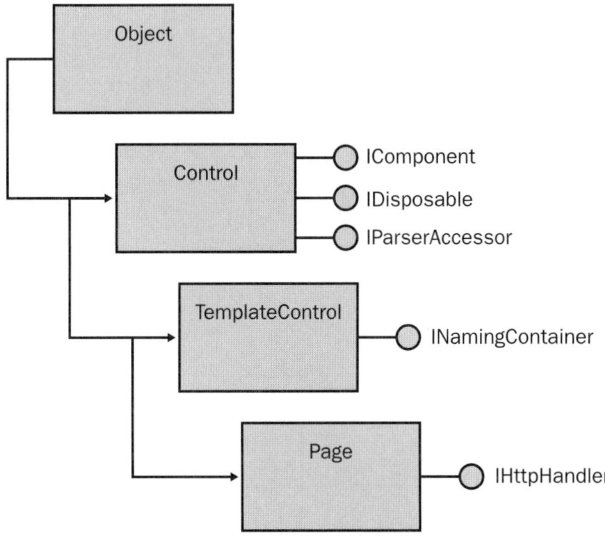

Figure 2-9 The hierarchy of classes from which *Page* inherits.

From the parent *Control* class, *Page* inherits the base behavior for interacting with all other components in the CLR—the *IComponent* interface—and for releasing unmanaged resources (the *IDisposable* interface). In addition, the *IParserAccessor* interface groups the methods that ASP.NET controls must implement to recognize parsed child elements. The *IParserAccessor* interface plays a key role in the implementation of the control tree in the dynamically generated source code for requested ASP.NET pages. (Actually, the *IParserAccessor* interface consists of the single *AddParsedSubObject* method we saw largely used in the code shown in "Reviewing the Class Source Code" section.)

> **Note** The *Control* class also implements the *IDataBindingsAccessor* interface. This interface, though, is not involved with the run-time behavior of server controls. The interface allows access to the collection of data-binding expressions on a control at design time.

Derived from a class—*TemplateControl*—that implements *INamingContainer*, *Page* also serves as the naming container for all its constituent controls. In the .NET Framework, the naming container for a control is the first parent control that implements the *INamingContainer* interface. For any class that implements the naming container interface, ASP.NET creates a new virtual namespace in which all child controls are guaranteed to have unique names in the overall tree of controls. (This is also a very important feature for iterative data-bound controls, such as *DataGrid*, and for user controls.)

The *Page* class also implements the methods of the *IHttpHandler* interface, thus qualifying as the handler of a particular type of HTTP requests—those for .aspx files. The key element of the *IHttpHandler* interface is the *ProcessRequest* method, which is the method the ASP.NET runtime calls to start the page processing that will actually serve the request.

> **Note** *INamingContainer* is a marker interface that has no methods. Its presence alone, though, forces the ASP.NET runtime to create an additional namespace for naming the child controls of the page (or the control) that implements it. The *Page* class is the naming container of all the page's controls, with the clear exception of those controls that implement the *INamingContainer* interface themselves or are children of controls that implement the interface.

Properties of the *Page* Object

The properties of the *Page* object can be classified in three distinct groups: intrinsic objects, worker properties, and page-specific properties. Tables 2-4, 2-5, and 2-6 enumerate and describe them.

Table 2-4 ASP.NET Intrinsic Objects in the *Page* Class

Property	Description
Application	Instance of the *HttpApplicationState* class, represents the state of the application. Functionally equivalent to the ASP intrinsic *Application* object.
Cache	Instance of the *Cache* class, implements the cache for an ASP.NET application. More efficient and powerful than *Application*, it supports item decay and expiration.
Request	Instance of the *HttpRequest* class, represents the current HTTP request. Functionally equivalent to the ASP intrinsic *Request* object.
Response	Instance of the *HttpResponse* class, sends HTTP response data to the client. Functionally equivalent to the ASP intrinsic *Response* object.

Table 2-4 ASP.NET Intrinsic Objects in the *Page* Class

Property	Description
Server	Instance of the *HttpServerUtility* class, provides helper methods for processing Web requests. Functionally equivalent to the ASP intrinsic *Server* object.
Session	Instance of the *HttpSessionState* class, manages user-specific data. Functionally equivalent to the ASP intrinsic *Session* object.
Trace	Instance of the *TraceContext* class, performs tracing on the page.
User	An *IPrincipal* object that represents the user making the request.

We'll cover *Request*, *Response*, and *Server* in Chapter 13; *Application*, *Cache*, and *Session* in Chapter 14; and *User* and security will be the subject of Chapter 15.

Table 2-5 Worker Properties of the *Page* Class

Property	Description
Controls	Returns the collection of all the child controls contained in the current page
ErrorPage	Gets or sets the error page to which the requesting browser is redirected in case of an unhandled page exception
IsPostBack	Indicates whether the page is being loaded in response to a client postback or whether it is being loaded for the first time
IsValid	Indicates whether page validation succeeded
NamingContainer	Returns *null*
Page	Returns the current *Page* object
Parent	Returns *null*
TemplateSourceDirectory	Gets the virtual directory of the page
Validators	Returns the collection of all validation controls contained in the page
ViewStateUserKey	String property used to assign an identifier to the view state variable for individual users. This trick is a line of defense against one-click attacks. *The property is not available with ASP.NET 1.0.*

In the context of an ASP.NET application, the *Page* object is the root of the hierarchy. For this reason, inherited properties such as *NamingContainer* and *Parent* always return *null*. The *Page* property, on the other hand, returns an instance of the same object (*this* in C# and *Me* in Visual Basic .NET).

A special note deserves the *ViewStateUserKey* property that has been added with version 1.1 of the .NET Framework. A common use for the user key would be to stuff user-specific information that will then be used to hash the contents of the view state along with other information. (See Chapter 14.) A typical value for the *ViewStateUserKey* property is the name of the authenticated user or the user's session ID. This contrivance reinforces the security level for the view-state information and further lowers the likelihood of attacks. If you employ a user-specific key, an attacker couldn't construct a valid view state for your user account unless he could also authenticate as you. That way, you have another barrier against on-click attacks. This technique, though, might not be really effective for Web sites that allow anonymous access unless you have some other unique tracking device running.

Note that if you plan to set the *ViewStateUserKey* property, you must do that during the *Page_Init* event. If you attempt to do it later (for example, when *Page_Load* fires), an exception will be thrown.

Table 2-6 Page-Specific Properties of the *Page* Class

Property	Description
ClientID	Always returns the empty string.
ClientTarget	Set to the empty string by default, allows you to specify the type of browser the HTML should comply with. Setting this property disables automatic detection of browser capabilities.
EnableViewState	Gets or sets whether the page has to manage view-state data. You can also enable or disable the view-state feature through the *EnableViewState* attribute of the *@Page* directive.
ID	Always returns the empty string.
SmartNavigation	Gets or sets a value indicating whether smart navigation is enabled. Smart navigation exploits a bunch of browser-specific capabilities to enhance the user's experience with the page. The feature works only with Internet Explorer 5.5 and newer versions. You can also enable or disable this feature through the *SmartNavigation* attribute of the *@Page* directive.
UniqueID	Always returns the empty string.
Visible	Indicates whether ASP.NET has to render the page. If you set *Visible* to *false*, ASP.NET doesn't generate any HTML code for the page. When *Visible* is *false*, only the text explicitly written using *Response.Write* hits the client.

The three ID properties (*ID*, *ClientID*, and *UniqueID*) always return the empty string from a *Page* object. They make sense only for server controls.

Methods of the *Page* Object

The whole range of *Page* methods can be classified in a few categories based on the tasks each method accomplishes. A few methods are involved with the generation of the HTML for the page (as shown in Table 2-7); others are helper methods to build the page and manage the constituent controls (as shown in Table 2-8). Finally, a third group collects all the methods that have to do with client-side scripting (as shown in Table 2-9).

Table 2-7 Methods for HTML Generation

Method	Description
DataBind	Binds all the data-bound controls contained in the page to their data sources. The *DataBind* method doesn't generate code itself but prepares the ground for the forthcoming rendering.
RegisterRequiresPostBack	Registers the specified control with the page so that the control will receive a post-back handling notice. In other words, the page will call the *LoadPostData* method of registered controls. *LoadPostData* requires the implementation of the *IPostBackDataHandler* interface.
RegisterRequiresRaiseEvent	Registers the specified control to handle an incoming postback event. The control must implement the *IPostBackEventHandler* interface.
RenderControl	Outputs the HTML text for the page, including tracing information if tracing is enabled.
VerifyRenderingInServerForm	Controls call this method when they render to ensure they are included in the body of a server form. The method does not return a value, but it throws an exception in case of error.

In an ASP.NET page, no control can be placed outside a *<form>* tag with the *runat* attribute set to *server*. The *VerifyRenderingInServerForm* method is used by Web and HTML controls to ensure they are rendered correctly. In theory, custom controls should call this method during the rendering phase. In many situations, the custom control embeds or derives an existing Web or HTML control that will make the check itself.

Table 2-8 Worker Methods of the *Page* Object

Method	Description
DesignerInitialize	Initializes the instance of the *Page* class at design time, when the page is being hosted by RAD designers like Visual Studio.
FindControl	Takes a control's ID and searches for it in the page's naming container. The search doesn't dig out child controls that are naming containers themselves.
GetTypeHashCode	Retrieves the hash code generated by *ASP.xxx_aspx* page objects at run time. (See the source code of the sample page class we discussed earlier in the "Reviewing the Class Source Code" section.) In the base *Page* class, the method implementation simply returns 0; significant numbers are returned by classes used for actual pages.
HasControls	Determines whether the page contains any child controls.
LoadControl	Compiles and loads a user control from a .ascx file, and returns a *Control* object. If the user control supports caching, the object returned is *PartialCachingControl*.
LoadTemplate	Compiles and loads a user control from a .ascx file, and returns it wrapped in an instance of an internal class that implements the *ITemplate* interface. The internal class is named *SimpleTemplate*.
MapPath	Retrieves the physical, fully qualified path that an absolute or relative virtual path maps to.
ParseControl	Parses a well-formed input string, and returns an instance of the control that corresponds to the specified markup text. If the string contains more controls, only the first is taken into account. The *runat* attribute can be omitted. The method returns an object of type *Control* and must be cast to a more specific type.
RegisterViewStateHandler	Mostly for internal use, the method sets an internal flag causing the page view state to be persisted. If this method is not called in the prerendering phase, no view state will ever be written. Typically, only the *HtmlForm* server control for the page calls this method. There's no need to call it from within user applications.
ResolveUrl	Resolves a relative URL into an absolute URL based on the value of the *TemplateSourceDirectory* property.
Validate	Instructs any validation controls included on the page to validate their assigned information.

The methods *LoadControl* and *LoadTemplate* share a common code infrastructure but return different objects, as the following pseudocode shows:

```
public Control LoadControl(string virtualPath) {
    Control ascx = GetCompiledUserControlType(virtualPath);
    ascx.InitializeAsUserControl();
    return ascx;
}
public ITemplate LoadTemplate(string virtualPath) {
    Control ascx = GetCompiledUserControlType(virtualPath);
    return new SimpleTemplate(ascx);
}
```

Both methods differ from *ParseControl* in that the latter never causes compilation but simply parses the string and infers control information. The information is then used to create and initialize a new instance of the control class. As mentioned, the *runat* attribute is unnecessary in this context. In ASP.NET, the *runat* attribute is key, but in practice, it has no other role than marking the surrounding markup text for parsing and instantiation. It does not contain information useful to instantiate a control, and for this reason can be omitted from the strings you pass directly to *ParseControl.*

Table 2-9 enumerates all the methods in the *Page* class that have to do with HTML and script code to be inserted in the client page.

Table 2-9 Script-Related Methods

Method	Description
GetPostBackClientEvent	Calls into *GetPostBackEventReference.*
GetPostBackClientHyperlink	Appends *javascript:* to the beginning of the return string received from *GetPostBackEventReference.* `javascript:__doPostBack('CtlID','')`
GetPostBackEventReference	Returns the prototype of the client-side script function that causes, when invoked, a postback. It takes a *Control* and an argument, and it returns a string like this: `__doPostBack('CtlID','')`
IsClientScriptBlockRegistered	Determines whether the specified client script is registered with the page.
IsStartupScriptRegistered	Determines whether the specified client startup script is registered with the page.
RegisterArrayDeclaration	Use this method to add an *ECMAScript* array to the client page. This method accepts the name of the array and a string that will be used verbatim as the body of the array. For example, if you call the method with arguments such as "*theArray*" and "'*a*', '*b*'", you get the following JavaScript code: `var theArray = new Array('a', 'b');`

(continued)

Table 2-9 Script-Related Methods *(continued)*

Method	Description
RegisterClientScriptBlock	An ASP.NET page uses this method to emit client-side script blocks in the client page just after the opening tag of the HTML *<form>* element.
RegisterHiddenField	Use this method to automatically register a hidden field on the page.
RegisterOnSubmitStatement	Use this method to emit client script code that handles the client *OnSubmit* event. The script should be a JavaScript function call to client code registered elsewhere.
RegisterStartupScript	An ASP.NET page uses this method to emit client-side script blocks in the client page just before closing the HTML *<form>* element.

Many methods listed in Table 2-9 let you emit script in the client page—either JavaScript or VBScript. When you use any of these methods, you actually tell the page to insert that script code when the page is rendered. So when any of these methods execute, the script-related information is simply cached in internal structures and used later when the page object generates its HTML text. The same pattern applies to hidden fields and *ECMAScript* arrays.

> **Note** JavaScript is the script language that virtually any available browser supports. For this reason, some of the methods in Table 2-9 default to JavaScript. However, when you register a script block, nothing really prevents you from using VBScript as long as you set the language attribute of the *<script>* tag accordingly. On the other hand, methods such as *RegisterOnSubmitStatement* and *RegisterArrayDeclaration* can be used only with JavaScript code.

Events of the *Page* Object

In addition to the events we mentioned earlier, the *Page* class fires a few extra events that are notified during the page life cycle. As Table 2-10 shows, some events are orthogonal to the typical life cycle of a page and are fired as extra-page situations evolve.

Table 2-10 Events That a Page Can Fire

Event	Description
AbortTransaction	Occurs for ASP.NET pages marked to participate in an automatic transaction when a transaction aborts.
CommitTransaction	Occurs for ASP.NET pages marked to participate in an automatic transaction when a transaction commits.
DataBinding	Occurs when the *DataBind* method is called on the page to bind all the child controls to their respective data sources.
Disposed	Occurs when the page is released from memory, which is the last stage of the page life cycle.
Error	Occurs when an unhandled exception is thrown.
Init	Occurs when the page is initialized, which is the first step in the page life cycle.
Load	Occurs when the page loads up.
PreRender	Occurs when the page is about to render.
Unload	Occurs when the page is unloaded from memory but not yet disposed.

The Code-Behind Technique

At the highest level of abstraction, an ASP.NET page is made of page layout information and code. The code for the page can be developed in two ways: inline through the *<script>* tag or by using a code-behind class. All inline code must be written in the same language declared for the page and will be copied verbatim in the source code of the dynamically generated class that represents the .aspx resource in execution.

A code-behind class inherits from *Page*, either directly or indirectly. As such, the code-behind class encapsulates in an object-oriented fashion all the functionalities you're building in the page—event handlers, method and property overrides, and new members. Visual Studio .NET takes advantage of code-behind classes to implement an efficient and effective code editor. As mentioned in Chapter 1, though, the code-behind syntax used by Visual Studio .NET is a bit unusual and to some extent undocumented. As a matter of fact, though, the resultant page architecture is even more efficient in practice.

In this section, we'll start with a review of the code-behind scheme of Visual Studio .NET, and then we'll move on to more general considerations of code-behind.

Code and Layout Separation

Code-behind is an architectural feature designed to clearly separate code and layout in an ASP.NET page. To achieve this, though, it exploits one of the cornerstones of object-oriented programming (OOP)—class inheritance. Just the capability to inherit pages from existing pages leads to even more attractive and compelling uses of the code-behind feature, such as visual inheritance and Web site master pages.

Code-Behind in Visual Studio .NET

When you create a new page in an ASP.NET project, Visual Studio .NET creates an .aspx file and a ghost file with the same name as the .aspx plus a .cs or .vb extension, depending on the project language. The .aspx file contains control declarations and other layout information. The .cs (or .vb) file contains all the code for the page. The page is seen as a class derived from *Page* with overrides and new members as appropriate.

When you build the Visual Studio .NET project, the page class is compiled into the project's assembly and the run-time link between the .aspx file and its base class is given by the value of the *Inherits* attribute in the *@Page* directive. The design-time link between the .aspx file and its code-behind class is given by the value of the *CodeBehind* attribute in the *@Page* directive. The *CodeBehind* attribute is blissfully ignored by the ASP.NET runtime and makes sense only to Visual Studio .NET.

The separation between code and layout is achieved by using two distinct files—the .aspx for the layout and the .cs (or whatever language you use) for the code—that the IDE manages transparently.

Code-Behind in Action at Run Time

For example, if the ASP.NET runtime receives a request for a page.aspx resource, the runtime creates an instance of a dynamically generated class named *ASP.Page_aspx*. By default, this class inherits from *Page* or from the class you specify in the configuration. The base class can be changed on a per-page basis also through the *Inherits* attribute in the *@Page* directive. The *Inherits* attribute contains only the fully qualified name of the class from which *ASP.Page_aspx* must derive. It doesn't say anything about the actual location of the class.

The ASP.NET runtime locates the base class assembly using the usual probing algorithm for missing assemblies. One of the directories scanned is the virtual folder's Bin directory, which is the location in which Visual Studio .NET places the project assemblies at development time.

For the code-behind feature to work, the *Inherits* attribute is always necessary, as it is the only supported way to inform the ASP.NET runtime to derive *ASP.Page_aspx* from a different and more specific page class. (The code-behind class itself must necessarily derive from *Page* or from a class that, in turn, inherits from *Page*.)

You can also deploy a code-behind class as plain source code. In this case, you use *Inherits* to indicate the name of the class and the *Src* attribute to specify the URL from which the class can be loaded and compiled, as shown in the following line of code:

```
<%@ Page Language="C#" Inherits="MyBasePageClass" Src="MyBasePage.cs" %>
```

The file pointed to by the *Src* attribute is automatically compiled on demand and recompiled in case of updates. It goes without saying that the class file used must match the language of the page.

> **Tip** Code-behind classes and inline code can happily cohabit within the same Web Forms page. Interestingly, this fact alone opens up the possibility of using multiple languages to develop the page. In fact, you could use one language to develop the code-behind class and then link it to the page using the *Inherits* attribute. You're responsible for compiling the class and deploying the class through an assembly. Next, you'd use the other language to set the *Language* attribute and develop inline code for the page. Finally, you should note that this programming style is not supported by Visual Studio .NET. If you like it, use Web Matrix or other third-party commercial products.

If you decide to use the *Src* attribute, you have to deploy the source code of the class, thus making the logic of your solution available on the Web server. On the other hand, this approach simplifies the maintenance of the Web site because you could modify the file (or better yet, a copy of it) on the Web server. Otherwise, you have to modify the source, rebuild the project yourself, and then deploy it again to the Web server.

> **Note** Visual Studio .NET does not support code-behind if it is implemented through the *Src* attribute. In this case, you can either resort to your own code editor or, better yet, download and install the free Web Matrix editor.

Moving to Code-Behind

A practical advantage of the code-behind approach is that it allows two programmers or programming teams to simultaneously work on the development of a Web page. After the structure of a page is defined in terms of the number, names, and types of constituent controls, HTML designers can work on the appearance of the page, determining the position, colors, and fonts of the controls; they can even determine the necessity for client-side scripting. At the same time, programmers can develop the code and event handlers required for the page to work properly and fulfill users' expectations.

Any existing ASP.NET page can migrate to code-behind with very few changes. The first step is writing a class that inherits, either directly or indirectly, from *Page*. Next, you add to the class, as a protected or public member, any control declared in the page layout that has the *runat* attribute set to *server*. Also, convert any global variable or procedure in the *<script>* section of the original ASP.NET page into a new member of the class with the scope and visibility you want.

Be sure to choose the right control type that will lie behind an ASP.NET or HTML tag. For example, an *<asp:textbox runat="server">* tag maps to a *TextBox* control, whereas an equivalent *<input type=text runat="server">* tag maps to *HtmlInputText*.

> **Caution** Because the actual page class being processed will inherit from the code-behind class, make sure you don't declare any control members as *private*. In this case, in fact, the actual derived class won't be able to access the control because of the protection level. Use the *public* modifier—or better yet, the *protected* modifier—instead.

Once you've accomplished this, you're almost done. A subtle design issue you might want to consider is the following. Typically, your Web page will have controls that fire server-side events—for example, a submit button:

```
<asp:button runat="server" id="TheButton" text="Submit" />
```

To make the control usable, you need to bind it to some code. You can do this in two ways. You could either add an *onclick* attribute to the tag or programmatically define an event handler in the code-behind class. In the former case, you end up having the following code:

```
<asp:button runat="server" id="TheButton" text="Submit"
    onclick="OnSubmitDocument" />
```

There's nothing bad about this code, at least in terms of overall functionality. However, it makes the ideal of neat separation between code and layout a bit less neat. The page layout, in fact, contains a reference to a piece of code. Among other things, this means HTML designers must remember to change the attribute should they decide to rename the handler.

From a design standpoint, a much better approach is to go the programmatic route and register the event handler with code. In C#, you would accomplish this with the following code:

```
override protected void OnInit(EventArgs e)
{
    this.TheButton.Click += new System.EventHandler(this.OnSubmitDocument);
}
```

In both cases, the *OnSubmitDocument* method should be defined in the code-behind class.

Page Inheritance

It's hard to say whether code-behind inspired the separation between code and layout or whether things happened the other way around—that is, code-behind was invented as a way to implement code and layout separation. Rather than concern ourselves with how it all developed, let's look at code-behind from another, more architectural, perspective.

At the end of the day, code-behind is just a fancy name for the ASP.NET feature that lets you explicitly set the base class for the dynamically created page class. And I think this feature alone is much more important to developers than the separation between code and layout. To achieve code separation, you don't need to know about the architecture of code-behind—just use Visual Studio .NET and you're done.

The capability of changing the base class of dynamic pages opens a new world of possibilities that can be described as the Web counterpart of the visual form inheritance we have in Windows Forms applications. For Windows Forms, visual inheritance indicates the .NET Framework ability to let you create new forms by inheriting from previously created forms. The .NET Framework provides you with a base *Form* class that you extend in user projects by adding child controls. Each application form is definitely an instance of some user-defined, *Form*-based class.

You normally inherit your custom forms always from the base class *Form*, but a smarter approach is possible. For example, to make all your applications share the same look and feel, you could create a form class inheriting from *Form*, add some features and controls, and compile the resultant class into a new assembly. Suppose you call this form class *AcmeForm*. Next, whenever you need to create a new Windows Forms application with the same characteristics, you simply derive the main window from *AcmeForm* and get a ready-to-use and feature-rich form window. Although it's impressive to show, this feature involves nothing that qualifies as rocket science; it's just the offspring of class inheritance. As such, it can be applied to ASP.NET pages as well. Code-behind and the *Inherits* attribute of the *@Page* directive are the underpinnings of this important feature.

A Server-Side Abstraction for Client-Side Events

To demonstrate a real-world application of the code-behind technique, let's consider the level of server-side abstraction that ASP.NET provides for client-side events such as setting the input focus. ASP.NET doesn't provide, and it is not supposed to provide, a rich object model for client-side scripting and page decoration. In other words, you have to write any JavaScript code you might need and attach it to the page using the *RegisterXXX* methods of the *Page* class.

That said, though, consider that almost every Web page displays some HTML control that would work much better if you could set the input focus. For example, a page that contains a list of text boxes for data entry would look much more user-friendly if the input focus was automatically placed on the first field. After all, it's not such a hard task; a few lines of JavaScript code would do the job quickly and effectively. You need to write a small script to set the focus and call it from the body's *onload* method. The following HTML page shows just that:

```
<html>
<script language="javascript">
function SetInputFocus() {
    if(document.__theForm["fname"] != null)
        document.__theForm["fname"].focus();
}
</script>

<body onload="SetInputFocus()">
<form name="__theForm">
    <input type="text" value="Joe" name="fname">
    <input type="text" value="Users" name="lname">
</form>
</body>
</html>
```

Although it's easy to understand and implement, the solution is still boring to code (or even to cut and paste) for each page of the application. The code-behind technique comes to the rescue. The idea is that you derive a new class from *Page* and make sure it contains the needed script code and runs it upon startup.

A Better Page Class

The following listing demonstrates an alternative *Page* class. It inherits from the *System.Web.UI.Page* class and exposes a *Focus* property that clients can set with the name of the HTML control with the input focus:

```
using System;
using System.Web.UI;
using System.Text;

namespace ProAspNet.CS.Ch02
{
    public class Page : System.Web.UI.Page
    {
        public Page()
        {
        }

        // Internals
        private const string FUNCTION_NAME = "__setFocus";
        private const string SCRIPT_NAME = "__inputFocusHandler";

        // Gets/Sets the name of the HTML control with the input focus
        public string Focus;

        // Registers client-side script
        protected override void OnPreRender(EventArgs e)
        {
            base.OnPreRender(e);
            AddStartupScript();
        }

        // Create the script strings
        private void AddStartupScript()
        {
            // Find the ID of the ASP.NET form
            string formName = "";
            foreach(Control ctl in this.Controls)
                if (ctl is HtmlForm)  {
                    formName = "\"" + ctl.UniqueID + "\"";
                    break;
                }

            // Add the script to declare the function
            StringBuilder sb = new StringBuilder("");
            sb.Append("\n<script language=javascript>\n");
            sb.Append("function ");
            sb.Append(FUNCTION_NAME);
            sb.Append("(ctl) {");
            sb.Append("\n  if (document.forms[");
            sb.Append(formName);
            sb.Append("][ctl] != null)  {");
            sb.Append("\n      document.forms[");
```

```
                sb.Append(formName);
                sb.Append("][ctl].focus();");
                sb.Append("\n  }");
                sb.Append("\n}\n");

                // Add the script to call the function
                sb.Append(FUNCTION_NAME);
                sb.Append("('");
                sb.Append(Focus);
                sb.Append("');\n<");
                sb.Append("/");
                sb.Append("script>");

                // Register the script (names are CASE-SENSITIVE)
                if (!IsStartupScriptRegistered(SCRIPT_NAME))
                    RegisterStartupScript(SCRIPT_NAME, sb.ToString());
            }
        }
    }
```

In the *PreRender* event, the page registers a startup script. If the server form is named *theForm* and the *Focus* property is set to *user*, the following script will be generated:

```
<script language=javascript>
function __setFocus(ctl) {
    if (document.forms["theForm"][ctl] != null)  {
        document.forms["theForm"][ctl].focus();
    }
}
__setFocus('user');
</script>
```

The *__setFocus* JavaScript function is first declared and then invoked with a particular argument. The script is registered using the *RegisterStartupScript* method. A startup script is placed exactly before closing the *<form>* tag and executed when the browser has finished with the rest of the form—in this sense, it is called a startup script and is functionally equivalent to setting the *onload* attribute of the page body.

Programmatically Set the Input Focus

Because the *ProAspNet.CS.Ch02.Page* class inherits from *Page*, you can use it wherever a page class is acceptable. To make sure that ASP.NET builds an .aspx page just from the *ProAspNet.CS.Ch02.Page* class, use this type with the *Inherits* attribute of the page directive. Of course, you need to have an assembly for the class in one of the paths the ASP.NET runtime can reach—typically the virtual folder's Bin directory. The following page automatically sets the input focus to the field named *user*. The code in boldface type is all you have to add to an existing page to support the feature, which sets a new base class and the input focus:

```
<%@ Page Language="C#" Inherits="ProAspNet.CS.Ch02.Page" %>

<script runat="server">
    public void Page_Load(object sender, EventArgs e)
    {
        if (!IsPostBack)
            this.Focus = "user";
    }
</script>

<html>
<head><title>Pro ASP.NET (Ch 02)</title></head>
<body>
    <h2>Log on to the System</h2>
    <form runat="server">
        <b>UserName</b><br>
        <asp:textbox runat="server" id="user" /><br>
        <b>Password</b><br>
        <asp:textbox runat="server" id="pswd" /><br>
        <asp:button id="go" runat="server" text="Connect" />
    </form>
</body>
</html>
```

The *IsPostBack* property is set to *true* if the page is being displayed after a postback. If you don't check against *IsPostBack*, the input focus will be set to the control named *user* each time the page is accessed; otherwise, it will be set only the first time the page is accessed in the session.

Changing the Default Page Base Type

As mentioned earlier, by default a page inherits from the *Page* class or from any other code-behind class specified in the *@Page* directive. If you need all pages in an application (or in a certain folder) to inherit from a common and user-defined class, you can override the base page type from the *System.Web.UI.Page* class to whatever class you want. Obviously, the new page class must in turn inherit from *System.Web.UI.Page*.

For example, to make all the pages in a Web application inherit the focus feature we discussed earlier, create a web.config file in the application's root folder and give it the following content:

```
<configuration>
    <system.web>
        <pages pageBaseType="ProAspNet.CS.Ch02.Page, Page" />
    </system.web>
</configuration>
```

The *pageBaseType* attribute must be set to a valid type name—that is, a comma-separated string formed by a type name and the assembly name. In the preceding code, the specified class is implemented in the page.dll assembly.

Note that the base page could also be changed for all the applications running on a server machine. In this case, you must edit the machine.config file, locate the *<pages>* section, and add the *pageBaseType* attribute. By default, the attribute is initialized implicitly and is not listed in the configuration file. To edit both web.config and machine.config, you need administrator privileges.

> **Note** In the next version of ASP.NET, the *WebControl* class and the *Page* class will provide a nearly identical feature through a method named *SetFocus*. The method takes the ID of a control and caches it internally. When the page is rendered to HTML, ad hoc script code will be generated to set the focus to the control.

Master Pages in ASP.NET

A large number of Web sites these days contain similar-looking pages that share the same header, footer, and perhaps some navigational menus or search forms. What's the recommended approach for reusing code across pages? One possibility is wrapping these user-interface elements in user controls and referencing them in each page. Although the model is extremely powerful and produces highly modular code, when you have hundreds of pages to work with, it soon becomes unmanageable.

An alternative approach entails using code-behind to aim at a kind of visual inheritance akin to that of Windows Forms. In this case, the custom base class programmatically generates user-interface elements such as the page header. In addition, the page class could expose custom objects as programmable entities—for example, a collection for the links to display on the header. To build a new page, you simply set the *Inherits* attribute with the class name. When part of the user interface (UI) is programmatically generated, merging the base elements and the actual content of the content page can be problematic unless absolute positioning is used. In the sample code of this chapter (located at ch02\Inherit), you find an application that solves this issue by forcing the client page to include an *<asp:placeholder>* control with a particular ID just where a particular parent UI element should appear.

In the next version of ASP.NET, the concept of the *master page* will be introduced. A master page is a distinct file referenced at the application level, as well as at the page level, that contains the static layout of the page. Regions that each *derived* page can customize are referenced in the master page with a special placeholder control. A derived page is simply a collection of blocks the run time will use to fill the holes in the master. Master pages in the next version of

ASP.NET are orthogonal to true visual inheritance. The contents of the master, in fact, are merged into the derived page rather than serving as a base class for the derived page.

Conclusion

ASP.NET is a complex technology built on top of a simple and, fortunately, solid and stable Web infrastructure. To provide highly improved performance and a richer programming tool set, ASP.NET builds a desktop-like abstraction model, but it still has to rely on HTTP and HTML to hit the target and meet end-user expectations.

There are two relevant aspects in the ASP.NET Web Forms model: the process model, including the Web server process model, and the page object model. ASP.NET anticipates some of the features of IIS 6.0—the new and revolutionary version of the Microsoft Web information services. ASP.NET applications run in a separate worker process (as all applications will do in IIS 6.0); ASP.NET applications support output caching (as IIS 6.0 will do on behalf of all types of Web applications); and finally, the ASP.NET runtime automatically recycles processes to guarantee excellent performance in spite of run-time anomalies, memory leaks, and programming errors. The same feature becomes a system feature in IIS 6.0.

Each request of a URL that ends with .aspx is assigned to an application object working within the CLR hosted by the worker process. The request results in a dynamically compiled class that is then instantiated and put to work. The *Page* class is the base class for all ASP.NET pages. An instance of this class runs behind any URL that ends with .aspx. The code-behind technique allows you to programmatically change the base class for a given .aspx resource. The net effect of code-behind is the possibility to implement very cool features such as code and layout separation and page inheritance.

In this chapter, we mentioned controls several times. Server controls are components that get input from the user, process the input, and output a response as HTML. In the next chapter, we'll explore various server controls, which include Web controls, HTML controls, validation controls, and data-bound controls.

Resources

- HTTP Architecture (*http://www.develop.com/conferences/conferencedotnet/materials/A4.pdf*)
- HTTP Pipeline (*http://www.develop.com/summercamp/conferencedotnet/materials/W2.pdf*)
- Securely Implement Request Processing, Filtering, and Content Redirection with HTTP Pipelines in ASP.NET (*http://msdn.microsoft.com/msdnmag/issues/02/09/HTTPPipelines*)
- Viewstate Optimization Strategies in ASP.NET (*http://www.webreference.com/programming/asp/viewstate*)
- KB306005 Repair IIS Mapping After You Remove and Reinstall IIS
- KB315158 ASP.NET Does Not Work with the Default ASPNET Account on a Domain Controller

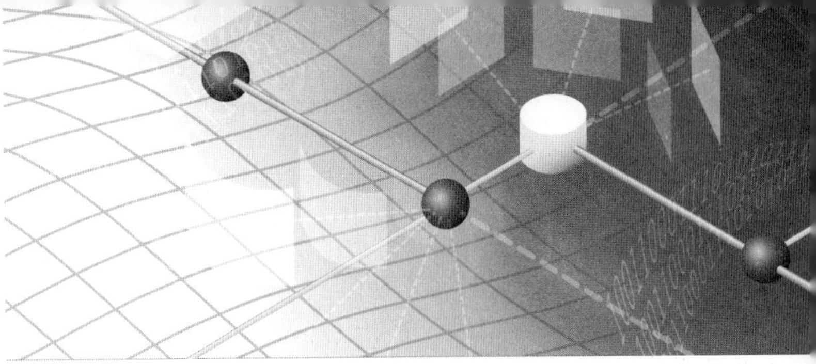

3

ASP.NET Core Server Controls

It does not matter how slowly you go so long as you do not stop.
—Confucius

ASP.NET pages are made of code, markup tags, literal text, and server controls. Based on the request, the server controls generate the right markup language. The ASP.NET runtime combines the output of all controls and serves the client a page to display in a browser.

The programming richness of ASP.NET springs from the wide library of server controls that covers the basic tasks of HTML interaction—for example, collecting text through input tags—as well as more advanced functionalities such as grid-based data display. In the ASP.NET world, more advanced and very specific controls ensure all basic tasks and common functionalities are available. The *AdRotator* and *Calendar* controls are two illustrious examples.

Key to ASP.NET control programming is the *runat* attribute. If a control is declared without the *runat* attribute, it is considered plain text and is output verbatim. If a control contains the *runat* attribute set to the value of "*server*", ASP.NET creates and handles an instance of the control while processing the page on the server. All this happens transparently to the user and the programmer as part of the ASP.NET runtime infrastructure.

In Chapter 1, we identified two main families of server controls—HTML server controls and Web server controls. In ASP.NET, these controls are typically referred to as HTML controls and Web controls. HTML controls map to HTML tags and are implemented through server-side classes whose programming interface faithfully represents the standard set of attributes for the corresponding HTML tag. Web controls, in turn, are a more abstract library of controls in which adherence to HTML syntax is much less strict. As a result, Web and HTML controls share a large common subset of functionalities and, in spite of a few exceptions, we could say that Web controls, functionally speaking, are a superset of HTML controls. Web controls also feature a richer development environment with a larger set of methods, properties and events.

As we'll see in more detail in the following pages, a second and more thoughtful look at the characteristics of the server controls in ASP.NET reveals the existence of more than just two families of controls. In real-world ASP.NET applications, you'll end up using controls from at least the following categories: HTML controls, Web controls, validation controls, data-bound controls, user controls, mobile controls, and custom controls. Validation controls are a special subset of Web controls and deserve to be treated in a separate section. Data-bound controls are not a category per se, with features that make them different from HTML or Web controls. Data-binding, instead, refers to the control's capability of connecting some of its properties to particular data sources. Hence, data-bound controls fall into any of the previously listed groups of server controls, but deserve a section of their own because of their importance and frequent use. User controls—also referred to as *pagelets* in relatively outdated literature—are visual aggregates of existing Web and HTML controls that appear as individual, encapsulated, programmable controls to external callers. Mobile controls are used when creating Web applications that target mobile devices. Custom controls refer to server controls you create that derive from a base control class.

In this chapter, we'll cover HTML controls, Web controls, validation controls, and data-bound controls. We'll cover user controls in Chapter 10, mobile controls in Chapter 11, and custom controls in Chapter 18 through Chapter 20.

Generalities of ASP.NET Server Controls

All ASP.NET server controls, including HTML and Web controls plus any custom controls you create or download, descend from the *Control* class. The class is defined in the *System.Web.UI* namespace and, as we discussed in Chapter 2, also represents the foundation of all ASP.NET pages. The *Control* class is declared as follows:

```
public class Control : IComponent, IDisposable, IParserAccessor,
    IDataBindingsAccessor
```

The *IComponent* interface defines the way in which the control interacts with the other components running in the common language runtime (CLR), whereas *IDisposable* implements the common pattern for releasing unmanaged resources. The *IParserAccessor* interface enables the control to work as the container of child controls. Finally, the *IDataBindingsAccessor* interface makes the control capable of supporting data-binding expressions at design time. The *IDataBindingsAccessor* interface defines a read-only collection—the *DataBindings* property—that contains all the data bindings for the controls available to rapid application development (RAD) designers such as Microsoft Visual Studio .NET. Note that the collection of data bindings exist only at design time and, as such, is useful only if you write a RAD designer for the control. (Design-time features are discussed further in Chapter 21.)

Properties of the *Control* Class

The properties of the *Control* class have no user interface–specific features. The class, in fact, represents the minimum set of functionalities expected from a server control. The list of properties for the *Control* class is shown in Table 3-1.

Table 3-1 Properties of a Server Control

Property	Description
ClientID	Gets the ID assigned to the control in the HTML page. The string is a slightly different version of the *UniqueID* property. *UniqueID* can contain the colon symbol (:), but this symbol is not allowed in *ClientID* and is replaced with the underscore (_).
Controls	Gets a collection filled with references to all the child controls.
EnableViewState	Gets or sets whether the control should persist its view state—and the view state of any child controls across multiple requests—to the configured location (for example, HTML hidden field, Web server memory, server-side databases or files).
ID	Gets or sets the name that will be used to programmatically identify the control in the ASP.NET page.
NamingContainer	Gets a reference to the control's naming container. A naming container is the namespace to which the control belongs. If the control doesn't define its own naming space, a reference to the parent control (or the page) is returned.

(continued)

Table 3-1 Properties of a Server Control *(continued)*

Property	Description
Page	Gets a reference to the *Page* instance that contains the control.
Parent	Gets a reference to the parent of the control in the page hierarchy.
TemplateSourceDirectory	Gets the virtual directory of the host page.
UniqueID	Gets a hierarchically qualified ID for the control.
Visible	Gets or sets whether ASP.NET has to render the control.

The *Control* class is the ideal base class for new controls that have no user interface and don't require style information.

Identifying a Server Control

The client ID of a control is generated from the value of the *UniqueID* property—the truly server-side identifier that ASP.NET generates for each control. The contents of the *ClientID* property differ from *UniqueID* simply in that all occurrences of the colon symbol (:) are replaced with the underscore (_). Colons in the *UniqueID* string are possible only if the control belongs to a naming container different than the current one—typically, the page.

ASP.NET generates the value for the *UniqueID* property based on the value of the *ID* property that the programmer indicates. If no ID has been specified, ASP.NET autogenerates a name such as *_ctlX*, where *X* is a progressive 0-based index. If the control's naming container is the host page, *UniqueID* simply takes the value of *ID*. Otherwise, the value of *ID* is prefixed with the string representing the naming container and the result is assigned to *UniqueID*.

> **Note** For performance reasons, ASP.NET caches into a static array defined on the *Control* class the strings ranging from *_ctl0* to *_ctl127*. These autogenerated and cached IDs will be used for the first 128 controls in the page defined with an empty ID string. If you have more than 128 controls with an empty ID, the ID string is generated on the fly for each control instance.

Visibility of a Server Control

If you set *Visible* to *false*, ASP.NET doesn't generate any HTML code for the control. However, having *Visible* set to *false* doesn't really mean the control's code can't output text. The control is still an active object that exposes methods and handles events. If a method, or an event handler, sends text directly to the output console through *Response.Write*, this text will be displayed to the user anyway. A control with the *Visible* attribute set to *false* is still part of the page and maintains its position in the control tree.

Methods of the *Control* Class

The methods of the *Control* class are listed and described in Table 3-2.

Table 3-2 Methods of a Server Control

Method	Description
DataBind	Fires the *OnDataBinding* event and then invokes the *DataBind* method on all child controls
Dispose	Gives the control a chance to perform clean-up tasks before it gets released from memory
FindControl	Looks for the specified control in the collection of child controls. Child controls belonging to a different naming container are not sought.
HasControls	Indicates whether the control contains any child controls
RenderControl	Generates the HTML output for the control
ResolveUrl	Resolves a relative URL to an absolute URL based on the value passed to the *TemplateSourceDirectory* property

At the *Control* class level, the *DataBind* method works recursively and simply loops through all the child controls and calls *DataBind* on each of them. On derived data-bound controls, the method resolves all data-binding expressions and updates the status of the control itself.

Events of the *Control* Class

The *Control* class also defines a set of base events that all server controls in the .NET Framework support, as described in Table 3-3.

Table 3-3 Events of a Server Control

Event	Description
DataBinding	Occurs when the *DataBind* method is called on a control and the control is binding to a data source
Disposed	Occurs when a control is released from memory—the last stage in the control life cycle
Init	Occurs when the control is initialized—the first step in the life cycle
Load	Occurs when the control is loaded into the page. Occurs after *Init*.
PreRender	Occurs when the control is about to render its content
Unload	Occurs when the control is unloaded from memory

All server controls are rendered to HTML using the *RenderControl* method and, when this happens, the *PreRender* event is fired.

HTML Controls

In ASP, HTML tags inserted in the layout of the server page were treated as opaque text and output to the client verbatim. This behavior has been entirely maintained in ASP.NET. A big difference, though, is that in ASP.NET, by simply adding the *runat* attribute with a value of "*server*", you can bring to life otherwise-dead HTML text. Once transformed into a living instance of a server-side component, the original tag can be configured programmatically using an object-oriented approach. By design, HTML controls expose a set of methods and properties that carefully reflect the HTML syntax. For example, to set the default text of an input form field, you use a property named *Value*—case does matter in C# but not in Microsoft Visual Basic .NET—instead of the more expressive *Text*. The name of the server control is determined by the value of the *id* attribute. The following code snippet shows how to define a server-side input tag named *lastName*:

```
<input runat="server" id="lastName" type="text" />
```

The tag declaration does not include an explicit and static value for the *Value* attribute, which can be configured programmatically as follows:

```
void Page_Load(object sender, EventArgs e)
{
    lastName.Value = "Esposito";
}
```

After being processed by the ASP.NET runtime, the preceding declaration generates the following HTML code:

```
<input name="myName" id="myName" type="text" value="Esposito" />
```

Notice that a server-side *id* attribute expands to a pair of HTML attributes—*name* and *id*. Be aware that this happens for browser compatibility. In no way, does this mean that on the server *name* and *id* can be interchangeably used to name the server instance of the control. The name of the server control instance is given by *id*. If you specify both *name* and *id* on a server-side tag, the value assigned to *name* will be silently overridden.

Generalities of HTML Controls

The .NET Framework provides predefined server controls for commonly used HTML elements such as *<form>*, *<input>*, and *<select>*, as well as for tables, images, and hyperlinks. All the predefined HTML server controls inherit from the same base class—the *HtmlControl* class. In addition, each control then provides its own set of specific properties and its own events.

Controls typically supply properties that allow you to manipulate the HTML attributes programmatically from within server code. HTML controls integrate well with data-binding and the ASP.NET state maintenance, and they also provide full support for postback events and client scripting. For example, for a button that gets clicked, you can have some JavaScript code running on the client responding to the *onclick* event as well as some code that handles the event on the server if the page posts back as the result of that event.

HTML controls are defined in the *System.Web.UI.HtmlControls* namespace. As mentioned, most HTML tags have a direct class counterpart in the .NET Framework, but not all do. HTML elements that don't map to a made-to-measure class are rendered through the *HtmlGenericControl* class and have attributes set using generic collections rather than direct properties. Generic controls include *<div>*, *<iframe>*, *<span>*, *<hr>*, *<font>*, and *<body>*. In general, you should bear in mind that every element that can appear in an HTML page can be marked as *runat="server"* and programmed and styled on the server.

The *HtmlControl* Base Class

The *HtmlControl* class inherits from *Control* and defines the methods, properties, and events common to all HTML controls. Actually, many properties and all methods and events are simply inherited from the base class. Table 3-4 shows the list of properties specific to HTML controls.

Table 3-4 Specific Properties of an HTML Control

Property	Description
Attributes	Gets a collection object representing all the attributes set on the control with the corresponding value
Disabled	Gets or sets a Boolean value, which indicates whether the HTML control is disabled
Style	Gets a collection object representing all CSS properties applied to the control
TagName	Gets the name of the HTML tag behind the control

A disabled HTML server control is visible and always gets generated as HTML code. If the *Disabled* property is set to *true*, the *disabled* HTML attribute is inserted in the HTML output for the control. As mentioned earlier, if the *Visible* property is set to *false*, HTML is not generated for the control.

Working with HTML Attributes

Each HTML control features more properties than those listed in Table 3-4. Properties of HTML server controls map to HTML attributes, and the values assigned to the properties are replicated in the HTML output. For controls that don't have an HTML direct counterpart, the *Attributes* collection is used to set attributes on the resulting HTML tag. This collection can also be used to set properties not mapped by the control's interface and, if needed, to define custom HTML attributes. Any content of the *Attributes* collection is managed as a string.

Given the following HTML code snippet, let's see how to programmatically set some attributes on the *<body>* tag:

```
<script>
function Init() {
    alert("Hello");
}
</script>

<script runat=server language="C#">
    void Page_Load(object sender, EventArgs e) {
        theBody.Attributes["onload"] = "Init()";
    }
</script>

<html>
    <body runat="server" id="theBody">
    </body>
</html>
```

You bind a JavaScript script to the *onload* attribute of the *<body>* tag. The resulting HTML code that the browser displays is as follows:

```
<script>
function Init() {
    alert("Hello");
}
</script>

<html>
    <body id="theBody" onload="Init()">
    </body>
</html>
```

The *Attributes* property is rendered through a special type of class named *AttributeCollection*. In spite of the name, the content of the class is not enumerable using the *for...each* statement because the *IEnumerable* interface is not supported. The content is instead stored in a *StateBag* object—the same class used for the ASP.NET view state—which is enumerable. However, the enumerability of the internal data container is exposed to the world. The *AttributeCollection* class provides ad hoc methods to render attributes of a text writer object and to add and remove elements. Interestingly, if you add an attribute named *Style*, the class is smart enough to reroute the assigned content to the *Style* collection.

Hierarchy of HTML Controls

HTML controls can be grouped into two main categories—container and input controls. One control, though, cannot be easily catalogued in either of the two groups—the *HtmlImage* control, which is the ASP.NET counterpart of the *<img>* tag. Figure 3-1 shows the tree of HTML controls.

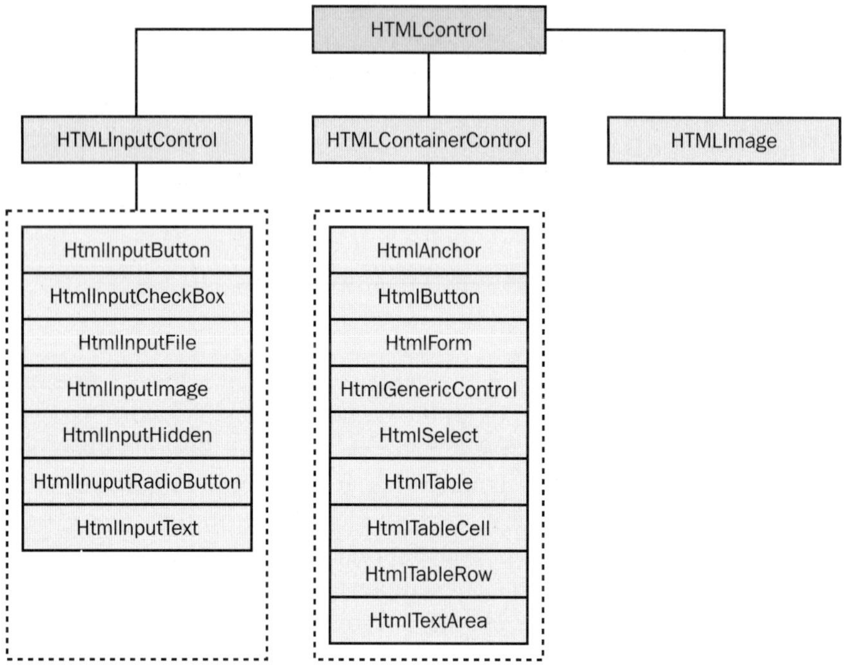

Figure 3-1 A diagram that groups all HTML controls.

Notice that the controls in the figure are not grouped based on discretionary and perhaps arguable rules; instead they are grouped simply by looking at the base class of each control. The *HtmlImage* control forms a group of its own because it inherits directly from *HTMLControl* without any other intermediary class.

The input controls category includes all possible variations of the *<input>* tag, from submit buttons to check boxes and from text fields to radio buttons. The container controls category lists anchors, tables, forms, and in general, all HTML tags that might contain child elements.

HTML Container Controls

The base class for container controls is the *HtmlContainerControl* class, which descends directly from *HtmlControl*. The HTML elements addressed by this tag are elements that must have a closing tag—that is, forms, selection boxes, and tables, as well as anchors and text areas. Compared to the *HtmlControl* class, a container control features a couple of additional string properties—*InnerHtml* and *InnerText*.

Both properties manipulate the reading and writing of literal content found between the opening and closing tags of the tag. Note that you cannot get the inner content of a control if the content includes server controls. *InnerHtml* and *InnerText* work only in the presence of all literal content. The tag itself is not considered for the output. Unlike *InnerText*, though, *InnerHtml* lets you work with HTML rich text and doesn't automatically encode and decode text. In other words, *InnerText* retrieves and sets the content of the tag as plain text, whereas *InnerHtml* retrieves and sets the same content but in HTML format.

Table 3-5 lists the HTML container controls defined in ASP.NET 1.1.

Table 3-5 HTML Container Controls

Class	Description
HtmlAnchor	Represents an HTML anchor—specifically, the *<a>* tag.
HtmlButton	Represents the HTML *<button>* tag. The *<button>* element is defined in the HTML 4.0 specification and supported only in Internet Explorer version 4.0 and later.
HtmlForm	Represents the *<form>* tag, but can be used only as a container of interactive server controls on a Web page. Cannot really be used to create HTML forms programmable on the server.
HtmlGenericControl	Represents an HTML tag for which the .NET Framework does not provide a direct class. Sample tags include *<span>*, *<font>*, *<div>*, *<hr>*, *<link>*, and *<iframe>*. You program these controls using the *Attributes* collection and set attributes indirectly.
HtmlSelect	Represents the *<select>* tag—that is, an HTML selection box.
HtmlTable	Represents an HTML table—specifically, the *<table>* tag.
HtmlTableCell	Represents the *<td>* HTML tag—that is, a cell in a table.
HtmlTableRow	Represents the *<tr>* HTML tag—that is, a row in a table.
HtmlTextArea	Represents a multiline text box, and maps the *<textarea>* HTML tag.

Note that the *HtmlButton* control is different than *HtmlInputButton*, which represents the button variation of the *<input>* tag. We'll say more about buttons in the next section while discussing the Web controls. Server-side forms play a key role in the economy of ASP.NET applications, as they are the means for implementing postbacks and guaranteeing state maintenance. For this reason, the *HtmlForm* control is not simply a form element you can program on the server. In particular, the *HtmlForm* hides the *Action* property and cannot be used to post content to a page different than the content that generated the HTML for the browser. We will cover HTML forms in great detail in Chapter 4.

Navigating to a URL

The *HtmlAnchor* class is the programmatic way of accessing and configuring the *<a>* tag. With respect to the other container controls, the *HtmlAnchor* class provides a few extra properties, such as *HRef*, *Name*, *Target*, and *Title*. The *HRef* property sets the target of the hyperlink and can be used to navigate to the specified location. The *Name* property names a section in the ASP.NET page that can be reached from anywhere on the same page through #-prefixed *HRefs*. The following code demonstrates a bookmarked anchor named *MoreInfo*:

```
<a name="MoreInfo" />
```

This anchor can be reached using the following hyperlink:

```
<a href="#MoreInfo">Get More Info</a>
```

The *Target* property identifies the target window or the frame where the linked URL will be loaded. Common values for *Target* are *_self*, *_top*, *_blank*, and *_parent*, as well as any other name that refers to a page-specific frame. Although the feature is mostly browser dependent, you should always consider these special names as lowercase. Finally, the *Title* property contains the text that is displayed as a ToolTip when the mouse hovers over the anchor's area.

Handling Events on the Server

In addition to being used for navigating to a different page, the anchor control—as well as the *HtmlButton* control—can be used to post back the page. Key to this behavior is the *ServerClick* event, which lets you define the name of the method that will handle, on the server, the event generated when the user clicks the control. The following code demonstrates an anchor in which the click event is handled on both the client and server:

```
<a runat=server onclick="Run()" onserverclick="DoSomething">Click</a>
```

The *onclick* attribute defines the client-side event handler written using JavaScript; the *onserverclick* attribute refers to the server-side code that will run after the page posts back. Of course, if both event handlers are specified, the client-side handler executes first before the post back occurs.

The *HtmlSelect* Control

The *HtmlSelect* control represents a list of options from which you choose one or more. You control the appearance and behavior of the control by setting the *Size* and *Multiple* properties. The *Size* property specifies the number of rows to be displayed by the control, whereas the *Multiple* property indicates whether more than one item can be selected in the control. Internal items are grouped in the *Items* collection, and each element is represented by a *ListItem* object. Interestingly, the *ListItem* class is not defined in the *HtmlControls* namespace but lives instead in the *WebControls* namespace. To specify the text for each selectable item, you can either set the *Text* property of the *ListItem* or simply define a series of *<option>* tags within the opening and closing tags of the *<select>* element.

By default, the *HtmlSelect* control shows up as a drop-down list. However, if multiple selections are allowed or the height is set to more than one row, the control is displayed as a list box. The index of the selected item in a single-selection control is returned through the *SelectedIndex* property. If the multiple selection is enabled, you just loop through the *Items* collection and check the *Selected* property on individual list items.

The *HtmlSelect* control supports data binding through additional properties. The *DataSource* property lets you set the data source, which can be any .NET object that implements the *ICollection* interface. If the data source contains multiple bindable tables (for example, a *DataSet* object), by using the *DataMember* property you can choose a particular one. Finally, the *DataTextField* and *DataValueField* properties are used to bind the list item's *Text* and *Value* properties to columns in the data source.

HTML Tables

In ASP.NET, HTML tables provide a minimum set of functions when rendered using the *HtmlTable* control. In most cases, you don't need to use server-side tables because you typically rely on richer list and grid controls to do the job of displaying tables or records. So you resort to tables when you need to define a fixed layout for graphical elements of the page, but this is not a feature that requires a server-side table.

However, server-side tables are not as powerful as pure HTML tables—which are created by using the *<table>* tag. The main limitation is that rich and complex tables are not supported. The *HtmlTable* class does not support HTML elements such as *<caption>*, *<col>*, *<colgroup>*, *<tbody>*, *<thead>*, and *<tfoot>*. If you use these elements in your ASP.NET code, no run-time exception or compile error is ever thrown. Nevertheless, those elements are silently removed from the HTML code being generated. For example, let's consider the following code:

```
<table runat="server">
    <thead><th>Name</th><th>Last Name</th></thead>
    <tr><td>Joe</td><td>Users</td></tr>
    <tr><td>Bob</td><td>Whosthisguy</td></tr>
</table>
```

As you can see in the following code, the HTML output that is generated by the preceding example does not include the *<thead>* element:

```
<table>
    <tr><td>Joe</td><td>Users</td></tr>
    <tr><td>Bob</td><td>Whosthisguy</td></tr>
</table>
```

By design, an *HtmlTable* control can have only children of the *HtmlTableRow* class. Any attempt to programmatically add other table elements, such as a *<thead>* or a *<tfoot>*, will generate an exception.

The *HtmlTextArea* Control

The *HtmlTextArea* control corresponds to the *<textarea>* HTML element and allows you to programmatically create and configure a multiline text box. The *HtmlTextArea* class provides the *Rows* and *Cols* properties to control the number of rows and columns of the text box. The *Value* property can be used to assign some text to display in the control area.

The *HtmlTextArea* class also provides a *ServerChange* event that fires during a postback and allows you to validate on the server the data contained in the control. Note that the *HtmlTextArea* control does not fire the event itself and does not directly cause the page to post back. Rather, when the page posts back in response to a click on a link or submit button, the *HtmlTextArea* control intervenes in the server-side chain of events and gives the programmer a chance to run some code if the internal content of the control is changed between two successive postbacks.

All ASP.NET controls that, like *HtmlTextArea*, implement the *IPostBackDataHandler* interface can invoke user-defined code when the control's internal state changes. In particular, controls can fire custom events by overriding the *RaisePostDataChangedEvent* method on the aforementioned interface. The following pseudocode shows what happens in the method's implementation of *HtmlTextArea*:

```
void System.Web.UI.IPostBackDataHandler.RaisePostDataChangedEvent() {
    this.OnServerChange(EventArgs.Empty);
}
```

Finally, note that the control raises the event only if the state has changed between two successive posts. To determine whether that has happened, the control needs to track the content it had the time before. This value can be stored only in the view state. Of course, the *ServerChange* won't even fire if you disable the view state for the host page or the control.

HTML Input Controls

In HTML, the *<input>* element has several variations and can be used to provide a submit button as well as a check box or text box. In ASP.NET, each possible instance of the *<input>* element is mapped to a specific class. All input classes derive from the *HtmlInputControl* class. *HtmlInputControl* is the abstract class that defines the common programming interface for all input controls. The class inherits from *HtmlControl* and simply adds three custom properties to the inherited interface: *Name*, *Type*, and *Value*.

The *Name* property returns the name assigned to the control. In ASP.NET, this property is peculiar because, although marked as read/write, it actually works as a read-only property. The *get* accessor returns the control's *UniqueID* property, while the *set* accessor is just void. As a result, whatever value you assign to the property, either programmatically or declaratively, is just ignored and no exception or compile error is ever thrown.

The *Type* property mirrors the *type* attribute of the HTML input elements. The property is read-only. Finally, the *Value* property is read/write and represents the content of the input field.

Table 3-6 lists the HTML input controls defined in ASP.NET 1.1.

Table 3-6 HTML Input Controls

Class	Description
HtmlInputButton	Represents the various flavors of a command button supported by HTML. Feasible values for the *Type* attribute are *button*, *submit*, and *reset*.
HtmlInputCheckBox	Represents an HTML check box—that is, the *<input>* tag with a type equal to *checkbox*.
HtmlInputFile	Represents the file uploader—that is, the *<input>* tag with a type equal to *file*.
HtmlInputHidden	Represents a hidden buffer of text data—that is, the *<input>* tag with a type equal to *hidden*.
HtmlInputImage	Represents a graphic button—that is, the *<input>* tag with a type equal to *image*. Note that this tag is supported by all browsers.
HtmlInputRadioButton	Represents a radio button—that is, the *<input>* tag with a type equal to *radio*.
HtmlInputText	Represents a text field—that is, the *<input>* tag with a type of either *password* or *text*.

The hidden and text-input controls are nearly identical, and the contents of both are posted back. They basically differ only in that hidden fields are not displayed and, subsequently, don't provide some UI-related properties such as *MaxLength* and *Size*.

Command Buttons

The *HtmlInputButton* class is the most flexible button class in the .NET Framework. It differs from the *HtmlButton* class we encountered earlier in that it renders through the *<input>* tag rather than the Internet Explorer–specific *<button>* tag. This fact ensures for the control much wider support from browsers.

The HTML input button controls support the *ServerClick* event, which allows you to set the code to run on the server after the button is clicked. Note that if you set the button type to *Button* and the *ServerClick* event handler is specified, the control automatically adds the postback script code to the *onclick* HTML attribute. In this way, any click causes the page to post back and the code to execute. Let's consider the following ASP.NET code:

```
<input runat="server" type="button" id="btn" value="Click"
    onserverclick="buttonClicked" />
```

The corresponding HTML code is as follows:

```
<input language="javascript" onclick="__doPostBack('btn','')" name="btn"
    type="button" value="Click" />
```

The client-side *__doPostBack* script function is the standard piece of code generated by ASP.NET to implement the postback. The code is actually emitted through a call to the *RegisterPostBackScript* method of the *Page* class. If the button type is set to *Submit*—that is, a value that would always cause a postback—no client-side script code is generated and the *onclick* attribute is not set.

> **Note** The *HtmlInputImage* control supports a nearly identical pattern for handling server-side events and validation. The *HtmlInputImage* control features a few more properties specific to the image it shows. In particular, you can set the alternate text for the image, the border, and the alignment with respect to the rest of the page. The *ServerClick* event handler has a slightly different form and looks like the following:
>
> ```
> void ImageClickEventHandler(object sender,
>     ImageClickEventArgs e);
> ```
>
> When an image button is clicked, the coordinates of the click are determined by using the *X* and *Y* properties of the *ImageClickEventArgs* data structure.

Controlling Validation

The *HtmlInputButton* class, as well as the *HtmlButton* class, support a Boolean property named *CausesValidation*. The property indicates whether the content of the input fields should be validated when the button is clicked. By default, the property is set to *true*, meaning the validation always takes place. We'll examine data validation later in the chapter. For now, it suffices to say, you can programmatically enable or disable the validation step by using the *CausesValidation* property.

Typically, you might want to disable validation if the button that has been clicked doesn't perform a concrete operation but simply clears the user interface or cancels an ongoing operation. By design, in fact, server-side page validation takes place just before the *ServerClick* event handler is executed. Setting the *CausesValidation* property to *false* is the only means you have to prevent an unnecessary validation.

Detecting State Changes of Controls

Earlier in this chapter, while discussing the features of the *HtmlTextArea* control, we ran into the *ServerChange* event and described it as the mechanism to detect and validate changes in the control's state between two successive postbacks. The *ServerChange* event is not an exclusive feature of the *HtmlTextArea* control but is also supported by other input controls such as *HtmlInputCheckBox*, *HtmlInputRadioButton*, *HtmlInputHidden*, and *HtmlInputText*. Let's look at an example in which we use the *ServerChange* event to detect which elements have been checked since last time the control was processed on the server.

We build a page with a list of check boxes and a button to let the user post back to the server when finished. Notice, in fact, that neither the *HtmlInputCheckBox* control nor any other input control except buttons, post back to the server when clicked. For this reason, you must provide another control on the Web page that supports posting to the server—for example, an *HtmlButton* or an *HtmlInputButton* control. The following code implements the page shown in Figure 3-2:

```
<%@ Page Language="C#" %>
<html>
<script runat="server">
public void DetectChange(object sender, EventArgs e) {
    HtmlInputCheckBox cb = (HtmlInputCheckBox) sender;
    Response.Write("Control <b>" + cb.UniqueID + "</b> changed<br>");
}
</script>

<body>
<form runat="server">
```

```
    <input runat="server" type="checkbox" id="one"
        OnServerChange="DetectChange">One<br>
    <input runat="server" type="checkbox" id="two"
        OnServerChange="DetectChange">Two<br>
    <input runat="server" type="checkbox" id="three"
        OnServerChange="DetectChange">Three<br>
    <input runat="server" type="submit" value="Submit" />
</form>
</body>
</html>
```

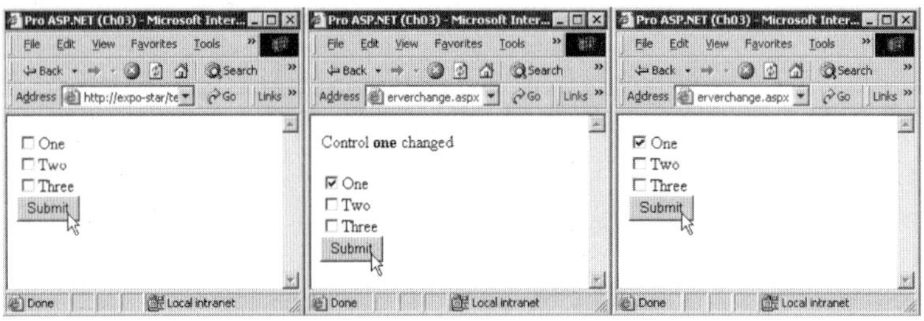

Figure 3-2 The *ServerChange* event fires only if the status of the control has changed since the last time the control was processed on the server.

The *ServerChange* event is fired only if the state of the control results changed after two postbacks.

By implementing the *IPostBackDataHandler* interface, each server control takes a chance to update its current state with data posted by the client. The ASP.NET runtime invokes *LoadPostData* on each control that implements the interface.

```
public bool LoadPostData(string postDataKey,
    NameValueCollection postCollection);
```

The first argument of *LoadPostData* is the client ID of the control; the second argument is a name-value collection that contains the posted data. Posted data can either be *Request.Form* or *Request.QueryString* depending on the form's method. Each control compares the value posted by an HTML element with the same ID with the contents of a particular property. It is *Value* for text boxes and *Checked* for check boxes. The posted value is obtained using the *postDataKey* string as a key to access the values stored in the collection.

Controls that implement the *IPostBackDataHandler* interface use a boilerplate piece of code to implement the *LoadPostData* method. Basically, the method updates the key property of the control with the posted value. The following code shows how *LoadPostData* works for the *HtmlInputText* control:

```
bool LoadPostData(string postDataKey, NameValueCollection postColl) {
    string oldValue;
```

```
    string postedValue;

    // At this point, the view state has been restored
    oldValue = this.Value;

    // Get the posted value for the HTML element with the same
    // ID as the control
    postedValue = postColl[postDataKey];

    // Compare the posted value with Text and updates if needed
    if (oldValue != postedValue) {
        this.Value = postedValue;
        return true;
    }

    // Return a Boolean value denoting whether the state has changed
    return false;
}
```

LoadPostData returns true if the state of the control changes as a result of the post back—that is, if the user generated a new state for the control. For this infrastructure to work, it is key that the value of the server control's *UniqueID* property be assigned to the name attribute of the HTML element. Otherwise, the ASP.NET runtime will not be able to handle postback data for that control.

The ASP.NET runtime tracks all the controls that return true to *LoadPostData* and then invokes the *RaisePostDataChangedEvent* method for each of them—the second method on the *IPostBackDataHandler* interface. The following code snippet reports what that method does for the *HtmlInputText* control:

```
// System.Web.UI.IPostBackDataHandler
void RaisePostDataChangedEvent() {
    this.OnServerChange(EventArgs.Empty);
}
```

For the *HtmlInputCheckBox* control in the preceding sample, a change of state occurs whenever the *Checked* property changes. Note that a nearly identical mechanism exists for Web controls.

Uploading Files

The *HtmlInputFile* control is the HTML tool for uploading files from a browser to the Web server. Note that file upload requires Internet Explorer version 3.0 or newer. To exploit the *HtmlInputFile* control in a form, you should first set the server form's *Enctype* property to *multipart/form-data.*

```
<form runat="server" enctype="multipart/form-data">
    <input runat="server" type="file" id="upLoader" >
    <input runat="server" type="submit" value="Upload..." />
</form>
```

The way in which the *HtmlInputFile* control is rendered to HTML is browser-specific, but it normally consists of a text box and a Browse button. The user selects a file from the local machine and then clicks the button to submit the page to the server. When this occurs, the browser uploads the selected file to the server. Prior to ASP.NET, a server-side process—the posting acceptor—was required to run in the background to handle multipart/form-data submissions. In ASP.NET the role of the posting acceptor is no longer necessary as it is carried out by the ASP.NET runtime itself.

On the server, the file is parked into an object of type *HttpPostedFile* and stays there until explicitly saved to disk. The *HttpPostedFile* object provides properties and methods to get information on an individual file and to read and save the file. The following code shows how to save a posted file to disk:

```
upLoader.PostedFile.SaveAs(serverFile);
```

You can also use the *InputStream* property of the *HttpPostedFile* object to read the posted data without creating a disk file. The *HtmlInputFile* control also allows you to restrict the file types that can be uploaded to the server. You do this by setting the *Accept* property with a comma-separated list of MIME types.

> **Caution** When you use the *SaveAs* method, you should pay attention to specify the full path to the output file. If a relative path is provided, ASP.NET attempts to place the file in the system directory. This practice might result in an access-denied error. Furthermore, make sure to provide write permission for the account used by ASP.NET for the directory where you want to store the file.

ASP.NET exercises some control on the amount of data being uploaded. The *maxRequestLength* attribute in the *<httpRuntime>* section of the configuration file sets the maximum allowable file size. An error is generated in the browser when the file exceeds the specified size—4 MB by default. Uploading large files might also generate another runtime error due to an excessive consumption of system memory. As we've seen in Chapter 2, when more than 60% of the available RAM is consumed the ASP.NET runtime recycles the worker process (aspnet_wp.exe). Of course, this fact breaks the upload process. To avoid this error, you should increase the value of the *memoryLimit* attribute in the *<processModel>* element of the configuration file for the application.

The *HtmlImage* Control

The *HtmlImage* class is the ASP.NET counterpart of the *<img>* tag. You can use it to configure on the server the display of an image. Possible parameters you can set are the size of the image, the border, and the alternate text. An instance of the *HtmlImage* is created only when the *runat* attribute is added to the *<img>* tag. If you simply need to display an image within a page, and the image is not dynamically determined or configured, there is no need to resort to the *HtmlImage* control, which would add unnecessary overhead to the page. The following code snippet shows how to configure a server-side *<img>* tag called to display an image whose name is determined based on run-time conditions.

```
theImg.Width = 100;
theImg.Height = 100;
theImg.Src = GetImageUrl(Request);
```

The *HtmlImage* control should be used to programmatically manipulate the image to change the source file, the width and height, or the alignment of the image relative to other page elements. The majority of properties of the *HtmlImage* control are implemented as strings, including *Src*—the URL of the image—and *Align*. Feasible values of *Align* are only a small set of words such as *left*, *right*, *top*, and so forth. These words would have been more appropriately grouped in a custom-enumerated type, thus providing for a strongly typed programming model. If you think so, too, you just grabbed the gist of the difference between HTML and Web server controls! HTML controls just mirror HTML tags; Web controls attempt to provide a more consistent and effective programming interface by exploiting the characteristics of the .NET Framework.

Literal Controls

Literal controls are a special type of server control that ASP.NET creates and uses whenever it encounters plain text that doesn't require server-side processing. In general, everything that appears in the context of an ASP.NET page is treated like a control. If a tag includes the *runat="server"* attribute, ASP.NET creates an instance of a specific class; otherwise, if no *runat* attribute has been specified, the text is compiled into a *LiteralControl* object. Literal controls are simple text holders that are added to and removed from pages using the same programming interface defined for other server controls.

Web Controls

Web controls are defined in the *System.Web.UI.WebControls* namespace and represent an alternative approach to HTML server controls. Like HTML controls, Web controls are server-side components that spring to life thanks to the *runat="server"* attribute. Unlike HTML controls, Web controls are designed from scratch without needing to be compliant with the HTML syntax, but generate valid HTML. For this reason, they sometimes appear to be more consistent and abstract in the API design and richer in functionality. When hosted in .aspx pages, Web controls are characterized by the *asp* namespace prefix.

To a large degree, Web controls and HTML controls overlap and generate almost the same client code, although they do it through different programming interfaces. For example, the Web controls namespace defines the *TextBox* control and makes it available through the *<asp:textbox>* tag; similarly, the HTML controls namespace provides the *HtmlInputText* control and declares it using the *<input>* tag. The output that both produce is nearly identical. Using either is mostly a matter of preference; only in a few cases will you run into slight functionality differences. Using Web controls gives you a far richer development model and exception management.

Generalities of Web Controls

The *WebControl* class is the base class from which all Web controls inherit. The class defines several properties and methods that are shared, but not necessarily implemented, by derived controls. Many of the properties have the look and feel of the controls and are subject to browser and HTML version. For example, although all Web controls provide the ability to define a border, not all underlying HTML tags actually support a border.

Properties of Web Controls

Table 3-7 lists the properties available on the *WebControl* class.

Table 3-7 Specific Properties of Web Controls

Property	Description
AccessKey	Gets or sets the letter to press (together with ALT) to quickly set focus to the control in a Web form. Supported on Internet Explorer 4.0 and newer.
Attributes	Gets the collection of attributes that do not correspond to properties on the control. Attributes set in this way will be rendered as HTML attributes in the resulting page.

Table 3-7 Specific Properties of Web Controls

Property	Description
BackColor	Gets or sets the background color of the Web control.
BorderColor	Gets or sets the border color of the Web control.
BorderStyle	Gets or sets the border style of the Web control.
BorderWidth	Gets or sets the border width of the Web control.
ControlStyle	Gets the style of the Web server control. The style is an object of type *Style*.
ControlStyleCreated	Gets a value that indicates whether a *Style* object has been created for the *ControlStyle* property.
CssClass	Get or sets the cascading style sheet (CSS) class associated with the client.
Enabled	Gets or sets whether the control is enabled.
Font	Gets the font properties associated with the Web control.
ForeColor	Gets or sets the foreground color of the Web control mostly used to draw text.
Height	Gets or sets the height of the control. The height is expressed as a member of type *Unit*.
Style	Gets a *CssStyleCollection* collection object made of all the attributes assigned to the outer tag of the Web control.
TabIndex	Gets or sets the tab index of the control.
ToolTip	Gets or sets the text displayed when the mouse pointer hovers over the control.
Width	Gets or sets the width of the control. The width is expressed as a member of type *Unit*.

The *ControlStyle* and *ControlStyleCreated* properties are used primarily by control developers, while the *Style* property is what application developers would typically use to set CSS attributes on the outer tag of the control. The *Style* property is implemented using an instance of the class *CssStyleCollection*. The class is a simple collection of string values—the values you set either declaratively or programmatically through the *Style* property. The *ControlStyle* property, on the other hand, evaluates to an object of type *Style*—a class that encapsulates the appearance properties of the control. In other words, the *Style* class works as the repository of the graphical and cosmetic attributes that characterize all Web controls. All properties are strongly typed. In contrast, the *CssStyleCollection* class is just the collection of CSS styles defined in the tags. The *Style* class groups together some of the properties that were shown in Table 3-7. The grouped properties are: *BackColor*, *BorderColor*, *BorderStyle*, *BorderWidth*, *CssClass*, *Font*, *ForeColor*,

Height, and *Width*. Note that style values set through the *CssStyleCollection* class are not automatically reflected by the (strongly typed) values in the *Style* object.

Styling a Web Control

The style properties of a Web control can be programmatically manipulated to some extent. For example, in the *Style* class, you can count on a *CopyFrom* method to duplicate the object and you can take advantage of the *MergeWith* method to combine two style objects.

```
currentStyle.MergeStyle(newStyle);
```

The *MergeWith* method joins the properties of both objects. In doing so, it does not replace any property that is already set in the base object but limits itself to defining uninitialized properties. Finally, the *Reset* method clears all current attributes in the various properties of the style object.

Methods of Web Controls

The *WebControl* class supports a few particular methods that are not part of the *Control* interface. These methods are listed in Table 3-8.

Table 3-8 Specific Methods of Web Controls

Method	Description
ApplyStyle	Copies any nonempty elements of the specified style to the control. Existing style properties are overwritten.
CopyBaseAttributes	Imports from the specified Web control the properties *AccessKey*, *Enabled*, *ToolTip*, *TabIndex*, and *Attributes*. Basically, it copies all the properties not encapsulated in the *Style* object.
MergeStyle	Like *ApplyStyle*, copies any nonempty elements of the specified style to the control. Existing style properties are *not* overwritten, though.
RenderBeginTag	Renders the HTML opening tag of the control into the specified writer. The method is called right before the control's *RenderControl* method.
RenderEndTag	Renders the HTML closing tag of the control into the specified writer. The method is called right after the control's *RenderControl* method.

All these methods are rarely of interest to application developers. They are mostly designed to help control developers.

Core Web Controls

The set of Web controls can be divided in four main categories: core controls, validators, data-bound controls, and list controls. A fifth category of Web controls—iterative data-bound controls—will be examined separately in future chapters. In addition, the .NET Framework also provides a few miscellaneous controls that provide ad hoc functionalities and are as common on the Web as they are hard to catalogue. We'll cover these controls in the section "Miscellaneous Web Controls." Let's start off with a look at the core Web controls, which are described in Table 3-9.

Table 3-9 Core Web Controls

Control	Description
Button	Implements a submit push button through the *<input>* tag.
CheckBox	Implements a check box through the *<input>* tag.
HyperLink	Implements an anchor *<a>* tag, and lets you specify either the location to jump to or the script code to execute.
Image	Implements a picture box through the *<img>* tag.
Label	Represents a static, nonclickable piece of text. Implemented through the *<span>* tag.
Panel	Implements an HTML container using the *<div>* block element. Note that in down-level browsers it is rendered as a *<table>*.
RadioButton	Implements a single radio button through the *<input>* tag.
Table	Implements the outer table container. Equivalent to the HTML *<table>* element.
TableCell	A table cell; is equivalent to the HTML *<td>* element.
TableRow	A table row; is equivalent to the HTML *<tr>* element.
TextBox	Implements a text box using the *<input>* or *<textarea>* tag as appropriate and according to the requested text mode. Can work in single-line, multiline, or password mode.

The *Table* class and its related classes allow you to build and configure an HTML table using the same abstract object model used for building other Web controls. The power of the *Table* class, though, is particularly evident when it comes to building tables programmatically with dynamic contents. No matter how complex the programming model is, all Web controls produce HTML for both up-level and down-level browsers.

Images and Image Buttons

The *Image* control displays an image on the Web page. The path to the image is set through the *ImageUrl* property. Image URLs can be either relative or absolute, with most programmers showing a clear preference for relative URLs, which make a Web site inherently easier to move. You can also specify alternate text to display when the image is not available. The property to use in this case is *AlternateText*. The image alignment with respect to other elements on the page is set by using the *ImageAlign* property. Feasible values are taken from the homonymous *enum* type.

The *Image* control is not a clickable component and is simply limited to displaying an image. If you need to capture mouse clicks on the image, use the *ImageButton* control instead. The *ImageButton* class descends from *Image* and extends it with a couple of events—*Click* and *Command*—that are raised when the control is clicked. The *OnClick* event handler provides you with an *ImageClickEventArgs* data structure that contains information about the coordinates for the location at which the image is clicked.

The *OnCommand* event handler makes the *ImageButton* control behave like a command button. A command button has an associated name that you can control through the *CommandName* property. If you have multiple *ImageButton* controls on the same page, the command name allows you to distinguish which one is actually clicked. The *CommandArgument* property can be used to pass additional information about the command and the control.

Check Boxes and Radio Buttons

Check boxes and radio buttons are implemented through the *<input>* tag and the *type* attribute set to *checkbox* or *radio*. Unlike using the HTML control versions, the Web control versions of check boxes and radio buttons let you specify the associated text as a property. The HTML elements and the corresponding HTML controls lack an attribute whose content becomes the text near the check box or radio button. In HTML, to make the text near the check box or radio button clickable, you have to resort to the *<label>* tag with the *for* attribute.

```
<input type="checkbox" id="ctl" />
<label for="ctl">Check me</label>
```

Neither the *HtmlInputCheckBox* nor the *HtmlInputRadioButton* control add a label, which leaves you responsible for doing that. These Web controls counterpart, on the other hand, are not bound to the HTML syntax and do precisely that—they automatically add a *Text* property, which results in an appropriate *<label>* tag. For example, consider the following ASP.NET code:

```
<asp:checkbox runat="server" id="ctl" text="Check me" />
```

It results in the following HTML code:

```
<input type="checkbox" id="ctl" />
<label for="ctl">Check me</label>
```

HyperLinks

The *HyperLink* control creates a link to another Web page and is typically displayed through the text stored in the *Text* property. Alternatively, the hyperlink can be displayed as an image; in this case, the URL of the image is stored in the *ImageUrl* property. Note that if both the *Text* and *ImageUrl* properties are set, the *ImageUrl* property takes precedence. In this case, the content of the *Text* property is displayed as a ToolTip when the mouse hovers over the control's area.

The *NavigateUrl* property indicates the URL the hyperlink is pointing to. The *Target* property is the name of the window or frame that will contain the output of the target URL.

Miscellaneous Web Controls

The *WebControls* namespace also includes a few controls that provide useful functionality that is common in Web applications. In particular, we'll examine the *AdRotator* control, which works like an advertisement banner, and the *Calendar* control, which is a flexible and highly interactive control used to specify a date.

The *AdRotator* Control

Abstractly speaking, the *AdRotator* control displays an automatically sized image button and updates both the image and the URL each time the page refreshes. The image to display and other information is read from an XML file written according to a specific schema. More concretely, you use the *AdRotator* control to create an advertisement banner on a Web Forms page. The control actually inserts an image and hyperlink in the page and makes them point to the advertisement page selected. The image is sized by the browser to the dimensions of the *AdRotator* control, regardless of its actual size. The following code shows a typical XML advertisement file:

```
<Advertisements>
<Ad>
    <ImageUrl>6235.gif</ImageUrl>
    <NavigateUrl>www.microsoft.com/MSPress/books/6235.asp</NavigateUrl>
    <AlternateText>Applied XML Programming with .NET</AlternateText>
    <Impressions>50</Impressions>
</Ad>
<Ad>
    <ImageUrl>5727.gif</ImageUrl>
```

```
    <NavigateUrl>www.microsoft.com/MSPress/books/5727.asp</NavigateUrl>
    <AlternateText>Building Web Solutions with ASP.NET</AlternateText>
    <Impressions>50</Impressions>
</Ad>
</Advertisements>
```

The *<Advertisement>* root node contains multiple *<Ad>* elements, one per each image to show. The syntax of the *AdRotator* control is as follows:

```
<%@ Page Language="C#" %>
<html>
<head><title>Pro ASP.NET (Ch03)</title></head>
<body>
    <form runat="server">
        <h1>Dino Esposito's Books</h1>
        <asp:AdRotator runat="server" id="bookRotator"
            AdvertisementFile="MyBooks.xml" />
    </form>
</body>
</html>
```

In the XML advertisement file, you use the *<ImageUrl>* node to indicate the image to load and the *<NavigateUrl>* node to specify where to go in case of a click. The *<AlternateText>* node indicates the alternate text to use if the image is unavailable. Finally, *<Impressions>* indicates how often an image should be displayed in relation to other images in the advertisement file.

Once per roundtrip, the *AdRotator* control fires the server-side *AdCreated* event. The event occurs before the page is rendered. The event handler receives an argument of type *AdCreatedEventArgs*, which contains information about the image, the navigation URL, and the alternate text. The *AdRotator* control exposes a few custom properties, including *Target* to set the target of the hyperlink and *AdvertisementFile* to set the file with image names.

The *Calendar* Control

The *Calendar* control displays a one-month calendar and allows you to choose dates and navigate backward and forward through the months of the year. The control is highly customizable both for appearance and functionality. For example, by setting the *SelectionMode* property, you can decide what the user can select—that is, whether a single date, week, or month can be selected. Figure 3-3 provides a view of the *Calender* control.

```
<asp:calendar runat="server" id="hireDate"
    BackColor="white" ForeColor="black" Font-Size="9px"
    SelectionMode="" DayHeaderStyle-Font-Bold="True" />
```

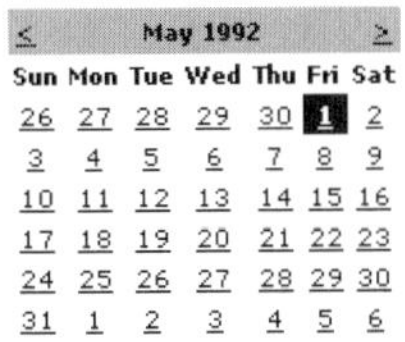

Figure 3-3 The *Calendar* control in action.

The *VisibleDate* property sets a date that must be visible in the calendar, while *SelectedDate* sets with a different style the date that is rendered as selected. The control also fires three ad hoc events: *DayRender*, *SelectionChanged*, and *VisibleMonthChanged*. The *DayRender* event signals that the control has just created a new day cell. You can hook the event if you think you need to customize the cell output. The *SelectionChanged* event fires when the selected date changes, while *VisibleMonthChanged* is raised whenever the user moves to another month using the control's selector buttons.

The *Calendar* control originates a roundtrip for each selection you make. Although it is cool and powerful on its own, for better performance you might also want to provide a plain text box for manually typing dates.

The *Xml* Control

The *Xml* control, defined by the *<asp:xml>* tag, is used to output the content of an XML document directly into an ASP.NET page. The control can display the source XML as-is or as the results of an XSL transformation (XSLT). The *Xml* control is a sort of declarative counterpart for the *XslTransform* class and can make use of the .NET Framework XSLT transform class internally.

You use the *Xml* control when you need to embed XML documents in a Web page. For example, the control is extremely handy when you need to create XML data islands for the client to consume. The control lets you specify a document to work with and, optionally, a transformation to apply. The XML document can be specified in a variety of formats—an XML document object model, string, or file name. The XSLT transformation can be defined through either an already configured instance of the .NET Framework *XslTransform* class or a file name.

```
<asp:xml runat="server"
    documentsource="document.xml"
    transformsource="transform.xsl" />
```

If you're going to apply some transformation to the XML data, you could also embed it inline between the opening and closing tags of the control. The control also makes it easier to accomplish a common ASP task: apply browser-dependent transformations to portions of the page expressed in an XML meta language. In this case, you exploit the programming interface of the control as follows:

```
<asp:xml runat="server" id="theXml" documentsource="document.xml" />
```

In the *Page_Load* event, you just check the browser capabilities and decide which transformation should be applied.

```
void Page_Load(object sender, EventArgs e) {
    if (IsInternetExplorer(Request.Browser))
        theXml.TransformSource = "ie5.xsl";
    else
        theXml.TransformSource = "downlevel.xsl";
}
```

The *PlaceHolder* Control

The *PlaceHolder* control is one of the few controls in the *WebControls* namespace that isn't derived from the *WebControl* class. It inherits from *Control* and is used only as a container for other controls in the page. The *PlaceHolder* control does not produce visible output of its own and is limited to containing child controls dynamically added through the *Controls* collection. The following code shows how to embed the *PlaceHolder* control in a Web page:

```
<asp:placeholder runat="server" id="theToolbar" />
```

Once you have a placeholder, you can add controls to it. As mentioned, the placeholder does not add extra functionality, but it provides for grouping and easy and direct identification of a group of related controls. The following code demonstrates how to create a new button and add it to an existing placeholder:

```
btn = new Button();
btn.Text = "Click me";
theToolbar.Controls.Add(btn);
```

The *PlaceHolder* control reserves a location in the control tree and can be extremely helpful in identifying specific areas of the page to customize and extend by adding controls programmatically.

Validation Controls

A key rule for writing more secure applications is to get the data right before you use it. Getting the data right requires you to apply a validation step to any external input. In ASP.NET, validator controls are used to verify the input of the form fields within a Web page. Validation controls provide an easy-to-use mechanism to perform a variety of validation tasks, including testing for valid types, values within a given range, or required fields.

The validator controls are Web server controls and inherit from the *BaseValidator* class which, in turn, descends from *Label*. All validator controls defined on a page are automatically grouped in the *Validators* collection of the *Page* class. You can validate them all in a single shot using the *Validate* method in the *Page* class or individually by calling the *Validate* method on each validator. The *Validate* method sets the *IsValid* property both on the page and on the individual validator. The *IsValid* property indicates whether the user's entries match the requirements of the validators.

> **Note** The *Validate* method on the validator control performs any needed checks on the associated control and, as a result, updates the control's *IsValid* property. The *Validate* method, when called on the page, cumulatively validates all validation controls defined within the page. The page's *IsValid* property is the logical AND of the values of *IsValid* on all embedded validation controls.

Other than explicitly using the *Validate* method, the user's entry is also automatically validated whenever the page posts back. In this case, validation is performed when a button control is clicked. The button controls that can automatically apply validation are *Button*, *HtmlButton*, *HtmlInputButton*, *HtmlInputImage*, *ImageButton*, and *LinkButton*. You can enable or disable a button's validation capability by using the *CausesValidation* Boolean property.

The .NET Framework also provides complete client-side implementation for validation controls. This allows Dynamic HTML–enabled browsers (such as Internet Explorer version 4.0 and later) to perform validation on the client as soon as the user tabs out of a monitored input field.

Types of Validation Controls

Each validation control references an input control located elsewhere on the page. When the page is going to be submitted, the contents of the monitored server control is passed to the validator for further processing. Each validator would perform a different type of verification. Table 3-10 shows the types of validation supported by the .NET Framework.

Table 3-10 Validator Controls in the .NET Framework

Validator	Description
CompareValidator	Compares the user's entry against a fixed value by using a comparison operator such as *LessThan*, *Equal*, or *GreaterThan*. Can also compare against the value of a property in another control on the same page.
CustomValidator	Employs a programmatically defined validation logic to check the validity of the user's entry. You use this validator when the other validators cannot perform the necessary validation and you want to provide custom code that validates the input.
RangeValidator	Ensures that the user's entry falls within a specified range. Lower and upper boundaries can be expressed as numbers, strings or dates.
RegularExpressionValidator	Validates the user's entry only if it matches a pattern defined by a regular expression.
RequiredFieldValidator	Ensures that the user specifies a value for the field.

Multiple validation controls can be used with an individual input control to validate according to different criteria. For example, you can apply multiple validation controls on a text box that is expected to contain an e-mail address. In particular, you can impose that the field is not skipped (*RequiredFieldValidator*) and that its content matches the typical format of e-mail addresses (*RegularExpressionValidator*).

Table 3-10 lacks a reference to the *ValidationSummary* control. The control does not perform validation tasks itself. It displays a label to summarize all the validation error messages found on a Web page as the effect of other validators. We'll cover the *ValidationSummary* control later in the chapter.

The *BaseValidator* Class

Figure 3-4 shows the relationship between the various validation controls and their parent classes.

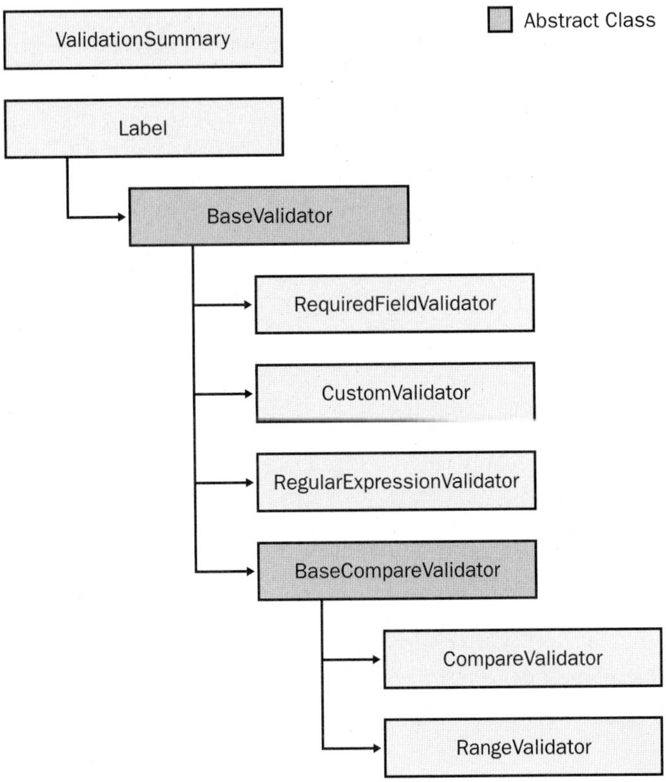

Figure 3-4 Diagram of validation controls in ASP.NET. Gray boxes represent abstract classes.

Table 3-11 details the specific properties of validation controls. Some properties, such as *ForeColor*, *Enabled*, and *Text*, are overridden versions of base properties on base classes.

Table 3-11 Basic Properties of Validators

Property	Description
ControlToValidate	Gets or sets the input control to validate. The control is identified by name—that is, by using the value of the *ID* attribute.
Display	If client-side validation is supported and enabled, gets or sets how the space for the error message should be allocated—either statically or dynamically. In case of server-side validation, this property is ignored. A *Static* display is possible only if the browser supports the *display* CSS style. The default is *Dynamic*.

(continued)

Table 3-11 Basic Properties of Validators *(continued)*

Property	Description
EnableClientScript	*True* by default; gets or sets whether client-side validation is enabled.
Enabled	Gets or sets whether the validation control is enabled.
ErrorMessage	Gets or sets the text for the error message.
ForeColor	Gets or sets the color of the message displayed when validation fails.
IsValid	Gets or sets whether the associated input control passes validation.
Text	Gets or sets the description displayed for the validator in lieu of the error message. Note, though, this text does not replace the contents of *ErrorMessage* in the summary text.

All validation controls inherit from the *BaseValidator* class except for compare validators, for which a further intermediate class—the *BaseCompareValidator* class—exists. The *BaseCompareValidator* class serves as the foundation for validators that perform typed comparisons. An ad hoc property, named *Type*, is used to specify the data type the values are converted to before being compared. The *CanConvert* static method determines whether the user's entry can be converted to the specified data type. Supported types includes string, integer, double, date, and currency. As shown in Figure 3-4, the classes acting as compare validators are *RangeValidator* and *CompareValidator*.

Associating Validators with Input Controls

The link between each validator and its associated input control is established through the *ControlToValidate* property. The property must be set to the ID of the input control. If you do not specify a valid input control, an exception will be thrown when the page is rendered. The association validator/control is between two controls within the same container—be it a page, user control, or template.

Not all server controls can be validated. Those which can be validated specify their validation property through an attribute named *[ValidationPropertyAttribute]*. The attribute takes the name of the property that contains the user's entry. For example, the validation property for a *TextBox* is *Text* and is indicated as follows:

```
[ValidationPropertyAttribute("Text")]
public class TextBox : WebControl {
    ⋮
}
```

The standard list of validating controls include *TextBox*, *DropDownList*, *HtmlInputFile*, *HtmlInputText*, *HtmlSelect*, *HtmlTextArea*, *ListBox*, and *RadioButtonList*. Custom controls can be validated too, as long as they are marked with the aforementioned *ValidationPropertyAttribute* attribute.

> **Note** If the validation property of the associated input control is left empty, all validators accept the value and pass the test. The *RequiredFieldValidator* control represents a rather natural exception to this rule, as it has been specifically designed to detect fields the user skipped and left blank.

The *CompareValidator* Control

The *CompareValidator* control lets you compare the value entered by the user with a constant value or the value specified in another control in the same naming container. The behavior of the control is characterized by the following additional properties:

- ***ControlToCompare*** Represents the ID of the control to compare with the current user's entry. You should avoid setting the *ControlToCompare* and *ValueToCompare* properties at the same time. They are considered mutually exclusive; if you set both, the *ControlToCompare* property takes precedence.
- ***Operator*** Specifies the comparison operation to perform. The list of feasible operations is defined in the *ValidationCompareOperator* enumeration. The default operator is *Equal*. Other operators are *NotEqual*, *LessThan*, *GreaterThan*, *GreaterThanEqual*, *LessThanEqual*, and *DataTypeCheck*. The last operator in particular is useful when you want to make sure certain input data can be converted to a certain type. When the *DataTypeCheck* operator is specified, both *ValueToCompare* and *ControlToCompare* are ignored. In this case, the test is made on the type of the input data and returns *true* if the specified data can be converted to the expected type. Supported types are expressed through the following keywords: *String*, *Integer*, *Double*, *Date*, and *Currency* (decimal).
- ***ValueToCompare*** Indicates the value to compare the user's input against. If the *Type* property is set, the *ValueToCompare* attribute must comply with it.

The following code demonstrates the typical markup of the *CompareValidator* control when the control is called to validate an integer input from a text box representing someone's age:

```
<asp:CompareValidator runat="server" id="ageValidator"
    ControlToValidate="ageTextBox"
    ValueToCompare="18"
    Operator="GreaterThanEqual"
    Type="Integer"
    ErrorMessage="Must specify an age greater than 17." />
```

The *CustomValidator* Control

The *CustomValidator* control is a generic and totally user-defined validator that uses custom validation logic to accomplish its task. You typically resort to this control when none of the other validators seems appropriate or, more simply, when you need to execute your own code in addition to that of the standard validators.

To set up a custom validator, you need to indicate a client-side function through the *ClientValidationFunction* property. If client-side validation is disabled or not supported, simply omit this setting. Alternatively, or in addition to client validation, you can define some managed code to execute on the server. You do this by defining a handler for the *ServerValidate* event. The code will be executed when the page is posted back in response to a click on a button control. The following code snippet shows how to configure a custom validator to check the value of a text box against an array of feasible values.

```
<asp:CustomValidator runat="server" id="membershipValidator"
    ControlToValidate="membership"
    ClientValidationFunction="CheckMembership"
    OnServerValidate="ServerValidation"
    ErrorMessage="Membership can be Normal, Silver, Gold, or Platinum." />
```

If specified, the client validation function takes a mandatory signature and looks like this:

```
function CheckMembership(source, arguments)
{ ... }
```

The *source* argument references the HTML tag that represents the validator control—usually, a *<span>* tag. The *arguments* parameter references an object with two properties, *IsValid* and *Value*. The *Value* property is the value stored in the input control to be validated. The *IsValid* property must be set to *false* or *true* according to the result of the validation. The *CustomValidator* control is not associated in all cases with a single input control in the current naming container. For this type of validator, setting the *ControlToValidate* property is not mandatory. For example, if the control has to validate the contents of multiple input fields, you just don't set the *ControlToValidate* property and the *arguments.Value* variable evaluates to the empty string. In this case, you write the validation logic so that any needed values are dynamically retrieved. With client-side script code, this can be done by accessing the members of the document's form, as shown in the following code:

```
function CheckMembership(source, arguments) {
    // Retrieve the current value of the element
    // with the specified ID
    var membership = document.forms[0]["membership"].value;
    ⋮
}
```

Setting only a client-side validation code opens a security hole because an attacker could work around the validation logic and manage to have invalid or malicious data sent to the server. By defining a server event handler, you have one more chance to validate data before applying changes to the back-end system. To define a server-side handler for a custom validator, use the *ServerValidate* event.

```
void ServerValidation(object source, ServerValidateEventArgs e) {
    <$VE;>
}
```

The *ServerValidateEventArgs* structure contains two properties—*IsValid* and *Value*—with the same meaning and goal as in the client validation function. If the control is not bound to a particular input field, the *Value* property is empty and you retrieve any needed value using the ASP.NET object model. For example, the following code shows how to check the status of a check box on the server:

```
void ServerValidation (object source, ServerValidateEventArgs e) {
    e.IsValid = (CheckBox1.Checked == true);
}
```

Note that the *CheckBox* control (as well as *HtmlInputCheckBox*) cannot be validated using the standard validators and the *CustomValidator* control is the only option.

The *RegularExpressionValidator* Control

Regular expressions are an effective way to ensure that a predictable and well-known sequence of characters form the user's entry. For example, using regular expressions you can validate the format of zip codes, Social Security numbers, client codes, e-mail addresses, telephone numbers, and so on. When using the *RegularExpressionValidator* control, you set the *ValidationExpression* property with the regular expression, which will be used to validate the input. (For more information about regular expressions, see the Visual Studio .NET documentation or the MSDN online documentation.)

The following code snippet shows a regular expression validator that ensures the user's entry is an e-mail address:

```
<asp:RegularExpressionValidator runat="server" id="emailValidator"
    ControlToValidate="email"
    ValidationExpression="[a-zA-Z_0-9.-]+\@[a-zA-Z_0-9.-]+\.\w+"
    ErrorMessage="Must be a valid email address." />
```

The regular expression just shown specifies that valid e-mail addresses are formed by two nonzero sequences of letters, digits, dashes, and dots separated by an @ symbol and followed by a dot (.) and an alphabetic string. (This might not be the perfect regular expression for e-mail addresses, but it certainly incorporates the majority of e-mail address formats.)

> **Note** The regular expression validation syntax is slightly different on the client than on the server. The *RegularExpressionValidator* control uses JScript regular expressions on the client and the .NET Framework *Regex* object on the server. Be aware that the JScript regular expression syntax is a subset of the *Regex* model. Whenever possible, try to use the regular expression syntax supported by JScript so that the same result is obtained for both the client and server.

The *RangeValidator* Control

The *RangeValidator* control lets you verify that a given value falls within a specified range. The type of the values involved in the check is specified dynamically and picked from a short list that includes strings, numbers, and dates. The following code shows how to use a range validator control. The key properties are *MinimumValue* and *MaximumValue*, which together clearly denote the lower and upper boundaries of the interval.

```
<asp:RangeValidator runat="server" id="hiredDateValidator"
    ControlToValidate="hired"
    MinimumValue="1999-1-1"
    MaximumValue="9999-12-31"
    Type="Date"
    ErrorMessage="Must be a date after <b>Jan 1, 1999</b>." />
```

Note that an exception is thrown if the strings assigned *MinimumValue* or *MaximumValue* cannot be converted to the numbers or dates according to the value of the *Type* property.

If the type is set to *Date*, but no specific culture is set for the application, you should specify dates using a culture-neutral format, such as *yyyy/MM/dd*. If you don't do so, the chances are good that the values will not be interpreted correctly. Also bear in mind that the *RangeValidator* control just extends the capabilities of the more basic *CompareValidator* control by checking for a value in a fixed interval. In light of this, the *RangeValidator* control might raise an exception if either *MinimumValue* or *MaximumValue* is omitted. Whether the exception is thrown or not depends on the type chosen and its inherent ability to interpret the empty string. For example, an empty string on a *Date* type causes an exception.

If you want to operate on an unbound interval—whether lower or upper unbound—either you resort to the *GreaterThan* (or *LessThan*) operator on the *CompareValidator* control or simply use a virtually infinite value such as the *9999-12-31* date.

> **Note** Properties on the validation controls can be configured programmatically—for example, in the *Page_Load* event. In particular, if you're going to define the boundaries of a *RangeValidator* control at run time, be aware that both *MinimumValue* and *MaximumValue* are string properties.

The *RequiredFieldValidator* Control

To catch when a user skips a mandatory field in an input form, you use the *RequiredFieldValidator* control to show an appropriate error message.

```
<asp:RequiredFieldValidator runat="server" id="lnameValidator"
    ControlToValidate="lname"
    ErrorMessage="Last name is mandatory" />
```

As long as you're using an up-level browser and client-side scripting is enabled for each validator, which is the default, invalid input will display error messages without performing a postback. Note that just tabbing through the controls is not a condition that raises an error; the validator gets involved only if you type blanks or if the field is blank when the page is posted back.

The control that requires input does not automatically display an asterisk or other character near the control to emphasize that it's required. Marking the field so that it stands out from the others is a good programming practice, but it is left up to the programmer to make controls that require input to stand out from the others.

How can you determine whether a certain field is really empty? In many cases, the empty string just pays the bill, but this is not a rule. The *InitialValue* property specifies the initial value of the input control. The validation fails only if the value of the control equals *InitialValue* upon losing focus. By default, *InitialValue* is initialized with the empty string.

Setting Up a Data Entry Page

Let's see how to build a form that makes intensive use of validators to ensure that the input is always well-formed. The following page contains a couple of mandatory text fields to specify first and last name. Both are associated with an instance of the *RequiredFieldValidator* control. Other controls are expected to accept a minimum age and a date. For them, we'll use *CompareValidator* and *RangeValidator*. An e-mail address is entered and validated using a *RegularExpressionValidator*. Finally, a membership level is validated using a *CustomValidator*.

```
<form runat="server">
    <h3>Fill the form out</h3>

    <table>
        <tr><td>Name</td><td>*</td>
            <td><asp:textbox runat="server" id="fname" />
                <asp:RequiredFieldValidator runat="server"
                    id="fnameValidator"
                    ControlToValidate="fname"
                    ErrorMessage="Name is mandatory" /></td></tr>
        <tr><td>Last Name</td><td>*</td>
            <td><asp:textbox runat="server" id="lname" />
                <asp:RequiredFieldValidator runat="server"
                    id="lnameValidator"
                    ControlToValidate="lname"
                    ErrorMessage="Last name is mandatory" /></td></tr>
        <tr><td>Age</td><td></td>
            <td><asp:textbox runat="server" id="age" />
                <asp:CompareValidator runat="server"
                    id="ageValidator"
                    ControlToValidate="age"
                    Operator="GreaterThanEqual"
                    ValueToCompare="18"
                    Type="integer"
                    ErrorMessage="Age must be at least 18." /></td></tr>
        <tr><td>Email</td><td></td>
            <td><asp:textbox runat="server" id="email" />
                <asp:RegularExpressionValidator runat="server"
                    id="emailValidator"
                    ControlToValidate="email"
                    ValidationExpression=
                        "[a-zA-Z_0-9.-]+\@[a-zA-Z_0-9.-]+\.\w+"
                    ErrorMessage="Must be an email address." /></td></tr>
        <tr><td>Hire Date</td><td></td>
            <td><asp:textbox runat="server" id="hired" />
                <asp:CompareValidator runat="server"
                    id="hiredValidator"
                    ControlToValidate="hired"
                    Display="Dynamic"
```

```
                    Operator="DataTypeCheck"
                    Type="date"
                    ErrorMessage="Must enter a date." />
                <asp:RangeValidator runat="server"
                    id="hiredDateValidator"
                    ControlToValidate="hired"
                    Display="Dynamic"
                    MinimumValue="1999-1-1"
                    MaximumValue="9999-12-31"
                    Type="Date"
                    ErrorMessage="Date after 1-1-99." /></td></tr>
        <tr><td>Membership Level</td><td></td>
            <td><asp:textbox runat="server" id="membership" />
                <asp:CustomValidator runat="server"
                    id="membershipValidator"
                    ControlToValidate="membership"
                    ClientValidationFunction="CheckMembership"
                    ErrorMessage="Must be Gold or Platinum." /></td></tr>
    </table>
</form>
```

By default, if the page runs on an up-level browser such as Internet Explorer 6.0, the validation is automatically enabled on the client as well. As you tab out of each form field, some automatically created Javascript code runs and checks the user input before it is sent to the server.

In the page just listed, each validator control is rendered to the right of the input field so that in case of an error, the error message is displayed to the right of the input field, as shown in Figure 3-5.

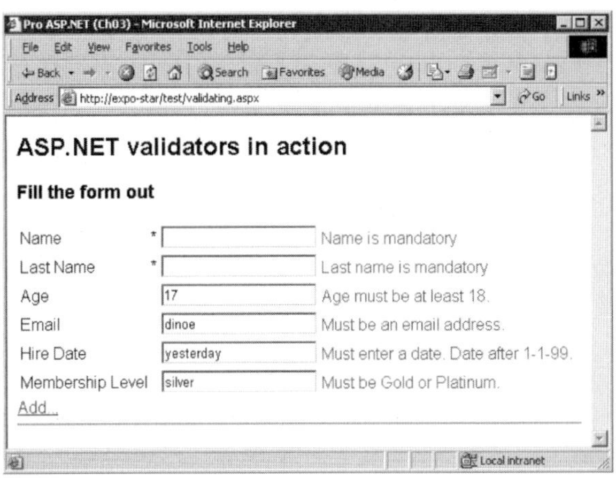

Figure 3-5 The input form with error messages signaled by validation controls.

If the client script support is disabled or the browser doesn't provide for it, no validation takes place until the page is posted back. In this case, nothing happens as you tab in and out of input fields, but after a postback the page is served with the proper error messages.

Displaying Error Information

The *ErrorMessage* property determines the static message that each validation control will display in case of error. Note that if the *Text* property is also set, it would take precedence over *ErrorMessage*. *Text* is designed to display inline where the validation control is located; *ErrorMessage* is designed to display in the validation summary. (Strategies for using *Text* and *ErrorMessage* will be discussed more in the next section, "The *ValidationSummary* Control.") Because all validation controls are labels, no other support or helper controls are needed to display any message. The message will be displayed in the body of the validation controls and, subsequently, wherever the validation control is actually placed. The error message is displayed as HTML, so it can contain any HTML formatting attribute.

Validators that work in client mode can create the *<span>* tag for the message either statically or dynamically. You can control this setting by using the *Display* property. When the display mode is set to *Static* (the default), the *<span>* element is given the following style:

```
style="color:Red;visibility:hidden;"
```

The CSS *visibility* style attribute, when set to *Hidden*, causes the browser not to display the element but reserves space for it. If the *Display* property contains *Dynamic*, the style string changes as follows:

```
style="color:Red;display:none;"
```

The CSS *display* attribute, when set to *none*, simply hides the element, which will take up space on the page only if displayed. The value of the *Display* property becomes critical when you have multiple validators associated with the same input control. For example, consider the following code excerpted from the previously considered page:

```
<asp:textbox runat="server" id="hired" />
    <asp:CompareValidator runat="server"
        id="hiredValidator"
        ControlToValidate="hired"
        Display="Dynamic"
        Operator="DataTypeCheck"
        Type="date"
        ErrorMessage="Must enter a date." />
    <asp:RangeValidator runat="server"
        id="hiredDateValidator"
```

```
    ControlToValidate="hired"
    Display="Dynamic"
    MinimumValue="1999-1-1"
    MaximumValue="9999-12-31"
    Type="Date"
    ErrorMessage="Date after 1-1-99." />
```

The value of the *hired* text box is first validated to ensure it contains a valid date and then to verify the specified date is later than 1-1-1999. If the *Display* property is set to *Static* and the date is outside the specified range, you get a page like the one shown in Figure 3-6.

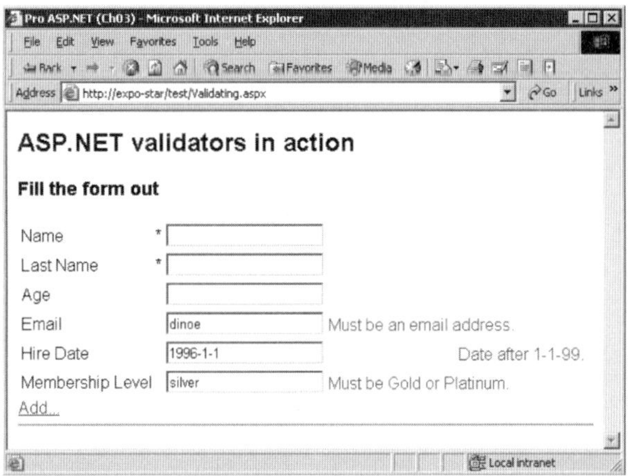

Figure 3-6 The first error message is not displayed, but it takes up space.

The *ValidationSummary* Control

The *ValidationSummary* control is a label that summarizes and displays all the validation error messages found on a Web page. The summary is displayed in a single location formatted in a variety of ways. The *DisplayMode* property sets the output format, which can be a list, a bulleted list, or a plain text paragraph. By default, it is a bulleted list. The feasible values are grouped in the *ValidationSummaryDisplayMode* enumeration.

Whatever the format is, the summary can be displayed as text in the page, in a message box, or in both. The Boolean properties *ShowSummary* and *ShowMessageBox* let you decide. The output of the *ValidationSummary* control is not displayed until the page posts back no matter what the value of the *EnableClientScript* property is. The *HeaderText* property defines the text that is displayed atop the summary.

```
<asp:ValidationSummary runat="server"
    ShowMessageBox="true"
```

```
ShowSummary="true"
HeaderText="The following errors occurred:"
DisplayMode="BulletList" />
```

This code snippet originates the screen shown in Figure 3-7.

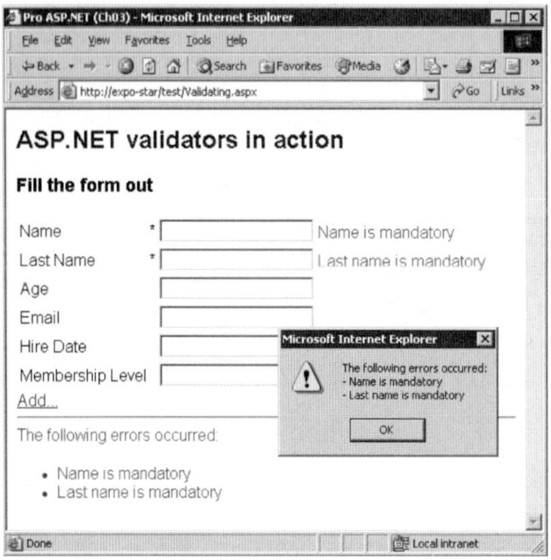

Figure 3-7 After the page posts back, the validation summary is updated and a message box pops up to inform the user.

The validation summary is displayed only if there's at least one pending error. Note that, in the default case, the labels near the input controls are updated anyway, along with the summary text. You can control the error information in the following ways:

- **Both in-place and summary information** This is the default scenario. Use the *ValidationSummary* control and accept all default settings on the validator controls. If you want to leverage both places to display information, a recommended approach consists of minimizing the in-place information by using the *Text* property rather than *ErrorMessage*. If you set both, *Text* is displayed in-place while *ErrorMessage* shows up in the validation summary. For example, you can set *Text* with a glyph or an asterisk and assign *ErrorMessage* with more detailed text. (This case is illustrated in Figure 3-8.)
- **Only in-place information** Do not use the *ValidationSummary* control, and set the *ErrorMessage* property in each validation control you use.

- **Only summary information** Use the *ValidationSummary* control, and set the *ErrorMessage* property on individual validation controls. Set the *Display* property of validators to *None* so that no in-place error message will ever be displayed.
- **Custom error information** You don't use the *ValidationSummary* control, and you set the *Display* property of the individual validators to *None*. In addition, you collect the various error messages through the *ErrorMessage* property on the validation controls and arrange your own feedback for the user.

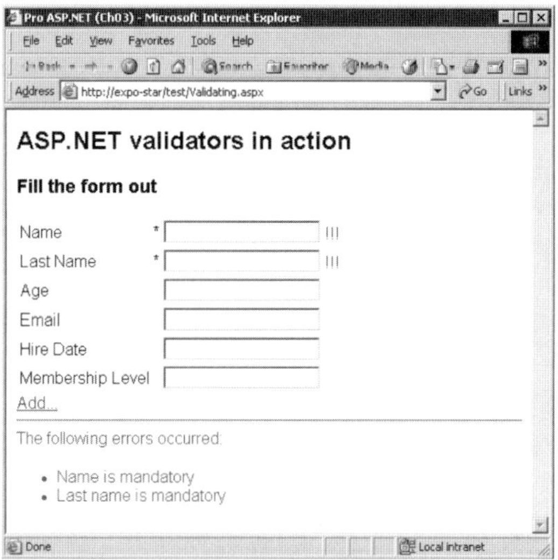

Figure 3-8 A glyph marks the input data as wrong, and the summary text details the errors.

Validating for Multiple Conditions

As mentioned earlier, you can associate multiple validators with a single input control. The validation takes place in order, and each validation control generates and displays its own error message. The content of the input control is considered valid if all the validators return *true*.

If an input control has multiple valid patterns—for example, an ID field can take the form of a Social Security number or a VAT number—you can either validate by using custom code or regular expressions.

Client-Side Validation

As mentioned earlier, the verification normally takes place on the server either after the *Validate* method is called or as the result of a postback event. If the browser supports Dynamic HTML, though, you can also activate the validation process on the client, with a significant gain in responsiveness. To be precise, ASP.NET automatically enables client-side validation if it detects a browser with enough capabilities.

If client-side validation is turned on, the page won't post back until all the input fields contain valid data. To run secure code and prevent malicious and underhanded attacks, you might want to validate data on the server too. Consider also that not all types of validation can be accomplished on the client. In fact, if you need to validate against a database, there's no other option than posting back to the server.

Enabling Client Validation

Client validation can be controlled on a per-validation control basis by using the *EnableClientScript* Boolean property. By default, the property is set to *true*, meaning client validation is enabled as long as the browser supports it. If you want to control the client validation at the page level, resort to the *ClientTarget* attribute on the *@Page* directive. The following code disables client validation by specifying that any code in the page should target a down-level browser:

```
<% @Page ClientTarget="DownLevel" %>
```

The *ClientTarget* attribute—also available as a property on the *Page* class—overrides the type of browser that ASP.NET should target when generating the page. If the *ClientTarget* attribute is set, ASP.NET doesn't detect the actual browser's capabilities but loads the capabilities for the specified browser from the machine.config file. Feasible values for the *ClientTarget* attribute include any value defined in the configuration *<clientTarget>* section. The standard content is as follows:

```
<clientTarget>
    <add alias="ie5" userAgent="Mozilla/4.0 (compatible; MSIE 5.5; ...)"/>
    <add alias="ie4" userAgent="Mozilla/4.0 (compatible; MSIE 4.0; ...)"/>
    <add alias="uplevel" userAgent="Mozilla/4.0 (compatible; MSIE 4.0;…)"/>
    <add alias="downlevel" userAgent="Unknown" />
</clientTarget>
```

If *ClientTarget* is not set, the browser's capabilities are detected through *Request.Browser* property. The *BaseValidator* class determines whether the browser is up-level or not. Only if the browser is considered up-level, will the client validation be implemented. Browsers and client devices that are considered up-level support at least the following:

- ECMAScript (including JScript and JavaScript) version 1.2
- HTML version 4.0
- The Microsoft Document Object Model
- Cascading style sheets

For down-level browsers, the only requirement is HTML version 3.2.

Implementing Client Validation

For situations in which validation can be applied on the client, a lot of JavaScript code is silently injected in the page. Let's consider a simple page like the following one:

```
<% @Page language="c#" %>
<script runat="server">
void DoClick(object sender, EventArgs e) {}
</script>

<html>
<body>
<form runat="server" id="theForm">
<asp:textbox runat="server" id="fname" />
<asp:RequiredFieldValidator runat="server" id="fnameValidator"
    ControlToValidate="fname"
    Text="*"
    ErrorMessage="Name is mandatory" />
<br>
<asp:linkbutton runat="server" Text="Click..." OnClick="DoClick" />
</form>
</body>
</html>
```

This page contains a single text box with a required field validator. When viewed through an up-level browser, the HTML output looks like the following code. The code in bold represents specific extensions due to the client validation.

```
<form name="theForm" method="post" action="Simple.aspx" id="theForm"
    language="javascript" onsubmit="ValidatorOnSubmit();">
<input type="hidden" name="__EVENTTARGET" value="" />
<input type="hidden" name="__EVENTARGUMENT" value="" />
<input type="hidden" name="__VIEWSTATE" value="..." />

<script language="javascript">
<!--
    function __doPostBack(eventTarget, eventArgument) {
        var theform = document.theForm;
        theform.__EVENTTARGET.value = eventTarget;
        theform.__EVENTARGUMENT.value = eventArgument;
        theform.submit();
    }
// -->
```

```
</script>

<script language="javascript"
    src="/aspnet_client/system_web/1_x_xxxx_0/WebUIValidation.js" />

<input name="fname" type="text" id="fname" />
<span id="fnameValidator"
    controltovalidate="fname"
    errormessage="Name is mandatory"
    evaluationfunction="RequiredFieldValidatorEvaluateIsValid"
    initialvalue=""
    style="color:Red;visibility:hidden;">*</span>
<br>
<a href="javascript:{if (typeof(Page_ClientValidate) != 'function' ||
    Page_ClientValidate()) __doPostBack('_ctl0','')} ">Click...</a>

<script language="javascript">
<!--
    var Page_Validators =
        new Array(document.all["fnameValidator"]);
// -->
</script>

<script language="javascript">
<!--
var Page_ValidationActive = false;
if (typeof(clientInformation) != "undefined" &&
clientInformation.appName.indexOf("Explorer") != -1) {
    if (typeof(Page_ValidationVer) == "undefined")
        alert("Unable to find script library ....");
    else if (Page_ValidationVer != "125")
        alert("This page uses an incorrect version ...");
    else
        ValidatorOnLoad();
}

function ValidatorOnSubmit() {
    if (Page_ValidationActive) {
        ValidatorCommonOnSubmit();
    }
}
// -->
</script>
</form>
</body>
</html>
```

When the page loads up, the *ValidatorOnLoad* JavaScript function executes and populates the *Page_Validators* array with instances of the JavaScript objects that represent the active validators. Another change to notice is the *onsubmit* client event handler that has been added to the *<form>* element. When the HTML form is going to be submitted, a piece of script code runs and checks the validity of all input fields. The *onsubmit* handler allows the actual post only when all the validators agree to commit.

All the client script functions are imported in the page from a well-known JavaScript file located under the Web server's root:

```
/aspnet_client/system_web/1_x_xxxx_0/WebUIValidation.js
```

The path of this file is controlled by the *<webControls>* section of the machine.config file.

Another interesting change to observe in the ASP.NET code when client validation is enabled is the insertion of extra attributes in the *<span>* tag that represents the validator. The preceding code reveals a couple of custom attributes named *evaluationfunction* and *initialvalue*. The former refers to the JavaScript function that performs the client-side validation. The function is defined in the WebUIValidation.js file. The other attribute, specific to the required field validator, refers to the value to check against—the empty string in this case. The script validator functions receive one argument, that being the JavaScript object representing the validator. Custom attributes are an effective way to pass external data to script objects based on HTML tags. The following code snippet from WebUIValidation.js shows the script implementation of the required field validator:

```
function ValidatorTrim(s) {
    var m = s.match(/^\s*(\S+(\s+\S+)*)\s*$/);
    return (m == null) ? "" : m[1];
}
function RequiredFieldValidatorEvaluateIsValid(val) {
    var t = ValidatorTrim(ValidatorGetValue(val.controltovalidate);
    return (t != ValidatorTrim(val.initialvalue))
}
```

Internet Explorer WebControls

Although they're not officially part of the .NET Framework and aren't included in the Web controls namespace, other Web controls have been around for some time to address the needs of developers who do a lot of client-side, Internet Explorer–specific Web programming. Unlike controls in the ASP.NET namespace, these controls extensively exploit the Dynamic HTML object model of Internet Explorer 5.x and newer versions. They perform a lot of tasks on the client and make provisions for Web versions of typical desktop controls such as the *TreeView* or *TabStrip*. You can download some of these controls from the control gallery at *http://www.asp.net*. Microsoft has released the following controls:

(continued)

Internet Explorer WebControls *(continued)*

- **IE TreeView** Facilitates rendering of hierarchical data, folder views, and other similar data structures. The control includes support for data binding and rich DHTML behaviors in Internet Explorer 5.5 and newer.

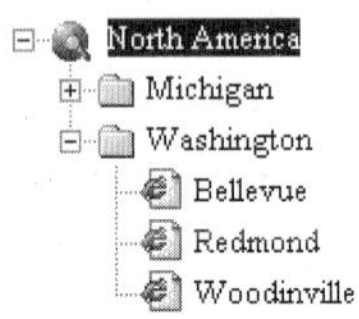

- **IE Toolbar** Web counterpart of the toolbar control commonly used in Microsoft Windows desktop applications.

- **IE TabStrip** Simplifies the authoring of tabbed menus, and is particularly useful for authoring user-interface elements that navigate site content.
- **IE MultiPage** Enables the definition of collections of child page elements. As in a desktop Windows tab control, the control lets you define the content of pages that are navigated.

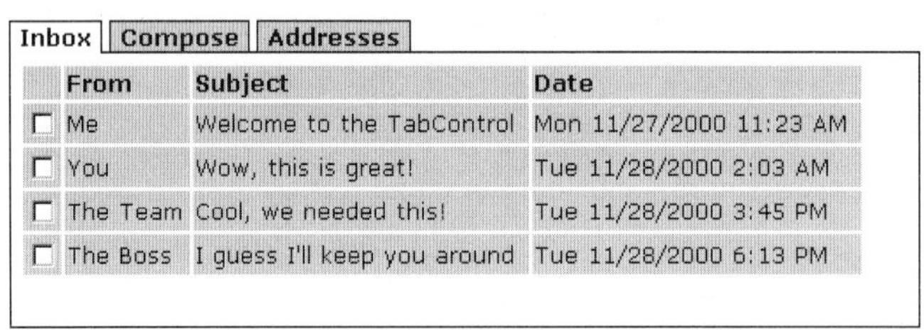

All Internet Explorer WebControls are tailored for both down-level browsers and up-level browsers and renders their advanced functionalities using client-side behaviors when the browser allows for that. In the same gallery of controls on the *http://www.asp.net* portal, you'll also find links to similar third-party products.

Data-Bound Controls

Web applications are, for the most part, just data-driven applications. For this reason, the ability to bind HTML elements like drop-down lists or tables to structured data represents a key feature for a development platform. Data-bound controls are the ASP.NET answer to the growing demand for automatic binding between data sources and graphical elements. Data binding is the process that retrieves data from a fixed source and dynamically associates this data to properties on server controls. Valid target controls are those that have been specifically designed to support data binding. Data-bound controls are not yet another family of controls. Data-bound controls are simply server controls that feature a few well-known data-related properties, including *Text*, *DataSource*, *DataTextField*, and *DataValueField*.

The *DataSource* property, in particular, lets you specify the data source object the control is linked to. Note that this link is logical and does not result in any overhead or underlying operation until you explicitly order to bind the data to the control. Not all properties in the Web control programming interface are data bindable. You activate data binding on a control by calling the *DataBind* method. When this method executes, the control actually loads data from the associated data source, evaluates the data-bound properties, and redraws its user interface to reflect changes.

Feasible Data-Binding Sources

Many .NET classes can be used as data sources—and not just those that have to do with database contents. In general, any object that exposes the *ICollection* interface is a valid bindable data source. The *ICollection* interface defines size, enumerators, and synchronization methods for all .NET collections. In particular, you can bind a Web control to the following classes:

- *DataTable*, *DataView*, and *DataSet*
- Data readers
- Dictionaries and arrays

In ASP.NET 1.1, XML documents are not directly bindable unless you load their content in one of the previously mentioned classes. You can do this by loading the XML document into a *DataSet* and then binding to the *DataSet*.

To be honest, I should note that the *DataSet* and *DataTable* classes don't implement *ICollection* or any other interface that inherit from it (for example, *IList*). However, both classes do store collections of data internally. These collections are accessed using the methods of an intermediate interface—*IListSource*—which performs the trick of making the *DataSet* and *DataTable* classes look like they implement a collection. In Chapter 20, we'll discuss in detail the mechanism that makes such ADO.NET objects bindable.

ADO.NET Classes

As we'll see in greater detail in Chapter 5, ADO.NET—and in particular the *System.Data* namespace—provides a bunch of data container classes that can be filled with any sort of data, including database information. Classes in the *System.Data* namespace are just in-memory caches of data and work disconnected from any database server. The data reader class, on the other hand, is specific to a managed provider and, as such, is tightly bound to a particular data source such as Oracle or Microsoft SQL Server.

Note that the *DataSet* class can contain more than one table; however, only one table can be associated with a data-bound control. In this case, you should assign the *DataSet* object to the *DataSource* property and the selected *DataTable* object to another property acting as a selector—the *DataMember* property.

Collection-Based Classes

At the highest level of abstraction, a collection serves as a container for instances of other classes. All collection classes implement the *ICollection* interface, which in turn implements the *IEnumerable* interface. As a result, all collection classes provide a basic set of functionalities.

All collection classes have a *Count* property to return the number of cached items; they have a *CopyTo* method to copy their items, in their entirety or in part, to an external array; they have a *GetEnumerator* method that instantiates an enumerator object to loop through the child items. *GetEnumerator* is the method behind the curtain whenever you call the *foreach* statement in C# and the *For...Each* statement in Visual Basic .NET.

IList and *IDictionary* are two interfaces that extend *ICollection*, giving a more precise characterization to the resultant collection class. *ICollection* provides only basic and minimal functionality for a collection. For example, *ICollection* does not have any methods to add or remove items. Add and remove functions are exactly what the *IList* interface provides. In the *IList* interface, the *Add* and *Insert* methods place new items at the bottom of the collection or at the specified index. The *Remove* and *RemoveAt* methods remove items, while *Clear* empties the collection. Finally, *Contains* verifies whether an item with a given value belongs to the collection, and *IndexOf* returns the index of the specified item. Commonly used container classes that implement both *ICollection* and *IList* are *Array*, *ArrayList*, and *StringCollection*. Previously mentioned ADO.NET classes—such as the *DataView* class—support data binding via the *ICollection* interface.

The *IDictionary* interface defines the API that represents a collection of key/value pairs. The interface exposes methods similar to *IList*, but with different signatures. Dictionary classes also feature two extra properties, *Keys* and *Values*. They return collections of keys and values, respectively, found in the dictionary. Typical dictionary classes are *ListDictionary*, *Hashtable*, and *SortedList*.

Simple Data Binding

In ASP.NET, there are two types of data binding—simple and complex. A simple binding is a connection between one piece of data and a server control property. It is established through a special expression and is evaluated when the code in the page calls the *DataBind* method either on the *Page* object or the control.

A data binding expression is any text wrapped by <% ... %> and prefixed by the symbol #. You can use data-binding expressions to set the value of an attribute in the opening tag of a server control. A data-binding expression is programmatically managed via an instance of the *DataBoundLiteralControl* class. The following code snippet shows how to set the text of a label with the current time:

```
<asp:label runat="server" Text='<%# DateTime.Now.ToString() %>' />
```

Within the delimiters, you can invoke user-defined page methods, static methods, and properties and methods of any other page components. The following code demonstrates a label bound to the name of the currently selected element in a drop-down list control:

```
<asp:label runat="server" Text='<%# dropdown.SelectedItem.Text %>' />
```

Note that if you're going to use quotes within the expression, you should wrap the expression itself with single quotes. The data-binding expression can accept a minimal set of operators, mostly for concatenating subexpressions. If you need more advanced processing and use external arguments, resort to a user-defined method. The only requirement is that the method must be callable within the page. If the code of the page is not resident in the .aspx page (for example, you're using code-behind), make sure the method is declared public or protected.

Simple Data Binding in Action

In the following example, you'll see how to use simple data binding with text boxes to arrange a form-based record viewer. The user interface of the page supplies three text boxes, one for each of the retrieved fields. The data source is the Employees table of the Northwind database in Microsoft SQL Server 2000.

The query that is run against the database selects three fields: employeeid, firstname, and lastname. The binding takes place between the text boxes and the fields. Only one record at a time is displayed, and Previous and Next buttons let you move through the data. You can see what the application looks like in Figure 3-9.

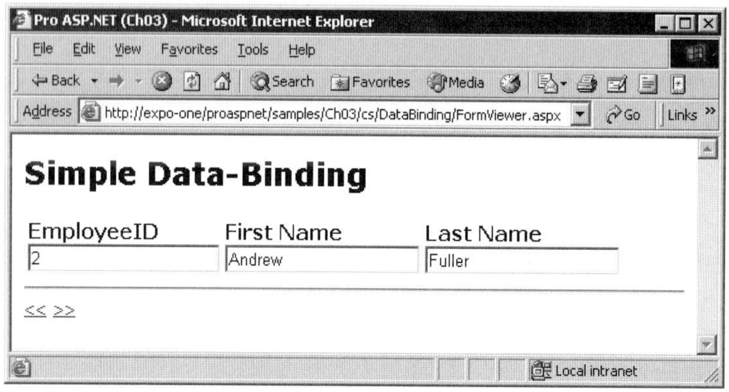

Figure 3-9 The text boxes in the figure are bound to fields in the Employees table from the SQL Server 2000 Northwind sample database.

The binding expression makes use of a user-defined method named *GetBoundData*.

```
<asp:textbox runat="server" id="txtID"
    Text = '<%# GetBoundData("employeeid") %>' />
```

The method takes the name of the field to display and retrieves the position of the current record from the ASP.NET *Session* object. It then reads the corresponding value and passes it to the ASP.NET runtime for actual rendering.

```
public string GetBoundData(String fieldName)
{
    DataSet ds = (DataSet) Session["MyData"];
    DataTable dt = ds.Tables["EmpTable"];
    int nRowPos = (int) Session["CurrentRecord"];

    String buf = dt.Rows[nRowPos][fieldName].ToString();
    return buf;
}
```

Implementation of Data-Bound Expressions

What really happens when a data-bound expression is found in a Web page? How does the ASP.NET runtime process it? Let's consider the following base code:

```
<asp:label runat="server" id="today"
    text='<%# DateTime.Now.ToString() %>' />
```

While compiling the source code for the page, the ASP.NET runtime writes a handler for the *DataBinding* event of the control—a *Label* in this case. The following pseudocode shown illustrates the generation of the label in the underlying class. (See Chapter 2 for more details on the compilation of the page.)

```
private Control __BuildControltoday() {
    Label __ctrl = new Label();
    this.today = __ctrl;
    __ctrl.ID = "today";


    __ctrl.DataBinding += new EventHandler(this.__DataBindtoday);
    return __ctrl;
}
```

Basically, the data-binding handler assigns the verbatim expression to the control's property.

```
public void __DataBindtoday(object sender, EventArgs e) {
    Label target;
    target = (Label) sender;
    target.Text = Convert.ToString(DateTime.Now.ToString());
}
```

The value returned by the data-binding expression must be convertible to a string. The code in the event handler does not change if the expression points to another control. The ASP.NET runtime assumes the control exists and is instantiated—which is *true* by design.

Complex Data Binding

Complex data binding occurs when you bind a list control or an iterative control to one or more columns of data. List controls include the *DropDownList*, *CheckBoxList*, *RadioButtonList*, and *ListBox*. Iterative controls are the *Repeater*, *DataList*, and *DataGrid* controls.

List controls have a more complex and richer user interface than labels and text boxes. They display (or at least need to have in memory) more items at the same time. That's the reason you should associate them explicitly with a collection of data—the data source. Depending on its expected behavior, the control will pick the needed items from memory and properly format and display them.

Iterative controls take a data source, loop through the items, and iteratively apply HTML templates to each row. This basic behavior is common to all three ASP.NET iterators. Beyond that, they differ in terms of layout capabilities and functionality they support. We'll cover iterative controls from various perspectives in Chapter 6 and Chapter 9.

Let's see how complex forms of data binding apply to key list controls. All list controls inherit from the base *ListControl* class.

The *DropDownList* Control

The *DropDownList* control enables users to select one item from a single-selection drop-down list. You can specify the size of the control by setting its height and width in pixels, but you can't control the number of items displayed when the list drops down. The *DropDownList* control can be filled through data binding. The following code provides an example:

```
<asp:DropDownList runat="server" id="theList"
    DataSource="<%# getData() %>"
    DataTextField="lastname"
    DataValueField="employeeid">
```

You can assign a data binding expression to the *DataSource* property but not to the *DataTextField* and *DataValueField* properties. Their value must match exactly the name of one of the columns in the data source. The properties specific to the *DropDownList* control are shown in Table 3-12.

Table 3-12 Properties of the *DropDownList* Control

Property	Description
AutoPostBack	Gets or sets whether the control should automatically post back to the server when the user changes the selection
DataMember	Gets or sets the name of the table in the *DataSource* to bind
DataSource	Gets or sets the data source that populates the items of the list
DataTextField	Gets or sets the name of the column in the data source that provides the text content of the list items
DataTextFormatString	Gets or sets the formatting string used to control how data bound to the list is displayed
DataValueField	Gets or sets the field of the data source that provides the value of each list item
Items	Gets the collection of items in the list control
SelectedIndex	Gets or sets the index of the selected item in the list
SelectedItem	Gets the selected item in the list

The programming interface of the *DropDownList* also features three properties to configure the border of the drop-down list—the *BorderColor*, *BorderStyle*, and *BorderWidth* properties. Although the properties are correctly transformed by style properties, most browsers won't use them to change the appearance of the drop-down list.

The *DataTextField* and *DataValueField* properties don't accept expressions, only plain column names. To combine two or more fields of the data source, you can use a calculated column. You can either use a column computed by the database or exploit the power of the ADO.NET object model (as explained in Chapter 5) and add an in-memory column. The following SQL query returns a column obtained by concatenating *lastname* and *firstname*.

```
SELECT lastname + ', ' + firstname AS 'EmployeeName'
FROM Employees
```

The same result can also be obtained, more efficiently, without the involvement of the database. Once you've filled a *DataTable* object with the result of the query, you add a new column to its *Columns* collection. The content of the column is based on an expression. The following code adds an *EmployeeName* column to the data source that concatenates the last name and first name:

```
dataTable.Columns.Add("EmployeeName",
    typeof(string),
    "lastname + ', ' + firstname");
```

An expression-based column does not need to be filled explicitly. The values for all the cells in the column are calculated and cached when the column is added to the table. The table tracks any dependencies and updates the calculated column whenever any of the constituent columns are updated.

The *CheckBoxList* Control

The *CheckBoxList* control is a single monolithic control that groups a collection of checkable list items, each of which is rendered through an individual *CheckBox* control. The properties of the child check boxes are set by reading the associated data source. You insert a check box list in a page as follows:

```
<asp:CheckBoxList runat="server" id="employeesList">
```

Table 3-13 lists the specific properties of the *CheckBoxList* control.

Table 3-13 Properties of the *CheckBoxList* Control

Property	Description
AutoPostBack	Gets or sets whether the control should automatically post back to the server when the user changes the selection
CellPadding	Gets or sets the pixels between the border and contents of the cell
CellSpacing	Gets or sets the pixels between cells
DataMember	Gets or sets the name of the table in the *DataSource* to bind

(continued)

Table 3-13 Properties of the *CheckBoxList* Control *(continued)*

Property	Description
DataSource	Gets or sets the data source that populates the items of the list
DataTextField	Gets or sets the name of the column in the data source that provides the text content of the list items
DataTextFormatString	Gets or sets the formatting string used to control how data bound to the list is displayed
DataValueField	Gets or sets the field of the data source that provides the value of each list item
Items	Gets the collection of items in the list control
RepeatColumns	Gets or sets the number of columns to display in the control
RepeatDirection	Gets or sets a value that indicates whether the control displays vertically or horizontally
RepeatLayout	Gets or sets the layout of the check boxes (table or flow)
SelectedIndex	Gets or sets the index of the selected item in the list
SelectedItem	Gets the selected item in the list
TextAlign	Gets or sets the text alignment for the check boxes

Unlike the *DropDownList* control, the *CheckBoxList* does not supply any properties that know which items have been selected. But this aspect is vital for any Web application that utilizes checkable elements. The *CheckBoxList* can have any number of items selected, but how can you retrieve them?

Any list control has an *Items* property that contains the collection of the child items. The *Items* property is implemented through the *ListItemCollection* class and makes each contained item accessible via a *ListItem* object. The following code loops through the items stored in a *CheckBoxList* control and checks the *Selected* property of each of them:

```
foreach(ListItem item in chkList.Items)
{
    if (item.Selected) {
        // this item is selected
    }
}
```

The *RadioButtonList* Control

The *RadioButtonList* control acts as the parent control for a collection of radio buttons. Each of the child items is rendered through a *RadioButton* control. By design, a *RadioButtonList* can have zero or one item selected. The *SelectedItem* property returns the selected element as a *ListItem* object. Note, though, that there is nothing to guarantee that only one item is selected at any time. For this reason, be extremely careful when you access the *SelectedItem* of a *RadioButtonList* control—it could be null.

The contents of the control can be fetched from a data source as follows:

```
<asp:RadioButtonList runat="server" id="employeesList"
    DataSource="<%# getData() %"
    DataValueField="EmployeeID"
    DataTextField="EmployeeName" />
```

The control supports the same set of properties as the *CheckBoxList* control and, just like it, accepts some layout directives. In particular, you can control the rendering process of the list with the *RepeatLayout* and *RepeatDirection* properties. By default, the list items are rendered within a table, which ensures the vertical alignment of the companion text. The property that governs the layout is *RepeatLayout*. The alternative is displaying the items as free HTML text, using blanks and breaks to guarantee some sort of minimal structure. *RepeatDirection* is the property that controls the direction in which, with or without a tabular structure, the items flow. Feasible values are *Vertical* (the default) and *Horizontal*. *RepeatColumns* is the property that determines how many columns the list should have. By default the value is *0*, which means all the items will be displayed in a single row, vertical or horizontal according to the value of *RepeatDirection*.

The *ListBox* Control

The *ListBox* control represents a vertical sequence of items displayed in a scrollable window. The *ListBox* control allows single-item or multiple-item selection and exposes its contents through the usual *Items* collection, as shown in the following code:

```
<asp:listbox runat="server" id="theListBox"
    rows="5" selectionmode="Multiple" />
```

You can decide the height of the control through the *Rows* property. The height is measured in number of rows rather than pixels or percentages. When it comes to data binding, the *ListBox* control behaves like the controls discussed earlier in the chapter. It supports properties such as *DataSource* and *DataMember*, and it can be bound to a data source and show its contents.

Two properties make this control slightly different than other list controls—the *Rows* property, which represents the number of visible rows in the control, and the *SelectionMode* property, which determines whether one or multiple items can be selected. The following code demonstrates how to write a comma-separated string with the values of the selected items:

```
public void ShowSelectedItems(object sender, EventArgs e)
{
    StringBuilder sb = new StringBuilder("");
    for (int i=0; i < theList.Items.Count; i++)
```

```
    {
        if (theList.Items[i].Selected)
        {
            sb.Append(theList.Items[i].Text);
            sb.Append(", ");
        }
    }
    Response.Write(sb.ToString());
}
```

This code is nearly identical to the one you would write to accomplish the same operation on a *CheckBoxList* control. The programming interface of the list box also contains a *SelectedItem* property that makes little sense when you work with a multiselection control. In this case, the *SelectedItem* property returns the selected item with the lowest index.

> **Note** All list controls support the *SelectedIndexChanged* event, which is raised when the selection from the list changes and the page posts back to the server. You can use this event to execute server-side code whenever a control is checked or unchecked.

Conclusion

In ASP.NET pages, server controls are vital components. Server-side controls alone—no matter their capabilities and flavors—constitute a huge difference between ASP and ASP.NET. Server-side controls transform the programming model of ASP.NET from a mere factory of HTML strings to a more modern and effective component-based model.

ASP.NET features a long list of control classes. Looking at the namespaces involved, we should conclude that only two families of controls exist—HTML and Web controls. Controls in the former group simply mirror the set of elements in the HTML syntax. Each constituent control has as many properties as there are attributes in the corresponding HTML tag. Names and behavior have been kept as faithful to the originals as possible. The ultimate goal of the designers of HTML controls is to make the transition from ASP to ASP.NET as seamless as possible—just add *runat="server"* and refresh the page.

The overall design of Web controls is more abstract and much less tied to HTML. In general Web controls do not provide a strict one-to-one correspondence between controls and HTML tags. However, the capabilities of Web and HTML controls overlap. All ASP.NET server controls render in HTML, but Web controls render to more complex HTML representation than HTML controls.

In the family of Web controls, we can identify interesting and powerful subsets of controls—for example, validators, list controls, and iterative controls. Data-bound controls, including list and iterative controls, represent a key enhancement in the ASP.NET programming model. The ability to bind data sources to controls—especially to disconnected and in-memory sources—adds spice to an already powerful model and significantly increases speed and productivity. Just consider the following example. Do you remember the typical check box and radio button code that countless ASP pages implemented? The code walks its way through all the records in a result set and generates a check box or radio button at each step. With this old model, state maintenance is in the care of the programmer, code has to be written over and over again, and extensibility and reusability is a mere dream. In ASP.NET—thanks to server controls—control list generation is as easy as using ad hoc data-bound list controls.

Resources

- Internet Explorer WebControls (*http://msdn.microsoft.com/workshop/webcontrols/overview/overview.asp*)
- Detect Control Changes (*http://www.aspnetpro.com/features/2003/03/asp200303de_f/asp200303de_f.asp*)
- ASP.NET Validation in Depth (*http://msdn.microsoft.com/library/en-us/dnaspp/html/aspplusvalid.asp*)
- Using the Internet Explorer WebControls (*http://msdn.microsoft.com/msdnmag/issues/03/02/ASPColumn*)

4

Working with the Page

Whatever you do will be insignificant, but it is very important that you do it.
—Mahatma Gandhi

Although formless pages are still accepted and correctly handled, the typical ASP.NET page is a single form page. The *HtmlForm* class defines the behavior of the server-side form when the *runat* attribute is set to *server*. The *HtmlForm* class acts as a container of server controls and wraps them in an HTML *<form>* element when the page is rendered. The obtained HTML form always posts to the same page and for this reason is said to be *reentrant*. The default method used to submit form data is POST but GET can be used as well.

In most cases, the server form is the outermost tag and is contained directly in *<body>*. In general, though, the server *<form>* tag can be the child of any other server container control such as *<table>*, *<div>*, *<body>*, and any other HTML generic control. (We covered HTML controls and Web controls in Chapter 3.) If any noncontainer controls (for example, a *TextBox*) are placed outside the form tag, an exception is thrown. Note, though, that no check is made at compile time. The exception is raised by the control itself when the host page asks to render. Noncontainer Web controls, in fact, check whether they are being rendered within the boundaries of a server form and throw an *HttpException* if they are not. A call to the *Page*'s *VerifyRenderingInServerForm* method does the job.

In this chapter, we'll examine some aspects of form-based programming in ASP.NET, including how to use multiple forms in the same page. We consider the use of pop-up windows and show how to inject script code in the body of the client page. We'll also consider the styling of the page and how a made-to-measure API, such as the ASP.NET globalization and localization classes, can in some situations help to easily and effectively change the look and feel of the page. When designing a Web site or any application to be consumed over the Web, you can't realistically pretend to keep it error-free! For this reason, debugging, tracing, and effective and user-friendly error handling are key aspects for top-notch ASP.NET developers.

Programming with Forms

One of the most common snags ASP developers face when they first approach the ASP.NET lifestyle is the fact that managed Web applications support the single-form interface (SFI) model.

> **Note** If you've never heard anyone use the SFI acronym, there's no reason for you to panic. It's an acronym I've created to mimic other more popular acronyms that, although used in different contexts, describe similar programming models—the single-document interface (SDI) and its opposite, the multiple-document interface (MDI).

In the SFI model, each page always posts to itself and does so through the POST or GET HTTP method. The HTTP method and the target frame of the post can be programmatically adjusted using ad hoc *HtmlForm* properties—*Method* and *Target*. The final destination of the postback can't be set in any way. What in HTML and ASP programming was the *Action* property of the form is simply not defined on the ASP.NET *HtmlForm* class. As a result, the SFI model is a built-in feature so much integrated with the ASP.NET platform that you can only take it or code the old ASP way without server forms.

Technically speaking, a kind of multiform interface (MFI) is still possible. Hold on, though. By MFI here, I simply mean the possibility of having multiple forms on the final HTML page. In no way does this mean you can have multiple *server-side* forms in an ASP.NET page. An ASP.NET page can host exactly one server form and as many HTML forms as needed. If you place two or more server forms in a page, you won't get any error at compile time. When processing the request, the *Page*-derived object examines markup blocks one at a time. The first *<form>* block is processed and rendered. After that, the page object sets an internal flag to remember that one form object has been processed for the page. Guess what happens next? When the second *<form runat="server">*

block is found, the page verifies that no other similar block has been processed earlier. If the flag is set, an *HttpException* is thrown. Later in this chapter, we'll discuss an example in which multiple forms—one server and one client—work together.

Multiple forms, though, are sometimes needed—although probably not frequently. You would need them, for example, for functionality hosted by the application pages, such as search or login capabilities.

The *HtmlForm* Class

The *HtmlForm* class inherits from *HtmlContainerControl* and implements the *IAttributeAccessor* interface. The base class provides *HtmlForm* with the capability of containing child controls. This capability is shared with other HTML control classes, such as *HtmlTable*, characterized by child elements and a closing tag. The *IAttributeAccessor* interface defines two methods—*GetAttribute* and *SetAttribute*—used to read attribute values out of the opening tag.

Properties of the *HtmlForm* Class

The *HtmlForm* class provides programmatic access to the HTML *<form>* element on the server through the set of properties shown in Table 4-1.

Table 4-1 Form Properties

Property	Description
Attributes	Gets a name/value collection with all the attributes declared on the tag.
ClientID	Gets the value of *UniqueID*.
Controls	Gets a collection object that represents the child controls of the form.
Disabled	Gets or sets a value indicating whether the form is disabled. Matches the *disabled* HTML attribute.
EnableViewState	Rarely used at this level, gets or sets a value indicating whether the state of child controls should be persisted.
Enctype	Gets or sets the encoding type. Matches the *enctype* HTML attribute.
ID	Gets or sets the programmatic identifier of the form.
InnerHtml	Gets or sets the markup content found between the opening and closing tags of the form.
InnerText	Gets or sets the text between the opening and closing tags of the form.

(continued)

Table 4-1 Form Properties *(continued)*

Property	Description
Method	Gets or sets a value that indicates how a browser posts form data to the server. The default value is POST. Can be set to GET if needed.
Name	Gets the value of *UniqueID*.
NamingContainer	Gets a reference to the form's naming container; typically the host page.
Page	Gets a reference to the host page.
Parent	Gets a reference to the parent object. The parent object is typically, but not necessarily, the page. Note that if the form is contained in a *<table>* or *<div>* element not marked *"runat=server"*, the parent object is still the page.
Site	Returns *null*.
Style	Gets a collection of all cascading style sheet (CSS) properties applied to the form.
TagName	Returns "form".
Target	Gets or sets the name of the frame or window to render the HTML generated for the page.
TemplateSource-Directory	Gets the virtual directory of the page that contains the form.
UniqueID	Gets the unique, fully qualified name of the form.
Visible	Gets or sets a value that indicates whether the form is rendered. If *false*, the form is not rendered to HTML.

The form must have a unique name. If the programmer doesn't assign the name, ASP.NET generates one using a built-in algorithm. The default name follows the pattern *_ctlX*, in which *X* is a unique integer—typically the index of the control in the page. The programmer can set the form's identifier by using either the *ID* or *Name* property. If both are set, the *ID* attribute takes precedence. Based on the value of *ID*, ASP.NET determines the values of *UniqueID* and *ClientID*. *UniqueID* is a fully qualified string based on the naming container of the form. *ClientID*, on the other hand, is used to identify a control for client-side operations, such as JavaScript functions.

The parent object of the form is the outer container control with the *runat* attribute. If such a control exists, the page object is set as the parent. Typical containers for the server form are *<table>* and *<div>* if they are marked as server-side objects.

By default, the *Method* property is set to POST. The value of the property can be modified programmatically. If the form is posted through the GET method, all form data is passed on the URL's query string. However, if you choose the GET method, make sure the limited size of a GET request does not affect the integrity of your application.

Methods of the *HtmlForm* Class

Table 4-2 lists the methods available on the *HtmlForm* class. All the methods listed in the table are inherited from the base *System.Web.UI.Control* class.

Table 4-2 Form Methods

Method	Description
DataBind	Calls the *DataBind* method on all child controls.
Dispose	Performs the final clean up before the object is freed.
FindControl	Retrieves and returns the control that matches the specified ID.
HasControls	Indicates whether the form contains any child controls.
RenderControl	Outputs the HTML code for the form. If tracing is enabled, caches tracing information to be rendered later, at the end of the page.
ResolveUrl	Ensures that the specified URL is absolute. Reads the base URL from the *TemplateSourceDirectory* property.

The *FindControl* method searches only in the form's naming container. Controls belonging to an inner or outer naming container are not found.

Multiple Forms

As mentioned, the SFI model is the default in ASP.NET and plays a key role in the automatic state management mechanism we described in Chapter 2. Some pages, though, would have a more consistent and natural design if they could define multiple *logical* forms. In this context, a *logical* form is a logically related group of input controls. For example, think of a login page for restricted areas of a Web site. Registered users just type in their user name and password and connect. Unregistered users need to fill out a form before they're given the parameters to connect. How do you code this? Let's review a few options.

In ASP, you can use two forms, each posting to a different page. The schema is outlined in Figure 4-1.

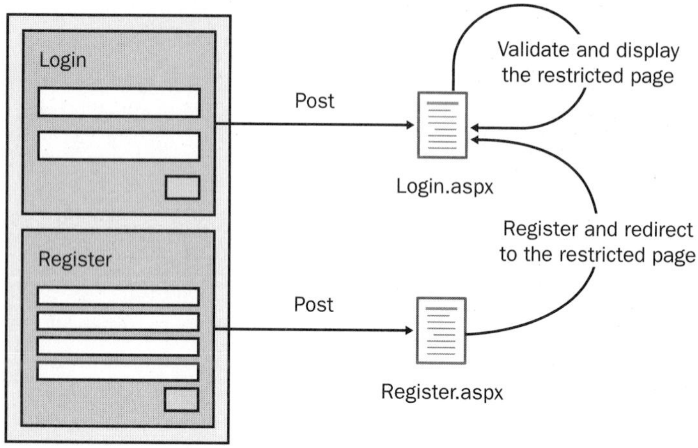

Figure 4-1 Each form posts to a different page.

This solution is impracticable in ASP.NET unless you resort to a kind of pseudo-trick that basically consists of not using ASP.NET server controls. (More on this in a moment.) More apt to the ASP.NET programming style is the solution depicted in Figure 4-2.

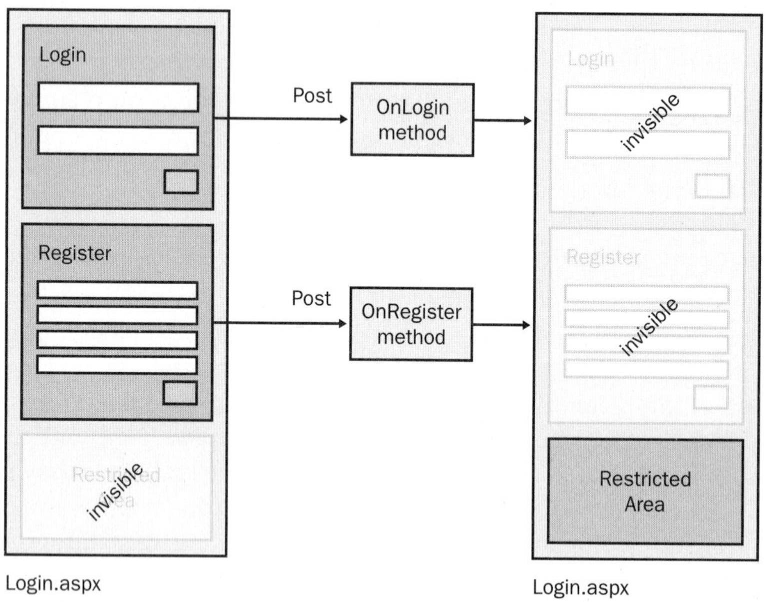

Figure 4-2 One physical *<form>* tag contains multiple logical forms. All logical forms post to the same page and hide any unneeded user interface element.

A unique page is involved and contains a single *<form>* tag. Within the opening and closing tags of the form, two or more groups of logically related controls find their place. Each group can post back using either a classic submit button or a hyperlink bound to some script code—the entity that ASP.NET renders as a link button. Although the various groups are not forms in the technical sense of the word, they do behave like forms. All groups post to the same page, but the ASP.NET infrastructure guarantees both state maintenance and the execution of a piece of code specific to the group that caused the post. Each link button is associated with a server-side method that runs when the page posts back as the result of a click. Functionally speaking, the mechanism is in no way different than the ASP implementation. Furthermore, the programming model enjoys a higher abstraction layer and handy features such as view state and server-side control programming.

Toggling the Control's Visibility

How can you update the user interface of the HTML being generated? You should know the answer immediately if you're somewhat familiar with Dynamic HTML (DHTML) and client-side programming. Otherwise, just read on.

ASP.NET server controls can programmatically be hidden from and restored to view. Controls with the *Visible* property set to *false* are ignored by the ASP.NET parser, and no HTML code will ever be generated for them. It turns out that this feature is key to dynamically creating the user interface of a page, piece by piece. So with reference to Figure 4-2, you design your login page to contain three blocks of HTML code: the login form, registration form, and restricted area. The first time you show the page—that is, when *IsPostBack* is set to *false*—the former two blocks are displayed while the restricted area remains invisible. Next, the user clicks to either log in or register. The page posts back to execute ad hoc code. Once you have registered the new user or checked the credentials of a known user, you simply toggle off the visibility of the forms and toggle on that of the restricted area. Et voilà!

> **Note** Playing with the visibility of controls is a key technique in Dynamic HTML and is the underpinning to many animation effects you see on Web sites when you navigate with Internet Explorer. Typically, cascading menus and collapsible views are obtained by putting a hidden *<div>* tag below the clickable text. When you click on the text, some script code simply toggles the display attribute of the *<div>* tag and the browser does the rest, refreshing the page.

Multiple *<form>* Tags on a Page

For completeness, let's see how to create an ASP.NET page that really contains multiple *<form>* tags. Of course, only one of these tags can have the *runat* attribute set to *server*, and only for the controls contained therein can ASP.NET provide view state management and postback events. Let's consider the following ASP.NET page:

```
<html>
<body>
    <form runat="server">
        <asp:textbox runat="server" id="theTextBox" />
        <asp:button runat="server" text="Post back" />
    </form>

    <form method="post" action="another.aspx">
        <input type="text" name="SecondField " />
        <input type="submit" id="submit1" value="another.aspx" />
    </form>

    <form method="post" action="multiforms.aspx">
        <input type="text" name="ThirdField" />
        <input type="submit" id="submit2" value="This page" />
    </form>
</body>
</html>
```

As you can see, the second and third *<form>* tags are not marked *runat*, meaning that ASP.NET will treat them as plain text to output verbatim. When you click on the *submit1* button, the browser navigates to another.aspx—a different ASP.NET page that knows nothing about the main page's controls. You can still retrieve values from the referrer page by using the old ASP programming style.

```
<% @Page Language="C#" %>
<script runat="server">
void Page_Load(object sender, EventArgs e)
{
    Response.Write(Request.Form["SecondField"]);
}
</script>
```

Note also that when you use the ASP.NET form to post back, the content of the other text boxes is cleared. The same thing happens when you submit form data using the third button—the submit button of an HTML form that posts to the same page. Why doesn't ASP.NET work as usual? It's simple: there's no view-state information for the controls in the third form. That's the importance of working the ASP.NET way.

> **Important** You can have multiple server-side forms in your ASP.NET page as long as only one at a time is visible. For example, a page with, say, three *<form>* tags marked to run at the server is allowed, but only one of them can be actually rendered. Given the dynamics of page rendering, an exception is thrown if more than one *HtmlForm* control attempts to render. By playing with the *Visible* property of the form controls, you can change the active server form during the page lifetime. This approach mimics that of ASP.NET mobile controls. (See Chapter 11.) This trick doesn't really solve the problem of having multiple active forms, but it can be helpful sometimes.

Passing Variables Across Pages

All in all, the HTML form mechanism is a way to invoke an external page to accomplish some specific tasks. When the form is posted, the browser packs the contents of the form fields in the body of the request. On the server, the target page retrieves those values and processes the request. In other words, you use the HTML *<form>* element when you need to execute some code on the server passing parameters.

Accomplishing this task with ASP.NET is straightforward if you use postback events and the SFI programming model. In this case, you implicitly assume that all the server-side code resides within the same reentrant page. Let's consider, though, the more general case in which you just want to spawn any external page and make sure it can get some parameters from the caller. Figure 4-3 explains a possible ASP.NET architecture to transfer the control from the caller page to external pages passing some context information. This multiple-form model is implemented within the default SFI model.

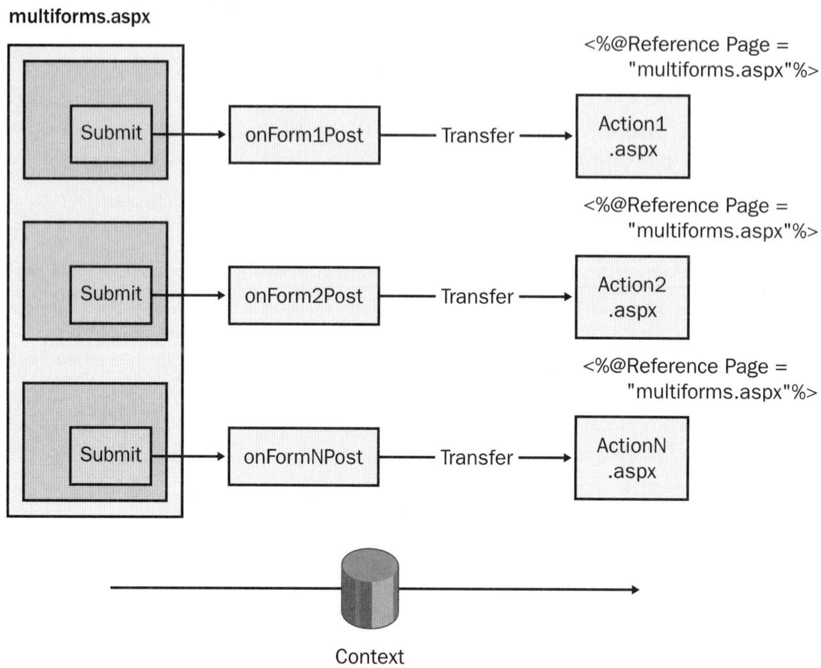

Figure 4-3 Passing values between Web Forms pages.

The base page contains multiple logical forms—that is, not real *<form>* tags but groups of input fields with each one having a submit button. Each group posts back to the same page, but then in the server-side event handler the page transfers the execution to another page—the actual action page. Should the action page access the context of the referrer by using the *Session* or *Application* objects?

Referencing Referrer Pages

In this model, the action page is activated through the *Server.Transfer* method. As will be discussed in Chapter 13, a page spawned through *Transfer* is processed in the same AppDomain and by the same *HttpApplication* object that was processing the referrer. The spawned page also inherits the original context of the request—the *HttpContext* object created upon startup.

In Chapter 13, we will learn that the *HttpContext* object has a property named *Handler* that returns the *IHttpHandler* object that is managing the request. When *Transfer* executes, the context of the original request is preserved and made available to the newly running page. Within the context, the *Handler* property in particular is not replaced and continues pointing to the handler that first received the HTTP request from the client. The spawned page can access the page object representing its referrer by using the *Handler* property as follows:

```
Page referrerPage = (Page) Context.Handler;
```

Because *Handler* returns a valid instance of the page object, the spawned page can access all its properties and methods. It cannot directly access the controls because of the protection level. In fact, if you look back at the source code for compiled pages in Chapter 2, you'll see that all page controls are mapped as protected members on the *ASP.Xxx_aspx* class. However, you could define ad hoc public properties on the caller page and expose to spawned pages all the data you want. For example, the following code exposes the content of the *RegUserName* text box through the *RegistrationUserName* public property:

```
<% @Page ClassName="MultiFormPage" %>
<script language="C#" runat="server">
public string RegistrationUserName
{
    get {return RegUserName.Text;}
}
:
</script>
```

Notice the *ClassName* attribute in the *@Page* directive. It lets you assign a user-defined alias to the page class. In practice, any spawned pages can access the referrer page as an instance of the class *MultiFormPage* rather than as an instance of the *ASP.Xxx_aspx* class.

Retrieving Values

As mentioned, the spawned page can access the instance of the parent page using the *Handler* property. However, this fact alone is not sufficient to enable access to additional properties. The value returned by *Handler* must be cast to the actual page type—*ASP.Xxx_aspx* or whatever the *ClassName* attribute specifies. But how can the page add a reference to the type? That's just what the *@Reference* directive is all about. Figure 4-4 shows a page with a couple of logical forms—each of which transfers execution to a different page.

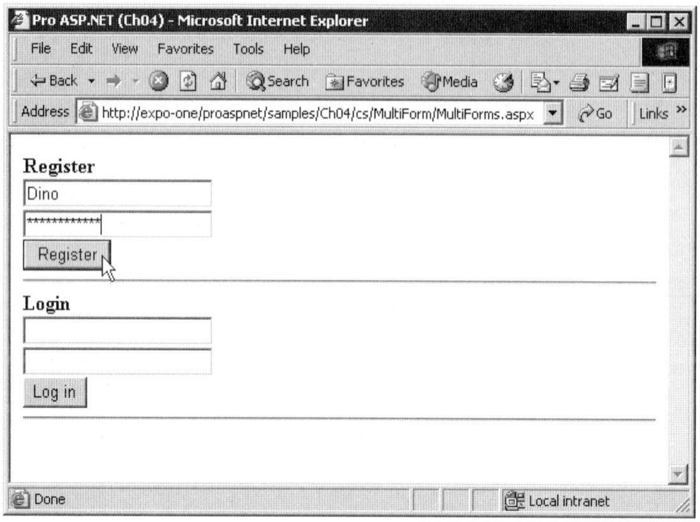

Figure 4-4 An ASP.NET page that contains multiple groups of logically related controls acting as independent forms.

When the user clicks the Register button, the page posts back and transfers to register.aspx. This page, in turn, retrieves the handler of the original request and casts it to an instance of the *MultiFormPage* class. After that, the register.aspx page can use any of the ad hoc properties defined by the caller page to expose its public data.

```
<!-- multiforms.aspx -->
<% @Page ClassName="MultiFormPage" %>

<script language="C#" runat="server">
    public string RegistrationUserName {
        get {return RegUserName.Text;}
    }
    public string RegistrationPassword {
        get {return RegPassword.Text;}
    }
    public string UserName {
        get {return LogUserName.Text;}
    }
    public string Password {
        get {return LogPassword.Text;}
    }
    void OnRegister(object sender, EventArgs e) {
        Server.Transfer("register.aspx");
    }
    void OnLogIn(object sender, EventArgs e) {
        Server.Transfer("login.aspx");
    }
</script>
```

```
<html>
<body>
<form runat="server">
    <b>Register</b><br>
    <asp:textbox runat="server" id="RegUserName" /><br>
    <asp:textbox runat="server" id="RegPassword" textmode="password" /><br>
    <asp:button runat="server" text="Register" onclick="OnRegister" />
    <hr>

    <b>Login</b><br>
    <asp:textbox runat="server" id="LogUserName" /><br>
    <asp:textbox runat="server" id="LogPassword" textmode="password" /><br>
    <asp:button runat="server" text="Log in" onclick="OnLogIn" />
    <hr>
</form>
</body>
</html>
```

The structure of register.aspx and login.aspx is nearly identical, although the two pages will do quite different things. Both pages access input data from the referrer using the *@Reference* directive and the *Context.Handler* property.

```
<% @Page Language="C#" %>
<% @Reference Page="MultiForms.aspx" %>

<script runat="server">
MultiFormPage refPage;
void Page_Load(object sender, EventArgs e) {
    refPage = (MultiFormPage) Context.Handler;
}
</script>

<html>
<body>
User <b><%= refPage.RegistrationUserName %></b> has been registered.
Password is <b><%= refPage.RegistrationPassword%></b>.
</body>
</html>
```

The model we discussed here has a couple of drawbacks that should be mentioned. First, it makes use of *Server.Transfer*, which is a server-to-server mechanism to transfer control. Although highly efficient in terms of performance, it does not notify the browser of the URL change. Second, the *Server.Transfer* method does not work across domains. In other words, you can't post to a page resident on another server. An alternative is using *Response.Redirect*, but in this case you must take care yourself of posting any relevant data to the target page. For more information and further references, see the "Resources" section at the end of the chapter.

Note From this example, it should be clear that having multiple server forms is not really impossible. The *<form runat="server">* tag will remain unique, but one could create custom, *form*-like container controls and use them within the single server form. The new control will have an *Action* property and manage to handle the submit post-back event on any of its buttons. The onclick handler would simply transfer the control to the page specified in *Action*. To establish uniformity in the way in which spawned pages retrieve input parameters, you could force the host page to implement a particular interface or take greater advantage of hidden fields. We'll return to this in Chapter 18 when discussing custom Web controls.

Caution Note that the approach previously described to pass values to other pages requires the callee to know about the type and the programming interface of the caller. When assuming this is not safe, you might want to consider an alternative scheme for passing values. You can copy relevant information to the *Context.Items* collection and use *Server.Transfer* to pass the control. Because the context for the request is the same, caller and callee share the same HTTP context. In this way, the callee reads input data from a common cargo collection rather than referencing a particular page class. In terms of programming, using the *Context.Items* collection is nearly identical to using *Request.Form* or *Request.QueryString*.

Pop-Up Forms

The HTML 4.0 object model allows you to use the *window.showModalDialog* method to show a modal window with a Web page inside. In some situations, this is a very viable approach for retrieving information from the user. ASP.NET pages can be used with pop-up windows. If the page has read-only contents, no particular care should be taken—just open the window with some client-side script code and let it go. On the other hand, if the page shown through a modal window is interactive and posts back, some measures should be taken to ensure that all the output goes through the modal dialog until the user closes it.

To show logically modal forms without using client-side modal dialogs, you could resort to the trick we discussed earlier and build multiple forms with 100 percent ASP.NET code. (See Figure 4-2.) Let's drill down a bit into creating modal windows.

Client Modal Dialogs

To perform a modal operation—that is, a blocking operation that prevents interaction with the main page until terminated—a Web page can resort to the following JavaScript code:

```
<script language="Javascript">
function ShowPopup() {
    window.showModalDialog("dialog.aspx", "Dialog",
        "dialogWidth:200px;dialogHeight:300px;");
}
</script>

<html>
<head><title>Pro ASP.NET (Ch04)</title></head>
<body>
    <input type="button" onclick="ShowPopup()" value="Popup" />
</body>
</html>
```

The *showModalDialog* method on the *window* object opens the specified page in a Windows dialog box with the given title and styles. (For more information about the styling options of the dialog, see the MSDN documentation.) The preceding code pops up a 200-by-300-pixel modal window filled with the HTML content generated by dialog.aspx. So far so good.

Suppose now that the dialog.aspx page contains some links and buttons you can click. Again, think of a modal page you want to pop up for users' registration and logging. The user enters some data and then clicks; the page posts back, but the new output is displayed in a new browser window. Any value you can assign to the form's *target* value seems to be ineffective. The behavior is by design, but is there a workaround? Yes, for the browsers that support it, you can use a wrapper inline frame. (The *<iframe>* tag is part of the HTML 4.0 specification.)

Instead of containing the code to display the window contents, dialog.aspx contains a properly sized *<iframe>* tag.

```
<iframe src="Pages/multiforms.aspx" name="embeddedFrame"
width="100%" height="100%" />
```

At this point, the target attribute set on the multiforms.aspx page is detected and properly handled, as shown in Figure 4-5.

```
<form runat="server" target="embeddedFrame">
    ⋮
</form>
```

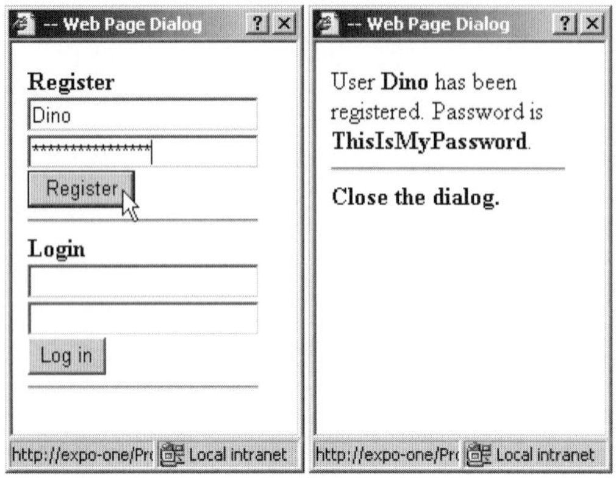

Figure 4-5 Navigable modal dialogs based on ASP.NET pages.

Using Embedded Forms

As mentioned earlier, by toggling on and off the visibility of blocks of related controls you can implement sort of pop-up forms as well. In the page, you define a logical form—that is, a block of controls acting as a real form—and hide and show it as needed. Basically, such a logical form would work with the rest of the page in a mutually exclusive way. The following code snippet shows a form with two logical subforms: one with a button and one with the typical login fields. Both are wrapped by a server-side <*div*> panel.

```
<form runat="server">
    <div runat="server" id="RunDlg">
        <asp:button runat="server" text="Login" onclick="OnShowLogin" />
    </div>

    <div runat="server" id="Login" visible="false">
        <hr>
        <b>Login</b><br>
        <asp:textbox runat="server" id="UserName" /><br>
        <asp:textbox runat="server" id="Pswd" textmode="password" /><br>
        <asp:button runat="server" text="Log in" onclick="OnLogIn" />
        <hr>
    </div>
</form>
```

When the button is clicked, the *RunDlg* block is hidden and *Login* is displayed. Note that when the *Visible* attribute is set to *false*, no code will be generated for any control.

```
<script runat="server">
void OnShowLogin(object sender, EventArgs e) {
    RunDlg.Visible = false;
    login.Visible = true;
}
```

```
void OnLogIn(object sender, EventArgs e) {
    RunDlg.Visible = true;
    login.Visible = false;
}
</script>
```

Using this approach, the form expected to work as a modal dialog is the only piece of the page's UI being displayed at a time. Note that for a better implementation of the solution, you can take advantage of user controls to wrap the contents of a server-side *<div>* block. We'll cover user controls in Chapter 10.

Working with Script Code

When you have input forms that need to be displayed only in certain situations (for example, when the user is not registered), a commonly used approach entails that you keep hidden the optional form and show the user a link to click. (See Figure 4-6.)

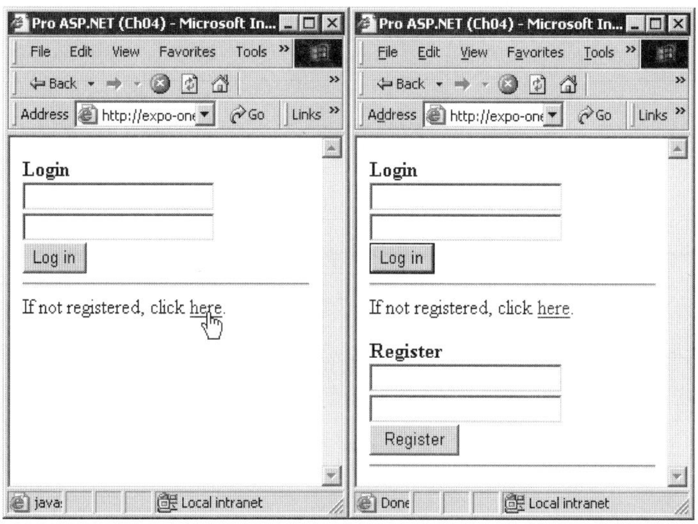

Figure 4-6 The optional dialog shows up only if the user explicitly requests it.

The overall user interface of the page is cleaner, and only information that's strictly needed is displayed. The downside of this approach is that you need an extra roundtrip to display the optional input form. In some cases, typically when an up-level browser is used, resorting to some client-side script code can be as much as twice effective, giving you a clean user interface and avoiding the extra roundtrip.

Supporting Multiple Browsers

Browser information is packed in the *HttpBrowserCapabilities* object returned by the *Request.Browser* property. Table 4-3 lists all the available properties.

Table 4-3 Browser Capabilities

Property	Description
ActiveXControls	Gets whether the browser supports ActiveX controls.
AOL	Gets whether the client is an America Online browser.
BackgroundSounds	Gets whether the browser supports background sounds.
Beta	Gets whether the browser is a beta release.
Browser	Gets the user agent string transmitted in the HTTP User-Agent header.
CDF	Gets whether the browser supports Channel Definition Format (CDF) for webcasting.
ClrVersion	Gets the *Version* object containing version information for the .NET common language runtime installed on the client.
Cookies	Gets whether the browser supports cookies.
Crawler	Gets whether the browser is a Web crawler search engine.
EcmaScriptVersion	Gets the version number of ECMA script supported by the browser.
Frames	Gets whether the browser supports HTML frames.
Item	Indexer property, gets the value of the specified browser capability.
JavaApplets	Gets whether the client browser supports Java applets.
JavaScript	Gets whether the browser supports JavaScript.
MajorVersion	Gets the integer number denoting the major version number of the browser.
MinorVersion	Gets the decimal number denoting the minor version number of the browser.
MSDomVersion	Gets the version of the Microsoft HTML (MSHTML) document object model that the browser supports.
Platform	Gets the name of the platform that the client uses.
Tables	Gets whether the client browser supports HTML tables.
Type	Gets a string made of the name and the major version number of the browser (for example, Internet Explorer 6 or Netscape 7).
VBScript	Gets whether the browser supports VBScript.
Version	Gets a string representing the full (integer and decimal) version number of the browser.

Table 4-3 Browser Capabilities

Property	Description
W3CDomVersion	Gets the version of the W3C XML Document Object Model (DOM) supported by the browser.
Win16	Gets whether the client is a Win16-based computer.
Win32	Gets whether the client is a Win32-based computer.

As a margin note, consider that if you're writing a mobile application, you must cast the *Request.Browser* return value to the *MobileCapabilities* object and work with that. The mobile capabilities object is supported only by version 1.1 of the .NET Framework. However, a separate download is available to enable mobile controls support for version 1.0 of the .NET Framework.

The *Browser* property returns the full string contained in the User-Agent header, and using it is probably the most flexible way to make sure the browser has just the characteristics you need to check. However, *Type* is another useful property for verifying the identity of the client browser. The following code shows how to make sure that the browser is Internet Explorer version 4.0 or newer:

```
bool upLevelBrowser = false;
HttpBrowserCapabilities caps = Request.Browser;
if (caps.Browser.ToUpper().IndexOf("IE") > -1) {
    // This is IE. Is version >3?
    upLevelBrowser = (caps.MajorVersion >3);
}
```

By putting this code in the *Page_Load* event, you enable yourself to modify the structure of the page according to the capabilities of the browser.

Note The *ClrVersion* property does not include build information, which means you can't track which service pack is installed on the client, if any. For the local machine, you can get full version information about the installed CLR using the following code:

```
Version v = Environment.Version;
Console.WriteLine("{0}.{1}.{2}.{3}", v.Major, v.Minor,
v.Build, v.Revision);
```

If the *Revision* property is *0*, no service pack is installed. If the revision number is *209*, service pack 1 is installed. The revision number for service pack 2 is *288*.

Now that we know a way to distinguish between browsers, let's use this technique to make up-level browsers show optional input forms via script. In the context of this example, an up-level browser is Internet Explorer 4.0 or a newer version.

Adding Client-Side Scripts

The idea is to obtain the effect shown in Figure 4-6 using client-side DHTML script code on up-level browsers and the classic postback event elsewhere. When the user clicks the hyperlink, what happens depends on the type of the browser. Although clear in the overall design, the solution is trickier to implement than one might think at first. The hidden difficulty revolves around the type of object the user really clicks on. Whatever the browser, the user always clicks a hyperlink with some client script code attached. Because we're talking about ASP.NET pages, any script code is associated with the hyperlink on the server. And this is exactly the issue.

If the browser is up-level, you need to render the clickable hyperlink by using a client-side HTML element—that is, an element without the *runat="server"* attribute.

```
Click <a href="javascript:YourFunc()">here</a>
```

If the browser is down-level, you need to use the ASP.NET *LinkButton* control as shown in the following code:

```
Click <asp:linkbutton runat="server" text="here" onclick="Clicked" />
```

How should you design the page layout to meet this requirement? Let's review a few possibilities, starting with ASP-style code blocks:

```
If not registered, click
<% if (upLevelBrowser) {%>
<a href="javascript:ShowRegisterDlg">here</a>.
<% } else {%>
<asp:linkbutton runat="server" text="here" onclick="ShowRegisterDlg" />.
<% } %>
<hr>
```

Although effective, the solution shown generates messy and rather unreadable code when used on a large scale. It also requires you to declare the *upLevelBrowser* variable as global. Finally, ASP-style code-blocks are deprecated, although ASP.NET fully supports them.

A second possibility entails the use of ASP.NET custom controls smart enough to detect the browser and produce appropriate HTML output. The key advantage of this approach is that you use a single tag and bury all necessary logic in the folds of its implementation. However, because we'll not cover custom controls until Chapter 18, we'll go for a third alternative that falls somewhere in the middle of the previous two.

You use a placeholder control to mark the place in which the hyperlink should appear in one form or the other. Next, in the *Page_Load* event handler, you populate the *Controls* collection of the *PlaceHolder* control with either plain text or a dynamically created instance of the *LinkButton* control. You use plain text—more exactly, a *LiteralControl* instance—if the client is up-level and client script code can be used. You use the *LinkButton* otherwise. The following code snippet shows the page layout:

```
<b>Login</b><br>
<asp:textbox runat="server" id="LogUserName" /><br>
<asp:textbox runat="server" id="LogPassword" textmode="password" /><br>
<asp:button runat="server" text="Log in" onclick="OnLogIn" />
<hr>
If not registered, click <asp:placeholder runat="server" id="theLink" />.
<hr>
```

In the *Page_Load* event handler, you first learn about the browser's capabilities and then configure the placeholder to host an HTML hyperlink or a server-side link button.

```
void Page_Load()
{
    // Check browser capabilities
    bool upLevelBrowser = false;
    HttpBrowserCapabilities caps = Request.Browser;
    if (caps.Browser.ToUpper().IndexOf("IE") > -1) {
        // This is IE. Is version >3?
        upLevelBrowser = (caps.MajorVersion >3);
    }

    // if downlevel (considering only IE4+ uplevel)
    if (upLevelBrowser) {
        AddDhtmlScriptCode(theLink);
        RegPanel.Visible = true;
        RegPanel.Style["display"] = "none";
    }
    else
        AddPostBackCode(theLink);
}
```

If the browser is up-level, the registration panel should be included as HTML but not displayed to the user. For this reason, you must set the *Visible* property to *true*—ensuring that the HTML code for the panel will be generated—and, at the same time, you need to hide the controls from view by resorting to CSS-style properties.

If the browser proves to be down-level—whatever this means to your application—you simply create and configure the link button control to receive the user's clicking and post back.

```
void AddDhtmlScriptCode(PlaceHolder ctl)
{
    // Name of the Javascript function
    string scriptFuncName = "ShowRegisterDlg";

    // Token used to register the Javascript procedure
    // with the instance of the Page object
    string scriptName = "__ShowRegisterDlg";

    // Create the hyperlink HTML code and add it to the placeholder
    string html = "<a href='javascript:{0}()'>{1}</a>";
    html = String.Format(html, scriptFuncName, "here");
    LiteralControl lit = new LiteralControl(html);
    ctl.Controls.Add(lit);

    // Create the Javascript function (must include <script>)
    StringBuilder sb = new StringBuilder("<script language=Javascript>\n");
    sb.Append("function ");
    sb.Append(scriptFuncName);
    sb.Append("() {\n");
    sb.Append("RegPanel.style['display'] = '';");
    sb.Append("\n}\n<");
    sb.Append("/");
    sb.Append("script>");

    // Register the Javascript function with the page so that it can be
    // flushed when the page is rendered
    if (!IsClientScriptBlockRegistered(scriptName))
            this.RegisterClientScriptBlock(scriptName, sb.ToString());
}

void AddPostBackCode(PlaceHolder ctl)
{
    LinkButton link = new LinkButton();
    link.ID = "showRegPanel";
    link.Text = "here";
    link.Click += new EventHandler(this.ShowRegisterDlg);
    ctl.Controls.Add(link);
}
```

There's no need for you to explicitly set the script for postback; adding a server-side control to the page fits the bill. The page will then call back the control to make it render its user interface as HTML.

In Figure 4-7, you can see how the sample page looks in Internet Explorer 6.0 and Netscape 4.7. To see the difference, look at the status bar of the browser windows when the mouse hovers over the hyperlink. Internet Explorer points to a local JavaScript procedure whereas Netscape points to the typical *__doPostBack* JavaScript function that implements the postback in ASP.NET.

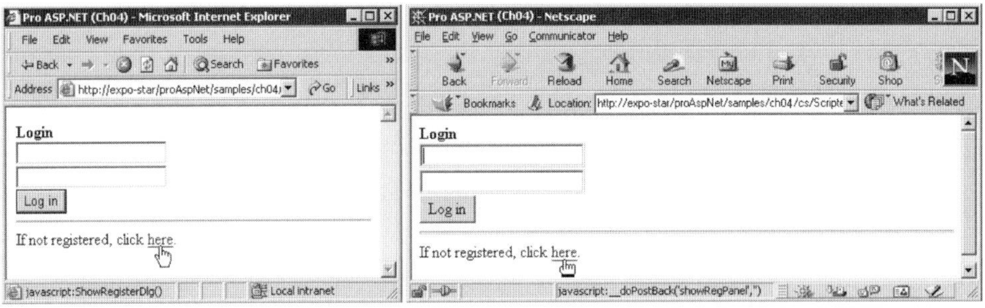

Figure 4-7 Internet Explorer 6.0 displays the input form using client script code, while Netscape 4.7 resorts to an event postback.

Registering Script Blocks

As discussed in Chapter 2, the *Page* object provides a couple of methods to inject client-side scripts in the body of the HTML page being generated. The methods are *RegisterClientScriptBlock* and *RegisterStartupScript*.

```
RegisterClientScriptBlock(scriptName, code);
RegisterStartupScript(scriptName, code);
```

Calling either method does not physically insert the JavaScript or the VBScript script code in the page's source code. The code injection takes place only as the final step in the ASP.NET page building process. So what happens to the scripts once either method is called? Look at the signature of both methods.

The latter argument is the string that contains the script code. The former, on the other hand, just names the script. The script code can be registered for output at any time in the page lifetime. Calling either registering method temporarily parks the script code into dedicated and case-sensitive name/value collections. The *scriptName* argument is used as the key to identify and track the script in the collection. The *code* argument, on the other hand, is just the content of the script stored as the value in the collection. Note that each registering method runs its own collection, so script names must be unique only within the scope of the method.

The content of script collections is flushed into the page output when the HTML code for the page is actually created, namely after the *PreRender* event. Each piece of script code must be wrapped by opening and closing *<script>* tags. However, more script functions can be declared in the same *<script>* block, but they will only count for a single entry in the collection.

The script collections are private fields of the *Page* class and are not programmatically accessible. You cannot walk your way through the collections, but you can check whether a script with a given name already exists. Each registering method also features a query counterpart that returns a Boolean value.

Checking the existence of a given named script is critical because duplicates are not allowed and any further attempt to add a script with an existing name will just be ignored. To check the script before registering, use the following code:

```
if (!IsClientScriptBlockRegistered(scriptName))
    RegisterClientScriptBlock(scriptName, code);
if (!IsStartupScriptRegistered(startupScriptName))
    RegisterStartupScript(startupScriptName, startupCode);
```

> **Tip** For your comfort, you might decide to keep the function declaration and the actual function call in different script blocks. You can use *RegisterClientScriptBlock* to declare the function and *RegisterStartupScript* to register the call. This approach perhaps results in more elegant code, but it requires the *Page* object to handle two nonempty collections instead of just one. This isn't really a big concern, but when you have to squeeze out every little bit of performance even that could help. Script collections are initialized only when the first item gets added.

It's also interesting to note that the actual collections classes used are of a special type—*HybridDictionary*. The class implements the methods of the *IDictionary* interface in a very flexible way. It utilizes a *ListDictionary* object as long as the number of items in the collection is relatively small (less than 10). When the size of the dictionary grows beyond the threshold, the class automatically switches to a *Hashtable* object, which manages large collections more efficiently.

Registering Startup Script Blocks

Where is a script block injected exactly? That mostly depends on which method you use to register the script with the page. If you use *RegisterClientScriptBlock*, the script block is placed right after the opening *<form>* tag. When the script executes, the content of the form has not been initialized. So if the script attempts to access any of the elements in the form, an exception is raised.

In contrast, *RegisterStartupScript* places its script code just before the closing *</form>* tag. In this way, the code runs after the form has been initialized and provides safe access to all constituent controls. In this sense, it is a startup script.

Registering Hidden Fields

As mentioned, hidden fields shouldn't be used to make context-specific information survive across different requests of the same page. ASP.NET provides more powerful and flexible tools to accomplish that and there's no need for you to resort to hidden fields.

Hidden fields, though, are still a viable tool to pass information to HTML elements defined on the client. You can either define them statically in the page layout or have the ASP.NET runtime create them at render time, in much the same way as the runtime does with script blocks. The method to use is *RegisterHiddenField*.

```
RegisterHiddenField("BookTitle", "Programming ASP.NET");
```

The method takes a couple of arguments: the name of the field and its content. When the method executes, ASP.NET tracks whether an extra hidden field should be created at render time. The previous line of code generates the following HTML code:

```
<input type="hidden" name="BookTitle" value="Programming ASP.NET" />
```

Page Localization

In the real world, several companies have different Web sites, one per each country in which they have subsidiaries or operate. In many cases, the localized Web site is only a branch of the main Web site located in a subdirectory; more often than not, the Web site is also accessible using the same domain but a local extension. For example, let's say that the Contoso, Ltd is on the Web at *http://www.contoso.com*. Its Italian subsidiary, if any, is normally reachable either at *http://www.contoso.com/italy* or, through a more direct local domain, at *http://www.contoso.it*. In all cases, the localization is achieved by replicating, translating, and adapting existing pages. Is this what ASP.NET page localization is all about? Not exactly.

Actually, ASP.NET page localization and, more generally, the .NET world-ready initiative is aimed at a different result: enabling the *same* application to morph user-interface (UI) and locale-sensitive resources into localized versions. Page localization simply provides a deeply automated mechanism to translate and localize a group of UI-related resources. In no way does page localization provide for overriding and customizing functions. In summary, if your subsidiaries need to create their own Web sites with localized content and structure, page localization is not the right tool. On the other hand, if you're just looking for an effective way to publish some locale-sensitive data in a way that reflects the current culture and sentiment, ASP.NET page localization is just right.

Culture and Locales

Localization—that is the application's ability to load resources specific to a culture—is only the final step of a more systemic process. To start out, you should be predisposing the application to use a localized user interface and strive to have it grow up independent from cultures and regional settings. In doing so, as the second step of the design process, you should ensure that all localizable resources are clearly isolated from the rest of the code. The idea is that locale-specific resources can be plugged in dynamically without affecting the overall functionality. The page localization finalizes the work and, by dynamically reading resources data, gives international users an interface they feel comfortable with.

Programming Cultures

In the .NET Framework, a culture is a logical container of information about a specific country culture. Typical culture information includes the writing system, the calendar used, formatting dates, currency, and sorting strings. Technically speaking, a culture is represented by the *CultureInfo* class. The .NET Framework provides a list of predefined cultures in the *System.Globalization* namespace. Cultures are given a name and an identifier and are classified by language and country. To enumerate all the available cultures, you can use the following code:

```
CultureInfo [] cults;
cults = CultureInfo.GetCultures(CultureTypes.AllCultures);
foreach (CultureInfo ci in cults) {
    Console.WriteLine(ci);
}
```

The *CultureInfo* class exposes its information through ad hoc classes such as *DateTimeFormatInfo*, *NumberFormatInfo*, *CompareInfo*, and *TextInfo*. Other .NET Framework classes use *CultureInfo* to accomplish locale-specific operations. For example, the *String* class and the *DataTable* classes use culture information to compare text and column values.

The culture names follow an international standard ratified in RFC 1766. A name is a dash-separated string made of two tokens: the language code and the region code. The language code is a lowercase two-letter code derived from ISO 639-1. The region code is an uppercase two-letter code derived from ISO 3166. A typical culture name is *en-US*, meaning that English is the language and US is the country. The same language can be accompanied with different regions or countries—for example, *en-GB* (United Kingdom) and *en-ZA* (South Africa). Likewise, the same country can have multiple languages—for example, *it-CH* and *fr-CH* identify the culture for Swiss people speaking Italian and French, respectively.

Invariant and Neutral Cultures

Along with specific cultures in which both the language and region information is known, the .NET Framework supports two other types of cultures. They are the invariant culture and neutral cultures. The invariant culture is represented by the *InvariantCulture* class and has the empty string as the name. This type of culture should be used by applications that have no locale-sensitive data to display or process. The invariant culture is associated with the English language but not with a particular country or region.

On the other hand, a neutral culture is a culture that is associated with a language but not with a country. Note that some classes don't accept neutral culture information. For example, in Chapter 1 we pointed out that the *Culture* attribute on the *@Page* directive must be set to a fully qualified culture name and neutral names are not accepted.

> **Note** A code page is a list of selected character codes ordered in a certain way. Code pages exist to support languages that share common writing systems. By convention, in most code pages the codes 0 through 127 represent the same characters, thus allowing for continuity. Normally, the characters corresponding to codes 128 through 255 differ significantly between code pages. In the .NET Framework, the widespread use of Unicode simplifies the development of globalized applications, eliminating the need to reference a code page. However, code pages are supported through the *Encoding* class.

```
Encoding enc = Encoding.GetEncoding(1252);
```

> The preceding code shows how to get the specified code page. After that, you can use the newly created object wherever encoding information is accepted.

The ASP.NET Resource Manager

Just like other applications, an ASP.NET application can, and often should, use resources. Resources are an effective way to isolate localizable portions of the application's user interface. In general, a resource is a nonexecutable text associated with the program. Typical resources are images, icons, and internal-use files, but any serializable object can be considered a resource. Application resources are stored outside the application so that they can be recompiled and replaced without affecting and recompiling the application itself.

An ASP.NET application needs to have a primary assembly to contain the default or neutral resources for the application. In addition, you create a number of satellite assemblies each containing localized resources for a particular culture you want to support. The primary resource assembly is installed into the application's Bin directory; the satellite assemblies go in their respective locale-specific subdirectory, as shown in Figure 4-8.

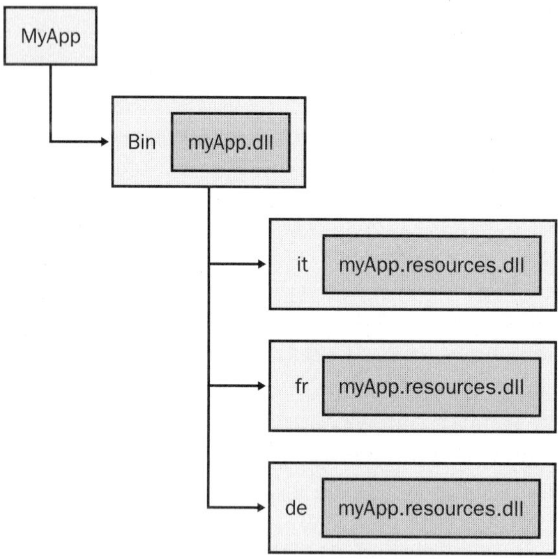

Figure 4-8 Satellite resource assemblies for an ASP.NET application.

Creating Satellite Assemblies

The resource file can take various forms, including that of a simple text file or the XML file created by Microsoft Visual Studio and saved with the *.resx* extension. However, only .resources files can be embedded in a .NET executable or compiled into satellite assemblies. You use the Resource File Generator (*resgen.exe*) utility to convert text and XML-based resource files into .resources. The resource file names follow the naming convention *baseName.cultureName.resources*. Typically, the base name is the name of the application.

```
resgen.exe myapp.resx myapp.it.resources
```

Once created, the .resources file should be embedded into an assembly or can even be used as-is as a resource container. To embed the resource file into a satellite assembly, you use the Assembly Linker tool (*al.exe*). On the command line, you indicate the culture (*it* in the next example) and the name of the assembly.

```
al /out:myapp.resources.dll /c:it /embed:myapp.it.resources
```

After you have compiled your satellite assemblies, they all have the same name. The default resource file should be named after the base name and have the .resources extension. The culture-specific files are packaged in satellite assemblies, one for each culture. The default resource file is commonly embedded in your main assembly.

> **Note** You should avoid deploying ASP.NET applications using individual .resources files. While this can be acceptable for other types of applications, it can break XCOPY deployment in ASP.NET. The files, in fact, will be locked until the application shuts down, thus causing locking issues and invalidating the XCOPY deployment. To avoid that, deploy ASP.NET resources in satellite assemblies.

If you develop your application using Visual Studio .NET, resources are managed automatically and compiled within the assembly if the Build Action property in the Properties window is set to Embedded Resource.

Retrieving Localized Information

The *ResourceManager* class provides access to culture resources at run time. You configure a new instance of the class to look up the resources stored in the satellite assemblies derived from the specified base name.

```
ResourceManager rm;
rm = new ResourceManager("myApp", this.GetType().Assembly);
```

The constructor also requires a second argument because it is the main assembly that contains the default resources. Each resource item is identified by a name, and that name is used to retrieve the value from the currently selected culture. The following code snippet shows how to retrieve the string named "welcome":

```
rm.GetString("welcome");
```

The value will be retrieved from the resource assembly that complies with the current UI culture. A fallback process is started to individuate the resource to use should the requested locale not be available.

The *CurrentUICulture* for the page, or for the current thread, determined what resource assembly the Resource Manager should check.

Note A best-practice for ASP.NET applications is setting the *Current-UICulture* property in the code of the page to ensure that the culture used to process the page matches that of the requesting user. The following code shows how to set the *CurrentUICulture* property to the culture associated with the browser's current settings:

```
Culture c = new CultureInfo(Request.UserLanguages[0]);
Thread.CurrentThread.CurrentUICulture = c;
```

Page Errors and Tracing

Just like other .NET applications, ASP.NET applications can take advantage of exceptions to catch and handle run-time errors that occur in the code. Exceptions, though, should be just what their name suggests—that is, exceptional events in the life of the application.

As a matter of fact, exceptions seriously affect the average performance of any application, and because ASP.NET applications are very critical and sensitive, you should handle exceptions with extreme care and limit their use as much as possible. A typical bad programming practice is to rely on exceptions to catch any possible error resulting from an operation. Admittedly, wrapping a piece of code with a *try/catch* block makes programming much simpler while offering a single point of control for errors. However, employing this technique on a large scale might result in a dramatic loss of performance. Exceptions are meant to target exceptional events that aren't predictable in other ways. Exceptions should not be used to control the normal flow of the program. If there is a way to detect possible inconsistent situations, by all means use that other method and keep exceptions as the last resort.

Note that a *try/catch* block in the code always causes extra code to be generated and executed. The impact on performance is minimal if the *try* branch executes. The performance hit is relevant if the *catch* block executes instead. For this reason, you should use exceptions only to handle exceptional events in your code.

> **Note** The *debug* attribute on the *@Page* directive forces the ASP.NET runtime to add debug information to the dynamically generated assembly for the page. That information is then used by Visual Studio .NET to debug the application. Outside the development and testing phase, though, debug information makes the assembly unnecessarily heavy and poorly responsive. Make sure you have no *debug=true* attribute left in .aspx when you actually deploy the site.

Defining Custom Error Pages

Although the concept of an error is nearly identical in all types of applications and platforms, the way in which errors manifest themselves to the users varies quite a bit in terms of context and application. When an unrecoverable error occurs in an ASP.NET page, the user always receives a page that, more or less nicely, informs that something went wrong at a certain point. ASP.NET catches any unhandled exception wandering around the page and transforms it into a page for the user, as shown in Figure 4-9.

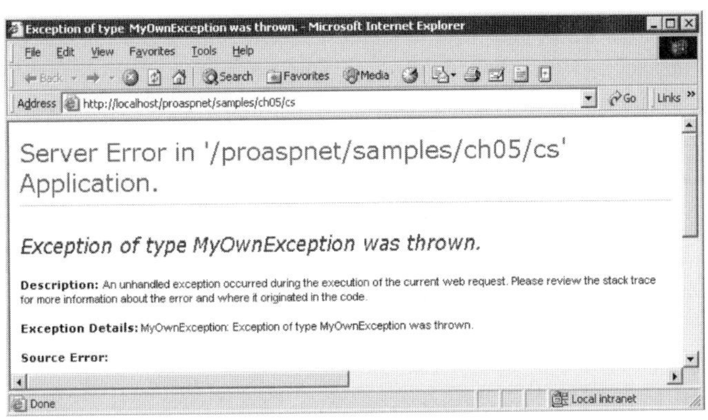

Figure 4-9 The error page generated by an unhandled exception.

The way in which ASP.NET displays error pages is controlled by the *<customErrors>* section in the configuration file. As we'll see in greater detail in Chapter 12, the section can be defined in the web.config file located in the root folder as well as in a child directory. The following code presents an excerpt from the web.config file created by Visual Studio .NET:

```
<configuration>
  <system.web>
    ⋮
```

```
    <customErrors mode="RemoteOnly" />
  </system.web>
</configuration>
```

When the *mode* property is set to *RemoteOnly* and an error occurs, users receive a generic error page that informs them that something went wrong on the server. The page is not like that in Figure 4-9 in that it doesn't contain stack trace and error details, but I wouldn't say it's really comfortable and user-friendly, as Figure 4-10 demonstrates.

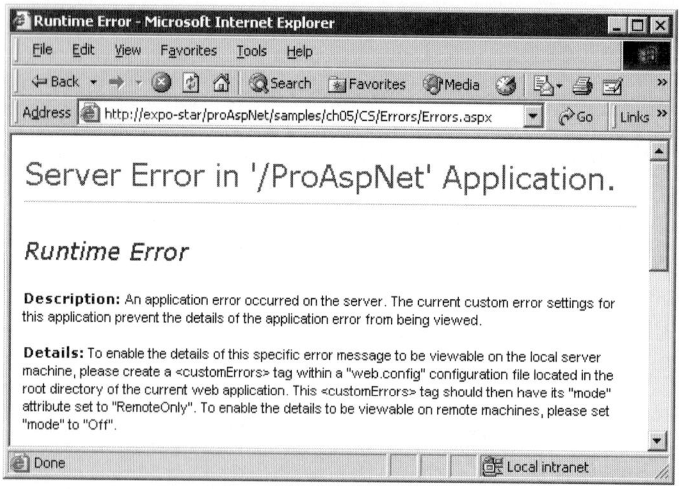

Figure 4-10 A runtime error occurred on the server. The page does not provide information about the error, but it still can't be said to be a user-friendly page!

The error page of Figure 4-9 is reserved only for the user working on the Web server machine—probably, just the developer whose code caused the error.

Using Custom Error Pages

The error-handling policy can be changed at will. In particular, ASP.NET can be instructed to always display custom pages to all users—local and remote. To obtain this, you change the *mode* attribute of the *<customErrors>* section to *On*. This is only half the task, though. All users now get a rather inexpressive and uninformative page. To display a more friendly and apologetic page (as shown in Figure 4-11), set web.config as follows:

```
<configuration>
  <system.web>
    <customErrors mode="On" defaultRedirect="GenericError.aspx" />
  </system.web>
</configuration>
```

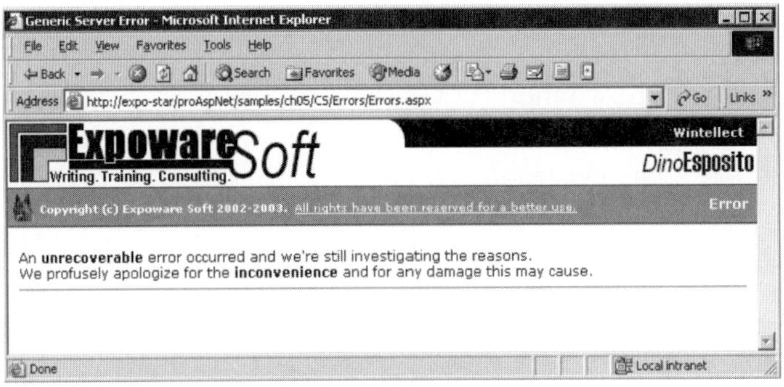

Figure 4-11 A nice and friendly error page.

In most cases, the error page is made of plain HTML so that no error could recursively be raised. However, should the error page, in turn, originate another error, the default generic page of ASP.NET will be shown. (See Figure 4-10.)

Keeping the mode set to *On* is not a recommended practice. *RemoteOnly* is preferable because it contributes to the Web site security by not showing application details to remote clients. The following code snippet shows the ideal combination that all Web sites should implement: remote users receive a nice message, while the Web master gets detailed information from the ASP.NET runtime.

```
<configuration>
  <system.web>
    <customErrors mode="RemoteOnly"
      defaultRedirect="GenericError.aspx" />
  </system.web>
</configuration>
```

Setting the mode *Off* is useful and recommended only during the development phase when the application runs internally and can help developers to figure out errors and problems more quickly and even remotely. Do not use it in production environments.

> **Caution** If you have plans to change the value of the *mode* attribute in the *<customErrors>* section, pay attention to the fact that the attribute is case sensitive and accepts only the following values spelled as shown: *On*, *Off*, and *RemoteOnly*.

HTTP Errors

In addition to the customization of application errors, ASP.NET enables you to customize pages to show when HTTP errors occurs. For example, the following web.config file provides a customized error page whenever the user types in the name of a nonexisting resource.

```
<configuration>
  <system.web>
    <customErrors mode="RemoteOnly" defaultRedirect="GenericError.aspx">
        <error statusCode="404" redirect="GenericError.aspx?errID=404" />
        <error statusCode="500" redirect="GenericError.aspx?errID=500" />
    </customErrors>
  </system.web>
</configuration>
```

The *<error>* element indicates the page to redirect the user to when the specified HTTP error occurs. The attribute *statusCode* denotes the HTTP error. Figure 4-12 shows what happens when the user mistypes the name of the URL and the error HTTP 404 (resource not found) is generated. Note that not all HTTP errors can be trapped in this way. Some HTTP errors are handled directly by IIS and never processed by ASP.NET.

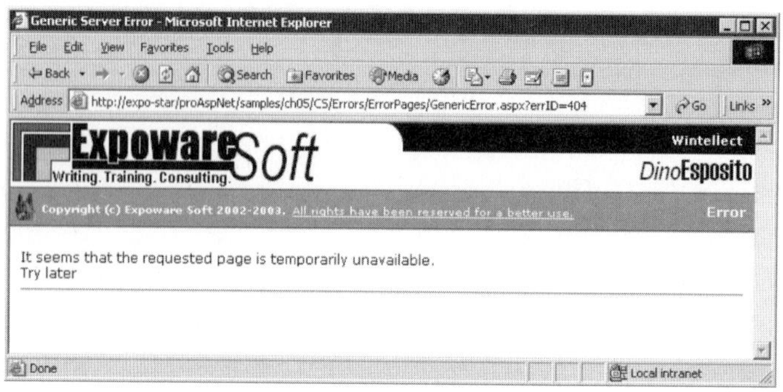

Figure 4-12 A custom page for the popular HTTP 404 error.

Tracing the Execution Flow in .NET

The .NET Framework comes with a rather feature-rich set of tools for debugging and tracing applications. In particular, the *Systems.Diagnostics* namespace defines two classes, named *Trace* and *Debug*, whose methods can be used to output messages commenting the execution of the code. This feature is extremely useful to track data inconsistencies, monitor the flow, assert conditions, and even to gather profiling information. The *Trace* and *Debug* classes are essentially identical and work on top of more specialized modules known as *listeners*.

The ASP.NET support for tracing is different and fairly disjointed. We'll first briefly overview the .NET Framework support for tracing and then move on to consider the peculiarity of ASP.NET.

The Listener Object

The listener acts like a driver and collects and stores tracing messages into a particular medium such as the Windows event log, an application window, or a text file. Each application can have its own set of listeners, which will receive all emitted messages. The application configuration file has a *<trace>* section under *<system.diagnostics>* to add and remove listeners. The .NET Framework provides three predefined listeners:

- ***DefaultTraceListener*** The listener emits messages to the Win32 *OutputDebugString* API function and to the *Debugger.Log* method. When the application runs within Visual Studio .NET, any message shows in the Output window. The *DefaultTraceListener* class is the only listener automatically included in every listeners collection.
- ***TextWriterTraceListener*** The listener redirects output to a *Stream* object, including the console or a file. If the target is a file, the name can be indicated in the configuration file via the *initializeData* attribute. (We'll discuss this more in a moment.) Otherwise, the listener is configured and attached programmatically. In this case, you set the target storage medium using the *Writer* property.
- ***EventLogTraceListener*** The listener redirects all its output to the Windows event log. The class provides the *EventLog* property to get and set the name of the event log. The event log can also be set at configuration time using the *initializeData* attribute.

Registering and Configuring Listeners

Listeners can be added to an application in two ways: programmatically through the *Listeners* collection of either the *Trace* or *Debug* class, and declaratively using the *<listeners>* subsection in the *<trace>* section of the configuration file. The following code snippet shows how to replace the default listener with the event log listener. In addition, the snippet sets the *autoflush* property to *true*, which means the listener is expected to flush the internal buffer after each write.

```
<system.diagnostics>
   <trace autoflush="true">
     <listeners>
        <add name="eventListener"
          type="EventLogTraceListener"
```

```
            initializeData="MyAppEventLog" />
         <remove type="DefaultTraceListener"/>
      </listeners>
   </trace>
</system.diagnostics>
```

Note that you can use a non–fully qualified name for the listener class as long as the calling application imports the *System.Diagnostics* namespace. To configure the event log tracer to work alone codewise, do as follows:

```
Trace.Listeners.Clear();
EventLogTraceListener evWriter;
evWriter = new EventLogTraceListener(MyAppEventLog);
Trace.Listeners.Add(evWriter);
```

As mentioned, *Debug* and *Trace* classes share the same collection of listeners. Neither of the two classes really owns the listener collection. The collection, instead, is maintained by an assemblywide internal class and accessed by both *Debug* and *Trace*. So if your application adds a listener object to the *Debug.Listeners*, it automatically becomes visible to the *Trace* class as well.

> **Note** Custom listeners can be defined by inheriting from the *TraceListener* base class and overriding methods. At a minimum, a new class would implement the *Write* and *WriteLine* methods. Additional overridable methods are *Fail*, *Close*, and *Flush*.

ASP.NET Tracing

The ASP.NET subsystem provides a specific and made-to-measure tracing mechanism. Regardless of whether you write messages to the page trace log, a trace-enabled page always contains a series of tables containing performance information about the request and the controls tree.

Although a *<trace>* configuration section does exist in the web.config file to let you configure tracing at the application level, you typically want to control tracing on a per-page basis. However, for large projects you can toggle on and off the trace attribute by using the following code in the application's web.config file:

```
<configuration>
  <system.web>
     <trace enabled="true" pageOutput="true" />
  </system.web>
</configuration>
```

The *enabled* attribute enables tracing on the application, while the *pageOutput* attribute permits output to appear in the page. If *pageOutput* is set to *false* (the default setting), the tracing output is automatically routed to the ASP.NET tracer tool—*trace.axd*. At the end of the project, you simply drop the <*trace*> element from the web.config file or set both attributes to *false*. In this way, you eliminate at the root the risk of inadvertently leaving tracing enabled on one of the application pages.

Enabling Page Tracing

The *trace* attribute in the *@Page* directive defaults to *false*; if set to *true*, it enables tracing information to appear at the bottom of the page, as shown in Figure 4-13.

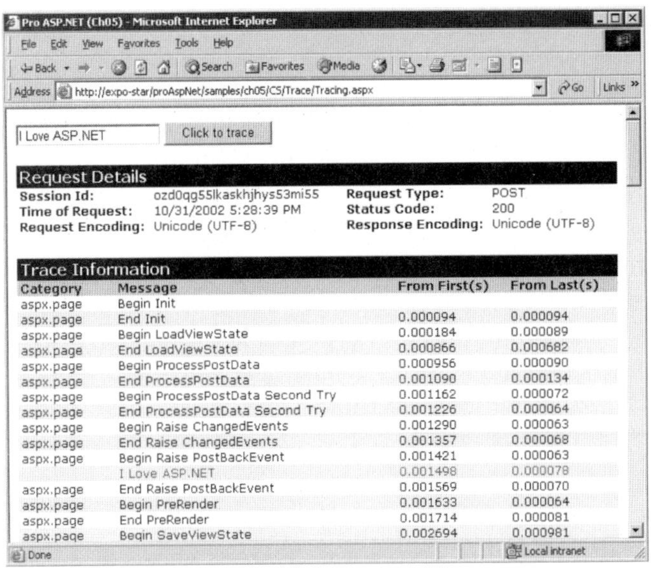

Figure 4-13 ASP.NET tracing in action.

The trace information is part of the page and, as such, displays through any type of browser that accesses the page. As you can see in the figure, several tables of information show up along with the trace information generated by the page. Additional tables display request details, the control tree, and some useful collections such as cookies, headers, form values, and server variables. If the session and the application state are not empty, the contents of the *Session*- and *Application*-intrinsic properties are also included in the view. In no case are the contents of the *Cache* object flushed to the trace log. (We'll return to this topic in Chapter 14.)

The *@Page* directive also supplies the *TraceMode* attribute to let you choose the order in which the information should be displayed. Feasible values are *SortByCategory* and *SortByTime*. By default, the trace messages appear in the order in which they are emitted. If you set the *TraceMode* attribute to the *SortByCategory* value, the rows appearing in the Trace Information section are sorted by category name. The category to which each row belongs is determined by the method used to emit the message.

Emitting Trace Messages

An ASP.NET page populates its trace log using methods on the *TraceContext* class. An instance of this class is created when the HTTP request is set up for execution. The trace object is then exposed through the *Trace* property of the *HttpContext* class and is also mirrored by the *Trace* property on the *Page* class.

The *TraceContext* class has a simple interface and features a couple of properties and as many methods. The properties are *IsEnabled* and *TraceMode*. The *IsEnabled* property is a read-only Boolean property that indicates whether tracing is enabled or not. The value that this property returns is affected by the *trace* attribute on the *@Page* directive as well as the *enabled* attribute in the *<trace>* section of the web.config file. The *TraceMode* property gets and sets the order in which the traced rows will be displayed in the page. The property is of type *TraceMode*—an enumeration that includes values such as *SortByCategory* and *SortByTime*.

To emit messages, you can use either of the two methods *Write* and *Warn*. Both methods have three overloads, which all behave in the same way. *Write* and *Warn* are nearly identical methods—the only visible difference is that *Warn* always outputs messages in red.

```
public void Write(string);
public void Write(string, string);
public void Write(string, string, Exception);
```

The simplest overload just emits the specified text in the Message column. (See Figure 4-13.) In the second overload, the first string argument represents the name of the category you want to use for the message—the second argument. The category name can be used to sort trace information and is any name that makes sense to the application to better qualify the message. Finally, the third overload adds an extra *Exception* object in case the message is tracing an error. In this case, the text in the Message column is the concatenation of the specified text and the exception's message.

Note Although the text being passed to both *Write* and *Warn* methods is meant to be displayed in HTML pages, no HTML formatting tag is ever processed. The text is written as plain text, so if you attempt to use boldface characters your only result is having a trace message with *<b>* and *</b>* substrings.

Tracing from External Classes

The ASP.NET *Trace* object is accessible without a fully qualified name from the source code of the .aspx page or from the code-behind class. Custom controls embedded in the page, and their code-behind classes, can also access the tracing subsystem directly. Other classes don't have the same possibility, though.

Suppose your code-behind class delegates an external class to accomplish some tasks. How can the worker class trace in the ASP.NET page? In the context of the worker class, the *Trace* object is unavailable, or at least not in its unqualified form. External classes that want to emit text in the trace log of the current HTTP request can do that using the following expression:

```
System.Web.HttpContext.Current.Trace.Write(category, msg);
```

By writing and registering a custom listener, you could also have the worker class write to the .NET tracing subsystem with the listener routing the text back to ASP.NET. This is probably a more elegant solution, but it's a bit twisted and less efficient. However, a custom listener is as easy to write as shown in the following code:

```
public class AspNetTraceListener : TraceListener
{
    public override void Write(string msg)
    {
        System.Web.HttpContext.Current.Trace.Write(msg);
    }
    public override void WriteLine(string msg)
    {
        System.Web.HttpContext.Current.Trace.Write(msg);
    }
}
```

The newly created listener must now be added to the collection of .NET listeners for the application. In the web.config file, add the following entry:

```
<system.diagnostics>
  <trace>
    <listeners>
      <add name="aspNetListener" type="AspNetListener, YourAssembly" />
```

```
    </listeners>
  </trace>
</system.diagnostics>
```

At this point, make sure the worker class traces text using either the *Debug* or *Trace* class in the *System.Diagnostics* namespace. The just-added ASP.NET listener will route the text to the ASP.NET tracing system.

> **Note** The ASP.NET tracing system does not support its own set of listeners, nor does it support those registered through the diagnostic's *<trace>* section. In addition, there's no known way to modify the output of the trace to show only a few of the standard tables of data.

The Trace Viewer

ASP.NET also supports application-level tracing through the trace viewer tool. Once tracing has been enabled for the application, each page request routes all the page-specific trace information to the viewer. You can view the trace viewer by requesting *trace.axd* from the root application directory. The trace viewer is shown in Figure 4-14.

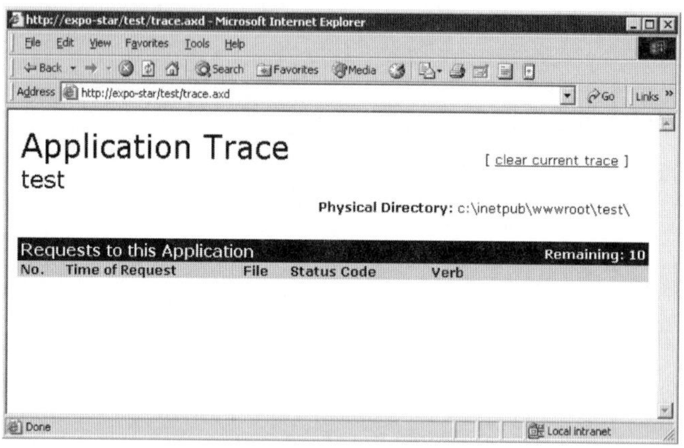

Figure 4-14 The trace viewer ready for action.

To enable the viewer, you need to have a *<trace>* section in your application web.config file—that is, the configuration file deployed in the root folder.

```
<configuration>
  <system.web>
     <trace enabled="true" />
  </system.web>
</configuration>
```

Actually, most of the settings we will discuss in Chapter 12 about the ASP.NET *<trace>* section apply to the trace viewer. The *pageOutput* attribute, for example, indicates whether the trace output should be visible to the individual pages too or only accessible through the viewer. By default, *pageOutput* is *false* and only the viewer receives trace information. However, each page can individually override this setting by using the trace attribute on the *@Page* directive. The trace viewer caches no more than the number of requests specified by thc *rcqucstLimit* attribute (10 by default).

In brief, the ASP.NET trace viewer acts as a centralized console and gathers all the trace information generated by the pages in a certain application. Each request, up to the maximum number fixed by *requestLimit*, is identified by a row in the viewer's interface and can be consulted until the viewer's cache is cleared, as shown in Figure 4-15.

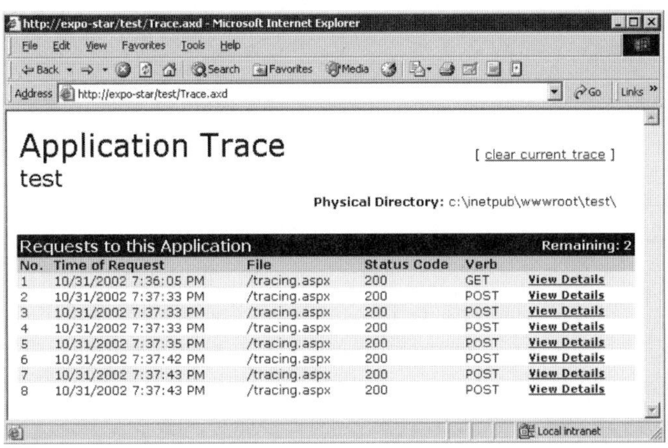

Figure 4-15 The trace viewer in action.

You activate the viewer by requesting the *trace.axd* URL on the root of the application. AXD is a special resource type that is resolved through the page shown in Figure 4-14. After that, the viewer automatically tracks all requests and caches the full trace for each. When the request limit is reached, no other request will be cached until the log is manually cleared.

Important Although you should pay careful attention not to deploy pages with the *trace* attribute turned on, tracing calls can be left in the code for further use. Both the *Write* and *Warn* methods, in fact, return immediately if tracing is not enabled. Although not null, the impact this might have on the performance is negligible. It is especially minor when considering that, in case of need, the tracing mechanism can be turned on declaratively and without touching the code. By simply changing the *<trace>*'s *enabled* attribute in the web.config file, you enable tracing through the viewer. In this way, you can monitor the application—for example, after some user feedback—without stopping it. For the viewer to work, though, trace information must be emitted.

Conclusion

In this chapter, we examined issues you might face when building pages and interacting with them. Form-based programming is fundamental in ASP.NET because it's the only way to have users and applications interact. ASP.NET pages can have only one server-side form with view-state and control support. To add more forms, you can either resort to old-style and stateless HTML programming or create some sort of logical form controls hosted by the single-server form, basically redirecting the user to the specified page.

Making different pages work together in exchanging data and arguments is the ultimate goal of the *@Reference* directive that allows pages to reference other pages as external libraries.

Often good programs do bad things and raise errors. In the Web world, handling errors is a task architecturally left to the run-time environment running the application. The ASP.NET runtime is capable of providing two types of error pages, both of which are simply impracticable for serious and professional applications. When a user who is locally connected to the application does something that originates an error, by default ASP.NET returns a "geek" page with the stack trace and the full transcript of the exception that occurred. The remote user, on the other hand, receives a less compromising page but certainly not a user-friendly one. Fortunately, though, the ASP.NET framework is flexible enough to let you change the error pages, even to the point of distinguishing between HTTP errors.

Localization is another aspect of page and user interaction that we covered, along with tracing. Unlike localization, tracing is not a feature directly aimed at end users, but when properly used it can make users' experiences much easier and enjoyable while giving programmers solid information to profile and track the application's behavior.

In the next chapter, we'll introduce how to add data to your ASP.NET pages. We'll start with a discussion of ADO.NET object model.

Resources

- Post Multiple Forms from a Single Page (*http://www.aspnetpro.com/features/2003/04/asp200304pw_f/asp200304pw_f.asp*)
- Build Generic Error Handlers (*http://www.aspnetpro.com/features/2003/05/asp200305dk_f/asp200305dk_f.asp*)
- Internationalize Your ASP.NET Applications (*http://www.devx.com/dotnet/Article/7000*)
- MyTracer Monitors and Traces ASP.NET Apps (*http://msdn.microsoft.com/msdnmag/issues/03/04/CuttingEdge/default.aspx*)
- Customize '404' Errors (*http://www.aspnetpro.com/features/2002/10/asp200210fj_f/asp200210fj_f.asp*)

Part II

Adding Data in an ASP.NET Site

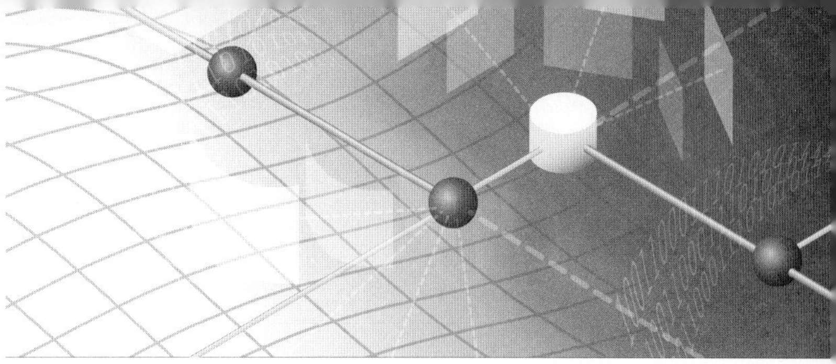

5

The ADO.NET Object Model

As a general rule, the most successful man in life is the man who has the best information.

—Benjamin Disraeli

ADO.NET is the latest in a long line of database-access technologies that began with the Open DataBase Connectivity (ODBC) API several years ago. Written as a C-style library, ODBC was designed to provide a uniform API to issue SQL calls to various database servers. In the ODBC model, database-specific drivers hide any difference and discrepancy between the SQL language used at the application level and the internal query engine. Next, COM landed in the database territory and started a colonization process that culminated with OLE DB.

OLE DB has evolved from ODBC and, in fact, the open database connectivity principle emerges somewhat intact in it. OLE DB is a COM-based API aimed at building a common layer of code for applications to access any data source that can be exposed as a tabular rowset of data. The OLE DB architecture is composed of two elements—a consumer and a provider. The consumer is incorporated in the client and is responsible for setting up COM-based communication with the data provider. The OLE DB data provider, in turn, receives calls from the consumer and executes commands on the data source. Whatever the data format and storage medium are, an OLE DB provider returns data formatted in a tabular layout—that is, with rows and columns.

Because it isn't especially easy to use and is primarily designed for coding from within C++ applications, OLE DB never captured the heart of programmers, even though it could guarantee a remarkable mix of performance and flexibility. ActiveX Data Objects (ADO)—roughly, a COM automation version of

OLE DB—came a little later just to make the OLE DB technology accessible from Microsoft Visual Basic and ASP applications. When used, ADO acts as the real OLE DB consumer embedded in the host applications. ADO was invented in the age of connected, two-tier applications, and the object model design reflects that. ADO makes a point of programming redundancy: it usually provides more than just one way of accomplishing key tasks, and it contains a lot of housekeeping code. For all these reasons, although it's incredibly easy to use, an ADO-based application doesn't perform as efficiently as a pure OLE DB application.

ADO.NET is a data-access layer tailor-made for the .NET Framework. It was heavily inspired by ADO, which has emerged over the past few years as a very successful object model for writing data-aware applications. The key design criteria for ADO.NET are simplicity and performance. Those criteria typically work against each other, but with ADO.NET you get the power and performance of a low-level interface combined with the simplicity of a modern object model. Unlike ADO, though, ADO.NET has been purposely designed to observe general, rather than database-oriented, guidelines.

Several syntactical differences exist between the object models of ADO and ADO.NET. In spite of this, the functionalities of ADO and ADO.NET look much the same. This is because Microsoft put a lot of effort in aligning some programming aspects of the ADO.NET object model with ADO. In this way, data developers don't need to become familiar with too many new concepts to use ADO.NET and can work with a relatively short learning curve. With ADO.NET, you probably won't be able to reuse much of your existing code. You'll certainly be able, though, to reuse all your skills.

The .NET Data Access Layer

The key improvements in ADO.NET are the rather powerful disconnected model exposed through the *DataSet* object, the strong integration with XML, and the seamless integration with the rest of the .NET Framework, including ASP.NET applications and Web services. Additionally, the performance of ADO.NET is very good, and the integration with Microsoft Visual Studio .NET is unprecedented. If you're writing a new application in the .NET Framework, deciding whether to use ADO.NET is a no-brainer.

> **Note** Using ADO in .NET applications is still possible, but for performance and consistency reasons its use should be limited to a very few and special cases. For example, ADO is the only way you have to work with server cursors, and ADOX is the variation of ADO that provides you with an object model for managing table structure and schema information. On the other hand, ADO recordsets can't be directly bound to ASP.NET or Microsoft Windows Forms databound controls. We'll cover data binding in Chapter 6 and Chapter 7.

A key architectural element in the ADO.NET infrastructure is the *managed provider*, which can be considered as the .NET counterpart of the OLE DB provider. A managed data provider enables you to connect to a data source and retrieve and modify data. Compared to the OLE DB provider, a .NET managed provider has a simplified data-access architecture made of a smaller set of interfaces and based on .NET Framework data types. Figure 5-1 illustrates the internal structure of a .NET data provider.

A COM-based OLE DB provider is a monolithic component. In contrast, a managed provider is made of a suite of classes, each of which represents a particular step in the connection model that a data-aware application implements. A managed provider is composed of classes used to connect to a particular data source, manage transactions, execute commands, and access result sets. For each of these steps, the managed provider supplies a particular class with its own set of properties, methods, and events. The union of these classes form the logical entity known as the managed provider for that data source.

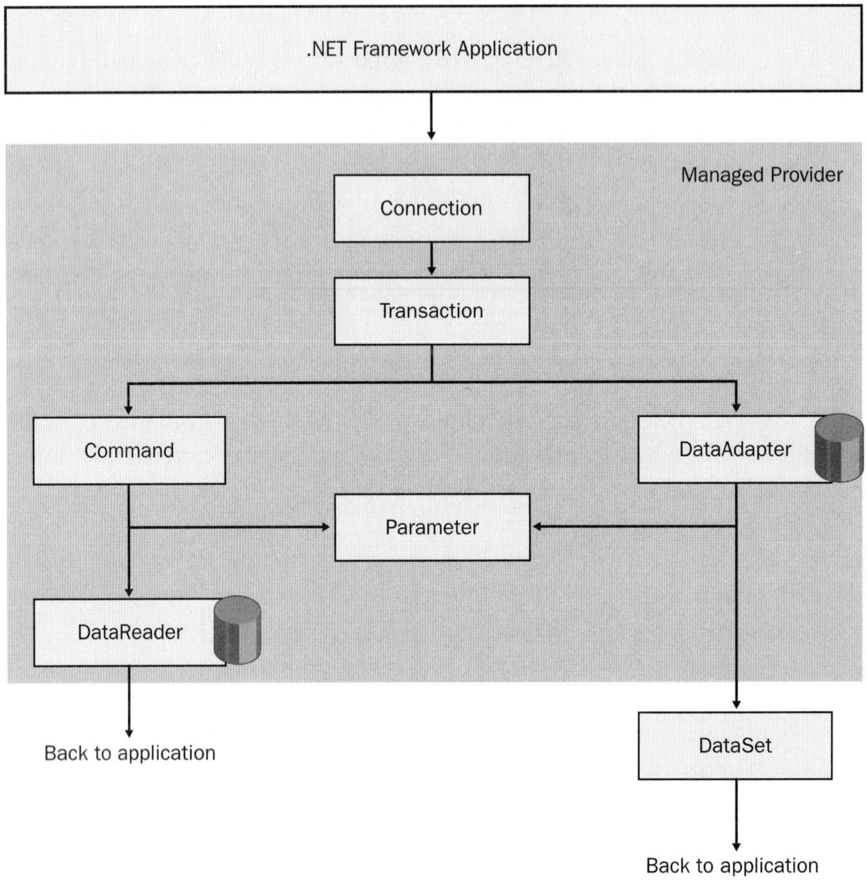

Figure 5-1 The connections between the .NET Framework classes that form a typical managed provider.

> **Note** In the .NET Framework, each managed provider is characterized by a prefix that qualifies the various classes of the same type. For example, the class that manages connections to Microsoft SQL Server is named *SqlConnection*, while the class that opens a connection to an Oracle database is *OracleConnection*. In the former case, the prefix *Sql* is used; in the latter case, the prefix used is *Oracle*.

Architecture of a .NET Managed Provider

The classes in the managed provider interact with the specific data source and return data to the application using the data types defined in the .NET Framework. The logical components implemented in a managed provider are those graphically featured in Figure 5-1 and detailed in Table 5-1.

Table 5-1 Logical Components of a .NET Data Provider

Component	Description
Command	Represents a command that hits the underlying database server
Connection	Creates a connection with the specified data source, including SQL Server, Oracle, and any data source for which you can indicate either an OLE DB provider or an ODBC driver
DataAdapter	Represents a database command that executes on the specified database server and returns a disconnected set of records
DataReader	Represents a read-only, forward-only cursor created on the underlying database server
Parameter	Represents a parameter you can pass to the command object
Transaction	Represents a transaction to be made in the source database server

The functionalities supplied by a .NET data provider fall into a couple of categories:

- Support for disconnected data—that is, the capability of populating the ADO.NET *DataSet* class with fresh data
- Support for connected data access, which includes the capability of setting up a connection and executing a command

Each managed provider that wraps a real-world database server implements all the objects in Table 5-1 in a way that is specific to the data source. The components listed in Table 5-1 are implemented based on methods and properties defined by the interface. Table 5-2 lists possible interfaces for data providers.

Table 5-2 Interfaces of .NET Data Providers

Interface	Description
IDataAdapter	Populates a *DataSet* object, and resolves changes in the *DataSet* object back to the data source
IDataParameter	Allows implementation of a parameter to a command
IDataReader	Reads a forward-only, read-only stream of data created after the execution of a command
IDbCommand	Represents a command that executes when connected to a data source
IDbConnection	Represents a unique session with a data source
IDbDataAdapter	Supplies methods to execute typical operations on relational databases (such as insert, update, select, and delete)
IDbTransaction	Represents a local, nondistributed transaction

Note that all these interfaces except *IDataAdapter* are officially considered to be optional. However, any realistic data provider that manages a database server would implement them all. Managed providers that implement only the *IDataAdapter* interface are said to be *simple managed providers*.

Managed Providers vs. OLE DB Providers

OLE DB providers and managed data providers are radically different types of components that share a common goal—to provide a unique and uniform programming interface for data access. The differences between OLE DB providers and .NET data providers can be summarized in the following points:

- **Component Technology** OLE DB providers are in-process COM servers that expose a suite of COM interfaces to consumer modules. The dialog between consumers and providers takes place through COM and involves a number of interfaces. More roughly, the dialog is fairly formal and based on a rigid etiquette. The OLE DB specification stems from the Universal Data Access (UDA) vision, a Microsoft white paper in which data was perceived as being made of building blocks that ad hoc tools normalized to a common tabular format—the rowset. For this reason, the specification for OLE DB components were rather formal and even a bit quirky. A few years of real-world experience showed the specification to be much too complex, quirky, and error-prone for being ported as is to a new framework—specifically, the .NET Framework.

A .NET data provider contains the gist of OLE DB providers, just as OLE DB providers were based on the battle-tested characteristics of ODBC drivers. A managed data provider is not a monolithic component, but a suite of managed classes whose overall design looks into one *particular* data source rather than blinking at an abstract and universal data source.

- **Internal Implementation** Both types of providers end up making calls into the data-source programming API. In doing so, though, they provide a dense layer of code that separates the data source from the calling application. Learning from the OLE DB experience, Microsoft designed .NET data providers to be more agile and simple. Fewer interfaces are involved, and the conversation between the caller and the callee is more direct and as informal as possible. In OLE DB, data-access components are designed to provide a database-independent layer for accessing generic databases. The value of such a generic layer is that it provides nearly universal access. Its major drawback is the difficulty to deliver database-specific optimizations. In .NET, data access components are simpler and less general, but they're also more practical and effective.
- **Application Integration** Another aspect in .NET that makes the conversation between caller and callee more informal is the fact that managed providers return data using the same data structures that the application would use to store it. In OLE DB, the data-retrieval process is more flexible but also more complex because the provider packs data in flat memory buffers and leaves the consumer responsible for mapping that data into usable data structures, such as the ADO *Recordset* or a user-defined class. In .NET, the integration with the application is total and the managed provider packs return data in a ready-to-use format using types from the .NET Framework.

Calling into an OLE DB provider from within a .NET application is even more expensive because of the type and data conversion necessary to make the transition from the managed environment of the common language runtime (CLR) to the COM world. Calling a COM object from within a .NET application is possible through the COM interop layer, but doing so comes at a cost. In general, to access a data source from within a .NET application, you should always use a managed provider instead of OLE DB providers or ODBC drivers. You should be doing this primarily because of the transition costs, but also because managed providers are normally more modern tools based on an optimized architecture.

Not all data sources, though, have a managed provider available. In these cases, resorting to old-fashioned OLE DB providers or ODBC drivers is a pure necessity. For this reason, the .NET Framework encapsulates in managed wrapper classes the logic needed to call into a COM-style OLE DB provider or a C-style ODBC driver.

> **Note** Data-driven .NET applications are in no way limited to managed providers. They can access virtually any data source for which any of the following data-access components exists: a managed provider, OLE DB provider, or ODBC driver. In terms of raw performance, a managed provider is the fastest approach, but functionally speaking, others are effective as well. Note that in general you'll have a choice of multiple providers from various vendors. They'll certainly supply a common subset of functionality, but they won't necessarily supply the same set of features or the same implementation.

Data Providers Available in the .NET Framework

The .NET Framework 1.0 supports only two managed providers—those for SQL Server 7.0 or later and those for the main OLE DB providers. A few months after the release of .NET Framework 1.0, Microsoft released as separate downloads a managed provider for ODBC data sources and for Oracle databases. In the .NET Framework 1.1, these additional data providers have been incorporated in the framework. Table 5-3 details the managed providers available in the .NET Framework 1.1.

Table 5-3 Managed Providers in .NET

Data Source	Namespace	Description
SQL Server	*System.Data.SqlClient*	Targets SQL Server 7.0 and 2000, including XML extensions. To maximize performance, hooks up the database at the wire level using optimized packets.
OLE DB providers	*System.Data.OleDb*	Targets OLE DB providers, including SQLOLEDB, MSDAORA, and the JET engine.

Table 5-3 Managed Providers in .NET

Data Source	Namespace	Description
ODBC drivers	*System.Data.Odbc*	Targets several ODBC drivers, including those for SQL Server, Oracle, and the Jet engine.
Oracle	*System.Data.OracleClient*	Targets Oracle 9i, and supports all of its data types.

The OLE DB and ODBC managed providers listed in Table 5-3 are not specific to a physical database server, but rather they serve as a bridge that gives instant access to a large number of existing OLE DB providers and ODBC drivers. When you call into OLE DB providers, your .NET applications jumps out of the managed environment and issues COM calls through the COM interop layer.

The managed providers for SQL Server and Oracle, on the other hand, hook up the database server directly to the wire level and obtain a substantial performance advantage. As of version 1.1 of the .NET Framework, Oracle and SQL Server are the only databases for which Microsoft supplies a direct data provider. Third-party vendors supply managed providers for a few other databases such as MySQL. For other major databases—such as IBM DB2, AS/400, Sybase, and Informix—managed providers have been announced and in some cases are already available in beta versions. Having them available on the market is only a matter of time.

Alternative Ways of Exposing Data

In .NET, managed providers are only the preferred way of exposing database contents—that is, data in a wire format or data that must be accessed concurrently and through transactions. If you just have generic data to publish (for example, a proprietary text or binary file), you should expose it as XML or by using a simple managed provider. If you have a store to expose, an OLE DB provider still makes sense because you plug into all the existing .NET and Win32 OLE DB consumers, from ADO-driven applications to the data transformation services and from SQL Server replication to the distributed query processor.

Data Sources You Access Through ADO.NET

The .NET data provider is the managed component of choice for database vendors to expose their data in an effective way. Ideally, each database vendor should provide a .NET-compatible API that is seamlessly callable from within managed applications. Unfortunately, this is not yet the case. At this time, only a few database servers can be accessed through ADO.NET and managed providers, but the situation is expected to improve over the next few months as .NET takes root as a platform in the software community. If you look back at the state of the art for ODBC in the early 90s and for OLE DB in the late 90s, you'll see the same clear signs of a technology that is slowly but steadily gaining widespread acceptance. Let's review the situation for the major database management systems (DBMS).

Accessing SQL Server

As mentioned, Microsoft supplies a managed provider for SQL Server 7.0 and newer versions. Using the classes contained in this provider is by far the most effective way of accessing SQL Server. Figure 5-2 shows how SQL Server is accessed by .NET and COM clients.

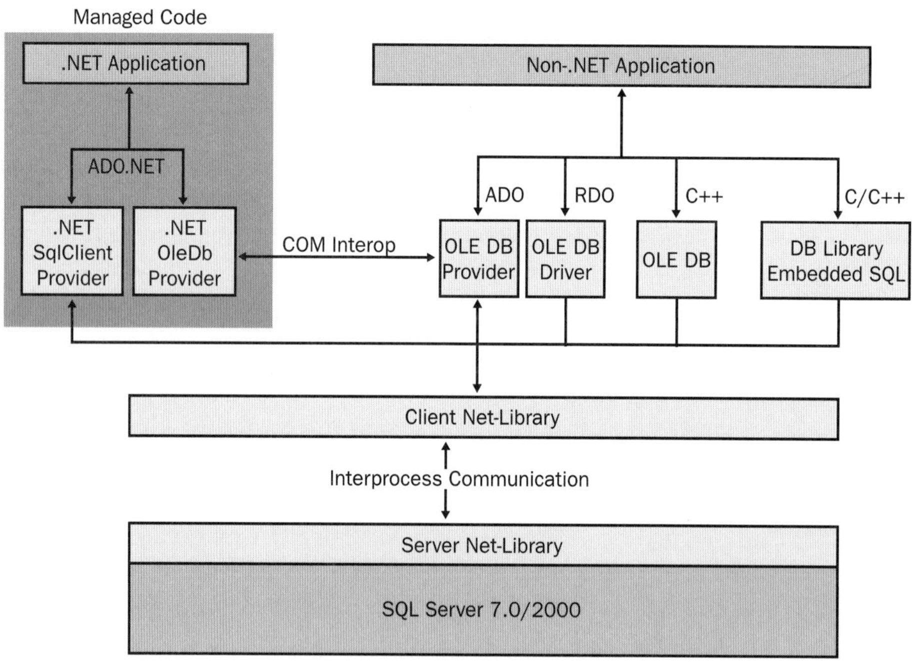

Figure 5-2 Accessing SQL Server by using the managed provider for OLE DB adds overhead because the objects called must pass through the COM interop layer.

A .NET application can access a SQL Server database by using either the native data provider or the COM OLE DB provider via the managed provider for OLE DB data sources. The rub is that the OLE DB provider—a component named SQLOLEDB—is a COM object that can be used only through the COM interop layer, which seamlessly provides for data and type marshaling. You should always use the native data provider. In general, you should have a good reason to opt for SQLOLEDB. A possible good reason is the need to use ADO rather than ADO.NET as the data-access library. As of version 1.1 of the .NET Framework, ADO.NET doesn't fully cover the same set of features available in ADO. For example, if you need to use server cursors, you must resort to ADO. In this case, you use OLE DB to read from and write to SQL Server.

The SQL Server native provider not only avoids paying the performance tax of going down to COM, it also implements some little optimizations when preparing the command for SQL Server. For example, suppose you need to run the following statement:

```
SELECT * FROM Employees
```

If you run the command using the native managed provider, the SQL code that actually hits the server is slightly different:

```
exec sp_executesql N'SELECT * FROM Employees'
```

The *sp_executesql* system stored procedure brings advantages when a Transact-SQL statement that has parameter values as the only variation is repeatedly executed. Because the statement itself remains constant, the SQL Server query optimizer is likely to reuse the execution plan it has generated for the first execution. Note, though, that for this feature to work better you should use fully qualified object names in the statement string.

In addition, a statement that goes through the managed provider executes as a remote procedure call (RPC). A statement processed by the OLE DB provider runs as a Transact-SQL batch. The RPC protocol increases performance by eliminating much of the parameter processing and statement parsing done on the server.

> **Note** SQL Server can also be accessed using the Microsoft ODBC driver and the classes in the .NET data provider for ODBC. The classes are located in the *System.Data.Odbc* namespace in the .NET Framework 1.1.

Accessing Oracle Databases

The .NET Framework 1.1 includes a managed provider for Oracle databases. The classes are located in the *System.Data.OracleClient* namespace in the System.Data.OracleClient assembly. Instead of using the managed provider, you can resort to the COM-based OLE DB provider (named MSDAORA) or the ODBC driver. Note, though, that the Microsoft OLE DB provider for Oracle does not support Oracle 9i and its specific data types. In contrast, Oracle 9i data types are fully supported by the .NET managed provider. So by using the .NET component to connect to Oracle you not only get a performance boost, but also increased programming power.

> **Note** The .NET data provider for Oracle requires that Oracle client software (version 8.1.7 or later) be installed on the system before you can use it to connect to an Oracle data source.

Microsoft is not the only company to develop a .NET data provider for Oracle databases. A few months ago, Core Lab was probably the first vendor to ship such a provider—named OraDirect—whose details can be discovered by stepping through the appropriate links at *http://www.crlab.com/oranet*. Oracle also couldn't resist jumping in and developing its own .NET data provider immediately after the official release of the .NET Framework 1.0. The latest updates for this component, named Oracle Data Provider for .NET (ODP.NET), can be found at *http://otn.oracle.com/tech/windows/odpnet*. ODP.NET features high performance access to the Oracle database while providing access to advanced Oracle functionality not otherwise available in .NET through OLE DB and ODBC layers. ODP.NET is part of the Oracle 9i Release 2 Client, but it can be used with any Oracle 8, Oracle 8i, or Oracle 9i database server. Unlike OLE DB and ODBC access layers, ODP.NET has many optimizations for retrieving and manipulating Oracle native types, such as any flavor of large objects (LOBs) and REF cursors. ODP.NET can participate in transactional applications with the Oracle database acting as the resource manager and the Microsoft Distributed Transaction Coordinator (DTC) coordinating transactions.

Using OLE DB Providers

The .NET data provider for OLE DB providers is a data-access bridge that allows .NET applications to call into data sources for which a COM OLE DB provider exists. While this approach is architecturally less effective than using native providers, it represents the only way to access those data sources when no managed providers are available.

The classes in the *System.Data.OleDb* namespace, though, don't support all types of OLE DB providers and have been optimized to work with only a few of them, as listed in Table 5-4.

Table 5-4 OLE DB Providers Tested

Name	Description
Microsoft.Jet.OLEDB.4.0	The OLE DB provider for the JET engine implemented in Microsoft Access
MSDAORA	The Microsoft OLE DB provider for Oracle 7 that partially supports some features in Oracle 8
SQLOLEDB	The OLE DB provider for SQL Server 6.5 and newer

The preceding list does not include all the OLE DB providers that really work through the OLE DB .NET data provider. However, only the components in Table 5-4 are guaranteed to work well in .NET. In particular, the classes in the *System.Data.OleDb* namespace don't support OLE DB providers that implement any of the OLE DB 2.5 interfaces for semistructured and hierarchical rowsets. This includes the OLE DB providers for Microsoft Exchange (EXOLEDB) and for Internet Publishing (MSDAIPP).

> **Caution** The OLE DB .NET data provider does not work with the OLE DB provider for ODBC (MSDASQL). To access an ODBC data source using ADO.NET, you should use the .NET data provider for ODBC. If you try to set the *Provider* attribute of the connection string to MSDASQL, a runtime error is thrown and no connection is ever attempted.

In general, what really prevents existing OLE DB providers from working properly within the .NET data provider for OLE DB is the set of interfaces they really implement. Some OLE DB providers—for example, those written using the Active Template Library (ATL) or with Visual Basic and the OLE DB Simple Provider Toolkit—are likely to miss one or more COM interfaces that the .NET wrapper requires.

As of version 1.1 of the .NET Framework, there's no native managed data provider for the Jet engine and Microsoft Access databases. As a result, you should use the OLE DB provider.

Using ODBC Drivers

The .NET data provider for ODBC lets you access ODBC drivers from managed, ADO.NET-driven applications. Although the ODBC .NET data provider is intended to work with all compliant ODBC drivers, it is guaranteed to work well only with the drivers for SQL Server, Oracle, and Jet. Although ODBC might appear to now be an obsolete technology, it's still used in several production environments and for some vendors still represents the only way to connect to their products.

As mentioned earlier, you can't access an ODBC driver through an OLE DB provider. There's no technical reason behind this limitation—it's just a matter of common sense. In fact, calling the MSDASQL OLE DB provider from within a .NET application would drive your client through a double data-access bridge—one going from .NET to the OLE DB provider and one going one level down to the actual ODBC driver.

Accessing Other Data Sources

The list of databases for which a native managed provider exists is not limited to SQL Server and Oracle. The list, in fact, also includes MySQL, the most popular open-source database server. For more information about MySQL, visit the *http://www.mysql.com* Web site. Recently, a third-party vendor—Core Lab—shipped MySqlDirect .NET, which is a managed provider that uses the native MySQL programming interface to access MySQL databases. The component is targeted to version 3.2 of MySQL and provides only a thin layer of code between ADO.NET and the database server. For more information about the product, go to *http://www.crlab.com/mysqlnet.*

The availability of managed providers is rapidly and constantly evolving, and almost every day we read press releases from database vendors and third-party tool vendors announcing beta versions or plans for supporting the .NET data provider architecture. At the time of this writing, it is amazing to see that in the list of the released .NET data providers we find an open-source database like MySQL but not yet more traditional database servers such as Sybase, Informix, AS/400, and IBM DB2. You can still access those database management systems from within your .NET application by using either the corresponding OLE DB provider or an ODBC driver. However, note that IBM is working on a native DB2 .NET data provider. (For more information, see *http://www7b.software.ibm.com/dmdd/downloads/dotnetbeta/index.html.*) In addition, DataDirect is expected to provide Sybase support soon. You should note that the key advantage of native .NET solutions is that no third-party drivers or bridge solutions are needed, which results in great performance.

Connecting to Data Sources

The beauty of the ADO.NET object model and managed data providers is that programmers always write their data-access code in the same way, regardless of whether the underlying data source is SQL Server, Oracle, or even MySQL. The programming model is based on a relatively standard sequence of steps that first creates a connection, then prepares and executes a command, and finally processes the data retrieved. In the rest of the chapter, we'll mostly discuss how data classes work with SQL Server 2000. However, we'll promptly point out any aspect that is significantly different than other .NET data providers. To start out, let's see how connections take place.

The *SqlConnection* Class

The first step in working with an ADO.NET-based application is setting up the connection with the data source. The class that represents a physical connection to SQL Server 2000 is *SqlConnection*, and it's located in the *System.Data.SqlClient* namespace. The class is sealed (that is, not inheritable), cloneable, and implements the *IDbConnection* interface. The class features two constructors, one of which is the default parameterless constructor. The second class constructor, on the other hand, takes a string containing the connection string:

```
public SqlConnection();
public SqlConnection(string);
```

The following code snippet shows the typical way to set up and open a SQL Server connection:

```
string nwind_string = "SERVER=localhost;DATABASE=northwind;UID=...;PWD=...";
SqlConnection nwind_conn = new SqlConnection(nwind_string);
nwind_conn.Open();
⋮
nwind_conn.Close();
```

Table 5-5 details the public properties defined on the *SqlConnection* class. The table also checks the properties the class provides through the *IDbConnection* interface. These properties are important because they form the subset of properties common to all connection classes in the .NET Framework.

Table 5-5 Properties of the *SqlConnection* Class

Property	*IDbConnection* Interface	Description
ConnectionString	Yes	Gets or sets the string used to open the database.
ConnectionTimeout	Yes	Gets the seconds to wait while trying to establish a connection.
Database	Yes	Gets the name of the database to be used.

(continued)

Table 5-5 Properties of the *SqlConnection* Class *(continued)*

Property	*IDbConnection* Interface	Description
DataSource		Gets the name of the instance of SQL Server to connect to. Normally corresponds to the *Server* connection string attribute.
PacketSize		Gets the size in bytes of network packets used to communicate with SQL Server. Set to 8192, it can be any value in the range from 512 to 32767.
ServerVersion		Gets a string containing the version of the current instance of SQL Server. The version string is in the form of *major.minor.release*.
State	Yes	Gets the current state of the connection: open or closed. Closed is the default.
WorkstationId		Gets the network name of the client, which normally corresponds to the *Workstation ID* connection string attribute.

The *SqlConnection* class is expected to signal any change of the internal state using the values in the *ConnectionState* enumeration. Many of the acceptable values, though, are reserved for future versions of the .NET Framework. The only state transitions that take place are from Closed to Open when the *Open* method is called, and from Open to Closed when *Close* is called.

An important characteristic to note about the properties of the connection classes is that they are all read-only except *ConnectionString*. In other words, you can configure the connection only through the tokens of the connection string, but you can read attributes back through handy properties. This characteristic of connection class properties in ADO.NET is significantly different than what you find in ADO, where many of the connection properties—for example, *ConnectionTimeout* and *Database*—were read/write.

Table 5-6 shows the methods available in the *SqlConnection* class.

Table 5-6 Methods of the *SqlConnection* Class

Method	*IDbConnection* Interface	Description
BeginTransaction	Yes	Begins a database transaction. Allows you to specify a name and an isolation level.
ChangeDatabase	Yes	Changes the current database on the connection. Requires a valid database name.
Close	Yes	Closes the connection to the database. Use this method to close an open connection.
CreateCommand	Yes	Creates and returns a *SqlCommand* object associated with the connection.
Dispose		Calls *Close*.
EnlistDistributed-Transaction		If auto-enlistment is disabled, the method enlists the connection in the specified transaction. *Supported only in version 1.1 of the .NET Framework.*
Open	Yes	Opens a database connection with the property settings specified by the *ConnectionString*.

Note that if the connection goes out of scope, it is not automatically closed. Later on, but not especially soon, the garbage collector picks up the object instance, but the connection won't be closed because the garbage collector can't recognize the peculiarity of the object and handle it properly. Therefore, you must explicitly close the connection by calling *Close* or *Dispose* before the object goes out of scope.

The *SqlConnection* class fires three events: *Disposed*, *InfoMessage*, and *StateChange*. The event *Disposed* fires when the connection object is being disposed of by the garbage collector. The event *InfoMessage* reaches the client whenever SQL Server has a warning or nonblocking error. Finally, *StateChange* accompanies any valid state transition.

Configuring Connection Properties

The *ConnectionString* property is the configuration string used to open a SQL Server database. Made of semicolon-separated pairs of names and values, a connection string specifies settings for the SQL Server runtime. Typical information contained in a connection string includes the name of the database, location of the server, and user credentials. Other more operational information, such as connection timeout and connection pooling settings, can be specified too.

> **Note** Although some particular connection strings for the SQL Server .NET data provider might be nearly identical to OLE DB connection strings, in general the list of acceptable properties in the two cases is different.

The *ConnectionString* property can be set only when the connection is closed. Many connection-string values have corresponding read-only properties in the connection class. These properties are updated when the connection string is set. The contents of the connection string are checked and parsed immediately after the *ConnectionString* property is set. Attribute names in a connection string are not case sensitive, and if a given name appears multiple times, the value of the last occurrence is used. Table 5-7 lists the keywords that are supported.

Table 5-7 Connection-String Keywords

Keyword	Description
Application Name	Name of the client application as it appears in the SQL Profiler. Defaults to *.Net SqlClient Data Provider*.
AttachDBFileName or *Initial File Name*	The full path name of the file (.mdf) to use as an attachable database file.
Connection Timeout	The number of seconds to wait for the connection to take place. Default is 15 seconds.
Current Language	The SQL Server language name.
Database or *Initial Catalog*	The name of the database to connect to.
Encrypt	Indicates whether SSL encryption should be used for all data sent between the client and server. Needs a certificate installed on the server. Default is *false*.
Integrated Security or *Trusted_Connection*	Indicates whether current Windows account credentials are used for authentication. When set to *false*, an explicit user ID and password need to be provided. The special value *sspi* equals *true*. Default is *false*.
Network Library or *net*	Indicates the network library used to establish a connection to SQL Server. Default is *dbmssocn*, which is based on TCP/IP.

Table 5-7 Connection-String Keywords

Keyword	Description
Packet Size	Bytes that indicate the size of the packet being exchanged. Default is 8192.
Password or *pwd*	Password for the account logging on.
Persist Security Info	Indicates whether the managed provider should include password information in the string returned as the connection string. Default is *false*.
Server or *Data Source*	Name or network address of the instance of SQL Server to connect to.
User ID or *uid*	User name for the account logging on.
Workstation ID	Name of the machine connecting to SQL Server.

The network DLL specified by the *Network Library* keyword must be installed on the system to which you connect. If you use a local server, the default library is *dbmslpcn*, which uses shared memory. For a list of options, consult the MSDN documentation.

Any attempt to connect to an instance of SQL Server should not exceed a given time. The *Connection Timeout* keyword controls just this. Note that a connection timeout of 0 causes the connection attempt to wait indefinitely rather than meaning no wait time.

You normally shouldn't change the default packet size, which has been determined based on average operations and workload. However, if you're going to perform bulk operations in which large objects are involved, increasing the packet size can be of help because it decreases the number of reads and writes.

Secure Connections

Depending on how you configure your instance of SQL Server, you can exploit trusted connections. When working with trusted connections, SQL Server ignores any explicit user ID and password set in the connection string. In this case, the current Windows account credentials are used to authenticate the request. Of course, you must have a login corresponding to those credentials. As we'll see in Chapter 15, for ASP.NET applications this means you must first add the ASPNET login for the databases you want to access programmatically.

When applications read the *ConnectionString* property, the *get* accessor of the property—that is, the piece of code that determines the value being returned—normally strips off any password information for security reasons. The *Persist Security Info* keyword allows you to change this setting. If you set it to *true* (which is strongly discouraged), the connection string is returned as-is and includes password information, if any.

Connection Pooling

Connection pooling is a fundamental aspect of high-performance, scalable applications. All .NET data providers support connection pooling as Table 5-8 illustrates.

Table 5-8 Connection Pooling in .NET Data Providers

Provider	Connection Pooling Managed By
SQL Server	Internal class
Oracle	Internal class
OLE DB	OLE DB Service component
ODBC	ODBC Driver Manager

The .NET data providers for SQL Server and Oracle manage connection pooling internally using ad hoc classes. Both support local and distributed transactions. For distributed transactions, they automatically enlist in a transaction and obtain transaction details from Windows 2000 Component Services. If automatic enlistment is disabled through the connection string, the method *EnlistDistributedTransaction* allows you to accomplish that manually.

For the OLE DB data provider, connection pooling is implemented through the OLE DB service infrastructure for session pooling. Connection-string arguments (for example, *OLE DB Service*) can be used to enable or disable various OLE DB services including pooling. A similar situation occurs with ODBC, in which pooling is controlled by the ODBC driver manager.

Configuring Pooling

Some settings in the connection string directly affect the pooling mechanism. The parameters you can control to configure the environment are listed in Table 5-9.

Table 5-9 Connection-Pooling Keywords

Keyword	Description
Connection Lifetime	Sets the maximum duration in seconds of the connection object in the pool. This value is used when the object is returned to the pool. If the creation time plus the lifetime is earlier than the current time, the object is destroyed.
Connection Reset	Determines whether the database connection is reset when being drawn from the pool. Default is *true*.
Enlist	Indicates that the pooler automatically enlists the connection in the creation thread's current transaction context. Default is *true*.

Table 5-9 Connection-Pooling Keywords

Keyword	Description
Max Pool Size	Maximum number of connections allowed in the pool. Default is 100.
Min Pool Size	Minimum number of connections allowed in the pool. Default is 0.
Pooling	Indicates that the connection object is drawn from the appropriate pool, or if necessary, is created and added to the appropriate pool. Default is *true*.

To disable connection pooling, you set *Pooling* to *false*. When changing connection-string keywords—including connection-pooling keywords—Boolean values can also be set by using *yes* or *no* instead of *true* or *false*.

Getting and Releasing Objects

Each connection pool is associated with a distinct connection string and the transaction context. When a new connection is opened, if the connection string does not exactly match an existing pool, a new pool is created. Once created, connection pools are not destroyed until the process ends. This behavior does not affect the system performance because maintenance of inactive or empty pools requires only minimal overhead.

When a pool is created, multiple connection objects are created and added so that the minimum size is reached. Next, connections are added to the pool on demand, up to the maximum pool size. When a connection object is requested, it is drawn from the pool as long as a usable connection is available. A usable connection must currently be unused, have a matching or null transaction context, and have a valid link to the server. If no usable connection is available, the pooler attempts to create a new connection object. When the maximum pool size is reached, the request is queued and served as soon as an existing connection object is released to the pool. Connections are released when you call methods such as *Close* or *Dispose*. Connections that are not explicitly closed might not be returned to the pool unless the maximum pool size has been reached and the connection is still valid.

A connection object is removed from the pool if the lifetime has expired or if a severe error occurred. In this case, the connection is marked as invalid. The pooler periodically scavenges the various pools and permanently removes invalid connection objects.

Caution Pay careful attention not to create a connection string programmatically by concatenating input data together. If you do, you should first validate the data you're putting in the connection string. This little precaution could save you from sneaky attacks through code injection. We'll say more about this in Chapter 15.

Generic Database Programming

In ADO.NET, data access is strongly typed, in the sense that you must know at all times what data source you're targeting. In ADO, you could write data-access code that worked in a generic way, regardless of the actual database server. For example, the ADO object model provides unique connection and command objects that hide the characteristics of the underlying DBMS. Once you've set the *Provider* property on the *Connection* object, you're pretty much done. At that point, in fact, creating a *Command* object for SQL Server or Oracle requires the same code.

In ADO.NET, you can retain the same behavior only if you choose to use the .NET data provider for OLE DB. In this case, the programming model is exactly that which you might have experienced with ADO. But what if you want to use the native .NET data providers?

In ADO.NET, the connection object must be data-source specific, and there's no way for you to create a connection in an indirect way. However, once you hold a connection object, you can create and execute a command in a generic way regardless of the actual data source in use. Let's take a look at the following code snippet:

```
IDbConnection conn;
if (useOracle)
    conn = (IDbConnection) new OracleConnection(oracle_conn_string);
else    // use SQL Server
    conn = (IDbConnection) new SqlConnection(sqlserver_conn_string);

// Create the command
IDbCommand cmd = conn.CreateCommand(cmd_text);
```

Based on a user setting, the code decides whether a connection to Oracle or SQL Server is to be used. Once created, the connection object is referenced through an interface type—the *IDbConnection* interface—which is common to all ADO.NET connection objects. To create a command—either an *OracleCommand* or *SqlCommand* object—you use the *CreateCommand* method and reference the command by using the *IDbCommand* interface.

After that, you can use the *ExecuteReader* or *ExecuteNonQuery* methods on the *IDbCommand* interface to execute the command. If you use *ExecuteReader*, you get back a sort of managed cursor—the data reader—and can access it generically using the *IDataReader* interface.

> **Note** You cannot fill a *DataSet* object by using a generic database programming pattern. In fact, you can't create the data adapter object in an indirect way as you can with a command. The reason is that, unlike the command object, in some cases the data adapter can create a connection internally and implicitly. To do so, though, it needs to work in a strongly typed way and know what the underlying database server is.

Other Connection Objects

So far we've discussed the features of the ADO.NET connection objects mostly from a SQL Server perspective. The programming interface of ADO.NET connection objects is similar but not identical. So let's review what the main differences are in the various cases.

Oracle Connections

The class that represents a physical connection to an Oracle 8.x database is *OracleConnection*, which is located in the *System.Data.OracleClient* namespace. As mentioned earlier, bear in mind that the Oracle managed provider is implemented in the System.Data.OracleClient assembly. All the others, on the other hand, live in the System.Data assembly.

The *OracleConnection* class differs from other connection classes in the .NET Framework because it does not support the *ConnectionTimeout* and *Database* properties. If you set a timeout in the connection string, the value is simply ignored. Likewise, the class doesn't support a *ChangeDatabase* method.

> **Note** The *PacketSize* and *WorkstationId* properties are specific to the SQL Server data provider and aren't available on any other connection class, including *OracleConnection*.

OLE DB Connections

The .NET data provider for OLE DB communicates to an OLE DB data source through both the OLE DB Service component, which provides connection pooling and transaction services, and the OLE DB provider for the data source. For this reason, the programming interface of the *OleDbConnection* class is slightly different and includes an extra property that just doesn't make sense for a DBMS-specific component. The property is read-only and named *Provider*. It returns the content of the *Provider* keyword in the connection string. The content of *Provider* is normally the program identifier (progID) of the OLE DB provider to use.

In addition, the *OleDbConnection* class features an OLE DB–specific method—*GetOleDbSchemaTable*—that returns a *DataTable* filled with schema information from a data source.

The data provider for OLE DB also provides a static method to release object pools that are in the process of being destroyed. The *ReleaseObjectPool* method gets into the game only after all active connections have been closed and the garbage collector has been invoked. At this time, the connection objects are released, but the resources reserved for the pools are not.

ODBC Connections

An *OdbcConnection* object represents a unique connection to a data source that is typically identified through an ODBC data source name (DSN) or a plain connection string. The class works by using resources such as ODBC environment and connection handles.

Unlike other connection classes, the *OdbcConnection* class features the *Driver* property to indicate the name of the driver in use and the *ReleaseObjectPool* static method to release the ODBC environment handle. After an environment handle is released, a request for a new connection creates a new environment.

Executing Commands

Once you have a physical channel set up between your client and the database, you can start preparing and executing commands. The ADO.NET object model provides two types of command objects—the traditional one-off command and the data adapter. The one-off command executes a statement (that is, a Transact-SQL command) or a stored procedure and returns a sort of cursor. Using that, you then scroll through the rows and read data. While the cursor is in use, the connection is busy and open. The data adapter, on the other hand, is a more powerful object that internally uses a command and a cursor. It retrieves and loads the data into a data container class—the *DataSet*. The client application can then process the data while disconnected from the source. The adapter can also be used to set up a batch update mechanism in which all the records changed in memory are submitted to the DBMS in a loop with autogenerated, but modifiable, commands.

The *SqlCommand* Class

The *SqlCommand* class represents a SQL Server statement or stored procedure. It is a cloneable and sealed class that implements the *IDbCommand* interface. A command executes in the context of a connection and, optionally, a transaction. This situation is reflected by the constructors available in the *SqlCommand* class:

```
public SqlCommand();
public SqlCommand(string);
public SqlCommand(string, SqlConnection);
public SqlCommand(string, SqlConnection, SqlTransaction);
```

The string argument denotes the text of the command to execute, whereas the *SqlConnection* parameter is the connection object to use. Finally, if specified, the *SqlTransaction* parameter represents the transactional context in which the command has to run. Unlike ADO command objects, ADO.NET command objects can never implicitly open a connection. The connection must be explicitly assigned to the command by the programmer and opened and closed with direct operations. The same holds true for the transaction.

Table 5-10 shows the attributes that comprise a command in the.NET data provider for SQL Server. The values in the *IDbCommand* Interface column indicate whether the property is part of the *IDbCommand* interface.

Table 5-10 Properties of the *SqlCommand* Class

Property	*IDbCommand* Interface	Description
CommandText	Yes	Gets or sets the statement or the stored procedure name to execute.
CommandTimeout	Yes	Gets or sets the seconds to wait while trying to execute the command. Default is 30.
CommandType	Yes	Gets or sets how the *CommandText* property is to be interpreted. Set to *Text* by default, which means the *CommandText* property contains the text of the command.
Connection	Yes	Gets or sets the connection object used by the command. Null by default.

(continued)

Table 5-10 Properties of the *SqlCommand* Class *(continued)*

Property	*IDbCommand* Interface	Description
Parameters	Yes	Gets the collection of parameters associated with the command. The actual type of the collection is *SqlParameterCollection*. Empty by default.
Transaction	Yes	Gets or sets the transaction within which the command executes. The transaction must be connected to the same connection as the command.
UpdatedRowSource	Yes	Gets or sets how query command results are applied to the row being updated. The value of this property is used only when the command runs within the *Update* method of the data adapter. Acceptable values are in the *UpdateRowSource* enumeration.

Commands can be associated with parameters, and each parameter is rendered using a provider-specific object. For the SQL Server managed provider, the parameter class is *SqlParameter*. The command type determines the role of the *CommandText* property. The possible values for *CommandType* are:

- ***Text*** The default setting, which indicates the property contains Transact-SQL text to execute directly.
- ***StoredProcedure*** Indicates that the content of the property is intended to be the name of a stored procedure contained in the current database.
- ***TableDirect*** Indicates the property contains a comma-separated list containing the names of the tables to access. All rows and columns of the tables will be returned. Note that *TableDirect* is supported only by the data provider for OLE DB.

Table 5-11 details the methods available on the *SqlCommand* class.

Table 5-11 Methods of the *SqlCommand* Class

Property	*IDbCommand* Interface	Description
Cancel	Yes	Attempts to cancel the execution of the command. No exception is generated if the attempt fails.
CreateParameter	Yes	Creates a new instance of a *SqlParameter* object.
ExecuteNonQuery	Yes	Executes a nonquery command, and returns the number of rows affected.
ExecuteReader	Yes	Executes a query, and returns a read-only cursor—the data reader—to the data.
ExecuteScalar	Yes	Executes a query, and returns the value in the 0,0 position (first column of first row) in the result set. Extra data is ignored.
ExecuteXmlReader		Executes a query that returns XML data and builds an *XmlReader* object.
Prepare	Yes	Creates a prepared version of the command in an instance of SQL Server.
ResetCommandTimeout		Resets the command timeout to the default.

If the *CommandType* property is set to *TableDirect*, the *Prepare* method does nothing. A *SqlCommand* object executes Transact-SQL code statements wrapping the user-specified text with the system *sp_executesql* stored procedure. The command is sent to SQL Server using tabular data stream (TDS) packets and the RPC protocol.

Using Parameters

Parameterized commands define their own arguments by using instances of the *SqlParameter* class. Parameters have a name, value, type, direction, and size. In some cases, parameters can also be associated with a source column. A parameter is associated with a command by using the *Parameters* collection.

```
SqlParameter parm = new SqlParameter();
parm.ParameterName = "@employeeid";
parm.DbType = DbType.Int32;
parm.Direction = ParameterDirection.Input;
cmd.Parameters.Add(parm);
```

The following SQL statement uses a parameter:

```
SELECT * FROM employees WHERE employeeid=@employeeid
```

The .NET data provider for SQL Server identifies parameters by name, using the @ symbol to prefix them. In this way, the order in which parameters are associated with the command is not determinant.

> **Note** Named parameters are supported by the managed provider for Oracle but not by the providers for OLE DB and ODBC data sources. The OLE DB and ODBC data sources use positional parameters identified with the question mark (?) placeholder. The order of parameters is important.

Ways to Execute

As Table 5-11 shows, a *SqlCommand* object can be executed in four different ways: *ExecuteNonQuery*, *ExecuteReader*, *ExecuteScalar*, and *ExecuteXmlReader*. The various executors work in much the same way, but they differ in the return values. Typically, you use the *ExecuteNonQuery* method to perform update operations such as those associated with statements like UPDATE, INSERT, and DELETE. In these cases, the return value is the number of rows affected by the command. For other types of statements, such as SET or CREATE, the return value is -1.

The *ExecuteReader* method is expected to work with query commands, and returns a data reader object—an instance of the *SqlDataReader* class. The data reader is a sort of read-only, forward-only cursor that client code scrolls and reads from. If you execute an UPDATE statement through *ExecuteReader*, the command is successfully executed but no affected rows are returned.

The *ExecuteScalar* method helps considerably when you have to retrieve a single value. It works great with SELECT COUNT statements or for commands that retrieve aggregate values. If you call the method on a regular query statement, only the value in the first column of the first row is read and all the rest are discarded. Using *ExecuteScalar* results in more compact code than you'd get by executing the command and manually retrieving the value in the top-left corner of the rowset.

These three executor methods are common to all command objects. The *SqlCommand* class also features the *ExecuteXmlReader* method. It executes a command that returns XML data, and it builds an XML reader so that the client application can easily navigate through the XML tree. The *ExecuteXmlReader* method is ideal to use with query commands that end with the FOR XML clause or with commands that query for text fields filled with XML data. Note that while the *XmlReader* object is in use, the underlying connection is busy.

Setting Up Transactions

A SQL Server native transaction is fully represented by an instance of the *SqlTransaction* class. The transaction object is obtained through the *BeginTransaction* method and can be given a name and an isolation level.

```
SqlTransaction tran;
tran = conn.BeginTransaction();
cmd.Connection = conn;
cmd.Transaction = tran;
⋮
tran.Commit();
```

You terminate a transaction explicitly by using the *Commit* or *Rollback* method. The *SqlTransaction* class supports named savepoints in the transaction that can be used to roll back a portion of the transaction. Named savepoints exploit a specific SQL Server feature—the SAVE TRANSACTION statement.

Other Command Objects

Let's look at the characteristics of other command objects that, for one reason or another, have not been covered so far.

Oracle Commands

Oracle commands don't support a timeout, and in fact, the *OracleCommand* object doesn't expose the *CommandTimeout* property. In addition, the class features two extra executor methods—*ExecuteOracleNonQuery* and *ExecuteOracleScalar*. *ExecuteOracleScalar* differs from *ExecuteScalar* only because it returns an Oracle-specific data type. The difference between *ExecuteNonQuery* and *ExecuteOracleNonQuery* is more subtle.

```
public int ExecuteOracleNonQuery(out OracleString rowid);
```

If you're executing an UPDATE statement that affects exactly one row, the *ExecuteOracleNonQuery* method returns a Base64 string as an output parameter. This value identifies the modified row in the database and allows you to write subsequent, related queries in a more powerful way.

OLE DB Commands

The *OleDbCommand* class does not support the *ExecuteXmlReader* method and limits its support to the three basic executor methods in the *IDbCommand* interface. In addition, it recognizes *TableDirect* as a valid command type. As mentioned earlier, the OLE DB .NET provider does not support named parameters for statements and stored procedures. If parameters are to be used, you should use the question mark (?) placeholder, as shown in the following command:

```
SELECT * FROM Customers WHERE CustomerID = ?
```

As a result, the order in which *OleDbParameter* objects are added to the collection of parameters must correspond to the position of the question mark placeholder for the parameter.

ODBC Commands

Just like *OleDbCommand*, the *OdbcCommand* class doesn't support named parameters and resorts to the question-mark placeholder and position-based arguments. To execute a stored procedure, the *OdbcCommand* class requires the *CommandText* property to be set using standard ODBC escape sequences for stored procedures. Note that simply setting the property to the name of the stored procedure does not work. Use the following escape sequence for ODBC stored procedures:

```
{call sp_name(?, ?, ?)}
```

In this example, *sp_name* is the name of the stored procedure while the ? placeholder represents an argument to the procedure.

ADO.NET Data Readers

In the .NET Framework, a reader is a generic type of object used to read data in a variety of formats. A reader is used to read bytes out of a binary stream, lines of text from a text writer, nodes from an XML document, and records from a database-provided stream of data. The data reader class is specific to a DBMS and works like a firehose-style cursor. It allows you to scroll through and read one or more result sets generated by a command. The data reader operates in a connected way and moves in a forward-only direction.

A data reader is instantiated during the execution of the *ExecuteReader* method. The results are stored in a buffer located on the client and are made available to the reader. The reader moves through the result set by using the *Read* method. By using the data reader object, you access data one record at a time as soon as it becomes available. An approach based on the data reader is effective both in terms of minimizing system overhead and improving performance. Only one record is cached at any time, and there's no wait time to have the entire result set loaded in memory. You should note that by default the cached record is accessible only after it has been completely loaded in memory. This might take a while and consume too much memory, if the query includes large binary large object (BLOB) fields. (More on this later in this chapter and also in Chapter 22.)

A data reader object is made of two interfaces—*IDataReader* and *IDataRecord*. *IDataReader* includes general-purpose properties and methods to read data. For example, it includes the methods *Read* and *Close*. *IDataRecord* supplies methods to extract values out of the current record. Table 5-12 shows the properties of the *SqlDataReader* class—that is, the data reader class for SQL Server.

Table 5-12 Properties of the *SqlDataReader* Class

Property	Description
Depth	Returns 0.
FieldCount	Gets the number of columns in the current row.
HasRows	Gets a value that indicates whether the data reader contains one or more rows. *This property is not supported in version 1.0 of the .NET Framework.*
IsClosed	Gets a value that indicates whether the data reader is closed.
Item	Indexer property. Gets the value of a column in the original format.
RecordsAffected	Gets the number of rows modified by the execution of a batch command.

The *Depth* property—a member of the *IDataReader* interface—is meant to indicate the level of nesting for the current row. The depth of the outermost table is always 0; the depth of inner tables grows by one. Most data readers, including the *SqlDataReader* and *OracleDataReader* classes, do not support multiple levels of nesting so that the *Depth* property always returns 0.

The *RecordsAffected* property cumulatively refers to the rows affected by any update statement executed in the command—typically, a batch or a stored procedure. The property, though, is not set until all rows are read and the data reader is closed. The default value of *RecordsAffected* is 1. Note that *IsClosed* and *RecordsAffected* are the only properties you can invoke on a closed data reader.

Table 5-13 lists the methods of the data reader.

Table 5-13 Methods of the Data Reader Class

Methods	Description
Close	Closes the reader object. Note that closing the reader does not automatically close the underlying connection.
GetBoolean	Gets the value of the specified column as a Boolean.
GetByte	Gets the value of the specified column as a byte.
GetBytes	Reads a stream of bytes from the specified column into a buffer. You can specify an offset both for reading and writing.
GetChar	Gets the value of the specified column as a single character.

(continued)

Table 5-13 Methods of the Data Reader Class *(continued)*

Methods	Description
GetChars	Reads a stream of characters from the specified column into a buffer. You can specify an offset both for reading and writing.
GetDataTypeName	Gets the name of the back-end data type in the specified column.
GetDateTime	Gets the value of the specified column as a *DateTime* object.
GetDecimal	Gets the value of the specified column as a decimal.
GetDouble	Gets the value of the specified column as a double-precision floating-point number.
GetFieldType	Gets the *Type* object for the data in the specified column.
GetFloat	Gets the value of the specified column as a single-precision floatingpoint number.
GetGuid	Gets the value of the specified column as a globally unique identifier (GUID).
GetInt16	Gets the value of the specified column as a 16-bit signed integer.
GetInt32	Gets the value of the specified column as a 32-bit signed integer.
GetInt64	Gets the value of the specified column as a 64-bit signed integer.
GetName	Gets the name of the specified column.
GetOrdinal	Given the name of the column, returns its ordinal number.
GetSchemaTable	Returns a *DataTable* object that describes the metadata for the columns managed by the reader.
GetString	Gets the value of the specified column as a string.
GetValue	Gets the value of the specified column in its original format.
GetValues	Copies the values of all columns in the supplied array of objects.
IsDBNull	Indicates whether the column contains null values. The type for a null column is *System.DBNull*.
NextResult	Moves the data reader pointer to the beginning of the next result set, if any.
Read	Moves the data reader pointer to the next record, if any.

The SQL Server data reader also features a variety of other DBMS-specific get methods. They include methods such as *GetSqlDouble*, *GetSqlMoney*, *GetSqlDecimal*, and so on. The difference between the *GetXXX* and *GetSqlXXX* methods is in the return type. With the *GetXXX* methods, a base .NET Framework type is returned; with the *GetSqlXXX* methods, a .NET Framework wrapper for a SQL Server type is returned—such as *SqlDouble*, *SqlMoney*, or *SqlDecimal*. The SQL Server types belong to the *SqlDbType* enumeration.

All the *GetXXX* methods that return a value from a column identify the column through a 0-based index. Note that the methods don't even attempt a conversion; they simply return data as is and just make a cast to the specified type. If the actual value and the type are not compatible, an exception is thrown.

The *GetBytes* method is useful to read large fields one step at a time. However, the method can also be used to obtain the length in bytes of the data in the column. To get this information, pass a buffer that is a null reference and the return value of the method will contain the length.

Reading Data with the Data Reader

The key thing to remember when using a data reader is that you're working while connected. The data reader represents the fastest way to read data out of a source, but you should read your data as soon as possible and release the connection. One row is available at a time, and you must move through the result set by using the *Read* method. The following code snippet illustrates the typical loop you implement to read all the records of a query:

```
while (reader.Read()) {
    // process record
}
```

You have no need to explicitly move the pointer ahead and no need to check for the end of the file. The *Read* method returns *false* if there are no more records to read. Unlike the ADO firehose-style cursor, the data reader features no bookmarks, no scrolling, and no bulk-reading methods such as ADO *GetString* and *GetRows*. In contrast, it provides a *GetValues* method to get all the column values in an array of objects.

Tip Null values in the returned stream of data can be checked using a handful of methods on the data reader object and row object itself. For example, you can check a column value against null as shown in the following code snippet:

```
if (reader.IsDBNull(colIndex)) {...}
```

To set a null value, use the *System.DBNull.Value* expression, as in the following code snippet:

```
param.Value = System.DBNull.Value;
```

Command Behaviors

When calling the *ExecuteReader* method on a command object—on any command object regardless of the underlying DBMS—you can require a particular working mode known as a command behavior. *ExecuteReader* has a second overload that takes an argument of type *CommandBehavior*:

```
cmd.ExecuteReader(CommandBehavior.CloseConnection);
```

CommandBehavior is an enumeration. Its values are listed in Table 5-14.

Table 5-14 Command Behaviors for the Data Reader

Behavior	Description
CloseConnection	Automatically closes the connection when the data reader is closed.
Default	No special behavior is required. Setting this option is functionally equivalent to calling *ExecuteReader* without parameters.
KeyInfo	The query returns only column metadata and primary key information. The query is executed without any locking on the selected rows.
SchemaOnly	The query returns only column metadata and does not put any lock on the database rows.
SequentialAccess	Enables the reader to load data as a sequential stream. This behavior works in conjunction with methods such as *GetBytes* and *GetChars*, which can be used to read bytes or characters having a limited buffer size for the data being returned. When this behavior is set, the record is not automatically and entirely cached in memory, but physical reading occurs as you access the various fields.
SingleResult	Only the first result set is returned.
SingleRow	The query is expected to return a single row.

The sequential-access mode applies to all columns in the returned result set. This means you can access columns only in the order in which they appear in the result set. For example, you cannot read column #2 before column #1. More exactly, if you read or move past a given location you can no longer read or move back. This happens because when the *SequentialAccess* behavior is selected, record contents aren't cached by the reader object. Caching the contents of the records is what enables, for most behaviors, random access to the fields. Combined with the *GetBytes* method, sequential access can be helpful when you must read binary large objects with a limited buffer.

Note You can specify *SingleRow* also when executing queries that are expected to return multiple result sets. In this case, all the generated result sets are correctly returned, but each result set has a single row.

Closing the Reader

The data reader is not a publicly creatable object. It does have a constructor, but not one that is callable from within user applications. The data-reader constructor is marked as internal and can be invoked only from classes defined in the same assembly—System.Data. The data reader is implicitly instantiated when the *ExecuteReader* method is called. Opening and closing the reader are operations distinct from instantiation and must be explicitly invoked by the application. The *Read* method advances the internal pointer to the next readable record in the current result set. The *Read* method returns a Boolean value indicating whether or not more records can be read. While records are being read, the connection is busy and no operation, other than closing, can be performed on the connection object.

The data reader and the connection are distinct objects and should be managed and closed independently. Both objects provide a *Close* method that should be called twice—once on the data reader (first) and once on the connection. When the *CloseConnection* behavior is required, closing the data reader also closes the underlying connection. In addition, the data reader's *Close* method fills in the values for any command output parameters and sets the *RecordsAffected* property.

Tip Because of the extra work *Close* always performs, closing a reader with success can sometimes be expensive, especially in cases of large and complicated queries. In situations in which you need to squeeze out every little bit of performance, and where the return values and the number of records affected are not significant, you can invoke the *Cancel* method of the associated *SqlCommand* object instead of *Close*. *Cancel* aborts the operation; however, if you call it after reading all rows, you can clean up the reader with less effort.

Accessing Multiple Result Sets

Depending on the syntax of the query, multiple result sets can be returned. By default, the data reader is positioned on the first of them. You use the *Read* method to scroll through the various records in the current result set. When the last record is found, the *Read* method returns *false* and does not advance further. To move to the next result set, you should use the *NextResult* method. The method returns *false* if there are no more result sets to read. The following code shows how to access all records in all returned result sets:

```
SqlDataReader reader;
reader = cmd.ExecuteReader();
do {
    // Move through the first result set
    while (reader.Read())
    {
        // access the row
    }
}
while (reader.NextResult())
reader.Close();
cmd.Connection.Close();
```

When reading the contents of a row, you can identify the column by either index or name. Using an index results in significantly faster code because the provider can go directly to the buffer. If the column name is specified, the provider uses the *GetOrdinal* method to translate the name into the corresponding index and then performs an index-based access. Note that for the SQL Server data reader, all the *GetXXX* methods actually call into the corresponding *GetSqlXXX* methods. A similar situation occurs for the Oracle data reader, in which the native data is always marshaled to the .NET Framework types. The OLE DB and ODBC readers have only a single set of *get* methods.

> **Note** The .NET Framework version 1.1 extends the programming interface of data readers by adding the *HasRows* method, which returns a Boolean value indicating whether or not there are more rows to read. However, the method doesn't tell anything about the number of rows available. Similarly, there is no method or trick to know in advance how many result sets have been returned.

Obtaining Schema Information

All data reader classes supply a *GetSchemaTable* method that retrieves metadata information about the columns the query is going to read. *GetSchemaTable* returns a *DataTable* object—that is, a table with one row for each retrieved column and a fixed number of informative columns.

The metadata available can be catalogued in three categories: column metadata, database characteristics, and column attributes. Table 5-15 details the columns. Note that the column metadata is listed in alphabetical order, which is not the order in which they appear in the result set.

Table 5-15 Metadata Column for a SQL Server Data Reader

Metadata Column	Description
AllowDBNull	Indicates whether the column allows null values.
BaseCatalogName	Set to null by default. Returns the name of the database that contains the table accessed by the query.
BaseColumnName	Set to null by default. Returns the original name of the column if an alias is used.
BaseSchemaName	Set to null by default. Returns the name of the owner (for example, *dbo*) of the database from which the column is retrieved.
BaseServerName	Set to null by default. Returns the name of the instance of DBMS used by the data reader.
BaseTableName	Returns the name of the table.
ColumnName	Name of the column as it appears in the query. If an alias has been used, the aliased name is returned.
ColumnOrdinal	0-based position of the column in the result set.
ColumnSize	Maximum size in bytes of the data allowed in the column.
DataType	Returns the .NET Framework type the column maps to.
IsAliased	Indicates whether the column is aliased in the result set. A column is aliased if renamed using the *AS* clause. The original name of aliased columns is stored in the *BaseColumnName* column.
IsAutoIncrement	Indicates whether the column is marked as auto-increment.
IsExpression	Indicates whether the content of the column is based on an expression.
IsHidden	Indicates whether the column is marked as hidden.
IsIdentity	Indicates whether the column is an identity column.
IsLong	Indicates whether the column contains BLOB data. Note, though, that the definition of a BLOB is provider-specific.
IsKey	Indicates whether the column is a key or part of a set of columns that together represent a key.
IsReadOnly	Indicates whether the column is read-only.

(continued)

Table 5-15 Metadata Column for a SQL Server Data Reader *(continued)*

Metadata Column	Description
IsRowVersion	Indicates whether the column has a unique identifier value—that is, a row GUID.
IsUnique	Indicates whether the column can contain duplicates.
NumericPrecision	Set to null by default. Indicates the maximum precision of the column data.
NumericScale	Set to null by default. Indicates the number of digits to the right of the decimal point if the column type allows.
ProviderType	Indicates the type of the column data. The type is expressed as a numeric value corresponding to the type in the database-specific enumeration. For example, an integer column in a SQL Server table returns the value of *SqlDbType.Int*.

Catalog and owner (schema) information can be retrieved only if explicitly mentioned in the command text. Writing the same query in the following ways affects the contents of the *BaseXXX* columns:

```
SELECT * FROM northwind.dbo.employees
SELECT * FROM employees
```

In the first query, *BaseCatalogName* would be set to *northwind* and *BaseSchemaName* to *dbo*. In the second query, the same information wouldn't be retrieved. Note that this is true only if you're also using the *KeyInfo* command behavior.

Tip The *GetSchemaTable* method for SQL Server returns more accurate data if you require the *KeyInfo* command behavior when calling *ExecuteReader*. The *KeyInfo* behavior can be combined with the default behavior so that you can execute a single command and obtain both schema and data:

```
reader = cmd.ExecuteReader(CommandBehavior.KeyInfo |
                           CommandBehavior.CloseConnection)
```

The fields whose values are correctly returned only if the *KeyInfo* behavior is required are: *IsKey*, *BaseTableName*, *IsAliased*, *IsExpression*, and *IsHidden*. Note also that if *KeyInfo* is required, the key columns (if any) are always added at the bottom of the result set but no data is returned for them.

Special Features of Data Readers

The characteristics of the various provider-specific data readers are nearly identical, with only some differences that are more architectural than functional. We've examined the *SqlDataReader* class, now let's examine the differences with other reader classes supported by the .NET Framework 1.1 data providers.

Oracle Data Readers

The *OracleDataReader* class provides a personal set of *GetXXX* methods for its own internal types. Some of its methods are *GetOracleBFile*, *GetOracleBinary*, and *GetOracleDateTime*. In Oracle database programming, multiple result sets returned by a query or stored procedure are handled through multiple REF CURSOR objects. For the *NextResult* method to work properly with Oracle databases, you must associate as many output parameters to the command as there are expected result sets. An ADO.NET result set coincides with an Oracle REF CURSOR in the command text. The output parameter names must match the name of the cursors, while their type must be *OracleType.Cursor*. The following code shows how to run a stored procedure (or the command text) that references a couple of cursors named Employees and Orders:

```
// cmd is an OracleCommand object that points to a command or a
// stored procedure. It executes code that creates two REF CURSORs
// called Employees and Orders. Names must match.
OracleParameter p1 = cmd.Parameters.Add("Employees", OracleType.Cursor);
p1.Direction = ParameterDirection.Output;
OracleParameter p2 = cmd.Parameters.Add("Orders", OracleType.Cursor);
p2.Direction = ParameterDirection.Output;
```

OLE DB Data Readers

The *OleDbDataReader* is the only data reader that fully supports the *Depth* property. It is the only provider that admits hierarchical rowsets (or OLE DB chapters). An example of a hierarchical result set is what you obtain by putting the *MSDataShape* OLE DB provider to work on a SHAPE query. A hierarchical query includes one or more columns that are in effect embedded result sets. Each of these columns is exposed as an *OleDbDataReader* object within the main *OleDbDataReader* object. Of course, rows in the child readers have a higher depth level.

Another little difference between *OleDbDataReader* and other reader classes is that when using the *OleDbDataReader* class in sequential access mode, you can reread the current column value until reading past it. This is not possible with other readers, in which you can read a column value only once.

Finally, when the reader works in *SingleRow* mode, the .NET data provider for OLE DB uses this information to bind data using the OLE DB *IRow* interface if it is available. Using *IRow* instead of the default *IRowset* interface results in faster code.

ADO.NET Data Adapters

In ADO.NET, the data adapter object acts as a two-way bridge between a data source and the *DataSet* object. The *DataSet* is a sort of disconnected, feature-rich container of data, and the adapter takes care of filling it and submitting its data back to the data source. Viewed from a higher level of abstraction, a data adapter is just a command. It differs from the data reader because it returns a disconnected set of records. In a certain way, the data reader and data adapter are the results of the ADO *Recordset* split into two. Born to be a simple COM wrapper around an SQL result set, the ADO *Recordset* soon became a rather bloated object incorporating three types of cursors—read-only, disconnected, and server.

Compared to ADO, the ADO.NET object model is simpler overall and, more importantly, made of simpler objects. Instead of providing a big monolithic object like the *Recordset*, ADO.NET supplies two smaller and highly specialized objects—the data reader and the *DataSet*. The data reader is generated by a direct query command; the *DataSet* is generated by a data adapter.

The big difference between commands and data adapters is mostly in the way each one returns the retrieved data. A query command returns a read-only cursor—the data reader. The data adapter performs its data access, grabs all the data, and packs it into an in-memory container—the *DataSet*. Under the hood, the data adapter is just an extra layer of abstraction built on top of the command/data reader pair. Internally, in fact, the data adapter just uses a command to query and a data reader to walk its way through the records and fill a user-provided *DataSet*.

The *SqlDataAdapter* Class

By definition, a data adapter is a class that implements the *IDataAdapter* interface. However, looking at the actual implementation of the adapters in the supported providers, you can see that multiple layers of code are used. In particular, all data adapter classes inherit from a base class named *DbDataAdapter* and implement the *IDbDataAdapter* interface. The relationship is shown in Figure 5-3.

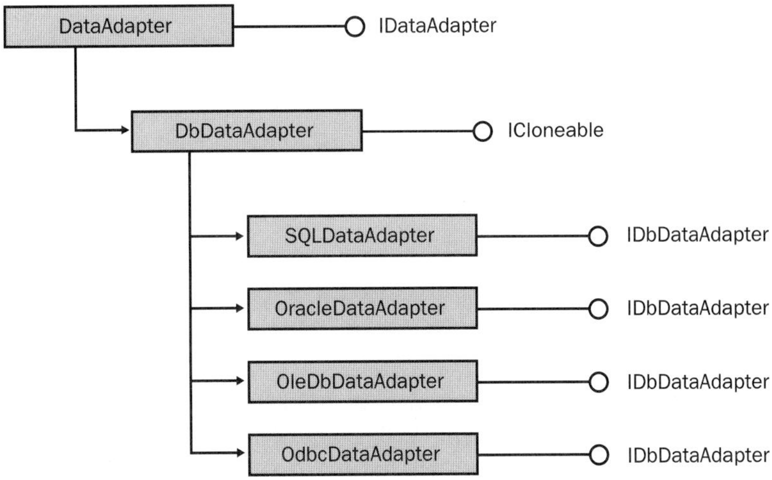

Figure 5-3 The hierarchy of data adapters and implemented interfaces.

The *DbDataAdapter* class provides the basic implementation of the members defined in the *IDataAdapter* interface. All data adapters implemented in the .NET Framework 1.1 inherit from *DbDataAdapter*.

Programming the SQL Server Data Adapter

Table 5-16 shows the properties of the *SqlDataAdapter* class—that is, the data adapter class for SQL Server.

Table 5-16 Properties of the *SqlDataAdapter* Class

Property	Description
AcceptChangesDuringFill	Gets or sets a value that indicates whether or not during the population of the in-memory row insertions must be committed. *True* by default.
ContinueUpdateOnError	Gets or sets a value that indicates whether in case of row conflicts the update continues or an exception is generated. Used during batch update.
DeleteCommand	Gets or sets a statement or stored procedure to delete records from the database. Used during batch update. Is a member of the *IDbDataAdapter* interface.
InsertCommand	Gets or sets a statement or stored procedure to insert new records in the database. Used during batch update. Is a member of the *IDbDataAdapter* interface.

(continued)

Table 5-16 Properties of the *SqlDataAdapter* Class *(continued)*

Property	Description
MissingMappingAction	Gets or sets a value that determines the action to take when a table or column in the source data is not mapped to a corresponding element in the in-memory structure. Is a member of the *IDataAdapter* interface.
MissingSchemaAction	Gets or sets a value that determines the action to take when source data does not have a matching table or column in the corresponding in-memory structure. Is a member of the *IDataAdapter* interface.
SelectCommand	Gets or sets a statement or stored procedure to select records from the database. During batch update, the method is used to download metadata; it is used to select records in a query statement. Is a member of the *IDbDataAdapter* interface.
TableMappings	Gets a collection that provides the mappings between a source table and an in-memory table. Is a member of the *IDataAdapter* interface.
UpdateCommand	Gets or sets a statement or stored procedure to update records in the database. Used during batch update. Is a member of the *IDbDataAdapter* interface.

A data adapter is a two-way channel used to read data from the data source into a memory table and to write in-memory data back to the data source. These two operations can be clearly identified in the list of properties. The four *xxxCommand* members of the *IDbDataAdapter* interface are used to control how in-memory data is written to the database. This is not really true of *SelectCommand*; although *SelectCommand* plays a role in the batch update process. The two *MissingXXX* properties and the *TableMappings* collection—the members of the *IDataAdapter* interface—represent how data read out of the data source is mapped onto client memory.

Once loaded in memory, the (disconnected) data is available for client-side updates. Batch update is the data-provider procedure that posts all the in-memory changes back to the data source. In doing so, a bunch of DBMS-specific commands are required to carry out the three basic operations—insert, update, and delete. The *InsertCommand*, *UpdateCommand*, and *DeleteCommand* properties are *SqlCommand* objects that do just this.

During the population step—that is, when the data adapter is used to load data into an ADO.NET container class—the state of the in-memory table (for example, a *DataTable* object) changes in response to the insertions. As we'll see in more detail in the "ADO.NET Container Objects" section, container objects implement a commit model and assign in-memory rows a state. The row state can be reset to *unchanged* by accepting the change. At least during the filling step, this setting can be controlled through the *AcceptChangesDuringFill* property. Table 5-17 lists the methods on the data adapter objects.

Table 5-17 Methods of the *SqlDataAdapter* Class

Method	Description
Fill	Populates an in-memory table with rows read from the source.
FillSchema	Configures an in-memory table so that the schema matches the schema in the data source.
GetFillParameters	Returns the parameters the user set on the query statement.
Update	Updates the data source based on the current content of the specified in-memory table. It works by calling the respective INSERT, UPDATE, or DELETE statements for each inserted, updated, or deleted row, respectively, in the table.

The data adapter uses the *SelectCommand* property to retrieve schema and data from the data source. The connection object associated with the *SelectCommand* does not need to be open. If the connection is closed before the reading occurs, it is opened to retrieve data and then closed. If the connection is open when the adapter works, it remains open.

Filling a *DataSet* Using a Data Adapter

A data adapter object uses the *Fill* method to populate an in-memory object with data retrieved through a query. The in-memory structure is a *DataSet* or *DataTable* object. As we'll see more clearly in a moment, the *DataSet* is the in-memory counterpart of a DBMS database. It might contain multiple tables (that is, multiple *DataTable* objects) and set up relationships and constraints between tables. Each table, in turn, is made of a number of columns and rows.

Filling a *DataSet* object ultimately means filling one of its tables. The data adapter can create a new table for each result set generated by the query. The table mapping code decides how. Mapping a result set to a *DataSet* is a process articulated in two phases: table mapping and column mapping. During the first step, the data adapter determines the name of the *DataTable* that will contain the rows in the current result set. By default, each *DataTable* is given a default name you can change at will. The default name of the *DataTable* depends on the signature of the *Fill* method that was used for the call. For example, let's consider the following two *Fill* calls:

```
DataSet ds = new DataSet();
adapter.Fill(ds);
adapter.Fill(ds, "MyTable");
```

In the first call, the name of the first result set generated by the query defaults to Table. If the query produces multiple result sets, additional tables will be named Table1, Table2, and so on, appending a progressive index to the default name. In the second call, the first result set is named MyTable and the others are named after it: MyTable1, MyTable2, and so forth. The procedure is identical; what really changes in the two cases is the base name.

The names of the tables can be changed at two different moments. You can change them after the *DataSet* has been populated or, when using table mapping, you can define settings that will be used to name the tables upon creation. You define a table mapping on a data adapter object using the *TableMappings* property.

> **Note** You can also use the *Fill* method to populate a single *DataTable*. In this case, only the first result set is taken into account and only one mapping phase occurs—column mapping.
>
> ```
> DataTable dt = new DataTable();
> adapter.Fill(dt);
> ```
>
> The preceding code shows how to use the *Fill* method to populate a *DataTable*.

The Table-Mapping Mechanism

The .NET data provider assigns a default name to each result set generated by the query. The default name is Table or any name specified by the programmer in the call to *Fill*. The adapter looks up its *TableMappings* collection for an entry that matches the default name of the result set being read. If a match is found, the data adapter reads the mapped name. Next, it attempts to locate in the *DataSet* a *DataTable* object with the name specified in the mapping, as shown in Figure 5-4.

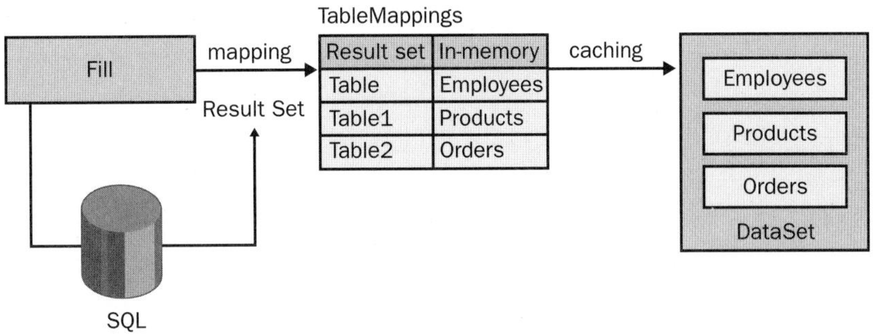

Figure 5-4 Mapping a result set onto a *DataSet* object.

If the result set named Table has been mapped to Employees, a table named Employees is searched in the *DataSet*. If no such *DataTable* object exists, it gets created and filled. If such a *DataTable* exists in the *DataSet*, its content is merged with the contents of the result set.

The *TableMappings* property represents a collection object of type *DataTableMappingCollection*. Each contained *DataTableMapping* object defines a pair of names: a source table name and an in-memory table name. Here's how to configure a few table mappings:

```
DataSet ds = new DataSet();
DataTableMapping dtm1, dtm2, dtm3;
dtm1 = adapter.TableMappings.Add("Table", "Employees");
dtm2 = adapter.TableMappings.Add("Table1", "Products");
dtm3 = adapter.TableMappings.Add("Table2", "Orders");
adapter.Fill(ds);
```

It goes without saying that the default names you map onto your own names must coincide with the default names originated by the call to the *Fill* method. In other words, suppose you change the last line of the previous code snippet with the following one:

```
adapter.Fill(ds, "MyTable");
```

In this case, the code won't work any longer because the default names will now be MyTable, MyTable1, and MyTable2. For these names, the *TableMappings* collection would have no entries defined. Finally, bear in mind you can have any number of table mappings. The overall number of mappings doesn't necessarily have to be related to the expected number of result sets.

The Column-Mapping Mechanism

If table mapping ended here, it wouldn't be such a big deal for us. In fact, if your goal is simply to give a mnemonic name to your *DataSet* tables, use the following code. The final effect is exactly the same.

```
DataSet ds = new DataSet();
adapter.Fill(ds);
ds.Tables["Table"].TableName = "Employees";
ds.Tables["Table1"].TableName = "Products";
```

The mapping mechanism, though, has another, rather interesting, facet: column mapping. Column mapping establishes a link between a column in the result set and a column in the mapped *DataTable* object. Column mappings are stored in the *ColumnMappings* collection property defined in the *DataTableMapping* class. The following code shows how to create a column mapping:

```
DataSet ds = new DataSet();
DataTableMapping dtml;
dtml = adapter.TableMappings.Add("Table", "Employees");
dtml.ColumnMappings.Add("employeeid", "ID");
dtml.ColumnMappings.Add("firstname", "Name");
dtml.ColumnMappings.Add("lastname", "FamilyName");
adapter.Fill(ds);
```

Figure 5-5 extends the previous diagram (Figure 5-4) and includes details of the column-mapping mechanism.

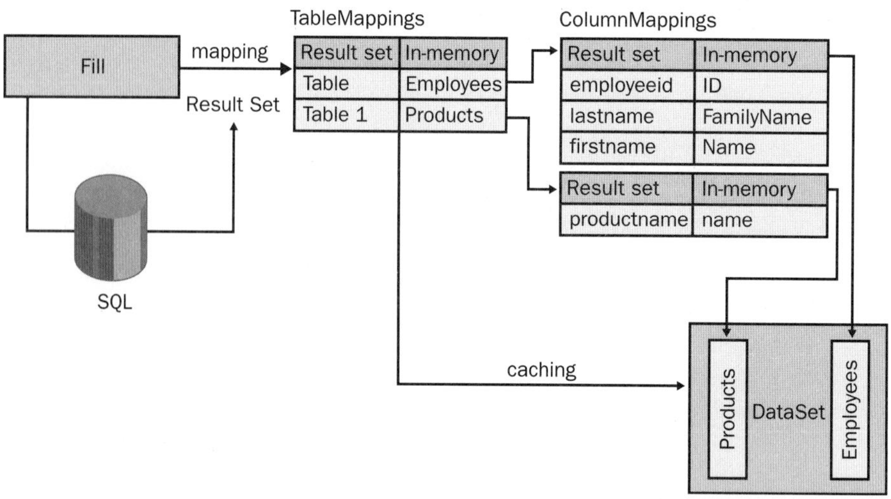

Figure 5-5 How the table and column mappings control the population of the *DataSet*.

In the preceding code, the source column *employeeid* is renamed to *ID* and placed in a *DataTable* named *Employees*. The name of the column is the only argument you can change at this level. Bear in mind that all this mapping takes place automatically within the body of the *Fill* method. When *Fill* terminates, each column in the source result set has been transformed into a *DataTable* column object—an instance of the *DataColumn* class.

Missing Mapping Action

The *Fill* method accomplishes two main operations. First, it maps the source result sets onto in-memory tables. Second, it fills the tables with the data fetched from the physical data source. While accomplishing either of these tasks, the *Fill* method could raise some special exceptions. An exception is an anomalous situation that needs to be specifically addressed codewise. When the adapter can't find a table or column mapping, or when a required *DataTable* or *DataColumn* can't be found, the data adapter throws a kind of lightweight exception.

Unlike real exceptions that must be resolved in code, this special breed of data adapter exceptions have to be resolved declaratively by choosing an action from a small set of allowable options. Data adapters raise two types of lightweight exceptions: missing mapping actions and missing schema actions.

A missing mapping action is required in two circumstances that can occur when the data adapter is collecting data to fill the *DataSet*. You need it if a default name is not found in the *TableMappings* collection, or if a column name is not available in the table's *ColumnMappings* collection. The data adapter's *MissingMappingAction* property is the tool you have for customizing the behavior of the data adapter in face of such an exception. Allowable values for the property, which are listed in Table 5-18, come from the *MissingMappingAction* enumeration.

Table 5-18 The *MissingMappingAction* Enumeration

Value	Description
Error	An exception is generated if a missing column or table is detected.
Ignore	The unmapped column or table is ignored.
Passthrough	Default option, add the missing table or column to the structure.

Unless you explicitly set the *MissingMappingAction* property prior to filling the data adapter, the property assumes a default value of *Passthrough*. As a result, missing tables and columns are added using the default name. If you set the *MissingMappingAction* property to *Ignore*, any unmapped table or column is simply ignored. No error is detected, but there will be no content for the incriminating result set (or one of its columns) in the target *DataSet*. If the *MissingMappingAction* property is set to *Error*, the adapter is limited to throwing a *SystemException* exception whenever a missing mapping is detected.

Once the data adapter is done with the mapping phase, it takes care of actually populating the target *DataSet* with the content of the selected result sets. Any required *DataTable* or *DataColumn* object that is not available in the target *DataSet* triggers another lightweight exception and requires another declarative action: the missing schema action.

Missing Schema Action

A missing schema action is required if the *DataSet* does not contain a table with the name that has been determined during the table-mapping step. Similarly, the same action is required if the *DataSet* table does not contain a column with the expected mapping name. *MissingSchemaAction* is the property you set to indicate the action you want to be taken in case of an insufficient table schema. Allowable values for the property come from the *MissingSchemaAction* enumeration and are listed in Table 5-19.

Table 5-19 The *MissingSchemaAction* Enumeration

Value	Description
Error	An exception is generated if a missing column or table is detected.
Ignore	The unmapped column or table is ignored.
Add	The default option. Completes the schema by adding any missing item.
AddWithKey	Also adds primary key and constraints.

By default, the *MissingSchemaAction* property is set to *Add*. As a result, the *DataSet* is completed by adding any constituent item that is missing—*DataTable* or *DataColumn*. Bear in mind, though, that the schema information added in this way for each column is very limited. It simply includes name and type. If you want extra information—such as the primary key, autoincrement, read-only, and allow-null settings—use the *AddWithKey* option instead.

Note that even if you use the *AddWithKey* option, not all available information about the column is really loaded into the *DataColumn*. For example, *AddWithKey* marks a column as autoincrement, but it doesn't set the related seed and step properties. Also the default value for the source column, if any, is not automatically copied. Only the primary key is imported; any additional indexes you might have set in the database are not. As for the other two options, *Ignore* and *Error*, they work exactly as they do with the *MissingMappingAction* property.

Prefilling the Schema

MissingMappingAction and *MissingSchemaAction* are not as expensive as real exceptions, but they still affect your code. Put another way, filling a *DataSet* that already contains all the needed schema information results in faster code. The advantage of this approach is more evident if your code happens to repeatedly fill an empty *DataSet* with a fixed schema. In this case, using a global *DataSet* object pre-filled with schema information helps to prevent all those requests for recovery actions. The *FillSchema* method just ensures that all the required objects are created beforehand.

```
DataTable[] FillSchema(DataSet ds, SchemaType mappingMode);
```

FillSchema takes a *DataSet* and adds as many tables to it as needed by the query command associated with the data adapter. The method returns an array with all the *DataTable* objects created (only schema, no data). The mapping-mode parameter can be one of the values defined in the *SchemaType* enumeration. The *SchemaType* enumeration values are listed in Table 5-20.

Table 5-20 The *SchemaType* Enumeration

Value	Description
Mapped	Apply any existing table mappings to the incoming schema. Configure the *DataSet* with the transformed schema. Recommended option.
Source	Ignore any table mappings on the data adapter. Configure the *DataSet* using the incoming schema without applying any transformations.

The *Mapped* option describes what happens when mappings are defined. *Source*, on the other hand, deliberately ignores any mappings you might have set. In this case, the tables in the *DataSet* retain their default name and all the columns maintain the original name they were given in the source tables.

How Batch Update Works

Batch update consists of the submission of an entire set of changes to the database. The batch update basically repeats the user actions that produced the changes but has the database—rather than the *DataSet*—as the target. Batch update assumes that the application enters its changes to the data set in an offline manner. In a multiuser environment, this might pose design problems if users concurrently access on the server the same data you're editing offline. When you post your changes on a record that another person has modified in the meantime, whose changes win out?

Data Conflicts and Optimistic Lock

The possibility of data conflicts represents a design issue, but it isn't necessarily a problem for the application. Batch update in a multiuser environment creates conflict only if the changes you enter are somewhat implied by the original values you have read. In such a case, if in the time elapsed between your fetch and the batch update someone else has changed the rows, you might want to reconsider or reject your most recent updates. Conflicts detected at update time might introduce significant overhead that could make the batch update solution much less exciting. In environments with a low degree of data contention, batch update can be effective because it allows for disconnected architectures, higher scalability, and considerably simpler coding.

To submit client changes to the server, use the data adapter's *Update* method. Data can be submitted only on a per-table basis. If you call *Update* without specifying any table name, a default name of Table is assumed. If no table exists with that name, an exception is raised.

```
adapter.Update(ds, "MyTable");
```

The *Update* method prepares and executes a tailor-made INSERT, UPDATE, or DELETE statement for each inserted, updated, or deleted row in the specified table. Rows are processed according to their natural order, and the row state determines the operation to accomplish. The *Update* method has several overloads and returns an integer, which represents the number of rows successfully updated.

When a row being updated returns an error, an exception is raised and the batch update process is stopped. You can prevent this from happening by setting the *ContinueUpdateOnError* property to *true*. In this case, the batch update terminates only when all the rows have been processed. Rows for which the update completed successfully are committed and marked as unchanged in the *DataSet*. For other rows, the application must decide what to do and restart the update if needed.

> **Note** The batch update is a loop that executes one user-defined database command for each inserted, modified, or deleted row in a *DataSet* table. In no way does the batch update process send the whole *DataSet* to the database for server-side processing.

Command Builders

The data adapter provides a bunch of command properties—*InsertCommand*, *DeleteCommand*, and *UpdateCommand*—to let the programmer control and customize the way in which in-memory updates are submitted to the database server. These properties represent a quantum leap from ADO, in which update commands were SQL commands silently generated by the library. If you don't quite see the importance of this change, consider that with ADO.NET you can use stored procedures to perform batch updates and even work with non-SQL data providers.

The commands can also be generated automatically and exposed directly to the data-adapter engine. Command-builder objects do that for you. A command-builder object—for example, the *SqlCommandBuilder* class—cannot be used in all cases. The automatic generation of commands can take place only under certain circumstances. In particular, command builders do not generate anything if the table is obtained by joining columns from more than one table and if calculated—or aggregate—columns are detected. Command builders are extremely helpful and code-saving only when they are called to deal with single-table updates. How can a command builder generate update statements for a generic table? This is where the fourth command property—the *SelectCommand* property—fits in.

A command builder employs *SelectCommand* to obtain all the metadata necessary to build the update commands. To use command builders, you must set *SelectCommand* with a query string that contains a primary key and a few column names. Only those fields will be used for the update, and the insertion and key fields will be used to uniquely identify rows to update or delete. Note that the command text of *SelectCommand* runs in the provider-specific way that makes it return only metadata and no rows.

The association between the data adapter and the command builder is established through the builder's constructor, as shown in the following code:

```
SqlCommand cmd = new SqlCommand();
cmd.CommandText = "SELECT employeeid, lastname FROM Employees";
cmd.Connection = conn;
adapter.SelectCommand = cmd;
SqlCommandBuilder builder = new SqlCommandBuilder(adapter);
```

The builder requests metadata and generates the commands the first time they are required and then caches them. Each command is also exposed through a particular method—*GetInsertCommand*, *GetUpdateCommand*, and *GetDeleteCommand*. Note that these methods return temporary command objects but *not* the real command objects that will be used to carry the batch update on. For this reason, any changes made to the command objects obtained in this way are lost. If you want to use the autogenerated commands as a base for your own further changes, you should first assign them to the corresponding *XXXCommand* properties of the data adapter and then enter changes. The command builder won't overwrite any command property that is not null.

> **Note** The behavior of data adapters and command builders for other managed providers does not differ in a relevant way from what we described here for the SQL Server .NET data provider.

The Case of Server Cursors

As of version 1.1 of the .NET Framework, ADO.NET does not support server cursors, such as the ADO *adOpenKeyset* and *adOpenDynamic* cursors. If you absolutely need that functionality in your application, there's probably no better choice than sticking to ADO. In a future version of the .NET Framework, the architecture of the .NET managed provider is expected to be enhanced to allow for server cursors. You should not expect it to be a general implementation of server cursors, though. Rather, it will be a database-specific implementation.

Server cursors will be exposed to applications through a new executor method in the provider's command class and return an instance of a new data-oriented class. For SQL Server, this class is tentatively named *SqlResultSet*.

ADO.NET Container Objects

The *System.Data* namespace contains several collection-like objects that, combined, provide an in-memory representation of the DBMS relational programming model. The *DataSet* class looks like a catalog, whereas the *DataTable* maps to an individual table. The *DataRelation* class represents a relationship between tables, and the *DataView* creates a filtered view of a table's data. In addition, the *System.Data* namespace also supports constraints and a relatively simple model of indexing.

The facilities of the memory-resident database model tout a programming model in which disconnection is a key feature rather than a precise requirement. Using the *DataSet* model, for example, you can filter and sort the data on the client before it gets to the middle tier. Having such facilities available within the *DataSet* means that once the data is there, you don't need to go back to the database to get a different view on the data. The data stored in the *DataSet* is self-sufficient, which makes the whole model inherently disconnected.

The *DataSet* is great for storing state that survives across page requests—for example, cached catalog information, a shopping cart, or similar kinds of data. Storing a *DataSet* in ASP.NET global objects such as *Session* or *Application* doesn't have the same scalability implications that it had in ASP. ADO.NET objects are thread safe for read operations, but they need to be explicitly synchronized for write operations. The *DataSet*, though—and more generally, the disconnected model—is not appropriate for just any sort of Web application.

> **Note** It can be argued that in a Web application, using the *DataSet* as the data container attached to a command object might be a solution. This solution, though, is problematic if you consider Windows Forms applications in which you can leverage the power of the client. Generally, an interesting use of the *DataSet* that makes sense both for Web and desktop scenarios is in moving data around between components and tiers. The *DataSet* is great at encapsulating tables of data and relationships. It can also be passed around between tiers as a monolithic object. Finally, it can be serialized into and out of XML, meaning that data and related schema can be moved between tiers in a loosely coupled manner.

The *DataSet* class is the principal component in the ADO.NET object model, but several others are satellite classes that play a fundamental role. ADO.NET container classes are listed Table 5-21.

Table 5-21 ADO.NET Container Classes

Class	Description
DataSet	An in-memory cache of data made of tables, relations, and constraints. Serializable and remotable, it can be filled from a variety of data sources and works regardless of which one is used.
DataTable	Logically equivalent to a disconnected ADO *Recordset*. Represents a relational table of data with a collection of columns and rows.
DataColumn	Represents a column in a *DataTable* object.
DataRow	Represents a row in a *DataTable* object.
DataView	Defined on top of a particular table. Creates a filtered view of data. Can be configured to support editing and sorting. The data view is not a copy of the data—just a mask.
DataRelation	Represents a relationship between two tables in the same *DataSet*. The relationship is set on a common column.
UniqueConstraint	Represents a restriction on a set of table columns in which all values must be unique.
ForeignKeyConstraint	Represents an action enforced on a set of table columns when a value or row is either deleted or updated. The columns must be in a primary key/foreign key relationship.

A key point to remember about ADO.NET container classes is that they work regardless of the data source used. You can populate the tables in a *DataSet* by using the results of a SQL Server query as well as file system information or data read out of a real-time device. Even more importantly, none of the ADO.NET container classes retains information about the source. Like array or collection objects, they just contain data. Unlike array or collection objects, though, they provide facilities to relate and manage data in a database-like fashion.

> **Note** Of all the ADO.NET container classes, only *DataSet* and *DataTable* can be serialized using the .NET Framework formatters—the *BinaryFormatter* and *SoapFormatter* classes. Only the *DataSet* can be serialized to XML. The *DataSet* class supports two flavors of XML serialization—through the *WriteXml* method and through the XML serializer.

The *DataSet* Object

The *DataSet* class inherits from the *MarshalByValueComponent* class and implements interfaces as shown in Figure 5-6.

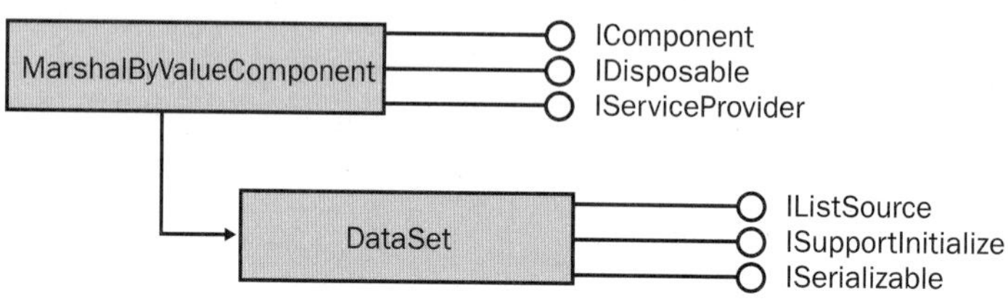

Figure 5-6 The structure of the *DataSet* class.

The parent class provides the *DataSet* with the capability of being marshaled by value, meaning that a copy of the serialized object is passed down to remote callers. Other base behaviors are provided by the implemented interfaces. The *IListSource* interface makes it possible to return a data-bound list of elements, while the *ISupportInitialize* interface allows for a *BeginInit* and *EndInit* pair of methods to bracket initialization of properties. Finally, *ISerializable* makes the class capable of controlling how its data is serialized to a .NET formatter. Table 5-22 lists the properties of the *DataSet* class.

Table 5-22 Properties of the *DataSet* Class

Property	Description
CaseSensitive	Gets or sets a value that indicates whether string comparisons within *DataTable* objects are case sensitive.
DataSetName	Gets or sets the name of the *DataSet*.
DefaultViewManager	Gets the default view manager object—an instance of the *DataViewManager* class—that contains settings for each table in the *DataSet*.
EnforceConstraints	Gets or sets a value that indicates whether constraint rules are enforced when attempting any update operation.
ExtendedProperties	Gets the collection of customized user information associated with the *DataSet*.
HasErrors	Gets errors in any of the child *DataTable* objects.
Locale	Gets or sets the locale information used to compare strings within the tables.
Namespace	Gets or sets the namespace of the *DataSet*.
Prefix	Gets or sets the prefix that aliases the namespace of the *DataSet*.
Relations	Gets the collection of the relations set between pairs of child tables.
Tables	Gets the collection of contained tables.

The *Namespace* and *Prefix* properties affect the way in which the *DataSet* serializes itself to XML. The name of the *DataSet* is also used to set the root node of the XML representation. If the *DataSetName* is empty, the *NewDataSet* string is used. The methods of the class are listed in Table 5-23.

Table 5-23 Methods of the *DataSet* Class

Method	Description
AcceptChanges	Commits all the changes made to all the tables in the *DataSet* since it was loaded or since the last time the method was called.
Clear	Removes all rows in all tables.
Clone	Copies the structure of the *DataSet*, including all table schemas, relations, and constraints. No data is copied.

(continued)

Table 5-23 Methods of the *DataSet* Class *(continued)*

Method	Description
Copy	Makes a deep copy of the object, including schema and data.
GetChanges	Returns a copy of the *DataSet* containing only the changes made to it since it was last loaded or since *AcceptChanges* was called.
GetXml	Returns the XML representation of the data stored.
GetXmlSchema	Returns the XSD schema for the XML string representing the data stored in the *DataSet*.
HasChanges	Indicates whether there are new, deleted, or modified rows in any of the contained tables.
InferXmlSchema	Replicates into the *DataSet* the table structure inferred from the specified XML document.
Merge	Merges the specified ADO.NET object (*DataSet*, *DataTable*, or an array of *DataRow* objects) into the current *DataSet*.
ReadXml	Populates the *DataSet* reading schema and data from the specified XML document.
ReadXmlSchema	Replicates into the *DataSet* the table structure read from the specified XML schema.
RejectChanges	Rolls back all the changes made to all the tables since it was created or since the last time *AcceptChanges* was called.
Reset	Empties tables, relations, and constraints, resetting the *DataSet* to its default state.
WriteXml	Serializes the *DataSet* contents to XML.
WriteXmlSchema	Writes the *DataSet* structure as an XML schema.

To make a full, deep copy of the *DataSet*, you must resort to the *Copy* method. Only in this case, you duplicate the object. The following code does not duplicate the object:

```
DataSet tmp = ds;
```

If you simply assign the current *DataSet* reference to another variable, you duplicate the reference but not the object. Use the following code to duplicate the object:

```
DataSet tmp = ds.Copy();
```

The *Copy* method creates and returns a new instance of the *DataSet* object and ensures that all the tables, relations, and constraints are duplicated. The *Clone* method is limited to returning a new *DataSet* object in which all the properties have been replicated but no data in the tables is copied.

Merging *DataSet* Objects

A merge operation is typically accomplished by a client application to update an existing *DataSet* object with the latest changes read from the data source. The *Merge* method should be used to fuse together two *DataSet* objects that have nearly identical schemas. The two schemas, though, are not strictly required to be identical.

The first step in the merge operation compares the schemas of the involved *DataSet* objects to see whether they match. If the *DataSet* to be imported contains new columns or a new table source, what happens depends on the missing schema action specified. By default, any missing schema element is added to the target *DataSet*, but you can change the behavior by choosing the *Merge* overload that allows for a *MissingSchemaAction* parameter.

As the second step, the *Merge* method attempts to merge the data by looking at the changed rows in the *DataSet* to be imported. Any modified or deleted row is matched to the corresponding row in the existing *DataSet* by using the primary key value. Added rows are simply added to the existing *DataSet* and retain their primary key value.

The merge operation is an atomic operation that must guarantee integrity and consistency only at its end. For this reason, constraints are disabled during a merge operation. However, if at the end of the merge the original constraints can't be restored—for example, a unique constraint is violated—an exception is thrown, but no uploaded data gets lost. In this case, the *Merge* method completely disables constraints in the *DataSet*. It sets the *EnforceConstraints* property to *false* and marks all invalid rows in error. To restore constraints, you must first resolve errors.

The *DataSet* Commit Model

When the *DataSet* is first loaded, all the rows in all tables are marked as unchanged. The state of a table row is stored in a property named *RowState*. Allowable values for the row state are in the *DataRowState* enumeration listed in Table 5-24.

Table 5-24 States of a Table Row

Value	Description
Added	The row has been added to the table.
Deleted	The row is marked for deletion from the parent table.
Detached	Either the row has been created but not yet added to the table or the row has been removed from the rows collection.
Modified	Some columns within the row have been changed.
Unchanged	No changes have been made since the last call to *AcceptChanges*. This is also the state of all rows when the table is first created.

The *AcceptChanges* method has the power to commit all the changes and accept the current values as the new original values of the table. After *AcceptChanges* is called, all changes are cleared. The *RejectChanges* method, on the other hand, rolls back all the pending changes and restores the original values. Note that the *DataSet* retains original values until changes are committed or rejected.

The commit model is applicable at various levels. In particular, by calling *AcceptChanges* or *RejectChanges* on the *DataSet* object, you commit or roll back changes for all the rows in all the contained tables. If you call the same methods on a *DataTable* object, the effect is for all the rows in the specified table. Finally, you can also accept or reject changes for an individual row in a particular table.

Serializing Contents to XML

The contents of a *DataSet* object can be serialized as XML in two ways, which I'll call *stateless* and *stateful*. Although these expressions are not common throughout the ADO.NET documentation, I feel that they perfectly describe the gist of the two possible approaches. A stateless representation takes a snapshot of the current instance of the data and renders it according to a particular XML schema—the ADO.NET normal form—as shown in the following code:

```
<MyDataSet>
    <Employees>
        <ID>...</ID>
        <Name>...</Name>
    </Employees>
    ⋮
    <Orders>
        <OrderID>...</OrderID>
        <OrderDate>...</OrderDate>
        <Amount>...</Amount>
    </Orders>
</MyDataSet>
```

The root node appears after the *DataSetName* property. Nodes one level deeper represent rows of all tables and are named as the table. Each row node contains as many children as there are columns in the row. This code snippet refers to a *DataSet* with two tables—Employees and Orders—with two and three columns, respectively. That kind of string is what the *GetXml* method returns and what the *WriteXml* method writes out when the default write mode is chosen.

```
dataSet.WriteXml(fileName);
dataSet.WriteXml(fileName, mode);
```

A stateful representation, on the other hand, contains the history of the data in the object and includes information about changes as well as pending errors. Table 5-25 summarizes the writing options available for use with *WriteXml* through the *XmlWriteMode* enumeration.

Table 5-25 The *XmlWriteMode* Enumeration

Write Mode	Description
IgnoreSchema	Writes the contents of the *DataSet* as XML data without schema.
WriteSchema	Writes the contents of the *DataSet*, including an inline XSD schema. The schema cannot be inserted as XDR, nor can it be added as a reference.
DiffGram	Writes the contents of the *DataSet* as a DiffGram, including original and current values.

IgnoreSchema is the default option. The following code demonstrates the typical way to serialize a *DataSet* to an XML file:

```
StreamWriter sw = new StreamWriter(fileName);
dataset.WriteXml(sw);    // defaults to XmlWriteMode.IgnoreSchema
sw.Close();
```

A DiffGram is an XML serialization format that includes both the original values and current values of each row in each table. In particular, a DiffGram contains the current instance of rows with the up-to-date values plus a section where all the original values for changed rows are grouped. Each row is given a unique identifier that is used to track changes between the two sections of the DiffGram. This relationship looks a lot like a foreign-key relationship. The following listing outlines the structure of a DiffGram:

```
<diffgr:diffgram
    xmlns:msdata="urn:schemas-microsoft-com:xml-msdata"
    xmlns:diffgr="urn:schemas-microsoft-com:xml-diffgram-v1">
    <DataSet>
    ⋮
    </DataSet>

    <diffgr:before>
    ⋮
    </diffgr:before>

    <diffgr:errors>
    ⋮
    </diffgr:errors>
</diffgr:diffgram>
```

The *<diffgr:diffgram>* root node can have up to three children. The first is the *DataSet* object with its current contents, including newly added rows and modified rows (but not deleted rows). The actual name of this subtree depends on the *DataSetName* property of the source *DataSet* object. If the *DataSet* has no name, the subtree's root is *NewDataSet*. The subtree rooted in the *<diffgr:before>* node contains enough information to restore the original state of all modified rows. For example, it still contains any row that has been deleted as well as the original content of any modified row. All columns affected by any change are tracked in the *<diffgr:before>* subtree. The last subtree is *<diffgr:errors>*, and it contains information about any errors that might have occurred on a particular row.

> **Note** The XML serialization of the *DataSet* object is a relatively large topic that deserves much more space than this section allows. The topic is covered in detail in Chapters 9 and 10 of my book, *Applied XML Programming for Microsoft .NET* (Microsoft Press, 2002).

The *DataTable* Object

The *DataTable* object represents one table of in-memory data. Mostly used as a container of data within a *DataSet*, the *DataTable* is also valid as a stand-alone object that contains tabular data. The internal structure of the class is identical to that depicted in Figure 5-6 for the *DataSet*. The *DataTable* and *DataSet* are the only ADO.NET objects that can be remoted and serialized.

Just as with a *DataSet*, a *DataTable* can be created programmatically. In this case, you first define its schema and then add new rows. The following code snippet shows how to create a new table within a *DataSet*:

```
DataSet ds = new DataSet();
DataTable tableEmp = new DataTable("Employees");
tableEmp.Columns.Add("ID", typeof(int));
tableEmp.Columns.Add("Name", typeof(string));
ds.Tables.Add(tableEmp);
```

The table is named Employees and features two columns—ID and Name. The table is empty because no rows have been added yet. To add rows, you first create a new row object by using the *NewRow* method:

```
DataRow row = tableEmp.NewRow();
row["ID"] = 1;
row["Name"] = "Joe Users";
tableEmp.Rows.Add(row);
```

The *DataTable* contains a collection of constraint objects that can be used to ensure the integrity of the data and signals changes to its data-firing events.

Let's have a closer look at the programming interface of the *DataTable*, beginning with properties. Table 5-26 lists the properties of the *DataTable* class.

Table 5-26 Properties of the *DataTable* Class

Property	Description
CaseSensitive	Gets or sets whether string comparisons are case-sensitive.
ChildRelations	Gets the collection of child relations for this table.
Columns	Gets the collection of columns that belong to this table.
Constraints	Gets the collection of constraints maintained by this table.
DataSet	Gets the *DataSet* this table belongs to.
DefaultView	Gets the default *DataView* object for this table.
DisplayExpression	Gets or sets a display string for the table. Used in the *ToString* method together with *TableName*.
ExtendedProperties	Gets the collection of customized user information.
HasErrors	Gets a value that indicates whether there are errors in any of the rows.
Locale	Gets or sets locale information used to compare strings.
MinimumCapacity	Gets or sets the initial starting size for the table.
Namespace	Gets or sets the namespace for the XML representation of the table.
ParentRelations	Gets the collection of parent relations for this table.
Prefix	Gets or sets the prefix that aliases the table namespace.
PrimaryKey	Gets or sets an array of columns that function as the primary key for the table.
Rows	Gets the collection of rows that belong to this table.
TableName	Gets or sets the name of the *DataTable* object.

The *ExtendedProperties* property is a collection shared by several ADO.NET objects, including *DataSet* and *DataColumn*. It manages name/value pairs and accepts values of object type. You can use this collection as a generic cargo variable in which to store any user information. Although the *ExtendedProperties* collection can accept any object, you should always store strings. If you use something other than strings, you might run into troubles if the *DataTable* gets serialized at some time. When the table is serialized, any item in the *ExtendedProperties* collection is serialized as a string using the output of the *ToString* method. This fact doesn't ensure that the object will be correctly restored during the deserialization step. The methods of the *DataTable* class are listed in Table 5-27.

Table 5-27 Methods of the *DataTable* Class

Method	Description
AcceptChanges	Commits all the pending changes made to the table.
BeginInit	Begins the initialization of the table. Used when the table is used on a form or by another component.
BeginLoadData	Turns off notifications, index maintenance, and constraints while loading data.
Clear	Removes all the data from the table.
Clone	Clones the structure of the table. Copies constraints and schema, but doesn't copy data.
Compute	Computes the given expression on the rows that meet the specified filter criteria. Returns the result of the computation as an object.
Copy	Copies both the structure and data for the table.
EndInit	Ends the initialization of the table. Closes the operation started with *BeginInit*.
EndLoadData	Turns on notifications, index maintenance, and constraints after loading data.
GetChanges	Gets a copy of the table containing all changes made to it since it was last loaded or since *AcceptChanges* was called.
GetErrors	Gets an array of all the *DataRow* objects that contain errors.
ImportRow	Performs a deep copy of a *DataRow*, and loads it into the table. Settings, including original and current values, are preserved.
LoadDataRow	Finds and updates a specific row. If no matching row is found, a new row is created using the given values. Uses the primary keys to locate the row.
NewRow	Creates a new *DataRow* object with the schema as the table.
RejectChanges	Rolls back all changes that have been made to the table since it was loaded or since the last time *AcceptChanges* was called.
Reset	Resets the *DataTable* object to its default state.
Select	Gets the array of *DataRow* objects that match the criteria.

Any row in the *DataTable* is represented by a *DataRow* object, whereas the *DataColumn* object represents a column. The *Select* method implements a simple but effective query engine for the rows of the table. The result set is an array of *DataRow* objects. The filter string is expressed in an internal language that looks like that used to build WHERE clauses in a SQL SELECT statement. The following line of code is a valid expression that selects all records in which the ID is greater than 5 and the name begins with A:

```
tableEmp.Select("ID >5 AND Name LIKE 'A%'");
```

Refer to the .NET Framework documentation for the full syntax supported by the *Select* method. Note that it's the same language you can use to define expression-based *DataTable* columns.

Performing Computations

The *Compute* method of the *DataTable* class calculates a value by applying a given expression to the table rows that match a specified filter. Expressions can include any sort of Boolean and arithmetic operators, but they can also include more interesting aggregate functions such as *Min*, *Max*, *Count*, and *Sum*, plus a few more statistical operators such as average, standard deviation, and variance. The following code counts the rows in which the Name column begins with A:

```
int numRecs = (int) tableEmp.Compute("Count(ID)", " Name LIKE 'A%'");
```

The *Compute* method has two possible overloads—one that takes only the expression to compute and one that also adds a filter string, as shown in the preceding code. Note that all aggregate functions can operate on a single column. This means you can directly compute the sum on two columns, as in the following pseudo-code:

```
Sum(quantity * price)
```

To compute functions on multiple columns, you can leverage the capabilities of the *DataColumn* object and, in particular, its support for dynamic expressions. For example, you can define an in-memory column named *order_item_price* as follows:

```
tableEmp.Columns.Add("order_item_price", typeof(double), "quantity*price");
```

At this point, you can compute the sum of that column using the following expression:

```
Sum(order_item_price)
```

Columns of a Table

A *DataColumn* object represents the schema of a column in a *DataTable* object. It provides properties that describe the characteristics and capabilities of the column. The *DataColumn* properties include *AllowDBNull*, *Unique*, *ReadOnly*, *DefaultValue*, and *Expression*. As discussed earlier, some of these properties are automatically set with the corresponding information read from the data source—at least when the data source is a database.

A *DataColumn* object has a name and type; sometimes it can also have an associated expression. The content of an expression-based column is a function of one or more columns combined with operators and aggregates to form a full expression. When an expression-based column is created, ADO.NET precalculates and caches all the values for the column as if they were native data. At the same time, ADO.NET tracks the columns involved and monitors them for changes. It does so by registering an internal handler for the *DataTable*'s *RowChanged* event. When a row changes in one of the columns involved in the expression, the computed column is automatically refreshed.

Expression-based columns are extremely powerful for setting up more effective and practical forms of data binding, as we'll see in the next chapter. In addition, expression-based columns work side by side with table relations and, using both, you can implement really powerful features. We'll demonstrate this later in the "Data Relations" section.

Rows of a Table

The data in a table is represented with a collection of *DataRow* objects. A row has a state, an array of values, and possibly error information. The *DataTable* maintains various versions of the row. You can query for a particular version at any time using the *Item* accessor property. The following code snippet shows how to read the original value of a column in a particular *DataRow* object. By default, you are returned the current value.

```
Response.Write(row["Name", DataRowVersion.Original].ToString());
```

All the values in a row can be accessed either individually or as a whole. When accessing all the values in a row, you use the *ItemArray* property, which passes you an array of objects, one for each column. The *ItemArray* property is a quick way to read values from a row and to set all the columns on a row in a single shot.

The *DataRow* class doesn't have a public constructor. As a result, a data row can be created only implicitly using the *NewRow* method on a base table. The *NewRow* method populates the *DataRow* object with as many entries as there are columns in the *DataTable*. In this case, the table provides the schema for the row, but the row is in no way a child of the table. To add a row to a *DataTable*, you must explicitly add it to the *Rows* collection.

```
tableEmp.Rows.Add(row);
```

Note that a *DataRow* object cannot be associated with more than one table at a time. To load a row into another table, you can use the *ImportRow* method, which basically duplicates the *DataRow* object and loads it into the specified table. A row can be detached from its parent table using the *Remove* method. If you use the *Delete* method, on the other hand, the row will be marked for deletion but still remain part of the table.

> **Note** Objects removed from a parent collection are not automatically destroyed or, at least, not until they go out of scope and become fodder for the garbage collector. This consideration holds true for several ADO.NET objects including, but not limited to, the *DataRow*. A *DataTable*, for example, can be detached from the *DataSet* by simply removing it from the *Tables* collection. However, this doesn't mean that the *DataTable* is automatically deleted as an object.

Table Constraints

A constraint is a logical rule set on a table to preserve the integrity of the data. For example, a constraint determines what happens when you delete a record in a table that is related to another one. The .NET Framework supports two types of constraints—*ForeignKeyConstraint* and *UniqueConstraint*.

In particular, the *ForeignKeyConstraint* class sets the rules that govern how the table propagates changes to related tables. For example, suppose you have two related tables, one with employees and one with orders. What happens when an employee is deleted? Should you delete all the related records too? The *ForeignKeyConstraint* object associated with the Employees table will determine what is related to it in the Orders table. You create a *ForeignKeyConstraint* object as shown below:

```
DataColumn c1 = tableEmp.Columns("empID");
DataColumn c2 = tableOrd.Columns("empID");
ForeignKeyConstraint fk = new ForeignKeyConstraint("EmpOrders", c1, c2);
// configure the constraint object
tableOrd.Constraints.Add(fk);
```

The *ForeignKeyConstraint* constructor takes the name of the object plus two *DataColumn* objects. The first *DataColumn* object represents the column (or the columns) on the parent table; the second *DataColumn* object represents the column (or the columns) in the child table. The constraint is added to the child table and is configured using the *UpdateRule*, *DeleteRule*, and *AcceptRejectRule* properties. While setting the *UpdateRule* and *DeleteRule* properties, you use values taken from the *Rule* enumeration. *AcceptRejectRule* is the enumeration used to look for the *AcceptRejectRule* property of the same name. For updates and deletions, the child table can cascade the change or set the involved rows to null or default values. Alternately, the child table can simply ignore the changes. The *AcceptRejectRule* property is processed when the *AcceptChanges* method is called on the parent row to commit changes. The choices for the constraint are limited to either cascading or ignoring changes.

The *UniqueConstraint* class ensures that a single column (or an array of columns) have unique, nonduplicated values. There are several ways to set a unique constraint. You can create one explicitly using the class constructor and adding the resulting object to the *Constraints* collection of the *DataTable*.

```
UniqueConstraint uc;
uc = new UniqueConstraint(tableEmp.Columns("empID"));
tableEmp.Constraints.Add(uc);
```

A unique constraint can also be created implicitly by setting the *Unique* property of the column to *true*. In contrast, setting the *Unique* property to *false* resets the constraint. In addition, adding a column to the in-memory primary key for a table would automatically create a unique constraint for the column. Note that a primary key on a *DataTable* object is an array of *DataColumn* objects that is used to index and sort the rows. The *Select* method on the *DataTable* exploits the index as well as other methods on the *DataView* class do.

> **Note** When you define a *DataColumn* as the primary key for a *DataTable* object, the table automatically sets the *AllowDBNull* property of the column to *false* and the *Unique* property to *true*. If the primary key is made of multiple columns, only the *AllowDBNull* property is automatically set to *false*.

Data Relations

A data relation represents a parent/child relationship between two *DataTable* objects in the same *DataSet*. In the .NET Framework, a data relation is represented by a *DataRelation* object. You set a relation between two tables based on matching columns in the parent and child tables. The matching columns in the two related tables can have different names, but they must have the same type. All the relations for the tables in a *DataSet* are stored in the *Relations* collection. Table 5-28 lists the properties of the *DataRelation* class.

Table 5-28 Properties of the *DataRelation* Class

Property	Description
ChildColumns	Gets the child *DataColumn* objects for the relation.
ChildKeyConstraint	Gets the *ForeignKeyConstraint* object for the relation.
ChildTable	Gets the child *DataTable* object for the relation.

Table 5-28 Properties of the *DataRelation* Class

Property	Description
DataSet	Gets the *DataSet* to which the relation belongs.
ExtendedProperties	Gets the collection that stores user information.
Nested	Gets or sets a value that indicates whether the relation should render its data as nested subtrees when the *DataSet* is rendered to XML. (More on this later in the "Serializing a Data Relation" section.)
ParentColumns	Gets the parent *DataColumn* objects for the relation.
ParentKeyConstraint	Gets the *UniqueConstraint* object that ensures unique values on the parent column of the relation.
ParentTable	Gets the parent *DataTable* object for the relation.
RelationName	Gets or sets the name of the *DataRelation* object. The name is used to identify the relation in the *Relations* collection of the parent *DataSet* object.

When a *DataRelation* is created, two constraints are silently created. A foreign-key constraint is set on the child table using the two columns that form the relation as arguments. In addition, the parent table is given a unique constraint that prevents it from containing duplicates. The constraints are created by default, but by using a different constructor you can instruct the *DataRelation* to skip that step. The *DataRelation* class has no significant methods.

Creating a Data Relation

The *DataRelation* class can be seen as the memory counterpart of a database table relationship. However, when a *DataSet* is loaded from a database, DBMS-specific relationships are not processed and loaded. As a result, data relations are exclusively in-memory objects that must be created explicitly with code. The following snippet shows how:

```
DataColumn c1 = tableEmp.Columns("empID");
DataColumn c2 = tableOrd.Columns("empID");
DataRelation rel = new DataRelation("Emp2Orders", c1, c2);
DataSet.Relations.Add(rel);
```

Given two tables, Employees and Orders, the preceding code sets up a relationship between the two based on the values of the common column *empID*. What are the practical advantages of such a relation? After the relation is set, the parent *DataTable* knows that each row might have a bunch of child related rows. In particular, each employee in the Employees table has an array of related rows in the Orders table. The child rows are exactly those where the value of the *Orders.empID* column matches empID column on the current Employees row.

ADO.NET provides an automatic mechanism to facilitate the retrieval of these related rows. The method is *GetChildRows*, and it's exposed by the *DataRow* class. *GetChildRows* takes a relation and returns an array filled with all the *DataRow* objects that match.

```
foreach(DataRow childRow in parentRow.GetChildRows("Emp2Orders"))
{
    // Process the child row
}
```

Another important facility ADO.NET provides for data relations has to do with table calculations and expression-based columns.

Performing Calculations on Relations

A common task in many real-world applications entails that you manage two related tables and process, given a parent row, the subset of child records. In many situations, processing the child rows just means performing some aggregate computations on them. This is just one of facilities that ADO.NET and relations provide for free. Let's suppose that, given the previous employees-to-orders relation, you need to compute the total of orders issued by a given employee. You could simply add a dynamically computed column to the parent table and bind it to the data in the relation:

```
tableEmp.Columns.Add("Total", typeof(int),
    "Sum(child(Emp2Orders).Amount)");
```

> **Caution** Although powerful and easy to use, ADO.NET disconnected features are not all extremely useful in ASP.NET applications. To exploit a relation to its fullest, you need to have full tables in memory or, at least, all the records in both tables that you need to display. As you surely understand, although this is possible, it makes the SQL code significantly more complex. But there's a subtler point to consider. A relation implies multiple tables, which implies multiple SELECT statements. In highly concurrent environments, this requires a rather heavy serializable transaction. Should you resort to an old-fashioned query using INNER JOIN in spite of the redundant data it returns? Not necessarily; returning multiple result sets in a single call would require less bandwidth and the same transactional penalty.

The new column Total contains, for each employee, a value that represents the sum of all the values in the Amount column for the child rows of the relation. In other words, now you have a column that automatically computes the total of orders issued by each employee. The keyword *child* is a special syntax element of the language that ADO.NET expressions support. Basically, the *child* keyword takes a relation name and returns an array of *DataRow* objects that is the child of that relation.

Serializing a Data Relation

The *Nested* property on the *DataRelation* object affects the way in which the parent *DataSet* is rendered to XML. By default, the presence of a relation doesn't change the XML schema used to serialize a *DataSet*. All the tables are therefore rendered sequentially under the root node. A nested relation changes this default schema. In particular, a nested relation is rendered hierarchically with child rows nested under the parent row.

A *DataSet* with Employees and Orders tables is rendered according to the following pattern:

```
<MyDataSet>
    <Employees empid="1" name="Joe Users" />
    ⋮
    <Orders empid="1" amount="6897" … />
    <Orders empid="1" amount="19713" … />
    ⋮
</MyDataSet>
```

If a relation exists between the tables and is set as nested, the XML schema changes as follows:

```
<MyDataSet>
    <Employees empid="1" name="Joe Users">
        <Orders empid="1" amount="6897" … />
        <Orders empid="1" amount="19713" … />
    </Employees>
    ⋮
</MyDataSet>
```

The child rows are taken out of their natural place and placed within the subtree that represents the parent row.

The *DataView* Object

The *DataView* class represents a customized view of a *DataTable*. The relationship between *DataTable* and *DataView* objects is governed by the rules of a well-known design pattern: the document/view model. The *DataTable* object acts as the document, whereas the *DataView* behaves as the view. At any moment, you can have multiple, different views of the same underlying data.

More importantly, you can manage each view as an independent object with its own set of properties, methods, and events.

The view is implemented by maintaining a separate array with the indexes of the original rows that match the criteria set on the view. By default, the table view is unfiltered and contains all the records included in the table. By using the *RowFilter* and *RowStateFilter* properties, you can narrow the set of rows that fit into a particular view. Using the *Sort* property, you can apply a sort expression to the rows in the view. Table 5-29 lists the properties of the *DataView* class.

Table 5-29 Properties of the *DataView* Class

Property	Description
AllowDelete	Gets or sets a value that indicates whether deletes are allowed in the view.
AllowEdit	Gets or sets a value that indicates whether edits are allowed in the view.
AllowNew	Gets or sets a value that indicates whether new rows can be added through the view.
ApplyDefaultSort	Gets or sets a value that indicates whether to use the default sort.
Count	Gets the number of rows in the view after the filter has been applied.
DataViewManager	Gets the *DataViewManager* object associated with this view.
Item	An indexer property. Gets a row of data from the underlying table.
RowFilter	Gets or sets the expression used to filter out rows in the view.
RowStateFilter	Gets or sets the row state filter used in the view.
Sort	Gets or sets the sorting of the view in terms of columns and order.
Table	Gets or sets the source *DataTable* for the view.

The filter can be an expression, the state of the rows, or both. The *RowStateFilter* property, in particular, takes its acceptable values from the *DataViewRowState* enumeration and allows you to filter based on the original or current values of the row, or on modified, added, or deleted rows. The *RowFilter* property supports the same syntax as the *DataTable*'s *Select* method.

A *DataView* does not contain copies of the table's rows. It is limited to storing an array of indexes that is updated whenever any of the filter properties is set. The *DataView* object is already connected to the underlying *DataTable*, of which it represents a possibly filtered and/or sorted view. The *AllowXXX* properties only let you control whether the view is editable or not. By default, the view is fully editable. Table 5-30 lists the methods of the *DataView* class.

Table 5-30 Methods of the *DataView* Class

Method	Description
AddNew	Adds a new row to the view and the underlying table.
BeginInit	Begins the initialization of the view.
CopyTo	Copies items from the view into an array.
Delete	Deletes the row at the specified index in the view. The row is deleted from the table too.
EndInit	Ends the initialization of the view.
Find	Finds a row in the view by the specified key value.
FindRows	Returns an array of row objects that match the specified key value.
GetEnumerator	Returns an enumerator object for the *DataView*.

Both the *AddNew* and *Delete* methods affect the underlying *DataTable* object. Multiple changes can be grouped using the pair *BeginInit/EndInit*.

Navigating the View

The contents of a *DataView* object can be scrolled through a variety of programming interfaces, including collections, lists, and enumerators. The *GetEnumerator* method, in particular, ensures that you can walk your way through the records in the view using the familiar *for...each* statement. The following code shows how to access all the rows that fit into the view:

```
DataView myView = new DataView(table);
foreach(DataRowView rowview in myView)
{
    // dereferences the DataRow object
    DataRow row = rowview.Row;
    ⋮
}
```

When client applications access a particular row in the view, the *DataView* class expects to find it in an internal cache of rows. If the cache is not empty, the specified row is returned to the caller via an intermediate *DataRowView* object. The *DataRowView* object is a kind of wrapper for the *DataRow* object that contains the actual data. You access row data through the *Row* property. If the row cache is empty, the *DataView* class fills it up with an array of *DataRowView* objects, each of which references an original *DataRow* object. The row cache is refreshed whenever the sort expression or the filter string are updated. The row cache can be empty either because it has never been used or because the sort expression or the filter string have been changed in the meantime. Figure 5-7 illustrates the internal architecture of a *DataView* object.

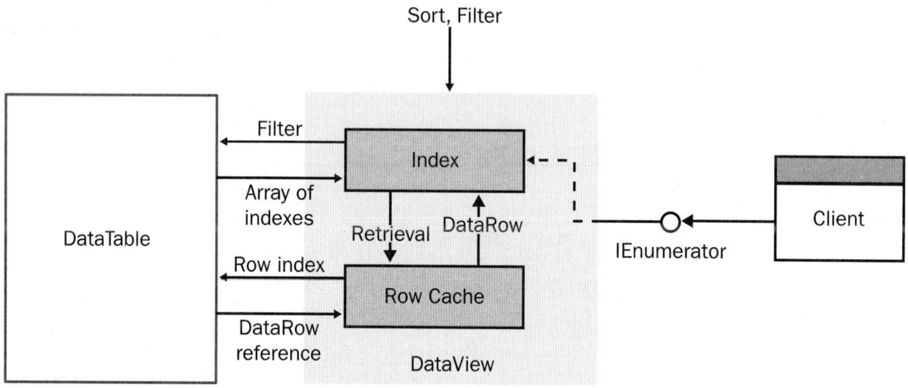

Figure 5-7 The internal structure of a *DataView* object.

Finding Rows

The link between the *DataTable* and the *DataView* is typically established at creation time through the constructor:

```
public DataView(DataTable table);
```

However, you could also create a new view and associate it with a table at a later time using the *DataView*'s *Table* property. For example:

```
DataView dv = new DataView();
dv.Table = dataSet.Tables["Employees"];
```

You can also obtain a *DataView* object from any table. In fact, the *DefaultView* property of a *DataTable* object just returns a *DataView* object initialized to work on that table.

```
DataView dv = dt.DefaultView;
```

Originally, the view is unfiltered and the index array contains as many elements as the rows in the table. To quickly find a row, you can either use the *Find* or *FindRows* method. The *Find* method takes one or more values and returns an array with the indexes of the rows that match. The *FindRows* method works in much the same way, but it returns an array of *DataRowView* objects rather than indexes. Both methods accept a sort key value to identify the rows to return.

> **Note** The contents of a *DataView* can be sorted by multiple fields by using the *Sort* property. You can assign to *Sort* a comma-separated list of column names, and even append them with *DESC* or *ASC* to indicate the direction.

Conclusion

The ADO.NET object model is made of two main subtrees—the managed providers and the database-agnostic container classes. Managed providers are the new type of data source connectors and replace the COM-based OLE DB providers of ADO and ASP. As of today, very few managed providers exist to connect to commercial DBMS. The .NET Framework version 1.1 includes two native providers—one for SQL Server and one for Oracle—and support for all OLE DB providers and ODBC drivers. Third-party vendors also support MySQL and provide alternative providers for Oracle. (Providers for other popular DBMS systems are in the works.)

A managed provider is faster and more apt than any other database technology for data access tasks. Especially effective with SQL Server, it hooks up at the wire level and removes any sort of abstraction layer. In this way, a managed provider makes it possible for ADO.NET to return to callers the same data types they would use to refresh the user interface. Functionally speaking, managed providers don't provide the same set of features as ADO. In particular, server cursors and the schema object model are not supported in this version of ADO.NET but are expected for the next major release.

A managed provider supplies objects to connect to a data source, execute a command, and then grab or set some data. The ADO.NET object model provides a special type of command—the data adapter—which is different because it returns a disconnected container object—the *DataSet*. Central to the ADO.NET infrastructure, the *DataSet* can be considered the in-memory counterpart of a DBMS catalog. Disconnected programming is useful and powerful but not always suited for simple and not too heavily layered Web applications.

In the next chapter, we'll see practical examples of how to bind data to user interface controls and we'll start seeing why disconnected data containers are not always the most effective tools to use over the Web to manage large quantities of data.

Resources

- *Microsoft ADO.NET*, by David Sceppa (Microsoft Press, 2002)
- *Pragmatic ADO.NET*, by Shawn Wildermuth (Addison-Wesley, 2002)
- *Applied XML Programming for Microsoft .NET*, by Dino Esposito (Microsoft Press, 2002)

6

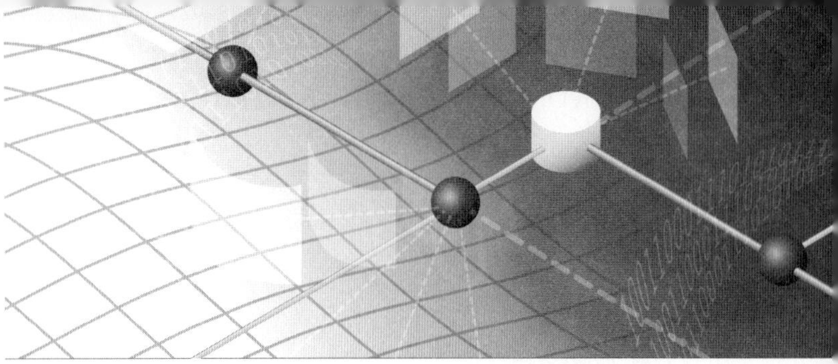

Creating Bindable Grids of Data

Imagination is more important than knowledge.

—*Albert Einstein*

Data-bound controls play a key role in the development of ASP.NET applications. Data-driven controls allow you to associate the whole interface, or individual properties, with one or more columns read out of a .NET-compliant data source. We already mentioned data-bound controls in Chapter 3 and reviewed their basics. In this chapter, we'll delve into the details of an extremely versatile data-bound control that is a fixed presence in any real-world ASP.NET application—the *DataGrid* control.

The *DataGrid* control renders a multicolumn, fully templated grid and provides a highly customizable, Microsoft Excel–like user interface. In spite of the rather advanced programming interface and the extremely rich set of attributes, the *DataGrid* simply generates an HTML table with interspersed hyperlinks to provide interactive functionalities such as sorting, paging, selection, and in-place editing.

According to the naming convention set in Chapter 3, the *DataGrid* control is said to be an iterative control and displays a list of records according to a given graphical template. Unlike other iterative controls, such as the *Repeater* and *DataList* controls that we'll dig out in Chapter 9, the *DataGrid* features a relatively rigid and inflexible graphical model. The data bound to a *DataGrid* is always rendered like a table, therefore, in terms of rows and columns. As we'll see later in the chapter, though, the contents of the cells in a column can be customizable to some extent using system-provided as well as user-defined templates.

The *DataGrid* Control

The *DataGrid* is a column-based control that supports various types of data-bound columns, including text columns, templated columns, and command columns. You associate the control with a data source by using the *DataSource* property. Just as for other data-bound controls, no data will be physically loaded and bound until the *DataBind* method is called. The simplest way of displaying a table of data using the ASP.NET grid is as follows:

```
<asp:DataGrid runat="server" id="grid" />
```

Once the control has been placed into the page, you bind it to the data source and display the resulting HTML code.

```
string connString = "SERVER=localhost;DATABASE=northwind;UID=sa;";
string cmdText = "SELECT firstname, lastname, title FROM employees";

void Page_Load(object sender, EventArgs e)
{
    // Run the query and get some data to display
    DataTable data = ExecuteQuery(cmdText, connString);

    // Bind the data to the grid
    grid.DataSource = data;
    grid.DataBind();
}

DataTable ExecuteQuery(string cmdText, string connString)
{
    SqlDataAdapter adapter = new SqlDataAdapter(cmdText, connString);
    DataTable data = new DataTable();
    adapter.Fill(data);
    return data;
}
```

Although it's effective in terms of retrieval and display, the preceding code is hardly usable in real applications because it's too minimal. Figure 6-1 shows the output.

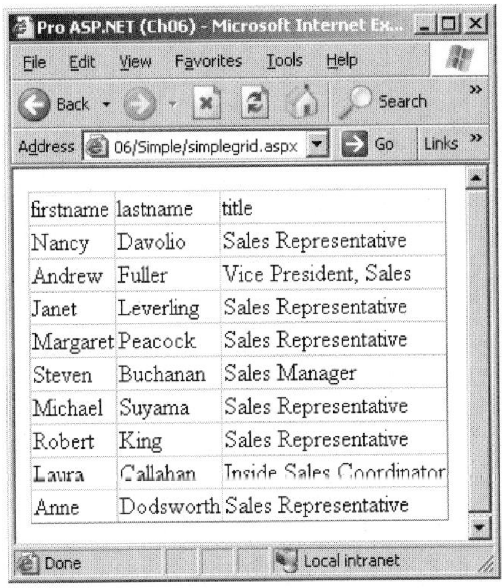

Figure 6-1 A too simple and minimal *DataGrid* control in action.

This simple *DataGrid* sample has the following drawbacks:

- **Poor user interface** A grid of data rows is aimed at the end user to make as seamless as possible her interaction with the application. For this reason, a clear and graceful combination of colors, styles, and fonts is an absolute must.
- **Data binding and caching** Performance-wise, the simple application just shown runs the query whenever the page is invoked. By design, the *DataGrid* control needs to be re-bound to its data at each request. Getting data repeatedly from the database is a necessity when the data gets stale frequently, but it's relatively ineffective in other situations. In this case, server-side caching techniques can make the difference.
- **Column mapping** In this sample, all the columns in the query are mapped to the grid and all have the same settings. A real-world grid, on the other hand, would bind each column independently using different settings and an individual user-interface pattern.
- **Scrolling and navigation** All the rows in the query resultset are included in the view regardless of the total number. In a more realistic scenario, only a relatively small number of rows are retrieved or just displayed. An effective support for data paging is essential for real-world grids.

- **Sorting and page interaction** Rarely is a grid of data read-only and completely static. More likely, you'll need to implement row selection and then drill-down and sort the records in various ways. None of these functionalities are supported in the sample code we've considered so far.

The *DataGrid* is a powerful and versatile control. Frankly, I admit that I have yet to find anything that can't be accomplished with an appropriate mix of methods and event handlers. Let's review the programming interface of the control.

Properties of the *DataGrid* Control

The *DataGrid* control inherits from the *BaseDataList* class and implements the *INamingContainer* interface. The *BaseDataList* abstract class provides a common set of functionality for all data listing controls, including *DataList* and *DataGrid*. As we saw in Chapter 2, the *INamingContainer* interface is a marker interface that doesn't require the implementation of any methods but only indicates that the class has some features. In particular, the interface marks the class as a naming container.

Table 6-1 lists the properties of the *DataGrid* class, but it doesn't include properties the control inherits from *Control* and *WebControl*.

Table 6-1 Properties of the *DataGrid* Class

Property	Description
AllowCustomPaging	Sets custom paging, or indicates whether it is enabled. *AllowPaging* must be set to *true* for this setting to work.
AllowPaging	Sets paging, or indicates whether paging is enabled.
AllowSorting	Sets sorting, or indicates whether sorting is enabled.
AlternatingItemStyle	Gets the style properties for alternating rows.
AutoGenerateColumns	Sets column objects to be automatically created and displayed for each field in the data source, or indicates whether this option is enabled. *True* by default.
BackImageUrl	Gets or sets the URL of the image to display as the background of the control.
CellPadding	Sets the space (in pixels) to remain between the cell's border and the embedded text, or indicates how much space remains.

Table 6-1 Properties of the *DataGrid* Class

Property	Description
CellSpacing	Sets the space (in pixels) to remain, both horizontally and vertically, between two consecutive cells, or indicates how much space remains.
Columns	Gets a collection of *DataGridColumn* objects that represent the columns in the *DataGrid* control.
Controls	Gets a collection of all the child controls in the grid.
CurrentPageIndex	Gets or sets the index of the currently displayed page.
DataKeyField	Gets or sets the key field in the bound data source.
DataKeys	Gets a collection that stores the key values of all records displayed as a row in the grid. The column used as the key is defined by the *DataKeyField* property.
DataMember	Gets or sets a string that indicates the specific table in a multimember data source to bind to the grid. The property works in conjunction with *DataSource*. If *DataSource* is a *DataSet* object, *DataMember* contains the name of the particular table to bind.
DataSource	Gets or sets the data source object that contains the values to populate the control.
EditItemIndex	Gets or sets the index of the grid's item to edit.
EditItemStyle	Gets the style properties for the item being edited.
FooterStyle	Gets the style properties for the footer section of the grid.
GridLines	Sets whether all cells must have the border drawn.
HeaderStyle	Gets the style properties for the heading section of the grid.
HorizontalAlign	Gets or sets the horizontal alignment of the text in the grid.
Items	Gets the collection of the currently displayed items.
ItemStyle	Gets the style properties for the items in the grid.
PageCount	Gets the number of pages required to display all bound items.
PagerStyle	Gets the style properties for the paging section of the grid.
PageSize	Gets or sets the number of items to display on a single page.
SelectedIndex	Gets or sets the index of the currently selected item.
SelectedItem	Gets a *DataGridItem* object that represents the selected item.
SelectedItemStyle	Gets the style properties for the currently selected item.
ShowFooter	Sets whether the footer is displayed. *False* by default.
ShowHeader	Sets whether the header is displayed.
VirtualItemCount	Gets or sets the virtual number of items in the *DataGrid* control when custom paging is used.

The characteristic traits of the *DataGrid* control are the *Columns* and *Items* collections, the *xxxStyle* properties, and the data-binding properties. All columns in the grid are represented by an object with its own set of properties and methods. Several types of columns are available to implement the most common tasks. In general, not all rows in the bound data source are included in the HTML code for the client. The *Items* collection returns only the displayed rows.

The *DataGrid* properties allow you to improve the grid's look and feel. You can set properties both declaratively through attributes set in the ASP.NET page layout and programmatically through properties set on the *DataGrid* control. When setting attributes, you can either set the property individually at the *<asp:datagrid>* level or group related properties on a per-item basis. For example, suppose you want to set the background color of the column headers to a particular color. You can do that through the headerstyle-backcolor attribute at the root level, as shown here:

```
<asp:DataGrid runat="server" id="grid"
    headerstyle-backcolor="brown">
```

However, you can also define the *<HeaderStyle>* child node within the *<asp:DataGrid>* declaration and set its *BackColor* attribute:

```
<asp:DataGrid runat="server" id="grid" ...>
    <HeaderStyle BackColor="brown">
    ⋮
</asp:DataGrid>
```

The effect is the same, but the second option looks more elegant and is easier to maintain. This is also the type of code that Microsoft Visual Studio .NET generates when you drop a *DataGrid* control on a Web form. The following schema illustrates the ASP.NET layout of the control:

```
<asp:DataGrid runat="server" ... >
    <AlternatingItemStyle ... />
    <EditItemStyle ... />
    <FooterStyle ... />
    <HeaderStyle ... />
    <ItemStyle ... />
    <PagerStyle ... />
    <SelectedItemStyle ... />
    <Columns>
    ⋮
    </Columns>
</asp:DataGrid>
```

Constituent Elements of a *DataGrid*

The output of a *DataGrid* control is made of several constituent elements grouped in the *ListItemType* enumeration. Each element plays a clear role and has a precise location in the user interface of the control, as Figure 6-2 shows.

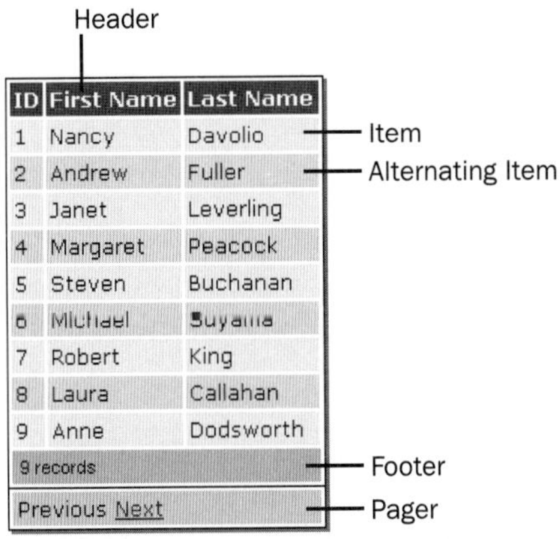

Figure 6-2 The layout of a *DataGrid* control.

The *DataGrid* user interface comprises the logical elements listed in Table 6-2. Each element has its own style property—that is, the set of graphical settings that are automatically applied by the control.

Table 6-2 Graphical Elements that Form a Data Grid

Item Type	Description
AlternatingItem	Represents a data-bound row placed in an odd position. Useful if you want to use different styles for alternating rows. *AlternatingItemStyle* is the property that lets you control the look and feel of the element.
EditItem	Represents the item, or alternating item, currently displayed in edit mode. *EditItemStyle* lets you control the look and feel of the element.
Footer	Represents the grid's footer. The element can't be bound to a data source and is styled using the settings in the *FooterStyle* property.
Header	Represents the grid's header. The element can't be bound to a data source and is styled using the settings in the *HeaderStyle* property.
Item	Represents a data-bound row placed in an even position. Styled through the *ItemStyle* property.

(continued)

Table 6-2 Graphical Elements that Form a Data Grid *(continued)*

Item Type	Description
Pager	Represents the pager element you use to scroll between pages. The element can't be bound to a data source and is styled using the settings in the *PagerStyle* property. The pager can be placed at the top or bottom of the grid's table and even in both places.
SelectedItem	Represents the item, or alternating item, currently selected. The property that defines its look and feel is *SelectedItemStyle*.

Each time one of the constituent elements is about to be created, the grid fires an *ItemCreated* event for you to perform some application-specific tasks. We'll examine the use of the *ItemCreated* event later in the chapter.

Data Source Rows and Displayed Rows

By design, the *DataGrid* control displays the data stored in a data source object. Each row in the data source is potentially a row in the grid. However, this one-to-one mapping doesn't always correspond to reality. The *DataSource* property contains the *ICollection*-based binding object; the *Items* property contains a collection of objects representing the rows of the grid. The *Items* collection is automatically filled when the *DataBind* method is called. Each element in the *Items* collection supplies a *DataItem* property that is set with the object that corresponds to the row in the data source. An item object is an instance of the *DataGridItem* class that inherits from *TableRow*.

The *Items* collection doesn't provide methods to add or remove items to the collection. However, the *ItemCreated* event provides a way for you to control when an item is added and determine its contents and configuration. Note that only bindable items are contained in the *Items* collection. The header, footer, and pager are not included in the collection.

The index properties of the *DataGrid* refer to the rows displayed rather than to the underlying data source. When the item with an index of 1 is selected, the second displayed item is selected, but this piece of information says nothing about the position of the corresponding source record. The data-source index for the item object is stored in the *DataSetIndex* property on the *DataGridItem* class. *DataSetIndex* returns the absolute position in the overall data source of the record represented by the current item. Although functional, this method isn't especially handy in some common scenarios, such as when you want to select a row and retrieve a bunch of associated records. In such a case, you need to know the value of the key field in the underlying data source row.

The *DataKeys* collection and the *DataKeyField* property provide an effective shortcut designed specifically to work in similar situations. When you configure a *DataGrid* control, you can store the name of a key field in the *DataKeyField* property. During the data-binding phase, the control extracts from the data source the values for the specified key field that correspond to the rows being displayed. As a result, the index of the selected row in the *Items* collection can be used with *DataKeys* to get the key value for the underlying data-source row. Let's consider the following declaration, which refers to a grid that displays information about the employees of a company:

```
<asp:DataGrid runat="server" id="grid" DataKeyField="employeeid" ... >
```

To get the ID of the selected employee—to be used to implement, say, a drill-down view—you simply use the following code:

```
int empID = grid.DataKeys[grid.SelectedIndex];
```

The *DataKeys* collection is automatically filled by the control based on the value of the *DataKeyField* property and the bound data source.

Events of the *DataGrid* Control

The *DataGrid* control has no specific methods worth mentioning. The control programming interface features a variety of methods, but all of them are inherited from various base classes—*Control*, *WebControl*, and *BaseDataList*. Table 6-3 lists the events that the control fires during its lifecycle.

Table 6-3 Events of the *DataGrid* Class

Event	Description
CancelCommand	The user clicked to cancel any updates made on the current item being edited.
DeleteCommand	The user clicked to start a delete operation on the current item.
EditCommand	The user clicked to put the current item in edit mode.
ItemCommand	The user clicked any command button within the grid control.
ItemCreated	The *DataGrid* control has created a new item during its initialization process.
ItemDataBound	This occurs after a grid item is bound to data.
PageIndexChanged	The user clicked to see a new page of data.
SelectedIndexChanged	The user clicked to select a different item.
SortCommand	The user clicked to start a sort operation on a column.
UpdateCommand	The user clicked to save any updates made on the item currently being edited.

The *CancelCommand* and *UpdateCommand* events are fired under special circumstances—that is, when an item is being edited. (We'll cover the *DataGrid* in-place editing capability later in the chapter.) The *CancelCommand* event signals that the user clicked the Cancel button to cancel all pending changes. The *UpdateCommand* event denotes the user's intention to persist all the changes. Note that any code necessary to update the underlying data source must be manually written by the programmer.

The other command events—*EditCommand*, *DeleteCommand*, and *SortCommand*—indicate that the user required a particular action by clicking on command buttons within the user interface of the grid. Typically, the user will click a link in the heading section to sort by a particular column and a row-specific button to delete or edit that row. If the grid contains multiple pages, *PageIndexChanged* signals when the user selects a new page. Note that all these events describe situations that the ASP.NET code is called to handle after a postback. For example, the *PageIndexChanged* event occurs when the user clicks and the page posts back to the server.

> **Note** In addition to the events just listed, the *DataGrid* control fires all the standard events of Web controls including *Load*, *Init*, *PreRender*, and *DataBinding*. In particular, you might want to write a handler for *PreRender* if you need to modify the HTML code generated for the grid. The *DataBinding* event, on the other hand, is the entry point in the grid's binding process. The event, in fact, is fired from within the *DataBind* method as the first step before the whole binding process begins.

The *DataGridItem* Object

A *DataGridItem* object represents a table row within a *DataGrid* control. A data grid item can be a data row, but it can also be the heading section, footer, or pager. All the data-bound items of a *DataGrid* control are grouped in a *DataGridItemCollection* and are programmatically accessed via the *Items* property. The programming interface of a data grid data item is the *DataGridItem* class. The class is characterized by the properties listed in Table 6-4.

Table 6-4 Properties of the *DataGridItem* Class

Property	Description
DataItem	Gets or sets the data item behind the row within the *DataGrid* control.
DataSetIndex	Gets the index number that characterized the object stored in the *DataItem* property in the bound data source.
ItemIndex	Gets the index of the item represented by the *DataGridItem* object in the *Items* collection of the *DataGrid* control.
ItemType	Gets the type of the item represented by the *DataGridItem* object in the *DataGrid* control.

Note that the table includes only the properties specific to the class. All properties inherited from parent classes haven't been listed.

The Data-Binding Process for the *DataGrid* Control

The data-binding process for a *DataGrid* control begins when the *DataBind* method is called. The *DataGrid* class doesn't really override the method but exploits the method as supplied by the *BaseDataList* class. This implementation is pretty simple and doesn't do more than raise the *DataBinding* event for the class. The internal handler of the *BaseDataList* class first clears all the child controls and the view state and then calls a protected method named *CreateControlHierarchy*, as in the following pseudo-code:

```
protected virtual void OnDataBinding(EventArgs e)
{
    // call the parent's event handler
    base.OnDataBinding(e);

    // Clear the collection of child controls
    Controls.Clear();

    // Clear the view state container
    ClearChildViewState();

    // Build the grid
    CreateControlHierarchy();

    // Monitor the view state for changes
    TrackViewState();
}
```

The *CreateControlHierarchy* method is responsible for setting up the hierarchy of controls and HTML code that actually makes up the final grid. The most important thing that happens within the body of *CreateControlHierarchy* is the creation of the various grid items. For each created item, a pair of correlated events are raised—*ItemCreated* and *ItemDataBound*.

ItemCreated and *ItemDataBound* Events

Whenever a new *DataGrid* item is created, an *ItemCreated* event is sent to applications. The event is fired immediately after the *DataGridItem* object is created and before it is added to the resulting HTML table. (The output of a *DataGrid* control is always a plain old HTML table.) The following delegate illustrates the prototype of the event handlers:

```
public delegate void DataGridItemEventHandler(
    object sender,
    DataGridItemEventArgs e
);
```

The event handler receives an argument of type *DataGridItemEventArgs*, which contains data related to the involved item. The *DataGridItemEventArgs* class features an extra *Item* property initialized with the freshly created *DataGridItem* object. When the *ItemCreated* event is raised, the binding between the underlying data row and the grid's row has not yet been set. The data binding takes place only when the *ItemDataBound* event reaches the application. The initialization step occurs in the following order:

- ***DataGridItem* creation** The new grid item object is created and initialized. At this point, it is a stand-alone object not bound yet to the grid and data.
- ***ItemCreated* event** The *ItemCreated* event is fired to let applications know that a new item has been created. The event data includes information about the new item. Once the event handler terminates, the item is added to the HTML table being generated.
- **Data binding** If the *DataGrid* item supports data binding, the underlying row is associated with the table row. The *DataItem* property on the new grid item object is set correctly.
- ***ItemDataBound* event** The *ItemDataBound* event is fired, and applications can read the actual values bound to normal and alternating rows.

Note that if you define a handler for the *ItemDataBound* event, it will also be called for the creation of nonbindable items, such as the header or footer. In this case, the *DataItem* property on the *DataGridItem* object is null, as expected.

Why Is *ItemCreated* Raised Twice?

When a page that includes a *DataGrid* control posts back, the *ItemCreated* event is raised twice. The event is first raised during the restoration of the page view state. The *DataGrid* control, in fact, stores its data row objects in the view state. When the view state is re-created, all items are instantiated and reinitialized.

Note that in this case, *ItemCreated* is raised for all the items stored in the view state, and therefore, for all the items displayed in the previous page. For example, suppose that the grid displays ten rows and you click to view another page. Suppose also that the new page would display, say, three rows. While processing the page request, the *DataGrid* control first fires *ItemCreated* ten times, one for each item cached in the view state that is restored. Next, while generating the output for the new page, the *DataGrid* fires the pair *ItemCreated* and *ItemDataBound* for each item to be displayed in the new page—three times only.

The second notification arrives when the page is being built and the *DataGrid* output code is ready to be generated. In this case only, *ItemCreated* is followed by an *ItemDataBound* event. Figure 6-3 shows the two moments in which the event is fired.

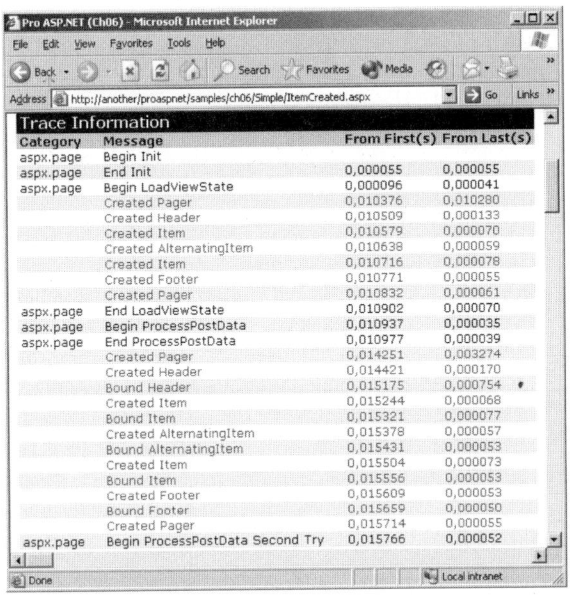

Category	Message	From First(s)	From Last(s)
aspx.page	Begin Init		
aspx.page	End Init	0,000055	0,000055
aspx.page	Begin LoadViewState	0,000096	0,000041
	Created Pager	0,010376	0,010280
	Created Header	0,010509	0,000133
	Created Item	0,010579	0,000070
	Created AlternatingItem	0,010638	0,000059
	Created Item	0,010716	0,000078
	Created Footer	0,010771	0,000055
	Created Pager	0,010832	0,000061
aspx.page	End LoadViewState	0,010902	0,000070
aspx.page	Begin ProcessPostData	0,010937	0,000035
aspx.page	End ProcessPostData	0,010977	0,000039
	Created Pager	0,014251	0,003274
	Created Header	0,014421	0,000170
	Bound Header	0,015175	0,000754
	Created Item	0,015244	0,000068
	Bound Item	0,015321	0,000077
	Created AlternatingItem	0,015378	0,000057
	Bound AlternatingItem	0,015431	0,000053
	Created Item	0,015504	0,000073
	Bound Item	0,015556	0,000053
	Created Footer	0,015609	0,000053
	Bound Footer	0,015659	0,000050
	Created Pager	0,015714	0,000055
aspx.page	Begin ProcessPostData Second Try	0,015766	0,000052

Figure 6-3 Tracing the events raised during the binding process of the *DataGrid*.

How can you avoid having your event handler called during the view-state restoration phase? The rub is that there's no specific information available with the event data structure that allows you to detect this situation. A possible trick is using a global state variable—a Boolean flag—to track whether the code is entered in the data-binding phase or not. If the *ItemCreated* is called when this flag is set to *false*, the call is because of view-state restoration. The beginning of the data-binding phase is signaled by the *DataBinding* event.

```
<asp:datagrid runat="server" id="grid"
    onitemcreated="ItemCreated"
    onitemdatabound="ItemDataBound"
    ondatabinding="TraceDataBinding" />
```

The handler of the *DataBinding* event has a simple structure, as shown below:

```
void TraceDataBinding(object sender, EventArgs e) {
    m_isBindingData =  true;
    Trace.Warn("Data binding...");
}
void ItemCreated(object sender, DataGridItemEventArgs e) {
    if (m_isBindingData)
        Trace.Warn("Created " + e.Item.ItemType.ToString());
}
```

Finally, note that the footer and header items are always created regardless of the setting of the *ShowFooter* and *ShowHeader* properties. The pager object, on the other hand, is created only if the *AllowPaging* property is set to *true*. It is interesting to note that the grid is composed of two pager objects—one on the first row and one on the last row. Using the *PagerStyle* property, you can decide how many pagers, or which one, are actually displayed. If needed, a *DataGrid* can also have two pager objects that work in synchronization. In any case, bear in mind that two *ItemCreated* events are fired for pagers.

Binding Data to the Grid

A *DataGrid* control is formed by data-bindable columns. By default, the control includes all the data-source columns in the view. You can change this behavior by setting the *AutoGenerateColumns* property to *false*. In this case, only the columns explicitly listed in the *Columns* collection are displayed. The *DataGrid* control supports a variety of column types, which differ from one another mostly in how each represents the data. You are required to indicate the type of the column if you add it to the *Columns* collection; otherwise, if automatic generation is used, all columns are of the simplest type—the *BoundColumn* column type. As Table 6-5 shows, a *BoundColumn* object displays the contents of the corresponding data source field by using labels.

Table 6-5 Types of Columns

Column Type	Description
BoundColumn	The contents of the column are bound to a field in a data source. Each cell displays as plain text.
ButtonColumn	This type displays a command button for each item in the column. The text of the button can be data-bound. The command name of the button must be common to all the items in the column. You can control the graphical style of the button—push button or link button.
EditColumn	This is a particular type of button column associated with a command named *Edit*. When in edit mode, the whole row is drawn using text boxes rather than literals.
HyperLinkColumn	This type displays the contents of each item in the column as a hyperlink. The text of the hyperlink can be bound to a column in the data source or it can be static text. The target URL can be data-bound too. Clicking a hyperlink column causes the browser to jump to the specified URL. Supports target frames.
TemplateColumn	This type displays each cell of the column following a specified ASP.NET template. It also allows you to provide custom behaviors.

Note that the *AutoGenerateColumns* property and the *Columns* collection are not mutually exclusive. If both properties are set to *true* and the collection is not empty, the *DataGrid* will first show the user-defined columns and then all the ones that autogeneration would produce.

You normally bind columns using the *<columns>* tag in the body of the *<asp:datagrid>* server control, as the following code demonstrates:

```
<asp:datagrid runat="server" id="grid" ... >
⋮
  <columns>
    <asp:BoundColumn runat="server" DataField="employeeid"
        HeaderText="ID" />
    <asp:BoundColumn runat="server" DataField="firstname"
        HeaderText="First Name" />
    <asp:BoundColumn runat="server" DataField="lastname"
        HeaderText="Last Name" />
  </columns>
</asp:datagrid>
```

Alternatively, you can create a new column of the desired class, fill its member properly, and then add the class instance to the *Columns* collection. Here is some code to add a *BoundColumn* object to a grid:

```
BoundColumn bc = new BoundColumn();
bc.DataField = "firstname";
bc.HeaderText = "First Name";
grid.Columns.Add(bc);
```

The order of the columns in the collection determines the order in which the columns are displayed in the *DataGrid* control.

Data-Bound Columns

All grid column types inherit from the *DataGridColumn* class and have a few common properties such as the header text, footer and item style, and visibility flag. Table 6-6 details the properties shared by all types of columns.

Table 6-6 Properties of the *DataGridColumn* Class

Property	Description
FooterStyle	Gets the style properties for the footer of the column.
FooterText	Gets or sets the static text displayed in the footer of the column.
HeaderImageUrl	Gets or sets the URL of an image to display in the header.
HeaderStyle	Gets the style properties for the header of the column.
HeaderText	Gets or sets the static text displayed in the header of the column.
ItemStyle	Gets the style properties for the item cells of the column.
SortExpression	Gets or sets the expression to pass to the *OnSortCommand* method when a column is selected for sorting.
Visible	Sets whether the column is visible in the *DataGrid* control.

The *BoundColumn* class represents a *DataGrid* column type that is bound to a data field. The specific properties available on the class are listed in Table 6-7.

Table 6-7 Properties of the *BoundColumn* Class

Property	Description
DataField	Gets or sets the data-source column to bind to.
DataFormatString	Gets or sets the string that specifies the display format for the cells in the column.
ReadOnly	Sets whether the items in the column can be edited. *False* by default.

The key properties to set up a grid column are *DataField*, which represents the name of the column to bind, and *DataFormatString*, which allows you to format the displayed text to some extent. The *ReadOnly* property has effect only if an edit command column is added to the grid. In this case, the cells in the column are switched to edit mode according to the value of the property.

The following code snippet adds two columns and specifies for each the header text and the source column. In addition, the second column is given a format string to make it look like a currency value with right alignment.

```
<asp:boundcolumn runat="server" datafield="quantityperunit"
    headertext="Packaging" />
<asp:boundcolumn runat="server" datafield="unitprice"
    headertext="Price" DataFormatString="{0:c}">
    <itemstyle width="80px" horizontalalign="right" />
</asp:boundcolumn>
```

Note that graphical settings for a column must be specified using a child style tag.

Configuring the Column Footer

As mentioned, the footer in a *DataGrid* control is hidden by default. To turn it on, you must set the *ShowFooter* property to *true*. As usual, you can do that either declaratively or programmatically. The footer style can be fully modified through the *FooterStyle* property at the grid level or on a per-column basis.

The footer, though, is not a bindable element and doesn't supply system-provided aggregate functions (for example, Count, Sum). The footer also doesn't provide a predefined way to modify its structure. The footer is rendered through an empty row, so it maintains the same column structure as other rows. If this suits you, use the column's *FooterText* property to assign it HTML content. If you want a footer with a different number of columns, write a handler for *ItemCreated* and hook up the moment in which the footer is created. The following code snippet shows how to make the footer display a single cell that spans the entire grid width:

```
void ItemCreated(Object sender, DataGridItemEventArgs e) {
    ListItemType elemType = e.Item.ItemType;
    if (elemType == ListItemType.Footer)
    {
        // Remove all the cells but one
        TableCellCollection tcc = e.Item.Cells;
        int nTotalCols = tcc.Count;
        for (int i=0; i<nTotalCols-1; i++)
            e.Item.Cells.RemoveAt(0);

        // Only 1 cell left at this time ...
        TableCell c = e.Item.Cells[0];
        c.ColumnSpan = nTotalCols;

        // Set any text to be displayed
        c.Text = "...";
    }
}
```

The footer is a *DataGridItem* object and, as such, a special type of table row. The *Cells* collection provides access to all the row cells you can modify at will as a *TableCell* object.

Using Cascading Style Sheets Styles

When creating a *DataGrid* control, you inevitably need to tune up some of its visual settings for a more user-friendly result. This normally means that you change the font family, font size, and width and color of the text and borders. The code necessary to obtain the desired graphical effect might be replicated for several other pages in the same application. Because many visual settings of a Web control are actually rendered as cascading style sheets (CSS)–style properties, you can group all of them into a CSS class. Next, you reference the style from the control (including *DataGrid* controls) by using the *CssClass* property.

Another, slightly more elegant, way to solve the issue is by deriving from the *DataGrid* a new control that simply uses the specified settings as the new default settings.

HyperLink Columns

The *HyperLinkColumn* class is a column type that contains a hyperlink for each cell. The programmer can control the text of the hyperlink and the URL to navigate. In particular, both fields can be bound to a column in the data source. Table 6-8 details the properties specific to the class.

Table 6-8 Properties of the *HyperLinkColumn* Class

Property	Description
DataNavigateUrlField	Gets or sets the data source column to bind to the URL of the hyperlinks in the column.
DataNavigateUrlFormatString	Gets or sets a parametric structure for the URL.
DataTextField	Gets or sets the data source column to bind to the text caption of the hyperlinks.
DataTextFormatString	Gets or sets the display format for the hyperlinks text.
NavigateUrl	Gets or sets the static URL to link to when a hyperlink in the column is clicked.
Target	Gets or sets the name of the target window or frame in which the linked page will be displayed.
Text	Gets or sets the static text caption to display for the hyperlinks in the column.

Note that if you set the *Text* property, the *NavigateUrl* property, or both, all hyperlinks in the column will share the same caption and URL. Use the *DataTextField* and *DataNavigateUrlField* properties to associate the text and URL of the hyperlink with columns in the database. Finally, note that if *DataNavigateUrlField* and *NavigateUrl* are both set at the same time, the *DataNavigateUrlField* takes precedence.

The following code snippet demonstrates how to create a column of product names that, if clicked, displays a product information page in a frame. The *DataTextField* property indicates the source column for the hyperlink caption. The *DataNavigateUrlFormatString* property defines the format of the URL to use. The final URL is the productinfo.aspx page with a query string in which the ID argument is automatically set with the information read from the *DataNavigateUrlField* property—that is, *productid* in the following code:

```
<asp:hyperlinkcolumn runat="server" datatextfield="productname"
    headertext="Product"
    datanavigateurlfield="productid"
    datanavigateurlformatstring="productinfo.aspx?id={0}"
    target="ProductView">
    <itemstyle width="200px" />
</asp:hyperlinkcolumn>
```

The color of the hyperlinks can be controlled using CSS styles. In particular, you can set up a hover color with the following style block:

```
<style>a:hover {color:red;}</style>
```

Formatting URLs and Column Names

There are some limitations in the use of column and URL names in *DataGrid* programming. In particular, the *DataField* and *DataTextField* properties don't allow you to combine more field names. Because of this restriction, you can have a single column displaying first and last name only if such a column is included in the underlying data source.

Even though the *DataField* and *DataTextField* properties don't support expressions, you can resort to dynamically created expression-based columns to work around the issue. In Chapter 5, we saw how to create such columns. The following code adds a *FullName* column to a *DataTable* object:

```
table.Columns.Add("FullName", typeof(string),
    "lastname + ', ' + firstname");
```

The newly created *FullName* column is then bound to the desired *DataGrid* column as you would do with any other column. This solution might be more effective than having the database management system (DBMS) return a calculated column. Later in the chapter, we'll examine an even more effective trick based on templated columns.

By using the *DataTextField* and *DataNavigateUrlField* properties together, you can make the URL of the hyperlink parametric. However, by default you are limited to just one parameter—the value bound to the *DataNavigateUrlField* field. To use a hyperlink bound to any number of arguments, you should resort to templated columns, as we'll see later in the section "Templated Columns."

Using Frames

When the cell of a hyperlink column is clicked, the browser jumps to the specified URL and displays the linked contents in the window specified by the *Target* property. Allowable values for the *Target* property are a few special names like *_self*, *_blank*, *_top*, *_parent*, and any name that individuates a frame window both inline and located in a frameset. If no target has been set, the current page is refreshed.

The following code shows how to display in an Internet Explorer inline frame window the output of a hyperlink column:

```
<iframe name="ProductView" frameborder="no"
    height="100%" style="border:solid 1px;" />
```

The various code snippets considered so far are all excerpts from the sample application shown in Figure 6-4.

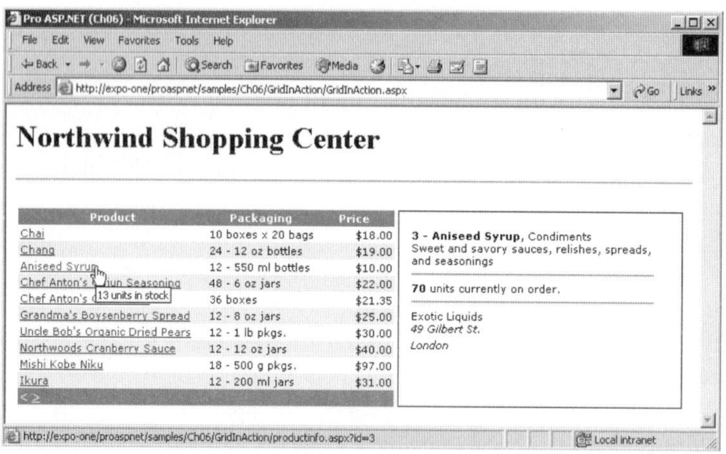

Figure 6-4 A realistic *DataGrid* control in action.

The white box on the right of the grid is an inline frame with a modified border named *ProductView*. Note that the name of the frame must begin with a letter and is case insensitive. The frame is refreshed whenever a hyperlink is clicked in the column.

> **Note** The *<iframe>* tag is part of the HTML 4.0 specification and is supported by Internet Explorer 4.0 and later. Downlevel Netscape browsers don't support it. Netscape 4.x browsers support a similar tag instead. The name of this browser-specific tag is *<layer>*.

Bindable ToolTips

As you can see in Figure 6-4, a ToolTip appears when the mouse hovers over the hyperlink. The ToolTip is not a bindable element in any type of column. However, with a relatively simple piece of code, you can make it bindable and use it to display extra fields on demand. In Figure 6-4, in fact, the ToolTip displays information about the number of items in stock for a given product.

To bind a data-source column to the *ToolTip* property of a Web control, you need a handler for the *ItemDataBound* event:

```
void ItemDataBound(object sender, DataGridItemEventArgs e) {
    ListItemType itemType = e.Item.ItemType;
    if (itemType == ListItemType.Item ||
        itemType == ListItemType.AlternatingItem)
    {
        DataRowView drv = (DataRowView) e.Item.DataItem;

        // Extract the first control in the first cell of the row
        WebControl webCtl = (WebControl) e.Item.Cells[0].Controls[0];
        WebCtl.ToolTip = drv["unitsinstock"] + " units in stock" ;
    }
}
```

In the handler, you first verify the type of the item being bound and then access the *DataItem* property. The test on the *ItemType* property serves to filter out the cases in which a selected or edited item is being bound to data. The *DataItem* property refers to the data object behind the particular row the grid is processing. As long as you use ADO.NET objects as the data source, the *DataItem* can be successfully cast to a *DataRowView* object.

> **Note** The *DataItem* property is set to a non-null object only during the *ItemDataBound* event. The same code won't work if attached to the *ItemCreated* event because at that time the *DataItem* property would be uninitialized.

You use the contents of the *DataItem* property to prepare a row-specific string and bind it to the *ToolTip* property of a particular control located anywhere in the row. In particular, the previous code snippet associates the ToolTip with the first control in the first cell—the <*a*> tag representing the hyperlink.

Command Columns

The *ButtonColumn* class represents a command column and contains a user-defined button for each cell in the column. Functionally similar to hyperlink columns, button columns are different because they generate a postback event on the same URL. To handle the click on a button, you write the *ItemCommand* event handler and check the *CommandName* property of the column button. Although the caption of each button can be bound to a data-source column, more often than not a button column has static text displayed through all the cells. Table 6-9 shows the properties that characterize the *ButtonColumn* class.

Table 6-9 Properties of the *ButtonColumn* Class

Property	Description
ButtonType	Gets or sets the type of button to display in the column—a link button or push button.
CommandName	Gets or sets a string that represents the command to perform during the postback after a button in the column is clicked.
DataTextField	Gets or sets a source column to bind to the caption of the button.
DataTextFormatString	Gets or sets the string that specifies the display format for the caption in each command button.
Text	Gets or sets the caption displayed in the buttons of the column.

The idea behind the button column is that you execute a particular action after the user clicks on a row. All buttons in the column are associated with some script code that posts the page back and executes the *ItemCommand* server-side procedure. Within that procedure, you use the command name to distinguish between multiple button columns and you use the *ItemIndex* property of the *DataGridItem* class to know about the particular row that was clicked.

Caution Unlike what happens with other actions related to button controls in ASP.NET pages, validation is not performed when buttons in a *ButtonColumn* are clicked. To perform validation in a *ButtonColumn*, use a templated column and add a *Button* or *LinkButton* control to it.

Handling a User's Clicking

To handle the user's clicking on the buttons in a *ButtonColumn*, you write a handler for the *DataGrid*'s *ItemCommand* event. The handler requires the following prototype:

```
void ItemCommandHandler(
    object sender,
    DataGridCommandEventArgs e);
```

The *DataGridCommandEventArgs* structure makes available three key properties: *Item*, which represents the grid item where the click occurred, plus *CommandName* and *CommandSource*. The *CommandName* property is the name of the command associated with the clicked button, whereas *CommandSource* is the button object that raised the click event. A fourth property is mentioned in the documentation—*CommandArgument*, which represents an argument for the command. This property, though, is not defined in the programming interface of the *ButtonColumn* class and subsequently is not used in the *ItemCommand* event handler.

The following code illustrates the typical structure of the *ItemCommand* handler:

```
void ItemCommand(object sender, DataGridCommandEventArgs e) {
    switch(e.CommandName)
    {
        case "AddToCart":
            AddToCart(e.Item.ItemIndex);
            break;
        ⋮
    }
}
```

In this sample, the *AddToCart* method is passed the ordinal position of the clicked item. In other cases, you might want to use that information to retrieve the key associated with the clicked row. As mentioned earlier, the *DataKeys* collection on the *DataGrid* does just that for you.

You can use a picture to define the caption of the button. The following code shows how to accomplish this by simply using an HTML string that includes a static *<img>* tag. This trick can be used, and works, with any type of column. However, it does not work if you change the button type from the default *linkbutton* to *pushbutton*.

```
<asp:buttoncolumn runat="server" headertext=""
    buttontype="linkbutton" commandname="AddToCart"
    Text="<img title='Add to cart...' border='no' src='images/cart.gif' />">
    <itemstyle width="30px" horizontalalign="right" />
</asp:buttoncolumn>
```

Figure 6-5 shows a grid with a button column that represents the user interface of a simple shopping cart.

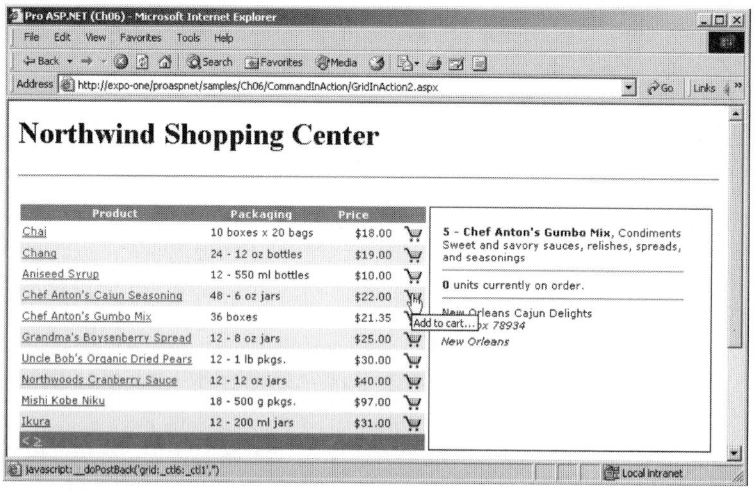

Figure 6-5 A *DataGrid* with a button column.

Implementing a Simple Shopping Cart

When the user clicks on the shopping cart button, the page posts back and requests the execution of the method, if any, associated with the *DataGrid*'s *ItemCommand* event. In the previous code snippet, this method is *AddToCart*. It takes the index of the clicked row, retrieves some information from the underlying data item, and then adds a new row to a memory-resident *DataTable* object. This data table is the effective shopping cart and is stored in *Session* to survive across page requests.

The shopping cart is set up the first time the page is accessed—that is, when *IsPostBack* returns *false*—and is retrieved from *Session* for successive requests. The underlying *DataTable* object contains three fields—*ProductName*, *Quantity*, and *Price*—and is bound to a second grid to let users view the current list of orders. As you can see in Figure 6-6, the shopping cart *DataGrid* shows a footer section in which the number of ordered items and the total price are computed and displayed. To make such calculations, we use the *Compute* method on the *DataTable* object.

```
// m_cart is the DataTable that contains the shopping cart
int totalItems = Convert.ToInt32(m_cart.Compute("Count(quantity)", ""));
int totalPrice = Convert.ToInt32(m_cart.Compute("Sum(price)", ""));

// Write the total number of items in the cart
e.Item.Cells[0].Text = totalItems.ToString();

// Write the total amount for the items in the cart
e.Item.Cells[2].HorizontalAlign = HorizontalAlign.Right;
e.Item.Cells[2].Text = String.Format("{0:c}", totalPrice);
```

The shopping cart grid also features a button column to remove an item from the cart. The associated code removes the clicked row from the *DataTable* that represents the shopping cart.

Figure 6-6 A simple shopping cart in action implemented using *DataGrid* controls.

The *Select* Button Column

A special type of button column is the select column. It is a normal *ButtonColumn* with a command name of *select*. When you click on such a column, the *DataGrid* automatically redraws the selected row using a different class of settings—those defined under the *<selecteditemstyle>* node. There is no need for you to write an *ItemCommand* handler; the described behavior is built in.

```
<asp:ButtonColumn runat="server" text="Select" CommandName="Select" />
```

The style of the selected row—at most one at a time—is set using the *SelectedItemStyle* property. It can be as easy as the following code:

```
<selecteditemstyle backcolor="cyan" />
```

The text of the button column can be replaced with a picture, as discussed earlier for the shopping cart. The change of the selected item is signaled with the *SelectedIndexChanged* event. However, before this event is fired, the application can handle the related *ItemCommand*. Note that the value of the *DataGrid*'s *SelectedIndex* property has not been changed yet when *ItemCommand* arrives. It is set to the new index when *SelectedIndexChanged* reaches the application.

This characteristic alone allows you to implement a nice feature—deselecting the item after two consecutive clicks. In this case, you first cache the old selected item in the *ItemCommand* event handler; then you compare this index with the new selected index within the *SelectedIndexChanged* event. If the two match, you're clicking on a selected item, which will then be unselected. To unselect a selected item, you set the *SelectedIndex* property to -1.

```
void ItemCommand(object sender, DataGridCommandEventArgs e) {
    // Command names ARE case-sensitive
    switch(e.CommandName) {
        case "select":
            m_currentSelectedIndex = grid.SelectedIndex;
            break;
        ⋮
    }
}
void SelectedIndexChanged(object sender, EventArgs e) {
    if (m_currentSelectedIndex == grid.SelectedIndex) {
        grid.SelectedIndex = -1;
        return;
    }
    ⋮
}
```

> **Note** The comparison of command names made within a *switch* statement is case-sensitive and must perfectly match the name of the command as specified in the column declaration. This said, the *select* command in the column declaration can be specified with any case and is understood by the *DataGrid* engine in a case-insensitive way.

If you want the clicked item to appear with the selected style while displaying the product information in a separate frame, you should switch to a button column instead of the hyperlink column.

```
<asp:buttoncolumn runat="server" DataTextField="productname"
    headertext="Product" commandname="select">
    <itemstyle width="200px" />
</asp:buttoncolumn>
```

When the *SelectedIndexChanged* fires, you change the *Src* attribute of the frame component and make it point to the given URL. You retrieve the key value associated with the selected row by using the *DataKeys* collection:

```
void SelectIndexChanged(object sender, EventArgs e)
{
    int productID = (int) grid.DataKeys[grid.SelectedIndex];
    string url = String.Format("productinfo.aspx?id={0}", productID);
    ProductView.Attributes["Src"] = url;
}
```

Note, though, that to programmatically configure the frame you must mark it as *runat=<;$QD>server<;$QD>*, as in the following code:

```
<iframe runat="server" id="ProductView" frameborder="no"
    height="100%" style="border:solid 1px;"></iframe>
```

Figure 6-7 shows the final result.

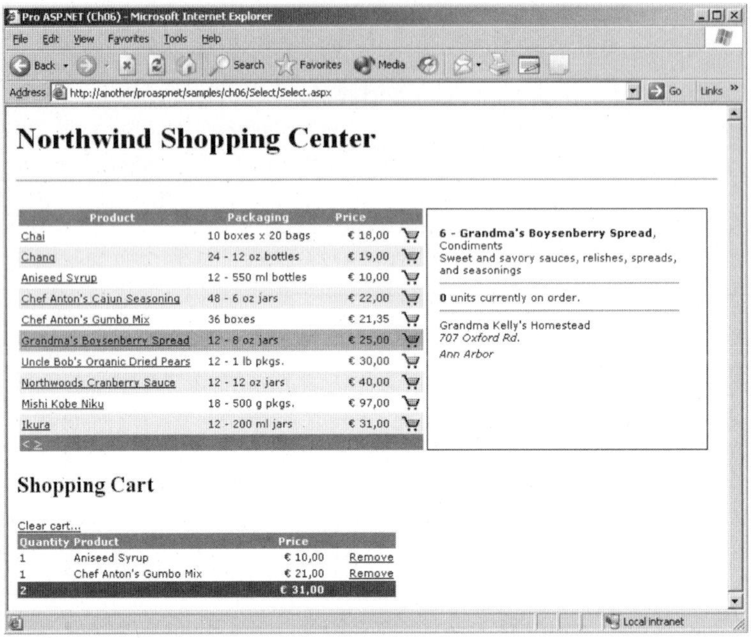

Figure 6-7 A shopping cart application in which the item being added or viewed is displayed with a selected style.

> **Caution** The selected item can be changed programmatically by setting the *SelectedIndex* property of the *DataGrid* control. Note, though, that if you select a new item through code, the *SelectedIndex-Changed* code is not automatically executed. As long as that code is important, you should add an explicit call in the method.

Enhancing the *DataGrid*

So far, we assumed that the *DataGrid* control was large enough to contain and display all the items in the data source. In a real-world scenario, though, a couple of additional functions are often needed—paging and sorting. The *DataGrid* control provides good built-in support for both functions. Also, the code you are required to write to implement these functions is limited and, more importantly, can be easily embedded in derived controls.

In this section, I'll focus the discussion on how to page and sort data through the grid. However, I'll do that paying particular attention to the programming interface of the control and blissfully skip over important aspects of data-driven applications, such as scalability and performance. Chapter 7 will be entirely devoted to rewriting the same application discussed here, but with more realistic considerations and optimization in mind. The content of this section focuses on the set of methods and events you can leverage on the *DataGrid* control.

Paging the Grid Content

In real-world scenarios, the size of a data source easily exceeds the real estate of the page. Data paging is the contrivance that many applications adopt to both gain in scalability and present a more helpful page to the user. Especially on the Web, displaying only a few rows at a time is a more effective approach than downloading hundreds of records that stay hidden most of the time. Setting up a data-paging mechanism requires a certain amount of work from both the control and the page side.

The *DataGrid* control provides some built-in facilities to let the programmer easily switch to a new page according to the user's clicking. The control needs to know how many items should be displayed per page, what type of functionality is required for the pager, and the data source to page through. In return for this, the control tracks the current page index, extracts the rows that fit into the particular page, and refreshes the user interface. Whenever the page index changes, an event is fired to the application—the *PageIndexChanged* event.

Caching the Data Source

The *DataGrid* control supports two types of paged data sources—built-in paging and custom paging. The standard way of paging is based on the assumption that all the records to scroll through are memory resident. The *DataGrid* is bound to the source all the time and extracts only the rows to display in each particular page. Note that the data source is not saved with the page's view state, so you are responsible for rebinding the data source at each postback.

Because the data source is lost at each response, caching is vital for effective standard paging. You download all the data the first time the page is accessed, store the data set into the application's *Cache* object or the session memory, and rebind until the application is closed or the session is over. In real-world applications, data caching is a double-edged sword. On one hand, it significantly speeds up data retrieval; on the other hand, it taxes the Web server's memory and potentially affects the overall scalability of the application. The scope of the data is another factor to consider carefully. If the data is shared by all sessions and doesn't get stale often, you can store it once in a global object. If you need to store a distinct copy of the data for each session, standard paging is probably not the smartest approach you can take, as it requires a lot of memory and, even worse, pushes an application architecture that doesn't scale really well. We'll delve much deeper into this topic in Chapter 7 when we'll introduce and discuss the second paging mechanism available—custom paging. For now, let's assume all the data is downloaded once and stored in the application's *Cache* object.

```
void Page_Load(object sender, EventArgs e) {
    if (!IsPostBack) {
        LoadDataFromDatabase();
        ⋮
    }
    ⋮
    BindData();
}
void LoadDataFromDatabase() {
    DataTable data = ExecuteQuery(cmdText, connString);
    Cache["AppData"] = data;
}
void BindData() {
    DataTable data = (DataTable) Cache["AppData"];
    ⋮
    grid.DataSource = data;
    grid.DataBind();
}
```

As this code demonstrates, the data is loaded only once and cached in memory. Whenever the page posts back, data is retrieved from the cache and bound to the *DataGrid* control.

Built-In Paging Support

To enable paging in a *DataGrid* control, you must set the *AllowPaging* property to *true*. When the property is turned on, the control user interface automatically acquires an extra component—the grid pager. The pager is a built-in toolbar with links to move from one page to the next or the previous. You normally configure the pager declaratively by specifying the working mode and a few visual settings. The maintenance of the component is in the care of the *DataGrid* control. The *PageSize* property lets you control the number of rows each page should contain. By default, this value is set to 10.

After turning the pager on, you're only halfway done. The pager is displayed and updated, but it's not functional until you write and register a handler for the *DataGrid*'s *PageIndexChanged* event.

```
<asp:datagrid runat="server" id="grid"
    ⋮
    allowpaging="true"
    onpageindexchanged="PageIndexChanged">
```

The delegate for the *PageIndexChanged* event is shown below. It passes down to the handler a data structure of type *DataGridPageChangedEventArgs*.

```
public delegate void DataGridPageChangedEventHandler(
    object source,
    DataGridPageChangedEventArgs e
);
```

The class inherits from *EventArgs* and features two extra properties—*CommandSource* and *NewPageIndex*. The former represents the source of the event. Because the event is fired only when a button in the pager is clicked, the event source is nothing more than the pager itself—a *DataGridItem* object. The *NewPageIndex* property contains the updated index of the page to show. The *DataGrid* internal engine calculates the correct index of the new page based on the button the user actually clicked.

The following code shows the typical (and minimal) page-changed handler for a *DataGrid* control. It sets the grid's *CurrentPageIndex* property with the new page index and rebinds to the data.

```
void PageIndexChanged(object sender, DataGridPageChangedEventArgs e)  {
    grid.CurrentPageIndex = e.NewPageIndex;
    BindData();
}
```

When the *DataGrid*'s *DataBind* method executes, the control extracts from the data source the subset of rows that fits into the current page. Those records are loaded into the *Items* collection and are used to generate the HTML output for the control.

Just as with row selection, you can programmatically change the page by updating the value of the *CurrentPageIndex* property. However, also in this case no related event is ever fired to the application. Another little gotcha you might want to be aware of occurs when you page a grid with a selected row or a row that is currently being edited. Changing the page doesn't reset the value of *SelectedIndex* and *EditItemIndex* properties. As a result, if you have selected, say, the third item on a page and move to the next page, the third item will also be selected on the new page. To avoid this, you can reset the *SelectedIndex* property to -1 in the *PageIndexChanged* event handler.

```
void PageIndexChanged(object sender, DataGridPageChangedEventArgs e)  {
    // Cancels the selection
    grid.SelectedIndex = -1;
    ProductView.Attributes["Src"] = "about:blank";

    grid.CurrentPageIndex = e.NewPageIndex;
    BindData();
}
```

The preceding code clears the selection index and frame upon page changes.

Customizing the Pager Component

The pager component is a table row made of a single cell that spans the whole width of the grid. You can obtain a reference to the pager in two ways—either through the *CommandSource* member of the *DataGridPageChangedEventArgs* data structure during the *PageIndexChanged* event or through the event data available within the *ItemCreated* event. In particular, the *ItemCreated* event is useful because it allows you to customize the pager structure beyond imagination. For example, you could add ToolTips to existing links, insert new link buttons, and even embed a completely user-defined pager. I'll demonstrate this in Chapter 7.

The *DataGrid* control provides some built-in properties to also let you declaratively customize the pager bar. In particular, you can choose between two display modes—numeric pages and next-prev mode. By default, the pager is made of two link buttons: one pointing to the previous page and one pointing to the next page. The default text that is associated with these links is < for the previous button and > for the next button. You can change the text for each link using the *PrevPageText* and *NextPageText* properties. The text replacement can occur both declaratively and programmatically. In the latter case, you do it through the *PagerStyle* property of the *DataGrid* control. The following code, on the other hand, shows how to proceed declaratively:

```
<pagerstyle backcolor="gray" forecolor="white" font-name="webdings"
    font-size="12pt" prevpagetext="3" nextpagetext="4" />
```

The font of the pager is set to *Webdings*, in which the strings 3 and 4 are equivalent to the characters ◀ and ▶.

The display mode of the pager is controlled by the *Mode* property, whose acceptable values are *NumericPages* and *NextPrev*. The *Mode* property takes its values from the *PagerMode* enumeration. The default setting is *NextPrev* and results in two buttons, one to move to the previous page and one to jump to the next page. The *DataGrid* control automatically enables and disables the links according to the current page.

When working in numeric pages mode, the pager displays as many links as there are pages in the data source. The *PageCount* read-only property informs you about the total number of available pages. Figure 6-8 shows the two pager modes.

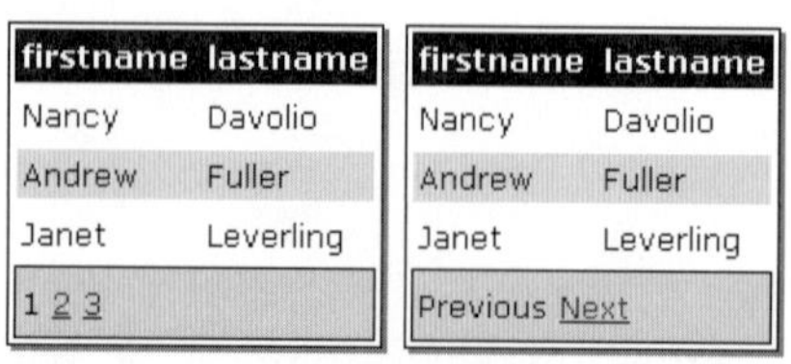

Figure 6-8 The two pager modes, face to face.

In numeric pages mode, the pager shows the index of the current page as plain, nonclickable text. On the other hand, there's no explicit information about the current page index in the default mode. This information can be added manually using the advanced customization mechanism supplied by the *ItemCreated* event. The following code inserts a new label control with page information between the page links:

```
if (e.Item.ItemType == ListItemType.Pager) {
    if (cartGrid.PagerStyle.Mode == PagerMode.NextPrev) {
        TableCell pager = e.Item.Cells[0];
        Label ctl = new Label();
        ctl.Font.Name = "verdana";
        ctl.Font.Size = FontUnit.Point(8);
        ctl.Text = String.Format(" <b>Page {0}</b> ",
            1 + cartGrid.CurrentPageIndex);
        pager.Controls.AddAt(1, ctl);
    }
}
```

The final results are shown in Figure 6-9.

Quantity	Product	Price	
1	Chang	€ 19,00	Remove
1	Chef Anton's Cajun Seasoning	€ 22,00	Remove
1	Northwoods Cranberry Sauce	€ 40,00	Remove
1	Uncle Bob's Organic Dried Pears	€ 30,00	Remove
5		€ 142,00	
◂ Page 1 ▸			

Figure 6-9 Page information dynamically inserted between the links of a pager.

Sorting the Data

To enable the *DataGrid*'s sorting capabilities, you set the *AllowSorting* property to *true*. When sorting is enabled, the *DataGrid* gains the ability of rendering the header text of columns as links. You can associate each column with a sorting expression by using the *SortExpression* property. A sorting expression is any comma-separated sequence of column names. Each column name can be enriched with an order qualifier such as DESC or ASC. DESC indicates a descending order, while ASC denotes the ascending order. The ASC qualifier is the default; if omitted, the column is sorted ascendingly. The following code sets up the *DataGrid* column for sorting on the *productname* data source column:

```
<columns>
    <asp:buttoncolumn runat="server"
        DataTextField="productname"
        HeaderText="Product"
```

```
            SortExpression="productname" />
    ⋮
</columns>
```

As Figure 6-10 shows, the header of the column is rendered as a link.

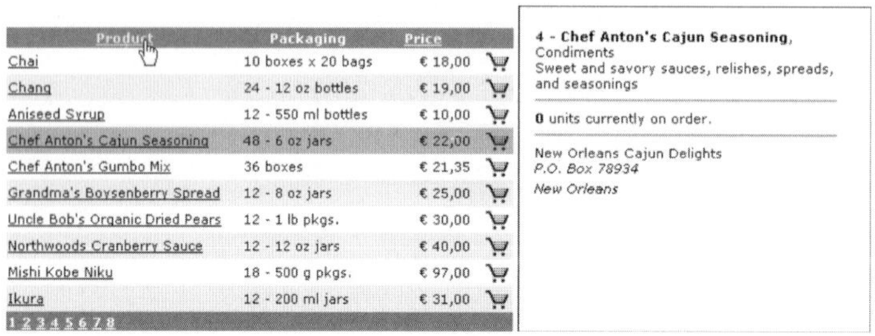

Figure 6-10 A *DataGrid* with a couple of sortable columns.

When you click the header of the column, the page posts back and runs the code associated with the *SortCommand* event.

```
<asp:datagrid runat="server"
    ⋮
    onsortcommand="SortCommand" />
```

The *DataGridSortCommandEventArgs* structure contains an extra property named *SortExpression*, which contains the sort expression of the column.

```
void SortCommand(object sender, DataGridSortCommandEventArgs e)
{
    // sort the data source
    // bind the data source
}
```

The event handler must accomplish two tasks—sorting the source and binding the data back to the grid. The sorting can take place in any way that is suitable to your application. Typically, if you're working with cached data (as we're doing now), you use the sorting capabilities of the ADO.NET objects. Otherwise, you can run another query against the DBMS and obtain a properly sorted recordset.

Let's modify the *BindData* method to make it capable of supporting sorted views of data. The code first retrieves the data from the *Cache* object and then sorts it using a *DataView* object. (See Chapter 5.)

```
void SortCommand(object sender, DataGridSortCommandEventArgs e) {
    ViewState["DataSortExpression"] = e.SortExpression;
    BindData();
}
void BindData() {
    DataTable data = (DataTable) Cache["AppData"];
```

```
    DataView dv = data.DefaultView;
    dv.Sort = (string) ViewState["DataSortExpression"];
    grid.DataSource = dv;
    grid.DataBind();
}
```

We need to pass the sort expression from the *SortCommand* method to the *BindData* method, which will actually prepare and bind the sorted view of data to the grid. Judging from the preceding code, there would be no need to use the view state. (As we'll discuss in more detail in Chapter 14, minimizing the use of the view state is a key factor in ASP.NET optimization.) You could actually pass the sort expression as an argument to the *BindData* method, but that would work only to sort data after a user click. If you don't save the sort expression in some sort of persistent location (*Session* is fine as well), that information would get lost with the next postback. In particular, you lose the sort as soon as you move to the next page.

> **Caution** Caching a *DataView* to feed the *DataGrid*'s built-in paging engine will not work because the *DataView* class does not store any data. Storing a *DataView* would simply cache the indexes of an underlying *DataTable* object. Unfortunately, though, there will be no track of that table across postbacks if you don't cache it too!

Auto-Reverse Sorting

Although functional, the sorting mechanism discussed so far is too simplistic and unusable for real-world applications. First, the user has no feedback about the column the data is sorted by. Second, users might want to reverse the order of the data while maintaining the same sort expression. Auto-reverse sorting is a feature that automatically switches from ascending to descending order, and vice versa, when you click a column that is already sorted.

The *ViewState*-based sorting mechanism we discussed earlier already provides a firm infrastructure to build auto-reverse sorting.

```
void SortCommand(object sender, DataGridSortCommandEventArgs e)
{
    // Cache the column sort expression
    string newExpr = e.SortExpression;

    // Compare the new and the cached sort expression. If the two
    // match, then a DESC qualifier is silently appended.
    string oldExpr = (string) ViewState["DataSortExpression"];
    if (oldExpr == newExpr)
```

```
        ViewState["DataSortExpression"] = newExpr + " DESC";
    else
        ViewState["DataSortExpression"] = newExpr;

    // Bind the data
    BindData();
}
```

Any information stored in the page's *ViewState* persists across two successive requests for the same page. In light of this, the current sort expression is available while processing the next request along with the expression associated with the clicked column. If the two expressions match, you're clicking on an already sorted column. This behavior is normally a prelude to reversing the order of the sort.

The code just shown does exactly that, at least in a good number of circumstances. There's an implicit assumption in the preceding listing. It tacitly assumes no sort expression in any columns would ever use the (redundant) keyword ASC to denote an ascending order; it also assumes no descending order is requested. As long as any sort expression is made of a single column name with no order qualifier, the code would work perfectly in providing auto-reverse sorting.

> **Caution** The sorting infrastructure described here needs some improvement to work in all cases regardless of the sort expressions used. In particular, it has a couple of shortcomings. It doesn't work well if multicolumn sorting is used and if a column must be sorted in a descending way by default. A more general approach entails writing a function to parse all the columns in the expression and invert the order for each of them. This approach is described in detail in my book *Building Web Solutions with ASP.NET and ADO.NET* (Microsoft Press, 2002).

Providing Feedback About Sorting

To give some feedback to the user about the sorted column, you need to programmatically modify the header of the column. You hook up the creation of the header by writing an *ItemCreated* event handler.

```
void ItemCreated(object sender, DataGridItemEventArgs e)
{
    switch(e.Item.ItemType){
        case ListItemType.Header:
            SetupHeader(e);
            break;
```

```
    }
}
void SetupHeader(DataGridItemEventArgs e)
{
    // Is the current sort expression descending?
    string sortExpr = (string) ViewState["DataSortExpression"];
    bool isDesc = sortExpr.EndsWith(m_DESC);

    // Remove the DESC keyword from the sort expression
    string pureSortExpr = sortExpr.Replace(m_DESC, "");

    // Loop through columns to find a matching expression
    for (int i=0; i<grid.Columns.Count; i++)
    {
        // Draw the glyph to reflect sorting direction. The
        // glyph is rendered through an extra label
        string colSortExpr = grid.Columns[i].SortExpression;
        if (pureSortExpr == colSortExpr && colSortExpr != "")
        {
            TableCell cell = e.Item.Cells[i];
            Label lblSorted = new Label();
            lblSorted.Font.Name = "webdings";
            lblSorted.Font.Size = FontUnit.XSmall;
            lblSorted.Text = (isDesc ? " 6" :" 5");
            cell.Controls.Add(lblSorted);
        }
    }
}
```

The label added alongside the header text is a webding glyph that represents a triangle pointed up (as in Figure 6-11) or down.

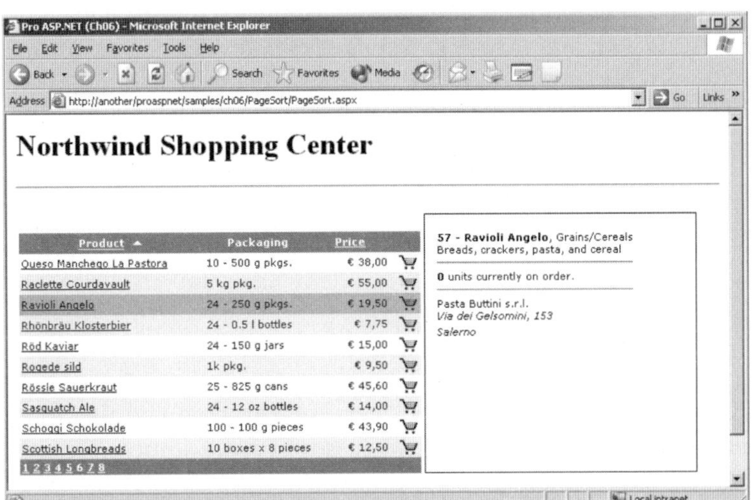

Figure 6-11 An auto-reverse *DataGrid* providing feedback about the current sort.

> **Note** How can you return to the original sort once you sorted the data source by clicking on column headers? To restore the original sort, you simply clear the current expression and refresh the data.

Templated Columns

Templated columns allow you to create combinations of HTML text and server controls to design a custom layout for any column. The controls within a templated column can be bound to any combination of fields in the data source. In particular, you can group more fields in a single expression and even embellish the expression with HTML attributes such as boldface or italic style. Templates are column-specific and cannot be applied to autogenerated columns. If you want more columns to share the same template, you can duplicate the code only in the ASP.NET page for each column.

A templated column is recognized by the <*TemplateColumn*> tag and rendered by the *TemplateColumn* class. The body of the tag can contain up to four different templates: *ItemTemplate*, *EditItemTemplate*, *HeaderTemplate*, and *FooterTemplate*. Just as any other column type, a templated column can have a header text and a sort expression. Templated columns, though, do not have an explicit data source field to bind. To bind a template column to one or more data fields, you use a data-binding expression and the *DataBinder* class. The *DataBinder* class provides a simpler syntax than data-binding expressions, but it doesn't let you obtain more than single-value data binding. In particular, you use the *DataBinder*'s *Eval* method to evaluate data-bound expressions at run time and return the value properly cast. For example, the following code snippet shows a templated column that mimics the behavior of a *BoundColumn* object associated with the *lastname* column:

```
<asp:templatecolumn runat="server" headertext="Last Name">
    <itemtemplate>
        <asp:label runat="server" Text='<%#
             DataBinder.Eval(Container.DataItem, "lastname") %>' />
    </itemtemplate>
</asp:templatecolumn>
```

By using *DataBinder.Eval*, you can access any number of fields in the currently bound data source. In addition, you can combine them in any order to obtain any sort of expression, which is otherwise impossible using a simpler bound or button column.

Available Templates

ItemTemplate is the property that lets you define the layout and content of each cell in the column. Other available templates would let you define the structure of the column header (*HeaderTemplate*) and footer (*FooterTemplate*). Furthermore, you can decide the behavior and appearance of the column when a cell is being edited through the *EditItemTemplate* template. I'll have more to say about column in-place editing in the later section "DataGrid In-Place Editing." Table 6-10 summarizes the available column templates and gives a hint about their usage.

Table 6-10 Supported Column Templates

Template Name	Usage

ItemTemplate	Contains the template for the items in a *DataGrid* column.
	`<ItemTemplate>`
	`  <asp:label runat="server" text= '<%# ... %>'`
	`</ItemTemplate>`
	You can use any combination of HTML text and ASP.NET controls to populate the column.

EditItemTemplate	Controls the contents of the item selected for editing in the column of the *DataGrid* control. Places the controls you need for editing the cell between the opening and closing *<EditItemTemplate>* tags.
	`<EditItemTemplate>`
	`  <asp:textbox runat="server" text= '<%# ... %>'`
	`</EditItemTemplate>`

HeaderTemplate	Contains the template for the heading section.
	`<HeaderTemplate>`
	`  <asp:label runat="server" text= "Header">`
	`</HeaderTemplate>`
	If you omit this template, the column header is rendered with a label, or with a hyperlink if sorting is enabled. By specifying a custom template, you make yourself responsible to provide the user interface needed to enable sorting on the column.

FooterTemplate	Contains the template for the footer section of the column. The default value is a null reference.
	`<FooterTemplate>`
	`  <asp:label runat="server" text= "...">`
	`</FooterTemplate>`
	The footer is displayed only if the *ShowFooter* property of the *DataGrid* is set to *true*.

The template properties in the table are exposed by the *TemplateColumn* class as data members of a type that inherits from the *ITemplate* interface. Template-based properties are declaratively set with plain text in the layout of ASP.NET pages. You can programmatically define a template property by writing and instantiating a class that implements the *ITemplate* interface.

In addition to templates, the *TemplateColumn* class provides a few style properties—*ItemStyle*, *HeaderStyle*, and *FooterStyle*—that you use to customize the appearance of items on a per-column basis. The usage of these properties is nearly identical to the same properties seen for other types of columns.

Combining Multiple-Source Columns

A template column is typically used to combine multiple data-source columns into a single *DataGrid* column. A template column allows you to bind, say, the last and first name of an employee to the same column using some HTML styles to make it even more compelling. The following code snippet demonstrates how to concatenate the first and last name:

```
<itemtemplate>
    <%# "<b>" + DataBinder.Eval(Container.DataItem, "lastname") +
        "</b>, " + DataBinder.Eval(Container.DataItem, "firstname") %>
</itemtemplate>
```

The *DataBinder.Eval* method takes two arguments, the second of which is the name of the data-source column. The first argument is the data object bound to the particular row being processed. The *Container.DataItem* expression returns the *DataItem* property on the underlying *DataGrid* item.

The item template can be described in terms of plain ASP.NET text as well as resorting to some ASP.NET layout code. The following code snippet rewrites the same code discussed a moment ago, but it uses a *Label* control and sets the *ToolTip* property:

```
<itemtemplate>
    <asp:label runat="server"
        text='<%# "<b>" + DataBinder.Eval(Container.DataItem, "lastname") +
        "</b>, " + DataBinder.Eval(Container.DataItem, "firstname") %>'
        tooltip='<%# "Born on " +
        DataBinder.Eval(Container.DataItem, "birthdate", "{0:d}") %>' />
</itemtemplate>
```

As you can see, the *DataBinder.Eval* method features a third argument, which is the format string for the bound value. The output generated by the code is shown in Figure 6-12.

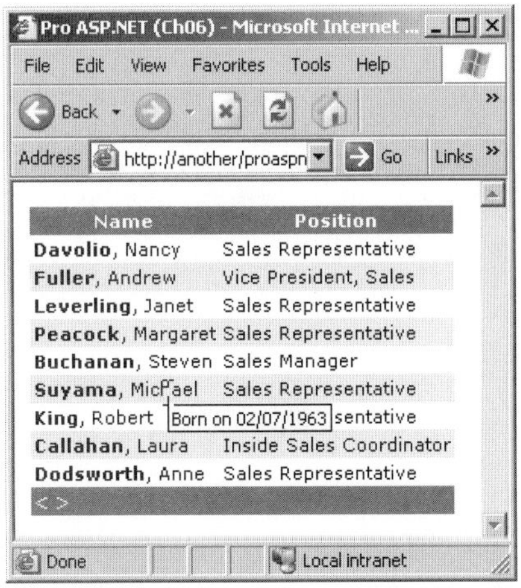

Figure 6-12 A templated column employs custom styles and bound ToolTips.

Using Multiple Arguments with HyperLink Columns

As we saw earlier, the *HyperLinkColumn* class can navigate to parametric and data-bound URLs. The column expands arguments automatically but doesn't let you specify more than one argument per URL. More often than not, you'll find this limitation too restrictive. Is there a way to have a hyperlink column with a URL that embeds multiple arguments? Templated columns make this possible. The HTML output of a *HyperLinkColumn* cell is an *<a>* tag. If you create a templated column and make it output an anchor element, you can closely control the structure of the resultant hyperlink and specify as many data-bound arguments as needed.

The following code defines a *DataGrid* templated column that provides the same functionality as a hyperlink column but supports up to four URL arguments:

```
<asp:TemplateColumn runat="server">
<itemtemplate>
    <a runat="server"
        target="frInfo"
        href='<%# "moreinfo.aspx" +
        "?id=" + DataBinder.Eval(Container.DataItem, "employeeid") +
        "&first=" + DataBinder.Eval(Container.DataItem, "firstname") +
        "&last=" + DataBinder.Eval(Container.DataItem, "lastname") +
        "&position=" + DataBinder.Eval(Container.DataItem, "title")
        %>'>More...
    </a>
</itemtemplate>
</asp:TemplateColumn>
```

The structure of the template is extremely simple and just builds up an anchor tag in which the *href* attribute and the text are data bound to as many fields as needed. Figure 6-13 shows the final results.

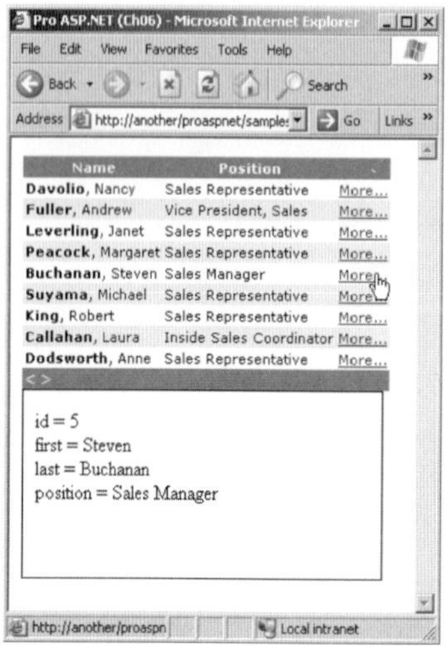

Figure 6-13 A templated column that acts as a multiparameter hyperlink column.

> **Note** To some extent, templated columns are functionally similar to hooking up the *ItemCreated* event and can modify the *DataGrid* items on the fly. Templates are extremely flexible, but with them you pay parsing costs that make them less efficient overall than hooking an event. Although the difference is not always relevant, you should avoid templates if you have another way to accomplish the same task.

Enhancing the Shopping Cart Application

A templated column allows you to enhance the shopping cart by adding the possibility of specifying how many items of a given product will be purchased. The idea is to replace the button column used for adding items to the shopping cart with a template column in which the button is preceded by a text box, as in Figure 6-14.

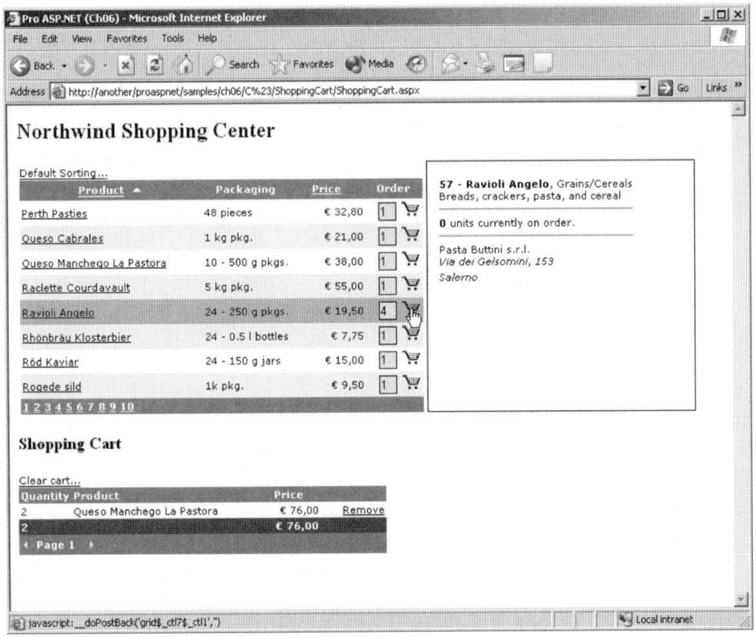

Figure 6-14 Using a templated column to enhance the shopping cart application.

The source code of the template looks like the following:

```
<asp:templatecolumn runat="server" headertext="Order">
    <itemstyle width="60px" horizontalalign="right" />
    <itemtemplate>
        <asp:textbox runat="server" id="qty" text="1"
            width="20px" maxlength="1"
            font-size="x-small" backcolor="yellow"
            style="border:solid 1px;" />
        <asp:linkbutton runat="server"
            commandname="AddToCart"
            text="<img title='Add to cart...' border='no'
                src='images/cart.gif' />" />
    </itemtemplate>
</asp:templatecolumn>
```

The template is composed of a text box and link button whose text is a static *<img>* tag. The procedure to handle the click doesn't need to change. Reading the value entered in the text box when the page posts back to add to the shopping cart is a bit more tricky. You must retrieve the text-box control in the subtree of controls rooted in the templated cell. You can do that either by index or by name. To find a control by name in its proper naming container, you use the *FindControl* method. Be sure the *FindControl* method is called on the *DataGrid* item object, not on the page or anywhere else. The following code shows how to rewrite the *AddToCart* method to add the specified number of items:

```
void AddToCart(DataGridItem item, int rowIndex)
{
    :
    int defaultQuantity = 1;
    TextBox ctl = (TextBox) item.FindControl("qty");
    if (ctl != null)
        defaultQuantity = Convert.ToInt32(ctl.Text);

    row["quantity"]= defaultQuantity;
    row["productname"] = tableRow["productname"];
    row["price"] = (decimal) (defaultQuantity *
        Convert.ToDecimal(tableRow["unitprice"]));
    m_cart.Rows.Add(row);
    :
}
```

The *DataGridItem* object that gets passed to *AddToCart* is the *e.Item* object taken from the event data:

```
void ItemCommand(object sender, DataGridCommandEventArgs e)
{
    // Command names ARE case-sensitive
    switch(e.CommandName)
    {
        case "AddToCart":
            AddToCart(e.Item, e.Item.ItemIndex);
            break;
        :
    }
}
```

DataGrid In-Place Editing

A *DataGrid* control displays mostly read-only data. If editing is needed, you select the row to update and post a request for another page. The new page contains an edit form with input fields and links to persist or reject the changes. This is probably the most effective pattern for editing data over the Web and certainly the pattern that provides the highest level of flexibility. With *DataGrid* controls, though, another simpler, but just as effective, model of data editing is possible. The new model is known as in-place editing and mimics the behavior of an Excel worksheet. When you trigger the event that begins the editing phase, the visible part of the grid is redrawn and—like cells in Excel—the row selected for editing is rendered in a different way, using text-box controls instead of literals and labels. At the same time, the *DataGrid* control completes its own user interface with a couple of button links to allow you to commit or rollback changes.

In-place editing doesn't require much work to be completely set up but, at the same time, is not appropriate for all types of applications and not functional in all operating contexts. All in all, if you have to edit the content of single and relatively small tables that have no special validation or business logic to apply, in-place editing is extremely handy and powerful.

Configuring the Built-In Edit Engine

The key object for in-place editing is the *EditCommandColumn* class. The column adds a link button to all rows of the grid. When the link is clicked, the page posts back and the cells of the row are drawn in edit mode. How a column behaves in edit mode depends on the column type. For example, button and hyperlink columns are completely ignored in edit mode. Bound and templated columns, on the other hand, change their rendering when the row is being edited. In particular, bound columns are rendered using text boxes in place of literals, whereas templated columns display the contents of the *<EditItemTemplate>* section, if any. Here is a typical declaration for an edit column:

```
<asp:editcommandcolumn runat="server"
    EditText="Edit" UpdateText="OK" CancelText="Cancel">
    <itemstyle width="30px" horizontalalign="center" backcolor="yellow" />
</asp:editcommandcolumn>
```

The properties specific to the *EditCommandColumn* class are listed in Table 6-11.

Table 6-11 Properties of the *EditCommandColumn* Class

Property	Description
ButtonType	Gets or sets the button type for the column. Acceptable values are defined in the *ButtonType* enumeration. Default is *LinkButton*.
CancelText	Gets or sets the text to display for the Cancel command button when the row is being edited.
EditText	Gets or sets the button text to display to let the user click and edit the contents of the row.
UpdateText	Gets or sets the text to display for the Update command button when the row is being edited.

The edit column initially displays a link (or a push) button to click to enter in the edit mode. The text displayed in each cell of the column is not data-bound but can only be a literal string (for example, Edit) or anything else you can define through HTML tags (for example, an image). The text to use is read through the *EditText* property. When the row enters in edit mode, the *EditItemIndex* property is automatically set to the 0-based index of the row, the cells are rendered using text boxes, and the Edit button is replaced with two new buttons—one to save the changes and one to cancel. The text for these two buttons can be controlled using the *UpdateText* and *CancelText* properties.

Clicking any edit buttons fires an ad hoc event—*EditCommand*, *UpdateCommand*, or *CancelCommand*—for which programmers should provide handlers.

```
<asp:datagrid runat="server" id="grid"
    ⋮
    oneditcommand="EditCommand"
    oncancelcommand="CancelCommand"
    onupdatecommand="UpdateCommand">
    ⋮
</asp:datagrid>
```

The *DataGrid* control provides a built-in mechanism for editing rows, but the programmer is still responsible for supplying the actual code that updates the underlying data source. Likewise, the programmer is responsible for any start-up or clean-up operation that needs to be accomplished when the editing begins or is canceled. The following code snippet shows typical event handlers for in-place editing:

```
void EditCommand(object sender, DataGridCommandEventArgs e) {
    // Set the current item to edit mode
    grid.EditItemIndex = e.Item.ItemIndex;

    // Refresh the grid
    BindData();
}

void CancelCommand(object sender, DataGridCommandEventArgs e) {
    // Cancel edit mode for the row
    grid.EditItemIndex = -1;

    // Refresh the grid
    BindData();
}

void UpdateCommand(object sender, DataGridCommandEventArgs e) {
    // Cancel edit mode for the row
    grid.EditItemIndex = -1;

    // Update the data source
    // *** do something here

    // Refresh the grid
    BindData();
}
```

Figure 6-15 shows the two phases of the row-editing process.

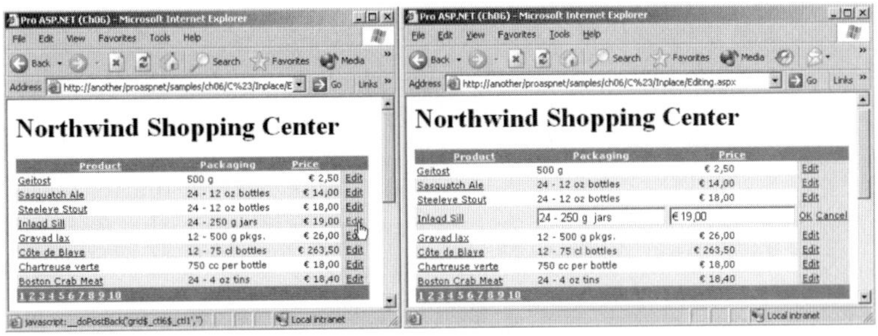

Figure 6-15 The in-place editing process in action.

Setting Up the Template of the Row

As you can see in Figure 6-15, there's a significant difference in the style of the row before and during the editing. Any visual setting you apply to the row in read mode is lost when the row enters the edit mode. To obtain a consistent user interface, there's no other way than intervening when the row is created—that is, when the *ItemCreated* event fires for an item of type *EditItem*.

```
void ItemCreated(object sender, DataGridItemEventArgs e) {
    ListItemType itemType = e.Item.ItemType;
    switch(itemType)
    {
        case ListItemType.EditItem:
            SetupEditItem(e);
            break;
        ⋮
    }
}
```

In this case, the *DataGridItem* is the table row that contains the row to edit. You can walk your way through the various cells and modify font and styles at your convenience. For example, the following code changes the style of the all text boxes:

```
void SetupEditItem(DataGridItemEventArgs e) {
    foreach(TableCell cell in e.Item.Cells)
    {
        // Skip if a readonly cell is found
        if (cell.Controls.Count <=0)
            continue;

        Control ctl = cell.Controls[0];
        if (ctl is TextBox)
        {
            TextBox t = (TextBox) ctl;
            t.BackColor = Color.Yellow;
            t.BorderStyle = BorderStyle.Outset;
            t.BorderColor = Color.BlueViolet;
            t.BorderWidth = Unit.Point(1);
            t.Width = Unit.Percentage(100);
```

```
                t.Font.Name = "verdana";
                t.Font.Size = FontUnit.Point(8);
            }
        }
    }
```

The text that characterizes the link buttons can be made of HTML-rich text and include formatting and images as well. For example, the following code uses a GIF file for the edit text:

```
EditText="<img src='edit.gif' border='no' align='absmiddle' alt='Edit'>"
```

The final results are shown in Figure 6-16.

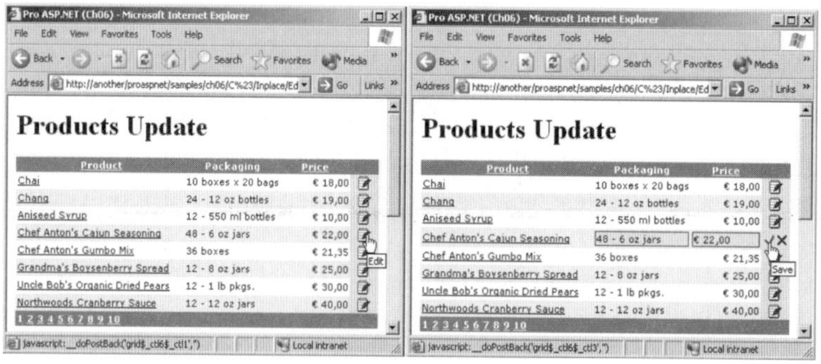

Figure 6-16 The in-place editing process in action after applying cosmetic changes.

Not all cells in a row are actually editable. As mentioned, cells belonging to hyperlink and button columns cannot be edited and cells of bound columns are editable by default. The *BoundColumn* class has a *Readonly* attribute that if set to *true* (*false* is the default) would make the cell read-only and leave it unaffected by the editing mode. By contrast, cells of templated columns are read-only by default and enter into edit mode only if you explicitly define an edit template.

> **Note** Just as for the row selection, the row editing mode is persisted across page changes. For example, suppose you are editing the third row on a page. If you jump to another page, the third row would automatically display in edit mode too. This happens because the *EditItemIndex* property—the property that determines which row is being edited—is never reset during the page changed postback. To avoid this behavior, reset the *EditItemIndex* property to -1 in your own *PageIndexChanged* event handler.

Validation and Edit Templates

The in-place editing, as we've built it so far, is simple and easy but comes with quite a long list of shortcomings. In particular, only the visible fields are updateable and the initial text of the text boxes defaults to the display text of the cell. As you can see in Figure 6-16, this is a bit impractical if you have formatting rules applied or computed columns. In addition, the use of automatically generated edit controls forces you to use indexes to retrieve the new values from text boxes and no validation or special input policies are possible. For example, you can't check whether a date or a ZIP code is really entered or figure out a way to force users to pick up values from a closed list.

All these issues are solved at the root if you don't use *DataGrid* in-place editing and resort to a more traditional approach based on ad hoc pages or user controls. However, by also using edit templates, the *DataGrid* in-place editing can be enhanced to some extent. Let's see how to edit the price of a product without formatting text and making sure that a valid price is entered.

The first step in accomplishing this is turning the unit price column into a templated column. The following code would do the job:

```
<asp:templatecolumn runat="server" headertext="Price">
    <itemstyle width="80px" horizontalalign="right" />
    <itemtemplate>
        <%# DataBinder.Eval(Container.DataItem, "unitprice", "{0:c}")%>
    </itemtemplate>
</asp:templatecolumn>
```

Replacing the original bound column with this one doesn't change the appearance of the page but produces one relevant effect—the Price column is no longer editable. Templated columns, in fact, are read-only by default. To make the price editable, we need to add an edit template, as shown here:

```
<asp:templatecolumn runat="server" headertext="Price">
⋮
<edititemtemplate>
    <asp:textbox runat="server" id="priceBox" backcolor="yellow"
        font-name="verdana" font-size="8pt" style="border:solid 1px;"
        text='<%#
          DataBinder.Eval(Container.DataItem, "unitprice", "{0:N}")%>'
    />
</edititemtemplate>
</asp:templatecolumn>
```

The column's edit template includes a text-box server control that we can configure as needed for fonts and styles. Not a minor point is the fact that we can now also explicitly set the ID of the control. The default text of the text box is set using the *DataBinder.Eval* method, for which we can choose the formatting rules that best apply. For example, *{0:N}* indicates that the price is displayed as a standard number with thousand separators and two decimal digits. Note that with templated columns, the *ItemCreated* trick we set up earlier for customizing the look and feel of the text box doesn't work any longer. If you want to control the visual settings of the text box, you can work on the control declaration in the template.

If validation is required, you simply add the validation control that best suits your needs. For example, you add a *RangeValidator* if you want to make sure the new value falls in a specified range:

```
<asp:RangeValidator runat="server" id="priceValidator"
    ControlToValidate="priceBox"
    Display="Dynamic"
    Text="<span title='Must be a price from 2,00 to 400,00.'>*</span>"
    MinimumValue="2,00" MaximumValue="400,00"
    Type="Currency" />
```

The type of the data in the control is set to *Currency* to allow for currency characters to be entered if needed. The *MinimumValue* and *MaximumValue* properties define the range of allowed values. As we saw in Chapter 3, the *Text* property indicates the short text to display alongside the text-box control should the validation not be successful. You normally set the *Text* property to an asterisk, an exclamation mark, or any expression that might serve to capture the user's attention. You might also set it to descriptive text, but this is sometimes impractical for space constraints. In this case, you store a short alert expression into *Text* and set the *ErrorMessage* property to a full description. *ErrorMessage* would be displayed only in the validation summary of the page, if any.

A smart trick to get the best of both solutions is associating an HTML ToolTip with the short alert text in the *Text* property. To obtain that, you can wrap the text in a *<span>* tag and set the *title* attribute as needed. When using a validation control in a *DataGrid* cell, you should always set the *Display* property to *Dynamic* to ensure that the label with the error message is created in the page only if strictly needed. This contrivance normally produces a better graphical result. Figure 6-17 shows the validation control in action.

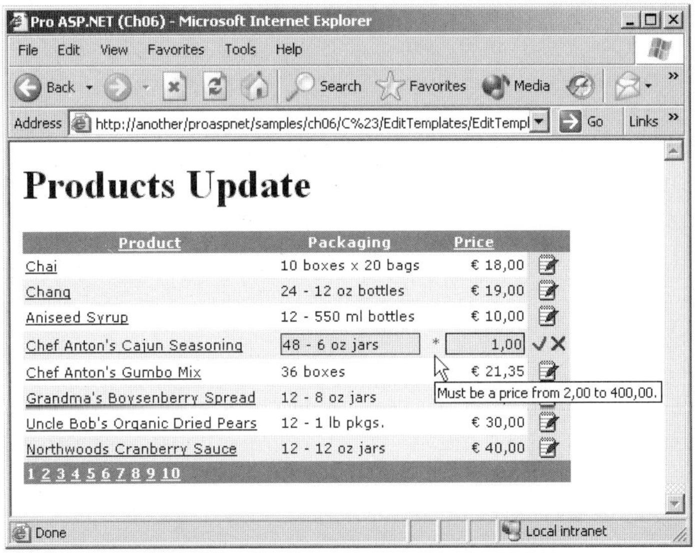

Figure 6-17 Validating the input values in a *DataGrid* control.

Note that validation on the page is performed only when the update command button is clicked.

Persisting Changes

The final step of in-place editing is persisting the changes to the underlying data source. Before performing the physical update, though, you must first retrieve the new values from the text boxes or drop-down lists in the editing cells. The code you use to retrieve values differs depending on whether the default or a custom edit template is used. When the user clicks to save the changes, the page posts back and executes any code associated with the *UpdateCommand* event.

To start out, the event handler resets to -1 the index of the row being edited and cancels the editing mode. Next, it retrieves the new values and prepares the commands needed to update the underlying data source. For Web applications, direct SQL commands are probably the fastest way to persist changes, at least when data conflicts are not critical events. On the other hand, when the logic of the application requires that the code update the *same* record read (that is, a record that has not been modified in the time between your reading and writing), then resorting to ADO.NET batch update allows you to exploit the framework facilities for data conflicts. (We covered batch updates in Chapter 5.)

Retrieving Input Values

To read the input values, you retrieve the instances of the corresponding controls and extract their contents. When the in-place editing feature is implemented in the default way—that is, without edit templates—the preferred way to retrieve the involved text boxes is by position.

```
// Retrieve the second column of the row
// (e is the event data (DataGridCommandEventArgs class))
Control = e.Item.Cells[1].Controls[0];
if (ctl == null)
    return;
string packaging = ((TextBox) ctl).Text;
```

The preceding code shows how to retrieve the value of the text box in the second column of the row. The index of the *Cells* collection is the 0-based position of the edited column. The index is absolute and doesn't consider any read-only column in the middle. Of the specified cell, you then take the first control, which is a *TextBox* control by design. Note that the value read out of the text box must be converted to the destination type—that is, the type of the corresponding source column. This feature alone makes it significantly more complex than using the default editing template with formatted columns. In fact, you must be able to read the column's value free of all formatting text (for example, the currency symbol).

You must identify input controls by position also because the text boxes are created by the *DataGrid* control and are given a predefined ID that you can only guess or determine empirically. All text boxes are created by the time the *ItemCreated* event fires, however. So by writing such an event handler, you could change the text-box ID on the fly and use a custom but unambiguous name. The following code snippet slightly enhances the code we discussed earlier to customize the style of the editing text boxes:

```
foreach(TableCell cell in e.Item.Cells)
{
    // Skip if a readonly cell is found
    if (cell.Controls.Count <=0)
        continue;

    Control ctl = cell.Controls[0];
    if (ctl is TextBox) {
        TextBox t = (TextBox) ctl;
        t.ID = "MyTextBox";
        ⋮
    }
}
```

The name of the underlying database column is a good (and unique) replacement for the system-provided ID.

If you use edit templates, things are easier because you use your own text boxes and give them your own IDs, which are fixed and unique. In this case, retrieving the input values is as easy as the following code:

```
// priceBox is the ID of the textbox in the edit template
ctl = item.FindControl("priceBox");
if (ctl == null)
    return;
double price = Convert.ToDouble(((TextBox) ctl).Text);
```

Using *FindControl* is easier to code and more readable, but slower than just using indexes and position-based access.

Updating the Data Source

Once you hold all the new data, updating the underlying data source is simply a matter of preparing and executing a SQL command. Using parameters makes code more clear and also constitutes an extra line of defense against malicious SQL attacks. Command parameters, in fact, are strongly typed and match exactly the database type. If you set up the command using parameters, a string would never be passed in place of a number, which is one of the typical ways SQL injections occur. (More on this in Chapter 15.)

```
// Prepare the command
string updText = "UPDATE products " +
                 "SET quantityperunit=@packaging, " +
                 "unitprice=@price WHERE productid=@productid";
SqlConnection cnn = new SqlConnection(connString);
SqlCommand cmd = new SqlCommand(updText, cnn);
cmd.Parameters.Add("@productID", SqlDbType.Int).Value = productID;
cmd.Parameters.Add("@packaging", SqlDbType.NVarChar).Value = packaging;
cmd.Parameters.Add("@price", SqlDbType.Money).Value = price;

// Execute the command
cnn.Open();
cmd.ExecuteNonQuery();
cnn.Close();
```

The command executes during the postback event that originates from the user's clicking of the Update link. After that, the data source must be re-bound to the *DataGrid* control for display purposes. However, an extra step might be needed this time. If you configured the grid to use cached data (as we did in this chapter), for the changes to show up you must invalidate and refresh the current cache. As a result, the complete code for the *UpdateCommand* event looks like the following:

```
void UpdateCommand(object sender, DataGridCommandEventArgs e)
{
    // Cancel edit mode for the row
    grid.EditItemIndex = -1;
```

```
    // Update the data source
    UpdateDataSource((int) grid.DataKeys[e.Item.ItemIndex], e.Item);

    // Reload the data and refresh the grid
    LoadDataFromDatabase();
    BindData();
}
```

The *DataGrid* in-place editing is quick and effective, but it also has the drawback of allowing for only one row at a time to be edited. If you want a full-page edit grid control, you must define all template columns and configure them to use data-bound text boxes rather than literals. If you do so, though, the update mechanism is entirely your own, but it doesn't require code different from the solutions we examined in this chapter.

Conclusion

In this chapter, we examined the *DataGrid* ASP.NET control, which is a type of component that all Web applications need to employ in one shape or another. All Web applications, in fact, at a certain point in their life cycle are called to display data. More often than not, this data is in tabular format.

As long as the data to display can be articulated in rows and columns, the *DataGrid* control is ideal to display it. The control provides facilities to select and edit single rows, page through a bound data source, and sort and filter views. In addition, you can customize all the cells in a column by using any data-bound template made of any combination of HTML and ASP.NET text. To top it off, a fair number of events signal to user applications the key events in the control's lifecycle. Good examples of such events are *ItemCreated* and *ItemDataBound*, just to name those that provide for the deepest types of customization. Other events such as *SelectedIndexChanged*, *ItemCommand*, and *PageIndexChanged* are more specific but equally useful.

The in-place editing feature is a piece of cake, as it is easy to configure and powerful to exploit. We could discuss the fact that this type of editing—designed to resemble Excel worksheets—is not appropriate for all applications and pages. However, as long as you can functionally afford the feature, in-place editing can save you a lot of coding and increase productivity by at least one order of magnitude.

So what should your opinion be about the *DataGrid* control after this chapter? The control is definitely the richest and most powerful of all ASP.NET Web controls. However, if you look at the amount of code we've put in all the pages we've built in this chapter, you can't help but have doubts. If the *DataGrid* is so powerful and feature-rich, why do we need to write all that code? The answer is not simple and probably touches Microsoft policies for public controls. Although incredibly rich with functions and settings, the *DataGrid* is only a small portion of a real-world control. For paging, editing, and sorting, it provides only an easily extensible infrastructure for which you have to write the missing, application-specific code.

Although the *DataGrid* control could be even richer than it is today in ASP.NET 1.1, no general-purpose control would ever be so perfect as to need virtually no customization code. The reason is that all applications have a grid of data to display, but all applications need their own grid. As a result, applications either use a generic grid to configure and customize programmatically or employ a tailor-made control in which extensions have been hard-coded once and for all. Fortunately, though, the *DataGrid* is part of an object-oriented framework, so deriving new classes is easier than ever before. Finally, note that we've used inline code for all the samples we developed in this chapter. Given the amount of code we had to write, a page code-behind class wouldn't have been a bad idea.

While introducing the chapter, we mentioned that the *DataGrid* is not the most flexible of all iterative data-bound controls. After that, we didn't do anything else but emphasize the flexibility of the control. What's up with that? The *DataGrid* is an extremely flexible control, but it can only display tables of data. Other components—the *DataList* and the *Repeater*—let you gain more precise control over the binding process and even produce a nontabular output. We'll examine other iterative controls in Chapter 9.

In the next chapter, we'll discuss ways to paginate and navigate through large amounts of data in a Web application. In particular, we'll focus on the importance of writing ad hoc SQL code to balance various contrasting requirements, such as minimizing the data to transfer, maximizing performance, and improving scalability.

Resources

- Building Web Solutions with ASP.NET and ADO.NET (Microsoft Press, 2002)
- Alternate by value (*http://www.aspnetpro.com/features/2003/02/asp200302de_f/asp200302de_f.asp*)
- Sort Data on the Fly (*http://www.aspnetpro.com/features/2002/12/asp200212wf_f/asp200212wf_f.asp*)
- Keep Your DataGrid Position (*http://www.aspnetpro.com/features/2002/12/asp200212ht_f/asp200212ht_f.asp*)
- Summary Rows in DataGrid Controls (*http://msdn.microsoft.com/library/en-us/dndive/html/data01102002.asp*)

7

Paging Through Data Sources

Men acquire a particular quality by constantly acting a particular way.... You become just by performing just actions, temperate by performing temperate actions, brave by performing brave actions.

—*Aristotle*

In real-world scenarios, pagination is an important issue when you have a lot of records to display. To preserve a good level of scalability and performance on the server, you might decide to show the records that form the key view of your application in equally sized pages. You would then want to create a pager bar that has a bunch of ad hoc buttons that allow users to navigate between pages. So with a data source, a sized view, and a pager bar, you are pretty much done; the *DataGrid* itself would do the job of paging the records.

As we saw in the previous chapter, setting up the *DataGrid* control to work in paging mode is easy and effective. First you enable data paging by setting the *AllowPaging* property to *true*. Next you decide the style for user-interface elements related to pagination. Internally, the *DataGrid* control takes care of extracting from the bound data source the records that fall in the range of the current page. When you work with large-sized data sources, the risk of taxing the Web server's memory too much is high. For mostly read-only data globally shared by all sessions, caching for pagination can be a feasible solution. However, the accuracy of this statement depends on the effective size of the data source. Caching a few dozen, or even hundreds, of records is much different than caching a few thousand!

If session-specific data is to be paged, binding and caching the entire data source should be avoided because the data would be loaded for each user, potentially degrading overall scalability. However, if you're determined to exploit the *DataGrid*'s built-in paging capabilities without caching data somewhere and somehow, you inevitably experience the paradox of pagination. The *DataGrid* control requires you to load and bind the data source at each request. If caching is not used, you execute a query at each request. You could end up querying for 1000 records (if that is the size of the entire data source) to display only the 20 that fit in the requested page.

Custom Paging with *DataGrid* Controls

In situations in which you have to display session-specific or highly volatile data, you can exploit another feature of the *DataGrid* control—custom pagination. When custom pagination is enabled, the control does not implement any algorithm to page over a bound data source. The *DataGrid* still supplies the built-in infrastructure for paging (the pager bar, informational properties, and events), but it expects the programmer to set the *DataSource* property with only the records to be displayed for a given page.

When working in custom-paging mode, the *DataGrid* control does not locate and extract the records that fall into the given page. It simply assumes all the records currently associated with the *DataSource* property form the page. The advantage is that only the records that fit into the page are held in memory, resulting in a significant savings in the amount of system resources used. Because the records are obtained by querying the database, you always display up-to-date data, which is a strict requirement for databases that get stale relatively quickly. A less pleasant side effect of this approach is that, depending on the database management system (DBMS) you're using and the style of the pager you expect to provide, coming up with a page-based query command might not be easy. In this chapter, though, we'll focus on providing basic strategies for custom paging.

The layout of the code you need to write is not significantly different whether you use default or custom pagination. You have to provide the content of the page in both cases—the whole source for built-in pagination, and only the current page if custom paging is turned on. There are clear differences in how the two approaches work in terms of overall performance and scalability. Factors that determine which method to use are (in order of priority):

1. How often your data gets stale and needs to be updated
2. The scope of the data, be it session or application
3. The size of the overall data source to page through

The more static your data is, the more you can exploit caching, both data and page-output caching. (We'll cover page-output caching in Chapter 14.) The more dynamic your data is, the more you should try to minimize the amount of data being read and stored. In systems that need to be highly–scalable, support a variable, and have a normally high number of concurrent users (not all Web systems are like this), you should also have a middle tier that can be scaled out to mitigate the impact that data retrieval has on performance.

Let's see how to turn custom pagination on for ASP.NET applications and examine the complications raised in real-world implementations.

Enabling Custom Pagination

To enable custom pagination for ASP.NET *DataGrid* controls, you must ensure that both *AllowPaging* and *AllowCustomPaging* properties are set to *true*. This can be done declaratively through the ASP.NET page layout using the following code:

```
<asp:datagrid runat="server" id="grid"
    ⋮
    AllowPaging="true"
    AllowCustomPaging="true"
    OnPageIndexChanged="PageIndexChanged">
```

Alternatively, you can programmatically set these properties to *true* during page loading or whenever it makes sense to your application:

```
void Page_Load(object sender, EventArgs e) {
    grid.AllowPaging = true;
    grid.AllowCustomPaging = true;
    PageIndexChanged += new DataGridPageChangedEventHandler(
        this.PageIndexChanged);
}
```

Setting the *AllowPaging* property to *true* tells the *DataGrid* control that the support for paging must be initialized (that is, the pager must be displayed). Setting the *AllowCustomPaging* property to *true* instructs the control not to page through the data source but to just read and display all the data items bound to the *DataSource* property.

In addition to enabling pagination, you must provide settings for the pager and the page size. This is the same as for normal pagination. The pager and the page size take default values, so it's not necessary to explicitly set them in your code—although you can if you don't like the standard settings. However, you must supply a valid handler for the *PageIndexChanged* event. This event is fired whenever the user clicks on a page button or in any way causes, even programmatically, the current page to change. The event handler to write is based on the *DataGridPageChangedEventHandler* delegate type. (For more information on default paging, see Chapter 6.)

Setting the Virtual Item Count

During the execution of the *DataBind* method, the *DataGrid* control extracts all the items from *DataSource* and copies them into the *Items* collection. This behavior is common to both paging scenarios. What differs in the two cases is the subset of data items extracted from *DataSource*. The *DataGrid* control determines the page count, dividing the total number of items by the page size. In the case of default pagination, the total number of items is given by the record count in the data source.

With custom pagination, on the other hand, the data source contains only the records that fit in the page being displayed. The total number of items to page through can't be inferred from any available data. For this reason, you must provide that number by using an ad hoc property—the *VirtualItemCount* property. The following code shows the typical way to retrieve a value to set the property. This sample procedure simply executes a SELECT COUNT query on the Northwind Products table.

```
public void SetVirtualItemCount()
{
    // Set up the connection
    string strConn = "...";
    SqlConnection conn = new SqlConnection(strConn);

    // Set up the command
    string strCmd = "SELECT COUNT(*) FROM products";
    SqlCommand cmd = new SqlCommand(strCmd, conn);

    // Execute the command
    conn.Open();
    int nItemCount = (int) cmd.ExecuteScalar();
    conn.Close();

    // Set the grid's virtual item count
    grid.VirtualItemCount = nItemCount;
    return;
}
```

Note the use of the command's *ExecuteScalar* method to retrieve a single, scalar value from a query. The *DataGrid* control uses the virtual item count information to properly set up the pager bar. Setting the *AllowCustomPaging* and *VirtualItemCount* properties are two requirements for the *DataGrid* custom pagination.

Paging Using Key Values

With custom pagination, the trick is to figure out a (customized) way to page through records using SQL commands. Because the contents of each page are retrieved with an individual query, the command text must be designed to return a precise subset of the records that match certain criteria. Data paging means that you have a base query command but need to scroll through its resultset one page at a time. How can you force the DBMS to return only a particular portion of the selected records? Unfortunately, there's no official answer to this question, but a few best practices have been identified over the years. More important, these best practices—usually, smart SQL tricks—are database specific.

> **Important** Generally, we could say the difficulty of getting pages of records out of a query can be traced back to the nature and design of the SQL language. Within SQL, there's no explicit notion of the record position. Any record can be identified through the value of any of its fields by using the WHERE clause or server cursors and the FETCH statement. Specific DBMS systems, then, might add custom features to support position-based row identification. Oracle, for example, does that through the ROWNUM keyword; Microsoft SQL Server uses different tools, which aren't, functionally speaking, completely equivalent.

To start experimenting with custom paging, let's consider a simple, maybe even simplistic, case. The assumption we make here is not unrealistic, but it's too strong a requirement for most real-world cases. In addition, it has a few shortcomings that make it suitable only for read-only tables. Let's suppose the table to page through has a column (not necessarily a key column) with numeric values unfolded in regular succession. By *regular succession*, we mean that given an index, the corresponding value can be determined algorithmically, just like a mathematical succession.

Figure 7-1 shows the rows that form the Products table in the Northwind database. Focus on the productid column and its sequence of values.

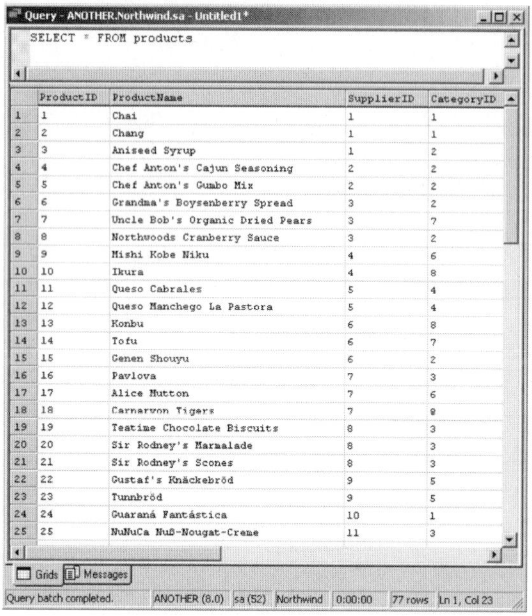

	ProductID	ProductName	SupplierID	CategoryID
1	1	Chai	1	1
2	2	Chang	1	1
3	3	Aniseed Syrup	1	2
4	4	Chef Anton's Cajun Seasoning	2	2
5	5	Chef Anton's Gumbo Mix	2	2
6	6	Grandma's Boysenberry Spread	3	2
7	7	Uncle Bob's Organic Dried Pears	3	7
8	8	Northwoods Cranberry Sauce	3	2
9	9	Mishi Kobe Niku	4	6
10	10	Ikura	4	8
11	11	Queso Cabrales	5	4
12	12	Queso Manchego La Pastora	5	4
13	13	Konbu	6	8
14	14	Tofu	6	7
15	15	Genen Shouyu	6	2
16	16	Pavlova	7	3
17	17	Alice Mutton	7	6
18	18	Carnarvon Tigers	7	8
19	19	Teatime Chocolate Biscuits	8	3
20	20	Sir Rodney's Marmalade	8	3
21	21	Sir Rodney's Scones	8	3
22	22	Gustaf's Knäckebröd	9	5
23	23	Tunnbröd	9	5
24	24	Guaraná Fantástica	10	1
25	25	NuNuCa Nuß-Nougat-Creme	11	3

Figure 7-1 A screen shot with some of the rows in the Northwind.Products table.

The productid column is made of integer, progressive values that start from 1. The regularity of the succession extends over the whole column and is never broken. In light of this, the value at row *n* is a function of a certain expression *F*:

```
value = F(n)
```

In particular, for the productid column the function is extremely simple and summarized by the following succession:

```
F(0) = 1
F(n+1) = F(n)+1
```

When the table provides a column with a regular succession of values, the following SQL code allows you to extract in a very flexible and generic way the rows that form a given page:

```
SELECT * FROM products WHERE
productid >= F(PageSize*(PageIndex-1)+1) AND
productid <= F(PageSize*PageIndex)
```

Because the size of the page is a fixed setting, the only variable parameter in the expression is the index of the page. The following listing shows a full application that pages through a list of products:

```
private SqlDataReader m_dataReader;
private string m_connString =
    "DATABASE=Northwind;SERVER=localhost;UID=sa;";
private string m_cmdCount = "SELECT COUNT(*) FROM products";
private string m_cmdQuery = "SELECT productid AS 'ID', " +
    "productname AS 'Product', quantityperunit AS 'Packaging' " +
    "FROM products " +
    "WHERE productid >=@minProductID AND productid <=@maxProductID";

void Page_Load(object sender, EventArgs e) {
    if (!Page.IsPostBack)
        SetVirtualItemCount();
    BindData();
}

SqlDataReader CreateDataSource(int nPageIndex) {
    // page index is assumed to be 0-based
    int pageSize = grid.PageSize;
    int minProductID = pageSize * nPageIndex + 1;
    int maxProductID = pageSize * (nPageIndex + 1);

    // Set up the command
    SqlConnection conn = new SqlConnection(m_connString);
    SqlCommand cmd = new SqlCommand(m_cmdQuery, conn);
    cmd.Parameters.Add("@minProductID", SqlDbType.Int).Value = minProductID;
    cmd.Parameters.Add("@maxProductID", SqlDbType.Int).Value = maxProductID;

    // Execute the command through a global data reader
    conn.Open();
    m_dataReader = cmd.ExecuteReader(CommandBehavior.CloseConnection);
    return m_dataReader;
}

void PageIndexChanged(object sender, DataGridPageChangedEventArgs e) {
    grid.CurrentPageIndex = e.NewPageIndex;
    BindData();
}

void BindData() {
    m_dataReader = CreateDataSource(grid.CurrentPageIndex);
    grid.DataSource = m_dataReader;
    grid.DataBind();
    m_dataReader.Close();
}

void SetVirtualItemCount() {
    SqlConnection conn = new SqlConnection(m_connString);
    SqlCommand cmd = new SqlCommand(m_cmdCount, conn);
```

```
        // Execute the command
        conn.Open();
        int nItemCount = (int) cmd.ExecuteScalar();
        conn.Close();

        grid.VirtualItemCount = nItemCount;
        return;
    }
```

Figure 7-2 shows the custom paging application in action.

Notice a couple of things in Figure 7-2. The pager bar is displayed on top of the grid, and the check box allows you to switch between the pager styles. The code discussed so far works regardless of the paging mode you opt for.

Fixed-Size *DataGrid* Controls

The *DataGrid* control is rendered as an HTML table, so the actual size of the HTML table depends on a number of factors, including the font, length of the text, and number of items displayed. Especially when you're paging through a data source using a grid control, it can be annoying to have the body of the page move up or down a few pixels each time the height of the grid changes. Setting the *Width* property to a specified maximum number of pixels allows you to maintain a fixed width for the grid. The same trick doesn't work for the height. In this case, the drawback is that the final page of the grid (which normally contains a smaller number of items) is stretched to occupy the fixed height. A possible workaround is padding the data source with empty rows prior to binding to the grid. An even better approach, one that doesn't require any programmatic work, is to wrap the *DataGrid* in a fixed-height HTML table with an empty row at the bottom:

```
<table style="..." bgcolor="...">
    <tr><td><asp:datagrid .../></td></tr>
    <tr><td height="100%"></td></tr>
</table>
```

The unique cell of the bottom row must have a 100 percent height so that it will automatically occupy any space left by the topmost grid. Combine this structure with some ad hoc visual settings and you'll have the grid paging always within the boundaries of the parent table. In particular, you might want to use a borderless *DataGrid* and define border settings on the table. Also, you should use the same background color for the table and the grid.

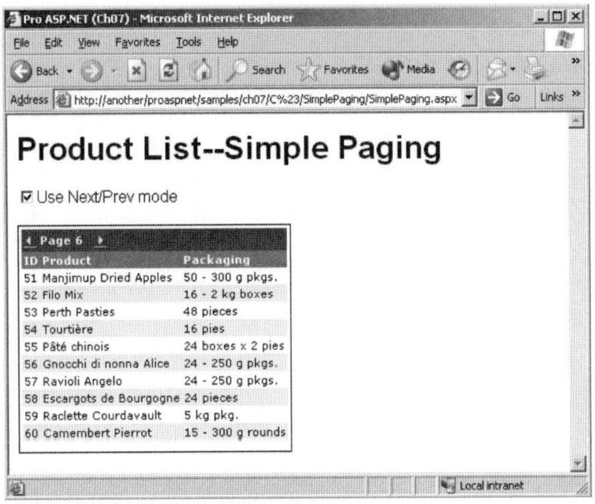

Figure 7-2 The grid exploits the characteristics of the productid column to page through records.

Shortcomings of the Key-Based Approach

There are pros and cons with this column-based approach. It is simple to code and effective in returning a compact resultset that is immediately bindable and requires no further preparation work. Column updates do not affect the functionality, and row insertion is a nonissue too, as long as you guarantee and preserve the regularity of the succession. On the downside, though, I should mention that this technique works only with primarily read-only, look-up tables.

Deletions are one type of operation that can really nullify the functionality of this technique. The deletion of a row creates a hole in the succession, which then breaks the arithmetic rule set up to identify the first record in the page. You can try to work around the issue by resorting to nonidentity, custom-made columns that can be programmatically updated. In other words, you must perform the deletion through a stored procedure that first executes the deletion and then reorders the index column. To make this approach more complex, though, consider that in some cases the stored procedure (or, in general, the sequence of statements involved) needs to be embedded in a transaction.

In the remainder of the chapter, we'll analyze more powerful approaches that work in a larger number of cases. We'll discuss the solutions based on the paging mode you want to support—for example, next/previous navigation and random access to pages. However, no matter which approach you choose to control paging, don't forget to set the virtual item count.

> **Note** The *DataGrid* is the only ASP.NET control that provides a built-in infrastructure for pagination. The *DataList* is the control that most closely resembles the *DataGrid* in terms of functionality. The key difference between the two is just pagination. However, if you use custom paging and don't mind using external link buttons to navigate, obtaining a pageable *DataList* is not a hard task at all. We'll examine the *DataList* in Chapter 9 and review how to extend it to support pagination.

Next/Previous Navigation

When we want to move to the next or previous page, a more general query command can be used to leverage any column that has unique values but which might not form a regular succession. The idea is that you cache the first and last key values in the currently displayed page and select the previous (or next) page based on that. If the page size is set to 10, moving to the previous page entails selecting the first 10 records whose key value is less than the cached value. If you move to the next page, the first 10 records with a key greater than the cached last key are selected.

Defining the SQL Code

With the *NextPrev* pager mode, you can view only pages close to the currently displayed one—that is, pages immediately previous to or following the page you are viewing. This constraint enables us to set up ad hoc SQL code that works regardless of the values in the key column. To sum it up, the pivot column doesn't have to be the key column—it only has to contain unique values. For the SQL code to work, you need to cache the value on this key column for the first and last items in the page. The values require persistent storage that survives across page requests. These key values can be stored in the view state:

```
ViewState["FirstKey"] = grid.DataKeys[0];
ViewState["LastKey"] = grid.DataKeys[grid.Items.Count-1];
```

This code stores in the view state the minimum and maximum key values in the page. The key values are retrieved from the *DataKeys* collection, and the name of the key column is set using the *DataKeyField* property. Prior to executing the query command, the value of the key is read back from the view state, as shown here:

```
// going to page back
int productID = Convert.ToInt32(ViewState["FirstKey"]);
// going to page ahead
int productID = Convert.ToInt32(ViewState["LastKey"]);
```

Let's have a look at the SQL code to move to the previous record and to move to the next record. Later in the "Adding First and Last Buttons" section, we'll discuss how to move to the first record and move to the last record.

Moving to the Previous Record

When the user clicks to view the previous page of a data source, the grid has cached the key values for the first and last records displayed in the current page. Assuming a default page size of 10, the records that fit in the previous page are the last 10 whose key value is less than the first key of the current page.

In SQL Server, the TOP *n* clause allows you to select the first *n* records that match. Unfortunately, though, there's no equivalent clause that lets you select the last *n* matching records. To obtain the same result, you must resort to a little trick and use a virtual table. You use the following Transact-SQL (T-SQL) code. The key column is productid.

```
SELECT * FROM
(SELECT TOP 10 productid, productname, quantityperunit
    FROM products WHERE productid <@productID ORDER BY productid DESC) AS t
ORDER BY productid
```

Before we discuss the query any further, a few general points need to be addressed. The code here is not standard SQL but is written in the SQL dialect that SQL Server supports—the Transact-SQL language. It can't be considered a general solution, as it exploits features of recent versions of SQL Server and might not be supported by other DBMS. Unlike the SQL code we considered for the application in Figure 7-2, the code shown here can't be used with just any database server. The features that make it to some extent unique and SQL Server–specific are the TOP *n* clause and the use of subqueries.

The T-SQL code used to query for the previous page is based on two nested queries. The innermost query selects the first 10 records that have a key value less than the first key displayed in the current page. Because the table is queried in descending order, the top 10 records are actually the last 10 but are listed from the highest to the lowest key. We name this in-memory table *AS t* and, through the outermost query, select all the records in it ordered by the key column. This final operation returns the last 10 records sorted in the natural ascending order.

Important Very few databases support the TOP *n* clause in the SELECT statement. The TOP clause was originally introduced in Microsoft Access and then imported into SQL Server beginning with version 7. It has no counterpart in SQL Server version 6.5 nor in any version of Oracle. Oracle, though, has an alternative mechanism that is in some aspects even more powerful. (We'll discuss this feature more in the "Selecting Records in Oracle" section later in the chapter.) Informix SQL does provide a TOP-like behavior through the FIRST clause. Generally, the SET ROWCOUNT statement, although a bit less flexible, can be used as a rougher counterpart when the TOP clause is not supported. The main difference is that the TOP clause is command specific, whereas the SET ROWCOUNT statement is a global environment setting.

Note Many T-SQL statements that include subqueries can sometimes be formulated as joins. Other statements, like ours here, can be posed only with subqueries. In T-SQL, there is usually no relevant performance difference between a statement that includes a subquery and a functionally equivalent command that does not. In some cases, though, a join gets slightly better performance. What's important to note for our purposes, though, is that subqueries can be significantly faster than server cursors and temporary tables. Server cursors, in particular, should always be your last resort.

Moving to the Next Record

Extracting the records to display in the next page is a bit easier and faster once you know the last key in the current page. In this case, the TOP *n* clause works just fine and without the need of other tricks. The following T-SQL code simply selects the top 10 records with a key value greater than the last key (the productid column) in the page.

```
SELECT TOP 10 productid, productname, quantityperunit
FROM products WHERE productid >@productID
```

Both the commands we've examined so far, for moving to the previous and next records, use a parameter named *@productID*. This parameter is set with the value retrieved from the view state for the first or last key according to the previous or next command to execute.

Setting Up the Next/Previous Navigation

The following code shows the initialization step of the sample application that demonstrates next/previous pagination:

```
void Page_Load(object sender, EventArgs e) {
    if (!Page.IsPostBack)
    {
        SetVirtualItemCount();
        ViewState["LastKey"] = 0;
        ViewState["FirstKey"] = 0;
        m_cmdText = m_cmdQueryNext;
        BindData();
    }
}
```

The default value of the view-state entries is 0, and the records that fit in the first page are retrieved as a next-page command with a *LastKey* value of 0.

The command to execute is decided by looking at which link the user clicked to page back or forth. The ASP.NET page is fired by the *PageIndexChanged* event when the user clicks to page back or forth. The event doesn't provide explicit information about the direction of the paging. However, you can easily figure it out by comparing the values of the *CurrentPageIndex* property and the *NewPageIndex* event data member.

```
if (grid.CurrentPageIndex > e.NewPageIndex)
    // moving forward
else
    // moving back
```

At the time the *PageIndexChanged* fires, the new page index has not yet been set. Moreover, you have to explicitly set it in the event handler.

Knowing whether you're moving to the next or previous record is important in this case because, based on it, we decide which query command to run. Another way to obtain that information is by exploiting the services of the *ItemCommand* event. The sample code discussed here implements this technique because it's more general and will work even with future extensions.

When the user clicks to change pages, regardless of whether it is to page back or forth, the *DataGrid* fires an *ItemCommand* event in which the *CommandName* member is set to *Page*. The *CommandArgument* member, on the other hand, is accordingly set to *Next* or *Prev*. All these keywords don't have to be addressed as literals—predefined constants should be used instead. The following code shows the *ItemCommand* event handler:

```
void ItemCommand(object sender, DataGridCommandEventArgs e)
{
    switch(e.CommandArgument.ToString())
    {
        case DataGrid.NextPageCommandArgument:
            m_direction = GridNavigation.Next;
            break;
        case DataGrid.PrevPageCommandArgument:
            m_direction = GridNavigation.Previous;
            break;
    }
}
```

The code stores in an application global variable a value that indicates the direction of the paging. The *GridNavigation* values belong to a user-defined type that has been defined mostly for clarity:

```
public enum GridNavigation : int
{
    First = -2,
    Previous = -1,
    Next = 1,
    Last = 2
}
```

Notice that the enumeration also includes command names to access the first and last pages of the data source. I'll discuss this feature in the next section, "Adding First and Last Buttons." The following listing illustrates the mechanism that allows the sample application to fetch records using the SQL commands discussed earlier. Note that the code employs a data reader (instead of a slower *DataTable*) to bind data to the *DataGrid*:

```
void BindData() {
    m_dataReader = CreateDataSource();
    grid.DataSource = m_dataReader;
    grid.DataBind();
    m_dataReader.Close();

    // Configure for the view state
    ViewState["FirstKey"] = grid.DataKeys[0];
    ViewState["LastKey"] = grid.DataKeys[grid.Items.Count-1];
}

SqlDataReader CreateDataSource() {
    // page size is assumed to be 10
    int productID = 0;
    string cmdText = "";
    switch(m_direction)
```

```
    {
        case GridNavigation.Previous:
            productID = Convert.ToInt32(ViewState["FirstKey"]);
            cmdText = m_cmdQueryPrev;
            break;
        case GridNavigation.Next:
            productID = Convert.ToInt32(ViewState["LastKey"]);
            cmdText = m_cmdQueryNext;
            break;
    }
    return ExecuteCommand(cmdText, productID);
}

SqlDataReader ExecuteCommand(string cmdText, int productID) {
    SqlConnection conn = new SqlConnection(m_connString);
    SqlCommand cmd = new SqlCommand(cmdText, conn);
    cmd.Parameters.Add("@productID", SqlDbType.Int).Value = productID;

    // Execute the command through a global data reader
    conn.Open();
    m_dataReader = cmd.ExecuteReader(CommandBehavior.CloseConnection);
    return m_dataReader;
}
```

As mentioned in Chapter 5, you can populate a list-bound control like the *DataGrid* using a data reader object. The data reader works connected to the data source. For this reason, you must close it after calling the control's *DataBind* method. The data reader is marked with the *CloseConnection* flag so that closing the reader would automatically close the underlying connection. The *CreateDataSource* method examines the determined direction and sets the command text to execute and the key value to use as a parameter.

Selecting Records in Oracle

Speaking of Oracle databases, you should note that named parameters in Oracle must be prefixed with a colon (:). In SQL Server, you precede the name of parameters by using the @ symbol. The SQL language supported by Oracle databases doesn't provide a facility like the TOP *n* clause for SELECT statements. However, particularly for data paging, the Oracle database provides an even more powerful feature than TOP—the ROWNUM operator.

The ROWNUM operator returns the ordinal position of a row in a resultset. In light of this, and given a page size of 10, moving to a page requires the following, surprisingly simple, query:

```
SELECT * FROM table WHERE
ROWNUM > (PageIndex*(PageSize-1)+1 AND ROWNUM > (PageIndex*PageSize)
```

The ROWNUM operator has a drawback that should be discussed. An Oracle database assigns the unique index before sorting the result set. So if you have a query that includes an ORDER BY clause, the sequence of ROWNUM values is not ordered as the clause indicates. To fix things up, you must use an outermost query that does not require sorting.

Adding First and Last Buttons

A next/previous navigation model can be made even richer by using a pair of extra links for the first and last pages of the data source. In this case, though, you can't count on any support from the *DataGrid* control. You must modify the pager bar on the fly to accommodate for the extra buttons, add a handler for the *Click* event, and update the view.

The following code shows how you can modify the pager bar by adding a text label displaying the number of the current page (as mentioned in Chapter 6) and the links for the first and last pages. The key procedure is the *ItemCreated* event handler:

```
void ItemCreated(object sender, DataGridItemEventArgs e) {
    if (e.Item.ItemType == ListItemType.Pager) {
        if (grid.PagerStyle.Mode == PagerMode.NextPrev) {
            TableCell pager = e.Item.Cells[0];
            AddPageLabel(pager);
            AddLinkFirstPage(pager);
            AddLinkLastPage(pager);
        }
    }
}
```

Creating Link Buttons Dynamically

The First and Last buttons are to be added as link buttons or labels, depending on the page index. If the link can be clicked to go to the first or last page, you render the button as a link; otherwise, you render it as a label or a disabled link. Because the standard pager renders disabled buttons as labels, we'll use this approach here too. Let's consider adding the First button. No significant changes are expected for the Last button.

The First button must be disabled only if the current page is the first. Put another way, the First button must be rendered as a link button only if the Previous button is a link. The Previous button is the first in the *Controls* collection. You check its type and then create a *LinkButton* or *Label* control accordingly:

```
void AddLinkFirstPage(TableCell pager)
{
    if(pager.Controls[0] is LinkButton) {
        LinkButton btnFirst = new LinkButton();
        btnFirst.Font.Name = grid.PagerStyle.Font.Name;
        btnFirst.Font.Size = grid.PagerStyle.Font.Size;
```

```
        btnFirst.ForeColor = grid.PagerStyle.ForeColor;
        btnFirst.Text = "<<";
        if (btnFirst.Font.Name == "webdings")
            btnFirst.Text = "7";
        btnFirst.Click += new EventHandler(GoToFirstPage);
        pager.Controls.AddAt(0, btnFirst);
    }
    else
    {
        Label btnFirst = new Label();
        btnFirst.Font.Name = grid.PagerStyle.Font.Name;
        btnFirst.Font.Size = grid.PagerStyle.Font.Size;
        btnFirst.ForeColor = grid.PagerStyle.ForeColor;
        btnFirst.Text = "<<";
        if (btnFirst.Font.Name == "webdings")
            btnFirst.Text = "7";
        pager.Controls.AddAt(0, btnFirst);
    }
}
```

You ensure that the font and color used for the First button are identical to those used for other buttons in the pager. You read the default settings from the *DataGrid*'s *PagerStyle* object. A nice feature you can add is setting the caption of the button to a Webdings symbol if Webdings is the current pager font. The value of 7 corresponds to the ⏪ symbol. For the Last page, you use the value 8, which corresponds to the ⏩ glyph.

You add the control to the *Controls* collection at a specified position, as shown in Figure 7-3.

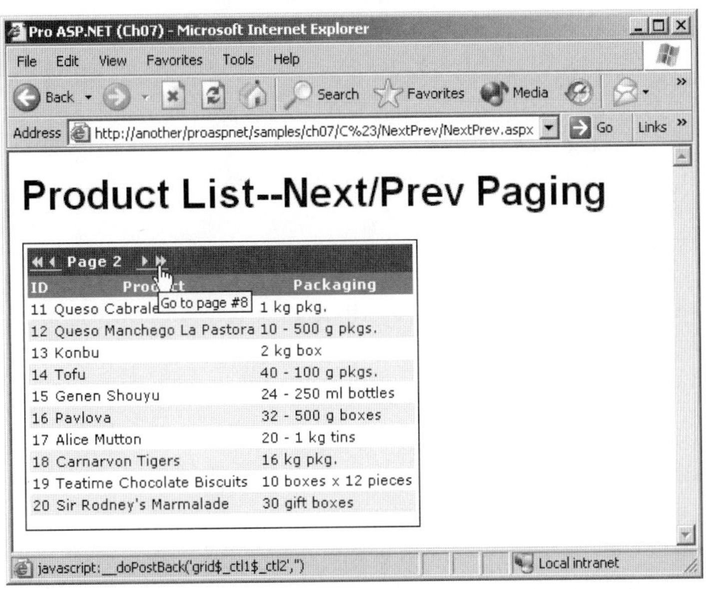

Figure 7-3 The new pager bar with a pair of First and Last buttons.

The command to select the records of the first page is straightforward and consists of a pretty simple SELECT command:

```
SELECT TOP 10 productid, productname, quantityperunit FROM products
```

Getting the records of the last page is a bit more involved. The problem has two facets. Because users can click on the Last button at any time, we can't assume we know the last key of the last page. Knowing this value would make the query trivial; unfortunately, we do not know it. The second issue to consider is that we don't know exactly how many records would fit in the last page, as that depends on the page size and the size of the data source. The following query would select the last *n* records in the data source with a key value greater than the specified value:

```
SELECT * FROM (
    SELECT TOP {0} productid, productname, quantityperunit
    FROM products
    WHERE productid >@productID ORDER BY productid DESC)
    AS t ORDER BY productid
```

The key value we use does not determine the resultset, but the higher value we use the smaller subset of records the query would process. The *{0}* placeholder in the query is dynamically replaced with the computed number of records in the last page. Here's the necessary code:

```
SqlDataReader CreateDataSource() {
    switch(m_direction) {
        ⋮
        case GridNavigation.Last:
            productID = Convert.ToInt32(ViewState["LastKey"]);
            int nRem = grid.VirtualItemCount % grid.PageSize;
            nRem = (nRem == 0 ?grid.PageSize :nRem);

            // Replaces the placeholder to include the effective
            // number of records in the last page
            cmdText = String.Format(m_cmdQueryLast, nRem);
            break;
    }
}
```

The nonzero modulus obtained by dividing the data source size by the page size is the number of rows to retrieve for the last page. If the modulus is zero, the last page is full and the number of rows to retrieve matches the page size.

Setting the Click Handler

What happens when the user clicks on the First or Last button? The action taken depends on the registered *Click* event handler:

```
btnFirst.Click += new EventHandler(GoToFirstPage);
btnLast.Click += new EventHandler(GoToLastPage);
```

In Microsoft Visual Basic .NET, you register handlers using the *AddHandler* keyword. The structure of both handlers is similar and refers to the code built in the *PageIndexChanged* event handler.

```
void GoToFirstPage(object sender, EventArgs e) {
    m_direction = GridNavigation.First;
    GoToPage(sender, 0);
}
void GoToLastPage(object sender, EventArgs e) {
    m_direction = GridNavigation.Last;
    GoToPage(sender, grid.PageCount-1);
}
void GoToPage(object sender, int nPageIndex) {
    // page number is 0-based
    DataGridPageChangedEventArgs evPage;
    evPage = new DataGridPageChangedEventArgs(sender, nPageIndex);
    PageIndexChanged(sender, evPage);
}
```

As the code illustrates, going to the first or last page is resolved in terms of a page transition accomplished through the standard pager buttons. The *GoToPage* method invokes the user's defined code for the *PageIndexChanged* event. The code assumes that such an event handler is defined—a reasonable assumption as we're speaking of code for paging.

Figure 7-4 shows the final page of the grid. Note that the height of the grid *seems* to be constant. As we explained in the sidebar "Fixed-Size *DataGrid* Controls," this is only a trick performed using a wrapper HTML table element.

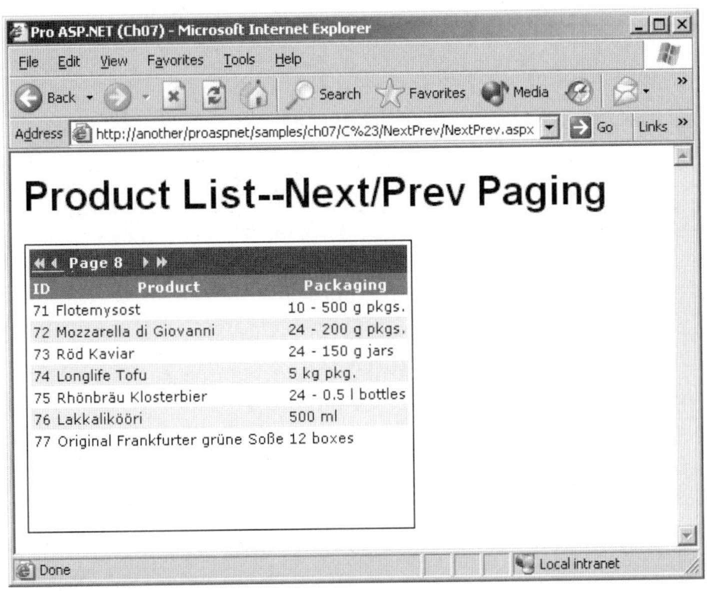

Figure 7-4 The final page of the grid.

Adding ToolTips to the Pager

As shown in Figure 7-3, the pager buttons include ToolTips. Each ToolTip indicates the number of the page the button would move you to. The index of the next or previous page is a fundamental piece of information if no other feedback is provided about the current page. With next/previous navigation, users don't know what page they're currently viewing, so ToolTips help considerably. In the sample code discussed here, the current page index is displayed through a label, so ToolTips aren't really necessary.

You can add ToolTips on the fly to pager buttons as well as header cells. In both cases, all you need to do is write a handler for the *ItemCreated* event. The following code shows how to proceed with the Previous button—the second button in the pager:

```
if (e.Item.ItemType == ListItemType.Pager) {
    if (grid.PagerStyle.Mode == PagerMode.NextPrev) {
        TableCell pager = e.Item.Cells[0];
        WebControl ctl = (WebControl) pager.Controls[1]);
        ctl.ToolTip = String.Format("Go to page #{0}",
        grid.CurrentPageIndex);
    }
```

Note that the *CurrentPageIndex* property returns 0-based values, whereas the displayed page indexes are 1-based. For this reason, the 1-based index of the previous page coincides with the *CurrentPageIndex* property. Similarly, the index of the next page is *CurrentPageIndex* plus 2.

Random Page Navigation

Let's examine the tricks of data pagination when the *NumericPages* pager mode is used. In this case, we can't rely on any features and values in the previously viewed page. Data access must be independent from external parameters and only a function of the page index and page size. The ROWNUM statement of Oracle databases is ideal for setting up a random-access paging mechanism. Unfortunately, other databases, including SQL Server, don't provide for that. In this section, we'll discuss and put to work an alternative trick based entirely on the SQL language.

A page that uses a grid in *NumericPages* pager mode has a much simpler layout (and involves less code) than a page based on the *NextPrev* pager mode. For one thing, a unique SQL command is needed and used regardless of the page to be accessed. Second, the direction of the navigation is unimportant and doesn't require ad hoc handling. Let's have a closer look at the necessary SQL statement.

Selecting a Specified Page of Records

To select from a SQL Server database only the records that fit into the specified page (identified by an index), a rather complex and nested query is necessary. The resultset is selected in three steps. First you get the smallest resultset that includes the desired records. Next you get rid of the additional records, and then you sort the remaining rows properly.

Suppose that, given a page size of 10, you want to obtain the records of page 3 according to a particular order. The last 10 rows of the first 30 are the rows you are looking for. How can you get them? Let's see what happens with the Products table in the Northwind database:

```
SELECT TOP 10 * FROM
    (SELECT TOP 30 * FROM products ORDER BY productid) AS t1
ORDER BY productid DESC
```

This nested query selects the correct subset of records but in the reverse order. It takes the first 10 rows out of the first 30 in descending order. A third query must be placed to wrap this code with the sole goal of sorting the previous resultset:

```
SELECT * FROM
    (SELECT TOP 10 * FROM
        (SELECT TOP 30 * FROM products ORDER BY productid) AS t1
    ORDER BY productid DESC) AS t2
ORDER BY productid
```

The following listing shows how this statement is turned into .NET executable code. Replace the numeric values with a pair of *{n}* placeholders, and run the following code:

```
string cmdText = String.Format(m_cmdQuery,
    grid.PageSize, grid.PageSize*pageIndex);
SqlConnection conn = new SqlConnection(m_connString);
SqlCommand cmd = new SqlCommand(cmdText, conn);
conn.Open();
m_dataReader = cmd.ExecuteReader(CommandBehavior.CloseConnection);
conn.Close();
```

One problem raised with this code is that the last page always shows up with 10 records—the regular records plus the last in the previous page. The culprit of this is the SELECT TOP 10 outer query. A simple way to work around this issue is by associating the TOP clause with the actual number of rows in the final page:

```
int recsInLastPage = grid.VirtualItemCount % grid.PageSize;
if (recsInLastPage == 0)
    recsInLastPage = grid.PageSize;
```

```
int sizeOfPage = grid.PageSize;
if (pageIndex == grid.PageCount)
    sizeOfPage = recsInLastPage;
string cmdText = String.Format(m_cmdQuery,
    sizeOfPage, grid.PageSize*pageIndex);
```

The code discussed so far includes two sorting operations that are not lightweight ones. However, indexes are just the right tool to leverage to make the query run faster. Using a clustered index on the ORDER BY field (productid, in the preceding example) speeds the query up immensely; using a clustered primary key index would speed things up even more—an order of magnitude faster.

For completeness, you might also want to consider the following, functionally equivalent, version of the query:

```
SELECT * FROM
    (SELECT TOP 30 * FROM products ORDER BY productid) AS t1
WHERE productid NOT IN
    (SELECT TOP 20 productid FROM products ORDER BY productid)
```

The idea is that you first select the minimum number of records that will contain the desired subset, and then you run an outer query in which you filter out the records that don't belong to the page. For example, if page #3 is to be retrieved, you discard the records of the first two pages. This second query also doesn't suffer from the last-page drawback we had to fix earlier. In terms of raw performance, the second query runs statistically slower than the first except in one circumstance—when you have additional criteria set on the table. If the main query, which was *SELECT * FROM products* in the previous example, contains a WHERE clause, especially for larger tables, the second query tends to run about 15 percent faster. The break-up point seems to be around 150,000 records. As a disclaimer, I want to recommend that you don't take this statistical analysis for pure gold but instead roll your own before you make a decision.

> **Note** The TOP clause doesn't accept parameters, so it's hard with this trick to use code from within a stored procedure. However, the SQL Server query engine can still do a good job reusing the execution plans of the subqueries.

Customizing the Structure of the Pager

When working in *NumericPages* pager mode, the pager bar is made of a single table cell populated with an alternate sequence of links and blank literals. One link is actually a nonclickable label control. By default, the links and the label have simple numeric captions, which makes the pager bar difficult to read.

Unfortunately, the *DataGrid* control doesn't support a format string for the links in the numeric pager bar. To customize the text of the buttons, you can only write the usual *ItemCreated* handler:

```
void ItemCreated(object sender, DataGridItemEventArgs e) {
    if (e.Item.ItemType == ListItemType.Pager) {
        if (grid.PagerStyle.Mode != PagerMode.NumericPages)
            return;

        TableCell pager = (TableCell) e.Item.Cells[0];
        for (int i=0; i<pager.Controls.Count; i+=2)
        {
            object o = pager.Controls[i];
            if (o is LinkButton) {
                LinkButton h = (LinkButton) o;
                h.Text = "[" + h.Text + "]";
            } else {
                Label l = (Label) o;
                l.Font.Bold = true;
                l.Text = "Page " + l.Text;
            }
        }
    }
}
```

The modified grid is shown in Figure 7-5.

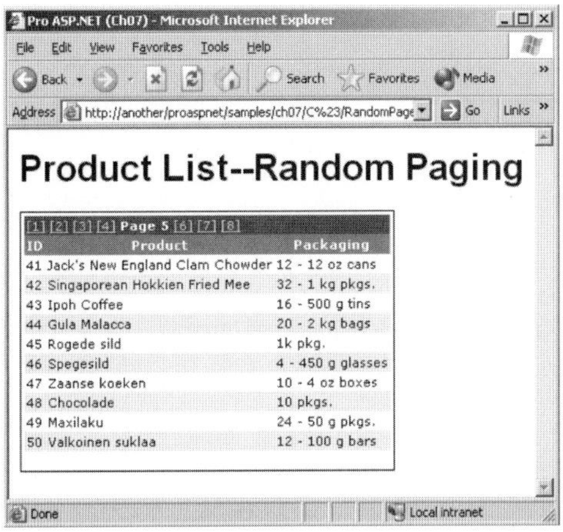

Figure 7-5 A *DataGrid* control with a customized numeric pager bar.

In some cases, a particularly large data source might lead to a too-long list of links for the real estate of the pager bar. The pager's *PageButtonCount* property lets you control how many links are to be displayed. By default, *PageButtonCount* is set to 10. If extra buttons are required, the *DataGrid* adjusts for extra pagination buttons, as shown in Figure 7-6.

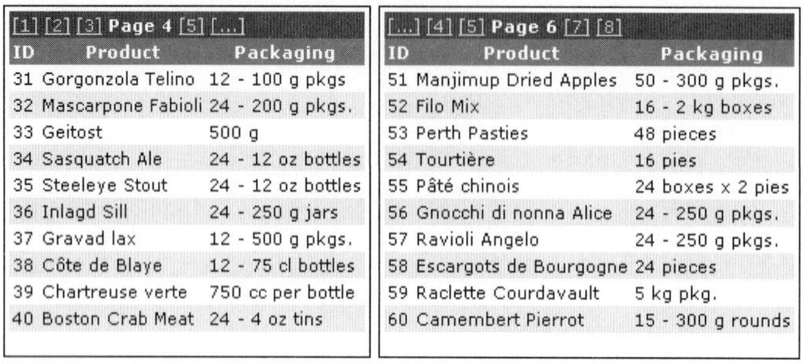

[1] [2] [3] Page 4 [5] [...]

ID	Product	Packaging
31	Gorgonzola Telino	12 - 100 g pkgs
32	Mascarpone Fabioli	24 - 200 g pkgs.
33	Geitost	500 g
34	Sasquatch Ale	24 - 12 oz bottles
35	Steeleye Stout	24 - 12 oz bottles
36	Inlagd Sill	24 - 250 g jars
37	Gravad lax	12 - 500 g pkgs.
38	Côte de Blaye	12 - 75 cl bottles
39	Chartreuse verte	750 cc per bottle
40	Boston Crab Meat	24 - 4 oz tins

[...] [4] [5] Page 6 [7] [8]

ID	Product	Packaging
51	Manjimup Dried Apples	50 - 300 g pkgs.
52	Filo Mix	16 - 2 kg boxes
53	Perth Pasties	48 pieces
54	Tourtière	16 pies
55	Pâté chinois	24 boxes x 2 pies
56	Gnocchi di nonna Alice	24 - 250 g pkgs.
57	Ravioli Angelo	24 - 250 g pkgs.
58	Escargots de Bourgogne	24 pieces
59	Raclette Courdavault	5 kg pkg.
60	Camembert Pierrot	15 - 300 g rounds

Figure 7-6 A pager bar with ellipsis buttons when too many links are required.

Building a Completely Customized Personal Pager

Although the *DataGrid* doesn't provide a built-in mechanism to plug in a custom pager, you can always replace the standard pager with your own. You can hide the pager by turning off its *Visible* attribute. However, nothing really prevents you from displaying both the ordinary pager and a personal pager:

```
<pagerstyle visible="false" />
```

The personal pager is any custom toolbar appended at the bottom of the grid. The *DataGrid* and your personal pager are two rows of the same table, as in the following schema:

```
<table>
<tr><td>
    <asp:datagrid ...> ... </asp:datagrid>
</td></tr>
<tr><td>
    personal pager goes here
</td></tr>
</table>
```

The following code shows how to transform the pager in a numeric text box with a button to jump to the specified page:

```
<asp:panel runat="server">
    <asp:label runat="server" text="Page" />
    <asp:textbox runat="server" id="txtGoto" width="20px" height="20px"
        text="1" style="border:solid 1px;" />
    <asp:button runat="server" Text="Go" height="20px" font-size="8pt"
        onclick="GoToPage" />
</asp:panel>
```

The code that actually moves to the specified page is as follows:

```
void GoToPage(object sender, EventArgs e) {
    int pageIndex = Convert.ToInt32(txtGoto.Text)-1;
    if (pageIndex >=0) {
        grid.CurrentPageIndex = pageIndex;
        BindData();
    }
}
```

The *GoToPage* method doesn't include any validation logic. You can either validate the content of the text box programmatically or resort to a range validator control. (See Chapter 3.)

```
<asp:rangevalidator runat="server" id="gotoValidator"
    ControlToValidate="txtGoto"
    ForeColor="white"
    Font-Size="8pt"
    Display="Dynamic"
    ErrorMessage="Page not found"
    MinimumValue="1"
    Type="Integer" />
```

The lower bound of the range can be set declaratively to 1. As for the upper bound, you have to set it dynamically—for example, in the *BindData* method.

```
gotoValidator.MaximumValue = grid.PageCount.ToString();
```

Figure 7-7 shows a grid control with a personal pager bar.

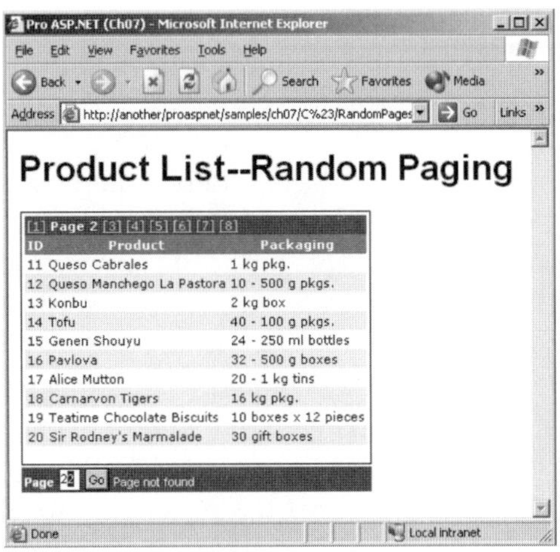

Figure 7-7 A *DataGrid* control with a personal pager along with the standard pager. The two work side by side without any conflicts.

Logical Navigation

So the *DataGrid* control—unique among the ASP.NET data-bound controls—provides two basic types of paging, which differ in the way in which the page content is retrieved. With default paging, you bind the control to the whole data set and then make it responsible for selecting the subset of records that fits in each displayed page. Custom paging, on the other hand, is based on the assumption that the programmer puts into the control's data source only the records that should be displayed in the current page. Does this cover all the possible needs you might have when it comes to planning navigation through a data set? The answer is debatable.

The types of paging you get for free from the *DataGrid* control certainly do not cover all the possible real-world scenarios you might be facing. On the other hand, by exploiting the *DataGrid* custom-paging infrastructure, you can easily build new paging engines that fit into your application's architecture.

To top off this chapter, we'll demonstrate how to use the *DataGrid* custom-paging mechanism to set up a sort of logical data navigation—that is, a navigation engine that displays variable-length pages that are selected based on a logical condition rather than a physical position.

Changing the Pager's Perspective

In the *DataGrid* control, all the pages except the last one are the same size, as specified through the *PageSize* property. You select each page to display from the links of the variable-length pager bar. The pager bar contains as many links as there are pages to display. With the help of a practical example, let's see how this model deals with a scenario in which you have a fixed number of pages, each with a variable length.

Suppose you have a query to select all the orders issued by customers in a given year. Using the paging approach discussed so far, you would have a long list of (possibly numbered) pages displayed to the users. Are you really sure that your users would love to scroll through a year's worth of orders by page? How could they orientate themselves in the results once you show them a menu of, say, 40 meaningless page indexes? Wouldn't it be much better if you grouped orders, say, by month or by company? In the traditional way of paging, you keep the page size constant but provide a variable-length pager bar. Logical navigation does just the opposite—it keeps the pager bar size constant but accepts pages of any length (almost any length, actually).

We'll discuss the underpinnings of logical navigation by grouping data by months. However, the mechanism we'll use here is rather general and applies to a number of everyday scenarios: grouping customers or contacts by initials, sales by year or quarters, and bills by weeks or days.

Is the *DataGrid* Appropriate for the Task?

Although we can successfully employ the *DataGrid* control for this type of navigation—a special case of custom paging—there's an upper bound we must set for the control to work. The limitation is in the maximum number of rows that can be displayed per page. This number can be any value—yet we have to set it and configure other parameters of the grid accordingly. (We'll discuss this further in the next section.)

Is there another control we can use instead? The *DataList* control is one of the few alternatives we can rely on. As we'll more clearly see in Chapter 9, the *DataList* is a data-bound list of rows, each sequentially displayed according to an ASP.NET template. The *DataList* doesn't pose any limitation on the number of items you can display in a page, but, on the other hand, this happens only because the *DataList* doesn't have the notion of paging and doesn't provide any built-in facilities.

In summary, you can use both the *DataGrid* and the *DataList* for the task, but neither of them is the perfect tool for a logical navigation of data. Both would work, but both require some adjustments.

Configuring the *DataGrid*

A *DataGrid* used to implement a logical navigation of data requires some ad hoc settings. First you might want to use a topmost pager bar because the list of items can be long and a topmost pager can simplify movements. For the same reason, a double pager bar would also be more useful. Next you should opt for a *NumericPages* pager mode and then write an *ItemCreated* handler to customize the text displayed. For example, you can turn 1 into January, 5 into May, and so forth.

Finally you should carefully choose the values for the *DataGrid*'s *PageSize* and *VirtualItemCount* properties and for the *PagerStyle*'s *PageButtonCount* property. These properties are key to forcing the *DataGrid* to support logical data navigation. By design, the control can't show more items than the number of *PageSize* states. You can set *PageSize* with any value. Let's assume we don't need to display more than 100 rows per page. The *PageButtonCount* property determines how many buttons are displayed in the pager bar. By default, this value is set to 10. Because we plan to have month names on the pager bar, we must raise this value to 12. Subsequently, the virtual item count is a computed value—1200 (that is, *PageSize* * *PageButtonCount*).

In this way, the grid will always display through 12 pages, each of which can have no more than 100 rows.

Binding the Data Source

As mentioned, logical navigation is a special case of custom paging. Whenever the user clicks to view a new page, an ad hoc data source is created based on the page index. You can use the page index directly to obtain the data source or, more generally, use it to reference another data structure (for example, a collection or an array) with more specific information. In the sample scenario we're considering now, the page index would suffice, as it directly represents the index of a month. Let's see how to modify the pager bar to reflect months rather than indexes.

Modifying the Pager Bar

To modify the pager bar of a *DataGrid*, you write an *ItemCreated* handler. The handler will process all nonliteral controls in the pager bar and transform the default text—a 1-based number—into a month name. To increase flexibility, the name of the month is generated through an intermediate *DateTime* object corresponding to the first day of that month in the current year. This date is then formatted into the month name. The *ItemCreated* handler is shown here:

```
void ItemCreated(object sender, DataGridItemEventArgs e) {
    if (e.Item.ItemType == ListItemType.Pager &&
        grid.PagerStyle.Mode == PagerMode.NumericPages)
    {
        TableCell pager = (TableCell) e.Item.Controls[0];
        for(int i=0; i<pager.Controls.Count; i+=2) {
            object o = pager.Controls[i];
            if (o is LinkButton) {
                // Text is the 1-based number of the month
                LinkButton lb = (LinkButton) o;
                DateTime dt = new DateTime(2003,
                    Convert.ToInt32(lb.Text), 1);
                lb.Text = " " + dt.ToString("MMM") + " ";
            }
            else
            if (o is Label) {
                Label l = (Label) o;
                DateTime dt = new DateTime(2003,
                    Convert.ToInt32(l.Text), 1);
                l.Text = " " + dt.ToString("MMMM") + " ";
                l.BackColor = grid.HeaderStyle.BackColor;
                l.ForeColor = grid.HeaderStyle.ForeColor;
            }
        }
    }
}
```

As mentioned earlier, a pager bar built in *NumericPages* pager mode is made of a sequence of link buttons and a single label, all interspersed with blank literal controls. To skip over literals, we use a step of 2 in the *for* loop. When the *i*-th control in the pager is a Label control, its value represents the currently selected month. To differentiate it even further, we use a distinct group of visual settings. In particular, we use the same font and colors of the grid's header and draw the month name in its full extension instead of abbreviating it. The final effect is shown in Figure 7-8, and the tab-style look is free!

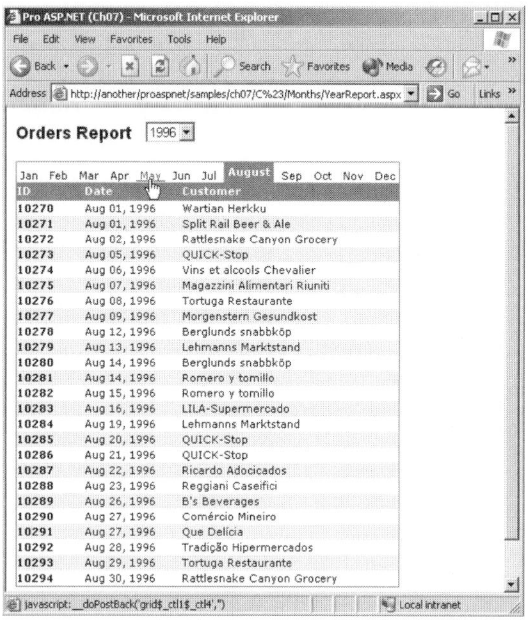

Figure 7-8 A customized grid that displays data grouped by months rather than by pages.

Selecting the Page's Rows

Each page in the grid displays the resultset generated by the following query with two parameters:

```
SELECT o.orderid, o.orderdate, c.companyname
FROM orders AS o
INNER JOIN customers AS c ON o.customerid=c.customerid
WHERE Year(orderdate)=@TheYear AND Month(orderdate)=@TheMonth
```

The year is selected only once per page through the drop-down list. The month is determined from the page index. The method that creates the data source is shown here:

```
DataTable CreateDataSource(int nYear, int nMonth) {
    SqlConnection conn;
    conn = new SqlConnection(m_connString);
    SqlCommand cmd = new SqlCommand(m_cmdQuery, conn);
    cmd.Parameters.Add("@TheYear", SqlDbType.Int).Value = nYear;
    cmd.Parameters.Add("@TheMonth", SqlDbType.Int).Value = nMonth;

    SqlDataAdapter da = new SqlDataAdapter(cmd);
    DataTable dt = new DataTable();
    da.Fill(dt);
    return dt;
}
```

In this case, the data source is fully identified by the page index. Generally, the page index is only the starting point to get any information useful for obtaining the final data source. For example, suppose you're paging through the customers of your company. In this case, a user interface in which pages are rendered as groups of initials (for example, A-D, E-H, and so forth) produces much more user-friendly results. To obtain that, only minimal changes to the discussed infrastructure are needed.

To start out, you define an array of information that will be accessed through the page index. In this case, you define each page with a string of initials and store the resulting array in the view state. (You can use any structure as long as it is serializable.)

```
void Page_Load(object sender, EventArgs e) {
    if (!IsPostBack) {
        ArrayList a = new ArrayList();
        a.Add("a-b-c-d");
        a.Add("e-f-g-h");
        a.Add("i-j-k-l");
        a.Add("m-n-o");
        a.Add("p-q-r");
        a.Add("s-t-u");
        a.Add("v-w-x-y-z");
        ViewState["PageMap"] = a;
        grid.VirtualItemCount = a.Count*100; //100 is max page size
        LoadData();
    }
}
```

The query that creates the data source adds a LIKE criterion to the WHERE clause for each letter in the selected string of initials:

```
private DataTable CreateDataSource() {
    // Retrieve the paging info
    ArrayList info = (ArrayList) ViewState["PageMap"];
    string strInitials = info[grid.CurrentPageIndex].ToString();
```

```
    // Prepare the SQL command to execute
    StringBuilder sb = new StringBuilder("");
    sb.Append(m_cmdQuery);

    // Append a WHERE clause for each initial in the comma-separated string
    string[] a = strInitials.Split('-');
    for(int i=0; i<a.Length; i++) {
        sb.Append("customerid LIKE '");
        sb.Append(a[i].ToUpper());
        sb.Append("%'");
        if (i < a.Length-1)
            sb.Append(" OR ");
    }
    string strCmd = sb.ToString();
    SqlDataAdapter da = new SqlDataAdapter(strCmd, m_connString);
    DataTable dt = new DataTable();
    da.Fill(dt);
    return dt;
}
```

Figure 7-9 shows the final results.

Figure 7-9 A customized grid that displays logically grouped data.

Conclusion

No matter what type of application you are building—whether it's a Web application, Microsoft Windows application, or Web service—you can rarely afford downloading and caching the whole data source you're expected to display. Sometimes, test environments might lead you to believe such a solution works great and is the preferable one. Even more often, test environments lie and mislead you. The size of the data source does matter, and the more the application must be scaled the more size does matter.

The *DataGrid* control has two ways of paging. In one case, you bind the control to the whole data source and let it go. For Web applications, this approach is twice as risky. For one thing, you must be sure you tested the application with sample databases of the proper order of magnitude. Also, a Web application loses its state across two successive requests and the *DataGrid* control doesn't employ countermeasures to avoid that. As a result, each time the page is requested, the data source must be restored. In summary, either you can afford caching the whole data source or opt for the second type of paging—custom paging. In addition, while computing the size of the data source, don't forget to multiply it by a factor if the data to cache is session specific!

Custom paging is a memory-effective technique. Only the data needed at a particular time is loaded into memory. If this approach sounds familiar—perhaps familiar even to the point of déjà vu—you're more than right. Custom paging is a common best practice for paging—integrated here with an ASP.NET server control and exposed by the framework. You should consider using custom paging for everything except small and global data with a low level of volatility.

A second problem to consider for data paging is the structure and the content of each page. What's a page in your particular context? Is it simply a sequence of data rows listed in any order? Or is a page a group of related records that respond to some criteria? In this chapter, we showed how to customize paging to make a *DataGrid* display rows grouped by months or name. SQL commands are key elements to setting up functional and effective pagination. Paging through the resultset returned by a query is not a feature the SQL language supports natively as part of the SQL-92 standard. For this reason, you should look carefully at the features of the SQL language for the particular DBMS you're using.

In the next chapter, we'll look at how to make the data-access layer more effective and data-driven applications more user-friendly. We'll consider compound queries and scalability, but also reporting and master/detail views.

Resources

- Data Paging: Display Your Data One Page at a Time (*http://www.aspnetpro.com/features/2002/05/asp200205wf_f/asp200205wf_f.asp*)
- Customizing Pagination (*http://www.aspnetpro.com/features/2002/03/asp200203de_f/asp200203de_f.asp*)
- Paging Results with ASP.NET's PagedDataSource (*http://www.sitepoint.com/article/921*)
- Paging with Repeater control in ASP.NET (*http://www.charon.co.uk/content.asp?CategoryID=4&ArticleID=21*)
- Design a Custom Paging Solution (*http://www.fawcette.com/dotnetmag/2002_10/magazine/columns/architecting*)

8

Real-World Data Access

Adults should put in their work the same seriousness that children put in their games.

—*Friedrich Nietzsche*

Almost all data-driven applications look alike. They need to fetch data across different tables, join columns, and filter data based on some user-specific criteria. Data-driven applications must also format data in such a way that it can be easily (and pleasantly) consumed by end-users. In this context, the organization of the output, pagination, and editing models are key issues. More often than not, data is made of cross-related tables in which parent/child relationships are necessary to define the data model and to extract a specific subset of information (for example, detail views and subtotals) quickly and easily.

All distributed applications must be scalable to some extent. In general, Web applications are more sensitive to the issue of scalability than desktop, client/server applications. If a Web application is deployed over the Internet and made open to anonymous users—for example, a shopping Web site—providing a good, if not optimal, level of scalability is a sort of survival test. Scalability is related to performance, but it can't be identified exclusively with that. Likewise, performance affects scalability. However, they're not synonymous. For example, an application with a long response time will often have an overall software architecture that scales well, either up or out, to avoid performance degradation as the number of users grows. On the other hand, you will often run across extremely fast and super-optimized applications whose designs are not very scalable. A general law of performance tuning states that you must know the underpinnings of a system to devise tricks to increase the throughput.

In summary, optimizing performance involves making assumptions and choosing average values as indicators of the typical workload. In contrast, scalability just refers to the system's ability of maintaining the same level of performance as the number of concurrent users and the workload grows.

In general, caching data does not seem to be an optimal choice for all Web applications because it consumes valuable resources on a per-user or per-application basis. As a result, having less memory available to the Web server might lead to performance degradation. An application that needs to be *only* fast should be as stateless as possible and, subsequently, avoid caching state information. On the other hand, if you're developing an application that needs to be both fast *and* scalable, you should carefully consider caching data at some level to reduce the workload on middle-tier processing components. In addition, the more tiered your system is, the more options you have to scale it out as long as disconnected caches of data can be moved across the tiers. In the area of speed and scalability, ADO.NET helps considerably. ADO.NET doesn't perform magic or provide a ready-to-use solution for every scenario. The true power of ADO.NET is the set of tools it supplies for you to build highly scalable and reasonably fast Web applications that are suited to your needs.

The *DataSet* and its satellite classes (*DataRelation* in particular) are efficient and effective tools that primarily offer options to accomplish common tasks in real-world, data-driven Web applications. After evaluating the characteristics and expectations of your particular application, you should choose the right combination of old-style and new-style programming. Do not trust those who depict ADO.NET as a magic wand that makes Web applications fast and scalable with nothing more than a simple touch. And also don't trust those who completely disregard ADO.NET. At a minimum, ADO.NET provides you with new and powerful tools. It's up to you, then, to decide in any given situation whether they can help or not.

This chapter is divided in three parts, the first of which is about the ADO.NET best practices for executing cross-table commands—the typical commands of a real Web application. The other parts tackle two specific issues—subtotaling and master/detail views—whose effective implementation depends to some extent on the execution of compound queries.

Compound Commands

Even the simplest Web application has a rather complex and interrelated structure of databases. While a database with dozens of related tables, views, constraints, and triggers is not that common, I have yet to see a (nontoy) Web application with less than a handful of related tables. As a result, the need for Web applications to execute commands against a multitude of tables is more concrete than ever and, therefore, must be properly addressed.

The problem with more complicated databases has to do with both queries and updates. Users should be able to access and filter related rows, such as all orders generated within a given period by a particular customer. They also must be able to update or delete rows in a way that does not violate the consistency and integrity of the database. Some databases resort to server-side constraints to block undesired changes. The fact that most database administrators use this strategy to stay on the safe side is not a good reason to avoid code that could potentially corrupt the database. Ideally, client applications should submit changes that respect the database structure and its internal update rules (for example, relationships and constraints).

Conducting Multiple Queries

In light of the ADO.NET capabilities, we can recognize two ways of conducting multiple queries that span across multiple tables—an old way and a new way. The old-fashioned way is typical of ADO and any former data-access technology. Based on the SQL JOIN command, this well-known programming technique returns a single data structure that is quite easy to filter but hard to update and is populated with redundant data.

The alternative approach, touted by the ADO.NET disconnected model, exploits the capabilities of the *DataSet* object—that is, a multitable cache of data. The idea is that you split the original query into two or more distinct queries and gather the results in separate tables within the same *DataSet* object. The queries can be run individually or grouped in a stored procedure or in a batch. Using split queries results in a much more compact data set that can be easily managed via the programming interface of the *DataSet* and *DataRelation* objects. Separate queries managed through ADO.NET support cascading changes and batch updates, and they don't require synchronization code to be written on your end to retrieve the children of a parent row. On the downside, filtering records over a relation is not particularly easy.

Using Joined Queries

Suppose you need to obtain, grouped by customer, all orders issued in a given year. You don't want all the orders, though, only those with at least 30 items. In addition, you want the name of the employee who processed the order and the name of the company that issued it. The query can be written like this:

```
SELECT o.CustomerID, od.OrderID, o.OrderDate, o.ShippedDate,
       SUM(od.Quantity * od.UnitPrice) AS price,
       c.CompanyName, e.LastName
FROM Orders o INNER JOIN
     Customers c ON c.CustomerID=o.CustomerID INNER JOIN
     Employees e ON e.EmployeeID=o.EmployeeID INNER JOIN
     [Order Details] od ON o.OrderID=od.OrderID AND o.OrderID=od.OrderID
```

```
WHERE (YEAR(o.OrderDate) = 1997)
GROUP BY o.CustomerID, c.CompanyName, od.OrderID, o.OrderDate,
        o.ShippedDate, e.LastName
HAVING (SUM(od.Quantity) > 30)
ORDER BY o.CustomerID, od.orderid
```

The query spans the Northwind tables—Orders, Order Details, Customers, and Employees. It retrieves all orders with more than 30 items and is grouped by customer and filtered by year. Viewed through Microsoft SQL Server Query Analyzer, the result set looks like Figure 8-1.

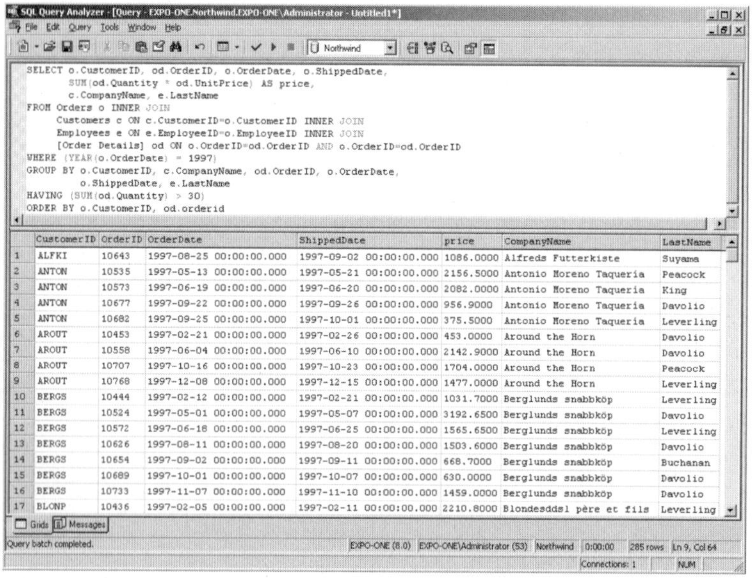

Figure 8-1 The result of a query that makes intensive use of JOIN statements.

You can immediately see how much redundant data the result set contains. The query counts about 300 records, and each of them has a high likelihood of containing a duplicate customer or employee name. The main characteristic of a join query is that it returns data as a monolithic block. As mentioned, this is good news and bad news at the same time. The good news is the data is held in the same block of memory, works great for presentation purposes, and can be further filtered by simply adding some criteria to the object that represents it—either an ADO *Recordset* or an ADO.NET *DataTable*. The bad news is, the result set does not make good use of memory and might raise scalability issues. Also, keeping changes synchronized with the database is not trivial. Finding a match between an element in the result set and a table record is challenging, and this makes it hard to keep the data synchronized and even to apply changes.

ADO hierarchical recordsets have been an attempt to better sort things out. They gave developers a chance to design a hierarchical query through a made-to-measure (and, frankly, horrible) syntax. As a result, a tree of parent and child *Recordset* objects reduced the redundancy of data and made synchronization simpler. The main drawbacks of ADO hierarchical recordsets are the inability to access more than one data source and the overly simple update model. To this list, we should then add the annoyance of working with the notorious SHAPE language, which is needed to build such recordsets.

Another subtle point in favor of joined queries is the inherent transaction support that SQL Server (and in general any database management system) guarantees to individual commands. A complex query, especially if it includes subqueries or views, is made of different low-level operations that run in the context of the same implicit transaction. This guarantees that no concurrency issue would ever be raised, even for highly volatile databases. We'll return to this point later in the chapter in the "Respecting Data Integrity" section.

Paging Through the Results of *Any* Query

In Chapter 7, "Paging Through Data Sources," we discussed various ways of paging through the results of a query. In particular, we focused on building queries that return a page of data. However, we used very simple commands to query just a single table. The paging techniques we discussed can be applied to any query, even though they might sometimes require adjustments. In general, the pattern used to retrieve a page is as follows:

```
SELECT * FROM
    (SELECT TOP PageSize * FROM
        (SELECT TOP PageSize*PageIndex * FROM (query) AS t1
    ORDER BY KeyColumn DESC) AS t2
ORDER BY KeyColumn
```

Note that if you're going to sort by multiple columns you must add the DESC qualifier to all column names. If the *query* placeholder is a subquery, it can contain an inner ORDER BY clause only if a TOP clause is present. If you don't actually need a TOP clause, use TOP 100 PERCENT.

To greatly simplify coding, you could also define a view. Adapting the random paging sample we saw in Chapter 7 to work on the aforementioned orders query requires only minor changes. (See joins.aspx in the book samples.)

Using Distinct Queries

An alternative approach made particularly attractive by ADO.NET is separating an otherwise nested and complex query into multiple simpler queries. There's a double advantage to doing so. First, the amount of data returned to the client is significantly smaller. Second, the functionality of the ADO.NET *DataSet* object makes managing multiple tables straightforward.

Next, I'll show you a way to split the preceding query into smaller and relatively independent pieces. The query consists of three subqueries: getting a filtered view of orders and details, plus getting a view of related employees and customers, respectively.

The first query (shown below) selects all orders containing at least 30 items. In this slightly revised version, the query doesn't join with the Customers and Employees tables to get *foreign* information about the customer and employee who participated in the order.

```
SELECT o.CustomerID, od.OrderID, o.OrderDate, o.ShippedDate,
       SUM(od.Quantity * od.UnitPrice) AS price
FROM Orders o INNER JOIN
     Customers c ON c.CustomerID=o.CustomerID INNER JOIN
     Employees e ON e.EmployeeID=o.EmployeeID INNER JOIN
     [Order Details] od ON o.OrderID=od.OrderID AND o.OrderID=od.OrderID
WHERE (YEAR(o.OrderDate) = 1997)
GROUP BY o.CustomerID, od.OrderID, o.OrderDate, o.ShippedDate
HAVING (SUM(od.Quantity) > 30)
ORDER BY o.CustomerID, od.orderid
```

The other two queries serve only the purpose of providing extra information about the involved employees and customers. In their simplest form, the queries are written as follows:

```
SELECT employeeid, lastname FROM employees
SELECT customerid, companyname FROM customers
```

Of course, in this case all employees and customers will be selected, which is not exactly what a joined query would return. However, depending on the structure and goals of the application, this shortcut might be acceptable. In general, employees and customers represent data that has low volatility and, as such, is ideal for caching. The issue here is the size of the tables. If your company has thousands of employees and customers, caching entire tables might not be the best approach.

A query that returns only the employees and the customers referenced by the first query might be much more complex to write, however. It mostly depends on the complexity of the search criteria. The more sophisticated the criteria is, the more complex the child queries are, and subsequently, the higher the price is for the query. As usual, fine-tuning the query subsystem of an application is a delicate art.

Let's continue with the example and analyze what's needed to obtain only the employees and customers involved with the orders selected by the first query. The criteria set for these queries require you to group the information by orders and compute the quantity of orders (at least 180 in the following sample). Given this subset of orders, you can then extract distinct employees or customers:

```
SELECT DISTINCT * FROM
    (SELECT c.customerid, c.companyname FROM Customers c INNER JOIN
            Orders o ON o.customerid=c.customerid INNER JOIN
            [Order Details] od ON o.OrderID=od.OrderID
    WHERE (YEAR(o.OrderDate) = 1997)
    GROUP BY o.orderid, c.customerid, c.companyname
    HAVING (SUM(od.Quantity) > 180)
    ) AS t1
```

Similarly, for employees you use the following third query:

```
SELECT DISTINCT * FROM
    (SELECT e.employeeid, e.lastname, e.title FROM employees e INNER JOIN
        Orders o ON o.employeeid=e.employeeid INNER JOIN
        [Order Details] od ON o.OrderID=od.OrderID
    WHERE (YEAR(o.OrderDate) = 1997)
    GROUP BY o.orderid, e.employeeid, e.lastname, e.title
    HAVING (SUM(od.Quantity) > 180)
    ) AS t1
```

As you can see, in this case we're going to run three complex queries rather than just one. In other circumstances, filtering the satellite tables is considerably easier and faster. As we'll also see throughout this chapter, ADO.NET is not a magic solution and effective SQL commands are now, more than ever, essential for creating effective applications.

> **Note** Many Web applications cache global data in global objects such as *Cache*, *Application*, or *Session*. (We'll review these objects in detail in Chapter 14, "ASP.NET State Management.") A warning, though, must be raised here. Suppose you decide to split a complex query into separate queries and also decide to keep child queries simple by creating look-up tables with employee and customer information. Where do you cache that data? If you store data in *Session* or *Cache*—it depends on the required scope—be aware that both objects might be subject to unexpected clean-up because of process recycling (see Chapter 2), low memory conditions, or both. You should always check whether the cache is still there and reload it if necessary. In summary, consider that look-up tables might need to be frequently refreshed.

All the queries you obtained can be grouped in a SQL batch or stored procedure and handed off to a data adapter for actual population. You get back a *DataSet* with as many tables as there are queries in the statement. You can access and index tables individually and create in-memory relations between tables. Note that relationships must be set up manually because no feature in ADO.NET provides for automatic reading and processing of database relationship objects and constraints. For more information about ADO.NET relations, see Chapter 5, "The ADO.NET Object Model."

Tip Relations also offer a quick way to simulate in-memory JOINs. Suppose you have two tables (named Orders and Employees) filled with information on orders and employees, respectively. To create a relation between the two tables based on the common field employeeid, you would use the following code:

```
DataRelation rel = new DataRelation("Emp2Ord",
    employees.Columns["employeeid"],
    orders.Columns["employeeid"]);
data.Relations.Add(rel);
```

Finally, to add a new column to the Orders table that points to the lastname column in the parent table according to the relation, you would use the following code:

```
orders.Columns.Add("EmployeeName",
    typeof(string), "Parent(Emp2Ord).lastname");
```

To read the last name of the employee, you would simply refer to the newly created EmployeeName column on the in-memory Orders table.

Respecting Data Integrity

Another issue to consider is data consistency. A complex query that runs as a single SELECT statement works in the context of an implicit transaction and looks like an atomic piece of code. When you split that into separate queries, you should also consider the impact that concurrency might have on the state of the database. What if a customer is concurrently deleted or an order is modified between the subqueries? It might or might not be a problem for the application. In case it is, though, you must consider protecting the subqueries in a transaction so that other users are prevented from updating or inserting rows while the queries are executing.

Transactions are a unit of work that execute according to four principles—atomicity, consistency, isolation, and durability—often cumulatively known as ACID. For our purposes, the key element is isolation. The isolation property refers to the database's ability to shield each running transaction from the effects of other concurrently running transactions. If a transacted query is running at the same time someone else is updating the database, the final results can vary depending on the level of isolation set. Normally each transacted operation can have the level of isolation it needs. If the application needs absolute data consistency and cannot afford phantom rows, the only appropriate isolation level is *serializable.* A serializable transaction unlocks the tables only upon completion. With this level of isolation, reading uncommitted data (a process known as *dirty reads*) and getting phantom rows is not possible. Phantom rows refer to any situation in which transactions work on misaligned sets of data. A phantom row is a row that one transaction added but is unknown to the other concurrent transaction. Likewise, a row visible in one transaction but physically deleted by another is an example of phantom rows. Serializable transactions should be the last resource in database programming because they seriously affect the overall concurrency of the system.

If you need the power of serializable transactions without its burden, you can opt for a sort of compromise between joined and distinct queries. You first run the query by using nested JOINs as needed. Next, once the result set has been downloaded in an ADO.NET environment, you process the original *DataTable* and split its contents into smaller tables. On the server, the query works as a monolithic piece of code; the application, though, sees it as the union of distinct but related tables.

```
SELECT o.customerid, c.companyname, e.employeeid, e.lastname,
       od.orderid, o.orderdate, o.shippeddate,
       SUM(od.quantity*od.unitprice) AS price
FROM Orders AS o
INNER JOIN Customers AS c ON c.customerid=o.customerid
INNER JOIN Employees AS e ON e.employeeid=o.employeeid
INNER JOIN [Order Details] AS od ON o.orderid=od.orderid
    WHERE Year(o.orderdate) = @TheYear AND od.orderid=o.orderid
    GROUP BY o.customerid, c.companyname, od.orderid,
        o.orderdate, o.shippeddate, e.employeeid, e.lastname
    HAVING SUM(od.quantity) >@TheAmount
ORDER BY o.customerid
```

The next listing shows the structure of the code that works on the preceding query:

```
DataSet SplitData(DataSet ds)
{
    // Assumes that the DataSet has one table named Orders. The 2nd
```

```
    // column is CompanyName; the 4th column is LastName
    DataSet _dataset = new DataSet();

    // Make a full worker copy of the DataSet
    _dataset = ds.Copy();

    // Extract tables
    CreateCustomers(_dataset, ds);
    CreateEmployees(_dataset, ds);

    // Remove columns from Orders(companyname [2] and lastname [4])
    // so that the original table doesn't contain any longer data
    // moved into distinct tables
    _dataset.Tables["Orders"].Columns.RemoveAt(1);
    _dataset.Tables["Orders"].Columns.RemoveAt(3);

    return _dataset;
}
```

The code makes a full deep copy of the source *DataSet*, which will be used as the Orders table in the resulting new *DataSet*. This new *DataSet* then adds dynamically created tables for customers and employees. Finally, the columns now included in child tables are removed from the Orders table. The following code shows how the satellite Customers table is created:

```
// Create Customers
static void CreateCustomers(DataSet _dataset, DataSet orig)
{
    DataTable _customers = orig.Tables["Orders"].Clone();
    _customers.TableName = "Customers";

    // Remove unneeded columns (no data is involved)
    // Only the first two columns (CustomerID and CompanyName) are kept
    for(int i=2; i<_customers.Columns.Count - 1; i++)
        _customers.Columns.RemoveAt(2);

    // Fill with data
    string customerKey = "";
    foreach(DataRow row in _dataset.Tables["Orders"].Rows)
    {
        // Already sorted by CustomerID
        if(customerKey != row["customerid"].ToString())
        {
            // select distinct
            _customers.ImportRow(row);
            customerKey = row["customerid"].ToString();
        }
    }
```

```
    // Add to the DataSet
    _dataset.Tables.Add(_customers);
}
```

> **Note** A similar approach can also be used if you have an existing stored procedure to retrieve the data and want to manage its return data through distinct in-memory tables. If you can't modify the existing stored procedure, this approach is a viable solution.

Conducting Cross-Table Updates

When it comes to updating cross-related tables, the order in which each constituent statement executes is critical. For example, you can't delete an order without also deleting all its details. Likewise, you aren't normally allowed to add an invoice detail row without first adding its parent row. When related tables are involved, changes flow from the parent to the children in different ways, depending on the type of change—update, delete, or insert.

In general, there are two ways of conducting table updates—through a direct connection or batch update. In the direct connection case, you typically open a connection and execute the stored procedure or the SQL batch with all the logic and data you need to apply. In the batch update case, you typically yield to a middle-tier component, which takes care of submitting data to the database, possibly in an asynchronous way. This approach in a Web scenario requires you to serialize the data to be submitted from the Web server layer down to an internal tier, which holds a physical connection to the database. The availability of an easy-to-serialize object such as the *DataSet* and the powerful batch update mechanism of data adapters give you the tools to build highly scalable applications. But how can you effectively use these tools?

Cascading Changes

As mentioned in Chapter 5, a foreign key constraint set on a *DataTable* restricts the action performed when a value in a column is either deleted or updated. In a parent/child relationship between two tables, deleting a value from the parent table can affect the child rows in various ways. Typically, the child rows are also deleted. However, in some cases, the cascading action sets the child rows to null or default values. The action that works best for you can be programmatically selected using the programming interface of the *ForeignKeyConstraint* class.

What really matters, though, is that ADO.NET provides the tools to configure the runtime environment to automatically cascade changes from parent to child rows. Such a mechanism is important because it allows you to work on a *DataSet* object, enter changes, and if needed, have them propagated through the tree. When you have gone through all the changes, ADO.NET guarantees that all the tables in the *DataSet* have been properly updated. In addition, the *DataSet* is a disconnected and serializable object and is ideal for delivering the new image of the data to the middle-tier component for physical updates.

The Batch Update

Data submission is the process in which all in-memory changes are passed on to the back-end system for permanent storage. In ADO.NET, submission does not consist of a block of data being sent to the database—Microsoft SQL Server 2000 or any other—in a single shot. An ADO.NET batch update just executes individual statements on the target system, one for each change that needs to be submitted. For the most part, statements will be SQL statements.

The *DataSet* object can submit data to the database in batch mode by using the data adapter's *Update* method. Data can be submitted only on a per-table basis. The *Update* method prepares and calls a tailor-made statement for each inserted, updated, or deleted row in the specified *DataTable* object.

```
adapter.Update(dataSet, tableName);
```

The cascading changes feature guarantees that all the tables in the *DataSet* are in sync and consistent. The batch update is its natural complement, as it allows you to submit changes, one table at a time, to the database.

Rows are scanned and processed according to their natural order (their position in the table's *Rows* collection). If you need to process rows in a particular order, you must split the overall update process into various subprocesses, each working on the selected bunch of rows you need. For example, if you have parent/child related tables, you might want to start by modifying rows in both tables. Next, you delete rows in the child table, and after that, you delete rows in the parent table. Finally, you insert new rows in the parent table and finish with insertions into the child table. The following code snippet shows how to select and submit only the rows that have been added to a table:

```
// Submit all the rows that have been added to a given table
DataRow[] arrayOfRows = table.Select("", "", DataViewRowState.Added);
adapter.Update(arrayOfRows);
```

This solution is made possible by the fact that one of the *Update* overloads takes an array of *DataRow* objects, an overload that provides for the greatest flexibility.

> **Important** When serializing a *DataSet* object across the tiers of a system for update purposes, you're much better off using the subset of the *DataSet* that contains the changed rows. You get this smaller version by using the *GetChanges* method. If you're batch-updating from within the same AppDomain, though, this technique won't result in a significant improvement in performance.

Detecting and Resolving Update Conflicts

Data updates are based on a decidedly optimistic vision of concurrency. What happens if, by the time you attempt to apply your changes to the back-end system, someone else has modified the same records? Technically speaking, in this case you have a *data conflict*. How to handle conflicts is strictly application-specific, but the reasonable options can be easily summarized in three points: the first-win, last-win, and ask-the-user options:

- **First-win** The conflict is resolved by silently and automatically dropping the latest change—that is, the one you were trying to submit. To implement a first-win approach, you simply set the *ContinueUpdateOnError* property on the data adapter to *true*. If *ContinueUpdateOnError* is set to *true*, no exception is thrown when an error occurs during the update of a row. The error information is stored in the *RowError* property of the corresponding row. The batch-update process continues with subsequent rows.

- **Last-win** Your changes are applied regardless of the current status of the row. To implement this approach, you have to ensure only that the SQL command used to carry the update is not too restrictive to generate a data conflict. A data conflict, in fact, is raised when the SQL command finds no row to affect. If you build the SQL command so that it updates or deletes rows that match a primary key field, no data conflict will ever be raised. Conflict-aware SQL code is code generated by ADO.NET command-builders in which the WHERE clause ensures that the current and original status of the row match prior to proceeding with the statement. In the last-win approach, a special case is represented by the situation in which another user deleted the row you are trying to update. In this case, you should drop your change.

- **Ask-the-user** You should choose this route when the other two options don't work in all cases you can foresee. By default, a data conflict raises a *DBConcurrencyException* exception. Note that the exception is not raised if you set the *ContinueUpdateOnError* property to *true*. The *Row* property on the exception class returns a reference to the row in error. By reading the properties of such a *DataRow* object, you have access to both proposed and original values. You have no access to the underlying value, but you can obtain that by issuing another query against the database. At the end of the day, resolving the conflict means opting either for a first-win or last-win approach. In this case, you let the user decide, but you must provide him or her with enough information.

For Web applications, you normally choose one of the first two options and try to ensure that the update always ends without going back to the user for further interaction.

> **Important** Conflicts are not detected automatically by some special feature built into the ADO.NET runtime. Conflicts are caught only if the commands used to carry the batch update have certain characteristics. In particular, conflict-aware commands have quite a long WHERE clause, one in which the primary key is first checked to verify the identity of the row and then a number of other columns are checked against the values they had when the *DataSet* was originally built. You control the columns in the WHERE clause in two ways: either by writing your own commands (as shown in the upcoming text) or by setting the *SelectCommand* property of the data adapter. (See Chapter 5.)
>
> An alternative way of detecting conflicts is by using a timestamp column. You add a timestamp column to a table and set it with the current time whenever you update the table. This trick greatly simplifies both the operations needed to check whether a conflict is going to happen (forward checking) and the command itself. Checking a single field is much easier than checking multiple columns!

Stored Procedures in Batch Updates

One of the biggest drawbacks of the ADO batch update was that it was impossible for the user to intervene and modify the commands being used for the update. As discussed in Chapter 5, ADO.NET allows you to configure the command—insert, update, or delete—to use for any event and gives you a chance to link it to source columns. The following code shows how to use a stored procedure for all the updated rows of the table:

```
adapter.UpdateCommand = new SqlCommand();
adapter.UpdateCommand.CommandText = "sp_myUpdate";
adapter.UpdateCommand.CommandType = CommandType.StoredProcedure;
adapter.UpdateCommand.Connection = conn;

p1 = new SqlParameter("@empID", SqlDbType.Int);
p1.SourceVersion = DataRowVersion.Original;
p1.SourceColumn = "employeeid";
adapter.UpdateCommand.Parameters.Add(p1);

p2 = new SqlParameter("@firstName", SqlDbType.NVarChar, 10);
p2.SourceVersion = DataRowVersion.Current;
p2.SourceColumn = "firstname";
adapter.UpdateCommand.Parameters.Add(p2);

p3 = new SqlParameter("@lastName", SqlDbType.NVarChar, 20);
p3.SourceVersion = DataRowVersion.Current;
p3.SourceColumn = "lastname";
adapter.UpdateCommand.Parameters.Add(p3);
```

Notice the pair of properties, *SourceColumn* and *SourceVersion*, that allows you to define what column and what version of the column should be bound to the parameter. The possibility of using a stored procedure adds an unprecedented level of flexibility to the batch update, especially when cross-referenced tables are involved.

Using Transactions in Batch Updates

To execute transacted commands, you can either use the transaction-related statements of the database management system (DBMS) you're working with or rely on the .NET data provider's abstraction of a transaction. There's virtually no difference between the two approaches, as the .NET abstraction of a transaction simply exists in a managed wrapper that triggers a call to the underlying transactional infrastructure. When you call the *BeginTransaction* method on the connection object of a .NET data provider, a new transaction command executes over the connection. Let's consider the following snippet:

```
conn.Open();
SqlTransaction tran = conn.BeginTransaction();
⋮
tran.Commit();
conn.Close();
```

If you spy on the process by using a profiler tool, you'll see the following sequence of commands hitting the database:

```
SET TRANSACTION ISOLATION LEVEL READ COMMITTED;BEGIN TRANSACTION
⋮
COMMIT TRANSACTION
```

So the ADO.NET transaction object is useful because it makes the code you're writing less dependent on the physical structure of the database, but no significant difference occurs under the hood.

Once created, the transaction must be associated with the command or the commands you are about to run. For batch updates, this means the *UpdateCommand*, *InsertCommand*, and *DeleteCommand* must share the same transactional context.

Retrieving Server-Generated Values

A frequent problem of cross-table updates is that you have to use some values generated by the database for further statements within the same stored procedure or SQL batch. A typical situation in which this problem arises is when triggers are involved as well as identity columns. If you're using direct commands or stored procedures, there's not much that ADO.NET does for you. You must address the issue using the tools the database provides you with. Typically, using a subsequent query that reads critical values back fits the bill. The values can be exposed through output parameters or additional result sets. If identity columns are involved, you use the identity functions of the DBMS to retrieve them. For example, with SQL Server 2000, you use the SCOPE_IDENTITY function.

If you're using batch updates, ADO.NET provides a couple of built-in mechanisms that enable you to know the values actually stored in the database as a result of the update. The first mechanism is based on the *UpdatedRowSource* property of the command object. The other mechanism leverages the *RowUpdated* event on the data adapter object. Let's examine how to use each to retrieve the value of an identity column when a new record is added.

The *UpdatedRowSource* property tells the command object to look for values returned by the INSERT and UPDATE statements and to assign them to the *DataRow* object being updated in the batch. The net effect of this property is that, at the end of the batch, each inserted or updated row in the *DataTable* contains exactly the values of its counterpart in the database. If identity columns or triggers are around, the original, in-memory values of the row are automatically updated with the actual values stored in the database. Sounds great? It is, indeed, but for it to happen, a bit of work is required on your side. In particular, you have to define the insert and the update commands as stored procedures or SQL batches so that they execute the appropriate query to read values back. In other words, the ADO.NET batch update provides some handy facilities but there's only way to get server-generated—by reading them back with a batch query.

The *UpdatedRowSource* property is designed to look for output parameters, the first row of the next query, both, or neither. By default, the option to look for both is selected. The following batch inserts a new row into the Employees database whose employeeid column is the identity. Next, it retrieves the last identity value generated in the scope.

```
INSERT INTO employees (lastname, firstname) VALUES (@LName, @FName)
SELECT SCOPE_IDENTITY() AS employeeid
```

If you assign the previous statements to the *InsertCommand* property of a data adapter, the *UpdatedRowSource* property will catch the newly generated identity value and pass it along to the *DataRow* object being updated. By setting the *UpdatedRowSource* property to *Both* (the default) or *FirstReturnedRecord*, each inserted row processed through the batch update will have its employeeid column updated. You don't have to write any additional code.

> **Caution** It's highly recommended that you *don't* use this technique if commands are to be autogenerated using a command builder. The statements generated by a command builder don't include the required additional query and are generated when the data adapter's *Update* method is called. At this time, it is too late for editing the command text to add the extra query. You should not use the *UpdatedRowSource* property if you are using command builders.

The SCOPE_IDENTITY function returns the last identity value inserted into an identity column in the same stored procedure, trigger, function, or batch. If you're using SQL Server 7.0 or earlier, use @@IDENTITY instead. SCOPE_IDENTITY, IDENT_CURRENT, and @@IDENTITY are similar functions in that they return values inserted into identity columns. For more information on the difference between these features, see the SQL Server Books Online.

Whenever the data adapter is going to update a row within a batch update, it fires a couple of events—*RowUpdating* and *RowUpdated*. *RowUpdating* fires before the update takes place and *RowUpdated* fires immediately after. The following code shows how to specify an event handler for the *RowUpdated* event.

```
adapter.RowUpdated += new SqlRowUpdatedEventHandler(RowUpdated);
```

The event passes back a data structure of type *SqlRowUpdatedEventArgs* in which the *Row* property returns an updated row. (We're using SQL Server as the data provider; the code would have to be adapted for other providers.) The *RowUpdated* event is provided mostly for databases that don't support stored procedures, multiple queries, and output parameters. Want an example? Microsoft Access.

> **Important** Bear in mind that the automatic update of the *DataRow* occurs only during batch updates and only if you add output parameters to the command (for example, a stored procedure) or additional queries to retrieve particular fields. Also note that the name of the retrieved column must match the name of the *DataTable* column. That's why we aliased SCOPE_IDENTITY in the earlier sample (on page 403).

Data Reporting and Subtotals

In ASP.NET, the *DataGrid* is the ideal tool for building feature-rich data reports. As we've seen in Chapter 6, "Creating Bindable Grids of Data," and Chapter 7, it provides for paging, sorting, and advanced customization of the data displayed. Despite its adeptness at building feature-rich reports, the *DataGrid* does not have an ad hoc feature to automatically compute functions on the values listed in a given column. In Chapter 6, we demonstrated how to add a footer to a table built with the *DataGrid* and how to modify the structure of the footer to display totals. In computing totals for a column, though, we exploited the programming interface of the *DataTable* and *DataRelation* objects.

Keep in mind that a total is a scalar value you display only in a single place—typically, a cell in the footer bar. Displaying a total doesn't in any way affect the rows you display in the grid. Unfortunately, the same can't be said for displaying column subtotals—they do affect rows you display in the grid.

A subtotal is a non–data-bound row that is interspersed with the data rows of the grid. Like a footer bar, it can have any structure and normally displays summary information that relates to the records found after the beginning of the table or the last subtotal. For example, if your grid displays orders grouped by customers, a subtotal row could count the number and total amount of all orders issued by each customer. The *DataGrid* control doesn't provide any built-in facility that works in this scenario, but with an appropriate combination of SQL and ASP.NET coding you can make it happen.

Summarizing or Aggregating Values

The key point to understand about *DataGrid* controls is that they don't distinguish between rows in the bound data source. All the bound rows are displayed and any attempt to insert fake rows programmatically is destined to fail or, even worse, to violate the consistency of the output. On the other hand, bound rows can be displayed with different styles, even radically different styles.

As a result, any subtotaling rows you want to display must be part of the data source you associate with the grid. These rows must be easily recognizable so that the *ItemDataBound* and *ItemCreated* event handlers can apply any necessary styling. How can you add summary rows to the data source? There are two possibilities. You can either ask the database to compute subtotal rows, or you can add blank rows and populate them with ad hoc data. In many cases, the database subtotaling capabilities will match your expectations. If you need to control the whole process of aggregation, or if the database you're targeting doesn't provide subtotaling support, you should opt for a pure ADO.NET approach.

The WITH ROLLUP Operator

Subtotaling makes particular sense if you're also grouping data. SQL Server provides the WITH ROLLUP operator as an extension to the GROUP BY clause of a SELECT statement. The operator works by adding summary rows to the result set according to a specified template. The summary row will have the same layout as all other columns, but you can customize the content of each column to some extent. Let's consider a sample query: getting all orders issued in a given year (say, 1997) grouped by customers. The SQL query to start with is the following:

```
SELECT o.customerid, od.orderid, SUM(od.quantity*od.unitprice) AS price
FROM Orders o, [Order Details] od
WHERE YEAR(o.orderdate)=1997 AND od.orderid=o.orderid
GROUP BY o.customerid, od.orderid
ORDER BY o.customerid, od.orderid
```

Figure 8-2 shows the results as they appear in SQL Query Analyzer. The arrows indicate where we would like to have subtotal rows.

Let's rewrite the query to use the WITH ROLLUP operator and compute order subtotals per customer:

```
SELECT
    o.customerid AS MyCustomerID,
    CASE GROUPING(od.orderid) WHEN 0 THEN od.orderid ELSE 99999 END
        AS MyOrderID,
    SUM(od.quantity*od.unitprice) AS OrderAmount
FROM Orders o, [Order Details] od
```

```
WHERE Year(orderdate) = 1997 AND od.orderid=o.orderid
GROUP BY o.customerid, od.orderid WITH ROLLUP
ORDER BY o.customerid, MyOrderID
```

	customerid	orderid	price	
1	ALFKI	10643	1086.0000	
2	ALFKI	10692	878.0000	
3	ALFKI	10702	330.0000	← Subtotal goes here
4	ANATR	10625	479.7500	
5	ANATR	10759	320.0000	← Subtotal goes here
6	ANTON	10507	881.2500	
7	ANTON	10535	2156.5000	
8	ANTON	10573	2082.0000	
9	ANTON	10677	956.9000	
10	ANTON	10682	375.5000	← Subtotal goes here
11	AROUT	10453	453.0000	
12	AROUT	10558	2142.9000	
13	AROUT	10707	1704.0000	
14	AROUT	10741	285.0000	
15	AROUT	10743	336.0000	
16	AROUT	10768	1477.0000	
17	AROUT	10793	191.1000	← Subtotal goes here
18	BERGS	10444	1031.7000	
19	BERGS	10445	174.9000	
20	BERGS	10524	3192.6500	
21	BERGS	10572	1565.6500	

Grids Messages

Figure 8-2 A result set that groups order information by customer.

The first thing to notice is that the GROUP BY clause has been extended to include the WITH ROLLUP operator. The second column—originally od.orderid—has been replaced with a more complex CASE...WHEN construct. The CASE...WHEN statement is a simple flow controller, however. The resulting column contains the corresponding od.orderid value if the guarded value is 0; otherwise, it contains 99999. This brings us to the role of the GROUPING function.

GROUPING is an aggregate function that takes the name of a column in the GROUP BY clause and returns an additional column with 0/1 values. A value of 0 means the row has been generated by the query; a value of 1 indicates the row is a summary row added by the ROLLUP operator. The following code snippet shows how to add an extra column to the query. The *IsSummary* column indicates whether the row is a subtotal.

```
SELECT GROUPING(od.orderid) IsSummary,
⋮
```

In the preceding statement, no extra column is actually returned to the user, but the orderid column in the regular query is assigned a special value (99999 or whatever value you decide to use) if the row contains summary values.

The result set of the WITH ROLLUP query contains summary rows characterized by the 99999 value in the MyOrderID field. (If you can't figure out a neutral value for a column, just add an additional 0/1 column based on the output of the GROUPING function.) An appropriate order in the query makes any summary rows appear as the last row of each group. Displaying subtotals is now a simple matter of styling the grid.

	MyCustomerID	MyOrderID	OrderAmount
1	NULL	99999	658388.7500
2	ALFKI	10643	1086.0000
3	ALFKI	10692	878.0000
4	ALFKI	10702	330.0000
5	ALFKI	99999	2294.0000
6	ANATR	10625	479.7500
7	ANATR	10759	320.0000
8	ANATR	99999	799.7500
9	ANTON	10507	881.2500
10	ANTON	10535	2156.5000
11	ANTON	10573	2082.0000
12	ANTON	10677	956.9000
13	ANTON	10682	375.5000
14	ANTON	99999	6452.1500
15	AROUT	10453	453.0000

Grids | Messages

Figure 8-3 Rollup information in a grouped query.

> **Note** The ROLLUP operator is not the only aggregator available in SQL Server 2000. SQL Server 2000 also supports COMPUTE BY, although it is used only for backward compatibility. Contentwise, the result set generated by a ROLLUP operation is identical to that returned by a COMPUTE BY statement. Other differences, though, tip the scales in favor of ROLLUP. For example, ROLLUP returns a single result set. In contrast, COMPUTE BY returns multiple result sets that increase the complexity of code necessary to handle the data. In addition, only ROLLUP can be used in a server cursor, and the query optimizer can sometimes generate more efficient execution plans for it.
>
> The CUBE operator, on the other hand, has programmatic characteristics that assimilate it with ROLLUP. The result set generated, though, is quite different because CUBE explodes data and produces a superset of groups with cross-tabulation of every column to the value of other columns.

A Pure ADO.NET Approach

If the database doesn't support any aggregate operator that groups data, you can calculate the needed values yourself and insert the summary rows manually with a bit of ADO.NET coding. A possible way of doing that entails the steps shown in the following paragraphs.

Fetch any needed data. You do this by executing a couple of queries against the database. The first retrieves all orders to be displayed but is limited to returning the customer ID, order ID, and total amount of the order.

```
SELECT customerid, od.orderid, SUM(od.quantity*od.unitprice) AS price
    FROM Orders o, [Order Details] od
    WHERE Year(orderdate) = @nYear AND od.orderid=o.orderid
GROUP BY od.orderid, o.customerid ORDER BY o.customerid
```

The second query selects all distinct customers and for each of them counts the orders and computes the total:

```
SELECT c.customerid, c.CompanyName,
    Total=SUM(od.quantity*od.unitprice),
    TotalOrders=COUNT(DISTINCT od.OrderID)
FROM Customers c, [Order Details] od, Orders o
WHERE Year(orderdate)=@nYear AND
      c.CustomerID=o.CustomerID AND
      o.OrderID=od.OrderID
GROUP BY c.CompanyName, c.CustomerID ORDER BY c.customerid
```

Once the two tables are in memory, you programmatically add empty rows to the orders table and create a sorted view of the table so that the empty rows show up as the last row of each customer group. Next, you can customize a little bit of the text shown by the additional rows so that the final output looks like Figure 8-4. The full source code for the Subtotal sample is available in the book samples.

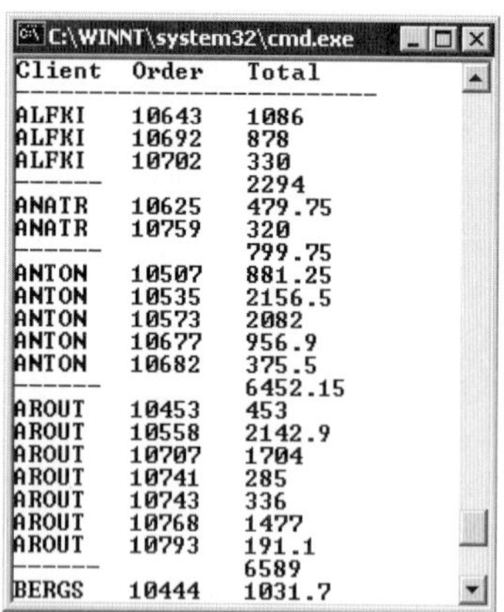

Figure 8-4 A console application that adds summary rows to the tables of a *DataSet*.

Setting Up the *DataGrid*

Let's take the result set shown in Figure 8-3 and display it through a *DataGrid* control. The output looks like Figure 8-5. The rows with a black background are the summary rows added by the ROLLUP operator. Notice, though, that the highlighted background in the figure is only a graphical effect on the picture. The *DataGrid* control has no built-in logic to detect a summary row. Adding such logic is exactly the goal of this section.

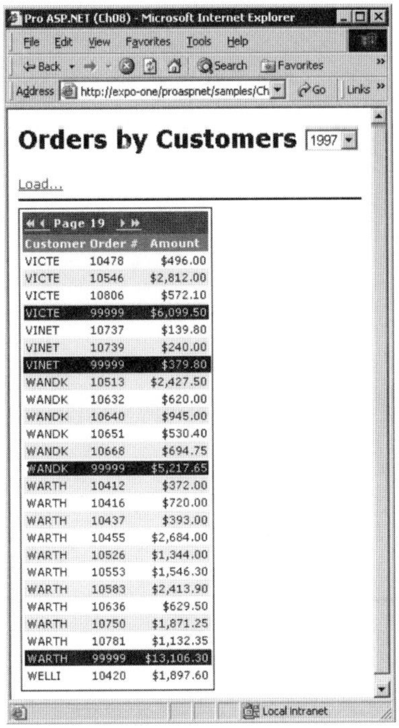

Figure 8-5 Displaying the output of a *ROLLUP* query using a *DataGrid* control.

Having summary rows in the data source is not enough. We must be able to distinguish summary rows from ordinary bound rows and render the summary rows with different visual styles.

When the *DataGrid* is rendered in HTML, it fires a couple of events to the page—*ItemCreated* and *ItemDataBound*. As we saw in Chapter 6, by hooking those events you can analyze the data object being drawn and set its styles. In doing so, you test the value of the MyOrderID column against the well-known value of 99999 and decide whether that row is to be rendered as a summary row.

Formatting the Summary Row

When the *ItemCreated* event fires, no data has yet been bound to the *DataGrid* item. You can apply visual styles only from within the *ItemCreated* event. However, before creating the appearance of a summary row, we first need to verify that it is a summary row. To verify that the current row is just a summary row, we need to access the underlying data object and check its MyOrderID column. *ItemCreated* is not the ideal place to check for this condition, so let's hook *ItemDataBound* instead. The following code shows the *ItemDataBound* event handler for the sample page shown in Figure 8-6.

```
void ItemDataBound(object sender, DataGridItemEventArgs e)
{
    CustomizeItem(e);
}

void CustomizeItem(DataGridItemEventArgs e)
{
    DataRowView drv = (DataRowView) e.Item.DataItem;
    if (drv != null)
    {
        // Current row is a summary row
        if ((int) drv["MyOrderID"] == 99999)
        {
            // Yellow background and bold font
            e.Item.BackColor = Color.Yellow;
            e.Item.Font.Bold = true;

            // Remove the cell with the Order ID
            e.Item.Cells.RemoveAt(1);

            // Span the Customer ID cell to cover two cells
            e.Item.Cells[0].ColumnSpan = 2;
            e.Item.Cells[1].HorizontalAlign = HorizontalAlign.Right;
        }
    }
}
```

Summary rows are given a different background color and a boldface font. In addition, we also modify the structure of the row by removing the second cell (the one containing the order ID) and enlarging the first to span over two logical cells. The last column, which contains the total amount of the order, is then right-aligned. Note that after a cell is removed, you must reassign any properties (for example, horizontal alignment) to all the cells.

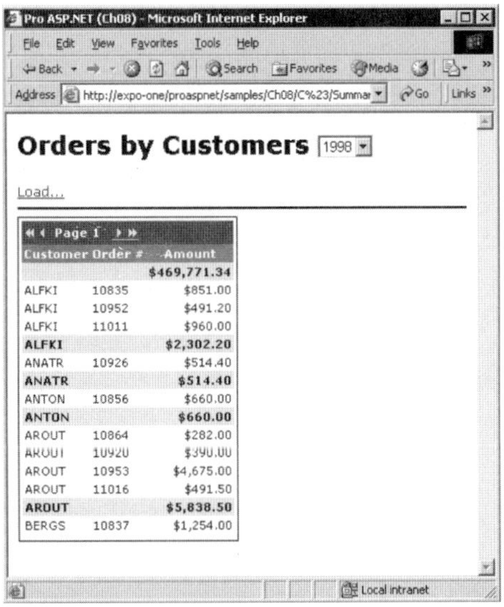

Figure 8-6 Summary rows display with different styles and a different layout.

Setting Up the Footer

As you can see in Figure 8-6, the first row in the result set contains the total of all orders selected by the query. If you're going to display a list of orders, keep in mind that information simply doesn't belong on the page. You can remove the first row of the *DataTable* at any time before you bind it to the *DataGrid*.

```
// Fill the DataSet
DataSet ds = new DataSet();
da.Fill(ds, "Orders");

// Remove the first row but cache the total of orders
decimal total = (decimal) ds.Tables["Orders"].Rows[0]["total"];
ds.Tables["Orders"].Rows.RemoveAt(0);
ViewState["TotalAmountOfOrders"] = total;
```

To remove a row within a table, you call the *RemoveAt* method on the *Rows* collection. The *RemoveAt* method can take either a *DataRow* object or the 0-based index of the row to remove. The row is physically detached from the table, but it's not destroyed as an object until it goes out of scope.

The Total column on the first row contains the total amount of all the orders issued by all customers in the specified year. That information might be valuable as well, but it's better to display it in the footer. To have it available for each request, we cache it in the page view state or in any other global repository:

```
void CustomizeFooter(DataGridItemEventArgs e)
{
    e.Item.Cells[2].HorizontalAlign = HorizontalAlign.Right;
    e.Item.Cells[2].Text = String.Format("{0:c}",
        ViewState["TotalAmountOfOrders"]);
}
```

Figure 8-7 shows the total of all orders displayed in the footer.

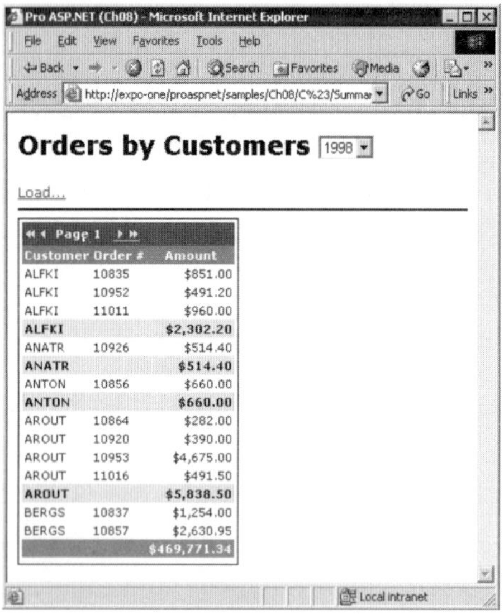

Figure 8-7 The footer shows the total of all orders.

Adding Statistical Information

So far we've used a summary row in which the customerid column dumbly repeated the ID of the above customer. While this is a possibility, more useful information can be provided. For example, you could count the orders that a given customer has issued in the year, and spice it up with some statistics, such as a calculation of the orders as a percentage of the total volume for the year:

```
void CustomizeItem(DataGridItemEventArgs e)
{
    DataRowView drv = (DataRowView) e.Item.DataItem;
    if (drv != null)
    {
        // current row is a summary row
        if ((int) drv["MyOrderID"] == 99999)
```

```
        {
            // Yellow background and bold font
            e.Item.BackColor = Color.Yellow;
            e.Item.Font.Bold = true;

            // Remove the cell with the Order ID
            e.Item.Cells.RemoveAt(1);

            // Set up the alignment for the last column
            e.Item.Cells[1].HorizontalAlign = HorizontalAlign.Right;

            // Count the orders for the customer
            DataTable dtOrders = drv.Row.Table;
            int orderCount = (int) dtOrders.Compute(
                "Count(customerid)",
                "customerid='"+drv["customerid"]+"'") -1;

            // Calculate the percentage of the total volume
            decimal amount = (decimal) drv["price"];
            decimal total = (decimal) ViewState["TotalAmountOfOrders"];
            decimal percent = 100 * amount / total;

            // Set up the first cell
            e.Item.Cells[0].ColumnSpan = 2;
            e.Item.Cells[0].Style["font-weight"] = "400";
            e.Item.Cells[0].Style["font-size"] = "80%";
            string msg = String.Format("{0} order(s) [{1:n}%]",
                orderCount, percent);
            e.Item.Cells[0].Text = msg
        }
    }
}
```

There are many ways to count the orders for each customer. Probably the most effective way consists of calculating them once and caching the few bytes somewhere in the view state or session state. In the following sample code, we count them each time using the *Compute* method of the *DataTable* object. (This is definitely not a smart choice for a real application, but it gives us a chance to show an interesting use of the ADO.NET model.)

```
int count = dtOrders.Compute("Count(customerid)",
    "customerid='" + drv["customerid"] + "'") -1;
```

Of course, you must subtract one from the total because it also includes the summary row.

Finally, as the code shows, you can use custom visual settings for each cell in the row. The first cell, in fact, is displayed without boldface type and with a font size 80 percent smaller than the default, as shown in Figure 8-8.

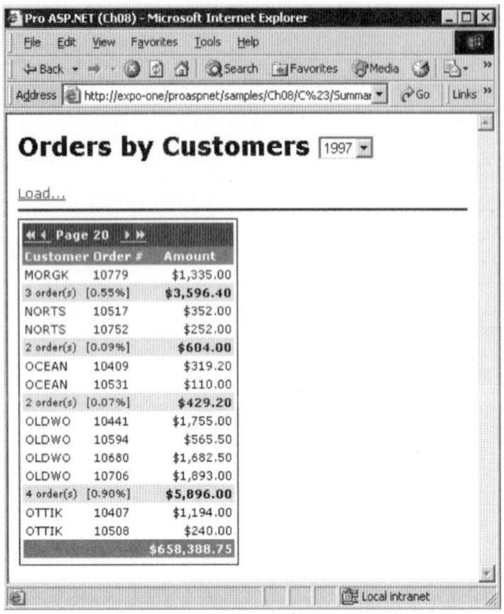

Figure 8-8 Statistical information shown in the summary row.

The summary information can take up any number of rows in the grid. However, if multiple rows are necessary, you should insert additional rows yourself using the approach discussed earlier.

Master/Detail Views

Applications based on interrelated tables often need to provide a hierarchical navigation mechanism to enable users to sort through various parent/child table relationships. For example, a user can pick a customer from a menu and then see all the orders the selected customer has issued. Next, the user can click on a particular order and have all its details displayed. When such parent/child relationships exist, a child table is always associated with a particular element on the parent table. What, then, would be an effective way of retrieving and displaying parent/child information in an ASP.NET application?

ADO.NET provides a rich in-memory, database-like infrastructure that makes it particularly easy to define relationships between tables and extract child rows from parent rows. The downside is that a roundtrip occurs whenever a user clicks on a row to go one level down or up. As a result, the page posts back and is completely rebuilt from scratch. The hierarchical data that is necessary to fill the page is either cached on the Web server or downloaded over and over again from the database. As discussed in Chapter 6 and Chapter 7, caching is an excellent choice if you can afford it. Otherwise, retrieving small pieces of data, and retrieving them only when you need them, is an alternative technique that consumes a minimum amount of server resources. If you're caching data across page requests, do it using the *DataSet* object and create as many relationships as needed. Doing this will allow you to retrieve the related rows quickly and effectively.

In the rest of this chapter, we'll build a master/detail application that addresses issues you'll encounter in the real world. The application contains three related grids that display customers, orders for a customer, and the details of an order. We'll use the *SelectedIndexChanged* event to command a more specific query and drill down into the data. We'll also use different techniques for paging and sorting the data. The different views of the data are implemented using inline frames.

Listing the Customers

The sample page we'll consider is made of a master grid that pages through a set of customers. We'll use custom paging and also add sorting capabilities to the *DataGrid*. Figure 8-9 shows the grid in action with an applied filter that selects only the customers based either in Italy or Spain.

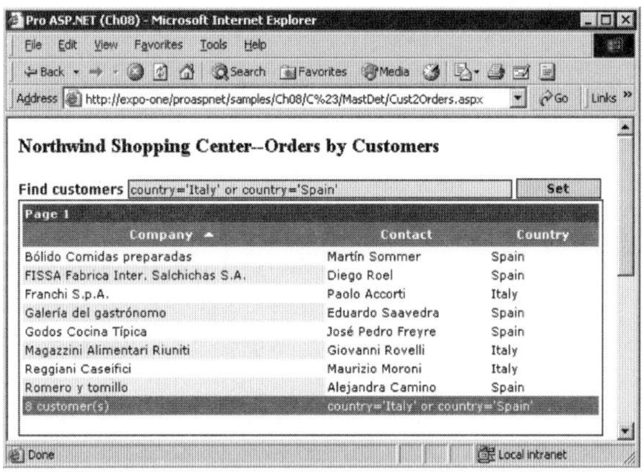

Figure 8-9 A sortable and pageable grid that lets you select a customer. By clicking on the customer name, you can see the orders the customer has issued.

The grid retrieves only the records that fit in the current page based on the sort expression. This is a combination of styles we didn't fully cover in Chapter 6 and Chapter 7 when we explored the paging and sorting mechanism of the grid. If you plan to use custom paging and sorting together, you can't use a client-side mechanism (for example, a *DataView*) to sort records. The *DataView* in fact has limited visibility over the set of records and would actually sort only records in the current page. Sometimes this feature is acceptable, sometimes not. If you want full sorting—that is, if you want to page through customers in a given order—the query command used to retrieve a page of records must be slightly enhanced.

Custom Paging and Sorting

To get a page of records, we use a query made of three nested SELECT statements that select the right subset and then re-order it. (See Chapter 7.) It's useful to recall the scheme we discussed earlier in this chapter in the "Paging Through the Results of Any Query" sidebar. The placeholders in boldface are elements you must configure properly.

```
SELECT * FROM
    (SELECT TOP size * FROM
        (SELECT TOP size*index *
            FROM (query ORDER BY KeyCol ASC) AS t0) AS t1
    ORDER BY KeyCol DESC) AS t2
ORDER BY KeyCol ASC
```

The *query* element is any SELECT statement that defines the set of records to be displayed. It can be as complex as needed and can include any clauses that make sense with a SELECT statement. In its simplest form, the *query* placeholder is the name of the table. As you can see, the *KeyCol* placeholder indicates the column (or the columns) to sort by. Each occurrence of the *KeyCol* placeholder is associated with a sort direction. If you request a default ascending order, only the second occurrence must be set to DESC. We fully explained the reason for this in Chapter 6. Of course, if you want to invert the direction, all direction placeholders must be reversed too. Note that if multiple columns are used, you must reverse the direction of each of them.

In this way, what you get from SQL Server is a properly sorted result set that can be bound to the grid without further manipulations. The following listing shows the new version of the *BindData* method:

```
void BindData() {
    string sortby = (string) ViewState["DataSortExpression"];
    DataTable _data = CreateDataSource(1 + grid.CurrentPageIndex, sortby);
    grid.DataSource = _data;
    grid.DataBind();
}
```

As we mentioned in Chapter 6, sorting is a subtle and complex operation that can add unnoticed overhead to your Web application. Going down to the database only for sorting is probably a bad hit to overhead, but if we're already using the database to page through a data set, asking it to return sorted data is a minor addition and probably the most effective approach.

> **Note** The Oracle ROWNUM operator numbers the rows in the result set before the sort is applied. So if you want rows sorted in some way, you must nest queries so that the innermost retrieves and sorts data and the outermost just ensures rows are correctly numbered. While I'm speaking of Oracle ROWNUM, I should mention that the next version of SQL Server is expected to support a similar feature but, at the time of this writing, the form, implementation, and syntax have not been decided upon.

The Selection Mechanism

When the user selects a row in the master grid, the *SelectedIndexChanged* event fires and updates the *SelectedIndex* property with the 0-based index of the row. As mentioned in Chapter 6, when the user clicks on a *DataGrid* column with a command name of *select*, two events are raised: *ItemCommand* and then *SelectedIndexChanged*. This sequence of events simplifies the implementation of the item deselection. While processing *ItemCommand*, the *SelectedIndex* property has not yet been updated. So you store the selected index in a global variable and compare it with the new selected index. If the two match, the user clicked two consecutive times on the same item. At this point, you deselect the item.

```
void ItemCommand(object sender, DataGridCommandEventArgs e) {
    switch(e.CommandName) {
        case "select":
            m_currentSelectedIndex = grid.SelectedIndex;
            break;
    }
}
void SelectedIndexChanged(object sender, EventArgs e) {
    if (m_currentSelectedIndex == grid.SelectedIndex) {
        UnselectItem();
        return;
    }
    SelectItem();
}
void SelectItem() {
    string custID = (string) grid.DataKeys[grid.SelectedIndex];
    string url = String.Format("orderslist.aspx?custid={0}", custID);
    ordersView.Attributes["Src"] = url;
}
```

When a customer is selected, the page refreshes the orders frame that points to a second page named orderslist.aspx. The page receives the ID of the customer as a query parameter, performs a query against the orders, and finally lists all the orders associated with that customer.

Note that if you can afford caching all the data, including customers and orders, you can easily retrieve the orders for a customer using a relation between the tables.

Using Inline Frames

Inline frames are browser windows that can be placed anywhere in the HTML code by using the *<iframe>* tag. The *<iframe>* tag is part of the HTML 4.0 standard. Note, though, that not all browsers support this element, which has been part of the Internet Explorer arsenal since version 4.0. Old Netscape Navigator 4.x browsers support a similar element, named *<layer>*, with a nearly identical overall goal and syntax.

There are no ASP.NET server controls to map the functionality of the *<iframe>* tag. If you mark it with the *runat* attribute, the ASP.NET runtime will render it using an instance of the *HtmlGenericControl* class. The following code declares a frame with a solid, single-line, flat border and no scrolling capabilities:

```
<iframe runat="server" id="ordersView"
    frameborder="no"
    scrolling="no"
    style="border:solid 1px;"
    width="100%"
    height="270px" />
```

To set the URL that the frame will display, you use the *Src* attribute. Note, though, that you can't set the *Src* attribute through a property because the *HtmlGenericControl* class doesn't provide for that. You must set it as an explicit HTML attribute using the *Attributes* collection.

```
ordersView.Attributes["Src"] = url;
```

To unselect a customer and clear the page with its orders displayed, you simply make the frame point to the *about:blank* URL. The *about* protocol is supported by most browsers, including old versions of Netscape browsers.

Listing the Orders

The orderslist.aspx page has a structure that is nearly identical to its parent page (cust2orders.aspx). It gets the customer ID from the query string and uses that to perform an ad hoc query against the database. The orders are then displayed through a pageable *DataGrid* control. One of the columns of the grid is a *But-*

tonColumn with a command name of *select*, which makes the items displayed truly selectable.

Normally the text of a *ButtonColumn* is a hyperlink element rendered with the default styles—that is, underlining and visited-link or active-link colors. To make it look like normal yet selectable text, you can resort to the following style declaration:

```
<style>
    a:hover {color:red;text-decoration:underline;}
    a       {text-decoration:none;}
</style>
```

The text will be underlined in red only when the mouse hovers over the text, as shown in Figure 8-10.

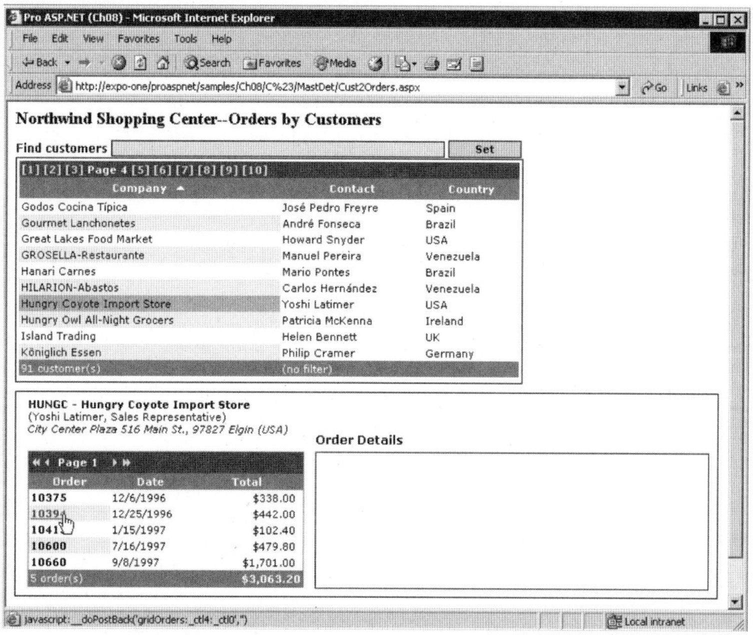

Figure 8-10 A pageable grid that shows the orders for a customer. By clicking on the order ID, you can see the details of that order.

Smart Caching

The orders *DataGrid* is pageable but does not use custom paging. It also does not cache all orders. It caches only the orders the grid needs to display—that is, the orders that relate to a given customer. The pagination takes place automatically within the *DataGrid* and is completely handled by the control.

Because the role of the grid is to display an unfiltered list of orders for a customer, chances are that concurrent users working in different sessions might be accessing the same set of records. For this reason, the population of the orders *DataGrid* occurs in two steps. First the code attempts to locate a slot in the ASP.NET global *Cache* object that contains the orders for the customers. If found, no database access is performed and the records are retrieved from memory. Otherwise, a query is run and the results are copied in to the *Cache* for further access by the same, or other, users.

```
void Page_Init(object sender, EventArgs e)
{
    // Store the current customer ID
    string tmp = (string) Request.QueryString["CustID"];
    m_currentCustomerID = tmp.Substring(0, 5);

    // Store the name of the DataSet as used within Cache
    m_dataSetName = String.Format(m_dataSetName, m_currentCustomerID);
}
```

The *Init* event fires at the beginning of the page request lifecycle. All the global data you set here is visible to all the other methods that are called as the request processing proceeds. In particular, we need to retrieve data from *Cache* to set up the footer. The footer is configured during the *DataGrid*'s *ItemCreated* event, which occurs before the page's *Load* event. For this reason, we need to store the name of the cache slot and the customer ID into global variables at the very beginning of the request processing.

> **Note** Each processing of a request results in a sequence of methods—event handlers, actually—being called one after the next. Any global variables you set at any point in this cycle work as expected. You can't, on the other hand, set global variables and expect that they will survive the request. If you need this to happen, use the *ViewState* object or any other global data container such as *Session* or *Cache*.

The naming convention used to recognize the slot within *Cache* that contains the orders of a particular customer is illustrated in the following line:

```
private string m_dataSetName = "Orders [{0}]";
```

The code in *Page_Init* replaces the placeholder with the actual customer ID read out of the query string. Also note that only the first five characters are taken into account—the known maximum length of a customer ID. As we'll see in Chapter 15, "ASP.NET Security," this simple trick can save you from a lot of trouble with malicious code and SQL injection attacks. The following code is used to populate the orders grid:

```
void DataFromSourceToMemory() {
    // Attempt to locate the orders from the cache in case other users
    // already retrieved them. Otherwise, read from the database
    DataSet ds;
    ds = (DataSet) Cache[m_dataSetName];
    if (ds == null)
        ds = PhysicalDataRead();

    // Stores orders in the cache
    Cache[m_dataSetName] = ds;
}
```

The *DataSet* we're caching for each accessed customer is made of two tables—the orders table and further customer information table. The second table holds only one record with registration data about the customer. Note that the *DataSet* is obtained using a SQL batch—that is, a couple of concatenated SQL statements. Both statements require the use of a parameter—the customer ID. Because the parameter is the same in both cases—and thanks to the SQL Server .NET provider's named parameters—you specify it only once. This wouldn't have been possible with position-based parameters.

Adding Templated Columns

In the Northwind database, orders are registered with a required date and a ship date. Users, though, might appreciate a simple flag positioned beside an order to denote whether the order shipped on time or not. Later, if needed, they could drill down and find date-related details. If you don't plan to show more than a Boolean flag to signify the delay of an order, you can modify the query to make SQL Server return a computed Boolean column. Otherwise, you query for both the *shippeddate* and *requireddate* columns and create an in-memory computed column to store the Boolean flag.

```
// Get the data
DataSet _data = new DataSet();
adapter.Fill(_data);
_data.Tables["Table"].TableName = "Orders";

// Add a custom column comparing ShippedDate and RequiredDate
_data.Tables["Orders"].Columns.Add("Delayed", typeof(bool),
    "shippeddate > requireddate");
```

How can you display this information? Although effective, a True or False string might not be a particularly friendly solution. In addition, rows with the most common value (say False, meaning that the order shipped on time) shouldn't be displayed. A better solution would be to display a new column that indicates when an order was delayed. What about templated columns? The following code shows the declaration of a templated column in which the contents of each cell is an elaboration of the newly added *Delayed* column:

```
<asp:TemplateColumn runat="server" HeaderText="Delay"
    ItemStyle-HorizontalAlign="center"
    ItemStyle-Font-Name="wingdings 2">
    <ItemTemplate>
        <%# ((bool)DataBinder.Eval(Container.DataItem,
            "Delayed") ?"P" :"") %>
    </ItemTemplate>
</asp:TemplateColumn>
```

In particular, the template displays a Wingdings symbol (the checkmark) or the empty string based on the Boolean value in the source column. Of course, for this to happen you must have the Wingdings 2 font installed.

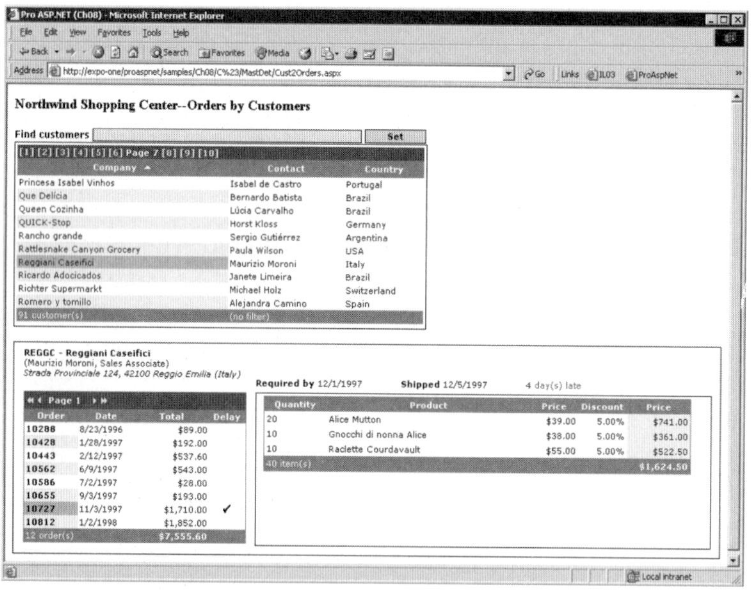

Figure 8-11 The last column shows a check symbol to indicate the corresponding order shipped after being delayed.

Listing the Order Details

The orderslist.aspx page contains a child frame that points to the orderdetails.aspx page. This page is aimed at showing the details of a particular order. The page receives the order ID through the query string, downloads the few records that describe the items in the order, and populates a nonpageable *DataGrid* control.

The orderdetails.aspx page is fired when the user clicks to select an order. When this happens, a label is also updated with further information about the ship date and the required date of shipment for the order. The difference between the two dates is expressed in terms of days.

The various totals you see on the footer of the grids are calculated using the *Compute* method on the *DataTable* object.

Conclusion

The complexity of the code we examined in this chapter is really close to the physical threshold beyond which one normally starts looking at ways to implement reusability and encapsulation. The master/detail views and subtotaling applications we've built so far make intensive use of certain features of the *DataGrid* control that I simply cut and pasted from one source file to the next. There has to be a better way of reusing code in ASP.NET! Actually, a (much) better way does exist, and we'll start looking at it in Chapter 10 and get into more detail in Chapter 18 and Chapter 19.

Real-world programming is a powerful mix of best practices, design patterns, and those finer touches that always marks the difference between good and not-quite-as-good applications. However, a deep knowledge and understanding of the platform is a must. Speaking of ASP.NET in particular, the required knowledge spans the world of .NET and touches on the land of SQL.

Many real-world applications are based on a web of interrelated and interconnected databases. Designing effective queries and update strategies is critical. Keeping an eye on the overall scalability is a must. Providing awesome, user-friendly features is just what you live (and work) for. Right? SQL is the glue that holds databases and data-driven applications together, but SQL—in the real world—is not a complete standard. Yes, there was once the SQL 92 platform, but since then each vendor has added feature upon feature to provide better functionality. So you should know the SQL engine you're using to write effective code. And in ASP.NET, you also must know the client-side engine that interacts with the back end. This engine is ADO.NET.

ADO.NET doesn't add magic to your arsenal of tricks and techniques. It doesn't reduce database programming to mere declarative programming, in which you build working code by simply pointing and clicking. Several times in this chapter (and even more often in ADO.NET books such as David Sceppa's *Microsoft ADO.NET* [Microsoft Press, 2002]), you find described tools and classes that kindly and generously do most of the work for you. In the same sources, you normally find notes that warn you against using those tools and classes in real-world applications. The command-builder object or even the batch update, for example, greatly simplify the update process, but you must know what they do and how they do it. Chances are that to fix your application you just need to work around their standard behavior. ADO.NET can do a lot of things for you, but it can do even more if you know how to instruct it.

This chapter discussed a few general points typical of all Web applications of some complexity. In the next chapter, we'll move away from the rather ubiquitous *DataGrid* control to consider more flexible alternatives, such as the *Repeater* and *DataList* controls. The next chapter opens Part III of the book, which is entirely devoted to system-provided ASP.NET rich controls.

Resources

- *Microsoft ADO.NET Core Reference*, by David Sceppa (Microsoft Press, 2002)
- *Programming Visual Basic .NET*, by Francesco Balena (Microsoft Press, 2002)—see the ADO.NET section
- Tackle Data Concurrency Exceptions Using the DataSet Object (*http://msdn.microsoft.com/msdnmag/issues/03/04/DataConcurrency/default.aspx*)
- Implement a Data Access Layer for Your App with ADO.NET (*http://msdn.microsoft.com/msdnmag/issues/03/04/DataAccessLayer/default.aspx*)

Part III

ASP.NET Controls

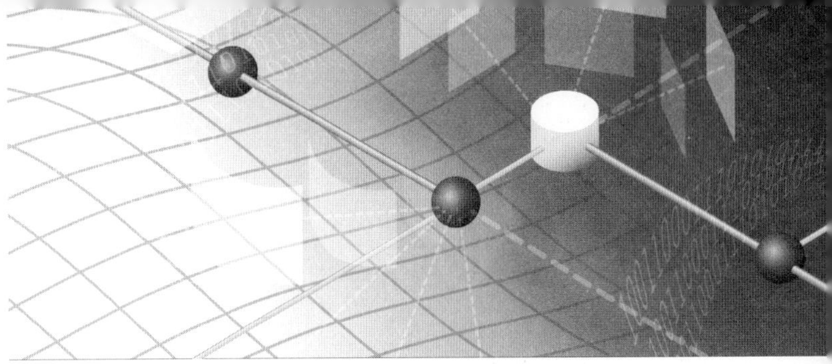

9

ASP.NET Iterative Controls

Be sincere; be brief; be seated.

—*Franklin D. Roosevelt*

Iterative controls are a special type of data-bound controls that combine two key capabilities. They support ADO.NET-compliant data sources and supply a template-based mechanism to create free-form user interfaces.

In Part II of the book, while covering database programming and techniques, we covered the *DataGrid* control in great detail. Technically speaking, the *DataGrid* control is certainly an iterative control in the sense that it iterates over a bound data source to generate its user interface, one row after the next. Although the *DataGrid* is highly customizable, it can't go beyond the boundaries of a column-based representation of the data. For example, the *DataGrid* supports templates, but only within the cells of a column. Other tasks are only for the bravest—for example, redesigning the layout of an individual row, or altering the default template of the control's output to employ multiple rows per record or multiple columns per data source. In some cases, by resorting to dirty and smart tricks you can customize the *DataGrid*, such as displaying subtotals as we did in Chapter 8, "Real-World Data Access." Generally, though, the *DataGrid* is not the ideal tool to use when you need a more free-form display of data. For this purpose, the *Repeater* and *DataList* controls, each with its own set of pros and cons, seem to be more appropriate.

What's an Iterative Control, Anyway?

Before looking under the hood of the *Repeater* and *DataList* controls, let's discuss in general terms the expected features of iterative and templated controls. A control is said to be *iterative* if it provides the ability to loop over a set of data items in order to apply some layout elements to each of them. In addition, an iterative control works by applying an ASP.NET template to each data item. It exposes the individual data item as a customizable and configurable stand-alone object that holds its own set of properties, methods, and events.

According to this definition, what is the role of all controls that show a list of data rows? Are the *DropDownList* and *CheckBoxList* controls, just to name a few, iterative controls? Is the *DataGrid* iterative as well?

Iterative Controls vs. List Controls

The big difference between, say, a *DropDownList* control and what we recognize here as iterative controls—that is, the *Repeater* and *DataList*—is all in how each control shows its contents. The *DropDownList* control uses a drop-down list and doesn't provide relevant facilities for you to change the user interface of each displayed item.

Similarly, the *CheckBoxList* control displays a list of selectable options whose value and displayed text can be bound to a data source. With this list control, you can apply some relatively simple HTML formatting to each item. However, you can't do that with a stand-alone object that represents the list item. More specifically, you have no object that is equivalent to the *DataGridItem* class of the *DataGrid* control. If you want to render, say, some items of the check-box list in boldface type, you can only modify the text of the single item being displayed and wrap it in a *<b>* element. Although this is (much) better than nothing, it's still too little for complex applications that need more advanced display features.

In summary, iterative controls differ from list controls because of their greater rendering flexibility. An iterative control lets you apply an ASP.NET template to each row in the bound data source. A list control, on the other hand, provides a fixed and built-in template for each data item. List controls are customizable to some extent, but you can't change anything other than the text displayed. No changes to layout are supported.

On the other hand, using a list control is considerably easier than setting up an iterative control, as we'll see in a moment. Defining templates requires quite a bit of declarative code, and if accomplished programmatically, it requires that you write a class that implements the *ITemplate* interface. A list control needs only data binding.

Iterative Controls vs. the *DataGrid* Control

The *DataGrid* is an iterative control because it displays the contents of a data source by using customizable templates in which the programmer can easily access and configure each constituent element—from the data rows to the header and from the footer to the pager. However, the *DataGrid* can also be considered a list control because the customization facilities it provides don't allow you to break the rigid scheme of a tabular, multicolumn representation of data.

The *DataGrid* has more advanced features than the *Repeater* and *DataList*—particularly, paging. On the other hand, it doesn't offer the same level of flexibility as iterative controls. In a certain sense, it's a sort of highly specialized, off-the-shelf version of an iterative control.

Using a *Repeater* control, and even more easily using a *DataList*, you can build a grid of data. Note also that you can't always use a *DataGrid* control to reproduce the same output you can with either a *Repeater* or *DataList*. Table 9-1 summarizes the differences among the *DataGrid*, iterative controls, and list controls.

Table 9-1 Outlining Iterative and List Controls

	Rendering	**Usage**
DataGrid Control	Loop over data, and create a tabular representation of data allowing for column-specific templates.	Use when you have tabular data to display. If the data is not naturally tabular but can be rendered as such, consider iterative controls too.
Iterative Controls	Loop over data-bound items, and apply a user-defined template.	Use when you have data to render as a monolithic structure in a free-form way.
List Controls	Loop over data-bound items, and apply an immutable, control-specific template.	Use when you don't need item-specific customization and you like the standard user interface.

The *Repeater* Control

The *Repeater* is a data-bound control that displays data using a custom layout. It works by repeating a specified ASP.NET template for each item displayed in the list. The *Repeater* is a rather basic templated data-bound control. It has no built-in layout or styling capabilities. All formatting and layout information must be explicitly declared and coded using HTML tags and ASP.NET classes.

Programming Interface of the *Repeater* Control

The *Repeater* class inherits from *Control* and acts as a naming container by implementing the marker interface *INamingContainer*. Table 9-2 lists the properties exposed by the control, not counting those inherited from the base class *Control*.

Table 9-2 Properties of the *Repeater* Control

Property	Description
AlternatingItemTemplate	Gets or sets the template that defines how every other item is to be rendered.
DataMember	Gets or sets the specific table in the *DataSource* that is to be bound to the control.
DataSource	Gets or sets the data source that provides any data for populating the list.
FooterTemplate	Gets or sets the template that defines how the footer is rendered.
HeaderTemplate	Gets or sets the template that defines how the header is rendered.
Items	Gets a *RepeaterItemCollection* object—that is, a collection of *RepeaterItem* objects. Each element of the collection represents a displayed data row in the *Repeater*.
ItemTemplate	Gets or sets the template that defines how items are rendered.
SeparatorTemplate	Gets or sets the template that defines how separators between items are rendered.

For the most part, properties are the template elements that form the control's user interface. Aside from that, the *Items* property contains the list of child items that are associated with each displayed data row. The *RepeaterItem* object is the *Repeater*'s counterpart of the *DataGridItem* object we discussed in earlier chapters. The *Repeater* populates the *Items* collection by enumerating all the data objects in its bound data source. In no way does the control filter the contents of the *Items* collection. All the rows contained in the data source are mapped onto a *RepeaterItem* object and inserted in the collection. The *RepeaterItemCollection* class is a plain collection class with no special or peculiar behavior.

Just as in the *DataGridItem* class, the *RepeaterItem* class is used to represent any type of constituent item and is not limited to data items. You distinguish between types using the familiar *ListItemType* enumeration. A few properties characterize the programming interface of the *RepeaterItem* class. The *RepeaterItem* class is self-explanatory once you know about the *DataGridItem* class and have a look at its properties—*ItemIndex*, *ItemType*, and *DataItem*.

Binding a *Repeater* to Data

Just like any other data-bound ASP.NET control, the *Repeater* generates its user interface only when a call to its *DataBind* method is made. *DataBind* is the only method in the control's interface aside from those directly inherited from parent classes. A call to *DataBind* causes the control to rebuild its control hierarchy and related view state. Before the whole process starts, the *DataBinding* event fires.

The call to *DataBind* is necessary to have the HTML code for the control be generated and added to the output stream. In addition to the events defined on the *Control* class, the *Repeater* exposes three additional events—*ItemCreated*, *ItemCommand*, and *ItemDataBound*. (See Table 9-3.) Their overall behavior is nearly identical to that of the analogous events in the *DataGrid*.

Table 9-3 Events of the *Repeater* Control

Event	Description
ItemCommand	Fires when a button is clicked within the *Repeater* control.
ItemCreated	Fires when a repeater item is being created.
ItemDataBound	Fires after an item in the *Repeater* has been bound to underlying data. The event occurs before the data item is added to the *Items* collection. (Note that only items and alternating items are bindable.)

The *DataBinding* event fires before all the events listed in Table 9-3. The sequence of data-binding events is triggered by the call to *DataBind*. As the very first step, the *Repeater* fires the *DataBinding* event and then begins building the control's hierarchy. Events in Table 9-3 occur only at this time, in the order we're going to discuss in the next section.

How the *Repeater* Builds the Output

An internal, protected method of the *Control* class named *CreateControlHierarchy* is responsible for the generation of the HTML code sent to the browser. This method connects to the data source and then runs a loop over the items in the bound collection. (See the "Resolving the Data Source" sidebar later in the chapter for more information on how the *Repeater* resolves the reference to the run-time data-bound object.)

The following pseudocode illustrates the process that leads to the creation of the *Repeater* output.

```
if (headerTemplate != null)
    CreateItem(ListItemType.Header);

int _counter = 0;
RepeaterItem _repItem;
```

```
foreach(object _dataItem in DataSource) {
    if (useSeparator && _counter > 0)
        CreateItem(ListItemType.Separator);
    if (_counter % 2)
        _repItem = CreateItem(_counter, ListItemType.Item, _dataItem);
    else
        _repItem = CreateItem(_counter, ListItemType.AlternatingItem,
            _dataItem);
    Items.Add(_repItem);

    _counter ++;
}

if (footerTemplate != null)
    CreateItem(ListItemType.Footer);
```

The *Repeater* first applies the header's template, if any. Next, it walks its way through the collection of bound objects and applies the *ItemTemplate* or the *AlternatingItemTemplate* as appropriate. Each item template might be interspersed with a separator template, if any has been provided. Finally, at the end of the loop, the footer's template is applied only once.

Within the *CreateItem* placeholder, a new *RepeaterItem* object is created and initialized to default values. Next, the *ItemCreated* event fires and then the object is added to the *Items* collection. As explained for *DataGrid* controls in Chapter 6, "Creating Bindable Grids of Data," the *ItemCreated* event occurs twice, the first time of which is before the whole data binding process begins. This just means that the *CreateItem* placeholder is invoked twice. The second time, the *DataBind* method is invoked on the newly created *RepeaterItem* object and then *ItemDataBound* fires. The following listing shows the pseudocode for the *CreateItem* placeholder.

```
RepeaterItem CreateItem(int index, ListItemType itemType,
    bool dataBind, object dataItem)
{
    RepeaterItem _repItem;
    RepeaterItemEventArgs e;

    _repItem = new RepeaterItem(itemIndex, itemType);
    e = new RepeaterItemEventArgs(_repItem);
    ApplyItemTemplate(_repItem);
    if (dataBind)
        _repItem.DataItem = dataItem;
    OnItemCreated(e);
    Controls.Add(_repItem);
    if (dataBind)
    {
```

```
            _repItem.DataBind();
            OnItemDataBound(e);
        }

        return _repItem;
    }
```

The *ApplyItemTemplate* placeholder renders a piece of code that instantiates all the controls and the literals contained in a bound template. This point leads us straight to the question: what's a template, anyway?

Templates of the *Repeater* Control

We've already met ASP.NET templates in Chapter 6 while examining the templated columns of *DataGrid* controls. Speaking abstractly, a template is a block of server controls, literals, and HTML text that is used as a monolithic output element. To some extent, you can think of a template as a dynamically defined ASP.NET control with a composite interface that can be defined either declaratively using client and server tags or programmatically via ad hoc classes.

At a minimum, the *Repeater* must provide the *ItemTemplate* template. Unspecified templates are simply ignored; however, if you also omit the *ItemTemplate* template, the *Repeater* will have blank output.

In most cases, you define a template using declarative code. For example, the following code shows how to generate output that looks like that of a *DataGrid*:

```
<asp:Repeater runat="server" id="Repeater1">
<HeaderTemplate>
    <table>
        <thead>
            <td> <b>ID</b> </td>
            <td> <b>First Name</b> </td>
            <td> <b>Last Name</b> </td>
        </thead>
</HeaderTemplate>

<ItemTemplate>
    <tr>
        <td bgcolor="white">
            <%# ((DataRowView)Container.DataItem)["EmployeeID"] %></td>
        <td bgcolor="white">
            <%# ((DataRowView)Container.DataItem)["FirstName"] %></td>
        <td bgcolor="white">
            <%# ((DataRowView)Container.DataItem)["LastName"] %></td>
    </tr>
</ItemTemplate>

<AlternatingItemTemplate>
    <tr>
```

```
            <td bgcolor="#eeeeee">
                <%# ((DataRowView)Container.DataItem)["EmployeeID"] %></td>
            <td bgcolor="#eeeeee">
                <%# ((DataRowView)Container.DataItem)["FirstName"] %></td>
            <td bgcolor="#eeeeee">
                <%# ((DataRowView)Container.DataItem)["LastName"] %></td>
        </tr>
</AlternatingItemTemplate>

<FooterTemplate>
    <tfoot style="color:white">
        <td bgcolor="gray" colspan="3">
            <%# "<b>" + ((DataView)Repeater1.DataSource).Count +
                "</b> employees found."%></td>
    </tfoot>
    </table>
</FooterTemplate>
</asp:Repeater>
```

Figure 9-1 shows what this *Repeater* control looks like.

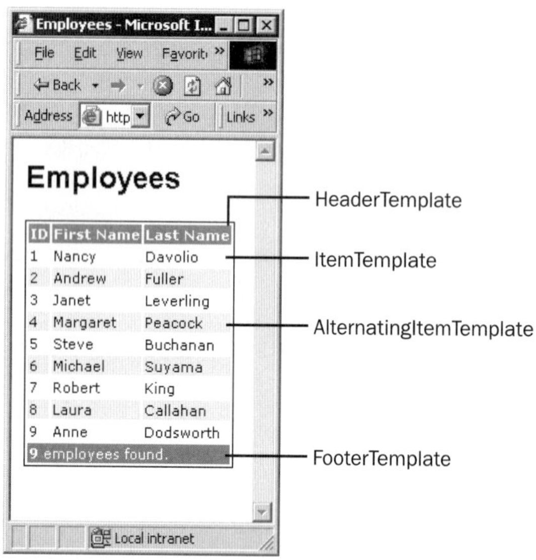

Figure 9-1 The *Repeater* control can do whatever a *DataGrid* can do, even though it might require a lot of coding. The opposite is not true.

In this case, the data source of the *Repeater* control is a *DataView* object.

```
DataSet _data = new DataSet();
string _conn = "SERVER=localhost;DATABASE=Northwind;UID=sa;";
string _query = "SELECT employeeid, firstname, lastname FROM employees";
SqlDataAdapter _adapter = new SqlDataAdapter( _query, _conn);
_adapter.Fill(_data);
```

```
Repeater1.DataSource = _data.Tables[0].DefaultView;
Repeater1.DataBind();
```

As you can see, a lot of casting is needed to keep the compiler quiet and avoid errors. Many of those explicit casts can be avoided if you resort to the *DataBinder* object and its late-binding *Eval* method.

The final output of the *Repeater* is simply the summation of the HTML generated by each involved template. As illustrated in the aforementioned example, the *Repeater* control allows you to split HTML tags across the various templates.

The *ITemplate* Interface

The *Repeater* class references a template through the *ITemplate* interface, meaning that a template is always treated as an instance of any class that implements the *ITemplate* interface. In spite of this, you are allowed to specify a template by using server-side tags and HTML tags. What's up?

When the page is compiled, all the fragments defined within a template block are compiled into an internal object that implements the *ITemplate* interface. Set the *debug* attribute of the *@Page* directive to *true*, and look into the actual code being generated for the page shown in Figure 9-1. (See Chapter 2, "Web Forms Internals," for instructions on how to do this and retrieve the correct source file.) The *Repeater* is built using the following code. Note that the code shown here is the same code generated by the ASP.NET compiler—it's just made more readable.

```
// Instantiate the Repeater object
Repeater __ctrl = new Repeater();
Repeater1 = __ctrl;
__ctrl.ID = "Repeater1";

// Build the template for the header
BuildTemplateMethod _builder;
_builder = new BuildTemplateMethod(__BuildControl__control3);
CompiledTemplateBuilder _template = new CompiledTemplateBuilder(_builder);
__ctrl.HeaderTemplate = _template;

// Build other templates
⋮
```

The *CompiledTemplateBuilder* class is listed in the ASP.NET documentation, but it's not documented. The same holds true for the *BuildTemplateMethod* delegate.

```
public delegate void BuildTemplateMethod(Control control);
```

The constructor of the *CompiledTemplateBuilder* class takes an instance of the delegate and calls it back to build a template class based on the source of the specified control. What's the *_control3* in the source code? It's simply the literal control that contains all the source code of the *<HeaderTemplate>* tag.

```
void __BuildControl__control3(Control __ctrl)
{
    IParserAccessor __parser = (IParserAccessor) __ctrl;
    LiteralControl _header = new LiteralControl("text of <headertemplate>");
    __parser.AddParsedSubObject(_header);
}
```

When a template is instantiated, all the child controls are instantiated and then rendered to HTML. This is what happens in the preceding procedure using the methods on the *IParserAccessor* interface. If you want to create templates programmatically, there are simpler ways, and we'll look at a couple of them in a moment. In the meantime, let's review the definition of the *ITemplate* interface.

The *ITemplate* interface consists of a single method, named *InstantiateIn*.

```
void InstantiateIn(Control container);
```

The expected behavior of *InstantiateIn* is intuitive: it programmatically creates all the child controls to be used in the template. All the controls are added to the container's *Controls* collection. If needed, the newly created controls can be bound to the data source by adding a handler for the *DataBinding* event.

Creating Templates Programmatically

There are basically two ways to set template properties programmatically. The simplest way is by using the *LoadTemplate* method of the *Page* class. *LoadTemplate* takes only one argument, that being the name of the .ascx file that describes the template. The file name must have an *.ascx* extension. .ascx is the typical extension of Web user control files. (We'll cover Web user controls in the Chapter 10, "Web Forms User Controls.") You create a file-based template using the following code:

```
Repeater1.ItemTemplate = Page.LoadTemplate("item_template.ascx");
```

The template file can be written in any .NET language and doesn't necessarily have to be written in the language of the page. The *LoadTemplate* method can be used to load the layout code for any template property, including *HeaderTemplate* and *FooterTemplate*. The following code shows how to write an .ascx control to emulate the behavior of the page shown in Figure 9-1:

```
<%@ Control Language="C#" %>
<tr>
    <td bgcolor="white">
    <%# DataBinder.Eval(((RepeaterItem)Container).DataItem,
"EmployeeID")%>
    </td>
    <td bgcolor="white">
    <%# DataBinder.Eval(((RepeaterItem)Container).DataItem, "FirstName")
 %>
```

```
    </td>
    <td bgcolor="white">
    <%# DataBinder.Eval(((RepeaterItem)Container).DataItem, "LastName") %>
    </td>
</tr>
```

The use of *DataBinder* in this case contributes significantly to clarifying the code. Without it, you would have to cast *Container* to *RepeaterItem* (unnecessary within the page) and then *DataItem* to *DataRowView*.

The second way to set template properties programmatically is by using a class that implements the *ITemplate* interface. Using a class that implements *ITemplate* achieves the same effect as using *LoadTemplate* and an .ascx file. Here is an example the class:

```
public class MyItemTemplate : ITemplate
{
    public void InstantiateIn(Control container)
    {
        // Create the <tr> element
        TableRow _row = new TableRow();

        // Add the employeeID <td>
        TableCell _empID = new TableCell();
        _empID.DataBinding += new EventHandler(BindEmpID);
        _row.Cells.Add(_empID);

        // Add the lastname <td>
        TableCell _lname = new TableCell();
        _lname.DataBinding += new EventHandler(BindLName);
        _row.Cells.Add(_lname);

        // Add the firstname <td>
        TableCell _fname = new TableCell();
        _fname.DataBinding += new EventHandler(BindFName);
        _row.Cells.Add(_fname);

        // Add the row to the container
        container.Controls.Add(_row);
    }

    public void BindEmpID(object sender, EventArgs e)
    {
        TableCell cell = (TableCell) sender;
        RepeaterItem container = (RepeaterItem) cell.NamingContainer;
        DataRowView _row = (DataRowView) container.DataItem;

        cell.Text = _row["EmployeeID"].ToString();
    }
```

```
    public void BindLName(object sender, EventArgs e)
    {
        TableCell cell = (TableCell) sender;
        RepeaterItem container = (RepeaterItem) cell.NamingContainer;
        DataRowView _row = (DataRowView) container.DataItem;

        cell.Text = _row["LastName"].ToString();
    }

    public void BindFName(object sender, EventArgs e)
    {
        TableCell cell = (TableCell) sender;
        RepeaterItem container = (RepeaterItem) cell.NamingContainer;
        DataRowView _row = (DataRowView) container.DataItem;

        cell.Text = _row["FirstName"].ToString();
    }
}
```

Resolving the Data Source

You should note that the *DataGrid* control, as well as the *Repeater* and the *DataList*, manage the data source through the generic interface of the *object* class. However, underneath this common and somewhat too simple interface, quite different objects can be used. How can iterative controls distinguish between *DataTable*, *DataSet*, *DataView*, and even custom collections?

Iterative controls use an internal class named *DataSourceHelper* to resolve any issues related to the actual data source to bind to. In a certain way, the helper class straightens differences out and normalizes all possible sources to the root collection interface *IEnumerable*. (*ICollection* descends from *IEnumerable*, and *IList*, in turn, inherits from *ICollection*.)

DataSet and *DataTable*, for example, don't implement *IList* directly. They implement *IListSource*, from which the helper class extracts an *IList*-compliant array. A similar pattern can be observed with the *DataView*, *DataViewManager*, and *PagedDataSource* classes. All these classes act as proxies between the control and an embedded object—for example, a *DataTable*. Although they implement *IList*, an intermediate interface is needed to bind and publish the schema of the underlying data source. The *ITypedList* interface provides the tools to extract a valid enumerable list from these objects too.

> In summary, iterative controls access and manipulate their data items through the *IEnumerable* interface. However, an extra step is necessary to normalize all possible data sources to *IEnumerable*. This is a subtle problem that arises if you're going to write a list-bound control yourself. We'll tackle this problem in Chapter 20, "Data-Bound and Templated Controls."

Note that the type of the data item depends on the data source that has been bound to the *Repeater*. The *sender* argument refers to the control that is being bound to the data—the *TableCell*. The *NamingContainer* property is only a shortcut to obtain a reference to the parent *Repeater*. In this case, the *Repeater* is the naming container of the cell; however, this technique should be used with a grain of salt. If the bound control or its parent is a naming container itself, the technique will fail.

Working with the *Repeater* Control

The output that a *Repeater* control can generate for you is any HTML code that can be obtained by repeating ASP.NET templates for all rows in a data source. The overall output can be bound within a table as well as flow as plain HTML text. The *Repeater* control doesn't provide any facility for formatting or styling the output, so whatever effect you need must be manually coded. Note also that you don't necessarily have to bind an ADO.NET object such as *DataTable* or *DataView*. Arrays of custom classes, hash tables, and, in general, any objects that implement the *IEnumerable* interface (or any of its derivates) are acceptable. Of course, you are responsible for casting the *Container.DataItem* expression to the right type.

Let's build a page that lists some information about the customers stored in the Microsoft SQL Server Northwind database. We did this several times in past chapters, but we did it by using a *DataGrid* control or a list control. In those cases, though, we were limited by the fixed template of the controls and could show only text. The greater flexibility of the *Repeater* control allows us to create a sort of Web form for each customer. In particular, our goal is to list minimal information about customers along with a check box. When the page is refreshed, all checked items will display with different colors and more information.

Designing the Templates

For a realistic *Repeater* control, the item template is a fundamental tool for showing the actual data. The *Repeater* also needs to have the header template, which is normally used to introduce the user to the information displayed below. The separator template is effective to graphically separate one item from the next. It's especially needed if you use the alternating item template. In this example, we provide a simple implementation of the separator, making it include only a thin horizontal ruler—an *<hr>* element. However, the separator template might be the ideal tool to use when you need to display summary rows or subtotals.

Building the Page

The following listing illustrates the underpinnings of the page shown in Figure 9-2. It contains a few templates for the header, data items, and separator.

```
<asp:repeater runat="server" id="Repeater1">
    <HeaderTemplate>
        <div style="background-color:yellow;">Customers</div>
        <small>Check to see more information</small><br><br>
    </HeaderTemplate>

    <ItemTemplate>
        <span style="display:none;">
            <%# m_checkBox = (CheckBox) FindCheckBox(Container) %>
    </span>

        <asp:checkbox runat="server" id="ExpandButton" />
        <%# ShowHeader(Container.DataItem) %><br>
        <%# ShowInfoBar(Container.DataItem) %>
        <%# ShowAddressBar(Container.DataItem) %>
    </ItemTemplate>

    <SeparatorTemplate>
        <hr style="border:solid 1px black;height:1px;" />
    </SeparatorTemplate>
</asp:repeater>
```

The header template is applied only once, whereas the separator is applied before every displayed item except the first. We modified the default style of the *<hr>* element to make it one-pixel thin. The core of the page is in the *<ItemTemplate>* section. Let's examine its constituent pieces.

You see that the item's template begins with a rather odd hidden *<span>* tag. Next, it includes a check box and three additional functions, each run within a data-bound code block, *<%# ... %>*. As clearly visible in Figure 9-2, address information is displayed for checked customers and all information appears in blue, even though this last effect is not perceivable from a grayscale picture.

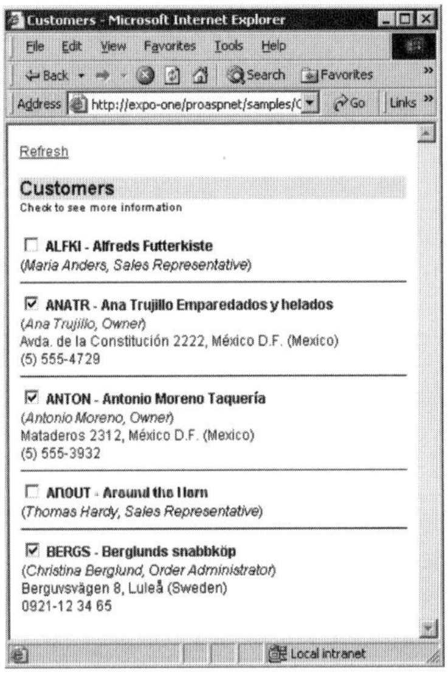

Figure 9-2 The *Repeater* in action, showing information about customers.

The *ShowHeader*, *ShowInfoBar*, and *ShowAddressBar* output the various blocks of information that make up the customer's form. *ShowHeader* outputs the boldface line with the customer code and name. *ShowInfoBar* generates the italicized line with contact details. Finally, *ShowAddressBar* shows the address of the customer and other personal information such as the phone number. All these functions take the data item and return the HTML-formatted string to add to the page's output stream.

```
private string ShowHeader(object dataItem)
{
    // Determine the color to use
    string color = (m_checkBox.Checked ?"blue" :"black");

    // Set up the pattern of the final HTML string
    string _output = "<b style='color:{0};'>{1} - {2}</b>";

    // Fill in the placeholders
    DataRowView _row = (DataRowView) dataItem;
    _output = String.Format(_output,
        color, _row["customerid"], _row["companyname"]);

    // Return the output string
    return _output;
}
```

The other helper routines have a similar structure. (See this book's sample code.) The key thing going on here is the how the function determines the color to use. Aside from that, it simply casts the *Container.DataItem* expression to the actual type—*DataRowView* in this case. Let's see the initialization code of the page.

```
CheckBox m_checkBox;

public void Page_Load(object sender, EventArgs e) {
    if (!IsPostBack)
        BindData();
}

private void BindData() {
    DataSet _data = new DataSet();

    string _conn = "SERVER=localhost;DATABASE=Northwind;UID=sa;";
    string _query = "SELECT TOP 5 * FROM customers";
    SqlDataAdapter _adapter = new SqlDataAdapter(_query, _conn);
    _adapter.Fill(_data);

    // Bind to a DataView
    // The type of the data item will be DataRowView
    Repeater1.DataSource = _data.Tables[0].DefaultView;
    Repeater1.DataBind();
}
```

The *m_checkBox* global variable is reinitialized whenever the item template is processed. As a global variable, it is visible and accessible from within any methods on the page. The check-box variable is initialized when the data item is created.

The Initialization Step

While the repeater's output is being generated, the check-box control is instantiated, but it has yet to be updated with the user's information. If you need to do something when an item is created, you could write either an *ItemCreated* or *ItemDataBound* handler. You can also resort to the following trick, in which we run initialization code at the beginning of the template.

```
<ItemTemplate>
    <span style="display:none;">
        <%# m_checkBox = (CheckBox) FindCheckBox(Container) %>
    </span>
    ⋮
</ItemTemplate>
```

The solutions are not completely equivalent because the various events occur at different times. During the initialization step, the first event that hits the page is *ItemCreated*. At this point, all controls in the templates have been created and initialized. However, they have yet to be bound to the data.

A detail that often goes unnoticed is that when *ItemCreated* fires, the ID of each child control has not yet been associated with the correct naming container—the *RepeaterItem*. If you watch the *UniqueID* property of, say, the check-box control during the *ItemCreated* event, you'll see that it equals *ExpandButton*. Later, when the *DataBind* method has been called on the *RepeaterItem* object, each child control is mapped to the actual container. The *UniqueID* property becomes *Repeater1:_ctlX:ExpandButton*, where *_ctlX* indicates the particular item. This is the situation observed from within the *FindCheckBox* helper function we used in the preceding code. Depending on what you really need to do during the initialization of data items, using *ItemCreated* or the tricks discussed might lead to significantly different results. On the other hand, the *ItemDataBound* event occurs as the final step in the initialization process and hits the application at the end of the template data binding.

Retrieving Child Controls

We need to know whether each item's *CheckBox* is checked, because this affects the way in which the item itself is rendered. At the time we need that information, the most reliable way to get it is by reading the value directly from *Request.Form*. To do this, we should know the unique ID of the check box.

The ID of the check box is not yet known when *ItemCreated* fires, and *ItemDataBound* occurs when the HTML output of the template has already been generated. (Look back at the "How the *Repeater* Builds the Output" section earlier, and you'll see that *OnItemBound* fires immediately after the call to *DataBind* for each repeater's item.) That's why a piece of code placed at the beginning of the item template is an effective trick. There might be other ways of accomplishing the same task, but I find this approach both easy to understand and functional.

The global variable *m_checkBox* is not strictly needed. However, if it's used, it optimizes your code because there's no need to call *FindControl* each time you need to access the item-specific instance of the *ExpandButton* check box.

Handling Postbacks

To retrieve the item-specific instance of a child control, you use the *FindControl* method from within the actual container—the *RepeaterItem* object.

```
CheckBox ctl = (CheckBox) container.FindControl("ExpandButton");
```

Note that calling the *FindControl* method exposed by the *Page* wouldn't work because *FindControl* explores only the subtree rooted in the naming container. You pass the identifier for the control to be found. Note that the identifier doesn't have to be the client-side and unique ID that is used within the page. The contents of the ASP.NET *ID* property is just fine. The following listing illustrates how we retrieve the item-specific instance of the *CheckBox* control and update its properties reading from the request's *Form* collection.

```
private CheckBox FindCheckBox(Control container)
{
    // Retrieve the item-specific instance of the checkbox
    CheckBox ctl = (CheckBox) container.FindControl("ExpandButton");
    if (ctl == null)
        return null;

    // Update the state of the control
    ctl.Checked = (Page.Request.Form[ctl.UniqueID]=="on");

    // Return the instance of the control
    return ctl;
}
```

Although at this time the state of the child controls has not been restored, the correct value is held in the *Request.Form* collection. The *FindCheckBox* method anticipates the restoration of the current logical state of the check-box field. In addition, it contributes to making the instance globally available within the template. Accessing the check box directly through the *m_checkBox* variable is faster than running *FindControl* each time.

A Scrollable List of Data Items

In Chapter 6 and Chapter 7 ("Paging Through Data Sources"), we discussed how to page through the records bound to a *DataGrid* control. Both the *Repeater* and *DataList* have no built-in support for pagination. However, the template-based nature of such controls lends itself well to implementing a scrolling mechanism. Bear in mind that any scrolling capabilities rely on the capabilities of the underlying browser and in particular are tied to the level of support the browser provides for version 2 of cascading style sheets (CSS2).

The page shown in Figure 9-3 employs two *Repeater* controls. The first one displays a push button for each customer initial; the other one populates the page with information about all the customers whose company name starts with the selected letter. The second *Repeater* is nearly identical to the one we discussed in the previous section. The only significant change has to do with the layout of the HTML output, which now supports text overflow.

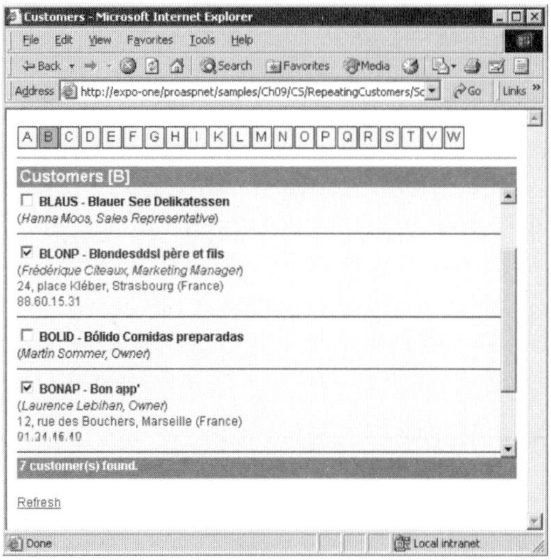

Figure 9-3 A page that features two *Repeater* controls; one to pick the initial and one to display the related customers in a scrollable area.

Handling the Click Event

As mentioned earlier, the *Repeater* control doesn't have any built-in mechanisms to render its contents according to special formatting rules. The resulting text, therefore, flows as you write it—either horizontally or vertically. In the previous example, we built a vertical list of data items. Let's see how to create a horizontal strip of data items. We display a push button for each distinct initial found in the companyname column of the Customers table.

```
SELECT DISTINCT substring(companyname, 1, 1) AS Initial FROM customers
```

To display items horizontally, the *Repeater* must build an HTML table with one row and as many cells as there are items in the query's result set.

```
<asp:repeater runat="server" id="Picker" OnItemCommand="ItemCommand">
<HeaderTemplate>
    <table border="0" cellspacing="1" cellpadding="0"><tr>
</HeaderTemplate>

<ItemTemplate>
    <td>
    <asp:button runat="server" style="border:solid 1px;width=20px;"
        BackColor='<%# GetBackColor(Container.DataItem) %>'
        Text='<%# DataBinder.Eval(Container.DataItem, "Initial")%>'
        CommandName='<%# DataBinder.Eval(Container.DataItem, "Initial")%>'
    />
    </td>
</ItemTemplate>
```

```
<FooterTemplate>
    </tr></table><hr>
</FooterTemplate>
</asp:repeater>
```

Each data item is rendered as a push button with a few parametric properties—*BackColor*, *Text*, and *CommandName*. *Text* and *CommandName*, in particular, are bound to the same value—the contents of the Initial column in the data set. The *CommandName* property represents the keyword associated with a command object within an iterative control.

Whenever the user clicks any of the letter buttons, the *ItemCommand* event fires. The sample page handles the *ItemCommand* event as follows:

```
private void ItemCommand(object sender, RepeaterCommandEventArgs e)
{
    BindData(e.CommandName);
}

private void BindData(string initial)
{
    // Store the current initial
    ViewState["Initial"] = initial;

    // Get the necessary data with a single SQL batch
    string _cmdText = m_cmdInitial + ";";
    _cmdText += String.Format(m_cmdCustmrs, initial);
    SqlDataAdapter _adapter = new SqlDataAdapter(_cmdText, m_connString);
    DataSet _data = new DataSet();
    _adapter.Fill(_data);

    // Rename tables
    _data.Tables[0].TableName = "Initials";
    _data.Tables[1].TableName = "Customers";

    // Bind data
    Picker.DataSource = _data.Tables["Initials"].DefaultView;
    Picker.DataBind();
    Customers.DataSource = _data.Tables["Customers"].DefaultView;
    Customers.DataBind();
}
```

The current initial letter is cached in the *ViewState* and persists across successive requests of the same page. Note that the result set with all the initials could have effectively been cached in *Cache* or *Application* because of its relatively low level of volatility.

Making the Control Scroll

The trick to making a portion of an HTML page scroll vertically and horizontally is the *overflow* CSS style. Most popular browsers recognize about a hundred style-sheet properties, most of which are CSS1 recommendations. The *overflow* attribute is specific to CSS2 and supported by Microsoft Internet Explorer 5.0 and later. The *overflow* attribute controls how a container element (for example, a *<div>*) displays its content if it's not the same size as the container.

```
<HeaderTemplate>
    <div style="background-color:gray;color:white;height:20px;">
        <%# SetHeader() %>
    </div>
    <div style="background-color:lightcyan;height:260px;overflow:auto;">
</HeaderTemplate>
```

Possible values for the *overflow* attribute are listed in Table 9-4.

Table 9-4 Possible Values for the *overflow* CSS Attribute

Value	Description
auto	Uses scrollbars only if needed.
hidden	Clips any text that exceeds the fixed container's size.
visible	Default value, ignores any difference between the fixed size of the container and the contained text.
scroll	Uses both horizontal and vertical scrollbars. A scrollbar that isn't really needed is disabled.

The header template defines two *<div>* tags, the latter of which is given a fixed height and will contain the output generated by the items. Nothing is to be changed in the *<ItemTemplate>* section. A *<FooterTemplate>* section, conversely, is needed to close the pending *<div>* tag and provide a footer for summary information.

```
<FooterTemplate>
    </div>
    <div style="background-color:gray;color:white;height:20px;">
        <%# SetFooter() %>
    </div>
</FooterTemplate>
```

The following code is used to show the count of customers displayed in the table:

```
private string SetFooter() {
    string _text = "{0} customer(s) found.";
    ICollection _coll = (ICollection) Customers.DataSource;
    return String.Format(_text, _coll.Count);
}
```

Repeating with Custom Classes

As mentioned earlier, you don't necessarily bind an ADO.NET object to an iterative control. If you use your own classes to store data, those classes can also be used to populate a *Repeater* as well as a *DataList* control. The data source must be an array of class instances. To access individual properties, you then use *DataBinder.Eval* as you would with a *DataTable*.

```
private void BindData()
{
    string _conn = "SERVER=localhost;DATABASE=Northwind;UID=sa;";
    string _query = "SELECT firstname, lastname FROM employees";
    SqlDataAdapter _adapter = new SqlDataAdapter(_query, _conn);
    DataTable _data = new DataTable();
    _adapter.Fill(_data);

    ArrayList values = new ArrayList();
    foreach(DataRow _row in _data.Rows)
        values.Add(new Employee(
            _row["LastName"].ToString(),
            _row["FirstName"].ToString()));

    Repeater1.DataSource = values;
    Repeater1.DataBind();
}
public class Employee
{
    private string _lastname;
    private string _firstname;

    public Employee(string lname, string fname) {
        _lastname = lname;
        _firstname = fname;
    }

    public string LastName {
        get {return _lastname;}
    }

    public string FirstName {
        get {return _firstname;}
    }
}
```

As you can guess, with the *DataBinder.Eval* method you can access only public properties on your class.

```
<ItemTemplate>
<tr>
```

```
    <td><%# DataBinder.Eval(Container.DataItem, "LastName") %></td>
    <td><%# DataBinder.Eval(Container.DataItem, "FirstName") %></td>
</tr>
</ItemTemplate>
```

If you bind an iterative control to an array of classes, you can't rely on any ready-made tool to sort data. You must sort the array yourself using the *IComparer* interface to define your own rules. (See the MSDN documentation for the *IComparer* interface.)

The *DataList* Control

Functionally speaking, the *DataList* is a data-bound control that falls somewhere in between the *Repeater* and the *DataGrid*. It begins where the *Repeater* ends and terminates a little before the starting point of the *DataGrid* control. In some unrealistically simple cases, you can even take some code that uses a *Repeater*, replace the control, and not even notice any difference. Looking at the programming interface, though, the *DataList* is much more similar to the *DataGrid*.

In spite of such deep similarities, the *DataList* is a control with its own personality and a set of features that make it unique and ideal in a number of situations. Compared to the *Repeater*, the *DataList* control comes with a full bag of goodies and new features, mostly in the area of graphical layout. The control overtakes the *Repeater* in several respects. For example, it supports directional rendering, meaning that items can flow horizontally or vertically to match a specified number of columns. Furthermore, just as with the *DataGrid*, it provides facilities to retrieve a key value associated with the current data row and has built-in support for selection and in-place editing. In addition, the *DataList* control supports more templates and can fire some extra events beyond those of the *Repeater*. Data binding and the overall behavior are nearly identical for the *Repeater* and *DataList* controls.

Programming Interface of the *DataList* Control

The *DataList* is smarter than the *Repeater* and works by making some assumptions about the expected results. This is good news and bad news for you as a programmer. It means that in some cases much less code is needed to accomplish the same effect; on the other hand, it also indicates that you should know the behavior of the control very well to govern it. For example, the *DataList* assumes that no HTML tag is split across templates. This fact isn't a problem per se, but it can result in badly formed or totally unexpected HTML output. In addition, by default the *DataList* renders its entire output as an HTML table, meaning that if this is exactly what you want, there's no need for you to comply with *<table>* or *<td>* elements.

Before we look in detail at the programming interface of the *DataList* control, let's see what we should do to make the previous example (the scrolling page) work with a *DataList*. Once you have replaced *<asp:repeater>* with *<asp:datalist>*, set the *RepeatDirection* property to *Horizontal* on the Picker control.

```
<asp:datalist runat="server" id="Picker"
    RepeatDirection="Horizontal"
    RepeatLayout="Flow"
    OnItemCommand="ItemCommand">
```

Both the Picker and Customers control also need to have the *RepeatLayout* property set to the value of *Flow*.

```
<asp:datalist runat="server" id="Customers"
    RepeatLayout="Flow">
```

Finally, modify the item template of the Picker control by removing any text other than the *<asp:button>* declaration. Likewise, remove the header and the footer template—the *DataList* will automatically provide the formatting features that you have to code yourself when the *Repeater* is used. The final result is shown in Figure 9-4.

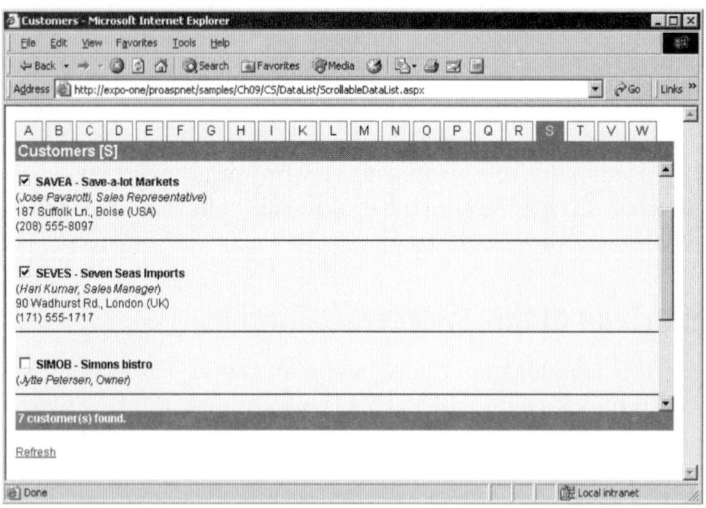

Figure 9-4 The previously discussed scrollable list implemented with *DataList* controls.

The *DataList* has no methods aside from those provided by parent controls. It features a lot of properties and fires quite a few events. The *DataList* control is declared as follows:

```
public class DataList : BaseDataList, INamingContainer, IRepeatInfoUser
```

Like the *DataGrid* control, it inherits from *BaseDataList* and implements the *INamingContainer* interface. In addition, the *DataList* class implements the *IRepeatInfoUser* interface. The *IRepeatInfoUser* interface defines the properties and methods that must be implemented by any list control that repeats a list of items. This interface is also supported by the *CheckBoxList* and *RadioButtonList* controls. However, all of its properties and methods are marked as private and, as such, are inaccessible from within the user code.

Properties of the *DataList* Control

Table 9-5 lists the properties of the *DataList* control. The table doesn't include properties inherited from *Control* and *WebControl*.

Table 9-5 Properties of the *DataList*

Property	Description
AlternatingItemStyle	Gets the style properties for alternating rows.
AlternatingItemTemplate	Gets or sets the template for alternating items.
CellPadding	Gets or sets the space (in pixels) between the cell's border and the embedded text.
CellSpacing	Gets or sets the space (in pixels) between two consecutive cells, both horizontally and vertically.
Controls	Gets the collection of all the child controls in the list.
DataKeyField	Gets or sets the key field in the bound data source.
DataKeys	Gets a collection that stores the key values of all the records displayed in the list. The column used as the key is the one stored in the *DataKeyField* property.
DataMember	Gets or sets a string that indicates the specific table in a multimember data source to bind. The property works in conjunction with *DataSource*. If *DataSource* is a *DataSet* object, then *DataMember* contains the name of a child table to bind.
DataSource	Gets or sets the data source object that contains the values to populate the control.
EditItemIndex	Gets or sets the 0-based index of the item to edit.
EditItemStyle	Gets the style properties for the item being edited.

(continued)

Table 9-5 Properties of the *DataList* *(continued)*

Property	Description
EditItemTemplate	Gets or sets the template for the item selected for editing.
ExtractTemplateRows	Gets or sets a value that instructs the *DataList* to extract the constituent rows from any HTML table in the templates. The extracted rows are then combined to create a single, all-encompassing HTML table. Set to *false* by default.
FooterStyle	Gets the style properties for the footer section.
FooterTemplate	Gets or sets the template for the footer section.
GridLines	Gets or sets a value that indicates whether all cells must have the border drawn. The property is ignored if the *RepeatLayout* property is set to *RepeatLayout.Flow*.
HeaderStyle	Gets the style properties for the heading section.
HeaderTemplate	Gets or sets the template for the heading section.
HorizontalAlign	Gets or sets the horizontal alignment of the text in the list.
Items	Gets the collection of the currently displayed items.
ItemStyle	Gets the style properties for the items in the list.
ItemTemplate	Gets or sets the template for the items in the *DataList*.
RepeatColumns	Gets or sets the number of columns to display.
RepeatDirection	Gets or sets a value that indicates whether the *DataList* control displays its items vertically or horizontally.
RepeatLayout	Gets or sets a value that indicates whether the output of the control is displayed within an automatically created table or by using a flow layout. In a flow layout, text is output in free form.
SelectedIndex	Gets or sets the index of the currently selected item.
SelectedItem	Gets the *DataListItem* object that represents the currently selected item.
SelectedItemStyle	Gets the style properties for the selected item.
SelectedItemTemplate	Gets or sets the template for the currently selected item.
SeparatorStyle	Gets the style properties of the separator used to break text between consecutive items.
SeparatorTemplate	Gets or sets the template for the separator.
ShowFooter	Gets or sets a value that indicates whether the footer section is to be displayed.
ShowHeader	Gets or sets a value that indicates whether the heading section is to be displayed.

The *ShowFooter* and *ShowHeader* properties are both set to *true* by default, but they're considered only if the *FooterTemplate* and *HeaderTemplate* properties, respectively, are non-null.

The data binding process of the *DataList* control is nearly identical to that of the *Repeater*, and the generation of the output also takes place according to the same rules. However, the *DataList* control has a richer programming interface that lets you handle two additional states—selected and editing. The currently selected item is tracked through the *SelectedIndex* and *SelectedItem* properties. The same occurs for the item being edited. In this case, the property is *EditItemIndex*. The in-place editing mechanism of a *DataList* is identical to that of a *DataGrid* control. (See Chapter 6.)

Events of the *DataList* Control

Table 9-6 lists the events that, under various circumstances, the *DataList* control can fire. The list doesn't include the base events (for example, *Load* and *DataBinding*) the class inherits from *Control* and *WebControl*.

Table 9-6 Events Fired by the *DataList*

Event	Description
CancelCommand	Fires when a button with a command name of *Cancel* is clicked for a displayed item.
DeleteCommand	Fires when a button with a command name of *Delete* is clicked for a displayed item.
EditCommand	Fires when a button with a command name of *Edit* is clicked for a displayed item.
ItemCommand	Fires when a button is clicked within the *DataList* control.
ItemCreated	Fires when a *DataList* item is being created.
ItemDataBound	Fires after an item in the *DataList* has been bound to its underlying data. The event occurs before the data item is added to the *Items* collection. (Note that only items and alternating items are bindable.)
SelectedIndexChanged	Fires when a new item is selected in the *DataList*.
UpdateCommand	Fires when a button with a command name of *Update* is clicked for a displayed item.

With the exception of *ItemCreated* and *ItemDataBound*, all the events relate to the execution of some sort of command. *ItemCommand* is the base command event and always fires before the more specific event, such as *EditCommand* or *DeleteCommand*. Regardless of the name, *SelectedIndexChanged* also is a command event that fires when a button with the command name of *Select* is clicked.

> **Note** Command buttons don't necessarily have to be item specific. Any button within the user interface of the *DataList* control can be given a special command name, such as Edit or Delete. The effect is always that of firing the related event. Of course, if the button is not item specific, the logic of the application must determine the affected item and decide the proper action.

The Update and Cancel command buttons are normally generated by the *DataList* itself when a particular item enters into edit mode. Finally, note that the *DataList* class provides constants to identify special command names in a parametric way. The constants are *CancelCommandName*, *DeleteCommandName*, *EditCommandName*, *SelectCommandName*, and *UpdateCommandName*. They are implemented as static properties (*shared properties* according to Microsoft Visual Basic .NET jargon).

Formatting Capabilities

As mentioned earlier, the *Repeater* control is a general-purpose iterator and is limited to generating templated text without applying any extra formatting rules. The *DataList* control, on the other hand, provides additional features specifically for controlling the layout of the list. In particular, the *DataList* can render surrounding table rows and cells around its template-defined elements. This capability allows you to build more advanced and user-friendly layouts with less code. Key elements for taking advantage of this enhanced set of capabilities are the *RepeatColumns*, *RepeatDirection*, and *RepeatLayout* properties. They let you specify the number of columns the output will span and the direction (vertical or horizontal) in which to render the data items.

Table and Flow Layout

The *RepeatLayout* property takes its values from the *RepeatLayout* enumeration, which consists of two possibilities—*Table* and *Flow*. The default is *Table*. If the layout is set to *Flow*, the *DataList* wraps any template element within a *<span>* tag. Next, it automatically adds a *
* element if the rendering direction is vertical. You should note that vertical is the default direction. If the direction is horizontal, the output text simply flows in a concatenated HTML string. The following *DataList* output is for a vertical *Flow* layout:

```
<span id="DataList1">
    <span> header template </span>
    <br>
```

```
    <span> item template </span>
    <br>
    <span> separator template </span>
    ⋮
    <span> footer template </span>
</span>
```

The *Table* mode saves you from a lot of HTML coding if you're just going to build an HTML table. The following *DataList* output is for a vertical *Table* layout:

```
<table id="DataList1">
    <tr>
        <td> header template </td>
    </tr>
    <tr>
        <td> item template </td>
    </tr>
    <tr>
        <td> separator template </td>
    </tr>
        ⋮
    <tr>
        <td> footer template </td>
    </tr>
</table>
```

If the direction is horizontal, the layout of the table is slightly different and is composed of only three table rows—the header, one row for all the items, and the footer.

```
<table id="DataList1">
    <tr>
        <td> header template </td>
    </tr>
    <tr>
        <td> item template </td>
        <td> separator template </td>
        ⋮
    </tr>
    <tr>
        <td> footer template </td>
    </tr>
</table>
```

When the *ExtractTemplateRows* property is set to *true*, the *DataList* control extracts table rows out of all declared templates and merges them into an all-encompassing table. The *ExtractTemplateRows* property allows you to create a single table from other smaller tables defined for each *DataList* template. The use of the property is subject to a few restrictions. In particular, you must provide a well-formed *Table* control (the *<asp:table>* tag) for each template you want to include in the output. An exception would be thrown if you specify the table using the HTML *<table>* element or the ASP.NET *HtmlTable* control—the *<table runat="server">* element. Note also that *all* templates must be expressed using the *Table* control and that only the rows of the tables will be displayed. All other content in the templates will be ignored. The following code shows how to define a table in an item template:

```
<ItemTemplate>
    <asp:table runat="server">
        <asp:tablerow runat="server">
            <asp:tablecell runat="server">
                <%# DataBinder.Eval(Container.DataItem, "Name") %>
            </asp:tablecell>
        </asp:tablerow>
    </asp:table>
</ItemTemplate>
```

The *ExtractTemplateRows* property is really helpful only when you're going to create quite a complex structure in which tables with different templates are to be merged together. You can use the *ColumnSpan* and *RowSpan* properties of the *TableCell* object to control the number of columns and rows the cell spans.

> **Note** When the *ExtractTemplateRows* property is set to *true*, the *RepeatColumns*, *RepeatDirection*, and *RepeatLayout* properties are ignored and do not affect the appearance of the *DataList* control.

Extracting Template Rows

Let's drill down into a common scenario in which *ExtractTemplateRows* proves extremely useful. Suppose that you need to create a report in which multiple rows for each data item should be displayed. Assuming that you want it to work with a table of customers, let's say that you want to display the customer ID and name on the first row and the address on the second.

With a *Repeater*, you could accomplish this by defining a table in the header template and then defining a couple of rows for each item. If you don't mind using a *Repeater*, this is just fine. However, the *DataList* control has styling and formatting capabilities that one wouldn't easily sacrifice. The *DataList*, though, doesn't let you break HTML elements across templates. In other words, this means that you cannot place the opening tag of a table in the header and close it in the footer.

The *DataList* control requires that you express the layout of each template using stand-alone tables. You can use, for instance, a table for the header and a table for the item template. However, if you set the *ExtractTemplateRows* property to *true*, all the rows of the various tables will automatically converge into a unique, all-encompassing table.

```
<asp:datalist runat="server" id="list" extracttemplaterows="true">
    <AlternatingItemStyle backcolor="palegoldenrod" />
    <headerstyle backcolor="brown" forecolor="white"
        font-size="larger" font-bold="true" horizontalalign="center" />

    <HeaderTemplate>
    <asp:table runat="server">
        <asp:tablerow runat="server">
            <asp:tablecell runat="server">Customer</asp:TableCell>
            <asp:tablecell runat="server">Contact</asp:TableCell>
        </asp:tablerow>
    </asp:table>
    </HeaderTemplate>

    <ItemTemplate>
    <asp:table runat="server">
        <asp:tablerow runat="server" font-bold="true">
            <asp:tablecell runat="server">
            <%# DataBinder.Eval(Container.DataItem, "CustomerID") %>
            </asp:tablecell>
            <asp:tablecell runat="server">
            <%# DataBinder.Eval(Container.DataItem, "ContactName") %>
            </asp:tablecell>
        </asp:tablerow>
        <asp:tablerow runat="server">
            <asp:tablecell runat="server" columnspan="2">
            <%# DataBinder.Eval(Container.DataItem, "Address") + " - " +
                DataBinder.Eval(Container.DataItem, "City")   %>
            </asp:tablecell>
        </asp:tablerow>
    </asp:table>
    </ItemTemplate>
</asp:datalist>
```

At display time, the *DataList* merges the two *Table* objects and removes any table element that is not an instance of the *TableRow* class. The final table contains two columns, and each record displays on two different rows, the second of which contains a single cell spanning two columns. The *DataList* control is smart enough to consistently manage visual settings (for example, the alternating item styles) for all table rows that actually participate in a data item row. The results are shown in Figure 9-5.

Figure 9-5 The *DataList* shows a data table in which all records display in two table rows.

> **Note** The need to merge multiple tables explains the strict requirement set on the use of the *<asp:table>* tag, which corresponds to the *Table* object. The *DataList* builds the resulting table object in memory. If you use a *<table>*, whether it's with or without the *runat* attribute, other objects are involved and the trick won't work.

Multicolumn Rendering

The output of a *DataList* control can be rendered over multiple columns whose number you specify by using the *RepeatColumns* property. By default, the text displays in one column. You can create multicolumn output by using either a flow or a table layout. However, the ideal way of repeating items over multiple columns is within a fixed table layout. Figure 9-6 shows the effect of the *RepeatColumns* property along with some possible shortcomings.

```
<asp:datalist runat="server" id="list" RepeatColumns="3">
    ⋮
</asp:datalist>
```

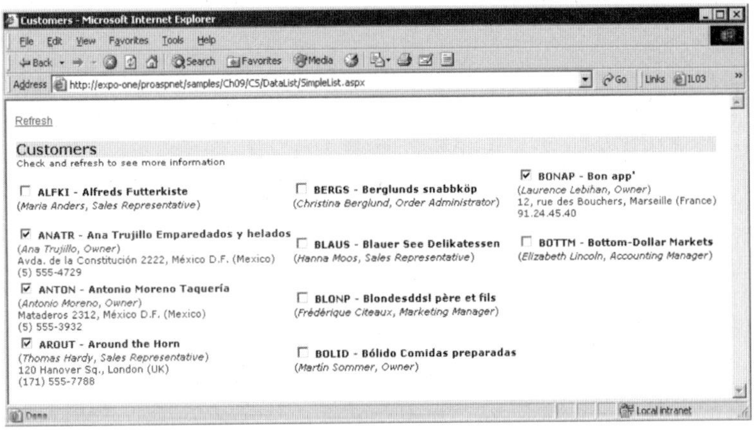

Figure 9-6 A *DataList* control that renders its output over three columns.

As you can see, the vertical alignment of the cells is the default and no properties are allowed to modify it programmatically.

Templates of the *DataList* Control

In addition to all the templates supported by the *Repeater* control, the *DataList* control supports two new templates—*SelectedItemTemplate* and *EditItemTemplate*. The *SelectedItemTemplate* template lets you control the contents and functionality of the selected item. The *EditItemTemplate* template takes care of in-place editing in much the same way as with *DataGrid* controls.

The *SelectedItemTemplate* Template

The appearance of the selected item is controlled by the *SelectedItemStyle* property. The following code changes the background color of the selected item to the specified color:

```
<SelectedItemStyle backcolor="cyan" />
```

As for the *DataGrid* control, you must trigger the selection process using a command button labeled with the *Select* command name. If you want to do more, such as adding information or controls to the currently selected item, you can even replace the default template with a new one. You specify a template for the selected item through the *<SelectedItemTemplate>* tag. A similar mechanism greatly simplifies the building of master/detail views. Once the row has been selected, in fact, you display an ad hoc template that includes any child tables that are needed.

If you need to programmatically access the currently selected item, you use the *SelectedItem* property. It returns the instance of the *DataListItem* object that corresponds to the specified index. For each displayed row, the *DataKeys* collection contains the source values stored in the column that the *DataKeyField* column specifies.

```
// Get the key of the currently selected record and
// drills down into the available data
int key = (int) list.DataKeys[list.SelectedIndex];
GetChildData(key);
```

Items can be selected programmatically by setting the *SelectedIndex* property to a 0-based value. A value of –1 means that no item is currently selected. Note that the value stored in the *SelectedIndex* property is persisted in the view state and survives across consecutive page requests. For this reason, you should reset it whenever a new page of data is displayed.

The *EditItemTemplate* Template

You use the *EditItemTemplate* property to control the contents of the item selected for editing in a *DataList* control. The look and feel of the item selected for editing is controlled by the *EditItemStyle* property. The *EditItemIndex* property contains the 0-based index of the item being edited. Also, this value is cached in the view state, so you should reset it whenever your data set is bound to the control changes.

The in-place editing feature of the *DataList* control is nearly identical to *DataGrid* in-place editing when all columns are based on templates. The *DataList* fires the *EditCommand* event when the user clicks a button associated with the *Edit* command. However, the control enters into edit mode only if the event handler sets the *EditItemIndex* to a 0-based value. When the user clicks to commit the changes, the *UpdateCommand* event fires. You retrieve the current values from input fields using the *FindControl* method and then proceed to persist those changes. The overall procedure is identical to what we saw in Chapter 6 regarding *DataGrid* controls.

Working with the *DataList* Control

Let's add item selection to the page shown in Figure 9-4. The idea is to transform the scrollable area of the *DataList* into something that closely resembles a custom list box. The *DataList* renders its contents vertically using the *Flow* layout. To start, let's remove the *<hr>* element from the separator template so that we save a few pixels of space.

```
<SeparatorTemplate>
</SeparatorTemplate>
```

Note that an empty *SeparatorTemplate* is not ignored but is rendered with an extra *
* element. To set up a functional and effective selection mechanism, we need to handle the *SelectedIndexChanged* event and define the *SelectedItemStyle*. In this case, we don't need to change the template of the item. That feature would be needed to make the component support drill-down functionality, however.

If you've played a little bit with the page shown in Figure 9-4, you should have noticed that whenever you refresh the view (for example, you checked a few items), the scrollbar is reset to its topmost position. This is boring, especially if you have a relatively long list of items; you scroll the view to locate the item to expand and then when the page is refreshed, the item of interest is out of view. This is another problem we'll address in a moment.

Adding Support for Selection

The first point to consider is, how can we make a displayed item selectable? We need to add a command button labeled with the special keyword *Select*. If, for some reason, you need more control over the whole process of selection, you could give the clickable element any command name. Next, when *ItemCommand* fires, you recognize the command and activate the selection yourself by setting the *SelectedIndex* property to a correct index. Note that the default process—applying a particular style and template—begins at this point. The trigger for the process is buried in the code that sets the *SelectedIndex* property.

Making an Item Selectable

The header of each item—that is, the customer's ID and company name—is a good candidate to become the trigger for the selection. Instead of rendering it as plain text, we surround it with a link button.

```
<asp:linkbutton runat="server"
    CommandName="Select"
    Text='<%# SetCustomerName(Container.DataItem) %>' />
```

The text of the link is defined by the following function that simply concatenates a couple of source columns:

```
private string SetCustomerName(object dataItem)
{
    DataRowView _row = (DataRowView) dataItem;
    string _output = "<b>{0} - {1}</b>";
    _output = String.Format(_output,
        _row["customerid"], _row["companyname"]);

    return _output;
}
```

The appearance of the link button is controlled by a couple of page-wide styles that we also used in previous chapters.

```
<style>
    a:hover {color:red;text-decoration:underline;}
    a       {text-decoration:none;}
</style>
<body vlink="black" link="black" ... />
```

The combined effect of these settings is that the link displays as normal text until the mouse moves over it. When that happens, the color switches to red and an underline appears to restore the typical look and feel of HTML clickable elements, as shown in Figure 9-7.

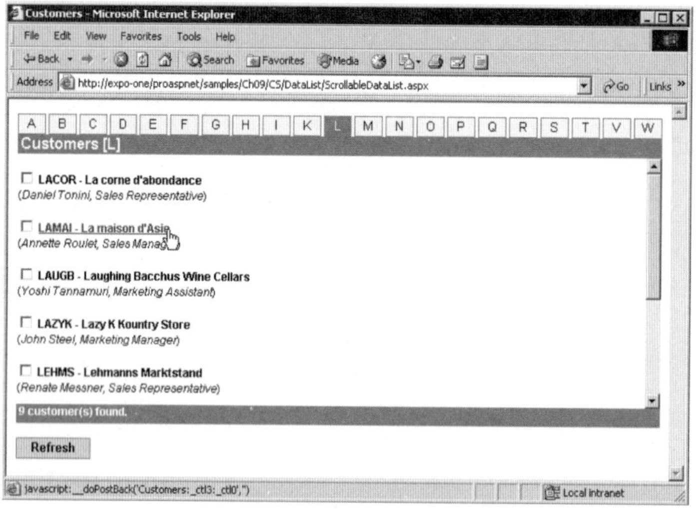

Figure 9-7 A selectable element in the output of a *DataList* control.

With *DataGrid* controls, the following tag would suffice to set the background color when a row is selected:

```
<SelectedItemStyle backcolor="cyan" />
```

If you use that tag with a *DataList* control, though, the graphical aspect of the selected row is not what you would expect. As Figure 9-8 shows, with a *Flow* layout only the individual controls have the background color changed.

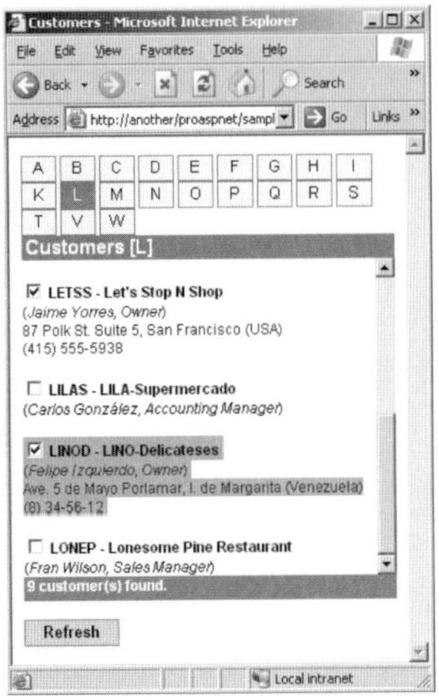

Figure 9-8 A selectable element in the output of a *DataList* control.

To extend the new background color to the whole row, use the following style declaration, which adds an explicit width. The result is shown in Figure 9-9.

```
<SelectedItemStyle backcolor="cyan" width="100%" />
```

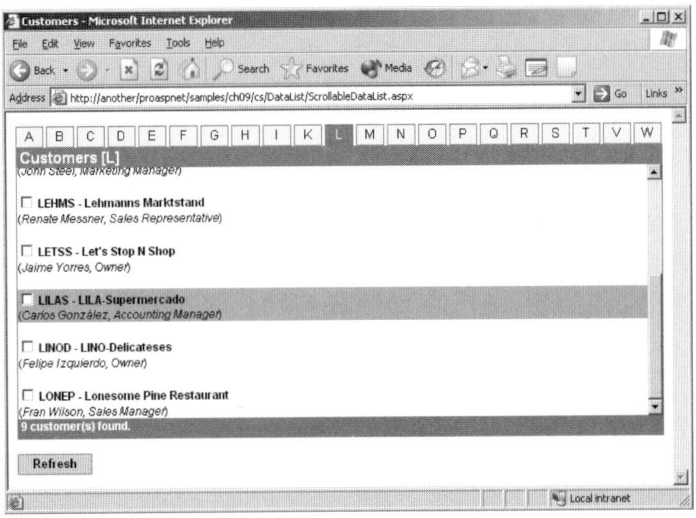

Figure 9-9 A listbox-like selection in a *DataList* control.

At this point, we have a fully functional infrastructure for handling the item selection event. To take a particular action on the selected item, register a handler for the *SelectedIndexChanged* event and update the user interface.

Keeping the Selected Item in View

The second problem—ensuring that the portion of the *DataList* output that contains the selected item is included in the current view—requires a more subtle solution. In this example, we made the *DataList* output scrollable by surrounding the data items with a *<div>* element and setting the *<div>* *overflow* style property to the value of *auto*.

However, when the page posts back, the scrollbar that lets you move back and forth over the *DataList* output is not automatically restored to the position occupied beforehand. Suppose that you scroll down and select one of the last customers in the list. When the page is re-created after the selection, the scrollbar is reset and the selected item is not in the default view. As a result, you have to scroll down again to see its updated content. Is there an automatic way to scroll a particular item into view?

The Dynamic HTML (DHTML) object model provides a large number of HTML elements with a method named *scrollIntoView*. The following JavaScript function illustrates the working of the *scrollIntoView* DHTML method:

```
<SCRIPT>
function ScrollToElem(ctlName)
{
    var elem = document.all(ctlName);
    if (elem == null)
        return;
    elem.scrollIntoView(true);
}
</SCRIPT>
```

The function takes the ID of an HTML element as its sole argument. Next, it attempts to locate the element in the page object model. If successful, it calls the *scrollIntoView* method to ensure the specified element is visible within its container. The container can be the page as well as a container tag such as *<div>*. The Boolean argument you pass to the method indicates whether the element must be shown at the top or the bottom of the view. Although this trick is not acceptable with all browsers, it represents the only possibility we have to scroll an HTML element into view. Let's see how to integrate this piece of code with the existing *DataList*.

To call the *scrollIntoView* method, we need to assign a unique HTML name to all the data items displayed by the *DataList*. Furthermore, the ID we assign to each item must be easily accessible from within the *SelectedIndexChanged* event handler. Whenever a new item is selected, we execute some

ASP.NET code that configures the HTML page's *onload* method. In particular, we link the page's *onload* method to the JavaScript function just shown. The function is passed as an argument the name of the DHTML object that represents the currently selected *DataList* item.

In the following code snippet, we surround the contents of an item with a *<span>* tag whose ID matches the value of the *customerid* column for the item being rendered:

```
<ItemTemplate>
    <span ID='<%# DataBinder.Eval(Container.DataItem, "customerid") %>'>
    ⋮
    </span>
</ItemTemplate>
```

In addition, we set the *DataKeyField* property of the *DataList* with the name of the *customerid* column and add a handler for the *SelectedIndexChanged* event.

```
<asp:datalist runat="server" id="Customers"
    RepeatLayout="Flow"
    DataKeyField="customerid"
    OnSelectedIndexChanged="SelectedIndexChanged">
⋮
```

When the user selects a new item, we retrieve the value of key field—the *customerid* column—and prepare the JavaScript call to link with the *onload* event on the HTML page.

```
public void SelectedIndexChanged(object sender, EventArgs e)
{
    // Get the customerid of the currently selected item
    string custID = (string) Customers.DataKeys[Customers.SelectedIndex];

    // Prepare the Javascript call.
    // For example, if the current item has an ID of ALFKI, the
    // Javascript call will be ScrollToElem('ALFKI')
    string js = "ScrollToElem('{0}')";
    js = String.Format(js, custID);

    // Register the Javascript call with the onload event
    TheBody.Attributes["onload"] = js;
}
```

The final step entails that we bind the JavaScript call to the *onload* event of the HTML page. There are two ways of accomplishing this from within ASP.NET code. You can either use the *Page RegisterStartupScript* method or set the *onload* attribute on the *<body>* tag. I have chosen the second option because it's clearer and more intuitive. As we saw in Chapter 1, "The Web

Forms Model," to programmatically assign a property on the body of the page, you must first give it an ID and mark it as *runat="server"*.

```
<body runat="server" id="TheBody" ...>
```

The net effect of these changes is that whenever the user selects a new item, the page posts back and executes the *SelectedIndexChanged* method. The method updates the JavaScript function call associated with the page's *onload* event to reflect the current item. Next, the page is rendered and sent back to the browser. On the client, the *onload* event scrolls into view the piece of HTML code that corresponds to the currently selected item of the server-side *DataList* control.

Adding Support for Paging

The *DataList* control has a more free-form user interface than the *DataGrid* control. This consideration alone makes the *DataList* control particularly compelling to many developers who have the need to create interactive reports outside the relatively standard visualization pattern employed by grids. For example, no matter how powerful and customizable a grid can be, you can hardly force it to display a data-source column in more columns or rows of data. By contrast, you can easily obtain that flexibility using *DataList* controls. However, the *DataList* control doesn't support pagination.

Pagination is the control's ability to display equally sized blocks of data according to an internal index the user can modify through links. The *DataGrid* user interface incorporates a pager bar element, which is nothing more than a table row with links to internal pieces of code that handle the page movements. The *DataList* user interface doesn't provide any predefined link bar for pagination, meaning that the host page can define anywhere in the body a couple of links to move the data source back and forth.

Rendering Pages of Data

The following code snippets illustrate the page-level code that controls the current index and the contents of the current page:

```
private void OnPreviousPage(object sender, EventArgs e)
{
    CurrentPageIndex -= 1;
    RefreshPage();
}

private void OnNextPage(object sender, EventArgs e)
{
    CurrentPageIndex += 1;
    RefreshPage();
}
```

The code adjusts the page index—a global variable named *CurrentPageIndex*—and binds the data to the *DataList* control. *RefreshPage* is a page-level helper routine that extracts the data to bind from the database or, more logically, from a server-side cache.

```
private void RefreshPage()
{
    DataTable _data = GetData();
    AdjustPageIndex(_data.Rows.Count);

    CurrentPage.Text = (CurrentPageIndex +1).ToString();
    list.DataSource = GetPage(_data, CurrentPageIndex);
    list.DataBind();
}
private DataTable GetData()
{
    // Try to get the data from the session cache
    DataTable _data = (DataTable) Session["MyData"];

    // If no data is available, read from the database
    if (_data == null)
        _data = LoadData();

    return _data;
}
```

The *GetPage* method is responsible for extracting the right subset of rows that fit into the current page. The page of data is returned as a *DataTable* object and is bound to the *DataList*.

```
private DataTable GetPage(DataTable dt, int pageIndex)
{
    if (dt==null)
        dt = LoadData();

    int firstIndexInPage = (CurrentPageIndex*PageSize);
    DataRowCollection rows = dt.Rows;

    DataTable target = dt.Clone();
    for (int i=0; i<PageSize; i++)
    {
        int index = i+firstIndexInPage;
        if (index < rows.Count)
            target.ImportRow(rows[i+firstIndexInPage]);
        else
            break;
    }

    return target;
}
```

The function clones the original table of data and creates a new, smaller table with only the rows that fit into the specified page index. The *Clone* method creates a new empty object with the same structure as the sample. The *ImportRow* method duplicates and copies a new row from one *DataTable* object to another. Note that a deep copy of the row is necessary because ADO.NET objects can't be contained in more than one parent object.

> **Note** As we saw in Chapter 6 and Chapter 7, the *DataGrid* control supports two flavors of pagination—automatic and custom. In automatic paging, you bind the control to a data source for the lifetime of the control and, while you page, the control itself takes care of extracting all the records that need to be displayed. Custom paging, on the other hand, loads in memory all the records to display. Implementing a form of custom paging for a *DataList* control is straightforward and, in a certain way, this is exactly what we did when we created a list of buttons with the initials of the available customers. The preceding code completes the demonstration showing how to extract records from a cache of rows. However, note that the *DataGrid* control relies on an ad hoc class to perform paging related tasks—the *PagedDataSource* class. You could rewrite this code using an instance of the *PagedDataSource* class for the actual pagination.

Tracking the Page Index

For effective pagination, at least a couple of properties are needed: *CurrentPageIndex* and *PageSize*. The sample page in Figure 9-10 defines them as global properties on the page. If you plan to incorporate the code discussed here in a self-contained control, *CurrentPageIndex* and *PageSize* have to be public properties on the new class.

The *CurrentPageIndex* property contains the 0-based index relative to the current page. The *PageSize* property defines the maximum number of rows permitted per page.

```
public int PageSize = 12;
public int CurrentPageIndex
{
    get {
        if (ViewState["CurrentPageIndex"] == null)
            return 0;
        int _tmp = (int) ViewState["CurrentPageIndex"];
```

```
        return _tmp;
    }
    set {ViewState["CurrentPageIndex"] = value;}
}
```

It's interesting to note that unlike *PageSize*, *CurrentPageIndex* must necessarily be persisted across multiple page requests. This can easily be done using the *ViewState* collection. As the preceding code clearly shows, the value of the property is not stored in a class member but in the page *ViewState* bag. This ensures that its value will always be up to date.

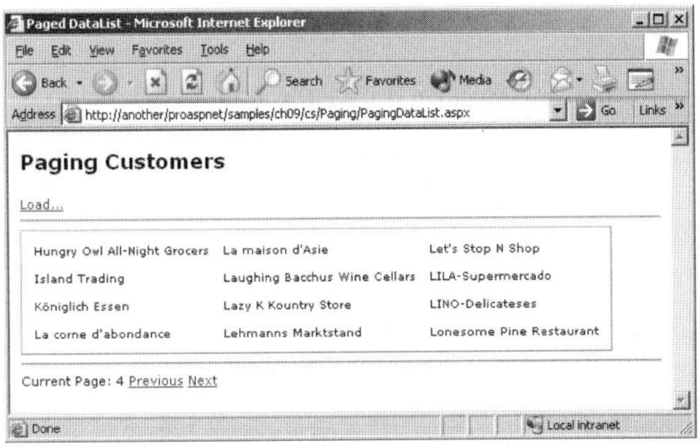

Figure 9-10 All the customers are displayed one page at a time in three columns of data. The link buttons provide for page movements and cause the *DataList* to refresh its contents.

Conclusion

In this chapter, we examined the characteristics of two iterative controls available with the ASP.NET programming platform. The two controls are the *Repeater* and *DataList* controls. A third iterative control—the *DataGrid*—has been widely covered in previous chapters. Iterative controls differ from list controls because of their native support for templates and their extremely flexible rendering engine. Iterative and list controls have some points in common too. Both can be bound to a data source and display a list of items. The key point is in the algorithm and the templates that each control, and category of controls, employs.

In an ideal scale, the *Repeater* is the simplest of all controls, but also the most flexible; the *DataGrid* has the richest set of features but is also the one that ties the developer to a multicolumn, tabular view. The *DataList* control falls somewhere in the middle, but it's logically closer to the *DataGrid* control. Just like the *Repeater*, the *DataList* displays the contents of a data-bound list through ASP.NET templates. But just like the *DataGrid*, it supports selecting and in-place editing and can have its look and feel customized using style properties.

Compared to the *Repeater* control, the *DataList* also shows off predefined layouts and more advanced formatting capabilities. Compared to the *DataGrid*, on the other hand, it lacks a key functionality: the ability to page through bound data. In this chapter, we've exploited the features of iterative controls, along with some HTML and JavaScript tricks, to build more effective and powerful components, and we discussed how to work around the lack of paging support in the *DataList* control.

In particular, we've seen how to build a sort of custom list box in which each item is free and based on a template. We wrote a lot of code in each page, both C# (or Visual Basic .NET) and ASP.NET layout code. It's about time we start practicing with more compact software elements that provide some level of code reusability. In Chapter 10, in fact, we'll cover Web user controls.

Resources

- Paging in DataList (*http://www.aspalliance.com/das/datalistpaging.aspx*)
- Creating Master-Detail Listings using ASP.NET controls (*http://www.dotnetbips.com/displayarticle.aspx?id=184*)
- Paging Results with ASP.NET's PagedDataSource (*http://www.sitepoint.com/article/921*)

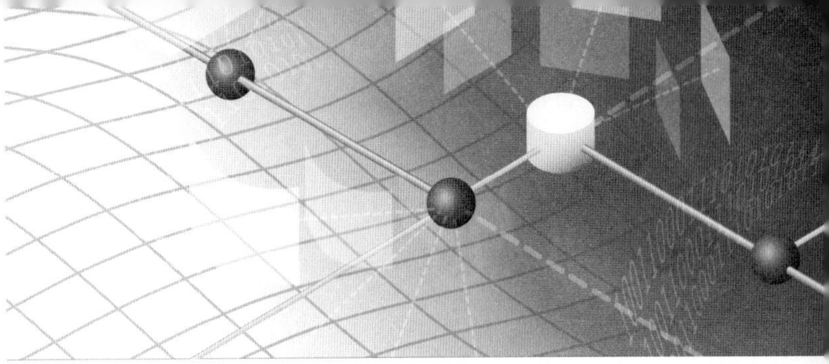

10

Web Forms User Controls

Divide and rule, a sound motto. Unite and lead, a better one.
—*Wolfgang Goethe*

While designing the new version of ASP, Microsoft spent a considerable amount of time developing a powerful and effective extensibility model. As a result, the old ASP was completely redesigned and made fully component-based. In doing this, Microsoft killed two birds with a single stone. For one thing, they could easily integrate the new Web platform—ASP.NET—with the surrounding and emerging .NET Framework. In addition, they came up with a stable and consolidated extensibility model based on inheritance and other object-oriented programming techniques. Enter ASP.NET and its families of controls.

At the highest level of abstraction, ASP.NET provides two types of component-based extensibility—custom controls and user controls. With custom controls, you create a new control inheriting from a base class (for example, *WebControl* or *Control*) or extend an existing class. A custom control is primarily a class built to behave like a control and provide a given set of functionalities—for example, a text box or a drop-down list. The user interface is a secondary aspect and is often created programmatically and rendered by concatenating HTML text. (We'll devote the entire Part V of the book to custom controls.) With user controls, you group a few controls together in a sort of embeddable child Web form. Although user controls can appear to be not particularly object-oriented at first, the class you come up with is built on top of a base class—the *UserControl* class.

What's a User Control, Anyway?

A user control is primarily a Web form made of any combination of server and client controls sewn together with server and client script code. A user control has a rich user interface, even though you can also program it as if it were an encapsulated component. As with Microsoft Visual Basic ActiveX controls, all constituent controls are protected and inaccessible if not made available through a public programming interface.

My favorite definition to describe a user control is that it's an embeddable Web form. The similarity between user controls and pages is not coincidental. (By the way, one of the first names assigned to this technology was *pagelets*.) You create a user control in much the same way you create a Web form. When you're done with code and layout, you give the resulting file a mandatory .ascx extension and then you can use the control with any ASP.NET page. Pages see the new control as a monolithic component and work with it as with any other built-in Web control. If you're familiar with Dynamic HTML (DHTML) scriptlets, look at user controls just as you look at their ASP.NET counterpart. Creating a Web user control is simpler and faster than creating a custom control.

The *UserControl* Class

User controls are server files with an .ascx extension that are referenced from within ASP.NET pages. They offer Web developers an easy way to capture and reuse common pieces of the user interface. Web user controls are compiled when first requested and cached in ways similar to *Page* objects. As with a page, you can develop them using code-behind or inline code. Unlike pages, though, user controls cannot be called independently. Internet Information Services (IIS), in fact, is configured to block and deny any requests directed at .ascx URLs. As a result, user controls can be called only from .aspx pages or other user controls that contain them.

> **Note** In their simplest form, user controls can be seen as a more flexible alternative to server-side includes (SSI). However, thinking of user controls only as a smarter form of SSI is highly reductive. User controls can expose their own object model instead of copying a piece of static HTML text. They're live objects and can be used just like any other ASP.NET server control.

UserControl is the .NET Framework class that represents an .ascx file when called from within an .aspx file. It inherits from *TemplateControl*, which is the base abstract class that provides a base set of functionality to both *Page* and *UserControl*. (This set of relationships is another element that marks the structural affinity between Web pages and user controls.)

```
public class UserControl : TemplateControl, IAttributeAccessor
```

The *TemplateControl* class implements the *INamingContainer* interface and adds to the programming interface of the *Control* class a few methods such as *LoadControl*, *LoadTemplate*, and *ParseControl*. The first two methods load a user control and a template from an external .ascx file. The *ParseControl* method parses an input string into an instance of a control or user control as appropriate.

Base Properties of User Controls

Table 10-1 lists the properties of the *UserControl* class, but it doesn't include those inherited from *TemplateControl*.

Table 10-1 Properties of the *UserControl* Class

Property	Description
Application	Gets the *HttpApplicationState* object for the current request.
Attributes	Gets the collection of all attributes declared in the user control tag.
Cache	Gets the *Cache* object associated with the current application.
IsPostBack	Gets whether the user control is being loaded for the first time or in response to a postback event.
Request	Gets the *HttpRequest* object for the current request.
Response	Gets the *HttpResponse* object for the current request.
Server	Gets the *HttpServerUtility* object for the current request.
Session	Gets the *HttpSessionState* object for the current request.
Trace	Gets the *TraceContext* object for the current request.

As you can see, the class provides properties to access all the intrinsic objects of an ASP.NET application plus the *IsPostBack* value, which is critical information to all ASP.NET components. A user control features all the various flavors of ID properties (*ID*, *ClientID*, and *UniqueID*) and acts as a naming container for all its child controls. As usual, the list of child controls is accessible via the *Controls* collection.

Base Methods of User Controls

The *UserControl* class features only a few methods in addition to those inherited from base classes. Inherited methods include commonly used functions such as *DataBind*, *FindControl*, and *LoadTemplate*. The methods of the *UserControl* class appear in Table 10-2.

Table 10-2 Methods of the *UserControl* Class

Property	Description
DesignerInitialize	Performs any initialization steps on the user control that are required by RAD designers.
InitializeAsUserControl	Completes the initialization of the *UserControl* object that has been created declaratively.
MapPath	Returns the physical file path that corresponds to the given virtual path. Note that the method maps the path from the .ascx file's location, not the page's location.

The *DesignerInitialize* and *InitializeAsUserControl* methods are rarely used in normal pages and are there mostly for internal use by the .NET Framework. In particular, the *InitializeAsUserControl* method makes sure the user control is initialized properly. The most important thing it does is hook up automatic event handlers. In other words, this method ensures methods named *Page_Load* or *Page_Init*, if present, are invoked during the control's *Load* and *Init* events. Table 10-3 shows the list of automatic event handlers that are supported.

Table 10-3 Automatic Event Handlers Hooked by the *UserControl* Class

Event Handler	Description
OnTransactionAbort, *Page_AbortTransaction*	Event *AbortTransaction*, occurs when a user aborts a transaction.
OnTransactionCommit, *Page_CommitTransaction*	Event *CommitTransaction*, occurs when a user commits a transaction in a transacted page. (See Chapter 1.)
Page_DataBind	Event *DataBind*, occurs when the control binds to a data source.
Page_Error	Event *Error*, occurs when an unhandled exception is thrown.
Page_Init	Event *Init*, occurs when the control is initialized.

Table 10-3 Automatic Event Handlers Hooked by the *UserControl* Class

Event Handler	Description
Page_Load	Event *Load*, occurs when the control is loaded into the page.
Page_PreRender	Event *PreRender*, occurs when the control is about to render its contents.
Page_Unload	Event *Unload*, occurs when the control is going to be unloaded from memory.

The events listed in this table are also the events supported by all user controls.

Converting Pages into User Controls

User controls and pages have so much in common that transforming one into the other is no big deal. However, in most cases you need to convert a page into a user control. As we'll see in a moment, it's a simple operation that takes only a few steps.

To start, make sure the user control does not contain any of the following tags: *<html>*, *<body>*, or *<form>*. Eliminating such tags will help to avoid conflicts, because the layout of the control will be merged with the layout of the hosting page and tags like *<html>* and *<body>* must be unique in the final page. As for the *<form>* tag, you can have as many form elements as needed, but only one can be marked with the *runat* attribute. So remove from the original page any reference you might have to a *<form runat="server">* element. If you have HTML forms, on the other hand, leave them on. (An HTML form is the *<form>* tag without the *runat* attribute.)

Once any offending HTML tags have been removed, rename the file with an .ascx extension. This is the key that will enable special treatment on the file. Furthermore, if the page you're converting contains an *@Page* directive, change it to an *@Control* directive.

The *@Control* Directive

The *@Control* and *@Page* directives share several attributes. The list of attributes supported by user controls is shown in Table 10-4.

Table 10-4 Attributes of the *@Control* Directive

Attribute	Description
AutoEventWireup	Indicates whether the control's events are automatically bound to methods with a particular name. The default is *true*.
ClassName	Indicates an alias for the name of the class that will be created to render the user control. This value can be any valid class name, but it should not include a namespace.
CompilerOptions	A sequence of compiler command-line switches used to compile the control's class.
Debug	Indicates whether the control should be compiled with debug symbols. If *true*, the source code of the class is not deleted and can be retrieved as discussed in Chapter 2.
Description	Provides a text description of the control.
EnableViewState	Indicates whether view state for the user control is maintained across page requests. The default is *true*.
Explicit	Determines whether the page is compiled using the Visual Basic *Option Explicit* mode. Ignored by languages other than Visual Basic .NET. *False* by default.
Inherits	Defines a code-behind class for the user control to inherit. Can be any class derived from *UserControl*.
Language	Specifies the language used throughout the control.
Strict	Determines whether the page is compiled using the Visual Basic *Option Strict* mode. Ignored by languages other than Visual Basic .NET. *False* by default.
Src	Specifies the source file name of the code-behind class to dynamically compile when the user control is requested.
WarningLevel	Indicates the compiler warning level at which you want the compiler to abort compilation for the user control.

From within a control, you cannot set any property that affects the overall behavior of the page. For example, you cannot enable or disable tracing, nor can you enable or disable session-state management.

You use the *Src* attribute of the *@Control* directive to develop the control using a code-behind schema. The *Src* attribute points to the C# or Visual Basic .NET class that contains the logic of the component. You should note, though, that the *Src* attribute is not recognized and supported by RAD designers such as Microsoft Visual Studio .NET. If you develop the control with Visual Studio .NET, in fact, the code-behind class is bound to the source file in a different way. The code of the class is compiled in the project assembly and made available to the ASP.NET runtime through the *Inherits* attribute. For editing purposes only, Visual Studio .NET tracks the name of the code-behind file using the custom attribute *CodeBehind*. If you use another editor, say Web Matrix, the *Src* attribute can be used to let the ASP.NET runtime know where the code of the component should be read from and dynamically compiled.

> **Note** The *@Control* directive makes it possible to use different languages for the user control and the page. For example, you can use Visual Basic .NET in the user control and C# in the calling page. The interaction between the two occurs at the level of compiled classes and therefore uses the common intermediate language (IL).

Finally, note that giving a user control an alias by using the *ClassName* attribute is not strictly necessary but is highly recommended. The *ClassName* attribute allows the user control to be strongly typed when it is added to a container programmatically.

Fragment Output Caching

User controls also provide an optimized version of a performance-related feature specific to Web Forms pages—output caching. We'll cover page output caching in great detail in Chapter 14, "ASP.NET State Management." Output caching is an ASP.NET system feature that caches the response of a page so that subsequent requests to the same URL can be satisfied without executing the page but simply by returning the cached output. (By the way, note that IIS 6.0 supports this feature at the Web-server level, thus supporting all types of Web applications.)

Output caching can take place at two levels—for the entire page or for a portion of a page. User controls are the smallest unit of a page whose output is cacheable. To make the entire page cacheable, you place an *@OutputCache* directive within the .aspx file. As a result, the whole output of the page will be cached according to the parameters you specify. To cache only a portion of the page, you first isolate that portion in a user control and then declare the *@OutputCache* directive in the .ascx file.

When caching the output of a user control, you must set at least a couple of attributes—*Duration* and *VaryByParam*. The following code snippet caches the output of the user control for 60 seconds:

```
<% @OutputCache Duration="60" VaryByParam="None" %>
```

Page and control output caching is smart enough to let you save distinct output, even output based on the parameters in a GET query string. See Chapter 14 for more details.

> **Important** Custom controls and user controls are two different and distinct ways to create user-defined controls for ASP.NET applications. Both have pros and cons, and each have advantages in particular scenarios. User controls are ideal if you have to encapsulate a rich and complex user interface and keep it separate from the page. A user control can also be separated into two files—the .ascx file representing the layout, and the file with the code (either a source file or an assembly).
>
> Custom controls are implemented in an assembly and expose both the user interface and the object model programmatically. Unlike user controls, custom controls better leverage the power of object-oriented programming (OOP) in the sense that they can be built from existing classes and new classes can be derived from them. Although user controls could technically be derived from existing controls, the presence of a distinct layout file makes inheritance a bit more problematic.

Developing User Controls

The structure of a user control is not much different than that of a regular Web page. It is composed of a directive section, inline code, and the graphical layout of the control. The inline code—that is, the *<script runat="server">* block—can be omitted if you use a code-behind file. Although nothing prevents you from writing user-interface-less user controls, the user interface (UI) is the most important part of the control and typically the most compelling reason for writing one. The typical structure of an .ascx file is shown as follows:

```
<%@ Control Language="C#" %>
<script runat="server">

    // Insert user control code here
    //

</script>
<!-- Insert content here -->
```

Many Web sites have pieces of the user interface that must be repeated in a large number of pages. Typical examples are: headers and footers, login and search forms, menus and panels. A login form doesn't need a complex object model and often doesn't need one at all. In other situations, you need to add a layer of logic on top of the control and make it programmable from within the host page. To start with user controls, let's see how to build a tab-strip control with a relatively simple object model.

Building a *TabStrip* User Control

A typical tab-strip control is made of a series of buttons laid out in a single row. When users click on a tab, the control selects the particular tab and fires an event to the host page. The page will in turn update and refresh its own user interface. Figure 10-1 shows the final form.

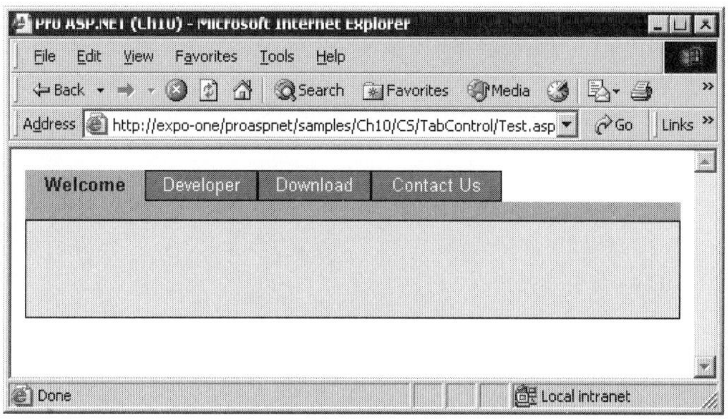

Figure 10-1 The *TabStrip* control in action within a sample page.

The user interface of the control is generated using a *Repeater* control and consists of a single-row HTML table in which each cell contains a button. Just below the table, an empty, tiny panel separates the tab strip from the rest of the page. The control acts as a simple selector and doesn't include any smart code to process the click event. Whenever the user clicks any of the tabs, a postback event is generated back to the page. The page is also responsible for creating the tabs to display. In this example, we represent a tab with a simple string. In more real-world scenarios, you might want to use an ad hoc class to describe a tab and include a key value, a ToolTip, a Boolean state (enabled/disabled), or maybe a URL.

```
<%@ Control Language="C#" ClassName="TabStrip" %>
<%@ Import Namespace="System.Drawing" %>

<script runat="server">
// Tabs to display
public ArrayList Tabs;
```

```
private void Page_Init(object sender, EventArgs e) {
    Tabs = new ArrayList();
}

private void Page_Load(object sender, EventArgs e) {
    if (!IsPostBack) {
        BindData();
    }
}

private void BindData() {
    __theTabStrip.DataSource = Tabs;
    __theTabStrip.DataBind();
}
</script>

<asp:Repeater runat="server" id="__theTabStrip">
    <headertemplate>
        <table cellpadding="0" cellspacing="0" border="0" ><tr>
    </headertemplate>

    <itemtemplate>
        <td>
            <asp:button runat="server" id="__theTab"
                style="border:solid 1px black"
            text='<%# Container.DataItem %>' />
        </td>
    </itemtemplate>

    <footertemplate>
        </tr></table>
    </footertemplate>
</asp:Repeater>
<asp:panel runat="server" id="__theSep" width="100%" backcolor="gray" />
```

The *Tabs* array contains the string to display as the caption of each tab. The object is initialized in the control's *Page_Init* event and consumed during the rendering phase of the control. The caller page typically populates the *Tabs* collection in its *Page_Load* event.

Before taking the *TabStrip* user control to the next level, let's see what's needed to include a user control in a Web page.

Including a User Control in a Page

A user control is inserted in a Web page by using a custom tag marked with the *runat* attribute. The control instance has an ID and can be programmed using that name. The server tag is divided in two parts—a tag prefix and a tag name. In the following code snippet, the tag prefix is *mspo* and the tag name is *tabstrip*.

```
<mspo:tabstrip runat="server" id="menu" />
```

If you give the control the asp prefix, or no prefix at all, the ASP.NET runtime will look for the needed class only in the *System.Web* assembly. Because the user control is not implemented there, an exception is thrown. How do you register a tag name and prefix for a user control? And how do you bind both with an .ascx file?

The *@Register* Directive

The *@Register* directive associates aliases with namespaces and class names to provide a concise notation to reference custom and user controls within Web pages. Table 10-5 details the attributes of the directive.

Table 10-5 Attributes of the *@Register* Directive

Attribute	Description
Assembly	The assembly in which the namespace associated with the tag prefix resides. The assembly name does not include a file extension.
Namespace	The namespace to associate with the tag prefix.
Src	The relative or absolute location of the user control file to associate with the tag prefix and name. The file name must include the .ascx extension.
TagName	A tag name to alias the custom or user control. (It is *tabstrip* in the code snippet shown previously.)
TagPrefix	A tag prefix to alias the namespace of the control, if any. (It is *mspo* in the code snippet shown previously.)

You use the *@Register* directive in one of two ways. The first way is to register a custom control—that is, a server control that you write as a class—and you use the following syntax:

```
<%@ Register tagprefix="..." namespace="..." assembly="..." %>
```

The second way is to register a user control. To do this, you use the following syntax:

```
<%@ Register tagprefix="..." tagname="..." src="..." %>
```

A server control is represented by two parts—a prefix and a tag name. The prefix identifies a namespace and subsequently the assembly in which the code for the user control is located. For user controls, the namespace defaults to *ASP* and the class name is the value of the control's *ClassName* attribute. For example, it is *ASP.TabStrip* for the sample code we just discussed. The assembly is dynamically created the first time the ASP.NET runtime accesses the resource. The tag name is any unique name you use to refer to the user control within a client page. Different pages can use different tag names for the same user control.

For a custom control, you indicate the namespace and assembly and specify any namespace prefix you like better. The tag name, on the other hand, is fixed and must match the custom control class name.

Setting Up a User Control

Although absolute path names can be used to register a user control, you should always use relative names. However, you should be aware that any code within a user control is always executed taking the URL of the control as the base URL. This means that if the user control needs to access an image in the application's Images folder, you can't just use a relative path like the following one:

```
<img src="images/logo.gif" />
```

To address the right location, you could either move one or more folders back or, better yet, indicate a relative path that begins from the root. In the former case, you use .. to move one level up in the virtual Web space; in the latter case, you use the tilde (~) character to indirectly refer the root directory of the application.

```
<img src="~/images/logo.gif" />
```

To register the *TabStrip* control, you use the following registration directive:

```
<%@ Register TagPrefix="mspo" TagName="TabStrip" Src="tabstrip.ascx" %>
```

An instance of the user control is created upon page loading. Just as for Web pages, a class that represents the control is created on the fly and cached in the ASP.NET temporary folders. Any updates to the source code of the .ascx file (or the code-behind class) are immediately detected and invalidate the existing assembly. In no case do you need to compile the user control to make it available to the page. (To sum it up, there's just one case in which you need to compile it first—when the control is included in code-behind pages. I'll say more about this in the "Getting Serious About User Controls" section later in this chapter.)

Building a User-Control Object Model

When running, a user control is an instance of a dynamically created class. The class derives from *UserControl* and belongs to the *ASP* namespace. The actual name of the user control class depends on whether or not you set the *ClassName* attribute in the *@Control* directive. If a class name was not specified, the ASP.NET runtime generates a default name based on the .ascx file name. For example, a user control defined in a sample .ascx file generates a class named *ASP.sample_ascx*.

For a user control, as well as for Web pages, every property or method that is marked as public is externally callable and, as such, part of the control's object model. The following code snippet declares a couple of read/write properties that represent the background and foreground color of the unselected tabs:

```
<script runat="server">
    public Color BackColor
    {
        get {return (Color) ViewState["BackColor"];}
        set {ViewState["BackColor"] = value;}
    }
    public Color ForeColor
    {
        get {return (Color) ViewState["ForeColor"];}
        set {ViewState["ForeColor"] = value;}
    }
    ⋮
</script>
```

The qualifier *public* is essential to make the property (or the method) externally visible and callable.

> **Note** To make sure the contents of a property are retrieved when the page posts back, you should store it in the control's *ViewState* collection. Basically, you use a slot in the *ViewState* as the storage medium of the property. However, note that if you're simply exposing at the user-control level the property of an embedded control, you don't need to resort to the view state. In that case, in fact, the embedded control takes care of the variable persistence.

Adding Properties

At a minimum, the *TabStrip* control should expose properties to let you add tabs, track the current index, and set background and foreground colors for selected and unselected tabs.

```
<script runat="server">
// Tabs to display
public ArrayList Tabs = new ArrayList();

// Current Tab (read-only)
```

```
public int CurrentTabIndex
{
    get {return (int) ViewState["CurrentTabIndex"];}
}

// Background color
public Color BackColor
{
    get {return (Color) ViewState["BackColor"];}
    set {ViewState["BackColor"] = value;}
}

// Selected background color
public Color SelectedBackColor
{
    get {return (Color) ViewState["SelectedBackColor"];}
    set {ViewState["SelectedBackColor"] = value;}
}

// Foreground color
public Color ForeColor
{
    get {return (Color) ViewState["ForeColor"];}
    set {ViewState["ForeColor"] = value;}
}

// Selected foreground color
public Color SelectedForeColor
{
    get {return (Color) ViewState["SelectedForeColor"];}
    set {ViewState["SelectedForeColor"] = value;}
}
⋮
</script>
```

A property on a user control is any publicly accessible variable. If you need to perform special tasks when reading or writing the value of the property, you can define *get* and *set* accessors. A *get* accessor is a special procedure that returns the value of the property. Likewise, the *set* accessor is a method that sets the value of the property. The lack of an accessor automatically disables the corresponding function, thus making the property read-only or write-only. In the preceding code, the *CurrentTabIndex* property is read-only.

All the properties except *Tabs* use accessors and persist their value to the control's view state. The contents of the *Tabs* collection are lost and must be rebuilt whenever the page posts back. As we'll see in more detail in Chapter 14, the view state might affect the download time of the page. All the information you store in the *ViewState* collection, in fact, is encoded as Base64 and transmitted back and forth between the Web server and the browser. Information that is not strictly tied to choices made by the user should not be stored in the view state. Following this guideline will keep Web pages lean and mean.

> **Note** According to the aforementioned guideline, color properties should not be stored in the view state because the page author is the only one responsible for their values. As such, you can explicitly hard-code the colors to use in the control's declaration within the host page. The same can't be said for the *CurrentTabIndex* property, whose value depends on what the user does.

User control properties can be set both declaratively and programmatically. If you opt for a declarative approach, the name of the property is used as a tag attribute.

```
<mspo:tabstrip runat="server" id="menu"
    selectedbackcolor="cyan" />
```

In this case, you can use strings only to specify the value. To set the background color, you use a string that represents the desired color. ASP.NET will attempt to convert the assigned string into a valid value of the expected type. On the other hand, if you set a property programmatically, you must pass values of the correct type.

```
void Page_Load(object sender, EventArgs e)
{
    // Since the Tabs collection is not stored in the view state,
    // you must populate it each time the page posts back. This code
    // must be placed outside the IsPostBack branch.
    menu.Tabs.Add("Welcome");
    menu.Tabs.Add("Developer");
    menu.Tabs.Add("Download");
    menu.Tabs.Add("Contact Us");

    if (!IsPostBack)
    {
        // Do here all the things that need to be done only the
        // first time the control is loaded in the page.
        // For example, select here the page to be displayed
        // by default.
        ⋮
    }

    // Set colors programmatically
```

```
    menu.SelectedBackColor = Color.Green;
    menu.SelectedForeColor = Color.White;
    menu.BackColor = Color.LightGray;
    menu.ForeColor = Color.Black;
}
```

The instance of the user control is identified using the ID of the control. If you're handling properties that do not rely on the view state, you should configure them each time the page posts back, without distinguishing between the first load and postbacks.

The selected tab is rendered with different colors, which are applied through data-bound expressions, as shown here:

```
<itemtemplate>
    <td>
        <asp:button runat="server" id="__theTab"
            BorderWidth="1px"
            BorderStyle="solid"
            BorderColor='<%# SetBorderColor(Container) %>'
            text='<%# Container.DataItem %>'
            font-bold='<%# (Container.ItemIndex == CurrentTabIndex) %>'
            backcolor='<%# SetBackColor(Container) %>'
            forecolor='<%# SetForeColor(Container) %>' />
    </td>
</itemtemplate>
```

The *SetXXX* functions are internal members that compare the current tab index with the index of the item being created and decide which color to apply.

```
private Color SetBackColor(object elem)
{
    RepeaterItem item = (RepeaterItem) elem;
    if (item.ItemIndex == CurrentTabIndex)
        return SelectedBackColor;
    return BackColor;
}
```

Initializing the User Control

When you create a user control with inline code—as we're doing here—you can't write code that executes in the user control class constructor. If you just add some code for the default constructor, you get a compile error because the ASP.NET runtime has already defined a constructor with the same parameter types.

```
public TabStrip()
{
    ⋮
}
```

Any constructor overloads you define will be ignored by the ASP.NET runtime. However, you can use such overloads if you create the user control dynamically. (We'll discuss this later in the section "Loading Controls Dynamically".) If the user control is developed with a code-behind, the constructor can be successfully managed. So what's the issue if you can't execute your own code in the default constructor?

Suppose you have a few properties that should take default values. Normally, you would initialize these values in the class constructor and set them to default values. In the case we're considering, we need to instantiate the *ArrayList* object that implements the *Tabs* collection and set the default page index and colors. If the properties do not make use of accessors, you simply assign a default value when declaring them.

```
public ArrayList Tabs = new ArrayList();
```

This is not possible, though, if you need accessors.

The *Page_Init* event is the first piece of the control's code in which you can insert your own instructions.

```
private void Page_Init(object sender, EventArgs e)
{
    // Check to see if defined declaratively or in
    // the page's Init event
    if (ViewState["SelectedBackColor"] == null)
        SelectedBackColor = Color.White;
    if (ViewState["SelectedForeColor"] == null)
        SelectedForeColor = Color.Blue;
    if (ViewState["BackColor"] == null)
        BackColor = Color.Gray;
    if (ViewState["ForeColor"] == null)
        ForeColor = Color.White;
    if (ViewState["CurrentTabIndex"] == null)
        ViewState["CurrentTabIndex"] = 0;
}
```

Note, though, that the control's *Page_Init* event fires when the ASP.NET runtime already did a lot of work constructing the page. In particular, it comes after the user control has been instantiated and configured with the properties declaratively set in the page layout. The *Init* event of the control precedes the page *Init* event. In contrast, the page *Load* event comes earlier than the *Load* event on child controls.

In short, you can't simply treat the *Page_Init* event of the control as a replacement for the constructor. If you do so, you'll overwrite any settings defined in the control's tag. So how can you assign default values to all properties without overwriting any values that might have been set declaratively?

You should set the default value only if the property is unassigned. The way in which you detect that the property is unassigned is application specific. For example, if the property is part of the view state, you can check the *ViewState* collection against null.

Adding Methods

The next step in the process of building a functional and reusable tab-strip control is adding a method to programmatically select a particular tab. So far, in fact, the selection can only be triggered by the user when she clicks a button. The *Select* method will do that programmatically. Here is the prototype of the *Select* method:

```
public void Select(int index)
```

The method takes an integer argument, which is the 0-based index of the tab to select. Internally, it sets the current tab index and rebinds the data.

```
public void Select(int index) {
    // Ensure the index is a valid value, otherwise select the first
    if (index <0 || index >Tabs.Count)
        index = 0;

    // Updates the current index. Must write to the view state
    // because the CurrentTabIndex property is read-only
    ViewState["CurrentTabIndex"] = index;

    // Ensure the bottom panel is of the selected color
    __theSep.BackColor = SelectedBackColor;

    // Refresh the user interface
    BindData();
}
```

A method on a user control is simply a public method defined either as inline code or in the code-behind class. Note that the *Select* method can't set the current tab index by using the public property. The reason is that the property is read-only (that is, it lacks a *set* accessor), and subsequently no code within the class can set it explicitly. The workaround is to directly access the *ViewState*, where the values of the property are actually stored.

The sample page can now offer some user-interface elements to let users select tabs programmatically. The following code snippet shows a text box in which you can type the index of the tab to select and a link button to execute the code:

```
<asp:textbox runat="server" id="tabIndex" width="30px" />
<asp:linkbutton runat="server" text="Select tab" onclick="OnSelectTab" />
```

The *OnSelectTab* event handler simply calls the *Select* method on the user control, as Figure 10-2 demonstrates.

```
void OnSelectTab(object sender, EventArgs e) {
    menu.Select(Convert.ToInt32(tabIndex.Text));
}
```

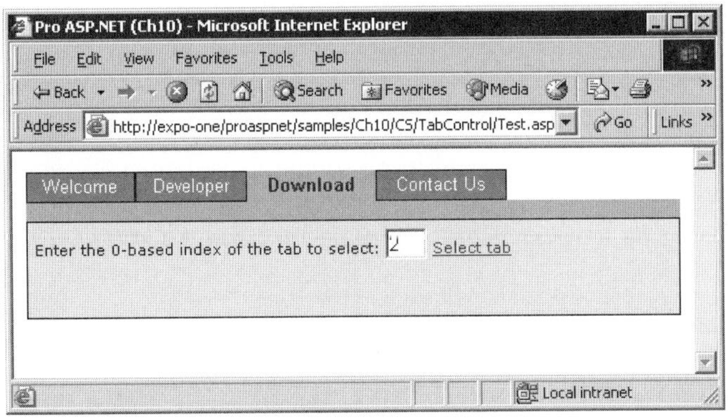

Figure 10-2 A new link button commands the selection of a particular tab.

The *Select* method acts as the *set* accessor of the *CurrentTabIndex* property. If you want to read the index of the current tab, you use the property; if you want to programmatically set a particular tab, you use the method.

Handling User-Control Events

So far we've built a user control that displays its own user interface and allows users to select tabs. For a control such as the *TabStrip*, though, the key feature has not been implemented yet. How can a page that hosts the control be notified of a user's clickings? A tab strip makes sense if the page can detect the selection changed event and properly refresh. For example, the page could generate different content according to the selected tab; alternatively, it can redirect the user to a child page within a frame or simply jump to a new URL. To let the page know about the selection, we must add an event to the user control.

Adding the *SelectionChanged* Event

Within the *TabStrip* control, the selection changes whenever the user clicks the buttons or when the page calls the *Select* method. Let's define an event named *SelectionChanged*.

```
public event SelectionChangedEventHandler SelectionChanged;
```

An event is a special property bound to a delegate. A delegate is a reference to a method signature. An instance of a delegate is actually a pointer to a function with a well-known signature. The .NET Framework provides a general-purpose delegate for event handlers—the *EventHandler* class. Here is the prototype of such event handlers:

```
public delegate void EventHandler(object sender, EventArgs e);
```

The *EventHandler* delegate represents all methods that take an *object* and an *EventArgs* argument and return *void*. This predefined delegate is good as long as you don't need to pass custom data back to the caller. You should use it only for events that work as simple notifications of some server-side event. In this case, we need to pass at least the index of the selected tab. So let's define a custom delegate and a custom event data structure.

```
public delegate void SelectionChangedEventHandler(
    object sender, SelectionChangedEventArgs e);
```

A custom delegate for the event differs from *EventHandler* for the custom data structure used to carry event arguments. The common naming convention for events entails using the name of the event (*SelectionChanged* in this case) to prefix both the delegate and the data structure name.

```
public class SelectionChangedEventArgs : EventArgs
{
    public int Position;    // 0-based index of the selected tab
}
```

The *SelectionChangedEventArgs* structure inherits from *EventArgs* and adds an integer property that represents the 0-based index of the selected tab. An instance of this data structure will be created and initialized when the event occurs within the user control.

Firing a Custom Event

To better handle custom events, you might want to define a helper routine like the one shown at the end of this paragraph. The name you choose for this routine is unimportant. Likewise, the method qualifiers (*protected*, *virtual*) are subject to your personal preferences. Let's say that declaring such a helper routine as protected and overridable is considered a best programming practice that is widely employed in the .NET Framework itself. My suggestion is that either you declare it as protected and virtual or don't declare it at all.

```
// Helper function that fires the event by executing user-defined code
protected virtual void OnSelectionChanged(SelectionChangedEventArgs e)
{
    // SelectionChanged is the event property. Check if the user defined it
```

```
    if (SelectionChanged != null)
        SelectionChanged(this, e);
}
```

The routine doesn't do much—it just ensures the event property is not null and makes the call. However, it adds an extra layer of code that, if made overridable, can help derived classes to customize the behavior more easily and effectively.

At this point, firing the event becomes simply a matter of initializing the data structure and calling the helper function. The event is fired by the *Select* method.

```
public void Select(int index) {
    // Ensure the index is a valid value
    if (index <0 || index >Tabs.Count)
        index = 0;

    // Updates the current index. Must write to the view state
    // because the CurrentTabIndex property is read-only
    ViewState["CurrentTabIndex"] = index;

    // Ensure the bottom panel is of the selected color
    __theSep.BackColor = SelectedBackColor;

    // Refresh the UI
    BindData();

    // Fire the event to the client
    SelectionChangedEventArgs ev = new SelectionChangedEventArgs();
    ev.Position = CurrentTabIndex;
    OnSelectionChanged(ev);
}
```

When the user clicks on the tabs, the underlying *Repeater* control we used to create the control's user interface fires an *ItemCommand* event. The embedded handler for the *ItemCommand* event just calls into *Select*.

```
private void ItemCommand(object sender, RepeaterCommandEventArgs e)
{
    // Select the tab that corresponds to the clicked button
    Select(e.Item.ItemIndex);
}
```

Now that the user control fires an event, let's see what's needed on the caller page to detect and handle it.

Handling a Custom Event

A .NET component that wants to sink events emitted by controls must write a handler whose prototype matches that of the event delegate. How you bind the handler with the event on a particular instance of the component is language specific. For example, in C#, you create a new instance of the event handler class and add it to the component's event property.

```
// YourHandler is the actual name of the handler in your code
menu.SelectionChanged += new SelectionChangedEventHandler(YourHandler);
```

In Visual Basic .NET, you can use the *AddHandler* keyword, as shown here:

```
' YourHandler is the actual name of the handler in your code
AddHandler menu.SelectionChanged, AddressOf YourHandler
```

This technique is not always necessary in ASP.NET applications. In ASP.NET, in fact, you can also register event handlers declaratively using the *OnXXX* attribute, where *XXX* stands for the actual name of the event property.

```
<mspo:menu runat="server" id="menu"
    SelectedBackColor="cyan"
    OnSelectionChanged="SelectionChanged" />
```

Here is the *SelectionChanged* event handler:

```
void SelectionChanged(object sender, TabStrip.SelectionChangedEventArgs e)
{
    msg.Text = "Selected tab #" + e.Position.ToString();
}
```

Note that the name of the custom event data class must be prefixed with the name of the user control class. The reason for this requirement is that the event data class is defined within the user control class. Figure 10-3 shows the *Tab-Strip* user control, which includes a *SelectionChanged* event handler.

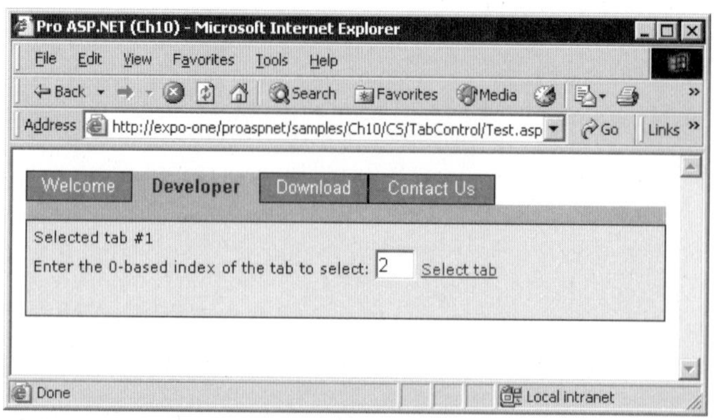

Figure 10-3 The user selects the second tab, and the application detects the change and properly refreshes.

Getting Serious About User Controls

In Chapter 9, "ASP.NET Iterative Controls," we created quite complex user interfaces by combining iterative controls and HTML advanced features such as text overflow. That code addresses common needs and, therefore, might be employed in other pages or applications. Unfortunately, as we wrote it, it's hardly reusable. To work around this issue, let's try to rewrite as a user control some of the *Repeater*-based code we discussed in Chapter 9. In doing so, we'll also address an interesting and real-world aspect of control development—data binding. Incidentally, data binding is also a reasonable next step for the user control we have just built. A data-bound version of the *TabStrip* user control would use the results of a SQL query to automatically generate the tabs.

Earlier in this chapter, we mentioned that user controls can be developed using inline code as well as a code-behind. For the sake of completeness, in the next sample, we'll use and examine the code-behind approach.

Building Data-Bound User Controls

In most cases, a data-bound user control is not really different than a data-free control. The only relevant difference is that a data-bound control features a few properties that bind it to an *ICollection*-based data source object—mostly, but not necessarily, an ADO.NET object. In Chapter 9, we used a *Repeater* control to build a list of buttons, each with a letter name. Such neat and handy functionality clashes with all the boilerplate code that is needed to set it up. With their powerful mix of user-interface and back-end code, user controls seem to be the right tool to leverage for reaching a satisfactory solution.

The *ButtonList* User Control

The *ButtonList* control is made of an .ascx file and a code-behind file. Its link is set in the *@Control* directive. The layout of the .ascx file is fairly simple and contains a *Repeater* control to enumerate all the bound items and create a push button for each. In addition, a thin one-row table is placed below the *Repeater* for a better graphical effect.

```
<%@ Control Language="C#" ClassName="ButtonList"
    Inherits="ProAspNet.CS.Ch10.ButtonList"
    Src="ButtonList.ascx.cs" %>

<asp:repeater runat="server" id="__theMenu">
    <HeaderTemplate>
        <table border="0" cellspacing="0" cellpadding="0"><tr>
    </HeaderTemplate>
```

```
    <ItemTemplate>
        <td valign="bottom">
            <asp:button runat="server" id="TheButton"
                style="border:solid 1px gray" />
        </td>
    </ItemTemplate>

    <FooterTemplate>
        </tr></table>
    </FooterTemplate>
</asp:repeater>
<asp:panel runat="server" id="__theSep" width="100%" />
```

Because the control is developed using a code-behind, you must use the *Inherits* attribute on the *@Control* directive. It tells the ASP.NET runtime what the base class is from which the dynamic control class is to be derived. You set *Inherits* with the fully qualified name of the code-behind class. If you use Visual Studio .NET, this happens by default; if you use Web Matrix, on the other hand, remember to set it yourself. If you omit the *Inherits* attribute, the ASP.NET runtime would ignore your code-behind class and use *UserControl* instead. In addition to using *Inherits*, you can specify *Src* to let ASP.NET know about the location of the source code to compile. If *Src* is omitted, ASP.NET assumes that the needed assembly is already available in one of the common paths and complains if the needed assembly isn't found.

The .ascx file contains only the skeleton of the control's user interface. As you can see, there's no data-binding expression and no event handlers. When you work with code-behind classes, isolating all executable code in the source file is considered a best practice because it guarantees full separation between code and layout.

The Programming Interface of the *ButtonList* Control

The *ButtonList* control exposes a few properties, as listed in Table 10-6. These properties are primarily related to the data-binding mechanism, which leverages the data binding of the underlying *Repeater* control.

Table 10-6 Properties of the *ButtonList* Control

Property	Description
ButtonWidth	Integer that indicates the width in pixels of the buttons
CurrentButtonCommand	Gets the command name of the currently selected button
CurrentButtonIndex	Gets the 0-based index of the currently selected button
DataSource	Indicates the data source used to populate the control

Table 10-6 Properties of the *ButtonList* Control

Property	Description
DataTextField	Indicates the name of the data source column used to render the caption of the buttons
DataValueField	Indicates the name of the data-source column used to express the command associated with the buttons

The *DataSource* property plays the same role as in other data-bound controls. It provides a collection of data items the control will use to populate its own user interface. A couple of columns from this data source are used to render the caption and the command name of each button. The command name of a *Button* object is a string that uniquely identifies that button and is used to detect events. When binding data to this control, you should set *DataValueField* to a column with unique values. Note that the value will be converted into a string, so be sure you choose a column that maintains unique values after being converted into a string. All the properties except *DataSource* are cached in the view state.

The contents of the *DataSource* are cached internally in the ASP.NET *Cache* object. This shouldn't be a big issue because the number of records bound to the *ButtonList* control is not expected to be high.

```
public object DataSource {
    get {return Cache[DataSourceName];}
    set {Cache[DataSourceName] = value;}
}
```

The data source is cached in a slot with a unique name. The name is determined using the ID of the control. This guarantees that multiple controls in the same page work correctly and without conflicts. As mentioned, all the other properties are cached in the control's view state, which, in turn, is flushed in the page's view state.

```
public string DataTextField {
    get {return (string) ViewState["DataTextField"];}
    set {ViewState["DataTextField"] = value;}
}
```

The view state is specific to the individual control, so there's no need to figure out a scheme for unique names. When writing a *get* accessor for a property, you should always make sure the value you read is not null. This is especially true if you deal with objects such as *Cache*, *Session* or *ViewState*.

The overall data-binding mechanism of the *ButtonList* control mirrors the data-binding engine of the *Repeater* control. In particular, the *DataBind* method is nothing more than a wrapper.

```
private void DataBind() {
    __theMenu.DataSource = DataSource;
    __theMenu.DataBind();
}
```

The *ButtonClicked* event completes the programming interface of the control. The event fires whenever the user clicks a button. The client page receives a custom structure containing the index and the command of the button. We'll return to this in the next section, "Generating the Output." The implementation of the event is identical to the event we discussed for the *TabStrip* user control earlier in this chapter.

> **Note** The slots in the *Cache* object are subject to be emptied if the system runs low on memory. It's a good practice to make sure you always check against null all the properties that depend on *Cache*. If the slot is null, your code should be smart enough to restore the correct value.

Generating the Output

When the control is initialized—that is, after the constructor is called—it hooks up its own set of events. In this case, we need to register handlers for some events fired by the embedded *Repeater* control.

```
private void HookUpEvents() {
    __theMenu.ItemCommand += new RepeaterCommandEventHandler(ItemCommand);
    __theMenu.ItemCreated += new RepeaterItemEventHandler(ItemCreated);
    __theMenu.ItemDataBound += new RepeaterItemEventHandler(ItemBound);
}
```

During the *ItemCreated* event, we take care of the appearance of each button and decide about colors, borders, and size. In particular, the selected button is larger than others and highlighted.

```
protected void ItemCreated(object sender, RepeaterItemEventArgs e)
{
    if (e.Item.ItemType != ListItemType.Item &&
        e.Item.ItemType != ListItemType.AlternatingItem)
        return;
```

```
    // Retrieve the item being created
    RepeaterItem item = e.Item;
    bool isSelected = IsSelectedItem(item);
    Button btn = (Button) item.FindControl("TheButton");

    // Customize the appearance
    if (isSelected) {
        btn.BackColor = SelectedBackColor;
        btn.ForeColor = SelectedForeColor;
        btn.Height = Unit.Pixel(23);
        btn.Width = Unit.Pixel(ButtonWidth*150/100);
    }
    else
    {
        btn.BackColor = BackColor;
        btn.ForeColor = ForeColor;
        btn.Height = Unit.Pixel(20);
        btn.Width = Unit.Pixel(ButtonWidth);
    }
}
```

Note that although the colors are not exposed as public properties, they are used as if they were. (If you want to enhance the *ButtonList* control, this feature shouldn't be too hard to add, especially in light of your previous experience with the *TabStrip* control.) Pay attention to the type of the item being created, and exit the *ItemCreated* event handler if the *Repeater* is not creating an item of type *Item* or *AlternatingItem*.

When *ItemCreated* fires, the item has not yet been bound to data. So, to adjust the caption and the command name for the button, we need to wait for the *ItemDataBound* event.

```
protected void ItemBound(object sender, RepeaterItemEventArgs e)
{
    if (e.Item.ItemType != ListItemType.Item &&
        e.Item.ItemType != ListItemType.AlternatingItem)
        return;

    // Retrieve the item being bound to data
    RepeaterItem item = e.Item;
    Button btn = (Button) item.FindControl("TheButton");

    // Bind to data
    btn.Text = DataBinder.Eval(item.DataItem,
        DataTextField).ToString();
    btn.CommandName = DataBinder.Eval(item.DataItem,
        DataValueField).ToString();
}
```

The *DataBinder* class is used to bind properties with data. Note that the code-behind class (from which all this code is excerpted) doesn't know anything about ADO.NET and doesn't even import the *System.Data* namespace.

Finally, when the user clicks one of the buttons, the *Repeater* fires the *ItemCommand* event.

```
protected void ItemCommand(object sender, RepeaterCommandEventArgs e)
{
    // Update the internal state
    CurrentButtonCommand = e.CommandName;
    CurrentButtonIndex = e.Item.ItemIndex;

    // Refresh the UI
    DataBind();

    // Fire the ButtonClicked event to the client
    ButtonClickedEventArgs ev = new ButtonClickedEventArgs();
    ev.ButtonCommand = CurrentButtonCommand;
    ev.ButtonIndex = CurrentButtonIndex;
    OnButtonClicked(ev);
}
```

The *RepeaterCommandEventArgs* class contains both the index of the clicked item and its command name. These two pieces of information are packed into a *ButtonClickedEventArgs* structure and passed to the client's handler, if any.

Setting Up a Client Page

So much for the *ButtonList* control, let's see how to set up a client page that intends to use the control. The following directive registers the control for use within the page:

```
<%@ Register TagPrefix="mspo"
TagName="ButtonList" Src="buttonlist.ascx" %>
```

Once more, note that you can change at will the content of the *TagName* and *TagPrefix* attributes. If the control has been developed using code-behind, chances are you have to also import the namespace of the control. This namespace might be needed to access any public element that is included in the package, such as enumeration and related classes. If you use code-behind, you can control the location of each public element in the namespace. If inline code is used, everything is the child of the user control class. Let's consider the following code snippet, which reflects the structure of the code-behind class:

```
namespace ProAspNet.CS.Ch10
{
    public class ButtonClickedEventArgs : EventArgs
    {
```

```
        public string ButtonCommand;
        public int ButtonIndex;
    }

    public class ButtonList : UserControl
    {
        ⋮
    }
}
```

In this case, the *ButtonClickedEventArgs* class is not a child of *ButtonList*. With inline code, the overall structure of the code would have been slightly different.

```
namespace ASP
{
    public class ButtonList : UserControl
    {
        ⋮

        public class ButtonClickedEventArgs : EventArgs
        {
            ⋮
        }
    }
}
```

Defining the *ButtonClickedEventArgs* class outside the user control class is just a matter of preference. If you want, you can certainly move that code as a subclass within the *ButtonList* definition. If you do this, there's no need to import the *ProAspNet.CS.Ch10* namespace, but you should prefix the class name with *ButtonList*. The following code declares a couple of *ButtonList* controls sharing the same handler for the *ButtonClicked* event:

```
<mspo:buttonlist runat="server" id="initialStrip"
    onbuttonclicked="ButtonClicked" />
<mspo:buttonlist runat="server" id="yearStrip"
    buttonwidth="50"
    onbuttonclicked="ButtonClicked" />
```

The page is responsible for downloading data from a data source and binding it to the controls.

```
void Page_Load(object sender, EventArgs e) {
    if (!IsPostBack) {
        BindInitials();
        BindYears();
    }
}
```

In the sample code we're considering, *BindInitials* and *BindYears* execute the following queries:

```
-- Get the first letter of all customer names
SELECT DISTINCT substring(companyname, 1, 1) AS Initial FROM customers
-- Get the years for which at least an order exists
SELECT DISTINCT year(orderdate) AS year FROM orders
```

The *ButtonList* controls are initialized with the following code:

```
initialStrip.DataSource = _data.Tables["Initials"];
initialStrip.DataTextField = "Initial";
initialStrip.DataValueField = "Initial";
initialStrip.DataBind();
```

Figure 10-4 shows the final results.

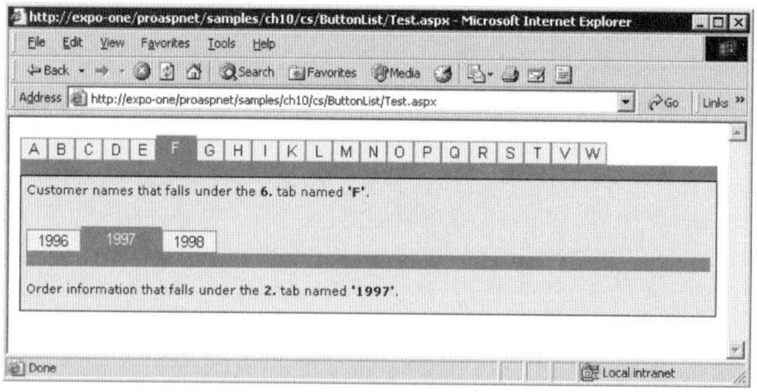

Figure 10-4 Two *ButtonList* controls in action within the same page.

The code that handles the *ButtonClicked* event for both controls is as follows:

```
// Namespace "ProAspNet.CS.Ch10" imported
void ButtonClicked(object sender, ButtonClickedEventArgs e)
{
    string t1 = "Customer names that falls under the <b>{0}.</b> " +
                "tab named <b>'{1}'</b>.";
    string t2 = "Order information that falls under the <b>{0}.</b> " +
                "tab named <b>'{1}'</b>."

    // Recognize the sender and update a label control
    if (sender.Equals(initialStrip))
        msg1.Text = String.Format(t1, 1 + e.ButtonIndex, e.ButtonCommand);
    else
        msg2.Text = String.Format(t2, 1 + e.ButtonIndex, e.ButtonCommand);
}
```

Loading Controls Dynamically

Just like any other ASP.NET server controls, user controls can be created programmatically. Unlike server controls, though, you normally don't use the *new* operator to instantiate user controls but resort to the *LoadControl* method on the containing page.

```
Control ctl = LoadControl("ButtonList.ascx");
```

LoadControl returns a generic reference to a *Control* object, so you need to cast the reference to the appropriate strong type to be able to set individual properties and use the control at its fullest. The *ClassName* attribute in the *@Control* directive represents the only means you have to name the user control class in a way that is both easy to remember and consistent with the expected behavior.

To cast an object to a user-control strong type, you need to have a reference to the assembly that contains the compiled code of the control. Doing this is precisely the role of the *@Reference* directive.

The *@Reference* Directive

When you create the user control programmatically, the strong type for the user control is available to the page only after you have created a reference to it. The following code creates a reference to the *ButtonList* user control created in the buttonlist.ascx file:

```
<%@ Reference Control="buttonlist.ascx" %>
```

The net effect of this directive is to make available in the context of the Web Forms page a reference to a type that represents the specified control. The type is named *ASP.buttonlist_ascx* if the user control doesn't contain a *ClassName* attribute; otherwise, it is named *ASP.XXX*, in which *XXX* is the content of the *ClassName* attribute.

The *@Reference* directive declaratively indicates that another user control or page should be dynamically compiled and linked against the current page or control. The directive supports only two, mutually exclusive, attributes—*Page* and *Control*. Both point to a URL and identify the Web element to bind to the current page or control. Once you hold a reference to the .ascx file, you can create instances of the user control programmatically.

```
ButtonList btn = (ButtonList) LoadControl("buttonlist.ascx");
```

In general, you use the *@Register* directive to register user controls that are declared in the page layout and instantiated by the system. You use the *@Reference* directive if you create the controls programmatically.

> **Note** If the user control has been developed using inline code, you need *@Reference* to reference to its strong type. However, if the user control has been authored using a code-behind class, *@Register* would also suffice. If both the caller page and the user control apply the code-behind model, yet another change is needed. We'll discuss this change later in the "Referencing User Controls from Code-Behind Pages" section.

Adding Dynamically Created Controls to the Page

Creating and casting the user control is only the first step. After setting all the individual properties you need to customize, you have the problem of adding the control to the container page. Doing this is as easy as adding the control to the *Controls* collection of the page.

```
ButtonList btn = (ButtonList) LoadControl("buttonlist.ascx");
// customize the ButtonList control
Page.Controls.Add(btn);
```

However, there's a more reliable approach to ensure the dynamically created control is placed exactly where you decided. You put a *PlaceHolder* marker control where you want the user control to display and then add the dynamic instance to the *Controls* collection of the *PlaceHolder*.

```
<asp:placeholder runat="server" id="YearStripPlaceHolder" />
```

At the beginning of the section, we mentioned that you normally don't use the *new* operator to instantiate user controls. This is only a common practice; no technical limitation forces you to do so. The following code demonstrates how to create a *ButtonList* control and bind it to a placeholder:

```
// Global variable
ButtonList yearStrip;

// Execute after the constructor when all declared controls
// have been initialized
public void Page_Init(object sender, EventArgs e)
{
    // Instantiate the user control. Might use a more
    // specialized constructor, if any
    yearStrip = new ButtonList();

    // Complete the initialization by adding default handlers
    yearStrip.InitializeAsUserControl(Page);
```

```
    // Set the ID of the control
    yearStrip.ID = "yearstrip";

    // Set some custom properties
    yearStrip.ButtonWidth = 70;

    // Add a handler for the user control's ButtonClicked event
    yearStrip.ButtonClicked += new ButtonClickedEventHandler(BtnClicked);

    // Must use a placeholder to make sure the control is added
    // within a runat=server area
    YearStripPlace.Controls.Add(yearStrip);
}
```

The *AddHandler* operator in Visual Basic .NET and the += operator in C# provide a way for you to add event handlers to control instances dynamically.

Referencing User Controls from Code-Behind Pages

To include a user control in a Web page, you must first register it so that the ASP.NET runtime can locate and dynamically bind the needed assembly to the page. In doing so, you also obtain a strong reference to the user control class that allows for programmatic creation of controls. However, so far we've been making decisions based on creating simple Web pages—that is, Web pages that don't have a code-behind class.

Examining things from a pure ASP.NET perspective, the situation in which both the page and the user control are written in code-behind mode is a special one and requires a little more care. Amazingly enough, though, if you always develop your ASP.NET applications with Visual Studio .NET, you'll probably never run into this gotcha.

The *@Register* and *@Reference* directives configure the runtime environment so that all the needed assemblies are linked to the ASP.NET page that contains a user control. As a result, any reference to the user control, even a strong-typed one, can be successfully resolved. Can we say the same for a C# class or a Visual Basic .NET class? When the caller is a code-behind page, you write all its code in, say, a C# class. How can you reference the *ButtonList* type from here? The C# language has no special construct that emulates the behavior of the ASP.NET directives. As a result, any reference to *ButtonList* in the class is destined to raise a compiler error.

To work around this obstacle, you must also write the user control in code-behind mode. When you're done, compile the class that represents the user control into an assembly. In practice, instead of relying on the ASP.NET runtime for a dynamic compilation, you deploy the control as a precompiled unit that C# classes can easily locate.

```
<%@ Control Language="C#"
    Classname="ButtonList"
    Inherits="ProAspNet.CS.Ch10.ButtonList" %>
```

Be aware that in this case the *Src* attribute in the *@Control* directive is redundant and even harmful and must be removed. As the declaration just shown indicates, the code of the *ButtonList* control is contained in the specified class implemented in one of the available assemblies. If you leave the *Src* attribute, the compiler raises an error because it finds two assemblies with the same set of public symbols—the one you created and the one ASP.NET creates on the fly while processing the *Src* attribute. In general, the *Inherits* and *Src* attributes can work together, but not if both represent the same class.

> **Note** Because Visual Studio .NET always uses the code-behind model for whatever ASP.NET component it creates, this issue passes unnoticed because it doesn't cause problems and doesn't require special care. There's a caveat though. If you, being unaware of the internal structure of the Visual Studio user controls, copy the source files of a running application into another virtual directory, it doesn't work until you also copy the binaries.

Conclusion

User controls are a type of ASP.NET server control you can easily create by using the same techniques you've learned for common Web pages. Little code is normally required for building a user control, but in some cases Web Forms user controls can also be codeless. However, there's no technical limitation to what a user control can do, and the amount and complexity of the embedded code depends only on the functionality you want to obtain.

User controls offer an easy way to partition and reuse common user-interface elements across applications. They are ideal whenever the reuse of layout and graphical functionality is critical. You can top off this component with some code that gets compiled on the fly like a Web page; however, quick and effective reuse of user-interface functionality is the primary objective of Web Forms user controls. Like pages, user controls can be developed with inline code as well as code-behind classes. User controls are not the ideal tool to leverage if you need to build a hierarchy of controls according to a pure object-oriented model. Although not impossible to obtain, inheritance is not the goal of user controls. Just the presence of a fair quantity of layout code makes user-control inheritance harder. You can stuff the code of a user control into a class and reuse it; but the associated layout information remains a separate entity that's a bit harder to manage programmatically. If you're going to build a control others can inherit from, you should drop user controls in favor of more flexible custom controls. We'll cover custom controls in Part V.

We started this chapter by building an interactive control just to emphasize how the user control technology can help you to reuse common pieces of a Web site. Next, we built an object model on top of it. The summation of an advanced user interface with a layer of business logic constitutes a powerful model that can be helpful in any scenario in which you need rich and reusable components.

In Chapter 11, "ASP.NET Mobile Controls," we'll complete our overview of ASP.NET controls by taking a look at mobile controls. The ASP.NET mobile controls are a set of ASP.NET server controls that can generate Wireless Markup Language (WML), compact HTML, and HTML content for a variety of devices. Note that the ASP.NET mobile controls have been integrated with the .NET Framework only since version 1.1.

Resources

- KB 316370—Visual Studio .NET Does Not Generate a Code-Behind Declaration for Web User Controls
- KB 308378—Perform Fragment Caching in ASP.NET by Using Visual C# .NET
- Creating a File-Upload User Control with ASP.NET (*http://www.15seconds.com/issue/010504.htm*)
- Create Localizable Web User Controls (*http://www.fawcette.com/vsm/2002_09/online/villeda*)
- Event Handling between Custom User Controls that are loaded at Run Time (*http://www.asptoday.com/catalogue/aspcontent/20021211_01.html*)

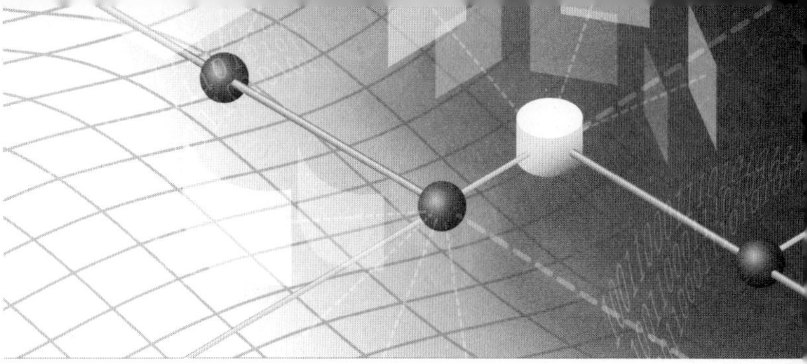

11

ASP.NET Mobile Controls

HTML and WML are similar markup languages, more or less like Italian and Spanish. As an Italian, you could grab the sense of what Spanish speaking people are saying, but if you need to write correct Spanish, then that's a totally different story.

—*Luca Passani, Openwave*

Years ago, one of the factors for the rapid adoption of ASP was the level of programmability it added on top of HTML. Not only could you apply some business logic to generate appropriate HTML tags, you could also straighten out the differences between the browsers. The overall architecture has been redesigned and empowered with ASP.NET, which provides a thicker abstraction layer and a richer object model fully integrated with the .NET Framework. In addition, ASP.NET 1.1 incorporates mobile controls. Mobile controls provide an abstracted programming model to build wireless Web applications. ASP.NET mobile controls are a revised version of the Microsoft Mobile Internet Toolkit (MMIT)—the SDK for mobile wireless devices. An integral part of the .NET Framework 1.1, the MMIT is available as a separate download for the .NET Framework version 1.0.

ASP.NET mobile controls enable you to build Web applications for wireless devices using the same rich application model that characterizes development for desktop browsers. Mobile controls target a variety of devices such as cell phones, pagers, the Pocket PC, and other personal digital assistants (PDA) such as Palm and BlackBerry devices. ASP.NET mobile controls extend the Web Forms model of ASP.NET in two ways—devices and ad hoc controls. All supported devices are listed in a new section of the machine.config file (discussed in Chapter 12, "Configuration and Deployment"). It's an extensible list open to the contribution of third parties, who can register new devices as well as new controls.

Registering a new device mostly means providing a list of characteristics (for example, screen size or markup language), and then one of the built-in adapters can be used by the .NET Framework to generate device-specific output. Less frequently, you need to write a new adapter too. You don't need to call into the adapter or manually write device-specific code; instead, you simply write mobile applications using the ASP.NET mobile controls and the ASP.NET object model. Based on the configuration information, Mobile Web Forms detect the underlying device and adaptively renders the output of controls by using the specific markup language and logic. ASP.NET mobile controls abstract a subset of ASP.NET server controls and intelligently render your application on the target device. In addition, several mobile-specific controls are provided, such as the *PhoneCall* control. The .NET Framework 1.1 provides a handful of built-in controls but remains open to third-party contributions.

Mobile Web applications can be developed using the Mobile Designer in Microsoft Visual Studio .NET as well as any other editor, such as Web Matrix or Notepad. Because ASP.NET mobile applications are .NET applications, you can develop them using any common language runtime (CLR)–compliant programming language.

In this chapter, we'll provide an overview of the ASP.NET mobile controls, discuss the basics of the mobile technology, and take a quick tour of the Visual Studio .NET mobile features.

Architecture of Mobile Controls

ASP.NET mobile controls are an extension of ASP.NET desktop server controls. Another way of characterizing mobile controls is to say they are the twin brother of desktop controls. Mobile controls add the capability of adapting to the device that is making the request. Automatic browser detection is a key aspect of mobile applications and controls and is probably a bit more important for them than for desktop controls.

Desktop controls are rendered in different modes to accommodate a few client targets (for example, Internet Explorer 5.0, HTML 3.2, and HTML 4.0). Although the final output can vary a lot from one target to the next, the area of markup most affected is style. Validation controls are controls whose output varies significantly from one target browser to another. Desktop server controls always generate HTML code. Although differences exist between the HTML 3.2 and HTML 4.0 standards, and between standards and the implementations of individual browsers, we're still far from the untangled mess of dialects and syntaxes that characterize the markup in the mobile world. For this reason, browser detection is implemented at a lower level than user code. Basically, the ASP.NET mobile runtime evaluates the browser's user agent and selects the appropriate device adapter object to use for any task that involves the request. (A user agent is a request header that contains information about the capabilities of the browser.) As a result, any mobile controls conform to the capabilities of the particular device it is running on.

The set of supported wireless devices is rather heterogeneous and ranges from full-featured browsers found on PDAs to small cell phone displays featuring WML browsers. As a result, not just the markup output but also the design of the application might significantly change from one device to the next. In general, a multiauthoring tool for mobile controls must abstract a number of aspects: different markup languages, vendor-specific implementations of the same markup, and different form factors (such as display size and programmable buttons). ASP.NET mobile controls internally handle much of the boring device-specific rendering and let you focus on the Web-application logic.

Multiple Markup Languages

ASP.NET mobile controls support a few types of markup languages, which are listed in Table 11-1. Acceptable values don't include all possible wireless markup languages, but they certainly include the most popular ones.

Table 11-1 Markup Languages in ASP.NET Mobile Controls

Markup	Description
Compact HTML 1.0	Subset of HTML 3.2, has been specifically designed for mobile phones and in general for battery-powered, low-memory devices. Abbreviated as cHTML. The language is widely used in Japanese I-Mode devices.
HTML 3.2	Relatively old version of HTML, is supported by high-end PDAs such as Pocket PC 2002, Palm, and BlackBerry devices.
WML 1.1, WML 1.2	The Wireless Markup Language (WML) is probably the most popular wireless language. It has been developed as a part of a larger initiative aimed at defining an application protocol for wireless devices—the Wireless Application Protocol (WAP). WML lets you program the keys of a mobile phone, such as softkeys and the numeric pad.
XHTML	XHTML is the XML reformulation of HTML and a key element of the WAP 2.0 standard. There are several flavors of XHTML out there. The Device Update 2.0 of ASP.NET Mobile Controls supports XHTML Mobile Profile. It is available for download at *http://msdn.microsoft.com/vstudio/device/mobilecontrols*.

The list has a couple of noticeable omissions—the Handheld Device Markup Language (HDML) and the newest version 1.3 of the Wireless Markup Language (WML). However, be aware that new devices—and possibly even new markup languages—can be added to the list of supported devices at any time.

The required markup language that the controls should generate is set through a read-only string property in the *MobileCapabilities* class—*PreferredRenderingType*.

Compact HTML

As the name implies, Compact HTML (cHTML) is a simplified version of HTML developed for less powerful browsers embedded in cell phones and other small-screen devices. The cHTML language consists of a mix of HTML 2.0 and HTML 3.2 tags optimized for navigation and text display.

The cHTML language supports hyperlinks, text scrolling, forms, and data submission. It doesn't provide much layout and formatting capabilities because of the rather spartan user interface (UI) of such devices. So tables, frames, cascading style sheets (CSS), fonts, and scripting are not supported. Just the lack of scripting support in cHTML provides a prime example of the great job done by ASP.NET device adapters. Adapters force the exclusive generation of server-side code for data validation, and they always implement postback events through a form's data submission. For more information on cHTML, take a look at *http://www.w3.org/TR/1998/NOTE-compactHTML-19980209*.

> **Note** The cHTML markup language is mostly used in Japan by I-Mode devices, although some experiments have been made in Europe, particularly in the Netherlands. Some browsers—specifically the newest Openwave XHTML browser—support cHTML internally to access I-Mode sites.

HTML 3.2

HTML 3.2 is a more basic version of HTML, whose latest version is numbered 4.0. HTML 3.2 is the markup language for most down-level browsers, such as Netscape Navigator 3.x. HTML 3.2 is also supported in Pocket Internet Explorer. Key differences between HTML 4.0 and 3.2 include the addition of cascading style sheets and the Dynamic HTML (DHTML) object model. In general, targeting HTML 3.2 is fair for many ASP.NET applications and doesn't constitute a restriction in the overall functionality. The HTML 3.2 specification is available at *http://www.w3.org/TR/REC-html32*.

Wireless Markup Language

Historically speaking, the WML language was the standard markup language that emerged as the result of joint efforts to standardize one proprietary language—the HDML. Created through an initiative of the WAP Forum (now renamed to Open Mobile Alliance, and which can be found at *http://www.openmobilealliance.org*), the WML language is founded on a strict XML syntax and shares only a few tags with HTML. Some examples of the shared tags are *<input>*, *<select>*, *<a>*, *<p>*, and *<img>*. However, even in the context of the same tag (for example, *<input>*), the intended behavior might be different. WML tags are case-sensitive, while HTML tags are not.

On a more technical note, WML pushes the idea of cards, which represent the various states of the application. A card is like a wizard page, and most of the application's life is spent navigating between cards. In addition, WML supports a form of exception handling to catch errors that occur in a card.

The Wireless Application Protocol

A key point with the mobile controls is that you don't need to worry about the markup language or transport mechanism used for the request. However, learning a little more about the WAP protocol is helpful anyway. The WML language was developed as part of a wider initiative aimed at ruling the world of wireless development. The WAP Forum was started in 1997 with the declared goal of defining the technologies that would unify the world of wireless applications. WAP is a suite of wireless-specific specifications adapted from open Web standards such as HTML and TCP/IP.

To access a Web site using a mobile device, you type the URL in the mobile browser and have the browser create an HTTP-like request (which can optionally be encrypted) that travels toward the back-end Web server over the Wireless Session Protocol (WSP). The WSP protocol uses packets whose overall semantics are similar to HTTP packets. Unlike HTTP, though, WSP transfers binary packets to save bandwidth. WSP packets are physically transported by the Wireless Transaction Protocol (WTP), the wireless counterpart of TCP, as shown in Figure 11-1.

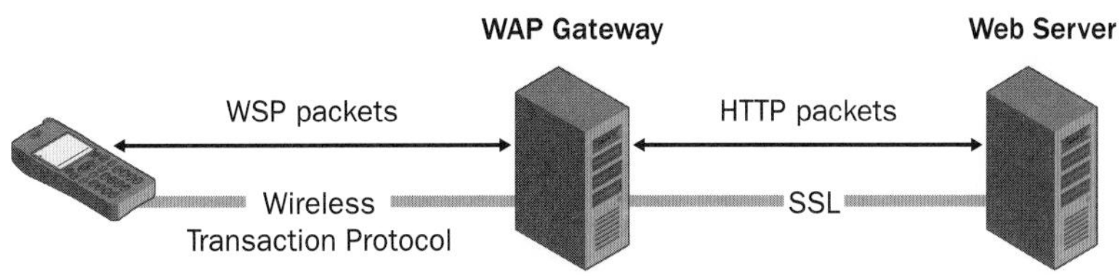

Figure 11-1 Architecture of wireless Web applications.

The connection between the mobile device and the WAP gateway can be secured using the Wireless Transport Layer Security (WTLS) protocol. The WAP gateway is a server that translates the WSP request into conventional HTTP and forwards it to the back-end Web server.

> **Note** The Open Mobile Alliance released the WAP 2.0 standard in September 2001. Although 100 percent backward compatibility is guaranteed, the new standard is geared toward a full convergence between the wireless Web and the conventional HTTP-based Web. The WAP 2.0 standard is heavily based on XHTML and brings the power of CSS to the wireless world by introducing WCSS, which is an abridged version of Web CSS for wireless devices.

The Web server receives the request and performs any needed operations. The returned output is an HTTP response that contains a WML document. After receiving the WML stream, the gateway removes any unneeded headers and translates it into binary packets. The response is then forwarded back to the device and displayed. (Actually, the WML-to-binary translation consists of a simple tokenization in which each tag and attribute is mapped to a single byte.)

Overview of Mobile Controls

ASP.NET mobile controls are server controls and thus require their *runat* attribute to be set to *server*. They execute on the server and for this reason can exploit the potential of the .NET Framework in spite of the modest amount of memory typically available on wireless devices. All mobile controls inherit from the *MobileControl* base class, which in turn inherits from *Control*. In this relationship, both server and mobile controls share a common set of properties, methods, and events. Mobile Web forms, on the other hand, inherit from the *MobilePage* class. Later in the chapter, we'll write a sample mobile application using Visual Studio .NET. In the meantime, let's learn more about the hierarchy of mobile controls and their internal plumbing.

Mobile Controls Hierarchy

ASP.NET mobile controls can be logically grouped in five categories: container, text, validation, list, and miscellaneous controls. Table 11-2 lists them all in alphabetical order. Some of these controls work in much the same way as ASP.NET Web Forms controls do. However, mobile controls also provide adaptive rendering for mobile devices. We'll discuss adaptive rendering more later in the "Adaptive Rendering" section.

Table 11-2 ASP.NET Mobile Controls

Mobile Control	Description
AdRotator	Provides advertisement rotation in the same way that the ASP.NET *AdRotator* control does.
Calendar	Provides date-picking functionality mimicking the behavior of the ASP.NET *Calendar* control.
Command	Similar to the ASP.NET *Button* control, causes a postback event after users click.
CompareValidator	Identical to the ASP.NET *CompareValidator* control.
CustomValidator	Identical to the ASP.NET *CustomValidator* control.
Form	The control is similar to the *HtmlForm* control of ASP.NET pages. However, multiple form controls are admitted on mobile pages.
Image	Identical to the ASP.NET *Image* control.
Label	Identical to the ASP.NET *Label* control.
Link	Represents a hyperlink to another form on a mobile page or an arbitrary URL. Similar to the ASP.NET *HyperLink* control.
List	Similar to the ASP.NET *Repeater* and *DataList* controls, applies templates to bound data. Supports device-specific templates.
ObjectList	Similar to the ASP.NET *DataGrid* control, displays multiple fields for each data item and supports multiple commands.
Panel	Provides grouping mechanism for organizing controls in much the way the ASP.NET *Panel* control does.
PhoneCall	For devices that support phone calls, the control represents a link to a phone number to call. Similar to the *mailto* tag of HTML hyperlinks.
RangeValidator	Identical to the ASP.NET *RangeValidator* control.
RegularExpression-Validator	Identical to the ASP.NET *RegularExpressionValidator* control.
RequiredFieldValidator	Identical to the ASP.NET *RequiredFieldValidator* control.
SelectionList	Displays a list of data-bound items with different styles. It can be configured to behave like a drop-down or check-box list. Selection, however, does not automatically cause the control to post back. The change of selection, though, will fire a server event with the next postback.
StyleSheet	Invisible control, can be used to organize styles to apply to other controls. Can contain multiple style definitions.

(continued)

Table 11-2 ASP.NET Mobile Controls *(continued)*

Mobile Control	Description
TextBox	Represents a single-line text-box control. Does not support read-only and multiline.
TextView	Used to display large blocks of text, supports basic text formatting and pagination.
ValidationSummary	Similar to the *ValidationSummary* control of ASP.NET, displays the results of the validation in a separate form.

Almost all mobile controls have a counterpart in the family of ASP.NET server controls or, at a minimum, a control that looks alike. *PhoneCall* and *TextView* are the only two without an equivalent control. Other controls, such as *SelectionList* and *Command*, group the functionality of multiple ASP.NET controls. The programming interface of validation controls, on the other hand, is nearly identical to ASP.NET; a key difference here is that not all devices support client-side validation. Figure 11-2 shows graphically the relationships between controls. Controls with a white background are abstract classes.

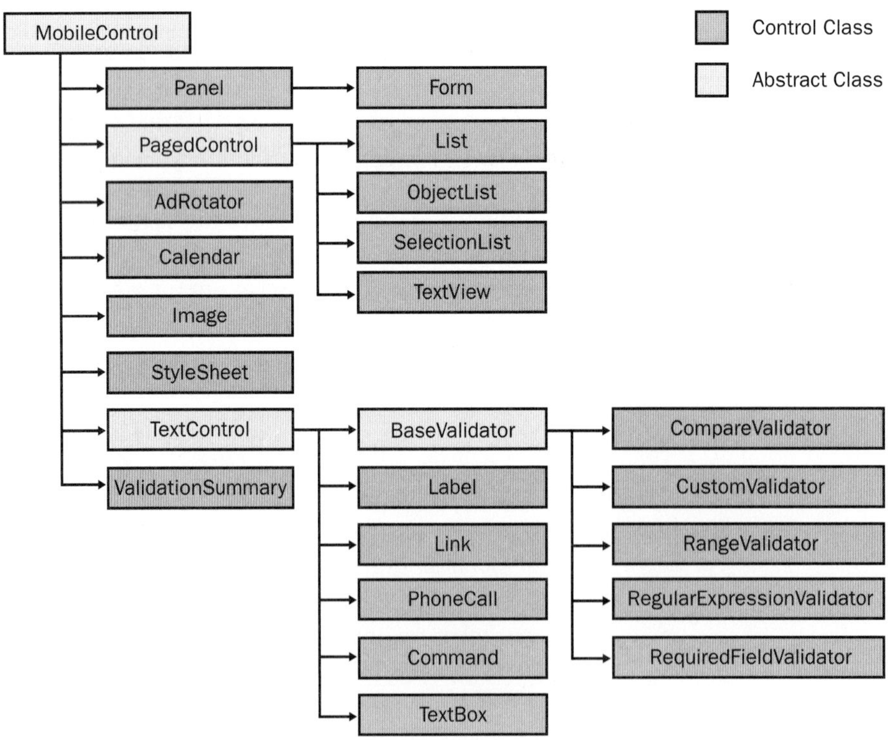

Figure 11-2 The ASP.NET mobile control class hierarchy.

Before taking a closer look at the characteristics of each group of controls, let's learn more about the structure of an ASP.NET mobile page.

ASP.NET Mobile Pages

The *MobilePage* class is the base class for all ASP.NET mobile Web pages and inherits from the ASP.NET *Page* class. In other words, a mobile page is in no way different from a user-defined page class such as a code-behind class. An .aspx page that intends to use ASP.NET mobile controls must declare its base class by using the *Inherits* attribute on the *@Page* directive.

```
<%@ Page Inherits="System.Web.UI.MobileControls.MobilePage" %>
```

In addition, all mobile controls are perceived as custom controls and must be explicitly registered in all pages. As we saw in the previous chapter, this can be done using the *@Register* directive.

```
<%@ Register TagPrefix="mobile"
    Namespace="System.Web.UI.MobileControls"
    Assembly="System.Web.Mobile" %>
```

> **Note** The prefix *mobile*, although extremely intuitive, is totally arbitrary and can be replaced with any other string. You should note, though, that the whole documentation of ASP.NET mobile controls uses the prefix *mobile*. If you're authoring the page using Visual Studio .NET, using the prefix *mobile* is mandatory. In fact, once a mobile project has been set up, Visual Studio .NET defaults to *mobile* and doesn't recognize any new prefix. As a result, either you manually update the prefix each time you drop a new control on the designer or the page won't compile!

The following listing shows a simple page that displays the name of the wireless language being used by the device:

```
<%@ Page Language="C#"
    Inherits="System.Web.UI.MobileControls.MobilePage" %>
<%@ Register TagPrefix="mobile"
    Namespace="System.Web.UI.MobileControls"
    Assembly="System.Web.Mobile" %>
<%@ Import Namespace="System.Web.Mobile" %>
```

```
<script runat="server">
void Page_Load(object sender, EventArgs e) {
    MobileCapabilities mobCaps = (MobileCapabilities) Request.Browser;
    theBrowser.Text = mobCaps.PreferredRenderingType;
}
</script>

<mobile:Form runat="server">
    Language is
    <mobile:Label runat="server" font-bold="true" id="theBrowser" />
</mobile:Form>
```

The page contains a *Label* control that renders with boldface type and some literal text. During the page *OnLoad* event, the code retrieves the preferred rendering type from the requesting device, reads related settings from the configuration file, and displays it. The *MobileCapabilities* class is defined in the *System.Web.Mobile* namespace; the controls, on the other hand, are all defined in the *System.Web.UI.MobileControls* namespace. When viewed through a device that incorporates the Openwave browser, the page looks like the one shown in Figure 11-3.

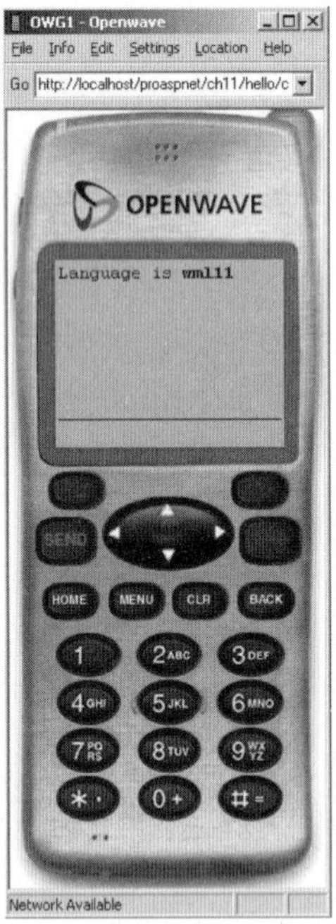

Figure 11-3 The first mobile application in action as seen through the Openwave emulator.

> **Note** The mobile samples in this chapter were tested with the Openwave emulator included with the Openwave SDK version 4.1.1. This SDK is free of charge and can be downloaded from Openwave (*http://developer.openwave.com/download*). Not all emulators are supported by the ASP.NET mobile controls. For a list of emulators to test your mobile applications, check out *http://www.asp.net/mobile/DeviceSimulators.aspx*. For a list of tested devices and emulators, check out *http://www.asp.net/mobile/testeddevices.aspx*.

The mobile page detected the device capabilities and generated the following WML 1.1 output:

```
<html>
  <head>
    <meta http-equiv="Cache-Control" content="max-age=0"/>
  </head>
  <p:card>
    <p:do type="accept">
      <p:noop/>
    </p:do>
    <p>Language is
      <b>wml11</b>
    </p>
  </p:card>
</html>
```

Interestingly, the same page is also viewable through Internet Explorer. In this case, the target language is HTML 3.2. Figure 11-4 shows the Internet Explorer version of the page.

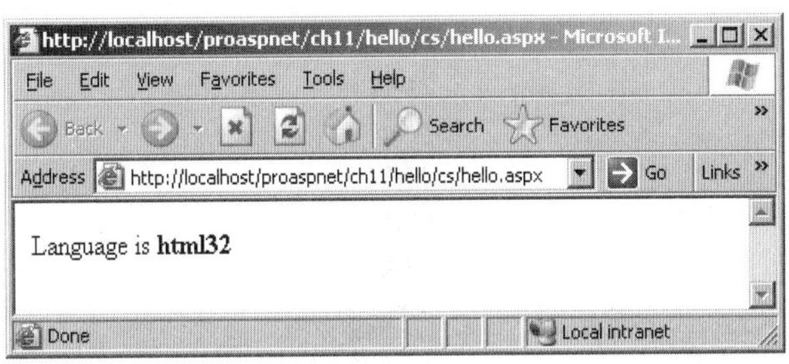

Figure 11-4 The same mobile application rendered by Internet Explorer.

In this case, the output sent to the device is completely different.

```
<html><body>
<form id="_ctl0" name="_ctl0" method="post"
    action="hello.aspx?__ufps=261294">
<input type="hidden" name="__VIEWSTATE" value="...">
<input type="hidden" name="__EVENTTARGET" value="">
<input type="hidden" name="__EVENTARGUMENT" value="">
<script language=javascript><!--
function __doPostBack(target, argument){
  var theform = document._ctl0
  theform.__EVENTTARGET.value = target
  theform.__EVENTARGUMENT.value = argument
  theform.submit()
}
// -->
</script>
Language is <b>html32</b></form></body></html>
```

Note A variety of emulators exist to test the interface of a mobile application at development time. Although you should never ship a wireless application without first seriously testing it on real devices, emulators are indeed extremely helpful to prototype the user interface. Visual Studio .NET lets you register browsers for mobile applications by selecting Browse With from the File menu.

A *MobilePage* object can contain only a *Form* or *StyleSheet* control. Literal text placed outside a form is ignored. If other controls are used outside the boundaries of a form, a compiler error is raised. All needed text and controls must always be placed within a form. A mobile page must contain at least one form; multiple forms are supported, but only one is visible at a time. A style sheet is not required for a mobile page. However, you can't indicate more than one style sheet per page.

Pagination in Mobile Pages

ASP.NET mobile controls provide a mechanism for automatically partitioning the form's contents into smaller portions of markup code. This mechanism is known as *pagination*. When you use pagination, these segments of content are automatically formatted to fit the target device. The final output is also completed with common user-interface elements that you can use to browse to other pages.

By default, pagination is not activated for a form. To activate pagination, you must set the *Paginate* property of the *Form* to *true*. You should note that although pagination can be enabled on individual controls, the setting has no effect if the *Paginate* property of the containing form is set to *false*. The *Form* control also provides other properties—such as *PageCount*, *CurrentPage*, and *PagerStyle*—that allow you to control pagination behavior. You can also specify pagination for a particular control on a form by using the *ControlToPaginate* property of the form with the ID of the control.

The main motivation for pagination is to not exceed the memory capabilities of the device with a too large page. Pagination is particularly effective for controls that display large amounts of data; it's often redundant for forms that display interactive and input controls. The pagination is implemented by sectioning the structure of the form or the control into pieces. Some controls (for example, the *List* control) handle pagination internally and decide themselves how to break their output. Other controls are managed by the container controls; to be effectively pageable, they must contain child controls or fit entirely in a single page.

The Life Cycle of a Mobile Page

The life cycle of an ASP.NET mobile page is nearly identical to the life cycle of a conventional Web Forms page. The events are the same, even though the system's behaviors before and after the various events are different. The phases in the cycle are summarized as follows:

- **Page initialization** At this phase, the page determines the device adapter to use and sets the *Adapter* property on the *MobilePage* class. The device adapter is an instance of one of the classes listed in the *<mobileControls>* section of the configuration files. Default adapters are registered in machine.config; in web.config, you could add application-specific adapters. The search for the adapter begins with the machine.config file and then proceeds to the root web.config and any innermost web.config that might have been defined. The adapter is picked up based on the detected characteristics of the underlying device. Note that the adapter is cached for performance so that the search is conducted only once per user agent. The event you can hook up at this time is the *Init* event both on the page and the adapter.
- **Loading the view state** During this phase, any saved state for the page is restored. There is no event associated with this phase. Gaining more control over this phase requires the override of the *LoadViewState* method of the page.

- **Loading postback data** The page loads all incoming *<form>* data cached in *Request* and updates the page properties accordingly. No user event is associated with this phase. Gaining more control over this phase requires the override of the *LoadPostData* method of the page.
- **Loading the user code** The page is ready to execute any initialization code related to the logic and behavior of the page. The page fires the *Load* event and performs device adapter–specific loading of information. To control this phase, you can handle the *Load* event both on the page and the adapter.
- **Send postback change notifications** Controls in the page raise change events in response to state changes between the current and previous postbacks. Any further change entered by the *Load* event handler is also taken into account to determine any difference. A control must implement the *IPostBackDataHandler* interface to get a chance from the page to fire a state change event during this phase. No user event is provided.
- **Handle postback events** The page executes the .aspx code associated with the client-side event that caused the postback. It's the heart of the ASP.NET Web Forms model.
- **Pre-rendering** The code can perform its last updates before the output is rendered. The event developers can hook up from a mobile page or the device adapter at this phase is *PreRender*. Pagination occurs at this time. During this phase, the output of the page is determined based on the pagination settings.
- **Saving the view state** During this phase, the page serializes its state to a string, which will then be persisted—typically, through a hidden field. No user event is associated with this phase.
- **Page rendering** The page generates the output to be rendered to the client. The adapter is responsible for accessing and rendering child controls in the appropriate order. The event is *Render* and is available on both the page object and the device adapter.
- **Page unload** This phase performs the device adapter–specific cleanup and unloading. The event is *Unload* and is available on both the page object and the device adapter.

In summary, mobile pages differ from conventional ASP.NET pages in particular because of the initialization step. At that phase, in fact, mobile pages and controls have to determine the device adapter to use from the list of registered objects. The adapter is exposed through the *Adapter* property, and pages and controls refer to it for rendering.

Device Adapters

Although the programmer writes ASP.NET mobile applications in a device-independent fashion, a set of device adapters take care of translating the high-level description of a user interface into the device-specific presentation layer. Interesting analogies exist between device drivers in Microsoft Windows and device adapters in ASP.NET mobile controls. Both control a device by generating device-specific command text; device adapters just generate that in the form of markup languages. Device adapters are the bridge between individual mobile controls and target devices. For any given device, each mobile control can have a unique adapter and each instance of a control is bound to a corresponding instance of an adapter. The availability of an adapter is critical for the appropriate rendering of mobile controls. In general, for each supported device, the following classes can be defined:

- **Page adapter** Associated with the page, this class provides view-state and postback functionality, as well as methods that save and load device-specific control-state information, such as pagination information and the currently active form. The page adapter is also responsible for preparing the response to the client and for rendering the skeleton of the page. The page adapter class implements the *IPageAdapter* interface.
- **Form adapter** Associated with the form control, this adapter provides methods that handle device-specific form-based interactivity. In addition, it should supply methods that adapt a generic form to the particular device. For example, the fields of the forms could be paginated or grouped into a menu. Finally, the form adapter must be able to render the skeleton of the form.
- **Control adapter** This is the base class for control adapters and is also the base class for page and form adapters. It provides methods for rendering control postback events and style properties.
- **Text writer** The text writer class is not an adapter class, but it works in conjunction with adapters. The text writer class inherits from the *HtmlTextWriter* class and performs all rendering for a control. An instance of the text writer class is created and passed through every adapter for rendering purposes. The text writer usually contains helper methods to perform tasks such as encoding data.

The ASP.NET Mobile Controls toolkit contains a few device adapters, one for each supported markup language—cHTML, XHTML, HTML, and WML. As mentioned, XHTML has been added to the list in the Device Update 2.0.

Container Controls

ASP.NET mobile controls include a couple of controls—*Panel* and *Form*—that act as containers of other controls. The *Form* control differs from *Panel* in that it supports posting of data, whereas the *Panel* represents a simple static group of related controls. Multiple panels can be nested and included in forms; forms, on the other hand, cannot be nested.

The *Panel* Control

The following code demonstrates a couple of panels containing plain text with minimal formatting. Note that not all attributes are supported on all devices. For example, background and foreground colors are ignored by cell phones.

```
<mobile:Form runat="server">
    <mobile:Panel runat="server" Font-Bold="true" Alignment="Right">
        <mobile:Label runat="server">Programming ASP.NET</mobile:Label>
    </mobile:Panel>
    <mobile:Panel runat="server" BackColor="yellow">
        <mobile:Label runat="server">Dino Esposito</mobile:Label>
    </mobile:Panel>
</mobile:Form>
```

A panel can contain any ASP.NET mobile control other than *MobilePage*, *Form*, or *StyleSheet* controls. Panel controls do not have a visual representation and cascade any style properties down to the individual controls. Both the layout and style of the child controls are mediated by the device adapter.

Note that the *Panel* control could be used to define pagination segments. In addition, a *Panel* control can also work as a sort of placeholder to contain dynamically generated child controls.

The *Form* Control

The *Form* control represents the outermost container of controls within a mobile page. The *Form* control features common-use properties such as *Action* and *Method*. In particular, *Action* defaults to the empty string, which causes a postback to the same URL. A form fires events when activated and deactivated.

A page can contain multiple forms, but only one form is rendered to the browser at a time. The currently active form can be set and retrieved through the *ActiveForm* property. When multiple forms are active on the same page, you can move from one to the other by using a *Link* control.

```
<mobile:Form id="Form2" runat="server">
    <mobile:Label runat="server"
        text="Second page of information" />
    <mobile:Link runat="server" NavigateURL="#Form1" text="Back" />
</mobile:Form>
```

To make a *Link* control point to an internal form, you set the *NavigateURL* property to the ID of the form prefixed with a # symbol.

List Controls

The *List*, *ObjectList*, and *SelectionList* controls are the mobile counterpart of ASP.NET list-bound and iterative controls. The *List* control looks like the *Repeater* and the *DataList*, and it displays a static or bound list of items. The *SelectionList* is helpful if you need the user to pick one or more items from a list. Finally, you should use the *ObjectList* control if you need to display database information in a tabular format. Note that the *ObjectList* control is strictly data-bound, while the other two can also display a list of items set either statically or programmatically.

The *List* Control

As mentioned, a *List* control renders a sequence of items to a device. The control can work in static or interactive mode. In static mode, the control generates a static list in which each item is plain text. In interactive mode, all items are rendered as clickable elements that generate an event if clicked. If an event handler for the *ItemCommand* event is present, the control works interactively; otherwise, it appears as a static option list. When set to *true*, the *ItemsAsLinks* property transforms the list items into hyperlinks. In this case, no *ItemCommand* event will ever be fired because the click is resolved by jumping to a new URL. You indicate the URL through the *DataValueField* property and the hyperlink text using *DataTextField*.

The following listing shows a sample application that displays a list of cities and lets users pick one. The page consists of two forms, one with the list of cities and one that shows the result of the choice.

```
<%@ Page Inherits= "System.Web.UI.MobileControls.MobilePage"
    Language="C#" %>
<%@ Register TagPrefix="mobile"
    Namespace="System.Web.UI.MobileControls"
    Assembly="System.Web.Mobile" %>

<script language="C#" runat="server">
void PickUpCity(object source, ListCommandEventArgs e) {
    string msg = String.Format("Going to {0} for {1}.",
```

```
        e.ListItem.Text, e.ListItem.Value);
    Info.Text = msg;
    ActiveForm = ResultsForm;
}
</script>

<mobile:Form id="IntroForm" runat="server">
    <b>Where do you want to go today?</b>
    <mobile:List runat="server" id="Cities" OnItemCommand="PickUpCity" >
        <item Text="Rome" Value="·10" />
        <item Text="New York" Value="$500" />
        <item Text="London" Value="·200" />
        <item Text="Paris" Value="·350" />
        <item Text="Sydney" Value="$1200" />
    </mobile:List>
</mobile:Form>

<mobile:Form runat="server" id="ResultsForm">
    <mobile:Label runat="server" id="Info"/>
</mobile:Form>
```

Figure 11-5 shows the application in action.

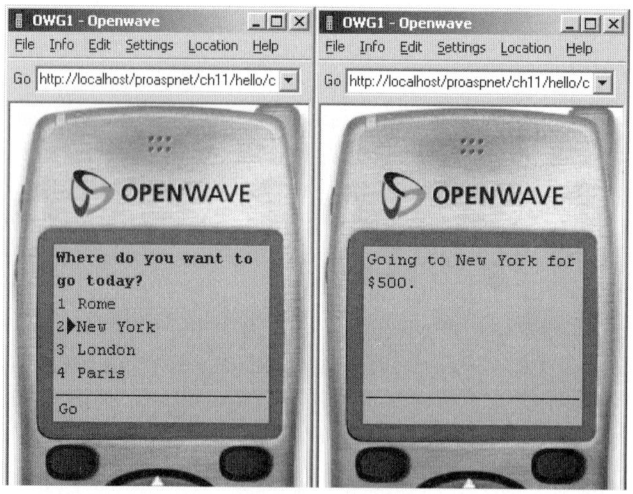

Figure 11-5 The list of cities as generated by the *List* control. The presence of the *ItemCommand* handler makes each item selectable.

> **Note** Pay attention when you use the $ symbol with mobile applications. In WML, the $ symbol has a special meaning and is used to identify variables. However, ASP.NET mobile controls automatically process occurrences of $ symbols in the source code and render them correctly using a double $$ symbol.

A *List* control can be bound to a data source by using the *DataSource* and *DataMember* properties, whose behavior is identical to what we saw for ASP.NET list-bound controls. It goes without saying that *DataSet*, *DataTable*, and *DataView* objects are good sources for a such a data-bound mobile control.

You should note that the *List* control can bind only to two columns on the specified data source—one for the *Text* property of the list item and one for the *Value* property. These values are set through the *DataTextField* and *DataValueField* properties of the *List* control. By defining a handler for the *ItemDataBind*, you can also set the text of a list item as the combination of more source fields.

```
void OnItemDataBind(object sender, ListDataBindEventArgs e) {
    e.ListItem.Text = String.Format ("{0} - ${1}",
        DataBinder.Eval(e.DataItem, "city"),
        DataBinder.Eval(e.DataItem, "price"));
}
```

On devices that support richer rendering, you can specify templates to customize the view of data items. In templated mode, the *List* control functions similarly to the *Repeater* ASP.NET server control.

The *ObjectList* Control

The *ObjectList* is the mobile counterpart of the ASP.NET *DataGrid* server control. In particular, the *ObjectList* can have two views—list and details. In list view, the control displays a sort of menu made of the values of a single field. This has been done to accommodate devices with small screens. The *LabelField* property lets you choose which bound field is to be used to populate the quick menu. Each displayed item is clickable and generates a detail view in which all the fields in the current data row are displayed. The way in which the item is made clickable is device specific.

The detail view can include a toolbar with all the commands specified using the *<command>* tag plus the back command, whose text is set through the *BackCommandText* property. Finally, the *AutoGenerateField* property (which is *true* by default) along with the *<fields>* elements let you decide which bound fields are to be actually displayed. As you can easily guess, this feature mimics the column auto-generation feature of ASP.NET *DataGrid* controls that we examined in Chapter 6, "Creating Bindable Grids of Data."

The *ObjectList* differs from the *List* control in some respects. One is that the *ObjectList* allows you to associate multiple commands with each item. The set of commands for an item can be either shared among all items or unique to the item. Other differences are that the *ObjectList* supports multiple views and doesn't support static items. Later on in this chapter, when building a sample application, we'll use an *ObjectList* control to display some data.

The *List* and *ObjectList* controls fully support internal pagination. Both controls also provide a feature known as *custom pagination*, which closely resembles the custom paging of Web *DataGrid* controls. Normally, paginated controls require that all the data they need be provided at once. Custom paginated controls, on the other hand, fire the *LoadItems* event when they display a new portion of the user interface. Developers specify the total number of items in the *ItemCount* property. Changing the value of the *ItemCount* property from its default value of zero to the total number of items indicates that the control is to be custom paginated. The *LoadItems* event handler is expected to retrieve the appropriate data and bind it to the control.

The *SelectionList* Control

In the gallery of mobile list-bound controls, the *SelectionList* control is unique in that it provides UI selection capability for a list of items. Like a drop-down list or a check-box list, it shows a list of items and can allow users to select one or more items. When an item is selected, no server-side event is automatically generated, as happens in certain Web list controls when the *AutoPostBack* property is set to *true*. The *SelectedIndexChanged* event is generated for the change of selection.

The *SelectionList* control can be rendered in five different selection types: drop-down (default), radio button, check box, list box, and multiselection list box. You choose the selection type by using the *SelectType* property. Not all devices support all these selection types. Typically, a cell phone will recognize only check-box and multiselection types, so radio button, list box, and drop-down are rendered with a pick list.

The following listing shows how to display a list of selectable items and how to retrieve all the selected items:

```
<%@ Page Inherits="System.Web.UI.MobileControls.MobilePage"
    Language="C#" %>
<%@ Register TagPrefix="mobile"
    Namespace="System.Web.UI.MobileControls"
    Assembly="System.Web.Mobile" %>

<script runat="server">
void Page_Load(object sender, EventArgs e) {
```

```
    if (!IsPostBack) {
        ArrayList values = new ArrayList();
        values.Add("ASP.NET");
        values.Add("ADO.NET");
        values.Add("XML");
        list.DataSource = values;
        list.DataBind();
    }
}

void Button_Click(object sender, EventArgs e) {
    string buf = "";
    foreach(MobileListItem item in list.Items)
        buf += (item.Selected ?" " + item.Text : "");
    Results.Text = buf;
}
</script>

<mobile:Form runat="server">
    Your skills?
    <mobile:Label runat="server" id="Results" />
    <mobile:SelectionList runat="server" id="list"
SelectType="checkbox" />
   <mobile:Command runat="server" OnClick="Button_Click" Text="Submit" />
</mobile:Form>
```

Figure 11-6 shows the application in action.

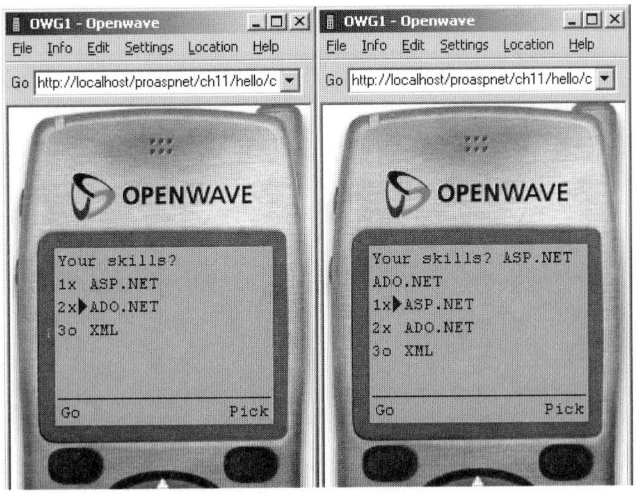

Figure 11-6 A check-box *SelectionList* control in action on a cell phone.

Text Controls

The *TextControl* class is an abstract class from which some navigation and input controls derive. All text-based controls have a *Text* property, which can be programmatically set and is usually used to render the output of the control. *Link*, *TextBox*, and *Label* are examples of controls derived from the *TextControl* class. The *Label* mobile control is similar to the ASP.NET *Label* control and the *Link* mobile control looks a lot like the ASP.NET *HyperLink* control. Other text controls are the *Command* control, which logically represents a command button, and the *PhoneCall* control.

The *TextBox* Control

The *TextBox* control generates a single-line text box and stores in the *Text* property the text that a user enters. The control can work in password or numeric mode, but it doesn't support multiline editing or the read-only attribute. Alignment and maximum length are other advanced characteristics of the control.

```
<mobile:TextBox runat="server" id="theUser" OnTextChanged="Alert" />
```

The *TextBox* control also supports the *OnTextChanged* server-side event, which executes the specified handler if the text changes between two successive postbacks of the same page.

The *Command* Control

The *Command* control sums up most of the characteristics of the ASP.NET *Button* and *LinkButton* controls. It can be rendered as a submit button (default) or as a hyperlink. It can also be rendered as an image. The *Format* property lets you choose between *Button* and *Link*; if the output format is *Link*, you can also choose an image to display as a clickable element. The image is set through the *ImageUrl* property. If the device supports softkeys, the output of the *Command* control can just be the label of one of the softkeys. (A *softkey* is a programmable button available on many cell phones.)

Any click on a *Command* control causes a postback event. You can set the server-side code in either of two ways—the *ItemCommand* or *OnClick* event handler. With the *ItemCommand* event handler, you must also give the control a command name and, optionally, a command argument. When the control is clicked, the *CausesValidation* Boolean property determines whether the control has to perform validation on all other controls in the same form.

The following listing shows how to use a *TextBox* and *Command* control:

```
<script runat="server">
void OnSearch(object sender, EventArgs e) {
    string msg = "Results for '{0}'";
    msg = String.Format(msg, theSubject.Text);
    theResults.Text = msg;
```

```
    // Set the new active form
    ActiveForm = ResultsForm;
}
</script>
<mobile:Form runat="server">
    Search for:
    <mobile:TextBox runat="server" font-bold="true" id="theSubject" />
    <mobile:Command runat="server" Text="GO" OnClick="OnSearch" />
</mobile:Form>

<mobile:Form runat="server" id="ResultsForm">
    <mobile:Label runat="server" id="theResults" />
</mobile:Form>
```

The *ActiveForm* property on a *Form* object programmatically gets or sets the form's currently active form. Figure 11-7 shows the application in action.

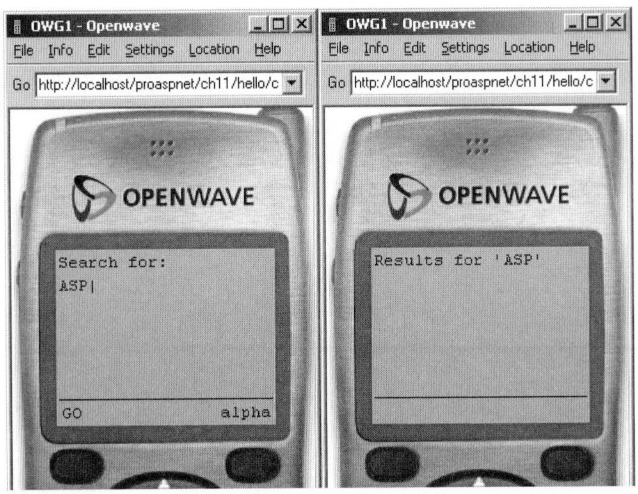

Figure 11-7 *TextBox* and *Command* controls in action.

The *PhoneCall* Control

The *PhoneCall* control is an output-only control that is used to represent a phone number to call. For devices that support placing phone calls (for example, cell phones), the control looks like an interactive element that makes a call when clicked. On other nonvoice devices, the phone number is displayed as a link to a URL or, optionally, as plain text.

```
<mobile:Form runat="server">
Phone numbers found for Joe:
    <mobile:PhoneCall runat="server"
```

```
        AlternateFormat="{0} at {1}"
        AlternateURL="http://www.acme.com"
        PhoneNumber="111-222-0000"
        Text="ACME Corp" />
    <mobile:PhoneCall runat="server"
        AlternateFormat="{0} at {1}"
        PhoneNumber="111-333-0000"
        Text="Home" />
</mobile:Form>
```

The *AlternateFormat* property can be any string and is used to represent the control on devices without telephony capabilities. It can accept two parameters, one having the value of *Text* and the other having the value of *PhoneNumber*. The alternate text is rendered as plain text unless the *AlternateURL* property is specified. In this case, the control generates a hyperlink that points to the specified URL. If the *Text* property is unspecified, the phone number is also used for display. Note that a large number of Nokia phones don't support this feature.

Validation Controls

All validation mobile controls inherit from an abstract class named *BaseValidator*, which in turn descends from the *TextControl* base class. All controls share a *Text* and *ErrorMessage* property. The *Text* property becomes the output of the control in case of an invalid entry. If the *Text* property is not set, the validator displays the value of the *ErrorMessage* property instead. The value stored in *ErrorMessage* is also the text that gets displayed in the *ValidationSummary* control. This behavior is identical to what we saw in Chapter 3, "ASP.NET Core Server Controls," for Web Forms validators. Mobile controls include five validators.

- ***CompareValidator*** This control compares the values of two controls by using the specified comparison operator. The *ControlToValidate* property indicates the ID of the control to validate. The value against which the validation should occur can be indicated either explicitly—the property *ValueToCompare*—or indirectly through the *ControlToCompare* property. This latter property contains the ID of the control to compare against the current ID. While setting up the validator, you can also indicate the type of the data being compared (for example, date, string, or integer) and the required operator (for example, greater-than or not-equal-to).

- ***CustomValidator*** This control allows you to validate the value of a control by using your own method. You use the *ControlToValidate* property to indicate the control being verified and write your own validation code handling the server-side *ServerValidate* event. To inform the run time about the outcomes of the process, you set the *IsValid* property of the event data structure to *true* or *false*, as appropriate.
- ***RangeValidator*** This control ensures that the values of another control fall within the specified range. The *MinimumValue* and *MaximumValue* properties set the bounds of the range. You can also indicate the type of the values being compared. You do this through the *Type* property. The range must include both bounds. If you need to check values without an upper or lower bound, use the *CompareValidator* instead.
- ***RegularExpressionValidator*** This control verifies that the value of a given control matches the specified regular expression. *ControlToValidate* indicates the control to keep under observation and *ValidationExpression* sets the pattern to match.
- ***RequiredFieldValidator*** This control makes an input control a required field. You should note, though, that a required field isn't necessarily an empty field. The concept of requirement applies to any value that is different from the contents of *InitialValue*. The validation is successful only if the value of the control is different from the initial value upon losing focus.

When validators are used within a page, ASP.NET can display a summary of the validation errors, if any. This task is accomplished by the *ValidationSummary* control. The control collects all the error messages set for the various validators, organizes them in an all-encompassing string, and displays the resulting text in a secondary form. The *BackLabel* property lets you set the text for the Back button that restores the failed form.

The *Command* control is the only mobile control that causes validation of input data in the form. *TextBox* and *SelectionList* are, on the other hand, the only mobile controls whose value can be validated. In particular, *Text* is the validation property of the *TextBox* control and *SelectedIndex* is the validation property of the *SelectionList* control. However, other controls (for example, custom and user controls) can participate in the validation process with their own properties. To do so, they need to be marked by the *ValidationPropertyAttribute* attribute.

The following listing shows how to set up a page that validates the user input. The page contains a *SelectionList* control that enumerates possible skills to communicate to the company. At least one skill must be specified, though. We use a *RequiredFieldValidator* control associated with the *SelectionList*. In this case, the *InitialValue* is automatically set to 1.

```
<script runat="server">
void Page_Load(object sender, EventArgs e) {
    if (!IsPostBack) {
        ArrayList values = new ArrayList();
        values.Add("ASP.NET");
        values.Add("ADO.NET");
        values.Add("XML");
        values.Add("WinForms");
        values.Add("Web Services");
        skills.DataSource = values;
        skills.DataBind();
    }
}

void Submit(object sender, EventArgs e) {
    // Check whether all validation controls in the page
    // validated successfully
    if (!Page.IsValid)
        return;

    string buf = "";
    foreach(MobileListItem item in skills.Items)
        buf += (item.Selected ?" " + item.Text :"");
    Results.Text = buf + skills.SelectedIndex.ToString();
        ActiveForm = ResultsForm;
}
</script>

<mobile:Form runat="server" id="Main">
    <mobile:RequiredFieldValidator runat="server"
        ErrorMessage="Must indicate a skill!"
        ControlToValidate="skills" />

    <b>Indicate your skills</b><br>
    <mobile:SelectionList runat="server" id="skills"
        SelectType="checkbox" />
    <mobile:Command runat="server" OnClick="Submit" Text="Send" />
</mobile:Form>

<mobile:Form runat="server" id="ResultsForm">
    <b>Recognized skills</b>
    <mobile:Label runat="server" id="Results" />
</mobile:Form>
```

When the user clicks to submit data, the page interrogates all the contained validators to see whether they have valid data. If the *IsValid* property of the *MobilePage* is set to *false*, the procedure aborts and the same form is rendered back to the client with the validator that now displays its error message. If one is needed, you can use a *ValidationSummary* control in a secondary form that can be activated on demand. Figure 11-8 shows the previous code in action.

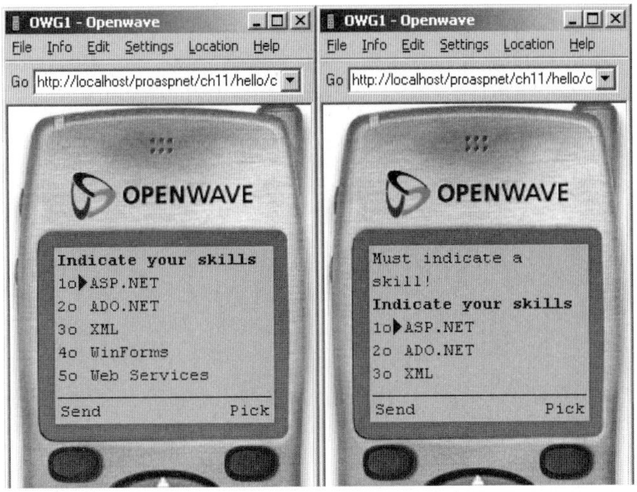

Figure 11-8 Validating the user input through mobile validation controls.

Developing Mobile Applications

To wrap up what we've learned so far about mobile controls and mobile pages, let's build an application that is representative of a typical wireless scenario. Depending on the capabilities of the device, you normally build a mobile application to cache information that will later be transmitted to a back-end system, or to interact in real time with the back-end system. The former scenario is more common for rich and smart devices such as the Pocket PC family of products. For their modest processing power and RAM, cell phones are typically used for interacting with systems. However, the limited hardware and software capabilities of such devices makes it challenging for developers to build effective and usable wireless applications. A typical scenario for mobile applications is the search of information. I've chosen to focus on this category of programs because of the repercussions it has on a critical aspect of wireless applications—usability.

Our goal in this section is building a mobile application that lets users retrieve information about a customer and perhaps place a call. Of course, the subject of the search—customers—is totally arbitrary. The pattern applies with any large database to be navigated through. The term *large* is used here in a relative sense—that is, the databases in question are large in the context of the display capabilities of mobile devices. If displaying 20 records at a time makes sense for conventional Web applications, you should never exceed a few units (and compact ones at that) of data for an application that is used through a small-screen cell phone. Another key point to consider is the input capabilities of the device. Again, while letting the user type a matching string to narrow the set of customers being retrieved is sensible in the Web world, in a wireless context such an action has to be reckoned with the (normally very limited) input capabilities of the device and subsequently with the high level of frustration the poor user might soon reach.

The CustomerFinder Application

Our goal is to build a customer finder application—that is, an application that lets you retrieve personal information about a particular customer you would like to call or visit if only you could remember her darn phone number. The rub, though, is that you can't afford to keep hundreds of addresses and phone numbers in your cell phone. If you're using a smarter device, well, then imagine that you simply forgot to synchronize it with the database before you left the office!

Devising the Application for Usability

Many Web and desktop applications let you perform searches in an incremental way. You enter a string that is a partial key and the system soon prompts you with all the keys that match. Next, you further narrow the list by using a less partial key or simply picking the right one from the displayed list. This way of working makes perfect sense as long as you have enough screen space and memory. But there's an extra, often unnoticed, asset you normally have if you're working at your desk—the keyboard. In general, with mobile devices you can easily enter numbers but not free text. So using a text box to type the key and a button to access the server is a rather unfair approach—easy for you as a developer, but annoying for the poor user who could be trying to use that application with only one hand while walking or eating.

A general guideline for wireless applications can be summarized in the following slogan: one more click is a more enjoyable torture than having to type text. In a wireless application, especially if you know it will be used through cell phones, data entry should be avoided altogether or, at least, limited only to when it's absolutely necessary. You should use any information you might have about the user (for example, name, e-mail address, profile, and even global position) to personalize the screen and present options in a way that is optimized for the specific user.

The structure of a form must be as terse as possible, with short but effective descriptions and just one way of accomplishing tasks. Data should be downloaded in small chunks for bandwidth reasons and using the application should be as easy as scrolling and clicking softkeys or numbers in the keypad.

A good design pattern for mobile applications that require input from the user is that of wizards. A tree-based representation of the tasks and the data to obtain is the key, as it makes it easier for you to submit a list of options to simply click or leave.

With this in mind, let's move on and build a serious mobile application using Visual Studio .NET and its pretty cool Mobile Designer.

The Mobile Designer in Visual Studio .NET

To build a true mobile application in Visual Studio .NET 2003, you should pick up an ASP.NET Mobile Web Application from the New Project dialog box, as shown in Figure 11-9.

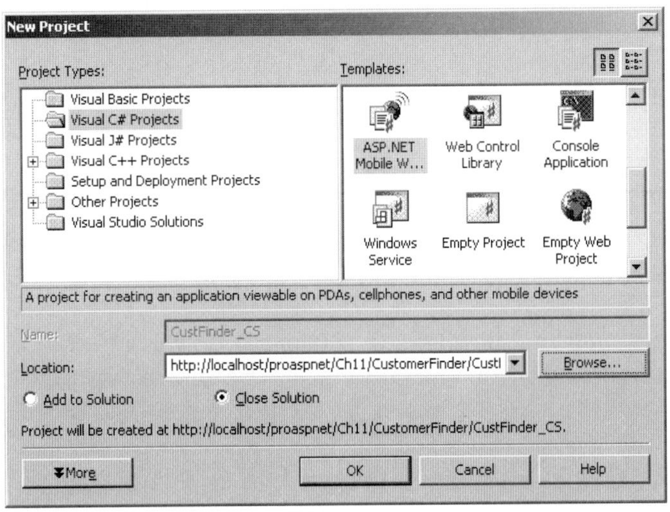

Figure 11-9 The first step in building an ASP.NET Mobile Web Application is choosing the right project type in Visual Studio .NET.

Beyond that, nothing is really different from building a conventional ASP.NET Web application. An ad hoc designer module—the ASP.NET Mobile Designer—appears to help you create mobile forms and fill them with controls and code. Controls cannot be resized because resizing is handled by ASP.NET when it generates the actual markup code for a particular device. You should try to organize the user interface of the application in forms, and provide commands to move from one form to the next.

The Mobile Designer offers an abstract representation of pages, meaning it does not emulate the rendering of any specific device. The page might appear quite differently at run time from how it appears at design time. Consider that the target device might not support every control property or the value you assigned. The *BackColor* property, for example, is supplied and can be set, but it's used only on smart devices, such as the Pocket PC. As we'll see later, developers can customize pieces of the application to control how it looks on a particular device.

Figure 11-10 shows the structure of the user interface we're going to build.

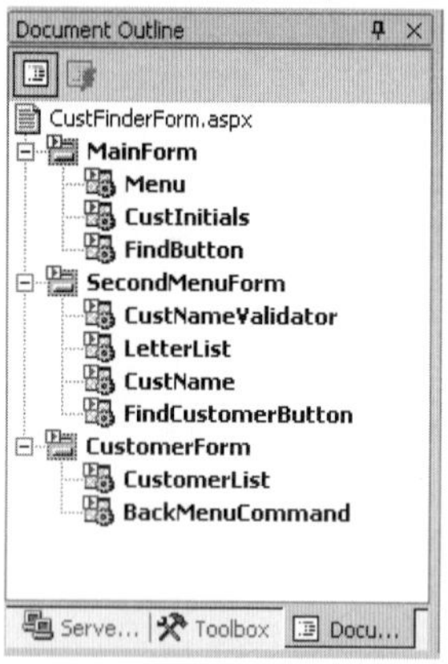

Figure 11-10 The outline of the CustomerFinder application. It consists of three forms. The first two let you navigate to the desired customer, whereas the third one displays information.

The CustomerFinder application consists of three forms. The first two forms (main form and second menu form) have a similar structure. Both display a list of options from which you can choose the customer to call. The first main form employs a *List* control to display a static list of options, each of which selects customers whose company name begins with any letter in a range (for example, A through F). In addition, a text box lets you enter a partial key to locate all the customers that match it.

The second menu form shows the results of the previous search. If you selected a range of letters, the second menu form displays all of them so that you can narrow the working set further by indicating the particular letter. This is probably a better option than presenting a long list of about 20 letters. (I say

20 because with a slightly smarter SQL query, you could, for example, skip letters for which there's no registered customer.) The second menu form also contains a text box and a command button to let you narrow further the list of customers. However, at this stage the content of the text box is validated and forced to be any string that starts with any of the displayed letters. For example, if you're viewing letters between A and F, you're not allowed to enter a partial key like GA. The validation is implemented using a *CustomValidator* control.

Finally, the third customer form displays the list of selected customers using an *ObjectList* control. Using and configuring all these controls is in no way different from using equivalent controls for an ASP.NET Web application. Figure 11-11 shows the main form of the application.

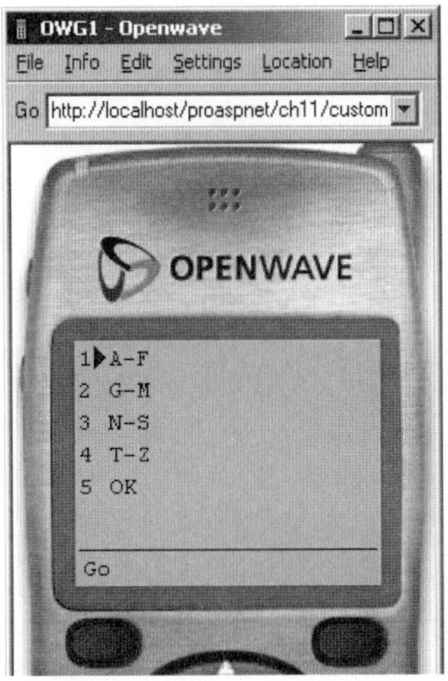

Figure 11-11 The main form of the CustomerFinder application as it appears in the Openwave emulator.

Working with Emulators

By default, Visual Studio .NET uses an internal browser to test and debug mobile applications. However, you can also install your own device emulator and use it to browse the application.

Once the emulator has been downloaded and installed on the machine, you can register it with Visual Studio .NET through the Browse With item under the File menu. When you select Browse With, the Browse With dialog box shown in Figure 11-12 appears. You locate the emulator executable, give it a friendly name, and you're done. Note that once the emulator has been added to the list, its settings cannot be edited further. You have to remove it and add it again with proper settings.

By selecting an emulator and clicking the Browse button in the Browse With dialog box, you can browse the current application using a particular device without leaving the development environment. If you set an emulator as the default browser, Visual Studio .NET will launch it whenever you debug an application.

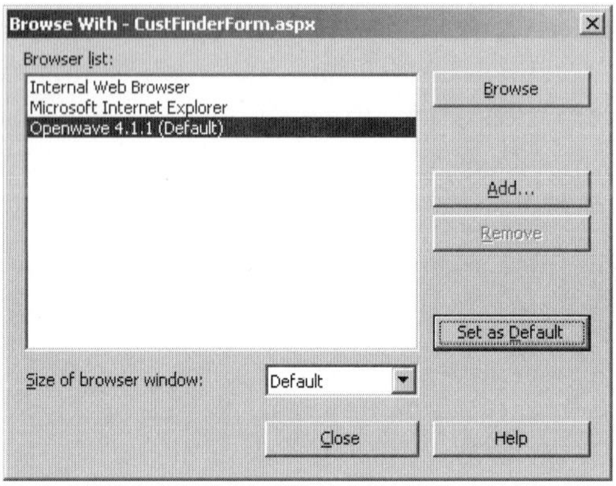

Figure 11-12 The dialog box used to install a browser emulator within Visual Studio .NET.

Openwave (which you can learn more about at *http://developer.openwave.com*) provides a handful of emulators, each with different characteristics for the WML language and a range of supported devices. Another suite you might want to try is YourWap. You can get it from *http://www.yourwap.com*. Of course, Mobile Internet Explorer and the Pocket PC emulator are other embedded tools you can use to quickly get an idea about the areas, if any, in which your mobile user interface is lame.

Suffice it to say that although ASP.NET mobile Web applications do a fantastic job of abstracting the various wireless markup languages and fusing them to the .NET Framework, a lot remains to be done. In particular, you should be aware that ASP.NET alone is not enough to build real-world mobile applications that work great on a wide range of devices. This is not because of flaws and shortcomings in the ASP.NET implementation, however. It's more the result of the deep differences, in both hardware and software, existing between devices. For this reason, you should carefully consider the possibility of extending the ASP.NET mobile code with device-specific extensions. We'll discuss device-specific extensions later in the "Adaptive Rendering" section.

The Navigation Model of the Application

As mentioned earlier, the CustomerFinder application is composed of three server-side forms. The first two forms let you narrow the set of customers to be displayed. When a reasonably small number of customers has been reached, the data is passed on to an *ObjectList* component for display.

If you look at this strategy from a pure Web perspective, you might find it questionable, to say the least. However, designed this way, a mobile application is easier to use because it requires the user only to push buttons to proceed. The overall set of data is seen as a tree and is traversed by making a logical choice at each step. Only small chunks of information need to be downloaded at any stage. Because the Customers table is likely to be used by all sessions, it needs to be downloaded only once and stored in the ASP.NET *Cache* object for better performance. The data is loaded when the application starts.

```
void Application_Start(object sender, EventArgs e) {
    DataSet data = LoadDataFromDatabase();
    Context.Cache["Customers"] = data;
}
```

The Main Form

The first form to display employs a *List* control to display four options that, when combined, cover the 26 letters of the alphabet. The *Text* property of the *ListItem* object indicates the range, while the *Value* property contains all letters included separated by a comma.

```
<mobile:form id="MainForm" runat="server">
    <mobile:List id="Menu" runat="server">
        <Item Value="A,B,C,D,E,F" Text="A-F" />
        <Item Value="G,H,I,J,K,L,M" Text="G-M" />
        <Item Value="N,O,P,Q,R,S" Text="N-S" />
        <Item Value="T,U,V,W,X,Y,Z" Text="T-Z" />
    </mobile:List>
    <mobile:TextBox id="CustInitials" runat="server" />
    <mobile:Command id="FindButton" runat="server" text="Find" />
</mobile:form>
```

The main form is completed with a text box and a command button. If the button is clicked, the text in the input field is used to select and display, in the customer form, a subset of customers. If you click on one of the list items, the following code executes:

```
void Menu_ItemCommand(object sender, ListCommandEventArgs e) {
    string[] menuItems = e.ListItem.Value.Split(",".ToCharArray());
    Session["AvailableInitials"] = menuItems;
    LetterList.DataSource = menuItems;
    LetterList.DataBind();
```

```
    // Move to the second form
    ActiveForm = SecondMenuForm;
}
```

The comma-separated list of letters is split into a string array and temporarily parked in the session cache. We might need to retrieve it later to validate any text the user should enter in the Find text box for a more direct search. The same array of strings is used to fill another *List* object. In this case, the instance of the *List* control is bound to dynamically generated data rather than to static data.

The *ActiveForm* property gets and sets the currently active form in a mobile page class. When a page is initially rendered, the first form in the page is automatically activated and displayed. On subsequent postbacks, another form might be brought to the foreground, either programmatically or as the result of user navigation. The *ActiveForm* property is a fundamental element for the implementation of wizard-like mobile user interfaces. In this case, the *ActiveForm* property is set to the second menu form.

The Second Menu Form

The second menu form (shown in Figure 11-13) shows all the letters that were listed in the *Value* property of the selected *ListItem* object.

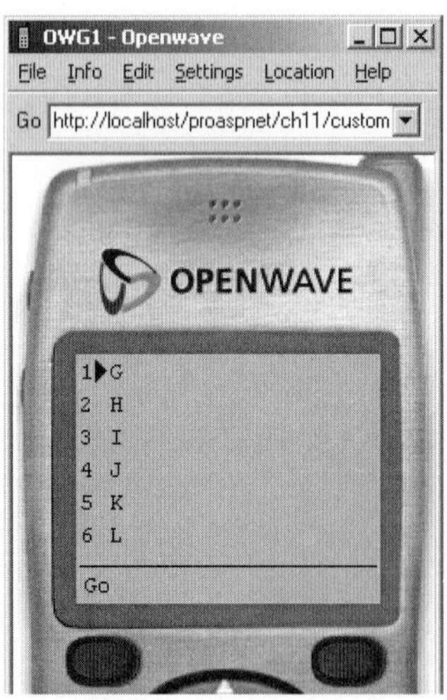

Figure 11-13 The second menu form with a restricted menu as it is displayed by the Openwave emulator.

You should note at this point how device output can differ even when the same markup is submitted. The Openwave browser uses a numbered list of options that can be selected by pushing numbers on the phone keypad. The Nokia browser, on the other hand, allows only position-based selection.

The code for the second menu form is shown here:

```
<mobile:form id="SecondMenuForm" runat="server">
    <mobile:CustomValidator id="CustNameValidator" runat="server"
        ControlToValidate="CustName"
        ErrorMessage="Must begin with next initials" />
    <mobile:List id="LetterList" runat="server" />
    <mobile:TextBox id="CustName" runat="server" />
    <mobile:Command id="FindCustomerButton" runat="server" text="Find" />
</mobile:form>
```

When the user clicks any of the individual letters displayed, the code prepares a sort of in-memory query and gets back with an ADO.NET *DataView* object with all customers whose name begins with the selected letters. The customers are listed using an *ObjectList* control.

If the user wants to type a string to restrict the search, there's a text box available at the bottom of the second menu form. The text you can type is subject to validation; only strings that start with any of the listed letters are acceptable. The following listing shows the code for the custom validator:

```
void ServerValidate(object source, ServerValidateEventArgs e) {
    e.IsValid = false;

    // Ensure that the contained value begins with any of the listed letters
    string[] menuItems = (string[]) Session["AvailableInitials"];
    string currentValue = e.Value.ToLower();
    foreach (string s in menuItems)
        if (currentValue.StartsWith(s.ToLower())) {
            e.IsValid = true;
            return;
        }
}
```

The effect of validation is shown in Figure 11-14. Note that, for usability reasons, you should place the validator at the very top of the form so that its error message is the first thing the user sees once the page posts back.

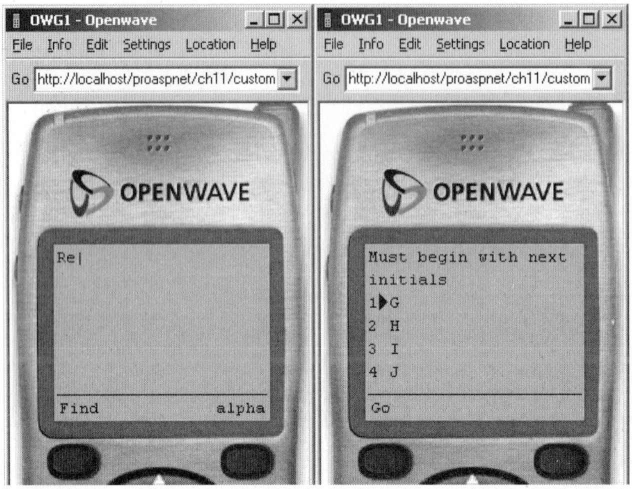

Figure 11-14 The user entered unexpected text, and the validator caught it.

The Customer Form

As the final step in our CustomerFinder application, let's display customers. We'll use an *ObjectList* control and bind it to the collection of rows selected by the following code:

```
DataView SelectCustomers(string filterString) {
    string cmdText = "";
    string[] initials = filterString.Split(",".ToCharArray());
    string opOR = "";

    // Build the filter string for ADO.NET view filters
    foreach(string s in initials) {
        cmdText += String.Format("{0} {2} LIKE '{1}%' ",
            opOR, s, "companyname");
        opOR = " OR ";
    }

    // Build the filtered view
    DataTable data = GetData();
    DataView view = new DataView(data);
    view.RowFilter = cmdText;
    return view;
}
```

The code sets up a view on top of the global table of customers that was downloaded upon startup. The filtered view is then assigned to the *DataSource* property of *ObjectList* control.

```
void LetterList_ItemCommand(object sender, ListCommandEventArgs e) {
    DataView view = SelectCustomers(e.ListItem.Value);
    CustomerList.DataSource = view;
    CustomerList.DataBind();

    ActiveForm = CustomerForm;
}
```

The customer form is shown in Figure 11-15.

Figure 11-15 The customer form showing the list of customers to select from.

The structure of the customer form is shown as follows:

```
<mobile:form id="CustomerForm" runat="server" paginate="true">
    <mobile:ObjectList id="CustomerList" runat="server"
        Wrapping="nowrap" AutoGenerateFields="False"
        LabelField="Company">
        <Field Name="Company" DataField="companyname" Visible="False" />
        <Field Name="Address" DataField="address" />
        <Field Name="City" DataField="city" />
        <Field Name="Country" DataField="country" />
        <Field Name="Phone" DataField="phone" />
    </mobile:ObjectList>
    <mobile:Command id="BackMenuCommand" runat="server" text="Back" />
</mobile:form>
```

The *ObjectList* control first displays a list of the values bound through the *LabelField* column. When you click any of these items, a detail view is provided that includes all the rows for which a *<field>* element exists. The collection of displayed fields must include the label field—*Company*, in the preceding example. If you don't want it to be displayed, set the *Visible* attribute to *false*. The *Name* attribute allows you to alias the physical data field. The detail view of the customer is shown in Figure 11-16.

Figure 11-16 The long-awaited information about the customer.

The detail view provided by the *ObjectList* control, as well as the *List* control, can be customized to some extent using templates.

> **Caution** In WML, a Web page is typically referred to as a card. A group of cards is called a deck. Most WML-based browsers have a limitation on the size of the deck they can receive. This is known as the deck size limit, and it can vary according to the individual device. Because the limit applies to content compiled at the WAP gateway, it's difficult to determine whether a WML deck is too large for a device. Exceeding the size limit could easily lead to a deck overflow error. This is particularly a risk for dynamic, data-bound pages.
>
> You should note that ASP.NET doesn't truncate pages to make decks fit within the deck size limit of a device. To be on the safe side, programmers should either use pagination within the form or consider approximately 1,200 characters as a realistic threshold for decks.

Adaptive Rendering

Mobile applications can adapt the appearance of controls to specific devices or to categories of devices. Because they are based on known device capabilities, you can vary the style of the controls as well as make the rendering of the control more or less rich to accommodate the device characteristics. Adaptive rendering is performed using device filters. A device filter is represented with a *<DeviceSpecific>* tag in the controls layout.

Understanding Device Filters

The ASP.NET runtime abstracts the .aspx code and generates appropriate markup for rendering on a variety of device types. However, when you need different code to be generated for the same control on a device by device basis, you should define a set of device filters for the application and then specify the code to generate for each filter. You express a device filter using the *<DeviceSpecific>* and *<Choice>* elements.

The *<DeviceSpecific>* element is merely a container that holds a number of choices. Choices represent pairs made from a device characteristic and the corresponding value. The device filters are defined in the web.config file. A choice is selected if the filter is verified—that is, if the attribute of the device and the value match. The following listing demonstrates some filters that can be defined in web.config:

```
<deviceFilters>
    <filter name="isHTML32"
        compare="PreferredRenderingType"
        argument="html32" />
    <filter name="isWML11"
        compare="PreferredRenderingType"
        argument="wml11" />
    <filter name="prefersGIF"
        compare="PreferredImageMIME"
        argument="image/gif" />
    ⋮
</deviceFilters>
```

The *<filter>* element has a name that is used to bind to the *<choice>* element. The *compare* attribute defines the capability of the device you want to test. The *argument* property is the value to match. For example, if you want a label to render in italic on HTML 3.2 devices and as normal text elsewhere, do the following:

```
<mobile:Form runat="server">
    <mobile:Label runat="server" text="Some text">
        <DeviceSpecific>
```

```
            <choice filter="isHTML32" font-italic="true" />
        </DeviceSpecific>
    </mobile:Label>
</mobile:Form>
```

Note that this technique works as long as you have the filter defined in the web.config file. Choices are evaluated in the order they appear in the *<DeviceSpecific>* construct. In practice, a device filter is a declarative way to test some capabilities of the device and configure the control properly.

Creating Control Templates

Device filters can also be used to change the default template used by list controls. For example, in the example just discussed we end up displaying the phone number of the selected customer. Wouldn't it be nice if we could automatically associate it with a *PhoneCall* control? In this way, in fact, our user could click and place a call. Both the *List* and *ObjectList* controls let you change the structure of the default template. The following code shows how to change the template used to render all the items of a *List* object using a *PhoneCall* control:

```
<mobile:List id="CustomerList" runat="server" OnItemCommand="ItemCommand">
    <DeviceSpecific>
    <Choice>
    <ItemTemplate>
        <mobile:PhoneCall runat="server"
            Text='<%# ((DataRowView) ((MobileListItem)
                Container).DataItem)["companyname"] %>'
            PhoneNumber='<%# ((DataRowView) ((MobileListItem)
                Container).DataItem)["phone"] %>'>
        </mobile:PhoneCall>
    </ItemTemplate>
    </Choice>
    </DeviceSpecific>
</mobile:List>
```

If the *Filter* property is omitted, the choice is picked by default, and this allows you to modify the output of some built-in controls using templates.

State Management

Most Web applications need state to be persisted between requests, and mobile applications are no exception. ASP.NET provides several services and facilities for state management, among which view state and session state play a primary role. View state is a page-level cache that is saved and loaded for each request of the page. This trick makes possible the development of stateful applications on top of a stateless protocol.

ASP.NET also provides a session-state object that can be used to save information across multiple requests. As we'll see more in detail in Chapter 14, "ASP.NET State Management," session management in ASP.NET is more scalable and robust than in previous versions of ASP and can also be used across Web farms.

The View State

On ASP.NET Web Forms pages, the view state is packed as a hidden variable in the unique server-side form object that is submitted. The view state is sent back and forth as part of every response and request being exchanged. The way in which applications interact with the view state is the same in ASP.NET mobile applications. The internal implementation is different, however.

To reduce bandwidth, ASP.NET does not send the view state of a mobile page to the client. Instead, the view state remains on the server and is saved as part of the user's session. The view state is cached in a slot named *ViewState* in which an object of type *SessionViewStateHistory* is saved. The *SessionViewStateHistory* type is a super-array of *SessionViewStateHistoryItem* objects in which the actual view state of the page—generated as in ASP.NET Web Forms—is stored. Because the view state is kept on the server, it's possible for the currently cached state and the currently displayed page to be out of sync. For example, suppose the user navigates to a given page and then moves back to another page by using the Back button. At this point, the current page doesn't match the view state on the server.

For this reason, ASP.NET maintains for mobile pages a history of view states on the server. Each page is assigned a numeric ID that corresponds to the position in the view-state history where information about that page is held. The size of the history array is set to 6 by default, but it can be changed in the web.config file, as shown in the following code. Of course too high a value might lead to unnecessary consumption of server memory.

```
<configuration>
    <system.web>
        <mobileControls sessionStateHistorySize="15" />
    </system.web>
</configuration>
```

Because the view state of mobile pages and controls is stored in *Session*, chances are that this information will get lost if the session expires or the process is recycled. When the view state can't be restored for a mobile page, the *ViewStateExpire* event is fired. The event normally results in an exception being thrown; however, if there's a way for the application to restore a consistent state on a view-state failure, you should override the method *OnViewStateExpire* on the *MobilePage* class and execute your recovery code there.

Just as for ASP.NET Web Forms, the use of the view state can be minimized and completely disabled if it's not really needed. You can disable the view state by using the *EnableViewState* attribute on the *@Page* directive; if you want to disable the view state for an individual control, use the *EnableViewState* property on the control's programming interface.

The Private View State

You should note, though, that even when the view state is disabled, mobile controls might save state information in a hidden field on the client. For example, a *MobilePage* control saves the index of the currently active form in a hidden field implemented in a way that closely resembles the Web Forms view state. The view-state history identifier is also saved in this sort of private view state.

The *ClientViewState* property returns a string that represents the serialized version of the private view state. Applications cannot add custom information to this table. The private view state should be used only for general state information, is always saved to the client, and cannot be disabled.

> **Note** The *HiddenVariables* collection of the *MobilePage* class provides a way to create hidden variables in the output. Although this feature has nothing to do with the private view state, it represents an easier-to-use alternative to the private view state.

The Session State

The session state is tied to an identifier that uniquely identifies the session within the application. By default, this identifier is stored in a client-side cookie and is retrieved across round-trips. Using cookies in mobile applications can be problematic because some devices and gateways do not support cookies.

ASP.NET supports cookieless sessions. A cookieless session relies on a special format of the URL to retrieve the identifier. When working in cookieless mode, ASP.NET redirects the browser to another page whose URL embeds the identifier, which is then parsed out of the actual URL. In this case, though, you should pay attention to devices that might experience difficulty if passed a URL with special formatting such as the URL of a cookieless application.

Hidden variables are a fair alternative to using the session state in the unfortunate case in which you can't afford it.

The Extensibility Model

The built-in set of mobile controls can be extended by using the same guidelines as for Web controls. Therefore, you can create user and custom controls. Mobile user controls inherit from the base class *MobileUserControl* and are stored in files with an .ascx extension. Unlike ASP.NET user controls, mobile user controls can contain child forms. To link to a form in a user control, you must use a combined ID made of the ID of the control and the ID of the embedded form—*UserControl:Form*. A child form can reference a form in the parent container simply by name. When this happens, ASP.NET recursively searches for a matching form, proceeding from the user control all the way up to the root page.

You can also create custom controls that inherit from existing mobile controls. You can add new properties, methods, and events and override existing elements. Custom controls can be created either to extend the capabilities of a single particular control or as a composite control. With composite controls, you programmatically combine existing controls and expose them as a new monolithic object. This is a slightly different procedure than with user controls. The key difference is that composite controls are deployed as assemblies, are inheritable, and enjoy full support from the Visual Studio .NET designers.

Extensibility in the .NET mobile world is not limited to controls but spans to cover new devices and new device adapters. You can add a new device browser by adding a new *<browserCaps>* entry to either the web.config or machine.config file. This is far easier than writing a new device adapter, which is a relatively complex class. However, in situations in which the particular capabilities of the device cannot be described declaratively, writing a new device adapter is necessary.

Conclusion

Developing mobile applications can be quite a complex task because of differences in browser presentation models and gateways. Like it or not, the market for wireless devices is fragmented, although this fragmentation is possibly stronger in Europe than in other parts of the world. So to be on the safe side and deploy effective applications, you should multi-author your application for each relevant class of devices. Writing multiple applications is not usually an attractive prospect to developers and managers, who are understandably reluctant to give the green light on such projects.

In the wireless world, though, the difference between devices is too large to be effectively addressed in all cases even by a well-written library such as the ASP.NET mobile controls. The need to deal with radically different sets of capabilities forces developers to implement navigation models, data entry capabilities, and strictly device-specific commands. If you're going to build mobile applications for multiple devices, your best chance is to endow yourself with a server-side programming library that abstracts the presentation of content from the underlying platform. ASP.NET mobile controls do just this and much more. There are several key plusses in ASP.NET mobile applications.

For one thing, ASP.NET mobile controls are fully integrated with the .NET platform, meaning that you can leverage the full potential of the .NET Framework with its over 7,000 ready-to-use classes. In addition, the Mobile Designer integrated with Visual Studio .NET 2003 lets you build mobile applications in an intuitive manner and with a very short learning curve if you're already a .NET developer. (Also Web Matrix supports mobile projects.) Finally, mobile development in the .NET world is language agnostic.

Aside from the .NET platform, other server-side libraries have been developed in the community with the declared goal of abstracting both the differences in the vendor's implementations of the WML language and the hardware device capabilities. An example of this approach is the Open Usability Interface (OUI) originally developed by Openwave and then transformed into an open-source project. With a more limited scope than ASP.NET, OUI is optimized for rendering on Nokia and Openwave browsers. OUI is available for download at *http://oui.sourceforge.net*.

In this chapter, we presented an overview of ASP.NET mobile controls, trying to emphasize all relevant aspects but not digging too deep into any of them. Building mobile applications, especially for multiple devices, is a huge topic that deserves an entire book of its own. This chapter concludes the overview of ASP.NET controls. In the next part of the book, we'll look at programming aspects that are essential for setting up real-world ASP.NET applications. We'll return to controls in Part V in time to cover custom controls.

Resources

- *Building Microsoft ASP.NET Applications for Mobile Devices, Second Edition*, by Andy Wigley and Peter Roxburgh (Microsoft Press, 2003)
- Mobile ASP.NET Web Applications (*http://www.asp.net/mobile/*)

Part IV

ASP.NET Application Essentials

12

Configuration and Deployment

Leave no stone unturned.

—Euripides

The .NET Framework provides an extensible infrastructure that enables you to define configuration settings for all types of applications including, but not limited to, ASP.NET applications. All applications, no matter the platform and the working model, should always be driven by configurable settings read from an external storage medium. Simply by updating the configuration file, developers and system administrators should be able to change the way in which the application works as well as the elements of the user interface. In other words, to the extent possible, applications should always be designed in a parametric way and according to the theoretical principles of attribute-based programming.

The .NET Framework defines a tailor-made, XML-based API to access configuration files and, in doing so, forces developers to adopt a common, rich, and predefined schema for storing application settings. In the more general context of the .NET configuration scheme, ASP.NET applications enjoy specific features such as a hierarchical configuration scheme that allows settings inheritance and overriding at various levels—machine, application, or specific directories.

Configuration files are typically created offline or during the development of the application. They are deployed with the application and can be changed at any time by administrators. Changes to such critical files are promptly detected by the ASP.NET runtime and cause all the pages to recompile. ASP.NET pages can use the classes in the *System.Configuration* namespace to read from configuration files but not to write back. The .NET Framework, in fact, provides no ad hoc API to create or edit configuration files. However, because configuration files are plain XML files, the XML API can be used to modify any contents. You should note, though, that by default ASP.NET applications have no permissions to write or create files.

In this chapter, after a bird's-eye look at the overall .NET Framework configuration engine, we'll specifically delve into the ASP.NET configuration machinery. We'll see how to fine-tune the ASP.NET runtime and review the whole collection of parameters you can set for an individual application. Finally, we'll see how to store custom data in a configuration file and top off the discussion by covering deployment issues.

Configuration in the .NET Framework

The .NET Framework provides three basic types of configuration files: machine, security, and application. Despite their different contents and goals, all configuration files are XML documents and share the same schema. For example, all configuration files begin with a *<configuration>* node and then differentiate their contents and child nodes according to the final goal and the information they contain.

The XML Schema of Configuration Files

Configuration files are standard XML files that follow a given schema. The schema defines all possible settings for machine, security, and application files. The .NET Framework provides made-to-measure classes to read configuration settings, but no writing facilities are provided. You need to be familiar with XML writers if you want to directly edit the configuration files. (In light of this, bear in mind that XML elements and attribute names are *strictly* case-sensitive.)

All configuration files have their root in the *<configuration>* element. Table 12-1 lists the first-level children of the *<configuration>* element. Each node has a specified number of child elements that provide a full description of the setting. For example, the *<system.web>* element optionally contains the *<authorization>* tag in which you can store information about the users who can safely access the ASP.NET application.

Table 12-1 Children of the *<configuration>* Element

Element	Description
<appSettings>	Contains custom application settings in the specified XML format.
<configSections>	Describes the configuration sections for custom settings. If this element is in a configuration file, it must be the first child of the *<configuration>* root.
<mscorlib> *<cryptographySettings>*	Cryptography schema; describes the elements that map friendly algorithm names to classes that implement cryptography algorithms.
<runtime>	Run-time settings schema; describes the elements that configure assembly binding and run time behavior such as probing and assembly redirect.
<startup>	Startup settings schema; contains the elements that specify which version of the common language runtime (CLR) must be used.
<system.diagnostics>	Describes the elements that specify trace switches and listeners that collect, store, and route messages.
<system.net>	Network schema; specifies elements to indicate how the .NET Framework connects to the Internet, including the default proxy, authentication modules, and connection parameters.
<system.runtime.remoting>	Settings schema; configures the client and server applications that exploit the .NET Remoting.
<system.web>	It's the ASP.NET-specific configuration section; contains the elements that control all aspects of the behavior of an ASP.NET application.

Because we're focusing on ASP.NET applications, only the *<system.web>* section has particular importance for us and only that will be covered in detail. However, this doesn't mean that, as an ASP.NET developer, you'll never be using other sections—most certainly you will!

For example, you'll need *<appSettings>* and *<configSections>* if you plan to persist user-profile information on the server, read working information such as connection strings, or specify advertising pictures to rotate. The *<configSections>* element defines the sections that will be used to group information in the rest of the document. The *<appSettings>* element contains user-defined nodes whose structure has been previously defined in the *<configSections>* node. You might need to interact with the *<system.diagnostics>* section if you want to use a custom trace listener that logs to an application-defined file.

You'll probably need *<runtime>* if some special rules for probing assemblies are required. Furthermore, if the ASP.NET application performs calls to some remote component, you must adjust settings in the *<system.runtime.remoting>* section.

The elements in Table 12-1 are used to compose the various .config files that all .NET applications are based on in some way. Let's learn a bit more about their internal structure.

The Machine Configuration File

The machine configuration file is named *machine.config* and is located in the CONFIG subdirectory of the .NET Framework installation path. The first path shown in the following code is typical of version 1.0 of the .NET Framework; the second path refers to version 1.1 of the .NET Framework:

```
C:\WINNT\Microsoft.NET\Framework\v1.0.3705\CONFIG
C:\WINNT\Microsoft.NET\Framework\v1.1.4322\CONFIG
```

The machine.config file contains machinewide settings that apply to assembly binding, built-in remoting channels, and the ASP.NET runtime. In particular, the machine.config file contains information about the browser capabilities, registered HTTP handlers, and page compilation. Here's an excerpt from machine.config that shows compilation and assembly default settings:

```
<?xml version="1.0" encoding="UTF-8"?>
<configuration>
    <configSections>
        ⋮
    </configSections>
    ⋮
    <system.web>
        ⋮
        <compilation debug="false" explicit="true" defaultLanguage="vb">
            <compilers>
                <compiler language="c#;cs;csharp"
                    extension=".cs" ... />
                <compiler language="vb;vbs;visualbasic;vbscript"
                    extension=".vb" ... />
                <compiler language="js;jscript;javascript"
                    extension=".js" ... />
                <compiler language="VJ#;VJS;VJSharp"
                    extension=".jsl" ... />
            </compilers>
        </compilation>
        <assemblies>
            <add assembly="mscorlib"/>
            <add assembly="System, Version=1.0.5000.0, ... " />
```

```
            <add assembly="System.Web, Version=1.0.5000.0, ... " />
            <add assembly="System.Data, Version=1.0.5000.0, ... " />
            <add assembly="System.Web.Services, Version=1.0.5000.0, ... />
            <add assembly="System.Xml, Version=1.0.5000.0, ... />
            <add assembly="System.Drawing, Version=1.0.5000.0, ... />
            <add assembly="System.EnterpriseServices, ... />
            <add assembly="System.Web.Mobile, ... />
            <add assembly="*" />
        </assemblies>
        ⋮
    </system.web>
    ⋮
</configuration>
```

> **Note** The lines in boldface type refer to changes in version 1.1 of the .NET Framework. Also, notice that the version number of the assemblies in version 1.1 is 1.0.5000.0.

Declaring a section in the machine.config file enables you to exploit those settings from within any ASP.NET application that runs on that computer. Note, though, that settings defined in machine.config can be overwritten and even canceled in the application configuration file (web.config). More on this later in the "ASP.NET Applications Configuration" section.

Security Configuration Files

Security configuration files contain information about the code groups and the permission sets associated with a policy level. A *code group* is a logical grouping of code that specifies certain conditions for membership. Any code that meets the given criteria can be included in the group. Code groups have associated permission sets. A permission set, in turn, defines the resources that can be accessed at execution time. A *policy level* describes all the security measures for the specified context—enterprise, machine, or user. The CLR grants permissions to an assembly based on the minimum set of permissions granted by any of the policy levels.

Security configuration files have names and locations that depend on the policy level. The configuration file for the enterprise policy level is named *enterprisesec.config* and resides in the same directory as the machine.config file. Contained in the same folder, the *security.config* file characterizes the machine policy level. The enterprise level groups security settings for the entire enterprise; the machine policy level, on the other hand, defines the security for the local machine. Both levels can be configured only by an administrator.

The user policy configuration file affects the code in all the processes associated with the user. Named *security.config*, the file resides in a folder under the user profile subtree. The path for a machine running version 1.1 of the .NET Framework is shown here.

```
C:\Documents and Settings\[UserName]\Application Data\Microsoft\
CLR Security Config\v1.1.4322
```

> **Caution** Editing the contents of the security files, and thereby modifying the security policies, is a potentially critical task that should be accomplished using the .NET Framework Configuration administrative tool (an MMC snap-in named mscorcfg.msc) or the Code Access Security Policy tool (a command-line tool named caspol.exe).

Application Configuration Files

Application-specific configuration files contain settings consumed by the CLR as well as by the application itself. The CLR reads information such as the assembly binding policy, the location of remote objects, and ASP.NET runtime settings. The application can read settings that correspond to the parameters it needs to work within. The name and location of the application configuration file depend on the application's model, which can be one of the following: Windows Forms or console executable, ASP.NET application or Web service, or Internet Explorer–hosted application. Table 12-2 shows the names used.

Table 12-2 Configuration Files for Applications

Application Type	Configuration File
Windows Forms	[ApplicationName].exe.config
Console	[ApplicationName].exe.config
ASP.NET	web.config
Web service	web.config
Hosted by Internet Explorer	The name of the file doesn't have to follow specific rules, but the location must be on the same virtual directory as the application.

More often than not, configuration files contain sensitive information the CLR and the ASP.NET runtime need to know and process. Both the CLR and the ASP.NET runtime treat XML files that have a particular name (for example, web.config) as special resources. For this reason, you can't really use different names for them. What you can do, instead, is move the application-specific information—the content of the *<appSettings>* section—to a distinct file. (More on this later in the "Persisting Application Settings" section.) If you move system information out of the web.config file, that information will easily be ignored by the ASP.NET runtime and might affect the overall functionality of the application.

Managing Configuration Settings

All sections used in a configuration file must be declared in the initial *<configSections>* section. The following code snippet demonstrates how the *<system.web>* section is declared in machine.config:

```
<configSections>
    ⋮
    <sectionGroup name="system.web">
        ⋮
        <section name="compilation"
            type="CompilationConfigurationHandler, System.Web, ... />
        <section name="pages"
            type="PagesConfigurationHandler, System.Web, ... />
        ⋮
    </sectionGroup>
    ⋮
</configSections>
```

The *<sectionGroup>* element has no other role than marking and grouping a few child sections, thus creating a sort of namespace for them. In this way, you can have sections with the same name living under different groups. The *<section>* element takes two attributes—*name* and *type*. The *name* attribute denotes the name of the section being declared. The *type* attribute indicates the name of the managed class that reads and parses the contents of the section from the configuration file. The value of the *type* attribute is a comma-separated string that includes the class and full name of the assembly that contains it.

The *<section>* element also has two optional attributes—*allowDefinition* and *allowLocation*—specifically targeted at ASP.NET applications. These two attributes are ignored by configuration readers controlled by other types of applications. The *allowDefinition* attribute specifies which configuration files the section can be used in. Feasible values for the *allowDefinition* attribute are in Table 12-3.

Table 12-3 Values for the *allowDefinition* Attribute

Value	Description
Everywhere	The section can be used in any configuration file. (Default.)
MachineOnly	The section can be used only in the machine.config file.
MachineToApplication	The section can be used in the machine.config file and in the application's web.config file. You cannot use the section in web.config files located in subdirectories of the virtual folder.

The *allowLocation* attribute determines whether the section can be used within the *<location>* section. The *<location>* section in a machine.config file allows you to apply the specified machinewide settings only to the resources below a given path. (More on the *<location>* element later in the "The *<location>* Section" section.)

Many sections in the configuration files support three special elements named *<add>*, *<remove>*, and *<clear>*. The *<add>* element adds a new setting to the specified section, while *<remove>* removes the specified one. The *<clear>* element clears all the settings that have previously been defined in the section. The *<remove>* and *<clear>* elements are particularly useful in ASP.NET configuration files in which a hierarchy of files can be created. For example, you can use the *<remove>* element in a child web.config file to remove settings that were defined at a higher level in the configuration file hierarchy.

The *<remove>* and *<clear>* elements don't affect the actual data stored in the configuration file. Removing a section doesn't erase the related data from the file, it simply removes the data from the in-memory tree of settings that ASP.NET builds and maintains for an application.

> **Note** Sections are a necessary syntax element in configuration files. However, you don't need to declare sections in all application-specific web.config files. When processing a web.config file, in fact, the reader builds a configuration tree starting from the root machine.config file. Because all standard sections are already declared in the machine.config that ships with the .NET Framework, your application needs to declare only custom sections you plan to use.
>
> Finally, bear in mind that an exception is thrown if a configuration section lacks a corresponding entry in the *<configSections>* section and when the layout of the data does not match the declaration.

The *ConfigurationSettings* Class

To programmatically read application settings, you use the *ConfigurationSettings* class from the *System.Configuration* namespace. *ConfigurationSettings* is a small, sealed class that simply provides one static method (*GetConfig*) and one static property (*AppSettings*).

The *AppSettings* property is a read-only *NameValueCollection* object designed to get the information stored in the *<appSettings>* section. If no setting is specified, or if no *<appSettings>* section exists, an empty collection is returned. The *GetConfig* method returns the configuration settings for the specified section, as shown here:

```
public static object GetConfig(string sectionName);
```

Although the method signature indicates an object return type, the actual return value you get from a call to *GetConfig* is determined by the handler class specified for the requested section. Internally, the *GetConfig* method first determines the name and location of the configuration file to access and then proceeds by creating a specialized XML text reader to operate on the XML document.

A more specialized tool for reading application settings is the *AppSettingsReader* class. This class provides a single method, named *GetValue*, for reading values of a particular type from the configuration file. The *GetValue* method takes two arguments—the name of the setting to retrieve and the type to return—as shown here:

```
public object GetValue(string key, Type type);
```

The *GetValue* method retrieves the value of the given setting using the *AppSettings* property and then performs an automatic cast to the specified type. Unlike the *AppSettings* property of the *ConfigurationSettings* object, the *GetValue* method works in a strongly typed way.

Section Handlers

A *section handler* is a .NET Framework class that implements the *IConfigurationSectionHandler* interface. It interprets and processes the configuration settings stored in a section and stores them in an appropriate object. The XML schema of the input data and the type of the returned object depend on the implementation of the section handler. A few predefined section handlers exist and are listed in Table 12-4. All these section handlers belong to the *System.Configuration* namespace and are implemented in the *System* assembly.

Table 12-4 Predefined Section Handlers

Class	Description
DictionarySectionHandler	Reads name/value pairs, and groups them in a hash-table object.
IgnoreSectionHandler	The *System.Configuration* classes ignore the sections marked with this handler because their contents will be processed by other components. This handler is an alternative to using and declaring custom handlers.
NameValueFileSectionHandler	Reads name/value pairs from a file referenced in the *<appSettings>* section, and groups them in a *NameValueCollection* object. This handler allows you to link an external, custom file to web.config.
NameValueSectionHandler	Reads name/value pairs, and groups them in a *NameValueCollection* object.
SingleTagSectionHandler	Reads settings from attributes stored in a single XML node. The data is returned as a hash table.

The *IgnoreSectionHandler* handler deserves a bit more attention. The handler simply tells the system's configuration reader to ignore any data stored under the specified section. It could be argued that one shouldn't flood a system's .config file with data that will be processed outside the standard configuration pipeline. Although this is a strong recommendation for user code, some system modules (for example,.NET Remoting) store some of their general settings in the machine.config file but then use internal readers to process the information. To preserve file consistency and avoid exceptions, the *IgnoreSectionHandler* handler is used. A better alternative is either using a custom configuration file or defining a custom section handler.

Later in this chapter in the "Creating New Configuration Sections" section, we'll discuss how to create custom sections and a custom section handler to manage the configuration of an ASP.NET application. By now, you should have enough background information to fully understand the details of the configuration machinery of ASP.NET applications.

ASP.NET Applications Configuration

Configuration in ASP.NET is based on the machine.config file plus any number of web.config files. The web.config file is in fact optional, and there's no need to have one in the virtual folder if nothing in the application is configurable. An application can also have multiple web.config files, deployed at any time in different subdirectories. Note that the settings stored in a web.config file apply to the pages contained in the same folder level and below. Any web.config file can extend, restrict, and override settings defined at an upper level, including the machine level. If no configuration file exists in an application folder, the settings that are valid at the upper level are applied.

A sapient use of the settings in machine.config and web.config files allows you to declaratively restrict access to given folders and even specify a different set of features. For example, the following web.config file restricts access to the folder that contains it to all users except the administrator.

```
<configuration>
    <system.web>
        <authorization>
            <allow users="YourDomain\Administrator" />
            <deny users="*" />
        </authorization>
    </system.web>
</configuration>
```

You simply have to add the code in boldface type to the web.config file in another directory to activate the same restriction.

> **Note** ASP.NET protects its configuration files from direct Web access by instructing Internet Information Services (IIS) to block browser access to configuration files. An HTTP access error 403 (forbidden) is returned to all browsers that attempt to request a .config as a URL.

The ASP.NET Configuration Hierarchy

The configuration machinery in ASP.NET is hierarchical by nature. Although, the application settings are located in different files—machine.config and web.config—they originate a single in-memory graph of settings that can take different forms on different directories. The machine.config file contains settings valid at the machine level—that is, for all .NET and ASP.NET applications running on that machine. You can imagine the configuration information in ASP.NET as given by a unique XML document with the schema outlined in Table 12-1. The nodes of this document are populated with the information read from both machine.config and all the web.config files available within the context of the application.

From an ASP.NET-only viewpoint, the contents of machine.config represent the tree of settings that all Web applications hosted on the machine initially share. You can customize and adapt the inherited machinewide settings for each application by creating one or more web.config files. In the end, the tree of settings for the application is unique even though it physically spans multiple files.

The syntax of machine.config and web.config files is identical—both are XML files based on the same schema. The ASP.NET runtime processes configuration information hierarchically, proceeding from a root common to all applications on the machine—machine.config—down to all the web.config files found in the various folders of the particular application. When an ASP.NET application starts, all configurable parameters are set to the default values defined in machine.config. These values can be overridden in the first place by a web.config file placed in the root folder. The web.config file can also add new application-specific settings. In theory, a root web.config file can also clear all the settings in the original machine.config and replace them altogether. You can also define extra web.config files in child folders to apply other settings to all the resources contained in the subtree rooted in the folder. Also in this case, the innermost web.config can overwrite, restrict, or extend the settings defined at upper levels. Figure 12-1 illustrates how ASP.NET processes system and application settings for each page in the Web site.

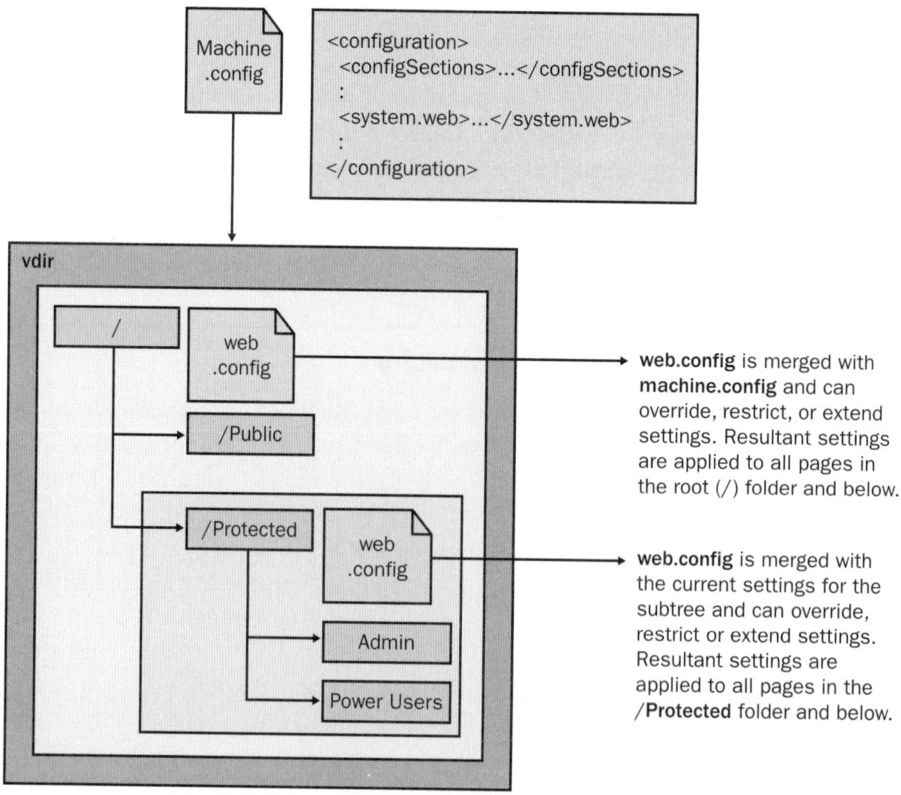

Figure 12-1 ASP.NET configuration is hierarchical by nature.

Applications don't need to read from machine.config. Configuring the machine file is an administrative task and should be performed offline when the application is deployed or during periodical maintenance. Applications, on the other hand, might have the need to read from web.config files—that is, the application-specific repository for configuration information. Data that applications might want to read from web.config is applicationwide data, such as connection strings to databases, URLs to connect to user-interface elements, and pieces of software that need to be enabled or disabled.

In no case should the application write to either machine.config or web.config. Unlike desktop applications, a typical Web application doesn't need to track on the server applicationwide and with dynamically changing settings. However, in some cases you might have the need to persist some noncritical and nonsensitive data on the server (for example, user profile data). A few severe drawbacks apply, though, if you use web.config instead of databases or custom files.

First, the web.config files require administrative privileges to be modified. In addition, consider that by default ASP.NET applications run under the ASPNET account, which provides no writing permissions. Furthermore, any modification made to web.config automatically invalidates all the dynamic assemblies created for the application. Hence, all the pages will be recompiled with the next request to reflect the changes in the configuration. You can understand, then, that especially for large-scale Web sites with hundreds of pages, repeated and generalized compilations are a serious issue that leads to dramatic performance hits. We'll return to this topic later in the "Persisting Application Settings" section.

> **Important** Bear in mind that the ASP.NET configuration system covers only ASP.NET-specific resources, which are not typically all types of resources employed in a Web site. ASP.NET-specific resources are only those registered to be handled by *aspnet_isapi.dll*—that is, .aspx, .ascx, .asmx, .ashx, and a few others. The complete list has been discussed in Chapter 2, in the "The IIS Resource Mappings" section.
>
> Note that the list doesn't include common resource types such as HTML, TXT, GIF, and JPEG files. All these resources, HTML pages for example, are always accessible by all users regardless of the contents of the *<authorization>* section. The reason for this behavior is that to improve performance IIS handles those resources internally without involving external modules such as the ASP.NET ISAPI extension.

The *<location>* Section

The *<location>* section provides an alternative technique to apply different settings to various subdirectories of the same application. Instead of defining child web.config files, you can create a single web.config file in the root folder and specify settings on a per-directory basis. Basically, the *<location>* element lets you create embedded configuration sections associated with a particular directory. From a functional point of view, this is equivalent to having a web.config file in each directory.

Centralized Configuration

The *<location>* element has two attributes: *Path* and *allowOverride*. *Path* represents the virtual path to which the embedded settings apply. The following snippet shows how it works:

```
<configuration>
    <system.web>
        <!-- Settings for the application go here -->
    </system.web>

    <location path="/protected">
        <system.web>
            <!-- Settings for the /protected folder go here -->
        </system.web>
    </location>
</configuration>
```

The defining characteristic of this approach is that you have a single, centralized web.config file to maintain. This feature saves you from the burden of maintaining several web.config files, but it also introduces some unpleasant side-effects that in the long run can turn out to be quite harsh. For example, any change to the file results in a new compilation for all the pages in the application. If you maintain distinct web.config files, the compilation occurs only for the pages really affected by the change.

Optimizing the distribution of pages and configuration files is a key aspect to improving the performance of ASP.NET Web sites. If some of your pages are subject to frequent configuration updates, you're probably better off isolating them in a subdirectory with a child web.config. Next, use the *<location>* element in the root file for all pages that are relatively static from the configuration point of view.

The *<location>* element can also be used within the machine.config file. Interestingly, in this case you can also specify different machinewide settings for various Web applications. In this case, though, you must indicate the application name prefixed by the IIS name of the Web site. (The Web site name is read in the IIS Manager.)

```
<location path="My Web Site/VirtualFolder">
    <system.web>
        <!-- Settings for the application folder go here -->
    </system.web>
</location>
```

We'll return to *<location>* and machine.config later in this chapter in the "Updating Configuration Options" section when discussing the deployment of ASP.NET applications.

Unmodifiable Settings

The second *<location>* attribute you can specify—*allowOverride*—allows you to lock some settings at both the machine level and application level. By grouping settings in a *<location>* element with the *allowOverride* attribute set to *false*, you tell the ASP.NET configuration system to raise an exception whenever a protected setting is overridden in a lower-level .config file.

```
<location path="My Web Site/VirtualFolder" allowOverride="false">
    <system.web>
        <!-- These settings cannot be overridden -->
    </system.web>
</location>
```

The ultimate goal of this feature is to enable administrators to control the settings of a server that provides ASP.NET hosting. When a new application is installed in production, changes might be required on the target machine to reflect the native environment of the application. Updating the machine.config file on the production machine is not an issue as long as yours is the only application running or if you can directly control and configure all the applications hosted on that machine. However, in an application-hosting scenario, the administrator might decide to lock some machine settings to prevent installed applications from modifying them.

Machine settings wrapped in a *<location>* element and adorned with the *allowOverride* attribute set to *false* cannot be modified in lower-level configuration files. In this way, the administrator can preserve, to the extent possible, the integrity of the hosting environment and guarantee that all applications run under the same conditions.

> **Note** By default, nearly all predefined sections can appear within a *<location>* section. The exceptions are *<runtime>*, *<mscorlib>*, *<system.runtime.remoting>*, and *<startup>*. In general, sections can be disallowed from any *<location>* section by using the *allowLocation* attribute. The *allowLocation* attribute of the *<section>* element determines the section's capability of being customized for a particular path. Set it to *false*, and the section is not allowed to be used within a *<location>* section.

The *<system.web>* Section

The *<system.web>* section contains all the configuration elements that set up the ASP.NET runtime environment and controls how ASP.NET applications behave. Table 12-5 shows all feasible first-level elements and their override level.

Table 12-5 Sections Allowed within *<system.web>*

Section	Overridable	Description
<authentication>	Machine, application	Sets the authentication mechanism.
<authorization>	Everywhere	Indicates authorized users.
<browserCaps>	Everywhere	Lists known browser capabilities.
<clientTarget>	Everywhere	Lists predefined client targets.
<compilation>	Everywhere	Settings for batch compilation.
<customErrors>	Everywhere	Settings for custom error pages.
<deviceFilters>	Everywhere	Lists known mobile browser capabilities. *Supported only in version 1.1 of the .NET Framework.*
<globalization>	Everywhere	Settings for application localization.
<httpHandlers>	Everywhere	Lists registered HTTP handlers.
<httpModules>	Everywhere	Lists registered HTTP modules.
<httpRuntime>	Everywhere	HTTP runtime settings.
<identity>	Everywhere	Sets impersonation.
<machineKey>	Everywhere	Encryption key for sensitive data.
<mobileControls>	Everywhere	Lists device-specific class adapters for Web controls. *Supported only in version 1.1 of the .NET Framework.*

Table 12-5 Sections Allowed within *<system.web>*

Section	Overridable	Description
<pages>	Everywhere	Controls features of ASP.NET pages.
<processModel>	Machine	Configures the process model.
<securityPolicy>	Machine, application	Defines allowed trust levels.
<sessionState>	Machine, application	Configures the *Session* object.
<trace>	Everywhere	Configures the tracing system.
<trust>	Machine, application	Defines the default trust level.
<webControls>	Everywhere	Locates client scripts.
<webServices>	Everywhere	Configures Web services.

Each of the elements listed in Table 12-5 features its own schema and provides attributes and enumerations to pick values from.

The *<authentication>* Section

The *<authentication>* section allows you to configure a Web site for various types of user authentication, including form-based authentication as well as Passport and IIS-driven authentication. This section has two mutually exclusive subsections—*<forms>* and *<passport>*—and the *mode* attribute to control the authentication mode requested by an application.

```
<authentication mode="forms">
    <forms name=".ASPXAUTH" loginUrl="login.aspx">
</authentication>
```

Allowable values for the *mode* attribute are shown in Table 12-6.

Table 12-6 Supported Authentication Modes

Value	Description
Forms	Makes use of a custom form to collect logon information.
Passport	Exploits the authentication services of Microsoft Passport.
None	Indicates ASP.NET should not enforce any type of authentication, which means only anonymous users can connect or the application itself provides a built-in mechanism.
Windows	Exploits any authentication services of IIS—basic, digest, NTLM\Kerberos, or certificates. This is the default mode.

When using the forms authentication, you should specify a few parameters: *name*, *loginURL*, *protection*, *timeout*, *path*. The *name* attribute refers to the name of the cookie that transmits logon information from the client. The default name is .ASPXAUTH, while the path to store the cookie is set in the *path* attribute. The cookie expires a few minutes after being issued. The *timeout* attribute (which has a default of 30) controls its lifetime. The cookie can be protected using encryption, a validation key attached to the data, or both. The *protection* attribute specifies how the protection is implemented. The default is *All*, which means both *Validation* and *Encryption* flags are used. The initial attempt to authenticate is conducted through the cookie. If it fails, a login page is displayed. The URL of the login page is returned by the *loginURL* attribute and is login.aspx by default.

> **Note** In version 1.1 of the .NET Framework, *requireSSL* (*false*) and *slidingExpiration* (*true*) are also supported. The former indicates whether the cookie should be sent only over SSL (Secure Sockets Layer). The latter specifies whether the cookie should automatically be reissued if it is about to expire.

The *<forms>* section supports the *<credentials>* element, which in turn has a nested *<user>* element. The *<credentials>* element lets you define the user credentials against which authentication should be performed. You should avoid using the *<credentials>* element because you end up having passwords stored in a text file. The *<credentials>* element features a *passwordFormat* attribute to set the encryption algorithm to use to protect the user's password.

```
<credentials passwordFormat="SHA1">
    <user name="joe" password="..." />
</credentials>
```

Finally, when the *Passport* mode is used, the entire burden of authentication is shifted to the *Passport* services. However, the *redirectURL* attribute on the *<passport>* element lets you specify the page to redirect to if authentication is required but the user is unknown to the *Passport* service.

The *<authorization>* Section

The *<authorization>* section is used to define a declarative filter to control access to the resources of the application. The *<authorization>* section contains two subsections named *<allow>* and *<deny>*, which can be used to allow and deny access to users. Both elements feature three attributes—*users*, *roles*, and *verbs*—filled with a comma-separated list of names, as the following code demonstrates:

```
<authorization>
    <allow users="comma-separated list of users"
           roles="comma-separated list of roles"
           verbs="comma-separated list of verbs" />

    <deny users="comma-separated list of users"
          roles="comma-separated list of roles"
          verbs="comma-separated list of verbs" />
</authorization>
```

The *<allow>* element authorizes access to any user whose name appears in the list—that is, to all users with any of the specified roles. Authorized users can execute only the HTTP verbs (for example, *POST* and *GET*) indicated by the *verbs* attribute.

Conversely, the *<deny>* element prohibits listed users from executing the specified actions. The default setting allows all users free access to the resources of the application. When specifying the user name, a couple of shortcuts are allowed. The asterisk (*) means all users, whereas the question mark (?) stands for the anonymous user.

The *<browserCaps>* Section

The *<browserCaps>* section enumerates the characteristics and capabilities of the supported browsers, including—in version 1.1 of the .NET Framework—mobile devices. The *<browserCaps>* section is tightly coupled with the *HttpBrowserCapabilities* class (and *MobileCapabilities* in version 1.1), which allows the ASP.NET runtime to gather technical information about the browser that is running on the client. An ASP.NET application identifies the browser through the *Browser* property of the intrinsic *Request* object. Internally, the *Request* object first looks at the user-agent information that comes with the HTTP request and then matches this information against the content of the *<browserCaps>* section. If a match is found, an instance of the *HttpBrowserCapabilities* class is created and filled with the available information. The newly created object is then made available to the application via the *Browser* property.

> **Note** To detect the capabilities of a mobile device, you use the same *Request.Browser* property. In this case, though, you might want to cast the return value to *MobileCapabilities*. The *MobileCapabilities* class inherits from and extends the *HttpBrowserCapabilities* class.

Under the *<browserCaps>* section, you find a fair number of commercial browsers described in terms of their run-time capabilities, such as cookies, tables and frames support, script languages accepted, XML DOM, and operating system. The element can be declared at any level in the application, thus making it possible for you to enable certain levels of browser support for certain applications. The list of available browsers can be updated as required to detect future browsers and browser capabilities.

The *<clientTarget>* Section

The *<clientTarget>* section adds aliases for specific user agents that ASP.NET pages can target through the *ClientTarget* property. In other words, the *<clientTarget>* section defines the allowable values for the *ClientTarget* property of the *Page*. By default, the following aliases are defined: *ie5*, *ie4*, *uplevel*, and *downlevel*. As the names suggest, the first two indicate Internet Explorer 5.5 and Internet Explorer 4.0, respectively. Note that in ASP.NET, an up-level browser is meant to be Internet Explorer 4.0 (the first browser to support Dynamic HTML), while a down-level browser is currently undefined.

```
<clientTarget>
    <add alias="ie5" userAgent="Mozilla/4.0 (compatible; MSIE 5.5; ...)"/>
    <add alias="ie4" userAgent="Mozilla/4.0 (compatible; MSIE 4.0; ...)"/>
    <add alias="uplevel" userAgent="Mozilla/4.0 (compatible; MSIE 4.0; ...)/>
    <add alias="downlevel" userAgent="Unknown"/>
</clientTarget>
```

Bear in mind that setting the *ClientTarget* property to one of the values listed by the *<clientTarget>* section forces the *HttpBrowserCapabilities* object for the page to return the capabilities of the specified browser, rather than the capabilities of the actual requesting client.

The *<compilation>* Section

The *<compilation>* section contains all the default settings the ASP.NET runtime uses when it compiles requested pages. In this section, you'll find information about automatically referenced assemblies, compiler options, and languages available for ASP.NET pages. The *<compilation>* section features the attributes shown in Table 12-7.

Table 12-7 Compilation Attributes

Attribute	Description
batch	Indicates whether page batch compilation is supported. Feasible values are *true* or *false*. The default is *true*.
batchTimeout	Indicates the time-out period (in seconds) for batch compilation. If batch compilation cannot be completed in 15 seconds, the current page is compiled to a single assembly. Previously compiled pages remain in the batched assembly.
debug	Indicates whether to include or not to debug information in the generated assemblies. The default is *false*.
defaultLanguage	Specifies the default programming language for ASP.NET pages. Feasible language names are defined in the *<compiler>* subtag. The default is *VB*.
explicit	Specifies the setting (*true* or *false*) of the Visual Basic *Explicit* compile option. The default is *true*.
maxBatchGeneratedFileSize	Specifies the maximum size (in KB) of the generated page class files that can fit in a batch compilation. The setting is meant to control the final size of the generated page assemblies. By default, this is set to *3000KB*.
maxBatchFileSize	Specifies the maximum number of pages per batch compilation. By default, this is set to *1000 pages*.
numRecompilesBeforeAppRestart	Indicates the number of page recompiles that can occur before the AppDomain is restarted to prevent performance degradation. The default is *15*. The attribute is not supported at the directory level—that is, in a child web.config file.
strict	Indicates the setting (*true* or *false*) of the Visual Basic *Strict* compile option. The default is *false*.
tempDirectory	Specifies the directory in which temporary files generated during compilation should be stored. By default, files are stored in the same directory as the generated assemblies.

The *<compilation>* tag contains two subtags—*<assemblies>* and *<compiler>*. The former tag defines all the assemblies that are automatically referenced by the page compiler. The latter tag enumerates the available ASP.NET compilers. To define the assemblies to reference or to remove an assembly from the list of references, you use *<add>*, *<remove>*, and *<clear>* tags and identify assemblies by name, not by path and extension. The asterisk (*) character denotes all assemblies in the application's Bin directory and in the .NET Framework installation path.

```
<assemblies>
    <add assembly="..." />
    <remove assembly="..." />
    <clear />
</assemblies>
```

The *<remove>* tag doesn't accept wildcards (*) for the *assembly* attribute. In addition, the assembly name must match the name of an assembly that has been previously added using *<add>*. The *<clear>* tag removes from compilation all assemblies defined in upper-level directories. The list of default assemblies has been discussed in the "The Processing Directives of a Page" section in Chapter 1. A new assembly is automatically linked in the .NET Framework version 1.1 for mobile controls. If you don't want to target those browsers, drop the assembly in the application's web.config file.

```
<compilation>
    <assembly remove="System.Web.Mobile ..." />
</compilation>
```

The *<compilers>* section defines the aliases you can use to specify the language of a page. The aliases are specified using the *language* attribute. The *extension* attribute denotes the file extensions allowed for that language. Finally, the *type* attribute indicates the name of the class that provides the compiler object model and the related assembly. In the .NET Framework version 1.1, the J# compiler has been added.

```
<compilers>
    <compiler language="c#;cs;csharp" extension=".cs"
        type="Microsoft.CSharp.CSharpCodeProvider, System,
            Version=1.0.5000.0, Culture=neutral,
            PublicKeyToken=b77a5c561934e089"
            warningLevel="1" />
    <compiler language="vb;vbs;visualbasic;vbscript" extension=".vb"
        type="Microsoft.VisualBasic.VBCodeProvider, System,
            Version=1.0.5000.0, Culture=neutral,
            PublicKeyToken=b77a5c561934e089" />
    <compiler language="js;jscript;javascript" extension=".js"
        type="Microsoft.JScript.JScriptCodeProvider, Microsoft.JScript,
            Version=7.0.5000.0, Culture=neutral,
            PublicKeyToken=b03f5f7f11d50a3a" />
    <compiler language="VJ#;VJS;VJSharp" extension=".jsl"
        type="Microsoft.VJSharp.VJSharpCodeProvider, VJSharpCodeProvider,
            Version=7.0.5000.0, Culture=neutral,
            PublicKeyToken=b03f5f7f11d50a3a" />
</compilers>
```

A couple of optional attributes for the <*compilers*> section are *warningLevel* and *compilerOptions*. You can use these attributes to specify the desired warning level and any other extra compiler options you need.

The <*customErrors*> Section

The <*customErrors*> section specifies the error-handling policy for an ASP.NET application. By default, when an error occurs on a page, the local host sees the detailed ASP.NET error page, while remote clients are shown a custom error page or a generic page if no custom page is specified. This policy is controlled through the *Mode* attribute. The *Mode* attribute can be set to *On*, *Off*, or *RemoteOnly*, which is the default. If set to *On*, custom error pages are displayed both locally and remotely; if set to *Off*, no special error-handling mechanism is active and all users receive the typical ASP.NET error page with the original runtime's or compiler's error message and the stack trace.

Error pages can be specified in two ways. You can provide a generic error page as well as error-specific pages. The custom but generic error page is set through the *defaultRedirect* attribute of the <*customErrors*> element. This setting is ignored if the mode is *Off*.

```
<customErrors defaultRedirect="Errors/appGenericErr.aspx" mode="On">
    <error statusCode="404" redirect="Errors/notfound.aspx" />
    <error statusCode="500" redirect="Errors/internal.aspx" />
</customErrors>
```

The <*customErrors*> section supports a repeatable child <*error*> tag that is used to associate a custom page with a particular error code. You should note that only certain status codes are supported. Some error codes, such as 403, might come directly from IIS and never get to ASP.NET. The <*error*> tag has two optional attributes, *redirect* and *statusCode*. The *redirect* attribute points to the URL of the page, whereas *statusCode* specifies the HTTP status code that will result in an error. If custom mode is enabled but no error-specific page is known, the default redirect is used. If custom mode is enabled but no custom page is specified, the ASP.NET generic error page is used.

The <*deviceFilters*> Section

This <*deviceFilters*> section is new to version 1.1 of the .NET Framework and is aimed at improving device-specific rendering of mobile Web Forms pages. The tight integration between mobile controls and the Web Forms architecture makes ASP.NET mobile pages capable of rendering to a variety of devices automatically. The settings in the <*mobileControls*> section of machine.config map some of the Web controls to device-specific classes through underlying driver classes known as *adapters*. This scheme works well as long as you can assume that a control, say a link, is always rendered with the same type of control on various devices. If this is not the case, and if on a certain device a link must be rendered differently, say by using a button, the developer must make a specific effort to render the link.

To customize a mobile Web Forms application for specific types of devices, you define a set of device filters for the application, and then in the code specify the filter to use for each type of device. For example, the following code uses the *<DeviceSpecific><Choice>* construct:

```
<mobile:Image runat=server ImageURL="bw.gif">
    <DeviceSpecific>
        <Choice Filter="isColor" ImageURL="colorImg.gif" />
        <Choice Filter="IsWML" ImageURL="myImage.wbmp" />
    </DeviceSpecific>
</mobile:Image>
```

The device-specific filters are defined in machine.config or web.config by using a syntax similar to the following:

```
<system.web>
    <deviceFilters>
        <filter
            name="filterName"
            compare="capabilityName"
            argument="argument" />
        <filter
            name="filterName"
            type="className"
            method="methodName" />
    </deviceFilters>
</system.web>
```

ASP.NET defines two types of device filters: comparison evaluators and evaluator delegates. With comparison evaluators, ASP.NET reads the *compare* attribute value from the connected device and compares it to the *argument* value. If the comparison to perform requires more complex code, you define an *evaluator* method in a class. The name of the class is set in the *type* attribute, whereas the name of the method is set in the *method* attribute. The signature of the method is as follows:

```
static bool EvaluatorMethod(
    MobileCapabilities capabilities,
    string compareArgument)
```

The *<globalization>* Section

The *<globalization>* section configures the globalization settings of ASP.NET applications, so that requests and responses take into account encoding and culture information. The attributes of the *<globalization>* section are shown in Table 12-8.

Table 12-8 Globalization Attributes

Attribute	Description
requestEncoding	Specifies the assumed encoding of each incoming request, including posted data and the query string; default is *UTF-8*.
responseEncoding	Specifies the content encoding of responses; default is *UTF-8*.
fileEncoding	Specifies the encoding for ASP.NET resource files (.aspx, .asmx, and .asax). Unicode and UTF-8 files saved with the byte order mark prefix are recognized regardless of the value of *fileEncoding*.
culture	Specifies the culture to be used to process requests.
uiCulture	Specifies the culture name the Resource Manager should use to look up locale-dependent resources at run time.

Note that, if specified, the *Accept-Charset* attribute in the request overrides the default *requestEncoding* setting. If you remove any encoding setting from the configuration files, ASP.NET defaults to the server's locale. In the majority of cases, *requestEncoding* and *responseEncoding* have the same value.

Valid names for the *culture* and *uiCulture* attributes are non-neutral culture names such as *en-US*, *en-AU*, and *it-IT*. A culture name is made of two elements—the language and country—and both are to be specified in this context.

The *<httpHandlers>* Section

The *<httpHandlers>* section lists all HTTP handlers currently registered to process incoming requests. This section supports *<add>*, *<remove>*, and *<clear>* tags. The *<add>* elements are processed sequentially. If an identical verb/path combination is specified at a lower configuration level (for example, in a child web.config), the last call wins and overrides the previous setting. To add a new HTTP handler, you must specify attributes as shown below:

```
<add verb="*" path="*.aspx" type="System.Web.UI.PageHandlerFactory"/>
```

Table 12-9 describes the *<add>* tag attributes.

Table 12-9 *<add>* Attributes for HTTP Handlers

Attribute	Description
path	Specifies the path to the resources on which the handler will operate. Typically, the path is either the name of a single resource or a wildcard expression such as *.aspx. All resources identified by the path will be handled by the specified class.
type	Comma-separated string that contains the name of the handler class and the assembly in which the class is defined.
validate	Optional attribute that controls the loading policy of the handlers. If set to *false*, the handler won't be loaded until strictly necessary to serve a request.
verb	Indicates the HTTP verbs that trigger the handler. It can be a comma-separated list of verbs (for example, "GET, PUT, POST") or the asterisk (*), which means all HTTP verbs.

To be effective, the *<remove>* directive must exactly match the verb and path of a previous *<add>* attribute. Wildcard characters are not supported.

The *<httpModules>* Section

The *<httpModules>* section lists all HTTP modules currently registered to hook up requests as they are processed by the ASP.NET pipeline. Similar to *<httpHandlers>*, the *<httpModules>* section supports *<add>*, *<remove>*, and *<clear>* tags. Also in this case, *<add>* elements are processed in a top-down fashion and settings defined at an upper level can be overridden in child configuration files.

The *<add>* element supports only the *name* and *type* attributes. The *name* attribute assigns a friendly and possibly evocative name to the module. This name is used to define ad hoc handlers for the module's events in the global.asax file. For example, the *Session_Start* event handler in the global.asax owes its name to the following declaration in the *<httpModules>* section:

```
<add name="Session" type="System.Web.SessionState.SessionStateModule" />
```

The name *Session* identifies the *SessionStateModule*. Such a module fires two events, named *Start* and *End*. Default handlers for those events in the global.asax follow a common naming convention that uses the name of the object plus an underscore (_) and the name of the event.

The *type* attribute on the *<add>* element points to a comma-separated string formed by the name of the class and the related assembly.

The *<httpRuntime>* Section

The *<httpRuntime>* section configures some run-time parameters for the ASP.NET pipeline. Interestingly enough, the section can be declared at any level, including subdirectory levels. This fact accounts for the great flexibility that allows you to set up the run-time environment with the finest granularity. Configurable attributes are listed in Table 12-10.

Table 12-10 ASP.NET Runtime Attributes

Attribute	Description
appRequestQueueLimit	Specifies the maximum number of requests the application is allowed to queue before returning error 503—Server too busy. The default is *100*.
enableKernelOutputCache	Enables the http.sys cache on IIS 6.0 and higher. The default is *true*. Ignored under IIS 5.0. *Supported only in version 1.1 of the .NET Framework.*
enableVersionHeader	Outputs a header with the ASP.NET version with each request. The default is *true*. *Supported only in version 1.1 of the .NET Framework.*
executionTimeout	Specifies the maximum number of seconds a request is allowed to execute before ASP.NET automatically times it out. The default is *90* seconds.
maxRequestLength	Indicates the maximum accepted size (in KB) of a Web request. No request is accepted if its overall length exceeds the threshold of 4 MB.
minLocalRequestFreeThreads	Indicates the minimum number of free threads to allow execution of new local requests. The default threshold value is set to *4*.
minFreeThreads	Indicates the minimum number of free threads needed to allow execution of new Web requests. The default threshold value is set to *8*.
useFullyQualifiedRedirectUrl	Indicates whether client redirects must be automatically converted to fully qualified URLs (*true*) or used as specified in the page source code (*false*). The default is *false*.

Note that ASP.NET won't process a request if not enough free threads are available in the thread pool. When this happens, the request is queued to the application until the threshold set by the *appRequestQueueLimit* is exceeded. But why, in the default case, does ASP.NET need at least 8 free threads to execute a request? These free threads are at the disposal of ongoing requests (for example, downloads of linked images, style sheets, and user controls) should they issue child requests to complete processing.

Another small number of threads (*4* by default) is kept reserved for child requests coming through the local host. If the request has been generated locally—that is, the client IP is 127.0.0.1 or matches the server IP—it is scheduled on one of the threads in the pool reserved for local calls. Often local requests originate as child requests—for example, when an ASP.NET page invokes a Web service on the same server. There's no need in this case to consume two threads from the pool to serve two related requests, one of which is waiting for the other to terminate. By using an additional thread pool, you actually assign local requests a slightly higher priority and reduce the risk of deadlocks.

The *<identity>* Section

The *<identity>* section controls the identity of the ASP.NET application. It supports three attributes: *impersonate*, *userName*, and *password*. The key attribute is *impersonate*, which is set to *false* by default, which means the application does not impersonate any client user.

```
<identity impersonate="true" />
```

When *impersonate* is set to *true*, each request is served by ASP.NET impersonating either the Windows user currently logged on or the user specified through the *userName* and *password* attributes.

The *<machineKey>* Section

Valid at the machine and application levels, the *<machineKey>* section configures the keys to encrypt and decrypt the data in the cookie used with forms authentication.

```
<machineKey
    validationKey="AutoGenerate"
    decryptionKey="AutoGenerate"
    validation="SHA1" />
```

Supported attributes are *validationKey*, *decryptionKey*, and *validation*. The first two attributes specify the encryption and decryption keys. An encryption key is a sequence of characters whose length ranges from a minimum of 40 to a maximum of 128 characters. The *validation* attribute, on the other hand, indicates the type of encryption used. Allowable values are *SHA1* (the default), *MD5*, and *3DES*.

By default, the validation keys are autogenerated at setup time and stored in the Local Security Authority (LSA). LSA is a protected subsystem of Windows NT–based operating systems that maintains information about all aspects of local security on a system.

The *<mobileControls>* Section

This *<mobileControls>* section is supported in version 1.1 of the .NET Framework and defines mappings between ASP.NET mobile controls and adapter classes. To support multiple devices, the mobile Web Forms architecture employs a driver-like model based on the concept of a device adapter. ASP.NET mobile pages and controls are totally device independent, but under the hood a set of ad hoc classes, called *device adapters*, provide a device-specific presentation layer. Let's consider the following excerpt from machine.config:

```
<device name="WmlDeviceAdapters"
    predicateClass="System.Web.UI.MobileControls.Adapters.WmlPageAdapter"
    predicateMethod="DeviceQualifies"
    pageAdapter="System.Web.UI.MobileControls.Adapters.WmlPageAdapter">
    <control name="System.Web.UI.MobileControls.Panel"
        adapter="System.Web.UI.MobileControls.Adapters.WmlPanelAdapter />
⋮
</device>
```

The output for WML-enabled devices (for example, cell phones) is generated by the *WmlPageAdapter* class, while the control *Panel* is rendered through the *WmlPanelAdapter* class. The classes involved change if you look at another type of device, but the high-level front-end—that is, the code you write in Visual Studio—is always the same. The *predicateClass* and *predicateMethod* attributes point to a static method in the specified class that is called to evaluate whether the adapter set is appropriate for the current device.

The *<pages>* Section

The *<pages>* section sets default values for many of the *@Page* directive attributes and declaratively configures the run-time environment for a Web page. Table 12-11 enumerates the supported attributes.

Table 12-11 Attributes to Configure ASP.NET Pages

Attribute	Description
autoEventWireup	Indicates whether page events are automatically assigned to event handlers with a particular name (for example, *Page_Load*). Set to *true* by default.
buffer	Indicates whether or not response buffering is enabled. Set to *true* by default.
enableSessionState	Indicates whether session state is enabled. Set to *true* by default; also accepts as values *false* and *ReadOnly*. The session state is disabled altogether if the attribute is set to *false*; it is accessible only for reading if set to *ReadOnly*.

(continued)

Table 12-11 Attributes to Configure ASP.NET Pages *(continued)*

Attribute	Description
enableViewState	Specifies whether view state is enabled. Set to *true* by default.
enableViewStateMac	Specifies whether the view state of a page should be checked for tampering on each page postback. Set to *true* by default.
pageBaseType	Indicates the base code-behind class that .aspx pages inherit by default—that is, unless a code-behind class is explicitly provided. The default class is *System.Web.UI.Page*. The new class name must include assembly information.
userControlBaseType	Indicates the code-behind class that .ascx user controls inherit by default. The default class is *System.Web.UI.UserControl*. The new class name must include assembly information.
validateRequest	Indicates that ASP.NET examines all input from the browser for potentially dangerous data. Set to *true* by default. *Supported only in version 1.1 of the .NET Framework.*

In particular, the *pageBaseType* attribute (and likewise the *userControlBaseType* attribute) is an extremely powerful setting you might want to leverage when all your application pages inherit from a common code-behind class. In this case, instead of modifying all the pages, you centralize the setting in the web.config file at the level (machine, application, or subdirectory) you want.

The *validateRequest* attribute is a new security-related feature of the .NET Framework version 1.1 designed to add a small line of defense against naïve implementations of Web applications. If set to *true*—the default—ASP.NET uses a regular expression to check form fields and query strings for potentially malicious values. If a match is found, ASP.NET rejects the request and raises an *HttpRequestValidationException* exception. Bear in mind that *validateRequest* is not a silver bullet that can stop all attacks. We'll return to security best-practices in Chapter 15, but for now realize that instead of relying on the services of *validateRequest*, a well-done application should implement a serious data-validation layer.

The *<processModel>* Section

This section configures the ASP.NET process model—that is, the procedure that brings an ASP.NET Web request to be processed in the ASP.NET HTTP pipeline. Note that under IIS 5.0 the attributes of the *<processModel>* section are actually read by unmanaged code—the *aspnet_isapi.dll* ISAPI extension. For this reason, you need to restart IIS to apply changes. For the same reason, you can never override any section attributes in a web.config file. The *<processModel>* section can exist only within a machine.config file.

Table 12-12 lists the parameters you can set to fine-tune the ASP.NET process model under IIS 5.0. Some of the following attributes might remind you of attributes we've already covered in other sections. Bear in mind, though, the attributes listed in Table 12-12 affect the ASP.NET worker process (*aspnet_wp.exe*) rather than a particular ASP.NET Web application.

Table 12-12 Configuring the IIS 5.0 ASP.NET Process Model

Attribute	Description
clientConnectedCheck	Indicates how long a request can stay in the queue before ASP.NET checks whether the client is still connected. The default is *5* seconds.
comAuthenticationLevel	Specifies the authentication level for DCOM security. Can be *Default*, *None*, *Connect*, *Call*, *Pkt*, *PktIntegrity*, or *PktPrivacy*. The default setting is *Connect*.
comImpersonationLevel	Specifies the impersonation level for COM security. Can be *Default*, *Anonymous*, *Identify*, *Impersonate*, or *Delegate*. The default setting is *Impersonate*.
cpuMask	Bitmask that indicates which CPUs can run worker processes in a multiprocessor environment. The attribute is used only if *webGarden* is *true*. The aspnet_isapi.dll schedules one process per each CPU set in the mask. By default, all CPUs are *enabled*.
enabled	Specifies whether the process model is enabled. The default is *true* on IIS 5.0 and *false* on IIS 6.0.
idleTimeout	Indicates the time after which the process is automatically terminated if idle. The default is *Infinite*.
logLevel	Specifies the type of events to be logged to the event log. Acceptable values include *All*, *None*, and the default *Errors*. When set to *All*, all events are logged; when set to *None*, no event is ever logged. When set to *Errors*, memory limits, deadlocks, and process-recycling shutdowns are recorded, in addition to unexpected failures.
maxWorkerThreads	Indicates the maximum number of worker threads per CPU in the thread pool. The default is *20* (a total of 20xN threads on a machine with N CPUs).
maxIoThreads	Indicates the maximum number of IO threads per CPU in the thread pool. The default is *20* (a total of 20xN threads on a machine with N CPUs).
memoryLimit	Indicates the percentage of the system's memory the process is authorized to consume before it is restarted. The default is set to *60%*.

(continued)

Table 12-12 Configuring the IIS 5.0 ASP.NET Process Model *(continued)*

Attribute	Description
password	Along with *userName*, determines the identity of the ASP.NET process. By default, it is set to *AutoGenerate*—a special keyword used in conjunction with the *userName* value of *Machine* to make the process run under the ASP-NET account.
pingFrequency	Indicates the frequency used by aspnet_isapi.dll to ping ASP.NET worker processes. By default, processes are pinged every *30* seconds.
pingTimeout	Indicates the time after which aspnet_isapi.dll restarts a nonresponsive process. By default, the process is given *5* seconds to respond if pinged.
requestLimit	Indicates the number of requests the ASP.NET worker process can serve before being shut down and replaced. The default is *Infinite*.
requestQueueLimit	Indicates the number of requests the ASP.NET process can queue before returning error 503 (Server too busy.) The default is *5000*.
responseDeadlockInterval	Indicates the time after which a process with queued requests that has not returned a response is considered deadlocked and is shut down. The default is *3* minutes.
responseRestartDeadlock-Interval	Indicates the time that must elapse between two successive process restarts due to deadlocks. This is set to *9* minutes by default.
restartQueueLimit	Indicates the number of requests kept in queue while the ASP.NET process is restarting. The default value is *10*.
serverErrorMessageFile	Indicates the name of the file whose contents will be used as the error message in case of fatal errors. If specified, the file must have a fully qualified path or a path relative to the location of machine.config. The attribute is not set by default, and the "Server Unavailable" message is used.
shutdownTimeout	Specifies the time allowed for the worker process to shut itself down once timed out. If the process fails, the aspnet_isapi.dll kills it. The default timeout is *5* seconds.
timeout	Specifies the allowed lifetime (in minutes) for the ASP.NET worker process. Once expired, the process is shut down and ASP.NET launches a new process. The default lifetime is *Infinite*.

Table 12-12 Configuring the IIS 5.0 ASP.NET Process Model *(continued)*

Attribute	Description
userName	Along with *password*, determines the identity of the ASP.NET process. By default, the attribute is set to *Machine*, which runs the process under the unprivileged ASPNET account. By changing this attribute, you can have the ASP.NET process impersonate a given Windows user (for example, *System*). If a domain is not specified, the current machine name is assumed to be the domain name.
webGarden	If set to *false*, indicates that a single worker process is used. On a Web garden machine, the CPU usage is scheduled by Windows. When set to *true*, the *cpuMask* attribute is used to indicate which CPUs can run ASP.NET processes. At most, one process per CPU is allowed. *webGarden* is set to *false* by default.

Note that time quantities are typically expressed in the HH:MM:SS format. For example, the 00:00:05 string is interpreted as 5 seconds. The word *Infinite* indicates an infinite time or an infinite number as appropriate.

When ASP.NET runs under IIS 6.0 in native mode, the IIS 6.0 process model is used. The net effect of this is that all settings in the *<processModel>* section are ignored in favor of similar settings entered in the IIS 6.0 metabase through ad hoc user interface (UI) tools.

The *<securityPolicy>* Section

In the *<securityPolicy>* section, you define xxxmappings between security levels and policy files. The section can be configured at the application level but not in subdirectories. The section contains one or more *<trustLevel>* elements with *name* and *policyFile* attributes.

```
<securityPolicy>
    <trustLevel name="Full" policyFile="internal" />
    <trustLevel name="High" policyFile="web_hightrust.config" />
    <trustLevel name="Medium" policyFile="web_mediumtrust.config"/>
    <trustLevel name="Low" policyFile="web_lowtrust.config" />
    <trustLevel name="Minimal" policyFile="web_minimaltrust.config"/>
</securityPolicy>
```

The *name* attribute can be set to *Full*, *High*, or *Low* in all versions of the .NET Framework. In version 1.1, *Minimal* and *Medium* levels are also allowed. The *None* level, on the other hand, is supported only in version 1.0 of the .NET Framework. Each trust level identifies a particular security level that you map to a policy file in a *<trustLevel>* element.

```
<trustLevel name="None" policyFile="web_notrust.config" />
```

Note that in ASP.NET the *Full* level of trust doesn't need to have an associated policy file full of permission sets and code-group definitions. The reason is that ASP.NET doesn't add extra security settings in case of *Full* trust, so in such cases the content of the *policyFile* attribute is ignored.

The *<sessionState>* Section

The *<sessionState>* section stores session-state settings for the current application. The section determines behavior and implementation details of the ASP.NET *Session* object. The *Session* object can work in different modes to accommodate the application's requirements for performance, robustness, and data reliability. The *mode* attribute determines the working mode of *Session*—one of the ASP.NET intrinsic objects we'll cover in greater detail in Chapter 14.

In Table 12-13, you can see the list of acceptable attributes for the element. The *mode* attribute is the only mandatory attribute. Some attributes are mutually exclusive.

Table 12-13 Session-State Attributes

Attribute	Description
cookieless	Boolean setting that specifies whether sessions should use cookies. By default, this is set to *false*, which means cookies are used to identify client sessions.
mode	Specifies the implementation mode of the *Session* object. Acceptable values are *Off*, *InProc*, *StateServer*, and *SQLServer*. When set to *Off*, session-state management is disabled and the *Session* object is not available to the application. *InProc* is the default working mode and stores session data locally in the Web server's memory. This behavior is identical to ASP applications. Alternatively, the session state can be stored on a remote server (*StateServer*) or in a SQL Server database (*SQLServer*).

sqlConnectionString	Used when *mode* is set to *SQLServer*; specifies the connection string for the SQL Server database to use for storing session data. The default connection string in machine.config can be one of the following:
	`data source=127.0.0.1;uid=sa;pwd=`
	`data source=127.0.0.1;Integrated Security=SSPI`

Table 12-13 Session-State Attributes

Attribute	Description
stateConnectionString	Used when *mode* is set to *StateServer*; specifies the server name and port where session state should be stored. The default string is: `tcpip=127.0.0.1:42424`
stateNetworkTimeout	Indicates the timeout in seconds for network operations when the mode is *StateServer*. By default, this is set to *10*.
timeout	Indicates how long a session can be idle before expiring. The timeout is expressed in minutes and is *20* by default.

The *<sessionState>* section contains declarations and configuration data, but more is needed to have the *Session* object work outside of the ASP.NET process. In Chapter 14, we'll cover the *Session* object in detail. We'll also review the steps necessary to set up and configure a remote server or SQL Server database to store session data.

The *<trace>* Section

Tracing refers to the program's capability of sending informative messages about the status of the execution. In general, *tracing* represents a way to monitor the behavior of an application in a production environment, whereas *debugging* is used for development time testing. We covered tracing and debugging in Chapter 4.

In the .NET Framework, tracing is provided through a unified, abstract API that utilizes ad hoc drivers to physically output the messages. These drivers are called *listeners* and redirect the tracing output to the specified target—typically a log file or an output stream. ASP.NET tracing is just an aspect of.NET Framework tracing. You can configure ASP.NET tracing at two levels and in two different group sections of the configuration files—*<system.diagnostics>* and *<system.web>*. In both cases, the actual section with configuration data is named *<trace>*.

In the *<system.diagnostics>* group section, the *<trace>* section features two attributes—named *autoflush* and *indentsize*—and a couple of child elements—*<listeners>* and *<switches>*. *autoflush* specifies whether all registered trace listeners automatically flush the buffer after every write operation. The default is *false*. *indentsize* simply indicates how many blanks are to be used to indent the output text. The default indentation size is four blanks.

Under the *<listeners>* element, you can register a particular listener class so that it will receive from any trace information that the pages generate. Listeners are registered using the familiar *<add>*, *<remove>*, and *<clear>* subelements.

```
<listeners>
    <add name="MyListener"
        type="System.Diagnostics.TextWriterTraceListener,System"
        initializeData="MyApp.log" />
</listeners>
```

To add a listener to the ASP.NET tracing system, you must give it a name and indicate the class and assembly in which it resides. In the preceding code snippet, we registered a listener that writes to the MyApp.log file. The listener is not based on a custom class but is simply an instance of one of the system-provided listeners—the class *TextWriteTraceListener*. Finally, *initializeData* is an optional attribute that must be set with any string you need to pass to the listener's constructor. Whether this attribute is optional or mandatory depends on the characteristics of the listener. The text writer listener needs it to be the name of the log file.

If you create custom listeners, the *<switches>* element lets you define dynamic parameters for controlling the activity of the listener at run time.

The *<trace>* element in the *<system.web>* section defines attributes that can modify the behavior of application-level tracing. The attributes are listed in Table 12-14.

Table 12-14 Application-Level ASP.NET Tracing Attributes

Attribute	Description
enabled	Set to *true* or *false*, depending on whether you want to enable tracing or not. The default is *false*.
localOnly	Setting of *true* makes the trace viewer application (trace.axd) available only on the local host; *false* makes it available also remotely. The default is *true*.
pageOutput	If *true*, trace output is displayed both in the trace viewer and in each requested page; if *false*, the output goes only to the viewer. The default is *false*. Regardless of this global setting, individual pages can enable tracing using the *Trace* attribute of the *@Page* directive.
requestLimit	Indicates the maximum number of trace results available in trace.axd. The default value is *10*.
traceMode	Indicates the criteria by which trace records are to be sorted and displayed. Acceptable values are *SortByTime* (the default) or *SortByCategory*. Sorting by time means that records are displayed in the order in which they are generated. A category, on the other hand, is a user-defined name that can be optionally specified in the trace text.

The *<trust>* Section

The *<trust>* section configures the trust level under which the application will be run and determines the code-access security restrictions applied to the application. The default value is *Full*, which means ASP.NET applications run on the Web server as fully trusted applications and are allowed to do whatever their account is allowed to do. In other words, the CLR is not sandboxing the code. The actual security restrictions applied to ASP.NET applications (for example, the inability to write files or write to the registry) are not a sign of partial trust, but more simply the effect of the underprivileged account (ASPNET) under which ASP.NET applications normally run.

The following code snippet shows the default *<trust>* setting in machine.config. Note that the *<trust>* section cannot be set at a subdirectory level:

```
<trust level="Full" originUrl="" />
```

Allowable values for the *level* attribute are all the *<trustLevel>* entries defined in the *<securityPolicy>* section. The *originUrl* attribute is a sort of misnomer. If you set it, what really happens is quite simple: the specified URL is granted the permission to access an HTTP resource using either a *Socket* or *WebRequest* class. The permission class involved with this is *WebPermission*. Of course, the Web permission is granted only if the specified *<trust>* level supports that. *Medium* and higher trust levels do.

> **Note** The *<trust>* section can be allowed only at the machine level and application level because of technical reasons, not because of security concerns. An ASP.NET application runs in its own AppDomain, and the trust level for that application is set applying the appropriate security policy to the AppDomain. Although policy statements can target specific pieces of code, the AppDomain is the lowest level at which a security policy can be applied. If the CLR has a policy level more granular than the AppDomain, you can define different trust levels for various portions of the ASP.NET application.

The *<webControls>* Section

The *<webControls>* section contains only the *clientScriptsLocation* attribute that specifies the default path to ASP.NET client script files. These files are included in the HTML code generated for .aspx pages when these pages require client-side functionalities such as smart navigation and client-side control validation.

```
<webControls clientScriptsLocation="/aspnet_client/{0}/{1}/" />
```

The preceding code snippet represents the default contents of the *<webControls>* section. The content of *clientScriptsLocation*, properly expanded, is the URL used for script includes. The aspnet_client directory is automatically created under the Web server's root when you install ASP.NET. The two placeholders in the string represent subdirectories whose name might change in future versions of ASP.NET. The first placeholder is always set to *system_web*. The second placeholder expands to a subdirectory name based on the version of the .NET Framework.

```
aspnet_client/system_web/1_0_3705_0
```

In version 1.0, the full path used at run time is the one just shown, and the folder contains the following JScript files: smartnav.js, smartnavie5.js, and webuivalidation.js. In version 1.1, only smartnav.js and webuivalidation.js are included, and the folder changes to this:

```
aspnet_client/system_web/1_1_4322_0
```

You can use the same folder to store script files employed by any custom ASP.NET control you might write. You can also change the default path to retrieve the system's client-side file, although I can't see any valid reason for doing so. If you do so, though, make sure you also move or copy the aforementioned .js files.

The *<webServices>* Section

The *<webServices>* section controls the settings of Web services created using ASP.NET. The section contains several subsections to configure the supported protocols, SOAP extensions that need to run, Web services help page, and more. The default content for the section is shown in the following code, and as you can see, contains only information about protocols and help pages:

```
<webServices>
    <protocols>
        <add name="HttpSoap1.2" />
        <add name="HttpSoap" />
        <!-- <add name="HttpPost"/> -->
        <!-- <add name="HttpGet"/> -->
        <add name="HttpPostLocalhost" />
        <add name="Documentation" />
    </protocols>
    <soapExtensionTypes />
    <soapExtensionReflectorTypes />
    <soapExtensionImporterTypes />
    <wsdlHelpGenerator href="DefaultWsdlHelpGenerator.aspx" />
    <serviceDescriptionFormatExtensionTypes />
</webServices>
```

Table 12-15 lists the supported subsections.

Table 12-15 Sections Available to Configure Web Services

Section	Description
protocols	Defines the transmission protocols that ASP.NET supports and can use to decrypt Web service client requests
serviceDescriptionFormatExtensionTypes	Defines additional classes that extend how a service description is generated for all Web services
soapExtensionTypes	Registers the SOAP extensions to run with all the Web services
soapExtensionImporterTypes	Registers the SOAP extensions to run when a service description for a Web service is accessed to create a proxy class
soapExtensionReflectorTypes	Registers the SOAP extensions to run when a service description is generated for all Web services
wsdlHelpGenerator	Specifies the .aspx page that generates the Web service help page displayed when a .asmx Web service is requested

In addition to using SOAP, a Web service can also be invoked through HTTP GET and POST commands. In ASP.NET 1.1, HTTP POST and GET are disabled by default. In version 1.0, if you want to disable HTTP-GET and HTTP-POST for a particular Web service, just remove the related rows in the *<protocols>* section. As an administrator, you might decide to disable HTTP-GET and HTTP-POST for Web only for a particular Web service or for all Web services. In the former case, put the following code in the application's web.config file:

```
<webServices>
    <protocols>
        <remove name="HttpPost" />
        <remove name="HttpGet" />
    </protocols>
</webServices>
```

To disable HTTP-GET and HTTP-POST for all Web services hosted on a Web server, comment the related *<add>* elements out.

```
<protocols>
    <add name="HttpSoap" />
        <!-- <add name="HttpPost" /> -->
        <!-- <add name="HttpGet" />  -->
    <add name="Documentation" />
</protocols>
```

The *Documentation* protocol is the key that enables the ASP.NET runtime to deliver a help page when you point your browser directly to an .asmx resource. If you disable the protocol, no help page will ever be generated when a user navigates to a Web service URL but a "Request format is unrecognized" error is displayed.

If you want to maintain the help page functionality but change the structure and contents of the page, modify the *href* attribute of the *<wsdlHelpGenerator>* element:

```
<webServices>
    <wsdlHelpGenerator href="YourNewGeneratorPage.aspx" />
</webServices>
```

Of course, the help page can be customized for all hosted Web services (by updating machine.config) or only for a particular Web service (by updating web.config).

Reading User Configuration Data

Custom configuration data for ASP.NET applications is normally stored in the *<appSettings>* section and read from there using the *AppSettings* object. The following code snippet shows a simple web.config file that contains the connection string of the application:

```
<configuration>
    <appSettings>
        <add key="ConnectionString" value="..." />
    </appSettings>
</configuration>
```

The syntax of the *<appSettings>* section is defined as follows:

```
<appSettings>
    <add key="..." value="..." />
    <remove key="..." />
    <clear />
</appSettings>
```

The *<add>* element adds a new setting to the internal collection. This new setting has a value and is identified by a unique key. The *<remove>* element removes the specified setting from the collection. The setting is identified using the key. Finally, the *<clear>* element clears all settings that have previously been defined in the section.

Using the *ConfigurationSettings* Class

The connection string is an example of the typical application-specific information you might want to store in web.config. As mentioned, *<appSettings>* is the section reserved for application-specific settings. Settings in *<appSettings>*—for example, a *ConnectionString* parameter—can be read using the following code:

```
string connStr = ConfigurationSettings.AppSettings["ConnectionString"];
```

As mentioned earlier, the *ConfigurationSettings* class is defined in the *System.Configuration* namespace and provides access to settings in a specified configuration section. The *AppSettings* property of the class is a read-only *NameValueCollection* object designed to get the information stored in the *<appSettings>* section. The use of a *NameValueCollection* object stems from the following section declaration in machine.config:

```
<section name="appSettings"
    type="System.Configuration.NameValueFileSectionHandler, System, ..."/>
```

The class responsible for reading the application settings is a section handler—*NameValueFileSectionHandler*—that specifically interprets and packages the read information as name/value pairs. If this scheme does not meet your needs, the most viable workaround is writing your own section handler.

The *NameValueFileSectionHandler* Class

Before going any further with the building of a custom section handler, let me clarify a point about the *<appSettings>* default section handler. The MSDN documentation mentions the *NameValueSectionHandler* class as the default reader of application configuration settings. If you snoop into the machine.config file, though, you'll see that the registered section handler is the *NameValueFileSectionHandler* class. What's up?

The MSDN documentation doesn't provide further information about the *NameValueFileSectionHandler* class; it notes only that the class is intended to be used only by the .NET Framework. The *NameValueFileSectionHandler* class is actually a wrapper for the *NameValueSectionHandler* class and provides an extra, although undocumented, feature. In particular, the *NameValueFileSectionHandler* section handler also allows the application settings to be stored in a separate file in accordance with the following syntax:

```
<configuration>
    <appSettings file="myfile.config" />
</configuration>
```

The contents of the file pointed to by the *file* attribute is read as if it is an *<appSettings>* section in the configuration file. Note that the root element of the file must match *<appSettings>*.

> **Tip** In general, you can use the *NameValueFileSectionHandler* class wherever a *NameValueSectionHandler* is acceptable. In doing so, you automatically inherit the ability of storing settings in an external file. Using external files is advantageous because although any changes will be effective for the application, they do not touch web.config and do not cause page recompilation.

The *NameValueFileSectionHandler* object processes the contents of the embedded file using the *NameValueSectionHandler* class. If no file is embedded in the *<appSettings>* section but the default documented schema is used, the two section handlers are functionally equivalent. Just the possibility of using a linked but external file opens up interesting opportunities to efficiently store ASP.NET user data. We'll return to this shortly in the "Persisting Application Settings" section.

Creating New Configuration Sections

The predefined XML schema for configuration files fits the bill in most cases, but when you have complex and structured information to persist, none of the existing schemas appear to be powerful enough. At this point, you have two possible workarounds. You can simply avoid using a standard configuration file and instead use a plain XML file written according to the schema you feel is appropriate for the data. Alternatively, you can embed your XML configuration data in the standard application configuration file but provide a tailor-made configuration section handler to read it.

Suppose you want to store in a .config file enough information to create a link collection for the page header. Each physical hyperlink is characterized by a URL, a display name, and possibly a ToolTip. You need a table row object to fully represent it. Subsequently, a collection of links becomes a collection of data rows—an ADO.NET *DataTable* object. In this version of the .NET Framework, no section handler object is capable of reading a *DataTable* object out of a .config file or XML stream. The only object that can be read is the *DataSet*. So our goal will be writing a *DataSet* section handler.

A Custom *DataSet* Section Handler

The *DatasetSectionHandler* class implements the *IConfigurationSectionHandler* interface and provides the default empty constructor. The most interesting part of the handler's code is the interface's *Create* method—the only method on the interface:

```
object Create(
    object parent,
    object configContext,
    XmlNode section
);
```

The *Create* method reads the contents specified through the *section* argument and then merges the resultant *DataSet* object with the *parent* object if a non-*null* parent object has been passed. Because configuration inheritance proceeds from top to bottom, the base *DataSet* object for merging is the parent.

The XML data to be parsed is passed via an *XmlNode* object—that is, an object that represents the root of an XML DOM subtree. To make an XML DOM subtree parsable by the *DataSet* object's *ReadXml* method, you must wrap it in an *XmlNodeReader* object—that is, an XML reader object capable of reading the .NET Framework implementation of the XML DOM. The full source code for the *DataSet* section handler is as follows:

```
using System;
using System.Data;
using System.Xml;
using System.Configuration;

namespace ProAspNet.CS.Ch12
{
    public class DatasetSectionHandler : IConfigurationSectionHandler
    {
        // Constructor(s)
        public DatasetSectionHandler()
        {
        }

        // IConfigurationSectionHandler.Create
        public object Create(
        object parent, object context, XmlNode section)
        {
            DataSet ds;

            // Clone the parent DataSet if not null
            if (parent == null)
                ds = new DataSet();
            else
                ds = ((DataSet) parent).Clone();

            // Read the data using a node reader
            DataSet tmp = new DataSet();
            XmlNodeReader nodereader = new XmlNodeReader(section);
            tmp.ReadXml(nodereader);
```

```
                // Merge with the parent and return
                ds.Merge(tmp);
                return ds;
            }
        }
}
```

You can use the *DatasetSectionHandler* class only with a custom section. To define a custom section in a web.config file you resort to the *<configSections>* initial section and define a *<sectionGroup>* and a *<section>*. Note that the *<sectionGroup>* element is optional but strongly recommended to avoid name conflicts. The *type* attribute of the *<section>* element indicates the class name and assembly of the section handler to use.

```
<configuration>
  <configSections>
    <sectionGroup name="MyAspNetApp">
      <section name="Links"
        type="ProAspNet.CS.Ch12.DatasetSectionHandler,
      DatasetSectionHandler_CS" />
    </sectionGroup>
  </configSections>

  <MyAspNetApp>
    <Links>
      <Link>
        <Text>MS Press</Text>
        <URL>http://mspress.microsoft.com</URL>
        <Tooltip>Go to the Microsoft Press Web site</Tooltip>
      </Link>
      <Link>
        <Text>Wintellect</Text>
        <URL>http://www.wintellect.com</URL>
        <Tooltip>Join the Wintellectuals</Tooltip>
      </Link>
    </Links>
  </MyAspNetApp>
</configuration>
```

The actual data finds its place within the MyAspNetApp/Links subtree. To programmatically retrieve this information, you use the *GetConfig* method of the *ConfigurationSettings* class.

```
void Page_Load(object sender, EventArgs e)
{
    DataSet ds;
    ds = (DataSet) ConfigurationSettings.GetConfig("MyAspNetApp/Links");
    BuildPageHeader(ds.Tables["Link"]);
}
```

In the preceding code snippet—an excerpt from the book samples—the internal *BuildPageHeader* procedure extracts the collection of *<link>* elements and processes them to create a tabstrip of hyperlinks as shown in Figure 12-2.

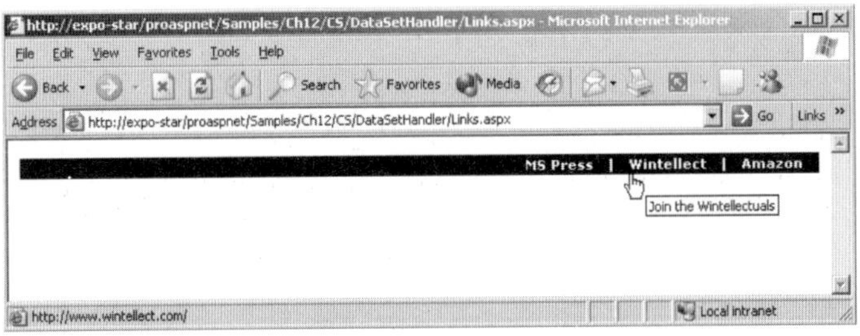

Figure 12-2 A page generated that reads link information from a local web.config file.

Persisting Application Settings

ASP.NET pages might need to persist some settings on the server, although this doesn't happen as frequently as with desktop applications. Keeping in mind that machine.config should never be touched, there are three possibilities for persisting settings on the server: using the *<appSettings>* section of the application's web.config, using a custom XML or text file, or storing information in a database. Determining the best option requires weighing a number of factors, including the amount of information to write, the API used to write, security implications, speed of retrieval, and miscellaneous undesired side-effects.

Writing to web.config

By default, an ASP.NET application has no permission to write to any server-side file, either existing or to be created, and this includes web.config. (As an aside, consider that by default web.config can be edited only by users in the Administrators group.) To be able to programmatically modify web.config, at least one of the two following requirements must be met: either your ASP.NET application is granted write permissions or the security settings of the web.config file are changed to enable full control by the account running the ASP.NET application.

One quick way to solve the issue is by adding the ASPNET user to the list of users that have full control over the file. (See Figure 12-3.) You first right-click the web.config file in the specified folder, and then select the Security tab. Click Add to show the list of all users, and select ASPNET. Next, enable the user to read or write the file.

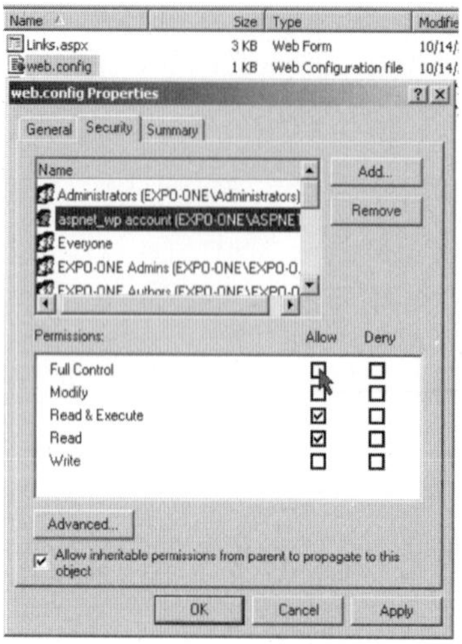

Figure 12-3 Changing the security settings of web.config, making it modifiable by ASP.NET applications.

At this point, you can programmatically overwrite web.config; but is it really worthwhile? The first consideration to make is that web.config is kept in memory, so the leaner you keep the file, the better. More important, any change to the file provokes all pages affected by that copy of web.config to be recompiled on next access. My recommendation is not to use web.config, especially if you're adding settings to the *<appSettings>* section. If the name/value scheme supported by *<appSettings>* suits your needs, you might want to resort to a linked external file. Look at the following file:

```
<configuration>
    <appSettings file="data.config" />
</configuration>
```

It is perfectly equivalent to the following, probably more common, format:

```
<configuration>
    <appSettings>
       <add key="ConnectionString"
          value="DATABASE=northwind;SERVER=localhost;UID=sa;" />
    </appSettings>
</configuration>
```

The content in boldface type is the actual content of the data.config file. You must be granted rights to write to the data.config, but at least changes don't affect web.config and don't cause pages to recompile. Interestingly enough, you don't need to change the API to access information in an external file. That you embed *<appSettings>* in web.config or move it to a linked file is completely transparent to the page. The following code does the same regardless of the physical location of the requested application setting:

```
string connStr = ConfigurationSettings.AppSettings["ConnectionString"];
```

The logic necessary to detect and handle the different situations is buried in the code of the *NameValueFileSectionHandler*.

In summary, as long as the scheme of *<appSettings>* fits your bill, there's really no reason for not using an external file.

Writing to Custom Files

Custom files, both XML or plain text, are a good solution when the name/value scheme of *<appSettings>* is too rigid for your data. In such cases, you might want to use a custom file to store data in a format that better fits your needs for example, a *DataSet* schema. Unfortunately, you can't use the standard configuration classes to do this and must resort to a custom I/O API as well. That's not too difficult, though. In most cases, in fact, ADO.NET and XML classes can easily do the job for you.

However, with a small refinement to the code of the aforementioned *DataSet* section handler, you can make it support an external file as well:

```
public object Create(object parent, object context, XmlNode section)
{
    DataSet ds;
    if (parent == null)
        ds = new DataSet();
    else
        ds = ((DataSet) parent).Clone();

    // If a "file" attribute exists, load the DataSet from there.
    string datasetFile = "";
    XmlAttribute a;
    a = (XmlAttribute) section.Attributes.RemoveNamedItem("file");
    if (a != null)
        datasetFile = a.Value;

    DataSet tmp = new DataSet();
    if (datasetFile != null && datasetFile != "")
    {
        // Read content from the file
        tmp.ReadXml(datasetFile);
    }
    else
    {
        // Read this section
        XmlNodeReader nodereader = new XmlNodeReader(section);
```

```
        tmp.ReadXml(nodereader);
    }

    // Merge with the parent if any
    ds.Merge(tmp);
    return ds;
}
```

The *DataSet* section handler now checks for a *file* attribute and, if any is found, loads the settings from there. In light of this, the MyAspNetApp section in web.config looks like the following:

```
<MyAspNetApp>
    <Links file="[full path]\data.config" />
</MyAspNetApp>
```

The contents of the data.config file is the XML normal form of the desired *DataSet*:

```
<Links>
    <Link>
        <Text>MS Press</Text>
        <URL>http://mspress.microsoft.com</URL>
        <Tooltip>Go to the Microsoft Press Web site</Tooltip>
    </Link>
    <Link>
        <Text>Wintellect</Text>
        <URL>http://www.wintellect.com</URL>
        <Tooltip>Join the Wintellectuals</Tooltip>
    </Link>
</Links>
```

Note that the data.config file (or whatever name you want to use) must be indicated with full path information. In this way, you can use a custom data schema without rejecting the configuration API and without causing too many page recompiles.

Writing to Databases

For a number of reasons, writing to databases is perhaps the best approach. First, neither the ASP.NET application nor files need to be granted special write permissions. Second, the database can easily handle concurrent accesses and ensure a much better speed when retrieving inserted information. In addition, you can set up and exploit the benefits of sorting, indexing, and filtering.

> **Note** Although the configuration system doesn't provide facilities to update, add, or remove settings, ADO.NET and XML do. ADO.NET commands or adapters let you update rows on the configuration database (whose schema is completely up to you), while the XML DOM is a great tool for working on XML data. Because configuration files are not expected to be very large, using XML DOM is preferable to XML writers for its higher level of abstraction.

ASP.NET Applications Deployment

One of the coolest features of .NET assemblies is that they are self-describing components. An application that wants to know about the internal characteristics of an assembly has only to ask! The .NET reflection API is the programming interface by which a client can interrogate an assembly. This fact eliminates the need of using the registry (or any other sort of centralized repository) to track paths and attributes of binary components. Another pleasant effect of the assembly's structure is that side-by-side execution is now a snap, and ASP.NET applications take advantage of it on a regular basis. In practice, whenever you update a page, two versions of the "same" assembly live side-by-side for awhile without interference and conflict.

Installing a .NET application in general, and an ASP.NET application in particular, is a matter of performing an *xcopy*—that is, a recursive copy of all the files to the target folder. Aside from some inevitable emphasis and promotion, the *xcopy deployment* is not pure hype—but it is not pure reality either. However, the *xcopy deployment* expression, which is often used to describe setup procedures in .NET, communicates the gist of .NET deployment: you don't need to do much more than copy files. In particular, there's no need to play with the registry, no components to set up, and no local files to create. Or at least, nothing of the kind is needed just because the .NET Framework mandates it.

Creating a Setup

An ASP.NET application is made of a bunch of ASP.NET resources (mostly *.aspx, *.asax, *.asmx, *.ascx, and *.ashx files), some assemblies, one or more configuration files, and other static resources such as HTML pages, images, style sheets, and client-side scripts. To set up an application, you need to accomplish the following simple steps:

- **(X)Copy the files** All files must be copied mirroring the tree you (with a little help from Visual Studio .NET) configured at development time. You create as many subdirectories as needed, plus a Bin subdirectory under the root folder of the application. If a web.config file is needed, place it in the root folder; make sure lower-level configuration files are copied where appropriate.
- **Set up the IIS virtual directory** The virtual folder is a fundamental piece in the deployment of an ASP.NET application. Typically, the virtual folder—an entry in the IIS metabase—is created by the setup application. However, you can also create it interactively through the IIS Manager or via a script.
- **Install assemblies in the global assembly cache (GAC)** In most cases, an ASP.NET application doesn't need to copy custom assemblies in the GAC. All the application-specific assemblies are to be copied in the Bin subfolder of the root. This is an important requirement to fulfill if you want the application to run correctly in production. To install an assembly in the GAC, you can use the gacutil.exe tool available with the .NET Framework SDK. Note also that GAC-enabled assemblies must have a strong name and be distributed with an extra .snk file.

While homemade setups can be easily and effectively created, in a real-world scenario you need a professional setup procedure. Visual Studio .NET can help a lot with this by providing an ad hoc project type. Typically, you add a setup project to the main project that builds an ASP.NET application; however, you can also create a setup as a standalone project and manually add all the files needed.

A Web Setup Project

As we saw in Chapter 1, a setup project creates a .msi (Windows Installer file) package plus a couple of executables. On those systems in which the Windows Installer is correctly installed and configured, you need to deploy only the .msi package. Generally, you should deploy all the files created by the setup. If the Windows Installer is not available on the target machine, the other executables generated will install it and then yield to the .msi file. The setup project also provides the option to create a cabinet (.cab) file. However, for ASP.NET applications you might want to create a .msi package, given the fact that the Windows Installer is normally installed together with the .NET Framework SDK.

Although the Visual Studio .NET UI presents a Web setup project as a particular type of setup project (as shown in Figure 12-4), it really differs from an ordinary setup only in the additional ability to create and configure IIS virtual folders.

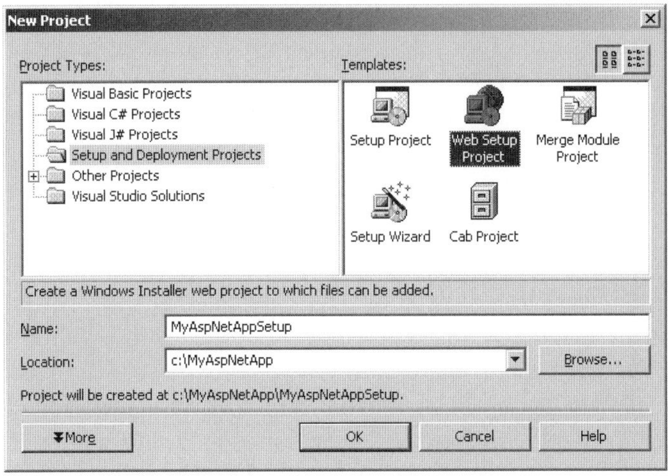

Figure 12-4 The New Project window of Visual Studio .NET.

A setup project modifies the toolbar of the Solution Explorer to let you specify custom actions, specify registry entries, modify user interface elements such as pages of the wizard, startup picture, and more. Figure 12-5 shows the Solution Explorer window.

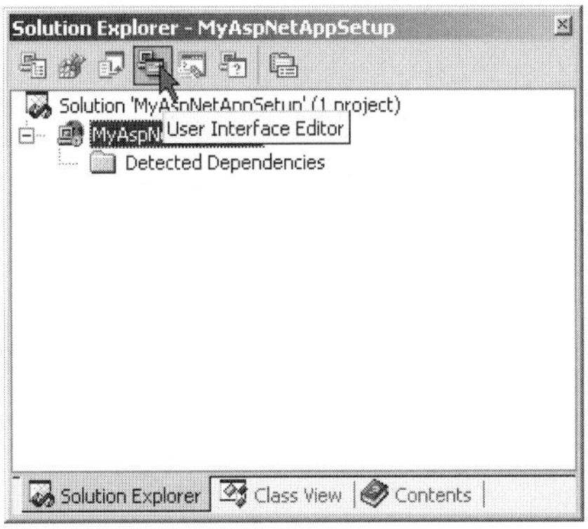

Figure 12-5 The Solution Explorer of a Web Setup Project.

Custom Actions

The setup can accept custom actions—that is, command-line executables that are called during the execution of the setup. The Custom Action Editor in the Solution Explorer lets you connect existing programs to the setup. The parameters you can pass to the custom executable must be static values and cannot be any information that the user specified at setup time.

For tighter integration between the base setup and custom modules, you might want to write an *installer class*. An installer class is a managed class that inherits from the *Installer* class defined in the *System.Configuration.Install* namespace. The class provides up to four overrides for typical setup events. By writing such a component, you could, for example, remove or initialize needed databases or files. The methods of the *Installer* class take a collection with as many dynamic parameters as you need to pass. (For more information on installers, refer to the .NET Framework documentation.)

> **Tip** The Web setup project lets you configure any new virtual directory you need to create through handy properties in the Properties window. However, if you don't need a setup because yours is an extremely simple ASP.NET application or because you need to pass only a ZIP to your ISP or client, you might want to use the following simple VBScript application to create an IIS virtual folder:

```
Set iis = GetObject("IIS://LocalHost/w3svc/1/Root")
Set vdir = iis.Create("IIsWebVirtualDir", vdirName)
vdir.AccessRead = True
vdir.AccessScript = True
vdir.Put "Path", vdirPath
Const POOLED = 2
vdir.AppCreate2 POOLED
vdir.Put "AppFriendlyName", vdirName
vdir.SetInfo
```

Programmatically Configuring the ACL of a File

As mentioned, for an ASP.NET application to write or create a file (including text and XML files and Microsoft Access databases), writing permissions should be granted. This can be accomplished by updating the worker process account from *ASPNET* to *System*, but it's an operation that hides some dark sides. First, by doing this, you significantly lessen your security level by allowing ASP.NET code to access all server resources, as in ASP. Second, for any updates to the *<processModel>* section to take effect, IIS must be restarted.

A less intrusive, but equally effective, approach entails changing the security settings on a single file. Of course, this can be done only on existing files. If you need to work on well-known files, add them to the setup with a zero length and avoid creating them from within ASP.NET code. In this way, you can adjust the security settings offline. If there's no other way than creating files dynamically, you must apply security changes at the directory level.

Earlier I described a manual procedure to give the ASPNET account write permissions on a given file or directory. In most cases, this is enough because the administrator wants to know exactly what's going on and doesn't allow you to run a regular setup. However, should you have the need to accomplish that task programmatically, how can you proceed?

The manual procedure edits the Access Control List (ACL) of the specified file by adding, in this case, a new entry. In version 1.1 of the .NET Framework, no class is provided to accomplish this task. The bad news is that you must resort to a managed class to wrap some calls to a bunch of Win32 API functions—in particular, to the *SetNamedSecurityInfo* API function available from advapi32.dll. The good news is that some sample code doing just that is already available at *http://www.gotdotnet.com/team/csharp/code/default.aspx.*

An even better approach to the problem—because it is simpler—is using an extremely handy utility available from the System32 folder of Windows 2000 and Windows XP operating systems. The utility is named cacls.exe (pronounced *cackles*) and does just what we need—edit the ACL of a given file or directory. The following command line shows how to configure data.config so that ASP.NET applications can write to it:

```
cacls.exe data.config /E /G ASPNET:F
```

The */E* switch indicates that you want to edit the security descriptor, not replace it as the default would do. The */G* switch indicates that you want to add a new user for the file with the specified privileges. If the specified user exists, the settings for the account are modified. The *ASPNET:F* argument indicates that you want to give the ASPNET user full control over the file. (For more options, see the command-line help of the utility.)

This trick is not just effective, but it is also easily plugged into a Visual Studio .NET setup project. This is accomplished through the mechanism of custom actions that just let the installer run an external executable with constant and statically determined arguments. If you have the need to set an ACL programmatically, don't be afraid of resorting to an external executable; cacls.exe is commonly used in the way we've seen here. In fact, because the access control API is notoriously difficult to use, even seasoned C/C++ developers of Win32 applications often prefer to give up on the API and just use this utility. Want an example of a very popular application that makes use of cacls.exe? ASP.NET, of course!

Updating Configuration Options

More often than not, you don't need really complex and sophisticated setup procedures for ASP.NET applications. In addition, in most hosted application environments, you don't get to run installers and even if you could, you must have administrative privileges to do so. Most administrators want, and probably with good reason, to hold a tight rein over what goes on. All this doesn't mean you should disregard and neglect the setup, however.

The key fact about setups is that .NET significantly simplifies the deployment of applications. No matter the details, and no matter how many complex features you can easily stuff into a .msi file, deploying .NET applications does not require much more than an xcopy. This fact really reduces the cost of setup for consulting companies.

Configuring the Machine

In ASP.NET, there's a subtle point you should pay more attention to than, say, custom actions or custom bitmaps in the startup box. When you develop the ASP.NET code, you test it on a machine with its own machine.config file. When you deploy the application on a production box, you might not be able to restore the same settings. One possible reason is that the administrator does not want you to modify the current settings because they proved to be great for other applications.

You can work around the issue by simply replicating any needed machine.config settings into the application's web.config. However, if you are deploying your code to a service provider, you might find that many machine.config settings have been locked down and cannot be overridden. In this case, you should ask (or beg) the administrator to create a new application-specific *<location>* section in the server's machine.config with all the machine settings needed for your application.

Replicating needed changes into the application's web.config is, however, preferable because it makes the entire application self-contained and hot-pluggable. It should always be the first option considered.

Deploying on a Web Farm

Deploying an ASP.NET application in a Web-farm scenario poses a few extra configuration issues you must be aware of. All machine.config files in the Web farm must be synchronized on the value of a few attributes. You can achieve this in two ways, the simplest of which is packing all attribute values in the application's web.config. This approach greatly simplifies the deployment because you only have to run the setup on all machines and no other changes are needed.

In an ISP scenario, though, in which some settings can be locked down at the machine.config level, the changes must be replicated in all the machine files of the farm. If multiple applications are configured to run, you create your own *<location>* section; otherwise, a plain copy of the machine.config file will work just fine. But what are the attributes that need to be kept in sync?

Measures of Performance

To monitor the health and responsiveness of ASP.NET applications, a few measures are commonly used: throughput, response time, and scalability. The throughput is the number of requests per second that a Web application can serve. As such, it is the most critical factor for performance. Response time is defined as the time that elapses between the request and the arrival of the data on the client. This time can be expressed in two ways: Time-to-First-Byte (TTFB) and Time-to-Last-Byte (TTLB). TTFB is the time elapsed when the first byte hits the client. TTLB is the time elapsed when all the data has been delivered. Response time tends to be inversely proportional to the throughput. A sign of good performance is when you have an acceptable throughput with an acceptable response time. Scalability measures the application's ability to maintain (or improve) the performance as the number of requests and resources allocated grows.

Another relevant metric to measure the performance is performance data gathered by performance counters. ASP.NET provides two groups of performance counter objects—system and application. Among the system objects, you find counters for queued, disconnected, rejected requests, application restarts, sessions active, and timed out. Application counters include total hits to the cache, resource compilations, errors, and debugging requests.

The *PerformanceCounter* class in the *System.Diagnostics* namespace can be used to reference a particular counter and read its performance data. The class can also be used to publish custom performance data—for example, the frequency or the execution time of a particular operation that is critical to your application.

There are three information types that must be configured in the same way across the farm: forms authentication cookies, view-state message authentication check (MAC) generation, and session state. The relevant sections are listed in Table 12-16.

Table 12-16 Sections to Synchronize in Web Farms

Section	Description
<machineKey>	The keys used for encryption (*validationKey* attribute) and decryption (*decryptionKey* attribute) of the form's authentication cookie data must be identical on all machines. The *validation* attribute must also be replicated if the authentication check is enabled for the view state of one or more pages. The message authentication check (MAC) takes place if the *@Page*'s *EnableViewStateMac* attribute is set to *true*.
<authentication>	Settings for the *<forms>* section must coincide across the farm to enable the correct treatment of the client cookie.
<sessionState>	All machines must handle session data in the same way, whether through SQL Server or a remote server.

Conclusion

The ASP.NET configuration system is based on a few XML files that are read when the application and the Web server start up. The ASP.NET ISAPI extension (aspnet_isapi.dll) hierarchically builds an in-memory tree of the configuration data and uses it to control the way in which a given application executes. Just the fact that an image of the configuration data is stored in memory since startup allows dynamic changes to the configuration that are promptly detected and applied to all related pages. Administrators have no need to restart the Web server for the new settings to apply—they just save the .config file and wait for users to renew their requests.

ASP.NET applications have many configurable settings. Also, the ASP.NET worker process exposes a fair number of accessible parameters—from the size of the thread pool to the frequency of process recycling, and from the maximum percentage of memory occupied to the number of pages that can be compiled into a single assembly. The various settings can all be controlled at different levels and overridden, extended, or restricted as appropriate. ASP.NET configuration is hierarchical by nature and lets you apply different configuration schemes at various levels of granularity—the machine, the Web site, or the folder.

Configuration files are probably the most critical aspect to consider when preparing the deployment of ASP.NET applications. Arranging a setup program has never been as easy as with Visual Studio .NET (not considering third-party products), but deciding how to replicate the settings of the native environment might not be trivial. ASP.NET applications, in fact, can be deployed on a Web farm or in an ISP scenario, which requires particular care of the machine.config and web.config files. All in all, though, the deployment at the time of ASP.NET is finally effective and time saving.

Finally, on the subject of performance, ASP.NET takes advantage of structural changes such as the just-in-time page compilation, process recycling, and various other caching mechanisms. It also provides a bunch of performance counters and utilities to measure the health and the performance of a Web site.

In the next chapter, we'll begin our in-depth exploration of the programming aspects of ASP.NET. The global.asax file and ASP-intrinsic objects such as *Request* and *Response* will constitute the bread and butter of Chapter 13.

Resources

- Top 10 Reasons for Systems Administrators to Use the .NET Framework (*http://msdn.microsoft.com/netframework/productinfo/topten/admins.asp*)
- Best Practices for Deploying Your Mobile Application and Services (*http://msdn.microsoft.com/library/en-us/dnmitta/html/bestpracdeplmob.asp*)
- Side-by-Side Execution of the .NET Framework (*http://msdn.microsoft.com/library/en-us/dnnetdep/html/sidexsidenet.asp*)
- *Microsoft ASP.NET Setup and Configuration Pocket Reference*, by James Avery (Microsoft Press, 2003)

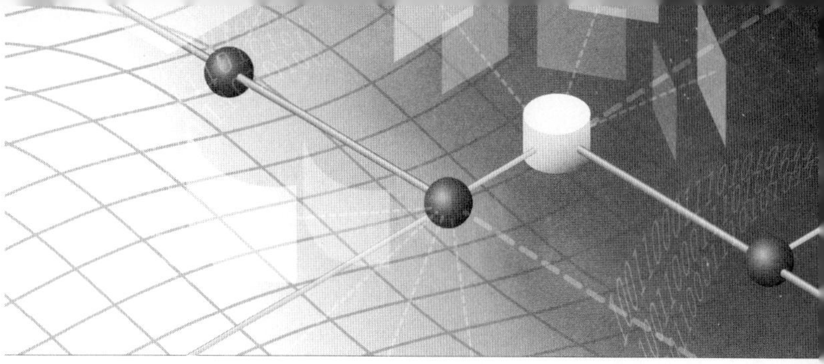

13

The HTTP Request Context

The nice thing about being a celebrity is that when you bore people, they think it's their fault.

—*Henry Kissinger*

In Chapter 2, I described in detail the various steps that take an incoming HTTP request to be served by the ASP.NET worker process. I'll summarize the process here. The request is assigned to the aspnet_isapi.dll ISAPI extension which, in turn, hands it over to the HTTP runtime pipeline. A new instance of the *HttpRuntime* class is created for each request and governs its overall execution. The *HttpRuntime* class represents the entry point in the ASP.NET pipeline that will generate the response text for the browser. Upon instantiation, the *HttpRuntime* class performs a number of initialization tasks, the first of which is the creation of a wrapper object to encapsulate all the HTTP-specific information available about the request. The newly created object—an instance of the *HttpContext* class—is then passed along to the pipeline and is used by the various modules to access intrinsic worker objects such as *Request*, *Response*, and *Server*.

In this chapter, we'll first review the startup process of the ASP.NET application and then move on to examine the various objects that form the context of the HTTP request. If you're a former ASP developer, the contents of this chapter might sound familiar as we discuss old acquaintances such as *Request*, *Response*, and *Server*. However, you need to notice up front that the role of these intrinsic ASP objects is different in ASP.NET. They are fully supported and fully backward-compatible with ASP, but their functionality is built on top of a completely redesigned server architecture.

Initialization of the Application

Once you've created the context for the request, the *HttpRuntime* class sets up an ASP.NET application object to carry out the request. An ASP.NET application consists of an instance of the *HttpApplication* class that we briefly discussed in Chapter 2. *HttpApplication* is a global.asax-derived object that handles all HTTP requests directed to a particular virtual folder.

An ASP.NET running application is wholly represented by its virtual folder and optionally by the global.asax file. The virtual folder name is a sort of key the HTTP runtime uses to selectively identify which of the running *HttpApplication* objects should take care of the incoming request. The global.asax file, if present, contains code for responding to application-level events raised by ASP.NET or by registered HTTP modules that affect the application. Figure 13-1 shows a detailed view of the process that creates a page for a request. You'll see that requests pass through the application factory that picks up (or creates) a valid *HttpApplication* object from a pool. The *HttpApplication* object, in turn, selects the proper resource handler based on the type of the request (.aspx, .asmx, or other type).

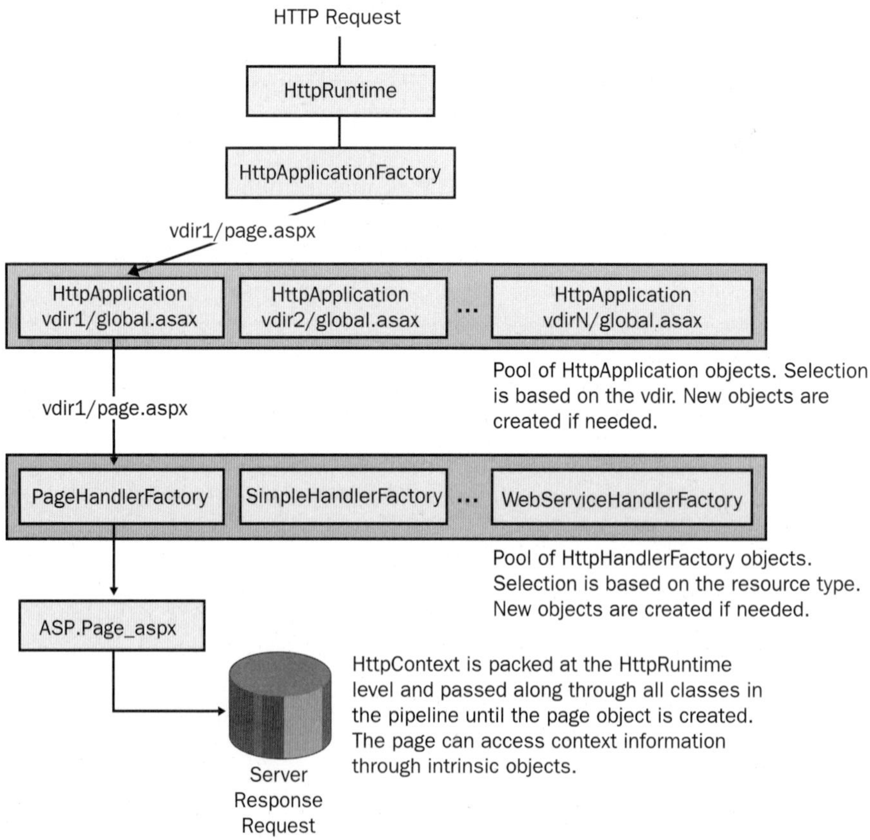

Figure 13-1 The process of creating a page for an HTTP request.

The particular *HttpApplication* selected is responsible for managing the entire lifetime of the request it is assigned to. That instance of *HttpApplication* can be reused only after the request has been completed. If no *HttpApplication* object is available, either because the application has not been started or all valid objects are busy, a new *HttpApplication* is created and pooled.

Properties of the *HttpApplication* Class

Although the *HttpApplication* class provides a public constructor, user applications never need to create instances of the *HttpApplication* class directly. The ASP.NET runtime infrastructure always does the job for you. As mentioned, instances of the class are pooled and, as such, can process many requests in their lifetime (but always one at a time). Should concurrent requests arrive for the same application, additional instances are created. Because the *HttpApplication* object serves just one request at a time, its member variables store per-request data. Table 13-1 lists the properties defined on the class.

Table 13-1 *HttpApplication* Properties

Property	Description
Application	Instance of the *HttpApplicationState* class, represents the global and shared state of the application. Functionally equivalent to the ASP intrinsic *Application* object.
Context	Instance of the *HttpContext* class, encapsulates in a single object all HTTP-specific information about the current request. Intrinsic objects (for example, *Application* and *Request*) are also exposed as properties.
Modules	Gets the collection of modules that affect the current application.
Request	Instance of the *HttpRequest* class, represents the current HTTP request. Functionally equivalent to the ASP intrinsic *Request* object.
Response	Instance of the *HttpResponse* class, sends HTTP response data to the client. Functionally equivalent to the ASP intrinsic *Response* object.
Server	Instance of the *HttpServerUtility* class, provides helper methods for processing Web requests. Functionally equivalent to the ASP intrinsic *Server* object.
Session	Instance of the *HttpSessionState* class, manages user-specific data. Functionally equivalent to the ASP intrinsic *Session* object.
User	An *IPrincipal* object that represents the user making the request.

A good question at this point of the discussion would be the following. Because the *HttpApplication* class is managed by the ASP.NET infrastructure, how can I take advantage of the fairly rich, public programming interface of the class? Properties, overridable methods, and class events, can be accessed and programmatically manipulated in the global.asax file. (We'll return to global.asax later in the section "The global.asax File.")

Application Modules

The *Modules* property returns a collection of applicationwide components providing ad hoc services. An HTTP module component is a class that implements the *IHttpModule* interface. Modules can be considered the managed counterpart of ISAPI filters; they are a kind of request interceptor with the built-in capability of modifying the overall context of the request being processed. The .NET Framework defines a number of standard modules as listed in Table 13-2. Custom modules can be defined too. We'll cover this particular aspect of HTTP programming in Chapter 23.

Table 13-2 Default ASP.NET Modules

Module	Description
DefaultAuthenticationModule	Ensures that an authentication object is present in the context.
FileAuthorizationModule	Verifies that the remote user has Windows NT permissions to access the requested resource.
FormsAuthenticationModule	Enables applications to use forms authentication.
OutputCacheModule	Manages the page output caching. *This class is not officially documented.*
PassportAuthenticationModule	Provides a wrapper around Passport authentication services.
SessionStateModule	Provides session-state services for the application.
UrlAuthorizationModule	Provides URL-based authorization services to access specified resources.
WindowsAuthenticationModule	Enables ASP.NET applications to use Windows and IIS-based authentication.

The list of default modules is defined in the machine.config file and can be modified to include new modules or exclude some of those shown in the preceding table. The modules listed in machine.config are available to all applications. By creating a proper web.config file, you can also create an application-specific list of modules. (See Chapter 12.)

It's worth noting that no class can be inherited. The reason is because all those classes are associated with the predefined mechanisms for authentication and authorization. Making those classes inheritable would have opened a potential security hole in ASP.NET. A derived class, in fact, often looks like the original but can provide significantly different good and bad features.

Methods of the *HttpApplication* Class

The methods of the *HttpApplication* class can be divided in two groups—operational methods and event handler managers. The *HttpApplication* operational methods are described in Table 13-3.

Table 13-3 *HttpApplication* Operational Methods

Method	Description
CompleteRequest	Sets an internal flag that causes ASP.NET to skip all successive steps in the pipeline and directly execute *EndRequest*. Mostly useful to HTTP modules.
Dispose	Overridable method, cleans up the instance variables of all registered modules once the request has been served. At this time, *Request*, *Response*, *Session*, and *Application* are no longer available.
GetVaryByCustomString	Overridable method, provides a way to set output caching based on a custom string for all pages in the application. (We'll say more on output page caching in Chapter 14.)
Init	Overridable method, executes custom initialization code after all modules have been linked to the application to serve the request. You can use it to create and configure any object you want to use throughout the request processing. At this time *Request*, *Response*, *Session*, and *Application* are not yet available.

Note that *Init* and *Dispose* are quite different from well-known event handlers such as *Application_OnStart* and *Application_OnEnd*. *Init* executes for every request directed at the Web application, whereas *Application_OnStart* fires only once in the Web application's lifetime. *Init* indicates that a new instance of the *HttpApplication* object has been created to serve an incoming request; *Application_OnStart* denotes that the first instance of *HttpApplication* has been created to start up the Web application and serve its very first request. Likewise, *Dispose* signals the next termination of the request processing but not necessarily the end of the application. *Application_OnEnd* is raised only once, when the application is being shut down.

> **Note** A similar difference exists between the pair *Init*/*Dispose* and *Session_OnStart* and *Session_OnEnd*. The latter two events are raised only once in the session lifetime, whereas methods *Init* and *Dispose* are invoked at each request.

You should also be aware that all resources you create that override the *Init* method are shared only with the current instance of modules, and in no way are those objects visible across multiple requests. Data that must survive multiple requests should be stored in instances of global state classes such as *HttpApplicationState* (the property *Application*) or *HttpSessionState* (the property *Session*). Any resource that gets created in *Init* should be cleaned up in *Dispose*.

In addition to the operational methods in Table 13-3, a few other *HttpApplication* methods are available and listed in Table 13-4. These methods are of no interest to user applications and are used only by HTTP modules to hook up the events generated during the request's chain of execution. The description of all methods is identical; what really changes is the name of the event that the handlers are attached to. All methods in Table 13-4 add the specified event handlers to the collection of handlers associated with the specified asynchronous application event. Event handlers are detached when the request is completed.

You should note that there are two versions of each application event, a synchronous version and an asynchronous version. The methods listed in Table 13-4 are for the asynchronous versions.

Table 13-4 Methods to Register Asynchronous Event Handlers

Method	Event
AddOnAcquireRequestStateAsync	*AcquireRequestState*
AddOnAuthenticateRequestAsync	*AuthenticateRequest*
AddOnAuthorizeRequestAsync	*AuthorizeRequest*
AddOnBeginRequestAsync	*BeginRequest*
AddOnEndRequestAsync	*EndRequest*
AddOnPostRequestHandlerExecuteAsync	*PostRequestHandlerExecute*
AddOnPreRequestHandlerExecuteAsync	*PreRequestHandlerExecute*
AddOnReleaseRequestStateAsync	*ReleaseRequestState*
AddOnResolveRequestCacheAsync	*ResolveRequestCache*
AddOnUpdateRequestCacheAsync	*UpdateRequestCache*

Each module is requested to indicate a begin handler and an end handler. The following code shows the prototype of the *AddOnAcquireRequestStateAsync* method. Other prototypes are nearly identical.

```
public void AddOnAcquireRequestStateAsync(
    BeginEventHandler bh,
    EndEventHandler eh
);
```

The *BeginEventHandler* is the delegate called at the start of the asynchronous event processing, while *EndEventHandler* is the delegate that gets into the game at the end of event processing.

Events of the *HttpApplication* Class

Table 13-5 describes the event model of the *HttpApplication* class—that is, the set of events that HTTP modules, as well as user applications, can listen to and handle.

Table 13-5 *HttpApplication* Events

Event	Description
AcquireRequestState	Occurs when the handler that will actually serve the request acquires the state information associated with the request.
AuthenticateRequest	Occurs when a security module has established the identity of the user.
AuthorizeRequest	Occurs when a security module has verified user authorization.
BeginRequest	Occurs as soon as the HTTP pipeline begins to process the request.
Disposed	Occurs when the *HttpApplication* object is disposed as a result of a call to *Dispose*.
EndRequest	Occurs as the last event in the HTTP pipeline chain of execution. The *EndRequest* event is always raised when *CompleteRequest* is called.
Error	Occurs when an unhandled exception is thrown. The exception object can be accessed through a call to the *Server*'s *GetLastError* method. If your application generates custom error output, use the *Server*'s *ClearError* method to suppress the default error message.
PostRequestHandlerExecute	Occurs when the HTTP handler of choice (.aspx, .asmx, .ashx, or other type) finishes execution. The response text has been generated at this point.
PreRequestHandlerExecute	Occurs just before the HTTP handler of choice (.aspx, .asmx, .ashx, or other type) begins to work.
PreSendRequestContent	Occurs just before the ASP.NET runtime sends the response text to the client.
PreSendRequestHeaders	Occurs just before the ASP.NET runtime sends HTTP headers to the client.
ReleaseRequestState	Occurs when the handler releases the state information associated with the current request.

(continued)

Table 13-5 *HttpApplication* Events *(continued)*

Event	Description
ResolveRequestCache	Occurs when the ASP.NET runtime resolves the request through the output cache, thus bypassing the regular handler (.aspx, .asmx, .ashx, or other type the requested resource was).
UpdateRequestCache	Occurs when the ASP.NET runtime stores the response of the current request in the output cache to be used to serve subsequent requests.

To handle any of these events asynchronously, an application will use the corresponding method in Table 13-4. To hook up some of these events in a synchronous manner, an application will define in the global.asax file event handler procedures with the following signature:

```
public void Application_XXX()
{
    // do something here
}
```

Of course the *XXX* placeholder must be replaced with the name of the event. All the events in the preceding table provide no event-specific data. You could also use the following syntax:

```
public void Application_XXX(object sender, EventArgs e)
{
    // do something here
}
```

This syntax, however, doesn't give you additional information and programming power. The *sender* argument evaluates to the sender object, which is always the *ASP.global_asax* class, with a couple of exceptions. The sender is *HttpApplicationFactory* when the application starts up and *SessionStateModule* when the session is started.

> **Note** In *Application_OnStart*, both *Response* and *Request* are not yet available in the context of the current application. They won't actually be linked until the request begins. This doesn't mean, though, that you can't access them. The trick is using the objects from the *Context* request, which, in contrast, has just been created by the HTTP runtime. In other words, resort to *Context.Response* and *Context.Request.* This approach is necessary only in the *Application_OnStart* handler.

In addition to the events of Table 13-5, in the global.asax file, an application can also handle *Application_OnStart* and *Application_OnEnd*. When ASP.NET is about to fire *BeginRequest* for the very first time in the application lifetime, it makes *Application_OnStart* precede it. *EndRequest* will happen at the end of every request to an application. *Application_OnEnd* occurs outside the context of a request, when the application is ending. Let's examine the order in which events are raised.

1. *BeginRequest*. The ASP.NET HTTP pipeline begins to work on the request. This event reaches the application after *Application_OnStart*.
2. *AuthenticateRequest*. The ASP.NET runtime has attempted to authenticate the user. All the information available is stored in the *HttpContext*'s *User* property. The user name is typically set to the empty string for anonymous, unauthenticated users.
3. *AuthorizeRequest*. The ASP.NET runtime has attempted to verify the user's authorization to access the resource.
4. *ResolveRequestCache*. The ASP.NET runtime verifies whether returning a previously cached page can resolve the request. If a previously cached page cannot resolve the request, the procedure continues. An HTTP handler corresponding to the requested URL is created at this point. If the requested resource is an .aspx page, an instance of a page class is created. Note that the *Session_OnStart* event (which occurs when the request starts a new session) is raised only at this point, following *ResolveRequestCache*.
5. *AcquireRequestState*. The newly created HTTP handler object that will handle the request is associated with state information (such as *Application*, *Session*, and other types).
6. *PreRequestHandlerExecute*. This event is fired just before calling the *ProcessRequest* method on the handler—a *Page*-derived class if the request targets an .aspx resource. The handler does its job and generates the output for the client.
7. *PostRequestHandlerExecute*. This event is raised when the handler has generated the response text.
8. *ReleaseRequestState*. This event is raised when the handler releases its state information and prepares to shut down. At this point, modules registered to filter the response text have their best chance to operate. The response text hasn't been sent yet.
9. *UpdateRequestCache*. The ASP.NET runtime determines whether the

generated output, now also properly filtered by registered modules, should be cached to be reused with upcoming identical requests.

10. *EndRequest.* This event fires as the final step of the HTTP pipeline. The control passes back to the *HttpRuntime* object, which is responsible for the actual forwarding of the response to the client. At this point, the text has not been sent yet.

Another pair of events can occur during the request, but in a nondeterministic order. They are *PreSendRequestHeaders* and *PreSendRequestContent*. The *PreSendRequestHeaders* event informs the *HttpApplication* object in charge of the request that HTTP headers are about to be sent. The event normally fires after *EndRequest* but not always. For example, if buffering is turned off, the event gets fired as soon as some content is going to be sent to the client. Finally, with the *PreSendRequestContent* event, the *HttpApplication* object in charge of the request learns that the response body is about to be sent.

In Figure 13-2, you can see a sample application (logevents.aspx) that uses global.asax to accumulate and display text for events as they are detected.

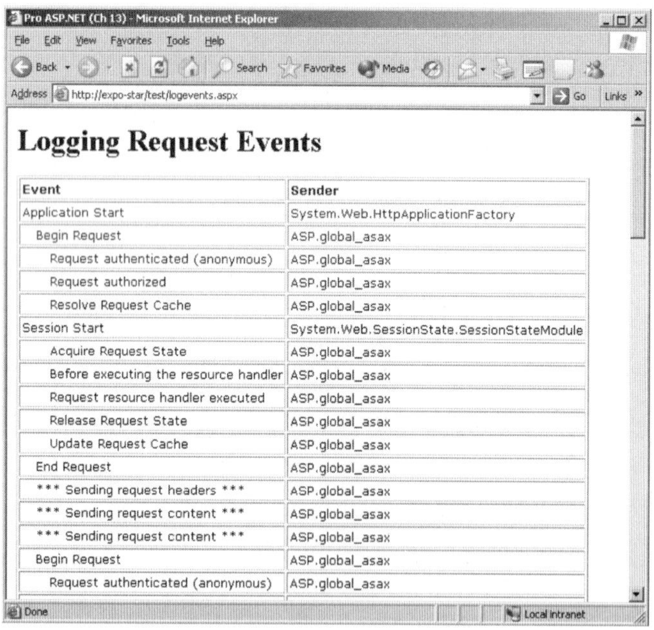

Figure 13-2 Logging the events raised while a request is being processed.

In all these event handlers, you can write code the same as in the context of an *HttpApplication* class, meaning you can access *Request*, *Response*, and *Server* without instance prefixes. You're just writing methods of a class that inherits from *HttpApplication*.

The global.asax File

The global.asax file is used by Web applications to handle some application-level events raised by the ASP.NET runtime or by registered HTTP modules. The global.asax file is optional. If missing, the ASP.NET runtime environment simply assumes you have no application or module event handlers defined. To be functional, the global.asax file must be located in the root directory of the application. Only one global.asax file per application is accepted. (global.asax files placed in subdirectories are simply ignored.)

> **Note** ASP.NET global.asax and ASP global.asax files can happily coexist in the same application. Of course, this consideration holds true even if you're going to have an application half ASP.NET-based and managed and half ASP-driven.

Compiling global.asax

When the application is started, the global.asax file, if present, is parsed into a source class and compiled. The resultant assembly is created in the temporary directory just as any other dynamically generated assembly would be. (See Chapter 2 for more information on this procedure.) The following listing shows the skeleton of the C# code that ASP.NET generates for any global.asax file:

```
namespace ASP
{
    public class global_asax : System.Web.HttpApplication
    {
        private static bool __initialized = false;

        //
        // The source code of "global.asax" file is flushed
        // here verbatim. For this reason, the following code
        // in global.asax would generate a compile error.
        //     int i;
        //     i = 2;  // can't have statements outside methods
        //
```

```
        public global_asax() {
            if ((ASP.global_asax.__initialized == false)) {
                ASP.global_asax.__initialized = true;
            }
        }
    }
}
```

The class is named *ASP.global_asax* and is derived from the *HttpApplication* base class. In most cases, you deploy global.asax as a separate text file; however, you can also write it as a class and compile it either in a separate assembly or within your project's assembly. The class source code must follow the outline shown earlier and, above all, must derive from *HttpApplication*. The assembly with the compiled version of global.asax must be deployed in the application's Bin subdirectory.

Note, though, that even if you isolate the logic of the global.asax file in a precompiled assembly, you still need to have a (codeless) global.asax file that refers to the assembly. (This is exactly what happens with Visual Studio .NET projects.)

```
<%@ Application Inherits="ProAspNet.Global" %>
```

We'll learn more about the syntax of global.asax in the next section, "Syntax of global.asax." With a precompiled global application file, you certainly don't risk exposing your source code over the Web to malicious attacks. However, even if you leave it as source code, you're somewhat safe.

The global.asax file, in fact, is configured so that any direct URL request for it is automatically rejected by IIS. In this way, external users cannot download or view the code it contains. The trick that enables this behavior is the following line of code, excerpted from machine.config:

```
<add verb="*" path="*.asax" type="System.Web.HttpForbiddenHandler" />
```

ASP.NET registers with IIS to handle .asax resouces, but then processes those direct requests through the *HttpForbiddenHandler* HTTP handler. As a result, when a browser requests a .asax resource, an error message is displayed on the page, as shown in Figure 13-3.

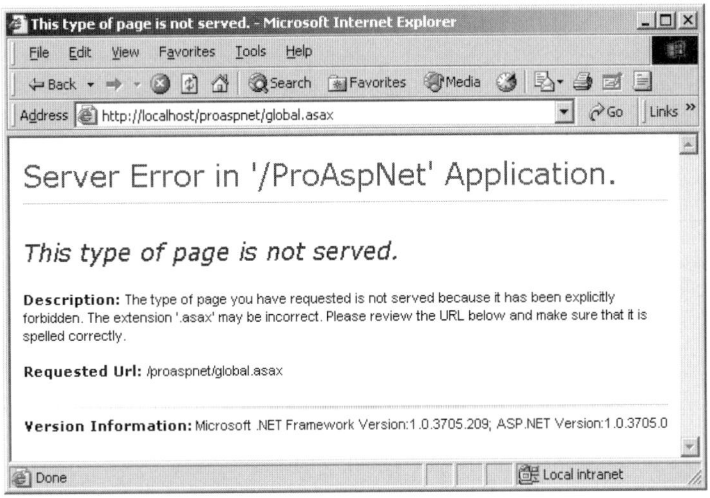

Figure 13-3 Direct access to forbidden resources, such as *.asax files, results in a server error.

Of course, you can duplicate that line in your machine.config file, or even in the application's web.config file, and block direct access to other types of resources specific to your application. For this trick to work, though, make sure that the resource type is redirected to ASP.NET at the IIS level. In other words, you must register aspnet_isapi.dll to handle those files in the IIS metabase.

> **Note** When the global.asax file of a running application is modified, the ASP.NET runtime detects the change and prepares to shut down and restart the application. It waits until all pending requests are completed and then fires the *Application_OnEnd* event. When the next request from a browser arrives, ASP.NET reparses and recompiles the global.asax file, and again raises the *Application_OnStart* event.

Syntax of global.asax

Four elements determine the syntax of the global.asax file. They are: application directives, code declaration blocks, server-side *<object>* tags, and server-side includes. These elements can be used in any order and number to compose a global.asax file.

Application Directives

The global.asax file supports three directives, two of which have been discussed in Chapter 1. The supported directives are: *@Application*, *@Import*, and *@Assembly*. The *@Import* and *@Assembly* directives work as we have seen in Chapter 1. The *@Import* directive imports a namespace into an application; the *@Assembly* directives links an assembly to the application at compile time.

The *@Application* directive supports a couple of attributes—*Description* and *Inherits*. *Description* can contain any text you want to use to describe the behavior of the application. This text has only a documentation purpose and is blissfully ignored by the ASP.NET parser. The *Inherits* attribute indicates a code-behind class for the application to inherit. It can be the name of any class derived from the *HttpApplication* class. The assembly that contains the class must be located in the Bin subdirectory of the application.

Just like the *@Page* directive, *@Application* accepts the *CodeBehind* attribute to allow for Visual Studio .NET editing. The attribute *CodeBehind* is ignored at run time.

Code Declaration Blocks

A global.asax file can contain code wrapped by a *<script>* tag. Just as for pages, the *<script>* tag must have the *runat* attribute set to *server*. The *language* attribute indicates the language used throughout. The value of this attribute determines the language used to create the source class for the file.

```
<script language="C#" runat="server">
    ⋮
</script>
```

If the *language* attribute is not specified, ASP.NET defaults to the language set in the configuration, which is Visual Basic .NET. As of version 1.1 of the .NET Framework, Visual Basic .NET, C#, JScript .NET, and J# are the only languages supported. (J# is supported only in version 1.1.)

The source code can also be loaded from an external file, whose virtual path is set in the *Src* attribute. The location of the file is resolved using *Server.MapPath*.

```
<script language="C#" runat="server" src="global.aspx.cs" />
```

In this case, any other code in the declaration *<script>* block is ignored. Notice that ASP.NET enforces syntax rules on the *<script>* tag. The *runat* attribute is mandatory, and if the block has no content the *Src* must be specified.

Server-Side *<object>* Tags

The server-side *<object>* tag lets you create new objects by using a declarative syntax. The *<object>* tag can take three forms, as shown in the following lines of code, depending on the specified reference type.

```
<object id="..." runat="server" scope="..." class="..." />
<object id="..." runat="server" scope="..." progid="..." />
<object id="..." runat="server" scope="..." classid="..." />
```

In the first case, the object is identified by the name of the class and assembly that contains it. In the last two cases, the object to create is a COM object identified by the program identifier (*progid*) and the 128-bit CLSID, respectively. As one can easily guess, the *classid*, *progid*, and *class* attributes are mutually exclusive. If you use more than one within a single server-side *<object>* tag, a compile error is generated. Objects declared in this way are loaded when the application is started.

The *scope* attribute indicates the scope at which the object is declared. The allowable values are defined in Table 13-6. Unless otherwise specified, the server-side object is valid only within the boundaries of the HTTP pipeline that processes the current request. Other settings that increase the object's lifetime are *application* and *session*.

Table 13-6 Feasible Scopes for Server-Side *<object>* Tags

Scope	Description
pipeline	Default setting, indicates the object is available only within the context of the current HTTP request
application	Indicates the object is added to the *StaticObjects* collection of the *Application* object and is shared among all pages in the application
session	Indicates the object is added to the *StaticObjects* collection of the *Session* object and is shared among all pages in the current session

When the ASP.NET parser encounters a server-side *<object>* in global.asax, it generates a slightly different source for the global.asax class. In particular, it adds a property on the class whose name is based on the value of the *id* attribute. Let's consider the following one-line global.asax:

```
<object runat="server" id="data"
    scope="application" class="System.Data.DataSet" />
```

The corresponding C# source code is as follows:

```
public class global_asax : System.Web.HttpApplication {
    private System.Data.DataSet cacheddata;
    private static bool __initialized = false;

    public global_asax() {
        if ((ASP.global_asax.__initialized == false)) {
            ASP.global_asax.__initialized = true;
        }
    }
```

```
        private System.Data.DataSet data {
            get {
                if (cacheddata == null) {
                    object o = Application.StaticObjects.GetObject("data");
                    cacheddata = (System.Data.DataSet) o;
                }
                return this.cacheddata;
            }
        }
    }
```

The newly added *DataSet* property is named *cachedXXX*, where *XXX* is the value of the *id* attribute in the *<object>* element. The property *get* accessor is configured to create an instance of the type the first time the property is referenced.

The structure of the generated code changes if the scope of the object is *session* or *pipeline*. If the scope is *session*, no internal placeholder (for example, the *cachedXXX* member) is used and the *get* accessor for a *sessionData* ID takes the following form:

```
private DataSet sessionData {
    get {
        return ((DataSet)(Session.StaticObjects.GetObject("sessionData")));
    }
}
```

If the server-side object is scoped to the pipeline, the *get* accessor takes yet another form:

```
public System.Data.DataSet localData {
    get {
        if ((this.cachedlocalData == null)) {
            this.cachedlocalData = new System.Data.DataSet();
        }
        return this.cachedlocalData;
    }
}
```

In this case, the value of the object is not cached and remains available only until the current request is up and running.

Server-Side Includes

A *#include* directive inserts the contents of the specified file as-is into the ASP.NET file that uses it. The directive for file inclusion can be used in global.asax as well as in .aspx pages. The directive must be enclosed in an HTML comment so that it isn't mistaken for plain text to be output verbatim.

```
<!-- #include file="filename" -->
<!-- #include virtual="filename" -->
```

The directive supports two mutually exclusive attributes—*file* and *virtual*. If the *file* attribute is used, the file name must be a relative path to a file located in the same directory or in a subdirectory; the included file cannot be in a directory above the file with the *#include* directive. With the *virtual* attribute, the file name can be indicated by using a full virtual path from a virtual directory on the same Web site.

Static Properties

If you define static properties in the global.asax file, they will be accessible for reading and writing by all pages in the application.

```
<script language="C#" runat="server">
    public static int Counter = 0;
</script>
```

The *Counter* property defined in the global.asax in the preceding code works like an item stored in *Application*. Consider that concurrent access to *Counter* is not serialized; on the other hand, you have a strong typed, direct global item whose access is much faster than retrieving the same piece of information from a generic collection such as *Application*.

To access the property from a page, you must use the *ASP.global_asax* qualifier, shown here:

```
Response.Write(ASP.global_asax.Counter.ToString());
```

If you don't particularly like the *ASP.global_asax* prefix, you can alias it as long as you use C#. Add the following code to a C#-based page (or code-behind class) for which you need to access the globals:

```
using Globals = ASP.global_asax;
```

The preceding statement creates an alias for the *ASP.global_asax* class (or whatever name your global.asax class has). The alias—*Globals* in this sample code—can be used throughout your code wherever *ASP.global_asax* is accepted.

```
Response.Write(Globals.Counter.ToString());
```

> **Note** You can use the global.asax file to handle any event exposed by the modules called to operate on the request. Handlers for events exposed by an HTTP module must have a name that conforms to the following scheme: *ModuleName_EventName*. The module name to use is defined in the machine.config *<httpModules>* section. Finally, bear in mind that you can handle the ASP-like *Session_OnStart* and *Session_OnEnd* events only because of this mechanism.

Tracking Errors and Anomalies

When an error occurs, displaying a friendly page to the user is only half the job a good programmer should do. The second half of the work consists in sending appropriate notifications to the system administrator—if possible, in real time. A great help is the *Error* event of the *HttpApplication* object. Write an *Application_Error* event handler in your global.asax file and the system will call it back whenever an unhandled error occurs in the application—either in the user code, a component's code, or ASP.NET code.

In the *Application_Error* event handler, you first obtain specific information about the error and then implement the tracking policy that best suits your needs—for example, e-mailing the administrator, writing to the Windows Event Log, or dumping errors to a text file. The *Server.GetLastError* method returns an *Exception* object that just represents the unhandled exception you want to track down. URL information is contained in the *Request* object and even session or application state is available.

The following code demonstrates how to write an *Application_Error* event handler in global.asax to report run-time anomalies to the Event Log. An example of this code in action is shown in Figure 13-4.

```
<%@ Import Namespace="System.Diagnostics" %>
<script language="C#" runat="server">
void Application_Error(object sender, EventArgs e)
{
    // Obtain the URL of the request
    string url = Request.Path;

    // Obtain the Exception object describing the error
    Exception error = Server.GetLastError();

    // Build the message --> [Error occurred. XXX at url]
    string buf = "Error occurred. ";
    buf += error.Message;
    buf += " at ";
    buf += url;

    // Write to the Event Log
    EventLog log = new EventLog();
    log.Source = "ProAspNet Log";
    log.WriteEntry(buf, EventLogEntryType.Error);
}
</script>
```

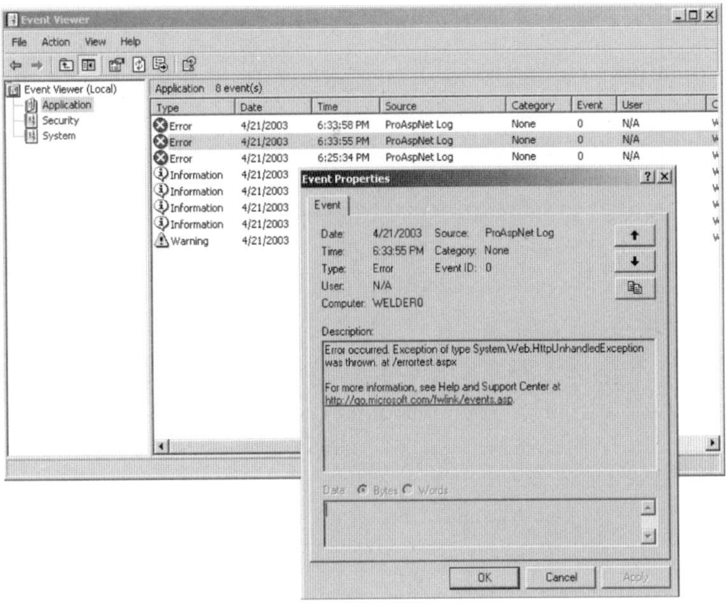

Figure 13-4 The Event Viewer tracks an error on an ASP.NET application.

Your code doesn't necessarily have to create the event source. If the source specified in the *Source* property does not exist, it will be created before writing to the event log. The *WriteEntry* method takes care of that. Windows provides three log files: Application, Security, and System, which is reserved for device drivers. The *Log* property of the *EventLog* class gets and sets the log file to use. It is Application by default.

Caution To create new event logs, applications should use the static method *CreateEventSource*. Note, though, that ASP.NET applications can't create new event logs because the running account (ASPNET) doesn't have enough permissions. One way to fix this is by having ASP.NET run as if it is the much more powerful SYSTEM account. As explained in Chapter 12, this can be done by changing the *userName* attribute in the *<processModel>* section of the machine.config file. On the other hand, running ASP.NET applications as SYSTEM opens serious security holes, which is the ultimate reason why Microsoft decided to use an account with limited privileges. If you want your ASP.NET application to use a custom log, create that at setup time.

The *HttpContext* Class

During the various steps of the request's chain of execution, an object gets passed along from class to class—this object is the *HttpContext* object. *HttpContext* encapsulates all the information available about an individual HTTP request that ASP.NET is going to handle. Defined in the *System.Web* namespace, the *HttpContext* class is instantiated by the *HttpRuntime* object while the request-processing mechanism is being set up. Next, the object is flowed throughout the various stages of the request's lifetime, as Figure 13-5 demonstrates.

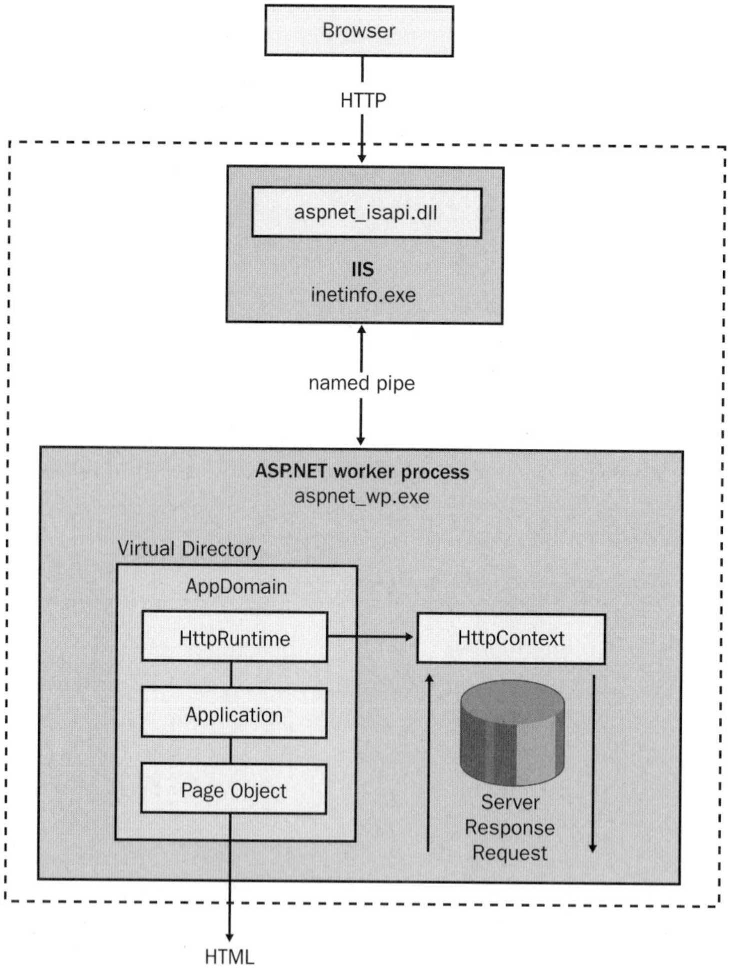

Figure 13-5 The *HttpContext* object, which encapsulates all the request information and gets flowed through the HTTP pipeline until the client response is generated.

Static Members

The programming interface of the *HttpContext* class includes two static members, one static property and one static method, to carry out general, noninstance-specific tasks. In the .NET Framework, a *static* member (a *shared* member in Visual Basic .NET jargon) of a class is a property or method that belongs to the type rather than to an instance of the type. All instances of the type share that same piece of code. To call static members, you must use the type name as the qualifier.

The *HttpContext* class has a static property named *Current* that returns the *HttpContext* object for the request being processed.

```
HttpContext cxt = HttpContext.Current;
```

In the *HttpContext* programming interface, you also find a static method. It is named *GetAppConfig* and returns configuration information for the specified section name. The information returned is read at the application level, which means it is a mix of machine.config and the application's main web.config file. The method returns an object whose actual type is determined by the characteristics of the section read.

Properties of the *HttpContext* Class

Table 13-7 enumerates all the properties exposed by the *HttpContext* class. The class represents a single entry point for a number of intrinsic objects such as ASP's *Server*, *Request*, and *Response* and new ASP.NET-specific *Cache* and *User* objects.

Table 13-7 *HttpContext* Properties

Property	Description
AllErrors	Gets an array of *Exception* objects, each of which represents an error that occurred while processing the request.
Application	Gets an instance of the *HttpApplicationState* class, which contains global and shared state of the application. Functionally equivalent to the ASP intrinsic *Application* object.
ApplicationInstance	Gets or sets the *HttpApplication* object for the current request. The actual type is *ASP.global_asax*. Use this cast to access public properties and methods you might have defined in global.asax.
Cache	Gets the ASP.NET *Cache* object for the current request.
Current	Gets the *HttpContext* object for the current request.

(continued)

Table 13-7 *HttpContext* Properties *(continued)*

Property	Description
Error	Gets the first *Exception* object (if any) that has been raised while processing the current request.
Handler	Gets or sets the *IHttpHandler* object for the current request.
IsCustomErrorEnabled	Gets whether custom error handling is enabled for the current request.
IsDebuggingEnabled	Gets whether the current request is in debug mode.
Items	Gets a name/value collection (hash table) that can be used to share custom data and objects between HTTP modules and HTTP handlers during the request lifetime.
Request	Gets an instance of the *HttpRequest* class, which represents the current HTTP request. Functionally equivalent to the ASP intrinsic *Request* object.
Response	Gets an instance of the *HttpResponse* class, which sends HTTP response data to the client. Functionally equivalent to the ASP intrinsic *Response* object.
Server	Gets an instance of the *HttpServerUtility* class, which provides helper methods for processing Web requests. Functionally equivalent to the ASP intrinsic *Server* object.
Session	Gets an instance of the *HttpSessionState* class, which manages user-specific data. Functionally equivalent to the ASP intrinsic *Session* object.
SkipAuthorization	Gets or sets a Boolean value that specifies whether the URL-based authorization module will skip the authorization check for the current request. This is *false* by default. Mostly used by authentication modules that need to redirect to a page that allows anonymous access.
Timestamp	Gets a *DateTime* object that represents the initial timestamp of the current request.
Trace	Gets the *TraceContext* object for the current response.
User	Gets or sets the *IPrincipal* object that represents the user making the request.

The *Items* property is a dictionary object—a hash table, to be exact—that can be used to share information between the modules and handlers involved with the particular request. By using this property, you can add your own information to the *HttpContext* object serving the request.

Methods of the *HttpContext* Class

Table 13-8 lists the methods specific to the *HttpContext* class. The table doesn't include methods inherited from the base *Object* class, such as *ToString*, *GetType*, and *Equals*.

Table 13-8 *HttpContext* Methods

Method	Description
AddError	Adds an exception object to the *AllErrors* collection.
ClearError	Clears all errors for the current request.
GetAppConfig	Returns requested configuration information for the current application. The information is collected from machine.config and the application's main web.config files.
GetConfig	Returns requested configuration information for the current request. The information is collected at the level of the requested URL, taking into account any child web.config files defined in subdirectories.
RewritePath	Mostly for internal use; overwrites path and query string of the current *Request* object.

In the all-encompassing container represented by the *HttpContext* object, a few popular objects also find their place. Among them are *Server*, *Request*, and *Response*. They are old acquaintances for ASP developers and indeed feature-rich elements of the ASP.NET programming toolkit. In ASP, the role of these objects was central, as they represented a large part of the ASP object model. The overall design of ASP.NET assigns to them a lower-level infrastructure role, but the set of properties and methods still makes these objects a fundamental resource for developers. Let's learn more about starting with the *Server* object.

The *Server* Object

The functionality of the ASP intrinsic *Server* object in ASP.NET is implemented by the *HttpServerUtility* class. An instance of the type is created when ASP.NET begins to process the request and is then stored as part of the request context. The bunch of helper methods that *HttpServerUtility* provides are publicly exposed to modules and handlers—including global.asax, pages, and Web services—through the *Server* property of the *HttpContext* object. In addition, to maintain ASP.NET coding as close as possible to the ASP programming style, several other commonly used ASP.NET objects also expose their own *Server* property. For example, both *Page* and *HttpApplication* show off a (technically speaking) redundant *Server* property. In this way, developers can use in the code, say, *Server.MapPath* without incurring compile errors. More important, they code exactly as they would have in ASP.

Intrinsic Objects? No, Intrinsic Properties

You should note that in ASP.NET, *Server*, *Request*, *Response*, and the like are in truth more *intrinsic properties* than intrinsic objects. In ASP, they were instances of COM components published to the ActiveX Scripting engine with easy-to-remember names such as *Server*, *Request*, and *Response*. To make them visible throughout all levels of code blocks, the objects were marked as globals, thereby gaining the label of intrinsically available objects.

The architecture is radically different in ASP.NET, in which the specific functionalities have been maintained and even enhanced but are integrated in the context of a true component-based model. The visibility of an object in a certain scope depends on strict syntax rules. Wide-range visibility, such as that of intrinsic objects in ASP, can be obtained only by replicating the objects in all scopes in which they are needed. Hence, the concept of *intrinsic properties*. Figure 13-6 compares the ASP and ASP.NET models.

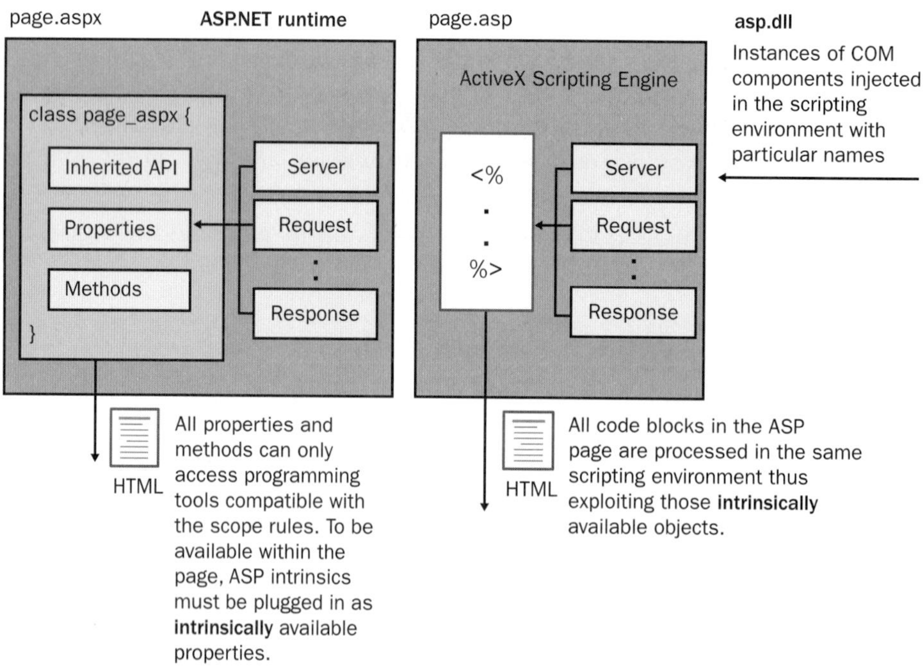

Figure 13-6 In ASP, intrinsic objects are published as globals in the ActiveX Scripting engine in which all code blocks are processed. In ASP.NET, the visibility of an object is determined by the syntax.

The ASP.NET *HttpServerUtility* class extends and enhances the set of properties and methods defined on the COM object working as the ASP *Server* intrinsic object. Let's look at the new programming interface in more detail.

Properties of the *HttpServerUtility* Class

This class provides two properties, named *MachineName* and *ScriptTimeout*. The *MachineName* property returns the machine name and raises an *HttpException* if the name of the Web server machine is not readable. The *ScriptTimeout* property gets and sets the time in seconds that a request is allowed to be processed. This property accepts integers and is populated with the value of the *executionTimeout* attribute in the *<httpRuntime>* section of the machine.config file. The default value is 90 seconds; however, it is set to a virtually infinite value if the page runs with the attribute *debug=true*.

```
this.Server.ScriptTimeout = 30000000;
```

The *ScriptTimeout* property is explicitly and automatically set in the constructor of the class that represents the page. (See Chapter 2.)

Methods of the *HttpServerUtility* Class

Table 13-9 lists all methods exposed by the *HttpServerUtility* class. As you can see, they constitute a group of helper methods that come in handy at various stages of page execution. The class provides a couple of methods to create instances of COM components and a few others to deal with errors. Another group of methods relates to the decoding and encoding of content and URL.

Table 13-9 *Server* Methods

Method	Description
ClearError	Clears the last exception that was thrown for the request.
CreateObject	Creates an instance of the specified COM object.
CreateObjectFromClsid	Creates an instance of the COM object identified by the specified CLSID. The class identifier is expressed as a string.
Execute	Passes control to the specified page for execution. The child page executes like a subroutine. The output can be retained in a writer object or automatically flushed in the parent response buffer.
GetLastError	Returns the last *Exception* object that was thrown.
HtmlDecode	Decodes a string that has been encoded to eliminate invalid HTML characters. For example, it translates *<* back into <.
HtmlEncode	Encodes a string to be displayed in a browser. For example, encodes < into *<*.

(continued)

Table 13-9 *Server* Methods *(continued)*

Method	Description
MapPath	Returns the physical path that corresponds to the specified virtual path on the Web server.
Transfer	Works as a kind of server-side redirect. It terminates the execution of the current page and passes control to the specified page. Unlike *Execute*, control is not passed back to the caller page. It is more effective than *Response.Redirect*.
UrlDecode	Decodes a string encoded for HTTP transmission to the server in a URL. The decoded string can be returned as a string or output to a writer.
UrlEncode	Encodes a string for HTTP transmission to a client in a URL. The encoded string can be returned as a string or output to a writer.
UrlPathEncode	Encodes only the path portion of a URL string, and returns the encoded string. This method leaves the query string content intact.

HTML and URL encoding are ways of encoding characters to ensure that the transmitted text is not misunderstood by the receiving browser. HTML encoding, in particular, replaces <, >, &, and quotes with equivalent HTML entities such as *<*, *>*, *&*, and *"*. It also encodes blanks, punctuation characters, and in general, all characters not allowed in an HTML stream. On the other hand, URL encoding is aimed at fixing the text transmitted in URL strings. In URL encoding, the same critical characters are replaced with different character entities than in HTML encoding.

Both HTML and URL encoding and decoding methods can return a string as well as output to any sort of *TextWriter* object—typically a *StringWriter* object. We'll talk about text writers in Chapter 16.

Embedding Another Page's Results

The *Execute* method allows you to consider an external page as a subroutine. When the execution flow reaches the *Server.Execute* call, control is passed to the specified page. The execution of the current page is suspended, and the external page is spawned. The response text generated by the child execution is captured and processed according to the particular overload of *Execute* that has been used.

```
public void Execute(string);
public void Execute(string, TextWriter);
```

If the first overload is used, the response text is automatically embedded in the response of the main page. (See Figure 13-7.) If a *TextWriter* object is specified, the response text of the child execution is accumulated into the writer object and left at the disposal of the main page.

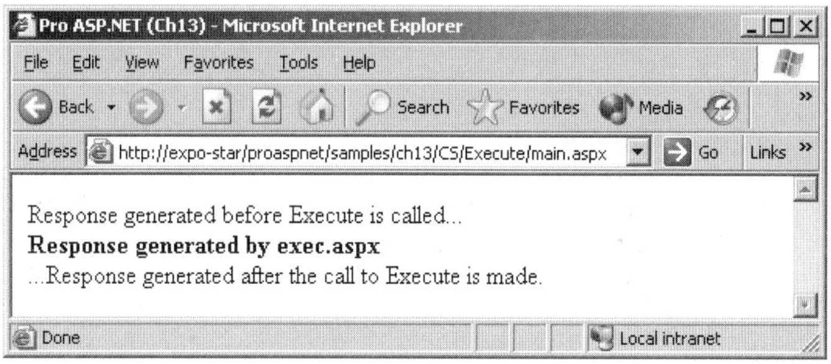

Figure 13-7 The response text generated by *Execute*, which can be automatically embedded in the main response or cached in a writer object.

The source code for the main page in Figure 13-7 is as follows:

```
<%@ Page Language="C#" %>
<script runat="server">
void Page_Load(object sender, EventArgs e) {
    Response.Write("Response generated before Execute is called...<br>");
    Server.Execute("exec.aspx");
    Response.Write("<br>...Response generated after the call to Execute.");
}
</script>
<html><title>Pro ASP.NET (Ch13)</title>
<body></body>
</html>
```

It's interesting to look at the internal implementation of the *Execute* method. Both the main and child pages are run by the same *HttpApplication* object as if they were the same request. What happens within the folds of *Execute* is a sort of context switch. First, the method obtains an HTTP handler from the application factory to serve the new request. The original handler of the main request is cached and replaced with the new handler. The spawned page inherits the context of the parent; when finished, any modification made to *Session* or *Application* is immediately visible to the main page.

The handler switching makes the whole operation extremely fast, as there's no need to create a new object to serve the request. When the child page returns, the original handler is restored. The execution of the main page continues from the point in which it was stopped but using the context inherited from the child page.

Server-Side Redirection

The *Transfer* method differs from the *Execute* method in that it terminates the current page after executing the specified page. The new page runs as if it was the originally requested one. The *Transfer* method has the following two overloads:

```
public void Transfer(string);
public void Transfer(string, bool);
```

The first overload simply redirects to the specified page. The second overload clears or preserves the *QueryString* and *Form* collections based on the value of the Boolean argument. When you call the first overload, the collections are always cleared unless the *IsPostBack* property on the original page is set to *true*.

The *Execute* and *Transfer* methods have a similar architecture. Both methods use the same internal procedure to perform the handler switch. In both cases, the same *HttpApplication* object is used to carry out the new request, as shown in Figure 13-8.

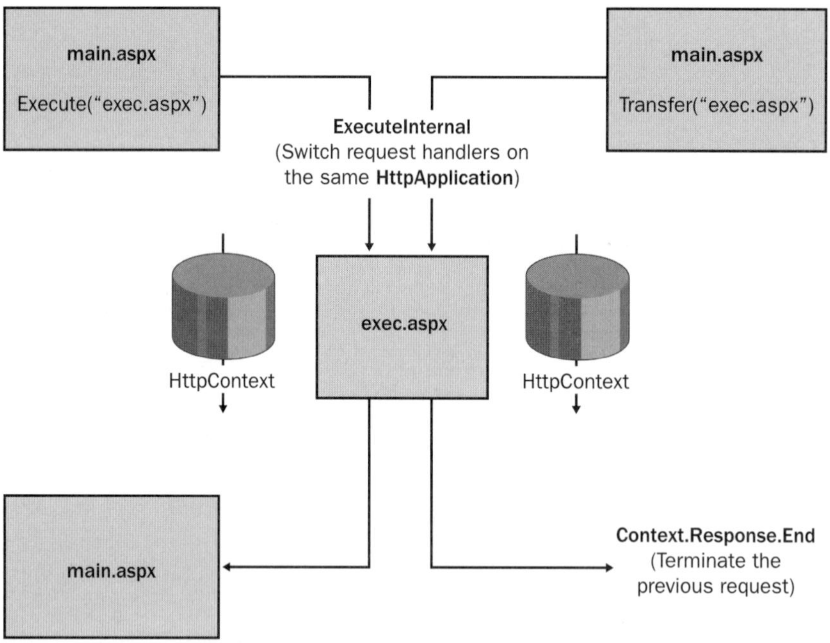

Figure 13-8 Comparing the internal architecture of the *Execute* and *Transfer* methods.

Note that when you call *Transfer*, the new page request is served immediately. However, the previous request is terminated only when the internal call to *Execute*, used to implement the redirect, has returned. The following pseudocode illustrates the behavior of the method:

```
public void Transfer(string path, bool preserveForm) {
    // the null argument indicates that no writer should
    // be used in the call to Execute
    ExecuteInternal(path, null, preserveForm);
    Context.Response.End();
}
```

All the code that might be following the call to *Transfer* in the main page is never executed. In the end, *Transfer* is just a page redirect method. However, it is particularly efficient for two reasons. First, no roundtrip to the client is requested as is the case, for example, with *Response.Redirect*. Second, the same *HttpApplication* that was serving the caller request is reused, thus limiting the impact on the ASP.NET infrastructure.

Late-Bound COM Objects

The *HttpServerUtility* class provides you with the ability to create late-bound COM objects in much the same way you do in ASP. The methods are *CreateObject* and *CreateObjectFromClsid*. They are marked to return a generic *Object* type. However, the actual type they return is *System.__ComObject*. Objects can be created either from the string representation of the class CLSID or from the progID. The following code creates an instance of a COM component using the CLSID:

```
Dim strClsid As String = "42754580-16b7-11ce-80eb-00aa003d7352"
Dim comObj As Object = Server.CreateObject(strClsid)
```

When assigned to a variable declared of type *Object*, an object is said to be late bound—as opposed to early-bound, strongly typed objects. Late-bound objects can hold references to any object, but they lack many advantages of early-bound objects. Early-bound objects should be used whenever possible because they are significantly faster than late-bound objects and make your code easier to develop, read, and maintain.

Primarily for backward-compatibility reasons, you might sometimes create late-bound instances of COM objects. Using COM objects in ASP.NET applications is a common necessity in real-world projects. The best way to import COM functionality in .NET applications entails the use of managed wrappers—special classes that expose the type library of the COM class as a .NET class. Managed wrappers are usually created by Visual Studio .NET when you reference a COM object in your project.

> **Note** A command-line utility is also available should you need to generate the class assembly using a particular namespace, language, or file name different from those automatically set by Visual Studio .NET. The utility is the Type Library Importer (tlbimp.exe) and is located in the installation path of Visual Studio .NET.

Although not especially effective as an approach, the *Server.CreateObject* method can be used to create a late-bound instance of a COM component. The ideal language for late binding is Visual Basic .NET; however, bear in mind that late binding is supported as long as the *Strict* option is *Off* (the default).

The following code shows how to fill an ADO *Recordset* object using the ASP programming style:

```
<%@ Page Language="VB" AspCompat="true" %>

<script runat="server">
Sub Page_Load(sender as object, e as EventArgs)
    Dim rs As Object = Server.CreateObject("ADODB.Recordset")
    rs.Open("SELECT firstname, lastname FROM employees", _
        "PROVIDER=sqloledb;DATABASE=northwind;SERVER=localhost;UID=sa;")

    Dim sb As StringBuilder = New StringBuilder("")
    While Not rs.EOF
        sb.Append(rs.Fields("lastname").Value.ToString())
        sb.Append(", ")
        sb.Append(rs.Fields("firstname").Value.ToString())
        sb.Append("<br>")
        rs.MoveNext
    End While

    Response.Write(sb.ToString())
End Sub
</script>
```

Note the use of the *AspCompat* attribute in the *@Page* directive. Apartment-threaded COM components can be created only in ASP.NET pages that have the *AspCompat* attribute set to *true*. Before an attempt to create the object is made, the *CreateObject* method checks the threading model of the component. If the page is already working in ASP compatibility mode—that is, the *AspCompat* attribute is *true*—the object is created, regardless of the threading model of the component. If the *AspCompat* attribute is set to *false* (the default), *CreateObject* reads the threading model of the COM component from the registry. If the threading model is *apartment*, or no threading model is specified, an exception is thrown; otherwise, the object is successfully created. The following pseudocode shows the internals of the *HttpServerUtility*'s *CreateObject* method:

```
public object CreateObject(string progID) {
    Type managedType = Type.GetTypeFromProgID(progID);
    if (!IsAspCompatMode) {
        string threadingModel = GetThreadingModel(managedType.GUID);
        if (threadingModel == "apartment")
            throw new HttpException("...");
    }
    return Activator.CreateInstance(managedType);
}
```

Note also that the use of the *AspCompat* attribute is not strictly necessary with the ADO library because the ADO library supports both the apartment and free-threading model.

> **Note** COM components developed using Visual Basic 6.0 need the *AspCompat* attribute to be used in ASP.NET pages because they typically use the single-threaded apartment model (STA). This situation is detected and throws an exception.
>
> Note, though, that if your code instantiates the COM object through a managed wrapper (instead of creating the instance using *CreateObject*), the runtime will no longer be able to detect the apartment nature of the component and does not throw an exception. A managed wrapper saves you from a run-time exception but not from the need of setting *AspCompat* to *true*.

The Importance of *AspCompat*

Running STA components in a multithreaded apartment environment (MTA) such as ASP.NET is strongly discouraged performance-wise. The *AspCompat* attribute is designed to avoid this critical situation. Let's see how and why.

To process HTTP requests, normally ASP.NET uses a pool of threads from an MTA. Objects in an MTA execute on any thread and allow any number of methods to occur simultaneously. Single-threaded apartment COM components (for example, all Visual Basic 6 COM components) execute on the particular thread in which they were created and allow only one method to execute at a time. Until special countermeasures are taken, when you run an STA component in an MTA environment continued thread switching is likely to happen.

More importantly, a thread switch can happen only when the particular thread in the pool that can serve the STA component is available. As you can see, this situation is heralding poor performance issues if not even deadlock.

By setting the *AspCompat* attribute to *true*, you force ASP.NET to use an STA thread pool to accommodate the COM object on a per-page basis. In this case, both the caller thread and the callee component live in the same apartment and no extra overhead is involved. As a matter of fact, ASP.NET pages that contain STA COM components run better in STA mode than in an, otherwise generally faster, MTA mode.

Because the *AspCompat* attribute is processed after the instance of the page class is created, you should also avoid creating instances of STA COM objects in the page constructor. If you don't avoid doing this, the page will be served by an MTA thread regardless of the value of *AspCompat* and probably incur poor performance.

Setting *AspCompat* to *true* also has another advantage—it makes ASP intrinsic objects (*ObjectContext*, *Request*, *Response*, and so forth) available to the COM component. ASP.NET creates unmanaged ASP intrinsic objects and passes them to the COM components used in the page.

The *Response* Object

In ASP.NET, the functionality of the ASP intrinsic *Response* object is provided through the *HttpResponse* class. An instance of the *HttpResponse* object is created when the HTTP pipeline is set up to serve the request. The instance is then linked to the *HttpContext* object associated with the request. The *HttpResponse* class defines methods and properties to manipulate the text that will be sent to the browser. Although user-defined ASP.NET code never needs to use the *HttpResponse* constructor, looking at it is still useful to get the gist of the class:

```
public HttpResponse(TextWriter writer);
```

As you can see, the constructor takes a writer object, which will then be used to accumulate the response text that controls the generated page. The actual writer used by *HttpResponse* is the *HttpWriter* class. All calls made to *Response.Write* are resolved in terms of internal calls to the *HttpWriter* object.

Properties of the *HttpResponse* Class

All properties of the class are grouped and described in Table 13-10. You set a few of these properties to configure key fields on the HTTP response packet, such as content type, character set, page expiration, and status code.

Table 13-10 ***HttpResponse*** **Properties**

Property	Description
Buffer	Gets or sets a Boolean value that indicates whether the response text should be buffered and sent only at the end of the request. This property is deprecated and provided only for backward compatibility with ASP. ASP.NET applications use *BufferOutput*.
BufferOutput	Gets or sets a Boolean value that indicates whether response buffering is enabled. The default is *true*.
Cache	Gets the caching policy set for the page. The caching policy is an *HttpCachePolicy* object that can be used to set the cache-specific HTTP headers for the current response.
CacheControl	Sets the *Cache-Control* HTTP header. Acceptable values are *Public* or *Private*. The property is deprecated in favor of *Cache*.
Charset	Gets or sets a string value for the HTTP character set of the output stream. If it's set after headers have been sent, it throws an exception. If it's set to *null*, it suppresses the *Content-Type* header.
ContentEncoding	Gets or sets an object of type *Encoding* for the character encoding of the output stream.
ContentType	Gets or sets the string that represents the MIME type of the output stream. The default value is *text/html*.
Cookies	Gets a collection (*HttpCookieCollection*) object that contains instances of the *HttpCookie* class generated on the server. All the cookies in the collection will be transmitted to the client through the *set-cookie* HTTP header.
Expires	Gets or sets the number of minutes before a page cached on a browser expires. Provided for compatibility with ASP, the property is deprecated in favor of *Cache*.
ExpiresAbsolute	Gets or sets the absolute date and time at which the page expires in the browser cache. Provided for compatibility with ASP, the property is deprecated in favor of *Cache*.
Filter	Gets or sets a filter *Stream* object through which all HTTP output sent by *Response.Write* passes.
IsClientConnected	Get a Boolean value that indicates whether the client is still connected.
Output	Gets a *TextWriter* object that is used to output text to the response stream.
OutputStream	Gets a *Stream* object that is used to output binary data to the response stream.
RedirectLocation	Gets or a sets a string for the value of the *Location* header.

(continued)

Table 13-10 *HttpResponse* Properties *(continued)*

Property	Description
Status	Sets the string returned to the client describing the status of the response. Provided for compatibility with ASP, the property is deprecated in favor of *StatusDescription*.
StatusCode	Gets or sets an integer value for the HTTP status code of the output returned to the client. The default value is *200 (OK)*. An exception is raised if the property is set after the HTTP headers have been sent.
StatusDescription	Gets or sets the HTTP status string, which is a description of the overall status of the response returned to the client. The default value is *OK*.
SuppressContent	Gets or sets a Boolean value that indicates whether HTTP content should be sent to the client. This is set to *false* by default; if set to *true*, only headers are sent.

As you can see, a few of the *HttpResponse* properties are provided only for backward compatibility with previous versions of ASP. In some cases (for example, *BufferOutput* and *StatusDescription*), the property has just been renamed; in other cases, the properties deprecated have been replaced by a more general and powerful API. This is certainly the case for cache and expiration properties.

Setting the Response Cache Policy

In ASP, the *Response* object has three properties dedicated to control the ability of the page being sent to the browser to be cached. The *Expires* and *ExpiresAbsolute* properties define relative and absolute times at which the page cached on the client expires and is no longer utilized by the browser to serve a user request. In fact, if the user navigates to a currently cached page, the cached version is displayed and no roundtrip occurs to the server.

A third property somehow related to page caching is *CacheControl*. The property sets a particular HTTP header—the *Cache-Control* header. The *Cache-Control* header controls how a document is to be cached across the network. Allowable values come from the *HttpCacheability* enumeration and are listed in Table 13-11.

Table 13-11 The *System.Web.HttpCacheability* Enumeration

Value	Description
NoCache	The page response is not cached on the client.
Private	The page response is cached only on the client and not on possible intermediate proxy servers. (This is the default setting.)
Public	The page response is cached both on the client and proxy servers.

The *HttpCacheability* enumeration has a few more members like *Server*. This member has nothing to do with HTTP caching and, in fact, sets the *Cache-Control* header to *no-cache*. However, it indicates that the page is cached on the origin server.

In ASP.NET, all caching capabilities are grouped in the *HttpCachePolicy* class. With regard to page caching, the class has a double role. It provides methods for both setting cache-specific HTTP headers and controlling the ASP.NET page output cache. In this chapter, we're mostly interested in the HTTP headers, and we'll keep page output caching warm for Chapter 14.)

To set the visibility of a page in a client cache, use the *SetCacheability* method of the *HttpCachePolicy* class with one of the values in Table 13-11. To set an expiration time, use the *SetExpires* method, which takes for input an absolute *DateTime* object. Finally, to set a lifetime for the cached page, pass to *SetExpires* the current time plus the desired interval.

> **Note** In the case of conflicting cache policies, ASP.NET maintains the most restrictive settings. For example, if a page contains two controls that set the *Cache-Control* header to *public* and *private*, the most restrictive policy will be used. In this case, *Cache-Control: Private* will be sent to the client.

Setting an Output Filter

In ASP.NET, a new component makes its debut—the *response filter*. A response filter is a *Stream*-derived object that can be associated with the *HttpResponse* object to monitor and filter any output being generated. If you set the *Filter* property with the instance of an object derived from *Stream*, all output being written to the underlying HTTP writer first passes through your output filter.

The custom filter, if any, is invoked during the *HttpResponse*'s *Flush* method before the actual text is flushed and then sent to the client. Building a response filter is a matter of creating a new class and making it inherit from *Stream* and override some of the methods. The class should have a constructor that accepts a *Stream* object. In light of this, a response filter class is more a wrapper stream class than a purely inherited stream class. If you try to set *Response.Filter* with a new instance of, say, *MemoryStream* or *FileStream*, an exception is thrown.

The following listing shows how to create a stream class that works as a response filter. For simplicity, the class inherits from *MemoryStream*. You might want to make it inherit from *Stream*, but in this case you need to override (because they are abstract) a number of methods, such as *CanRead*, *CanWrite*, *CanSeek*, and *Read*. The class converts lowercase characters to uppercase.

```
public class MyFilterStream : MemoryStream
{
    private Stream m_Stream;

    public MyFilterStream(Stream filterStream) {
        m_Stream = filterStream;
    }

    // The Write method actually does the filtering
    public override void Write(byte[] buffer, int offset, int count)
    {
        byte[] data = new byte[count];
        Buffer.BlockCopy(buffer, offset, data, 0, count);

        // Change lowercase chars to uppercase.
        for (int i = 0; i < count; i++)  {
            if (data[i] >= 'a' && data[i] <= 'z')
                data[i] -= ('a'-'A');
        }

        m_Stream.Write(data, 0, count);
    }
}
```

Use the following code to associate this output filter with the *Response.Filter* property. Here's a sample page:

```
<script runat="server" language="C#" >
void Page_Load(object sender, EventArgs e) {
    Response.Filter = new MyFilterStream(Response.Filter);
    Response.Write("hello, world...<br>");
}
</script>
```

Methods of the *HttpResponse* Class

Table 13-12 lists all the methods defined on the *HttpResponse* class. The class contains one deprecated method added only for compatibility with previous versions of ASP. This method is *AddHeader*.

Table 13-12 *HttpResponse* Methods

Method	Description
AddCacheItemDependencies	Adds an array of items in the output cache the current page is dependent upon. When any of the specified items is removed from the cache, the cached output of the current page becomes invalid.
AddCacheItemDependency	Adds a single cache key the current page is dependent upon. When the specified key is removed from the cache, the cached output of the current page becomes invalid.
AddFileDependencies	Adds a group of file names to the collection of file names on which the current page is dependent. When any of the files is modified, the cached output of the current page is invalid.
AddFileDependency	Adds a single file name to the collection of file names on which the current page is dependent. If the file is modified, the cached output of the current page becomes invalid.
AddHeader	Adds an HTTP header to the output stream. It is provided for compatibility with previous versions of ASP. In ASP.NET, use *AppendHeader*.
AppendHeader	Adds an HTTP header to the output stream.
AppendToLog	Adds custom log information to the IIS log file.AppendToLog.
ApplyAppPathModifier	Adds a session ID to the specified virtual path and returns the result. It is mostly used with cookieless sessions to construct an absolute HREF.
BinaryWrite	Writes binary characters to the HTTP output stream.
Clear	Clears all content output from the buffer stream.
ClearContent	Calls into *Clear*.
ClearHeaders	Clears all headers from the buffer stream.
Close	Closes the socket connection with the client.
End	Sends all buffered text to the client, stops execution, and raises the *Application_EndRequest* event.
Flush	Sends all currently buffered output to the client.

(continued)

Table 13-12 *HttpResponse* Methods *(continued)*

Method	Description
Pics	Appends a PICS-Label HTTP header to the output. PICS stands for Platform for Internet Content Selection and is a W3C standard for rating pages. Any string is acceptable, and ASP.NET does not validate the text as long as it doesn't exceed 255 characters. The header is added through *AppendHeader*.
Redirect	Redirects a client to a new URL. Needs a roundtrip.
RemoveOutputCacheItem	A static method that takes a file system path and removes from the cache all cached items associated with the specified path.
Write	Writes content to the underlying output stream. The method can write a string, a single character, an array of characters, as well as an object. In this case, though, what gets written is the output of the object's *ToString* method.
WriteFile	Writes the specified file (or a portion of it) directly to the output stream. The file can be identified with its path or a Win32 handle (an *IntPtr* object).

The *Redirect* method causes the specified page to execute. However, the trick used in this case is less efficient than with *Server.Execute* or *Server.Transfer*. The method sends a response that the browser interprets as an invitation to request the specified page. Although the final effect is always that of redirecting the user to a different page, the way in which this effect is obtained requires a roundtrip. The *HttpResponse*'s *Redirect* method has two overloads:

```
public void Redirect(string);
public void Redirect(string, bool);
```

The second overload lets you specify whether the execution of the current page should terminate. By default, the redirection is unconditional and the execution of the current page is stopped.

The *Request* Object

The *HttpRequest* object groups all the information contained in the HTTP packet that represents the incoming Web request. The contents of the various HTTP headers, the query string, or the form's input fields, path, and URL information are organized in a series of collections and other ad hoc objects for easy and effective programmatic access. The *HttpRequest* object is populated as soon as ASP.NET begins working on a Web request and is made available through the *Request* property of *HttpContext*.

HttpRequest exposes a fair number of properties and is one of the objects that has been more significantly enriched in the transition from ASP to ASP.NET.

Properties of the *HttpRequest* Class

The class properties can be classified in three groups based on the type of information they contain: type of the request, client data, and connection. Table 13-13 lists the properties that define the type of request being issued.

Table 13-13 Properties Describing the Request Type

Property	Description
AcceptTypes	Gets an array of strings denoting the list of MIME types supported by the client for the specified request.
Browser	Gets an *HttpBrowserCapabilities* object that contains information about the capabilities of the client's browser.
ContentEncoding	Gets or sets an *Encoding* object that represents the client's character set. If specified, this property overrides the ASP.NET default encoding.
ContentLength	Gets the length in bytes of the content sent by the client.
ContentType	Gets or sets the MIME content type of the incoming request.
CurrentExecutionFilePath	Gets the current virtual path of the request even when the client is redirected to another page via *Execute* or *Transfer*. *FilePath*, instead, always returns the path to the originally requested page.
FilePath	Gets the virtual path of the current request. The path doesn't change in cases of server-side page redirection.
HttpMethod	Gets a string that denotes the HTTP method used for the request. Values are GET, POST, or HEAD.
RequestType	Gets or sets a string that denotes the HTTP command used to issue the request. Can be GET or POST.

(continued)

Table 13-13 Properties Describing the Request Type *(continued)*

Property	Description
TotalBytes	Gets the total number of bytes in the input stream. This property differs from *ContentLength* in that it also includes headers.
UserAgent	Gets a string that identifies the browser. This property gets the raw content of the user agent header. Note that the Internet Explorer user agent string contains version information about COM+ and the .NET common language runtime (CLR). (The CLR version does not contain build information to recognize installed service packs.)

Initially, *CurrentExecutionFilePath* and *FilePath* share the same content—the requested URL. However, in cases of server-side redirects, the value of *CurrentExecutionFilePath* is automatically updated. You should check *CurrentExecutionFilePath* for up-to-date information about the target URL.

The *HttpBrowserCapabilities* object groups in a single place values that identify a fair number of browser capabilities, including support for ActiveX controls, scripting languages, frames, cookies, and more. (Browser capabilities was discussed in Chapter 4.) When the request arrives, the user agent information is used to identify the requesting browser and a new empty instance of the *HttpBrowserCapabilities* class is created. The instance is then populated with browser-specific information read from the machine.config file. The information returned through *HttpBrowserCapabilities* is in no way dynamically set by the browser. The browser sets only the user agent string, and ASP.NET uses that small piece of information as a key to retrieve statically set information from the configuration.

The *HttpRequest*'s *Browser* property also supports mobile scenarios in version 1.1 of the .NET Framework. In this case, the actual object returned is of class *MobileCapabilities*—a *HttpBrowserCapabilities*-derived class. When you obtain the *Browser* property reference you should cast it as a *MobileCapabilities* class.

Table 13-14 lists the *HttpRequest* properties that expose the client data that ASP.NET pages might want to use for server-side processing. The following table includes, for example, cookies, forms, and query string collections.

Table 13-14 Properties Describing the Client Data

Property	Description
ClientCertificate	Gets an *HttpClientCertificate* object containing information on the client's security certificate settings, if any. The *HttpClientCertificate* object wraps up information such as number, validity, and issuer of the certificate.
Cookies	Gets an *HttpCookieCollection* object representing all cookies sent by the client. A cookie is identified by the *HttpCookie* object.
Files	Gets an *HttpFileCollection* object representing a collection of client-uploaded files. The *Files* property requires the HTTP *Content-Type* header to be set to *multipart/form-data*.
Filter	Gets or sets a *Stream*-based object through which all HTTP input passes when received.
Form	Gets a *NameValueCollection* object filled with the values of the input fields in the form posted. The collection is populated when the *Content-Type* header is either *application/x-www-form-urlencoded* or *multipart/form-data*.
Headers	Gets a *NameValueCollection* object filled with all the header values in the request.
InputStream	Gets a *Stream* object representing the contents of the incoming HTTP content body.
Params	Gets a *NameValueCollection* object that is a union of four other similar collections: *QueryString*, *Form*, *ServerVariables*, and *Cookies*.
QueryString	Gets a *NameValueCollection* object containing all the query string variables sent by the client.
ServerVariables	Gets a *NameValueCollection* object filled with a collection of Web server–defined variables.
UserHostAddress	Gets the IP address of the remote client.
UserHostName	Gets the Domain Name System (DNS) name of the remote client.
UserLanguages	Gets an array of strings denoting the list of the languages accepted by the client for the specified request. The languages are read from the *Accept-Language* header.

The *Params* collection combines four different but homogeneous collections—*QueryString*, *Form*, *ServerVariables*, and *Cookies*—and replicates the information contained in each of them. Although not particularly high, the risk of creating conflicting names does exist especially because the entries in *Form*, *QueryString*, and *Cookies* are decided by the programmers. The collections are added in the following order: *QueryString*, *Form*, *Cookies*, and finally *ServerVariables*.

Table 13-15 lists the properties that relate to the open connection.

Table 13-15 Properties Describing the Connection

Property	Description
ApplicationPath	Gets the virtual path of the current application.
IsAuthenticated	Gets a Boolean value that indicates whether or not the user has been authenticated.
IsSecureConnection	Gets a Boolean value that indicates whether the connection is taking place over a Secure Sockets Layer (SSL) using HTTPS.
Path	Gets the virtual path of the current request.
PathInfo	Gets additional path information for the requested resource, if any. The property returns any text that follows the URL.
PhysicalApplicationPath	Gets the file system path of the current application's root directory.
PhysicalPath	Gets the physical file system path corresponding to the requested URL.
RawUrl	Gets the raw URL of the current request.
Url	Gets the *Uri* object that represents the URL of the current request.
UrlReferrer	Gets the *Uri* object that represents the URL from which the current request originated.

The *Uri* class provides an object representation of a Uniform Resource Identifier (URI)—a unique name for a resource available on the Internet. The *Uri* class provides easy access to the parts of the URI as well as properties and methods for checking host, loopback, ports, and DNS.

The server variables set in the *ServerVariables* collection are decided by the run-time environment that processes the request. The information packed in the collection is for the most part excerpted from the HTTP worker request object; another part contains Web server–specific information. The *ServerVariables* collection is just a friendly name/value model to expose that information.

In ASP.NET applications, the usefulness of *ServerVariables* is limited, as a large number of variables are also exposed as individual properties. For example, the URL and path information—whose corresponding variables are *URL* and PATH_INFO—are also available through more direct properties on the *HttpRequest* object, such as *Url* and *PathInfo*. (See Table 13-15.) However, some information is not available to Web applications other than through server variables. A few examples are the name of the Web server software (SERVER_SOFTWARE) and the meta path of the current instance of the application in IIS (INSTANCE_META_PATH).

Methods of the *HttpRequest* Class

Table 13-16 lists all methods exposed by the *HttpRequest* class. The list doesn't include methods such as *Equals* and *ToString*, which are inherited from *Object*.

Table 13-16 *HttpRequest* Methods

Method	Description
BinaryRead	Performs a binary read from the current input stream. The method lets you specify the number of bytes to read and returns an array of bytes. The method is provided for compatibility with ASP. ASP.NET applications should read from the stream associated with the *InputStream* property.
MapImageCoordinates	Maps an incoming image-field form parameter to x/y coordinate values.
MapPath	Maps the specified virtual path to a physical path on the Web server.
SaveAs	Saves the current request to a file disk with or without headers. This method is especially useful for debugging purposes.

The *SaveAs* method lets you create a file to store the entire content of the HTTP request. Note that the storage medium can only be disk file; no stream or writer can be used. Since ASP.NET by default isn't granted write permissions, this method causes an access denied exception unless you take ad hoc measures. Granting the ASPNET account full control over the file to create (or over the whole folder) is one of the possible ways to successfully use the *SaveAs* method. The following listing shows possible content that *SaveAs* writes to disk.

```
GET /test/main.aspx HTTP/1.1
Connection: Keep-Alive
Accept: */*
Accept-Encoding: gzip, deflate
Accept-Language: en-us
Cookie: ASP.NET_SessionId=3ogcmn550gnzl4zlao5h3545
Host: expo-star
User-Agent: Mozilla/
4.0 (compatible; MSIE 6.0; Windows NT 5.0; COM+ 1.0.2204; .NET CLR 1.1.4322)
```

Conclusion

In this chapter, we covered some basic objects that are the foundation of ASP.NET programming—*Server*, *Response*, *Request*, and others. An ASP.NET application is represented by an instance of the *HttpApplication* class properly configured by the contents of the global.asax file. And both the *HttpApplication* class and the global.asax files found their space in this chapter, too.

In ASP.NET, as well as in ASP, you can use an unqualified *Server* object in the source of the page. The context that allows you to execute that code is different in the two models, though. In ASP, *Server* is the name that identifies an instance of a COM component globally available in the scripting environment. In ASP.NET, *Server* is simply a property exposed by the page class. We summarized this key architectural difference with the expression *intrinsic properties* to distinguish it from the intrinsic objects of ASP.

While discussing the interface of the objects that generate the context of an HTTP request, we reviewed in detail some specific programming issues such as the instantiation of late-bound COM objects, server-side page redirection, and the setup of response filters. In the next chapter, we'll discuss an important topic related to Web applications and ASP.NET—state management. Fundamentally, Web applications are stateless, but ASP.NET provides various mechanisms for maintaining application state and caching pages.

Resources

- A Matter of Context (*http://msdn.microsoft.com/library/en-us/dnaspnet/html/asp01242002.asp*)
- ASP.NET Internals Chat (*http://msdn.microsoft.com/chats/vstudio/vstudio_061302.asp*)
- HTTP Modules (*http://msdn.microsoft.com/msdnmag/issues/02/05/asp/asp0205.asp*)
- Setting Up Global Objects with the global.asax File (*http://www.csharphelp.com/archives/archive206.html*)
- Happy Hunting Extend the ASP.NET page output cache and get inside AspCompat (*http://www.aspnetpro.com/features/2003/03/asp200303jp_f/asp200303jp_f.asp*)

14

ASP.NET State Management

The cause is hidden. The effect is visible to all.

—*Ovid*

All real-world applications of any shape and form need to maintain their own state to serve users' requests. ASP.NET applications are no exception, but unlike other types of applications, they need special system-level tools to achieve the result. The reason for this peculiarity lies in the stateless nature of the underlying protocol that Web applications still rely upon. As long as HTTP remains the transportation protocol for the Web, all applications will run into the same problem—they need to figure out the most effective way to persist state information.

Application state is a sort of blank container each application and programmer can fill with whatever piece of information makes sense to persist: from user preferences to global settings, from worker data to hit counters, from lookup tables to shopping carts. This extremely variegated mess of data can be organized and accessed according to a number of usage patterns. Typically, all the information contributing to the application state is distributed in various layers, each with its own set of settings for visibility, programmability, and lifetime.

ASP.NET provides state management facilities at four levels: application, session, page, and request. Each level has its own special container object, which is a topic we'll cover in this chapter. In particular, we'll explore the *HttpApplicationState*, *HttpSessionState*, and *ViewState* objects, which provide for application, session, and page state maintenance, respectively. In Chapter 13, we covered the *HttpContext* object, which is the primary tool used to manage information across the entire request lifetime. The context of the request is different from all other state objects in that the request has a limited lifetime but passes through the entire pipeline of objects processing an HTTP request. Table 14-1 summarizes the main features of the various state objects.

Table 14-1 State Management Objects at a Glance

Object	Lifetime	Data Visibility	Location
Cache	Implements an automatic scavenging mechanism, and periodically clears least-used contents	Global to all sessions	Does not support Web farm or Web garden scenarios
HttpApplicationState	Created when the first request hits the Web server, and released when the application shuts down	Same as for *Cache*	Same as for *Cache*
HttpContext	Spans the entire lifetime of the individual request	Global to the objects involved with the request	Same as for *Cache*
HttpSessionState	Created when the user makes the first request, and lasts until the user closes the session	Global to all requests issued by the user who started the session	Configurable to work on Web farms and gardens
ViewState	Represents the calling context of each page being generated	Limited to all requests queued for the same page	Configurable to work on Web farms and gardens (see Chapter 12)

In spite of their quite unfamiliar names, the *HttpApplicationState* and *HttpSessionState* objects are state facilities totally compatible with ASP intrinsic objects such as *Application* and *Session*. Ad hoc properties known as *Application* and *Session* let you use these objects in much the same way you did in ASP.

> **Note** In this chapter, we'll review several objects involved, at various levels, with the state management. We won't discuss cookies in detail, but cookies are definitely useful for storing small amounts of information on the client. The information is sent with the request to the server and can be manipulated and re-sent through the response. The cookie is a text-based structure with simple key/value pairs and consumes no resources on the server. In addition, cookies have a configurable expiration policy. The downside of cookies is their limited size (which is browser-dependent, but seldom greater than 8 KB) and the fact that the user can disable them. In e-commerce applications, for example, cookies are the preferred way of storing persistent user-specific data such as the content of the shopping cart.

The Application State

The *HttpApplicationState* object makes a dictionary available for storage to all request handlers invoked within an application. In ASP, only pages have access to the application state; this is no longer true in ASP.NET, in which all HTTP handlers and modules can store and retrieve values within the application's dictionary. The application state is accessible only within the context of the originating application. Other applications running on the system cannot access or modify the values.

An instance of the *HttpApplicationState* class is created the first time a client requests any resource from within a particular virtual directory. Each running application holds its own global state object. The most common way to access application state is by means of the *Application* property of the *Page* object. Application state is not shared across either a Web farm or Web garden.

Properties of the *HttpApplicationState* Class

The *HttpApplicationState* class is sealed and inherits from a class named *NameObjectCollectionBase*. In practice, the *HttpApplicationState* class is a sorted collection of pairs, each made of a string key and an object value. Such pairs can be accessed by using either the key string or the index. Internally, the base class employs a hash table with an initial capacity of zero that is automatically increased as required. The class makes no use of special hash code providers or particular comparers. In both cases, the default objects for a name/value collection are used—*CaseInsensitiveHashCodeProvider* and *CaseInsensitiveComparer*. Table 14-2 lists the properties of the *HttpApplicationState* class.

Table 14-2 *HttpApplicationState* Properties

Property	Description
AllKeys	Gets an array of strings containing all the keys of the items currently stored in the object.
Contents	Gets the current instance of the object. But wait! What this property returns is simply a reference to the application state object, not a clone. Provided for ASP compatibility.
Count	Gets the number of objects currently stored in the collection.
Item	Indexer property, provides read/write access to an element in the collection. The element can be specified either by name or index. Accessors of this property are implemented using *Get* and *Set* methods.
StaticObjects	Gets a collection including all instances of all objects declared in global.asax using an *<object>* tag with the *scope* attribute set to *Application*.

Note that static objects and actual state values are stored in separate collections. The exact type of the static collection is *HttpStaticObjectsCollection*.

Methods of the *HttpApplicationState* Class

The set of methods that the *HttpApplicationState* class features are mostly specialized versions of the typical methods of a name/value collection. As Table 14-3 shows, the most significant extension includes the locking mechanism necessary to serialize access to the state values.

Note that the *GetEnumerator* method is inherited from the base collection class and, as such, is oblivious to the locking mechanism of the class. If you enumerate the collection using this method, each returned value is obtained through a simple call to the *BaseGetKey* method—one of the methods on the base *NameObjectCollectionBase* class. Unfortunately, that method is not aware of the locking mechanism needed on the derived *HttpApplicationState* class because of the concurrent access to the application state. As a result, your enumeration would not be thread-safe. A better way to enumerate the content of the collection is by using a *while* statement and the *Get* method to access an item. Alternatively, you could lock the collection before you enumerate.

Table 14-3 *HttpApplicationState* Methods

Method	Description
Add	Adds a new value to the collection. The value is boxed as an *object*.
Clear	Removes all objects from the collection.

Table 14-3 *HttpApplicationState* Methods

Method	Description
Get	Returns the value of an item in the collection. The item can be specified either by key or index.
GetEnumerator	Returns an enumerator object to iterate through the collection.
GetKey	Gets the string key of the item stored at the specified position.
Lock	Locks writing access to the whole collection. No concurrent caller can write to the collection object until *UnLock* is called.
Remove	Removes the item whose key matches the specified string.
RemoveAll	Calls *Clear*.
RemoveAt	Removes the item at the specified position.
Set	Assigns the specified value to the item with the specified key. The method is thread-safe, and access to the item is blocked until the writing is completed.
UnLock	Unlocks writing access to the collection.

State Synchronization

Note that all operations on *HttpApplicationState* require some sort of synchronization to ensure that multiple threads running within an application safely access values without incurring deadlocks and access violations. The writing methods, such as *Set* and *Remove*, as well as the *set* accessor of the *Item* property implicitly apply a writing lock before proceeding. The *Lock* method ensures that only the current thread can modify the application state. The *Lock* method is provided to apply the same writing lock around portions of code that need to be protected from other threads' access.

You don't need to wrap a single call to *Set*, *Clear*, or *Remove* with a lock/unlock pair of statements—those methods, in fact, are already thread-safe. Using *Lock* in these cases will only have the effect of producing additional overhead, which will increase the internal level of recursion.

```
// This operation is thread-safe
Application["MyValue"] = 1;
```

Use *Lock* instead if you want to shield a group of instructions from concurrent writings.

```
// These operations execute atomically
Application.Lock();
int val = (int) Application["MyValue"];
if (val < 10)
  Application["MyValue"] = Application["MyValue"] + 1;
Application.UnLock();
```

Reading methods such as *Get*, the *get* accessor of *Item*, and even *Count* have an internal synchronization mechanism that, when used along with *Lock*, will protect them against concurrent and cross-thread readings and writings.

```
// The reading is protected from concurrent read/writes
Application.Lock();
int val = (int) Application["MyValue"];
Application.UnLock();
```

You should always use *Lock* and *UnLock* together. However, if you omit the call to *UnLock*, the likelihood of incurring a deadlock is not high because the .NET Framework automatically removes the lock when the request completes or times out, or when an unhandled error occurs.

Tradeoffs of Application State

Instead of writing global data to the *HttpApplicationState* object, you could use public members within the global.asax file. Compared to entries in the *HttpApplicationState* collection, a global member is preferable because it is strongly typed and does not require hash-table access to locate the value. On the other hand, a global variable is not synchronized per se and must be manually protected.

Whatever form you choose to store the global state of an application, some general considerations apply regarding storing data globally. For one thing, global data storage results in permanent memory occupation. Unless explicitly removed by the code, any data stored in the application global state is removed only when the application shuts down. On one end, putting a few megabytes of data in the application's memory speeds up access; on the other hand, doing this occupies valuable memory for the entire duration of the application.

Storing data globally is also problematic because of locking. Synchronization is necessary to ensure that concurrent thread access doesn't cause inconsistencies in the data. But locking the application state can easily become a performance hit that leads to nonoptimal use of threads. The application global state is held in memory and never trespasses the machine's boundaries. In multimachine and multiprocessor environments, the application global state is limited to the single worker process running on the individual machine or CPU. As such, it isn't something that is really global. Finally, the duration of the data in memory is at risk because of possible failures in the process or, more simply, because of ASP.NET process recycling. If you're going to use the application state feature and plan to deploy the application in a Web farm or Web garden scenario, you're probably better off dropping global state in favor of database tables.

The Session State

The *HttpSessionState* class provides a dictionary-based model of storing and retrieving session-state values. Unlike *HttpApplicationState*, this class doesn't expose its contents to all users operating on the virtual directory at a given time. Only the requests that originate in the context of the same session—that is, generated across multiple page requests made by the same user—can access the session state. The session state can be stored and published in a variety of ways, including in a Web farm or Web garden scenario. By default, though, the session state is held within the ASP.NET worker process.

Compared to *Session*, which is the intrinsic object of ASP, the ASP.NET session state is nearly identical in use, but it's significantly richer in functionality and radically different in architecture. In addition, it provides some extremely handy facilities—such as support for cookieless browsers, Web farms, and Web gardens—and the capability of being hosted by external processes, including Microsoft SQL Server. In this way, ASP.NET session management can provide an unprecedented level of robustness and reliability. The programming interface of the *HttpSessionState* looks similar to ASP but, more importantly, the internal architecture has been tuned to provide the best throughput in what, according to reports and statistics, appears to be the most common usage scenario. The ASP.NET session-state mechanism is optimized for situations in which reading and writing operations are well balanced and occur with roughly the same frequency.

The Session-State HTTP Module

The ASP.NET module in charge of setting up the session state for each user connecting to an application is an HTTP module named *SessionStateModule*. We already encountered this module in Chapter 12 and Chapter 13. Structured after the *IHttpModule* interface, the *SessionStateModule* object provides session-state services for ASP.NET applications.

Although the module has a poor programming interface—the *IHttpModule* interface contracts only for *Init* and *Dispose* methods—it does perform a number of quite sophisticated tasks, most of which are fundamental for the health and functionality of the Web application. The session-state module is invoked during the setup of the *HttpApplication* object that will process a given request and is responsible for either generating or obtaining a unique *SessionID* string and for storing and retrieving state data from an external state provider—for example, SQL Server.

State Client Managers

When invoked, the session-state HTTP module reads the settings in the *<sessionState>* section of the web.config file and determines what the expected state client manager is for the application. As Table 14-4 shows, there are three possibilities. The session state can be stored locally in the ASP.NET worker process; the session state can be maintained in an external, even remote, process named aspnet_state.exe; or finally, the session state can be managed by SQL Server and stored in an ad-hoc database table. Table 14-4 briefly discusses the various options.

Table 14-4 State Client Providers

Mode	Description
InProc	Session values are kept as live objects in the memory of the ASP.NET worker process (aspnet_wp.exe or w3wp.exe in Windows Server 2003). This is the default option.
StateServer	Session values are serialized and stored in the memory of a separate process (aspnet_state.exe). The process can also run on another machine. Session values are deserialized into the session dictionary at the beginning of the request. If the request completes successfully, state values are serialized into the process memory and made available to other pages.
SQLServer	Session values are serialized and stored in a SQL Server table. The instance of SQL Server can run either locally or remotely.

The *InProc* option is by far the fastest possible in terms of access. However, bear in mind that the more data you store in a session, the more memory is consumed on the Web server, which increases the risk of performance hits. If you plan to use any of the out-of-process solutions, the possible impact of serialization and deserialization should be carefully considered. We'll discuss this aspect in detail later in the chapter starting in the "Persist Session Data to Remote Servers" section.

The session-state module instantiates the state provider for the application and initializes it using the information read out of the web.config file. Next, each provider continues its own initialization, which varies depending on the type. For example, the SQL Server state manager opens a connection to the given database, whereas the out-of-process manager checks the specified TCP port. The *InProc* state manager, on the other hand, stores a reference to the callback function that will be used to fire the *Session_OnEnd* event. (I'll cover this in more detail in the section "Lifetime of a Session.")

All the actual state provider objects implement a common interface, named *IStateClientManager*, and by means of that interface, the session module polymorphically communicates with the provider in charge. The schema is outlined in Figure 14-1.

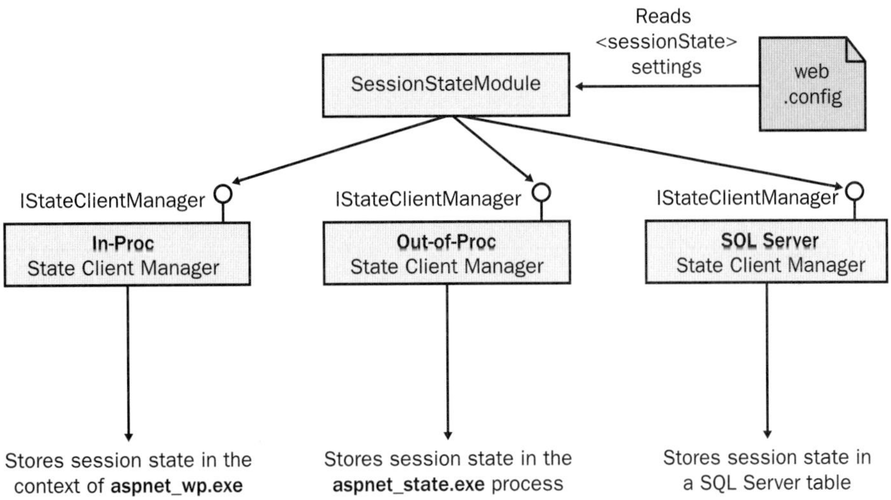

Figure 14-1 *SessionStateModule* and its child-state client managers.

Creating the *HttpSessionState* Object

The state module is also responsible for retrieving and attaching the session state to the context of each request that runs within the session. The session state is available only after the *HttpApplication.AcquireRequestState* event fires and gets irreversibly lost after the *HttpApplication.ReleaseRequestState* event. Subsequently, this means that no state is still available when *Session_OnEnd* fires. (For more information on the *HttpApplication* class and its events, see Chapter 13.)

The session module creates the *HttpSessionState* object for a request while processing the *HttpApplication.AcquireRequestState* event. At this time, the *HttpSessionState* object is given its *SessionID* and the session dictionary. The session dictionary is the actual collection of state values that pages will familiarly access through the *Session* property.

If a new session is being started, such a data dictionary is simply a newly created empty object. If the module is serving a request for an existing session, the data dictionary will be filled by deserializing the contents of the currently active state provider. At the end of the request, the current content of the dictionary, as modified by the page request, is flushed back to the state provider through a serialization step.

Synchronizing Access to the Session State

So when your Web page makes a call into the *Session* property, it's actually accessing a local, in-memory copy of the data. What if other pages attempt to concurrently access the session state? In that case, the current request might end up working on inconsistent data or data that isn't up to date.

To avoid that, the session-state module implements a reader/writer locking mechanism and queues the access to state values. A page that has session-state write access will hold a writer lock on the session until the request finishes. A page gains write access to the session state by setting the *EnableSessionState* attribute on the *@Page* directive to *true*. A page that has session-state read access—for example, when the *EnableSessionState* attribute is set to *ReadOnly*—will hold a reader lock on the session until the request finishes.

If a page request sets a reader lock, other concurrently running requests cannot update the session state but are allowed to read. If a page request sets a writer lock on the session state, all other pages are blocked regardless of whether they have to read or write. For example, if two frames attempt to write to *Session*, one of them has to wait until the other finishes. Figure 14-2 shows the big picture.

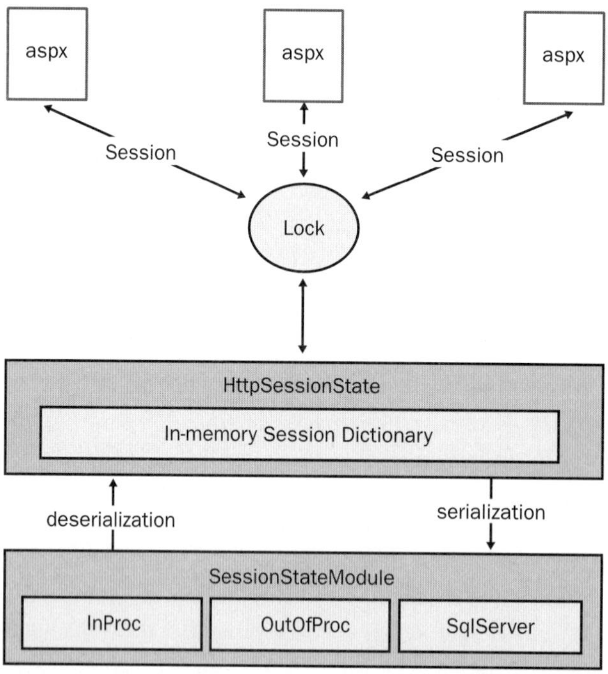

Figure 14-2 Page access to the session state is synchronized, and a serialization/deserialization layer ensures that each request is served an up-to-date dictionary of values, stored at the application's convenience.

Properties of the *HttpSessionState* Class

The *HttpSessionState* class is defined in the *System.Web.SessionState* namespace. It is a generic collection class and implements the *ICollection* and *IEnumerable* interfaces. Unlike *HttpApplicationState*, the *HttpSessionState* class does not inherit from an existing specialized collection class. The state values are held in an internal dictionary class named *SessionDictionary*. (In the .NET Framework, all dictionary classes are based on hash tables.) The properties of the *HttpSessionState* class are listed in Table 14-5.

Table 14-5 *HttpSessionState* Properties

Property	Description
CodePage	Gets or sets the code page identifier for the current session.
Contents	Gets the current instance of the object. But wait! What this property returns is simply a reference to the application state object, not a clone. Provided for ASP compatibility.
Count	Gets the number of items currently stored in the session state.
IsCookieless	Gets a value that indicates whether the session ID is embedded in the URL or stored in an HTTP cookie.
IsNewSession	Gets a value that indicates whether the session was created with the current request.
IsReadOnly	Gets a value that indicates whether the session is read-only. The session is read-only if the *EnableSessionState* attribute on the *@Page* directive is set to the keyword *ReadOnly*.
IsSynchronized	Returns *false*. (This will be discussed more later in the section.)
Item	Indexer property, provides read/write access to a session-state value. The value can be specified either by name or index.
Keys	Gets a collection of the keys of all values stored in the session.
LCID	Gets or sets the locale identifier (LCID) of the current session.
Mode	Gets a *SessionStateMode* value denoting the state client manager being used. Acceptable values are *InProc*, *StateServer*, *SQLServer*, and *Off*.
SessionID	Gets a string with the ID used to identify the session.
StaticObjects	Gets a collection including all instances of all objects declared in global.asax by using an *<object>* tag with the *scope* attribute set to *Session*. Note that you cannot add objects to this collection from within an ASP.NET application—that is, programmatically.
SyncRoot	Gets an instance of this object. (This will be discussed more later in the section.)
Timeout	Gets or sets the minutes that the session module should wait between two successive requests before terminating the session.

The *HttpSessionState* class is a normal collection class because it implements the *ICollection* interface, but synchronization-wise it's a very special collection class. As mentioned, the synchronization mechanism is implemented in the *SessionStateModule* component, which guarantees that at most one thread will ever access the session state. However, because *HttpSessionState* implements *ICollection* interface, it must provide an implementation for both *IsSynchronized* and *SyncRoot*. Note that *IsSynchronized* and *SyncRoot* are collection-specific properties for synchronization and have nothing to do with the session synchronization discussed previously. They refer to the ability of the collection class (*HttpSessionState* in this case) to work synchronized. Technically speaking, the *HttpSessionState* is not synchronized as a collection class, but access to the session state is.

Methods of the *HttpSessionState* Class

Table 14-6 shows all the methods available in the *HttpSessionState* class. They are primarily involved with the typical operations of a collection. In this sense, the only exceptional method is *Abandon*, which causes the session to be canceled.

Table 14-6 *HttpSessionState* Methods

Method	Description
Abandon	Sets an internal flag that instructs the session module to cancel the current session.
Add	Adds a new item to the session state. The value is boxed in an *Object* type.
Clear	Clears all values from the session state.
CopyTo	Copies the collection of session-state values to a one-dimensional array, starting at the specified index in the array.
GetEnumerator	Gets an enumerator to loop through all the values in the session.
Remove	Deletes an item from the session-state collection. The item is identified by the key.
RemoveAll	Calls *Clear*.
RemoveAt	Deletes an item from the session-state collection. The item is identified by position.

When running the procedure to terminate the current request, the session-state module checks an internal flag to verify whether the user ordered that the session be abandoned. If the flag is set—that is, the *Abandon* method was called—any response cookie is removed and the procedure to terminate the session is begun. Note, though, that this does not necessarily mean that a *Session_OnEnd* event will fire. First, the *Session_OnEnd* event fires only if the session mode is *InProc*; second, the event does not fire if the session dictionary is empty and no real session state exists for the application. In other words, at least one request must have been completed for the *Session_OnEnd* event to fire when the session is closed either naturally or after a call to *Abandon*.

Identifying a Session

Each active ASP.NET session is identified using a 120-bit string made only of URL-allowed characters. Session IDs are guaranteed to be unique and randomly generated to avoid data conflicts and prevent malicious attacks. Obtaining a valid session ID algorithmically from an existing ID is virtually impossible. The *SessionID* string is communicated to the browser and then returned to the server application in either of two ways: by using cookies or a modified URL. By default, the session-state module creates an HTTP cookie on the client, but a modified URL can be used—especially for cookieless browsers—with the *SessionID* string embedded. Which approach is taken depends on the configuration settings stored in the application's web.config file. To configure session settings, you use the *<sessionState>* section. We fully described this configuration section in Chapter 12, but a quick refresher is in order.

```
<sessionState mode="Off|InProc|StateServer|SQLServer"
        cookieless="true|false"
        timeout="number of minutes"
        stateConnectionString="tcpip=server:port"
        sqlConnectionString="sql connection string" />
```

By default, the *cookieless* attribute is *false*, meaning that cookies are used. A cookie is really nothing more than a text file placed on the client's hard disk by a Web page. In ASP.NET, a cookie is represented by an instance of the *HttpCookie* class. Typically, a cookie has a name, a collection of values, and an expiration time. In addition, you can configure the cookie to operate on a particular virtual path and over secure connections (for example, HTTPS).

When the *cookieless* attribute setting is *false*, the session-state module actually creates a cookie with a particular name and stores the session ID in it. The cookie is created as the following pseudocode shows:

```
HttpCookie sessionCookie;
sessionCookie = new HttpCookie("ASP.NET_SessionId", sessionID);
sessionCookie.Path = "/";
```

ASP.NET_SessionId is the name of the cookie and the *sessionID* string is its value. The cookie is also associated with the root of the current domain. The *Path* property describes the relative URL that the cookie applies to. A session cookie is given a very short expiration term and is renewed at the end of each successful request. The cookie's *Expires* property indicates the time of day on the client at which the cookie expires. If not explicitly set, as is the case with session cookies, the *Expires* property defaults to *DateTime.MinValue*—that is, the smallest possible unit of time in the .NET Framework.

> **Note** A server-side module that needs to write a cookie adds an *HttpCookie* object to the *Response.Cookies* collection. Cookies associated with the requested domain are also available for reading through the *Request.Cookies* collection.

Cookieless Sessions

To disable session cookies, you set the *cookieless* attribute to *true* in the configuration file, as shown here:

```
<configuration>
  <system.web>
    <sessionState cookieless="true" />
  </system.web>
</configuration>
```

At this point, suppose that you request a page at the following URL:

```
http://www.contoso.com/test/sessions.aspx
```

What is really displayed in the browser's address bar is slightly different and now includes the session ID, as shown here:

```
http://www.contoso.com/test/(5ylg0455mrvws1uz5mmaau45)/sessions.aspx
```

When instantiated, the session-state module checks the value of the *cookieless* attribute. If *true*, the request is redirected (HTTP 302 status code) to a modified virtual URL that includes the session ID just before the page name. When processed again, the request embeds the session ID. The session ID is also stored in an extra HTTP header, named *AspFilterSessionId*, and in an *HttpContext* slot named *AspCookielessSession*. The following listing shows the HTTP packets exchanged between the browser and the ASP.NET runtime when a page is requested for a cookieless application:

```
GET /test/sessionanalyzer.aspx HTTP/1.1
Accept: */*
Accept-Language: en-us
Accept-Encoding: gzip, deflate
User-Agent: Mozilla/4.0 (compatible; MSIE 6.0; Windows NT 5.0; ...)
Host: expo-star
Connection: Keep-Alive

HTTP/1.1 302 Found
Server: Microsoft-IIS/5.0
Date: Mon, 04 Nov 2002 22:33:16 GMT
Location: /test/(vz0wc1buubvzfr252f3yrqe0)/sessions.aspx
Cache-Control: private
```

```
Content-Type: text/html; charset=utf-8
Content-Length: 170

GET /test/(vz0wc1buubvzfr252f3yrqe0)/sessions.aspx HTTP/1.1
Accept: */*
Accept-Language: en-us
Accept-Encoding: gzip, deflate
User-Agent: Mozilla/4.0 (compatible; MSIE 6.0; Windows NT 5.0; ...)
Host: expo-star
Connection: Keep-Alive

HTTP/1.1 200 OK
Server: Microsoft-IIS/5.0
Date: Mon, 04 Nov 2002 22:33:16 GMT
Cache-Control: no-cache
Pragma: no-cache
Content-Type: text/html; charset=utf-8
Content-Length: 14090
```

Figure 14-3 reveals the existence of the *AspFilterSessionId* header. Note, though, that this header doesn't really travel over the HTTP connection. The header is simply an extra element added to the *Headers* collection of the *Request* during the setup phase. Incidentally, the same information is also available as a server variable named HTTP_ASPFILTERSESSIONID.

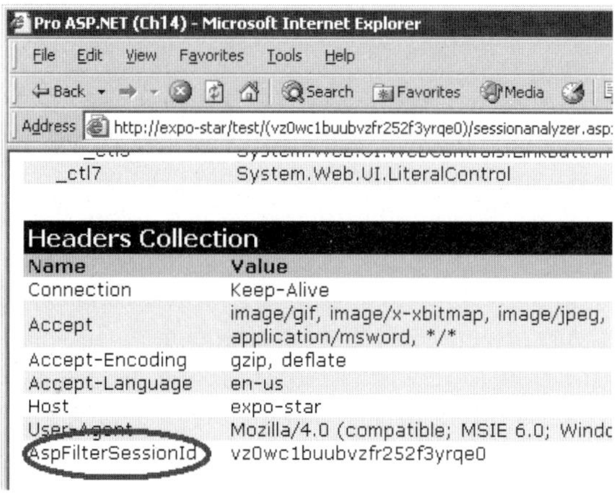

Figure 14-3 The trace of a cookieless session unveils the existence of the *AspFilterSessionId* header. The header is not transferred back and forth with the HTTP code but is entirely managed in memory when the *HttpRequest* object is set up.

Cookieless sessions cause a redirect when the session starts and whenever an absolute URL is invoked. When cookies are used, you can clear the address bar, go to another application, and then return to the previous one and retrieve the same session values. If you do this when session cookies are disabled, the session data is lost. This feature is not problematic for postbacks, which are automatically implemented using relative URLs, but it poses a serious problem if you use links to absolute URLs. In this case, a new session will always be created. The following code breaks the session:

```
<a runat="server" href="/test/sessions.aspx">Click</a>
```

To use absolute URLs, resort to a little trick that uses the *ApplyAppPathModifier* method on the *HttpResponse* class:

```
<a runat="server"
  href=<% =Response.ApplyAppPathModifier("/test/page.aspx")%> >Click</a>
```

The *ApplyAppPathModifier* method (which was listed in Chapter 13) takes a string representing a URL and returns an absolute URL that embeds session information. For example, this trick is especially useful in situations in which you need to redirect from an HTTP page to an HTTPS page.

Generating the Session ID

A session ID is 15 bytes long by design (15x8 = 120 bits). The session ID is generated using the Random Number Generator (RNG) cryptographic provider. The service provider returns a sequence of 15 randomly generated numbers. The array of numbers is then mapped to valid URL characters and returned as a string.

> **Important** If the session contains nothing, a new session ID is generated for each request and the session state is not persisted to the state provider. However, if a *Session_OnStart* handler is used, the session state is always saved, even if empty. For this reason, and especially if you're not using the in-process session provider, define *Session_OnStart* handlers with extreme care and only if strictly necessary.
>
> In contrast, the session ID remains the same after a nonempty session dictionary times out or is abandoned. By design, even though the session state expires, the session ID lasts until the browser session is ended. This means that the same session ID is used to represent multiple sessions over time as long as the browser instance remains the same.

Lifetime of a Session

The life of a session state begins only when the first item is added to the in-memory dictionary. The following code demonstrates how to modify an item in the session dictionary. "MyData" is the key that uniquely identifies the value. If a key named "MyData" already exists in the dictionary, the existing value is overwritten.

```
Session["MyData"] = "I love ASP.NET";
```

The *Session* dictionary generically contains *Object* types; to read data back, you need to cast the returned values to a more specific type.

```
string tmp = (string) Session["MyData"];
```

When a page or a session-enabled Web service saves data to *Session*, what really happens is that the value is loaded into an in-memory dictionary—an instance of an internal class named *SessionDictionary*. (See Figure 14-2.) Other concurrently running pages cannot access the session until the ongoing request completes.

The *Session_OnStart* Event

The session startup event is unrelated to the session state. The *Session_OnStart* event fires when the session-state module is servicing the first request for a given user that requires a new session ID. The ASP.NET runtime can serve multiple requests within the context of a single session, but only for the first of them does *Session_OnStart* fire. As pointed out in Chapter 13, the *Session_OnStart* event fires in between *BeginRequest* and *AcquireRequestState*.

A new session ID is created and a new *Session_OnStart* event fires whenever a page is requested that doesn't write data to the dictionary. The architecture of the session state is quite sophisticated because it has to support a variety of state providers. The overall schema entails that the content of the session dictionary be serialized to the state provider when the request completes. However, to optimize performance, this procedure really executes only if the content of the dictionary is not empty. As mentioned earlier, though, if the application defines a *Session_OnStart* event handler, the serialization takes place anyway.

The *Session_OnEnd* Event

The *Session_OnEnd* event signals the end of the session and is used to perform any clean-up code needed to terminate the session. Note, though, that the event is supported only in *InProc* mode—that is, only when the session data is stored in the ASP.NET worker process.

For *Session_OnEnd* to fire, the session state has to exist first. That means you have to store some data in the session state and you must have completed at least one request. When the first value is added to the session dictionary, an item is inserted into the ASP.NET cache—the aforementioned *Cache* object that we'll cover in detail later in the "The ASP.NET Caching System" section. The item is given a particular name and value. The name is a colon-separated string made of *System.Web.SessionState.SessionStateItem* and the session ID. For example, it might look like this:

```
System.Web.SessionState.SessionStateItem:3ov5q2550u4oxprmqyrolb55
```

The value of the cache entry is an internal object of type *SessionStateItem* (version 1.0) or *InProcSessionState* (version 1.1). The behavior is specific to the in-process state provider; neither the out-of-process state server nor the SQL Server state server works with the *Cache* object.

However, much more interesting is that the item added to the cache—only one item per active session—is given a special expiration policy. You'll learn more about the ASP.NET cache and related expiration policies in the section "The ASP.NET Caching System." For now it suffices to say that the session-state item added to the cache is given a sliding expiration, with the time interval set to the session timeout. As long as there are requests processed within the session, the sliding period is automatically renewed. The session-state module does this while processing the application's *EndRequest* event. The technique used to reset the timeout is pretty simple and intuitive—the session module just performs a read on the cache! Given the internal structure of the ASP.NET *Cache* object, this evaluates to renew the sliding period. As a result, when the cache item expires, the session has timed out.

An expired item is automatically removed from the cache. As part of the expiration policy for this item, the state-session module also indicates a remove callback function. The cache automatically invokes the remove function which, in turn, fires the *Session_OnEnd* event.

> **Caution** The items in *Cache* that represent the state of a session are not accessible from outside the *System.Web* assembly and can't even be enumerated. In other words, you can't access the data resident in another session or even remove it. Note that in version 1.0 of the .NET Framework, session items, as well as some other system items, are dangerously exposed to applications. Version 1.1 of the .NET Framework is more secure and does not expose these items.

Why Does My Session State Sometimes Get Lost?

Values parked in a *Session* object are removed from memory either programmatically by the code or by the system when the session times out or is abandoned. In some cases, though, even when nothing of the kind seemingly happens, the session state gets lost. Is there a reason for this apparently weird behavior?

When the working mode is *InProc*, the session state is mapped in the memory space of the AppDomain in which the page request is being served. In light of this, the session state is subject to process recycling and AppDomain restarts. As we discussed in Chapter 2, the ASP.NET worker process is periodically restarted to maintain an average good performance; when this happens, the session state is lost. Process recycling depends on the percentage of memory consumption and maybe the number of requests served. Although the process is cyclic, no general consideration can be made regarding the interval of the cycle. Be aware of this when designing your session-based, in-process application. As a general rule, bear in mind that the session state might not be there when you try to access it. Use exception handling or recovery techniques as appropriate for your application.

In Knowledge Base article Q316148, Microsoft suggests that some antivirus software might be marking the web.config or global.asax file as modified, thus causing a new application to be started and subsequently causing the loss of the session state. This holds true also if you or your code modify the timestamp of those files. Also, any addition to or removal from the Bin directory causes the application to restart.

> **Note** What happens to the session state when a running page hits an error? Will the current dictionary be saved or is it just lost? The state of the session is not saved if, at the end of the request, the page results in an error—that is, the *GetLastError* method of the *Server* object returns an exception. However, if in your exception handler you reset the error state by calling *Server.ClearError*, the values of the session are saved regularly as if no error ever occurred.

Detecting Expired Sessions

So what's the best thing to do when a session expires, and more importantly, is there a way to detect whether a session has expired? Redirecting to an error page is probably the most reasonable thing to do, unless the characteristics of the application allow for an even more graceful recovery. Normally, applications know that a session has expired only through an exception, and therefore, when it's too late.

Unfortunately, as of version 1.1, in ASP.NET there are no built-in features to quickly and effectively let applications know about expired sessions so that they could redirect users to other pages. One trick you can try entails the use of cookies. The idea is that you write a cookie when the session starts in the *Session_OnStart* event handler. At a certain point, the session times out or is recycled. As mentioned earlier, even though the session has expired, the session ID remains in use until the browser is closed. With the next access to the page, a new session is started, but this time the cookie is already there. This is a signal meaning that ASP.NET is reusing the same session ID but the previous session has expired. As the final step, you redirect to another page. The following code shows how to achieve this:

```
void Session_OnStart(Object sender, EventArgs e)
{
  HttpContext context = HttpContext.Current;
  HttpCookieCollection cookies = context.Request.Cookies;

  if (cookies["started_at"] == null)
  {
    HttpCookie cookie;
    Cookie = new HttpCookie("started_at", DateTime.Now.ToString());
    cookie.Path = "/";
    context.Response.Cookies.Add(cookie);
  }
  else
  {
    context.Response.Redirect("session_expired.aspx");
  }
}
```

Persist Session Data to Remote Servers

The session state loss problem we mentioned earlier for *InProc* mode can be neatly solved by employing either of the two out-of-process state providers—*StateServer* and *SQLServer*. In this case, though, the session state is held outside the ASP.NET worker process and an extra layer of code is needed to serialize and deserialize it to and from the actual storage medium. This operation takes place whenever a request is processed.

The need for copying session data from an external repository into the local session dictionary might tax the state management process to the point of causing a 15 percent to 25 percent decrease in performance. Note, though, that this is only a rough estimate, but it's closer to the minimum impact than to the maximum impact. The estimate, in fact, doesn't fully consider the complexity of the types actually saved into the session state.

State Serialization and Deserialization

When you use the *InProc* mode, objects are stored in the session state as live instances of classes. No real serialization and deserialization ever take place, meaning that you can actually store in *Session* whatever objects (including COM objects) you have created and access them with no significant overhead. The situation is less favorable if you opt for an out-of-process state provider.

In an out-of-process architecture, session values are to be copied from the native storage medium into the memory of the AppDomain that processes the request. A serialization/deserialization layer is needed to accomplish the task and represents one of the major costs for out-of-process state providers. How does this affect your code? First, you should make sure that only serializable objects are ever stored in the session dictionary; otherwise, as you can easily guess, the session state can't be saved.

> **Note** In ASP.NET 1.0, if you try to save a nonserializable object (for example, a COM object) in the session dictionary using SQL Server, the problem can go unnoticed. If you're working in *StateServer* mode, an exception is thrown instead.

To perform the serialization and deserialization of types, ASP.NET uses two methods, each providing different results in terms of performance. For basic types, ASP.NET resorts to an optimized internal serializer; for other types, including objects and user-defined classes, ASP.NET makes use of the .NET binary formatter, which is slower. Basic types are *string*, *DateTime*, *Boolean*, *byte*, *char*, and all numeric types.

The optimized serializer—an internal class named *AltSerialization*—employs a *BinaryWriter* object and writes out one byte to denote the type and then the value. While reading, the *AltSerialization* class first extracts one byte, detects the type of the data to read, and then resorts to a type-specific *ReadXxx* method on the *BinaryReader* class. The type is associated with an index according to an internal table, as shown in Figure 14-4.

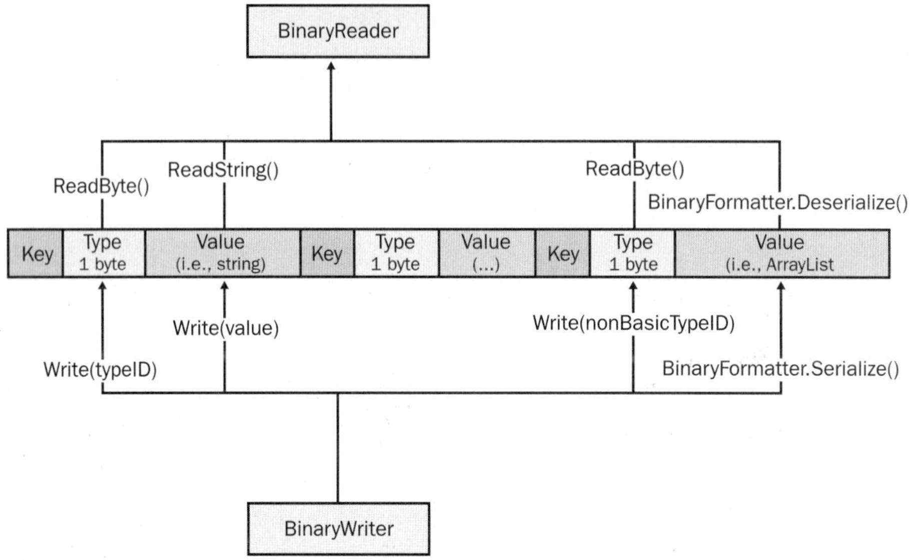

Figure 14-4 The serialization schema for basic types that the internal *AltSerialization* class uses.

> **Note** While Booleans and numeric types have a well-known size, the length of a string can vary quite a bit. How can the reader determine the correct size of a string? The *BinaryReader.ReadString* method exploits the fact that on the underlying stream the string is always prefixed with the length, encoded as an integer seven bits at a time. Values of the *DateTime* type, on the other hand, are saved by writing only the total number of ticks that form the date and are read as an *Int64* type.

As mentioned, more complex objects are serialized using the *BinaryFormatter* class as long as the involved types are marked as serializable. Both simple and complex types use the same stream, but all nonbasic types are identified with the same type ID. The performance-hit range of 15 percent to 25 percent is a rough estimate based on the assumption that basic types are used. The more you use complex types, the more the overhead grows, but reliable numbers can be calculated only by testing a particular application scenario.

In light of this, if you plan to use out-of-process sessions, make sure you store data effectively. For example, if you need to persist an instance of a class with three string properties, performancewise you are *probably* better off using three different slots filled with a basic type rather than one session slot for which the binary formatter is needed. However, understand that this is merely a guideline to be applied case by case and with a grain of salt. If you have a class with 100 string properties, you should probably store it as an object!

Storing Session Data

When working in *StateServer* mode, the entire content of the *HttpSessionState* object is serialized to an external application—a Microsoft Windows NT service named aspnet_state.exe. The service is called to serialize the session state when the request completes. The service internally stores each session state as an array of bytes. When a new request begins processing, the array corresponding to the given session ID is copied into a memory stream and then deserialized into an internal *SessionStateItem* object. This object really represents the session state. The *HttpSessionState* object that pages actually work with is only its application interface.

In Figure 14-5, you can see the overall format of a serialized session state as saved into the aspnet_state.exe Windows NT service.

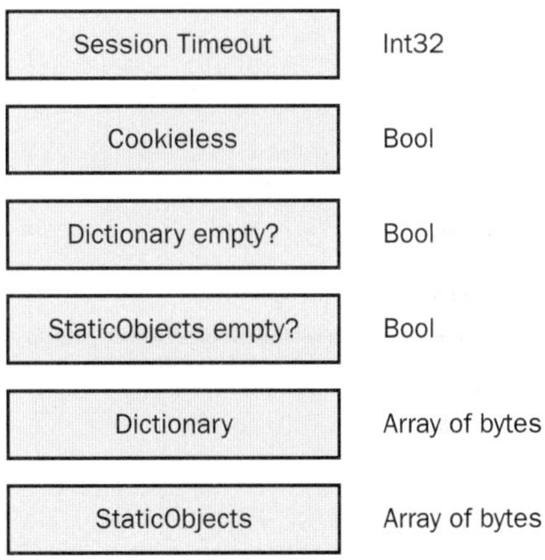

Figure 14-5 The session state as persisted in an out-of-process state provider.

The array of bytes contains an integer denoting the timeout of the session and whether the session is cookieless, a couple of Boolean values indicating whether the session has a nonempty dictionary, and at least one static object. The bytes that follow represent the dictionary (with the previously described format) and the list of serialized static objects.

Static objects are objects—both COM and managed—that are statically declared in the global.asax file with a session scope. Figure 14-6 illustrates the binary layout of the *StaticObjects* collection of the session. The first bytes indicate how many objects are going to be serialized. Next, each object is serialized in a structure that includes: the abbreviated name; a Boolean value indicating whether the object has been instantiated, the serialization of the instance, and the .NET full name of the object; and a final Boolean value indicating whether or not the object is late bound.

Note though that you cannot have static COM objects declared with a session scope if you're using an out-of-process state provider.

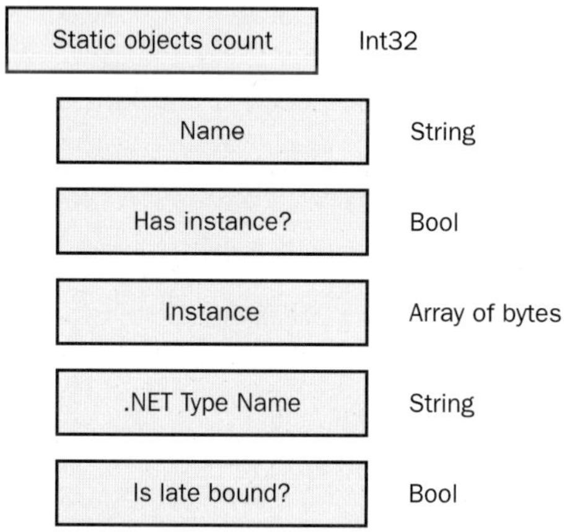

Figure 14-6 The persistence schema of the *StaticObjects* collection.

Configuring the *StateServer* Provider

Using out-of-process storage scenarios, you give the session state a longer life and your application greater robustness. Out-of-process session-state storage basically protects the session against Internet Information Services (IIS) and ASP.NET process failures. By separating the session state from the page itself, you can also much more easily scale an existing application to Web farm and Web garden architectures. In addition, the session state living in an external process eliminates at the root the risk of periodically losing data because of process recycling.

As mentioned, the ASP.NET session-state provider is a Windows NT service named aspnet_state.exe. It normally resides in the following folder:

```
C:\WINNT\Microsoft.NET\Framework\v1.1.4322
```

As usual, notice that the final directory depends on the .NET Framework version you're actually running. Before using the state server, you should make sure the service is up and running on the local or remote machine used as the session store. The state service is a constituent part of ASP.NET and gets installed along with it, so you have no additional setup to run.

By default, the state service is stopped and requires a manual start. You can change its configuration through the property dialog box of the service, as shown in Figure 14-7.

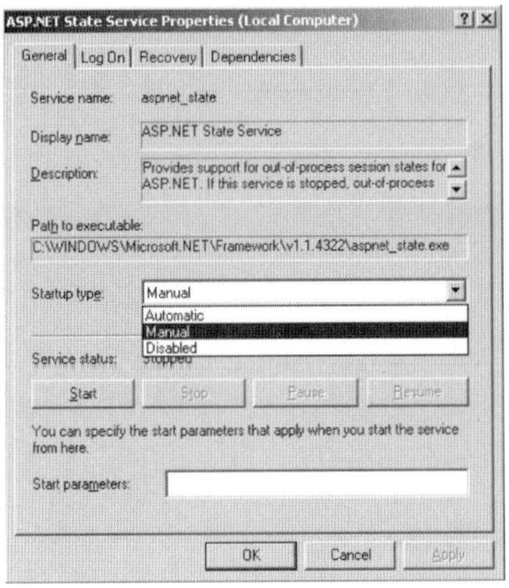

Figure 14-7 The property dialog box of the ASP.NET state server.

An ASP.NET application needs to specify the TCP/IP address of the machine hosting the session-state service. The following listing shows the changes needed to the web.config file to enable the remote session state:

```
<configuration>
  <system.web>
    <sessionState
      mode="StateServer"
      stateConnectionString="tcpip=expo-star:123" />
  </system.web>
</configuration>
```

Note that the value assigned to the *mode* attribute is case sensitive. The format of the *stateConnectionString* attribute is shown in the following line of code. The default machine address is 127.0.0.1, while the default port is 42424.

```
stateConnectionString="tcpip=server:port"
```

The server name can be either an IP address or a machine name. In this case, though, non-ASCII characters in the name are not supported. Finally, the port number is mandatory and cannot be omitted.

The ASP.NET application attempts to connect to the session-state server immediately after loading. The aspnet_state service must be up and running, otherwise an HTTP exception is thrown. By default, the service is not configured to start automatically.

> **Caution** When the session state is stored out of process, COM objects cannot be stored in the *Session* object because they aren't serializable. This limitation isn't specific to COM objects, however. Any nonserializable object cannot be stored in *Session* when the application session-state service works out of process.

Persist Session Data to SQL Server

Maintaining the session state in an external process certainly makes the whole ASP.NET application more stable. Whatever happens to the aspnet_wp.exe worker process, the session state is still there, ready for further use. If the service is paused, the data is preserved and automatically retrieved when the service resumes. Unfortunately, if the state provider service is stopped or if a failure occurs, the data is lost. If robustness is key for your application, drop the *StateServer* mode in favor of *SQLServer*.

Performance and Robustness

When ASP.NET works in *SQLServer* mode, the session data is stored in a made-to-measure database table. As a result, the session data survives even SQL Server crashes, but you have to add a higher overhead to the bill. *SQLServer* mode allows you to store data on any connected machine, as long as the machine runs SQL Server 7.0 or later. Besides the different medium, the storage mechanism is nearly identical to that described for remote servers. In particular, the serialization and deserialization algorithm is the same, only a bit slower. When storing data of basic types, the time required to set up the page's *HttpSessionState* object is normally at least 25 percent higher than in an *InProc* scenario. Also in regard to this issue, the more complex types you use, the more time will probably be required to manage the session data.

Creating and Configuring the Database

To use SQL Server as the state provider, enter the following changes in the *<sessionState>* section of the web.config file:

```
<configuration>
  <system.web>
    <sessionState
      mode="SQLServer"
      sqlConnectionString="server=127.0.0.1;uid=sa;pwd=;" />
  </system.web>
</configuration>
```

In particular, you need to set the *mode* attribute (which is case sensitive) to *SQLServer* and specify the connection string through the *sqlConnectionString* attribute. Notice that the *sqlConnectionString* attribute string must include user ID, password, and server name. It cannot contain, though, tokens such as *Database* and *Initial Catalog*. User ID and passwords can be replaced by integrated security.

ASP.NET provides two pairs of scripts to configure the database environment. The first pair of scripts are named InstallSqlState.sql and UninstallSqlState.sql. They create a database named ASPState and several stored procedures. The data, though, is stored in a couple of tables in the TempDB database. In SQL Server, the TempDB database provides a storage area for temporary tables, temporary stored procedures, and other temporary working storage needs. This means that the session data is lost if the SQL Server machine is restarted.

The second pair consists of InstallPersistSqlState.sql and UninstallPersistSqlState.sql. An ASPState database is created in this case also, but the tables are persistent because they are created within the same database. All scripts are located in the following path:

```
%SystemRoot%\Microsoft.NET\Framework\v1.1.4322
```

> **Note** Note that in ASP.NET 1.0 only the first pair of scripts were installed. Soon after, though, Microsoft addressed the issue of persistent SQL Server session state with Knowledge Base article Q311209.

The tables that get created are named ASPStateTempApplications and ASPStateTempSessions. Figure 14-8 shows a view of the session database in SQL Server.

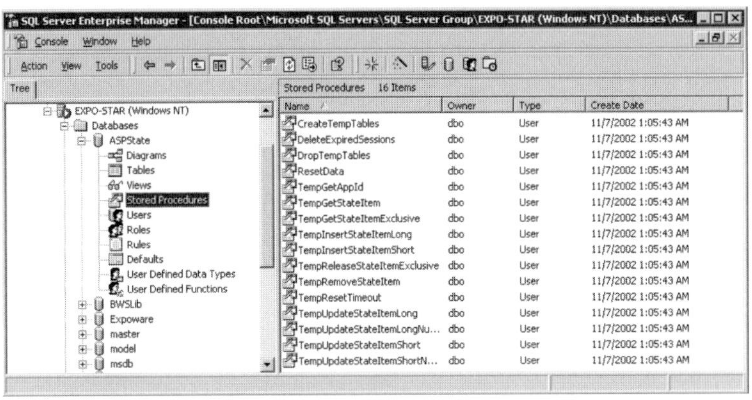

Figure 14-8 The ASPState database in SQL Server 2000.

The ASPStateTempApplications table defines a record for each currently running ASP.NET application. The table columns are listed in Table 14-7.

Table 14-7 The ASPStateTempApplications Table

Column	Type	Description
AppId	*Int*	Indexed field, represents a sort of autogenerated ID identifying a running application using the *SQLServer* session mode.
AppName	*Char(280)*	Indicates the application ID of the AppDomain running the application. Matches the *HttpRuntime.AppDomainAppId* property.

The ASPStateTempSessions table stores the actual session data. The table contains one row for each active session. The structure of the table is outlined in Table 14-8.

Table 14-8 The ASPStateTempSessions Table

Column	Type	Description
SessionId	*Char(32)*	Indexed field, represents the session ID.
Created	*DateTime*	Indicates the time in which the session was created. Defaults to the current date.
Expires	*DateTime*	Indicates the time in which the session will expire. This value is normally the time in which the session state was created plus the number of minutes specified in *Timeout*. Note that *Created* refers to the time at which the session started. On the other hand, *Expires* adds minutes to the time in which the first item is added to the session state.
LockDate	*DateTime*	Indicates the time in which the session was locked to add the last item.
LockCookie	*Int*	Indicates the number of times the session was locked—that is, the number of accesses.
Timeout	*Int*	Indicates the timeout of the session in minutes.
Locked	*Bit*	Indicates whether the session is currently locked.
SessionItemShort	*VarBinary(7000)*	Nullable field, represents the values in the specified session. The layout of the bytes is identical to the layout discussed for *StateServer* providers. If more than 7000 bytes are needed to serialize the dictionary, the *SessionItemLong* field is used instead.
SessionItemLong	*Image*	Nullable field, represents the serialized version of a session longer than 7000 bytes.

In spite of the baffling type name, the column *SessionItemLong*, contains a long binary block of data. Although the user always works with image data as if it is a single, long sequence of bytes, the data is not stored in that format. The data is stored in a collection of 8-KB pages that aren't necessarily located next to each other. (For more information, see SQL Server's Books Online.)

When installing the SQL Server support for sessions, a job is also created to delete expired sessions from the session-state database. The job, which is shown in Figure 14-9, is named ASPState_Job_DeleteExpiredSessions, and the default configuration makes it run every minute. You should note that the SQLServerAgent service needs to be running for this to work.

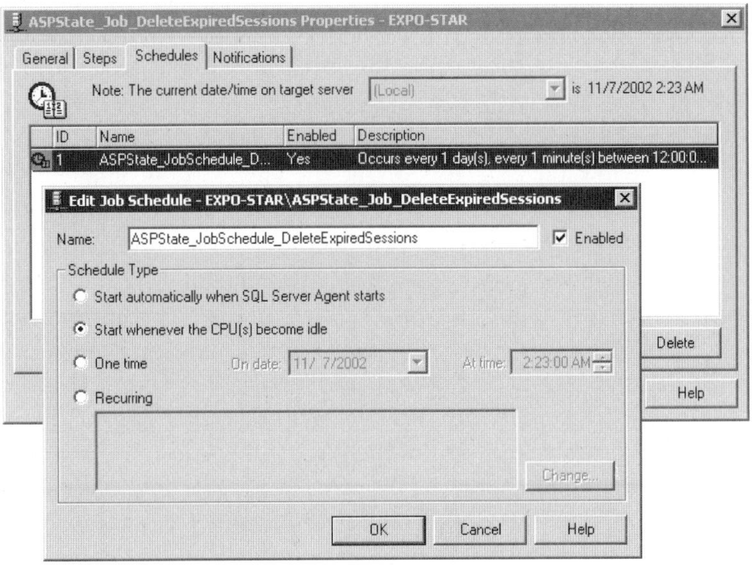

Figure 14-9 The SQL Server job to delete expired sessions.

Working in a Web Farm Scenario

ASP.NET applications designed to run in a Web farm or Web garden hardware configuration cannot implement an in-process session state. The *InProc* mode won't work on a Web farm because a distinct aspnet_wp.exe process will be running on each connected machine, with each process maintaining its own session state. It doesn't even work on a Web garden because multiple aspnet_wp.exe processes will be running on the same machine.

Keeping all states separate from worker processes allows you to partition an application across multiple worker processes even when they're running on multiple computers. In both Web farm and Web garden scenarios, there can be only one *StateServer* or *SQLServer* process to provide session-state management.

As mentioned in Chapter 12, if you're running a Web farm, make sure you have the same *<machineKey>* in all your Web servers. (More details can be found in Knowledge Base article Q313091.) In addition, for the session state to be maintained across different servers in the Web farm, all applications should have the same application path stored in the IIS metabase. This value is set as the AppDomain application ID and identifies a running application in the ASP.NET state database. (See Knowledge Base article Q325056 for more details.)

The View State of a Page

ASP.NET pages supply the *ViewState* property to let applications build a call context and retain values across two successive requests for the same page. The view state represents the state of the page when it was last processed on the server. The state is persisted—usually, but not necessarily, on the client side—and is restored before the page request is processed. We analyzed the overall page life cycle in Chapter 2. By default, the view state is maintained as a hidden field added to the page. As such, it travels back and forth with the page itself. Although sent to the client, the view state does not represent, nor does it contain, any information specifically aimed at the client. The information stored in the view state is pertinent only to the page and some of its child controls.

Using the view state has advantages and disadvantages you might want to carefully balance prior to making your state management decision. First, the view state doesn't require any server resources and is simple to implement and use. Because it's a physical part of the page, it's fast to retrieve and use. This last point, which in some respects is a strong one, turns into a considerable weakness as soon as you consider the page performance from a wider perspective.

Because the view state is packed with the page, it inevitably charges the HTML code transferred over HTTP with a few extra kilobytes of data—useless data, moreover, from the client's perspective. A complex real-world page, especially if it does not even attempt to optimize and restrict the use of the view state, can easily find 10 KB of extra stuff packed in the HTML code sent out to the browser. Finally, security is another hot topic for view states. Although you're not supposed to store sensitive data in the view state (for example, credit card numbers, passwords, or connection strings), the view state can still be a victim of malicious code. We'll return to security topics later in the "Common Issues with View State" section.

In summary, the view state is one of the most important features of ASP.NET, not so much because of its technical relevance but because it allows most of the magic of the Web Forms model. Used without strict criteria, the view state can easily become a burden for pages. Security issues also stand out, but countermeasures are in place, thus making the "real" risk of getting damaged much less significant than one might think at first.

The *StateBag* Class

The *StateBag* class is the class behind the view state that manages the information that ASP.NET pages and controls want to persist across successive posts of the same page instance. The class works like a dictionary and, in addition, implements the *IStateManager* interface. The *Page* and *Control* base classes expose the view state through the *ViewState* property. So you can add or remove items from the *StateBag* class as you would with any dictionary object, as the following code demonstrates:

```
ViewState["FontSize"] = value;
```

You should start writing to the view state only after the *Init* event fires for the page request. You can read from the view state during any stage of the page lifecycle, but not after the page enters rendering mode—that is, after the *PreRender* event fires.

View State Properties

Table 14-9 lists all the properties defined in the *StateBag* class.

Table 14-9 Properties of the *StateBag* Class

Property	Description
Count	Gets the number of elements stored in the object
Item	Indexer property, gets or sets the value of an item stored in the class
Keys	Gets a collection object containing the keys defined in the object
Values	Gets a collection object containing all the values stored in the object

Each item in the *StateBag* class is represented by a *StateItem* object. An instance of the *StateItem* object is implicitly created when you set the *Item* indexer property with a value or when you call the *Add* method. Items added to the *StateBag* object are tracked until the view state is saved to the storage medium using the page's *SaveViewState* protected method. *StateItem* objects not saved yet have the *IsDirty* property return *true*.

View State Methods

Table 14-10 lists all the methods you can call on the *StateBag* class.

Table 14-10 Methods of the *StateBag* Class

Method	Description
Add	Adds a new *StateItem* object to the collection. If the item already exists, it gets updated.
Clear	Removes all items from the current view state.
GetEnumerator	Returns an object that scrolls over all the elements in the *StateBag*.
IsItemDirty	Indicates whether the element with the specified key has been modified during the request processing.
Remove	Removes the specified object from the *StateBag* object.

The *IsItemDirty* method represents an indirect way to call into the *IsDirty* property of the specified *StateItem* object.

> **Note** The view state for the page is a cumulative property that results from the contents of the *ViewState* property of the page plus the view state of all the controls hosted in the page.

Common Issues with View State

Architecturally speaking, the importance of the view state cannot be denied, as it is key to setting up the automatic state-management feature of ASP.NET. A couple of hot issues are connected to the usage of the view state, however. Most frequently asked questions about the view state are related to security and performance. Can we say that the view state is inherently secure and cannot be tampered with? How will the extra information contained in the view state affect the download time of the page? Let's find out.

Encrypting and Securing

Many developers are doubtful about using view state just because it's stored in a hidden field and left on the client at the mercy of potential intruders. As Figure 14-10 demonstrates, the information can be read if the page output source is viewed directly. While this action alone is certainly not a threat to the application (although it violates data confidentiality), having the view state on the client side does represent a potential security issue. Although the data is stored in a hashed format, there's no absolute guarantee that it cannot be tampered with.

Although freely accessible in a hidden field named __VIEWSTATE, the view state information is hashed and Base64 encoded. To decode it, a number of steps must be completed and a number of circumstances must occur. In addition, consider that a tampered view state is normally detected on the server and an exception is thrown. Finally, and most importantly of all, the view state contains data, not code. What a hacker could perhaps do is modify the data that represents the state of the page to restore. This results in open holes for attacks only if basic rules of data validation and data checking are not enforced. But this, you understand, is a more general problem that affects writing secure code.

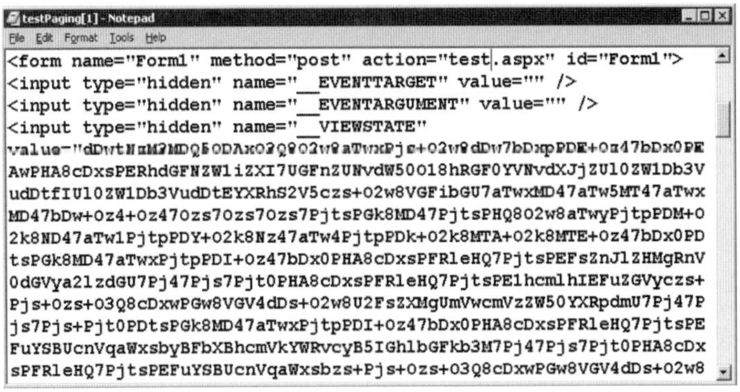

```
testPaging[1] - Notepad
File Edit Format Tools Help
<form name="Form1" method="post" action="test.aspx" id="Form1">
<input type="hidden" name="__EVENTTARGET" value="" />
<input type="hidden" name="__EVENTARGUMENT" value="" />
<input type="hidden" name="__VIEWSTATE"
value="dDwtNzM3MDQ5ODAxO3Q8O2w8aTwxPjs+O2w8dDw7bDxpPDE+Oz47bDx0PE
AwPHA8cDxsPERhdGFNZW1iZXI7UGFnZUNvdW50O18hRGF0YVNvdXJjZU10ZW1Db3V
udDtfIU10ZW1Db3VudDtEYXRhS2V5czs+O2w8VGFibGU7aTwxMD47aTw5MT47aTwx
MD47bDw+Oz4+Oz47Ozs7Ozs7Ozs7PjtsPGk8MD47PjtsPHQ8O2w8aTwyPjtpPDM+O
2k8ND47aTw1PjtpPDY+O2k8Nz47aTw4PjtpPDk+O2k8MTA+O2k8MTE+Oz47bDx0PD
tsPGk8MD47aTwxPjtpPDI+Oz47bDx0PHA8cDxsPFRleHQ7PjtsPEFsZnJlZHMgRnV
0dGVya2lzdGU7Pj47Pjs7Pjt0PHA8cDxsPFRleHQ7PjtsPE1hcmlhIEFuZGVyczs+
Pjs+Ozs+O3Q8cDxwPGw8VGV4dDs+O2w8U2FsZXMgUmVwcmVzZW50YXRpdmU7Pj47P
js7Pjs+PjtOPDtsPGk8MD47aTwxPjtpPDI+Oz47bDx0PHA8cDxsPFRleHQ7PjtsPE
FuYSBUcnVqaWxsbyBFbXBhcmVkYWRvcyB5IGhlbGFkb3M7Pj47Pjs7PjtOPHA8cDx
sPFRleHQ7PjtsPEFuYSBUcnVqaWxsbzs+Pjs+Ozs+O3Q8cDxwPGw8VGV4dDs+O2w8
```

Figure 14-10 A view of the hashed and encoded view state for a not-too-complex page.

Machine Authentication Check

As mentioned in Chapter 1, the *@Page* directive contains an attribute named *EnableViewStateMac*, whose only purpose is making the view state a bit more secure by detecting any possible attempt to corrupt the original data. When serialized, and if *EnableViewStateMac* is set to *true*, the view state is appended with a validator hash string based on the algorithm and the key defined in the *<machineKey>* section of the machine.config file. The resulting array of bytes, the output of the *StateBag*'s binary serialization plus the hash value, is Base64 encoded. By default, the encryption algorithm to calculate the hash is SHA1 and the encryption and decryption keys are auto-generated and stored in the Web server machine's Local Security Authority (LSA) subsystem. The LSA is a protected component of Windows NT, Windows 2000, and Windows XP. It provides security services and maintains information about all aspects of local security on a system.

If *EnableViewStateMac* is *true*, the hash value is extracted when the page posts back and is used to verify that the returned view state has not been tampered with on the client. If this is the case, an exception is thrown. The net effect is that you might be able to read the contents of the view state, but to replace it you need the encryption key, which is in the Web server's LSA.

The *MAC* in the name of the *EnableViewStateMac* property stands for *Machine Authentication Check* and, in spite of what some old documentation claims, it is enabled by default. The *EnableViewStateMac* attribute corresponds to a protected *Page* member with the same name.

If you disable the attribute, an attacker could crack the view state on the client and send a modified version to the server and have ASP.NET blissfully use that tampered-with information. To reinforce the security of the view state, in ASP.NET 1.1 the *ViewStateUserKey* property has also been added to the *Page* class. The property evaluates to a user-specific string (for example, the session ID or the user name) that is known on the server. ASP.NET uses the content of the property as an input to the hash algorithm that generates the MAC code.

Size Thresholds and Page Throughput

My personal opinion is that you should be concerned about the view state, but not because of the potential security holes it might open in your code—it can only let hackers exploit existing holes. You should be more concerned about the overall performance and responsiveness of the page. Especially for feature-rich pages that make use of plenty of controls, the view state can reach a considerable size, measured in KB of data. Such an extra burden taxes all requests and ends up being a serious overhead for the application as a whole.

The use of the view state feature should be carefully monitored because it can hinder your code. By default, the view state is enabled for all server controls; this doesn't mean that you strictly need it all the time. View state saves you from a lot of coding and, more importantly, makes coding simpler and smarter. However, if you find you're paying too much for this feature, drop view state altogether and reinitialize the state of the server controls at every postback. In this case, disabling view state saves processing time and speeds up the download process.

You can disable the view state for an entire page by using the *EnableViewState* attribute of the *@Page* directive. While this is not generally a recommended option, you should definitely consider it for read-only pages that either don't post back or don't need state to be maintained.

```
<% @Page EnableViewState="false" %>
```

A better approach entails disabling the view state only for some server controls hosted in the page. To disable it on a per-control basis, set the *EnableViewState* property of the control to *false*, as shown here:

```
<asp:datagrid runat="server" EnableViewState="false">
  ⋮
</asp:datagrid>
```

While developing the page, you can keep the size of the view state under control by enabling tracing on the page. Once you have set the *@Page trace* attribute to *true*, look under the Viewstate Size Bytes column of the control tree, as shown in Figure 14-11.

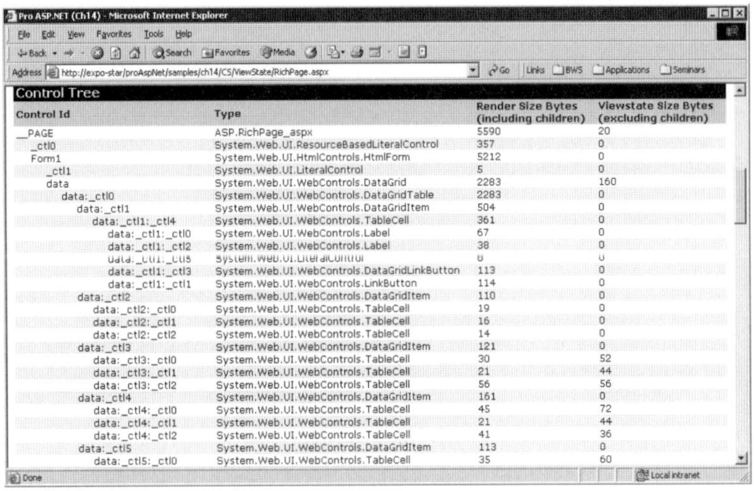

Control Id	Type	Render Size Bytes (including children)	Viewstate Size Bytes (excluding children)
__PAGE	ASP.RichPage_aspx	5590	20
_ctl0	System.Web.UI.ResourceBasedLiteralControl	357	0
Form1	System.Web.UI.HtmlControls.HtmlForm	5212	0
_ctl1	System.Web.UI.LiteralControl	5	0
data	System.Web.UI.WebControls.DataGrid	2283	160
data:_ctl0	System.Web.UI.WebControls.DataGridTable	2283	0
data:_ctl1	System.Web.UI.WebControls.DataGridItem	504	0
data:_ctl1:_ctl4	System.Web.UI.WebControls.TableCell	361	0
data:_ctl1:_ctl0	System.Web.UI.WebControls.Label	67	0
data:_ctl1:_ctl2	System.Web.UI.WebControls.Label	38	0
data:_ctl1:_ctl5	System.Web.UI.LiteralControl	8	0
data:_ctl1:_ctl3	System.Web.UI.WebControls.DataGridLinkButton	113	0
data:_ctl1:_ctl1	System.Web.UI.WebControls.LinkButton	114	0
data:_ctl2	System.Web.UI.WebControls.DataGridItem	110	0
data:_ctl2:_ctl0	System.Web.UI.WebControls.TableCell	19	0
data:_ctl2:_ctl1	System.Web.UI.WebControls.TableCell	16	0
data:_ctl2:_ctl2	System.Web.UI.WebControls.TableCell	14	0
data:_ctl3	System.Web.UI.WebControls.DataGridItem	121	0
data:_ctl3:_ctl0	System.Web.UI.WebControls.TableCell	30	52
data:_ctl3:_ctl1	System.Web.UI.WebControls.TableCell	21	44
data:_ctl3:_ctl2	System.Web.UI.WebControls.TableCell	56	56
data:_ctl4	System.Web.UI.WebControls.DataGridItem	161	0
data:_ctl4:_ctl0	System.Web.UI.WebControls.TableCell	45	72
data:_ctl4:_ctl1	System.Web.UI.WebControls.TableCell	21	44
data:_ctl4:_ctl2	System.Web.UI.WebControls.TableCell	41	36
data:_ctl5	System.Web.UI.WebControls.DataGridItem	113	0
data:_ctl5:_ctl0	System.Web.UI.WebControls.TableCell	35	60

Figure 14-11 The view state size, control by control.

The tracer doesn't show the total amount of the view state for the page, but it lets you form a precise idea of what each control does. In Figure 14-11, the page contains a relatively simple *DataGrid* control. As you can see, the cells of the grid take up a large part of the view state. The *TableCell* control, in particular, saves the view state of all its user interfaces, including text, column, and row span style attributes.

> **Note** Contrary to what many developers think, the *DataGrid* server control doesn't store its data source in the view state. The *DataGrid* control per se caches almost all its public properties, but the amount of space required is not related to the data source. However, the *DataGrid* uses child controls—for example, the *TableCell*—which also store their text and style in view state. The text displayed in the cells is part of the *DataGrid* data source.

In Figure 14-12, you see the same page with a client-side button that retrieves the view state string and calculates its length. The JavaScript code needed is pretty simple:

```
<script language="javascript">
  function ShowViewStateSize() {
    var buf = document.forms[0]["__VIEWSTATE"].value;
    alert("View state is " + buf.length + " bytes");
  }
</script>
```

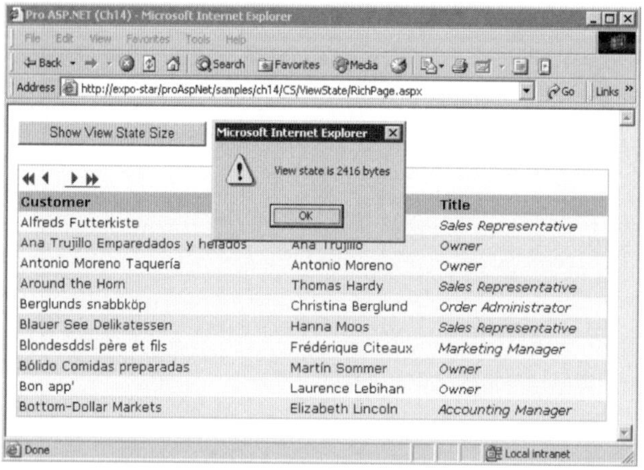

Figure 14-12 The overall view state size obtained scriptwise.

Programming Web Forms Without View State

Let's briefly recap what view state is all about and what you might lose if you ban it from your pages. View state represents the current state of the page and its controls just before the page is rendered to HTML. When the page posts back, the view state—a sort of call context for the page request—is recovered from the hidden field, deserialized, and used to initialize the server controls in the page and the page itself. However, as pointed out in Chapter 2, this is only the first half of the story.

After loading the view state, the page reads client-side information through the *Request* object and uses those values to override most of the settings for the server controls. In general, the two operations are neatly separated and take place independently. In particular, though, the second operation—reading from *Request.Form*—in many situations ends up just overriding some of the settings read out of the view state. You understand that in this case the view state is only an extra burden.

Let's examine a typical case and suppose you have a page with a text box server control. What you expect is that when the page posts back, the text box server control is automatically assigned the value set on the client. Well, to meet this rather common requirement, you *don't* need view state. Let's consider the following page:

```
<% @Page language="c#" EnableViewState="false" %>
<script runat="server">
void OnPost(object sender, EventArgs e) {
  Response.Write(theInput.Text);
}
</script>

<form runat="server">
  <asp:textbox runat="server"
    id="theInput" readonly="false" text="Type here" />
  <asp:checkbox runat="server" id="theCheck" text="Check me" />
  <asp:linkbutton runat="server" text="Click" onclick="OnPost" />
</form>
```

The behavior of the page is stateful even if view state is disabled. The reason lies in the fact that you are using two server controls—*TextBox* and *CheckBox*—whose key properties are updated according to the values set by the user. These values will override any setting view state might have set. As a result, as long as you're simply interested in persisting properties such as *Text* or *Checked*, you don't need view state at all.

> **Note** You don't need view state for the properties of a control whose value is ultimately determined by the posted data. For example, this is what happens for the *Text* property of a *TextBox* but not for *ReadOnly* or *MaxLength*.

All the properties declared as tag attributes are automatically restored as specified during the initialization of the control. As long as these extra properties are not expected to change during the session, you don't need view state at all. So when is view state really necessary?

Suppose that your text box can be edited only if the user has certain privileges. A possible implementation entails that you declare the text box as read-only and turn off the attribute the first time the page is loaded after checking the user's credentials. The code might be as follows:

```
<% @Page language="C#" %>
<script runat="server">
void Page_Load(object sender, EventArgs e) {
```

```
  if (!IsPostBack)
    theInput.ReadOnly = !IsUserAdmin();
}
bool IsUserAdmin() {
  return true;
}
void OnPost(object sender, EventArgs e) {
  Response.Write(theInput.Text);
}
</script>

<form runat="server">
  <asp:textbox runat="server" id="theInput" readonly="true"
    text="Type your UID here" />
  <asp:linkbutton runat="server" text="Click" onclick="OnPost" />
</form>
```

This programming style is inherently stateful and works as expected as long as you have view state enabled. Try setting the *EnableViewState* attribute to *false* and then re-run the page. In the *OnInit* page event, the text box is instantiated as declared in the page layout—that is, with the *ReadOnly* property equal to *true*. The first time the page is processed (*IsPostBack* returns *false*), the attribute is programmatically turned on according to the user's role. So far so good.

The preceding code, though, is stateful in the sense that it assumes that after the first access to the page, the run time can remember all settings. This is no longer the case if you turn view state off. In this case, because *IsPostBack* now returns *true*, the *Page_Load* event never has a chance to modify the text box *ReadOnly* property. Because the view state is disabled, the *ReadOnly* property remains set to *true* whatever the user's role is. By choosing an alternative programming style, you can obtain the same function without resorting to view state, thus saving 40 bytes of HTML for each instance of a *TextBox* control. The following code shows in boldface type the changes needed to disable view state for the page:

```
<% @Page language="c#" EnableViewState="false" %>
<script runat="server">
void Page_Load(object sender, EventArgs e) {
  if (IsPostBack)
    theInput.ReadOnly = !IsUserAdmin();
}
bool IsUserAdmin() {
  return true;
}
void OnPost(object sender, EventArgs e) {
  Response.Write(theInput.Text);
}
</script>
```

```
<form runat="server">
  <asp:textbox runat="server" id="theInput" readonly="false"
    text="Type your UID here" />
  <asp:linkbutton runat="server" text="Click" onclick="OnPost" />
</form>
```

In some cases, you can disable view state and still have the page run unchanged. In other cases, some minor changes must be entered to the code to make sure all properties of all controls are properly initialized. In general, you can do without view state whenever the state can be deduced either from the client or from the runtime environment (for example, by determining whether the user has certain privileges). In contrast, doing without view state is hard whenever state information can't be dynamically inferred. For example, if you want to track the sort order of a pageable *DataGrid*, you can cache it only in the view state.

Keeping the View State on the Server

As discussed so far, there are a couple of good reasons to keep the view state off the client browser. First, the view state can be tampered with, at least in theory. Second, the more stuff you pack into the view state, the more time the page takes to download. These two apparently unrelated issues have a common root—the view state is stored on the client through a hidden field. However, the client-side hidden field is not set in stone and is simply the default storage medium where the view state information can be stored. Let's see how to proceed to save the view state in a file on the Web server.

The *LosFormatter* Class

To design an alternative storage scheme for the view state, we need to put our hands on the string that ASP.NET stores in the hidden field. The string will be saved in a server-side file and read from where the page is being processed. When it comes to doing this, there is bad news and good news. The bad news is that the Base64 view state string is not publicly exposed to the code running within the page. The good news is that, although officially undocumented, the class that the .NET Framework actually uses to serialize and deserialize the view state is configured as a public type (as opposed to an internal type), and as such it can be called from user applications. The class is named *LosFormatter*.

The *LosFormatter* class has a simple programming interface made of only two publicly callable methods—*Serialize* and *Deserialize*. The *Serialize* method writes the final Base64 representation of the view state to a *Stream* or *TextWriter* object.

```
public void Serialize(Stream stream, object viewState);
public void Serialize(TextWriter output, object viewState);
```

The *Deserialize* method builds a *StateBag* object from a stream, a *TextReader* object, or a plain Base64 string.

```
public object Deserialize(Stream stream);
public object Deserialize(TextReader input);
public object Deserialize(string input);
```

The *LosFormatter* class is the entry point in the view state internal mechanism. By using it, you can be sure everything will happen exactly as in the default case.

> **Note** The *LosFormatter* class features a read/write property named *EnableViewStateMac*, whose role is exactly that of enabling hashing on the Base64 string. The variable cannot be accessed because it's marked as internal, meaning that only classes in the same assembly can work with it. However, because we're simply plugging our code into the ASP.NET view state pipeline, we can control the machine authentication check by using the high-level tools discussed earlier.

Creating a View-State-Less Page

The *Page* class provides a couple of protected virtual methods that the run time uses when it needs to deserialize or serialize the view state. The methods are named *LoadPageStateFromPersistenceMedium* and *SavePageStateToPersistenceMedium*.

```
protected virtual void SavePageStateToPersistenceMedium(object viewState);
protected virtual object LoadPageStateFromPersistenceMedium();
```

If you override both methods, you can load and save view state information from and to anything other than a hidden field. By the way, you cannot override only one method. Because the methods are defined as protected members, the only way to redefine them is by creating a new class and making it inherit from *Page*. The following code just gives you an idea of the default behavior of *LoadPageStateFromPersistenceMedium*:

```
string m_viewState = Request.Form["__VIEWSTATE"];
LosFormatter m_formatter = new LosFormatter();
StateBag viewStateBag = m_formatter.Deserialize(m_viewState);
```

The structure of the page we're going to create is as follows:

```
public class AltViewStatePage : Page
{
  protected override
```

```
    object LoadPageStateFromPersistenceMedium()
  { ... }
  protected override
    void SavePageStateToPersistenceMedium(object viewState)
  { ... }
}
```

Saving the View State to a Web Server File

The tasks accomplished by the *SavePageStateToPersistenceMedium* method are easy to explain and understand. The method takes a string as an argument, opens the output stream, and calls into the *LosFormatter* serializer.

```
protected override
void SavePageStateToPersistenceMedium(object viewStateBag)
{
  string file = GetFileName();
  StreamWriter sw = new StreamWriter(file);
  LosFormatter m_formatter = new LosFormatter();
  m_formatter.Serialize(sw, viewStateBag);
  sw.Close();
  return;
}
```

How should we choose the name of the file to make sure that no conflicts arise? The view state is specific to a page request made within a particular session. So the session ID and the request URL are pieces of information that can be used to associate the request with the right file. Alternatively, you could give the view state file a randomly generated name and persist it in a custom hidden field within the page. Note that in this case you can't rely on the __VIEWSTATE hidden field because when overriding the methods, you alter the internal procedure that would have created it.

The *GetFileName* function in the preceding code gives the file a name according to the following pattern:

```
SessionID_URL.viewstate
```

Figure 14-13 (presented a bit later) shows one of these files created in a temporary directory. Note that for an ASP.NET application to create a local file, you must give the ASPNET account special permissions on a file or folder. I suggest creating a new subfolder to contain all the view state files. Deleting files for expired sessions can be a bit tricky, and a Windows NT service is probably the tool that works better.

Loading the View State from a Web Server File

In our implementation, the *LoadPageStateFromPersistenceMedium* method determines the name of the file to read from, extracts the Base64 string, and calls *LosFormatter* to deserialize.

```
protected override object LoadPageStateFromPersistenceMedium()
{
  object viewStateBag;

  string file = GetFileName();
  StreamReader sr = new StreamReader(file);
  string m_viewState = sr.ReadToEnd();
  sr.Close();
  LosFormatter m_formatter = new LosFormatter();

  try {
    viewStateBag = m_formatter.Deserialize(m_viewState);
  }
  catch {
    throw new HttpException("The View State is invalid.");
  }
  return viewStateBag;
}
```

To take advantage of this feature to keep view state on the server, a page needs only to inherit from the *AltViewStatePage* class defined here. The following header will suffice:

```
<% @Page Language="C#" Inherits="ProAspNet.CS.Ch14.AltViewStatePage" %>
```

Figure 14-13 shows the view state files created in a temporary folder on the Web server machine.

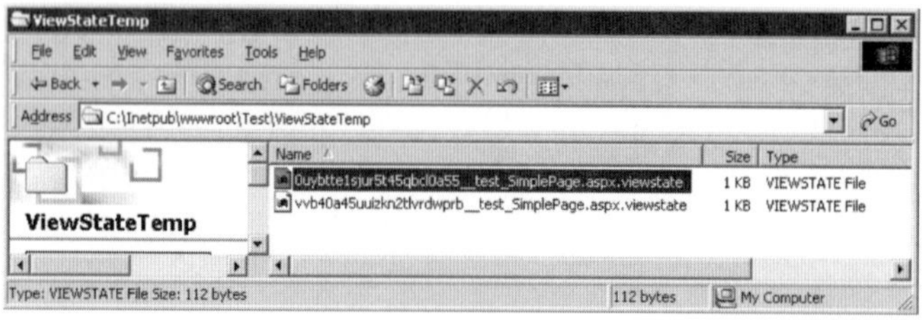

Figure 14-13 View state files created on the server. The folder must grant write permissions to the ASPNET account.

The page shown in Figure 14-13 (simplepage.aspx) enables view state, but no hidden field is present in its client-side code.

The ASP.NET Caching System

By definition, caching is the system's, or the application's, ability to save frequently used data to an intermediate storage medium. An intermediate storage medium is any support placed in between the application and its primary data source that lets you persist and retrieve data more quickly than with the primary data source. In a typical Web scenario, the intermediate storage medium is the Web server's memory, whereas the data source is the back-end data management system.

The ability to store in memory chunks of frequently accessed data can become a winning factor in the building of scalable Web applications. Instead of continuously connecting to the database server, locking records, and consuming one of the available connection channels, you can simply read the results needed from the local memory or maybe a disk file. This scenario delineates caching as an asset for any application. Well, not just any. Be aware that caching is rather a double-edged sword, and if abused or misused, it can easily morph into an insidious weakness. This typically happens when the quantity of memory-held information grows beyond a reasonable threshold. In a Web scenario, you should also distinguish between the session state and the application state and their actual size.

In general, caching as a *tout-court* solution does not necessarily guarantee better performance and is not quite a magic wand. However, if used in the context of an appropriate applicationwide strategy, it can result in a terrific boost for all kinds of applications—Web applications in particular.

In ASP.NET, caching comes in two independent but not exclusive flavors. One option is known as *output page caching* and consists of persisting the output of generated pages, thus having the system return the pages instead of processing them over and over again. We'll discuss this feature in the final part of the chapter "Caching ASP.NET Pages," paying special attention to the circumstances in which it is really useful. The second caching option takes place at the application level and is based on the new *Cache* object, which works side by side with the *Session* and *Application* objects. Let's start learning more about the *Cache* class.

The *Cache* Class

The *Cache* class is exposed by the *System.Web.Caching* namespace and represents a new entry in the set of tools that provide for state management in ASP.NET. The *Cache* class works like an applicationwide repository for data and objects, but this is the only aspect that it has in common with the *HttpApplicationState* class.

The *Cache* class is safe for multithreaded operations and does not require you to place locks on the repository prior to reading or writing. Next, what is stored in the *Cache* object is managed by the application, but under some circumstances it can automatically be invalidated, and then freed, by the system.

Some items stored in the application cache can be bound to the timestamp of one or more files or directories. Thus, when incoming changes to disk break this link, cached items are marked as invalid and made no longer available to the application. The *Cache* object is equipped with a scavenging tool that periodically clears stored data that hasn't been used lately or has timed out.

An instance of the *Cache* class is created on a per-AppDomain basis and remains valid until that AppDomain is up and running. The current instance of the application's ASP.NET cache is returned by the *Cache* property of the *HttpContext* object or the *Cache* property of the *Page* object.

Cache and Other State Objects

As mentioned, the *Cache* class lives side by side with the *HttpApplicationState* class. The two classes, though, are quite different. *Cache* is a thread-safe object and does not require you to explicitly lock and unlock before access. All critical sections in the internal code are adequately protected using synchronization constructs. Another key difference with the *HttpApplicationState* class is that data stored in *Cache* doesn't necessarily live as long as the application does. The *Cache* object lets you associate a duration as well as a priority with any of the items you store.

Any cached item expires after the specified number of seconds, freeing up some memory. By setting priority, you can control the memory occupation and help the object control that on your behalf. Both *Cache* and *HttpApplicationState* are globally visible classes and span all active sessions. However, neither works in a Web farm or Web garden scenario; in general, they don't work outside the current AppDomain.

The *Cache* object is unique in its capability to automatically scavenge the memory and get rid of unused items. Aside from that, it provides the same dictionary-based and familiar programming interface as *Application* and *Session*. Unlike *Session*, the *Cache* class does not store data on a per-user basis. Furthermore, when the session state is managed in-process, all currently running sessions are stored as distinct items in the ASP.NET *Cache*.

> **Note** If you're looking for a global repository object that, like *Session*, works across a Web farm or Web garden architecture, your expectations can be frustrated. No such object exists in the .NET Framework, but building an ad hoc one can be much easier than you might think. Web services, for example, provide a good infrastructure to devise and build such a made-to-measure component.

Properties of the *Cache* Class

The *Cache* class provides a couple of properties and a couple of public fields. The properties let you count and access the various items. The public fields are internal constants used to configure the expiration policy of the cache items. Table 14-11 lists and describes them all.

Table 14-11 *Cache* Class Properties and Public Fields

Property	Description
Count	Gets the number of items stored in the cache
Item	Indexer property, provides access to the cache item identified by the specified key
NoAbsoluteExpiration	Static constant, indicates a given item will never expire
NoSlidingExpiration	Static constant, indicates sliding expiration is disabled for a given item

The *NoAbsoluteExpiration* field is of the *DateTime* type and is set to the *DateTime.MaxValue* date—that is, the largest possible date defined in the .NET Framework. The *NoSlidingExpiration* field is of the *TimeSpan* type and is set to *TimeSpan.Zero*, meaning that sliding expiration is disabled. We'll say more about sliding expiration shortly. The *Item* property is a read/write property that can also be used to add new items to the cache. If the key specified as the argument of the *Item* property does not exist, a new entry is created. Otherwise, the existing entry is overwritten.

```
Cache["MyItem"] = value;
```

The data stored in the cache is generically considered to be of type *object*, whereas the key must be a case-sensitive string. When you insert a new item in the cache using the *Item* property, a number of default attributes are assumed. In particular, the item is given no expiration policy, no remove callback, and a normal priority. As a result, the item will stay in the cache indefinitely, until programmatically removed or until the application terminates. To specify any extra arguments and exercise closer control on the item, use the *Insert* method of the *Cache* class instead.

Methods of the *Cache* Class

The methods of the *Cache* class let you add, remove, and enumerate the items stored. As we'll see in a moment, insertion and removal of cached items can be quite a complex operation that involves the operating system as well. Methods of the *Cache* class are listed and described in Table 14-12.

Both the *Add* and *Insert* methods don't accept null values as the key or the value of an item to cache. If null values are used, an exception is thrown. If you're going to set the sliding expiration for an item, make sure it's not more than one year. Otherwise, an exception will be raised. Finally, bear in mind that you cannot set both sliding and absolute expirations on the same cached item.

Table 14-12 *Cache* Class Methods

Method	Description
Add	Adds the specified item to the cache. It allows you to specify dependencies, expiration and priority policies, and a remove callback. The call fails if an item with the same key already exists. The method also returns an item of the object being added.
Get	Retrieves an item from the cache. The item is identified by key. The method returns *null* if no item with that key is found.
GetEnumerator	Returns a dictionary enumerator object to iterate through all the valid items stored in the cache.
Insert	Inserts the specified item into the cache. *Insert* provides several overloads and allows you to specify dependencies, expiration and priority policies, and a remove callback. The method is void and, unlike *Add*, overwrites an existing item having the same key as the item being inserted.
Remove	Removes the specified item from the cache. The item is identified by the key. The method returns the instance of the object being removed or *null* if no item with that key is found.

> **Note** *Add* and *Insert* work in much the same way, but a couple of differences make it worthwhile to have both. *Add* fails (but no exception is raised) if the item already exists, whereas *Insert* overwrites the existing item. In addition, *Add* has just one signature, while *Insert* provides several different overloads.

Working with the ASP.NET Cache

An instance of the *Cache* object is associated with each running application and shares the associated application's lifetime. The cache holds references to data and proactively verifies their validity and expiration. When the system runs short of memory, the *Cache* object automatically removes some little-used items and frees valuable server resources. Each item when stored into the cache can be given special attributes that determine a priority and an expiration policy. All these are system-provided tools to help programmers control the scavenging mechanism of the ASP.NET cache.

Inserting New Items in the Cache

A cache item is characterized by a handful of attributes that can be specified as input arguments of both *Add* and *Insert*. In particular, an item stored in the ASP.NET *Cache* object can have the following properties:

- ***Key*** A case-sensitive string, represents the key used to store the item in the internal hash table the ASP.NET cache relies upon. If this value is null, an exception is thrown. If the key already exists, what happens depends on the particular method you're using: *Add* fails, while *Insert* just overwrites the existing item.
- ***Value*** A non-null value of type *Object* that references the information stored in the cache. The value is managed and returned as an *Object* and needs casting to become useful in the application context.
- ***Dependencies*** Object of type *CacheDependency*, tracks a physical dependency between the item being added to the cache and files, directories, or other objects in the application's cache. Whenever any of the files or the directories are modified, or the specified objects in the cache change, the newly added item is marked obsolete and automatically removed.
- ***Absolute Expiration Date*** A *DateTime* object that represents the absolute expiration date for the item being added. When this time arrives, the object is automatically removed from the cache. Items not subject to absolute expiration dates must use the *NoAbsoluteExpiration* constants representing the farthest allowable date. The absolute expiration date doesn't change after the item is used in either reading or writing.
- ***Sliding Expiration*** A *TimeSpan* object, represents a relative expiration period for the item being added. When you set the parameter to a non-null value, the expiration-date parameter is automatically set to the current time plus the sliding period. If you explicitly set the sliding expiration, you cannot set the absolute expiration date too. From the user's perspective, these are mutually exclusive parameters. If the item is accessed before its natural expiration time, the sliding period is automatically renewed.
- ***Priority*** A value picked out of the *CacheItemPriority* enumeration, denotes the priority of the item. It is a value ranging from *Low* to *NotRemovable*. The default level of priority is *Normal*. The priority level determines the importance of the item; items with a lower priority are removed first.

- ***Removal Callback*** If specified, indicates the function that the ASP.NET *Cache* object calls back when the item will be removed from the cache. In this way, applications can be notified when their own items are removed from the cache no matter what the reason is. As we mentioned earlier in the chapter, when the session state works in *InProc* mode, a removal callback function is used to fire the *Session_OnEnd* event. The delegate type used for this callback is *CacheItemRemoveCallback*.

There are basically three ways to add new items to the ASP.NET *Cache* object—the *set* accessor of *Item* property, the *Add* method, and the *Insert* method. The *Item* property allows you to indicate only the key and the value. The *Add* method has only one signature that includes all the aforementioned arguments. The *Insert* method is the most flexible of all options and provides the following four overloads:

```
public void Insert(string, object);
public void Insert(string, object, CacheDependency);
public void Insert(string, object, CacheDependency, DateTime, TimeSpan);
public void Insert(string, object, CacheDependency, DateTime, TimeSpan,
CacheItemPriority, CacheItemRemovedCallback);
```

The following code snippet shows the typical call that is performed under the hood when the *Item* set accessor is used:

```
Insert(key, value, null, Cache.NoAbsoluteExpiration,
  Cache.NoSlidingExpiration, CacheItemPriority.Normal, null);
```

If you use the *Add* method to insert an item whose key matches that of an existing item, no exception is raised, nothing happens, and the method returns *null*.

Removing Items from the Cache

All items marked with an expiration policy, or a dependency, are automatically removed from the cache when something happens in the system to invalidate them. To programmatically remove an item, on the other hand, you resort to the *Remove* method. Note that this method can remove any item, including items marked with the highest level of priority (*NotRemovable*). The following code snippet shows how to call the *Remove* method:

```
Cache.Remove("MyItem");
```

Normally, the method returns the object just removed from the cache. However, if the specified key is not found, the method fails and null is returned, but no exception is ever raised.

When items with an associated callback function are removed from the cache, a value from the *CacheItemRemovedReason* enumeration is passed on to the function to justify the operation. The enumeration includes the values listed in Table 14-13.

Table 14-13 The *CacheItemRemovedReason* Enumeration

Reason	Description
DependencyChanged	Removed because a file or a key dependency changed.
Expired	Removed because expired.
Removed	Programmatically removed from the cache using *Remove*. Note that a *Removed* event might also be fired if an existing item is replaced either through *Insert* or the *Item* property
Underused	Removed by the system to free memory.

If the item being removed is associated with a callback, the function is executed immediately after having removed the item.

Tracking Item Dependencies

Items added to the cache through the *Add* or *Insert* method can be linked to an array of files and directories as well as to an array of existing cache items. The link between the new item and its cache dependency is maintained using an instance of the *CacheDependency* class. The *CacheDependency* object can represent a single file or directory or an array of files and directories. In addition, it can also represent an array of cache keys—that is, keys of other items stored in the *Cache*. The dependency list of a cached item can also be composed of both files or directories and cache keys.

The *CacheDependency* class has quite a long list of constructors that provide for the possibilities listed in Table 14-14.

Table 14-14 The *CacheDependency* Constructor List

Constructor	Description
String	A file path—that is, a URL to a file or a directory name
String[]	An array of file paths
String, DateTime	A file path monitored starting at a specified time
String[], DateTime	An array of file paths monitored starting at a specified time
String[], String[]	An array of file paths, and an array of cache keys
String[], String[], CacheDependency	An array of file paths, an array of cache keys, and a separate *CacheDependency* class

(continued)

Table 14-14 The *CacheDependency* Constructor List *(continued)*

Constructor	Description
String[], String[], DateTime	An array of file paths and an array of cache keys monitored starting at a specified time
String[], String[], CacheDependency, DateTime	An array of file paths, an array of cache keys, and a separate instance of the *CacheDependency* class monitored starting at a specified time

Any change in any of the monitored objects invalidates the current item. It's interesting to note that you can set a time to start monitoring for changes. By default, monitoring begins right after the item is stored in the cache. A *CacheDependency* object can be made dependent on another instance of the same class. In this case, any change detected on the items controlled by the separate object results in a broken dependency and the subsequent invalidation of the present item.

In the following code snippet, the item is associated with the timestamp of a file. The net effect is that any change made to the file that affects the timestamp invalidates the item, which will then be removed from the cache.

```
CacheDependency dep = new CacheDependency(filename);
Cache.Insert(key, value, dep);
```

Bear in mind that the *CacheDependency* object needs to take file and directory names expressed through absolute file system paths.

> **Note** As of ASP.NET 1.1, the *Cache* object doesn't support dependencies set on database items. While Microsoft is considering this feature for a future version of ASP.NET, there's something you can do right now. You can define a trigger on the database and make it create or modify a file whenever executed. Next, you bind the cache item with this file. See the "Resources" section at the end of the chapter for a link to an MSDN article that demonstrates this technique.

Defining a Removal Callback

Item removal is an event independent from the application's behavior and control. The difficulty with item removal is that because the application is oblivious to what has happened, it attempts to access the removed item later and gets only a null value back. To work around this issue, you can either check for the item's existence before access is attempted or, more effectively, register a removal callback and reload the item if it's invalidated. This approach makes particular sense if the cached item just represents the content of the tracked file.

The following sample page demonstrates how to read the contents of a Web server's file and cache it with a key named "MyData." The item is inserted with a removal callback. The callback simply re-reads and reloads the file if the removal reason is *DependencyChanged*. Otherwise, the item just deleted is restored.

```
<%@ Page Language="C#" %>
<%@ Import Namespace="System.IO" %>

<script runat="server">
void OnLoadData(object sender, EventArgs e) {
  AddFileContentsToCache("data.xml");
}
void AddFileContentsToCache(string fileName) {
  string file = Server.MapPath(fileName);
  StreamReader reader = new StreamReader(file);
  string buf = reader.ReadToEnd();
  reader.Close();

  // Create and display the content
  CreateAndCacheItem(buf, file);
  contents.Text = Cache["MyData"].ToString();
}
void CreateAndCacheItem(object buf, string file) {
  CacheItemRemovedCallback onRemove;
  onRemove = new CacheItemRemovedCallback(ReloadItemRemoved);

  CacheDependency dep = new CacheDependency(file);
  Cache.Insert("MyData", buf, dep, Cache.NoAbsoluteExpiration,
    Cache.NoSlidingExpiration, CacheItemPriority.Normal, onRemove);
}
void ReloadItemRemoved(string key, object value,
  CacheItemRemovedReason reason)
{
  if (reason == CacheItemRemovedReason.DependencyChanged) {
    // Reload the file
    AddFileContentsToCache("data.xml");
  } else {
    // Just restore the item
    CreateAndCacheItem(value, "data.xml");
  }
}
</script>

<form runat="server">
  <asp:button runat="server" text="Load data" onclick="OnLoadData" />
```

```
  <hr>
  <b>Contents of the cache</b><br>
  <asp:label runat="server" id="contents" />
</form>
```

Note that the item removal callback is a piece of code defined by a user page but automatically run by the *Cache* object as soon as the removal event is fired. If the removal event has to do with a broken dependency, the *Cache* object will execute the callback as soon as the file change notification is detected. In other words, for the cache to be updated, you don't need to refresh the page. Of course, you need to refresh the page to see the changes (if there were any) reflected. To test the page just discussed, point the browser to the URL and modify the underlying file. Next, refresh the page, and if everything worked fine, you should see the updated contents of the dependency file.

> **Note** If you add an object to the *Cache* and make it dependent on a file, directory, or key that doesn't exist, the item is regularly cached and marked with a dependency as usual. If the file, directory, or key is created later, the dependency is broken and the cached item is invalidated. In other words, if the dependency item doesn't exist, it's virtually created with a null timestamp or empty content.

To define a removal callback, you first declare a variable of type *CacheRemovedItemCallback*. Next, you instantiate this member with a new delegate object with the right signature.

```
CacheItemRemovedCallback onRemove;
onRemove = new CacheItemRemovedCallback(ReloadItemRemoved);
```

The *CacheDependency* object is simply passed the *onRemove* delegate member, which carries out the actual function code for the *Cache* object to call back.

Setting the Item Priority

Each item in the cache is given a priority—that is, a value picked up from the *CacheItemPriority* enumeration. A priority is a value ranging from *Low* (lowest) to *NotRemovable* (highest) with the default set to *Normal*. The priority is supposed to determine the importance of the item for the *Cache* object. The higher the priority is, the greater the effort to keep the object in memory. Also in critical and stress conditions when the system resources are going dangerously down, priority will be used to determine which objects are kept in memory.

If you want to give a particular priority level to an item being added to the cache, you have to use either the *Add* or *Insert* method. The priority can be any value listed in Table 14-15.

Table 14-15 Priority Levels in the *Cache* Object

Priority	Value	Description
Low	*1*	Items with this level of priority are the first items to be deleted from the cache as the server frees system memory.
BelowNormal	*2*	Intermediate level of priority between *Normal* and *Low*.
Normal	*3*	Default priority level, is assigned to all items and is added using the *Item* property
Default	*3*	Same as *Normal*.
AboveNormal	*4*	Intermediate level of priority between *Normal* and *High*.
High	*5*	Items with this level of priority are the last items to be removed from the cache as the server frees memory.
NotRemovable	*6*	Items with this level of priority are never removed from the cache. Use this level with extreme care.

The *Cache* object is designed with two goals in mind. First, it has to be an efficient and easy-to-program global repository of application data. Second, it has to be smart enough to detect when the system is running low on memory resources and to clear elements to free memory. This trait clearly differentiates the *Cache* object from *HttpApplicationState*, which instead maintains its objects until the end of the application (unless the application itself frees those items). The technique used to eliminate low-priority and seldom-used objects is known as *scavenging*.

Controlling Data Expiration

Priority and changed dependencies are two causes that could lead a cached item to be automatically garbage-collected from the *Cache*. Another possible cause for a premature removal from the *Cache* is infrequent use associated with an expiration policy. By default, all items added to the cache have no expiration date, neither absolute nor relative. If you add items by using either the *Add* or *Insert* method, you can choose between two mutually exclusive expiration policies: absolute and sliding expiration.

Absolute expiration is when a cached item is associated with a *DateTime* value and is removed from the cache as the specified time is reached. The *DateTime.MaxValue* field, and its more general alias *NoAbsoluteExpiration*, can be used to indicate the last date value supported by the .NET Framework and to subsequently indicate that the item will never expire.

Sliding expiration implements a sort of relative expiration policy. The idea is that the object expires after a certain interval. In this case, though, the interval is automatically renewed after each access to the item. Sliding expiration is rendered through a *TimeSpan* object—a type that in the .NET Framework represents an interval of time. The *TimeSpan.Zero* field represents the empty interval and is also the value associated with the *NoSlidingExpiration* static field on the *Cache* class. When you cache an item with a sliding expiration of 10 minutes, you use the following code:

```
Insert(key, value, null, Cache.NoAbsoluteExpiration,
  TimeSpan.FromMinutes(10), CacheItemPriority.Normal, null);
```

Internally, the item is cached with an absolute expiration date given by the current time plus the specified *TimeSpan* value. In light of this, the preceding code could have been rewritten as follows:

```
Insert(key, value, null, DateTime.Now.AddMinutes(10),
  Cache.NoSlidingExpiration, CacheItemPriority.Normal, null);
```

However, a subtle difference still exists between the two code snippets. In the former case—that is, when sliding expiration is explicitly turned on—each access to the item resets the absolute expiration date to the time of the last access plus the time span. In the latter case, because sliding expiration is explicitly turned off, any access to the item doesn't change the absolute expiration time.

Statistics About Memory Usage

Immediately after initialization, the *Cache* collects statistical information about the memory in the system and the current status of the system resources. Next, it registers a timer to invoke a callback function at one-second intervals. The callback function periodically updates and reviews the memory statistics and, if needed, activates the scavenging module. Memory statistics are collected using a bunch of Win32 API functions, including the *GlobalMemoryStatusEx* API used to obtain information about the system's current usage of both physical and virtual memory.

The *Cache* object classifies the status of the system resources in terms of low and high pressure. Each value corresponds to a different percentage of occupied memory. Typically, low pressure is in the range of 15 percent to 40 percent, while high pressure is measured from 45 percent to 65 percent of memory occupation. When the memory pressure exceeds the guard level, seldom-used objects are the first to be removed according to their priority.

Building a Cache Viewer

Enumerating the items in the *Cache* is as easy as walking through a collection of objects using an ad hoc enumerator. Unlike *Session* and *Application* objects, though, there's no graphical way to see the contents of the *Cache*, not even when tracing is turned on. In this section, we'll build a simple user control that reads the items in the cache and displays them in a grid. We covered user controls in Chapter 10. You register the *CacheViewer* user control with your application by using the following code:

```
<%@ Register TagPrefix="expo" TagName="CacheViewer"
  Src="CacheViewer.ascx" %>
```

To embed an instance of the control, you resort to the following tag in the body of the ASP.NET page:

```
<expo:CacheViewer runat="server" id="viewer" />
```

The control incorporates a *DataGrid* control and exposes one method named *Refresh* to populate the internal grid with an information readout of the *Cache*.

Enumerating Items in the Cache

The *CacheViewer* control creates and displays a *DataTable* with two columns—one for the key and one for the value of the item stored. The value is rendered using the *ToString* method, meaning that the string and numbers will be loyally rendered but objects will typically be rendered through their class name. The following code shows the implementation of the *Refresh* method:

```
public void Refresh() {
  DataTable dt = GetCacheContents();
  grid.DataSource = dt;
  grid.DataBind();
}
private DataTable GetCacheContents() {
  DataTable dt = CreateDataTable();
  foreach(DictionaryEntry elem in Cache) {
        AddItemToTable(dt, elem);
  }
  return dt;
}
private DataTable CreateDataTable() {
  DataTable dt = new DataTable();
  dt.Columns.Add("Key", typeof(string));
  dt.Columns.Add("Value", typeof(string));
  return dt;
}
private void AddItemToTable(DataTable dt, DictionaryEntry elem) {
  DataRow row = dt.NewRow();
```

```
    row["Key"] = elem.Key.ToString();
    row["Value"] = elem.Value.ToString();
    dt.Rows.Add(row);
  }
```

Figure 14-14 shows a typical output of the *CacheViewer* control.

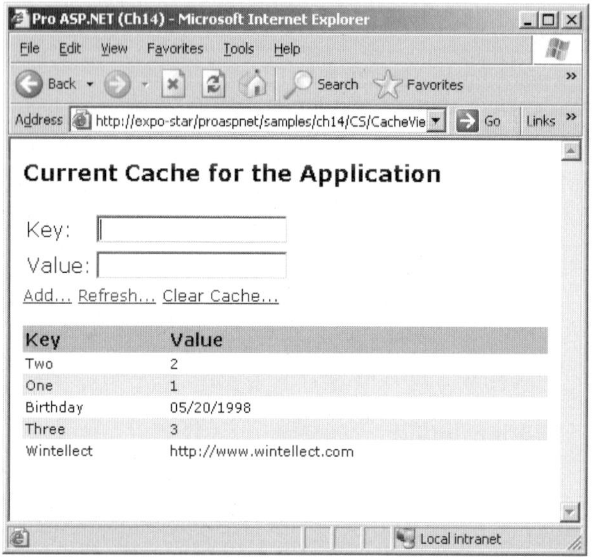

Figure 14-14 The content of the *Cache* object in a sample application.

The *Cache* class is a collection class that is instantiated within the *Http-Runtime* object. More exactly, an internal class named *CacheInternal* is used and its content is partitioned in public and private items. The set of public items is exposed to user applications through the *Cache* object. The rest of the HTTP runtime cache—the private items—contains system information, including objects that represent the state of all active sessions. Private items are inaccessible from user applications because of the protection level.

Clearing the Cache

The .NET Framework provides no method on the *Cache* class to programmatically clear all the content. The following code snippet shows how to build one:

```
public void Clear() {
  foreach(DictionaryEntry elem in Cache) {
    string s = elem.Key.ToString();
    Cache.Remove(s);
  }
}
```

The *CacheViewer* control provides a *Clear* method that removes all public items in the cache.

> **Important** The grid created by the *CacheViewer* control contains only a couple of columns because there's no other way to retrieve the additional information about an item in the cache. In particular, there's no way to know about the expiration policy, dependency, or removal callback. When you enumerate the contents of the *Cache* object, a generic *DictionaryEntry* object is returned with no property or method pointing to more specific information.
>
> Also note that because the *Cache* object stores data internally using a hash table, the enumerator returns contained items in an apparently weird order, neither alphabetical nor time-based. The order in which items are returned, instead, is based on the internal hash code used to index items.

Caching ASP.NET Pages

Output caching is an ASP.NET feature that allows you to store dynamic page responses so that next requests can be satisfied without executing the page but simply by returning the cached output. Output caching can take place at two levels—entire pages or portions of the page. In the latter case, the portion of the page to be cached is an embedded user control. Page caching is smart enough to let you save distinct output based on the requesting URL, query string, or form POST parameters, and even custom strings. Output caching can be configured either declaratively through the *@OutputCache* directive or programmatically through an API built around the *HttpCachePolicy* class.

The *@OutputCache* Directive

The *@OutputCache* directive can be used with both ASP.NET pages and user controls to declaratively control the caching capabilities of the resource. The directive accepts a handful of attributes. A couple of these attributes—*Duration* and *VaryByParam*—are mandatory. The *Duration* attribute indicates in seconds how long the system should cache the page output. The *VaryByParam* attribute allows you to vary the cached output depending on the GET query string or form POST parameters. The following declaration will cache the page for one minute regardless of any GET or POST parameters:

```
<%@ OutputCache Duration="60" VaryByParam="None" %>
```

The *@OutputCache* directive is made up of six attributes that indicate the location of the cache, its duration, and the arguments to use to vary page caching. The list of supported attributes is shown in Table 14-16.

Table 14-16 Attributes of the *@OutputCache* Directive

Attribute	Description
Duration	The time, in seconds, that the page or user control is cached.
Location	Specifies a valid location to store the output of a page. The attribute takes its value from the *OutputCacheLocation* enumeration. The default is *Any*.
VaryByCustom	A semicolon-separated list of strings that lets you maintain distinct cached copies of the page based on the browser type or user-defined strings.
VaryByHeader	A semicolon-separated list of HTTP headers.
VaryByParam	A semicolon-separated list of strings representing query string values sent with GET method attributes, or parameters sent using the POST method.
VaryByControl	A semicolon-separated list of strings representing fully qualified names of properties on a user control. Only valid for caching user controls; don't use it with ASP.NET pages.

Note that the *VaryByParam* attribute is mandatory. If you omit it, a runtime exception is always thrown. However, if you don't need to vary by parameters, set the attribute to *None*. The empty string is not an acceptable value for the *VaryByParam* attribute.

Choosing a Duration for the Output Cache

When the output caching service is active on a page—that is, the *@OutputCache* directive has been specified—the *Duration* attribute indicates the seconds that the ASP.NET system will maintain an HTML-compiled version of the page. Next, requests for the same page, or for an existing parameterized version of the page, will be serviced while bypassing the page handler.

The request is still assigned to an *HttpApplication* object and begins the normal processing by firing the *BeginRequest* event. The ASP.NET caching system includes an HTTP module—the *OutputCacheModule*—that registers its own handlers for the two application-level events related to output caching—*ResolveRequestCache* and *UpdateRequestCache*. In particular, the *ResolveRequestCache* event handler is used to short-circuit the processing of requests that have been cached. When the page is being generated, the output cache module grabs the output of the pages marked with the *@OutputCache* directive and stores it internally for further use.

Setting the *Duration* attribute on a page sets an expiration policy for the HTTP response generated by the ASP.NET runtime. The output is cached by the module for exactly the specified number of seconds. In the meantime, all the incoming requests that hit one of the cached pages are serviced by the module rather than by the ASP.NET pipeline.

A fair value for the *Duration* attribute depends on the application, but it normally doesn't exceed 60 seconds and works great, especially if the page doesn't need to be updated frequently.

> **Note** In ASP.NET 1.1, the output page-caching mechanism still requires that a new HTTP application be created, although for only a short time. With Microsoft Windows Server 2003 and the IIS 6.0 process model (discussed in Chapter 2), the output caching is integrated in the Web server, resulting in much better performance and responsiveness.

Choosing a Location for the Output Cache

The output cache can be located in various places, either on the client that originated the request or the server. It can also be located on an intermediate proxy server. The various options are listed in Table 14-17.

Table 14-17 Output Cache Locations

Location	Cache-Control	Description
Any	*Public*	The HTTP header *Expires* is set accordingly to the duration set in the *@OutputCache* directive. A new item is placed in the ASP.NET *Cache* object representing the output of the page. The type of this object is *CachedRawResponse*.
Client	*Private*	The HTTP header *Expires* is set accordingly to the duration set in the *@OutputCache* directive. No item is created in the ASP.NET *Cache* object.
DownStream	*Public*	The HTTP header *Expires* is set accordingly to the duration set in the *@OutputCache* directive. No item is created in the ASP.NET *Cache* object.
None	*No-Cache*	The HTTP header *Expires* is not defined. The *Pragma* header is set to *No-Cache*. No item is created in the ASP.NET *Cache* object.
Server	*No-Cache*	The HTTP header *Expires* is not defined. The *Pragma* header is set to *No-Cache*. A new *CachedRawResponse* item is placed in the ASP.NET *Cache* object to represent the output of the page.

Most browsers and intermediate proxies exploit any expiration information the Web server embeds in the HTML page being generated. A few HTTP 1.1 headers relate to page caching; they are *Expires* and *Cache-Control*.

In particular, the *Expires* HTTP header is used to specify the time when a particular page on the server should be updated by the client. Until that time, any new request the browser receives for the resource is served using the local, client-side cache and no server round-trip is ever made. When specified and not set to *No-Cache*, the HTTP 1.1 *Cache-Control* typically takes values such as *public* or *private*. A value of *public* means that both the browser and the proxy servers can cache the page. A value of *private* prevents proxy servers from caching the page; only the browser will cache the page. The *Cache-Control* is part of the HTTP 1.1 specification and is supported only by Internet Explorer 5.5 and higher.

If you look at the HTTP headers generated by ASP.NET when output caching is enabled, you'll notice that sometimes the *Pragma* header is used—in particular, when the location is set to *Server*. In this case, the header is assigned a value of *No-Cache*, meaning that client-side caching is totally disabled both on the browser side and the proxy side. As a result, any access to the page is resolved through a connection. To be precise, the *Pragma* header set to *No-Cache* disables caching only over HTTPS channels. If used over nonsecure channels, the page is actually cached but marked as expired.

Let's examine the client and Web server caching configuration when each of the feasible locations is used:

- **Any** Default option, means that the page can be cached everywhere, including in the browser, the server, and any proxies along the way. The *Expires* header is set to the page's absolute expiration time as determined by the *Duration* attribute; the *Cache-Control* is set to *Public*, meaning that the proxies can cache if they want and need to. On the Web server, a new item is placed in the *Cache* object with the HTML output of the page. In summary, with this option the page output is cached everywhere. As a result, if the page is accessed through the browser before it expires, no roundtrip is ever made. If, in the same timeframe, the page is refreshed—meaning that server-side access is made anyway—the overhead is minimal, the request is short-circuited by the output cache module, and no full request processing takes place.
- **Client** The page is cached only by the browser because the *Cache-Control* header is set to *Private*. Neither proxies nor ASP.NET stores a copy of it. The *Expires* header is set accordingly to the value of the *Duration* attribute.
- **DownStream** The page can be cached both on the client and in memory of any intermediate proxy. The *Expires* header is set accordingly to the value of the *Duration* attribute, and no copy of the page output is maintained by ASP.NET.

- **None** Page output caching is disabled both on the server and on the client. No *Expires* HTTP header is generated, and both the *Cache-Control* and *Pragma* headers are set to *No-Cache*.
- **Server** The page output is exclusively cached on the server and its raw response stored in the *Cache* object. The client-side caching is disabled. No *Expires* header is created and both the *Cache-Control* and *Pragma* headers are set to *No-Cache*.
- **ServerAndClient** The output cache can be stored only at the origin server or at the requesting client. Proxy servers are not allowed to cache the response.

> **Note** The ASP.NET output caching API affects caching both on the client and the Web server. You can control the caching mechanism by using a bunch of ASP.NET attributes such as *Location* and *Duration*. Note, though, that the *Location* attribute is not supported for *@OutputCache* directives included in user controls.

The *HttpCachePolicy* Class

The *HttpCachePolicy* class represents a programming interface alternative to using the *@OutputCache* directive. It provides direct methods to set cache-related HTTP headers such *Expires* and *Cache-Control*, which you could control to some extent anyway by using the interface of the *HttpResponse* object.

Properties of the *HttpCachePolicy* Class

Table 14-18 shows the properties of the *HttpCachePolicy* class.

Table 14-18 *HttpCachePolicy* Class Properties

Property	Description
VaryByHeaders	Gets an object of type *HttpCacheVaryByHeaders*, representing the list of all HTTP headers that will be used to vary cache output.
VaryByParams	Gets an object of type *HttpCacheVaryByParams*, representing the list of parameters received by a GET or POST request that affects caching.

When a cached page has several headers or parameters, a separate version of the page is available for each HTTP header type or parameter name.

Methods of the *HttpCachePolicy* Class

Table 14-19 shows the methods of the *HttpCachePolicy* class.

Table 14-19 *HttpCachePolicy* Class Methods

Method	Description
AddValidationCallback	Registers a callback function to be used to validate the page output in the server cache before returning it.
AppendCacheExtension	Appends the specified text to the *Cache-Control* HTTP header. The existing text is not overwritten.
SetCacheability	Sets the *Cache-Control* HTTP header to any of the following values: *NoCache*, *Private*, *Public*, *Server*, *ServerAndNoCache*, *ServerAndPrivate*. The allowable values are taken from the *HttpCacheability* enumeration type.
SetETag	Sets the *ETag* header to the specified string. The *ETag* header is a unique identifier for a specific version of a document.
SetETagFromFileDependencies	Sets the *ETag* header to a string built by combining and then hashing the last modified date of all the files upon which the page is dependent.
SetExpires	Sets the *Expires* header to an absolute date and time.
SetLastModified	Sets the *Last-Modified* HTTP header to a particular date and time.
SetLastModifiedFromFileDependencies	Sets the *Last-Modified* HTTP header to the most recent timestamps of the files upon which the page is dependent.
SetMaxAge	Sets the *max-age* attribute on the *Cache-Control* header based on the specified *TimeSpan* value. The sliding period cannot exceed one year.
SetNoServerCaching	Disables server output caching for the current response.
SetNoStore	Sets the *Cache-Control: no-store* directive.
SetNoTransforms	Sets the *Cache-Control: no-transform* directive.
SetProxyMaxAge	Sets the *Cache-Control: s-maxage* header based on the specified *TimeSpan*.
SetRevalidation	Sets the *Cache-Control* header to either the *must-revalidate* or *proxy-revalidate* directive.
SetSlidingExpiration	Sets cache expiration to sliding. When cache expiration is set to sliding, the *Cache-Control* header is renewed at each response.
SetValidUntilExpires	When *SetValidUntilExpires* is set to *true*, ASP.NET ignores the cache invalidation header sent by the browser. The page remains in the cache until it expires.
SetVaryByCustom	Sets the *Vary* HTTP header to the specified text string.

Most methods of the *HttpCachePolicy* class let you control the values of some HTTP headers that relate to the browser cache. The *AddValidationCallback* method, on the other hand, provides a mechanism to programmatically check the validity of page output in the server cache before it is returned from the cache.

Server Cache-Validation Callback

Before the response is served from the ASP.NET cache, all registered handlers are given a chance to verify the validity of the cached page. If at least one handler marks the cached page as invalid, the entry is removed from the cache and the request is served as if it were never cached. The signature of the callback function looks like this:

```
public delegate void HttpCacheValidateHandler(
  HttpContext context,
  object data,
  ref HttpValidationStatus validationStatus
);
```

The first argument denotes the context of the current request, whereas the second argument is any user-defined data the application needs to pass to the handler. Finally, the third argument is a reference to a value from the *HttpValidationStatus* enumeration. The callback sets this value to indicate the result of the validation. Acceptable values are *IgnoreThisRequest*, *Invalid*, and *Valid*. In the case of *IgnoreThisRequest*, the cached resource is not invalidated but the request is served as if no response was ever cached. If the return value is *Invalid*, the cached page is not used and gets invalidated. Finally, if the return value is *Valid*, the cached response is used to serve the request.

Caching Multiple Versions of a Page

Depending on the application context from which a certain page is invoked, the page might generate different results. The same page can be called to operate with different parameters, can be configured using different HTTP headers, can produce different output based on the requesting browser, and so forth.

ASP.NET allows you to cache multiple versions of a page response; you can distinguish versions by GET and POST parameters, HTTP headers, browser type, custom strings, and control properties.

Vary by Parameters

To vary output caching by parameters, you can use either the *VaryByParam* attribute of the *@OutputCache* directive or the *VaryByParams* property on the *HttpCachePolicy* class. If you proceed declaratively, use the following syntax:

```
<% @OutputCache Duration="60" VaryByParam="employeeID" %>
```

Note that the *VaryByParam* attribute is mandatory; if you don't want to specify a parameter to vary cached content, set the value to *None*. If you want to vary the output by all parameters, set the attribute to *. When the *VaryByParam* attribute is set to multiple parameters, the output cache contains a different version of the requested document for each specified parameter. Multiple parameters are separated by a semicolon. Valid parameters to use are items specified on the GET query string or parameters set in the body of a POST command.

If you want to use the *HttpCachePolicy* class, first set the expiration and the cacheability of the page using the *SetExpires* and *SetCacheability* methods. Next, set the *VaryByParams* property as shown here:

```
Response.Cache.VaryByParams["employeeid;lastname"] = true;
```

This code snippet shows how to vary page output based on the employee ID and the last name properties. Note that the *Cache* property on the *HttpResponse* class is just an instance of the *HttpCachePolicy* type.

Vary by Headers

The *@OutputCache* directive *VaryByHeader* attribute and the *HttpCachePolicy VaryByHeaders* property allow you to cache multiple versions of a page, according to the value of one or more HTTP headers that you specify.

If you want to cache pages by multiple headers, include a semicolon-delimited list of header names. If you want to cache a different version of the page for each different header value, set the *VaryByHeader* attribute to an asterisk *. For example, the following declaration caches for one minute pages based on the language accepted by the browser. Each language will have a different cached copy of the page output.

```
<%@ OutputCache Duration="60" VaryByParam="None"
  VaryByHeader="Accept-Language" %>
```

If you opt for a programmatic approach, here's the code to use that leverages the *VaryByHeaders* property of the *HttpCachePolicy* class:

```
Response.Cache.VaryByHeaders["Accept-Language"] = true;
```

> **Note** The *VaryByHeader* attribute enables caching items in all HTTP 1.1 caches, not just the ASP.NET cache. Whether the setting also applies to the browser cache depends on the value of the *Location* attribute.

If you want to vary the pages in the cache by all HTTP header names, use the *VaryByUnspecifiedParameters* method of the *HttpCacheVaryByHeaders* class. It's the same as using the asterisk with the *VaryByHeader* attribute. As a final note, consider that the *VaryByHeader* attribute is not supported for *@OutputCache* directives defined in user controls.

Vary by Custom Strings

The *VaryByCustom* attribute in the *@OutputCache* directive allows you to vary the versions of page output by the type of browser that requests the page. To obtain this information, you simply give the attribute the special value of *browser*.

```
<%@ OutputCache Duration="60" VaryByParam="None"
  VaryByCustom="browser" %>
```

Browser name and major version number are the pieces of information used to build a custom string to vary cached output by. In particular, the string is what returns the *Type* property of the *HttpBrowserCapabilities* object. You use the *SetVaryByCustom* method on the *HttpCachePolicy* class if you don't like the declarative approach.

```
Response.Cache.SetVaryByCustom("browser");
```

You can set both the *VaryByCustom* attribute and the *SetVaryByCustom* method to work on custom strings. In this case, you need to override the *GetVaryByCustomString* method of the *HttpApplication* object and make it return the actual vary string. The following pseudocode represents the standard implementation of *GetVaryByCustomString*:

```
string GetVaryByCustomString(HttpContext context, string custom) {
  if (custom == "browser")
    return context.Request.Browser.Type;
  return null;
}
```

You should make the method return a non-null string when the custom argument matches the string passed to the *VaryByCustom* attribute or the *SetVaryByCustom* method. Note that the string returned by the *GetVaryByCustomString* method must refer to some easily identifiable property of the browser or the application—for example, the minor version number or the title of the page.

Caching Portions of ASP.NET Pages

The capability of caching the output of Web pages adds a lot of power to your programming arsenal, but sometimes caching the entire content of a page is not possible or is just impractical. Some pages, in fact, are made of pieces with radically different features as far as cacheability is concerned. In these situations, being able to cache portions of a page is an incredible added value. Enter user controls.

Caching the Output of User Controls

As we saw in Chapter 10, user controls are good at a number of things, including caching portions of Web pages. Once you have identified a section of a page that is both heavy to compute and not subject to frequent updates, you build a user control and make it produce that output. The user control is a sort of embedded page and, as such, shares some of the directives of the Web page. One shared directive is just *@OutputCache*. As a result, when you have a page with multiple user controls, you can control page caching on a per-control basis rather than a per-page basis.

To make a user control cacheable, you declare the *@OutputCache* attribute by using almost the same set of attributes we discussed earlier for pages. For example, the following code snippet caches the output of the control that embeds it for one minute:

```
<% @OutputCache Duration="60" VaryByParam="None" %>
```

A few of the *@OutputCache* attributes I listed in Table 14-16 are not supported when the directive works within a user control. For example, the *Location* attribute is not supported because all controls in the page share the same location. So if you need to specify the cache location, do that at the page level and for all embedded controls. The same holds true for the *VaryByHeader* attribute.

The output of a user control can vary by custom strings and by parameters. More often, though, you'll want to vary the output of a control by property values. In this case, use the new *VaryByControl* attribute.

Vary by Controls

The *VaryByControl* attribute allows you to vary the cache for each specified user control property. The property is mandatory unless the *VaryByParam* attribute has been specified. You can indicate both *VaryByParam* and *VaryByControl*, but at least one of them is needed.

```
<%@ OutputCache Duration="60" VaryByControl="Text" %>
```

This directive caches a different copy of the control output based on the different values of the *Text* property.

Implementing Partial Caching

The following page demonstrates two user controls whose output varies by the value of the *Text* property. The ASPX page hosts two instances of the user control with different values in the *Text* property, and two different copies of the output will be stored in the output cache.

```
<%@ Page Language="C#" %>
<%@ Register TagPrefix="e" TagName="UserControl" Src="UserControl.ascx" %>

<script runat="server">
void Page_Load(object sender, EventArgs e) {
```

```
  Response.Write("Page created at " + DateTime.Now.ToString());
}
</script>

<html><body>
<form runat="server">
  <e:UserControl runat="server" Text="First control" />
  <hr>
  <e:UserControl runat="server" Text="Second control" />
</form>
</body></html>
```

The user control contains a label set with the value of the *Text* property.

```
<% @Control Language="C#" %>
<% @OutputCache Duration="10" VaryByControl="Text" %>
<script runat="server">
public string Text = "Simple User Control";
</script>
<asp:panel runat="server" backcolor="yellow">
  <span runat="server"><h2><%=Text%></h2></span><hr>
  <small><i>Cached at <%=DateTime.Now.ToString()%></i></small>
</asp:panel>
```

Figure 14-15 shows the output of the page. Notice the timestamps of the page and the controls.

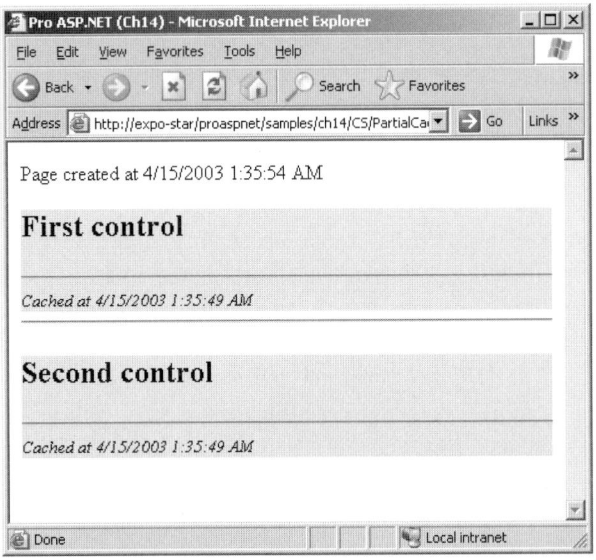

Figure 14-15 An ASP.NET page with two user controls implementing partial caching. The page is not cached while the two controls have a cache duration of 10 seconds.

The output text cached for each instance of the control is still stored in the ASP.NET *Cache* object, in the private portion.

> **Note** If you plan to cache user controls—that is, you're trying for partial caching—you probably don't want to cache the entire page. However, a good question to ask is: what happens if user controls are cached within a cacheable page? In this case, the page *@OutputCache* wins. Both the page and the controls are cached individually, and the ASP.NET *Cache* object contains both the page's raw response and the control's HTML responses. However, if the duration is different, the controls are refreshed only when the page needs to be refreshed. A cacheable user control can be embedded both in a cacheable page and in a wrapper cacheable user control.

The *PartialCachingControl* Class

When a *PartialCachingControl* cacheable user control is used within a Web Forms page, the base of the control being instantiated is *PartialCachingControl*. A user control is made cacheable in either of two ways: by using the *@OutputCache* directive or the *PartialCaching* attribute. The *PartialCaching* attribute—an instance of the *PartialCachingAttribute* class—is especially useful in code-behind user controls. You use the attribute as follows:

```
[PartialCaching(60)]
```

You can declare this attribute in a class derived from the *UserControl* class to specify settings for the user control output cache. Note that the *PartialCaching* attribute allows you to specify the duration only in seconds.

Whatever protocol is used to create an instance of the user control, an instance of the *PartialCachingControl* class is returned as long as the control is declared cacheable. The class has nearly the same programming interface as *UserControl*. The difference is in a couple of extra properties—*Dependency* and *CachedControl*. The *Dependency* property manages the instance of the *CacheDependency* class associated with the cached user control output. The property allows you to remove user control output from the output cache when a file or key dependency changes. The *CachedControl* property returns an instance of the control. However, if the output of the control is retrieved from the cache, no instance of the control is ever created and the property returns null.

Caution If you're building a page made of cacheable controls, you should pay a lot of attention to the code that manages the control ID. Note especially that if the page is using a cached copy of the control output, no control is ever instantiated and subsequently any access to the control ID results in a null object reference.

Conclusion

State management is a hot topic for all real-world Web applications. Setting up an effective and efficient solution for state management is often the difference between an application being scalable or nonscalable. In ASP, state management was offered through a couple of objects—*Application* and *Session*. The *Application* object is a global repository of data, whereas the *Session* object works on a per-session basis. ASP.NET provides a richer set of tools, including the *Cache* and *ViewState* objects. In addition, the architecture of the session state object has been revolutionized and made flexible as never before. You can store session data in the memory of the ASP.NET worker process as well as in external processes, and even in a SQL Server table. In spite of the radically different options, the programming interface is nearly identical. More importantly, the ASP.NET session state can be persisted in a Web farm or Web garden scenario as well.

In the internal implementation of the ASP.NET *Session* object, a key role is played by the *Cache* object. It is a global, application-specific repository of data with advanced capabilities such as priority, file dependencies, removal callbacks, and expiration dates. In addition, the *Cache* object periodically monitors memory consumption. When the memory pressure exceeds a certain threshold, a sort of internal garbage collector module is run to remove seldom-used items. When the session state is held in the ASP.NET worker process, the physical container for the session state is just the *Cache* object.

The *Cache* object is also key to the output caching mechanism—another powerful feature of ASP.NET. The typical situation in which output caching is great is when you know that many users will be accessing the same page or the same range of pages in a short time. In this case, you might decide to cache the HTML output of the page to save time by not reworking the page for all the requests that arrive in the fixed period. The tradeoff is between memory occupation and page responsiveness. The caching machinery can be adapted to work also on the client exploiting HTTP headers such as *Cache-Control* and *Expires*.

If caching the entire page is impractical, you can always opt for partial caching. Partial caching leverages the concept of user controls—that is, small, nested pages that inherit several features of the page. In particular, user controls can be cached individually based on the browser, GET and POST parameters, and the value of a particular set of properties.

As we thoroughly discussed in Chapter 4, an ASP.NET page is designed around a single server-side form with an automatic scheme for persisting the context of the specific page request. The call context is normally stored in the *ViewState* structure, namely an encoded collection stored in a hidden field and transmitted back and forth between the browser and the Web server. Having the view state implemented in the default way might pose some performance and security issues. In this chapter, we also discussed how to persist the view state on the server, thus significantly reducing both the security concerns and improving the usage of the bandwidth. Security, a topic in the software industry that can never be discussed too much, will be the subject of the next chapter.

Resources

- Supporting Database Cache Dependencies in ASP.NET (*http://msdn.microsoft.com/msdnmag/issues/03/04/WickedCode/default.aspx*)
- ASP.NET: Nine Options for Managing Persistent User State in Your ASP.NET Application (*http://msdn.microsoft.com/msdnmag/issues/03/04/ASPNETUserState/default.aspx*)
- ViewState: All You Wanted to Know (*http://www.aspalliance.com/PaulWilson/Articles/?id=7*)
- How to Share Session State Between Classic ASP and ASP.NET (*http://msdn.microsoft.com/library/en-us/dnaspp/html/converttoaspnet.asp*)
- *Developing Microsoft ASP.NET Server Controls and Components*, by Nikhil Kothari and Vandana Datye (Microsoft Press, 2002)

15 ASP.NET Security

If anyone tells you that security ends with the OS, they are dead wrong. Many times excellent network and host-based security has been bypassed exposing the very heart of the enterprise: all because of poor SQL Server configuration. That said...there is no "patch" for stupidity.

—*from www.sqlsecurity.com*

Many developers have learned on their own that security is not a feature that can be easily added to existing applications or introduced late in the development stage. Security is inherently tied to the functions of an application and should be planned as one of the first features, very early at the design level. As is the case with scalability, security has become much more important in the past few years because of the success of the Internet.

By nature, Web applications are subject to several types of attacks whose damage and impact can vary quite a bit, depending on the characteristics of the application itself. The most secure Web application is the application that actually resists attacks, not the application just designed to. Security is a rather intricate puzzle whose solution varies from one application to another. The important thing to remember is that, more often than not, security is manifested through a successful mix of application-level and system-level measures.

How can we design and code secure ASP.NET applications? First of all, the code can be secure or insecure regardless of the hosting platform. In addition, security is not a physical quantity subject to absolute measurement. Security is strictly related to the application's usage, its popularity, and the type of users who connect to it and work with it. Paradoxically, a poorly secured application that isn't attractive to hackers can be perceived as being much more secure than a well-armored application with just one loophole or two. Successful attacks are possible through holes in the system-level and application-level security apparatus. When it comes to security, don't look for a magic wand to do the job for you. Security is a state of mind, and insecurity is often the result of loose coding styles if not true programming laziness.

That said, ASP.NET simplifies programming secure applications by providing a built-in infrastructure that supplies application-level protection against unauthorized access to Web pages. Be aware, though, that this kind of security is only one side of the coin. A really secure Web site is especially well protected against server attacks, which can sneakily be used to bypass the highest walls of the application logic.

In this chapter, we will discuss both server-side IIS authentication mechanisms (such as Integrated Windows, Basic, and Digest) and ASP.NET application-side authentication mechanisms (such as Windows, Forms, and Passport).

Writing Secure Code

Writing secure Web applications is definitely a complicated task, at least as complex and variegated as writing a scalable application can be. The best word I can think of to describe the articulated topology of the subject is *multidimensional.* Security is multidimensional because it's not a physical quantity like RAM memory or hard-drive space. It cannot be measured in absolute terms because it mostly depends on the type and the frequency of attacks, and it is also a relative concept in terms of the possible consequences and the impact it might have on the target of the attack. Security is not the same for all applications and does come at a cost.

The only certain thing about security is that all attacks are conducted to exploit a hole in the system. Let's review the most common types of attacks and then look at a few golden rules to proactively defend your code.

Types of Web Attacks

Web attacks can be catalogued in two main groups: passive and active. Passive attacks are limited to monitoring information being exchanged between trusted sides acting over a network. Packets are sniffed and grabbed, and the contained information is consumed outside the native, legitimate environment. Confidentiality is broken, and the stolen information is often used to build the foundation of new and more intrusive attacks.

Active attacks work to alter and forge the information being exchanged, to inject false data, and to corrupt existing data. Other typical goals of active attacks are blocking the service and the network itself. To block a service, intruders can kill threads, violate the memory, isolate the machine on the network, or flood the server with fake requests.

Security is important because of the physical damage resulting from the theft or corruption of the data. In some cases, though, security is even more important to preserve the reputation of the company that is the target of the attack.

Passive Attacks

Let's review the most common types of passive attacks your network might be subject to and the countermeasures needed to defend.

- **Eavesdropping** A large part of network communications are still based on clear text, which makes it easy for an attacker to eavesdrop and read the packets of information being exchanged. Detecting eavesdroppers is generally one of the hardest security problems that an administrator faces in a corporate network. Typical eavesdropping attacks are conducted using sniffers—that is, ad hoc tools or devices capable of reading unencrypted network packets as they are transported on the network. There is only one solution to this problem: encryption. Strongly encrypted data makes it extremely hard and expensive for the intruder to decode an ongoing communication. Of course, the problem could also be addressed at its root by reinforcing the firewall around the enterprise to prevent sniffers from operating.
- **Man-in-the-Middle** In the man-in-the-middle attack scenario, a third user is silently and transparently filtering information two other users are exchanging. This attack is more active than eavesdropping and can include the attacker, for example, redirecting packets. Man-in-the-middle attacks are insidious because the attacker acts on behalf of you and actively communicates with other members of the network while passively listening to the information traveling on the wire.

Active Attacks

As you can easily understand, active attacks are much more dangerous because they configure an active role by attackers. In most cases, active attacks are preceded by passive monitoring and are often planned using critical information that was stolen during these prior passive, and perhaps unnoticed, attacks.

- **Data Modification** Data modification is the typical next step of a man-in-the-middle attack. The intruder sits between two sides and modifies data in the packet being transferred. Data modification often occurs blindly—that is, without the attacker knowing who the sender or receiver is.
- **IP Address Spoofing** Identity spoofing consists of using special programs to build IP packets that apparently originate from valid and trusted addresses inside the enterprise. Once the attacker has used the counterfeit packets to gain access to the network, he can simply eavesdrop or even proceed with deeper attacks.
- **Password Attack** Another alternative for an attacker is identity spoofing, which allows an attacker to exploit weak passwords to gain entry into a system. In many systems, access is granted by identity—that is, after a user name and a password are entered and verified. When an attacker finds a valid user account, she automatically gains the same rights as the real user. In the very unfortunate, but not unlikely, case in which the cloned account has administrative privileges, the attacker has made a huge score. She can obtain lists of valid user and computer names and network information; modify server and network configurations; and alter, reroute, or delete data.
- **Compromised Key** Encrypted communications are based on a key that is used to camouflage the information being exchanged. Normally, obtaining a key is a resource-intensive process, but depending on the value of the information being sought, an attacker might still see the effort as worthwhile. With the compromised key, the attacker can decrypt sensitive data and compute additional keys to unprotect other secured communications.
- **Denial-of-Service** The denial-of-service (DoS) attack is aimed at stopping a particular service from running, thus preventing valid users from accessing the network. Once an attacker has gained access to a system, he could circulate invalid data, which might ultimately cause the abnormal termination of applications and services. The attacker can flood the network with fake requests, thus overloading the system and blocking regular traffic. The attack rarely produces serious damage to the network itself, but it decreases user productivity and can seriously hurt the reputation of the company.
- **Web Server Attacks** A Web server normally implements a firewall to defend the internal applications from external attacks. An application-layer attack violates the defensive system of the server and lets the attacker bypass normal access controls. Once in the demilitarized

zone, the attacker can virtually do everything. She can introduce and propagate viruses, install a sniffer to analyze the network, terminate applications, and disable security controls to set the ground for future attacks.

Golden Rules for Secure Coding

As mentioned, Web attacks always originate from holes in the security apparatus. Holes can be caused by a number of circumstances and behaviors. Sometimes the attack is made possible by unknown and unrevealed bugs in the Web server core code; sometimes, though, the attack exploits an outdated version of the system code in which recent patches and hotfixes have not been applied. In other situations, attacks find fertile ground in naïve implementations of Web applications or careless use (or should I have said *misuse*) of built-in functions.

The following sections discuss a few golden rules every developer should be aware of. Even the strictest implementation of these security rules can't guarantee a bullet-proof Web site. However, by following these rules, you certainly make it harder for hackers to break in and crack your system.

Don't Trust

The first rule in security is, *don't trust*. Speaking of software security, this general-purpose rule translates to a more precise and definite adage, *don't trust user input*. User input is the main form of interaction for applications in general and Web applications in particular. If you don't strictly validate the data you're going to bring in, you automatically become a prime candidate to be the victim of a number of attacks.

Buffer Overruns

Any code that is going to accept input from an external source—that is, any method or function that takes a variable-length argument—should have clear *in advance* the characteristics and the size of the incoming information. When the method is finally called, it should validate the data first, before doing anything else. You should make sure that the string is not too long or too short for the use you're making of it. You should ensure that no disallowed character is included and, whenever possible, that the overall format of the string is compatible with a well-known pattern.

SQL Injections

SQL injection is a blanket term used to describe the act of passing SQL code into an application in a format that goes far beyond the original intentions of the developer. SQL injections are the perfect example of a creative use of buffer overruns. It is a common practice in applications to build SQL commands by concatenating constant strings and user arguments. Typically, the user argument has to be a key value needed to select one or more records. However, if not strongly validated, an innocuous key value can easily become malicious code when padded with extra statements. Let's consider the following code snippet:

```
void RunCommand(string empID)
{
    StringBuilder sb = new StringBuilder();
    sb.Append("SELECT * FROM customers WHERE customerid='");
    sb.Append(empID);
    sb.Append("'");
    :
}
```

The method takes a string argument that, in the developer's mind, is expected to be a plain ID. Assume for a moment that the *empID* argument contains more code, as shown here:

```
ALFKI' DROP TABLE employees --
```

The final SQL statement looks like the following:

```
SELECT * FROM customers WHERE customerid='ALFKI'
DROP TABLE employees --
```

As you can see, a second command has been added and will be blissfully executed. Notice that the -- comment symbol just tells the database to ignore what will then be added by the rest of the code.

A simple trick to somewhat mitigate, but not eliminate, the impact of SQL injection is passing quoted key values. Suppose you're using the following base command:

```
"SELECT * FROM customers WHERE customerid="
```

Note that the final quote is missing because you now assume that quotes will be provided by the key value. In this case, the quote character the attacker would add will break the SQL code and no code will be run. Don't think that you've eliminated SQL attacks, however. This is a very small line of defense. Much more effective would be avoiding rich accounts and stratifying the data access code by using business objects and stored procedures. In ADO.NET, enforcing strong typing in the parameters of the command objects is another fundamental security tip.

Another key aspect to consider is the account that is used to perform any database operation. SQL injections are especially harmful if combined with a lazy choice of user accounts. The more the running account is allowed to do, the more you're exposing your system to attacks. You should always use an ad hoc account with exactly the privileges needed to accomplish the particular task it's assigned. In real-world applications, the use of the *sa* (system administrator) user account is terribly dangerous because it would give attackers the power to conquer the database.

> **Caution** In this book, admittedly, we're not always practicing security as we preach it. In many examples, we're using the *sa* account to connect to the database. (In addition, we also use the blank password.) While these methods are strongly discouraged for any sort of production environment, they still make sense in the demos of a book. Using *sa* and the blank password, in fact, makes it much easier for you to run the samples without the need to configure anything. This is the only acceptable exception to the law. In real-world scenarios, saving configuration work might lead straight to security holes.

Detecting SQL injections is difficult, and you usually detect it when it's too late. Code review is the only effective precaution. Using code generators to write *Create*, *Read*, *Update*, and *Delete* methods can also be useful to some extent. Although generators are often limited, in general it's much better to use them to save time than to save development time by skipping security reviews. Finally, note that SQL injections are not an exclusive feature (so to speak) of Microsoft SQL Server. Any database can be subject to SQL injections. For more information on SQL and SQL Server security, visit *http://www.sqlsecurity.com*.

Keep a Low Profile

In software, and especially when security is involved, keeping a low profile is key to reducing the likelihood of being attacked. Any piece of software exposed to the Internet (even if it's only through e-mail) should have restrictive security policies. Translated into practice, this recommendation says you should always grant the least possible amount of privileges to any user. If a user is given rights to write and he needs only to read, he will probably never exploit the write capability, but some malicious code, paradoxically, could on behalf of him.

The low profile rule pays off also when you look at it from the server code perspective. If you don't need a certain service to be up and running all the time to serve 80 percent or more of the clients, by all means, you should disable it. Unmonitored—because they are rarely used—running services are an ideal platform for intruders to gain entrance. Take some time to review all the code on the Web server machine, and make sure you shut down all utilities and services you don't really need.

Cross-Site Scripting

Another common security error is outputting unfiltered request data to the browser. If your pages retrieve data directly from the *Request* object, you should avoid writing that text directly to *Response*. If not validated, one of the query strings could contain dangerous script code, which could easily access your cookie data and post it to another external Web site. In this case, data validation is a key countermeasure. For example, you can implement validation using regular expressions to ensure the text has the right length and does not include potentially dangerous characters. If you can't avoid using input as direct output, at least get in the habit of encoding text in HTML before sending it out to the browser.

In ASP.NET 1.1, the machine.config file defines in the *<pages>* section a new attribute named *ValidateRequest*. The goal of this attribute is raising a (not too high) barrier against potentially dangerous script-code injections. The *ValidateRequest* option is turned on by default and can be controlled on a per-page basis using a new *@Page* attribute—*ValidateRequest*. (Note that this won't work for version 1.0 of ASP.NET.)

For performance reasons, *ValidateRequest* is realized through a hard-coded parser that basically passes the contents of cookies, form fields, and query strings through a regular expression. If a potentially dangerous client input value is detected, the processing of the request is aborted and an HTTP security exception is thrown. Let's consider the following page called, say, test.aspx:

```
<html>
<body>
    <% Response.Write(Request.QueryString("Code")) %>
</body>
</html>
```

Try calling the page by passing some script code embedded in the URL, as shown here:

```
http://expo-two/test.aspx?code=<script>alert('Hello')</script>
```

In this case, ASP.NET 1.1 detects a potentially dangerous situation and raises an *HttpRequestValidationException* exception, as shown in Figure 15-1.

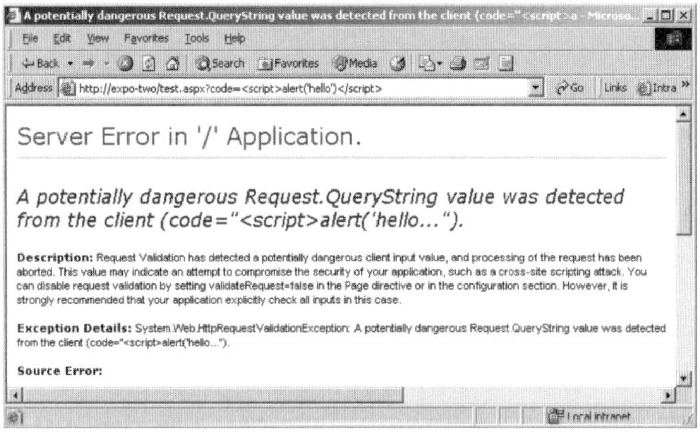

Figure 15-1 The ASP.NET runtime engine detected a potentially dangerous query string.

If for some reason your application legitimately needs to process script code that is passed through the URL, you can disable request validation. You accomplish this by setting the *ValidateRequest* attribute to *false* in the *@Page* directive or in the configuration file. However, it is strongly recommended, in this case, that you replace the standard code with some sort of application-specific validation code to block code-injection attempts. (Replacing *ValidateRequest* with a more specific barrier is generally a good thing to do to increase security.)

For more information about cross-site scripting, visit the following Web site: *http://www.cert.org/advisories/CA-2000-02.html.*

Configuring ASP.NET Applications for Security

The rules and warnings discussed so far are general-purpose pills of wisdom that apply to all types of Web applications and, in some cases, to all software applications. Having an up-to-date server configuration in which patches and hot-fixes are regularly applied is the first step in the building of a solid and secure system. The server configuration should also be as lean as possible, with all unused services stopped and the minimum set of privileges granted to all that have to run.

A consistent and effective set of policies should be applied to security. Using a couple of configuration snap-ins such as the Security Templates and Security Configuration And Analysis, you can define your own security templates and apply them to the various machines in the network.

> **Note** You can install the aforementioned tools by running the Microsoft Management Console (mmc.exe) from the command line and then selecting Add/Remove Snap-in from the File menu. Add the tools you need from the list of available snap-ins, and save the changes.

Using the Security Configuration And Analysis tool, you can define policies for passwords, account lockout, and auditing. A good starting point is the Security Configuration Template for High Security Web Server shown in Figure 15-2. It is named hisecweb.inf, and you can download it from the following URL: *http://www.microsoft.com/downloads/*.

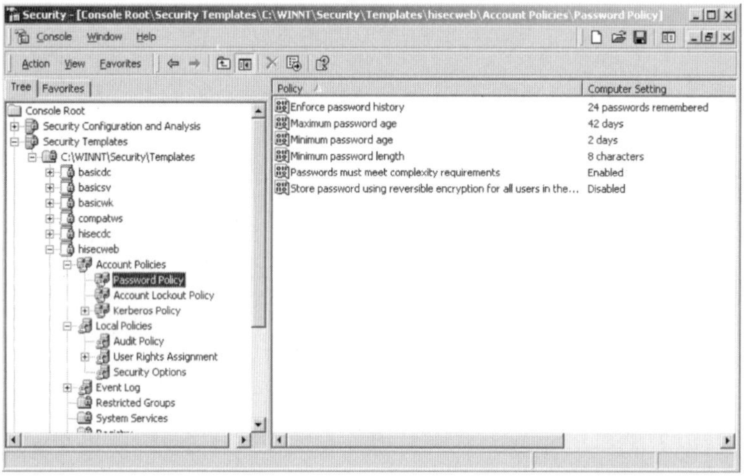

Figure 15-2 The hisecweb.inf file and its default settings for strong passwords.

When setting up the system software, you should look at the overall configuration of the application infrastructure. This entails looking at password definition and storage, database security configuration, and user accounts.

Choosing Strong Passwords

Do not undervalue the importance of using strong passwords. Passwords are sometimes the only barrier between hackers and a series of potentially harmful operations. Strong passwords meet at least the following requirements:

- Must be at least eight characters long

- Contain elements from any of the following groups: lowercase letters, uppercase letters, nonalphanumeric symbols (punctuation, *, #, $, and so forth), and digits
- Expire frequently; at least every 90 days

As a policy, you could also impose that a password history is maintained to avoid the same password being renewed over and over again. Other stricter rules are also possible, such as requiring certain elements fall within a certain range of positions. That said, remember that longer or complex passwords do not entirely eliminate the risk of brute-force attacks—attacks in which hackers try all possible combinations of characters to guess the right password. However, the longer and more articulated the password is, the more time it will take an attacker to decrypt it. Secure passwords, combined with an effective auditing policy, should significantly increase the likelihood of detecting an attack.

Storing Passwords

Let's say it upfront: there's no absolutely safe place in which critical data such as a password can be stored. In normal conditions, having the password stored as plain text in a file is not a problem per se. However, in the event of a successful attack, your critical password would be easily stolen.

If the password serves to connect to SQL Server, you might want to opt for trusted connections and Microsoft Windows and SQL Server integrated security. In this case, you need to configure the ASPNET account as a valid SQL Server login (more on this later in the "ASP.NET and SQL Server" section). Otherwise, you can store the password in a database or in a file located outside the Web application subtree. Again, this would not give you a 100 percent guarantee of inviolability, but it would certainly make it harder for anyone to hack the system.

Passwords and Encryption

Encrypting the password is certainly helpful in that it would add yet another layer of complexity. Do not try, though, to run your own homemade encryption algorithms. Serious hackers would break naïve schemes in a few hours. If you opt for encryption, don't be afraid to use the .NET Framework cryptography model. You don't have to be an expert to use those classes, which have proven to be more effective than homemade algorithms.

The .NET Framework provides implementations of many standard cryptographic algorithms. To encrypt and decrypt data, you must use a key with an encryption algorithm that transforms the data. The use of the key lets us distinguish two main families of algorithms: symmetric and asymmetric.

Symmetric algorithms have a single key and use this key for both encryption and decryption. The key must be known only to the sender and the receiver. The *DESCryptoServiceProvider* class is an implementation of a symmetric algorithm.

Passwords and Basic Combinatorial Calculus

If you're not too convinced about the importance of strong passwords, have a look at the coming list, which describes the possible permutations of strings that a brute-force attack has to walk through to guess a password. To start out, let's suppose you decided that a five-characters password made of only lowercase or uppercase letters would suffice. Given an alphabet containing 26 letters, the number of five-character substrings is obtained through the following formula, in which the exclamation point (!) denotes the factorial of the number:

26! / (26-5)!

As alphabet and password length vary, the number of permutations changes as follows:

- *Alphabet:* Only lowercase (or only uppercase). 26 characters; *Length:* 5; *Permutations:* 7,893,600
- *Alphabet:* Only lowercase (or only uppercase). 26 characters; *Length:* 6; *Permutations:* 165,765,600
- *Alphabet:* Lowercase and uppercase. 52 characters; *Length:* 5; *Permutations:* 311,875,200
- *Alphabet:* Lowercase and uppercase. 52 characters; *Length:* 6; *Permutations:* 14,658,134,400

A hacker would probably employ an optimized combinatorial algorithm so that the effective number of attempts is smaller. However, my only goal here is to show the order of magnitude your password security grows just by making the password longer or adding an extra group of characters.

Asymmetric, or *public-key, algorithms* require that both sender and receiver maintain a pair of keys: a private key and a public key. The public key can be made available to anyone and is used for encoding data that is sent to a receiver. The private key must be safely stored and used only for decoding messages encoded using the receiver's public key. *RSACryptoServiceProvider* is an implementation of a public-key algorithm.

Typically, symmetric encryption is performed on streams and is therefore useful to encrypt large amounts of data. Asymmetric encryption is performed on a small number of bytes and is therefore only useful for small amounts of data such as a password.

The ASPNET Account

Once the system has been configured for security, you can start considering how to configure the ASP.NET runtime engine for security. The ASP.NET worker process does not run under the aegis of the almighty SYSTEM account and does not impersonate by default. As we saw in Chapter 12, "Configuration and Deployment," you can configure the ASPNET account through the *<processModel>* section in the machine.config file. The following code snippet shows the default settings:

```
<processModel enable="true" userName="machine"
    password="AutoGenerate" ... />
```

The user name *machine* is a nickname for a specific account named ASPNET, which is created when the .NET Framework is installed. A 14-byte password is autogenerated and stored in the Web server's machine LSA. The ASPNET user account can be changed, just like any other configuration setting. Note, though, that the attributes of the *<processModel>* section cannot be overridden in a web.config file. The section is supported only in the machine.config file, and changes are not applied until Internet Information Services (IIS) is restarted.

Figure 15-3 shows that the ASPNET account belongs to the Users group and, as such, can leverage limited capabilities when processing Web pages. This fact alone makes certain programming tricks much harder to accomplish, but from the security standpoint, it's certainly good news.

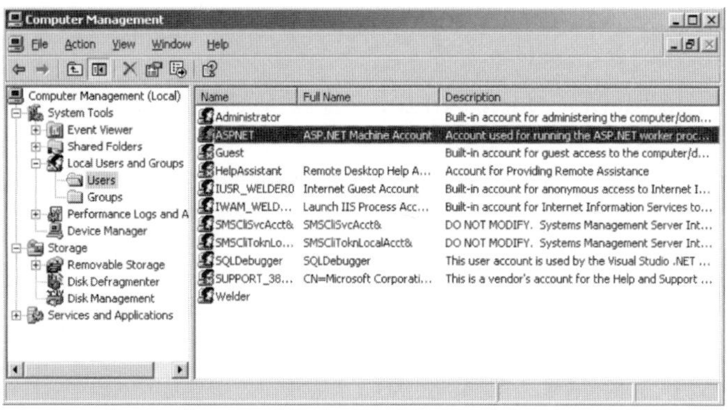

Figure 15-3 The ASPNET account shows up in the Users group.

> **Note** One particular limitation of an ASP.NET page is that it might lack the privileges to create or edit a local file. We'll see later in the "Enabling ASP.NET to Manage Local Files" section why this is so and how to work around the limitation. In my experience, though, this is the limitation that most frequently shows up in the development of serious ASP.NET applications. The bottom line is that we don't need overpowering accounts to write and run effective Web applications. More (unnecessary) privileges serve primarily to increase the risk of attacks.

Privileges of the ASPNET Account

The ASPNET account is created in the Users group, is given a nonmodifiable and nonexpiring strong password and a minimum set of privileges. Of all the possible user rights assignments, ASPNET is granted only the following five:

- Access this computer from the network
- Deny logon locally
- Deny logon through Terminal Services
- Log on as a batch job
- Log on as a service

In addition, the account is given some NTFS permissions to operate on certain folders and create temporary files and assemblies. The folders involved are:

- **.NET Framework Root Folder** This folder contains some .NET Framework system assemblies that ASP.NET must be able to access. The physical folder is normally *Microsoft.NET\Framework\v.1.x.xxxx* and is located under the Windows folder. ASP.NET has only read and list permissions on this folder. Permissions on this folder are granted both to the ASP.NET worker-process account and the impersonated user, if any.
- **Temporary ASP.NET Files** This folder represents the file system subtree in which all temporary files are generated. ASP.NET is granted full control over the entire subtree. Permissions on this subtree are granted both to the ASP.NET worker-process account and the impersonated user, if any.

- **Global Assembly Cache** ASP.NET needs to gain read permissions on the assemblies in the global assembly cache (GAC). Permissions on this subtree are granted both to the ASP.NET worker-process account and the impersonated user, if any. The GAC is located in the Windows\Assembly\GAC folder. The GAC folder is not visible in Windows Explorer, but you can view the installed assemblies by opening the Windows\Assembly folder.
- **Windows System Folder** The ASP.NET process needs to access and read the System32 Windows folder to load any necessary Win32 DLLs.
- **Application Root Folder** The ASP.NET process needs to access and read the files that make up the Web application. The folder is typically located under Inetpub\Wwwroot.
- **Web Site Root** ASP.NET might have the need to scan the root of the Web server—typically, Inetpub\Wwwroot—looking for configuration files to read.

Some of the permissions are automatically inherited because the folder grants those privileges to everyone or to all the members of the Users group. Some are specifically set during the installation stage using the cacls.exe tool.

Who Really Runs ASP.NET Applications?

ASPNET is actually only the default account that is used to run ASP.NET pages. The role of the ASPNET account spins off as the combined effect of two settings in machine.config.

```
<processModel enable="true" userName="machine"
    password="AutoGenerate" ... />
<identity impersonate="false" />
```

When impersonation is disabled, ASP.NET applications execute under the ASPNET account or under the account otherwise specified. If impersonation is permitted, ASP.NET applications are controlled by the Windows account authenticated through either Integrated Windows, Digest, or Basic methods. Otherwise, if anonymous access is used, ASP.NET runs under the IIS-defined account for anonymous access—typically, the *IUSR_*Machine account. The *<identity>* section in a configuration file controls the identity of the ASP.NET application. Unlike the *<processModel>* section, the *<identity>* section can be set in a local web.config file. In all cases, local resources can be accessed only if the resource itself has an access control list (ACL) for the caller identity.

To change the account that executes ASP.NET applications, you can either define a custom account or impersonate a fixed identity. In the former case, you need to define a new account, possibly in the Users group. You should assign it a strong password and try to grant no more permissions than the set we discussed earlier for ASPNET. When you're done, you register the account in the machine.config file as shown here:

```
<processModel userName="MyAspNetAccnt" password="ILoveA$p*SinceVer3.0" ... />
```

Storing credentials as clear text is not recommended, even though the machine.config file is considered significantly more secure than other resources because it's located outside the Web application space.

Secure Storage of Passwords

In ASP.NET 1.0, to change the ASP.NET worker process identity, to impersonate a fixed identity, or even to specify a connection string for the SQL Server session state, you need to store a password as clear text. Starting with the .NET Framework Service Pack 3, and of course in ASP.NET 1.1, you can use an encrypted password stored in the registry instead of plain text stored in a configuration file. This feature is supported by the following sections: *<processModel>*, *<identity>*, and *<sessionState>*.

You can use the ASP.NET Set Registry tool (aspnet_setreg.exe) to encrypt the credentials and store them in the registry. The tool creates registry keys under the *HKEY_LOCAL_MACHINE* subtree and stores the encrypted user name and password there. By default, only administrators can create keys under this hive. For example, to create encrypted registry keys for the user name and password you need to store in *<processModel>*, do the following:

```
aspnet_setreg.exe
    -k:"Software\Protected ASP.NET\ProcessModel"
    -u:userID
    -p:password
```

Figure 15-4 shows the settings in the registry after you execute the command just shown. Note that the aspnet_setreg.exe tool always creates an extra key named *ASPNET_SETREG* and, below that, the attributes *userName* and *password* contain encrypted data. You can change key and attribute names in the registry as needed to better camouflage them.

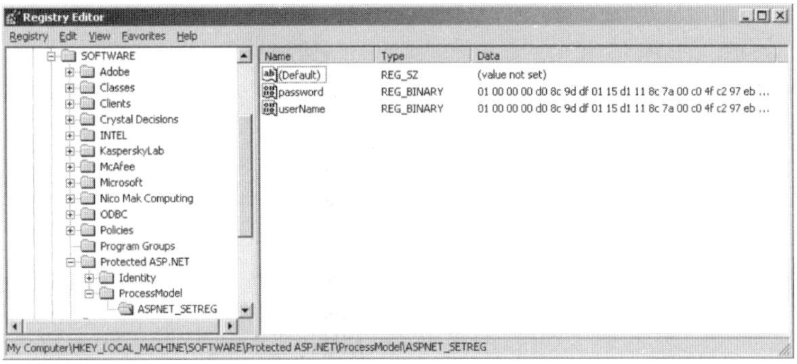

Figure 15-4 Newly created registry keys contain encrypted versions of the user ID, the password, or both for any of the critical configuration sections.

> **Note** Microsoft made available the aspnet_setreg.exe tool as part of a hotfix, as described in Knowledge Base article Q329290. The recommended way to get it, though, is through Service Pack 3 or ASP.NET 1.1. Getting the aspnet_setreg.exe tool alone is not sufficient because updates to aspnet_isapi.dll are needed too.

The *<processModel>* registry key is accessed by the aspnet_isapi.dll module which runs under the system account and as such can safely read the user name and password. The default ACL on the registry key, in fact, grants full control to System, Administrators, and Creator Owner accounts.

The *<identity>* and *<sessionState>* sections are processed by the ASP.NET worker process, whose identity might change and which is set to ASPNET by default. If you're going to have encrypted credentials for those sections, ensure that the actual ASP.NET worker process has read access to the registry keys. You can use regedt32.exe to set registry key permissions. (With Windows XP and Windows Server 2003, administrators can set registry permissions with a simple right-click in the Registry Editor (regedit.exe).)

Once the registry is set, you enter some changes into the involved configuration files (machine.config or web.config) and make the critical elements point to the registry for user ID, password, or both. You assign the *userName* and *password* attributes as shown in the following snippet. The sample text refers to the *<identity>* section.

```
registry:HKLM\SOFTWARE\Protected ASP.NET\identity\ASPNET_SETREG,userName
registry:HKLM\SOFTWARE\Protected ASP.NET\identity\ASPNET_SETREG,password
```

Basically, you make the attribute point to the registry path where the encrypted credentials have been stored. Note that you must explicitly mention the hive using the *HKLM* abbreviation. (*HKLM* stands for *HKEY_LOCAL_MACHINE*.) If you modified the default registry path, indicate the new one in the .config files. For this feature to work, you need updated versions of the aspnet_isapi.dll and the system.web assembly.

Enabling ASP.NET to Manage Local Files

In some situations, an ASP.NET application might have the need to create or edit a local file—for example, a configuration file. Let's consider the following simple code that opens a file for writing:

```
<%@ Page Language="C#" %>
<%@ Import Namespace="System.IO" %>
<script runat="server">
void Page_Load(object sender, EventArgs e) {
    StreamWriter file = new StreamWriter(serverFile);
    ⋮
    file.Close();
}
</script>
```

Try running this or similar code, and an unauthorized access exception will normally be thrown, as seen in Figure 15-5.

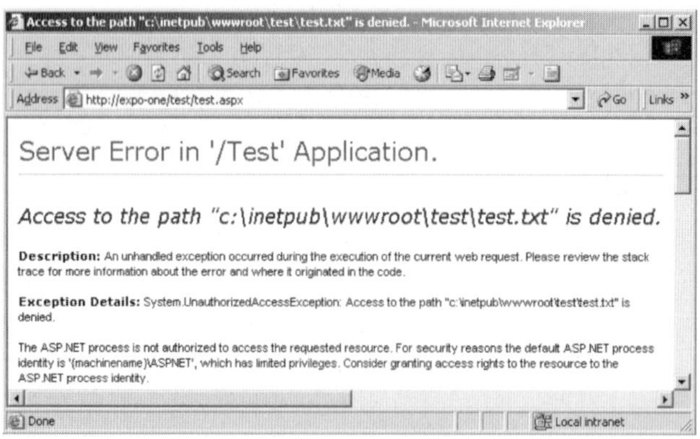

Figure 15-5 The ASPNET account has limited privileges and is not authorized to access the requested resource.

Avoiding the exception is simple. The only action to take is adding the ASPNET account to the list of accounts that have full control on the specific file or folder. In more technical terms, this action is defined as adding or editing an appropriately configured ACL on the file or folder.

If your application manages a well-known and constant number of files, you can deploy them with the needed security settings already in place. If the number and the names of the files being created is not known in advance, you could create a subdirectory, manage to put all the editable files there, and grant ASPNET write permissions on the folder.

But why can't ASP.NET applications create local files? By default, ASP.NET does not impersonate any user, and as a result, all local resources are accessed using the ASP.NET process identity—the ASPNET account. In light of this, Windows resources must have an ACL that grants access to the ASP.NET process account. When this is not the case, the exception in Figure 15-5 is generated. That's why you don't have to modify security configuration to work around the issue; you simply enable the ASPNET account to work in writing mode on the necessary resources.

> **Note** Writing to Microsoft Access .mdb files can often be problematic from within ASP.NET applications. The reason is always related to the fact that the default ASPNET account might not have sufficient permissions to connect to, or write to, an Access database. An Access database is treated as a standalone file; so from this standpoint, a .mdb database is in no way different from a plain text file. To work around the issue, you should grant read and write permissions to the ASPNET account to work on the database file. Finally, notice that the error message you get is different as you are trying to connect (without read permissions) or write (without write permissions).

Changing the Identity of the ASP.NET Process

In a situation in which you want to change the default ASPNET account to give it more or fewer privileges, how should you proceed? Is it preferable to create a custom account and use it for the worker process (via the *<processModel>* section), or should you force the ASP.NET worker to impersonate a given identity through the *<identity>* section?

Setting the Process Account

Using the *<processModel>* section is the only way to change the real identity of the ASP.NET process. You do this using the following setting:

```
<processModel userName="..." password="..." />
```

If you set the process identity in the *<processModel>* section, all threads in the process will use this as the base identity and no extra work is needed on thread switches. You should make sure the new account has at least full permissions on the Temporary ASP.NET Files folder. (Review carefully the minimum list of privileges required by the ASPNET account in "The ASPNET Account" section.)

Alternatively, you could require the worker process to impersonate a fixed identity. In this case, setting the *<identity>* section just sets up an impersonation. Note that the identity is tied to the process for the life of the process, while impersonations come and go and can be reverted too. As we'll see shortly, fixed impersonation might pose security issues too.

Unlike *<processModel>*, the *<identity>* section can be used on a per-folder basis. This is a common approach when you run multiple Web applications on the same machine and need to give them different identities. Application hosting is one of these scenarios.

Note that when fixed impersonation is used, every thread processing a request needs to impersonate the specified account. Impersonation must be performed for each asynchronous call or thread switch because all these events take you back to the process ID. The impersonated account must have full permissions on the Temporary ASP.NET Files folder.

Impersonating an Identity

Impersonation is a trickier point that deserves some further explanation. To start out, let's say that to impersonate a fixed identity, you first define the user account and then add a setting to the web.config or machine.config file. The following snippet shows an example:

```
<identity impersonate="true"
    userName="MyAspNetAccnt" password="ILoveA$p*SinceVer3.0" />
```

As mentioned earlier, impersonation doesn't really change the *physical* identity of the process running ASP.NET. More simply, the same ASP.NET process impersonates another user. The issue is that impersonating a fixed identity is possible only under certain conditions and configures potential security risks. Note that per-request impersonation (for example, impersonating the identity of the caller making the request) is always possible, but the extended form of the *<identity>* section, where an explicit account is set, must be handled with care.

A process running under a nonadministrator account—for example, ASPNET—cannot impersonate a specific account on Windows 2000 unless you grant it appropriate privileges. Obtaining a new logon session for the specified account requires the process to have the Act As Part Of The Operating System privilege, which is indeed a strong and powerful privilege that a nonadministrator process account like ASPNET generally will not have. The reason why the per-request impersonation still works is that IIS—which runs with administrative privileges—creates the session and passes the token to ASP.NET through the standard ISAPI protocol.

Note The limitation discussed here disappears with Windows XP and Windows Server 2003, which will make it possible for you to create logon sessions without the *SE_TCB_NAME* privilege—that is, the Act As Part Of The Operating System privilege.

Fixed impersonation requires a couple of unmanaged calls. The first is aimed at getting the impersonation token and requires the *LogonUser* Win32 API function. The second call is for the *CreateProcessAsUser* Win32 function, which is meant to create the process using the impersonated account. Both API functions are located in the system DLL advapi32.dll. The two calls require the following privileges to be granted to the ASPNET account or any other account attempting the impersonation. Table 15-1 lists the privileges required for impersonating a fixed identity.

Table 15-1 Privileges Required to Impersonate a Fixed Identity

Privilege	Description
SE_TCB_NAME	Act as part of the operating system
SE_ASSIGNPRIMARYTOKEN_NAME	Replace a process-level token
SE_INCREASE_QUOTANAME	Increase quotas

In particular, the *SE_TCB_NAME* privilege might have serious security implications because of two factors: the inherent power of the privilege itself (which makes the account as powerful as that of an administrator), and the fact that in ASP.NET 1.0 applications run fully trusted.

Although the requirement for the *SE_TCB_NAME* privilege is an operating system feature that is removed from Windows XP and Windows Server 2003, the ASP.NET 1.1 runtime plays some tricks to re-vector the call back to the aspnet_isapi.dll module, which is running on the system account. Basically, the ASP.NET 1.1 ISAPI extension creates the security token and duplicates it in the memory space of the worker process. In this way, ASP.NET 1.1 supports fixed impersonation without requiring the *SE_TCB_NAME* privilege on the worker process account.

> **Note** Impersonation can apply to either an authenticated user or an anonymous user. Impersonation is optional in ASP.NET: the default behavior is to run everything in the context of the worker process—whether it's aspnet_wp.exe running as the ASPNET account, or in the IIS 6.0 process model, w3wp.exe running as the Network Service account. Impersonation can be configured at the machine, site, or application level.

As long as you're running Windows 2000, fixed impersonation works as long as the worker process runs under an account that is granted the *SE_TCB_NAME* privilege. This process, of course, cannot be ASPNET.

Impersonating Through the Anonymous Account

To change the identity of the ASP.NET process, intervening at the *<processModel>* level remains the most viable approach. A third possibility is impersonating through the anonymous account. The idea is that the ASP.NET application grants access to anonymous users, and the anonymous account is configured to be the desired account for the application.

In this case, the application uses per-request impersonation and the managed code executes as the impersonated account. The process account remains set to ASPNET, and it still compiles pages and reads configuration files using the ASPNET account. Impersonation is used only with the code executed within the page and not for all the preliminary steps that happen before the request is handed to the HTTP page handler.

Impersonation and Web Application Isolation

The impersonation model is thread local, meaning that the system places the token for the request on the thread that executes the request. ASP.NET—generally, the .NET Framework—supports an asynchronous programming model and enables developers to consume services processed by different threads. The common language runtime (CLR), though, does not save and restore the native thread security context across asynchronous calls. The net effect of this is that applications do not really run isolated from one another. Impersonation is therefore effective for those Web applications that can't rely on, or exploit, thread switching.

The managed code of an ASP.NET application can easily switch threads so that other mechanisms of isolation are required for applications. Alternative mechanisms include process-level isolation and the use of .NET code access security. With code access security, in particular, you restrict access to resources based on the intersection of both the identity of the calling thread and the identity of the calling code.

Code Access Security and the CLR

Code access security is a set of services that the CLR provides to control access to managed resources. The CLR provides four separate levels of policy that can be used to control access to managed resources. The levels are Enterprise, Machine, User, and AppDomain. The first three levels of policy can be administered by using the Microsoft .NET Framework Configuration tool available in Administrative Tools or a command-line tool named caspol.exe. The AppDomain policy is only configurable programmatically by CLR hosts.

In the CLR, running code is assigned to a security zone based on the evidence it provides about its origin—for example, the originating URL. Each security zone corresponds to a set of permissions. Actual permissions are intersected across policy levels so that effective permissions granted to an assembly can only be further reduced moving from the Enterprise level to the AppDomain level. By default, ASP.NET applications run from the MyComputer zone with full trust. If you want, you can change the level of trust of ASP.NET applications by changing the *<trust>* section in the web.config file.

Implementing the *<trust>* Section

ASP.NET uses the AppDomain policy to implement the *<trust>* section defined in the machine.config file. By default, applications run as fully trusted. In other words, ASP.NET does not restrict security policy in any way, but you can choose among a few other modes using the *<trust>* section.

The *<trust>* section can be used to configure permissions for a Web application and decide whether it has to run fully or partially trusted. Table 15-2 describes the levels of trust available in ASP.NET 1.1.

Table 15-2 Levels Permitted in the *<trust>* Section

Level	Description
Full	Applications run fully trusted and can execute arbitrary native code in the process context in which they run. This is the default setting.
High	Code can use most permissions that support partial trust. Appropriate for applications you want to run with least privilege to mitigate risks.
Medium	Code can read and write its own application directories and can interact with SQL databases. Supported only in ASP.NET 1.1.
Low	Code can read its own application resources but can't interact with resources located outside of its application space.

(continued)

Table 15-2 Levels Permitted in the *<trust>* Section *(continued)*

Level	Description
Minimal	Code can't interact with any protected resources. Appropriate for non-professional hosting sites that simply intend to support generic HTML code and highly isolated business logic. Supported only in ASP.NET 1.1.
None	This code won't be loaded or run.

Note that the *Full* trust level is not necessarily appropriate for shared servers (for example, UNC shares) unless process isolation is used and individual accounts are used to isolate applications. Applications available over a shared server also run from the intranet zone with a restricted permission set.

ASP.NET Permissions

In version 1.1, ASP.NET implements a custom permission known as *AspNet-HostingPermission*, which has a named level corresponding to each default level described in Table 15-2. All public types defined in the *System.Web* and *System.Web.Mobile* namespaces are protected with a requirement for the *Minimal* level of permission. This is a risk mitigation strategy that ensures Web application code can't be used unless an administrator, or a trusted host, explicitly grants the permission. Key ASP.NET permissions for each trust level are outlined in Table 15-3.

Table 15-3 Main Permissions in ASP.NET Trust Levels

	High	Medium	Low	Minimal
AspNetHosting	High	Medium	Low	Minimal
FileIO	Unrestricted	Read/Write to application's space	Read	None
IsolatedStorage	Unrestricted	ByUser	ByUser (max 1 MB)	None
Printing	DefaultPrinting	*Same as High*	None	None
Security	Assertion, Execution, ControlThread, ControlPrincipal	*Same as High*	Execution	Execution
SqlClient	Unrestricted	Unrestricted (no blank password allowed)	None	None
Registry	Unrestricted	None	None	None
Environment	Unrestricted	None	None	None

Table 15-3 Main Permissions in ASP.NET Trust Levels

	High	Medium	Low	Minimal
Reflection	ReflectionEmit	None	None	None
Socket	Unrestricted	None	None	None
Web	Unrestricted	Connect to origin host, if configured	*Same as High*	None

More detailed information about the permissions actually granted to the default trust levels are available in the security configuration files for each policy. The name of the file for each level is stored in the *<trustLevel>* section.

Full-trust applications run unrestricted. High-trust applications have read/write permission for all the files in their application space. However, the physical access to files is still ruled by the NTFS access control list on the resource. High-trust applications have unrestricted access to SQL Server but not, for example, to OLE DB classes. (The *OleDbPermission*, and other managed provider permissions, are denied to all but fully trusted applications.) Reflection calls are denied with the exception of those directed at classes in the *System.Reflection.Emit* namespace.

Meta Variables in Security Configuration Files

While reading the contents of security .config files, you might run into a few particular names having the form of *xxx*. They are meta variables used to indicate absolute path names in the .config file. The contents of these sort of macros are calculated by ASP.NET at run time and described here:

- ***$AppDir$*** The root application directory of a given Web application.
- ***$CodeGen$*** The directory used for dynamic compilation by ASP.NET for a given application.
- ***Gac*** The location of the global assembly cache on a given machine.
- ***$ASP.NET$*** The current set of permissions based on the *<trust>* directive.

In any partial trust mode, any code running from both the *$AppDir$* and *$CodeGen$* directories is partially trusted and appropriately restricted based on the *<trust>* section.

Medium applications have unrestricted access to SQL Server, but only as long as they do not use blank passwords for accounts. The *WebPermission* is granted to both medium- and low-trust applications but requires that the URL be configured in the *<trust>* section of the web.config. Low-trust applications have read-only permission for files in their application directories. Isolated storage is still permitted but limited to a 1-MB quota.

Alternative Strategies for Isolating Applications

As long as your Web application runs under the IIS 5 process model, code access security is the most effective way to isolate applications from one another. By using a combination of separate accounts, access control lists and code access security policies, you prevent applications from accessing resources that belong to other applications. However, although separated to a great extent, ASP.NET applications are still all running in the context of a single worker process.

An even better way of isolating applications comes with IIS 6.0 and the new process model (w3wp.exe) on Windows Server 2003. IIS 6.0 supports application pools that run as distinct processes, each with its own set of security settings. If an application, for some reason, takes a Web process down, it will have an impact only on other applications within the process but not other application pools. In addition, with multiple processes running, an administrator can more easily figure out what resources a given process is consuming. Getting the same information is significantly harder if you're dealing with multiple AppDomains inside of a single process.

Using process isolation versus code access security-only isolation also poses some tradeoffs in terms of overall performance and scalability. More running processes result in more memory and system resources being used. For example, each process will have its own thread pool. This extensive resource consumption means that a finite number of concurrent application pools can be active at the same time. A reasonable estimate of this number ranges from 20 to 60 concurrent application pools.

User Authentication and Authorization

From an application point of view, security is mostly a matter of authenticating users and authorizing actions on the system's resources. ASP.NET provides a range of authentication and authorization mechanisms implemented in conjunction with IIS, the .NET Framework, and the underlying security services of the operating system.

When a client issues a Web request, the following sequence of authentication and authorization events occurs:

- **IIS Authentication** If the page can be viewed and the request comes from a nonrestricted IP address, IIS authenticates the caller using any of the predefined authentication mechanisms (Basic, Digest, or Integrated Windows).
- **ASP.NET Authentication** If ASP.NET is configured for Windows authentication (more on this later in the "Windows Authentication" section), no additional steps are needed and ASP.NET just accepts any security token it receives from IIS. If ASP.NET is configured for Forms authentication (more on this later in the "Forms Authentication" section), then the user is prompted for credentials using an HTML form. User ID and password are authenticated against a stored list of valid users. The application is free to choose the storage mech anism that best suits, including a SQL Server database or Active Directory services. Finally, if ASP.NET is configured for Passport authentication (more on this later in the "Passport Authentication" section), then the user is redirected to a Passport Web site and authenticated by the Passport service.
- **ASP.NET Authorization** ASP.NET verifies that the caller is authorized to access the requested resource to execute the operation. A few HTTP modules provide for this service; they are *UrlAuthorizationModule* and *FileAuthorizationModule*. The *UrlAuthorizationModule* class ensures that the authorization rules set in the *<authorization>* element of the web.config file are fulfilled. The *FileAuthorizationModule* class gets into the game when Windows authentication is used and verifies that the caller has the necessary permission to access the requested resource. The verification is performed by comparing the ACL of the resource against the caller's token. At this stage of the process, .NET roles can also be used to verify the caller's authorization to work on a resource. (More on .NET roles and code access security at the end of this chapter.)

IIS Authentication

When a request hits IIS, IIS first ensures that the request comes from a trusted IP address. If it doesn't come from a trusted IP address, the request is rejected with an HTTP error 403.6. A second preliminary check is then made regarding whether the requested resource is available for reading or browsing. If it isn't, the request is rejected with an HTTP error 403.2.

Next, IIS attempts to authenticate the caller by using the Integrated Windows, Digest, or Basic authentication method. If Integrated Windows authentication is used, either Kerberos or NTLM is used.

> **Note** Windows NT Challenge/Response (NTLM) is the authentication protocol used on networks based on Windows NT. NTLM stands for Windows NT LAN Manager. For the same purpose, in Windows 2000 Microsoft introduced Kerberos, a more powerful and flexible alternative.

In situations in which the resource is protected with an ACL, the user permissions are carefully verified. If the Web application includes pages that don't need authentication, IIS can be configured for anonymous access. In either case, at the end of the authentication phase IIS creates a Windows access token for the caller. The token refers to the authenticated user or, if anonymous authentication is enabled, IIS creates an access token for the predefined anonymous account. By default, this account is called *IUSR_*Xxx where Xxx is the machine name. You can change the anonymous user account in IIS as shown in Figure 15-6.

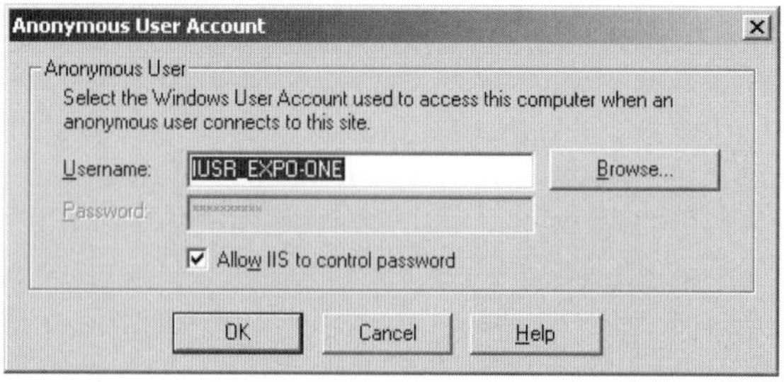

Figure 15-6 Configuring the Internet anonymous account in IIS.

ASP.NET Authentication Types

Depending on the type of the requested resource, IIS might or might not be able to handle the request itself. If the resource needs the involvement of ASP.NET (for example, an .aspx file), IIS hands the request over to ASP.NET along with the security token of the authenticated, or anonymous, user. What happens next depends on the ASP.NET configuration.

As mentioned earlier, ASP.NET supports three types of authentication methods: Windows, Passport, and Forms. A fourth possibility is None, meaning that ASP.NET does not attempt to perform its own authentication and completely relies on the authentication already carried out by IIS. In this case, anonymous users can connect and resources are accessed using the ASP.NET account. You choose the ASP.NET authentication mechanism using the *<authentication>* section in the web.config file. By default, the authentication mode is set to Windows.

The authentication mode can be set in the machine.config or, better yet, in the application-level web.config file. Child subdirectories inherit the authentication mode chosen for the application.

ASP.NET Authorization Rules

The goal of the authorization mechanism is allowing or denying user access to particular pages of the application. You set authorization rules by using the *<authorization>* section in the web.config file.

The authorization rules consist of two distinct blocks of information regarding what is allowed and what is denied. The child *<allow>* tag defines users, roles, and actions allowed; by contrast, the child *<deny>* tag indicates which users, roles, or actions are not permitted.

We'll cover authorization rules in greater detail later in this chapter.

ASP.NET and SQL Server

To access a SQL Server database from within an ASP.NET application, you use the ADO.NET objects and specify a connection string. Depending on the SQL Server security configuration, the connection string might require a user name and a password. As you know, the password is sensitive information that you must hard-code in the software or read dynamically from some, more or less secure, location. To avoid all the risks connected with this operation, you might want to opt for a SQL Server trusted connection.

A trusted connection entails assuming the identity of the user or caller making the request to access SQL Server. In this case, it isn't necessary to specify a user ID and password in the connection string. SQL Server revalidates the account name and password by calling back to Windows for the information.

Setting Up Trusted Connections

When connecting to SQL Server, you request a trusted connection by using the *trusted_connection* token in the connection string, as shown here:

```
string connString = "SERVER=localhost;...;TRUSTED_CONNECTION=true;";
SqlConnection conn = new SqlConnection(connString);
conn.Open();
⋮
conn.Close();
```

Note that to indicate a trusted connection in ADO.NET connection strings, you can interchangeably use the keywords *trusted_connection* and *integrated_security*. Both names are case insensitive. Valid values for the keywords are *true*, *false*, or *sspi* (which is equivalent to *true*).

If you run the code just shown, the chances are good that it will throw an exception because of a failed login for the ASP.NET user—typically, ASP-NET. In other words, SQL Server behaves as if the following connection string was specified:

```
SERVER=localhost;...;UID=ASPNET;PWD=...;
```

Unless ASPNET is really a valid SQL Server login name, an exception is thrown. To set up the ASPNET account as a SQL Server login, you open the SQL Server Enterprise Manager, select the Logins items under the Security node, and then select the New Login item from the Action menu. A dialog box pops up to let you choose the user account to associate with a particular database, as shown in Figure 15-7.

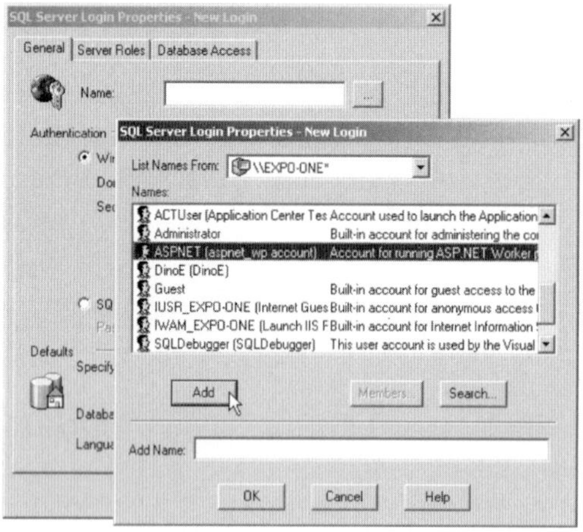

Figure 15-7 Setting up the ASPNET account as a SQL Server login.

On the Database Access tab, you specify which databases can be accessed using the login, as shown in Figure 15-8. You can check as many databases as needed and set up database roles as appropriate.

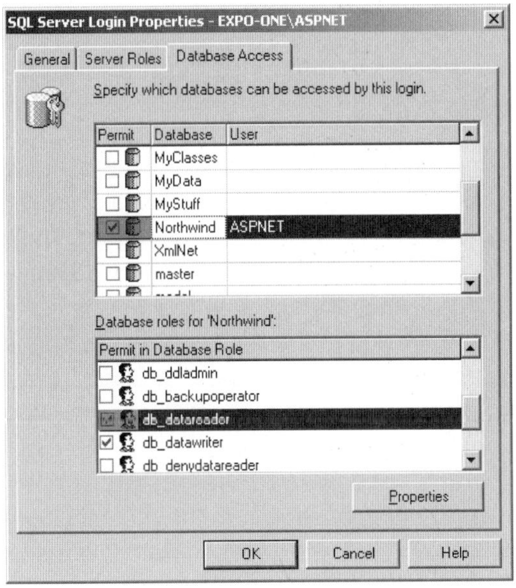

Figure 15-8 Setting up the database roles for the ASPNET account.

At this point, if you attempt to connect to SQL Server from within an ASP.NET application using the trusted connection mechanism, no exception will be thrown.

> **Note** Users who connect through a Windows user account can make use of trusted connections only if SQL Server is configured in Windows Authentication Mode or Mixed Mode. If SQL Server is configured to operate in SQL Server Authentication mode, trusted connections are not possible.

Working with Untrusted Connections

Having SQL Server and ASP.NET configured for trusted connections doesn't mean that you must always connect through a trusted channel. When you don't require a trusted connection, and connect using a string as below, there are two possible scenarios.

```
SERVER=localhost;...;UID=dino;PWD=...;
```

If SQL Server was installed to use Windows Authentication, the connection just fails. If SQL Server was installed to use Mixed-Mode Authentication, the authentication is performed using the User ID and the password contained in the connection string.

> **Note** A general rule for choosing between trusted and untrusted connections is that you should opt for trusted connections if you're mainly relying on SQL Server, and the data tier, for securing the application. Because SQL Server needs more time to handle a trusted connection, you might want to opt for a different approach. One alternative is to implement any security restriction in the business tier so that you can be sure that only trusted and verified modules can ever access SQL Server. After that, you go with untrusted, but faster, connections and still preserve a reasonable degree of safety.
>
> In this case, you still need to read the password from some trusted location; the *<appSettings>* section in the machine.config is a valid option. To reinforce security at this level, you could also restrict access to the machine.config file by using an ACL.

Windows Authentication

Let's start our examination of the ASP.NET authentication modes with the default one—Windows authentication. When using Windows authentication, ASP.NET works in conjunction with IIS. The real authentication is performed by IIS, which uses one of its three authentication methods: Basic, Digest, or Integrated Windows. When IIS has authenticated the user, it passes the security token on to ASP.NET. When in Windows authentication mode, ASP.NET does not perform any further steps and limits its use of the IIS token to authorizing access to the resources.

Typically, you use the Windows authentication mode in intranet scenarios when the users of your application only have Windows accounts that can be authenticated by the Web server. In most cases, Windows authentication is used in conjunction with file authorization—the *FileAuthorizationModule* HTTP module. The module does an ACL check to determine which user can access what resource. However, Windows authentication also works with URL authorization implemented by the HTTP module named *URLAuthorizationModule*. This module allows or denies access to URL resources to certain users and roles.

Authenticating Users Through IIS

As mentioned, there are three main ways in which IIS can authenticate the user making the request: Basic, Digest, and Integrated Windows. All techniques attempt to map callers to accounts available on the Web server machine. Of course, each of them accomplishes the same task in a different way.

Basic Authentication

Basic authentication is an HTTP standard supported by virtually any browser available on the face of the earth. If a user requests a page on a site where anonymous access has been disabled and Basic authentication has been configured, an HTTP 401 status code is returned, which instructs the browser to retry with credentials

```
HTTP/1.1 401 Access Denied
Server: Microsoft-IIS/5.0
WWW-Authenticate: Basic realm="expo-one"
Connection: close
⋮
Content-Type: text/html
```

The browser prompts the user with a dialog box and gets the user name and password, as shown in Figure 15-9.

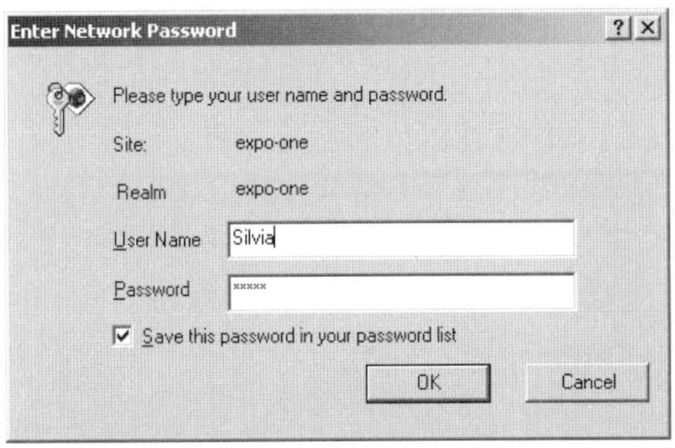

Figure 15-9 Basic authentication with Internet Explorer.

The information gathered is sent to IIS, which attempts to match it with any of the Web server's accounts. The following HTTP script illustrates the next request:

```
GET /intranet/ HTTP/1.1
⋮
Host: expo-one
Connection: Keep-Alive
Authorization: Basic QWRtaW5pc3RyYXRvcjpqZXJyeQ==
```

Basic authentication works by transmitting the user name and password as clear text, encoded as Base64.

The Basic authentication mode works well with all browsers and does not pose any issue if firewalls or proxies are present. Because user credentials are transmitted in clear text, you might want to limit its use to HTTPS-encrypted channels or to any context in which security is not a critical issue.

Digest Authentication

Digest authentication differs from Basic authentication mostly because it does not transmit credentials (for example, user names and passwords) in clear text. Credentials, in fact, are hashed using a Web server–provided code. As with Basic authentication, a user's request for a page on a site where anonymous access has been disabled bounces back the first time with a status code of 401. The *WWW-Authenticate* header contains the code to use to encrypt the credentials. The user is prompted with a dialog box and asked to enter her credentials.

Next, the browser creates the *message digest*—that is, a nondecipherable version of the credentials—and prepares a new request. The message digest is passed back to the Web server using the *Authorization* HTTP header.

Digest authentication is usable across proxy servers, firewalls, and Web Distributed Authoring and Versioning (WebDAV). On the downside, we find that Digest authentication is a new HTTP 1.1 feature and, as such, is not supported by all browsers. For example, in the Internet Explorer family of browsers only Internet Explorer 5.0 and newer versions support it. If a noncompliant browser makes a request on a server that requires Digest authentication, the server will reject the request and send the client an error message. In addition, Digest authentication requires the password to be stored as clear text on the Web server and is supported only for domains with a Windows 2000 domain controller.

Integrated Windows Authentication

Unlike the other two modes, when Integrated Windows authentication is configured the user doesn't need to explicitly enter a user name and password. Instead, when a Windows user requests a resource on the Web server, a conversation is set up between the browser and the Web server. The browser passes the credentials of the currently logged-on user. The user needs to have a valid account on the server to be successfully authenticated. The authentication can take place through the NTLM challenge/response method or by using Kerberos.

The technique is not supported outside the family of Internet Explorer browsers (although it works with versions as far back as Internet Explorer 2.0) and is impracticable in the presence of firewalls.

> **Note** A fourth type of authentication mode exists and is based on certificates. You can use the Secure Sockets Layer (SSL) security features of IIS and use client certificates to authenticate users requesting information on your Web site. SSL checks the contents of the certificate submitted by the browser for the user during the logon. Users obtain client certificates from a trusted third-party organization.

The Windows Authentication Provider

In ASP.NET, the Windows authentication mode is ruled by an HTTP module class named *WindowsAuthenticationModule*. During the authentication process, the module fires the *Authenticate* event that can be caught from within the global.asax file.

```
void WindowsAuthentication_OnAuthenticate(
    object sender,
    WindowsAuthenticationEventArgs e)
{
    ⋮
}
```

The event data is represented by the *WindowsAuthenticationEventArgs* structure and contains the following members: *Context*, *Identity*, and *User*.

Context is an instance of the *HttpContext* object and represents the HTTP context of the request. *Identity* is an object of type *WindowsIdentity* and represents an authenticated Windows user. Finally, *User* is a wrapper object that includes the identity and lets you check for the role of the identity. The *User* property can be used to get or set the identity object to be associated with the request. The identity object is also referred to as the *principal*.

How to Verify the Identity of the User

Let's assume that you configured the Web server to work with the Integrated Windows authentication mode and that you disabled anonymous access. The ASP.NET application works in Windows authentication mode. What happens when a user connects to the application?

First, IIS authenticates the user (popping up a dialog box if the account of the local user doesn't match any accounts on the Web server) and then hands the security token over to ASP.NET. The ASP.NET page shown in Figure 15-10 retrieves and displays the name of the connected user and the specific authentication mode used.

```
<%@ Page Language="C#" %>
<script runat="server">
void Page_Load(object sender, EventArgs e) {
    if (User.Identity.IsAuthenticated) {
        Response.Write("Welcome, <b>" + User.Identity.Name + "</b>!<br>");
        Response.Write("(" + User.Identity.AuthenticationType + ")<br>");
    }
    else
        Response.Write("Welcome, anonymous user!");
}
</script>
```

You use the *User* property on the *Page* class to access the identity of the current principal.

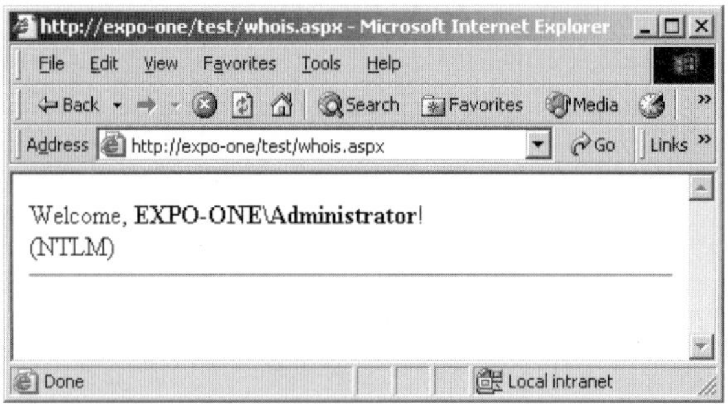

Figure 15-10 The page welcomes users by name.

You can use this technique to build user-specific pages in which profile information is used or different functionalities are enabled. However, if you plan to differentiate pages based on the user's role, you're better off using URL authorization (more on this later in the "URL Authorization and User-Based Security" section).

Using ACLs to Authorize Access

User-specific pages in the Web application can be protected from unauthorized access using ACLs on the file. When ASP.NET is about to access a resource, the *FileAuthorizationModule* HTTP module is called into action. File authorization performs an ACL check on ASP.NET files using the caller's identity. This means that the user Joe will never be able to access an .aspx page whose ACL doesn't include an entry for him.

Note, though, that file authorization does not require impersonation and, more importantly, works regardless of whether the impersonation flag is turned on. There's good news and bad news in this statement. The good news is that once you've set an appropriately configured ACL on an ASP.NET resource, you're pretty much done. Nobody will be able to access the resource without permission. But what about non-ASP.NET resources such as local files?

Enabling Impersonation

In ASP.NET, impersonation is disabled by default. Impersonation refers to the ASP.NET capability of accessing pages and running code on behalf of the impersonated identity. You control the impersonation flag on a per-application basis using the following snippet in the web.config file:

```
<configuration>
    <system.web>
        <identity impersonate="true" />
    </system.web>
</configuration>
```

As mentioned earlier, the *<identity>* section also lets you indicate a particular identity in terms of user name and password. If none of this information is specified, ASP.NET attempts to impersonate the server user that IIS has authenticated.

> **Note** Impersonating a fixed identity makes more sense in an application-hosting scenario, in which different applications have to run with different identities on the same machine. Using simple impersonation, in which no user is statically set, is particularly helpful to let the ASP.NET code serve personalized pages based on the user's identity.

The key thing to consider about ASP.NET impersonation is that, when enabled, the Web application accesses *any* resource using the caller's identity. Without impersonation, you can control which pages are served to which user, but you cannot control whether a page, for some reason, serves the user content that she's not authorized to view. In other words, direct access to ASP.NET resources is controlled by the *FileAuthorizationModule* and ACL-based security is enforced. By default, though, all the code executed within the request runs as ASPNET unless impersonation is enabled. This means that ACLs set on a resource not directly handled by ASP.NET—for example, an Access database, a text file, an image, or an XML document—are not enough to protect against programmatic access performed by pages that are authorized to run for a certain user. To ensure that the code within the page runs under the same account that was authorized to access the page, you need to enable impersonation.

URL Authorization and User-Based Security

URL authorization is governed by the *UrlAuthorizationModule* HTTP module. The behavior of the module is driven by the settings stored in the *<authorization>* section of the web.config file. From there, the module reads users, roles, and actions allowed or denied and then behaves accordingly.

The following configuration snippet authorizes only the DinoE user to connect to the application. This snippet translates to: the DinoE user is allowed to connect while all other users are denied.

```
<configuration>
    <system.web>
        <authorization>
            <allow users="domain\DinoE" />
            <deny users="*" />
        </authorization>
    </system.web>
</configuration>
```

Unlike *<authentication>*, the *<authorization>* section can be specified for each folder in the Web application, thus giving you a great chance to control access on a per-folder basis. On the downside of URL authorization, I should list the fact that only ASP.NET resources are monitored. On the other hand, this is in the natural order of things when you consider that, say, requests for HTML files and JPEG images are not processed by aspnet_isapi.dll but resolved directly by IIS. In this case, the URL authorization module has not even had a chance to get into the game.

In general, URL-based authorization is rarely used with Windows authentication. URL authorization is more effective with Forms authentication, and for this reason, we'll describe it in more detail later in the "URL Authorization" section.

> **Note** How can you protect an HTML page from unauthorized access? The first consideration is that an HTML page rarely needs to be protected against access. If you need to protect a page, the page very likely also needs to execute some server-side code. Implementing it as .aspx is more useful anyway. That said, by design HTML pages are not protected from unauthorized access and the best thing you can do is rename the page to .aspx so that it is processed by the ASP.NET runtime.
>
> As an alternative, you can rename the page to a custom extension and write a lightweight ISAPI extension (or a managed HTTP handler) to implement a made-to-measure authorization mechanism.

Passport Authentication

Passport authentication is a Microsoft-centralized authentication service. Passport provides a way to authenticate users coming across all the sites that participate in the initiative. Users need to do a single logon and, if successfully authenticated, they can then freely move through all the member sites. In addition to the single logon service, Passport also offers core profile services for member sites.

ASP.NET provides the *PassportAuthenticationModule* to set up authentication for Web applications hosted by Passport member sites.

Understanding the Passport Initiative

In a certain sense, the Passport authentication mode is the Web-wide counterpart of the Integrated Windows mode or the SQL Server Mixed mode. In all cases, security and identity tokens are shared between participating entities in a way that is totally transparent to the user and improves her experience. The code running in the Web applications resorts to the Passport single sign-in service to get information about the user making the request. As mentioned, all this happens transparently for the user, who just signs in once and jumps from one site to the next until she signs out.

The Passport profile information for each user is severely protected and managed according to a strict privacy policy. Each participating site guarantees that personal customer information will be kept in a secure environment and implements security measures such as using SSL and deleting any cookies that contain Personally Identifiable Information (PII) during sign out.

The .NET Passport SDK is required to implement the .NET Passport single sign-in and other profile-related services on your Web site. The SDK is freely available for developing and testing purposes. However, to run a Passport-enabled Web site, you must submit an official request, adhere to the Passport software licensing and service agreements, and swear that you'll comply with all the strict standards for privacy and security. Only then will you be allowed to obtain encryption keys and other start-up elements to move the Web site into a production environment.

ASP.NET has built-in support for Passport, which saves you from having to interact with the Passport SDK to activate the authentication service and then implement single sign-in.

The Passport Authentication Provider

In the .NET Framework, the *PassportAuthenticationModule* class carries out the Passport authentication. Passport authentication is enabled by the following text in the application's configuration file:

```
<configuration>
    <system.web>
        <authentication mode="Passport" />
    </system.web>
</configuration>
```

When an HTTP request hits a Passport-enabled Web site, the HTTP module verifies whether or not the request contains a valid Passport ticket. If not, the Web server returns the status code 302 and redirects the client to the Passport Logon service. The query string contains properly encrypted information about the original request. The client issues a *GET* request to the logon server and passes the supplied query string. At this point, the Passport logon server prompts the client with an HTML logon form. After the user has filled out the form, the form is posted back to the logon server over an SSL-secured channel.

The logon server utilizes the form information to authenticate the user and, if successful, creates a Passport ticket. Next, the user is redirected to the original URL and the ticket is passed, encrypted, in the query string. Finally, the browser follows the redirect instruction and requests again the original Passport protected resource. This time, though, the request contains a valid ticket so that the *PassportAuthenticationModule* can make the request pass.

Passport utilizes the Triple DES encryption algorithm. Each member site receives its own encryption key upon registration. In ASP.NET, an identity recognized by Passport is represented by a *PassportIdentity* object. The class contains ad hoc methods and properties that represent the Passport ticket and the key operations such as sign-in and sign-out. The Passport server controls the lifetime of the ticket and makes decisions about expiration and reuse on other member sites.

> **Note** The Passport SDK version 2.1 can be downloaded from the Microsoft Web site at *http://www.microsoft.com/net/services/passport/*. Older versions are supported but not recommended. Note that Windows XP supports only Passport 2.0 and newer versions.

Forms Authentication

If you're a former Web developer, regardless of the platform you used, you'll agree that both Windows and Passport authentication are seldom practical for real-world Internet applications. Windows authentication is based on Windows accounts and NTFS ACL tokens and, as such, assumes that clients are connecting from Windows-equipped machines. Useful and effective in intranet and possibly extranet scenarios, Windows authentication is simply unrealistic in more common situations. The same conclusion applies to Passport authentication, although for different reasons. Passport is not free, requires the implementation of serious security measures (which are not free and that you don't necessarily need in all sites), and makes sense mostly for e-commerce and co-branded Web sites.

So what is the ideal authentication mechanism for real Web developers? A Web programming best-practice recommends that you place some relatively boilerplated code on top of each nonpublic page and redirect the user to a login page. In the login page, the user is prompted for his credentials, which are verified, authenticated, and then, if all went fine, redirected to the originally requested page. All this code is not exactly rocket science, but it's still code that you have to write yourself and use over and over again.

Forms authentication is just the ASP.NET built-in infrastructure that greatly simplifies the implementation of the aforementioned pattern for login. Forms authentication is the ideal choice whenever you need to collect user credentials and process them internally—for example, against a database of login names. To some extent, the authentication pattern implemented by Forms authentication doesn't look radically different from Windows and Passport authentication. The key difference is that with Forms authentication everything happens under the strict control of the application.

The Forms Authentication Provider

The module that governs the forms-based authentication is an HTTP module implemented by the *FormsAuthenticationModule* class. The behavior of the component is driven by the contents of the various web.config files that make up the application. First, you enable Forms authentication by putting the following code in the application's web.config file:

```
<configuration>
    <system.web>
        <authentication mode="Forms">
            <forms loginURL="login.aspx" />
        </authentication>
    </system.web>
</configuration>
```

This code alone doesn't cause significant changes in your application as long as anonymous access to the pages is allowed. If some pages in your application must be made available only to well-known users, you might want to indicate which users are not directly admitted. You can do this by using the *<authorization>* section in the web.config file. For example, the following code blocks direct access to the all the pages for all users:

```
<authorization>
    <deny users="*" />
</authorization>
```

A protected resource is any ASP.NET resource (.aspx, .asmx, .ashx, and so forth) located in a folder in which Forms authentication and URL authorization is requested.

Accessing Protected ASP.NET Resources

When the browser attempts to access a protected resource, the Forms authentication module kicks in and attempts to locate an authentication ticket for the caller. A ticket is merely a cookie with a particular name. If no ticket is found, the module redirects the request to a login page. The login page is chosen by the programmer and hard-coded in the *loginUrl* attribute of the *<forms>* section.

The Forms authentication module intercepts the call and checks to see whether the request has an associated authentication ticket (much like Passport). If not, the module reads the login page URL and redirects the user there. The browser receives a response with a status code of HTTP 302 and the new location to query for. The user is prompted with the user-defined login page as shown in Figure 15-11.

Figure 15-11 The user is attempting to access a protected resource and is not authenticated. The Forms module redirects the user to a user-defined login page.

It's interesting to take a closer look at the URL being used for redirection. Assuming that the originally requested page is *http://expo-one/test/whois.aspx*, the redirection URL looks like this:

```
/Test/login.aspx?ReturnUrl=%2ftest%2fWhoIs.aspx
```

The URL of the login page has a query string appended to it with a *ReturnUrl* parameter set to the original URL.

Validating User Credentials

The user enters her credentials (name and password) into the logon form and clicks a button to have them processed by the system. We'll review this process in detail later in the "The Login Process" section. For now, it suffices to say that either the Forms authentication module or the application itself can validate the credentials against a list of valid accounts. If the authentication process ends successfully, you call a method on the Forms provider to redirect the browser to the original page.

In doing so, the Forms authentication module also creates a cookie known as the authentication ticket. The cookie is given a particular name and duration. When the browser issues a new request for the same original page, the module gets involved again but this time the cookie is there and the call is successfully resolved.

Attributes of the *<authentication>* Section

We already covered the fundamentals of the *<authentication>* section in Chapter 12; in this section, though, we briefly revisit the concepts and the features in the context of the Forms authentication model.

Forms authentication is driven by the contents of the *<forms>* section of the *<authentication>* section. The overall syntax is shown here:

```
<forms name="cookie"
       loginUrl="url"
       protection="All|None|Encryption|Validation"
       timeout="30"
       requireSSL="true|false"
       slidingExpiration="true|false">
       path="/" >
   <credentials passwordFormat="format" />
</forms>
```

The various attributes are described in Table 15-4.

Table 15-4 Attributes for Forms Authentication

Attribute	Description
loginUrl	Specifies the URL to which the request is redirected for logon if no valid authentication cookie is found.
name	Specifies the name of the HTTP cookie to use for authentication. The default name is *.ASPXAUTH*.
path	Specifies the path for the authentication cookies issued by the application. The default value is a slash (/). Note that some browsers are case-sensitive and will not send cookies back if there is a path case mismatch.
protection	Indicates how the application intends to protect the authentication cookie. The Forms provider supports two methods—validation and encryption. The protection attribute can take any of the following values: *All*, *Encryption*, *None*, and *Validation*. The default and recommended value is *All*.
requireSSL	Indicates whether a secure connection (SSL) is required to transmit the authentication cookie. The default is *false*. If *true*, ASP.NET sets the *Secure* property for the authentication cookie and a compliant browser does not return the cookie unless the connection is using SSL. *This attribute is supported only on ASP.NET 1.1.*
slidingExpiration	Indicates whether sliding expiration is enabled. The default is *false*, meaning that the cookie expires at a set interval from the time it was originally issued. The interval is determined by the *timeout* attribute. *This attribute is supported only on ASP.NET 1.1.*
timeout	Specifies the amount of time, in minutes, after which the cookie expires. The default value is 30.

Note that if multiple applications are running on a single server and more than one application is using Forms authentication, you are responsible for ensuring that each application ends up using a unique cookie name. You configure the cookie name in each application's web.config file.

Managing the Authentication Cookie

The contents of the cookie is also known as the authentication ticket and is represented by the *FormsAuthenticationTicket* class. It can be encrypted and/or validated. If encryption is specified, the cookie is encrypted using the Triple-DES (3DES) algorithm. Encryption is much more effective if combined with data validation. Data validation verifies that the contents of an encrypted cookie have not been tampered with along the way. Encryption and validation algorithms are controlled through the *<machineKey>* section. When encryption is

3DES, data validation for forms authentication defaults to the SHA1 algorithm. If the protection level for the cookie is set to *All* (both validation and encryption), the cookie data is concatenated with a validation key and a message authentication code (MAC) is computed and appended to the outgoing cookie. Encryption and validation take some CPU time; for this reason, if you're going to use HTTPS channels you might want to drop cookie security entirely, setting the protection attribute to *None*.

To use authentication cookies over HTTPS channels, you must indicate a secure URL for the login page and, of course, make sure that your Web server supports HTTPS in the folder in which the page resides.

In ASP.NET 1.1, the cookie by default expires after the specified timeout. In ASP.NET 1.0, on the other hand, the default behavior was that of a sliding expiration policy. Each request that involves the cookie resets the expiration of an active ticket to the specified number of minutes ahead of the current time. Note that the cookie is renewed only if half of its lifetime is already over. The method involved with this expiration policy is *RenewTicketIfOld*.

The *<credentials>* Section

The *<credentials>* section of the *<forms>* tag is not something that real-world applications will ever use. Basically, the section is expected to contain the credentials of the users enabled to access the application.

```
<credentials passwordFormat="mode">
    <user name="..." password="..." />
    ⋮
    <user name="..." password="..." />
</credentials>
```

If the *<credentials>* section is specified, only the users listed will be granted the permission to access the protected resources. The section is optional, but if you omit it you should provide an alternative and custom authentication scheme. Each child *<user>* element describes a user in terms of his name and password. The *passwordFormat* attribute specifies the encryption format for storing passwords. Possible values are *Clear*, *MD5*, and *SHA1*. By default, the password is stored as clear text, but if you specify the MD5 or SHA1 value you can store passwords as encrypted text obtained by running the MD5 or SHA1 hash algorithm.

There is good news and bad news about the *<credentials>* section. The good news is that in this way the authentication process is highly automated and looks like a declarative feature. The bad news is that storing users and passwords (even hashed) in a simple text file is neither secure nor practical. How could you cope with it when you have hundreds of users to manage? And what if a user changes her password? (Actually a user should change the password every few weeks.) What if a new user must be added or an existing one deleted? All these changes would occur on the web.config file and cause the entire subtree of pages to be invalidated and recompiled with the next access.

Although it's helpful for toy projects and good for demonstrating the extreme flexibility of the ASP.NET architecture, the *<credentials>* section is scarcely useful in real-world scenarios. In a real-world application, you need to take total control of the login process and verify the user-typed credentials against a database. In some other cases, typically when the number of users is high and the security policies are strict and articulated, you might want to consider role-based authentication. In this case, after the user logs in, you attach to the principal object representing the user's identity a string describing the role of the user. Next, you let the Forms authentication provider verify authorized users and block the request if no match is found. Let's see both aspects more in detail.

The Login Process

Let's consider a scenario in which you don't want users to connect anonymously to the application. The following web.config file sets up the Forms authentication and denies access to anonymous users. Note that a question mark (?) within the *<authorization>* section indicates the anonymous user; an asterisk (*) on the other hand indicates all users.

```
<configuration>
    <system.web>
        <authentication mode="Forms">
            <forms loginUrl="login.aspx" />
        </authentication>
        <authorization>
            <deny users="?" />
        </authorization>
    </system.web>
</configuration>
```

As a result, users for which an authentication ticket does not exist are redirected to the login page by the *Forms* module. The sample application, named MyCompany, provides the login page shown in Figure 15-12.

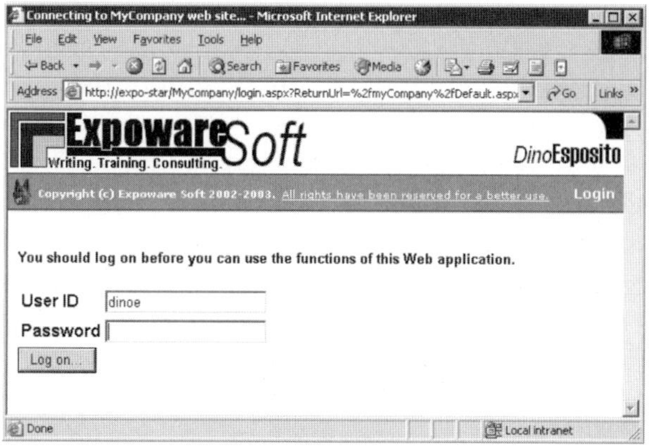

Figure 15-12 The login page of the sample application.

Collecting Credentials Through Login

The user enters the credentials, typically in a case-sensitive way, and then clicks the button to log on. When the login page posts back, the following code runs:

```
void LogonUser(object sender, EventArgs e)
{
    string user = userName.Text;
    string pswd = passWord.Text;

    // Custom authentication
    bool bAuthenticated = AuthenticateUser(user, pswd);
    if (bAuthenticated)
        FormsAuthentication.RedirectFromLoginPage(user, false);
    else
        errorMsg.Text = "Sorry, yours seems not to be a valid account.";
}
```

The event handler retrieves the strings typed in the user name and password fields and calls into a custom function named *AuthenticateUser*. The function returns a Boolean value. If the user has been successfully authenticated, the code invokes the *RedirectFromLoginPage* static method on the *FormsAuthentication* class to inform the browser it's about time that a new request is made to the original page.

The *RedirectFromLoginPage* method redirects an authenticated user back to the originally requested URL. It has two overloads with the following prototypes:

```
public static void RedirectFromLoginPage(string, bool);
public static void RedirectFromLoginPage(string, bool, string);
```

The first argument is the name of the user to store in the authentication cookie; this name will also be used by the URL Authorization module to deny or grant access based on the *<authorization>* section of the web.config file. The second argument is a Boolean value that denotes the duration of the authentication cookie being created. If *false*, the cookie is given the normal duration—that is, the number of minutes set by the *timeout* attribute (30 minutes by default). If this argument is *true*, the cookie is given a much longer lifetime. Finally, the third argument specifies the cookie path. Note that if no login page is indicated, the authentication mechanism defaults to a page named default.aspx.

Authenticating the User

If you can afford to keep the user list in the web.config file, you can simply call the *Authenticate* method on the *FormsAuthentication* class. The method validates the user credentials against those contained in the *<credentials>* section. The following code calls a function named *AuthenticateUser* that returns a Boolean value indicating if the user is authenticated.

```
void LogonUser(object sender, EventArgs e)
{
    string user = userName.Text;
    string pswd = passWord.Text;

    // Custom authentication
    bool bAuthenticated = AuthenticateUser(user, pswd);
    ⋮
}
```

If you want to check the credentials against a database or any other user-defined storage device, just write your own function and make it return a Boolean value. The following listing shows the aforementioned *AuthenticateUser* function, which accesses a SQL Server table named Users in the ProAspNet database. The Users table contains three string columns: *ID*, *pswd*, and *role*.

```
bool AuthenticateUser(string username, string pswd)
{
    string connString, cmdText;
    connString = "SERVER=localhost;DATABASE=proaspnet;UID=sa;";
    cmdText = "SELECT COUNT(*) FROM users WHERE id=@user AND pswd=@pswd";

    SqlConnection conn = new SqlConnection(connString);
    SqlCommand cmd = new SqlCommand(cmdText, conn);
    cmd.Parameters.Add("@theUser", SqlDbType.VarChar, 25).Value = username;
    cmd.Parameters.Add("@thePswd", SqlDbType.VarChar, 12).Value = pswd;
```

```
    conn.Open();
    int found = (int) cmd.ExecuteScalar();
    conn.Close();
    return (found >0);
}
```

The query is configured to return an integer that represents the number of rows in the table that match the specified user name and password. Notice the use of typed and sized parameters in the SQL command as a line of defense against possible injection of malicious code. Notice also that the SQL code just shown does not support strong passwords because the = operator doesn't perform case-sensitive comparisons. To make provisions for that, you should rewrite the command as follows:

```
SELECT COUNT(*) FROM users WHERE
    CAST(RTRIM(id) AS VarBinary)=CAST(RTRIM(@theUser) AS VarBinary)
    AND
    CAST(RTRIM(pswd) AS VarBinary)=CAST(RTRIM(@thePswd) AS VarBinary)
```

The *CAST* operator converts the value into its binary representation, while the *RTRIM* operator removes trailing blanks.

Figure 15-13 shows the page of the application once the user has been successfully authenticated.

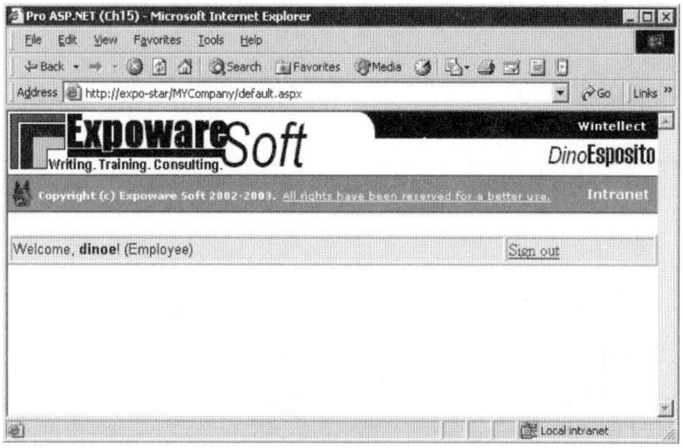

Figure 15-13 The user has been authenticated and his name and role show up in the user interface.

Accessing the Authentication Cookie Programmatically

By default, the authentication cookie lives for 30 minutes, or for whatever timeout value is on the *<forms>* element. The cookie lifetime is independent from the duration of the browser session. By varying the *timeout* attribute, you can change the cookie lifetime for all the pages in the application. To programmatically access the cookie being generated for an authenticated user, you must drop the *RedirectFromLoginPage* method and create your own equivalent method.

```
void CustomRedirectFromLoginPage(string userName, int minutes)
{
    // The false argument means that no persistent cookie is created

    // Get the redirect URL
    string redirectURL;
    redirectURL = FormsAuthentication.GetRedirectUrl(userName, false);

    // Create the cookie
    FormsAuthentication.SetAuthCookie(userName, false);

    // Retrieve the cookie
    string cookieName = FormsAuthentication.FormsCookieName;
    HttpCookie c = Response.Cookies[cookieName];
    c.Expires = DateTime.Now.AddMinutes(minutes);

    // Redirect
    Response.Redirect(redirectURL);
}
```

The method shown in the preceding code performs four basic operations: obtain the redirect URL, create the authentication cookie, retrieve and modify the cookie from the *Response* object, and finally redirect to the original URL. The basic tasks are accomplished through ad hoc methods on the *FormsAuthentication* class. In particular, the *SetAuthCookie* method creates and attaches the cookie to the cookie's collection of the outgoing response. The method is void and does not perform a redirect. To retrieve and programmatically access the cookie, you simply extract it by name from the *Cookies* collection of the *HttpResponse* class.

If you use a Boolean value of *true* as the second argument of the method *RedirectFromLoginPage*, you create a persistent cookie totally unaffected by *timeout* attribute. A *persistent* cookie is simply a cookie with a very long expiration date—50 years. You can't change this trait of the system declaratively. However, you can rewrite the redirect method and put your hands on the physical cookie.

Signing Out

While an explicit sign-in is always required by Web sites that need authentication, an explicit sign-out is less common but legitimate nonetheless. The Forms authentication module provides an explicit method to sign out. The *SignOut* method on the *FormsAuthentication* class takes no argument and resets the authentication cookie. In particular, the *SignOut* method removes the current ticket from the *Cookies* collection of the *HttpResponse* object and replaces it with an empty and expired cookie.

After you call *SignOut*, you might want to redirect the application to another page—for example, the home page or the login page. To do this, you don't have to redirect the browser, but as long as the page is publicly accessible, you can use the more efficient *Server.Transfer* method that we described in Chapter 4, "Working with the Page."

```
void Signout(object sender, EventArgs e)
{
    FormsAuthentication.SignOut();
    Server.Transfer("login.aspx");
}
```

Role-Based Authentication

So far, we have authenticated users by name and haven't put a lot of attention on the building of the actual site. If you have the need to authenticate users, the chances are good that you also need to serve them personalized pages. When it comes to this, there are basically two possibilities: either you implement a profile system and store configuration information for each user, or you define roles and map users to one or more of these categories.

In the case of a profile system, you maintain a lot of profile records that probably need to store user interface items as well as references to functions to enable or disable. While designing the page, you access the profile record for the current user and be sure to find in it any needed information.

If you don't have to maintain user-specific information but simply need to catalog groups of users and maintain profile information on a per-group basis, then roles are a better approach. A role is a name that identifies a set of functions, user interface elements, and permissions that the page grants to each user who plays that role.

Defining Roles

Defining roles is a two-step procedure. First, you define all the possible roles and give each user one or more roles. This association is normally done at the database level. In fact, our sample ProAspNet database of users purposely contains a Role column. Second, you need to figure out a way to retrieve this information at the page level to draw controls properly.

One possible approach entails you loading the table of users in memory when the application starts. After that, whenever you're in the process of designing a page, you access the table from *Application* and read the role based on the authenticated name. In global.asax, you put the following code:

```
<%@ Import Namespace="System.Data" %>
<%@ Import Namespace="System.Data.SqlClient" %>

<script runat="server" language="C#">
void Application_OnStart() {
    string connString = "SERVER=localhost;DATABASE=proaspnet;UID=sa;";
    string cmdText = "SELECT * FROM users";
    SqlDataAdapter data = new SqlDataAdapter(cmdText, connString);

    DataSet ds = new DataSet();
    data.Fill(ds);
    Application["MyData"] = ds;
}

void Application_OnEnd() {
    Application["MyData"] = null;
}
</script>
```

Each page that needs to be personalized based on the user's role will retrieve the role from the table using the user name as the key. The following listing shows how to proceed:

```
string GetRole(string name)
{
    DataSet ds = (DataSet) Application["MyData"];
    DataRow[] rows = ds.Tables[0].Select("ID='" + name + "'");
    if (rows.Length >0)
        return rows[0]["role"].ToString();
    else
        return "";
}
```

The role string can be a comma-separated string indicating more roles. In this case, you use the *IndexOf* method of the role string to check for a particular role. For example:

```
if (role.IndexOf("Employee") != -1)
{
    LinkButton l = new LinkButton();
    l.Text = "Employee task #1";
    RoleEmployee.Controls.Add(l);
    RoleEmployee.Controls.Add(new LiteralControl("<br>"));
    l = new LinkButton();
    l.Text = "Employee task #2";
    RoleEmployee.Controls.Add(l);
}
```

This code generates controls dynamically and binds them to a particular placeholder control specific to the role. Note that this code lacks the event handler for each newly created link button.

Serving Personalized Pages

There might be other ways to design the user interface of a page so that it accommodates controls and links specific to certain users. An alternative to dynamically creating controls is to simply declare on the .aspx file all the controls you plan to use regardless of the role, and then hide all those that do not belong to the current roles. To hide controls, you can use the *Visible* property, which also has the advantage of not generating HTML code for that control.

Figure 15-14 shows a list of links that has been dynamically created to reflect the capabilities of the role of the currently logged user.

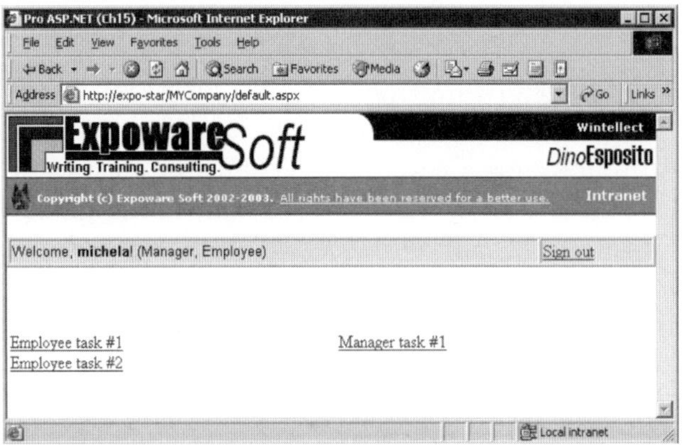

Figure 15-14 A page personalized for a user who acts as employee and manager.

URL Authorization

Whether you need to design pages, or simply authorize access to them, using roles gives you a significant level of flexibility and allows you to work with more coarse-grained entities—groups of users instead of individual users—which can be a determining factor in the success of an application with a high volume of users. In this case, reasoning in terms of roles is more natural and, above all, greatly simplifies the maintenance of the code.

In the previous section, we analyzed the implementation of user-specific pages based on roles. To top off the discussion, let's review how to use roles to authorize access to pages. Earlier in this chapter, we saw that blocking unauthenticated users solves only the first half of the more general problem of controlling access to pages. In other words, the following configuration script guarantees that no anonymous users will ever access a given page; it doesn't guarantee, though, that authenticated users can access it.

```
<authorization>
    <deny users="?" />
</authorization>
```

To limit access to only authorized and authenticated users, we need to implement another layer of code, and URL authorization comes to the rescue.

The *<authorization>* Section

The *<authorization>* tag controls client access to URL resources. It's made of two subtrees—one to allow users, and one to deny access. Both the *<allow>* and *<deny>* child nodes have the same structure and use the same methods to identify callers by name, role, or action.

```
<authorization>
    <allow users="..." roles="..." verbs="..." />
    <deny users="..." roles="..." verbs="..." />
</authorization>
```

The *users* attribute represents a comma-separated list of authenticated users that are granted access to the resources under the jurisdiction of the web.config file. A question mark (?) allows or denies anonymous users; an asterisk (*) allows or denies all users. The Forms authentication module uses this information to block incoming requests after the caller has been successfully identified. The following code grants access only to *dinoe* and *silviac* and denies all other users.

```
<authorization>
    <allow users="dinoe, silviac" />
    <deny users="*" />
</authorization>
```

The *roles* attribute represents a comma-separated list of roles that are granted or denied access to the resources. To use this information for authorization purposes, the Forms module needs to associate an authenticated user with a role. In the previous example, we did it by using the *Application* object. However, in this case we need a more general approach that enables an external tool to retrieve application and user-specific information.

Finally, the *verbs* attribute is a comma-separated list of HTTP methods that can be used to access a resource. Verbs registered to ASP.NET are *GET*, *HEAD*, *POST*, and *DEBUG*.

Note that you can combine *<allow>* and *<deny>* tags in any way or order. For example, you could allow users and deny roles, or allow a few roles and deny all the other users. Bear in mind that the nodes are processed in a top-down fashion, so the first directive is stronger than the ones that follow. In the sample just shown, the users *dinoe* and *silviac* are authorized first, so they are out of the range of users affected by the successive statement that denies access to all users.

Binding Roles and Identity Objects

By the time a user is authenticated, no role information is associated with the identity. There is, however, a function to check whether a given identity plays a certain role. The following code snippet shows how to check whether the current user is in a certain role:

```
if (User.IsInRole("Boss"))
    Response.Write("The user is the boss");
```

The *IsInRole* function is defined on the *GenericPrincipal* class, which represents a generic principal object describing a user. Other principal classes exist for the various authentication modes discussed in this chapter. They are *WindowsPrincipal*, *PassportPrincipal*, and *FormsPrincipal*. Side by side with principals are identity objects, which represent the identity of the user.

To associate a role with an authenticated user, you must create a new principal object, either generic or of the same type of the authentication. After you hold an instance of the new principal, you set the role and then attach it to the context of the request. The best place in which you can do this is the *AuthenticateRequest* event fired by the *Application* object and caught in the global.asax file.

```
void Application_OnAuthenticateRequest()
{
    if (!Request.IsAuthenticated)
        return;
    string roleString = GetRole(User.Identity.Name);
    string[] roles = roleString.Split(',');
    Context.User = new GenericPrincipal(User.Identity, roles);
}
```

The *GetRole* function is used to retrieve the role string for the current user from a database or from an in-memory lookup table. In the most general case, the string is a comma-separated sequence of roles. We transform it into an array of strings and pass the array to the constructor of the *GenericPrincipal* class. We build a new user object with the same identity as the current user but a different set of roles. The new user object replaces the current *User* object in the context of the request.

At this point, the authentication module can check the role of the user against the *<authorization>* section of the local web.config file. For example, a folder whose web.config file contains the following snippet would make its pages accessible only to users belonging to the *Boss* role:

```
<authorization>
    <allow roles="Boss" />
    <deny users="*" />
</authorization>
```

The authentication module uses the *IsInRole* function to authorize access by role. Figure 15-15 shows a user in the Boss role that is allowed access to a protected page.

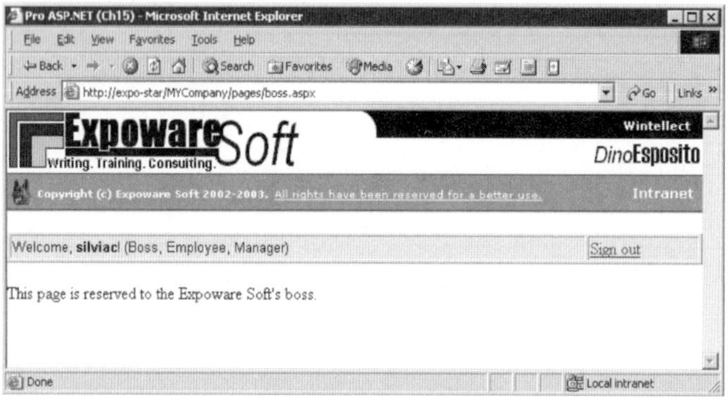

Figure 15-15 Only a user belonging to the Boss group can access this page. Other users not in the role are redirected to the login page.

A signed-in user can jump to protected pages and be authorized as long as the role provides for that. Any direct or indirect access to the page made by users not in the role cause the Web server to redirect the browser to the login page. If you design the user interface of the page to display to the user only the links and controls she needs to use, you significantly reduce the attempts to jump to reserved areas of the Web site and subsequently reduce the chances of overloading the system.

Conclusion

For Web applications, security is a two-headed animal. Securing a Web application entails protecting the Web server against a variety of attacks, including packet and port sniffing, denial of service, and sensitive data stealing. In addition, a secure Web application implements effective policies to prevent illicit access to its pages. ASP.NET provides some built-in layers of code to authenticate and authorize users and actions. Configuring the Web server to limit loopholes and applying patches and hot-fixes constitute another kind of security job that involves system administrators more than developers.

Developers, though, should pay more attention to buffer overruns, malicious SQL injections, and data validation. Interestingly, ASP.NET 1.1 introduces the *ValidateRequest* option in the machine.config file, which is better than nothing but is certainly not the silver bullet to stop all sorts of attacks of the present and the future.

In this chapter, we reviewed some best practices for writing more secure code—that is, code that is less subject to common types of attacks. We applied some of these practices to ASP.NET applications and exploited the built-in features for authentication and authorization. Finally, we spent some time discussing security aspects that involve the configuration of the ASP.NET runtime and the worker process.

In summary, ASP.NET defines three different security contexts at different levels—IIS, the worker process, the HTTP pipeline. The token generated by IIS for the request is passed on to the worker process and contributes to determine the account under which the request is serviced. Once the user has been authenticated, we enter in the realm of the ASP.NET application-specific security. ASP.NET provides three providers for authentication—Windows, Passport, and Forms. Forms authentication is the one that seems more suitable for real-world applications. Authentication is often combined with authorization and file access control. Accessing files on disk is not an easy operation in ASP.NET because of the various security constraints. In the next chapter, we'll tackle file I/O in the ASP.NET.

Resources

- *Writing Secure Code, Second Edition*, Michael Howard and David LeBlanc (Microsoft Press, 2003)
- Essential .NET Security: ASP.NET (*http://www.develop.com/kbrown/book/html/asp.html*)
- ASP.NET Security Chat (*http://msdn.microsoft.com/chats/vstudio/vstudio_091202.asp*)
- Add Custom Info to Authentication Cookies (*http://www.aspnetpro.com/features/2003/05/asp200305jp_f/asp200305jp_f.asp*)
- Building Secure ASP.NET Applications: Authentication, Authorization, and Secure Communication (*http://msdn.microsoft.com/library/en-us/dnnetsec/html/secnetlpMSDN.asp*)

- Forms Authentication with ACL Authorization (*http://www.aspnetpro.com/features/2002/07/asp200207rb_f/asp200207rb_f.asp*)
- Stop SQL Injection Attacks (*http://www.aspnetpro.com/features/2003/02/asp200302jp_f/asp200302jp_f.asp*)
- Authentication in ASP.NET: .NET Security Guidance (*http://msdn.microsoft.com/library/en-us/dnbda/html/authaspdotnet.asp*)
- Authenticate Users with Microsoft Passport (*http://www.aspnetpro.com/features/2002/07/asp200207st_f/asp200207st_f.asp*)

16

Working with the File System

Everything happens to everybody sooner or later if there is time enough.

—George Bernard Shaw

One reason I welcome the .NET Framework is because it reworks, rationalizes, and simplifies a large part of the old, and still underlying, Win32 API. Within the .NET Framework, the whole Win32 API—with very few exceptions—has been redesigned and made available to programmers in an object-oriented fashion. Not only do you have more effective and handy programming tools, but the object orientation of the .NET Framework makes programming easier, and makes code more reusable than ever.

ASP.NET applications are not specifically related to file-system functions; however, many ASP.NET applications happen to work with local files and need to explore the contents of folders. In this chapter, we'll review the main aspects of file-system programming using ASP.NET. By reading on, you'll see how to (finally) manage path names with ad hoc methods and properties, how to extract as much information as possible about files and directories, and how to read and write files, including XML files.

The file system is definitely a huge topic. So let's start by grouping the main categories of functionality in the API that you're most likely to encounter.

File I/O in the .NET Framework

The key namespace for operations and classes that relate to file-system activity is *System.IO*. Within this namespace, you find four logical groups of specialized types. These classes allow programmers to:

- Get information and perform basic operations on files and directories
- Perform string-based manipulation on path names
- Read and write operations on data streams and files
- Be notified of dynamic changes that occur to files and folders in a given directory tree

A bunch of classes let you access each of these features through methods, properties, and fairly easy-to-use enumeration types.

Working with Files

To manage the contents of files and directories, the .NET Framework provides two global static classes, named *File* and *Directory*. To use them, you don't need to create specific instances of the classes. *File* and *Directory* are just the repository of global, type-specific functions that you call to create, copy, delete, move, and open files and directories. All these functions require a file or a directory name to operate. Table 16-1 shows the methods of the *File* class.

Table 16-1 Methods of the *File* Class

Method Name	Description
AppendText	Creates and returns a stream object for the specified file. The stream allows you to append UTF-8 encoded text.
Copy	Copies an existing file to a new file. The destination cannot be a directory name or an existing file.
Create	Creates a new file.
CreateText	Creates (or opens if one exists) a new file for writing UTF-8 text.
Delete	Deletes the file specified.
Exists	Determines whether the specified file exists.
GetAttributes	Gets the attributes of the file.
GetCreationTime	Returns the creation date and time of the specified file.
GetLastAccessTime	Returns the last access date and time for the specified file.

Table 16-1 Methods of the *File* Class

Method Name	Description
GetLastWriteTime	Returns the last write date and time for the specified file.
Move	Moves a specified file to a new location. Also provides the option to specify a new file name.
Open	Opens a file on the specified path.
OpenRead	Opens an existing file for reading.
OpenText	Opens an existing UTF-8 encoded text file for reading.
OpenWrite	Opens an existing file for writing.
SetAttributes	Sets the specified attributes for the given file.
SetCreationTime	Sets the date and time the file was created.
SetLastAccessTime	Sets the date and time the specified file was last accessed.
SetLastWriteTime	Sets the date and time that the specified file was last written.

The path parameter that all methods require can indicate a relative or absolute path. A relative path is interpreted as relative to the current working directory. To obtain the current working directory, you use the *GetCurrentDirectory* method on the *Directory* class. Path names are case insensitive and can also be expressed in the Universal Naming Convention (UNC) format if they contain a server and share name. Writing methods create the specified file if it doesn't exist; if the file does exist, it gets overwritten as long as it isn't marked read-only.

Note Most path names contain a backslash (\) character, which has a special meaning to C-based languages such as C#. In C#, the backslash is used in conjunction with other characters to specify escape sequences, such as the tab character. To indicate that a single backslash character is needed, you can use a double backslash (\\). C# also provides a more elegant solution—prefixing the path name with the @ symbol. The following two path names are equivalent within a C# source file:

```
string path1 = "c:\\path\\file.txt";
string path2 = @"c:\path\file.txt";
```

The @ character tells the C# compiler to consider the following string as literal text and to process it verbatim.

The global *Directory* class exposes static methods for creating, copying, and moving directories and for enumerating their files and subdirectories. Table 16-2 lists the methods of the *Directory* class.

Table 16-2 Methods of the *Directory* Class

Method Name	Description
CreateDirectory	Create all directories and subdirectories as specified by the path.
Delete	Deletes a directory and, optionally, all of its contents.
Exists	Determines whether the given directory exists.
GetCreationTime	Gets the creation date and time of the specified directory.
GetCurrentDirectory	Gets the current working directory of the application.
GetDirectories	Returns an array of strings filled with the names of the child subdirectories of the specified directory.
GetDirectoryRoot	Gets volume and root information for the specified path.
GetFiles	Returns the names of files in the specified directory.
GetFileSystemEntries	Returns an array of strings filled with the names of all files and subdirectories contained in the specified directory.
GetLastAccessTime	Returns the date and time the specified directory was last accessed.
GetLastWriteTime	Returns the date and time the specified directory was last written.
GetLogicalDrives	Returns an array of strings filled with the names of the logical drives found on the computer. Strings have the form "<drive letter>:\".
GetParent	Retrieves the parent directory of the specified path. The directory is returned as a *DirectoryInfo* object.
Move	Moves a directory and its contents to a new location. An exception is thrown if you move the directory to another volume or if a directory with the same name exists.
SetCreationTime	Sets the creation date and time for the specified directory.
SetCurrentDirectory	Sets the application's current working directory.
SetLastAccessTime	Sets the date and time the specified file or directory was last accessed.
SetLastWriteTime	Sets the date and time a directory was last written to.

You should note that the *Delete* method has two overloads. By default, it deletes only empty directories and throws an *IOException* exception if the directory is not empty or marked as read-only. The second overload includes a Boolean argument that, if set to *true*, enables the method to recursively delete the entire directory tree.

```
// Clear a directory tree
Directory.Delete(dirName, true);
```

The global classes *File* and *Directory* provide you with a lot of helpful methods. However, many of those methods are also available on helper data structures that collect information about a particular file or directory. These classes are named *FileInfo* and *DirectoryInfo*.

> **Caution** Each time a method of the *Directory* or *File* class is invoked, a security check is performed on the involved file-system elements. The check is aimed at verifying that the current user has the permission to operate. This might result in a slight performance hit, especially if you use the same files or directories several times. In similar situations, consider using the corresponding instance method of the *FileInfo* or *DirectoryInfo* class. In this case, in fact, the security check would occur only once. In contrast, for single, one-shot use the global classes are preferable because their internal implementation results in more direct code.

The *FileInfo* Class

If you look at the overall functionality, the *FileInfo* class looks very similar to the static *File* class. However, the internal implementation and the programming interface is slightly different. The *FileInfo* class works on a particular file and requires that you first instantiate the class to access methods and properties.

```
FileInfo fi = new FileInfo("info.txt");
```

When you create an instance of the class, you specify a file name, either fully or partially qualified. The file you indicate is checked only for the name consistency and not for existence. The class, in fact, can also be used to create a new file, as shown here:

```
FileInfo fi = new FileInfo("info.txt");
FileStream stream = fi.Create();
```

If the file name you indicate through the class constructor is clearly an unacceptable name, an exception is thrown. Common pitfalls are colons in the middle of the string, invalid characters, blank names, and path and file names that exceed the maximum length. Table 16-3 lists the properties of the *FileInfo* class.

Table 16-3 Properties of the *FileInfo* Class

Property Name	Description
Attributes	Gets or sets the attributes of the current file.
CreationTime	Gets or sets the time when the current file was created.
Directory	Gets a *DirectoryInfo* object representing the parent directory.
DirectoryName	Gets a string representing the directory's full path.
Exists	Gets a value that indicates whether a file with the current name exists.
Extension	Gets the string representing the extension of the file name, including the period (.).
FullName	Gets the full path name of the current file.
LastAccessTime	Gets or sets the time when the current file was last accessed.
LastWriteTime	Gets or sets the time when the current file was last written.
Length	Gets the size in bytes of the current file.
Name	Gets the name of the file.

The methods available for the *FileInfo* class are summarized in Table 16-4. As you can see, methods can be grouped in two categories: methods to perform simple stream-based operations on the contents of the file, and methods to copy or delete the file itself.

Table 16-4 Methods of the *FileInfo* Class

Method	Description
AppendText	Creates and returns a stream object for the current file. The stream allows you to append UTF-8 encoded text.
CopyTo	Copies the current file to a new file.
Create	Creates a file. It's a simple wrapper for the *File.Create* method.
CreateText	Creates a file, and returns a stream object to write text.
Delete	Permanently deletes the current file. Fails if the file is open.
MoveTo	Moves the current file to a new location, providing the option to specify a new file name.
Open	Opens the file with various read/write and sharing privileges.
OpenRead	Creates and returns a read-only stream for the file.

Table 16-4 Methods of the *FileInfo* Class

Method	Description
OpenText	Creates and returns a stream object to read text from the file.
OpenWrite	Creates and returns a write-only stream object that can be used to write text to the file.
Refresh	Refreshes the information that the class can have about the file.
ToString	Returns a string that represents the fully qualified path of the file.

The *FileInfo* class represents a logical wrapper for a system element that is continuously subject to concurrent changes. Can you be sure that the information returned by the *FileInfo* object is always up to date? Properties such as *Exists*, *Length*, *Attributes*, and *LastAccessTime* can easily contain inconsistent values if other users can concurrently access the machine and modify files.

Keeping File Information In Sync

When you create an instance of *FileInfo*, no information is actually read from the file system. As soon as you attempt to read the value of one of the aforementioned critical properties, the class invokes the *Refresh* method, reads the current state of the file, and caches that information. For performance reasons, though, the *FileInfo* class doesn't automatically refresh the state of the object each time properties are read. It does that only the first time one of the properties is read.

To counteract for this built-in behavior, you should call *Refresh* whenever you need to read up-to-date information about the attributes or the length of a file. However, you don't necessarily need to do that all the time. Whether you need it or not mostly depends on the characteristics and requirements of the application.

The *Refresh* method makes a call to a Win32 API function—*FindFirstFile*—and uses the information contained in the returned *WIN32_FIND_DATA* structure to populate the properties of the *FileInfo* class.

Copying and Deleting Files

To make a copy of the current file, you use the *CopyTo* method. *CopyTo* comes with two overloads. Both copy the file to another file, but the first overload disallows overwriting, while the other gives you a chance to control overwriting through a Boolean parameter.

```
FileInfo fi = fi.CopyTo("NewFile.txt", true);
```

Note that both overloads consider the file name argument as a file name. You cannot pass just the name of a directory where you want the file to be copied. If you do so, the directory name will be interpreted as a file name.

The *Delete* method permanently deletes the file from disk. Using this method, there is no way to programmatically send the deleted file to the recycle bin. To accomplish this, you must resort to creating a .NET wrapper for the Win32 API function designed to do that. The API function needed is named *SHFileOperation*.

Attributes of a File

The *Attributes* property indicates the file system attributes of the given file. For an attribute to be read or set, the file must exist and be accessible. To write an attribute value to a file, you must also have write permissions; otherwise, a *FileIOPermissionAccess* exception is raised. The attributes of a file are expressed using the *FileAttributes* enumeration. Table 16-5 lists the values for the *FileAttributes* enumeration.

Table 16-5 The *FileAttributes* Enumeration

Attribute	Description
Archive	Indicates that the file is an archive.
Compressed	The file is compressed.
Device	Not currently used. Reserved for future use.
Directory	The file is a directory.
Encrypted	The file or directory is encrypted. For a file, this means that all data in the file is encrypted. For a directory, this means that encryption is the default for newly created files and directories but all current files are not necessarily encrypted.
Hidden	The file is hidden and doesn't show up in directory listings.
Normal	The file has no other attributes set. Note that this attribute is valid only if used alone.
NotContentIndexed	The file should not be indexed by the system indexing service.
Offline	The file is offline and its data is not immediately available.
ReadOnly	The file is read-only.
ReparsePoint	The file contains a reparse point, which is a block of user-defined data associated with a file or a directory. *Requires an NTFS file system.*
SparseFile	The file is a sparse file. Sparse files are typically large files whose data are mostly zeros. *Requires an NTFS file system.*

Table 16-5 The *FileAttributes* Enumeration

Attribute	Description
System	The file is a system file, part of the operating system, or used exclusively by the operating system.
Temporary	The file is temporary and can be deleted by the application when it is no longer needed.

Note that not all attributes in Table 16-5 are applicable to both files and directories.

> **Note** The *FileAttributes* type is an enumerated type marked with the *[Flags]* attribute.
>
> ```
> [Flags]
> public enum FileAttributes {...}
> ```
>
> The *[Flags]* attribute set for an enumeration type allows programmers to use a bitwise combination of the member values as if the resultant value were itself a native member of the enumeration.

You set attributes on a file by using code as in the following code snippet:

```
// Make the file read-only and hidden
FileInfo fi = new FileInfo("info.txt")
fi.Attributes = FileAttributes.ReadOnly | FileAttributes.Hidden;
```

Note that not all attributes listed in Table 16-5 can be set through the *Attributes* property. For example, the *Encrypted* and *Compressed* attributes can be assigned only if the file is contained in an encrypted folder or is programmatically encrypted. Likewise, a file can be given a reparse point or can be marked as a sparse file only through specific API functions and only on NTFS volumes.

The *FileAttributes* type has another nice feature. When you call the *ToString* method, the class returns a string with a description of the attributes. The returned text consists of a comma-separated string in which each attribute is automatically translated into descriptive text. This following text shows the output of *ToString* when called to operate on a read-only and hidden file:

```
Readonly, Hidden
```

Working with Directories

To manage a directory as an object, you resort to the *DirectoryInfo* class. The class supplies methods and properties to read attributes and performs basic operations on directories. Let's look at it in a bit more detail.

The *DirectoryInfo* Class

The *DirectoryInfo* class represents the instance-based counterpart of the *Directory* class we explored earlier. The class works on a particular directory.

```
DirectoryInfo di = new DirectoryInfo(@"c:\");
```

To create an instance of the class, you specify a fully qualified path name. Just as for *FileInfo*, the path name is checked for consistency but not for existence. Note that the path name can also be a file name or a UNC name. If you create a *DirectoryInfo* object passing a file name, the directory that contains the specified file will be considered for use. Table 16-6 shows the properties available with the *DirectoryInfo* class.

Table 16-6 Properties of the *DirectoryInfo* Class

Property	Description
Attributes	Gets or sets the attributes of the current directory
CreationTime	Gets or sets the creation time of the current directory
Exists	Gets whether the directory exists
Extension	Gets the extension (if any) in the directory name
FullName	Gets the full path of the directory
LastAccessTime	Gets or sets the time when the current directory was last accessed
LastWriteTime	Gets or sets the time when the current directory was last written
Name	Gets the name of the directory bound to this object
Parent	Gets the parent of the directory bound to this object
Root	Gets the root portion of the directory path

Note that the *Name* property of the file and directory classes is read-only and can't be used to rename the corresponding file system's element.

The methods you can use in the *DirectoryInfo* class are listed in Table 16-7.

Table 16-7 Methods of the *DirectoryInfo* Class

Method Name	Description
Create	Creates a directory. It's a simple wrapper for the *Directory.Create* method.
CreateSubdirectory	Creates a subdirectory on the specified path. The path can be relative to this instance of the *DirectoryInfo* class.
Delete	Deletes the directory.
GetDirectories	Returns an array of *DirectoryInfo* objects, each pointing to a subdirectory of the current directory.
GetFiles	Returns an array of *FileInfo* objects, each pointing to a file contained in the current directory.
GetFileSystemInfos	Retrieves an array of *FileSystemInfo* objects representing all the files and subdirectories in the current directory.
MoveTo	Moves a directory and all of its contents to a new path.
Refresh	Refreshes the state of the *DirectoryInfo* object.

The method *GetFileSystemInfos* returns an array of objects, each pointing to a file or a subdirectory contained in the directory bound to the current *DirectoryInfo* object. Unlike the *GetDirectories* and *GetFiles* methods, which simply return the names of subdirectories and files as plain strings, *GetFileSystemInfos* return a strongly typed object for each entry—either *DirectoryInfo* or *FileInfo*. The return type of the method is an array of *FileSystemInfo* objects.

```
public FileSystemInfo[] GetFileSystemInfos()
```

FileSystemInfo is the base class for both *FileInfo* and *DirectoryInfo*. *GetFileSystemInfos* has an overloaded version that can accept a string with search criteria.

Listing the Contents of a Directory

Let's see how to use the *FileInfo* and *DirectoryInfo* classes to write a small application that creates a navigation mechanism across Web folders. Figure 16-1 shows the page in action.

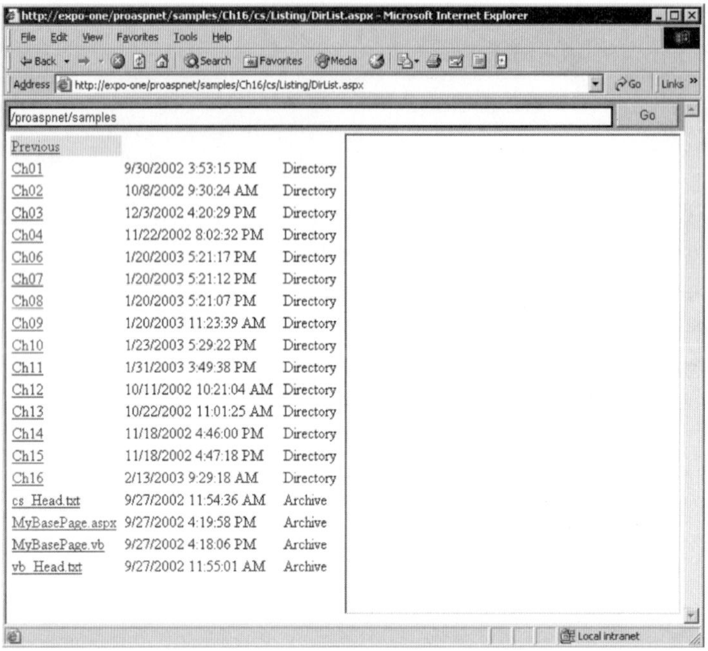

Figure 16-1 An ASP.NET application that navigates through Web folders.

The user interface consists of a text box, in which the user enters the virtual path to search in, and a button to start the search. The results are displayed using a *Repeater* control within a scrollable area. (We're reusing some of the tricks we've learned in Chapter 9, "ASP.NET Iterative Controls.") Finally, an inline frame is used to display the contents of listed .aspx pages.

When the user clicks on the Go button, the following code runs and displays all the files and subdirectories contained in the physical folder that maps to the given virtual path.

```
public void OnGo(object sender, EventArgs e) {
    // Reset the current URL
    SetFullUrl("");

    // Command to list the contents of the directory
    string url = folderName.Text;
    ListDirectory(url);
}
```

The *ListDirectory* method retrieves all the information available using the *GetFileSystemInfos* method. As mentioned, the *GetFileSystemInfos* method returns an array of *FileSystemInfo* objects. The array is then bound to the *Repeater*.

```
private void ListDirectory(string url) {
    // Build an absolute URL using the cached "current URL"
    string tmp = GetFullUrl(url);

    // Refresh the address bar
    folderName.Text = tmp;

    // Set this URL as the new "current URL"
    SetFullUrl(tmp);

    // Reset the contents of the frame (in case a page was displayed)
    SetView(null);

    // Obtain a physical path from the URL and instantiate the
    // DirectoryInfo class
    string path = Server.MapPath(tmp);
    DirectoryInfo di = new DirectoryInfo(path);

    // Bind to data
    Listing.DataSource = di.GetFileSystemInfos();
    Listing.DataBind();
}
```

Any public property on the *FileSystemInfo* object can be accessed through *DataBinder.Eval* and used in the resulting user interface. The following code snippet shows the *<ItemTemplate>* template of the *Repeater*.

```
<ItemTemplate>
<tr>
    <td><asp:linkbutton runat="server"
        commandname='<%# GetCommandName(Container.DataItem) %>'
        commandargument='<%# DataBinder.Eval(Container.DataItem, "Name")
        %>'
        >
            <%# DataBinder.Eval(Container.DataItem, "Name") %>
        </asp:linkbutton></td>
    <td><%# DataBinder.Eval(Container.DataItem, "LastWriteTime") %></td>
    <td><%# DataBinder.Eval(Container.DataItem, "Attributes") %></td>
</tr>
</ItemTemplate>
```

The template generates a link button for each selected file or directory. Directories are given a command name of *SELECT*, whereas files are associated with the *OPEN* command. When the user clicks on any of them, the page responds by either recursively running the *ListDirectory* method or updating the frame view. The first option is chosen when the user clicks on a directory; the second option is reserved for when the click hits an .aspx page. The following code illustrates the process that updates the user interface of the application.

```
string GetCommandName(object fsInfo) {
    FileSystemInfo fsi = (FileSystemInfo) fsInfo;
    if (fsi is DirectoryInfo)
        return "Select";
    else
        return "Open";
}

void ItemCommand(object sender, RepeaterCommandEventArgs e) {
    switch(e.CommandName) {
        case "Select":
            ListDirectory(e.CommandArgument.ToString());
            break;
        case "Open":
            SetView(GetFullUrl(e.CommandArgument.ToString()));
            break;
    }
    return;
}

void SetView(string url) {
    if (url == null)
        view.Attributes["src"] = "about:blank";
    else
        view.Attributes["src"] = url;
}
```

Filtering the Contents of a Directory

The *GetFileSystemInfos* method accepts a filter string by means of which you set some criteria. The filter string can contain commonly used wild-card characters such as *?* and ***. The *?* character is a placeholder for any individual character, while *** represents any string of one or more characters. Characters other than the wild-card specifiers just represent themselves. The following statement demonstrates how to scan a given directory searching for text files only:

```
foreach(FileSystemInfo fsi in di.GetFileSystemInfos("*.txt"))
{
    ⋮
}
```

A bit more problematic is selecting all files that belong to one group or another. Likewise, there's no direct way to obtain all directories plus all the files that match certain criteria. In similar cases, you must query each result set individually and then combine them in a single array of *FileSystemInfo* objects. The following code snippet shows how to select all the subdirectories and all the .aspx pages in a given folder:

```
FileSystemInfo fsiDirs = (FileSystemInfo[]) di.GetSubdirectories();
FileSystemInfo fsiAspx = (FileSystemInfo[]) di.GetFiles(".aspx");
```

You can fuse the two arrays together using the methods of the *Array* class.

Working with Path Names

Although path names are nothing more than strings, it's widely agreed that they deserve their own tailor-made set of functions for easier and handy manipulation. This old dream of programmers finally came true with the .NET Framework, particularly thanks to the *Path* class. The *Path* type provides programmers with the unprecedented ability to perform operations on instances of a string class that contain file or directory path information. *Path* is a single-instance class that contains only static methods. A path can contain either absolute or relative location information for a given file or folder. If the information about the location is incomplete and partial, the class completes it using the current location, if applicable.

The Programming Interface of the *Path* Class

The members of the *Path* class let you perform, quickly and effectively, everyday operations such as determining whether a given file name has a certain extension, changing only the extension and leaving the remainder of the path intact, combining partial path strings into one valid path name, and more. The *Path* class doesn't work in conjunction with the operating system and should be simply viewed as a highly specialized string manipulation class.

No members of the class ever interact with the file system to verify the correctness of a file name. From this point of view, you simply manipulate a string of text. So even though you successfully verified that a fully qualified file name has a given extension, nothing could give you the certainty that the file really exists. Likewise, even though you can combine two strings to get a valid directory name, that would not be sufficient to actually create that new directory. On the other hand, the members of the *Path* class are smart enough to throw an exception if they detect that a path string contains invalid characters. Table 16-8 summarizes the public fields of the class.

Table 16-8 Public Fields of the *Path* Class

Property Name	Description
AltDirectorySeparatorChar	The alternate character used to separate directory levels in a path. It is the forward slash (/) in Windows.
DirectorySeparatorChar	The platform-specific character used to separate directory levels in a path. It is the backslash (\) in Windows.
InvalidPathChars	Array of characters that are not permitted in a path string on the current platform.
PathSeparator	The character used to separate path strings in environment variables. It is the semicolon (;) in Windows.
VolumeSeparatorChar	The character used to separate a volume from the remainder of the path. It is the colon (:) in Windows.

Table 16-9, on the other hand, lists the methods of the *Path* class.

Table 16-9 Methods of the *Path* Class

Method Name	Description
ChangeExtension	Changes the extension of the specified path string.
Combine	Concatenates two path strings together.
GetDirectoryName	Extracts and returns the directory information for the specified path string.
GetExtension	Returns the extension of the specified path string.
GetFileName	Returns the file name and extension of the specified path string.
GetFileNameWithoutExtension	Returns the file name of the specified path string without the extension.
GetFullPath	Returns the absolute path for the specified path string.
GetPathRoot	Returns the root directory for the specified path.
GetTempFileName	Returns a unique temporary file name, and creates a zero-byte file by that name on disk.
GetTempPath	Returns the path of the temporary folder.
HasExtension	Determines whether the specified path string includes an extension.
IsPathRooted	Returns a value that indicates whether the specified path string contains an absolute path.

It's interesting to note that any call to *GetTempFileName* promptly results in a zero-length file actually being created on disk, and specifically in the user's temporary folder. This is the only case in which the *Path* class happens to interact with the operating system.

Combining Paths

A couple of considerations apply to the behavior of the *Combine* method, whose prototype is as follows:

```
public static string Combine(string path1, string path2)
```

If one of the specified arguments is an empty string, the method returns the other argument. If any of the arguments contains an absolute path, the first argument with an absolute path is returned. If any of the two arguments is a null string, the *ArgumentNullException* exception is thrown. Generally, the exception is thrown whenever a member of the *Path* class happens to work with a null argument.

In addition, if the first argument does not terminate with a valid separator, the character is appended to it before the concatenation takes place. A valid separator is either the character that *DirectorySeparatorChar* indicates or the character returned by *AltDirectorySeparatorChar*. In all other cases, the *Combine* method fuses the two strings together. However, under some circumstances (such as spaces and UNC paths in the second argument), the *Combine* method does not throw any exception, but the result should be programmatically verified prior to making use of it.

> **Note** Although useful and effective, the *Path* class doesn't seem to have a method to verify whether a given path is a URL. A similar method exists in Win32 API and in particular in the Shell Lightweight API (shlwapi.dll). The function is named *PathIsURL* and has the following prototype:
>
> ```
> bool PathIsURL(string path)
> ```
>
> To make use of it in managed code, you must resort to the P/Invoke platform and connect to the DLL from within managed code.

Readers and Writers

In the .NET Framework, the classes in the *System.IO* namespace provide for both synchronous and asynchronous operations (for example, reading and writing) on two distinct categories of data: streams and files. A file is an ordered and named collection of bytes and is persistently stored to a disk. A stream represents a block of bytes that is read from and written to a data store, which can be based on a variety of storage media. So a stream is a kind of superset of a file, or, if you prefer, a stream is just a file that can be saved to a variety of storage media, including memory. To work with streams, the .NET Framework defines reader and writer classes.

Readers and writers are generic software components that provide a common programming interface for both synchronous and asynchronous operations on streams and files. Readers and writers work in isolated compartments in the sense that readers work in a read-only fashion while writers operate in writing only. A reader works in much the same way as a client-side database cursor. The underlying stream is seen as a logical sequence of units of information whose size and layout depend on the particular reader. The reader moves through the data in a read-only, forward-only way. Just as a database cursor reads one record at a time and stores the content in some internal data structure, a reader working on a disk file stream would consider as its own atomic unit of information the single byte, whereas a text reader would perhaps specialize in extracting one row of text at a time.

To work with streams, the .NET Framework defines several flavors of reader and writer classes. Figure 16-2 shows how each class relates to the others.

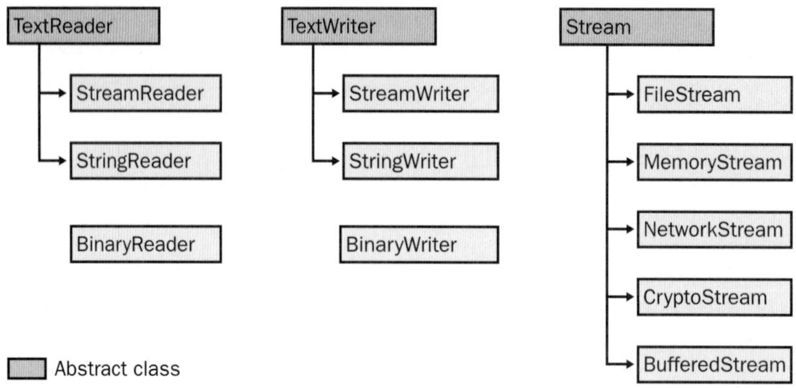

Figure 16-2 Various reader, writer, and stream classes.

The base classes are *TextReader*, *TextWriter*, *BinaryReader*, *BinaryWriter*, and *Stream*. *TextReader*, *TextWriter*, and *Stream* are marked abstract and cannot be directly instantiated in code. You can use abstract classes, though, to reference living instances of derived classes.

Working with Streams

The *Stream* class supports three basic operations: reading, writing, and seeking. Reading and writing operations entail transferring data from a stream into a data structure and vice versa. Seeking consists of querying and modifying the current position within the stream of data.

The .NET Framework provides a number of predefined stream classes, including *FileStream*, *MemoryStream*, and the fairly interesting *CryptoStream*, which automatically encrypts and decrypts data as you write or read. As you can see, the .NET Framework lacks a compressed stream class, but some third-party vendors already provide that. Overall, the methods and properties of the *Stream* base class are designed for a byte I/O. The *Read* and *Write* methods that you find in any derived class have the following signatures:

```
public abstract int Read(
    in byte[] buffer,
    int offset,
    int count
);
public abstract void Write(
    byte[] buffer,
    int offset,
    int count
);
```

A stream class works on top of a back-end storage medium, such as a disk or memory. Each different storage medium implements its own stream as an implementation of the *Stream* class. Each stream type reads and writes bytes from and to its given backing store. The constructors of a *Stream* class have the parameters necessary to connect the stream to the backing store. For example, *FileStream* has constructors that specify a path, whereas the *CryptoStream* class requires information about the cryptographic transformation to apply.

An interesting aspect of .NET streams is that they can be composed and piled up. Base streams can be attached to one or more pass-through streams that provide the desired functionality. Base streams are those which provide connectivity with the physical data source; pass-through streams are those which connect to an existing stream, modify data, and expose the new contents as a stream. A typical example of a pass-through stream is *CryptoStream*. You can't create a *CryptoStream* directly from a file; however, you can encrypt the contents of any object exposed as a stream. While composing streams, you end up building a chain of objects at the end of which there's the calling application. For the application's ease, a reader or writer can be attached to the end of the chain so that the desired types can be read or written more easily. The overall architecture is depicted in Figure 16-3.

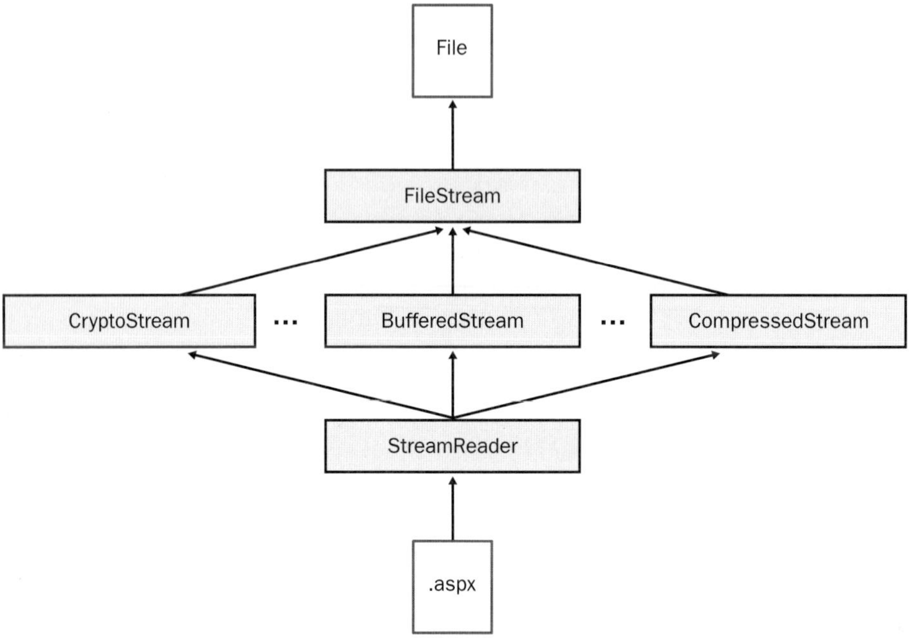

Figure 16-3 Composing streams to connect an ASP.NET page with a target file.

Working with Readers and Writers

The *TextReader* and *TextWriter* classes are designed to be the base classes for specialized readers and writers. In particular, they are designed for character I/O and, especially, to handle Unicode characters. For example, using the *TextReader* class, you can read an entire line of text in a single shot. The method that does this is *ReadLine*. A line of characters is intended as the sequence that flows from the current position to the end of the line. The end of the line is marked by a carriage return (0x000d), a line feed (0x000a), or the physical end of stream.

Along with *ReadLine*, the *TextReader* class provides a couple of more specialized methods for reading. They are *ReadBlock* and *ReadToEnd*. *ReadBlock* reads a given number of characters from the current stream and writes them to the specified buffer beginning at the given index. *ReadToEnd*, on the other hand, just reads from the current position to the end of the stream. To write text, you use either the *Write* method of the *TextWriter* class or the more specialized, and extremely handy, *WriteLine* method.

Specialized Readers and Writers

The *TextReader* and *TextWriter* classes act as the foundation for more specialized readers and writers. The *StreamReader* and *StreamWriter* classes are just examples of classes that provide a unified programming interface to read and write the contents of a stream. The .NET Framework also provides the *StringReader* and *StringWriter* classes to let you read and write characters on strings.

The .NET Framework uses the concept of reader and writer classes extensively. So you find ad hoc writer classes such as *HttpWriter* and *HtmlWriter*, which write bytes from ASP.NET pages to the browser and prepare HTML pages, respectively. Other ad hoc reader and writer classes exist throughout the framework, although they have a different programming interface and do not directly inherit from *TextReader* or *TextWriter*. In this category you find a pair of classes for binary data management: *BinaryReader* and *BinaryWriter*. These classes read and write primitive data types as binary values in the specified encoding. Other reader and writer classes can be found in particular areas of the framework, including XML (*XmlReader* and *XmlWriter*) and ADO.NET (*DataReader*).

We've already met ADO.NET data readers in Chapter 5, "The ADO.NET Object Model." We'll discuss XML readers and writers with practical examples later in this chapter.

Reading Local Files

In the .NET Framework, all files can be read and written only through streams. You transform the contents of a file into a stream by using the *FileStream* class. The following code shows how to open a file for reading:

```
FileStream fs = new FileStream(filename, FileMode.Open, FileAccess.Read);
```

Streams supply a rather low-level programming interface which, although functionally effective, is not always an appropriate interface for classes that need to perform more high-level operations such as reading the entire content or an entire line. For this reason, the .NET Framework provides you with reader classes. In particular, two types of file readers are available—text readers and binary readers.

To manipulate the contents of a file as a binary stream, you just pass the file stream object down to a specialized reader object that knows how to handle it.

```
BinaryReader bin = new BinaryReader(fs);
```

If you want to process the file's contents in a text-based way, you can use the *StreamReader* class. Note that unlike *BinaryReader*, the *StreamReader* class can be directly instantiated on a file, thus saving one step of programming. So if your goal is manipulating text files, you might find the following code more compact:

```
StreamReader reader = new StreamReader(fileName);
```

Finally, you should note that all the *File* and *FileInfo* methods that allow for data manipulation return stream objects. This code snippet shows how to get a stream reader directly from a *FileInfo* object using the *OpenText* method.

```
FileInfo fi = new FileInfo(fileName);
StreamReader reader = fi.OpenText();
```

The *StreamReader* Class

The *StreamReader* class inherits from *TextReader* and is designed for character input in a particular encoding scheme. You use it to read lines of information from a text file. *StreamReader* defaults to UTF-8 encoding unless otherwise specified. UTF-8 has the advantage of managing Unicode characters, which allows it to provide consistent results on localized versions of the operating system. The source that *StreamReader* works on doesn't have to be a disk file; it can be any store that supports access via streams.

Streams can be null objects. A quick test to see whether you're using a reader built around a null stream involves the static *Null* field.

```
StreamReader reader = new StreamReader(fileName);
if (!reader.Equals(StreamReader.Null)) {
    reader.BaseStream.Seek(0, SeekOrigin.Begin);
    string text = reader.ReadToEnd();
    ⋮
}
reader.Close();
```

The *StreamReader* class defines several constructors and can be created on top of a disk file or an existing stream. Other parameters you can specify are the character encoding, byte-order mark, and buffer size.

> **Note** When instantiating the *StreamReader* class, you can indicate whether to look for byte-order marks at the beginning of the file. The class automatically recognizes UTF-8, little-endian Unicode, and big-endian Unicode text if the file starts with the appropriate byte-order marks. Otherwise, the user-provided encoding is used.

The *StreamReader* class exposes only two properties—*BaseStream* and *CurrentEncoding*. The *BaseStream* property returns the underlying stream the class is working on; the *CurrentEncoding* property gets the current character encoding being used.

Accessing the Underlying Stream

The programming interface of the *StreamReader* class doesn't include any method to seek data or perform position-based reading. Similar functions are, instead, available on the underlying stream object. You use the method on the *BaseStream* object to move the internal pointer to a particular position.

```
// Skip the first 14 bytes
StreamReader reader = new StreamReader(fileName);
reader.BaseStream.Seek(14, SeekOrigin.Begin);
```

Note that reading methods on the *StreamReader* class doesn't update the pointer on the stream class. For this reason, the position of the underlying stream normally doesn't match the *StreamReader* position. The *StreamReader* maintains the current position internally, but this information is not made public and can be reset using the *DiscardBufferedData* method. To keep the pointers in sync, you must manually move the base stream pointer ahead after each reading. The following code snippet shows how to proceed:

```
StreamReader reader = new StreamReader(fileName);

// Set the file pointer to the beginning
reader.BaseStream.Seek(0, SeekOrigin.Begin);
reader.BaseStream.Position = 0;

// Read one character at a time
char[] buffer = new char[1];
while(reader.BaseStream.Position < reader.BaseStream.Length) {
    reader.Read(buffer, 0, 1);
    reader.BaseStream.Position ++;
    DoSomething(buffer[0].ToString());
}

// Reset and close
reader.DiscardBufferedData();
reader.Close();
```

If you continue reading from the reader after a call to *DiscardBufferedData* is made, you read back from the origin of the stream.

Character Encoding

The *CurrentEncoding* property returns the current character encoding the reader is using. The encoding scheme is expressed through an object that inherits from the *Encoding* class. Characters are abstract entities that can be represented using many different character schemes or code pages. An encoding scheme is a way of mapping source characters to an effective representation that the application understands.

In the .NET Framework, specifically in the *System.Text* namespace, the encoding classes that are defined are shown in Table 16-10.

Table 16-10 Encoding Schemes in the .NET Framework

Class	Description
ASCIIEncoding	Encodes Unicode characters as single 7-bit ASCII characters. Supports character values between 0 and 127.
UnicodeEncoding	Encodes each Unicode character as two consecutive bytes (16-bit). Both little-endian (code page 1200) and big-endian (code page 1201) byte orders are supported. Also known as UTF-16.
UTF7Encoding	Encodes Unicode characters using the UCS Transformation Format, 7-bit form (UTF-7) encoding. Supports all Unicode character values, and can also be accessed as code page 65000.
UTF8Encoding	Encodes Unicode characters using the UTF-8 encoding. Supports all Unicode character values, and can also be accessed as code page 65001.

If the *StreamReader* object is created using one of the constructors with the byte-order detection option turned on, the actual encoding scheme is determined only the first time you read from the stream. In this case, the encoding class you pass to the constructor is considered as a default scheme and can be different from the actual encoding detected looking at the first three bytes in the stream.

Methods of the *StreamReader* Class

The methods of the *StreamReader* class are detailed in Table 16-11.

Table 16-11 Methods of the *StreamReader* Class

Method	Description
Close	Closes the *StreamReader* object, and releases any system resources associated with the reader.
DiscardBufferedData	Resets all internal variables that track the current position and buffered data.
Peek	Reads the next available character, but does not consume it. The next reading operation returns only this character. The method acts as a preview and always forward-checks one character.
Read	Reads the next character or next set of characters from the input stream.
ReadBlock	Reads up to the specified maximum of characters from the current stream and writes the data to buffer, beginning at a given index.
ReadLine	Reads a line of characters from the current stream, and returns the data as a string.
ReadToEnd	Reads characters from the current position to the end of the stream. Returns a string.

The preview capabilities of the *Peek* method can be used to control the loop that is typically used to scan a stream.

```
// Loop until the end of the stream is reached
while (reader.Peek() > -1) {
    ⋮
}
```

The *Peek* method returns 1 if there's nothing else to read or if the stream does not support seeking.

Reading a Text File

If an ASP.NET application deals with a text file, chances are good that the file contains configuration data. As we saw in Chapter 12, "Configuration and Deployment," ASP.NET touts the use of .config files with an XML syntax. However, many developers feel quite comfortable with probably less expressive but terrifically handy INI files. The typical syntax of an INI file is as follows:

```
Server=http://localhost
Machine=expo-one
Options=Debug, Trace
```

Introduced with Windows 3.x, the INI syntax has never changed over time and has resisted change in spite of the invention of the registry and then XML configuration stores. In the simplest case, an INI file consists of any number of lines of text expressed in the form of *key=value*.

As we mentioned in Chapter 12, a similar collection of key/value pairs can be easily managed using the *AppSettingsReader* class and a .config file. However, with the tools available in the .NET Framework, even the old-fashioned, but still effective, pure INI approach becomes straightforward to implement. Let's see how to read from an INI-like file and build a key/value collection to display in a *DataGrid* control.

```
void Page_Load(object sender, EventArgs e)
{
    // File to process
    string path = Server.MapPath(@"info.txt");

    // Read and caches the contents
    StreamReader reader = new StreamReader(path);
    string text = reader.ReadToEnd();
    reader.Close();

    // Split data and builds a name/value collection
    string[] tokens = text.Split('\n');
    NameValueCollection coll = new NameValueCollection();
    foreach(string s in tokens) {
        string[] parts = s.Split('=');
        coll.Add(parts[0], parts[1]);
    }

    // Print data
    grid.DataSource = coll;
    grid.DataBind();
}
```

The contents of the file are read in a single shot thanks to the *ReadToEnd* method and cached in a local string variable. By using the *Split* method of the *String* class, we can tokenize the original string in individual substrings by using the specified character as the separator. We use the newline (*\n*) character and obtain an array of strings, each of which represents a line of text. (Note that you can obtain the same result by reading one line at a time, but this would probably lock the file for a longer time.)

The next step consists in calling *Split* on each line of text using the equal (=) symbol. The two parts of the string—left and right of the = symbol—are copied into a newly created *NameValueCollection* object as the key and the value, respectively. Finally, the collection is bound to a *DataGrid* control for display.

Binding the Contents of a File to a *DataGrid*

If automatically bound, a *DataGrid* control displays only the Name column of a name/value collection. To display it correctly, use a couple of templated columns.

```
<asp:datagrid runat="server" id="grid" autogeneratecolumns="false">
    <headerstyle font-bold="true" />
    <columns>
        <asp:templatecolumn runat="server" headertext="Key">
            <itemtemplate>
                <%# Container.DataItem %>
            </itemtemplate>
        </asp:templatecolumn>

        <asp:templatecolumn runat="server" headertext="Value">
            <itemtemplate>
                <%# ExtractData(Container.DataItem) %>
            </itemtemplate>
        </asp:templatecolumn>
    </columns>
</asp:datagrid>
```

The *Container.DataItem* expression evaluates to a string—specifically, the string that represents the key. To extract the physical data, you must access the key within the collection, as shown here:

```
string ExtractData(object dataItem) {
    // Get the collection object
    NameValueCollection coll = (NameValueCollection) grid.DataSource;

    // Get the text to display
    string displayText = coll[dataItem.ToString()];

    // Map the contents to a custom enum type
    if ((string) dataItem == "Options") {
        MyOptions opt;
        opt = (MyOptions) Enum.Parse(typeof(MyOptions), displayText);
        displayText = String.Format("{0} ({1})", displayText, (int) opt);
    }

    return displayText;
}
```

The collection is just what the *DataSource* property of the *DataGrid* returns. Once you hold the collection, getting the value is a child's game. The preceding code also demonstrates a very nice feature about enumeration and the persistence of the enumeration values.

Suppose you need to configure some options for your application. In practice, you never use strings to indicate features; instead, you use numbers. Subsequently, when you persist those settings, only numbers are saved to a file. This wouldn't be a big deal except for the fact that it makes it harder for administrators and developers to edit settings offline. Look at the *Options* element in the sample file we just discussed—wouldn't it be more confusing if we used, say, 3 instead of descriptive and human-readable text like "Debug, Trace"? How can you translate that easily editable string into a number? Let's start by defining a custom enumeration type named *MyOptions*.

```
[Flags]
enum MyOptions {
    Debug = 1,
    Trace = 2
}
```

Once the enumeration is defined, you can have the static *Enum.Parse* method parse any string trying to match it to a combination of values in the enumeration. A comma-separated list of strings that represent elements of the enumeration is automatically recognized as the AND of the corresponding values. *Enum.Parse* returns an object that evaluates to an element (or a combination of elements) in the enumeration. Figure 16-4 shows the output of the sample page we have built so far.

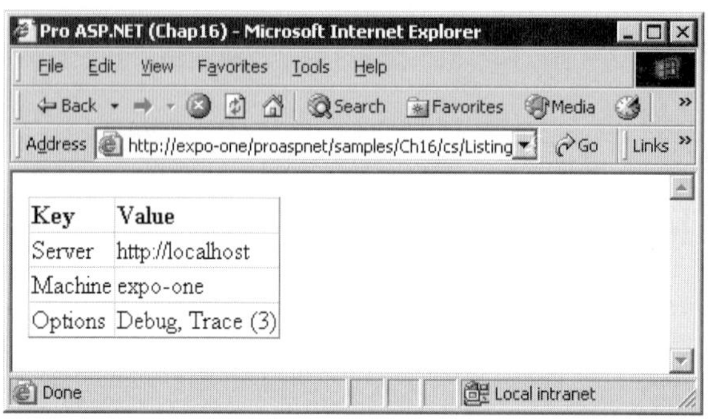

Figure 16-4 The contents of a text file that has been read, copied into a collection, and displayed using a *DataGrid* control.

The *BinaryReader* Class

A binary reader works by reading primitive data types from a stream with a specific encoding. The default encoding is UTF-8. The set of methods includes *Read*, *PeekChar*, and a long list of *ReadXxx* methods specialized to extract data of the given type. The generic *Read* method works by extracting only one character from the stream and moving the internal pointer ahead according to the current encoding.

Reading Binary Information

Binary readers are ideal for extracting information out of a binary file. The following code snippet shows how to read width, height, and color depth for a .bmp file.

```
void DisplayBmpInfo(string bmpFile) {
    FileStream fs = new FileStream(bmpFile, FileMode.Open,
        FileAccess.Read);
    BinaryReader reader = new BinaryReader(fs);

    // Skip the file header (14 bytes)
    reader.ReadBytes(14);

    // Skip the structure's size
    reader.ReadUInt32();

    // Read width and height of the BMP file
    int width = reader.ReadInt32();
    int height = reader.ReadInt32();

    // Skip info about BMP planes of colors
    Int16 planes = reader.ReadInt16();

    // Read color depth (bit per pixel)
    Int16 bitsPerPixel = reader.ReadInt16();

    // Clean-up
    reader.Close();
    fs.Close();

    // Print information
    Response.Write(width + " x " + height + " x " + bitsPerPixel * planes);
}
```

If you want to skip over the specified number of bytes, you just indicate the number of bytes explicitly.

```
reader.ReadBytes(14);
```

However, this is not always a smart approach. If you know what data structure the bytes represent, you can just skip the size of the type. For example, the file header of a .bmp file is given by a structure named *BITMAPFILEHEADER*, which counts a total of 14 bytes: three *UInt16* and two *UInt32*. How can you indicate the number of bytes in a parametric way?

Skipping Bytes While Reading

You cannot rely on handy functions such as *sizeof* (in C#) or *Len* (in Visual Basic) to indicate the number of bytes to skip in a parametric way. The *sizeof* function, in particular, works only on unmanaged resources. A more viable alternative would be to use the *Marshal.SizeOf* function, which works on a type or an object. In any case, you must import the type declaration straight from the Win32 API.

```
// Must import System.Runtime.InteropServices

// Skip the BITMAPFILEHEADER BMP's file header
reader.ReadBytes(Marshal.SizeOf(typeof(BITMAPFILEHEADER)));
```

When imported in the managed world, the *BITMAPFILEHEADER* structure looks like the following class:

```
[StructLayout(LayoutKind.Sequential, Pack=1)]
public class BITMAPFILEHEADER {
    public UInt16 bfType;
    public UInt32 bfSize;
    public UInt16 bfReserved1;
    public UInt16 bfReserved2;
    public UInt32 bfOffBits;
}
```

Pay attention to the role of the *Pack* attribute, which is set to 8 by default. The attribute determines the size of the minimum block of memory that is allocated for the structure. In other words, the size of the class can only be a multiple of the *Pack* value. It goes without saying that setting *Pack* to 1 is the only way to get an exact size with a byte precision.

More important than how you get the size to skip, though, is the fact that as long as you use a *ReadXxx* method, the bytes are read and not skipped. To really jump over the specified number of bytes, you must resort to the methods of the underlying stream object. You get the current stream by using the *BaseStream* property. Here is how you skip the header of a .bmp file:

```
int bytesToSkip = Marshal.SizeOf(typeof(BITMAPFILEHEADER));
reader.BaseStream.Seek(bytesToSkip, SeekOrigin.Begin);
```

You can also choose to move a given offset from the bottom of the stream or from the current position. The following code shows how to actually skip a short integer:

```
reader.BaseStream.Seek(2, SeekOrigin.Current);
```

Finally, if you need to read a complex structure from a binary stream, you must do that sequentially on a per-field basis.

Writing Local Files

All reader classes have a writing counterpart that works according to the same model. To write a text file, you use the *StreamWriter* class. To create a binary file, you use the *BinaryWriter* class. Writing local files is a bit more problematic than just reading in ASP.NET because of the default security model. Personally, I consider the need to create a local file as an alarm bell, which prompts me to think about possible alternatives. Let's quickly review a couple of common scenarios.

If you need to persist user settings, you're better off using a database, which provides more speed and flexibility in terms of search and manipulation. As for global settings, they are a type of information individual users should never access and modify. ASP.NET applications can be programmatically driven by a configuration file, but you will likely edit that file offline and not through an ASP.NET front-end.

The *StreamWriter* Class

The *StreamWriter* class implements a text writer and outputs characters to a stream in a particular encoding. The default encoding is UTF-8. The constructor of the class lets you specify the output stream as a *Stream* object or a file name. If you indicate a file name, you're also given a chance to specify whether you want to write it from scratch or just append text.

The Programming Interface of the *StreamWriter* Class

Table 16-12 details the properties available on the *StreamWriter* class.

Table 16-12 Properties of a *StreamWriter*

Property	Description
AutoFlush	Gets or sets whether the writer will flush its buffer to the underlying stream after every call to a writing method.
BaseStream	Gets the underlying stream that interfaces with a backing store.
Encoding	Gets the encoding scheme in which the output is written.
FormatProvider	Gets an object that controls formatting for the text according to a specific culture.
NewLine	Gets or sets the line terminator string used by the writer. The default string is a carriage return followed by a line feed (*\r\n*).

When *AutoFlush* is set to *true*, only the data is flushed from the buffer to the stream. The encoder state is retained so that it can encode the next block of characters correctly. Especially when working with UTF-8 and UTF-7 encodings, the writer might happen to manage characters that can only be encoded when having adjacent characters available. The *AutoFlush* state is checked at the bottom of all *WriteXXX* methods defined on the class. Setting *AutoFlush* to true should be used when the user expects immediate feedback on the output device, such as the console. In ASP.NET, you might get better performance by setting *AutoFlush* to *false* and calling *Close* (or at least *Flush*) when you're done writing.

The line terminator string is appended to the output stream whenever the *WriteLine* method is called. Although in theory you can use any string to terminate the line, be aware that the resulting text would be correctly readable through a *StreamReader* only if either *\n* or *\r\n* is used. If you set *NewLine* to null, the default new line sequence is used. If you're using *StreamWriter* to dynamically create, say, HTML pages, you can use the HTML break tag *
* instead.

Table 16-13 details the methods exposed by the *StreamWriter* class.

Table 16-13 Methods of a *StreamWriter*

Method	Description
Close	Closes the current writer and the underlying stream
Flush	Clears all buffers for the current writer, and causes any buffered data to be written to the underlying stream
Write	Writes data to the stream
WriteLine	Differs from *Write* because it always adds a line terminator

Both *Write* and *WriteLine* have several overloads, each of which enables you to write data of a particular value type—Boolean, character, string, decimal, and so forth. In all cases, what the methods really write is a textual representation of the value. For example, if you write a Boolean, the whole *False* or *True* strings are written, not a single byte!

Persisting a Collection of Data

Let's see how to write a sample text file. If you're going to write a text file from within an ASP.NET application, chances are that you are just persisting a collection of data. So to exemplify, let's dump the contents of the *Request.ServerVariables* collection.

```
<script runat="server">
void Page_Load(object sender, EventArgs e) {
    string file = Server.MapPath(@"servervars.txt");
    SaveFile(file);
}
```

```
void SaveFile(string file) {
    StreamWriter writer = new StreamWriter(file);
    foreach(string elem in Request.ServerVariables) {
        string buf;
        buf = String.Format("{0}={1}", elem,
            Request.ServerVariables[elem]);
        writer.WriteLine(buf);
    }
    writer.Close();
    Response.Write("Done");
}
</script>
```

Note that for this code to work, the account running the ASP.NET service must have writing permissions on the folder. If not, writing permissions must be granted. You can do that either manually, through the Explorer's Properties dialog box, or programmatically using the cacls.exe utility. (See Chapter 15, "ASP.NET Security.")

Writing Binary Files

There are a couple of interesting scenarios in ASP.NET in which you might need to write binary files. The first scenario has to do with the creation of dynamic images—that is, images that are created while users work with the application. Dynamic images are typically obtained from the contents of binary large object (BLOB) fields in a database or from the output of charting applications. In many cases, it's dynamically generated output that doesn't necessarily need to be cached. For this reason, you implement the generation of the image as a new page with a graphical content type. In this case, page output caching is the only possibility you have to reuse an image over and over again. In some cases, if the number of images is not that big, and the likelihood of reusing them is quite significant, you can persist the dynamically generated stream of bytes to a disk file.

Creating Images Dynamically

Suppose that you manage a Web site for registered users. Whenever a user is authenticated and connected to the system, you might want to display a welcome message. You can compose the message by using static graphics and rich-formatted HTML text, or you could generate the message dynamically, obtaining effects not otherwise possible with the normal tools. For example, if you use GDI+ you can easily draw any text using a gradient brush. (You'll probably never use this technique in a real-world application to generate messages, but persisting dynamically generated images can be a useful technique to know.)

In the current directory, the following method creates a GIF file that is the graphical representation of the specified text. The text is written using a cyan-to-yellow gradient of colors on a black background.

```
void CreateWelcomeBitmap(string userID, string file) {
    // Prepare the drawing context
    Rectangle area = new Rectangle(0,0,200,30);
    Font f = new Font("Verdana", 12);
    Bitmap bmp = new Bitmap(200, 30);
    Graphics g = Graphics.FromImage(bmp);

    // Prepare the text
    StringFormat sf = new StringFormat();
    sf.Alignment = StringAlignment.Center;
    sf.LineAlignment = StringAlignment.Center;

    // Draw the text
    LinearGradientBrush brForeColor = new LinearGradientBrush(area,
        Color.SkyBlue, Color.Yellow, LinearGradientMode.Horizontal);
    g.DrawString(userID, f, brForeColor, area, sf);

    // Create the file
    FileStream fs = new FileStream(file, FileMode.Create);
    bmp.Save(fs, ImageFormat.Gif);
    fs.Close();

    // Clean-up
    brForeColor.Dispose();
    f.Dispose();
    bmp.Dispose();
    g.Dispose();
}
```

The picture is created executing a few GDI+ operations on a logical canvas represented by a *Bitmap* object. The content of the object is then saved to the specified stream compressed as a GIF stream. The *FileStream* class is used to create and fill the new file. A reference to the stream is passed to the *Save* method of the *Bitmap* class for the actual writing. For the sake of completeness, you should note that the *Bitmap Save* method can also accept a direct file name, which would save you from creating a file stream. Figure 16-5 shows an example of the output.

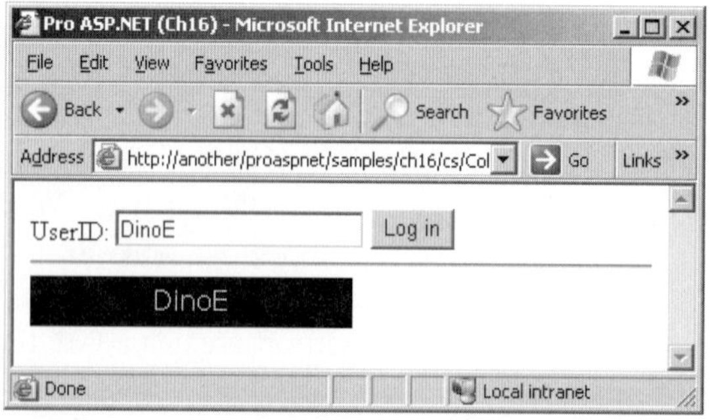

Figure 16-5 A dynamically generated image.

The user enters the user ID and clicks to log in. The system looks at the user ID and determines whether an appropriate bitmap is already present. If not, a new GIF file is generated and displayed through a server-side *<img>* tag.

```
void OnWelcome(object sender, EventArgs e)
{
    string userID = theUserID.Text;
    string file = Server.MapPath(userID + ".gif");
    if (!File.Exists(file))
        CreateWelcomeBitmap(userID, file);
    picture.Src = file;
}
```

The layout of the sample page is as follows:

```
<form runat="server">
    UserID: <asp:textbox runat="server" id="theUserID" />
    <asp:button runat="server" onclick="OnWelcome" text="Log in" />
    <hr>
    <img runat="server" id="picture" />
</form>
```

Caution Before attempting to create a new file, the *Save* method of the *Bitmap* class demands the write permission on the resource. It does that by calling the *Demand* method on a file-specific instance of the *FileIOPermission* class. The method forces a security exception at run time if all callers higher in the call stack (including your code) have not been granted the permission requested. Normally, though, no callers would prevent the GDI+ method from writing, so the *Save* method successfully passes the common language runtime (CLR) permission check and yields to a COM library, which is actually in charge for creating the file. At this point, the COM library operates on behalf of the ASP.NET account, and if no write permissions have been granted to that account, a system exception is raised. The module that catches the exception is the COM Interop infrastructure, which bubbles it up as an *ExternalException* exception because of some generic failure in the underlying COM code. The GDI+ layer can't translate that exception into a more meaningful message, and all that you get is a "Generic GDI+ Error". There might be several reasons for that message, one of which is the lack of write permissions.

In Chapter 22, "Working with Images in ASP.NET," we'll return to image processing in ASP.NET and cover the topic of dynamic images more in detail.

The *BinaryWriter* Class

The *BinaryWriter* class is another alternative to writing binary data to a stream or a file. The class writes primitive types in a binary format according to the specified encoding. *BinaryWriter* doesn't have a complex and rich programming interface. It features only one property—*BaseStream*—and a few methods, including *Close*, *Flush*, and *Write*. The *BinaryWriter* class also exposes the *Seek* method, which allows you to set the current position within the stream. As usual, you set the position by indicating a byte position and an origin—beginning, current position, or end of the stream.

Serializing Data Structures

Persisting binary data is a problem that can be approached in at least two different ways. You can write all the necessary pieces of data to disk one after the next, or you can group them all into a more manageable, all-encompassing data structure and save it to disk in a single step. The difference between the two approaches is not particularly relevant in terms of the file creation. The final output, in fact, is nearly identical. More significant is the difference when reading data back. When reading binary data in pieces, you are responsible for transforming all the pieces of data into a common memory structure that represents the data. When reading binary data in one chunk, the transformation step is unnecessary, as you can read data directly into a new instance of the class.

Working with objects and binary data exploits a key feature of the .NET Framework—run-time object serialization and deserialization. Object serialization and deserialization is offered through the classes exposed by the *System.Runtime.Serialization* namespace. It allows you to store public, protected, and private fields, and it automatically handles circular references. A circular reference occurs when a child object references a parent object, and the parent object also references the child object.

Serialization can generate output in multiple formats by using different formatter modules. A formatter is a sort of pass-through stream that accepts raw data and formats it for storage in a particular scheme. The .NET Framework comes with two predefined formatters—the *BinaryFormatter* and *SoapFormatter* classes—which write the object's state in binary format and SOAP format, respectively.

The run-time serialization engine works only with classes explicitly declared as serializable. Classes make themselves serializable in two ways. They can either support the *[Serializable]* attribute or implement the *ISerializable* interface. If the class supports the *[Serializable]* attribute, the class doesn't need to do anything else, and the serialization takes place automatically through reflection. The *ISerializable* interface, on the other hand, lets the class author exercise closer control on how the bits of the living object are actually persisted. Object serialization is a large topic that deserves much more space than is available in this context. In the rest of the section, we'll examine serialization only from the perspective of an ASP.NET application that wants to persist information in a format that is both compact and easy to manage.

The *BinaryFormatter* Class

To serialize an object to a file, you first select a serialization formatter. This is normally the binary or the SOAP formatter. Each formatter has its own class.

```
IFormatter binFormatter = new BinaryFormatter();
IFormatter soapFormatter = new SoapFormatter();
```

Once you hold a living instance of the serializer, you simply call the *Serialize* method, passing the stream to write to and the object to save.

```
MyClass obj = new MyClass();
⋮
binFormatter.Serialize(stream, obj);
```

Rebuilding objects from a storage medium is easy too. You simply call the *Deserialize* method on the specified formatter.

```
MyClass obj = (MyClass) binFormatter.Deserialize(stream);
```

It goes without saying that you cannot serialize to, say, SOAP and then deserialize through the binary formatter.

An object can only be serialized to, and deserialized from, a stream. However, a stream can be, in turn, attached to a disk file, a more specialized stream, a memory buffer, and even to a string.

Serializing Data Through Classes

Let's go through a practical example to see how the contents of a data structure can be serialized to a binary file. We'll consider the following class—*MenuItem*—which represents a menu item to display on the page.

```
[Serializable]
public class MenuItem {
    private int _key;
    private string _displayText;

    public MenuItem(string text, int value) {
        _key = value;
        _displayText = text;
    }
```

```
    public string DisplayText {
        get {return _displayText;}
    }

    public int Key {
        get {return _key;}
    }
}
```

The page reads out of a disk file the structure of its menu. The disk file simply consists of an array of *MenuItem* objects.

```
void Page_Load(object sender, EventArgs e) {
    string fileName = Server.MapPath(@"menu.dat");
    if (!File.Exists(fileName))
        BindMenu();
    else {
        ArrayList values = LoadFromFile();
        BindMenu(values);
    }
}

private void BindMenu() {
    ArrayList values = new ArrayList();
    values.Add(new MenuItem("File", 1));
    values.Add(new MenuItem("Tools", 2));
    values.Add(new MenuItem("Help", 3));

    Repeater1.DataSource = values;
    Repeater1.DataBind();

    SaveToFile(values);
}

private ArrayList LoadFromFile() {
    string fileName = Server.MapPath(@"menu.dat");
    FileStream stream = new FileStream(fileName, FileMode.Open,
        FileAccess.Read);
    BinaryFormatter reader = new BinaryFormatter();
    ArrayList values = (ArrayList) reader.Deserialize(stream);
    stream.Close();

    return values;
}
```

The deserialization process is straightforward once you know the structure of the disk file. The first time the page is accessed, it creates and persists the default menu. The menu is serialized as an array of *MenuItem* objects. You can also edit the structure of the menu, and any changes will be promptly detected.

```
private void SaveToFile(ArrayList values) {
    string fileName = Server.MapPath(@"menu.dat");
    FileStream stream = new FileStream(fileName, FileMode.Create);
    BinaryFormatter writer = new BinaryFormatter();
    writer.Serialize(stream, values);
    stream.Close();
}
```

Figure 16-6 shows the page in action.

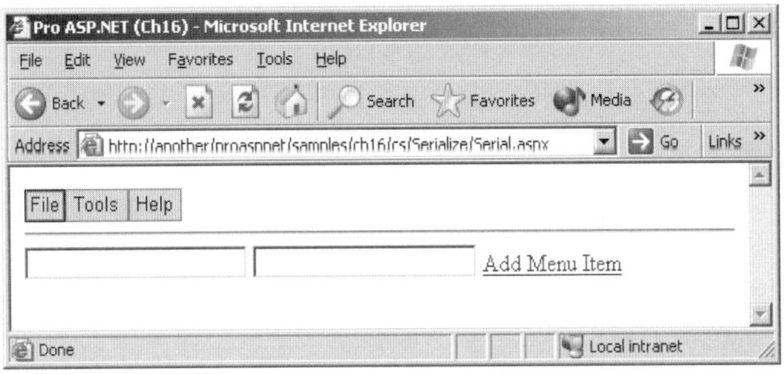

Figure 16-6 The structure of the menu is serialized to disk using a binary formatter.

Each class involved in the serialization process must be serializable; otherwise, a run-time exception is thrown. In this case, the rule applies to both *ArrayList* and *MenuItem*. *ArrayList* is serializable by design.

The resulting file contains more than just the class information. The .NET Framework, in fact, also inserts a signature and information about the assembly from which the class was read. Using the binary formatter is helpful because it lets you save and restore data using the same memory pattern. On the other hand, the layout of the data follows a well-known pattern decided by the .NET Framework and requires more space than if you write the data yourself.

Watching for File Changes

It's not uncommon that ASP.NET applications based on local files have to update their user interface and behavior if one of those files changes. Since Windows 95, the operating system has offered a feature that can be extremely useful in many situations in which you need to detect changes in a certain portion of the file system. This feature is called *file notification* and basically consists of the system's ability to notify through events several types of changes that affect files and folders under a given tree. ASP.NET exploits this feature extensively to detect changes in the source .aspx files.

The file notification mechanism works in a slightly different manner under the operating systems of the Windows 9x (including Windows ME) and Windows NT, Windows 2000, and Windows XP families. Under Windows 9x, the notification mechanism does not provide information about the actual files or directories involved in the change. What the programmer gets is the notification that a certain change occurred. To detect what really changed, you must scan the contents of the watched tree of directories and figure it out yourself. Windows NT 4.0 added an extra bunch of API functions to read the details of any directory changes. The whole notification mechanism was extended in particular by the *ReadDirectoryChangesW* function.

There's good news and bad news about the integration of the file notification mechanism in .NET. The good news is that all the intricacies of the underlying *ReadDirectoryChangesW* function have been straightened out and wrapped into an easy-to-use and elegant class named *FileSystemWatcher*. The bad news is that the file notification support built into .NET is completely based on the features of the *ReadDirectoryChangesW* function. This means that you can use the *FileSystemWatcher* class only if your code runs on a Windows NT 4.0, Windows 2000, or Windows XP machine. This is not an issue for ASP.NET code, though.

The *FileSystemWatcher* Class

The *FileSystemWatcher* class watches a specified directory for changes that involve contained files and subdirectories. The class can monitor what happens to the file system of a local computer, network drive, or remote computer. The *FileSystemWatcher* class does not raise events for CD and DVD drives because nothing can happen on these drives to change contents or timestamps.

You can initialize the *FileSystemWatcher* class using three possible constructors. You can use the default, parameterless constructor, but you can also create a new instance of the *FileSystemWatcher* class indicating the directory to watch and even the search string for the files to watch.

```
FileSystemWatcher fsw = new FileSystemWatcher(path, "*.txt");
```

Table 16-14 lists the properties of the class.

Table 16-14 Properties of the *FileSystemWatcher* Class

Property Name	Description
EnableRaisingEvents	Gets or sets a value that indicates whether the component is watching
Filter	Gets or sets the filter string used to determine what files are monitored in a directory

Table 16-14 Properties of the *FileSystemWatcher* Class

Property Name	Description
IncludeSubdirectories	Gets or sets a value that indicates whether subdirectories should be monitored too
InternalBufferSize	Gets or sets the size of the internal buffer used to retrieve file system information
NotifyFilter	Gets or sets the type of changes to watch for
Path	Gets or sets the path of the directory to watch

You set up a file system watcher in three steps. First, you define the root directory to monitor and the criteria for the files to watch for. Next, you indicate the events you want to be notified of and write event handlers accordingly. Finally, you start watching.

The *Path* property defines the root directory to watch for. Unless you also set the *IncludeSubDirectories* property to *true*, only the directory assigned to *Path* will be monitored. By default, *IncludeSubDirectories* is set to *false*. When *true*, *IncludeSubDirectories* works recursively through the entire sub tree and not just the immediate child directories. Of course, setting *IncludeSubDirectories* to *true* might significantly increase the number of notifications you get.

To filter out some notifications, you can specify search criteria for files and directories. You do this by setting the *Filter* property with a wild card expression such as *.txt. Interestingly, the default value for *Filter* is *.*, which means that all files without an extension are not processed. To process all files, set the *Filter* property to the empty string.

What are the events you can be notified of? The whole set of potential events you can watch for are defined in the *NotifyFilters* enumeration type, as described in Table 16-15.

Table 16-15 The *NotifyFilters* Enumeration

Member	Notifies when a change is detected on...
Attributes	The attributes of the file or folder
CreationTime	The time the file or folder was created
DirectoryName	The name of the directory
FileName	The name of the file
LastAccess	The date the file or folder was last opened
LastWrite	The date the file or folder last had anything written to it
Security	The security settings of the file or folder
Size	The size of the file or folder

The next code snippet shows how to use a file system watcher.

```
FileSystemWatcher fsw = new FileSystemWatcher();
fsw.Path = @"c:\";
fsw.Filter = "*.txt";
fsw.NotifyFilter = NotifyFilters.FileName |
                   NotifyFilters.LastWrite |
                   NotifyFilters.LastAccess;
```

Once you've finished with the preliminaries, you set up the object to work by setting the *EnableRaisingEvents* property to *true*. Setting *EnableRaising-Events* to *false* would stop the monitoring activity for the current directory.

Hooking Up Events

The *FileSystemWatcher* class has only one significant method: *WaitForChanged*. This method works synchronously and waits indefinitely until the first change occurs. Once the first change has been detected, the method returns. *Wait-ForChanged* also has an overload that accepts the number of milliseconds to wait prior to time out. When one of the events you registered for occurs, the *FileSystemWatcher* class raises an event to the application. The list of events is shown in Table 16-16.

Table 16-16 Events of the *FileSystemWatcher* Class

Event Name	Description
Changed	Occurs when a file or directory is modified (by date, security, size, or content)
Created	Occurs when a file or directory is created
Deleted	Occurs when a file or directory is deleted
Error	Occurs when the internal buffer overflows
Renamed	Occurs when a file or directory is renamed

The following code shows how to register events and then begin watching:

```
fsw.Changed += new FileSystemEventHandler(OnChanged);
fsw.Created += new FileSystemEventHandler(OnChanged);
fsw.Deleted += new FileSystemEventHandler(OnChanged);
fsw.Renamed += new RenamedEventHandler(OnRenamed);
fsw.EnableRaisingEvents = true;
```

An event handler routine for the *Changed* event would look like this:

```
void OnChanged(object sender, FileSystemEventArgs e) {
    // what to do
}
```

The event data structure might change according to the particular event. Events such as *Changed*, *Created*, and *Deleted* use the *FileSystemEventHandler* delegate, which results in the signature just shown.

The *FileSystemEventArgs* structure has three extra properties: *ChangeType*, *FullPath*, and *Name*. *ChangeType* gets the type of event that occurred, *FullPath* returns the fully qualified path of the affected file or directory, and *Name* contains the name of the affected file or directory. If the event is *Renamed*, you must use a different delegate—*RenamedEventHandler*.

The argument class for the event handler is *RenamedEventArgs*. The *RenamedEventArgs* class extends *FileSystemEventArgs* by adding two more properties—*OldFullPath* and *OldName*. As the names suggest, the properties let you know about the old path and file names that have just been renamed.

Isolated Storage and ASP.NET

Isolated storage is a .NET security feature designed to enable data storage for partially trusted applications in general and network-deployed client components in particular. Isolated storage assigns each application a unique storage area that is fully isolated from other applications and essentially private. It provides true isolation in the sense that the identity of an application or a component uniquely determines the root of a virtual, sandboxed file system that only that application or component can access.

The isolated storage is accessible from user code through tailor-made streams. When you open such streams, you can't indicate absolute file names, though. Your application is assigned a distinct and identity-based portion of the file system and can't cross its boundaries.

As of version 1.1, ASP.NET applications don't support isolated storage. However, Microsoft is considering some extensions to the current isolated storage model to make it suitable for the next generation of ASP.NET applications.

Loading XML Documents

XML documents are a special type of text file. They are text-based and human-authorable files in which each piece of information can be given a particular meaning and role using a descriptive syntax. XML documents are written using a markup language made of a vocabulary of terms and a few strict rules. Just the markup nature of the XML language raises the need for a worker tool capable of analyzing and understanding the schema and the contents of the documents. This tool is the XML parser—a sort of black box component that reads in markup text and returns platform-specific objects.

All the XML parsers available to programmers fall into one of two main categories: tree-based and event-based. The most popular implementations of both types of parsers are the XML Document Object Model (DOM) and Simple API for XML (SAX). The XML DOM parser is a generic tree-based API that renders an XML document as an in-memory structure. The SAX parser, on the other hand, provides an event-based API for processing each significant element in a stream of XML data. SAX parsers control the whole process and push data to the application which, in turn, is free to accept or just ignore it. The model is extremely lean and features very limited memory occupation. The .NET Framework provides full support for the XML DOM parsing model, but not for SAX.

The lack of support for SAX parsers doesn't mean you have to renounce the functionality that a SAX parser can bring. All the functions of a SAX parser can be easily, and even more effectively, implemented using an XML reader—the second parsing model within the .NET Framework. Unlike a SAX parser, a .NET reader works under the total control of the client application. In this way, the application itself can pull out only the data it really needs and skip over the remainder of the XML stream. A SAX parser, on the other hand, will read the entire file and push the whole stream, one piece at a time, to the application.

Readers are based on streams and work in much the same way as a database cursor. Reading and writing are two completely separated functions that require different and unrelated classes—*XmlReader* and *XmlWriter*.

So in the .NET Framework, you have two possible approaches when it comes to processing XML data. You can either use any classes directly built on top of the base *XmlReader* and *XmlWrite* classes or expose information through the XML DOM.

Reading XML Files

An XML reader supplies a programming interface that callers use to connect to XML documents and pull out all the data they need. *XmlReader* is an abstract class that provides the foundation for all XML reader classes. You'll never use it in your code except to simply reference more specific and richer classes. User applications are normally based on any of the following three derived classes: *XmlTextReader*, *XmlValidatingReader*, and *XmlNodeReader*. All these classes share a common set of properties and methods.

The Programming Interface of XML Readers

Table 16-17 lists the properties defined for the *XmlReader* base class. Concrete classes such as *XmlTextReader* can add more properties specific to their way of working.

Table 16-17 Properties of an XML Reader

Property	Description
AttributeCount	Gets the number of attributes on the current node.
BaseURI	Gets the base URI of the current node.
CanResolveEntity	Gets a value indicating whether the reader can resolve entities.
Depth	Gets the depth of the current node in the XML document.
EOF	Gets whether the reader has reached the end of the stream.
HasAttributes	Gets whether the current node has any attributes.
HasValue	Gets whether the current node can have a value.
IsDefault	Gets whether the current node is an attribute that originated from the default value defined in the DTD or schema.
IsEmptyElement	Gets whether the current node is an empty element with no attributes or value.
Item	Indexer property that returns the value of the specified attribute.
LocalName	Gets the name of the current node with any prefix removed.
Name	Gets the fully qualified name of the current node.
NamespaceURI	Gets the namespace URI of the current node. Relevant to *Element* and *Attribute* nodes only.
NameTable	Gets the name table object associated with the reader.
NodeType	Gets the type of the current node.
Prefix	Gets the namespace prefix associated with the current node.
QuoteChar	Gets the quotation mark character used to enclose the value of an attribute.
ReadState	Gets the state of the reader from the *ReadState* enumeration.
Value	Gets the text value of the current node.
XmlLang	Gets the *xml:lang* scope within which the current node resides.
XmlSpace	Gets the current *xml:space* scope from the *XmlSpace* enumeration (*Default*, *None*, or *Preserve*).

Table 16-18 details the methods common to all XML reader classes in the .NET Framework.

Table 16-18 Methods of an XML Reader

Method	Description
Close	Closes the reader, and sets the internal state to *Closed*.
GetAttribute	Gets the value of the specified attribute. An attribute can be accessed by index or by local or qualified name.
IsStartElement	Indicates whether the current content node is a start tag.
LookupNamespace	Returns the namespace URI to which the given prefix maps.
MoveToAttribute	Moves the pointer to the specified attribute. An attribute can be accessed by index or by local or qualified name.
MoveToContent	Moves the pointer ahead to the next content node or to the end of file. The method returns immediately if the current node is already a content node such as non–white space text, CDATA, *Element*, *EndElement*, *EntityReference*, or *EndEntity*.
MoveToElement	Moves the pointer back to the element node that contains the current attribute node. Relevant only when the current node is an attribute.
MoveToFirstAttribute	Moves to the first attribute of the current *Element* node.
MoveToNextAttribute	Moves to the next attribute of the current *Element* node.
Read	Reads the next node, and advances the pointer.
ReadAttributeValue	Parses the attribute value into one or more *Text*, *EntityReference*, or *EndEntity* nodes.
ReadElementString	Reads and returns the text from a text-only element.
ReadEndElement	Checks that the current content node is an end tag and advances the reader to the next node. Throws an exception if the node is not an end tag.
ReadInnerXml	Reads and returns all the content below the current node, including markup information.
ReadOuterXml	Reads and returns all the content of the current node, including markup information.
ReadStartElement	Checks that the current node is an element and advances the reader to the next node. Throws an exception if the node is not a start tag.
ReadString	Reads the contents of an element or text node as a string. The method concatenates all the text until the next markup. For attribute nodes, it is equivalent to reading the attribute value.
ResolveEntity	Expands and resolves the current entity reference node.
Skip	Skips the children of the current node.

To process an XML document, you normally use an instance of the *XmlTextReader*. You can create it in a number of ways and from a variety of sources, including disk files, URLs, streams, and text readers.

```
XmlTextReader reader = new XmlTextReader(file);
```

Once the reader object is up and running, you have to explicitly open it using the *Read* method. To move from any node to the next, you can continue using *Read* as well as a number of other more specialized methods, including *Skip* and *MoveToContent*. The *Read* method, in fact, returns *false* when nothing else is left to read and *true* otherwise. The following code snippet shows the typical .NET way to process the contents of an XML file:

```
XmlTextReader reader = new XmlTextReader(file);
while (reader.Read())
{
    // Verify the type of the current node
    if (reader.NodeType == XmlNodeType.Element)
    { ... }
}
reader.Close();
```

A lot of XML documents begin with several tags that don't represent any informative content. The reader's *MoveToContent* method lets you skip all the heading nodes and position the pointer directly onto the first content node. In doing so, the method skips over nodes such as *ProcessingInstruction*, *DocumentType*, *Comment*, *Whitespace*, and *SignificantWhitespace*.

Reading Attributes

Attribute nodes are not automatically visited by a reader that moves ahead through *Read*. To visit the set of attributes of the current node, you must use a loop controlled by the *MoveToNextAttribute* method. The following code snippet accesses all the attributes of the current node—the one you selected with *Read*—and concatenates their names and values into a comma-separated string.

```
if (reader.HasAttributes)
    while(reader.MoveToNextAttribute())
        buf += reader.Name + "=\"" + reader.Value + "\",";
reader.MoveToElement();
```

Once you're done with node attributes, consider calling *MoveToElement* on the reader object. The *MoveToElement* method moves the internal pointer back to the element node that contains the attributes. To be precise, the method does not really "move" the pointer because the pointer never moved away from that element node during the attributes navigation. The *MoveToElement* method simply refreshes some internal variables, making them expose values read from the element node rather than the last attribute read. For example, the *Name* property returns the name of the last attribute read before you call *MoveToElement* and the name of the parent node afterward. If you just need to proceed with the next element once finished with the attributes, you don't really need to call *MoveToElement*. Instead, you need it if you have more work to do on the node before you move to the next one.

In most cases, but not always, the content of an attribute is a simple string of text. Sometimes, the attribute value consists of the string representation of a more specific type (for example, a date or a Boolean) that you then convert into the native type using the methods of the static class *XmlConvert* or *System.Convert*. The two classes perform nearly identical tasks, but the *XmlConvert* class works according to the XML Schema Definition (XSD) data type specification and ignores the current locale. Suppose you have an XML fragment such as the following:

```
<person birthday="5-20-1998" />
```

Let's also assume that, according to the current locale, the birth date is May 20, 1998. If you convert the string into a specific .NET type (the *DateTime* type) using the *System.Convert* class, all will work as expected and the string is correctly transformed into the expected date object. In contrast, if you convert the string using *XmlConvert*, you'll get a parse error because the *XmlConvert* class doesn't recognize a correct date in the string. The reason is that in XML, a date must have the YYYY-MM-DD format to be understood. In summary, the *XmlConvert* class works as a translator to and from .NET types and XSD types. When the conversion takes place, the result is rigorously locale independent.

Validating Readers

The *XmlTextReader* class only checks the input document for well-formedness. In no case can the class validate the document against a schema. The *XmlValidatingReader* class is the XML reader class that provides support for several types of XML validation: DTD, XSD, and XML-Data Reduced (XDR) schemas. DTD and XSD are official recommendations issued by the W3C, whereas XDR is Microsoft's implementation of an early working draft of XML Schemas. It's supported only for backward compatibility.

The *XmlValidatingReader* class works on top of an XML reader—typically an instance of the *XmlTextReader* class. The text reader is used to walk through the nodes of the document, whereas the validating reader is expected to validate each piece of XML according to the requested validation type. The validator class implements internally only a small subset of the functionalities that an XML reader must expose. The class always works on top of an existing XML reader and simply mirrors many methods and properties. The dependency of validating readers on an existing text reader is particularly evident if you look at the class constructors. An XML validating reader, in fact, cannot be directly initialized from a file or a URL. The list of available constructors is composed of the following overloads:

```
public XmlValidatingReader(XmlReader);
public XmlValidatingReader(Stream, XmlNodeType, XmlParserContext);
public XmlValidatingReader(string, XmlNodeType, XmlParserContext);
```

A validating reader can parse any XML document for which a reader is provided as well as any XML fragments accessible through a string or an open stream. Table 16-19 details the properties of the *XmlValidatingReader* class.

Table 16-19 Properties of the *XmlValidatingReader* Class

Property	Description
CanResolveEntity	Gets a value indicating whether this reader can parse and resolve entities. Always returns *true* because the XML validating reader can always resolve entities.
EntityHandling	Gets or sets a value that indicates how entities are handled. Acceptable values for this property come from the *EntityHandling* enumeration type. The default value is *ExpandEntities*, which means that all entities are expanded. If set to *ExpandCharEntities*, only character entities are expanded (for example, *'*). General entities are returned as *EntityReference* node types.
Namespaces	Gets or sets a value that indicates whether namespace support is requested.
NameTable	Gets the name table object associated with the underlying reader.
Reader	Gets the *XmlReader* object used to construct this instance of the *XmlValidatingReader* class. The return value can be cast to a more specific reader type, such as *XmlTextReader*. Any change entered directly on the underlying reader object can lead to unpredictable results. Use the *XmlValidatingReader* interface to manipulate the properties of the underlying reader.
Schemas	Gets an *XmlSchemaCollection* object that holds a collection of preloaded XDR and XSD. Schema preloading is a trick used to speed up the validation process. Schemas, in fact, are cached, and there's no need to load them every time.
SchemaType	Gets the schema object that represents the current node in the underlying reader. This property is relevant only for XSD validation. The object describes whether the type of the node is one of the built-in XSD types or a simple or complex type.

Table 16-19 Properties of the *XmlValidatingReader* Class

Property	Description
ValidationType	Gets or sets a value that indicates the type of validation to perform. Acceptable values come from the *ValidationType* enumeration: *Auto*, *None*, *DTD*, *XDR*, and *Schema*.
XmlResolver	Sets the *XmlResolver* object used for resolving external DTD and schema location references. The *XmlResolver* is also used to handle any import or include elements found in XML Schema Definition language (XSD) schemas.

Just like a nonvalidating reader, the *XmlValidatingReader* class provides methods to navigate over the source document. The difference is that any movement methods validate the text. For example, the *Skip* method jumps over the children of the currently active node in the underlying reader. It's worth noting that you cannot skip over badly formed XML text. The *Skip* method, in fact, also attempts to validate the skipped contents and raises an exception in case of unexpected data.

The validation occurs incrementally, and no method is provided to tell you in a single shot whether the given document is valid or not. You move around the input document using the *Read* method. At each step, the structure of the currently visited node is validated against the specified schema and an exception is raised if an error is found. The following code shows how you can validate an XML document.

```
void Validate(String fileName) {
    // Prepare for validation
    XmlTextReader _coreReader = new XmlTextReader(fileName);
    XmlValidatingReader reader = new XmlValidatingReader(_coreReader);
    reader.ValidationType = ValidationType.Auto;
    reader.ValidationEventHandler += new ValidationEventHandler(Handler);

    // Validate (any errors results in a call to the handler)
    while (reader.Read()) {}

    _coreReader.Close();
    reader.Close();
}
```

The *ValidationType* property sets the type of validation you want—DTD, XSD, XDR, or none. If no validation type is specified (the *ValidationType.Auto* option), the reader automatically applies the validation it reckons to be most appropriate for the document. The caller application is notified of any error through a *ValidationEventHandler* event. If you fail to specify a custom event handler, an XML exception is thrown against the application.

The XML DOM Parser

Although stored as flat text in a linear text file, XML content is inherently hierarchical. Readers just parse the text as it is read out of the input stream. They never cache read information and work in a sort of stateless fashion. As a result, you can neither edit nodes nor move backward. The limited navigation capabilities also prevent you from implementing node queries of any complexity. The XML DOM philosophy is diametrically opposed to readers. XML DOM loads all the XML content in memory and exposes it through a suite of collections that, overall, offer a tree-based representation of the original content. In addition, the supplied data structure is fully searchable and editable.

Advanced search and editing are the primary functions of the XML DOM, while readers (and SAX parsers as well) are optimized for document inspection, simple searches, and any sort of read-only activity.

Loading and Caching XML Documents

The central element in the .NET XML DOM implementation is the *XmlDocument* class. The class represents an XML document and makes it programmable by exposing its nodes and attributes through ad hoc collections. The *XmlDocument* class represents the entry point in the binary structure and the central console that lets you move through nodes reading and writing content. Each element in the original XML document is mapped to a particular .NET class with its own set of properties and methods. Each element can be reached from the parent and can access all of its children and siblings. Element-specific information such as content and attributes are available via properties.

Any change you enter is applied immediately but only in memory. The *XmlDocument* class, though, provides an I/O interface to load from, and save to, a variety of storage media, including disk files. Subsequently, all the changes to constituent elements of an XML DOM tree are normally persisted all at once. When you need to load an XML document into memory for full-access processing, you start by creating a new instance of the *XmlDocument* class.

The following code snippet demonstrates how to load an XML document into an instance of the *XmlDocument* class:

```
XmlDocument doc = new XmlDocument();
doc.Load(fileName);
```

The *Load* method always works synchronously; so when it returns, the document has been completely mapped to memory and is ready for further processing. The *XmlDocument* class internally uses an XML reader to perform any reading operation and build the final tree structure for the source document.

To locate one or more nodes in an XML DOM object, you can use either the *ChildNodes* collection or the *SelectNodes* method. In the *ChildNodes* collection, you are given access to the unfiltered collection of first-level child nodes. The *SelectNodes* (and the ancillary *SelectSingleNode*) method exploits the XPath query language to let you extract nodes based on logical conditions. In addition, XPath queries can go deeper than one level as long as you specify the path to the node as the root of the search.

Walking Your Way Through Documents

The *ChildNodes* collection connects each node to its children. As mentioned earlier, though, the collection returns only the direct children of a given node. Of course, this is not enough to traverse the tree from the root to the leaves. The following code snippet demonstrates how to recursively walk through all the nodes in an XML document.

```
void ProcessData(string fileName) {
    XmlDocument doc = new XmlDocument();
    doc.Load(fileName);
    XmlElement root = doc.DocumentElement;
    LoopThroughChildren(root);
    return;
}

void LoopThroughChildren(XmlNode root) {
    foreach(XmlNode n in root.ChildNodes)
    {
        if (n.NodeType == XmlNodeType.Element)
            LoopThroughChildren(n);
    }
    // Process the node here
    // root represents the current node
    ⋮
}
```

The *LoopThroughChildren* method goes recursively through all its child nodes whose type is *Element*. The order in which you execute node-specific processing, before or after looping through children, determines the visiting algorithm for the document.

Validating Documents Through XML DOM

The XML document loader checks input data only for well-formedness. In the case of parsing errors, an *XmlException* exception is thrown and the resulting *XmlDocument* object remains empty. To load a document and validate it against a DTD or a schema, you must use the *Load* overload that accepts an *XmlReader* object. You pass it a properly initialized instance of the *XmlValidatingReader* class and proceed as usual.

```
XmlTextReader _coreReader;
XmlValidatingReader reader;
_coreReader = new XmlTextReader(fileName);
reader = new XmlValidatingReader(_coreReader);
doc.Load(reader);
```

Any schema information found in the file is taken into account, and the content is validated. Parser errors, if any, are passed on to the validation handler you might have defined. If your validating reader doesn't have an event handler, the first error stops the loading and throws an exception.

Creating XML Documents

Creating XML documents programmatically doesn't seem to be a hard task to accomplish. You just concatenate a few strings into a buffer and flush them out to a storage medium when you're done. XML documents, though, are mostly made of markup text, and complying with markup text is boring—and more importantly, error prone. The XML DOM supplies a more abstract way of creating elements, but it requires you to accumulate the entire document in memory before saving.

XML writers are the writing counterpart of the cursor-like parsing model we discussed earlier. The underlying engine takes care of the markup details, while you focus on the data to write and the structure to lay out.

Using XML Writers

An XML writer is a component that provides a fast, noncached, forward-only way of outputting XML data to streams or files. More importantly, an XML writer guarantees—by design—that all the XML data it produces conforms to the W3C XML 1.0 and Namespaces recommendations.

A writer features ad hoc write methods for each possible XML node type and makes the creation of XML output more logical and much less dependent on the intricacies, and even the quirkiness, of the markup languages. The following code shows how to write the content of an array of strings to disk using XML writers:

```
// Open the XML writer (default encoding charset)
XmlTextWriter writer = new XmlTextWriter(filename, null);
writer.Formatting = Formatting.Indented;

writer.WriteStartDocument();
writer.WriteStartElement("array");
foreach(string s in theArray) {
```

```
        writer.WriteStartElement("element");
        writer.WriteAttributeString("value", s);
        writer.WriteEndElement();
    }
    writer.WriteEndDocument();

    // Close the writer
    writer.Close();
```

Newline and indentation characters are inserted automatically. An XML writer is based on the *XmlWriter* abstract class. The *XmlWriter* class is not directly creatable from user applications, but it can be used as a reference type for objects that happen to be living instances of derived classes. Actually, the .NET Framework provides just one class that provides a concrete implementation of the *XmlWriter* interface—the *XmlTextWriter* class.

Using the XML DOM Writer

To create an XML document using the XML DOM API, you must first create the document in memory and then call the *Save* method or one of its overloads. This gives you great flexibility because no changes you make are set in stone until you save. In general, though, using the XML DOM API to create a new XML document is often overkill, unless the creation of the document is driven by a really complex and sophisticated logic.

In terms of the internal implementation, it's worth noting that the XML DOM *Save* method makes use of an XML text writer to create the document. So unless the content to generate is really complex and subject to a lot of conditions, using an XML text writer to create XML documents is faster. The following code shows how to use the *Save* method to save a changed document.

```
// Load the document
XmlDocument doc = new XmlDocument();
doc.Load(fileName);

// Retrieve a particular node and update an attribute
XmlNode n = root.SelectSingleNode("PageStructure");
n.Attributes["backcolor"] = "white";

// Save the document
doc.Save();
```

The *XmlDocument* class provides a bunch of factory methods to create new nodes. These methods are named consistently with the writing methods of the *XmlTextWriter* class. You'll find a *CreateXXX* method for each *WriteXXX* method provided by the writer. Actually, each *CreateXXX* method just creates a new node in memory, while the corresponding *WriteXXX* method on the writer just writes it to the output stream. Once created, a node must be bound to its parent using the *AppendChild* method, as shown here:

```
XmlDocument doc = new XmlDocument();
XmlNode n;

// Write and append the XML heading
n = doc.CreateXmlDeclaration("1.0", "", "");
doc.AppendChild(n);

// Write a node with one attribute
n = doc.CreateElement("info");
XmlAttribute a = doc.CreateAttribute("path");
a.Value = path;
n.Attributes.SetNamedItem(a);
doc.AppendChild(n);
```

Bear in mind that nodes and attributes, although created, are not automatically bound to the XML document tree until the *AppendChild* (for nodes) or *SetNamedItem* (for attributes) method are called.

Tip To insert many nodes at the same time and to the same parent, you can exploit a little trick based on the concept of a document fragment. You concatenate all the necessary markup into a string and then create a document fragment.

```
XmlDocumentFragment frag = doc.CreateDocumentFragment();
frag.InnerXml = "<extra>1</extra><extra>2</extra>";
parentNode.AppendChild(frag);
```

Set the *InnerXml* property of the document fragment node with the string and then add the newly created node to the parent. The nodes defined in the body of the fragment will be inserted one after the next in the parent node of the XML DOM.

XML Documents in ASP.NET

XML writers are more efficient than XML DOM writers. They require far less memory and run faster. It's not coincidental that XML DOM writers are implemented through XML writers. In general, XML writers are appropriate in all those situations in which the application needs to create documents from scratch, even when overwriting existing documents.

The approach based on XML DOM is more suited to when the application must logically edit the content of an existing document. In this case, in fact, an XML DOM parser can save you from having an intimate knowledge of the overall document structure. You must know only the details that you need to modify. All the rest can be automatically managed by the XML DOM infrastructure. Likewise, reading complex configuration documents using XML DOM can save a lot of development time and reduce the possibility of errors. Parsing and representing large documents with custom in-memory structures can be significantly worse than employing a more greedy component such as the XML DOM parser.

Server-Side XML Transformations

Many ASP pages describe portions of their user interface through XML documents, which are then dynamically processed and translated into HTML. To accomplish this task, you must write all the code necessary to perform the XML-to-HTML transformation and then append the resulting text to the output stream. In ASP.NET, an ad hoc control has been designed specifically to simplify this task—it's the *Xml* control, which uses the *<asp:xml>* tag.

The control is the declarative counterpart of the *XslTransform* class—that is, the .NET Framework class that performs style sheet transformations. You use the XML server control when you need to embed XML documents in a Web page either verbatim (for example, a data island) or transformed (for example, a browser-dependent piece of user interface). The XML data can be included inline within the HTML, or it can be in an external file. By combining this control's ability with a style sheet that does browser-specific transformations, you can transform server-side, XML data into browser-proof HTML.

> **Note** The *Xml* control comes in extremely handy when you need to create XML data islands for the client to consume. In particular, you can write an XSLT transformation capable of rendering ADO.NET *DataSet* objects in the XML representation of ADO *Recordset* objects. By combining the capabilities of the XML server control with such a style sheet, you can make the contents of a *DataSet* available on the client to some client script procedures.

Programming the *Xml* Server Control

In addition to the typical and standard properties of all server controls, the *Xml* control provides the properties listed in Table 16-20. The document properties represent the source XML data, while the transform properties handle the instance of the *XslTransform* class to be used and the style sheet.

You can specify a source document in various ways: using a file, a string, or an XML DOM. A style sheet, on the other hand, can be specified by file or using a preconfigured *XslTransform* object. The output of the transformation, if any, is the Web page output stream.

Table 16-20 Properties of the *Xml* Control

Property	Description
Document	Gets or sets the XML source document using an *XmlDocument*
DocumentContent	Gets or sets the XML source document using a string
DocumentSource	Gets or sets the XML source document using a file
Transform	Gets or sets the *XslTransform* class to use for transformations
TransformArgumentList	Gets or sets the argument list for transformations
TransformSource	Gets or sets the style sheet to use for transformations

The settings are mutually exclusive and the last setting wins. For example, if you set both *Document* and *DocumentSource*, no exception is thrown but the first assignment is overridden. The *DocumentContent* property can be set programmatically using a string variable or declaratively by placing text between the opening and closing of the control.

```
<asp:xml runat="server" id="xmlData">
    ⋮
</asp:xml>
```

You can optionally specify an XSL style sheet document that formats the XML document before it is written to the output. The output of the style sheet must be HTML, XML, or plain text. It cannot be, for example, ASP.NET source code or a combination of ASP.NET layout declarations.

Working with the *Xml* Server Control

The following listing demonstrates a simple but effective way to describe a portion of your Web page using XML code. The actual XML-to-HTML transformation is automatically and silently performed by the style sheet.

```
<!-- Show top bar menu -->
<asp:xml runat="server" TransformSource="Menu.xsl">
    <MyMenu>
    <Popup Text="Developers">
        <MenuItem Text="Tools" />
        <MenuItem Text="Downloads" />
    </Popup>
    <MenuItem Text="Job Opportunities" />
    <MenuItem Text="Contact Us" />
    </MyMenu>
</asp:xml>
```

The *Xml* control can have an ID and can be programmatically accessed. This opens up a new possibility. You can check the browser's capabilities and decide dynamically which style sheet best suits it.

You could also describe the whole page with XML and employ a style sheet to translate it to HTML. This is not always, and not necessarily, the best solution to gain flexibility, but the *Xml* control definitely makes implementing that solution considerably easier.

```
<asp:xml runat="server"
    DocumentSource="Menu.xml"
    TransformSource="Menu.xsl" />
```

If you need to pass in some argument, just create and populate an instance of the *XsltArgumentList* class and pass it to the control using the *TransformArgumentList* property.

Conclusion

The structure of the Windows file system has not radically changed in the past few years. With Windows 2000, Microsoft introduced some new features in the NTFS file system, but the most significant changes we observed remain those related to the infrastructure that has been built to keep up with the shell enhancements—for example, the desktop.ini file to assign additional attributes to folders. Significant changes to the file system are slated only for the next major Windows release.

Although the substance of the underlying file system is not something that changed with .NET (.NET is a development platform and not an operating system), .NET significantly changed the way you work with the constituent elements of a file system—the files and the directories.

The introduction of streams is a key step in the sense that it unifies the API necessary to perform similar operations on a conceptually similar storage medium. Another key enhancement is the introduction of reader and writer objects. They provide a kind of logical API by means of which you read and write any piece of information. The .NET Framework also provides a lot of facilities to perform the basic management operations with files and directories. Although managing files and directories is probably not the primary task of a typical ASP.NET application, many ASP.NET applications need to do it.

Reading and writing files is another file system–related activity that is common to many ASP.NET applications. Creating and editing files is subject to account restrictions and should be considered as the last resort. Databases are probably the first option to consider for Web applications that need to manage persistent and programmatically updateable data.

Text, XML, or binary files are all good choices when you're implementing a file-based solution. XML files are the most expressive option, and thanks to XSLT transformations, the *Xml* server control, and XML data islands, they are also the option that is best integrated with the rest of the .NET Framework. This chapter offered an overview of file management, with a discussion of XML files. However, both the file system API and the XML API are topics that deserve much more coverage.

Resources

- *Applied XML Programming with Microsoft .NET*, by Dino Esposito (Microsoft Press, 2002)

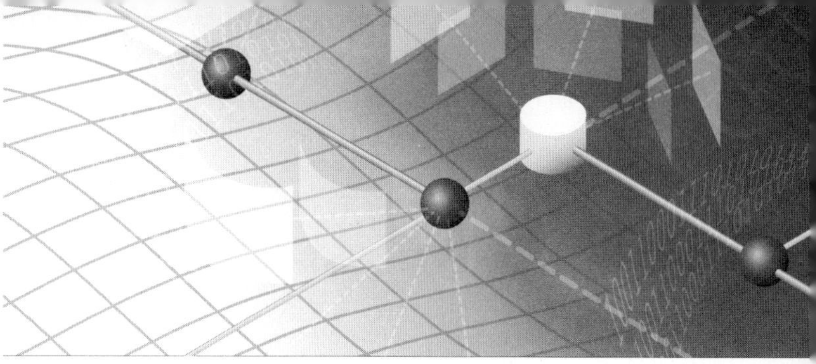

17

Working with Web Services

One thing life has taught me: if you are interested, you never have to look for new interests. They come to you. When you are genuinely interested in one thing, it will always lead to something else.

—Eleanor Roosevelt

Web services (sometimes called XML Web services) are software components that provide some type of service over the Internet. Just like a conventional Web site, a Web service is reachable through a public URL and is subject to the same security restrictions of an HTML-based Web site. Unlike ordinary Web sites, though, Web services don't have a user interface. Web services are programmable entities that expose callable functions.

The caller can certainly be a human, but it will more likely be an application. From a developer's perspective, a Web service is a sort of platform-independent dynamic-link library (DLL). A Web service is hosted by a Web site and exposes a number of functions with well-known signatures. These exposed functions are known as *Web methods*. By sending proper HTTP requests, and as long as the security layer of the site lets your request pass, you execute Web methods and get results back.

A number of standards are involved with Web services, the first in line being an Internet protocol, most commonly HTTP. The presence of such a ubiquitous transportation protocol is the key element that guarantees the platform-independence of Web services. Note that, architecturally speaking, Web services are not strictly tied to HTTP as the protocol. Web services can be devised and implemented on top of a number of transportation protocols, including SMTP, FTP, and message queues. HTTP is the most popular of all and the only one supported by the .NET Framework. For this reason, it's unlikely that you'll ever use another one even though other protocols could be used. Other fundamental standards in the Web service infrastructure are XML and the Simple Object Access Protocol (SOAP). XML comes up as the universal language to describe the data being exchanged. SOAP is an XML dialect and provides a universal syntax to define a Web method call. Any data returned by a Web service is defined by an XML schema, which makes it consumable on a large number of platforms. The availability of HTTP listeners and XML parsers on virtually any current software platform gives Web services tremendous implementation and deployment power. A Web service can be installed on any platform and be accessed from any other platform. These days, as a human user, you'll experience no difficulty at all connecting to a Web site hosted on a Linux-based machine. Likewise, for your client software, calling a Web service hosted on a Linux machine is no big deal, as long as a public URL and a public Web method signature are provided.

Web services are not an exclusive feature of the .NET platform. The .NET platform was one of the first platforms to provide programmers with significant and powerful support to call and create Web services. ASP.NET applications are just one possible client of Web services, along with Windows Forms, consoles, and even mobile and smart-device applications. The ASP.NET runtime is deeply involved in the implementation of Web services on the .NET platform. As we'll see later, .NET Web services are just a special case of an ASP.NET application.

In this chapter, we'll cover the .NET infrastructure that allows the creation of .NET Web services, how to build Web services, and how to call them. In doing so, we'll touch on critical aspects of Web programming such as security and state management.

The Infrastructure for Web Services

The infrastructure of Web services embraces some open Internet standards, such as HTTP, XML, SOAP, and the Web Services Description Language (WSDL). The combined use of such open standards makes Web services accessible and consumable from any client or Internet-enabled device. We know about HTTP from discussions in earlier chapters and we discussed XML in Chapter 16, so let's start by taking a quick tour of SOAP and WSDL.

SOAP provides the official XML-based syntax to be used for exchanging structured and typed information between peers in a distributed environment. The SOAP syntax defines how the client of the Web service can specify the method to execute, related parameters, and how the service will return the data. The Web service resides on a Web server, which recognizes and understands SOAP packets.

WSDL is the XML-based language that describes a Web service. In particular, a WSDL document indicates the location of the service and the methods the service exposes with their parameters. The WSDL document represents the type library of the Web service and is sometimes useful to clients for understanding how to call a given service.

> **Note** This book does not cover SOAP and WSDL in detail. While this chapter might be enough to refresh concepts you've already learned or to get you started, I doubt that it will give you a comprehensive understanding of the standards. I suggest you read more specific books such as *SOAP: Cross Platform Web Services Development Using XML* by Scott Seely and Kent Sharkey (Prentice Hall, 2001) or *Building XML Web Services for the Microsoft .NET Platform* by Scott Short (Microsoft Press, 2002).

Figure 17-1 shows how the various Internet open standards are related to each other in a Web service architecture.

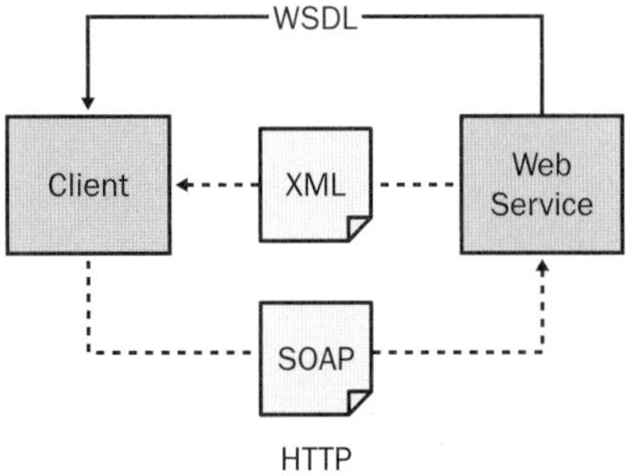

Figure 17-1 The Web service architecture and the role of the Internet open standards.

The SOAP Protocol

A good definition for the SOAP protocol is the following: SOAP is an XML-based protocol for invoking methods on a remote server component. So SOAP is an encoding mechanism that combined with a transport protocol links nodes of a distributed environment. Unlike other remoting protocols such as Distributed COM (DCOM), Java Remote Method Invocation (RMI), and the CORBA Internet InterORB Protocol (IIOP), SOAP is more lightweight. More exactly, SOAP is merely a wire protocol and would need a distributed environment built around it to be fully comparable with DCOM or RMI.

The inherent simplicity of SOAP doesn't equate to a lack of key features, however. SOAP is designed to provide developers with the most frequently used set of functionality, using a general-purpose protocol meant to extend current Internet protocols. The goal of SOAP is invoking remote methods. What is really needed to do this? We simply need a protocol capable of serializing a method call in a format that is transportable and recognizable on a variety of platforms. In addition, we need a transportation protocol to deliver method calls and return results. This is the essence of SOAP.

The SOAP Payload

SOAP commonly uses HTTP as the transportation protocol. This means that invoking a method on a Web service is a matter of sending a SOAP-formatted XML to a Web service using the HTTP POST command. The following code snippet shows a typical SOAP request:

```
POST /samples/services/MathService/MathService.asmx HTTP/1.1
Host: samples.gotdotnet.com
Content-Type: text/xml; charset=utf-8
Content-Length: length
SOAPAction: "http://tempuri.org/Multiply"

<?xml version="1.0" encoding="utf-8"?>
<soap:Envelope
  xmlns:xsi="http://www.w3.org/2001/XMLSchema-instance"
  xmlns:xsd="http://www.w3.org/2001/XMLSchema"
  xmlns:soap="http://schemas.xmlsoap.org/soap/envelope/">
  <soap:Body>
    <Multiply xmlns="http://tempuri.org/">
      <A>2</A>
      <B>3</B>
    </Multiply>
  </soap:Body>
</soap:Envelope>
```

In particular, the request is directed at a Web service named MathService.asmx and located on the host *http://samples.gotdotnet.com* in a given path. The method to invoke is *Multiply*, and the parameters are two float numbers, such as 2 and 3. As you can see, the Web service provides some rather simple mathematical services. The script just shown requests that the Web service executes 2 times 3 and returns the value. The computed value of the operation is returned to the client in a response packet like the following one:

```
HTTP/1.1 200 OK
Content-Type: text/xml; charset=utf-8
Content-Length: length

<?xml version="1.0" encoding="utf-8"?>
<soap:Envelope
  xmlns:xsi="http://www.w3.org/2001/XMLSchema-instance"
  xmlns:xsd="http://www.w3.org/2001/XMLSchema"
  xmlns:soap="http://schemas.xmlsoap.org/soap/envelope/">
  <soap:Body>
    <MultiplyResponse xmlns="http://tempuri.org/">
      <MultiplyResult>6</MultiplyResult>
    </MultiplyResponse>
  </soap:Body>
</soap:Envelope>
```

Let's examine more closely the format of the request/response packets. A SOAP request is made of an HTTP header, a SOAP action, a blank line, and a SOAP envelope.

- **HTTP Header** A SOAP request commonly uses a POST command in which the content type is set to *text/xml*. However, if the Web server returns a "510 Not Extended" error, the client should reiterate the request using the M-POST command from the HTTP Extension Framework. (For more information on the HTTP Extension Framework, see *http://www.w3.org/Protocols/HTTP/ietf-http-ext.*)

- **SOAP Action** *SOAPAction* is a mandatory field that indicates the ultimate goal of the payload—executing a method call. *SOAPAction* contains the name of the method to execute optionally prefixed by the method URI. If the method URI is specified, it has to match the URI of the method call in the envelope. If the two don't match, the Web server returns an error code.

- **SOAP Envelope** The SOAP envelope defines a unidirectional message and is the atomic unit of exchange between SOAP senders and receivers. Within the envelope tag, you can find an optional *<Header>* tag containing custom protocol header extensions. The method to call is described within the *<Body>* tag through a subtree rooted into a node with the method's name. Child nodes describe the arguments to pass. Each child node has the name of the formal parameter.

The body of the envelope contains a child node whose name is *XXX-Response*, where *XXX* is the name of the method. The node contains a child element named *XXXResult*, where again *XXX* stands for the actual name of the method invoked.

> **Note** The SOAP data model relies on the XML Schema type system. You can use a number of primitive types, including *String*, *Char*, *Byte*, *Boolean*, *Int16*, *Int32*, *Int64*, *UInt16*, *UInt32*, *UInt64*, *Single*, *Double*, *Guid*, *Decimal*, and *DateTime*. In addition, SOAP supports enumeration types, class and struct types with public properties, and arrays of the above. Complex data is serialized to XML text by using a combination of elements and attributes.

Architectural Issues

Because SOAP is intended to be a simple wire protocol, important features that would normally be found in other distributed architectures are unspecified in SOAP. While SOAP doesn't preclude supporting these features—such as security, object activation, state management, and garbage collection—neither does SOAP have built-in mechanisms for them. Some higher-level system must provide these features, using SOAP as the means to transport the underlying data to and from client and server. This is a fundamental difference between SOAP and fully featured distributed environments such as DCOM, CORBA, or RMI. SOAP carries the information—it doesn't process it.

SOAP specifically declines any liability for security aspects. SOAP does not provide its own security layer, but it can work with any infrastructure you provide. For example, you can send SOAP packets over secure sockets or HTTPS. The Web Services Enhancements for Microsoft .NET (WSE) kit also allows developers to incorporate security, routing, and attachment features in their .NET Framework applications. See the "Resources" section at the end of the chapter for more information.

Likewise, the activation of the remote object to serve the call is left to the server-side infrastructure. How and when the object is instantiated, how its memory is managed, and how its life cycle is monitored are all issues that are deliberately left uncovered in the SOAP specification.

Finally, because SOAP works mostly on top of HTTP, which is a stateless protocol, it doesn't supply any facility for maintaining the state of an object across invocations. This is still possible, but implementation details are left to the distributed model in use.

To learn more about the SOAP specification, take a look at the W3C Web site at *http://www.w3.org/TR/soap*.

The WSDL Language

WSDL is a specification to describe the structure and features of Web services. By looking at the WSDL description of a Web service, a potential client learns about the exposed methods, their signatures, and their return values. WSDL is a key part of the Universal Description, Discovery, and Integration (UDDI) initiative aimed at building a public, cross-platform directory of available Web services.

WSDL defines an XML grammar to describe Web services as collections of network endpoints, or ports, capable of exchanging messages. In WSDL, endpoints and messages are separated from any concrete reference to protocols and data formats. As a result, the specification makes intensive use of a few general terms (for example, messages, ports, bindings, and operations) to abstract what in practice becomes a Web service method call operated through SOAP and HTTP.

Elements of the WSDL Syntax

To describe a network service, a WSDL document uses the elements listed in Table 17-1.

Table 17-1 Abstract Elements of a WSDL Document

Element	Description
binding	Represents a concrete protocol and data format specification for a particular port type
message	Is an abstract definition of the data being exchanged, and is used to represent the input and output of a method
operation	Is an abstract description of an action supported by the service, and is used to represent a callable method
port	Is defined as a combination of a binding and a URL, and represents the callable Web service
portType	Represents an abstract set of operations supported by one or more services defined in the document
service	Is a collection of related endpoints that indicates how many and which Web services have been found at the specified URL
types	Is a container for data type definitions expressed using XSD

To better understand the relationship and the role of these abstract elements, take a look at Figure 17-2.

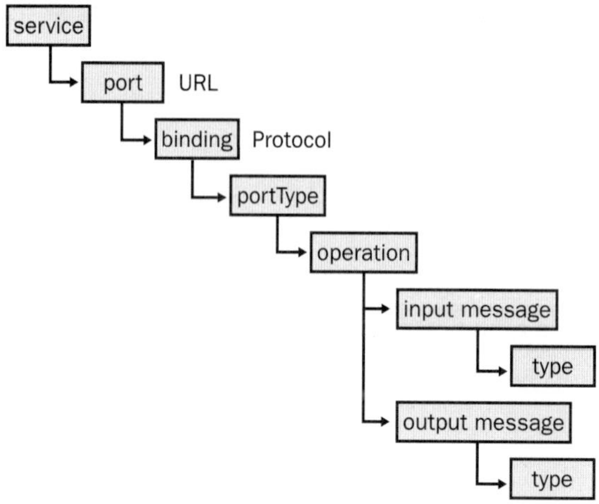

Figure 17-2 A hierarchical representation of the syntactical elements of a WSDL document.

The logical root of a WSDL document is the *<service>* tag, which lists all the callable endpoints found at the processed URL. You find an endpoint for each possible way of calling the Web service—typically through SOAP packets or direct HTTP-POST or HTTP-GET commands. In this case, three *<port>* elements will be found, each pointing to the physical URL to use.

Each Web service can have one or more bindings. You should think of a binding as a possible way to consume a Web service. As mentioned previously, you can consume a Web service by using various protocols. Each of them requires a binding to specify details. For example, the binding to the HTTP-POST protocol will explicitly indicate that the MIME content type of the input parameter is *application/x-www-form-urlencoded* and the verb to use is POST.

Each *<binding>* node refers to a port type to list all operations supported by the Web service. At this level, the operations are described in a rather abstract way, using messages instead of information about input and output parameters. In this context, a port type resembles an interface—an abstract set of logically related methods. Finally, any message points directly or indirectly to a name for the formal parameter and a type definition. A port type bound to SOAP will use a type definition within the *<types>* block. A port type bound to HTTP-POST or HTTP-GET will define the name and type within the *<message>* element.

A Sample WSDL Document

Let's consider a sample WSDL document; admittedly not a really complex one. However, once you understand this document, you'll be ready to tackle others with much more articulated structures. Consider the sample Web service available at *http://apps.gotdotnet.com/QuickStart/HelloWorld/HelloWorld.asmx*. It's made of a single method named *SayHelloWorld* having the following signature:

```
public string SayHelloWorld()
```

The WSDL for such a Web service is as follows:

```
<?xml version="1.0" encoding="utf-8"?>
<definitions
  xmlns:http="http://schemas.xmlsoap.org/wsdl/http/"
  xmlns:soap="http://schemas.xmlsoap.org/wsdl/soap/"
  xmlns:s="http://www.w3.org/2001/XMLSchema"
  xmlns:s0="http://tempuri.org/"
  xmlns:soapenc="http://schemas.xmlsoap.org/soap/encoding/"
  xmlns:tm="http://microsoft.com/wsdl/mime/textMatching/"
  xmlns:mime="http://schemas.xmlsoap.org/wsdl/mime/"
  targetNamespace="http://tempuri.org/"
  xmlns="http://schemas.xmlsoap.org/wsdl/">
  <types>
    <s:schema elementFormDefault="qualified"
      targetNamespace="http://tempuri.org/">
      <s:element name="SayHelloWorld">
        <s:complexType />
      </s:element>
      <s:element name="SayHelloWorldResponse">
        <s:complexType>
          <s:sequence>
            <s:element minOccurs="0" maxOccurs="1"
              name="SayHelloWorldResult" type="s:string" />
          </s:sequence>
        </s:complexType>
      </s:element>
    </s:schema>
  </types>

  <message name="SayHelloWorldSoapIn">
    <part name="parameters" element="s0:SayHelloWorld" />
  </message>
  <message name="SayHelloWorldSoapOut">
    <part name="parameters" element="s0:SayHelloWorldResponse" />
  </message>

  <portType name="HelloWorldSoap">
    <operation name="SayHelloWorld">
      <input message="s0:SayHelloWorldSoapIn" />
      <output message="s0:SayHelloWorldSoapOut" />
    </operation>
  </portType>
```

```
  <binding name="HelloWorldSoap" type="s0:HelloWorldSoap">
    <soap:binding transport="http://schemas.xmlsoap.org/soap/http" />
    <operation name="SayHelloWorld">
      <soap:operation soapAction="http://tempuri.org/SayHelloWorld" />
      <input>
        <soap:body use="literal" />
      </input>
      <output>
        <soap:body use="literal" />
      </output>
    </operation>
  </binding>

  <service name="HelloWorld">
    <port name="HelloWorldSoap" binding="s0:HelloWorldSoap">
      <soap:address
        location="http://apps.gotdotnet.com/... /HelloWorld.asmx" />
    </port>
  </service>
</definitions>
```

Looking at Figure 17-3, you can easily find a match between the abstract structure of Figure 17-2 and the listing just shown.

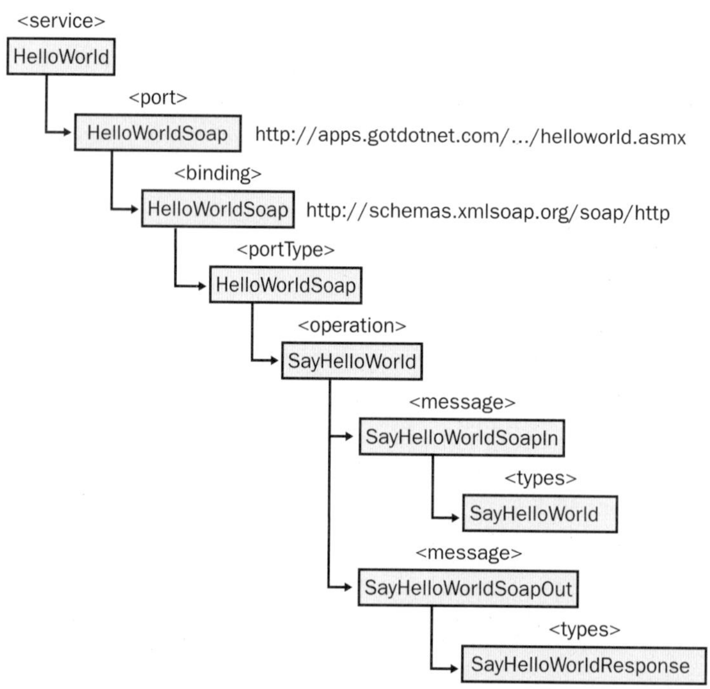

Figure 17-3 Mapping the actual nodes of the sample WSDL document to the abstract structure.

If you still find the WSDL language intimidating, don't worry. It's very unlikely that you'll have to create or consume WSDL on your own. Web Service platforms today generally have handy tools, system facilities, or utilities to consume and process WSDL automatically for you.

> **Note** To get the WSDL for a Web service based on the .NET Framework, you can invoke the URL of the Web service from your browser by appending *?wsdl* to the query string.

The .NET Infrastructure for Web Services

Historically speaking, Web services and the .NET Framework were introduced at roughly the same time in the summer of 2000, when SOAP was already taking root in the industry. Although it might be easy to associate Web services with the .NET platform, there is no strict dependency between them. As mentioned earlier, the .NET Framework is simply one of the platforms that support Web services—probably the first to integrate Web services in the framework from the ground up.

These days all major software vendors are rapidly transforming the raw idea of *software callable by other software* into a feature that fits seamlessly into the respective development platforms. A Web service can be created in a platform-specific manner, but the way in which it's exposed to the public is standard and universal. Let's examine the support that the .NET platform provides for building and running Web services.

IIS Support

Because a Web service is accessible through a public URL, it requires some sort of support from the Web server. In particular, the Web server must include a module capable of handling and parsing SOAP packets. The way in which this module gets into the game might vary with different Web servers. However, the availability of a SOAP parser within a Web server is a must for any server platform (for example, IIS or Apache) that wants to support Web services.

In .NET with IIS acting as the Web server, a Web service is an ASP.NET application saved with an .asmx extension. As Figure 17-4 demonstrates, IIS is configured to pass any requests for .asmx resources to the same ISAPI module that processes .aspx files. Instructions to handle Web services are stored in the IIS metabase during the installation of the .NET Framework.

> **Tip** For this reason, it's recommended that you install the .NET Framework after installing IIS. If you install IIS at a later time, you should run a utility to ensure that all configuration work is done. The utility is aspnet_regiis.exe, and you can find it in the C:\...\Microsoft.NET\Framework\v1.x.xxxx directory. The tool supports a variety of arguments on the command line. Use the following syntax:
>
> ```
> aspnet_regiis.exe -i
> ```

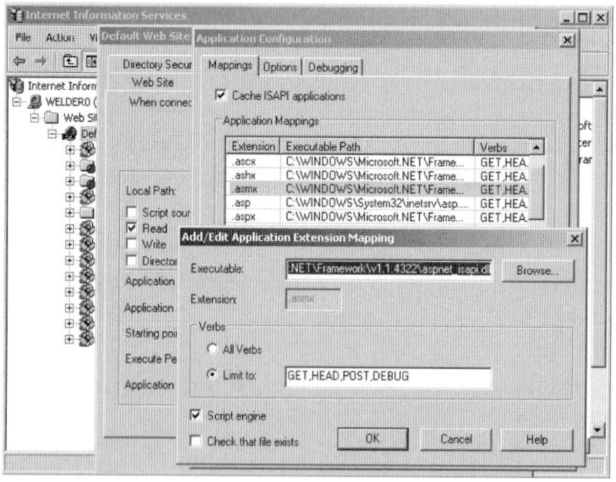

Figure 17-4 The IIS mapping between .asmx files and the ASP.NET runtime module.

Calls for Web services always come through port 80 as conventional HTTP requests. IIS intercepts these calls, looks at the extension of the resource, and hands the request over to the registered handler—the ASP.NET runtime. What happens next is described in Chapter 2 and is nearly identical to the request of a Web page. The ASP.NET worker process receives the request and routes it to an HTTP handler module specialized to handle Web service calls. The class is named *WebServiceHandler* and is defined within the *System.Web.Services.Protocols* namespace. The architecture is shown in Figure 17-5.

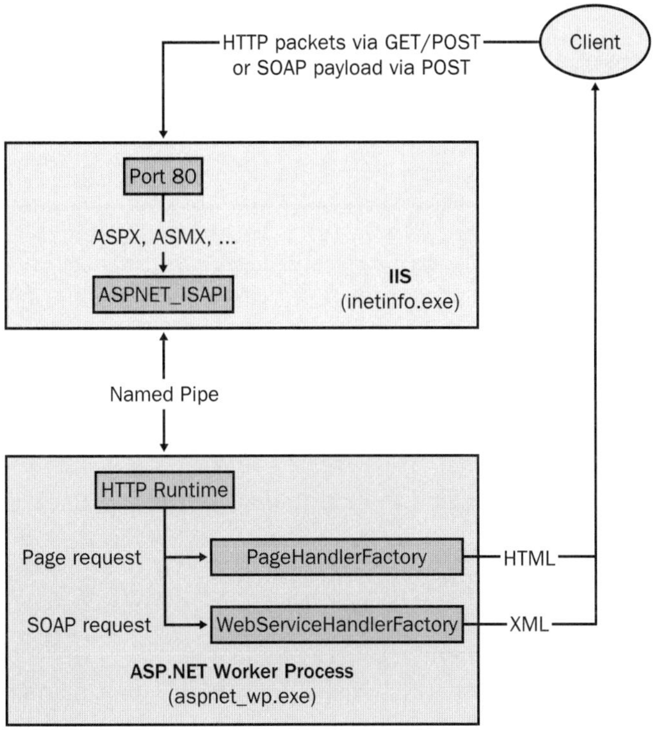

Figure 17-5 The ASP.NET architecture to process page and Web service requests.

Web Services Hosted by Apache Servers

In the Apache world (see *http://ws.apache.org*), Axis is the cutting-edge implementation of the SOAP specification. Based on Java, Axis requires the use of a servlet engine such as Tomcat (see *http://jakarta.apache.org/tomcat*). Once installed on the Web server machine, Axis is the server-side handler for Web service calls. Axis is a SOAP implementation that can host your own Web services but can also be added to your own Web application to expose it as a Web service.

Generally speaking, an Axis Web service consists of a plain Java class visible in the Web application space. You'll use an XML configuration file to specify which methods you want to expose, which security constraints are needed, and other useful information. A simpler alternative is renaming the Java class that represents the Web service, giving it a .jws extension, and putting it in a publicly accessible Web folder. When someone asks for the .jws resource, the Web server hands the request out to Axis. The class is then compiled and executed (much like a Java Server Page), exposing its public methods as Web methods.

The *WebService* Class

In the .NET Framework, a Web service is an ordinary class with public and protected methods. Web service files contain a directive that informs the ASP.NET runtime about the nature of the file, the language in use throughout, and the main class that implements the service:

```
<%@ WebService Language="C#" Class="MyWebService" %>
```

The main class must match the name declared in the *Class* attribute and must be public:

```
public class MyWebService : WebService {
    ⋮
}
```

Indicating the base class for a .NET Web service is not mandatory. A Web service can also be architected starting from the ground up by using a new class. Inheriting the behavior of the *WebService* class has some advantages, though. A Web service based on the *System.Web.Services.WebService* class gets direct access to common ASP.NET objects, including *Application*, *Request*, *Cache*, *Session*, and *Server*. These objects are packed into an *HttpContext* object, which also includes the time when the request was made. By using the *WebService* base class, a Web service also sees the ASP.NET server *User* object, which under certain conditions can be employed to verify the credentials of the user (often the anonymous user) who is executing the methods. If you don't have any need to access the ASP.NET object model, you can do without the *WebService* class and simply implement the Web service as a class with public methods.

Note Even if you don't inherit the Web service from the *WebService* class, you can still access ASP.NET intrinsic objects by using the *HttpContext.Current* static property, which gets the *HttpContext* object for the current HTTP request. The *HttpContext* class is defined in the *System.Web* namespace.

Building an ASP.NET Web Service

So you want to build your first Web service. Where do you start? Within the .NET Framework, a Web service is simply a class that can optionally inherit from *WebService*. As such, the class can implement any number of interfaces and can inherit from other user-defined classes. Moreover, when designing a real-world Web service, you're encouraged to employ standard object-oriented programming practices—such as inheritance and polymorphism—to reuse code and simplify the design. If you proceed this way, you derive the root class of the hierarchy from *WebService* and have the base class behavior inherited by all actual services you build.

Writing a Web Service Class

The Web service class is normally coded in an .asmx file. The file is made available to potential clients through a Web server virtual directory and is actually reached using a URL. Any client that can issue HTTP commands can actually connect to the Web service.

Let's create a Web service that accesses the Northwind database and provides information about customers and orders. The main class inherits from *WebService* and is named *NorthwindAnalysisService*.

```
<%@ WebService Language="C#" Class="NorthwindAnalysisService" %>
using System.Web.Services;

public class NorthwindAnalysisService : WebService {
    ⋮
}
```

You add an *@WebService* directive to the top of the file to indicate the class implementing the Web service and the programming language used in the implementation. The *Class* attribute can be set to a class residing in the same file or to a class within a separate assembly (more on this later in the "Precompiled Web Services" section). The *Class* attribute is important because it indicates which class is to be treated as the Web service class when there is more than one public class defined in the .asmx file.

The *Language* attribute can be set to a valid ASP.NET language, which as of ASP.NET 1.1 can be C#, Visual Basic .NET, JScript .NET, or J#. (See Chapter 1.) A third attribute can be specified—*Debug*—which works like Web-page enabling debuggers to step through the source code of the Web service.

The *WebService* Attribute

The Web service class is normally marked with the *WebService* attribute. The attribute is optional but should be considered a must for any serious Web service. It allows you to change three default settings for the Web service: the namespace, name, and description.

Within the body of the *WebService* attribute, you simply insert a comma-separated list of names and values. The keyword *Description* contains the description of the Web service, whereas *Name* points to the official name of the Web service.

```
[WebService(
    Name="Northwind Analysis Service",
    Description="Returns customers and orders information")]
public class NorthwindAnalysisService : WebService {
    ⋮
}
```

Changing the name and description of the Web service is mostly a matter of consistency. If you don't provide a more descriptive name, the name of the implementing class is assumed as the name of the Web service; no default description is provided.

The *Name* attribute is used to name the service in the WSDL document that explains its behavior to prospective clients. The description is not used in the WSDL document but is only retrieved and displayed by the IIS default page for URLs with an .asmx extension.

Changing the Default Namespace

Each Web service should have a unique namespace that makes it clearly distinguishable from others. By default, the .NET Framework gives each new Web service the same default namespace: *http://tempuri.org*. The default namespace should be replaced as soon as possible and certainly prior to publishing the service on the Web.

Note that using a temporary name doesn't affect overall functionality, but it will affect consistency and violate a Web service common naming convention. The only way you have to change the default namespace of an ASP.NET Web service is by setting the *Namespace* property of the *WebService* attribute, as shown in the following example:

```
[WebService(
    Namespace="ProAspNet/0-7356-1903-4",
    Name="Northwind Analysis Service",
    Description="Returns customers and orders information")]
public class NorthwindAnalysisService : WebService {
    ⋮
}
```

As discussed earlier, the namespace information is used extensively in the WSDL document that describes the Web service. In the preceding example, I've used the ISBN of this book.

Precompiled Web Services

If you have a precompiled class that you want to expose as a Web service, or if you want to write a Web service using a code-behind class, you can create an .asmx file that contains only the following line:

```
<%@ WebService Class="ProAspNet.CS.Ch17.NorthwindAnalysisService" %>
```

The value of the *Class* attribute denotes the class that implements the Web service. The class must be contained in the Bin subdirectory of the ASP.NET application. The advantage of using precompiled assemblies is that you don't need to deploy a file that contains the source code of the Web service.

Exposing Web Methods

In an ASP.NET Web service, a public method is not accessible to external clients over the network by default. To be accessible over the Internet, a method must be declared public and marked with the *[WebMethod]* attribute. In practice, the *[WebMethod]* attribute represents another member modifier like *public*, *protected*, or *internal*. Clients that access the Web service class locally see all the public members; clients accessing the class through the Web service infrastructure see only the methods marked as Web methods. Any attempt to invoke untagged methods via a URL results in a failure.

Note that if the requested method—the *SOAPAction* attribute of the payload generated by .NET Web services—is not available or not accessible, the HTTP return code is HTTP 500 Internal Error.

The *[WebMethod]* attribute features a variety of attributes that can be helpful to optimize the interaction with the method. We'll examine the attributes of a Web method later in the chapter in the "Attributes of Web Methods" section.

Defining a Web Method

Let's add a Web method to the *NorthwindAnalysisService* class. The method is named *GetCustomersOrders* and has the following prototype:

```
[WebMethod]
public DataSet GetCustomersOrders(string custID, int year)
```

The input parameters are primitive types—*string* and *integer*—but the return type of the method is a .NET Framework type—a *DataSet*. As we'll see in the next section, return types of Web service methods can always be complex types as long as they can be serialized to XML. The input types are subject to the protocol used to invoke the Web service. If the call goes through the SOAP protocol, complex types such as the *DataSet*, or custom classes, can be seamlessly used. If the HTTP-POST or the HTTP-GET protocols are used, input types are limited to primitive types.

The *GetCustomersOrders* method executes a query against the SQL Server Northwind database and returns all the orders that the specified customer issued in the given year. The SQL query is as follows:

```
SELECT o.customerid, od.orderid, SUM(quantity*unitprice) AS price,
       o.orderdate, o.shipcountry
FROM Orders o, [Order Details] od
WHERE o.orderid=od.orderid AND
      o.customerid=@theCust AND
      YEAR(orderdate)=@theYear
GROUP BY o.customerid, od.orderid, o.orderdate, o.shipcountry
```

The method uses a data adapter to execute the query. The two parameters of the query—the customer ID and the year—are set through parameters. The source code of the method is shown here:

```
[WebMethod]
public DataSet GetCustomersOrders(string custID, int year)
{
    // Check if a valid custID has been provided
    if (!IsValidCustomerID(custID))
        return null;

    // Prepare the query
    string _cmd = String.Format(m_cmdCustOrders, custID, year);
    SqlDataAdapter _adapter = new SqlDataAdapter(_cmd,
        m_connectionString);

    // Add parameters
    SqlParameter p1 = new SqlParameter("@theCust", SqlDbType.NChar, 5);
    p1.Value = custID;
    _adapter.SelectCommand.Parameters.Add(p1);
    SqlParameter p2 = new SqlParameter("@theYear", SqlDbType.Int);
    p2.Value = year;
    _adapter.SelectCommand.Parameters.Add(p2);

    // Execute the query
    DataSet _data = new DataSet("NorthwindAnalysis");
    _adapter.Fill(_data, "Orders");

    return _data;
}
```

Any method in any class, but especially a method in a Web service, should apply the golden rule of secure coding—don't trust user input. In this case, we can be sure about the year argument because the Web service infrastructure will try to convert it to an integer, failing if it contains strings. Can we say the same about the customer ID argument?

To stay on the safe side, we implement a quick validation test. The first time the method is accessed, the whole list of customers is loaded into *Application*. The passed customer ID is matched against the memory resident list. If no match is found, a null value is returned.

```
protected virtual bool IsValidCustomerID(string custID)
{
    // Get the list of customers if not available
    if (Application["CustomerList"] == null) {
        // Get the list of customers
        SqlDataAdapter _adapter;
        _adapter = new SqlDataAdapter("SELECT * FROM customers",
            m_connectionString);
        DataSet _customers = new DataSet();

        // Creates an in-memory index on the same field
        // indexed on the database table. An in-memory index
        // will allow the use of the (fast) Find method to retrieve rows
        _adapter.MissingSchemaAction = MissingSchemaAction.AddWithKey;

        _adapter.Fill(_customers, "Customers");
        Application["CustomerList"] = _customers;
    }

    // Try to find a match for the specified customer ID
    DataSet _tmp = (DataSet) Application["CustomerList"];
    DataTable _table = _tmp.Tables["Customers"];
    DataRow _row = _table.Rows.Find(custID);
    return (_row != null);
}
```

The *DataSet* type works well with Web services because of its inherently disconnected nature. *DataSet* objects can store complex information and relationships in an intelligent structure. By exposing *DataSet* objects through a Web service, you can limit the database connections your data server is experiencing. You should note, though, that the *DataSet* type cannot be used with input parameters if the request is not made through SOAP packets.

To deploy the Web service, you create a new virtual directory and copy the .asmx file in it. A quick but effective way to test a Web service consists in pointing the browser to the .asmx URL. In this case, IIS provides a default page to let you test the service. The page is shown in Figures 17-6.

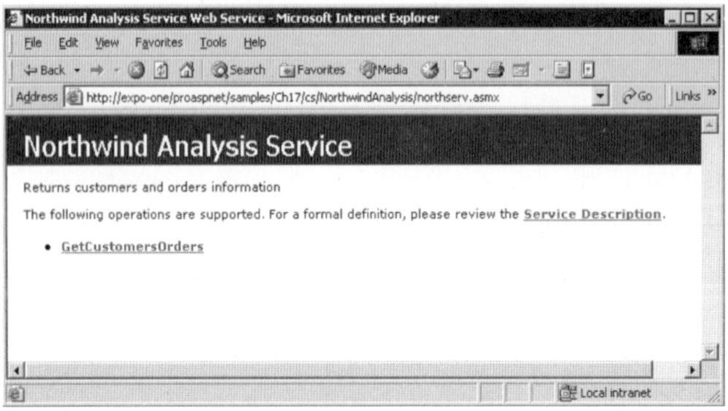

Figure 17-6 The test page that IIS displays when you request a Web service from the local machine.

Once you select the method to test, the form in Figure 17-7 pops up.

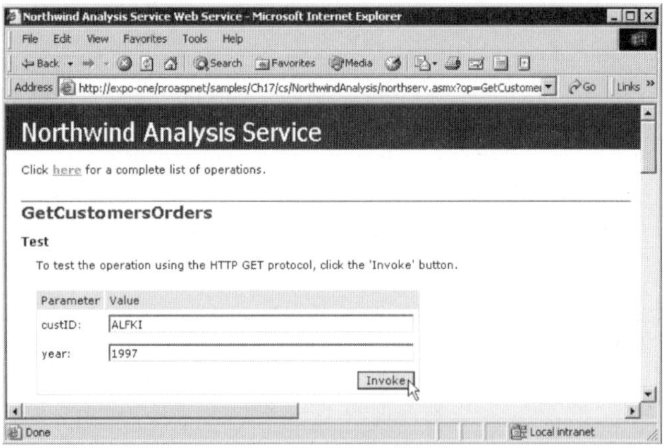

Figure 17-7 You enter parameters and invoke the method. The page works only through the HTTP-GET protocol. If the method can't be called through HTTP-GET, no form will be displayed.

The XML text returned by the Web method is shown using a new browser window, as in Figure 17-8.

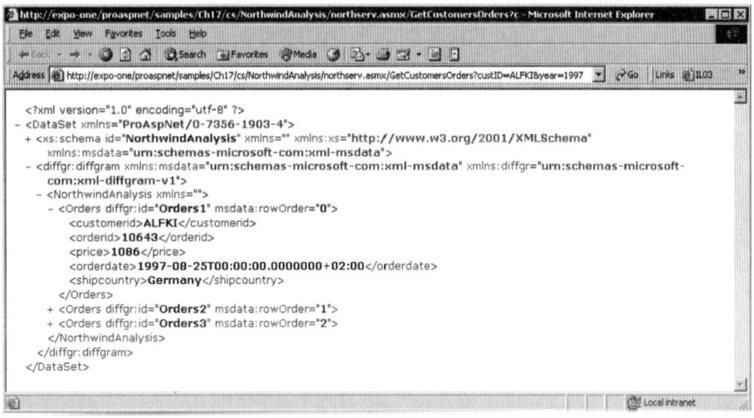

Figure 17-8 The return value for the previous call.

Type Marshaling

Various data types can be passed to and returned from Web service methods. In the .NET Framework, the Web services type marshaling extensively uses the XML serializer—the *XmlSerializer* class defined in the *System.Xml.Serialization* namespace. With some limitations that we'll discuss in a moment, all the following types can be used with Web services:

- **Primitive Types** Standard primitive types including *String*, *Char*, *Byte*, *Boolean*, *Int16*, *Int32*, *Int64*, *UInt16*, *UInt32*, *UInt64*, *Single*, *Double*, *Guid*, *Decimal*, and *DateTime*.
- **Enum Types** System and user-defined enumeration types. The enumeration must be defined as public within the Web service and can be used as a return value. A less than public enumeration would cause the XML serializer to fail. The definition of the enumeration will be included in the WSDL document for the Web service and automatically imported in the .NET client through either Microsoft Visual Studio .NET or proxy classes manually generated (more on building proxy classes later in the "Referencing Web Services from ASP.NET" section). Note that any nondefault value of the enumeration type will be lost. In other words, only the mnemonic names are returned, not the value behind. From the client's perspective, enumeration types become classes with a static *const* string for each value.
- **Classes and Structs** Class and struct types with public fields or properties. Only the public properties and fields are serialized. Any private and protected members the type might have will be ignored.

In addition, if the type features a circular reference, the serializer fails and so does the method call. The *DataSet* type is an illustrious exception to this rule. Noticeably, the class doesn't have to be serializable in the sense of the runtime object serialization that we briefly discussed in Chapter 16.

- **DataSet** Web services can work with the ADO.NET *DataSet* type. However, the *DataSet* is supported by the XML serializer as an exception to the rule that classes with circular references aren't serialized. A circular reference is a double link between classes, in which both contain a member of the other type. Almost all ADO.NET objects have circular references, but the XML serializer makes an exception only for the *DataSet*. As a result, you cannot return or pass a *DataTable* to a Web method.
- **XmlNode** The *XmlNode* class represents a single node in the XML document, and as such, it's an in-memory representation of an XML fragment. You can pass *XmlNode* objects as parameters, and they are added to the rest of the XML being passed to the Web service (the other parameters) in a SOAP-compliant manner. The same is true for return values. This allows you to pass or return XML whose structure changes from call to call, or work with XML when you might not know all the types being passed. *XmlNode* objects can also appear as fields in structs or classes. The *XmlNode* class is the second (and last) exception to the rule of circular references.
- **Arrays** Web methods support arrays of any of the aforementioned types. You can return arrays of primitive types, such as an array of strings, as well as arrays of *XmlNode* and *DataSet* objects and arrays of classes.

The class working behind type marshaling in the Web service architecture is *XmlSerializer*. Unlike the runtime serialization formatters, the class doesn't ensure true type fidelity, but simply an effective XSD (or SOAP-encoded) representation of the data being passed back and forth. Thanks to the combined effect of the XML serializer and the proxy classes, the marshaling of data types is transparent to the client application that consumes a Web service.

For example, a .NET client that invokes our Web service gets back a string that is the XML representation of the *DataSet* class. The string includes the XSD schema of the class. However, the XML representation of the *DataSet* is a schema that the XML serializer knows because it's part of the .NET Framework. Subsequently, the proxy class that client applications need to effectively call into Web services takes care of the deserialization step and provides the application with a ready-to-use instance of a *DataSet* object.

If a Linux client attempts to access this Web service, it still gets the same XML representation of the *DataSet*. In this case, the *DataSet* schema is likely to be just an unknown schema to the Linux application. As a result, the client application is responsible for parsing its contents and builds any useful representation of the data stored. Depending on the Web service support that the target platform provides, chances are that the *DataSet* can be automatically mapped to a dynamically generated class that the application can handle. (We'll see more about *DataSet* and Web services later.)

> **Note** For example, on a Java platform proxy classes can be statically generated by the wsdl2Java tool, which works in much the same way as the wsdl.exe utility does for .NET Web services. Interestingly, for an Axis Web service there is also a dynamic call option, similar to .NET Remoting proxies, which makes use of a reflection-like mechanism to detect methods and validate calls.

A .NET client is a bit more fortunate because the proxy class imports the XML schema returned by the method and transforms it into a brand new .NET Framework class.

Note that all the aforementioned types are supported as return values of Web methods whether the Web service is invoked using SOAP, HTTP-GET, or HTTP-POST. As for parameters, the types we just discussed can be used if the protocol is SOAP but not if the method is invoked using HTTP-GET or HTTP-POST. In these cases, in fact, the supported types are only primitives, enumeration types, and arrays of primitives.

Under the Hood of a Web Method Call

Any call made to a Web service method is resolved by an HTTP handler module tailor-made for Web services. Once the incoming call has been recognized as a Web service call and dispatched to the ASP.NET runtime, an instance of the *WebServiceHandlerFactory* class is created. The factory object compiles the Web service class into an assembly (only the first time) and parses the SOAP headers and contents. If the parse step is successful, the request is transformed into method information. An ad hoc data structure is created to contain information such as the name of the method, the list of formal and actual parameters, whether the method is void, and the returned type.

The method information is then passed to a call handler that will actually take care of executing the method. According to the information specified in the request, the call handler can contain context information (for example, *Session*) and work either synchronously or asynchronously. Finally, the server object is instantiated, the method is invoked, and the return value gets written to the output stream. Figure 17-9 illustrates the various steps of the process.

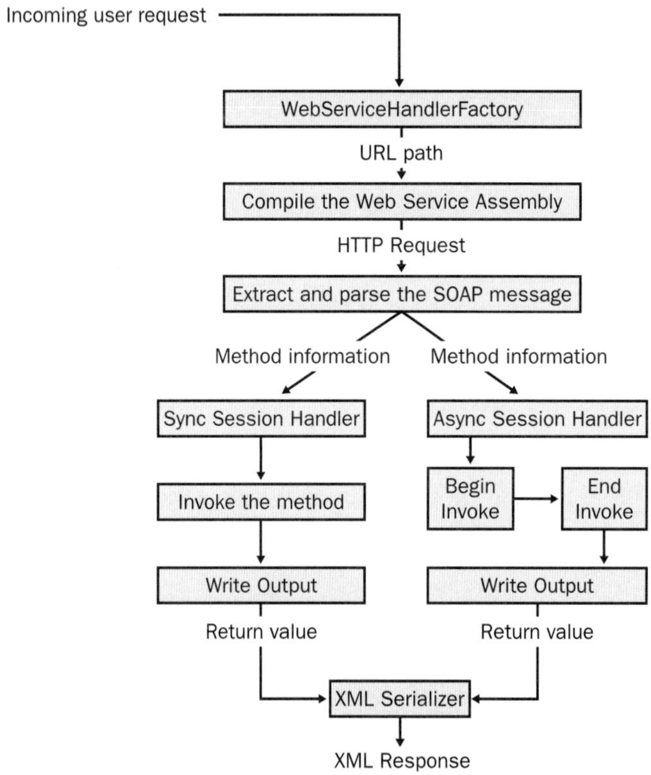

Figure 17-9 The steps needed to process a Web service call.

Referencing Web Services from ASP.NET

You can invoke a Web service in either of two ways. One possibility requires you to connect to the URL and get back the XML document with the embedded results. The second possibility involves proxy classes. A proxy class is an intermediate class that represents a local intermediary object that mirrors the programming interface of the remote Web service. The proxy class is added to the client project and bridges the local application with the remote server. The proxy can employ a variety of protocols to invoke the Web service, including SOAP and HTTP-POST. The proxy class is most often generated by a system utility and contains an infrastructure to call Web methods both synchronously and asynchronously, and to handle the parameter serialization and return value deserialization.

Building a Proxy Class

If you develop your ASP.NET application using Visual Studio .NET, you'll see that adding a reference to a Web service is not any more complex than adding a reference to a local assembly. You right-click the project node and choose to add a new Web reference. Next, you are shown a search dialog box that allows you to browse for Web services on the local machine, as well as in local and remote UDDI directories. If you know the URL of a particular Web service, you can enter it directly in the dialog box address bar and click to continue. If the Web service is found, a screen that looks like Figure 17-10 will appear.

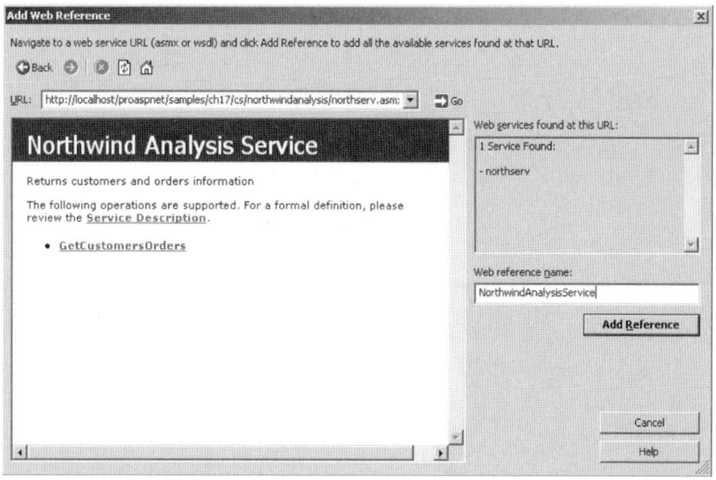

Figure 17-10 Browsing for Web services and adding references to Visual Studio .NET projects.

When you add a reference to a Web service, Visual Studio .NET generates a proxy class and automatically adds it to the project. The class is created using the language of the project and is given a default name (reference.cs if the project is a C# project). The proxy class defaults to the SOAP protocol to invoke the Web service and hard-codes the URL of the Web service.

> **Note** Although Visual Studio .NET by default hides the proxy reference file from view—and in spite of the warnings contained in the source file itself—the file can be modified without any particular concerns. Of course, take this last statement with a grain of salt. It actually means that the file can be modified without worries if you know what you're doing. Safe actions you can take on the reference file are changing the URL, adding some code to methods, adding new methods, and changing the namespace or the base class for the protocol. Altering the structure of the file incorrectly might result in a loss of functionality. In that case, a new reference file must be generated by removing and re-adding the Web reference.

If you're not using Visual Studio .NET, or if you want to keep the proxy class under strict control, you can generate one using the wsdl.exe utility. The utility is located in the C:\Program Files\Microsoft Visual Studio .NET 2003\SDK\v1.1\Bin directory. This application is the same tool that Visual Studio .NET utilizes to generate the proxy class. The command line of the utility is as follows:

```
wsdl.exe [options] url
```

Table 17-2 details the various switches you can use.

Table 17-2 Switches Supported by the wsdl.exe Utility

Option	Description
/language:<language>	The language to use for the generated proxy class. Choose from *CS*, *VB*, *JS*, and *VJS* (J#). The default is *CS*. Short form is */l:xxx*.
/namespace:<namespace>	The namespace for the generated proxy class. The default namespace is the global namespace. Short form is */n:xxx*.
/out:<fileName>	The filename for the generated proxy class. The default name is derived from the service name. Short form is */o:xxx*.
/protocol:<protocol>	The protocol to implement. Choose from *SOAP* (default), *HttpGet*, and *HttpPost*. You can also choose a custom protocol as specified in the web.config file of the Web service. SOAP 1.2 is expected to be supported in a future release of the .NET Framework.

Table 17-2 Switches Supported by the wsdl.exe Utility

Option	Description
/username:<username> */password:*<password> */domain:*<domain>	The credentials to use when connecting to a server that requires authentication. Short forms are */u:xxx*, */p:xxx* and */d:xxx*.
/proxy:<url>	The URL of the proxy server to use for HTTP requests. The default is to use the system proxy setting.
/proxyusername:<username> */proxypassword:*<password> */proxydomain:*<domain>	The credentials to use when connecting to a proxy server that requires authentication. Short forms are */pu:xxx*, */pp:xxx* and */pd:xxx*.
/appsettingurlkey:<key>	The name of the web.config key from which the proxy class reads the URL of the Web service. By default, the URL is hard-coded. Short form is */urlkey:xxx*.
/appsettingbaseurl:<baseurl>	The base URL to use when calculating the URL of the Web service. This option must be used in conjunction with the *appsettingurlkey* option. Short form is */baseurl:xxx*.

Called the default way, the WSDL utility generates the following proxy class for the Northwind Analysis Web Service. The command line is:

```
using System.Diagnostics;
using System.Xml.Serialization;
using System;
using System.Web.Services.Protocols;
using System.Web.Services;

[System.Diagnostics.DebuggerStepThroughAttribute()]
[System.ComponentModel.DesignerCategoryAttribute("code")]
[System.Web.Services.WebServiceBindingAttribute(
    Name="Northwind Analysis ServiceSoap",
    Namespace="ProAspNet/0-7356-1903-4")]
public class NorthwindAnalysisService : SoapHttpClientProtocol
{
    public NorthwindAnalysisService() {
        Url = "http://localhost/.../northserv.asmx";
    }

    [System.Web.Services.Protocols.SoapDocumentMethodAttribute(
        "ProAspNet/0-7356-1903-4/GetCustomersOrders",
        RequestNamespace="ProAspNet/0-7356-1903-4",
        ResponseNamespace="ProAspNet/0-7356-1903-4",
```

```
        Use=System.Web.Services.Description.SoapBindingUse.Literal)]
    public DataSet GetCustomersOrders(string custID, int year) {
        object[] results = Invoke("GetCustomersOrders",
        new object[] {custID, year});
        return (DataSet) (results[0]);
    }

    public IAsyncResult BeginGetCustomersOrders(string custID, int year,
        AsyncCallback callback, object asyncState) {
        return this.BeginInvoke("GetCustomersOrders",
            new object[] {custID, year}, callback, asyncState);
    }

    public DataSet EndGetCustomersOrders(IAsyncResult asyncResult) {
        object[] results = EndInvoke(asyncResult);
        return (DataSet) (results[0]);
    }
}
```

To communicate with a Web service, you must create a proxy class deriving indirectly or directly from the base class *HttpWebClientProtocol*. Typical classes you base your proxy on are *SoapHttpClientProtocol* if you want to go with SOAP packets or *HttpPostClientProtocol* if you want to go with HTTP-POST commands.

> **Note** The base class for a proxy class is different if you're using Web Services Enhancements (WSE) for Microsoft .NET. In this case, the base client protocol class is *WebServicesClientProtocol*.

When a proxy class is generated for the SOAP protocol, synchronous calls to Web service methods are made via the *Invoke* method, whereas asynchronous calls are made via *BeginInvoke* and *EndInvoke*. The proxy class supports asynchronous calls only if SOAP is used as the protocol. (HTTP-GET and HTTP-POST aren't supported, for example.) The *Invoke* method prepares the SOAP packets necessary to handshake with the Web service. It takes the name of the method and an array of objects in which elements represent individual method parameters.

Setting the URL of a Web Service

The URL of a Web service is just a public read/write property exposed by the protocol class—the *Url* property. In situations in which the URL cannot be determined univocally, or might change on a per-user basis or because of other runtime factors, you can ask the wsdl.exe utility not to hard-code the URL in the source. By using the */urlkey* command-line switch, you instruct the utility to dynamically read the Web service URL from the application's configuration file. If you use a switch such as */urlkey:ActualUrl*, the proxy class constructor changes as follows:

```
public NorthwindAnalysisService () {
    string urlSetting = ConfigurationSettings.AppSettings["ActualUrl"];
    if ((urlSetting != null))
        Url = urlSetting;
    else  // defaults to the URL used to build the proxy
        Url = "http://localhost/.../northserv.asmx";
}
```

The URL is read from the web.config file by using the *AppSettings* collection.

Disabling HTTP-POST and HTTP-GET

While HTTP-POST and HTTP-GET make accessing a Web service easier than ever, they leave the Web service door open to any HTTP packets. The SOAP protocol for the filtering capabilities of the *SOAPAction* attribute—especially when considering the syntax of the payloads—is inherently more resistant to malicious attacks than HTTP-POST and HTTP-GET. For this reason, you might want to configure your Web service so that its results are accessible only through the SOAP protocol.

If you want to disable HTTP-POST and HTTP-GET support, make sure the local web.config file contains the following text:

```
<configuration>
  <system.web>
    <webServices>
      <protocols>
        <remove name="HttpPost" />
        <remove name="HttpGet" />
      </protocols>
    </webServices>
  </system.web>
</configuration>
```

The HTTP-POST and HTTP-GET protocols will remain enabled for all Web services except the one that explicitly disables them. To disable them for all Web services on the machine, you must update the machine.config file instead. Under the same path, you should simply comment out the *<add>* nodes that relate to POST and GET.

Note If you look at the *<webServices>* section in web.config, you can't help but notice the special *Documentation* protocol. The protocol is the key that enables the ASP.NET runtime to deliver a test page when you point your browser to a .asmx resource. The default page is generated by a file named DefaultWsdlHelpGenerator.aspx located in the same folder as machine.config. The page can be replaced through the following configuration code:

```
<webServices>
    <wsdlHelpGenerator href="YourGeneratorPage.aspx"/>
</webServices>
```

Of course, the help page can be customized for all Web services or only for a particular Web service. In the latter case, you should enter the previous changes in the local web.config file.

Note that ASP.NET 1.1 enables an extra protocol named *HttpPostLocal*. This protocol automatically enables posting to the Web service through the .asmx URL only from the local machine. If you want the ASP.NET engine to show the test user interface of .NET Web services to remote users, you must disable the *HttpPostLocal* protocol in the web.config file.

Invoking Methods on a Web Service

Let's see how to build a sample ASP.NET page to consume the Web service. Once you created the proxy class, you should make it available to the ASP.NET application. If the application is being developed through a Visual Studio .NET project, you simply add the file to the project or, better yet, import the Web service automatically by using the Add Web Reference menu. If you're not using Visual Studio, you must compile the proxy class into an assembly and make the assembly available in the Bin subdirectory of the Web application.

For example, you can manually compile a C# proxy class by using the following command:

```
csc  /out:northservproxy.dll
     /t:library
     /r:System.Xml.dll, System.Web.Services.dll
     NorthwindAnalysisService.cs
```

The resultant assembly is named northservproxy.dll and references internally the *System.Xml* and *System.Web.Services* assemblies. Note that csc.exe is the C# compiler provided with the .NET Framework.

If the assembly with the proxy class is available in the Web space of the application, the ASP.NET page can use the proxy class as if it were an ordinary class of the .NET Framework. The following source code depicts a Web page with a couple of drop-down lists to pick up customer and year and a link button to retrieve orders:

```
<%@ Page Language="C#" %>
<%@ Import Namespace="System.Data" %>
<%@ Import Namespace="System.Data.SqlClient" %>

<script runat="server">
void Page_Load(object sender, EventArgs e) {
    if (!IsPostBack) {
        yearList.Items.Clear();
        yearList.Items.Add("1996");
        yearList.Items.Add("1997");
        yearList.Items.Add("1998");

        SqlDataAdapter adapter;
        adapter = new SqlDataAdapter("SELECT customerid FROM customers",
            "DATABASE=northwind;SERVER=localhost;UID=sa;");
        DataSet data = new DataSet();
        adapter.Fill(data);

        customerList.DataSource = data.Tables[0];
        customerList.DataTextField = "customerid";
        customerList.DataValueField = "customerid";
        Page.DataBind();
    }
}

// WARNING: SelectedValue is specific of ASP.NET 1.1
void GetData(object sender, EventArgs e) {
    NorthwindAnalysisService serv = new NorthwindAnalysisService();
    DataSet data = serv.GetCustomersOrders(customerList.SelectedValue,
        Convert.ToInt32(yearList.SelectedValue));
    grid.DataSource = data.Tables[0];
    grid.DataBind();
}
</script>

<html>
<body>
<form runat="server">
    <asp:dropdownlist runat="server" id="customerList" />
    <asp:dropdownlist runat="server" id="yearList" />
    <asp:linkbutton runat="server" text="Go get data" onclick="GetData" />
```

```
    <hr>
    <asp:datagrid runat="server" id="grid" />
</form>
</body>
</html>
```

The output of the page is shown in Figure 17-11.

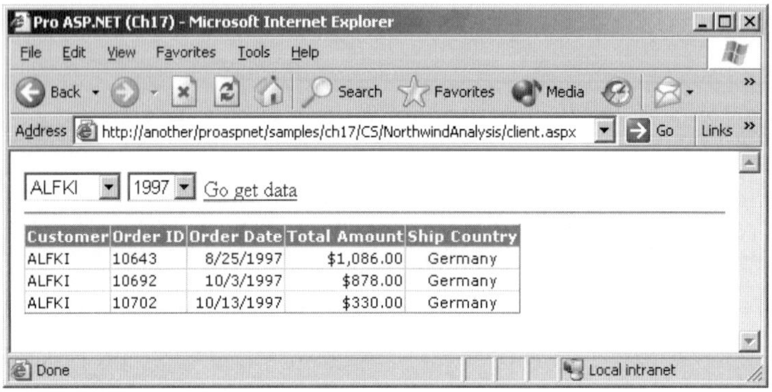

Figure 17-11 A sample page using a Web service.

> **Caution** In the preceding code, we used the *SelectedValue* property of the *DropDownList* Web control. You should note that the property is supported only in ASP.NET 1.1. The *SelectedValue* is exposed by the *ListControl* class from which *CheckBoxList*, *RadioButtonList*, and *ListBox* also inherit. The property is read/write and, as such, can be used to get and set the currently selected value (not the text). To make the preceding code work with ASP.NET 1.0, replace *SelectedValue* with *SelectedItem.Value*.

Web Methods Best Practices

While exposing a Web method is an easy task to accomplish, blending method attributes well to set up an effective call is not always easy. The execution of a Web method is a function of several parameters and can be optimized in many ways. Regardless of the magic performed by the proxy class, which gives the illusion of a local call, a Web method is a very special breed of code. It executes remotely, and it carries parameters and return values back and forth on top of a transportation protocol. This characteristic raises a few issues.

A Web method can certainly throw exceptions, but how do you handle them on the client? A Web method can execute in the context of a transaction, but can you realistically think of enlisting a Web service in a distributed transaction? A Web method call goes through the Internet and is likely to take seconds to complete. How can you minimize the impact of this structural aspect, though? Let's examine a few best practices for designing and implementing Web methods.

Attributes of Web Methods

The *[WebMethod]* attribute supports some properties that can be used to tune the behavior of the method. Table 17-3 lists the properties.

Table 17-3 Properties of the *WebMethod* Attribute

Property	Description
BufferResponse	Set to *true* by default, this property indicates that IIS should buffer the method's entire response before sending it to the client. Even if set to *false*, the response is partially buffered; however, in this case, the size of the buffer is limited to 16 KB.
CacheDuration	Specifies the number of seconds that IIS should cache the response of the method. This information is useful when you can foresee that the method will handle several calls in a short period of time. Set to *0* by default (meaning no caching), the caching engine is smart enough to recognize and cache page invocations that use different parameter values.
Description	Provides the description for the method. The value of the property is then embedded into the WSDL description of the service.
EnableSession	Set to *false* by default, this property makes available to the method the *Session* object of the ASP.NET environment. Depending on how *Session* is configured, using this property might require cookie support on the client or a SQL Server 2000 installation on the server. (See Chapter 14.)
MessageName	Allows you to provide a publicly callable name for the method. When you set this property, the resulting SOAP messages for the method target the name you set instead of the actual name. Use this property to give distinct names to overloaded methods.
TransactionOption	Specifies the level of COM+ (local) transactional support you want for the method. A Web service method can have only two behaviors, regardless of the value assigned to the standard *TransactionOption* enumeration you select: either it does not require a transaction or it must be the root of a new transaction.

The following code snippet shows how to set a few method attributes:

```
[WebMethod(
    CacheDuration=60,
    Description="Return orders for a customer in a given year")]
public DataSet GetCustomersOrders(string custID, int year)
{
    ⋮
}
```

Attributes must be strongly typed in the declaration. In other words, the value you assign to *CacheDuration* must be a number and not a quoted string containing a number.

Caching the Output of a Web Method

The *CacheDuration* property is implemented using the ASP.NET *Cache* object, which proves once again the tight integration between Web services and the ASP.NET runtime. Just before instantiating the Web service class, the Web service handler configures the *Cache* object. In particular, the handler sets the cache to work on the server, as shown here:

```
Response.Cache.SetCacheability(HttpCacheability.Server);
```

In addition, the handler sets the expiration time and configures the caching subsystem for parametric output, as follows:

```
Response.Cache.VaryByHeaders["SOAPAction"] = true;
Response.Cache.VaryByParams["*"] = true;
```

As we saw in Chapter 14, the *VaryByHeaders* property enables you to cache multiple versions of a page, depending on the value of the HTTP headers you specify (in this example, the header value is *SOAPAction*)—that is, the method invoked. The *VaryByParams* property, on the other hand, lets you maintain different caches for each set of distinct values of the specified parameter. In this case, using the asterisk (*) indicates that all parameters must be considered and cached separately.

As shown in an earlier *CacheDuration* code snippet, IIS maintains the output of calls for each distinct pair of customer ID and year. The cache is global and accessible to different sessions. An easy way to verify that the output of the method is being cached is storing somewhere in the *DataSet* the time at which the returned data is collected. The *DataSet ExtendedProperties* collection seems to be the ideal place for this kind of information.

```
// Fill the DataSet and store the time the query occurred
DataSet _data = new DataSet("OrderList");
_data.ExtendedProperties["QueryTime"] = DateTime.Now.ToString("hh-mm-ss");
_adapter.Fill(_data, "Orders");
```

Unfortunately, there's no automatic and generic way for a client page to detect whether the output it gets is cached or not. Figure 17-12 shows output being cached, but we're simply assuming the page knows about the information stored in the *ExtendedProperties* collection. Also, because the output cache is managed outside the Web service class, the client has no way to specify that it requires fresh data.

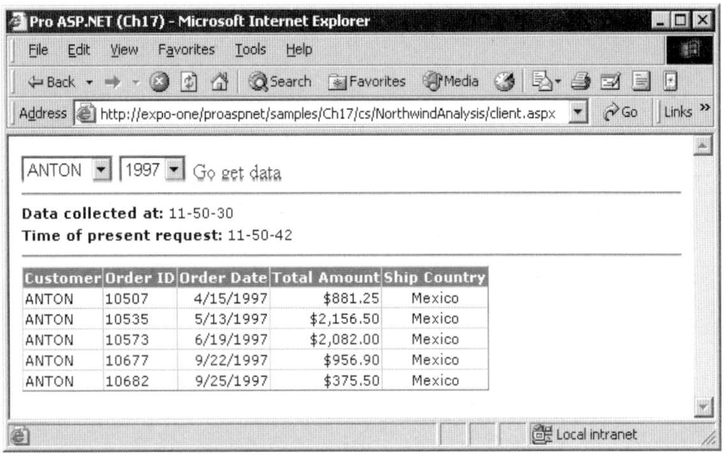

Figure 17-12 The client page demonstrates that the Web service returns cached output.

Under certain conditions, the *CacheDuration* attribute can constitute a significant improvement for your Web services. Ideally, you might want to set this attribute when your method queries for data and adds a database overhead. Using output caching amortizes the cost of retrieving data over more user calls, thus increasing the efficiency.

Minimizing the Data Transferred

When you have to return data objects, the *DataSet* seems to be the most flexible data container you can ever dream of. However, consider that the *DataSet* serializes in the DiffGram format plus the XSD schema. (See Chapter 5.) Although rich and flexible, a DiffGram is also quite verbose. The same information packed in a *DataSet* could be returned in a much more compact format if only you drop the *DataSet* class in favor of an array of custom classes. Let's see how.

The *OrderInfo* class is defined in the Web service as a public class. It maps through public properties the columns of the query run against the database. In other words, it looks like an extremely lightweight *DataRow* object.

```
// Helper class used to minimize the amount of data returned to the client
public class OrderInfo {
```

```
    public string CustomerID;
    public int OrderID;
    public DateTime OrderDate;
    public float Total;
    public string ShipCountry;
}
```

The new method *GetCustomersOrdersInfo* first calls the *GetCustomersOrders* method, gets a *DataSet*, and then packs all the contained info into an array of *OrderInfo* classes. (Of course, you could also optimize the code that executes the query.)

```
[WebMethod]
public OrderInfo[] GetCustomersOrdersInfo(string custID, int year)
{
    // Get the data to return
    DataSet _data = GetCustomersOrders(custID, year);
    if (_data == null)
        return null;
    DataRowCollection _rows = _data.Tables[0].Rows;

    // Allocate the array
    OrderInfo[] info = new OrderInfo[_rows.Count];

    // Fill the array (assume no DBNull values are found)
    int i=0;
    foreach(DataRow _row in _rows) {
        OrderInfo o = new OrderInfo();
        o.CustomerID = _row["CustomerID"].ToString();
        o.OrderID = Convert.ToInt32(_row["OrderID"]);
        o.OrderDate = DateTime.Parse(_row["OrderDate"].ToString());
        o.Total = Convert.ToSingle(_row["Total"]);
        o.ShipCountry = _row["ShipCountry"].ToString();
        info[i++] = o;
    }

    return info;
}
```

The client application doesn't know anything about the *OrderInfo* class. However, the proxy class reads its definition out of the WSDL document and creates an equivalent in the specified language. As a result, the ASP.NET client page can happen to work with a structure it was not designed to handle! You should note, though, that it's far more common to establish Web services between the client and middle-tier components in a single distributed application, or between federated applications. In these cases, the communicating sides share object definitions (assemblies if the .NET Framework is used) and are built with knowledge of the data they receive.

Figure 17-13 shows the client page for the NorthwindAnalysisService Web service. The first table uses the *GetCustomersOrders* method, which returns a *DataSet*. The second table uses the *GetCustomersOrdersInfo* method, which returns an array of *OrderInfo* classes.

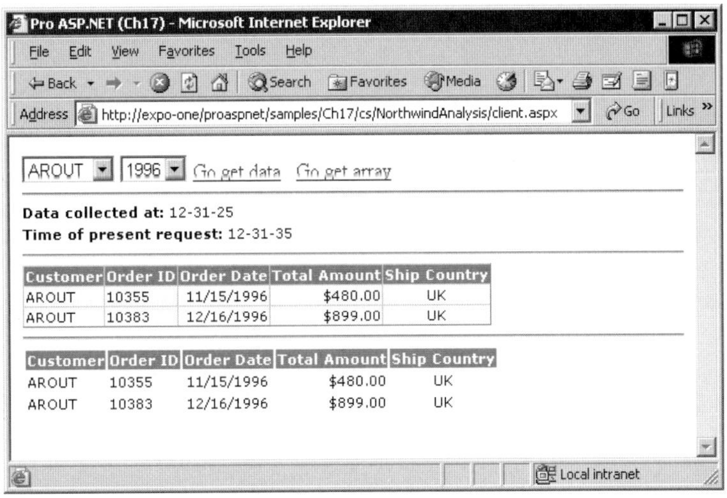

Figure 17-13 The client page extended to support the new *GetCustomersOrdersInfo* Web method. The second table has been created using a *Repeater* bound to the array of *OrderInfo* classes.

> **Note** It's rather obvious that when a class defined within the Web service file is returned (for example, a Java class if the Web service is hosted on Apache and run by Axis), the proxy class can only build a client-side representation of it. In other words, the serializer simply reproduces the public programming interface of the class limited to public properties. No code the class might originally contain is replicated.

You should use the *DataSet* only if you return multiple tables with relations, indexes, extended properties, and the like. As long as you use the *DataSet* only to contain a single read-only table, an array of custom structures is more effective in terms of bandwidth usage.

The Debate Around Web Services and *DataSets*

In many respects, working with the *DataSet* class is like having a simple, in-memory version of a relational database. You have tables and relations, indexes and views, and constraints. Could you ask for more? Furthermore, the class works disconnected from any data source you might have used to fill it and is totally serializable. When serialized, the *DataSet* returns a DiffGram XML schema that also allows you to maintain the story of the changes entered to the data. What's wrong with the *DataSet* class in the context of Web services?

Well, there are two things, one of which we already mentioned a moment ago—the size of the data is rather bloated. The second aspect is complexity. Imagine what happens when the *DataSet* is returned to clients running on other platforms. For sure, those clients have all that is needed to make sense of the data, but this alone doesn't mean that those clients are going to have an easy time parsing and extracting data. What seems to be the most savvy approach is overloading those methods that have to return database-like data so that they return the same data in three equivalent formats—a *DataSet*, an array of custom types, or even raw XML. In any case, an output alternative to *DataSet* objects can easily be built from the *DataSet* itself.

Throwing Exceptions

Any exception a Web service method might throw on the server is received on the client as an exception of a fixed type. If the client accessed the method over SOAP, a *SoapException* exception is raised on the client. If HTTP-POST or HTTP-GET was used, the type of the exception is *WebException*. Both exceptions wrap the original exception that was caught on the server, thus providing a uniform programming interface. The original exception object, though, won't be available on the client. To get more information, you can only rely on the properties exposed by the two exception classes.

If the client is known to issue calls through SOAP, there's a better way to throw exceptions. In this case, the Web method throws a *SoapException* and fills some of its properties. Some of the properties of the *SoapException* class are listed in Table 17-4.

Table 17-4 Properties of the *SoapException* Class

Property	Value
Actor	Indicates the actor that caused the SOAP fault. Typically, in the current implementation of the .NET Framework, the actor is the URL of the Web service method. In the SOAP specification, the actor is an intermediary in the message processing chain. The message jumps from one actor to the next until the final destination—another actor—is reached. Along the way, one actor could find an error and throw an exception. That object would be referenced by this property. As of today, the .NET Framework doesn't fully support actors yet.
Code	Indicates the type of the SOAP fault. When set, *ServerFaultCode* denotes an error occurred during the processing of a client call on the server—not an error due to a badly formed SOAP message. Other fault codes are *ClientFaultCode*, *VersionMismatchFaultCode*, and *MustUnderstandFaultCode*.
Detail	Gets an *XmlNode* representing the application-specific error information.
Message	The *Message* property of the original exception.

The following code illustrates the recommended way of throwing an exception from a Web service method:

```
if (_data == null)
{
    SoapException se = new SoapException("Invalid Customer ID",
        SoapException.ServerFaultCode,
        Context.Request.Url.AbsoluteUri);
    throw se;
}
```

Figure 17-14 shows how an exception appears on the client.

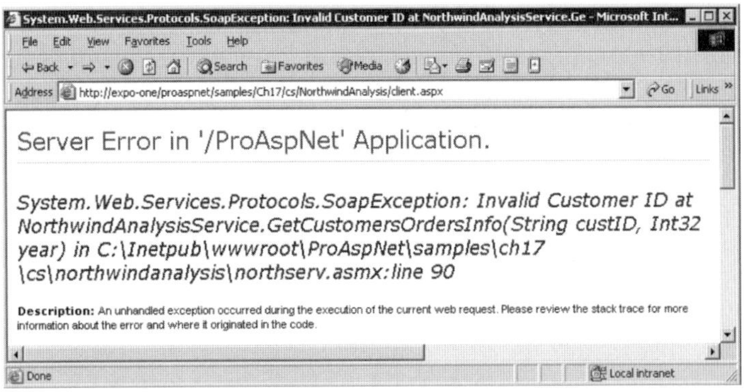

Figure 17-14 An unhandled SOAP exception raised by a Web method call.

In the code life cycle, exceptions should just be exceptional events. Working with exceptions is particularly easy, and the resulting code is significantly more readable. So what's wrong with exceptions? Generally speaking, exceptions are quite expensive in terms of CPU involvement. More importantly, whenever an exception is inserted in the code, the CLR does some extra work simply because an exception construct is met. When an exception is finally caught, that's the peak of pressure on the CPU. I could agree that this extra burden is less relevant in the context of a Web service call, which is a "*slow*" call by design. However, as a general guideline, you should throw exceptions just in exceptional circumstances when no other static way exists to trap the error.

> **Note** This advice about being careful with exceptions is simply a warning about the possible performance hit that result from the abuse of exceptions. In no way should it sound like an encouragement to trap errors through cryptic HRESULT codes.

Transactional Methods

The behavior of a Web service method in the COM+ environment deserves a bit of attention. The inherent reliance of Web services on HTTP inevitably prevents them from being enlisted in running transactions. In the case of a rollback, in fact, it would be difficult to track and cancel performed operations because HTTP is stateless, the network is unreliable, and latency introduces too much nondeterministic behavior. For this reason, a Web method can do one of two things: it can work in nontransacted mode, or it can start a nondistributed transaction.

For consistency, the *TransactionOption* property of the *WebMethod* attribute takes values from the .NET Framework *TransactionOption* enumeration. Some of the values in this enumeration have a different behavior than is expected or documented, however. In particular, the *Disabled*, *NotSupported*, and *Supported* values from the *TransactionOption* enumeration always cause the method to execute without a transaction. Both *Required* and *RequiresNew*, on the other hand, create a new transaction.

You can use the *ContextUtil* class from the *System.EnterpriseServices* namespace to explicitly commit or abort a transaction. The class exposes the *SetComplete* and *SetAbort* methods. In general, *SetComplete* indicates that the caller votes to commit its work, whereas *SetAbort* indicates that the object encountered a problem and wants to abort the ongoing transaction. When these methods are used from within a transacted Web service, the vote has an immediate effect and the transaction is committed or aborted, as required.

> **Note** When a transactional method throws an exception or an externally thrown exception is not handled, the transaction automatically aborts. If no exceptions occur, the transaction automatically commits at the end of the method being called.

Asynchronous Methods

Web services support both synchronous and asynchronous invocation. Under synchronous communication, the client sends a request for a method and waits for the response. While waiting for the results, the client can't perform other operations. In an asynchronous scenario, on the other hand, the client can continue with other tasks as it waits for a response on a different thread. The proxy class contains both synchronous versions and asynchronous versions of the methods in a Web service.

The asynchronous versions consist of two methods named *BeginXXX* and *EndXXX*, where *XXX* is the name of the method. The *BeginXXX* method is used to initiate the Web service, while the *EndXXX* method retrieves the results. The following code snippet shows how to set up an asynchronous call of a method that adds two integers:

```
// Calling Add(2,2)
int a=2, b=2;
IAsyncResult result = service.BeginAdd(a, b, null, null);

// Wait for asynchronous call to complete.
result.AsyncWaitHandle.WaitOne();

// Complete the asynchronous call to Web service method
int total = service.EndAdd(result);
```

How does the client know when the operation completed? There are two methods used to determine this. The first method entails that a callback function be passed into the *BeginXXX* method. The Web service infrastructure will then call this function back when the method has completed processing. The second method (shown previously) is that a client waits for the method to complete using the *WaitOne* method of the *WaitHandle* class. The *AsyncWaitHandle* property exposed by the *IAsyncResult* interface is just a member of the *WaitHandle* type.

> **Note** Regardless of whether the method is invoked synchronously or asynchronously, the SOAP messages sent and received are identical in the two cases.

Securing Web Services

In Chapter 15, we already covered several aspects of ASP.NET security. To briefly summarize, any request that hits IIS is first processed by the Web server. If the request is legitimate, the control passes to the ASP.NET application. The ASP.NET application can decide whether to rely on the IIS response and allow the user to operate or implement a more restrictive policy.

If the ASP.NET application is configured for Windows authentication, the security token received by IIS is considered valid. Next, ASP.NET looks at whether the authenticated user is authorized to access the requested resource. Users can be allowed or denied access to a resource by using the *<authorization>* section in the web.config file. The following code snippet details users that can access a particular resource:

```
<configuration>
  <system.web>
    <authentication mode="Windows" />
  </system.web>

  <location path="secureservice.asmx">
    <system.web>
      <authorization>
        <allow users="Administrator"/>
        <allow users="DOMAIN\Bradley"/>
        <deny roles="BUILTIN\Power Users"/>
      </authorization>
    </system.web>
  </location>
</configuration>
```

Web services are just a special flavor of ASP.NET applications; subsequently, the implementation of a security layer exploits many of the concepts we examined in Chapter 15. Access to Web services can be controlled in two ways—through a Windows user account and through a custom authentication scheme that can be considered as the Web service counterpart of the ASP.NET Forms authentication. Let's consider Windows authentication first.

Important The built-in security mechanism provided by the .NET Framework for Web services is sometimes limiting in the real-world. For a much more robust security framework, have a look at the Web Services Enhancements for Microsoft .NET.

HTTP User Authentication

To require Windows authentication on a given Web service, first ensure that anonymous access is disabled. Next, you enable Integrated Windows authentication for the .asmx resource. Figure 17-15 shows the properties and Authentication Methods dialog boxes for the Web service obtained within the IIS Manager.

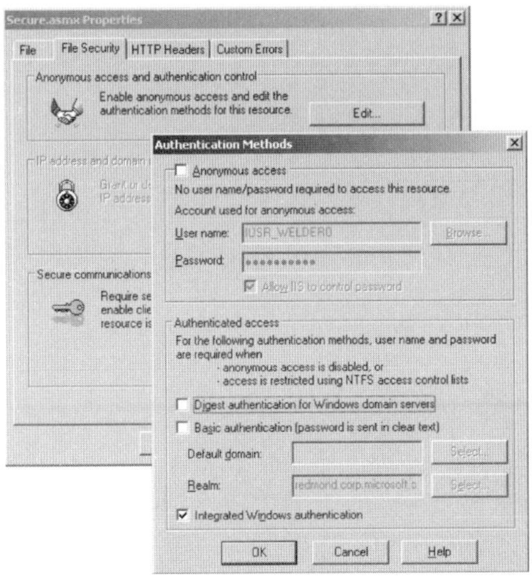

Figure 17-15 The first thing to do to secure a Web service is disable anonymous access and enable Integrated Windows authentication.

To allow or deny specific users access to the Web service, use the ASP.NET configuration system or set access control lists (ACLs) on the .asmx file itself. The web.config snippet shown previously is a good starting point.

Making a Secure Call

So much for the configuration of the environment, let's see in which way a client page can invoke a secured Web service. There are two possibilities. If the page invokes a method as usual—that is, without taking any measures—the call is successful as long as the client Windows account of the user is authenticated on the Web server and authorized by the Web service web.config file. As you can see, in this case everything happens in a codeless way.

Another scenario is when there's no correspondence between the Windows account of the calling machine and the credentials submitted to the Web service. In this case, the caller page operates as another user. The *NetworkCredential* class in the *System.Net* namespace acts as a credentials container. It can be used to provide credentials for password-based authentication schemes such as Basic, Digest, NTLM, and Kerberos authentication. The code of the client page is as follows:

```
<%@ Page Language="C#" %>
<%@ Import Namespace="System.Net" %>

<script runat="server">
public void Page_Load(object sender, EventArgs e)
{
    // Instantiate the proxy class (derived from WebClientProtocol)
    SecureService serv = new SecureService();
    serv.Credentials = new NetworkCredential("John", "LoveAspNet");
    msg.Text = serv.GuessWhoIs();
}
</script>

<html>
<title>Pro ASP.NET (Ch17)</title>
<body>
    <h2><asp:Label id="msg" runat="server" /><h2>
</body>
</html>
```

A good question is, where does the *Credentials* property come from? The property is exposed by the *WebClientProtocol* class from which any Web service proxy class inherits. The credentials stored in the proxy class are silently used when it is time to connect to the Web service.

Detecting the Connected User

The Web service can grab information about the connected user thanks to the *User* property of the HTTP context. The following code shows a simple Web service that just says hello to each authorized connected user:

```
<%@ WebService Language="C#" Class="SecureService" %>
using System.Web.Services;
using System;
```

```
class SecureService : WebService {
    [WebMethod]
    public string GuessWhoIs() {
        return "Welcome " + User.Identity.Name;
    }
}
```

Figure 17-16 shows this code in action.

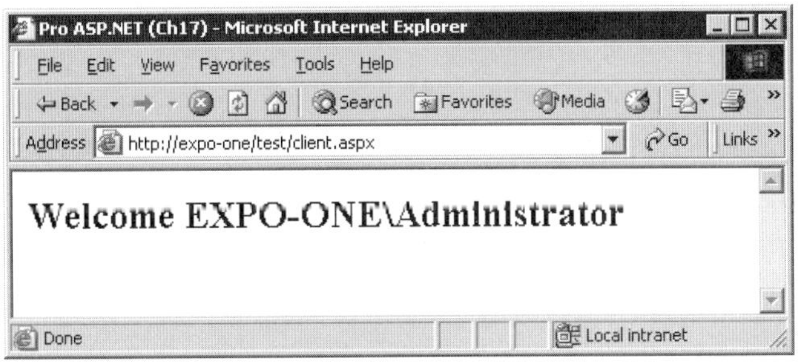

Figure 17-16 A sample Windows-based secure Web service.

In general, Windows authentication is mostly appropriate for intranet applications that authenticate users in the current domain. On the Internet, though, you need to use a SQL database to store user names and passwords. Forms authentication that works great for conventional ASP.NET applications is not a model that works for Web services because of its inherent interactivity. An alternative scheme for custom authentication and authorization can be performed making use of SOAP headers.

Custom User Authentication

To authenticate the user that is going to execute a Web method, credentials must be passed along with the request. The format you use for the credentials is custom and service-specific. In general, valid credentials are any sequence of values that the Web service can validate and successfully transform in a user identity. At a minimum, valid credentials include a user ID and a password.

As mentioned earlier in "The SOAP Payload" section, a SOAP message can optionally contain headers. This means that a SOAP header is ideal for transmitting free information not strictly related to the semantics of a Web service. A Web service that intends to use the custom SOAP authentication must do a couple of things. First, it must indicate that the SOAP header is expected to contain the authentication credentials. Second, it must process the credentials and determine whether or not the request can be authorized.

Embedding Credentials in the SOAP Payload

Let's create a new class to hold the credentials of the connecting user. In the Web service source code, we derive a new class from *SoapHeader*.

```
// UserInfoHeader represents the custom SOAP header
public class UserInfoHeader : SoapHeader
{
    public string UserName;
    public string Password;
}
```

The class represents the custom SOAP header we're going to use to hold the credentials for any secure method we define. The second step consists of declaring a publicly accessible member of the *UserInfoHeader* type.

```
// Must use a namespace different from that of the proxy class
namespace ProAspNet.CS.Ch17
{
    public class SecureNorthwindAnalysisService : WebService
    {
        // Custom authentication header
        public UserInfoHeader UserInfoHeaderValue;

        [WebMethod]
            [SoapHeader("UserInfoHeaderValue", Required=true)]
            public DataSet GetCustomersOrders(string custID, int year)
        {
            ⋮
        }
        ⋮
    }
}
```

The *UserInfoHeaderValue* property is exposed in the WSDL document for the service and made available to the client when the proxy is created. Any method that you want to protect against unauthorized callers features an extra *[SoapHeader]* attribute. Table 17-5 shows the properties of this attribute.

Table 17-5 Properties of the *[SoapHeader]* Attribute

Property	Description
Direction	Gets or sets whether the SOAP header is intended for the Web service, the Web service client, or both. By default, the header is for the Web service only.

Table 17-5 Properties of the *[SoapHeader]* Attribute

Property	Description
MemberName	Gets or sets the member of the Web service class representing the SOAP header contents. This is the default property of the attribute.
Required	Gets or sets a value indicating whether the SOAP header must be understood and processed by the recipient Web service or Web service client. *True* by default.

The *MemberName* of the attribute is set with the public property of the Web service class that will be filled with the contents of the header. Because this is the default property, you don't need to indicate it by name. In the preceding code snippet, we just set *userInfo* as the member associated with the header. Note that you can use multiple headers and a different header for each method to secure.

In light of the custom header, the SOAP envelope for the *GetCustomersOrders* method of our example Web service is slightly different.

```
<soap:Envelope
  xmlns:xsi="http://www.w3.org/2001/XMLSchema-instance"
  xmlns:xsd="http://www.w3.org/2001/XMLSchema"
  xmlns:soap="http://schemas.xmlsoap.org/soap/envelope/">
  <soap:Header>
    <UserInfoHeader xmlns="ProAspNet/0-7356-1903-4">
      <UserName>string</UserName>
      <Password>string</Password>
    </UserInfoHeader>
  </soap:Header>
  <soap:Body>
    <GetCustomersOrders xmlns="ProAspNet/0-7356-1903-4">
      <custID>string</custID>
      <year>int</year>
    </GetCustomersOrders>
  </soap:Body>
</soap:Envelope>
```

Important The SOAP header is sent over the network in clear text. The fact that a custom header is used doesn't automatically enable any protection mechanism. It's obvious that transmitting passwords as clear text is not a good practice, especially if you're just trying to make the Web service more secure. To encrypt transmitted data, add an encryption algorithm using the .NET Framework cryptographic API. For example, you could pass the password as a SHA1 hashed value and compare it against an identically hashed value retrieved from the database:

```
byte[] pswd = new byte[PSWD_SIZE];
:
byte[] hashedPswd;
SHA1 sha = new SHA1CryptoServiceProvider();
hashedPswd = sha.ComputeHash(pswd);
```

Authenticating the User

The proxy class generated for the Web service includes a definition for the *UserInfoHeader* class. To avoid run-time name conflicts, make sure the definition of the *UserInfoHeader* class in the proxy class and the Web service belong to different namespaces.

The client page first fills a new instance of the SOAP header class with its credentials. Next, it associates the custom header with the property of type *UserInfoHeader* on the Web service proxy.

```
// Instantiate the Web service proxy class
SecureNorthwindAnalysisService serv = new SecureNorthwindAnalysisService();

// Instantiate the SOAP header class
UserInfoHeader user = new UserInfoHeader();

// Store credentials
user.UserName = "joeusers";
user.Password = "loveAspNet";

// Bind the proxy class with the header
serv.UserInfoHeaderValue = user;
```

When a call is made, the invoked Web method will find its public member of type *UserInfoHeader* set with the credentials. Of course, the credentials are needed only for the methods marked with the *[SoapHeader]* attribute. The Web method will use the information stored in the credentials class to authenticate the user.

```
public DataSet GetCustomersOrders(string custID, int year) {
    // Authenticate the user
    if (!AuthenticateUser())
    {
        // or throw an exception...
        return null;
    }
```

AuthenticateUser is a local function you can implement as needed. The typical implementation is nearly identical to the authentication function we considered in Chapter 15 within the context of form-based authentication.

```
protected virtual bool AuthenticateUser()
{
    // ProAspNet database, Users table
    string connString, cmdText;
    connString = "SERVER=localhost;DATABASE=proaspnet;UID=sa;";
    cmdText = "SELECT COUNT(*) FROM users WHERE id=@User AND pswd=@Pswd";

    SqlConnection conn = new SqlConnection(connString);
    SqlCommand cmd = new SqlCommand(cmdText, conn);

    SqlParameter p1 = new SqlParameter("@User", SqlDbType.VarChar, 25);
    p1.Value = UserInfoHeaderValue.UserName;
    cmd.Parameters.Add(p1);
    SqlParameter p2 = new SqlParameter("@Pswd", SqlDbType.VarChar, 12);
    p2.Value = UserInfoHeaderValue.Password;
    cmd.Parameters.Add(p2);

    conn.Open();
    int found = (int) cmd.ExecuteScalar();
    conn.Close();

    return (found >0);
}
```

Managing Roles

Once the user has been authenticated, a new principal can be created and bound to the *Context.User* property. In doing so, you could also retrieve and store the roles associated with the user, if any. The following code snippet shows how to rewrite the *AuthenticateUser* method so that it checks for any role information in the database and sets the new user identity.

```
protected virtual bool AuthenticateUser()
{
    string connString, cmdText;
    connString = "SERVER=localhost;DATABASE=proaspnet;UID=sa;";
    cmdText = "SELECT role FROM users WHERE id=@theUser AND pswd=@thePswd";

    SqlConnection conn = new SqlConnection(connString);
    SqlCommand cmd = new SqlCommand(cmdText, conn);

    SqlParameter p1 = new SqlParameter("@User", SqlDbType.VarChar, 25);
    p1.Value = UserInfoHeaderValue.UserName;
    cmd.Parameters.Add(p1);
```

```
    SqlParameter p2 = new SqlParameter("@Pswd", SqlDbType.VarChar, 12);
    p2.Value = UserInfoHeaderValue.Password;
    cmd.Parameters.Add(p2);

    int found = 0;
    string[] roles = null;

    conn.Open();
    SqlDataReader _reader = cmd.ExecuteReader();
    while(_reader.Read())
    {
        found ++;
        string roleString = _reader["role"].ToString();
        roles = roleString.Split(',');
    }
    _reader.Close();
    conn.Close();

    bool isAuth = (found >0);

    // Set the new user identity
    if (isAuth)
    {
        GenericIdentity ident;
        ident = new GenericIdentity(UserInfoHeaderValue.UserName);
        Context.User = new GenericPrincipal(ident, roles);
    }

    return isAuth;
}
```

Associating the principal with roles information lets you distinguish the results of each method based on the role of each user.

```
[WebMethod(CacheDuration=30)]
[SoapHeader("UserInfoHeaderValue", Required=true)]
public DataSet GetCustomersOrders(string custID, int year)
{
    // Authenticate the user
    if (!AuthenticateUser())
    {
        // or throw an exception...
        return null;
    }

    // Check the role. If the role is Employee, then
    // no more than 3 rows should be returned
    string _cmd;
```

```
if (User.IsInRole("Employee"))
    _cmd = String.Format(m_cmdCustOrders, 3);
else
    _cmd = String.Format(m_cmdCustOrders, "100 PERCENT");

// Should check if a valid custID is provided
if (!IsValidCustomerID(custID))
    return null;

// Prepare the query
⋮
```

The method *GetCustomersOrders* now performs three different checks. First, it ensures that the user has the rights to do what she's trying to do. Second, it adapts the output to the role of the user. Finally, it validates the input parameters.

Using Application-Specific Tokens

The Web service infrastructure does not mandate that you implement authentication and authorization by using a made-to-measure API or approach. The implementation of authentication and authorization is left up to the application, which sets up an effective scheme exploiting the capabilities of the application's platform and protocol. The approaches to Web service security we discussed so far are extensively based on characteristics of the Windows platform and SOAP.

In the Windows authentication case, you can configure your security layer in a rather codeless way but at the price of forcing users to have a user account on the Web service machine. The second approach, based on custom SOAP headers, is more flexible but requires that credentials are passed for each method invocation. Also note that by default credentials are passed as clear text unless you manually encrypt them.

A consolidated scheme for authenticating users of a remote service is described next. Instead of passing credentials every time a Web service call is made, users manage to obtain a token (either statically or dynamically) and then pass it along with other parameters when making a call. The advantage is that you can more easily control the validity of the token, implement expiration policies, and provide encryption without encrypting credentials every time.

Getting the Token

You can design your Web service so that it requires all clients to log on prior to calling any methods. The signature of the method for logging on might look like the following:

```
long Login(string userName, string pswd)
```

The method returns a value that works as a token to call other methods. The information stored in the token, as well as its data type, is completely up to you. You can use a number, GUID, or string. The token should be several bytes long, unique, random, and overall hard to remember for humans. In addition, you should be able to extract from it all the information needed to verify the authenticity of the token and the user prior to calling the requested method. This can be obtained by either hashing the supplied credentials in a bijective mapping or, more simply, using a key value and database to track map tokens and users.

The following pseudocode shows how it works, assuming that the token is a long:

```
// Credentials should be encrypted when logging in
long token = MyService.Login(uid, pswd);

// Add the token to all successive calls
MyService.GetEmployee(token, nEmpID);
```

The *Login* method must authenticate the user against a database or any persistent support you might want to consider. It then creates and returns a token that summarizes information about the user and the time the token was generated. Each method that requires the token first checks its validity before resuming execution.

The Amazon Case

In the summer of 2002, Amazon (*http://www.amazon.com*) released the first version of its Web services, which allowed users to programmatically search for prices, products, and availability information as well as to manage shopping carts. The Amazon Web Services Developer's Kit can be downloaded from *http://associates.amazon.com/exec/panama/associates/join/developer/kit.html*. The developer's kit contains documentation as well as code samples for Java, Perl, SOAP, XML, and XSLT. No .NET samples are provided. The Amazon Web Services Developer's Kit, or the similar kit released by Google, is useful because it provides a concrete, real-world service to experiment with.

You can get the WSDL for the Amazon Web Services from the following URL: *http://soap.amazon.com/schemas2/AmazonWebServices.wsdl*. The proxy class can be generated with the following script:

```
wsdl.exe /out:aws.cs amazonwebservices.wsdl
```

For more details about programming with the Amazon Web Service, take a look at the documentation, but first make sure you have at least a working knowledge of the data structures involved.

However, what's interesting about the Amazon Web Services is the architecture of security. To call into the Amazon Web Services, you must first get your token by registering with the site. You can get your developer's token by visiting the following URL: *https://associates.amazon.com/exec/panama/associates/join/developer/application.html.*

The token is generated offline and handed to users in a static manner, as opposed to the programmatic login we considered earlier. That token, though, must be added as an argument to each method call. The Amazon token is an alphanumeric string.

Managing the State of Web Services

Web services can access the same state management features as other ASP.NET applications. For this to happen, though, the Web service class must derive from the *WebService* class, which contains many common ASP.NET objects, including the *Session* and *Application* objects. Classes that inherit from *WebService* don't need to take particular measures to access global state objects such as the *Application* or *Cache* object. Working with the session state is a bit trickier.

Enabling Session State

As mentioned, ASP.NET session support for Web methods is turned off by default. To use session state within a Web method, you must first set the *EnableSession* property of the *[WebMethod]* attribute to *true*. Note that support for the session state must be enabled on a per-method basis. If the Web service exposes two methods that need to deal with the session memory, the *EnableSession* property must be turned on for both.

Note that the requirement of session state is a transitive property. If, say, method A doesn't require session state directly but internally calls into method B that, on the other hand, does require state management, then sessions must be enabled for both methods.

Note If session support is disabled at the web.config level, then regardless of the value of *EnableSession*, the session state is always inaccessible to all pages affected by the web.config, including Web services. For more information on configuration files, see Chapter 12.

The value of the *CacheDuration* property affects the management of the session state in Web methods. When *CacheDuration* is set to a value greater than zero, the output of the method is cached for the specified number of seconds. This means that for the given duration any request for the method is served by returning the cached XML text rather than executing the code of the method. As a result, as long as the cached output is valid, the session state is not updated. This behavior affects both ASP.NET pages and Web services.

Using Cookie Containers

Unless you change the ASP.NET default settings, session state is implemented by using cookies and storing the collection of data items within the *Cache* object. When a Web method is called that uses session state, a cookie is passed back to the client in the response headers. The cookie uniquely identifies the session state as maintained by ASP.NET for that Web service.

The Importance of a Cookie Container

Suppose that a Web method contains code as in the following listing. The method updates an internal counter whenever called. With reference to the role discussion of the previous example, you could use this counter to stop requests from users with less privileges.

```
// Count accesses
if (Session["Counter"] == null)
    Session["Counter"] = 1;
else
    Session["Counter"] = ((int) Session["Counter"]) + 1;
```

Let's consider what happens the first time the method is invoked. The ASP.NET client issues the request; the Web method executes, and it sets the counter to 1. The Web response contains the cookie that represents the Web service session state. Unless the browser itself manages to send the request and get the response, the cookies in the response are lost. If you test the Web service using the browser-based sample test page, everything works great from the beginning. However, as long as the effective client of the Web service becomes a proxy class (either a Windows Forms or Web Forms class), a made-to-measure cookie container is needed.

Building a Persistent Cookie Container

It's not coincidental that the proxy class—specifically, the base class *HttpWebClientProtocol*—exposes a *CookieContainer* property. For the Web service client to receive the session cookie, a new instance of *CookieContainer* must be created and assigned to the *CookieContainer* property before calling the stateful

Web service method. This will ensure that the cookie is properly included in all subsequent requests.

In this way, when handling the successive Web method request, the ASP.NET runtime finds in the attached cookie list one that represents the session to bind to the Web service context. As a result, a session-state instance with a matching ID is loaded from the storage medium (cache, server, or SQL Server) and bound to the HTTP context. The Web service, therefore, retrieves the *right* session state.

Not only must a cookie container be used, but if the Web service client is an ASP.NET page, it has to be persistent too. The methods that follow illustrate how to bind the cookie container to the proxy class and how to save it for future retrieval by client session:

```
void BindCookieContainer(HttpWebClientProtocol proxy, string sessionSlot)
{
    CookieContainer cc;

    // Retrieve the cookie container from the page's Session state
    if (Session[sessionSlot] == null)
        cc = new CookieContainer();
    else
        cc = (CookieContainer) Session[sessionSlot];

    // Bind the cookie container to the proxy
    proxy.CookieContainer = cc;
}

void SaveCookieContainer(HttpWebClientProtocol proxy, string sessionSlot)
{
    Session[sessionSlot] = proxy.CookieContainer;
}
```

The cookie container we bind to the proxy class must be persisted across postbacks to provide an effective storage mechanism analogous to that of the browser, which uses an internal folder. In particular, we store the previous instance of the *CookieContainer* class in a session slot with a unique name. When binding the cookies to the proxy class, you call the method *BindCookieContainer*; when done with the method, the proxy *CookieContainer* property contains all the cookies that arrived with the response. They must be cached for further use by the client.

The following code snippet shows how the client should wrap a call to a stateful Web method. Figure 17-17 illustrates how the counter changes after two invocations of stateful methods.

```
// CookieJar is simply the (fancy) name of the session slot
// where the cookie container is persisted
BindCookieContainer(serv, "CookieJar");
serv.StatefulMethod(...);
SaveCookieContainer(serv, "CookieJar");
```

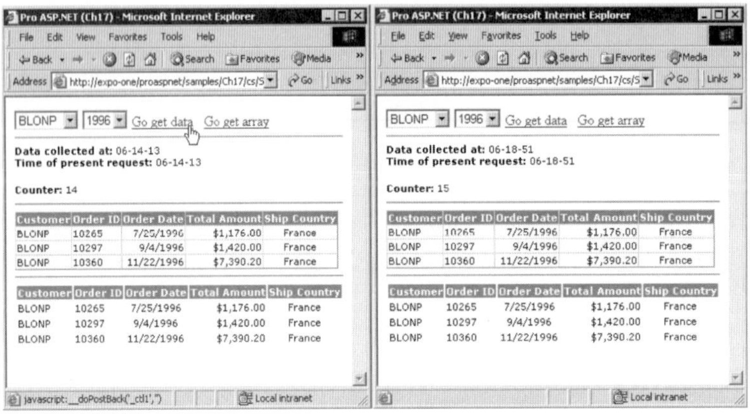

Figure 17-17 An ASP.NET client calling stateful methods on a Web service.

Conclusion

The world of Web services is evolving very quickly. Over the past couple of years, specifications have been first defined, then revised, and in some cases, even deprecated. Web service toolkits have shipped, and developers have tried to use them to build systems. In doing so, they discovered a number of issues that, unlike what often happens with ordinary code, reinforced the positive feeling toward the technology and self-propelled its progress.

A lot of work has been done with Web services over the past few years, but even more remains to be done. And should the remaining work be abandoned, the feeling is that the whole Web service technology would starve in a matter of months. What does this mean to you? It means you can't give up at this time. If you're going to build Web service–based systems, you should understand where the platform is today and what the future has in store for us all.

Today, the work and research are geared in two directions. While W3C focuses on new versions of the core Web service specifications, a separate organization focuses more on interoperability. The Web Services Interoperability

Organization (WS-I) is committed to defining a series of best practices for making services work seamlessly.

So far the experience of working with Web services proved the need of a standard way to secure Web services, route messages reliably, and define transactional semantics. These are just a few structural issues that apply to all domains of applications and business implemented through Web services. The Global XML Web Service Architecture (GXA) initiative is aimed at defining specifications for these infrastructure-related services—a sort of abstract virtual machine for Web services.

In this chapter, we focused on Web services from the .NET perspective and also limited our look at ASP.NET clients. However, all the key issues and caveats have been discussed. If you would like to learn more about SOAP and Web services in general, many wonderful resources are available on the Web. Here are a few recommended links:

- *http://www.webservices.org*
- *http://www.ibm.com/developerworks/webservices/*
- *http://msdn.microsoft.com/soap*
- *http://www.soapware.org/*

For a developer with .NET-oriented vision, nothing is better than the Microsoft XML Web service home at *http://msdn.microsoft.com/webservices*. Although we haven't covered it here, a technology preview that covers Web services on the .NET platform was made available a while ago. The Microsoft Web Service Enhancements provide early support for the WS-Security, WS-Routing, and DIME specifications and lets you experiment with newer specifications from within .NET applications.

Resources

- *SOAP: Cross Platform Web Services Development Using XML*, by Scott Seely and Kent Sharkey (Prentice Hall, 2001)
- *Building XML Web Services for the Microsoft .NET Platform*, by Scott Short (Microsoft Press, 2002)
- Web Services Enhancements for Microsoft .NET (*http://msdn.microsoft.com/webservices/building/wse/*)

Part V

Custom ASP.NET Controls

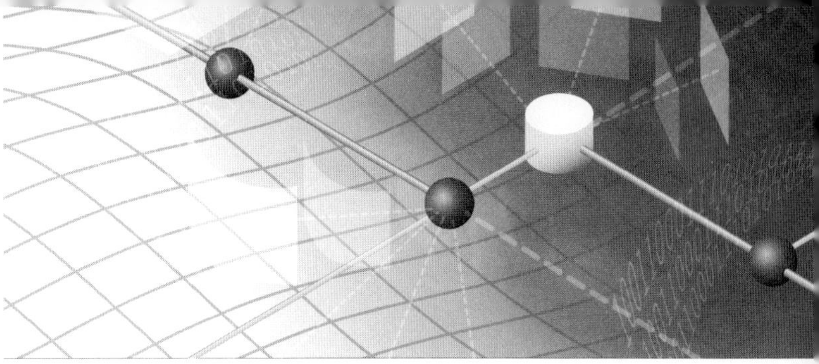

18

Extending Existing ASP.NET Controls

Nothing in all the world is more dangerous than sincere ignorance and conscientious stupidity.

—Martin Luther King

ASP.NET custom controls are compiled, server-side components that encapsulate user-interface and other functionality into reusable packages. Custom controls are no different than standard ASP.NET server controls except that they are bound to a different tag prefix and must be registered and deployed explicitly. Aside from that, custom controls can have their own object model, fire events, and support all the design-time features of Microsoft Visual Studio .NET, such as the Properties window, the visual designer, property builders, and the Toolbox.

Custom controls are not to be confused with Web user controls that we covered in Chapter 10. Web user controls are dynamic-compile components and cannot be added to the Toolbox. For the same reason, their design-time support is limited and so is their visual feedback when added to a page, where user controls simply display with a placeholder glyph. In addition, user controls, even if precompiled, cannot be separate from the .ascx source file that contains the layout. As a result, the only way to share the user control between applications is to put a separate copy in each application, which makes maintenance and deployment a little harder.

ASP.NET custom controls are compiled code. However, once you have compiled the control, you can add it to the Toolbox and take advantage of the rich visual environment of Visual Studio .NET. Because of their compiled nature, custom controls can be installed in a single copy in the global assembly cache (GAC) and be available to all applications, or deployed to the \Bin directory for a single application.

There are basically two ways of creating custom controls. If you find that an existing control meets your requirements only partially and lacks some key features, the simplest thing you can do is extend the control by deriving a new class from it. You can override specific properties, methods, and events as well as add new features. This is the approach we'll examine in this chapter. Another derived approach that we'll extensively examine in the next chapter entails the creation of composite controls. A composite control is a new control created by combining other existing controls.

If none of the existing Web server controls meet your requirements, consider creating a custom control from scratch by deriving from one of the base control classes—*Control* and *WebControl*. These classes provide all the basic functionality of ASP.NET server controls, so you can focus on just programming the extended features. Note that ASP.NET controls are limited in their overall functionality by the target markup language. For Web pages, the HTML language and HTML object model of the browser delimit the upper bound of implementable functionality. When you need a certain functionality that no existing control provides, you should first ask whether that functionality can be obtained from an HTML environment at all and what support it expects from the browser. For example, there's no standard ASP.NET control that provides a drop-down menu *à la* Windows Forms; however, while this feature can be implemented—and, indeed, several third-party vendors do it—it requires a rich Dynamic HTML (DHTML) object model on the client.

In this chapter, we'll dig around techniques that extend the standard features provided by existing controls. In the next chapter, we'll discuss how to create a new control from the ground up. The first control candidate to receive some sort of "*genetic*" manipulation is the simplest of all—the *Label* control.

A Better *Label* Control

The ASP.NET *Label* control provides a way to display text programmatically in a Web Forms page. The use of this control is a bit controversial in the sense that, if overused, it can slightly slow down the performance of the application. You should note that you don't always need a server control to display text. Static text within a server page, in fact, can be presented using plain HTML, resulting in more lightweight code. Also using *Response.Write* can be a more effective way of outputting dynamically generated text. Compared to *Response.Write*, a *Label* control provides a great deal of flexibility, more functionality, and encapsulation that makes it preferable in the majority of cases.

The main characteristic of the *Label* control—which also should be used to determine whether or not it is needed—is that it provides the ability of formatting and displaying text dynamically. The control displays HTML text, meaning that any HTML tag you put in the text is recognized and properly handled. The downside of this is that you are responsible for embedding any formatting tags you might need. This can quickly become quite boring, especially if you want to add hyperlinks. Once you've finished the job, wouldn't it be best if you could use it over and over again? I'm sure I know your answer.

The *LinkLabel* Server Control

The Windows Forms namespace defines a rather interesting control named the *LinkLabel*. It's similar to a *Label* control except that it can display multiple hyperlinks. The control works by letting you indicate one or more substrings in the bound text that must be rendered as hyperlinks. The control takes care of associating those substrings with URLs and fires an event each time the user clicks on one. Each hyperlink can perform a different task within an application. In Web Forms, it would be even easier to code and still just as helpful to developers.

We'll build the ASP.NET *LinkLabel* control, deriving it from *Label* and overriding its *Text* property to accommodate hyperlinks. In particular, whenever the *Text* property is assigned, we'll look into the specified value and search for URL-sensitive substrings to wrap in anchor tags. In doing so, we'll use regular expressions to do pattern matching.

Setting Up the New *LinkLabel* Class

As mentioned, the *LinkLabel* derives from *Label* and overrides the *Text* property. In particular, we want hyperlinking features be totally transparent to users. Users should be able to get and set the text as usual; therefore, rich text will be cached internally into a new protected field and used only at rendering time. To accomplish this, we need to override the *Text* property to generate the rich text whenever the text of the label is assigned. Furthermore, the *RenderControl* protected method, responsible for rendering the output of the control, must be overridden so that it can actually write the rich text. Finally, like icing on the cake, we could also expose a new property to let interested users know about the rich text being used.

The following listing details the core code of the new *LinkLabel* control:

```
namespace ProAspNet.CS.Ch18
{
    public class LinkLabel : Label
```

```
    {
        // Overrides the Text property
        public override string Text
        {
            get {
                return base.Text;
            }
            set {
                base.Text =  value;
                RichText = ActivateHyperLinks(value);
            }
        }

        // Expose the rich text
        protected string RichText
        {
            get {
                string richText = (string) ViewState["RichText"];
                return (richText!= null ? richText :String.Empty);
            }
            set {
                ViewState["RichText"] = value;
            }
        }

        // Overrides the RenderContents method
        protected override void RenderContents(HtmlTextWriter writer) {
            writer.Write(RichText);
        }
    }
}
```

The key event in the life of the *LinkLabel* control is when the inherited *Text* property is assigned. In general, you can catch this moment for any public property in any public class by overriding the property in a derived class. In the property's *set* accessor, you use the *value* keyword to reference the value being assigned and refer to the parent property through the *base* keyword in C# and the *MyBase* keyword in Microsoft Visual Basic .NET.

> **Note** An alternative to overriding a property is to choose to replace the property of the base class with a new one that has the same name and type. You would normally do this when you want to restrict or enlarge the visibility of the property—for example, when exposing a read/write property as read-only. To shadow a base property, use the *new* keyword instead of *override*. In Visual Basic .NET, you use *Shadows* instead of *Overrides*.

The *Text* property of the *LinkLabel* control works like its parent when it is being read. When a client attempts to read the property, the control simply invokes the *get* accessor of its parent *Label* class. When a client assigns a new value to the *Text* property, the first thing the *LinkLabel* control does is invoke the parent's *set* accessor. In this way, it ensures that the *Text* property is managed as usual. In particular, this means the view state is correctly updated to reflect the new value. After that, the *LinkLabel* control calls an internal method—*ActivateHyperLinks*—and saves its return value to the new *RichText* property.

> **Caution** Note that overriding the *Text* property is not necessarily the most efficient model. If you set the property several times in the same request, you pay the extra cost of a few unnecessary operations. A better model for implementing the *LinkLabel* control would be calculating the rich text whenever the output is rendered or whenever the *RichText* property is set.

The *ActivateHyperLinks* method takes the value of *Text* and inserts as many anchor tags as there are URLs in the text. The new richly formatted string is assigned to a protected member named *RichText*. Because this rich text is just what the control will show, we need to make this piece of state persistent. The view state is the most obvious and effective solution.

```
protected string RichText
{
    get {
        string buf = (string) ViewState["RichText"];
        return (buf != null ?buf :String.Empty);
    }
    set {
        ViewState["RichText"] = value;
    }
}
```

In the sample code, we declared the *RichText* property as protected. However, this is a totally arbitrary choice. Public or private would have worked as well. In general, if you mark a property as protected, you anticipate that developers who extend the class will want to override the particular property. If this is not the case, mark the property as private.

The formatted text is then cached and used when the control is requested to render its output.

How Controls Render Their Output

For Web controls, the entry point in the rendering process is the *RenderControl* method. The *RenderControl* method is declared public in the *Control* class and inherited by all ASP.NET controls. The method outputs the content of the control to a provided *HtmlTextWriter* object and, if tracing is enabled, stores tracing information about the control.

```
public void RenderControl(HtmlTextWriter writer);
```

The ASP.NET rendering mechanism is extremely layered and involves several methods at various levels. Figure 18-1 summarizes the process and the involved methods.

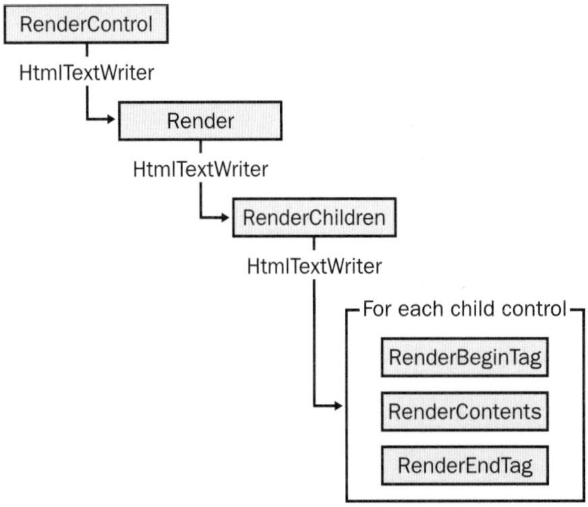

Figure 18-1 Architecture of the rendering mechanism for ASP.NET controls.

The base implementation of the *RenderControl* method calls a protected overridable method named *Render*. In the base implementation that provides the *Control* class, the *Render* method calls into another protected member named *RenderChildren*. As the name suggests, *RenderChildren* loops through the contents of the control's *Controls* collection and calls the *RenderControl* method on any child controls.

The *WebControl* class, which is a first-level child of *Control*, overrides *RenderControl* and implements it in three steps that recall the structure of the final HTML output—begin tag, contents, and end tag.

As a result, if you want to modify the output of a control, you should look at *RenderContents* and override it. If you need to handle the creation of the text for the opening and closing tags, override the *RenderBeginTag* and *RenderEnd-*

Tag methods. Unlike *RenderContents*, which is protected, *RenderBeginTag* and *RenderEndTag* are declared public (other than overridable). They render the opening and ending tags of the HTML text for the control.

> **Note** *RenderBeginTag*, *RenderContents*, and *RenderEndTag* are not available if you derive your custom control from *Control*. The methods, in fact, are defined by the *WebControl* class.

The *LinkLabel* control must modify the base rendering mechanism by replacing the text being written—that is, using *RichText* instead of *Text*. We don't need to change the way in which the opening and closing tags are rendered, so let's focus on *RenderContents*.

```
protected override void RenderContents(HtmlTextWriter writer)
{
    writer.Write(RichText);
}
```

As you can see, the output generated by a *Label* control is not particularly complex.

Finding Web-Sensitive Elements

The *ActivateHyperLinks* function takes the text assigned to the label for display and expands all the fragments that lend themselves to be e-mail addresses or Web sites. The method works by scanning the text and wrapping any Web-sensitive elements within an *<a>* tag. Regular expressions are used to quickly identify matching elements.

The method defines a couple of pattern strings that describe e-mail addresses and Web sites (URLs). I couldn't swear that all possible e-mail addresses and Web sites are included, but it will certainly work for most cases.

```
private string ActivateHyperLinks(string theText)
{
    Regex re;
    string buf = theText;

    // Handle email addresses
    string emailPattern = @"[a-zA-Z_0-9.-]+\@[a-zA-Z_0-9.-]+\.\w+";
    re = new Regex(emailPattern);
    if (re.IsMatch(buf))
        buf = re.Replace(buf, new MatchEvaluator(EmailMatchEvaluator));

    // Handle Web sites
    string websitePattern = @"\w*[\://]*\w+\.\w+\.\w+[/\w+]*[.\w+]*";
```

```
    re = new Regex(websitePattern);
    if (re.IsMatch(buf))
        buf = re.Replace(buf, new MatchEvaluator(WebSiteMatchEvaluator));

    return buf;
}
```

Defined in the *System.Text.RegularExpressions* namespace, the *Regex* object is an evaluator of regular expressions. You instantiate it by passing the desired pattern string. The *IsMatch* method indicates whether the regular expression finds a match in the input string. All matching substrings are replaced with the text supplied by the *MatchEvaluator* delegate.

```
public delegate string MatchEvaluator(Match match);
```

The *Replace* method has several overloads to replace all the substrings in the expression that comply with the pattern. The overload based on a *MatchEvaluator* delegate is the most flexible of all, as it lets you replace matching text with dynamically generated text. Let's see the source code for the evaluators that replace Web site names and e-mail addresses with related HTML anchors.

```
private string EmailMatchEvaluator(Match m)
{
    string format = "<a href='mailto:{0}'>{0}</a>";
    return String.Format(format, m.Value);
}

private string WebSiteMatchEvaluator(Match m)
{
    string format = "<a href='{0}'>{0}</a>";
    return String.Format(format, m.Value);
}
```

The *Match* class represents the results from a single regular expression match. Its *Value* property contains the effective text that matches the pattern. The net effect of the two routines just shown is illustrated by the following example. Suppose that you assign the following text to the *LinkLabel* control:

```
Contact Dino at dinoe@wintellect.com.
```

The e-mail pattern string will isolate the e-mail address in the text and pass it, wrapped in a *Match* class, to the *EmailMatchEvaluator* function. As a result, the original text is formatted as follows:

```
Contact Dino at <a href='mailto:dinoe@wintellect.com'>dinoe@wintellect.com</a>.
```

Similar operations are performed when the text contains URL-like strings.

Using the *LinkLabel* Control

As we've seen in Chapter 10, a custom ASP.NET control must be registered with the page by using the *@Register* directive. Unlike Web user controls, a custom

ASP.NET control can be deployed only through an assembly copied in the Bin directory of the virtual folder or to the GAC.

```
<%@ Register TagPrefix="mspo" Namespace="ProAspNet.CS.Ch18"
    Assembly="LinkLabel" %>
```

While registering a custom control, you set the *TagPrefix* attribute as a shortcut for the specified namespace.

```
<mspo:LinkLabel id="LinkLabel1" runat="server"  />
```

The *TagName* attribute is not used here because for custom controls it defaults to the name of the class. So for a *LinkLabel* control, the name of the tag can only be *linklabel*—whatever case you use.

Configuring the Control at Design-Time

The *LinkLabel* can be added to the Toolbox and dragged and dropped onto the designer. Within the designer, the behavior of the *LinkLabel* control is nearly identical to that of the parent *Label* control. The Web form displayed in Figure 18-2 contains two instances of the *LinkLabel* control.

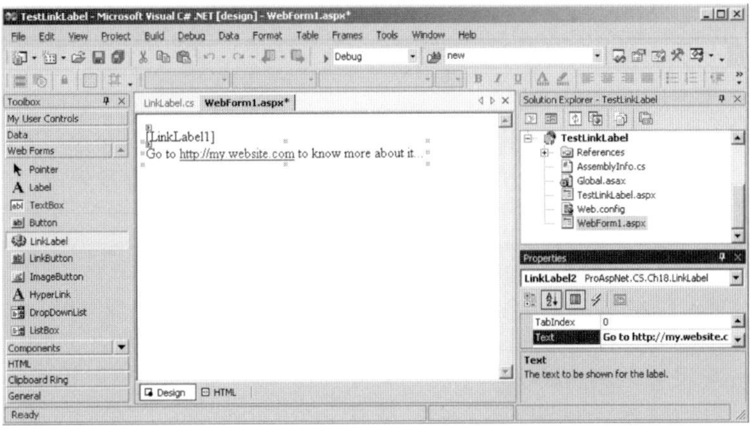

Figure 18-2 Using the *LinkLabel* control within Visual Studio .NET.

To let you experiment with the control (and possibly figure out bugs in the regular expressions used), let's create a more interactive application, like the one shown in Figure 18-3.

When you click the Test link button, the following code executes:

```
private void LinkButton1_Click(object sender, System.EventArgs e)
{
    LinkLabel1.UseBoldForEmail = CheckBox1.Checked;
    LinkLabel1.BeginNewParagraph = CheckBox2.Checked;
    LinkLabel1.Text = TextBox1.Text;
}
```

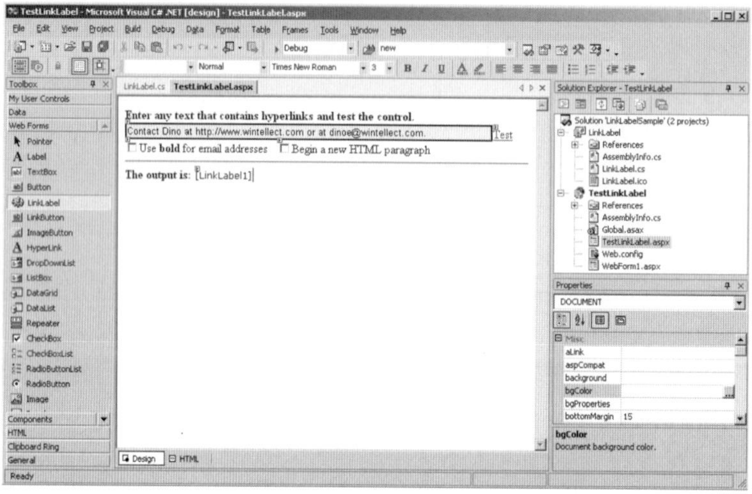

Figure 18-3 Type any text, click the button, and see whether the control detects any Web-sensitive elements.

As you can see, the preceding code contains a couple of new properties we haven't discussed yet—*UseBoldForEmail* and *BeginNewParagraph*.

Want to Be Spammed?

All *<a>* tags that appear in HTML pages are potential victims of Web robots that scan sites to see whether they have e-mail addresses embedded. Robots locate the *<a>* tag in the page being analyzed, look for the *mailto* prefix, and grab the attached e-mail address. You understand that a control like *LinkLabel* certainly doesn't do much to slow down spammers.

The *UseBoldForEmail* property is a Boolean property that affects the way in which the e-mail match evaluator works. If the *UseBoldForEmail* property is set to *true*, the evaluator formats the e-mail address as boldface text rather than as a hyperlink, which could potentially limit spam.

```
private string EmailMatchEvaluator(Match m) {
    string format = "<a href='mailto:{0}'>{0}</a>";
    if (UseBoldForEmail)
        format = "<b>{0}</b>";

    return String.Format(format, m.Value);
}
```

Figure 18-4 shows how the *LinkLabel* control looks when the *UseBoldForEmail* property is set to *true*.

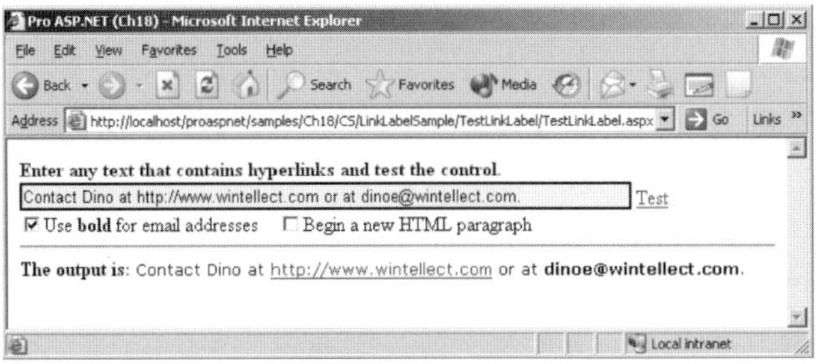

Figure 18-4 The *LinkLabel* control can render e-mail addresses in bold.

Modifying the Opening Tag

The *Label* control renders the text wrapped in a *<span>* tag. All the graphical properties you can set (for example, font and colors) are converted to cascading style sheet (CSS) properties and bound to the *style* attribute. The opening *<span>* tag and the style properties are set up during the *RenderBeginTag* method. In HTML, the *<span>* tag flows with the rest of the text in the page. This means that if you want to display a label on the next row of text, you must add a *
* tag or something like that.

The *<div>* tag has characteristics similar to the *<span>* tag and acts as a generic HTML container. Unlike the *<span>* tag, though, *<div>* represents a distinct block within the page and breaks the flow of the HTML text. In other words, if we could render the *LinkLabel* using a *<div>* instead of the default *<span>* tag, the text would be displayed below the existing output. The *BeginNewParagraph* property just specifies whether a *<div>* or *<span>* tag should be used. By overwriting the *RenderBeginTag* method, we can also add this feature to the *LinkLabel* control.

```
public override void RenderBeginTag(HtmlTextWriter writer)
{
    if(!BeginNewParagraph) {
        // Go the default way
        base.RenderBeginTag(writer);
        return;
    }

    // Write attributes
    AddAttributesToRender(writer);

    // Write the opening tag
    writer.RenderBeginTag("div");

    // The closing tag is automatically managed by the writer
}
```

The *AddAttributesToRender* method is a protected member included with all Web controls. The method adds HTML attributes and styles that need to be rendered to the specified HTML writer. The *RenderBeginTag* method on the writer writes the opening tag using the specified tag. The use of the *BeginNewParagraph* property is shown in Figure 18-5.

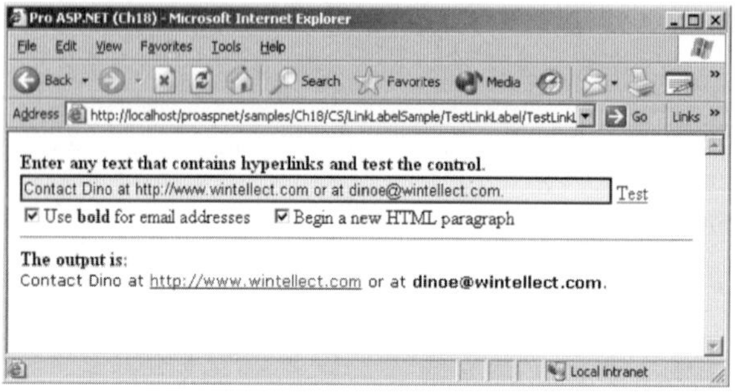

Figure 18-5 The HTML text generated by the *LinkLabel* is now wrapped by a *<div>* tag and begins on a new line.

> **Caution** At design time in Visual Studio .NET, the code always runs fully trusted. This means that the custom control might work properly when you are testing it on your own computer, but it might fail in a production environment because it lacks adequate permissions (for example, it could be called by a partially trusted client). Be sure to test your controls in the security context in which they will run in real-world applications.

A Better *DataGrid* Control

In Chapter 6 and Chapter 7, we worked to demonstrate a variety of features of the *DataGrid* control, including pagination, sorting, templates, and in-place editing. Even though the *DataGrid* is one of the most powerful ASP.NET controls, the amount of relatively boilerplate code you have to write in real-world scenarios is still significant. The control is designed to help developers display data in a way that's more productive for them and more enjoyable for users. The *DataGrid* control, though, is not supposed to be the ultimate grid, one that's good for everybody. By design, the control provides a rich and effective infrastructure, but it leaves developers responsible for fleshing it out with application-specific and scenario-specific code.

Technically speaking, it's not entirely true that the *DataGrid* supports paging or sorting. The control supplies an infrastructure that makes it simple for developers to build applications capable of paging and sorting data. The fact is that to fully set up these features, you need to write code. The code for paging or sorting cuts across the problem domain, so you need it regardless of what the logic is behind the data you're paging or sorting through.

One good reason to customize the *DataGrid* control, therefore, is the need to make it fit into a particular scenario—not just paging or sorting but also master/details views, two-way data-binding, selection, searching, and filtering. Incidentally, this is also the direction that Microsoft is geared toward for the next version of the .NET Framework. The second good reason to extend the *DataGrid* control is just to make the control work better and look nicer.

In this section, we'll consider a custom *DataGrid* control with an enhanced engine for pagination.

Improving the Pager Bar

The pager bar of a *DataGrid* supports two working modes, *NextPrev* and *NumericPages*. In *NextPrev* mode, two link buttons are displayed that move you one page back or forth. In *NumericPages* mode, each page boasts its own link button, up to a maximum number of page buttons. Both pager bars have pros and cons, and both can be customized at will by hooking the *ItemCreated* event. (See Chapter 7 for details.)

When a *DataGrid* pages in *NextPrev* mode, there's no visual feedback about the current page. I confess that I didn't notice it until one of my most attentive users raised the issue. The user can move back and forth, but nothing in the default user interface of the control tells her what portion of the data she's scrolled already. In addition, there's no way to jump to the first or last page in a single shot, a very desirable feature in many applications. Let's see how to extend the *DataGrid* to incorporate these features. In the past few months, I've developed so many types of custom grids that I've exhausted all the possible fancy names for it. Names like PowerGrid, SuperGrid, MyDataGrid, DataGridEx all look repetitive. So let's just maintain the original name but, of course, change the namespace.

Refining the *NextPrev* Mode

As mentioned, when working in *NextPrev* mode, the *DataGrid* control displays only a couple of link buttons to move to the next and previous pages. The two link buttons are created during the initialization step of the grid. Before the HTML output of the grid is generated, the programmer is given a chance to modify something in the item's layout. In Chapter 6, we already discussed many aspects of the *ItemCreated* event. In this chapter, what remains to do is simply incorporate the aforementioned tricks into an all-encompassing, reusable control.

Our *DataGrid* class derives from the ASP.NET *DataGrid* control and registers an internal handler for the *ItemCreated* event.

```
public class DataGrid : System.Web.UI.WebControls.DataGrid
{
    // Class constructor
    public DataGrid() : base()
    {
        ItemCreated += new DataGridItemEventHandler(DataGrid_ItemCreated);
    }

    // Handler of the ItemCreated event
    void DataGrid_ItemCreated(object sender, DataGridItemEventArgs e)
    {
        // Creating the pager
        if (e.Item.ItemType == ListItemType.Pager)
            SetupNextPrevPager(e);

        // Creating the footer
        if (e.Item.ItemType == ListItemType.Footer)
            SetupFooter(e);
    }
}
```

At this point, any feature that we discussed in previous chapters can be easily plugged in and made reusable. The *SetupNextPrevPager* method creates a new *Label* control and places it in between the two link buttons.

```
private void SetupNextPrevPager(DataGridItemEventArgs e)
{
    // Only if the pager mode is NextPrev
    if (this.PagerStyle.Mode != PagerMode.NextPrev)
        return;

    // Grab a reference to the pager (the first and unique cell of the row)
    TableCell pager = e.Item.Cells[0];

    // Create and configure a new label
    Label ctl = new Label();
    ctl.Font.Name = "verdana";
    ctl.Font.Size = PagerStyle.Font.Size;
    ctl.ForeColor = PagerStyle.ForeColor;
    ctl.Text = String.Format("<b>Page {0}</b>", 1 + CurrentPageIndex);

    // Add after the first control
    pager.Controls.AddAt(1, ctl);
}
```

Because the new feature of the control is set up at run time, the Visual Studio .NET designer can't handle it. For this reason, if you look at the new *DataGrid* at design time in a sample application, you won't notice any new features, as you can see in Figure 18-6.

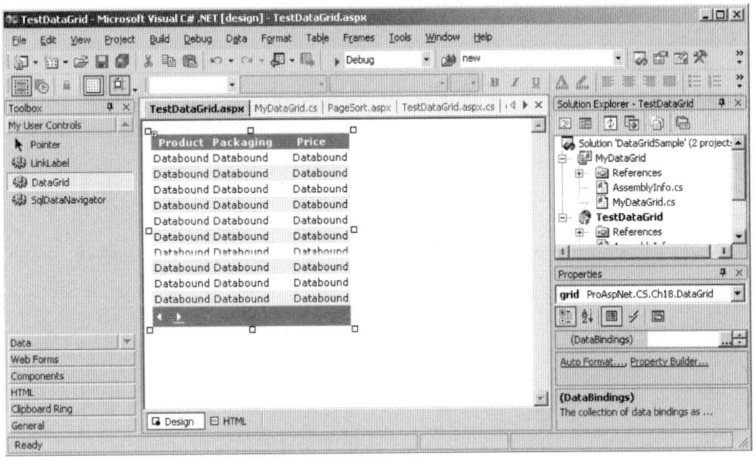

Figure 18-6 The new *DataGrid* control doesn't show any new special features when viewed through the Visual Studio .NET designer.

The dynamically created label shows up once the page that contains the grid is sent to the browser. Note that the *Label* control should have its own font to avoid unpleasant results if the font of the pager is set to Webdings or similar font families. The font size and colors, on the other hand, should be copied from the *PagerStyle* object of the parent grid. Figure 18-7 shows the *DataGrid* control in *NextPrev* mode.

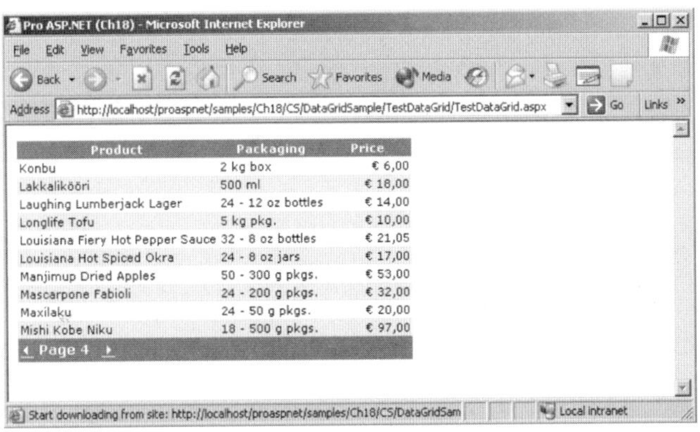

Figure 18-7 When working in *NextPrev* mode, the new *DataGrid* control displays the index of the currently selected page.

A Tab-Style Pager

In Chapter 7, we discussed how to extend the *DataGrid* control to make it support variable-length pages. In doing so, we also slightly modified the pager so that page numbers would display as tabs. Let's take that approach a little further by making it a configurable property of our new *DataGrid* control.

Let's add a couple of properties—*AllowTabbedPager* and *UnselectedTabColor*. The *AllowTabbedPager* property enables the new tabbed pager mode; the *UnselectedTabColor* property indicates the background color of unselected tabs. For the sake of simplicity only, we'll make the foreground color of unselected tabs default to the foreground color of the pager.

What's exactly a tab in this context? A tab is a control in the table row that represents the pager bar. To give the pager a tab-style look and feel, we simply need to adapt colors and borders a little bit. No change is needed in the built-in logic of the grid navigation.

```
public bool AllowTabbedPager
{
    get {return Convert.ToBoolean(ViewState["AllowTabbedPager"]);}
    set
    {
        ViewState["AllowTabbedPager"] = value;
        if (value)
        {
            // Force some layout properties
            CellSpacing = 0;
            CellPadding = 0;

            // Force the pager to be numeric and stay on top
            PagerStyle.Mode = PagerMode.NumericPages;
            PagerStyle.Position = PagerPosition.Top;
        }
    }
}

public Color UnselectedTabColor
{
    get {return (Color) ViewState["UnselectedTabColor"];}
    set {ViewState["UnselectedTabColor"] = value;}
}
```

When setting the *AllowTabbedPager* property, we need to force some settings on other properties. In particular, the pager mode must be *NumericPages* and the pager must be in top position. Furthermore, we also need zero cell padding and spacing for better graphical results. Because cell padding and spacing are properties that work throughout the grid, if you have them set to non-null values, the *AllowTabbedPager* might raise graphical issues. You can try to partially make up for it by using width, height, and margin style properties on individual columns.

Supporting the new pager style also implies some slight changes in the *ItemCreated* event handler.

```
private void DataGrid_ItemCreated(object sender, DataGridItemEventArgs e)
{
    if (e.Item.ItemType == ListItemType.Pager)
        CustomizePager(e);
    if (e.Item.ItemType == ListItemType.Footer)
        SetupFooter(e);
}

private void CustomizePager(DataGridItemEventArgs e)
{
    if (this.PagerStyle.Mode == PagerMode.NextPrev) {
        SetupNextPrevPager(e);
        return;
    }

    if (this.AllowTabbedPager) {
        SetupTabbedPager(e);
        return;
    }
}
```

The core of the code that transforms the numeric pager bar into a tab strip is located in the *SetupTabbedPager* method, as shown in the following code:

```
private void SetupTabbedPager(DataGridItemEventArgs e)
{
    TableCell pager = (TableCell) e.Item.Controls[0];

    // Enumerates all the items in the pager...
    for (int i=0; i<pager.Controls.Count; i++)
    {
        object o = pager.Controls[i];

        // Unselected tabs
        if (o is LinkButton) {
            LinkButton lb = (LinkButton) o;

            // Modify text
            lb.Text = "<span style=margin:2>Page " + lb.Text +
                "</span>";

            // Modify styles
            lb.BorderWidth = Unit.Pixel(1);
            lb.BorderColor = Color.White;
            lb.BackColor = UnselectedTabColor;
            lb.BorderStyle = BorderStyle.Outset;

            // Use hard-coded height (should be changed!)
            lb.Height = Unit.Pixel(18);
```

```
            }
            else
            {
                // Selected tab
                if (o is Label) {
                    Label l = (Label) o;

                    // Modify text
                    l.Text = "<span style=margin:2>Page " + l.Text +
                        "</span>";

                    // Modify styles
                    l.Font.Bold = true;
                    l.BackColor = HeaderStyle.BackColor;
                    l.BorderWidth = Unit.Pixel(1);

                    // Must express a .NET color as an HTML string
                    string htmlColor = HeaderStyle.BackColor.Name;
                    if (htmlColor.StartsWith("ff"))
                        htmlColor = htmlColor.Replace("ff", "#");

                    // Draw border around the selected page
                    string borderString = htmlColor + " outset 1px";
                    l.Style["border-top"] = borderString;
                    l.Style["border-left"] = borderString;
                    l.Style["border-right"] = borderString;
                    l.Style["border-bottom-color"] = htmlColor;

                    // Use hard-coded height (should be changed!)
                    // Make the current tag slightly taller
                    l.Height = Unit.Pixel(20);
                }
                else
                {
                    if (o is LiteralControl)
                    {
                        // Remove unneeded spacing
                        LiteralControl lc = (LiteralControl) o;
                        lc.Text = "";
                    }
                }
            }
        }
}
```

The *SetupTabbedPager* method loops through all the child controls of the unique *<td>* element that represents the pager of a *DataGrid* control. The *Controls* collection can contain controls of three different types—*LinkButton*, *Label*, and *LiteralControl*. In particular, we'll have as many *LinkButton* objects as there are pages to visit (all but the current one); one *Label* control representing the currently selected page; blank literal controls to separate other controls. We render link buttons as unselected tabs and change the text of literal controls to the empty string to keep tabs closer for a nicer output.

A little caveat worth noting has to do with HTML color strings. To make the selected tab look like a real tab, we need to create a continuous region including the *DataGrid* header and the selected tab. However, because they are different HTML elements, a trick is required. We draw the bottom border of the *<span>* tag representing the label with the same background color of the header. Working the ASP.NET way, though, there's no way for us to set the bottom border style of a control. We must resort to CSS settings in the *Style* collection. The rub is that the background color of the header is a .NET Framework class named *Color*. If a conventional color is used, we can easily convert it to a string usable with HTML browsers. However, if the background color has been specified using RGB factors—a #rrggbb string—the string returned by *Color.Name* property has the following format: *ff*rrggbb. As is, the string is not understood by browsers, so we need to strip the *ff* prefix off. Figure 18-8 shows the *DataGrid* in tab-style mode.

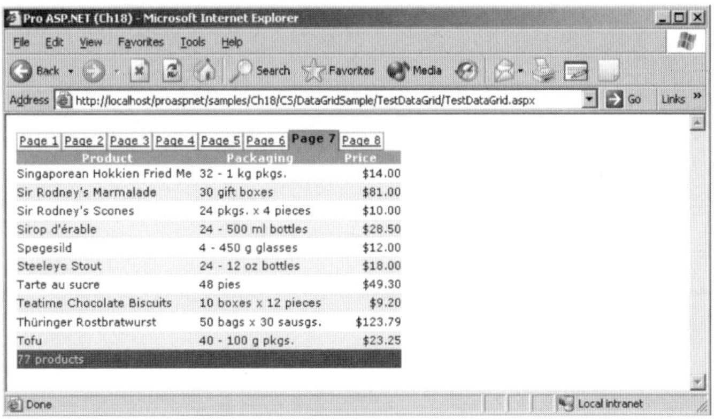

Figure 18-8 The tab-style pager of our *DataGrid* control.

Improving the Footer

The original *DataGrid* control doesn't display the footer by default. To make it appear, you must toggle the *ShowFooter* property on. The footer is displayed immediately after the last row of the page and above the pager, if any. A footer bar doesn't make sense in all cases. In particular, you might want to use it if you have some sort of summary data to display.

The *DataGrid* footer bar, though, is a simple extra table row being displayed with custom and customizable settings. The control doesn't provide any support for the implementation of subtotals and counters. The footer can be given any layout and doesn't necessarily need to have the same structure as preceding columns. By hooking up the *ItemCreated* event, you can modify both the structure of the footer (adding or removing cells) and populate the cells with freshly computed data.

Computing Expressions Dynamically

As mentioned in Chapter 5, the *DataTable* class of the ADO.NET namespace provides an extremely handy method—*Compute*—to calculate totals, subtotals, and other functions on a group of in-memory columns. The most interesting aspect of *Compute*, though, is that it supports a simple but functional and effective language for expressions.

By means of this internal language, you can count the rows that support a certain condition, sum up values in a column, or calculate the average number in a succession of values. If you're going to display the details of an order, you probably want to count the items as well as provide the total of the order. No controls in .NET Framework support summary rows; however, by intercepting the creation of the footer row and leveraging the power of ADO.NET objects, you can succeed as demonstrated in Chapter 6. How can we add support for summary rows in our new *DataGrid* control?

A programmable footer requires three types of information: the expression to compute, the position where the summary value should be displayed, and a formatting string. At first glance, it seems that the most complicated part of the puzzle is the expression. However, in ADO.NET an expression to compute is a plain string like the following ones:

```
sum(price)
count(itemID)
avg(price)
```

More important is the fact that the *Compute* method works only if the data source of the grid is a *DataTable* object. In light of this, the internal method called from within the *ItemCreated* handler to set up the footer must first check the type of the grid's data source.

```
private void SetupFooter(DataGridItemEventArgs e)
{
    if (!(this.DataSource is DataTable))
        return;

    DataTable data = (DataTable) this.DataSource;
    ⋮

    return;
}
```

> **Note** You can still compute a total on the items of an array or a generic collection. However, in this case the burden of looping and summing values is entirely your own. The *DataTable* class, conversely, provides a ready-to-use method. If you're going to use subtotaling footers in a real-world control, spending some time adapting the present solution to a more general case would certainly pay off.

The following code illustrates how the *ItemCreated* handler reads the *DataTable* object and computes the subtotals:

```
void DataGrid_ItemCreated(object sender, DataGridItemEventArgs e) {
    if (e.Item.ItemType == ListItemType.Footer)
        SetupFooter(e);
}

void SetupFooter(DataGridItemEventArgs e) {
    if (!(this.DataSource is DataTable))
        return;

    DataTable data = (DataTable) this.DataSource;

    foreach(FooterColumnData fcd in this.FooterItems)
    {
        decimal num;
        num = Convert.ToDecimal(data.Compute(fcd.Expression, ""));
        string buf = String.Format(fcd.FormatString, num);
        e.Item.Cells[fcd.ColumnPosition].Text = buf;
    }
    return;
}
```

The Programming Interface of the Footer

All the information that you need to pass to create a summary cell is described in the following classes:

```
public class FooterColumnData
{
    public int ColumnPosition;
    public string Expression;
    public string FormatString;
}

public class FooterColumnDataCollection : ArrayList
{
}
```

The *FooterColumnData* class represents a cell on the footer destined to contain a total. It needs to know the 0-based position of the cell to fill, the expression to use to calculate the total, and the needed formatting settings to render the total. Because in general you can have more than one summary cell, let's define a collection of *FooterColumnData* objects. For brevity, our collection class simply derives from *ArrayList*. In a real-world scenario, consider creating a more effective strong-typed collection class.

The property that gathers all the summary cells is named *FooterItems* and is implemented as follows:

```
public DataGrid() : base()
{
    FooterItems = new FooterColumnDataCollection();

    // Event handlers
    this.ItemCreated += new DataGridItemEventHandler(DataGrid_ItemCreated);
}

public FooterColumnDataCollection FooterItems
{
    get {return (FooterColumnDataCollection) ViewState["FooterItems"];}
    set {ViewState["FooterItems"] = value; }
}
```

To use a footer with summary information, a client page has just one thing to do—populate the *FooterItems* collection with as many *FooterColumnData* objects as there are summary cells to display.

The following code snippet, excerpted from the *ItemCreated* event handler, illustrates how the control manages the information about the footer:

```
foreach(FooterColumnData fcd in this.FooterItems)
{
    decimal num = Convert.ToDecimal(data.Compute(fcd.Expression, ""));
    string buf = String.Format(fcd.FormatString, num);
    e.Item.Cells[fcd.ColumnPosition].Text = buf;
}
```

Note that internally all the calculations are done using decimals. The format string determines how the data should be displayed.

A *DataGrid* with Summary Information

In the following code snippet, you see how to configure the footer of the new *DataGrid* control so that it automatically computes and displays totals:

```
private void Configure()
{
    FooterColumnData fcd = new FooterColumnData();
    fcd.ColumnPosition = 0;
    fcd.Expression = "count(productname)";
```

```
    fcd.FormatString = "{0} products";
    grid.FooterItems.Add(fcd);
    ⋮
}
```

The result of the code, shown in Figure 18-9, is that the summary cell will be displayed at the bottom of the first column and formatted as *{0} products*. In this case, the expression simply counts the rows in the data source.

> **Note** The built-in functions you can use within ADO.NET expressions accept only one field name. To work around the issue, you could either add a dynamic column to the data source, formatted as needed, or use an expression of expressions.

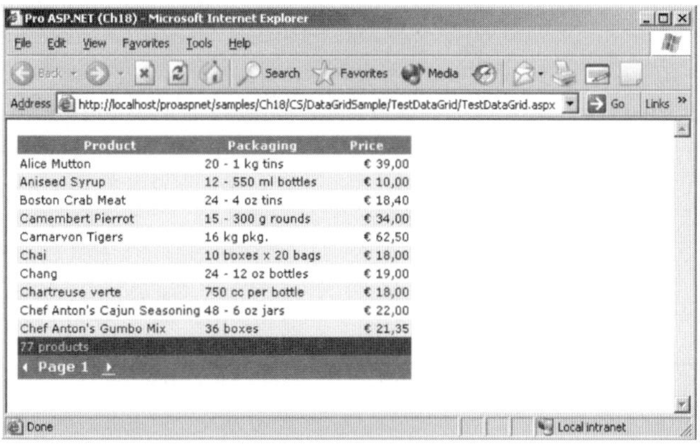

Figure 18-9 The *DataGrid* in action with its programmable footer.

Another interesting scenario for extending controls is represented by control containers—that is, ASP.NET server-side controls that contain child controls. The most popular, because it's required by all nontrivial Web Forms pages, is the *HtmlForm* control.

A Better Server-Side Form Control

In Chapter 4, we dug out many capabilities of the *HtmlForm* control, paying particular attention to the single-form programming model of ASP.NET. By design, an ASP.NET page can host exactly one server form, although you can add any number of HTML *<form>* tags without the *runat="server"* attribute.

If you place two or more server forms in a page, you won't get any error at compile time. The request for the page is processed as usual, and the temporary class for the page is generated, successfully compiled, and finally loaded. Next, the ASP.NET runtime begins processing the page request and regularly fires the *Init*, *Load*, and *PreRender* events. All these events are handled seamlessly. After that, the page enters its rendering phase, which is where the murder will out.

Supporting Multiple Server Forms

Let's briefly review the rendering process of Web pages to understand why multiple server forms are not permitted. The ASP.NET *Page* class calls the *RenderControl* method on all the controls it contains. So the first *<form>* block is successfully processed and rendered. After that, the page class sets an internal flag to track that one form object has been processed for the page. Can you guess what happens next?

Whenever a *<form runat=server>* block is found, the page first verifies that no other similar block has been processed earlier. If the aforementioned internal flag is set, an *HttpException* exception is thrown. As of ASP.NET 1.1, there's no compile-time control on multiple server-side forms. You could include as many server-side forms as you need in a Web Forms page, as long as you ensure that at most one is visible at any time. In practice, if you set the *Visible* attribute of all server-side forms but one to *false*, the page will render just fine.

It goes without saying that you can control the *Visible* attribute of forms programmatically and decide which one to show based on run-time conditions. Incidentally, a similar approach is comparable to that of ASP.NET mobile forms (as seen in Chapter 11), in which multiple server-side forms can be defined but only one at a time is visible.

Generally speaking, giving up multiple forms is not a big sacrifice. However, multiple forms are sometimes useful—although probably not as frequently as one might think. A scenario in which you would find multiple server forms helpful is when you implement a form-based functionality in a large number of pages—typically, search and login pages.

Devising Logical Forms

Some pages need to have multiple logical forms. A *logical form* is not necessarily a form as we normally define it based on the common HTML definition. A logical form is simply a logically related group of input controls whose contents can be submitted in a single shot to a piece of code that can handle it. Using the familiar *<form>* tag is only the simplest way to obtain these results. ASP.NET doesn't let you use multiple server-side *<form>* tags. However, you can figure out alternative ways to implement a "logical form."

One possibility is to embed logical forms within panels or Web user controls and include them in the same ASP.NET page. Some glue code will then take care of hiding and showing the blocks according to the particular state of the page. Within these logical forms, you can easily add link buttons that transfer execution to external pages, thus emulating the functionality of a true HTML form. The key advantage in this case is that you still exploit the state maintenance services of ASP.NET.

> **Note** In ASP.NET, you should think in terms of classes and functionality rather than in terms of HTML forms. However, especially if you're engaged in the migration of a complex Web site (for example, a portal), resorting to multiple forms might be the fastest way to be on time and on budget. In many cases, making better use of the power of ASP.NET will allow you to rearchitect the application without multiple HTML forms.

In Chapter 4, we demonstrated this architecture with plain inline code that looks similar to the following code snippet:

```
<form runat="server">

<!-- Logical Form #1 -->
<div>
<b>Register</b><br>
<asp:textbox runat="server" id="RegUserName" /><br>
    <asp:textbox runat="server" id="RegPassword" textmode="password" /><br>
    <asp:button runat="server" text="Register" onclick="OnRegister" />
</div>

<!-- Logical Form #2 -->
<div>
<b>Login</b><br>
<asp:textbox runat="server" id="LogUserName" /><br>
    <asp:textbox runat="server" id="LogPassword" textmode="password" /><br>
    <asp:button runat="server" text="Login" onclick="OnLogin" />
</div>

</form>
```

In this code, *OnRegister* and *OnLogin* methods transfer control to external pages in much the same way the browser does when processing the submission of a form. Instead of using plain *<div>* tags as containers, you can use Web user controls, as in the following code snippet:

```
<form runat="server">
    <mspo:MyRegForm runat="server" id="formReg" action="register.aspx" />
    <hr>
    <mspo:MyLogForm runat="server" id="formLog" action="login.aspx" />
</form>
```

An ever cleaner and more elegant solution would be defining a base class for these user controls. The base class will provide a basic set of properties such as the *Action* property. The big drawback of Web user controls is that they require an external .ascx page to hold the layout. This means that you can't define the contents of a user control inline in the host page as if it were a *<form>* or *<div>* tag.

What's needed to build a logical form that is authorable like a true form? Let's derive a new class from the ASP.NET control that represents the *<div>* tag and make it expose an *Action* property and a *Submit* method.

A Control Representing a Logical Form

The *<div>* tag has the built-in capability of parsing any child tags. By deriving a new class, you can acquire the same capability. The *<div>* tag is represented on the server through a generic class named *HtmlGenericControl*. This class is generic because it doesn't provide a programming interface tailor-made to the features of the *<div>* control.

ASP.NET utilizes the *HtmlGenericControl* to render a handful of HTML tags when these are used with the *runat* attribute. Generic HTML controls include the *<div>*, *<font>*, *<span>*, and *<body>* elements. By default, the constructor of the *HtmlGenericControl* class generates a *<span>* tag. If you want it to create another HTML container, use the proper constructor overload. The following code snippet shows the blueprint of a custom *Form* class that can be used any number of times within an ASP.NET server form:

```
public class Form : HtmlGenericControl, INamingContainer
{
    public Form(string tag) : base("div")
    {...}
    ⋮
}
```

The new *Form* control can contain any combination of HTML text and ASP.NET controls. It exposes the *Action* property to let you indicate the page to jump to when a submit button within the control is clicked. The submit button of this *Form* control is any button or link button that is bound to the *Submit* method of the *Form* class. The following listing shows the source code of the *Form* class that inherits from *HtmlGenericControl*:

```
namespace ProAspNet.CS.Ch18
{
    public class Form : HtmlGenericControl, INamingContainer
    {
        public Form(string tag) : base("div")
        {
        }

        // Indicate the URL to jump tp
        public string Action;

        // The Request.Form members that relate to the controls in the
        // form are packed in the HttpContext of the request
        public virtual void Submit(object sender, EventArgs e)
        {
            foreach(object o in Page.Request.Form)
            {
                string ctlName = o.ToString();
                if (!ctlName.StartsWith(UniqueID + ":"))
                    continue;

                // Split the ID in two parts, prefix:rest_of_the_ID
                string[] parts = ctlName.Split(':');
                Context.Items[parts[1]] = Page.Request.Form[ctlName];
            }

            Page.Server.Transfer(Action);
        }
    }
}
```

When the user clicks on the submit button of the logical form, a predefined *Submit* method executes. The method has a delicate task—making the contents of the logical form available to the action page.

Packing the Form's Contents

When the submit button is clicked, it passes the control to the action page using the *Server.Transfer* method. By default, the *Transfer* method clears the *Form* collection associated with the current request before yielding. We could override this behavior, and leave the *Form* collection intact by calling the overload of the *Transfer* method that accepts a Boolean value. (It's important to see Chapter 13 for more information about the *Transfer* method.)

```
// Preserve the contents of the Form collection
// and the query string
Page.Server.Transfer(Action, true);
```

However, if we leave the *Form* collection intact, the action page would receive the whole collection and not just the controls specific of the logical form. The *Submit* method looks up all the input controls in the logical form and copies their values in the HTTP context. To easily identify the correct subset of controls, we look at the prefix of the controls ID and select only the controls whose ID starts with the ID of the *Form* control. To implement this feature, the role of the *INamingContainer* interface is essential.

INamingContainer is a marker interface that exposes no methods but enjoys special treatment from the ASP.NET framework. In particular, child controls included in a naming container have their *UniqueID* property automatically prefixed with the ID of the parent.

Creating Multiple Form-Like Controls

Let's see how to employ our *Form* control in a test Web page. The control doesn't require any special treatment, and you actually work with it the usual way. You first register it and then create elements prefixed with the specified tag name.

```
<%@ Register tagprefix="mspo" Namespace="ProAspNet.CS.Ch18"
    Assembly="MyForm" %>
```

Pages with Multiple Forms

The following code snippet illustrates the structure of a page that includes one regular server-side form and as many logical server-side forms as needed:

```
<form runat="server">
    <mspo:form id="myRegForm" runat="server" action="register.aspx">
        <b>Register</b><br>
        <asp:textbox runat="server" id="RegUserName" /><br>
        <asp:textbox runat="server" id="RegPassword"
            textmode="password" /> <br>
        <asp:button runat="server" text="Register"
            onclick="myRegForm.Submit" />
    </mspo:form>

    <mspo:form id="myLogForm" runat="server" action="login.aspx">
        <b>Login</b><br>
        <asp:textbox runat="server" id="LogUserName" /><br>
        <asp:textbox runat="server" id="LogPassword"
            textmode="password" /> <br>
        <asp:button runat="server" text="Log in"
            onclick="myLogForm.Submit" />
    </mspo:form>
</form>
```

If you click on the submit buttons of logical forms, the control passes to the specified action page, giving the illusion of a true multiform server page. In this way, you write pages and forms exploiting the full potential of ASP.NET without sacrificing functionalities or giving up any features.

Retrieving Form Values

In pure HTML, when a form submits its contents, the browser collects current values from all input controls. These values are packed into a *POST* or *GET* command and forwarded to the server. From the browser perspective, the ASP.NET page is made of a unique, all-encompassing form. The custom *Form* control gets into the game when the page posts back, retrieves its own subset of input values, copies them into the *HttpContext* object, and transfers the control to the action page.

How can the action page retrieve the values sent by the caller form? These values are no longer available through the *Request.Form* collection because that collection is cleared before transferring the control. The page gets input data by reading from the context of the request.

```
<html>
<body>
User <b>
  <%= Context.Items["RegUserName"] %></b> has been registered.
Password is <b>
  <%= Context.Items["RegPassword"] %></b>.
</body>
</html>
```

In terms of programming style, you use *Context.Items* in much the same way you used *Request.Form* in ASP pages. *Context* is more efficient than *Session* because it doesn't persist longer than the page instance. *Context.Items* is an effective and quite generic way of passing parameters to pages that are run using *Server.Transfer* or *Server.Execute*.

> **Note** A control derived from *HtmlGenericControl* cannot be added to the Visual Studio .NET toolbox. This in no way jeopardizes the usability of the control in an ASP.NET application. The control must be registered and added manually to the Web Forms page.

Composite Controls

So far in this chapter, we emphasized the concept of reusability and customization obtained through inheritance. However, you can author new controls by combining existing controls and thus exploiting aggregation instead of inheritance. A composite control can extend its own object model by mirroring the properties of its child controls and handle events raised by its child controls. A composite control must meet a couple of requirements. First, authors of composite controls must override the protected *CreateChildControls* method. The method is exposed from *Control* and must be used to create instances of the child controls and add them to the new control's *Controls* collection.

The second requirement is that the control implement the *INamingContainer* interface to create a new naming scope for its children. You do not have to override the *Render* method because child controls provide the rendering logic. By overriding *Render*, you can inadvertently override the constituent controls too. We'll see more about composite controls in the next chapter.

Conclusion

ASP.NET comes with a full suite of goodies for developers. A large part of these goodies relate to controls and control development. Although the .NET Framework deploys a significant number of controls, there might be situations in which you need controls that do not exist. Sometimes the ideal control must be built from scratch, assembling pieces of HTML code under the umbrella of an object model. In many other situations, though, what you need is simply a slightly enhanced version of an existing control. A pageable *DataList*, a more specialized grid, and a rich textbox are examples of controls not defined within the .NET Framework but that can be built on top of existing controls.

To build new custom controls, you can use two well-known techniques—inheritance and aggregation. Composite controls are the result of aggregation and basically consist of various controls combined by using class composition. Functionally speaking, composite controls are similar to Web user controls, which we thoroughly examined in Chapter 10. However, many key differences exist under the hood, the first of which is that composite controls can be deployed only through assemblies. In the next chapter, we'll cover composite controls in detail.

In this chapter, though, we mostly focused on custom controls built by exploiting inheritance. You create a class that inherits from an existing ASP.NET control class and add functionality by overriding existing members or by creating new properties, methods, and events. Inheriting from existing controls cuts development time and increases productivity and the quality of the code. When a good base exists for the control you have in mind, it's easy to think bigger and devise functionality better and from a wider perspective.

As the three examples discussed in this chapter prove—*LinkLabel*, *DataGrid* and *SubForm*—to get the most out of control inheritance a deep knowledge of the surrounding framework is required. Inheritance supplies a control that works, but modifying the default behavior might not be straightforward. You must know very well the guts of the control and have a good understanding of any protected and overridable members. Also when building controls from scratch, keep in mind that not all controls lend themselves well to being used as a base for new controls. Inheritance can decrease your development time when used across projects, but it's a quick-sharpening, double-edged sword.

In the next chapter, we'll continue our exploration of ASP.NET custom controls by looking at completely new controls that you write from the ground up and which inherit from the base class *Control*.

Resources

- *Developing Microsoft ASP.NET Server Controls and Components*, by Nikhil Kothari and Vandana Datye (Microsoft Press, 2002)
- Post Multiple Forms from a Single Page (*http://www.aspnetpro.com/features/2003/04/asp200304pw_f/asp200304pw_f.asp*)
- ASP.NET Control Gallery (*http://www.asp.net/ControlGallery/default.aspx?tabindex=2*)
- In-depth: Creating Custom ASP.NET Controls in VS.NET (*http://www.dotnet247.com/247reference/articles/0/2019.aspx*)

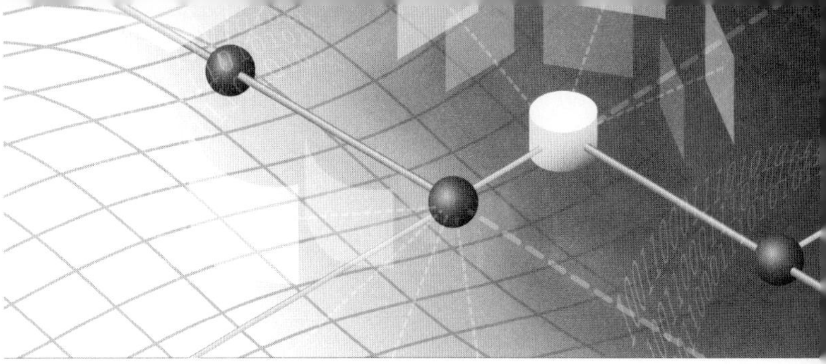

19

Creating New ASP.NET Controls

Appreciation is a wonderful thing: It makes what is excellent in others belong to us as well.

—Voltaire

If none of the existing Web server controls meet your requirements, you can create your own control by deriving from one of the control base classes—*Control* and *WebControl*. Even in this case, though, you don't have to build your control completely from scratch. The *Control* and *WebControl* classes provide all the basic functionality of a Web server control and let you focus mostly on the specific features you need to implement.

In its simplest form, a Web server control is a software component that abstracts a piece of HTML markup and exposes it through an object model. You can write controls using any .NET-compliant language and accessing the entire .NET Framework; however, a Web server control still works within the boundaries of an ASP.NET page and, as such, must output HTML markup. A Web server control encapsulates native or composite functionality that you can obtain through HTML and script code. If the functionality you have in mind cannot be obtained with a combination of HTML and client script code, we seriously doubt you'll ever make it work over the Web. An ASP.NET custom control is a class with public methods, properties, and events that renders through an HTML text writer. The final output of an ASP.NET Web server control is HTML text. Keep this in mind as you make your way through this chapter. In general, though, ASP.NET controls can output to other markup languages. For example, ASP.NET mobile controls generate WML.

In this chapter, we'll first demonstrate how to build controls from scratch that implement a simple object model and render it to HTML. Then we'll examine *composite controls*—a sort of middle way between derived and new controls.

Base Control Classes and Interfaces

Several programming aspects support the development of a custom control in ASP.NET. First, there are the two base classes, *Control* and *WebControl*. Each class provides a common set of base properties that address and fit into a particular use case. In addition to base classes, interfaces help you to better characterize the behavior and programming model of the control. Three interfaces are worth mentioning. They are *INamingContainer*, *IPostBackDataHandler*, and *IPostBackEventHandler*. We've already encountered them repeatedly throughout the book. In this chapter, we'll see them in action from the perspective of a control's developer. Finally, styles and the HTML writer are fundamental components to define and enhance the look and feel of the control and render it to the output stream. We'll review them too.

Control vs. *WebControl*

The *Control* class defines the properties, methods, and events common to all ASP.NET server controls. These include the methods and events that determine and govern the lifecycle of the control plus a few properties such as *ID*, *UniqueID*, *Parent*, *ViewState*, and the collection of child controls named *Controls*.

The *WebControl* class derives from *Control* and adds extra properties and methods, mostly regarding control styles which affect rendering. These properties include *ForeColor*, *BackColor*, *Font*, *Height*, and *Width*. *WebControl*, in particular, is the base class for the family of Web server controls in ASP.NET.

In Chapter 3, "ASP.NET Core Server Controls," we provided a detailed description of the properties and methods of the *WebControl* and *Control* classes and discussed how HTML and Web controls inherit from them. In this chapter, we'll focus on understanding which class you should consider when developing a brand new ASP.NET control.

When developing a new ASP.NET control, there's just one guideline to follow. If your control renders a user interface (UI), you should derive it from *WebControl*. If you're authoring a component that doesn't provide specific user-interface features, you're better off using *Control* as your base class. Although these rules are effective in most cases, there might be exceptional situations in which you would reasonably do otherwise. For example, you can derive from *Control* also if you want to provide a subset of the UI features or when you are combining multiple controls. When using these derived controls—known as *composite controls*—typical user-interface properties such as *BackColor* should be duplicated to let users address the background of individual controls. In similar situations, you might want to get rid of the typical programming interface and build your own completely from scratch. Note that you should never use *UserControl* as a base class for a custom control.

Related Interfaces

Depending on the functionality of your control, you might have to implement additional interfaces. Typically, a server control will implement some of the following three interfaces.

- ***INamingContainer*** This interface, also referred to as a marker interface, doesn't contain methods, it simply notifies the ASP.NET runtime that the control that exposes it should be considered as a naming container. Child controls contained within a naming-container control have their *UniqueID* property prefixed with the ID of the container. The naming container, therefore, acts as a namespace and guarantees the uniqueness of the control IDs within the specified naming scope. The use of the *INamingContainer* interface is essential if you're writing iterative or templated controls such as *Repeater* and *DataList*.
- ***IPostBackDataHandler*** The *IPostBackDataHandler* interface is needed whenever your control has to examine postback data. If the user can execute actions that affect the state of the control, you need to look into the postback data. For example, a *TextBox* control stores its configuration in the view state but also needs to read what the user typed in through the browser. This scenario is just where the *IPostBackDataHandler* interface fits in. The *LoadPostData* method lets controls examine posted values. The interface is also helpful if you need to raise events on the server based on changes to the data (using the *RaisePostDataChanged* method). Again, the *TextBox* is the perfect sample control; if the data changed between postbacks, the *TextChanged* event is also raised.
- ***IPostBackEventHandler*** The *IPostBackEventHandler* interface serves to capture a client-side postback event (for example, a click). Upon postback, after raising data change events, the ASP.NET runtime looks for a server control whose *UniqueID* property matches the name of a posted value (for example, the name of the clicked button). If a match is found and the control implements *IPostBack-EventHandler*, ASP.NET invokes the *RaisePostBackEvent* method on the control. *RaisePostBackEvent* is the only method defined on the

IPostBackEventHandler interface. What a particular control does within the *RaisePostBackEvent* method can vary quite a bit. The *Button* control—a simple control that implements this interface—fires its *Click* event when ASP.NET invokes the *RaisePostBackEvent* method.

The HTML Text Writer

The *HtmlTextWriter* is a helper class that turns out to be quite useful in the development of custom controls. You seldom use the writer if you derive controls from existing ones. However, when you build the control from the ground up, you inevitably need to write the HTML output to the stream.

The *HtmlTextWriter* class writes a sequential series of HTML-specific characters and text on an ASP.NET page. The class also provides formatting capabilities that ASP.NET server controls can take advantage of when rendering HTML content to clients. If you're familiar with XML writers (discussed in Chapter 16, "Working with the File System"), you'll find nothing new about the programming model of HTML writers. The class provides a bunch of methods that you use as ad hoc tools to handcraft the HTML code. Here's how to write a table using an *HtmlTextWriter*.

```
// outputs <table><tr>
writer.WriteFullBeginTag("table");
writer.WriteFullBeginTag("tr);

// outputs <td valign="top">
writer.WriteBeginTag("td");
writer.WriteAttribute("valign", "top");
writer.Write(HtmlTextWriter.TagRightChar);

// outputs Hello</td>
writer.Write("Hello");
writer.WriteEndTag("td");

// outputs </tr></table>
writer.WriteEndTag("tr");
writer.WriteEndTag("table");
```

The *WriteFullBeginTag* and *WriteBeginTag* methods perform a similar task and differ in that *WriteBeginTag* does not write the closing character (>) of the opening tag. In this way, attributes can be appended to the tag by other methods such as *WriteAttribute*. To close the tag, you write the *TagRightChar* constant, or the *SelfClosingTagEnd* constant if the element is a self-closing one (/>).

Writing Attributes

To render the attributes of a Web server control in HTML client code, you typically use the *WriteAttribute* method of the *HtmlTextWriter* object. The method takes the name of the attribute and its value and writes both to the output stream, adding a blank and using the common syntax of attributes.

```
// Generates border="1"
output.WriteAttribute(border, "1");
```

The value of the attribute must be a string, and the method takes care of quotes too.

An alternative technique you can use to add attributes is based on the combined use of the *AddAttribute* and *RenderBeginTag* methods. The *AddAttribute* method adds the value to the list of attributes for the outermost element. When the *RenderBeginTag* method is finally called, any attributes in the internal stack are popped out and rendered to the opening tag of the element. The list of attributes is then cleared. Generally, the pattern is to add attributes to the element, call *RenderBeginTag*, render the contents, and then call the *RenderEndTag* method. This technique is used internally in many standard ASP.NET controls.

Working with Styles

A bit more specific than *AddAttribute* is the *AddStyleAttribute* method. The two methods work in roughly the same way, but *AddAttribute* can manage any attribute whereas *AddStyleAttribute* is specific to the *Style* attribute.

```
// Generates style="font-name:verdana;font-size:10pt;"
output.AddStyleAttribute("font-name", "verdana");
output.AddStyleAttribute("font-size", "10pt");
```

The most commonly used style properties are grouped by name in the *HtmlTextWriterStyle* enumeration. By using a particular overload of the *AddStyleAttribute* method, you can take values from this type to indicate the style properties to render to the element.

> **Important** It might seem rather bizarre that while emphasizing the role of components in general and the ASP.NET object model in particular, Microsoft recommends the use of stream writers to let server controls generate their output. Objects are important and fundamental for a number of reasons. However, rendering controls to HTML is one of the common tasks that ASP.NET applications accomplish repeatedly, one request after the next. It goes without saying that such tasks are to be optimized as much as possible. Writing to the response stream—the HTML writer works on top of the response stream—is much faster than creating an object-based representation of the output and then asking the root control to render itself (and the children) to HTML. Using the HTML text writer is a matter of optimizing performance.

The way in which a style is rendered in ASP.NET varies according to the selected client target—a downlevel or uplevel browser. ASP.NET addresses differences between HTML 4.0 and HTML 3.2 by employing two distinct rendering engines—the *HtmlTextWriter* and *Html32TextWriter* classes. In particular, the *Html32TextWriter* class converts HTML 4.0 style attributes into the equivalent tags and attributes compatible with HTML 3.2 and ensures that attributes, like colors and fonts, are consistently and correctly propagated to older browsers. The version and the capabilities of the underlying browser are detected by looking at the *HttpBrowserCapabilities* class.

Building a Gauge Control

ASP.NET controls are made of two logical components—an object model and a rendering engine—that can be, in turn, implemented through various layers of code and topped with handlers for the events fired by the container and registered HTTP modules. When building a new control (as opposed to deriving a control), the most relevant difference lies in the fact that you have to render any needed HTML yourself. In a derived control, as we've seen in Chapter 18 ("Extending Existing ASP.NET Controls"), you normally don't need to provide HTML rendering and deal with text writers.

To get a grip on building new ASP.NET controls, let's start by creating a simple control with a limited state and a not-too-complex rendering engine. The control, named *GaugeBar*, represents a gauge and can be used to implement a rating system that represents the progress made for certain tasks, or in general it could be used to give a friendly user interface to measurable quantities.

Defining the Object Model

A gauge control needs to have at least two properties—one to indicate the value being rendered and one that provides the scale. In addition, we also give users a chance to control the ruler and the descriptive text for the gauge. Table 19-1 lists the properties of a gauge control.

Table 19-1 Properties of a Gauge Control

Property	Description
FormatString	Formats the string that the control will render alongside the control. The string can contain up to two placeholders. The first placeholder is set with the value; the second placeholder is set with the scale. The default string has the following form: *{0}out of{1}*.
Maximum	Indicates the maximum value the gauge can represent. Set to 100 by default.

Table 19-1 Properties of a Gauge Control

Property	Description
Segments	Indicates the number of notches to draw on the gauge ruler. Set to 4 by default.
Value	Indicates the value to represent. Set to 0 by default, and cannot be higher than the scale.

The *set* accessor of the *Value* properties cuts any value set that exceeds the current *Maximum*. The value stored in *Maximum* is the highest value you can assign to *Value*. The format string should be formed using two parameters in a fixed order—value and maximum. In the format string, you can use any HTML formatting and even reference the parameters in the reverse order. The following code snippet shows possible ways of setting the format string:

```
GaugeBar1.FormatString = "{0} ({1})";
GaugeBar2.FormatString = "Maximum is {1}. Value is <b>{0}</b>";
```

The gauge control has no methods and doesn't fire any events.

Implementing the Object Model

Internally, the control renders the gauge using an HTML table. The *Value* and *Maximum* pair are translated in percentages, and the ruler is drawn using table cells. Figure 19-1 shows the control within the Microsoft Visual Studio .NET designer.

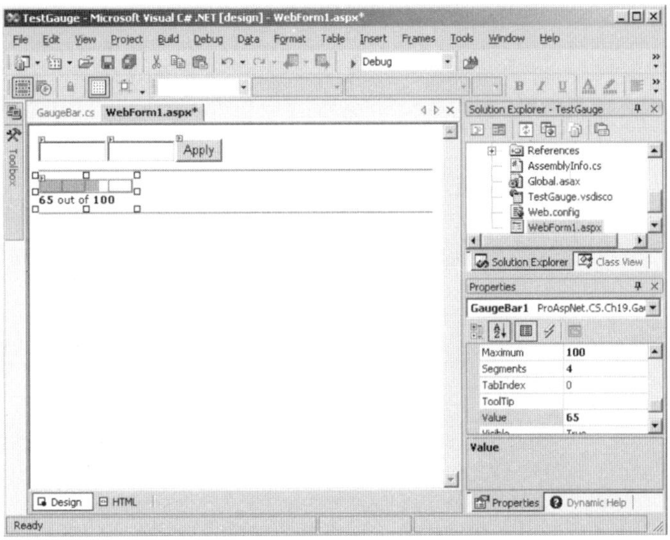

Figure 19-1 The *GaugeBar* control in action in the Visual Studio .NET designer.

The notches on the ruler are obtained simply by adding as many cells to the underlying table as there are units in the *Segments* property. The following listing shows the C# source code of the control:

```
using System;
using System.Web.UI;
using System.Web.UI.WebControls;
using System.ComponentModel;
using System.Drawing;

namespace ProAspNet.CS.Ch19
{
    public class GaugeBar : WebControl
    {
        public GaugeBar() : base() {
            ForeColor = Color.Orange;
            BackColor = Color.LightYellow;
            Width = 100;
            Height = 15;
            Maximum = 100;
            Value = 0;
            Segments = 4;
            FormatString = "<b>{0}</b> out of <b>{1}</b>";
        }

        public float Value {
            get {return (float) ViewState["Value"];}
            set {
                float f = (value > Maximum ? Maximum :value);
                ViewState["Value"] = f;
            }
        }

        public float Maximum {
            get {return (float) ViewState["Maximum"];}
            set {ViewState["Maximum"] = value;}
        }

        public int Segments {
            get {return (int) ViewState["Segments"];}
            set {ViewState["Segments"] = (value <1 ? 1 :value);}
        }

        public string FormatString {
            get {return ViewState["FormatString"].ToString();}
            set {ViewState["FormatString"] = value;}
        }

        protected override void Render(HtmlTextWriter output) {
            // Calculate the value to represent
            float valueToRepresent = 100f*Value/Maximum;

            // Begin the rendering of the table
```

```
            output.WriteBeginTag("table");
            output.WriteAttribute("bgcolor", "gray");
            output.WriteAttribute("border", "1");
            output.WriteAttribute("cellspacing", "0");
            output.WriteAttribute("cellpadding", "0");
            output.WriteAttribute("width", Width.ToString());
            output.WriteAttribute("height", Height.ToString());
            output.Write(HtmlTextWriter.TagRightChar);
            output.WriteFullBeginTag("tr");

            // Draw segments (cells of the table)
            DrawRuler(output, valueToRepresent);

            // Draw the text below (use another table)
            output.WriteEndTag("tr");
            output.WriteEndTag("table");
            output.AddStyleAttribute("font-family", "verdana");
            output.AddStyleAttribute("font-size", "8pt");
            output.RenderBeginTag("span");
            output.Write(FormatString, Value, Maximum);
            output.RenderEndTag();
        }
    }
}
```

Note In the previous code, we set default values for the various properties in the constructor. However, all standard ASP.NET controls follow a different but equivalent design pattern. Each property is assigned the default value in the *get* accessor. Consider this when designing your own controls.

The control maintains some state by using the view state collection. All the properties, in fact, are persisted using *ViewState*. Because all the persistent properties are marked as public, you can disable the view state altogether and still keep the control fully functional by explicitly setting properties upon page loading.

Caution A page can disable the view state for all embedded controls or for individual controls. Note, though, that disabling the view state for a control results in a loss of functionality if the control stores in the view state private or protected properties. Unlike public properties, in fact, private or protected properties cannot be programmatically set from within a host page.

As you can see, the *GaugeBar* control features a few properties that form its object model and override the protected member *Render*. As the name and the implementation suggest, the *Render* method generates the HTML output of the control. The control is actually rendered as a table built by outputting raw text to the system-provided HTML text writer.

Setting Up the Ruler

The ruler divides the area of the control in segments, which are filled proportionally based on the current value of the gauge. Each segment of the ruler corresponds to a cell in the underlying table. If no ruler is used, rendering the control consists of creating a single row table with two cells. The first cell is given a different color and a width expressed as a percentage. The second cell has the default background color and a width that denotes how much is still left to do to reach the maximum. The following HTML code snippet shows the code needed to render a value of 80 out of 100:

```
<table><tr>
    <td bgcolor=orange width=80%></td>
    <td bgcolor=white width=20%></td>
</tr></table>
```

When more than one segment is used, each segment renders its portion of the bar and displays the value (or its portion of the value) in a cell. The cell is totally filled if the gauge value is greater than the portion the segment represents. For example, suppose that we use four segments to represent a total value of 100. In this case, the logical width of each segment is 25. If the gauge value is, say, 60, the first two segments are filled up, the third segment is divided in two, and the last one is empty, as shown in the following code:

```
<table><tr>
    <td bgcolor=orange width=25%></td>
    <td bgcolor=orange width=25%></td>
    <td width=25%>
    <table><tr>
        <td bgcolor=orange width=10%></td>
        <td bgcolor=white width=15%></td>
    </tr></table>
    </td>
    <td bgcolor=white width=25%></td>
</tr></table>
```

Figure 19-2 shows how this gauge will look (four segments displaying a value of 60 out of 100). Figure 19-2 also shows gauges with different ruler settings.

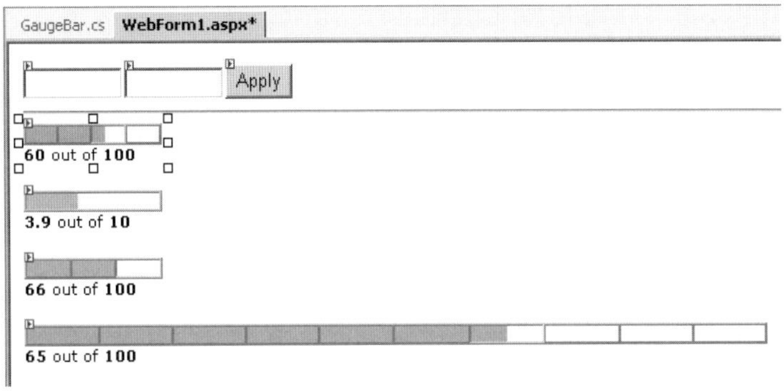

Figure 19-2 The effect of different settings on the gauge ruler.

Setting Up the Control's Site

As you might have guessed already from the preceding figures, other properties get into the game aside from those discussed in Table 19-1. Admittedly, the grayscale rendering used in this book doesn't do justice to the actual capabilities of the *GaugeBar* control in terms of color support. However, the control exploits a few color-related properties defined on the base class. These properties are *BackColor*, *ForeColor*, *Width*, and *Height*.

Width and *Height* are used to delimit the control's site—that is, the area within the container the control is assigned for rendering. The control is assigned a default size that can be changed either programmatically or through the Visual Studio .NET Properties window.

The value of the *ForeColor* property is used to render the text of the label that accompanies the gauge. The value of the *BackColor* property determines the color to be used for the progress bar. Note that the implementation we just discussed assumes that only known colors can be used. In other words, if you set any color properties to a custom value such as *#eeeeee*, the final result you get is radically different than what you'd expect. We'll dig into this topic in detail in Chapter 21, "Design-Time Support for Custom Controls," while covering design-time features of custom controls.

Rendering the Control

The user interface of a Web control is pure HTML, sometimes topped off with a bit of client script. There are basically two ways in which this HTML can be generated. You can compose the HTML code in the supplied writer, or you can build an in-memory representation of the output using existing HTML and Web server controls and then have them recursively render their contents to the writer. Let's discuss these two options in more detail.

Generating the HTML for a Custom Control

Earlier in this chapter, we discussed the capabilities of the HTML text writer object and how it simplifies the creation of complex HTML structures. However, the downside of this approach you should consider is that you end up making several calls to the writer. This has repercussions in terms of both the performance and the size of the code. Let's consider a quick but significant example.

To write the content of a string in a table cell, you would need the following code if you decide to opt for the rich interface of the writer:

```
output.WriteFullBeginTag("table");
output.WriteFullBeginTag("tr");
output.WriteFullBeginTag("td");
output.Write(text);
output.WriteEndTag("td");
output.WriteEndTag("tr");
output.WriteEndTag("table");
```

However, as long as you don't have a full bag of attributes to render, or a really complex structure to build, the following code is equally effective and even slightly faster:

```
output.Write("<table><tr><td>");
output.Write(text);
output.Write("</td></tr></table>");
```

In general, neither of these two approaches is always the best possible approach. A good compromise between the two is recommended to optimize performance while producing compact code. Taking the first approach to the limit, you end up with tons of lines of code. Taking the second approach further, you resort to building the control using strings, which is indeed not the best thing you can do.

In ASP.NET, every piece of HTML code can be managed on the server as an instance of a class. This pattern results in extreme flexibility and ease of development. However, it doesn't come free of problems either. The rub lies in the fact that you instantiate lots of controls, which always impact performance.

> **Tip** In general, in ASP.NET using controls is the first option; you shouldn't use them though in situations in which the control is just overkill. If you need to output constant text, there's no reasonable justification for using a *Label* control instead of a simpler *Response.Write*.

Using Child Controls For Rendering

Sometimes the custom control needs to build up a complex infrastructure with nested tables and elements. In this case, it makes sense to build an in-memory representation of the overall tree and then render everything to HTML using the *RenderControl* method of individual controls. We'll demonstrate this technique in detail later in the "Rendering the Control" section while discussing a more complex bar chart example.

To obtain and, optionally, manipulate the HTML text for a particular control, you can proceed as illustrated in the following code snippet:

```
StringWriter writer = new StringWriter();
HtmlTextWriter output = new HtmlTextWriter(writer);
GaugeBar1.RenderControl(output);
display.Text = writer.ToString();
```

The *RenderControl* method of Web controls needs an HTML text writer to generate the output. A writer, though, is only the topmost layer of a pile of objects at the bottom of which there's always a stream. In the simplest case, the HTML writer just lies on the top of the response output stream. In other cases, you can use intermediate writers such as a string writer. In the code just shown, you first create a string writer object and then create an instance of the *HtmlTextWriter* class that writes to the parent writer, which in turn, outputs to the backing store of the *StringWriter* class—a memory stream. The net effect of the code is that *RenderControl* just writes its output to a memory string. The string is then accessible using the *ToString* method.

> **Tip** The trick just described greatly simplifies the development of custom controls because it gives you a quick way to snoop into the actual HTML being generated for your control. (Sometimes the resulting HTML is not obvious if you generate rather entangled markup.) Alternatively, you can use the View Source menu of the browser to see the whole generated HTML. But the trick just described shows you only a small portion of HTML—usually just what really matters.

The Gauge in Action

Once compiled, the gauge control can be installed in the Visual Studio .NET toolbox and dragged and dropped onto any Web Forms page you're developing. The control is automatically registered and provides a preview of its final output.

```
<cc1:gaugebar id="GaugeBar1" runat="server" width="500px" height="15px"
    FormatString="<b>{0}</b> out of <b>{1}</b>"
    Segments="10"
    Value="65" />
```

The properties of the control that feature simple types can be set using the Properties window; for complex types, such as classes, you need to write a type converter and configure the property for the design-time environment of Visual Studio .NET. (We'll discuss this in Chapter 21.)

The following code shows how to set properties on the gauge control programmatically. You should try to set the *Maximum* property first because, in this way, the control automatically validates the value. However, by also adding some validation code to the *set* accessor of the *Maximum* property, you can perform a cross-check of the two values and always stay on the safe side.

```
private void Button1_Click(object sender, System.EventArgs e)
{
    GaugeBar1.Maximum = Convert.ToSingle(TheMax.Text);
    GaugeBar1.Value = Convert.ToSingle(TheVal.Text);
}
```

Maximum and *Value* are stored in the view state and are automatically restored when the page posts back. If the host page disables the view state, you should modify the code that relates to the control so that the needed properties are set on each request. Figure 19-3 shows a *GaugeBar* control in action.

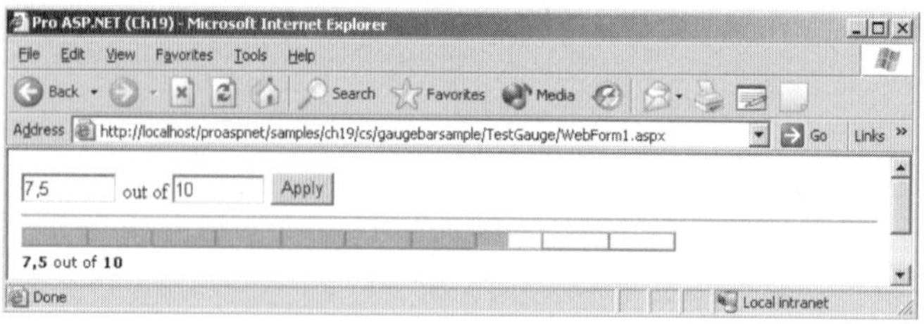

Figure 19-3 A page that makes use of the *GaugeBar* control.

Building a Chart Generator Control

Several third-party controls provide highly specialized charting components for use with Web pages. In addition, the new features built into the *System.Drawing* namespace make it possible for you to exploit GDI+ to create your own graphics and output them as images. If you don't need to create special types of charts, a lightweight but equally effective alternative exists—use HTML tables. As long as you content yourself with a plain two-dimensional bar chart, a pure HTML solution is possible and, to the extent possible, even snazzy and elegant. Let's discover how to build such a solution.

Defining the Object Model

Our HTML bar chart control is made of a sequence of table elements with two rows and one cell. The height and colors of each row are calculated in such a way that the resultant output looks like a vertical gauge. The control, named *BarChart*, features a few properties and one method—*Add*—that you'll use to bind data to the control.

Table 19-2 shows the properties exposed by the control.

Table 19-2 Properties of the *BarChart* Control

Name	Description
BackImageUrl	Indicates the URL of the image to use to tile the background of the control.
BarCount	Read-only property, gets the number of bars that form the chart.
Caption	The string that represents the title of the chart.
ChartColor	The default color used to fill the bars in the chart.
Maximum	The maximum value the chart can represent. Set to 100 by default.
SubTitle	The subtitle of the caption. Displayed below the caption with a smaller font.

The *Maximum* property is nearly identical to that defined on the *GaugeBar* control. It gets and sets the maximum value the control can represent. In addition to the properties listed here, the control will use *ForeColor* and *BackColor* as well as *Width*, *Height*, and *Font*.

Binding Data

To draw a chart, in whatever form or shape, you need data. A chart control lends itself very well to be data-bound. However, in the implementation discussed here, we will not use a data-bound control—at least not in the traditional sense of the word. You won't find a public *DataSource* property accompanied with ancillary properties such *DataMember*, *DataTextField*, and *DataValueField*. We'll discuss data-bound controls in Chapter 20, "Data-Bound and Templated Controls." For now, let's limit ourselves to passing data through a method, named *Add*, that acts as a data accumulator.

```
public void Add(string theLabel, float theValue);
```

The *Add* method has three overloads and allows you to define information about a single bar. The minimum amount of information you must specify includes the text to draw below the bar and the value to represent. Additional parameters are the bar's ToolTip and color. The data you specify is gathered in a custom data structure and copied into an *ArrayList*.

The *ArrayList* is the internal data repository used by the *BarChart* control and is cached in the control's view state. Because of this behavior, you don't need to rebind the control to its data any time the page posts back. Keeping the data source out of the view state is the usual behavior for data-bound controls. The *BarChart* control, at least in this implementation, is built in a different way. The difference shouldn't affect performance too much, as the quantity of data you cache in the view state is limited to very few columns.

The Bar Chart Item

Each bar of the chart is logically represented by a custom data structure known as *BarChartItem*. A new instance of this class is created whenever you call any overload of the *Add* method.

```
[Serializable]
protected class BarChartItem
{
    public string Text;
    public float Value;
    public string ToolTip;
    public Color BackColor;
}
```

Note that the class must be marked as serializable if you want to cache instances of it in the ASP.NET control's view state. The following code snippet shows what happens when a new bar chart item is added to the control:

```
public void Add(string theLabel, float theValue,
    string toolTip, Color barColor)
{
    // Initialize the bar chart object
    BarChartItem bci = new BarChartItem();
    bci.Text = theLabel;
    bci.Value = theValue;
    bci.ToolTip = toolTip;
    bci.BackColor = barColor;

    // Copy data to the view state for persistence
    if (_barChartData != null)
        _barChartData.Add(bci);
    DataSource = _barChartData;
}
```

The source code of the *BarChart* control is as follows:

```
using System;
using System.Web.UI;
using System.Web.UI.WebControls;
using System.ComponentModel;
using System.Drawing;
using System.Collections;

namespace ProAspNet.CS.Ch19
{
    public class BarChart : WebControl {
        public BarChart() : base() {
            _barChartData = new ArrayList();
            DataSource = _barChartData;

            Caption = "";
            SubTitle = "";
            BackImageUrl = "";
            BackColor = Color.White;
            ForeColor = Color.Black;
            ChartColor = Color.Orange;
            Maximum = 100;
            Font.Name = "verdana";
            Font.Size = FontUnit.Point(8);
        }

        public string BackImageUrl {
            get {return ViewState["BackImageUrl"].ToString();}
            set {ViewState["BackImageUrl"] = value;}
        }

        public int BarCount {
            get {
                if (DataSource != null)
                    return DataSource.Count;
                return 0;
            }
        }

        public Color ChartColor {
            get {return (Color) ViewState["ChartColor"];}
            set {ViewState["ChartColor"] = value;}
        }

        public string Caption {
            get {return (ViewState["Caption"].ToString();}
            set {ViewState["Caption"] = value;}
        }

        public string SubTitle {
            get {return ViewState["SubTitle"].ToString();}
            set {ViewState["SubTitle"] = value;}
        }
```

```
        public float Maximum {
            get {return Convert.ToSingle(ViewState["Maximum"]);}
            set {ViewState["Maximum"] = value;}
        }

        private ArrayList _barChartData;
        public void Add(string theLabel, float theValue) {
            Add(theLabel, theValue, "", ChartColor);
        }
        public void Add(string theLabel, float theValue, string toolTip) {
            Add(theLabel, theValue, toolTip, ChartColor);
        }
        public void Add(string theLabel, float theValue, string toolTip,
               Color barColor) {
            BarChartItem bci = new BarChartItem();
            bci.Text = theLabel;
            bci.Value = theValue;
            bci.ToolTip = toolTip;
            bci.BackColor = barColor;

            // Copy data
            if (_barChartData != null)
                _barChartData.Add(bci);
            DataSource = _barChartData;
        }

        protected virtual ArrayList DataSource {
            get {return (ArrayList) ViewState["DataSource"];}
            set {ViewState["DataSource"] = value;}
        }
    }
}
```

The preceding listing doesn't include the rendering code, which we'll discuss in a moment. The *DataSource* property is marked as protected and used to cache in the view state an *ArrayList* built with the data passed by the client application. In particular, the *DataSource* property is a wrapper for an entry in the *ViewState* collection. All the client data is temporarily parked in an *ArrayList* and then added to the view state. Note that the *ArrayList* must be explicitly associated with the *DataSource* property after each insertion or deletion. Simply obtaining a reference and then adding data to *DataSource* just won't make data persistent across postbacks.

The View State from the Control's Perspective

ViewState, which is a collection of name/value pairs, is serialized to a string at the end of the page pipeline. The final string, properly hashed and encoded as Base64, is sent to the client as a hidden variable. As we've seen in Chapter 14, "ASP.NET State Management," the view state of the page is the summation of the view state collections of all constituent controls. Each control governs the serialization and deserialization process for its own data.

Associating the HTML source of the page with the view state is a univocal way of binding together the page and its state. Other techniques can be employed, such as storing the view state on the server in disk files, databases, or memory, but each has pros and cons. As a matter of fact, the overall view state can grow up to several KB of data that is completely useless on the client but terribly helpful once the page posts back. It should be made clear, though, that the usefulness of the view state is primarily for the developer; there's no added value for users in the view state. But without view state, managing state would be significantly more complex. Well, just as complex as in old ASP.

Upon postback, the ASP.NET runtime reads and parses the content of the view state and gives any controls a chance to repopulate their *ViewState* bag. Thanks to this mechanism, controls that use *ViewState* to store property data (instead of a private member) have their state automatically persisted across round-trips. The following code fragment shows a property that is saved in *ViewState*:

```
public string Caption {
    get {return Convert.ToString(ViewState["Caption"]);}
    set {ViewState["Caption"] = value;}
}
```

Note that properties not persisted in the view state should be initialized and set to a default value in the class constructor, the *get* accessor, or in the handler for the page's *Init* event.

> **Note** As a general guideline, you should persist in the view state properties that cannot be easily restored or recalculated. Properties whose overall size can measure a few KBs (for example, the data source) should be kept off the view state too. Finally, bear in mind that if you persist internal properties (protected or private members) that would make your control strictly dependent on the value of the control's *EnableViewState* property, your control won't work as expected if the view state is disabled.

To be persisted in the view state, a type must either be serializable or have a *TypeConverter* object defined. Of the two possibilities, having a type converter is the most efficient from the view state perspective. You should look at type converters as sort of lightweight and highly specialized type serializers.

Storing in the view state a serializable type that doesn't provide a converter results in slower code and generates a much larger output. Type converters are also useful to give a design-time behavior to controls; we'll look at type converters in Chapter 21.

The view state is serialized using a custom ASP.NET object serialization format. It's optimized for a few common types, including primitive types, strings, arrays, and *HashTable* types. As a result, either you write a type converter or use those simple types.

> **Tip** A control can customize how property data is stored in the *ViewState*. To accomplish this, the control must override a couple of methods on the *Control* class. The methods are *SaveViewState* and *LoadViewState* and have the following signatures:
>
> ```
> protected virtual object SaveViewState();
> protected virtual void LoadViewState(object savedState);
> ```

Rendering the Control

The HTML structure of the *BarChart* control is a bit complex and is composed of a few nested tables. The outline is depicted in Figure 19-4.

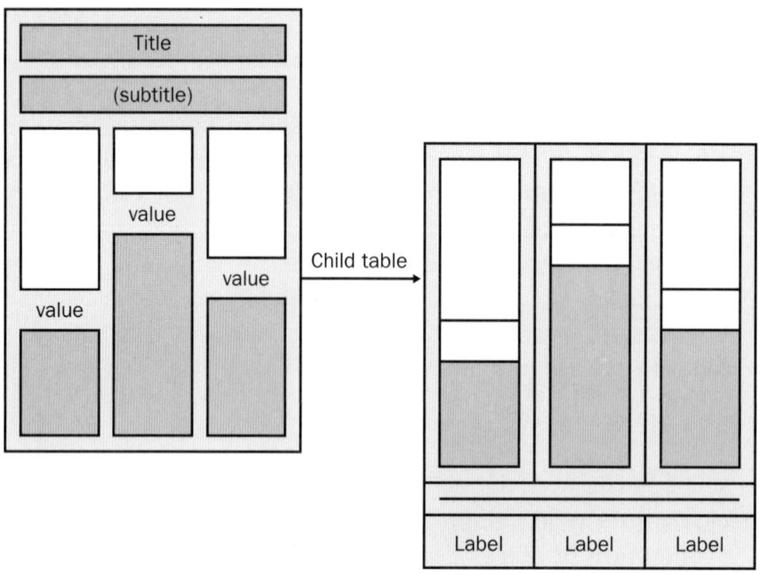

Figure 19-4 The outline of the *BarChart* control.

The outermost table counts three rows—title, subtitle, and chart table. The chart table comprises three rows—the chart, the separator, and the labels. Each bar in the chart table is rendered as a stand-alone table with three cells. The bottom-most cell represents the value of the bar; the middle cell is the value; the topmost cell is empty to denote what is left.

The *BarChart* control renders its output by building a graph of *Table* objects and rendering the output to HTML using the *RenderControl* method. As mentioned earlier, this is not necessarily the most efficient way in terms of raw performance but results in more manageable code. We're using this approach mostly for completeness, as we think that in real-world cases, and especially for controls, performance is a critical factor.

The Title Area

The following code demonstrates the main stream of the *Render* method that the control overrides to produce its output. Note that in building the main and outermost table we mirror in the *Table* object many of the base properties of the *WebControl*, including colors, borders, and font.

```
protected override void Render(HtmlTextWriter output)
{
    // Create the outermost table
    Table outer = new Table();
    outer.BorderColor = BorderColor;
    outer.BackColor = Color.White;
    outer.BorderStyle = BorderStyle;
    outer.BorderWidth = BorderWidth;
    outer.GridLines = GridLines.None;
    outer.CssClass = CssClass;
    outer.ForeColor = ForeColor;
    outer.Font.Name = Font.Name;
    outer.Font.Size = Font.Size;
    outer.BorderStyle = BorderStyle.Solid;

    // Create the caption row
    TableRow captionRow = new TableRow();
    if (!Caption.Equals(String.Empty))
    {
        TableCell captionCell = new TableCell();
        captionCell.ColumnSpan = BarCount;
        captionCell.HorizontalAlign = HorizontalAlign.Center;
        captionCell.Font.Bold = true;
        captionCell.Font.Size = FontUnit.Larger;
        captionCell.Text = Caption;
        captionRow.Cells.Add(captionCell);
    }
    outer.Rows.Add(captionRow);
```

```
    // Create the subtitle row
    TableRow subtitleRow = new TableRow();
    if (!SubTitle.Equals(String.Empty))
    {
        TableCell subtitleCell = new TableCell();
        subtitleCell.ColumnSpan = BarCount;
        subtitleCell.HorizontalAlign = HorizontalAlign.Center;
        subtitleCell.Font.Size = FontUnit.Smaller;
        subtitleCell.Text = SubTitle;
        subtitleRow.Cells.Add(subtitleCell);
    }
    outer.Rows.Add(subtitleRow);

    // Create the chart row
    if (DataSource != null)
    {
        TableRow chartRow = new TableRow();
        TableCell chartCell = new TableCell();
        CreateBarChart(chartCell);
        chartRow.Cells.Add(chartCell);
        outer.Rows.Add(chartRow);
    }

    // Render the output
    outer.RenderControl(output);
}
```

The title row uses a larger font and bold typeface, while the subtitle resorts to a smaller font. Note that *FontUnit.Larger* and *FontUnit.Smaller* return a font size one unit larger or smaller than the base font size, which is hard-coded to Verdana 8 but can be changed through the *Font* property.

Building the Chart

An internal method actually generates the chart—the *CreateBarChart* protected method. Also the child table mirrors many of the base properties of the Web control. The *WebControl* class just defines properties as a common interface; the developer, though, is responsible for mapping the values of those properties to the constituent elements of the control you're building. In particular, the *BackColor* property of the *BarChart* control is mapped to the *BackColor* property of the table being used to draw the chart. The same occurs with the font, width, height, and CSS style class.

For each element in the internal *DataSource* array, the *CreateBarChart* method generates a vertical table with one row and three cells. The height of the cells is determined by looking at the value and the scale to represent.

```
protected virtual void CreateBarChart(TableCell parent)
{
    // Create the child table
    Table chart = new Table();
    chart.ForeColor = ForeColor;
```

```
chart.CssClass = CssClass;
chart.GridLines = GridLines.None;
chart.BackColor = BackColor;
chart.Font.Name = Font.Name;
chart.Font.Size = Font.Size;
chart.CellPadding = 2;
chart.CellSpacing = 0;
chart.BackImageUrl = BackImageUrl;
chart.Style["background-position"] = "bottom";
chart.Width = Width;
chart.Height = Height;

// Create the chart row
TableRow rowChart = new TableRow();
rowChart.VerticalAlign = VerticalAlign.Bottom;
foreach(BarChartItem bci in DataSource)
{
    TableCell barCell = new TableCell();
    CreateSingleChart(barCell, bci);
    rowChart.Cells.Add(barCell);
}
if (DataSource.Count == 0)
    rowChart.Cells.Add(new TableCell());
chart.Rows.Add(rowChart);

// Create the separator row
TableRow rowSeparator = new TableRow();
rowSeparator.VerticalAlign = VerticalAlign.Bottom;
rowSeparator.Height = 2;
TableCell separatorCell = new TableCell();
separatorCell.BackColor = Color.Black;
separatorCell.ColumnSpan = BarCount;
rowSeparator.Cells.Add(separatorCell);
chart.Rows.Add(rowSeparator);

// Create the footer row
TableRow rowFooter = new TableRow();
rowFooter.Height = 10;
rowFooter.VerticalAlign = VerticalAlign.Bottom;
rowFooter.BackColor = Color.LightYellow;

// Draw the label
foreach(BarChartItem bci in DataSource)
{
    TableCell footerCell = new TableCell();
    footerCell.HorizontalAlign = HorizontalAlign.Center;
    footerCell.Text = bci.Text;
    rowFooter.Cells.Add(footerCell);
}
if (DataSource.Count == 0)
    rowFooter.Cells.Add(new TableCell());
```

```
    chart.Rows.Add(rowFooter);

    // Connect the chart to the parent
    parent.Controls.Add(chart);
}
```

The values inherent in the individual bar are packed in the *BarChartItem* structure and are used to draw and configure the chart table. The following listing shows how the single bar is built. The ratio between the value and the *Maximum* is protracted in a 0 to 100 scale so that it can be conveniently rendered with percentages.

```
protected virtual void CreateSingleChart(TableCell parent,
    BarChartItem bci)
{
    // Calculate the value to represent in a 0-100 scale
    float valueToRepresent = 100*bci.Value/Maximum;

    // Create the bar
    Table t = new Table();
    t.Font.Name = Font.Name;
    t.Font.Size = Font.Size;
    t.Width = Unit.Percentage(100);
    t.Height = Unit.Percentage(100);

    // The still-to-do area
    TableRow todoArea = new TableRow();
    todoArea.Height = Unit.Percentage(100-valueToRepresent);
    todoArea.Cells.Add(new TableCell());
    t.Rows.Add(todoArea);

    // The row with the value
    TableRow valueArea = new TableRow();
    valueArea.Height = 10;
    TableCell cell = new TableCell();
    cell.HorizontalAlign = HorizontalAlign.Center;
    cell.Text = bci.Value.ToString();
    valueArea.Cells.Add(cell);
    t.Rows.Add(valueArea);

    // The row with bar
    TableRow barArea = new TableRow();
    barArea.ToolTip = bci.ToolTip;
    barArea.Height = Unit.Percentage(valueToRepresent);
    barArea.BackColor = bci.BackColor;
    barArea.Cells.Add(new TableCell());
    t.Rows.Add(barArea);

    // Connect to the parent
    parent.Controls.Add(t);
}
```

When finished, the new table is connected to the parent table's cell that will actually contain it. Figure 19-5 shows how the control looks at the end of game.

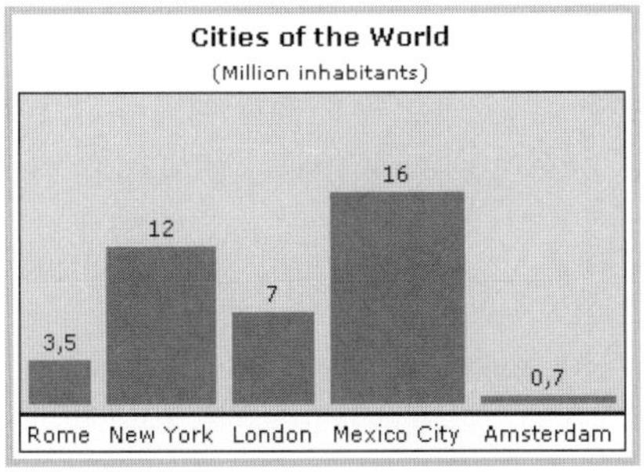

Figure 19-5 The various tables that form the *BarChart* control work together to generate an effective bar chart.

The *CreateSingleChart* method is marked as protected and overridable to allow potential derived classes to modify the way in which the control is rendered. Declaring protected and virtual methods is a good technique to allow customization from derived classes. Alternatively, you can consider firing ad hoc events in much the same way as the *DataGrid*, and other iterative controls, do. For example, you could fire a *ChartTableCreated* event when the chart table is created and *BarChartItemCreated* when the individual bar has been created.

```
public event BarChartEventHandler ChartTableCreated;
public event BarChartEventHandler BarChartItemCreated;
```

Both events will pass references to tables and rows allowing users to achieve more specific customization, such as specifying more attractive styles or deciding colors according to run-time conditions.

The Background of the Table

Because the *BarChart* control is made of HTML tables, and because HTML tables can contain a background image, we can transitively make our control support the same feature. The *BackImageUrl* property serves this purpose. In addition to improving the graphical quality of the control, the background image represents a powerful way to add a ruler to the chart.

The background image of a table is usually tiled to cover the entire area, but can be controlled in the number and direction of the repetition. As Figure 19-6 proves, a small and simple GIF can be iterated to cover the background of the table emulating a ruler.

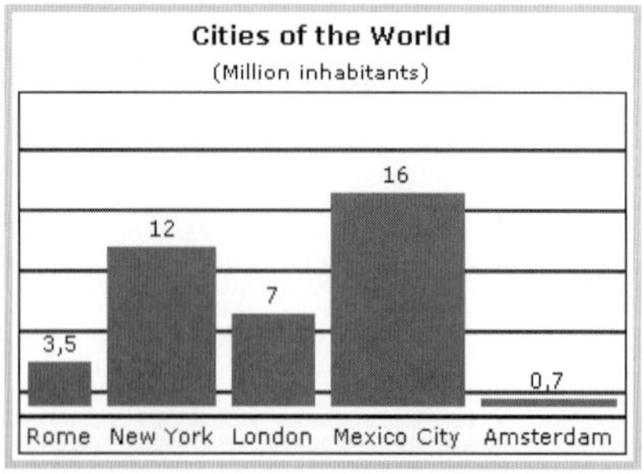

Figure 19-6 A *BarChart* control with a background image that provides a sort of ruler.

The image can have a transparent background, which will be reflected. By default, the control draws the background image from the bottom.

The *BarChart* Control in Action

To use the *BarChart* control, it must be bound to some data. Before Chapter 21 (in which we'll review techniques to enable this feature from the Properties window), let's assume data binding must be performed from code.

```
private void Chart_Click(object sender, System.EventArgs e)
{
    //
    // Other properties set through the Properties window
    //

    BarChart1.Add("Rome", 3.5f, "Italy");
    BarChart1.Add("New York", 12,  "USA");
    BarChart1.Add("London", 7,  "UK");
    BarChart1.Add("Mexico City", 16,  "Mexico");
    BarChart1.Add("Amsterdam", 0.7f, "The Netherlands");
    BarChart1.Maximum = 20;
}
```

The *Add* method has three overloads to indicate the label, value, ToolTip, and background color of each bar. In addition, the *BarChartItemCreated* event gives you a hook to intervene and modify the chart dynamically. As mentioned, the *BarChartItemCreated* event fires whenever the individual bar chart is created. For example, the following code shows how to render in red only bars whose value is greater than 10:

```
void BarChart1_ChartTableCreated(object sender, BarChartEventArgs e)
{
    // Renders a blue-to-white gradient using DHTML (IE50+)
    string style = "";
```

```
    style += "progid:DXImageTransform.Microsoft.Gradient(";
    style += "startColorstr='deepskyblue',endColorstr='white');"

    // ChartTableCreated event
    if (!e.IsBarChartCreated)
        e.ChartTable.Style["filter"] = style;
    else  // BarChartItemCreated event
    {
        if (e.Item.Value > 10)
            e.BarChart.BackColor = Color.Red;
    }
}
```

This code is used to handle both the *ChartTableCreated* and *BarChartItemCreated* events. It intercepts the *ChartTableCreated* event and renders the background of the main table with a gradient. Both events require a custom delegate—the *BarChartEventHandler* type. The event takes a custom event data structure—the *BarChartEventArgs* class—described as follows:

```
public delegate void BarChartEventHandler(object sender,
    BarChartEventArgs e);
public class BarChartEventArgs : EventArgs
{
    // Whether the bar or the table is being created
    public bool IsBarChartCreated;

    // The outermost table
    public Table ChartTable;

    // The bar being created
    public TableRow BarChart;

    // The data structure with item information
    public BarChartItem Item;
}
```

The same data structure is used for the *ChartTableCreated* and the *BarChartItemCreated* events. The *IsBarChartCreated* property indicates whether a bar chart or the underlying table is being created. The properties that do not apply to whichever event is fired are simply set to null. As usual, you can define event handlers either programmatically or declaratively by using the *OnBarChartItemCreated* and *OnChartTableCreated* attributes. The following code demonstrates the programmatic event binding:

```
BarChart1.BarChartItemCreated += new
    BarChartEventHandler(BarChart1_ChartTableCreated);
BarChart1.ChartTableCreated += new
    BarChartEventHandler(BarChart1_ChartTableCreated);
```

Figure 19-7 shows the *BarChart* control in action.

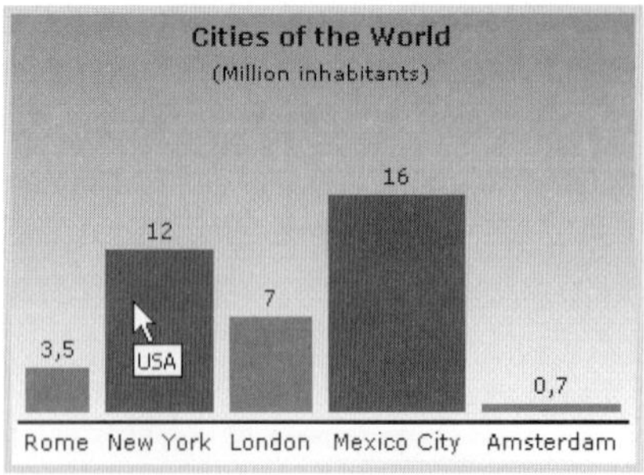

Figure 19-7 A dithered background, ToolTips, and bars of different colors adorn the *BarChart* control.

Building Composite Controls

As we briefly mentioned in Chapter 18, in addition to creating new and derived controls, you can also author Web server controls by combining existing controls into a new monolithic component. The set of methods and properties of a composite control is frequently, but not necessarily, composed from the methods and properties of constituent controls plus new members. A composite control can fire custom events, and it can also handle and bubble up events raised by child controls.

Structure of Composite Controls

The .NET Framework provides some facilities for the development of composite controls. This special support comes in the form of the *Controls* property and the protected overridable member named *CreateChildControls*. The *CreateChildControls* method is inherited from *Control* and is called when server controls have to create child controls after a postback.

```
protected virtual void CreateChildControls();
```

Another interesting method is *EnsureChildControls*. This method first checks the current value of the internal, protected *ChildControlsCreated* property. If this value is false, the *CreateChildControls* method is called to create all needed child controls. The *ChildControlsCreated* property is set to true only once all child controls have been successfully created.

ASP.NET calls *EnsureChildControls* when it needs to make sure that child controls have been created. In most cases, custom server control developers do not need to override this method. If you do override this method, you should use it in a similar fashion as its default behavior. If you provide different behavior, you risk violating the internal logic of standard controls, which can result in buggy applications.

In addition to creating its child controls, a composite component should also implement the *INamingContainer* interface so that the ASP.NET runtime can create a new naming scope for it. This ensures that all controls in the composite control have a unique name. This will also ensure that child controls' postback data is handled automatically.

Another important aspect of composite controls is that they normally don't require custom logic for rendering, unless the author has to include literal text or dynamically generated elements to enrich the overall user interface. The decision to optimize the performance of a control by using direct rendering instead of composition works for composite controls too. However, for composite controls, using direct rendering can be problematic if embedded controls are custom components whose logic is not completely clear or documented. For example, imagine you build a custom control by aggregating a third-party control. If the internal logic of the control is not well-documented, chances are that you will experience unexpected control behavior.

Designing a Composite Control

Let's have a closer look at composite controls. We'll build a simple component by assembling a label and a text box. Incorporating a text box in a composite control also poses additional questions. Would postback data be handled automatically for all child controls? And what about bubbling up events raised by child controls?

We'll build a *LabelTextBox* control made of a *Label* control and a *TextBox* control. The label displays left of the text box in bold. The text of the label is controlled by the *Caption* property; the *Text* property of the new composite control maps to the *Text* property of the embedded (and externally invisible) *TextBox* control. The *LabelTextBox* control derives from *Control* and implements *INamingContainer*.

Creating Child Controls

The structure of the control is defined in the *CreateChildControls* method, as shown in the following listing:

```
// Can inherit from WebControl too
namespace ProAspNet.CS.Ch19
{
    public class LabelTextBox : Control, INamingContainer
    {
        public LabelTextBox() : base()
        {
        }
```

```
        // Internal members
        protected TextBox __theTextBox;
        protected Label __theLabel;

        // Gets and sets the caption of the label
        public string Caption {
            get {return Convert.ToString(ViewState["Caption"]);}
            set {ViewState["Caption"] = value;}
        }

        // Gets and sets the text of the textbox
        public string Text {
            get {return Convert.ToString(ViewState["Text"]);}
            set {ViewState["Text"] = value;}
        }

        // Create the child controls of the control
        protected override void CreateChildControls() {
            // First clear the child controls
            Controls.Clear();
            // Add the label
            __theLabel = new Label();
            __theLabel.EnableViewState = false;
            __theLabel.Text = Caption;
            __theLabel.Font.Name = "verdana";
            __theLabel.Font.Bold = true;
            __theLabel.Font.Size = FontUnit.Point(8);
            Controls.Add(__theLabel);

            // Add a blank literal control for spacing
            Controls.Add(new LiteralControl("  "));

            // Add the textbox
            __theTextBox = new TextBox();
            __theTextBox.EnableViewState = false;
            __theTextBox.Text = Text;
            __theTextBox.BorderStyle = BorderStyle.Solid;
            __theTextBox.BorderWidth = 1;
            __theTextBox.BorderColor = Color.Black;
            Controls.Add(__theTextBox);
        }
    }
}
```

After creation, the *Label* control is given a default font and style and is then added to the *Controls* collection of the parent. The same treatment occurs for the *TextBox* control, which displays with a solid thin black border. The two controls are separated with a literal control containing a couple of blanks.

The *Caption* and *Text* properties cache their values in the control's view state. By default, *Label* and *TextBox* also cache some of their properties in their own view state. To avoid useless redundancy of data, we explicitly disable the view state for the embedded controls.

```
__theLabel.EnableViewState = false;
__theTextBox.EnableViewState = false;
```

You should note that *CreateChildControls* is invoked by the ASP.NET control infrastructure at the last minute during the prerendering stage in the control's lifecycle. You can easily verify this by adding a trace statement in the body of the method and running the sample page with tracing on. *CreateChildControls* is invoked from within *EnsureChildControls* whenever the internal flag—the *ChildControlsCreated* property—indicates the control is not completely set up. In general, *CreateChildControls* is not called until absolutely necessary. Figure 19-8 shows the trace output.

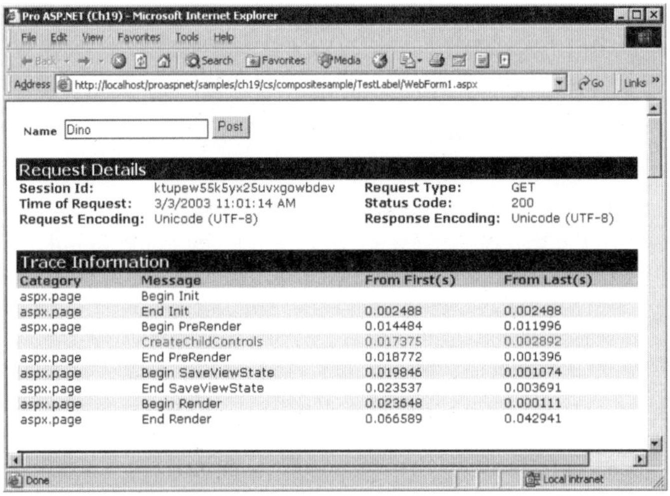

Figure 19-8 The *CreateChildControls* method is called during the prerendering stage.

The Importance of Being a Naming Container

If we omit marking the *LabelTextBox* control with the *INamingContainer* interface, the child controls will be given a simple, unqualified control ID or the ID that you could assign programmatically. If the composite control doesn't work as a naming container, the child ID will be identical for all child controls, in case you host multiple *LabelTextBox* controls within the same page. As a result, you experience a run-time error because ASP.NET requires that control IDs be unique. Using a naming container, you have to ensure only that composite controls have a unique ID. (And to say the least, Visual Studio .NET can guarantee this.)

But there's another, subtler reason to mark a composite control as a naming container. The implementation of the interface guarantees that the postback state restoration for the text box (and other controls that expose *IPostBack-*

DataHandler) works automatically and transparently with your code. Figure 19-9 illustrates the hierarchy of controls generated for a page that hosts the *LabelTextBox* control compiled with (the top box) and without (the bottom box) the *INamingContainer* interface.

Form1	System.Web.UI.HtmlControls.HtmlForm
_ctl1	System.Web.UI.LiteralControl
LabelTextBox1	ProAspNet.CS.Ch19.LabelTextBox
LabelTextBox1:_ctl0	System.Web.UI.WebControls.Label
LabelTextBox1:_ctl2	System.Web.UI.LiteralControl
LabelTextBox1:_ctl1	System.Web.UI.WebControls.TextBox
_ctl2	System.Web.UI.LiteralControl
Button1	System.Web.UI.WebControls.Button

Form1	System.Web.UI.HtmlControls.HtmlForm
_ctl3	System.Web.UI.LiteralControl
LabelTextBox1	ProAspNet.CS.Ch19.LabelTextBox
_ctl0	System.Web.UI.WebControls.Label
_ctl4	System.Web.UI.LiteralControl
_ctl1	System.Web.UI.WebControls.TextBox
_ctl5	System.Web.UI.LiteralControl
Button1	System.Web.UI.WebControls.Button

Figure 19-9 The top box shows the control names when the *INamingContainer* interface is implemented for the *LabelTextBox* control. The bottom box shows the control names when *INamingContainer* is not implemented.

During the post-back data-handling step (before the *Page_Load* event arrives), the ASP.NET runtime attempts to find a match between names in the *Request.Form* collection and controls in the *Controls* collection of the page. The ID of the HTML input control is *LabelTextBox:_ctl1* or *_ctl1*, depending on whether you implemented the *INamingContainer* interface or not. So far so good. The rub, though, is in the search algorithm that the ASP.NET runtime employs to find a control in a page. The algorithm is hard-coded in the *FindControl* method of the *Control* class. If you specify a control name with one or more occurrences of the colon symbol (:), the search is based in the *Controls* collection of the control whose name matches the prefix before the symbol. In practice, if the interface is implemented, the ASP.NET runtime searches for a *_ctl1* control within the *Controls* collection of a control named *LabelTextBox1*. In this case, the control is successfully located and the *Text* property of the child text box gets properly updated. If the composite control is not a naming container, then the run time assumes it has to find a *_ctl1* control within the outermost naming container—the page itself or any other container control. Because no such control exists, the *Text* property of the text box is not updated, and any other postback state is ignored. However, in this case you can perform the update yourself by implementing the *IPostBackDataHandler* interface and reading the client value directly from *Request.Form* using the *_ctl1* ID as the key. The value, in fact, is still there, but ASP.NET can't automatically catch its server-side counterpart.

Handling PostBacks

By storing *Text* and *Caption* in the local *ViewState* collection, we can successfully track the previous text value of the *Label* and *TextBox* child controls. By making the control a naming container, we also ensure that postback data is correctly detected and assigned to our child controls. Are we completely set up? Well, not completely.

So far we've ensured only that the *Text* property of the *LabelTextBox* control is restored from the view state. In addition, we've prepared things so that ASP.NET updates the *Text* property of the internal *TextBox*. The two values, though, are not in sync. We must copy the value of the *TextBox* in the *Text* property of the composite control.

The *TextBox* control fires an appropriate event—*TextChanged*. The idea, therefore, is handling the event internally, set the *TextBox* and then bubble the event up to the client of the *LabelTextBox* control.

```
// Register an internal handler for TextChanged
__theTextBox.TextChanged += new EventHandler(InternalTextChanged);
```

The *InternalTextChanged* method looks like the following code snippet:

```
protected void InternalTextChanged(object sender, EventArgs e)
{
    // Update the Text property with the value of the control
    Text = __theTextBox.Text;

    // Bubble up the TextChanged event (optional)
    if (TextChanged != null)
        TextChanged(this, e);
}
```

The method first synchronizes the internal text box with the *Text* property of the composite control and then, optionally, fires the same *TextChanged* event up to the rest of the hierarchy. For the event to reach the clients of the *LabelTextBox* controls, we need to publicly declare the event.

```
public event EventHandler TextChanged;
```

Notice that we can't use the predefined bubble-up interface because the *TextChanged* event doesn't link to the default mechanism. To do so, a control must call the method *RaiseBubbleEvent* after firing the event. The *TextBox* control just doesn't do this. The following pseudo-code shows how a control can bind one of its events to the default bubbling mechanism.

```
protected virtual void OnTextChanged(EventArgs e) {
    if (TextChanged != null)
        TextChanged(this, e);
```

```
        // Needed to link to the default bubble-up mechanism
        RaiseBubbleEvent(this, e);
    }
```

Using the *LabelTextBox* Control

Using a *LabelTextBox* control in a client page is in no way different than using any other control. The control can be registered with the Visual Studio .NET toolbox and dragged onto the form being developed.

```
<cc1:LabelTextBox id="LabelTextBox1" runat="server" />
```

The following code shows a sample page that makes use of the *LabelTextBox* control.

```
private void InitializeComponent() {
    this.Button1.Click += new System.EventHandler(this.Button1_Click);
    this.Load += new System.EventHandler(this.Page_Load);

    this.LabelTextBox1.TextChanged +=
        new System.EventHandler(this.LabelTextBox1_TextChanged);
}

private void Page_Load(object sender, System.EventArgs e) {
    LabelTextBox1.Caption = "Name";
    LabelTextBox1.Text = "Dino";
}

private void LabelTextBox1_TextChanged(object sender, System.EventArgs e) {
    Response.Write("Text changed to: <b>" + LabelTextBox1.Text);
}
```

The output is shown in Figure 19-10.

Figure 19-10 The *LabelTextBox* control in action.

Conclusion

Literally translated, an old Italian adage states that if you want a thing done, and you do it yourself, you can do as much as three people can. The motto applies to new ASP.NET controls as we described in this chapter.

The .NET Framework provides a wealth of server controls from which you can likely choose exactly the control you are looking for. If this is not the case, and the control simply doesn't exist, you can create your own control from the ground up and obtain incredibly powerful results. Writing a control from scratch is a matter of defining an appropriate object model and providing an effective rendering algorithm. Aside from these two points, other equally important aspects of control development are containment, naming, and integration with the engine that supplies state management.

In this chapter, we've built three controls and learned how to design a rendering engine by choosing between the pure HTML and the control-based approach. The HTML approach provides speed and sacrifices a bit of readability and ease of code maintenance. The control-based approach applies different priorities and chooses code modularity over raw speed of rendering. To say it all, there would be a third case in which you use existing controls for their rendering but not their functionality. In other words, you use controls internally to generate complex HTML markup but don't employ them as child controls. We covered this aspect of programming earlier in the "Using Child Controls For Rendering" section.

Composite controls are a special case of new controls. They exploit the principle of aggregation versus inheritance that we largely explored in Chapter 18. You create a composite control by assembling multiple, distinct controls and synthesizing a new object model on top of them. The resulting object model can be the summation of all elements or, more simply, can be built by taking what is really needed out of constituent elements. For composite controls, being a naming container is a critical point. The behavior of new components can be kept under strict control while resorting to the methods of a couple of interfaces—*IPostBackDataHandler* and *IPostBackEventHandler*. The *IPostBackDataHandler* interface is more useful if the control you're building behaves like an HTML input field (for example, the *<input>* tag). The *IPostBackEventHandler* interface, on the other hand, is the tool that allows ASP.NET controls to fire server-side events to notify clients of state changes.

In the next chapter, we'll take a look at even more complex types of controls—data-bound and templated controls. In particular, we'll explore ways to make the *BarChart* control we created here data-bindable and extensible through templates.

Resources

- *Developing Microsoft ASP.NET Server Controls and Components*, by Nikhil Kothari and Vandana Datye (Microsoft Press, 2002)

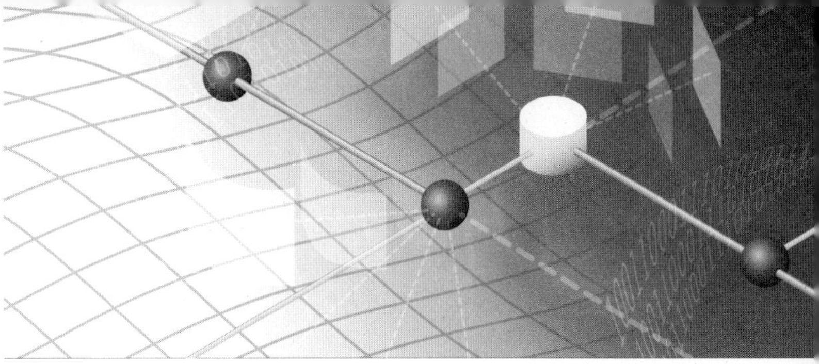

20

Data-Bound and Templated Controls

Life grants nothing to us mortals without hard work.

—*Horace*

In the previous chapter, we built a few controls completely from scratch—that is, not inheriting from existing Web controls, but simply using the base class for ASP.NET server controls as a starting point. Although they are effective and functional, both the *GaugeBar* and *BarChart* controls lack a few key features. More often than not, real-world controls need to be data-bindable and support templates. The importance of being a data-bindable control surfaced clearly in Chapter 6 ("Creating Bindable Grids of Data") and Chapter 9 ("ASP.NET Iterative Controls"), in which we thoroughly discussed and explored the *DataGrid*, *Repeater*, and *DataList* controls.

For an ASP.NET programmer, a control that can be bound to a collection of data is an essential aid that smooths development and significantly increases both personal and team productivity. Similarly helpful is built-in support for templates, which makes the control much more flexible and reduces by an order of magnitude the need for further customization. It's not infrequent, even when you buy a third-party control, that you're not completely satisfied with its user interface and overall set of capabilities and functions. Many software houses buy only components that come with full (and commented) source code primarily so that they can solve any issues that derive from the integration between the component and the core application. Templates provide a way to customize controls. Templates don't ensure that you'll never want something more or different from a component; however, templates have been introduced mainly as a way to make portions of the user interface as generic and parametric as possible. To fully understand the power of templates, think of templates as placeholders for a combination of child controls that the programmer defines and the ASP.NET runtime transparently manages and displays.

In this chapter, we'll take the *BarChart* control introduced in Chapter 19, "Creating New ASP.NET Controls," to the next level. In particular, we'll first add data binding capabilities to it and then extend its user interface with a couple of templates. To top off the chapter, and the more general topic of controls development, we'll take a look at control builders. Control builders support the ASP.NET page parser in building an instance of a server control from the declarative markup in the .aspx source and the child controls it contains.

Designing a Data-Bound Control

A data-bound control is mainly characterized by a data-source property of type *ICollection* or *IEnumerable*. In addition, the control provides its own override of the *DataBind* method and a few satellite properties to let developers better configure the mapping between data and control properties. The number and the type of these properties depend on the specific control features you're implementing.

When overriding the *DataBind* method, a data-bound control must call the base implementation on the parent class, import data from the source, and prepare for rendering. The same method is called to a more delicate role if the control you're developing is also based on templates. In this case, your own override must also clear the collection of child controls and the view state of child controls, and it must create the hierarchy of controls as needed. As long as you limit yourself to building data-bindable controls, probably the most tricky part of development will not be in how you bind data but more in how you resolve the data-source type.

Let's see how to modify the *BarChart* control we've developed in Chapter 19 to make it work like a data-bound control.

Making the *BarChart* Control Data Bound

As we've designed it in Chapter 19, the *BarChart* control is not purely data bindable. It can be configured to display virtually any data and from any data source, but the process of binding is manual and must be coded explicitly. For example, in the following code snippet, we link some data to the control, but the association is done on a per-record basis:

```
void Button1_Click(object sender, System.EventArgs e) {
    BarChart1.Maximum = 8;
    BarChart1.Add("Rome", 4);
    BarChart1.Add("Sydney", 2.5f);
    BarChart1.Add("London", 7);
}
```

Instead of using constant data, we could populate the control with data coming from a database query. However, in this case, the binding occurs through repeated calls to the *Add* method rather than being accomplished through a data-source property. As long as you build yourself a loop, you are *filling* or *populating* the control with data rather than *binding* it to a data source.

Data population and data binding can happily coexist, and there's no need for you to drop direct filling in favor of data binding. Providing two interfaces for managing data makes the control more useful without adding significant overhead. Furthermore, consider that depending on how you actually implement the two data features, they could also work together and allow programmers to bind a data source and then add explicit records.

Defining Data-Bound Properties

The typical name for the property that contains the data source is *DataSource*. Bear in mind that this is only a naming convention; no syntax rules ever dictate that you do this. The *DataSource* property represents the collection of data you want to display through the control. You can force it to be of any particular type that suits your needs; however, to comply with the .NET Framework standard, you should allow users to use an instance of a type that implements the *IEnumerable* or *ICollection* interface, an array, or a type that exposes the *ITypedList* or *IListSource* interface.

Admittedly, this definition might sound as if it's in conflict with definitions we provided in earlier chapters, in which we identified ADO.NET objects and collections of data as the only feasible data sources. This definition is correct overall, but it's not very precise. The definition we presented in the previous paragraph reflects much more closely the way in which the .NET Framework really works to resolve data sources. (More on this later.)

To add data-binding capabilities to the *BarChart* control, we add the properties listed in Table 20-1.

Table 20-1 Data-Binding Properties for the *BarChart* Control

Property	Description
DataSource	Represents the data source object bound to the control
DataTextField	Name of the field in the data source that will be used to render the label of each bar
DataValueField	Name of the field in the data source that will be used to render the value of each bar

In the .NET Framework, some data-bound controls cache the data source in the view state and some do not. The choice can depend on a number of factors; one of the most important is the expected size of the data source. A control such as the *DropDownList* is rarely called to display a large number of elements. For this reason, it caches the data source in the view state. The *DataGrid* control, conversely, doesn't cache the data source and requires you to always rebind it after each postback. You should note that this is only the default behavior and that you can change it at your convenience. You could, for instance, disable the view state for the drop-down list (by using the *EnableViewState* property) or override the *DataGrid* control to make it persist the data source.

The *BarChart* control is more like the drop-down list control than the data grid. The expected number of bars is limited for the simple reason that a bar chart is useful as long as users can see it quickly and without scrolling or paging. The following code shows the implementation details of data-binding properties in the *BarChart* control:

```
private object __dataSource;
public object DataSource {
    get {return __dataSource;}
    set {__dataSource = value;}
}

public string DataTextField {
    get {return Convert.ToString(ViewState["DataTextField"]);}
    set {ViewState["DataTextField"] = value;}
}

public string DataValueField {
    get {return Convert.ToString(ViewState["DataValueField"]);}
    set {ViewState["DataValueField"] = value;}
}
```

Unlike *DataTextField* and *DataValueField*, the *DataSource* property is not stored in view-state. The reason is that our goal is to link the property to the existing rendering engine so that we can both reuse as much code as possible and, more importantly, make the *DataSource* property and the back-end data store of the *Add* method work together.

Overriding the *DataBind* Method

The *DataBind* method represents the entry point in the binding mechanism of ASP.NET. The method is responsible for firing the *DataBinding* event and for preparing the control for rendering. To make sure the *DataBinding* event is properly raised, you only have to issue a call to the base method.

```
public override void DataBind()
{
    // Call the base method
    base.DataBind();

    // Import bound data into internal structures
    LoadBarChartData();
}
```

The *LoadBarChartData* method imports the bound data into the internal structure where the *Render* method expects to find it. This trick alone lets us save development time and combine two programming interfaces for binding data.

```
protected virtual void LoadBarChartData()
{
    // Obtain a generic object reference to manage the data source
    IEnumerable data = ResolveDataSource(DataSource, "");
    if (data == null)
        return;

    // Enumerate the data items
    IEnumerator e = data.GetEnumerator();
    while (e.MoveNext()) {
        object dataItem = e.Current;
        string theLabel = (string) DataBinder.Eval(dataItem,
            DataTextField);
        float theValue = Convert.ToSingle(DataBinder.Eval(dataItem,
            DataValueField));
        Add(theLabel, theValue);
    }
}
```

The *ResolveDataSource* method (which we'll discuss more in a moment) returns a generic object reference to let the code manage data through a common programming interface. As we briefly discussed in Chapter 9, the actual objects you can use for binding can be quite different objects indeed—arrays, collections, *DataSet*, *DataTable*, and *DataView*. The *DataSet* object, for instance, doesn't implement the *IEnumerable* interface, yet it contains data that can be enumerated and processed as a collection. The same can be said for the *DataTable* class. The *DataView* object, on the other hand, is a collection of data and can be referenced as an *IEnumerable* component.

The call to *ResolveDataSource* normalizes all possible differences between the feasible data sources and gives the data-bound control a chance to process data in a uniform manner. The code of the method gets an enumerator for the data source and walks its way through the data.

Information from individual records is extracted using the *DataBinder.Eval* method. The values of the *DataTextField* and *DataValueField* properties are used at this time to obtain the label and the value for the bar. The two objects are then passed to the *Add* method and copied into an internal *ArrayList* persisted to the view state. (See Chapter 19.)

Resolving Data Sources

The algorithm that resolves a data-source object to an *IEnumerable* object reference can be written in many ways. The difference between implementations would be given by the order in which you check for types. Here's a possible way of proceeding:

```
IEnumerable ResolveDataSource(object dataSource) {
    IListSource listSource;
    IList list;

    if (dataSource == null)
        return null;

    // First try: IListSource (i.e., DataSet, DataTable)
    listSource = (dataSource as IListSource);
    if (listSource != null)
    {
        // Get an object that represent the list
        list = listSource.GetList();
        return list;
    }

    // Does the source implement IEnumerable?
    // (i.e., DataView, array, collections)
    if ((dataSource as IEnumerable) != null)
        return (IEnumerable) dataSource;
    return null;
}
```

The code first attempts to cast the data source object to *IListSource*. The interface is designed to allow objects that do not implement *ICollection* to return a bindable list of data for data-bound controls. In the entire .NET Framework, only two classes implement this interface. They are *DataSet* and *DataTable*.

Objects that implement *IListSource* provide a method named *GetList*. The method returns the internal list of data that makes the object a bindable source. The *DataSet* returns the contents of its *DataViewManager* property; the *DataTable* returns its default view, which is the contents of the *DefaultView* property.

> **Note** In general, the *GetList* method can return a collection of *IList* objects. This is the case when a *DataSet* object is used as the data source and a data-member property indicates which table is to be used. The *ContainsListCollection* Boolean property specifies whether the *IList* object is a simple list or a collection of lists. If *IList* is a collection of lists, more work is needed to match the member name with the contained tables.

The *DataView* objects, as well as arrays and collections, are cast directly to *IEnumerable*. Note the use of the C# *as* operator. The *as* operator is like a cast except that it returns null if the conversion can't be accomplished, instead of raising an exception. A similar operator doesn't exist in Microsoft Visual Basic .NET, but can be simulated using the *TypeOf..Is* construct.

Using the Data-Bound *BarChart* Control

You can now execute a query against a Microsoft SQL Server database and bind the results to the new *BarChart* control. Let's consider the following SQL query:

```
SELECT e.lastname AS Employee, SUM(price) AS Sales FROM
    SELECT o.employeeid, od.orderid, SUM(od.quantity*od.unitprice) AS price
    FROM Orders o, [Order Details] od
    WHERE Year(o.orderdate)=@TheYear AND od.orderid=o.orderid
    GROUP BY o.employeeid, od.orderid ) AS t1
    INNER JOIN Employees e ON t1.employeeid=e.employeeid
    GROUP BY t1.employeeid, e.lastname
```

This SQL query returns a result set made of two columns—Employee and Sales. The Employee column contains the last name of the employee; the Sales column stores the amount of dollars sold in a given year by the employee. The following code binds this result set to the *BarChart* control:

```
private void Button2_Click(object sender, System.EventArgs e)
{
    // Configure the control
    BarChart1.Maximum = 150000;
    BarChart1.Caption = "Northwind Sales";
    BarChart1.SubTitle = "(Year 1997)";

    // Execute the query
    DataTable data = ExecuteQuery(1997);

    // Bind the data
    BarChart1.DataSource = data;
```

```
    BarChart1.DataTextField = "Employee";
    BarChart1.DataValueField = "Sales";
    BarChart1.DataBind();
}
```

The *DataSource* property is set with the *DataTable* that results from the query execution. The *DataTextField* and *DataValueField* properties are set with the names of the fields to use for the label and the value. Make sure you set the *Maximum* property with a value capable of providing a good representation of the quantities. Figure 20-1 shows a test page in action.

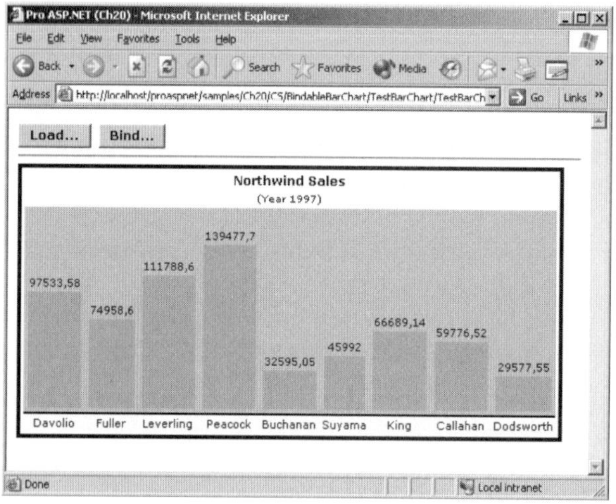

Figure 20-1 The *BarChart* control now supports data binding.

> **Note** The two ways of binding data can be combined. For example, you could first bind to a data source and then add a few records manually; or vice versa. Here's how to proceed:
>
> ```
> BarChart1.DataSource = data;
> BarChart1.DataTextField = "Employee";
> BarChart1.DataValueField = "Sales";
> BarChart1.DataBind();
> BarChart1.Add("Esposito", 100000);
> ```
>
> The last item will be added at the end of the collection. If you place the call before the call to *DataBind*, the record will display as the first record.

Just by looking at sample charts like the one in Figure 20-1, you can see the importance of text formatting. Wouldn't the picture look better if the values on top of the bars were properly formatted? By adding a couple of extra properties—*DataTextFormatString* and *DataValueFormatString*—you can easily implement this feature too.

```
public string DataTextFormatString {
    get {return Convert.ToString(ViewState["DataTextFormatString"]);}
    set {ViewState["DataTextFormatString"] = value;}
}

public string DataValueFormatString {
    get {return Convert.ToString(ViewState["DataValueFormatString"]);}
    set {ViewState["DataValueFormatString"] = value;}
}
```

You use both properties within the *Render* method in conjunction with the *String.Format* method.

```
// Displays the value on top of the bar
cell.Text = String.Format(DataValueFormatString, theValue);
```

Similar code is needed to format the label. Note that you can initialize both properties to *{0}* in the control constructor. The following code and Figure 20-2 illustrate the new look of the control:

```
BarChart1.DataValueFormatString = "{0:c}";
```

Note that you can make use of any HTML tag within the format string.

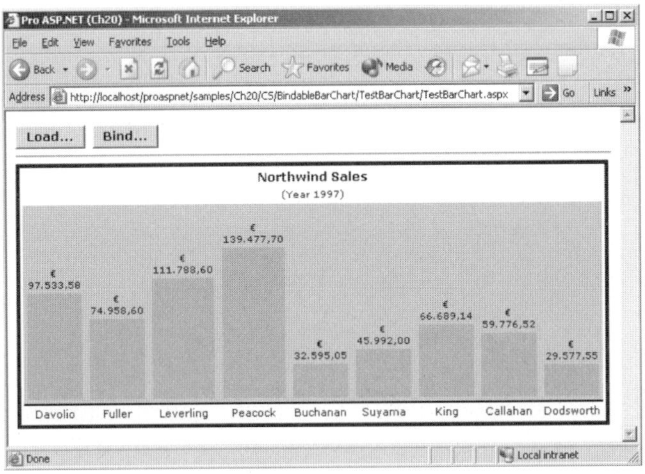

Figure 20-2 The *BarChart* control now supports data binding and text formatting.

Designing a Templated Control

Format strings are helpful in many cases but are a limited tool. You can enrich the format string with HTML tags, but in the long run, this would result in hardly manageable code. A much better approach for deep customizations of the user interface are templates.

In ASP.NET, you can import templates in two ways—through properties of type *ITemplate* or by dynamically loading user controls. As we've seen in Chapter 10, "Web Forms User Controls," a Web user control is a custom component that can be used wherever a server control is valid. You can import such a user-defined control into the layout of the main control and make the interface more flexible and generic. You put a *PlaceHolder* control in the location in which you want custom contents to be injected, and then at run time you create an instance of the user control and add it to the *Controls* collection of the placeholder.

```
placeHolder.Controls.Add(Page.LoadControl("usercontrol.ascx"));
```

The right time to call this code is early in the control life cycle—that is, in an *Init* event handler. When you use the *LoadControl* method, the code of the template is insulated in a separate file. This can be a good thing or a bad thing, depending on the context. If the template you want to implement is complex, keeping it off the main page is positive. Otherwise, it would certainly add a layer of unnecessary complexity. Having the template directly available in the source code of the page makes authoring the page much more intuitive and fast because you don't have to follow code into a separate file. There's a sort of compromise between the two approaches. You could define an *ITemplate* property and set it using the contents of an .ascx file.

Suppose the main control has a template property named *HeaderTemplate*. You can set this property with a dynamically generated template using the page's *LoadTemplate* method.

```
myCtl.HeaderTemplate = Page.LoadTemplate("usercontrol.ascx");
```

Let's see how to implement a templated property for an ASP.NET server control.

A Templated *BarChart* Control

Adding templates to the *BarChart* control would help us to more effectively customize some parts of the user interface for which different users might have different and conflicting requirements. The alternative is offering up dozens of properties that fit all the user scenarios—definitely not an enticing scenario.

By default, the *BarChart* control contains a header and a footer with standard formats. The header is made of text displayed in two rows with slightly different settings for font and size. The footer is limited to displaying the labels at the base of each bar. If you want a richer caption bar, or you want to add information that helps people to read the chart, the *BarChart* control can't be of much help.

The problem has little to do with the *BarChart* control itself, but more with the fact that different users might have different needs and even the same user can require different behaviors at different times. In the *BarChart* control, there are a few parts of the user interface that should be customized on a per-usage basis. This is just the context where templates fit in.

General Rules for Templated Controls

A templated control must follow a few practical rules. First, it must implement the *INamingContainer* interface so that any child controls can be given a unique name and thereby have their postback data handled properly. A second aspect to consider for template-based control is the *ParseChildrenAttribute* attribute. You should apply the *ParseChildrenAttribute* attribute to your control so that the page parser knows that all child tags are to be parsed.

```
[ParseChildren(ChildrenAsProperties = true)]
public class MyTemplatedControl : Control, INamingContainer
{
    ⋮
}
```

However, if you derive the control from *WebControl*, using the *ParseChildrenAttribute* is unnecessary because the *WebControl* class is already marked with this attribute.

A templated control must have one or more properties of type *ITemplate*. As we've seen in Chapter 9, for system-provided template controls these properties can be programmatically set using an instance of a class that implements the interface or a user control loaded by the page's *LoadTemplate* method. A template property, though, can also be set declaratively, which is exactly our main interest here.

A template property represents a collection of text and controls that is hosted within a container. The container is also responsible for exposing properties that page authors can use to create data-bound expressions. The following code snippet shows how to define a template property named *CaptionTemplate*:

```
[TemplateContainer(typeof(ChartTemplateContainer))]
public ITemplate CaptionTemplate {...}
```

The argument of the *TemplateContainer* attribute is the name of the class that represents the logical container of the template. The container control is a control other than the templated control you are building. It makes some of the templated control properties available to the child controls that form the template. A container that is independent from the main templated control lets you iterate the template many times using different data. The template container must be a naming container too. All the public properties of the template container can be called from within data-bound expressions. We'll discuss the *ChartTemplateContainer* class for the *BarChart* control later in the "The Template Container Class" section.

Finally, a templated control should override *CreateChildControls* and instantiate at this time the template within the container. The container class is then added to the root control. A local event handler for the *DataBinding* event is also necessary to ensure that all child controls are created before the ASP.NET runtime attempts to process data-bound expressions. Again, note that overriding *CreateChildControls* is not mandatory but certainly represents a best programming practice.

Parsing Nested Tags

The *ParseChildrenAttribute* is a metadata attribute that applies to control classes. It enables a control to specify how the page parser should interpret any nested elements within the control's declaration in an ASP.NET page. The attribute supports two properties—*ChildrenAsProperties* and *PropertyName*. The *ChildrenAsProperties* property represents a Boolean value; the *PropertyName* property is a string and represents the name of a control's property.

When *ChildrenAsProperties* is set to *true* (the default setting), the parser expects that any nested elements correspond to a public property of the control, and generates an error otherwise. When *ChildrenAsProperties* is *false*, the page parser assumes that child tags are ASP.NET server controls. The page parser creates the child controls and calls the *AddParsedSubObject* method on the control. Controls can override the default implementation of *AddParsedSubObject*—a protected overridable method of *Control*. By default, the method adds the child controls to the *Controls* collection of the parent. Literal text found between tags is parsed as instances of the *LiteralControl* class.

> **Note** As we'll see in the final section of this chapter, if a control is bound to a control builder class, the default logic for parsing child tags can be completely redefined in the custom implementation of the control builder class.

The *<CaptionTemplate>* Section

The *BarChart* control defines two template properties—*CaptionTemplate* and *FooterTemplate*. The *CaptionTemplate* property is aimed at providing a custom representation of the top-most part of chart; the *FooterTemplate* property provides the same capability for the bottom part of the table. If no templates are specified, the caption is composed using the values of the *Caption* and *SubTitle* properties; the footer is empty.

The *CaptionTemplate* property is declared and implemented as follows:

```
private ITemplate __captionTemplate = null;
[TemplateContainer(typeof(ChartTemplateContainer))]
public ITemplate CaptionTemplate
{
    get {return __captionTemplate;}
    set {__captionTemplate = value;}
}
```

The instantiation of the template takes place in the *CreateChildControls* overridden method.

```
// Declare the template container (defined later)
private ChartTemplateContainer _captionTemplateContainer;
protected override void CreateChildControls()
{
    // Instantiate the template in the container and add the
    // container to the Controls collection of the templated control
    if (CaptionTemplate != null) {
        _captionTemplateContainer = new ChartTemplateContainer(this);
        CaptionTemplate.InstantiateIn(_captionTemplateContainer);
        Controls.Add(_captionTemplateContainer);
    }
}
```

The method creates a new instance of the container and instantiates the template within. Next, the container is added to the *Controls* collection of the *BarChart* control.

When the control is ready for rendering, the just-created instance of the template container class is linked to its physical container—the table cell just above the bars.

```
protected virtual void CreateTemplatedCaption(Table parent)
{
    TableRow captionRow = new TableRow();
    TableCell captionCell = new TableCell();
    captionCell.ColumnSpan = BarCount;

    // Bind the template to the table cell for display
    if (CaptionTemplate != null)
        captionCell.Controls.Add(_captionTemplateContainer);
```

```
    // Insert the cell with the template into the main table
    captionRow.Cells.Add(captionCell);
    parent.Rows.Add(captionRow);
}
```

The *CreateTemplatedSection* method is invoked from within the *Render* method and links the template container class with the chart table.

The final item to note is in regard to the *DataBinding* event, which issues a call to another protected method of the *Control* class—*EnsureChildControls*. As the name suggests, the method just verifies that all child controls have been created.

```
protected override void OnDataBinding(EventArgs e) {
    EnsureChildControls();
    base.OnDataBinding(e);
}
```

Before we see how to use templates with the *BarChart* control, let's quickly create another template to make the control more usable and powerful than ever.

The *<FooterTemplate>* Section

The footer template is the area of the *BarChart* control that is displayed just below the labels. For a real-world usage of the control, that area is important because you could place specific information there that help people read the chart. You could, for instance, create a legend in the footer area. For example, if you're using the *BarChart* control to display a sales report, you could display bars of different colors indicating whether the employee met or missed her sales goal. In doing so, you need an area around the chart to tell the user that, say, the color red is used to indicate the sales for a given employee are short of her goal.

In terms of implementation, the *FooterTemplate* property is in no way different than *CaptionTemplate*. We don't need to define yet another container class; instead, we can use the same one as above—the *ChartTemplateContainer* class. The footer template is instantiated within the *CreateChildControls* method.

```
private ChartTemplateContainer _captionTemplateContainer;
private ChartTemplateContainer _footerTemplateContainer;
protected override void CreateChildControls()
{
    if (CaptionTemplate != null)
    {
        _captionTemplateContainer = new ChartTemplateContainer(this);
        CaptionTemplate.InstantiateIn(__captionTemplateContainer);
        Controls.Add(__captionTemplateContainer);
    }
```

```
    if (FooterTemplate != null) {
        _footerTemplateContainer = new ChartTemplateContainer(this);
        FooterTemplate.InstantiateIn(_footerTemplateContainer);
        Controls.Add(_footerTemplateContainer);
    }
}
```

The template is bound to the rest of the *BarChart* control when the *Render* method is called to produce the HTML output for the control.

```
protected virtual void CreateFooterSection(Table parent)
{
    // Add an extra templated row (mostly for information)
    if (FooterTemplate != null)
    {
        TableRow rowInfo = new TableRow();
        rowInfo.VerticalAlign = VerticalAlign.Bottom;
        TableCell infoCell = new TableCell();
        infoCell.Font.Name = parent.Font.Name;
        infoCell.Font.Size = FontUnit.Smaller;

        infoCell.ColumnSpan = BarCount;
        infoCell.Controls.Add(_footerTemplateContainer);
        rowInfo.Cells.Add(infoCell);
        parent.Rows.Add(rowInfo);
    }
}
```

The templates, both caption and footer, are inserted in the existing framework that generates the output of the *BarChart* control. Because the final structure is extensively based on HTML tables, both templates end up actually being hosted within table cells and rows.

The Template Container Class

The template container is a wrapper control class used to decouple the root templated control—the *BarChart* in this case—from the template classes behind template properties. Instead of instantiating the template directly within the root control, you use this intermediate class—the template container. In doing so, you gain the ability to repeat the template multiple times with different data.

In a relatively simple case like that of the *BarChart* control, there's no real need for iterating templates. In other scenarios, though, you can have repeated templates that can't just be handled without a container class. For example, imagine the following *List* control:

```
<cc1:List runat="server" id="myList">
    <MenuItem>...</MenuItem>
    <MenuItem>...</MenuItem>
    <MenuItem>...</MenuItem>
    ⋮
</cc1:List>
```

Even if it's not strictly required by the circumstances, using a template container class is considered a best practice. The following listing shows the source code of the *ChartTemplateContainer* class that we're using for both the *CaptionTemplate* and *FooterTemplate* properties:

```
public class ChartTemplateContainer : WebControl, INamingContainer
{
    private BarChart __parent;
    public ChartTemplateContainer(BarChart parent) {
        __parent = parent;
    }
    public BarChart BarChart {
        get {return __parent;}
    }
}
```

You should derive the template container class from *WebControl* and make it implement the *INamingContainer* interface. (Note that making it a naming container is strictly necessary only if you're hosting multiple templates of the same type.) The structure of the class is completely up to you. Let's say that a reasonable structure is that which we just depicted. The constructor takes a reference to the parent control—the *BarChart* in this case—and exposes another ad hoc public property that represents the templated control in its entirety or simply mirrors some of its properties.

Only the public properties of the container class can be callable from the data-bound expressions you might use within the templates. Keep this in mind when implementing your own container classes.

Using the Templated *BarChart* Control

Using the templated *BarChart* control within a Web page is not much more complicated than it was before. You drop the control onto the form and edit the ASP.NET markup that the control generates for you. Unless the control provides its own template editor, Microsoft Visual Studio .NET doesn't let you visually edit the contents of the control. So you must switch to the HTML view to create your own templates.

The following code demonstrates how simple it is to create a custom header for a *BarChart* control:

```
<cc1:BarChart id="BarChart1" runat="server"
    BackColor="LightGray" BorderColor="#0000C0" ChartColor="yellow"
    Height="256px" Width="472px"
    Caption="Northwind Sales">
    <CaptionTemplate>
        I'm a <b>BarChart</b> Control
    </CaptionTemplate>
</cc1:BarChart>
```

The output is shown in Figure 20-3.

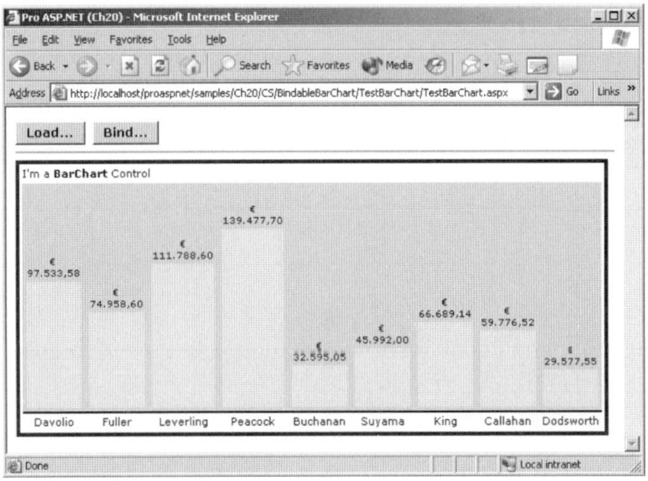

Figure 20-3 The *BarChart* control with a custom header.

Note that the *CaptionTemplate* property takes precedence over the *Caption* property. This behavior is consistent with ASP.NET controls and is considered a best practice. However, it is totally arbitrary and can be freely modified in alternative implementations. If the *FooterTemplate* is not specified, the extra row that will contain it is not added to the main table that represents the chart.

Within the <*CaptionTemplate*> tag, you can place virtually anything. All the markup code found is instantiated within the table cell that represents the table caption. The following example shows a caption that's a bit more complicated, made of a single row table with two cells. Furthermore, the content of the cells isn't constant but is determined by data-bound expressions.

```
<CaptionTemplate>
    <table width="100%" style="font-name:verdana;">
    <tr>
        <td><%# "<b>" + Container.BarChart.Caption + "</b> " +
            Container.BarChart.SubTitle %></td>
        <td align="right"><%# "Scale Factor <b>" +
            Container.BarChart.Maximum + "</b>"%></td>
    </tr>
    <table>
</CaptionTemplate>
```

The first cell displays the contents of the *Caption* and *SubTitle* properties; the second cell is right-aligned and indicates the maximum displayable value—the *Maximum* property.

You use the *Container* property of the template to return the instance of the *ChartTemplateContainer* class. Any public properties exposed by the class can be used in data-bound expressions. The *ChartTemplateContainer* class exposes only a *BarChart* property that represents the parent control. As a result, you can use a *Container.BarChart* expression to access any public properties of the hosting control. Figure 20-4 shows the results.

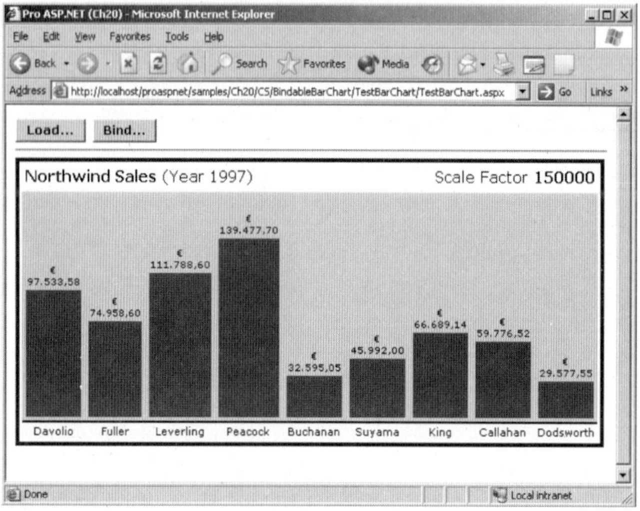

Figure 20-4 A more complex, and data-bound, custom header for the *BarChart* control.

Using the *FooterTemplate* is easy, too. The following ASP.NET fragment demonstrates how to create a footer that explains what each bar color indicates:

```
<FooterTemplate>
    <hr>
    <table width="100%" style="font-name:verdana;font-size:8pt;"><tr>
    <td>
        <table bgcolor="yellow" width="20" height="20"><tr>
        <td></td></tr></table>
        Sales</td>
    <td>
        <table bgcolor="green" width="20" height="20"><tr>
        <td></td></tr></table>
        Sales over goal</td>
    <td>
        <table bgcolor="red" width="20" height="20"><tr>
        <td></td></tr></table>
        Sales below goal</td>
    </tr></table>
</FooterTemplate>
```

Note that by default, all the bars have the same color when you obtain them from a data source. On the other hand, when you create the bar chart using direct data passed through the *Add* method, you can also indicate the color on a per-column basis. If you need to decide the color based on run-time conditions, define a *BarChartItemCreated* event (discussed in Chapter 19), as follows. The following event handler uses different colors depending on whether the employee sold over or below his or her goal. The colors employed are used to create the legend in the footer template.

```
void BarChart1_ChartTableCreated(object sender,
    ProAspNet.CS.Ch20.BarChartEventArgs e)
{
    if (e.IsBarChartCreated)
    {
        if (e.Item.Value > 80000)
            e.BarChart.BackColor = Color.Green;

        if (e.Item.Value < 50000)
            e.BarChart.BackColor = Color.Red;
    }
}
```

The final results are shown in Figure 20-5.

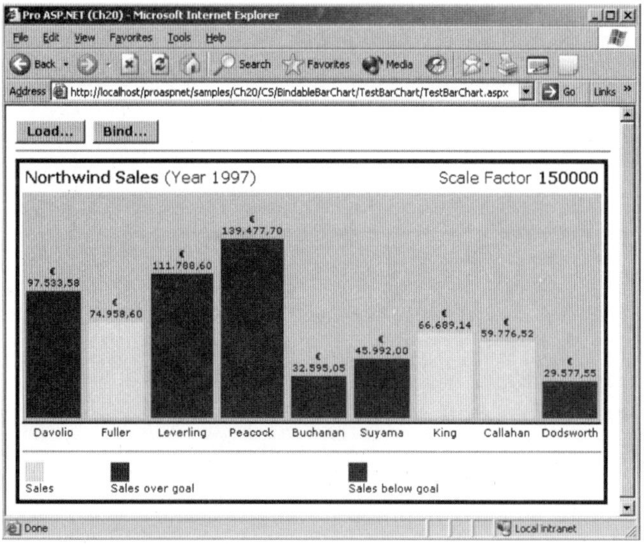

Figure 20-5 The *BarChart* control with custom header and footer.

The Control Builder Class

By default, every control on a page is associated with a default control builder class. A control builder works side by side with the page parser and helps to analyze the markup for the control and to build all the necessary child controls. The control builder class is responsible for handling any child markup element that the main tag of a control contains. The base class for control builders is *ControlBuilder*.

The default *ControlBuilder* class adds a child control to the *Controls* collection for every nested element it encounters within the control's tags. In addition, it creates literal controls for the text located between nested control tags. Custom controls are processed by the default control builder. If you don't like the way in which the *ControlBuilder* class works, replace the default control builder with a custom one. In most cases, you'll use a custom control builder if the control has a complex layout or contains child tags that require ad hoc parsing.

The control builder class is automatically replaced when you apply the *ControlBuilder* attribute to a custom control, as follows:

```
[ControlBuilderAttribute(typeof(ControlBuilderType))]
public class MyControl
{
    ⋮
}
```

Let's see how to write a custom control that can include custom child tags. In doing so, we'll build a custom control builder to handle the otherwise unknown layout.

Designing the *TextBoxList* Control

Especially when I'm building quick or test pages, I often have the need to display a few text boxes with a descriptive label. So I normally define an HTML table, add as many rows as there are text boxes to display, and create two cells in each row—one for the label and one for the editable text. The solution is neat, works great, and has no drawbacks. So what's wrong with this approach? Nothing is wrong, I simply find it tiresome!

In Chapter 19, we created the *LabelTextBox* control, which is obtained simply by composing a *Label* control with a *TextBox* control. Can we simply use a collection of such controls? We could do it that way, but the results wouldn't be particularly attractive. The difficulty lies in the fact that the *LabelTextBox* control is a juxtaposition of two controls separated with non-breaking spaces. Using non-breaking spaces would not provide a perfectly aligned table. To obtain the same results we would get using a plain old *<table>* tag, we must use a custom schema and modify the way in which the control is parsed. The following pseudo-code represents a possible good schema for such a control:

```
<TextBoxList>
    <FormField Label="..." Text="..." />
    <FormField Label="..." Text="..." />
```

```
    ⋮
</TextBoxList>
```

The *TextBoxList* control is rendered as an HTML table in which each *FormField* element generates a row with two cells.

Implementing the *TextBoxList* Control

To implement a control in accordance with the schema just mentioned, three classes are needed—the *TextBoxList* class for the control, the *FormField* class for the child element, and the control builder class to control the page parser. You can code them in the same file or in distinct files and possibly under the same namespace.

The Custom Control Builder Class

The control builder class is rarely a very complex piece of code. Its structure is extremely simple and agile and basically consists of a series of overrides. The only method you absolutely need to override for a significant and functional implementation is *GetChildControlType*.

The *GetChildControlType* method returns the type of the control's children tags. The default implementation of the base class simply returns null. The method takes two arguments: the name of the child tag found, and its collection of attributes. What programmers should do to implement the method depends mostly on the schema they have in mind. The method is responsible for getting the type that a particular child tag represents. If you need to map the nested markup to some custom structures, the *GetChildControlType* method is critical.

In our control builder, the *GetChildControlType* method should take into account any tag named *<FormField>* and force the run time to create an instance of the *FormField* type.

```
public class TextBoxListControlBuilder : ControlBuilder
{
    public override Type GetChildControlType(string tagName,
        IDictionary attributes)
    {
        if (tagName.ToLower() == "formfield")
            return typeof(ProAspNet.CS.Ch20.FormField);

        return null;
    }
}
```

The previous implementation and ones similar to it will handle only recognized tags. All other tags will be treated by the page parser as literal markup and converted to literal controls that are added to the control's child control tree. Note that this implementation matches the tag name in a case-insensitive manner.

The *TextBoxList* Class

The *TextBoxList* control has a rather simple programming interface that consists of a public property—named *HeaderText*—and an internal array of *FormField* instances. A couple of overrides and a few event handlers complete the structure of the class.

```
[ControlBuilderAttribute(typeof(TextBoxListControlBuilder))]
[ParseChildrenAttribute(false)]
public class TextBoxList : WebControl
{
    // Contains the instances of the FormField control class
    private ArrayList m_formFields = new ArrayList();
    public ArrayList Items {
        get {return m_formFields;}
    }
    ⋮
}
```

The *ControlBuilderAttribute* attribute indicates the type of the control builder that must be used for this control. The *ParseChildrenAttribute* attribute explicitly states that the general rule that child tags map to properties is not true in this case. Earlier in this chapter, we said that the *ParseChildrenAttribute* attribute defaults to *true* for all controls that inherit from *WebControl*. This means that, unless the attribute is disabled, the ASP.NET runtime will try to resolve any *<FormField>* tags to a FormField property on the control. If you use *Control* as the base class, you don't need to set the *ParseChildrenAttribute* attribute, but you'll lose some useful base style properties such as *BackColor*, *Width*, and *Height*.

The following code shows the rest of the code for the *TextBoxList* control:

```
public TextBoxList() : base() {
    Font.Name = "verdana";
    Font.Size = FontUnit.Point(8);
}

public string HeaderText {
    get {return Convert.ToString(ViewState["HeaderText"]);}
    set {ViewState["HeaderText"] = value;}
}

protected override void AddParsedSubObject(object obj) {
    if (obj is ProAspNet.CS.Ch20.FormField)
        m_formFields.Add(obj);
}
```

The constructor simply sets some font properties, and the *HeaderText* property gets and sets a string destined to be the title of the resulting table. More critical is the role played by the *AddParsedSubObject* method. Any tag that the *Get-ChildControlType* method recognizes is transformed into a living instance of the specified type. This object is then passed to the *AddParsedSubObject* method for further processing. If the object is of the correct type, it's added to the internal collection of *FormField* objects. At this point, once the *FormField* class is defined, the control is ready for rendering.

The *FormField* Class

The *FormField* class is another control class that gathers information about the text boxes to create within the main control. The class features a couple of string properties named *Label* and *Text*. The *Label* property indicates the text for the label; the *Text* property indicates the default text for the text box. The text box is created and configured when the *FormField* class is instantiated.

```
namespace ProAspNet.CS.Ch20
{
    public class FormField : Control
    {
        private TextBox __theTextBox;
        public FormField() {
            __theTextBox = new TextBox();
            __theTextBox.ID = this.ID;
            Controls.Add(__theTextBox);
        }

        public string Label {
            get { return Convert.ToString(ViewState["Label"]); }
            set { ViewState["Label"] = value; }
        }

        public string Text {
            get {return __theTextBox.Text;}
            set {__theTextBox.Text = value;}
        }
    }
}
```

The control is arbitrarily given the same ID of the *FormField* class and added to the collection of controls. The *Label* property is stored in the view state, whereas the *Text* property is implemented around the *Text* property of the text box.

Rendering the Control

The *TextBoxList* control is a composite control, and it overrides the *Create-ChildControls* method to build the hierarchy of its constituent controls. The HTML output of the *TextBoxList* control is structured like a table with as many rows as there are *<FormField>* tags. The table might have an extra, surrounding row if the *HeaderText* property has been set to a nonblank value.

```
protected override void CreateChildControls()
{
    // Create the main table
    Table t = new Table();
    t.BackColor = BackColor;
    t.BorderWidth = BorderWidth;
    t.BorderStyle = BorderStyle;
    t.BorderColor = BorderColor;
    t.Width = Width;
    t.Font.Name = Font.Name;
    t.Font.Size = Font.Size;

    // Add the header row if any caption has been specified
    if (HeaderText != "") {
        TableRow row = new TableRow();

        TableCell cell = new TableCell();
        cell.ColumnSpan = 2;
        cell.HorizontalAlign = HorizontalAlign.Center;
        cell.Font.Name = Font.Name;
        cell.Font.Size = FontUnit.Larger;
        cell.Font.Bold = true;
        cell.Text = HeaderText;
        row.Cells.Add(cell);

        t.Rows.Add(row);
    }

    // Loops through the FormField(s) children and adds TR/TD tags
    foreach(FormField ff in m_formFields) {
        TableRow row = new TableRow();

        // Create the Label cell
        TableCell cellLabel = new TableCell();
        cellLabel.VerticalAlign = VerticalAlign.Top;
        cellLabel.Text = "<b>" + ff.Label + "</b>";
        row.Cells.Add(cellLabel);

        // Create the TextBox cell
        TableCell cellTextBox = new TableCell();
        cellTextBox.Width = Unit.Percentage(75);
        cellTextBox.VerticalAlign = VerticalAlign.Top;

        // Import the TextBox defined within the FormField control
        TextBox txt = ff.Controls[0];
        txt.Font.Name = Font.Name;
        txt.Font.Size = Font.Size;
        txt.Width = Unit.Percentage(100);
        txt.ID = ff.ID;
        txt.BorderWidth = 1;
```

```
            txt.BorderStyle = BorderStyle.Solid;
            txt.BorderColor = Color.Black;
            cellTextBox.Controls.Add(txt);
            row.Cells.Add(cellTextBox);

            // Add the row to the parent table
            t.Rows.Add(row);
        }

        // Add the table to the Controls collection of the
        // TextBoxList control so that it can be rendered
        Controls.Add(t);
    }
```

The table inherits some visual styles from the parent control. The text box is given a fixed one-pixel solid border, and the label is always rendered in boldface type. The header text is centered in the table and drawn using a larger font. Finally, it's important to notice that each *TextBox* control is given the same ID as the *FormField* component. That ID is the only way to retrieve the text box from client code.

The *Render* method is limited to rendering the children of the *TextBoxList* control.

```
protected override void Render(HtmlTextWriter output) {
    this.RenderChildren(output);
}
```

Using the *TextBoxList* Control

Once successfully compiled, the *TextBoxList* control can be placed in the Visual Studio .NET toolbox and dragged on a new Web Forms page. By default, the Visual Studio .NET control designer does not give you much support for this type of control. However, the RAD designer could do much better if only we tell it about the right schema and specify the right attributes. (We'll learn how to configure the control designer in Chapter 21, "Design-Time Support for Custom Controls.")

In particular, the designer doesn't recognize the schema of the control and warns about the use of the *<FormField>* tag. The currently active schema for the markup language doesn't include *<FormField>*—and with good reason because nobody ever told it about the tag. (See Figure 20-6.) In addition, and always for the same reason, the designer doesn't prompt us with suggestions when we try to edit the source code of the control in the HTML designer. This is indeed a common problem that affects all the custom controls we developed so far. As mentioned, this problem will find its solution in Chapter 21.

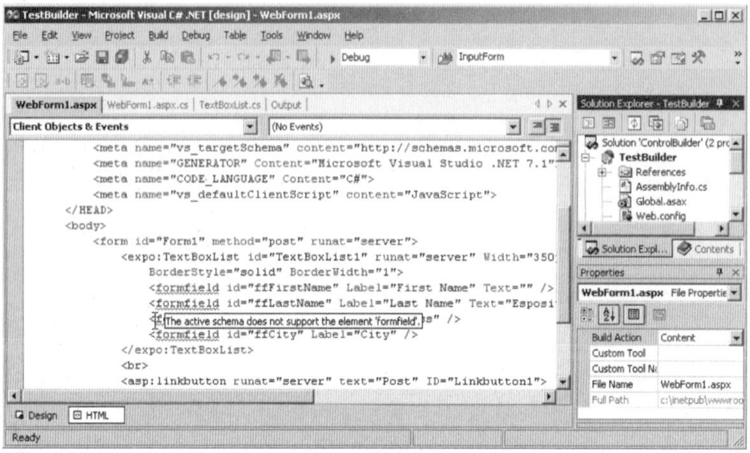

Figure 20-6 The Visual Studio .NET designer doesn't recognize the *<FormField>* tag.

As long as you type the code manually, you can use the *TextBoxList* control with no particular worries. Also pay attention not to set control attributes through the Properties window. With the current configuration, if you do so, all the nested *<FormField>* tags will be deleted. The following code declares a *TextBoxList* control:

```
<expo:TextBoxList id="TextBoxList1" runat="server"
    Width="350px" HeaderText="Data Entry"
    BackColor="PaleGreen" BorderStyle="solid" BorderWidth="1">
    <formfield id="ffFirstName" Label="First Name" Text="Dino" />
    <formfield id="ffLastName" Label="Last Name" Text="Esposito" />
    <formfield id="ffAddress" Label="Address" />
    <formfield id="ffCity" Label="City" />
</expo:TextBoxList>
```

Figure 20-7 shows the control in action in a sample page.

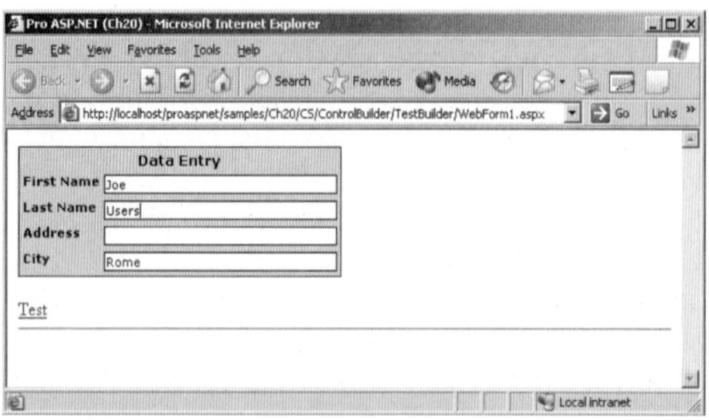

Figure 20-7 The *TextBoxList* control in action.

In the code-behind file, you need to manually declare the *FormField* members you want to code against. If needed, you can also set some of the text boxes at run time within the *Page_Load* event.

```
using ProAspNet.CS.Ch20;
:
protected TextBoxList TextBoxList1;
protected FormField ffAddress;
protected FormField ffCity;

private void Page_Load(object sender, System.EventArgs e)
{
    if (!IsPostBack)
        ffCity.Text = "Rome";
}
```

If you click the Test link in Figure 20-7, the page with the *TextBoxList* control posts back. To retrieve the posted data, you use the ID of the various *FormField* elements or a 0-based index on the *Items* collection. The following listing shows the source code, and Figure 20-8 shows the results.

```
private void Linkbutton1_Click(object sender, System.EventArgs e)
{
    msg.Text = "<b>Current Address is </b> " + ffAddress.Text;
    msg.Text += "<br><b>Current City is </b> ";

    // City is the 4th item
    msg.Text += ((FormField)TextBoxList1.Items[3]).Text;
}
```

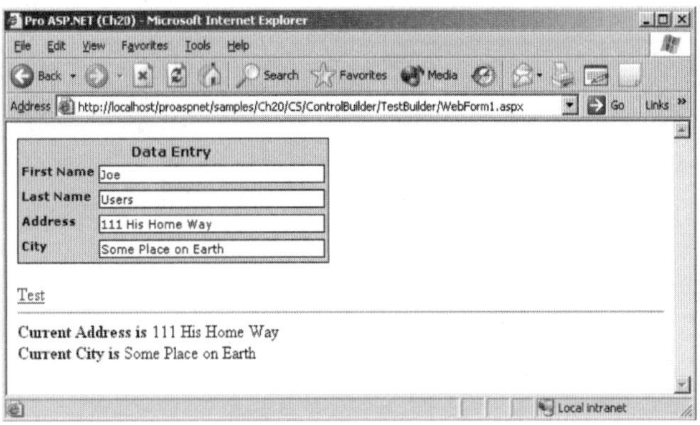

Figure 20-8 The *TextBoxList* control after a post back.

As you might have noticed, we have implemented the *Items* collection as an *ArrayList*—that is, a simple collection of objects. As a result, we need to cast the object to *FormField* before we can access any properties. Using a strong-typed array, or collection, would solve this issue.

Conclusion

The development of real-life controls is a task made easier by the wonders of the .NET Framework and Visual Studio .NET. Several aspects of developing a control will determine the quality of your work, the usability of the control, and its effective power.

Real-world controls must be data bound or, at least, must be able to accept data in a variety of formats. In addition, controls must be flexible enough to let people customize the user interface. These goals can be accomplished either through a rich set of properties or, better yet, through templates.

Finally, not all controls express their full potential using a single tag or free-form templates. In some cases, you want a rigid syntax and a well-known schema. In other words, you need to replace ASP.NET in parsing the source markup code of those controls. Here is where control builders fit in. A control builder lets you govern and monitor several aspects of the embryonic life of a control—that is, what happens before the control is actually created and enters into the HTTP runtime pipeline.

However, once you've learned about data-bound and templated controls—and even about control builders—you realize that all the powerful programmatic features you might have cooked into the control count for little if there's no decent support from the Visual Studio .NET design-time environment. Setting up a control for declarative programming is the next (and final) step in server control development and is the topic of the next chapter.

Resources

- *Developing Microsoft ASP.NET Server Controls and Components*, by Nikhil Kothari and Vandana Datye (Microsoft Press, 2002)

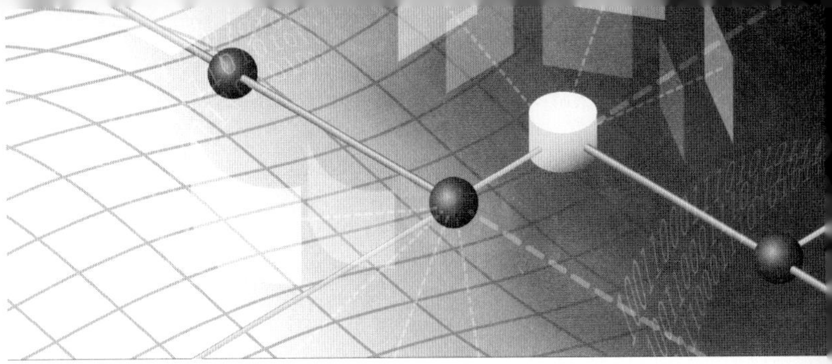

21

Design-Time Support for Custom Controls

What you cannot enforce, do not command.

—*Sophocles*

A server control has two distinct sets of functionality—run-time and design-time capabilities. The run-time capabilities show up when the control is embedded in a page and served to the browser. The design-time capabilities integrate with a visual designer such as Microsoft Visual Studio .NET and let the programmer configure the appearance and behavior of the control in a declarative manner. ASP.NET custom controls can be architected to integrate with the designer just like standard and built-in controls.

A control inherits some basic design-time capabilities from the base class *Control*. All controls can be dragged from the toolbox and dropped onto a Web Form, and all controls, when selected within the designer, cause their properties to display in the Properties window. The design-time behavior of a control can be enhanced in three ways: setting predefined attributes, defining custom editors for properties, and creating custom designers. We'll review the characteristics and the caveats of these three types of extensions in the context of a sample control.

Before going any further, though, it's important to remark that adding design-time features to a server control is optional. The *Control* class, from which all controls inherit directly or indirectly, already provides a base set of capabilities. These features are enough to make controls usable within a visual designer, but they're not necessarily enough to provide a rich user experience and to make the controls look like professional components.

The Design-Time Architecture in .NET

In the .NET Framework, a designable component is a class that implements the *IComponent* interface—for example, the *Control* class. The *IComponent* interface has just one property—named *Site*—which corresponds to an object that implements the *ISite* interface. Sites bind a component to a container and enable communication between them. In addition, a site provides a way for the container to manage its components and acts as a repository for container-specific, per-component information, such as the component name and attributes.

Components, Sites, Containers, and Controls

The *Component* class in the *System.ComponentModel* namespace implements the *IComponent* interface and acts as the base for all managed components. Generally speaking, a component is a reusable, black-box object that can interact and communicate with other objects. The definition has been extended a bit in the .NET Framework. A .NET Framework component can also control the life cycle of external resources and provide design-time support.

The *IComponent* interface extends the *IDisposable* interface and implements the *Dispose* method. The *Dispose* method is available to components to release external resources explicitly. Note that the *Dispose* method represents a deterministic way to free resources, in contrast to the default nondeterministic cleanup performed by the garbage collector. Design-time support for classes that implement the *IComponent* interface is built into the .NET Framework and makes it possible for the classes to be manipulated on a design surface.

The design-time support basically consists of the component's ability to be hosted in a container. When hosted in a site, the component interacts with the container through the methods of the *ISite* interface. The component can access the services that the container publishes through the site. Table 21-1 lists the members of the *ISite* interface.

Table 21-1 Members of the *ISite* Interface

Property	Description
Component	Gets the component associated with the class that implements the *ISite* interface.
Container	Gets the *IContainer* object associated with the class that implements the *ISite* interface.
DesignMode	Gets whether the component is in design mode.
Name	Gets or sets the name of the component associated with the site.

A control is a designable component that provides its own user interface (UI). This definition applies to both Windows Forms and ASP.NET server controls. In particular, the ASP.NET *Control* class implements *IComponent* and provides the infrastructure atop of which the user interface is added. Note that a control is always a component; a component, on the other hand, is not necessarily a control.

The container for ASP.NET server controls is the visual designer. At design time, the designer offers services to controls and controls consume these services through the site's interface.

Controls and Designers

The Visual Studio .NET design-time architecture is designed according to a guideline that establishes an important difference with earlier environments. In the .NET Framework, the design-time capabilities of a control are not implemented within the control but in separate classes. Design-time classes and controls are then declaratively linked using attributes.

Keeping run-time and design-time code separate has two advantages. First, the code that makes the control has a smaller footprint and makes the control itself more manageable at run time. Second, insulating design-time functionality in external classes results in a much more flexible and easily extensible architecture.

You can extend the base design-time support for controls in various ways, the simplest of which is mostly declarative and consists of setting a few metadata attributes. More advanced design-time support requires additional work. First, you need to import the *System.ComponentModel* namespace. Next you need to include the creation of components such as type converters, UI type editors, designers, and component designers. The various types of design-time functionality are summarized in Table 21-2.

Table 21-2 Design-Time Functionalities for a Control

Function	Description
Designer	Class that takes care of the appearance and behavior of the control when hosted in a .NET visual designer.
Editor	Class that provides a convenient way of editing the properties of the associated control. For example, a component editor is associated with the *AutoFormat* button that appears when you drop a *DataGrid* control on a Web Form.
Type Converter	Class that performs conversions to represent values of arbitrary types as strings. Used by the Properties window.
UI Type Editor	Class that provides a convenient way of editing the values of a certain type. For example, a UI type editor is used to select a color from a palette.

> **Note** The design-time mechanism we'll discuss here for ASP.NET server controls is just an instance of the more general design-time mechanism available in the .NET Framework. In ASP.NET, the designable components are classes that inherit from *Control* hosted by a class that derives from *ControlDesigner*. Generally, the container is a class that implements *IDesigner* and the designable component is any class that implements *IComponent*.

The *GraphicPanel* Control

To see the design-time functionality of the .NET Framework in action in a realistic scenario, let's begin by building a custom control that contains many of the features that justify extensive use of design-time features. We'll create a panel-like control completely from scratch, making use of templates, enumerated types, colors, and custom types. The control derives from *WebControl* and works like a *Panel* control, except that it surrounds all its contents with a thin border mimicking the Microsoft Windows XP group boxes.

```
public class GraphicPanel : WebControl
{
    ⋮
}
```

Figure 21-1 shows the control in the Visual Studio .NET designer.

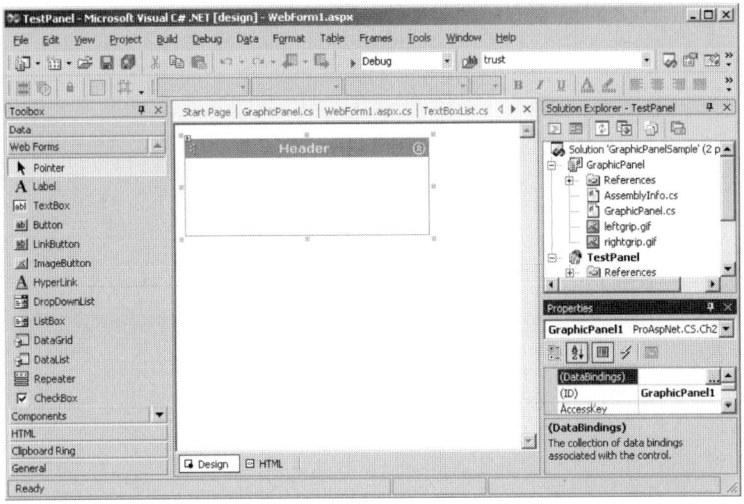

Figure 21-1 The *GraphicPanel* control in action in a sample project.

The control has a template property named *ItemTemplate*, which defines the contents of the panel. This content can be generated in various ways. The user can just specify controls declaratively or provide a data source. If a data source is provided, the control can arrange for a couple of specialized views such as a bullet list or a list of hyperlinks. The following listing shows the constructor and the properties of the control. The output for the control is generated within the *Render* method.

```
public class GraphicPanel : WebControl
{
    public GraphicPanel() : base()
    {
        BackColor = Color.SkyBlue;
        ForeColor = Color.Black;
        Font.Name = "verdana";
        Font.Size = FontUnit.Point(8);
        PanelStyle = GraphicPanelStyle.FreeForm;
        ItemTemplate = null;
    }

    public GraphicPanelStyle PanelStyle
    {
        get {return (GraphicPanelStyle) ViewState["PanelStyle"];}
        set {ViewState["PanelStyle"] = value;}
    }

    public string HeaderText
    {
        get {return Convert.ToString(ViewState["HeaderText"]);}
```

```
        set {ViewState["HeaderText"] = value;}
    }

    public ITemplate ItemTemplate
    {
        get {return __itemTemplate;}
        set {__itemTemplate = value;}
    }

    ⋮
}
```

The *PanelStyle* property contains values taken from the following enumeration:

```
public enum GraphicPanelStyle : int
{
    FreeForm = 0,
    HyperLinkList = 1,
    BulletList = 2
}
```

By default, all properties are browsable and the control provides minimal support for design-time use. If you select the control in Visual Studio .NET, you'll be able to see all properties in the Properties window and set values declaratively.

When you drop a custom control onto a Web Form, the designer generates some markup code. In particular, it first registers the control by using the *@Register* directive and next adds a tag to the .aspx source file. The new tag must have a tag prefix and a tag name. By default, the name of the control class is used to name the tag and *cc1* is used as the prefix.

```
<%@ Register TagPrefix="cc1"
    Namespace="ProAspNet.CS.Ch21"
    Assembly="GraphicPanel" %>
```

The name and prefix can certainly be changed manually; however, some design-time attributes let you configure what names should be used for a given control. In particular, the *ToolboxData* attribute on the class declaration sets the tag name and any default setting you might want to indicate.

```
[ToolboxData("<{0}:GraphicPanel runat=server></{0}:GraphicPanel>")]
public class GraphicPanel : WebControl
{
    ⋮
}
```

When a control is added to the toolbox, it's given the default icon. However, the control can provide a custom icon by following some simple steps. The control project must include a bitmap file with the same name as the control class—say, GraphicPanel.bmp. The bitmap file must have a 16-by-16 size, and the 0-by-0 pixel (lower-left corner) determines its transparent color. This bitmap file must be embedded as a resource in the project. This can be achieved by selecting the bitmap item in the Solution Explorer and setting the Build Action property to Embedded Resource, as shown in Figure 21-2.

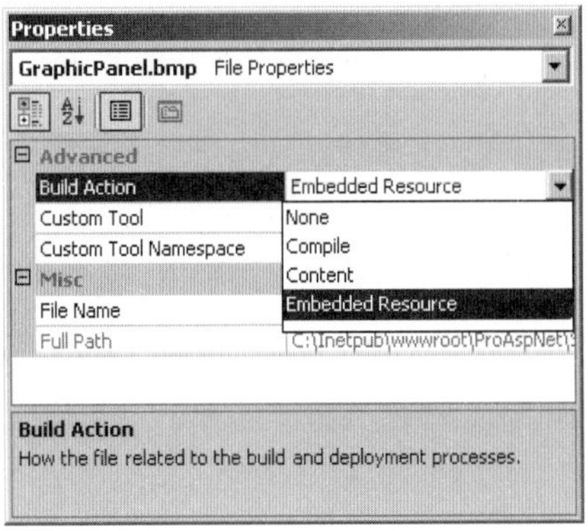

Figure 21-2 Setting the Build Action property to embed a bitmap into an assembly.

To get the custom icon to display, you might also have to specify the namespace to locate the bitmap. You can specify namespace a couple of ways. You can set the default namespace in the project properties or you can name the bitmap using the namespace (for example, ProAspNet.CS.Ch21.Graphic-Panel.bmp).

Design-Time Attributes

Generally speaking, metadata attributes are additional descriptive elements that modify the run-time behavior of types and members. In particular, though, the information contained in certain metadata attributes is also queried by design-time tools such as Visual Studio .NET. Metadata attributes are used to drive the representation and programmability of controls when sited in visual designers.

By convention, the name of a class that represents an attribute ends with the word *Attribute*, such as *BrowsableAttribute* and *DefaultValueAttribute*. When declaring an attribute in the control's source code, the suffix *Attribute* is normally omitted.

As we talk about attributes for controls, we should distinguish between design-time and run-time attributes. Both types of attributes can be applied to ASP.NET server controls—and should be used in real-world scenarios—but with different goals and outcomes. Run-time attributes affect the way in which the control works within the ASP.NET environment and, in particular, can modify the request/response cycle. Design-time attributes have no impact on the run-time behavior of the control but simplify the control configuration in Visual Studio .NET.

Using Design-Time Attributes

Table 21-3 details the design-time attributes for a control. In most cases, attributes can be assigned to properties, events, or both. Some attributes, though, are specific to the control class.

Table 21-3 Common Design-Time Attributes for Server Controls

Attribute	Description
Bindable	Indicates whether a property can be bound to data.
Browsable	Indicates whether a property or an event should be displayed in the Properties window.
Category	Provides the name of the category in which a property or an event belongs. This allows for logical grouping of properties and events.
DefaultEvent	Indicates the default event for the control. This is the event that is handled when users double-click the control in the designer.
DefaultProperty	Indicates the default property for the control. The default property is selected in the Properties window when users click the control in the designer.
DefaultValue	Used to provide a default value for a control property. If the property doesn't have a simple type, a type converter is needed.
Description	Provides a description of a property or an event. The text is displayed at the bottom of the Properties window when the user selects a property or event.
Editor	Specifies the editor to use for modifying a property in a visual designer.
Localizable	Indicates that a property can be localized. Any properties that have this attribute are automatically persisted into the resources file when a user chooses to localize a form.
TypeConverter	Indicates the type converter class to use to convert the type of the property to text.

The *Bindable* attribute tells the designer whether or not the property can be bound to data. Note that the attribute, which takes a Boolean value, doesn't really control the data-binding capabilities of the property but simply marks it for display in the *DataBindings* dialog box. Properties with the *Bindable* attribute set to *false* can still be associated with data sources programmatically using data-bound expressions.

A Commonly Used Set of Attributes

The *DefaultProperty* and *DefaultEvent* attributes apply to the control class rather than an individual property or event. The default property attribute, in particular, refers to the property that gets selected in the Properties window when the user clicks to select the control in the design surface. Likewise, the default event attribute indicates the event that is handled when users double-click the control in the designer, as shown in Figure 21-3.

```
[
    DefaultProperty("HeaderText"),
    DefaultEvent("PanelCreated"),
    ToolboxData("<{0}:GraphicPanel runat=server></{0}:GraphicPanel>")
]
public class MyPanel : WebControl
{
    ⋮
}
```

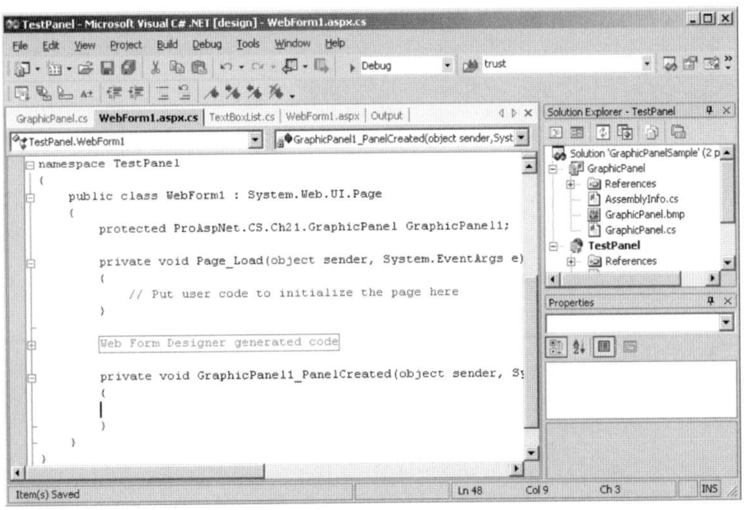

Figure 21-3 When users double-click the control in the designer, a handler for the default event is created.

As mentioned earlier, all properties are browsable until you explicitly disable the feature by setting the *Browsable* attribute to *false*. Unless you have good reasons not to permit design-time editing of a property, you shouldn't touch the *Browsable* attribute. You might want to set it to *false* for read-only properties, however.

```
[Browsable(false)]
public int Count
{
```

```
        get {return _count;}
}
```

Category and *Description* are other attributes you normally set for each property or event. The *Category* attribute indicates the category to which the property logically belongs; the *Description* attribute provides short descriptive text to display at the bottom of the Properties window. The category information is used only if the user selects Categorized View in the Properties window (shown in Figure 21-4). Default categories are Appearance, Behavior, Data, Layout, and Misc. If you indicate a different name, a new category is created. By default, custom properties go under the Misc category.

```
[
    Bindable(true)
    Browsable(true),
    Category("Layout"),
    Description("Gets and sets the title of the panel"),
]
public string HeaderText {
    ⋮
}
```

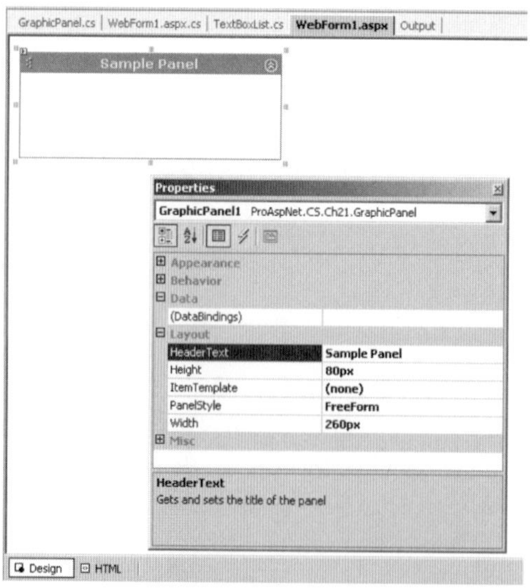

Figure 21-4 Categorized view of the Properties window in which the *HeaderText* property displays its own description under the Layout category.

Enumeration and Color Types

In addition to primitive types and strings, the design-time environment provides special support also for a few extra types—colors and enumerations. A property of type *Color* automatically supports using a color palette. (See Figure 21-5.)

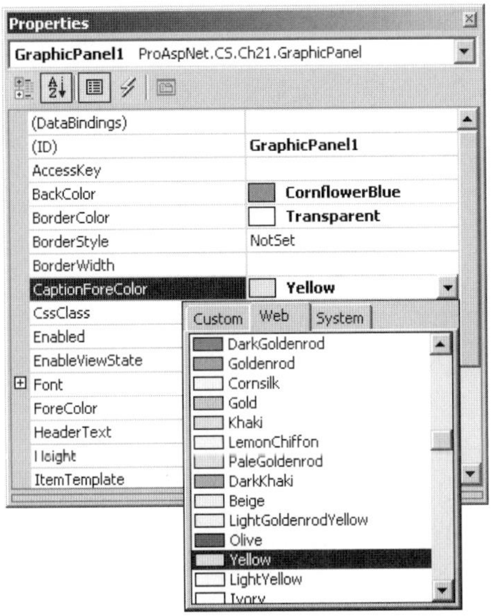

Figure 21-5 Properties of type *Color* can be edited using a color palette window.

Likewise, properties whose type is an enumeration can be edited using a drop-down list with all possible enumeration values. To achieve this capability, you don't have to make any extra effort. Everything is built into the visual designer. Figure 21-6 shows how to edit the *PanelStyle* enumeration property of the *GraphicPanel* control.

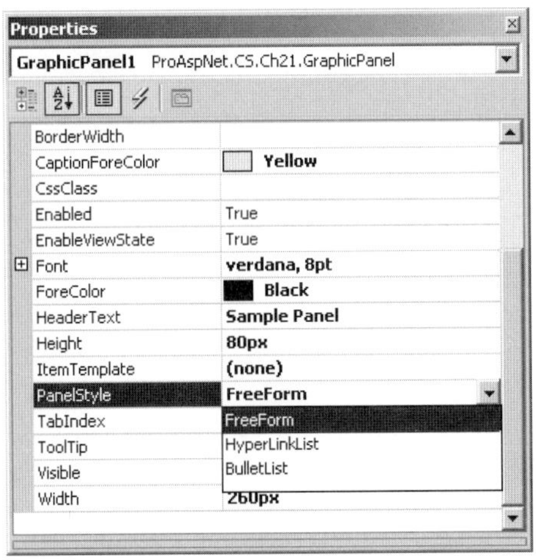

Figure 21-6 The values for the *PanelStyle* enumeration property are available in a drop-down list.

Attributes that Affect Run-Time Behavior

When developing a server control, you normally use attributes to indicate design-time functionality. However, there are a few attributes that, although used with design-time attributes, affect the run-time behavior of the control. These attributes instruct the page parser how to proceed during the examination of the .aspx source code. These attributes are listed in the Table 21-4.

Table 21-4 Attributes that Affect Run-Time Behavior

Attribute	Description
ControlBuilder	Indicates the control builder class for a given control. We demonstrated a custom control builder class in Chapter 20, "Data-Bound and Templated Controls."
ParseChildren	Tells the ASP.NET runtime how to parse the nested content of a control. The attributes takes a Boolean value that indicates whether the nested content should be parsed as properties or child controls.
TemplateContainer	Indicates the container class that wraps a given template. (See Chapter 20.)

Extending IntelliSense Support

Once the control has been dropped on a Web Form and configured via the Properties window, you can write some code that handles events or calls into its methods. In doing so, you take full advantage of IntelliSense and are shown handy lists of methods, events, and values whenever you're completing a statement. However, it often passes unnoticed that you get IntelliSense support only while writing C# or Visual Basic .NET in the code-behind class. What if you want IntelliSense to help also when typing markup text manually in the HTML view of the .aspx page?

The IntelliSense features you enjoy in code-behind mode are rooted in the reflection technology and exploit information stored in referenced assemblies. In other words, in code-behind mode the schema information is easily accessible. The same can't be said when you edit the page in HTML view mode. For IntelliSense to provide the same, enormously helpful support you need to bring some schema information in.

Writing the Schema of a Control

If you switch to the HTML view of a Web Forms page, IntelliSense recognizes all ASP.NET standard controls and properly provides attribute lists and auto-completion. The same doesn't happen if custom controls are involved. The problem lies in the fact that in HTML edit mode, the IntelliSense engine has no way to access the run-time code of the control and reflect its programming interface. To add IntelliSense support to the HTML view of the visual designer, you need to provide the schema of the control—an XSD file.

This XSD file must define the markup interface of the control and specify how many attributes it supports, their name and type, child elements, events, and enumerations. The following listing shows a sample XSD file for the *GraphicPanel*:

```
<?xml version="1.0" encoding="utf-8" ?>
<xsd:schema
    targetNamespace='http://schemas.microsoft.com/proaspnet'
    elementFormDefault='qualified'
    xmlns:xsd='http://www.w3.org/2001/XMLSchema'
    xmlns:vs='http://schemas.microsoft.com/Visual-Studio-Intellisense'
    xmlns='http://schemas.microsoft.com/proaspnet'
    vs:defaultnsprefix='expo'
    vs:ishtmlschema='false'
    vs:iscasesensitive='false'
    vs:friendlyname='Graphic Panel Control'
    vs:requireattributequotes='true'>
    <xsd:annotation>
        <xsd:documentation>GraphicPanel Control</xsd:documentation>
    </xsd:annotation>

    <!-- < Control attributes > -->
    <xsd:attributeGroup name="ControlAttributes">
        <xsd:attribute name="Visible" type="xsd:boolean" />
        <xsd:attribute name="ID" type="xsd:string" />
        <xsd:attribute name="EnableViewState" type="xsd:boolean" />
        <xsd:attribute name="OnLoad" vs:omtype="event" />
        <xsd:attribute name="OnDataBinding" vs:omtype="event" />
        <xsd:attribute name="OnPreRender" vs:omtype="event" />
        <xsd:attribute name="OnInit" vs:omtype="event" />
        <xsd:attribute name="OnUnload" vs:omtype="event" />
        <xsd:attribute name="OnDisposed" vs:omtype="event" />
    </xsd:attributeGroup>

    <!-- < WebControl attributes > -->
    <xsd:attributeGroup name="WebControlAttributes">
        <xsd:attribute name="BorderWidth" type="ui4" />
        <xsd:attribute name="BorderColor" type="xsd:string"
            vs:builder="color" />
        <xsd:attribute name="BorderStyle" type="BorderStyle" />
        <xsd:attribute name="Width" type="ui4" />
        <xsd:attribute name="Height" type="ui4" />
        <xsd:attribute name="AccessKey" type="xsd:string" />
        <xsd:attribute name="ForeColor" type="xsd:string"
            vs:builder="color" />
        <xsd:attribute name="ToolTip" type="xsd:string"
            vs:nonbrowseable="true" />
        <xsd:attribute name="TabIndex" type="xsd:integer" />
        <xsd:attribute name="BackColor" type="xsd:string"
```

```
            vs:builder="color" />
        <xsd:attribute name="CssClass" type="xsd:string" />
        <xsd:attribute name="Font-Size" type="ui4" />
        <xsd:attribute name="Font-Overline" type="xsd:boolean" />
        <xsd:attribute name="Font-Underline" type="xsd:boolean" />
        <xsd:attribute name="Font-Names" type="xsd:string" />
        <xsd:attribute name="Font-Italic" type="xsd:boolean" />
        <xsd:attribute name="Font-Name" type="xsd:string" />
        <xsd:attribute name="Font-Bold" type="xsd:boolean" />
        <xsd:attribute name="Font-Strikeout" type="xsd:boolean" />
        <xsd:attribute name="Style" type="xsd:string"
            vs:nonbrowseable="true" />
        <xsd:attribute name="Runat">
            <xsd:simpleType>
                <xsd:restriction base="xsd:string">
                    <xsd:enumeration value="server" />
                </xsd:restriction>
            </xsd:simpleType>
        </xsd:attribute>
        <xsd:attributeGroup ref="ControlAttributes" />
    </xsd:attributeGroup>

    <!-- GraphicPanel -->
    <xsd:element name="GraphicPanel" type="GraphicPanelDef" />
    <xsd:complexType name="GraphicPanelDef"
        vs:noambientcontentmodel="true">
        <xsd:choice>
            <xsd:element name="ItemTemplate" form="unqualified"
                type="ItemTemplateDef" />
        </xsd:choice>
        <xsd:attribute name="HeaderText" type="xsd:string" />
        <xsd:attribute name="CaptionForeColor" type="xsd:string"
            vs:builder="color" />
        <xsd:attribute name="PanelStyle" type="GraphicPanelStyle" />
        <xsd:attributeGroup ref="WebControlAttributes" />
    </xsd:complexType>

    <!-- ItemTemplate -->
    <xsd:complexType name="ItemTemplateDef">
    </xsd:complexType>

    <!-- GraphicPanelStyle -->
    <xsd:simpleType name="GraphicPanelStyle">
        <xsd:restriction base="xsd:string">
            <xsd:enumeration value="FreeForm" />
            <xsd:enumeration value="HyperLinkList" />
            <xsd:enumeration value="BulletList" />
        </xsd:restriction>
    </xsd:simpleType>
</xsd:schema>
```

The schema file contains three pieces of information that need further explanation. First, the schema file targets a namespace and a default prefix. In this case, we used *http://schemas.microsoft.com/proaspnet* and *expo* as the prefix. This information is important because it represents the link between this file and any page within Visual Studio .NET.

The attribute groups named *WebControlAttributes* and *ControlAttributes* are standard blocks that represent the schema of the *WebControl* and *Control* classes. They define the schema of the properties the *GraphicPanel* control inherits from the base classes.

Finally, the third block of code represents the specific properties and child tags of the *GraphicPanel* control.

Registering a Custom Schema with Visual Studio .NET

The trick to getting IntelliSense support for custom controls is making the just-created XSD file visible to Visual Studio .NET. This operation requires two steps. First, you copy the XSD file in the root of the Web application; next, you link the target namespace of the schema to the ASP.NET page.

The following line binds the namespace of the XSD file to the page. The prefix of the control's tag must match the prefix of the namespace.

```
<HTML xmlns:expo="http://schemas.microsoft.com/proaspnet">
   ⋮
</HTML>
```

Figure 21-7 shows the list of properties and events you can set as attributes in the markup code of a *GraphicPanel* control.

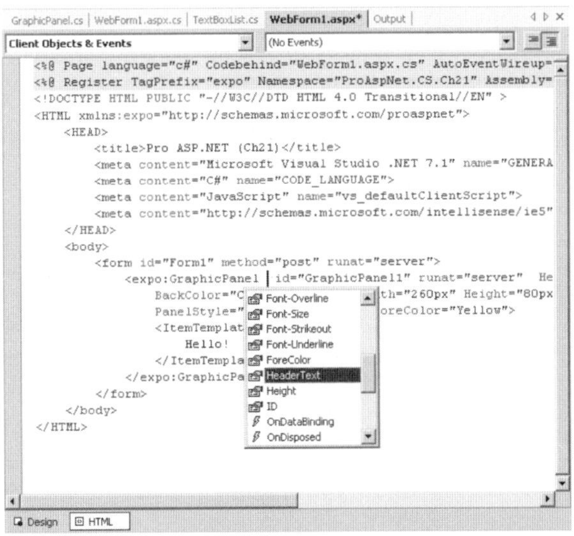

Figure 21-7 Attributes of the *GraphicPanel* control available through IntelliSense.

Also the child tags of the *GraphicPanel* control are available through IntelliSense. As Figure 21-8 demonstrates, the XSD schema informs IntelliSense that only *ItemTemplate* is a valid child tag for the *GraphicPanel* element.

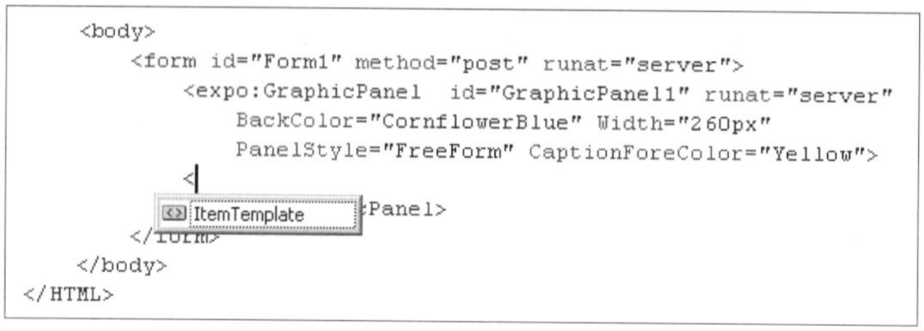

Figure 21-8 Creating the child elements of the *GraphicPanel* control.

If you omit the namespace declaration or don't create the XSD file for the control, users of your control will experience a warning, as shown in Figure 21-9.

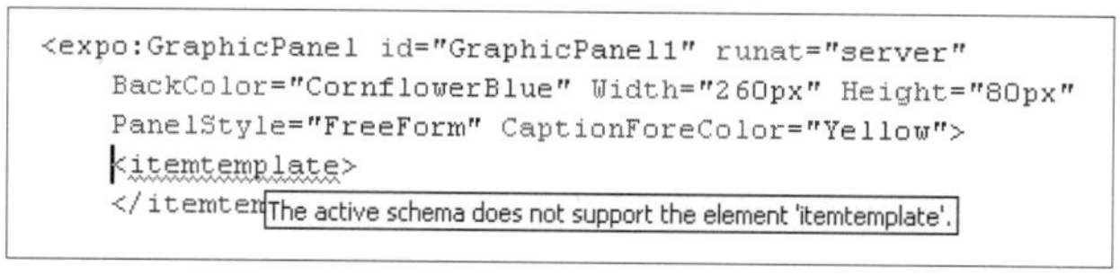

Figure 21-9 Without schema information, Visual Studio .NET doesn't recognize the *<ItemTemplate>* because it's not part of the default schema.

If you can place the XSD file in the root folder of the Web application, it will affect only that application. Generally, if you want to use that schema for all applications you develop, you can copy it in the following folder under the Visual Studio .NET installation:

```
C:\Program Files\Microsoft Visual Studio .NET 2003\ Common7\
    Packages\schemas\xml
```

If you snoop around this folder, you'll find a schema file named asp.xsd. That rather large file contains schema information for all standard ASP.NET controls. If you're going to write an XSD file for a control, you can paste common pieces from there.

Rendering Types

Any information you enter in the Properties window is persisted to disk as attributes of the control. This serialization mechanism works seamlessly as long as strings and primitive types are involved. However, not all information persisted in a block of markup code is really a string. Let's consider the *Width* property of a control.

```
<expo:MyControl runat="server" width="200px" />
```

The value of the *width* attribute looks definitely like a string—*200px*—but the type of the underlying control property—the *Width* property—is not *String*. The *Width* property, in fact, is declared of type *Unit*. So what happens to make the string *200px* understandable by the control?

The page parser makes use of special modules—known as *type converters*—to convert to and from other types into a given type. In this case, the *UnitConverter* class transforms strings into *Unit* values and serializes *Unit* values into a string.

Implementing a Type Converter

To write a type converter, you derive a class from *TypeConverter* and override a few methods. Let's see how it works for a property named *Caption* and implemented through the *PanelCaption* class. The *Caption* property groups some attributes that relate to the title bar of the panel.

```
public class PanelCaption {
    private string _text;
    private Color _backColor;
    private Color _foreColor;
    private int _cellSpacing;
    private int _cellPadding;

    public PanelCaption() {
        Text = "Panel";
        BackColor = Color.DodgerBlue;
        ForeColor = Color.Yellow;
        CellPadding = 1;
        CellSpacing = 0;
    }

    [Description("Title of the caption")]
    public string Text {
        get {return _text;}
        set {_text = value;}
    }

    [Description("Background color of the caption")]
    public Color BackColor {
    get {return _backColor;}
        set {_backColor = value;}
    }
```

```
    [Description("Foreground color of the caption")]
    public Color ForeColor {
    get {return _foreColor;}
        set {_foreColor = value;}
    }

    [Description("Pixels used to space the caption")]
    public int CellSpacing {
        get {return _cellSpacing;}
        set {_cellSpacing = value;}
    }

    [Description("Pixels used to pad the caption")]
    public int CellPadding {
        get {return _cellPadding;}
        set {_cellPadding = value;}
    }
}
```

As you can see, these properties are not persisted to the view state. Because these attributes are created to be set at design-time, you will reasonably give them default values and change these values programmatically. So, in this context, not using the view state just represents a form of optimization.

Deriving from *TypeConverter*

A type converter needs to override a few members of its base class. In particular, the converter must declare whether the conversion is permitted to and from a given type (for example, *string*). The members you override for this goal are *CanConvertTo* and *CanConvertFrom*. They simply check the destination and the source type with the list of types the converter supports. The list of supported types includes at least the type *string*.

Other members to override are *ConvertFrom* and *ConvertTo*. As the names suggest, the methods perform the actual transformation from *PanelCaption* to string and vice versa. Typically, the serialization process consists of creating a comma-separated string in which the value of each property is rendered as a string. The way in which each property is serialized is completely up to the programmer.

The following listing shows the full implementation of the type converter:

```
public class PanelCaptionConverter : TypeConverter
{
    public PanelCaptionConverter()
    {
    }

    public override bool CanConvertFrom(ITypeDescriptorContext
        context, Type sourceType)
    {
```

```
        if (sourceType == typeof(string))
            return true;

        return base.CanConvertFrom (context, sourceType);
    }

    public override bool CanConvertTo(ITypeDescriptorContext context,
        Type destinationType)
    {
        if (destinationType == typeof(string))
            return true;

        return base.CanConvertTo (context, destinationType);
    }

    public override object ConvertFrom(ITypeDescriptorContext context,
        CultureInfo culture, object value)
    {
        if (value == null)
            return new PanelCaption();

        // Deserialize from a string representation
        if (value is string)
        {
            // Get the source string
            string data = (string) value;

            if (data.Length == 0)
                return new PanelCaption();


            // Split the string into parts
            // (must be 5 parts--one per each property)
            string[] parts;
            parts = data.Split(culture.TextInfo.ListSeparator[0]);
            if (parts.Length != 5)
                throw new ArgumentException("Invalid object", "value");

            // Create a new PanelCaption object
            PanelCaption caption = new PanelCaption();

            // Part 0 is a string representing the Text property
            caption.Text = parts[0];

            // Part 1-2 represent the BackColor and ForeColor properties
            TypeConverter colorConv;
            colorConv = TypeDescriptor.GetConverter(typeof(Color));
            Color c = (Color) colorConv.ConvertFromString(context,
            culture, parts[1]);
            caption.BackColor = c;
            c = (Color) colorConv.ConvertFromString(context,
            culture, parts[2]);
            caption.ForeColor = c;
```

```
            // Part 3-4 represent CellPadding and CellSpacing properties
            TypeConverter intConv;
            IntConv = TypeDescriptor.GetConverter(typeof(int));
            int pixel = (int) intConv.ConvertFromString(context,
            culture, parts[3]);
            caption.CellSpacing = pixel;
            pixel = (int) intConv.ConvertFromString(context,
            culture, parts[4]);
            caption.CellPadding = pixel;

            return caption;
        }

        return base.ConvertFrom (context, culture, value);
    }

    public override object ConvertTo(ITypeDescriptorContext context,
        CultureInfo culture, object value, Type destinationType)
    {
        // Ensure the value is a PanelCaption object
        if (value != null) {
            if (!(value is PanelCaption))
                throw new ArgumentException("Invalid object", "value");
        }

        // If null, return the empty string
        if (destinationType == typeof(string))
        {
            if (value == null)
                return String.Empty;

            // Get the object to serialize and necessary converters
            PanelCaption caption = (PanelCaption) value;
            TypeConverter intConv;
            intConv = TypeDescriptor.GetConverter(typeof(int));
            TypeConverter colorConv;
            colorConv = TypeDescriptor.GetConverter(typeof(Color));

            // Create the string
            string[] parts = new string[5];
            parts[0] = caption.Text;
            parts[1] = caption.BackColor.ToArgb().ToString();
            parts[2] = caption.ForeColor.ToArgb().ToString();
            parts[3] = caption.CellSpacing.ToString();
            parts[4] = caption.CellPadding.ToString();
            return String.Join(culture.TextInfo.ListSeparator, parts);
        }

        return base.ConvertTo (context, culture, value, destinationType);
    }
}
```

The converter is not effective until you associate it with the *PanelCaption* class.

```
[TypeConverter(typeof(PanelCaptionConverter))]
public class PanelCaption
{
    ⋮
}
```

The Properties window now displays an entry for the *Caption* property. The value of the property is a list of strings, as shown in the following code. The colors, in particular, are rendered with an integer that indicates the RGB representation of the color.

```
// colors are CadetBlue and AliceBlue
Sample Panel,-10510688,-984833,0,3
```

To edit properties, you must type the new value directly in the text box. Admittedly, this is not very practical and indeed a more user-friendly solution exists. However, before we discuss a better solution, let's examine how the values of the convertible properties are serialized. You control the serialization and deserialization of properties by using metadata and a bunch of new attributes.

Serialization Attributes

The attributes in Table 21-5 tell the designer how to serialize the control and its properties. The serialization process is important because it governs the creation of the HTML code for the control.

Table 21-5 Design-Time Serialization Attributes for Server Controls

Attribute	Description
DesignerSerializationVisibility	Specifies whether (and how) a property displayed in the Properties window should be persisted into code.
NotifyParentProperty	Specifies whether or not changes to subproperties should be bubbled up to the parent property. This attribute is used when the converted property is derived from *ExpandableObjectConverter*. (We'll discuss *ExpandableObjectConverter* later in the "Deriving from *ExpandableObjectConverter*" section.)
PersistChildrenAttribute	Indicates whether the nested contents of a control should be interpreted as properties or child controls.
PersistenceMode	Specifies whether a property should be persisted as an attribute on the control's tag or as nested content.

The *DesignerSerializationVisibility* attribute can take any of the values listed in Table 21-6:

Table 21-6 Values for the *DesignerSerializationVisibility* Attribute

Value	Description
Content	This option causes the contents of the property (for example, *Caption*) to be serialized as a whole. All subproperties will be serialized using an ad hoc naming convention. The subproperties of a property are the child members of a complex type. For example, *Text* and *BackColor* are subproperties of the property *Caption*. For the *Text* subproperty, an attribute named *Caption-Text* will be created.
Hidden	This option hides the property from serialization. The property will simply not be persisted in the markup code of the control.
Visible	Default value, causes the top-level property to be serialized. When this option is set, the *Caption* property will be serialized as a comma-separated list of child values. All subproperties will not be saved individually but within a unique, all-encompassing attribute named *Caption*.

The *PersistChildren* attribute is set to *false* for a control derived from *WebControl* and to *true* if the control inherits from *Control*. When set to *false*, the nested contents of a control are handled as properties. Each child tag is mapped to a property with the same name as the tag. For example, a child tag named *<ItemTemplate>* must have a corresponding *ItemTemplate* property. If this automatic mapping is disabled—that is, if *PersistChildren* is *true*—the child tag is considered an HTML element and a custom builder is required to properly handle its content. We examined this case in Chapter 20.

The *PersistenceMode* attribute indicates how to persist the content of a property. You can decide whether you want a given property to be serialized as a tag level attribute or as a child tag. Acceptable values for the attribute are listed in Table 21-7.

Table 21-7 Values for the *PersistenceMode* Attribute

Value	Description
Attribute	The property is persisted as a tag's attribute. This is the default option.
EncodedInnerDefaultProperty	The property is persisted as the only content of the tag. The content is HTML encoded.

Table 21-7 Values for the *PersistenceMode* Attribute

Value	Description
InnerDefaultProperty	The property is persisted as the only content of the tag. The content is not encoded.
InnerProperty	The property is persisted as a child tag along with any other properties of the control.

If your control has template properties, you should change the default value of the *PersistenceMode* attribute to prevent the designer from wiping out any nested contents whenever a property in the Properties window is saved.

```
[
    TemplateContainer(typeof(ItemTemplateContainer)),
    Description("Defines the contents of the panel"),
    DefaultValue(null),
    PersistenceMode(PersistenceMode.InnerProperty),
    Category("Layout")
]
public ITemplate ItemTemplate {
    get {return __itemTemplate;}
    set {__itemTemplate = value;}
}
```

The preceding code indicates that the *ItemTemplate* property must be saved as a nested tag with all the other properties of the control.

Deriving from *ExpandableObjectConverter*

In Figure 21-10, you see the *Caption* property selected in the Properties. Like *Caption*, the *Font* property—defined on the *WebControl* class—is also an expression of a complex type. The type in question is *FontInfo*. The representation of the type in the Properties window is different, however.

The *Font* property is expandable and exposes all its subproperties as individual properties in the same window. How can we obtain the same behavior for a custom property? The type converter for the property must inherit from a more specialized base class. The new base class is *ExpandableObjectConverter*.

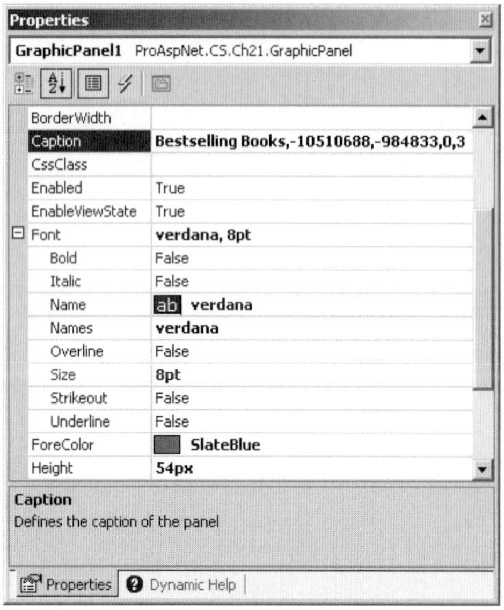

Figure 21-10 The *Caption* and *Font* properties in the Properties window.

The *ExpandableObjectConverter* class inherits from *TypeConverter* and provides a couple of additional overrides—*GetProperties* and *GetPropertiesSupported*. By simply replacing the base class, the type converter code shown previously in the "Deriving from *TypeConverter*" section provides a behavior identical to that of the *Font* property. This is demonstrated in Figure 21-11.

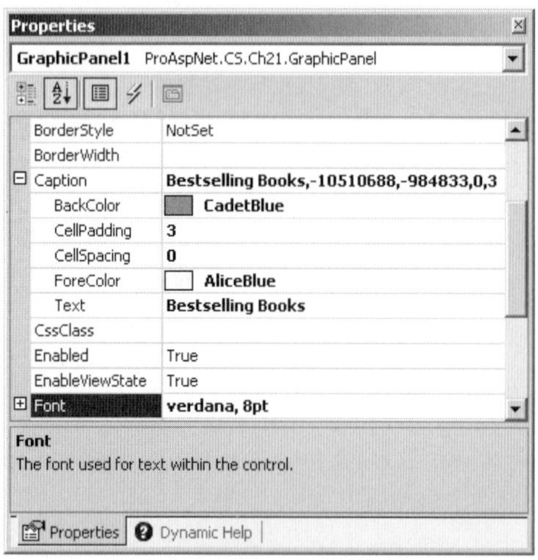

Figure 21-11 The *Caption* property just made expandable.

Each property in the expandable class should also be marked with the *NotifyParentProperty* attribute to notify the parent property (for example, *Caption*) of any changes. The following code snippet illustrates the metadata for the *Text* subproperty:

```
[NotifyParentProperty(true), Description("Title of the caption")]
public string Text {
    get {return _text;}
    set {_text = value;}
}
```

Creating a Type Editor

The Properties window doesn't provide much flexibility for editing values. If a text box is not ideal for editing the value of your properties, you can create a made-to-measure editor and link it to the designer. The base class for type editors is *UITypeEditor*. You define a custom type editor class and use metadata attributes to inform the designer that a given property must be edited through the specified form. A type editor is a Windows Forms dialog box managed through an interface. The dialog box supplies controls and facilities to make data editing as seamless as possible, and it fills a buffer with the string value for the Properties window.

Let's examine a simple case—an About dialog box.

The *About* Property Editor

To start, you define a read-only property named *About*. The following code shows how to proceed:

```
[Editor(typeof(AboutEditor), typeof(UITypeEditor)), Category("About")]
public string About {
    get {return "Courtesy of Programming ASP.NET";}
}
```

The *Editor* attribute indicates the dialog box to use to edit the value of the specified property. In this case, we're going to use the *AboutEditor* class. The second argument to the attribute is the type of the base class for the editor. The .NET Framework defines several editor classes from which you can choose the predefined one that already provides the features you're looking for.

The *UITypeEditor* class is a base class that can be extended to provide custom editing capabilities for a particular property. Other built-in editors exist for collections, URLs, colors, and dates, just to name a few.

When a property is marked with the *Editor* attribute, the designer shows an ellipsis button close to the default text box (shown in Figure 21-12). By clicking that button, the user-defined dialog box shows up and the user can edit the value using a more comfortable user interface. The *About* property is a particularly simple case in that it doesn't need real editing. However, the infrastructure you have to set up for this custom editor is in no way different than that of a more realistic scenario.

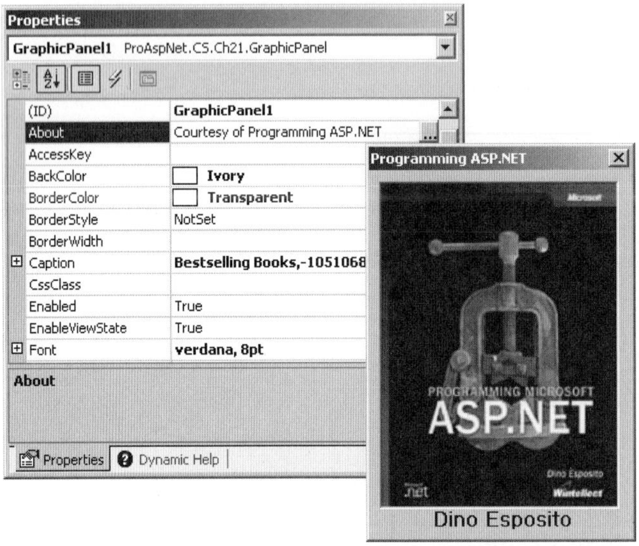

Figure 21-12 The *About* property and the ellipsis button that brings up the custom editor.

Designing a Custom Type Editor

To create a custom type editor, you start by deriving a new class from *UITypeEditor* or from any other type editor. Next, you add a form class to the project and define the user interface of the dialog box. In doing so, you'll probably need to import one or more namespaces that relate to Windows Forms. For example, you'll certainly reference the following namespace:

```
using System.Windows.Forms.Design;
```

Referencing Windows Forms classes, even from within an ASP.NET Web control project, is necessary to extend the user interface of the visual designer. A type editor class will at least override the *GetEditStyle* and *EditValue* methods. The *GetEditStyle* method indicates the style of the editing required. Acceptable values are *DropDown* and *Modal*. The *EditValue* method takes care of displaying the dialog box and retrieves the value to pass on to the Properties window. The following listing details the code for the *AboutEditor* class:

```
public class AboutEditor : UITypeEditor
{
    public override UITypeEditorEditStyle GetEditStyle(
        ITypeDescriptorContext context)
    {
        return UITypeEditorEditStyle.Modal;
    }

    public override object EditValue(ITypeDescriptorContext context,
        IServiceProvider provider, object value)
    {
        // Show the custom dialog box
        About dlg = new About();
        dlg.ShowDialog();

        // Set the value to return to the Properties window
        value = "Courtesy of 'Programming ASP.NET'";

        return value;
    }
}
```

If the *GetEditStyle* method returns the *UITypeEditorEditStyle.DropDown* value, the designer gets ready to display the specified control just below the property text box. If the modal style is set, the designer expects to have a modal dialog box to display. The *EditValue* method is called to enable editing. In the preceding code, a new dialog window is created and displayed. When the window is dismissed, you can use global fields on the dialog class to retrieve user information and store that to an internal variable. The value returned from the *EditValue* method is assigned to the property.

If you opt for a drop-down user interface, you must use the methods of the *IWindowsFormsEditorService* interface to display a custom control in the Properties window. In this case, a down-arrow button is displayed instead of an ellipsis.

```
public override object EditValue(ITypeDescriptorContext context,
    IServiceProvider provider, object value)
{
    object o = provider.GetService(typeof(IWindowsFormsEditorService));
    IWindowsFormsEditorService srv = (IWindowsFormsEditorService) o;
    if (srv != null) {
        // Display a custom control and retrieve the value
        MyControl myCtl = new MyControl(value);
        srv.DropDownControl(myCtl);
    }
}
```

You can also implement an owner-drawn mechanism by overriding the *GetPaintValueSupported* and *PaintValue* methods. The *GetPaintValueSupported* method just returns a Boolean value; the *PaintValue* method is passed a rectangle that represents the area of the Properties window where a representation of the value is to be drawn. The *PaintValue* method also receives a *Graphics* object and can use all the power of GDI+ to create owner-drawn output.

Writing Custom Designers

The appearance of the control in the visual environment is decided by the control's designer. Every control in ASP.NET has its own designer that provides a sort of preview of the control hosted in the page. The base class for a Web control designer is *ControlDesigner* and is located in the *System.Web.UI.Design* namespace. The class defines a common behavior for designers and supplies methods that the design-time environment can call for a variety of purposes. *ControlDesigner* is the first concrete class in the hierarchy that you can use in your code. All designers for ASP.NET controls actually inherit from an abstract class named *HtmlControlDesigner*, which marks the difference between Web and Windows control designers.

HTML Control Designers

When hosted in a visual environment, a Web server control is not very interactive, does not fire postback events, and is limited to generating HTML output. If you want the control to provide a truly what-you-see-is-what-you-get (WYSIWYG) view, you should implement the rendering engine of the control directly in the *Render* method. Only this method, in fact, is called from within the visual designer to obtain the HTML of the control. If you create a hierarchy of child controls overriding the *CreateChildControls* method, the control will work great at run time but not at design time. In the designer, the sequence of calls is different and, in the end, a control structured in this way returns an empty HTML string to the designer.

Note You can detect whether a component is running in design mode by using the *DesignMode* property on the *ISite* interface.

```
if(this.Site.DesignMode) {
    // design mode
}
```

You should note that a component's site is not available at run time; therefore, the *Site* property always returns null.

To control the appearance of the control in the visual designer, you can override a few methods, such as *GetDesignTimeHtml*. Writing a custom designer for a control is the most effective and efficient way to provide special design-time features without affecting the run-time behavior. As mentioned earlier, in the .NET Framework, design-time and run-time functions are neatly separated and implemented in separate classes. Because design-time classes are never invoked at run time, you should insulate all functions that relate to the composition of the Web Forms.

Creating a Control Designer

A typical control designer derives from *ControlDesigner* and overrides a few methods to control the HTML code displayed in the designer.

- ***GetDesignTimeHtml*** This method returns the HTML markup code that is used to represent the control at design time. By default, the method returns the output generated by the *Render* method. By overriding this method, you can enhance that string or even provide a fixed representation for the control.
- ***GetEmptyDesignTimeHtml*** This protected overridable method gets the HTML markup code that is used to represent an empty control at design time. The base implementation of this method returns a string that contains the name of the control class and the ID.
- ***GetErrorDesignTimeHtml*** This protected overridable method provides the HTML markup code that is displayed when a design-time error occurs in the control. The returned text typically provides information about the specific exception.

Other methods you can override or use in a custom control designer class are *AllowResize* and *CreatePlaceHolderDesignTimeHtml*. The *AllowResize* method returns a Boolean value that informs the designer about the availability of the control to be resized. Normally, there's no reason not to make a control resizable. However, in some situations you might decide for a fixed size—for example, when a templated control has an empty template.

The *CreatePlaceHolderDesignTimeHtml* method takes a message string and returns a block of HTML text with a look and feel consistent with that of standard ASP.NET controls. For example, you can use the method to provide an error message, as shown in the following code snippet (and in Figure 21-13):

```
protected override string GetErrorDesignTimeHtml(Exception e)
{
    return CreatePlaceHolderDesignTimeHtml("There was an error");
}
```

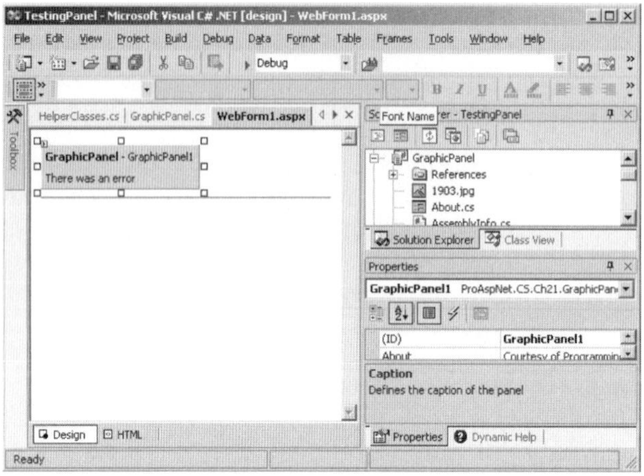

Figure 21-13 A design-time error message for a control.

If you don't like the standard user interface or you just want to customize it further, you can simply return ad hoc HTML code, as discussed in the following example.

Generating Design-Time HTML

The following listing shows a sample implementation of a designer for the *GraphicPanel* control. The class overrides three methods—*GetDesignTimeHtml*, *GetEmptyDesignTimeHtml*, and *GetErrorDesignTimeHtml*. The *GetDesignTime-Html* method takes the output of the control and inserts it in a table along with a copyright note. The same extra table with copyright information is maintained for error messages and for the standard, empty user interface.

```
public class GraphicPanelDesigner : ControlDesigner {
    public override string GetDesignTimeHtml() {
        string designTimeHtml = null;

        try {
            StringBuilder sb = new StringBuilder("");
            sb.Append("<table bgcolor=gainsboro><tr><td>");

            // The default design-time HTML code
            sb.Append(base.GetDesignTimeHtml());

            sb.Append("</td></tr><tr><td align=center>");
            sb.Append("<span>");
            sb.Append("Switch to HTML view to edit the template.<br>");
            sb.Append("Courtesy of <b>Programming ASP.NET</b></span>");
```

```
            sb.Append("</td></tr></table>");
            designTimeHtml = sb.ToString();
        }
        catch (Exception ex) {
            designTimeHtml = GetErrorDesignTimeHtml(ex);
        }

        if (designTimeHtml == null || designTimeHtml.Length==0)
            designTimeHtml = GetEmptyDesignTimeHtml();

        return designTimeHtml;
    }

    protected override string GetEmptyDesignTimeHtml() {
        StringBuilder sb = new StringBuilder("");
        sb.Append("<table bgcolor=gainsboro><tr><td>");
        sb.Append("This is a <b>GraphicPanel</b> control");
        sb.Append("</td></tr><tr bgcolor=white><td align=center>");
        sb.Append("<span style='font-family:verdana;font-size:10px;'>");
        sb.Append("Courtesy of <b>Programming ASP.NET</b></span>");
        sb.Append("</td></tr></table>");

        return sb.ToString();
    }

    protected override string GetErrorDesignTimeHtml(Exception e) {
        StringBuilder sb = new StringBuilder("");
        sb.Append("<table bgcolor=gainsboro><tr><td align=center>");
        sb.Append("This is a <b>GraphicPanel</b> control");
        sb.Append("</td></tr><tr><td>");
        sb.Append("<span style='font-weight:700;color:red;'>");
        sb.Append(e.Message);
        sb.Append("</span></td><tr bgcolor=white><td align=center>");
        sb.Append("<span style='font-family:verdana;font-size:10px;'>");
        sb.Append("Courtesy of <b>Programming ASP.NET</b></span>");
        sb.Append("</td></tr></table>");

        return sb.ToString();
    }
}
```

Figure 12-14 shows the *GraphicPanel* control in the Visual Studio .NET designer.

Note that the design-time HTML is composed of two parts—the effective output of the control and a part with information and copyright. The information and copyright will not show up at run time.

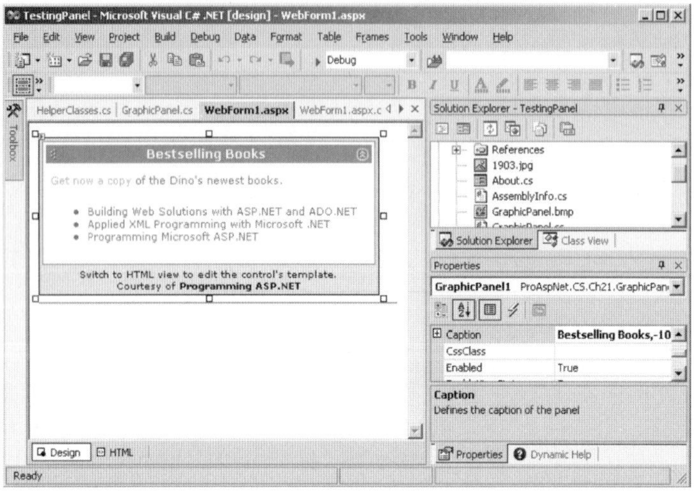

Figure 21-14 The *GraphicPanel* control in action sited in the Visual Studio .NET environment.

As mentioned, the *GetEmptyDesignTimeHtml* method is invoked whenever the design-time HTML for the control is empty. Figure 21-15 shows the results in this case.

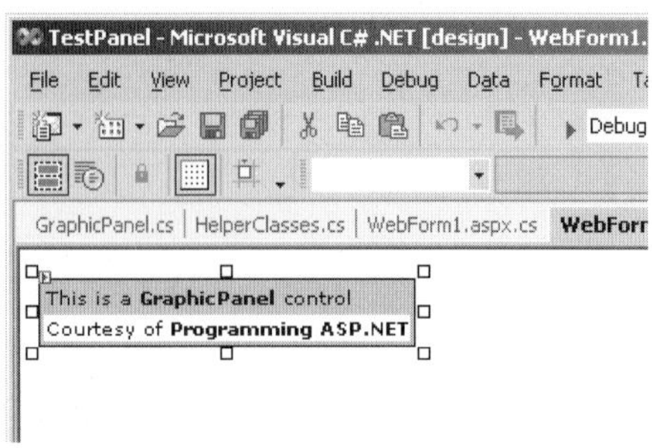

Figure 21-15 The design-time output of the *GraphicPanel* control displayed in lieu of the empty string.

The *GetErrorDesignTimeHtml* method is helpful to display friendly messages in case of design-time errors. The designer traps any exceptions and displays messages like the one shown in Figure 21-16.

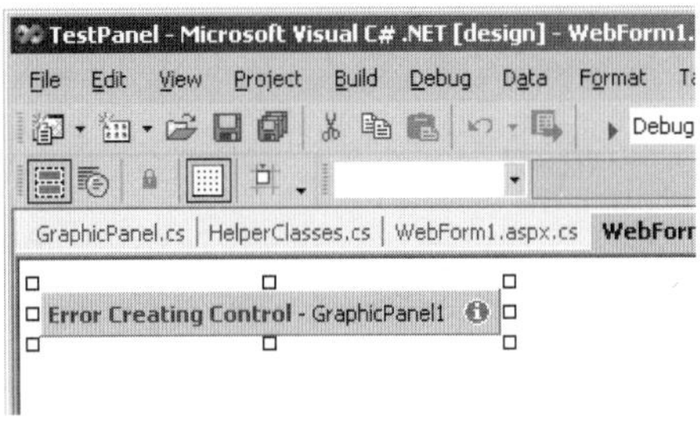

Figure 21-16 The standard error message displayed by the designer.

By overriding the *GetErrorDesignTimeHtml* method, you can format the HTML to look different and provide more information, as shown in Figure 21-17.

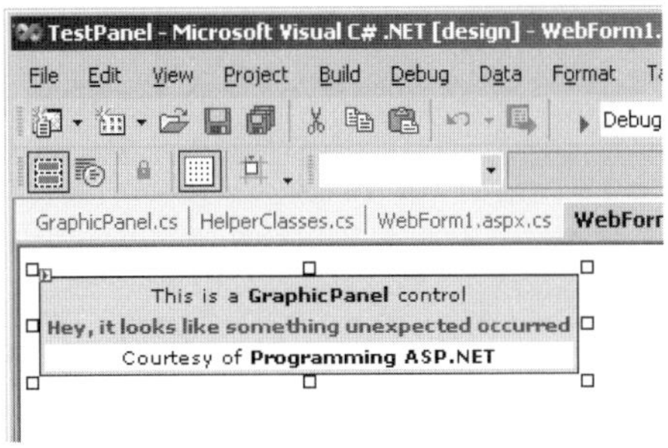

Figure 21-17 A customized error message displayed by the custom designer of the *GraphicPanel* control.

You associate a custom designer with a control using the *Designer* attribute, as shown in the following code snippet:

```
[Designer(typeof(GraphicPanelDesigner))]
public class GraphicPanel : WebControl {
    ⋮
}
```

The designer class will be loaded when the control is dropped onto a Web Form and its methods are called back by the visual designer.

Conclusion

Applications written for the .NET Framework are for the most part component-based applications. ASP.NET applications are no exceptions, and several controls can be found working under the hood of Web pages. If you choose Visual Studio .NET as your development environment, you end up assembling pages by using a visual designer. Controls are picked from a palette and dropped onto a design surface. Once instantiated, controls can be configured declaratively through the Properties window. ASP.NET controls know how to integrate themselves into this environment, but their behavior can be further enhanced by resorting to a number of extensions.

In this chapter, we discussed three ways to improve the design-time capabilities of ASP.NET controls. You can assign a few metadata attributes to each property so that the property displays with an ad hoc description and in the most appropriate category. Setting attributes works great if the property value is of a simple type, such as string, integer, or enumeration types.

Properties with custom types need more work and possibly a type converter. A type converter is a sort of special serializer that renders the state of a class as a string. Normally, a type converter returns a comma-separated string in which each token is the value of a public property. A property associated with a converter can be rendered as an expandable object in the Properties window. To achieve that, you simply need to inherit the custom type converter from a more specialized class such as *ExpandableObjectConverter*.

In all these cases, though, the user interface employed for editing properties consists of a simple text box control. If a plain text box is inadequate for your values, you can create a type or even a component editor. Editors are Windows Forms classes that are bound to the Properties window and shown when the user chooses to edit the value. A type editor class edits a particular property, whereas a component editor looks like a property page for the control and provides a single user interface to edit all properties in a more convenient way.

Finally, to control the aspect of the component in the designer, you can create a made-to-measure designer class. A designer class consists of a few overrides aimed at controlling the HTML text being displayed in the environment for the control. By default, the design-time aspect of the control is nearly identical to its run-time look. However, there might be situations in which you want the control to provide a different output that is not a function of the current properties. In these cases, using a custom designer can do the trick.

Resources

- *Developing Microsoft ASP.NET Server Controls and Components*, by Nikhil Kothari and Vandana Datye (Microsoft Press, 2002)

Part VI

Advanced Topics

22

Working with Images in ASP.NET

Difficulties strengthen the mind, as labour the body.

—*Seneca*

As we all know, the World Wide Web wouldn't be the same without the images. Effective browser support for images was one key to the rapid success of the Web because it sanctioned the Web platform as a new multimedia channel. Many Web pages today are topped with so many images and are so well conceived and well designed that an overall page looks more like a magazine advertisement than an HTML page. Looking at the current pages displayed by portals, it's rather hard to imagine there was a time—and it was only six or seven years ago—when one could create a Web site by using only a text editor and some assistance from a friend who had some familiarity with Adobe PhotoShop.

These days, although images are a common presence in Web pages, their use is still largely limited to art designers and other specialized professional figures. Programmers are rarely involved with images because although many images are the fruit of intense work and planning, they are nearly always deployed as static files. When static JPEG or GIF images are involved, a programmer can't do much to add more spice to the final page served to the user.

Over the Web, images are not merely and not always used as a publishing tool. In many applications, images play a much more active role and are as significant as data. Examples of this include image data banks, photographic galleries, museums, and also financial and business analysis applications. In all these cases, the application might need to work with dynamically generated images (for example, charts) or images that must undergo special treatment before display (for example, adding a watermark or copyright message).

Several third-party vendors provide powerful and professional tools to perform charting and image processing over the Web. Prior to the release of the .NET Framework, the need to resort to these tools was a foregone conclusion. Thanks to GDI+, ASP.NET applications can sometimes accomplish a variety of tasks in-house without requiring additional tools and libraries. You'll be surprised to see how many tasks can be accomplished with the wise use of GDI+ and other .NET Framework facilities.

Accessing Images from Web Pages

There is just one way in which Web pages can reference an image—by using the HTML *<img>* tag. By design, this tag points to a URL. As a result, to be displayable within a Web page, an image must be identifiable through a URL and its bits should be contained in the output stream returned by the Web server for that URL. In many cases, the URL points to a static resource such as a GIF or JPEG file. In this case, the Web server takes the request upon itself and serves it without invoking external components.

The fact that many *<img>* tags on the Web are bound to a static file does not mean there's no other way to include images in Web pages. Let's start with a few basic points on this topic and briefly recall the main points of Web image access.

The *<img>* Element

The HTML *<img>* element is used to display an image within an HTML page. It supports a few attributes such as width, height, and alternate text to display if the image is not available. The HTML definition of the element is as follows:

```
<img id="control ID"
     alt="alternate text"
     align="top | middle | bottom | left | right"
     border="border width"
     height="image height"
     src="URL"
     width="image width">
```

Note that the element does not require a closing tag. In ASP.NET, the *<img>* tag is rendered through the *HtmlImage* class. The *Image* control represents another way of generating the *<img>* tag. *HtmlImage* belongs to the *HtmlControls* namespace, whereas *Image* is a member of the *WebControls* namespace and provides a more abstract programming interface but no extra features.

Although it's good that two controls are provided to create a server-side representation of the *<img>* tag, a highly optimized ASP.NET application will not use any. Even though server controls are extremely easy to use, they're not always the best choice for a relatively simple task such as showing an image, because they consume server resources without really needing to. In many cases, a simple rendering or data-binding substitution will nicely and more efficiently do the job of showing an image.

The following code snippet successfully displays an image but doesn't require the creation of a server-side control:

```
<img src='<%# expression that evaluate to the image URL %>' />
```

When the *<img>* tag is configured on the server, you should pay careful attention to the URL you output, especially if the URL is in some way a function of the user input. The URL associated with the *<img>* element can be tampered with by a malicious user and result in undesired script code that runs on the client. Also, to validate the URL you don't necessarily have to resort to a server control. A call to a local function within the data-bound expression can also do the job.

Although the *<img>* element is mostly used with static files, it can easily display images stored on other storage media—for example, a database or even the Web server's memory. The key structure of the element doesn't change to support this feature. What changes, instead, is the extension of the URL and the content type of the HTTP response. If you make the *<img>* tag point to an .aspx page, the Web server will run the specified page and send the resultant output to the tag. As long as the output can be recognized as a valid image format, it is displayed. Let's see how.

Referencing Nonfile Images

From the browser's perspective, a Web page is nothing more than a long strip of characters to be processed sequentially. The browser displays some characters and interprets some others, such as *<b>*, according to special rules. When an *<img>* tag is found, the browser knows that it has to open another download channel and request the specified URL. To the browser's eyes, the type of the URL and the protocol have no importance. What matters is that the expected output matches a given format—the MIME type.

The browser requests the image URL and processes the returned output as the expected MIME type dictates. If the bytes form an image of the correct type, the picture is displayed with the attributes set in the *<img>* tag; otherwise, an error is raised and a standard bitmap is displayed. For a better understanding of the whole process, let's see the steps needed to send an image to the browser from within an .aspx page.

Setting the Content Type

All the response packets that reach the browser contain a *Content-Type* header that provides information about the type, and subsequently the format, of the incoming data. The browser looks at that value to decide how to process the data. The following snippet shows the Internet Information Services (IIS) response to a browser that requested a JPEG image:

```
HTTP/1.1 200 OK
Server: Microsoft-IIS/5.1
Date: Thu, 13 Mar 2003 14:30:12 GMT
X-Powered-By: ASP.NET
X-AspNet-Version: 1.1.4322
Cache-Control: private
Content-Type: image/jpeg
Content-Length: 28521
```

In ASP.NET, the *HttpResponse* object is responsible for setting the *Content-Type* header in the response packet. By default, the *ContentType* property of the *HttpResponse* object is set to *text/html*. Accepted values for the property are all HTTP MIME types. Of course, for the success of the download, the content type must be set only once in the page and before having sent some data to the output stream.

```
Response.ContentType = "image/jpeg";
```

This code illustrates how to set the *ContentType* property of a page that returns a JPEG image.

Flushing to the Output Stream

The following code demonstrates a simple page that requires an image from an ASP.NET page:

```
<html>
<body>
<form runat="server">
    <img src="image.aspx" />
</form>
</body>
</html>
```

The image.aspx page will first gain access to the bytes of the image and then serialize them all to the output stream.

```
<%@ Page Language="C#" %>
<%@ Import Namespace="System.IO" %>

<script runat="server">
void Page_Load(object sender, EventArgs e) {
```

```
    IntPtr fileHandle;
    long startPos = 0, fileSize;
    string fileName = Server.MapPath("bluehills.jpg");

    FileStream fs = new FileStream(fileName, FileMode.Open);
    fileHandle = fs.Handle;
    fileSize = fs.Length;

    // Send the output
    Response.ContentType = "image/jpeg";
    Response.WriteFile(fileHandle, startPos, fileSize);

    fs.Close();
}
</script>
```

In their overall simplicity, this pair of pages illustrate well the pattern needed to obtain and manipulate images dynamically. The client page sets the *src* attribute of the *<img>* tag to an .aspx resource. The server page, in turn, will retrieve or generate the bytes of the image and write them to the output stream along with the proper content type.

Accessing Database Images

The use of the database as the storage medium for images is controversial. Some people have good reasons to push it as a solution; others tell you bluntly they would never do it and that you shouldn't either. Some people could tell you wonderful stories of how storing images in a properly equipped database was the best experience of their professional life. With no fear that facts could prove them wrong, other people would confess that they would never use a database again for such a task.

I have had some experience in the past working with images and database systems, but I'll tell you that story later. In the meantime, let's go by facts. The facts say that all database management systems (DBMS) of a certain reputation and volume have supported binary large objects (BLOB) for quite some time. A BLOB field doesn't necessarily contain an image, but it can contain a multimedia file or a long text file. There must be a good reason for having this BLOB support!

Working with Binary Fields

To read a binary database field, you use ADO.NET classes as you would for any other database query. At the end of the day, in fact, a BLOB field is only a database column of a special type and of a reasonably large size. If you know that the size of the object is not excessive (say, tens of kilobytes), you can go for a single-step read; otherwise, you might want to opt for sequential access and read one chunk of information at a time.

The data reader is the tool that proves most useful for reading information out of a BLOB field. This doesn't mean you can't store large binary content in a *DataSet*. It's only that the *DataSet* is an in-memory cache of data, and caching data of that size in the memory of the Web server is rarely a great solution. BLOB fields are the type of data that should be read, consumed, and disposed of as soon as possible, without the programmer being tempted by the siren of caching techniques.

For now, consider we'll store BLOB fields in Microsoft SQL Server; later on, I'll share some thoughts about Oracle.

Reading Images from BLOB Fields

To read an image from a BLOB field with ADO.NET, you execute a SELECT statement on the column and use the *ExecuteScalar* method to catch the result and save it in an array of bytes. Next, you send this array down to the client through a binary write to the response stream. The following code shows how to proceed:

```
// photo.aspx file
void Page_Load(object sender, EventArgs e)
{
    // Ensure the parameter is a number
    int id = Convert.ToInt32(Request.QueryString["id"]);

    string connString = "SERVER=localhost;DATABASE=northwind;UID=sa;";
    string cmdText = "SELECT photo FROM employees WHERE employeeid=" +
        id.ToString();

    // Get an array of bytes from the BLOB field
    SqlConnection conn = new SqlConnection(connString);
    SqlCommand cmd = new SqlCommand(cmdText, conn);
    conn.Open();
    byte[] img = (byte[]) cmd.ExecuteScalar();
    conn.Close();

    // Prepare the response for the browser
    Response.ContentType = "image/jpeg";
    Response.BinaryWrite(img);
}
```

In this code, we assume that the field named *photo* contains image bits and that the format of the image is JPEG. Notice the attempt to convert the value of the *id* query parameter to an integer before proceeding. This simple check significantly reduces the surface attack for malicious users by verifying that what is going to be used as a numeric ID is really a numeric ID. Especially when you're inoculating user input into SQL query commands, filtering out extra characters and wrong data types is a fundamental measure for preventing attacks.

The *BinaryWrite* method of the *HttpResponse* object writes an array of bytes to the output stream. In addition to writing arrays of bytes, the *BinaryWrite* method also differs from the *Write* method because it writes directly to the output stream. All other writing methods of the *Response* object output data through the services of an HTTP writer object, which, in particular, provides buffering capabilities.

Note If the database you're using is Northwind (as in the preceding example), an extra step is required to ensure that the images are correctly managed. For some reason, the SQL Server version of the Northwind database stores the images in the *photo* column of the Employees table as OLE objects. This is probably due to the conversion that occurred when the database was upgraded from the Microsoft Access version. As a matter of fact, the array of bytes you receive contains a 78-byte prefix that has nothing to do with the image. Those bytes are just the header created when the image was added as an OLE object to the first version of Access. While the preceding code would work like a champ with regular BLOB fields, it must undergo the following modification to work with the *photo* field of the Northwind.Employees database.

```
Response.OutputStream.Write(img, 78, img.Length);
```

Instead of using the *BinaryWrite* call, which doesn't let you specify the starting position, use the code shown here.

A sample page to test BLOB field access is shown in Figure 22-1.

```
<asp:textbox runat="server" id="theID" type="text" />
<asp:linkbutton runat="server" text="Download" onclick="DownloadFile" />
<hr />
<img src='<%# "photo.aspx?id=" + theID.Text %>'>
```

Figure 22-1 Downloading images stored within the BLOB field of a database.

Uploading Images to BLOB Fields

Uploading an image to a database is simply a matter of preparing and executing an INSERT or UPDATE statement with the right set of parameters. You can use a single SQL statement or even a stored procedure. If the BLOB field is a column of type *Text*, you can pass the value as a string parameter. If the BLOB is expected to contain an image—the SQL Server type *Image*—you set the specific parameter by using an array of bytes.

In Figure 22-2, you can see a sample page that lets you upload a local file to the Web server and from there into a SQL Server database.

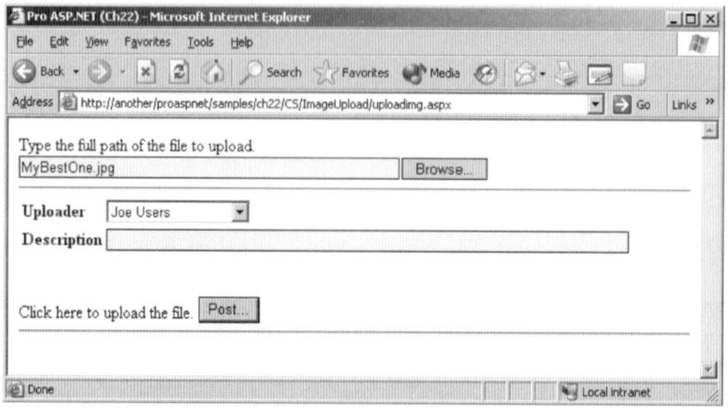

Figure 22-2 Users select a local image file and upload it to the Web server where the image is further processed and copied into a SQL Server database.

The structure of the database table is described in Table 22-1.

Table 22-1 The Schema of the Sample Table

Column	Type
Bits	BLOB field of type *Image* contains the bits of the image.
Description	Contains a short description of the image.
ImageSize	Size in bytes of the image.
MIME	String that represents the MIME type of the image.
Uploader	Foreign-key reference to the user who uploaded the image.
UploadTime	Time at which the upload occurred.

The sample page contains an *HtmlInputFile* control that is normally used to upload files.

```
<form runat="server" enctype="multipart/form-data">
    <input runat="server" id="theFile" type="file" />
    ⋮
</form>
```

The uploaded file is made available on the server through the *PostedFile* property of the *HtmlInputFile* control. The *PostedFile* property is an object of type *HttpPostedFile* and features interesting properties such as *ContentLength*, *ContentType*, and *InputStream*. The first two properties indicate the length and MIME type of the posted file; the third property exposes the posted file as a stream object, making it easy for the application to transform it into an array of bytes.

The following code shows how to upload an image directly into SQL Server. The content of the posted file is accessed through the *InputStream* property of the *HttpPostedFile* class. The stream is read into an array of bytes, and the array is used as the value for the command parameter that will fill the BLOB field. Information about the content type and the length of the posted file are inferred from the file itself.

```
void UploadFile(object sender, EventArgs e)
{
    int sizeOfFile = theFile.PostedFile.ContentLength;

    // Prepare for the SQL command
    string conn_string = "SERVER=localhost;DATABASE=proaspnet;UID=sa;";
    SqlConnection conn = new SqlConnection(conn_string);
    string cmd_text = "INSERT INTO images " +
           "(bits, description, uploader, uploadtime, imagesize, mime) " +
           "VALUES (@imageBits, @description, @uploader, @uploadTime, " +
```

```
            "@imageSize, @mimeType)";
    SqlCommand cmd = new SqlCommand(cmd_text, conn);

    // Set parameters
    SqlParameter p1, p2, p3, p4, p5, p6;
    p1 = cmd.Parameters.Add("@imageBits", SqlDbType.Image);
    p2 = cmd.Parameters.Add("@description", SqlDbType.NVarChar);
    p3 = cmd.Parameters.Add("@uploader", SqlDbType.Int);
    p4 = cmd.Parameters.Add("@uploadTime", SqlDbType.DateTime);
    p5 = cmd.Parameters.Add("@imageSize", SqlDbType.Int);
    p6 = cmd.Parameters.Add("@mimeType", SqlDbType.NVarChar);
    p1.Value = GetImageBits(theFile.PostedFile.InputStream, sizeOfFile);
    p2.Value = theDesc.Value;                         // name of the file
    p3.Value = theUploader.SelectedItem.Value;        // code of the uploader
    p4.Value = DateTime.Now;                          // time of upload
    p5.Value = sizeOfFile;                            // size of the image
    p6.Value = theFile.PostedFile.ContentType;        // MIME type

    // Copy the bits into the table
    cmd.Connection.Open();
    int recAffected = cmd.ExecuteNonQuery();
    cmd.Connection.Close();
    return;
}

private byte[] GetImageBits(Stream fs, int size)
{
    byte[] img = new byte[size];
    fs.Read(img, 0, size);
    return img;
}
```

Note Prior to ASP.NET, a server-side process was required to run in the background to handle a file upload to the server. The background application—the posting acceptor—is called to handle *multipart/form-data* submissions. IIS and ASP applications use the Microsoft Posting Acceptor, but other tools (mostly CGI applications) are available over the Web. In ASP.NET, the role of the posting acceptor is no longer necessary, as it is carried out by the ASP.NET runtime.

Real-World Scenarios

In the code discussed so far, we silently made a couple of assumptions which, in many cases, is the difference between good and not-so-good applications. More often than not, you need to retrieve information about a certain entity defined in the domain of the problem. The information might include both text and binary fields. As we architected the solution, a distinct database access is necessary to retrieve the BLOB and no special countermeasures are taken to minimize the memory footprint if the images are particularly large.

Optimizing the Database Query

It's clear that images, because of their potentially large size, need to be handled with care and should be cached sparingly. However, be aware that an .aspx resource bound to an *<img>* tag generates a distinct and extra call to the database. In practice, you make one call to retrieve all the text-based information and one call to fill each image bound to a Web page.

If you decide this model is not what you want, consider the following alternatives to optimize database access. First, you could create copies of the image in a temporary directory and look for local files before you embark into a database query. Especially if the size of the image is considerable, at a minimum you save a segment of the bandwidth. Because database fields are global resources shared by all sessions, figuring out an effective naming convention for these images shouldn't be an issue. In addition, you can also modify the source code of the calling page so that it points to an existing image file rather than to a server-side page. In this case, you also gain faster access because IIS will resolve the call to the image without posting the request to ASP.NET.

If the size and number of images allow for it, a second alternative to optimize database access is to use caching. This entails that you make a full query of all fields and cache the BLOB field temporarily, just long enough for the successive request for the image to be served. To make sure the object is not maintained in memory for long, you can store it in *Cache* and define a short-term expiration policy.

Optimizing Memory Usage

The *ExecuteScalar* method we used to read BLOB contents works by loading the incoming data as soon as it becomes available. In other words, the BLOB is read in a single shot, along with the rest of the data row, potentially consuming a lot of memory. Such large objects should be treated in a different way, in particular when you know they might contain hundreds of megabytes of data. For this reason, *ExecuteScalar*, or the default data reader, are not always the best approach.

In Chapter 5, "The ADO.NET Object Model," while discussing the data reader object, I mentioned the *CommandBehavior* enumeration, in particular its *SequentialAccess* value. When specified in a call to *ExecuteReader*, the sequential access attribute changes the standard behavior of the reader and makes it return data as it is received instead of one complete row at a time.

> **Note** This sequential access behavior will vary depending on your data source. For example, returning a BLOB from Access will result in the entire BLOB being loaded into memory rather than data being loaded sequentially, as it is received.

If you configure the reader for sequential reading, the order in which you access fields is important. The data reader, in fact, is a forward-only cursor and can't move back to consider bytes it has read past. For example, once you have accessed the third field, it's too late to access the first and the second fields.

When accessing the data in the BLOB field, you should use the *GetBytes* method of the data reader and fill an array with data.

```
bytesRead = reader.GetBytes(colIndex, startPos, buf, 0, bufSize);
while (bytesRead == bufSize)
{
    // Process the bytes
    ProcessBytes(buf);

    // Reposition the start index
    startPos += bufSize;
    bytesRead = reader.GetBytes(colIndex, startPos, buf, 0, bufSize);
}

// Process the remaining buffer
ProcessBytes(buf);
```

GetBytes accepts a starting position and a buffer size and returns the number of bytes effectively read. Using sequential access and *GetBytes* for reading allows you to conserve system resources, which could be compromised by too large of a BLOB value.

Should You Really Store Images in the Database?

About eight years ago, I started on one of the first Internet projects—an image data bank. We were supposed to deliver images of various size and resolution to registered users. Each image was designed as a collection of images, from the thumbnail to the highest resolution. The largest image available was about 4 megabytes. Each image stored in the archive took up a total of 6 megabytes of space.

The back-end database was not running on a Microsoft platform but provided support for BLOB fields. Without much debate, we decided to store descriptions and other catalog information in the database and to store images as individual files under a well-known path. We also stored in the database enough information for the software to retrieve the file. Being designed for a relatively small number of registered users, the application never showed scalability problems and at no time did anyone on the team or any users complain about performance.

Can this brief experience—especially an experience from a relatively old age of software and database technologies—be used as an example of the superiority of file-based storage over database storage? Certainly not, but reading between the lines of how modern DBMS systems implement BLOB fields, I've used this experience to formulate an idea about image storage and databases.

As long as the image size doesn't exceed a critical and mostly application-specific threshold, storing images in the database is fine. Images are treated as data, and access is protected and subject to locking in case of concurrent access. However, you might feel less comfortable if you need to edit images or in any way retouch them frequently. The importance of smart tools for inserting and extracting images from the database is significant. As things currently stand, in many cases the programmer must build these tools himself.

SQL Server stores images in a field of type *Image*, which should be used for any binary content exceeding 8 kilobytes and up to 2 gigabytes. Regardless of the availability of smart and to-the-point T-SQL commands such as UPDATETEXT, READTEXT, and WRITETEXT, working with large images (several megabytes each) is complex and difficult.

Oracle supplies two different data types to deal with large binary objects—the BFILE and the LOB data type. Both reference binary data with a maximum size of 4 gigabytes. A BFILE differs from a LOB data type in that its data is stored in a physical file in the operating system instead of within the database. Other characteristics distinguish BFILEs from LOBs. In particular, the BFILE uses *reference copy semantics*, meaning that if you perform a copy operation on a BFILE, only the reference to the file is copied, not the data in the file.

The BFILE data type should be used for referencing binary objects that are very large in size and, therefore, not practical to store in the database. On the other hand, using a BFILE introduces a slight increase in overhead because of the extra communication necessary to synchronize the database engine, the file, and the client application. In general, it's more efficient to access a BFILE if you need to obtain only a small amount of data. It's preferable to access a database-resident LOB if you need to obtain all the data.

In short, should you consider storing images in a database? If you need to frequently edit the images, I suggest storing the images as separate files. If the size of the images are very large (for example, hundreds of megabytes), I suggest storing the images as separate files. If your images are essentially read-only and relatively static, and if you measure the size in kilobytes or a few megabytes, you can consider storing your images in the database.

Generating Images Dynamically

Some Web sites offer a nice feature: you ask for something, and they return your request graphically. A lot of financial Web sites do this to satisfy their users. Isn't it true that an image is worth dozens of words? Web-deployed charts are often dynamically generated on the server and served to the browser as a stream of bytes traveling over the classic response output stream.

So far we've returned images read from a file or a database. In the end, the key thing with dynamically generated images is not so much the ability to return pictures from the Web server—that is nothing new and can be accomplished with almost all languages and over almost all platforms. The real issue is how easily you can create and manipulate server-side images. For these tasks, Web applications normally rely on ad hoc libraries or the graphics engine of other applications (for example, Microsoft Office applications). ASP.NET applications are different and, to some extent, luckier. ASP.NET applications, in fact, can rely on a powerful and integrated graphics engine capable of providing an object model for image generation. This back-end system is GDI+.

A Quick Tour of GDI+ Classes

GDI+ is the graphics engine of Windows XP made available also for other 32-bit and 64-bit platforms such as Windows 2000. As its name suggests, GDI+ is the successor of GDI, the Graphics Device Interface included with earlier versions of the Windows operating system. GDI+ is a programming interface exposed through a set of managed classes. The .NET Framework encapsulates the key GDI+ functionalities in a handful of namespaces and makes those functions available to Web, Windows Forms, and Web service applications.

Most of the GDI+ services belong to the following categories: 2D vector graphics and imaging. 2D vector graphics involves drawing simple figures such as lines, curves, and polygons. Under the umbrella of imaging are functions to display, manipulate, save, and convert bitmap and vector images. Finally, a third category of functions can be identified—typography, which has to do with the display of text in a variety of fonts, sizes, and styles.

Having the goal of creating images dynamically, we are most interested in drawing figures and text and in saving the work as JPEGs or GIFs.

The *Graphics* Class

The central element in the Win32 GDI programming model is the *device context*. The device context is a data structure that stores information about the capabilities of a particular display device. A device context is associated with a drawing surface such as a window, printer, or block of memory. Win32 programs obtain a handle to a device context and pass that handle to all GDI functions they call. A device context also maintains a list of the graphics attributes that are set—background and foreground color, pen, brush, and font. The device context is the connecting link between the high-level front-end API and the underlying device drivers.

GDI+ replaces the concept of a device context and its child handle-based programming style with a truly object-oriented approach. In GDI+, the role of the central console for drawing is played by the *Graphics* object. A big step forward is that graphics surfaces (such as the window and the printer) and graphics objects (such as the pen or the brush) are independent entities. GDI+ drawing methods take graphics objects only as an argument, whereas in Win32 you have to select those objects in the device context.

The first step for a GDI+ application is creating, or obtaining, a new graphics context. The *Graphics* class has no constructor; a new *Graphics* object can be obtained using any of the following methods:

- ***Control.CreateGraphics*** You use this method to create a *Graphics* object that draws to a Windows Forms control or form background. This method is one of the few that, on a control or a form, is safe to call from any thread.
- ***Graphics.FromHdc*** Designed for use within Windows Forms applications, this method creates a new *Graphics* object from the specified handle to a Win32 device context.
- ***Graphics.FromHwnd*** Designed for use within Windows Forms applications, this method creates a new *Graphics* object from the specified handle to a Win32 window.
- ***Graphics.FromImage*** This is the only creator method that makes sense in the context of ASP.NET applications. It creates a *Graphics* object from an instance of a .NET graphic object. Any operation performed on the *Graphics* is recorded in the associated image.

No matter how you obtain it, when a *Graphics* object is no longer needed, it must be disposed of through a call to the *Dispose* method.

The *Bitmap* Class

The *Bitmap* class encapsulates a GDI+ bitmap, which consists of the pixel data for a graphics image plus some attributes. A bitmap object is an object used to work with images defined by pixel data. In GDI+, we have three types of images—bitmaps, icons, and metafiles. All three classes derive from a common abstract class named *Image*. Note that an instance of the *Bitmap* class doesn't necessarily represent a .bmp file. It is, instead, a generic container of pixel data that could be saved as a .bmp or .jpg image, as required.

When you create a *Graphics* object, you associate it with a particular canvas. As mentioned, for a Web application an in-memory bitmap is the only viable option. The following code shows how to instantiate a *Bitmap* object of the desired size and creates a drawing context from it:

```
Bitmap bmp = new Bitmap(100, 100);
Graphics g = Graphics.FromImage(bmp);
```

From now on, any graphics primitives called to operate on the *Graphics* object will affect the underlying *Bitmap* object. Once you're done with the graphics work, a *Bitmap* object can be saved to a number of formats, including Portable Network Graphics (PNG), JPEG, BMP, and GIF. Note also that the *Bitmap* class supplies methods to rotate and flip the image and that you can also instantiate a bitmap from an existing file.

Filling Rectangles

To fill a rectangle, you need only a brush, aside from the dimensions of the rectangle to paint. The method to use is *FillRectangle*, and the area to work on can be indicated using coordinates or a *RectangleF* structure.

```
g.FillRectangle(brush, area);
```

The brush is the object you use to paint the rectangle. GDI+ supports different types of brushes, including solid, gradient, and textured brushes. A solid brush fills the region with a uniform color; a gradient brush uses a dithered combination of two or more colors. Finally, a textured brush tiles the rectangle with the specified image. The following code snippet shows how to draw and fill a rectangle:

```
// Draw the border
Pen p = new Pen(Color.Black);
g.DrawRectangle(p, 0, 0, width, height);

// Fill the interior
Brush brInterior = new SolidBrush(Color.SkyBlue);
g.FillRectangle(brInterior, 1, 1, width-2, height-2);
```

GDI+ also provides a tailor-made method to draw the border of a rectangle. Instead of a brush, the *DrawRectangle* method takes a pen object.

A gradient is a special brush you use to fill a shape with a gradually changing color. GDI+ supports two breeds of gradients: linear and path gradients. A linear gradient is fully identified with two colors and two points. The actual filling varies from the starting color to the final color, as you move from the initial point to the final point. The *LinearGradientBrush* class implements the functionality of a linear gradient. The following code snippet shows how to create and fill a rectangle with a linear and horizontal gradient:

```
// Fill the interior using a gradient
Rectangle area = new Rectangle(0, 0, width, height);
LinearGradientBrush brInterior;
brInterior = new LinearGradientBrush(area, Color.SkyBlue,
    Color.AntiqueWhite, LinearGradientMode.Horizontal);
brInterior.Dispose();
p.Dispose();
```

In a linear gradient, the color changes linearly, but you can adjust how the color intensity varies from one edge of the gradient to the next. To do that, you use the *Blend* property to set arrays of color intensities and corresponding positions in a 0-1 range.

```
// Set intensities and relative positions
float[] relativeIntensities = {0.0f, 0.6f, 1.0f};
float[] relativePositions   = {0.0f, 0.1f, 1.0f};

// Create a Blend object and assign it to the brush
Blend blend = new Blend();
blend.Factors = relativeIntensities;
blend.Positions = relativePositions;
brInterior.Blend = blend;
```

The gradient will have three key intensity points, two of which are clearly the starting and the ending points of filling. The default blending for a linear gradient is expressed by the following code:

```
float[] relativeIntensities = {0.0f, 1.0f};
float[] relativePositions   = {0.0f, 1.0f};
```

The code just shown indicates that the minimum and maximum intensities are reached at the beginning and end of the filling. The code we looked at prior to this states that 60 percent (the value 0.6 in a 0-1 range) of the color transition must be accomplished within the first 10 percent of the area to cover (the value 0.1 in a 0-1 range). Figure 22-3 shows the effect of the code. The top rectangle shows the default gradient; the bottom rectangle shows what happens when blending is used.

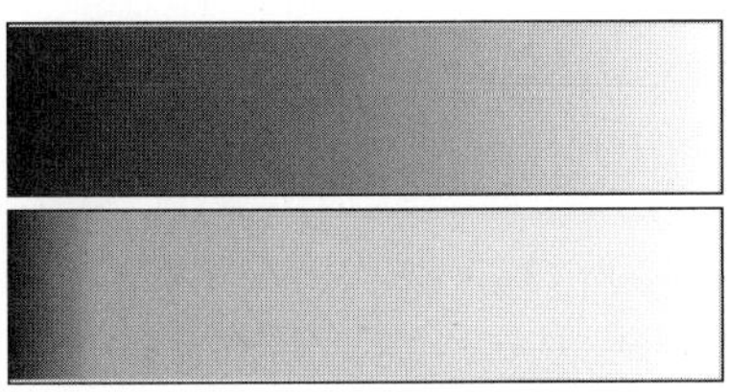

Figure 22-3 Gradient brushes with different settings for blending.

The third type of brush is the textured brush. A textured brush lets you fill a shape with a pattern stored in a bitmap. You can use a textured brush to draw lines, draw figures, and even write text.

```
Graphics g = this.CreateGraphics();
Image img = Image.FromFile("pattern.bmp");
TextureBrush brInterior = new TextureBrush(img);
g.FillRectangle(brInterior, area);
```

Drawing Text

The *DrawString* method on the *Graphics* object accepts the string to write, the font object, and the brush to color the text. Another block of arguments you can pass on to *DrawString* allows you to specify the rectangle within which the text should fit. You can decide the vertical and horizontal alignment and whether the text can exceed the assigned area or must be trimmed if too long. The *StringFormat* structure lets you set all these parameters in a single shot.

```
StringFormat sf = new StringFormat();
sf.Alignment = StringAlignment.Center;
sf.LineAlignment = StringAlignment.Center;

// Draw the text
Font f = new Font("Tahoma", 16);
g.DrawString("Hello, world", f, new SolidBrush(Color.White),
    new Rectangle(0, 0, width, height), sf);
```

GDI+ is much more than just these simple operations. Covering all the capabilities of GDI+ is beyond the goal of this book. A good resource to see GDI+ in action within the context of .NET applications is *Programming Microsoft Windows with C#,* by Charles Petzold (Microsoft Press, 2002).

Writing Images to Memory

As we already hinted at in Chapter 15, "ASP.NET Security," and Chapter 16, "Working with the File System," writing images—that is, creating disk files—from within an ASP.NET application might require some security adjustments. Normally, the ASP.NET worker process runs under the aegis of the user ASPNET account. In case of anonymous access with impersonation disabled—these are the default settings in ASP.NET—the worker process lends its own identity and security token to the thread that executes the user request of creating the file. Always with regard to the default scenario, an access denied exception is thrown because ASPNET doesn't normally have writing permissions on virtual directories.

To implement a file-based cache of images, you can create a new folder and give ASPNET, or any other account you use to run the application, full control over that folder. In this way, files can be created seamlessly. ASP.NET and

GDI+ provide an interesting alternative to writing files on disk. The dynamically generated image can be saved directly to the output stream in the needed image format or in a memory stream. (I'll say more about this in a moment.)

Supported Image Formats

GDI+ supports quite a few image formats, including JPEG, GIF, BMP, and PNG. The whole collection of image formats is in the *ImageFormat* structure. You can save a memory-resident *Bitmap* object to any of the supported formats by using one of the overloads of the *Save* method.

```
bmp.Save(outputStream, ImageFormat.Gif);
```

When you attempt to save an image to a stream or a disk file, the system attempts to locate an encoder for the requested format. The encoder is a GDI+ module that converts from the native format to the specified format. Note that the encoder is a piece of unmanaged code that lives in the underlying Win32 platform. For each save format, the *Save* method looks up the right encoder by using an internal method named *FindEncoder* and calls into another more general overload for the *Save* method.

```
// Can't call FindEncoder from ASP.NET code due to the
// protection level. FindEncoder is marked "internal" and
// is usable only within the same assembly where it is declared
bmp.Save(outputStream, ImageFormat.Gif.FindEncoder(), null);
```

Getting the encoder for a particular type is important because it can allow you to change settings for that type. For example, if you want to control the compression ratio of a dynamically created JPEG image, you must obtain the GDI+ encoder for the JPEGs. We'll return to the subject of encoders later in the "Controlling the Compression Ratio of JPEG Images" section.

Writing Copyright Notes on Images

The next example wraps up all the points we touched on. This example shows how to load an existing image, add some copyright notes, and serve the modified version to the user. In doing so, we'll load an image into a *Bitmap* object, obtain a *Graphics* for that bitmap, and use graphics primitives to write. When finished, we'll save the result to the page's output stream and indicate a particular MIME type.

The sample page that triggers the example is easily created, as shown in the following listing:

```
<html>
<title>Pro ASP.NET (Ch22)</title>
<body>
    <img id="picture" src="bluehills.aspx" />
</body>
</html>
```

The page contains no ASP.NET code and displays an image through an HTML <*img*> tag. The source of the image, though, is an .aspx resource with the same name as the target image but a different extension. The idea is that whenever you need an image.gif image, you reference an image.aspx page.

The server-side page is built around its *Page_Load* event handler. The physical path of the URL is translated into a JPG extension to obtain the file system path to an existing resource. Next, once it's ascertained that the file exists, the image is loaded into memory, processed, and returned to the user as a GIF.

```
void Page_Load(object sender, EventArgs e) {
    string msg = "Courtesy of 'Programming ASP.NET'";

    // The name of the image is same name of the page with jpg extension
    string file = Path.ChangeExtension(Request.PhysicalPath, ".jpg");

    if (File.Exists(file)) {
        Bitmap bmp = AddCopyright(file, msg);
        Response.ContentType = "image/gif";
        bmp.Save(Response.OutputStream, ImageFormat.Gif);
        bmp.Dispose();
    }
}
```

Note that the server-side page performs two different tasks indeed. First, it writes copyright text on the image canvas; next, it converts the original format (JPEG) into another format (GIF).

```
Bitmap AddCopyright(string file, string msg) {
    // Load the file and create the graphics
    Bitmap bmp = new Bitmap(file);
    Graphics g = Graphics.FromImage(bmp);

    // Define text alignment
    StringFormat strFmt = new StringFormat();
    strFmt.Alignment = StringAlignment.Center;

    // Write the topmost note, horizontally centered
    SolidBrush topColor = new SolidBrush(Color.Black);
    Rectangle area = new Rectangle(0, 0, bmp.Width, bmp.Height);
    Font f = new Font("Verdana", 8);
    g.DrawString(msg, f, topColor, area, strFmt);
    topColor.Dispose();
    f.Dispose();

    // Create brushes for the bottom writing
    // (green text on black background)
    SolidBrush btmForeColor = new SolidBrush(Color.PaleGreen);
    SolidBrush btmBackColor = new SolidBrush(Color.Black);

    // To calculate writing coordinates, obtain the size of the text
```

```
        // given font typeface and size
        Font btmFont = new Font("Verdana", 3);
        string author = "written by Dino Esposito";
        SizeF textSize = new SizeF();
        textSize = g.MeasureString(author, btmFont);

        // Calculate the output rectangle and fill
        float x = ((float) bmp.Width-textSize.Width-3);
        float y = ((float) bmp.Height-textSize.Height-3);
        float w = ((float) x + textSize.Width);
        float h = ((float) y + textSize.Height);
        RectangleF textArea = new RectangleF(x, y, w, h);
        g.FillRectangle(btmBackColor, textArea);

        // Draw the text and free resources
        g.DrawString(author, btmFont, btmForeColor, textArea);
        btmForeColor.Dispose();
        btmBackColor.Dispose();
        btmFont.Dispose();
        g.Dispose();

        return bmp;
    }
```

Figure 22-4 shows the final results.

Figure 22-4 A server-resident image has been modified before display.

It is worth noting that the text and copyright note is part of the image the user receives. If the user saves the picture by using the Save Picture As menu from the browser, the text and copyright will be saved with the image.

Generating Thumbnails

GDI+ also provides other handy facilities, such as the ability to generate thumbnails. Although browsers have no particular problem stretching and shrinking images to make them fit into the assigned space, if a small-sized image is needed there's no reason to return a big one. In doing so, you pay a double price: first you consume more bandwidth, and second you require the browser to do extra work to shape up the image.

A Web site that makes its bread and butter from images will probably conserve predefined thumbnails for each displayable image. In other circumstances, a thumbnail can be generated on the fly using the *GetThumbnailImage* method on the *Bitmap* class.

```
Bitmap GetThumbnail(string file) {
    Bitmap bmp = new Bitmap(file);
    Bitmap newImg = (Bitmap) bmp.GetThumbnailImage(bmp.Width/3,
        bmp.Height/3, null, IntPtr.Zero);
    return newImg;
}
```

You decide the scale factor to use, and you can also indicate fixed measures. Pay attention, though, that your width and height values are taken as absolute values, meaning that no aspect ratio is guaranteed if your parameters don't ensure that.

Controlling the Compression Ratio of JPEG Images

JPEG images are the result of a lossy compression algorithm. To save more space, a JPEG compressed image discards some raw information during the compression. A decompressed image, therefore, is different from the original. However, because the JPEG format is mostly used to store photographic images, the effective loss often passes unnoticed to the human eye. JPEGs store 24 bits per pixel and are capable of displaying 16 million colors, but they don't support transparency or animation. The level of compression in JPEG images is configurable. You should note that higher compression levels result in smaller files, but only because more data is discarded and therefore lost. Subsequently, the quality of the decompressed image might be bad. It's hard to indicate a compression ratio that fits every scenario. In general, a 15 to 1 ratio is acceptable and generates an imperceptible loss of data. This doesn't mean you can't compress at 30 to 1 with good results.

Choosing the compression ratio for a JPEG image using GDI+ is a bit tricky because you need to deal with the JPEG encoder, which is not easily found. To find the encoder for a particular image format, you must loop through the collection of supported encoders and find one whose *MimeType* property matches that of the type you're interested in.

```
// Search for the JPEG encoder
string mimeType = "image/jpeg";
ImageCodecInfo[] encoders;
ImageCodecInfo jpegEncoder = null;

// Loop through all GDI+ encoders
encoders = ImageCodecInfo.GetImageEncoders();
for(int j=0; j < encoders.Length; j++) {
    if(encoders[j].MimeType == mimeType)
        jpegEncoder = encoders[j];
}
```

Once the encoder has been found, you set some of its parameters. In particular, you create an encoder parameter that affects the quality of the final image.

```
// Create an encoding parameter for the expected quality
EncoderParameter paramRatio;
paramRatio = new EncoderParameter(Encoder.Quality, ratio);
```

The ratio value you pass to the constructor indicates the quality you want for the image. It is not a mere compression ratio. The higher the value, the better the quality and the larger the size of the image.

```
// Add the just created encoding param to the collection of
// parameters for the encoder
EncoderParameters jpegParams;
jpegParams = new EncoderParameters(1);    // only one param
jpegParams.Param[0] = paramRatio;

// Send the image
Response.ContentType = "image/jpeg";
bmp.Save(Response.OutputStream, jpegEncoder, jpegParams);
bmp.Dispose();
```

Saving to Larger Formats

For quite some time, using the aforementioned techniques I had been able to save images only to GIF and JPEG formats. Whenever I tried to save as the BMP, TIFF, or PNG formats from within an ASP.NET application, I regularly encountered a GDI+ generic error message. The exception was always raised as the code attempted to write to the stream. The GDI+ unmanaged code caught some sort of anomalous situation and bubbled the exception up to ASP.NET as an *ExternalException* error. This resulted in what was frankly not a very helpful error message.

After a few unfortunate attempts, I decided to make one last attempt using a different approach. I used an intermediate *MemoryStream* object to hold the image bits and *BinaryWrite* to flush the response back to the browser. Well, believe it or not, the pair *MemoryStream* and *BinaryWrite* did the trick.

```
Response.ContentType = "image/png";
MemoryStream ms = new MemoryStream();
bmp.Save(ms, ImageFormat.Png);
Response.BinaryWrite(ms.GetBuffer());
```

My hunch is that the GDI+ exception has something to do with the size of the images—PNG, TIFF, and BMP images are normally 10 times larger at a minimum than JPEG and GIF images. However, this is just a supposition not supported by clear evidence. To add one more thrill to this winning story, let me say that *BinaryWrite* doesn't perform any special trick such as buffering or caching data to minimize the memory footprint. The behavior of *BinaryWrite*, in fact, is all in this somehow trivial pseudo-code:

```
public void BinaryWrite(byte[] buffer) {
    OutputStream.Write(buffer, 0, (int) buffer.Length);
}
```

An even slightly faster code can be obtained by omitting the call to *BinaryWrite* and using the *WriteTo* method of the *MemoryStream* class.

```
Response.ContentType = "image/png";
MemoryStream ms = new MemoryStream();
bmp.Save(ms, ImageFormat.Png);
ms.WriteTo(Response.OutputStream);
```

Incidentally, I've received several messages from readers lately about this point and such undocumented behavior. I know that if you use an intermediate *MemoryStream* object it works. If you know why, please, let me know!

The *MemoryStream* Class

Because the *MemoryStream* class proved so helpful in saving large image files through the ASP.NET response stream, it might be worthwhile to take a closer look inside it. The *MemoryStream* class represents a stream of data completely held in memory. When you instantiate the class, it's normally created with an expandable capacity initially set to zero. Typical methods of a stream class are available to read, seek, and write content. In the end, *MemoryStream* is just a nice stream-like wrapper for an array of unsigned bytes. The *GetBuffer* method simply returns the contents as a byte array. The capacity of the current stream automatically increases when you use the *SetLength* method to set the length to a value larger than the capacity of the current stream.

The encapsulated data is directly accessible in memory at any time. Such memory-resident streams can reduce the need for temporary buffers and files in an application. More importantly, the *Bitmap* class accepts a *MemoryStream* object as a constructor argument, meaning that a graphic object can be created using the bytes stored in a memory stream.

Building Chart Generator Pages

Let's put the various pieces of the puzzle together and build a sample page that exploits the aforementioned techniques to generate and display graphics charts. To start, build a page that contains a couple of child *<img>* tags and make each tag point to an ASP.NET page that returns a chart image.

```
<table>
    <tr><td><img runat="server" id="bar"></td></tr>
    <tr><td><img runat="server" id="pie"></td></tr>
</table>
```

The *<img>* tags are configured during the page loading to point to a particular URL. Dynamic binding is needed to pass required arguments to the page. Note that instead of using server *HtmlImage* controls, you could more effectively use data-bound expressions. The following code snippet shows how the image controls are actually initialized:

```
void Page_Load(object sender, EventArgs e) {
    if (!IsPostBack) {
        ddYears.Items.Add("1998");
        ddYears.Items.Add("1997");
        ddYears.Items.Add("1996");
    }
    bar.Src = "__BarChartGen.aspx?Year=" + ddYears.SelectedItem.Text;
    pie.Src = "__PieChartGen.aspx?Year=" + ddYears.SelectedItem.Text;
}
```

The chart generator pages include all the logic necessary to fetch data and create the chart. In general, you should pass any required argument, including data, through the query string.

Drawing a Pie Chart

Once you hold the data to create the chart, drawing a pie chart is a matter of running a couple of loops. To draw a wedge, you need the sweep angle, the color, and the whole area of the pie. The loop begins with a sweep angle of zero and is increased, at any step, by the angle that is proportional to the value to represent.

```
// Get the total of sales from the DataTable
float maxValue = Convert.ToSingle(data.Compute("Sum(sales)", ""));

// Calculate the sweep angle for the value to represent in the wedge
float sweep = Convert.ToSingle(value) / maxValue * 360;
```

To draw the wedge, you use the *FillPie* method, whereas the *DrawEllipse* method can be used to give it a border. Both methods are exposed by the *Graphics* object.

```
g.FillPie(new SolidBrush(wedgeColor), rcChart, angle, sweep);
g.DrawEllipse(new Pen(Color.DarkGray, 1), rcChart);
```

If you want to make things look finer, add a shadow. Because of the lack of specific support from the graphics system, the shadow can be obtained only by drawing the wedge many times with a different offset. To improve the graphics result, we also use a hatch brush. The following listing shows the source code that draws a pie chart with a 3D shadow:

```
for(int j=ShadowDepth; j>0; j--)
{
    for(int i=0; i<dt.Rows.Count; i++)
    {
        // Angle for the value
        float sweep = Convert.ToSingle(dt.Rows[i]["Sales"])/maxValue*360;

        // Pick up a color
        wedgeColor = colors[i];

        // Draw the shadow
        Rectangle shadowArea = new Rectangle(area.Location, area.Size);
        shadowArea.Offset(j, j);
        g.FillPie(new HatchBrush(HatchStyle.Percent50, wedgeColor),
            shadowArea, angle, sweep);

        // Draw the wedge
        g.FillPie(new SolidBrush(wedgeColor), area, angle, sweep);
        g.DrawEllipse(new Pen(Color.DarkGray, 1), area);

        // Calculate the center of the wedge to use later to draw labels
        Point center = GetPoint(angle + sweep/2, area.Width, area.Height);
        center.X = (int) ((area.Right - area.Left) / 2 + center.X) / 2;
        center.Y = (int) ((area.Bottom - area.Top) / 2 + center.Y) / 2;
        centers[i] = center;

        // Increase the sweep angle for the next iteration
        angle += sweep;
    }
}
```

For pie charts, choosing the wedge color and drawing a descriptive label are two nontrivial problems. Choosing the color, in particular, is a relatively simple instance of a complex problem—the map coloring problem. It's been proven that you never need more than four colors to fill a map so that adjacent regions have different colors. In this case, two colors might be enough, but not if the total number of wedges is odd. Three colors would suffice, but that amount doesn't ensure a good graphical result. A better approach is defining a relatively large subset of colors, say 10 colors, and iterating through them, paying attention to pick up a color that has not been used for the previous wedge or the first wedge. In case of conflict, you resort to an extra color not included in the list or just pick up a nonconflicting color from the same list.

To draw the label within the wedge, you need to know the point at the center of the area. This requires just a little bit of trigonometry. Assuming that the pie is a circle, you obtain the coordinates of the point using the following formulas:

```
// width is the width of the smallest rectangle that contains the pie
int radius = width / 2;

// Get the radiant. The variable angle is angle of wedge
double rad = Math.PI * 2 * angle / 360;

// Get the coordinates of the point, including an offset
Point pt = new Point();
pt.X = (int) (radius * Math.Cos(rad)) + radius;
pt.Y = (int) (radius * Math.Sin(rad)) + radius;
```

The point you obtain in this way is located on the arc that represents the pie wedge. To move it to the center of the wedge, do the following:

```
pt.X = (int) ((rcChart.Right - rcChart.Left) / 2 + pt.X) / 2;
pt.Y = (int) ((rcChart.Bottom - rcChart.Top) / 2 + pt.Y) / 2;
centers[i] = pt;
```

The center is calculated during the generation of the pie, but no label is drawn at this time. The points are stored in an array and used to render text later. Because labels could likely exceed the space of the wedge, drawing them within the loop would truncate the text. For this reason, we draw the labels only when the pie has been created.

```
for(int i=0; i<dt.Rows.Count; i++)
{
    g.DrawString(dt.Rows[i]["Employee"].ToString(),
        new Font("Tahoma", 8),
        new SolidBrush(Color.Black),
        centers[i].X, centers[i].Y);
}
```

Figure 22-5 shows the final results.

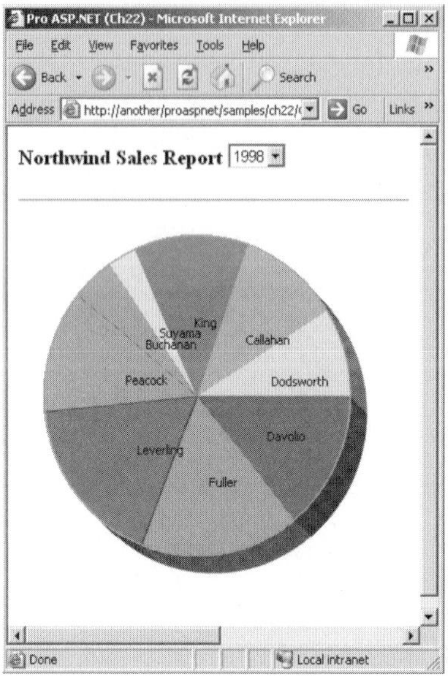

Figure 22-5 A dynamically generated 3D pie chart with inside labels.

Drawing a Bar Chart

Drawing a bar chart is slightly simpler than drawing a pie chart because you don't have to deal with sweep angles, radius, and other trigonometry tidbits. A bar chart is made of two labels and a rectangle to fill. The top label represents the value; the bottom label shows the legend for the chart.

Assuming that all the x,y coordinates for the various elements have been set up, the following code demonstrates how to create a 3D-like bar chart with a shadow effect:

```
// Draw the top label with the value
g.DrawString(String.Format("{0:c}", dt.Rows[i]["Sales"]),
    new Font("Tahoma", 8), new SolidBrush(Color.Blue),
    xBarPos, yCaptionPos);

// Calculate the bar
Rectangle rcBar = new Rectangle(xBarPos, yBarPos, barWidth, barHeight);

// Draw the shadow
Rectangle rcShadow = new Rectangle(rcBar.Location, rcBar.Size);
rcShadow.Offset(j, -j);
g.FillRectangle(new HatchBrush(HatchStyle.Percent50, Color.Orange),
    rcShadow);

// Draw the bar
```

```
g.FillRectangle(new LinearGradientBrush(rcBar, Color.Orange, Color.Yellow,
    LinearGradientMode.Horizontal), rcBar);

// Draw the bottom bar
Font fnt = new Font("Tahoma", 8, FontStyle.Bold);
g.DrawString(dt.Rows[i]["Employee"].ToString(), fnt,
    new SolidBrush(Color.Blue), xBarPos, yBarBottom);
```

The final result is shown in Figure 22-6.

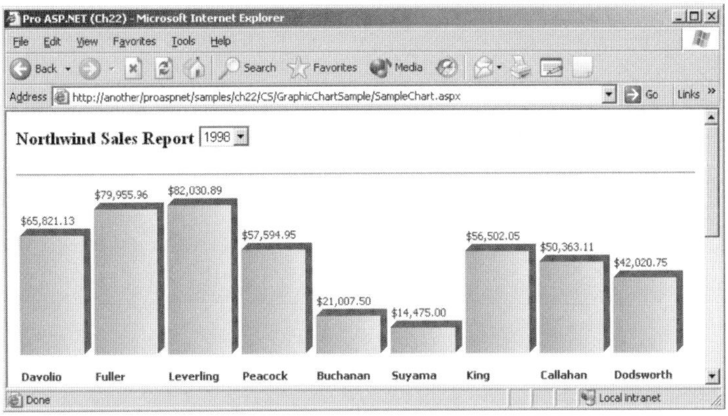

Figure 22-6 A dynamically generated 3D bar chart with top and bottom labels.

Conclusion

These days, it's unquestionable that images are fundamental elements of the Web. They aren't part of the infrastructure and don't contribute to the functionality of sites, yet they are a critical element for the success of the Web as an extremely powerful and expressive medium. In spite of the key role images play, the HTML language doesn't provide support that goes beyond the *<img>* tag. The *<img>* tag can be bound only to a URL and requires an extra roundtrip for the download.

If you bind the *<img>* tag to an .aspx page, you can gain some level of flexibility and use any needed logic to generate the image dynamically or to read it out of a database. To generate an image dynamically, you simply set the content type of the HTTP response and flush the bits of the image to the output stream. In ASP.NET, the process of generating images is extremely simplified and empowered with the addition of GDI+.

GDI+ is the graphics library of Windows XP and has been made available for other 32-bit and 64-bit Windows platforms. In the .NET Framework, GDI+ is offered as a set of managed wrapper classes that define drawing surfaces and tools for you to create images algorithmically.

In this chapter, we demonstrated various techniques to edit and create images and serve them to a Web browser. In particular, we discussed how to add watermarks and copyright notes on existing images, how to extract images out of the BLOB fields of a database, and how to create images dynamically. The typical example of a dynamically generated image is the chart. We created a couple of charts—3D pie charts and bar charts. An interesting follow-up for chart generators can be found in the ASP.NET Starter Kits available at *http://www.asp.net*.

In the next chapter, we'll analyze HTTP handlers and modules, which among other things, can be used to generate images even more effectively than .aspx pages.

Resources

- *Programming Microsoft Windows with C#*, by Charles Petzold (Microsoft Press, 2002)
- *GDI+ Programming in C# and VB.NET*, by Nick Symmonds (APress, 2002)
- Generate and Modify Images with GDI+ (*http://www.devx.com/dotnet/Article/10031*)
- Modify Image Data (*http://www.fawcette.com/vsm/2003_01/magazine/columns/aspnet*)
- KB 322796—HOW TO: Pass a BLOB as a Parameter to an Oracle Package by Using the .NET Managed Provider for Oracle
- KB 317043—HOW TO: Read and Write a File to and from a BLOB Column by Using Chunking in ADO.NET and Visual C# .NET

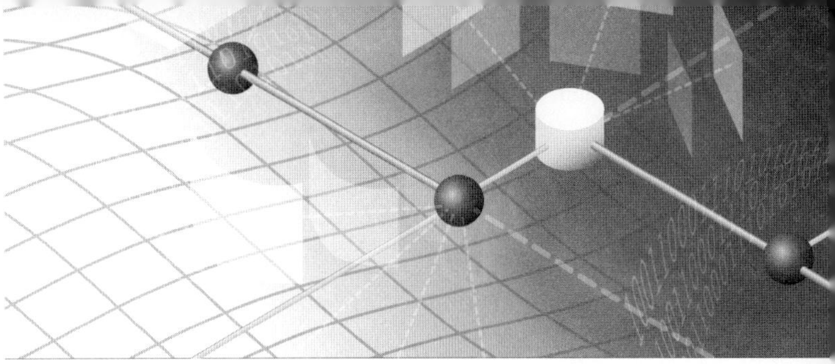

23

HTTP Handlers and Modules

Well done is better than well said.

—Benjamin Franklin

In various passages throughout this book, I've mentioned HTTP modules and HTTP handlers and introduced them as fundamental pieces of the ASP.NET architecture. HTTP handlers and modules are truly the building blocks of the .NET Web platform. While a request for a page or a Web service is being processed, it passes through a pipeline of HTTP modules, such as the authentication module and the session module, and is then processed by a single HTTP handler. After the handler has processed the request, the request flows back through the pipeline of HTTP modules and is finally transformed into HTML code for the browser.

An HTTP handler is the component that actually takes care of serving the request. It is an instance of a class that implements the *IHttpHandler* interface. The *ProcessRequest* method of the interface is the central console that governs the processing of the request. For example, the *Page* class implements the *IHttpHandler* interface, and its *ProcessRequest* method is responsible for loading and saving the view state and for firing the events such as *Init*, *Load*, *PreRender*, and the like.

ASP.NET maps each incoming HTTP request to a particular HTTP handler. A special breed of component—named the *HTTP handler factory*—provides the infrastructure for creating the physical instance of the handler to service the request. For example, the *PageHandlerFactory* class parses the source code of the requested .aspx resource and returns a compiled instance of the class that represents the page. An HTTP handler is designed to process one or more URL extensions. Handlers can be given an application or machine scope, meaning that they can process the assigned extensions within the context of the current application or all applications installed on the machine.

HTTP modules are classes that implement the *IHttpModule* interface and handle runtime events. There are two types of public events that a module can deal with. They are the events raised by *HttpApplication* (including asynchronous events) and events raised by other HTTP modules. For example, the *SessionStateModule* is provided by ASP.NET to supply session state services to an application. It fires the *End* and *Start* events that other modules can handle through the familiar *Session_End* and *Session_Start* signatures.

HTTP handlers and HTTP modules have the same functionality as ISAPI extensions and ISAPI filters, respectively, but with a much simpler programming model. ASP.NET allows you to create custom handlers and custom modules. Before we get into this rather advanced aspect of Web programming, a review of the Internet Information Services (IIS) extensibility model is in order because this model determines what modules and handlers can do and what they cannot do.

Quick Overview of the IIS Extensibility API

A Web server is primarily a server application that can be contacted using a bunch of Internet protocols such as HTTP, File Transfer Protocol (FTP), Network News Transfer Protocol (NNTP), and the Simple Mail Transfer Protocol (SMTP). IIS—the Web server included with the Windows operating system—is no exception.

A Web server also provides a documented API for enhancing and customizing the server's capabilities. Historically speaking, the first of these extension APIs was the Common Gateway Interface (CGI). A CGI module is a brand new application that is spawned from the Web server to service a request. Nowadays CGI applications are almost never used in modern Web applications because they require a new process for each HTTP request. As you can easily understand, this approach is rather inadequate for high-volume Web sites and poses severe scalability issues. IIS supports CGI applications, but you seldom exploit this feature unless you have serious backward compatibility issues. More recent versions of Web servers supply an alternative and more efficient model to extend the capabilities of the module. In IIS, this alternative model takes the form of the Internet Server Application Programming Interface (ISAPI).

The ISAPI Model

When the ISAPI model is used, instead of starting a new process for each request, IIS loads an ISAPI component—namely, a Win32 DLL—into its own process. Next, it calls a well-known entry point on the DLL to serve the request. The ISAPI component stays loaded until IIS is shut down and can service requests without any further impact on the Web server activity. The downside to such a model is that because components are loaded within the Web server process, a single faulty component can tear down the whole server and all installed applications. Starting with IIS 4.0, though, some countermeasures have been taken to alleviate this problem. As a result, while installing a Web application, you can control the protection level through the dialog box shown in Figure 23-1.

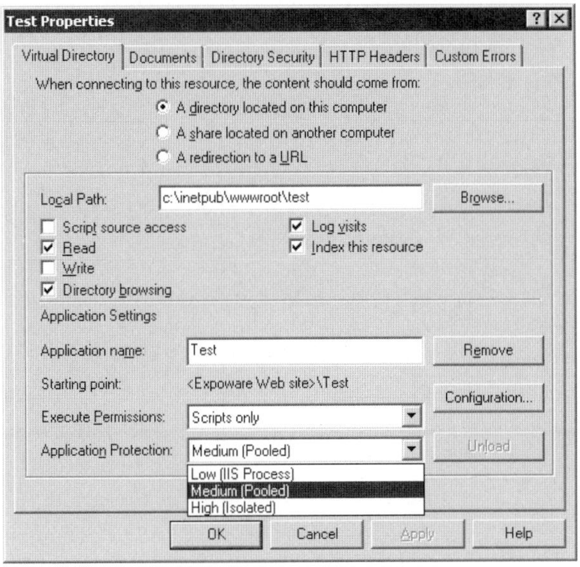

Figure 23-1 Configuring the protection level of a Web application in IIS 5.0.

If you choose a low protection, the application (and its extensions) will be run within the Web server process (Inetinfo.exe). If you choose medium protection, applications will be pooled together and hosted by an instance of a different process (Dllhost.exe). If you chooses high protection, each application set to High will be hosted in its own individual process (Dllhost.exe). Figure 23-2 shows the same dialog box in IIS 6.0 and Windows Server 2003.

As we mentioned in Chapter 2, Web applications under IIS 6.0 are grouped in pools and the choice you can make is whether you want to join an existing pool or create a new one. (See Figure 23-3.)

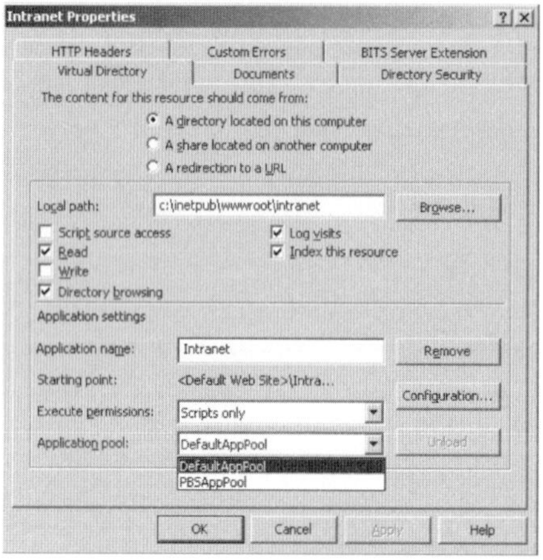

Figure 23-2 Configuring the protection level of Web applications in IIS 6.0 under Windows Server 2003.

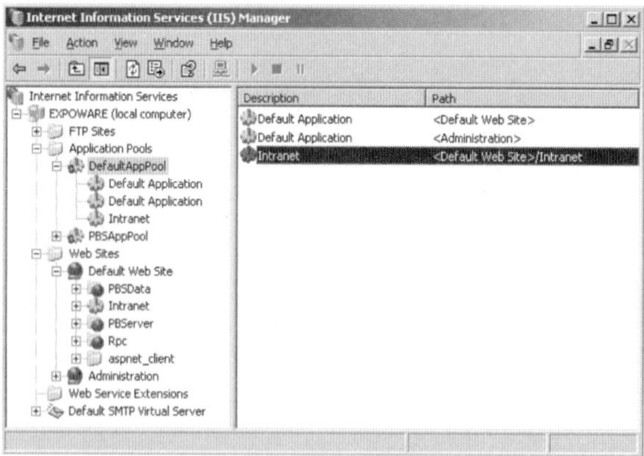

Figure 23-3 A view of the application pools in IIS 6.0.

Illustrious Children of the ISAPI Model

Aside from performance and security considerations, the ISAPI model has another key drawback—the programming model. An ISAPI component represents a compiled piece of code—a Win32 DLL—that retrieves data and writes HTML code to an output console. It has to be developed using C or C++, it should generate multithreaded code, and it must be written with extreme care because of the impact that bugs or runtime failures can have.

Microsoft attempted to encapsulate the ISAPI logic in the Microsoft Foundation Classes (MFC) but, although creditable, that effort didn't pay off very well. Active Server Pages (ASP), the predecessor of ASP.NET, is indeed an example of a well-done ISAPI application. ASP is implemented as an ISAPI DLL (named asp.dll) registered to handle HTTP requests with an .asp extension. The internal code of the ASP ISAPI parses the code of the requested resource, executes any embedded script code, and builds the page for the browser.

Any functionality built on top of IIS must be coded using the ISAPI model. ASP and ASP.NET are no exceptions. The ASP.NET worker process—the module that hosts the common language runtime (CLR) and the runtime pipeline (see Chapter 2)—is an executable connected to IIS by an ISAPI component—the aspnet_isapi.dll. When a request for .aspx or .asmx resources comes in, IIS passes the control to the ISAPI module which, in turn, hands the request to the worker process. As of this writing, to extend IIS you can only write a Win32 DLL with a well-known set of entry points.

Structure of ISAPI Components

An ISAPI extension is invoked through a URL that ends with the name of the DLL library that implements the function, as shown in the following URL:

```
http://www.contoso.com/apps/hello.dll
```

The DLL must export a couple of functions—*GetExtensionVersion* and *HttpExtensionProc*. The *GetExtensionVersion* function sets the version and the name of the ISAPI server extension. When the extension is loaded, the *GetExtensionVersion* function is the first function to be called. *GetExtensionVersion* is invoked only once and can be used to initialize any needed variables. The function is expected to return true if everything goes fine. In case of errors, the function should return false and the Web server will abort loading the DLL and put a message in the system log.

The core of the ISAPI component is represented by the *HttpExtensionProc* function. The function receives basic HTTP information regarding the request (for example, the query string and the headers), performs the expected action, and prepares the response to send back to the browser.

> **Important** Certain handy programming facilities, such as the session object, are abstractions the ISAPI programming model lacks. The ISAPI model is a lower-level programming model than, say, ASP or ASP.NET scripting.

The ISAPI programming model is made of two types of components—ISAPI extensions and ISAPI filters.

ISAPI Extensions

ISAPI extensions are the IIS in-process counterpart of CGI applications. As mentioned, an ISAPI extension is a DLL that is loaded in the memory space occupied by IIS or another host application. Because it is a DLL, only one instance of the ISAPI extension needs to be loaded at a time. On the downside, the ISAPI extension must be thread-safe so that multiple client requests can be served simultaneously. ISAPI extensions work in much the same way as an ASP page does. It takes any information about the HTTP request and prepares a valid HTTP response.

Because the ISAPI extension is made of compiled code, it must be recompiled and reloaded at any change. If the DLL is loaded in the Web server's memory, this means that the Web server must be stopped. If the DLL is loaded in the context of a separate process, only that process must be stopped. Of course, when an external process is used, the extension doesn't work as fast as it could when hosted in-process, but at least it doesn't jeopardize the stability of IIS.

ISAPI Filters

While ISAPI extensions are the counterpart of CGI applications, ISAPI filters can be considered a relatively new concept in Web server extensibility. ISAPI filters are components that intercept specific server events before the server itself handles them. Upon loading, the filter indicates what event notifications it will handle. If any of these events occur, the filter can process them or pass them on to other filters.

You can use ISAPI filters to provide custom authentication techniques or to automatically redirect requests based on HTTP headers sent by the client. Filters are a delicate gear in the IIS machinery. They can facilitate applications but also degrade performance if not written carefully. Filters, in fact, can only run in-process. With IIS 5.0, filters can be loaded for the Web server as a whole or for specific Web sites.

ISAPI filters can accomplish tasks such as implementing custom authentication schemes, compression, encryption, logging, and request analysis. The ability to examine, and if necessary modify, both incoming and outgoing streams of data makes ISAPI filters very powerful and flexible. This last sentence gives the measure of the strength of ISAPI filters but also indicates the potential weakness of them.

Writing HTTP Handlers

ASP.NET can be seen as a microcosm within the universe of IIS. The point of contact between the two worlds is the aspnet_isapi.dll component. The component is a Win32 DLL acting as an ISAPI extension. It handles requests for .aspx and .asmx resources (and a few more indeed) and then sets up the ASP.NET pipeline to service them. The ASP.NET pipeline, hosted by the ASP.NET worker process aspnet_wp.exe, consists of managed code and implements its own extensibility model made of HTTP handlers and HTTP modules. Although HTTP handlers look like ISAPI extensions, and HTTP modules are the managed counterpart of ISAPI filters, the resemblance makes sense only at a high level of abstraction, as Figure 23-4 shows.

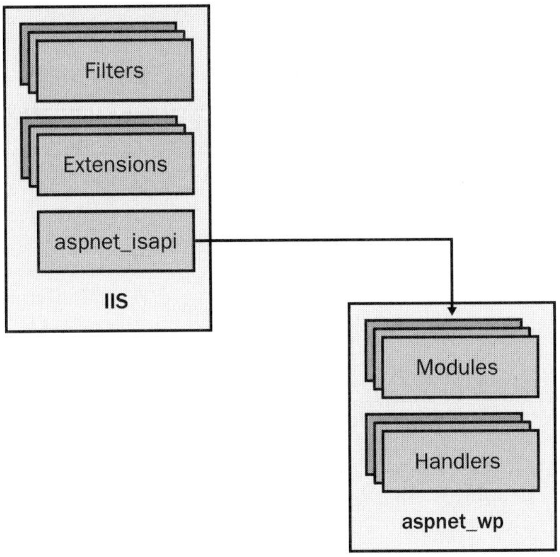

Figure 23-4 ISAPI components and HTTP handlers and HTTP modules.

HTTP handlers and HTTP modules never directly interact with IIS. They are made of managed code, live within the space of the ASP.NET worker process, and can only affect ASP.NET applications. For example, using an HTTP module, you can't implement a custom authentication scheme for an ASP application. Likewise, if you want to define a custom type of resource (say, a family of URLs with the .sqlx suffix), you can use HTTP handlers as long as you bind it to aspnet_isapi. Any request to an .sqlx resource will be funneled to aspnet_isapi and from there to your handler.

An HTTP handler can work either synchronously or operate in an asynchronous way. When synchronous, a handler doesn't return until it's done with the HTTP request. An asynchronous handler, on the other hand, launches a potentially lengthy process and returns immediately after.

Conventional ISAPI extensions and filters must be registered within the IIS metabase. In contrast, HTTP handlers must be registered with aspnet_isapi using the application's or machine's configuration file.

The *IHttpHandler* Interface

Want to take the splash and dive into HTTP handler programming? Well, your first step is getting the hang of the *IHttpHandler* interface. An HTTP handler is just a managed class that implements that interface. More exactly, a synchronous HTTP handler implements the *IHttpHandler* interface; an asynchronous HTTP handler, on the other hand, implements the *IHttpAsyncHandler* interface. Let's tackle synchronous handlers first.

The contract of the *IHttpHandler* interface defines the actions that a handler needs to take to process an HTTP request synchronously. In the .NET Framework, three classes implement the interface, as shown in Table 23-1.

Table 23-1 Classes that Implement *IHttpHandler*

Handler	Description
HttpApplication	Base class for ASP.NET applications that implements both the synchronous and asynchronous interfaces. Instances of this class are created only by the ASP.NET runtime, not by user code, and are used to process all the requests for the application, but one at a time. Note that although the class implements *IHttpHandler*, it always serves requests asynchronously. The implementation of *IHttpHandler* doesn't result in operative code.
HttpRemotingHandler	Implements an ASP.NET handler that forwards requests to the remoting HTTP channel. This handler is registered to process requests for URLs that end with .soap or .rem. These are fake resources that identify a method call on a remote object when IIS is used as the .NET Remoting application host.
Page	Represents an .aspx file requested from a server that hosts an ASP.NET application.

A noticeable absence in this table is that of a class that supports Web services. The reason such classes don't appear in the table is that they are nonpublic. However, Web services calls are handled by a bunch of internal handler classes—*SyncSessionHandler* and *AsyncSessionHandler*, which manage session-aware Web services, and *SyncSessionlessHandler* and *AsyncSessionlessHandler*, which serve requests for sessionless Web services.

Members of the *IHttpHandler* Interface

The *IHttpHandler* interface defines only two members—*ProcessRequest* and *IsReusable*, as shown in Table 23-2. *ProcessRequest* is a method whereas *IsReusable* is a Boolean property.

Table 23-2 Members of the *IHttpHandler* Interface

Member	Description
IsReusable	Gets a Boolean value indicating whether another request can use the current instance of the HTTP handler.
ProcessRequest	The method enables processing of HTTP requests.

The *IsReusable* property on the *Page* class returns false, meaning that a new instance of the HTTP request is needed to serve a page request. The *ProcessRequest* method has the following signature:

```
void ProcessRequest(HttpContext context);
```

It takes the context of the request as the input and ensures that the request is serviced. In case of synchronous handlers, when *ProcessRequest* returns, the output is ready for being forwarded to the client.

ASP.NET Request Processing

Now that we know a little more about HTTP handlers, it would be useful to look back at some of the topics we covered in Chapter 2—in particular, the steps involved in the actual processing of an ASP.NET request. The entry point in the ASP.NET pipeline is the *HttpRuntime* object. The class has a static method named *ProcessRequest*, which drives the execution of all ASP.NET requests.

The *ProcessRequest* method receives information about the request packed in an *HttpWorkerRequest* class. This abstract class defines the base worker methods and enumerations used by ASP.NET managed code. In most cases, user code will not deal with *HttpWorkerRequest* directly but access request and response data through the *HttpRequest* and *HttpResponse* classes. However, if your code implements its own hosting environment, it will need to extend this class to call the *ProcessRequest* method. (We'll cover ASP.NET hosting in the next chapter.)

The HTTP runtime first updates the performance counter and then processes the request. Processing a request entails performing the following steps.

1. **Creating the HTTP context** The worker request class is used as an argument to instantiate the *HttpContext* class for the request. When this happens, the objects behind the *Request* and *Response* intrinsics are created and populated with the posted data. The output stream is not yet initialized.

2. **First request for the resource** If this is the first time the resource is accessed in the application, some preliminary tests occur. In particular, the configuration data is read, changes to the files are

detected and properly handled, and assemblies are loaded. Generally, the environment is set up for execution. For example, culture information is associated with the thread serving the request and the output stream is initialized.

3. **Obtaining the handler** The application factory class is used to resolve the request and return the HTTP handler to process it. The application factory figures out the type of the object (that is, the name of the class that implements the page) and the assembly and creates an instance of it. By design, the returned object is a synchronous or asynchronous HTTP handler.
4. **Processing the request** The HTTP runtime invokes the *ProcessRequest* method on the handler if the handler is synchronous. It calls the *BeginProcessRequest* method if the handler is asynchronous. In the asynchronous case, it also supplies an adequate asynchronous callback function to detect the completion of the operation and finish the request.
5. **Finalizing the request** At this time, the output generated for the request is flushed to the response stream. If any exception was thrown, the error message is reported to the user. Finally, the performance counter is updated with information about the time it took to complete the request.

In brief, HTTP handlers are just what their name clearly states—managed components designed to handle HTTP requests and carry them out. HTTP handlers are invoked whatever the type of the requested resources is, as long as IIS routes the request to aspnet_isapi. Now let's examine the structure of a very simple synchronous HTTP handler.

A Very Simple HTTP Handler

As mentioned earlier, an HTTP handler is simply a class that implements the *IHttpHandler* interface. The output for the request is built within the *ProcessRequest* method, as shown in the following code:

```
using System.Web;
namespace HandlerExample
{
    public class SimpleHttpHandler : IHttpHandler
    {
        // Override the ProcessRequest method
        public void ProcessRequest(HttpContext context) {
            context.Response.Write("<H1>Hello, I'm an HTTP handler</H1>");
        }
```

```
        // Override the IsReusable property
        public bool IsReusable {
            get { return true; }
        }
    }
}
```

We need an entry point to be able to call the method. In this context, an entry point into the code is nothing more than an HTTP endpoint—that is, a public URL. The URL must be a unique name that IIS and the HTTP runtime map to this code. The mapping between an HTTP handler and a Web server resource is established through the web.config file.

```
<configuration>
    <system.web>
        <httpHandlers>
            <add verb="*" path="myHandler.aspx"
                type="HandlerExample.SimpleHttpHandler,SimpleHandler"/>
        </httpHandlers>
    </system.web>
</configuration>
```

The *<httpHandlers>* section lists the handlers available for the current application. If you enter the settings just shown in the machine.config file, you will register the myHandler.aspx URL, which is callable from within all Web applications in the machine. These settings indicate that any incoming requests for myHandler.aspx must be handled by the specified HTTP handler. The URL myHandler.aspx doesn't have to be a physical resource; it's simply a public resource identifier. The type attribute references the class and assembly that contains the handler. If you invoke the myHandler.aspx URL, you obtain the results shown in Figure 23-5.

Figure 23-5 A sample HTTP handler that answers requests for myHandler.aspx.

The technique discussed here is the quickest and simplest way of putting an HTTP handler to work, but there is more to know about registration of HTTP handlers and there are more options to exploit. Now let's consider a more complex example of an HTTP handler.

A Synchronous HTTP Handler for Quick Data Reports

With its relatively simple programming model, HTTP handlers give you a means of interacting with the low-level request and response services of IIS. In the previous example, we only returned constant text and made no use of the request information. In the next example, we'll configure the handler to intercept and process only requests of a particular type and generate the output based on the contents of the requested resource.

The idea is to build an HTTP handler for custom .sqlx resources. A SQLX file is an XML document that represents a SQL query. The handler grabs the information about the query, executes it, and finally returns the result set formatted as a grid. Figure 23-6 shows the expected outcome.

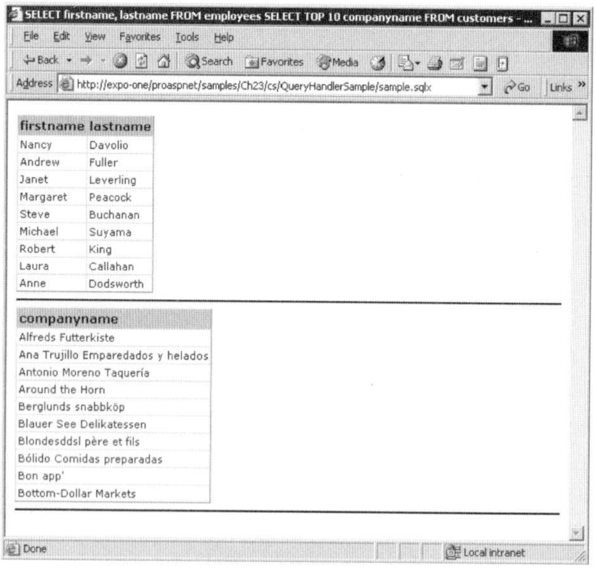

Figure 23-6 A custom HTTP handler in action.

To start, let's examine the source code for the *IHttpHandler* class.

Building a Query Manager Tool

The HTTP handler should get into the game whenever the user requests an .sqlx resource. Assume for now that this aspect has been fully configured, and focus on what's needed to execute the query and pack the results into a grid. To execute the query, at a minimum, we need the connection string and the command text. The following text illustrates the typical contents of an .sqlx file:

```
<query connString="DATABASE=northwind;SERVER=localhost;UID=sa;">
    SELECT firstname, lastname FROM employees
    SELECT TOP 10 companyname FROM customers
</query>
```

The XML document is formed by a unique node—the *<query>* node—that contains the *connString* attribute. The attribute stores the connection string, whereas the text of the node represents the query command.

The *ProcessRequest* method of the handler needs to extract this information before it can proceed with executing the query and generating the output.

```
class SqlxData
{
    public string ConnectionString;
    public string QueryText;
}

public class QueryHandler : IHttpHandler
{
    // Override the ProcessRequest method
    public void ProcessRequest(HttpContext context)
    {
        // Parses the SQLX file
        SqlxData _data = ParseFile(context);

        // Create the output as HTML
        string html = CreateOutput(_data);

        // Output the data
        context.Response.Write("<html><head><title>");
        context.Response.Write(_data.QueryText);
        context.Response.Write("</title></head><body>");
        context.Response.Write(html);
        context.Response.Write("</body></html>");
    }

    // Override the IsReusable property
    public bool IsReusable
    {
        get { return true; }
    }

    :
}
```

The *ParseFile* helper function uses an XML reader to scan the source code of the .sqlx resource.

```
private SqlxData ParseFile(HttpContext context) {
    SqlxData _data = new SqlxData();

    // Get the name of the file to process
    string _file = context.Server.MapPath(context.Request.Path.ToString());
```

```
    // Go to node <query> and get the connection string
    string _connString = null;
    XmlTextReader _reader = new XmlTextReader(_file);
    _reader.Read();
    _reader.MoveToContent();
    _connString = _reader["connString"];
    if (_connString == null) {
        _reader.Close();
        context.Response.Write(ErrorMessage(_file));
    }

    // Go to the content node and get the command text
    string _queryText = null;
    _reader.Read();
    _queryText = _reader.Value;
    if (_queryText == null) {
        _reader.Close();
        context.Response.Write(ErrorMessage(_file));
    }

    // Close the reader
    _reader.Close();

    // Pack the data
    _data.ConnectionString = _connString;
    _data.QueryText = _queryText;
    return _data;
}
```

The *SqlxData* internal class groups the connection string and the command text. The information is passed to the *CreateOutput* function, which will actually execute the query and generate the grid.

```
private string CreateOutput(SqlxData data)
{
    // Run the query
    DataSet ds = new DataSet();
    SqlDataAdapter adapter = new SqlDataAdapter(data.QueryText,
        data.ConnectionString);
    adapter.Fill(ds);

    // Prepare a distinct grid for each result set
    StringWriter sw = new StringWriter();
    HtmlTextWriter writer = new HtmlTextWriter(sw);
    for(int i=0; i<ds.Tables.Count; i++)
    {
        DataGrid grid = new DataGrid();
        grid.CellPadding = 2;
        grid.Font.Name = "verdana";
        grid.Font.Size = FontUnit.Point(8);
```

```
            grid.HeaderStyle.BackColor = Color.SkyBlue;
            grid.HeaderStyle.Font.Size = FontUnit.Larger;
            grid.HeaderStyle.Font.Bold = true;
            grid.ItemStyle.BackColor = Color.Ivory;
            grid.DataSource = ds.Tables[i];
            grid.DataBind();

            // Get the HTML out of the grid
            grid.RenderControl(writer);

            // Add a separator
            writer.WriteLine("<hr style='border:solid 1px black;'>");
        }

        return sw.ToString();
    }
```

After executing the query, the method populates a dynamically created *DataGrid* control. In ASP.NET pages, the *DataGrid* control, like any other control, is rendered to HTML. However, this happens through the care of the special HTTP handler that manages .aspx resources. For .sqlx resources, we need to provide that functionality ourselves. Obtaining the HTML for a Web control is as easy as calling the *RenderControl* method on an HTML text writer object. This is just what the page HTTP handler does by using the response stream as the underlying data store. In this case, though, we need to obtain the output as a string; so you use a *StringWriter* object as the back-end data store. This technique to obtain the HTML text generated for a control is quite general and can be used in a variety of circumstances and with all Web controls.

The handler generates a grid for each result set returned by the query in the .sqlx file.

> **Note** An HTTP handler that needs to access session state values must implement the *IRequiresSessionState* interface. Like *INamingContainer*, it's a marker interface and requires no method implementation. Note that the *IRequiresSessionState* interface indicates that the HTTP handler requires read and write access to the session state. If read-only access is needed, use the *IReadOnlySessionState* interface instead.

Registering the Handler

An HTTP handler is a class and must be compiled to an assembly before you can use it. The assembly must be deployed to the Bin directory of the application. If you plan to make this handler available to all applications, you can copy it to the global assembly cache (GAC). The next step is registering the handler with an individual application or with all the applications running on the Web server. You register the handler in the configuration file.

```
<configuration>
    <system.web>
        <httpHandlers>
            <add verb="*"
                path="*.sqlx"
                type="ProAspNet.CS.Ch23.QueryHandler,QueryHandler"/>
        </httpHandlers>
    </system.web>
</configuration>
```

You add the new handler to the *<httpHandlers>* section of the local or global web.config file. The section supports three actions: *<add>*, *<remove>*, and *<clear>*. You use *<add>* to add a new HTTP handler to the scope of the .config file. You use *<remove>* to remove a particular handler. Finally, you use *<clear>* to get rid of all the registered handlers. To add a new handler, you need to set three attributes: *verb*, *path*, and *type*, as shown in Table 23-3.

Table 23-3 Attributes Needed to Register an HTTP Handler

Attribute	Description
verb	Indicates the list of the supported HTTP verbs. For example, *GET*, *PUT*, and *POST*. The wildcard character (*) is an acceptable value and denotes all verbs.
path	A wildcard string, or a single URL, that indicates the resources the handler will work on. For example, *.aspx.
type	Specifies a comma-separated class/assembly combination. ASP.NET searches for the assembly DLL first in the application's private Bin directory and then in the system global assembly cache.

These attributes are mandatory. An optional attribute is also supported—*validate*. When *validate* is set to *false*, ASP.NET will delay as much as possible loading the assembly with the HTTP handler. In other words, the assembly will be loaded only when a request for it arrives. ASP.NET will not try to preload the assembly, thus catching any error or problem with it. The configuration script previously shown registers the *QueryHandler* class in the QueryHandler.dll assembly to handle all HTTP verbs that involve *.sqlx resources.

So far you have correctly deployed and registered the HTTP handler, but if you try invoking an .sqlx resource, the results you produce are not what you'd expect. The problem lies in the fact that so far you configured ASP.NET to handle only .sqlx resources; but IIS still doesn't know anything about them!

A request for an .sqlx resource is managed by IIS in the first place. If you don't register an ISAPI extension to handle that, IIS will treat it as a static resource and serve the request by sending back the source code of the file. The extra step required is registering the .sqlx extension with the IIS metabase, as shown in Figure 23-7.

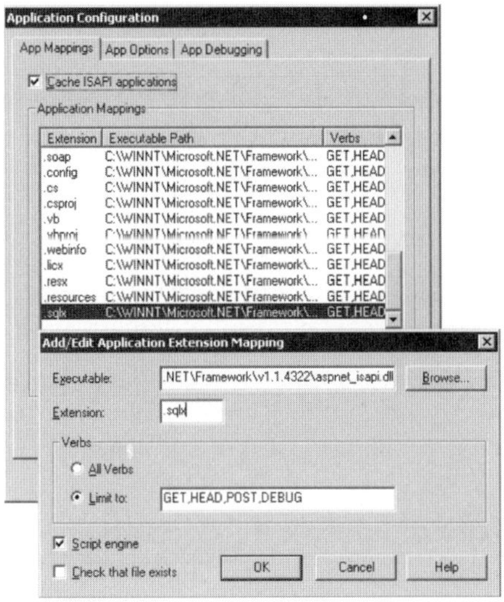

Figure 23-7 Registering the .sqlx extension with the IIS metabase.

To involve the HTTP handler, you must choose aspnet_isapi.dll as the ISAPI extension. In this way, all .sqlx requests are handed out to ASP.NET and processed through the specified handler.

Note If your Web application manages resources of a type that you don't want to make publicly available over the Web, you must instruct IIS not to display those files. A possible way to accomplish this consists of forwarding the request to aspnet_isapi and then binding the extension to one of the internal handlers—the *HttpForbiddenHandler* class.

```
<add verb="*" path="*.xyz"
     type="System.Web.HttpForbiddenHandler" />
```

Any attempt to access an .xyz resource results in an error message being displayed.

Deploying as an ASHX Resource

An alternative way to define an HTTP handler is through an .ashx file. When a request for a specified .ashx resource is received, the handler will get executed. The association between the HTTP handler and the .ashx resource is established within the .ashx source file by using a special directive: *@WebHandler*. All .ashx files must begin with a directive like the following:

```
<%@ WebHandler Language="C#" Class="Namespace.MyHandler" %>
```

When the URL that corresponds to the .ashx resource is invoked, the *MyHandler* class is automatically invoked.

When .ashx resources are used to implement an HTTP handler, no deployment setup is needed. In particular, you don't need to arrange for a web.config file and for a new *<httpHandlers>* section. You just deploy the source file, and you're done. Just as for Web services, the source file will be loaded and compiled only on demand. Because ASP.NET adds a special entry to the IIS metabase for .ashx resources, you don't even need to enter changes to the Web server configuration.

As we discussed in Chapter 2, the machine.config file defines a few standard HTTP handlers for commonly accessed resource types. In particular, handlers for .aspx, .asmx, and .ashx resources are defined. The former two types serve requests for Web pages and Web services. The latter type is handled by an HTTP handler class named *SimpleHandlerFactory*. Figure 23-8 illustrates the role of the *SimpleHandlerFactory* class in the processing of .ashx resources. Note that *SimpleHandlerFactory* is actually an HTTP handler factory class, not a simple HTTP handler class. We'll discuss handler factories in a moment.

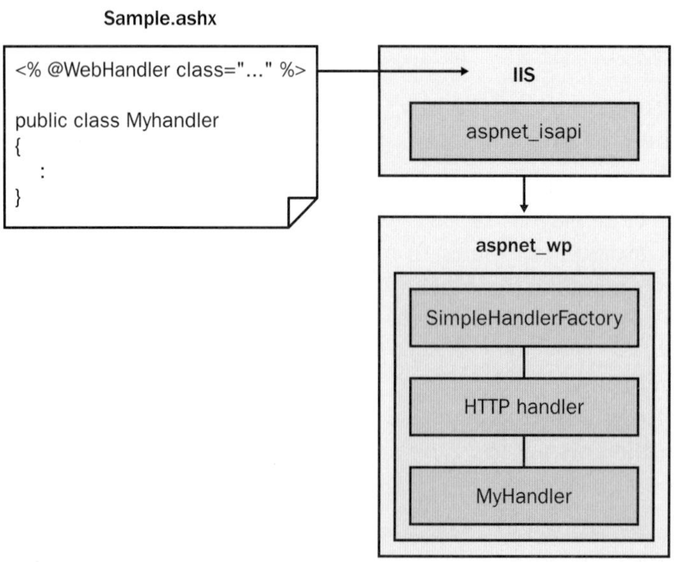

Figure 23-8 The *@WebHandler* directive within an .ashx resource tells the HTTP handler factory about the HTTP handler class to instantiate.

The *SimpleHandlerFactory* class looks for the *@WebHandler* directive at the beginning of the file. The *@WebHandler* directive tells the handler factory the name of the HTTP handler class to instantiate once the source code has been compiled.

> **Important** You should resort to .ashx resources to implement application-specific functionality that needs to be processed faster than regular Web pages. In any case, an HTTP handler returns a valid HTTP response with a content type and a body. Serving an .ashx request results in faster code than serving an .aspx resource. Processing an .ashx resource is faster because no intermediate events are raised to the user code (for example, *Init*, *Load*), no view state is managed, and no postback mechanism is supported. Roughly speaking, an .ashx request is like an .aspx resource in which only the rendering step ever takes place.
>
> Should you use generic .ashx resources or go for a custom extension? That mostly depends on the function you want to implement. The ASHX approach is designed for relatively simple scenarios in which you have few parameters to pass (or no parameters at all) and for which you use the query string to bring them in. A custom extension is preferable if you have a custom document to process with a variety of information organized in a nonflat layout.

Advanced HTTP Handler Programming

In a conventional HTTP handler, the *ProcessRequest* method takes the lion's share of the overall set of functionality. The second member of the *IHttpHandler* interface—the *IsReusable* property—is used only in particular circumstances. By calling *IsReusable*, an HTTP handler factory can query a handler to determine whether the same instance can be used to service multiple requests.

The Boolean value returned by *IsReusable* also indicates whether the handler object can be pooled. This is certainly true for *HttpApplication* objects called to serve a request, but it's patently false for handlers representing a Web Forms page. If you set the *IsReusable* property to return true, the handler is not unloaded from memory after use.

In all the cases considered so far, we never had the need to distinguish between two or more distinct handlers for a request. In situations in which the HTTP handler for a request is not uniquely identified, you might want to use an HTTP handler factory object.

HTTP Handler Factories

An HTTP request can be directly associated with an HTTP handler or with an HTTP handler factory object. An HTTP handler factory is a class that implements the *IHttpHandlerFactory* interface and is in charge of returning the actual HTTP handler to use to serve the request. For example, the *SimpleHandlerFactory* class handles requests for .ashx resources and determines the right handler to use by looking at the *@WebHandler* directive in the source file.

In the .NET Framework, HTTP handler factories are used to perform some preliminary tasks on the requested resource prior to passing it on to the handler. A typical handler factory object is represented by the internal class named *PageHandlerFactory*. It figures out the name of the handler to use and, if possible, loads it up from an existing assembly. In the SQLX example, we could use a handler factory class to insulate the code necessary to process the file and extract the contained information.

HTTP handler factories are classes that implement a couple of methods on the *IHttpHandlerFactory* interface—*GetHandler* and *ReleaseHandler*, as shown in Table 23-4.

Table 23-4 Members of the *IHttpHandlerFactory* Interface

Method	Description
GetHandler	Returns an instance of an HTTP handler to serve the request.
ReleaseHandler	Takes an existing HTTP handler instance and frees it up or pools it.

The *GetHandler* method has the following signature:

```
public virtual IHttpHandler GetHandler(HttpContext context,
    string requestType, string url, string pathTranslated);
```

The *requestType* argument is a string that evaluates to *GET* or *POST*—the HTTP verb of the request. The last two arguments represent the raw URL of the request and the physical path behind it. The *ReleaseHandler* method is a mandatory override for any class that implements *IHttpHandlerFactory*; in most cases, it will just have an empty body.

The following listing shows an example HTTP handler factory that returns different handlers based on the HTTP verb (*GET* or *POST*) used for the request:

```
namespace ProAspNet.CS.Ch23
{
    class MyHandlerFactory : IHttpHandlerFactory
    {
        public IHttpHandler GetHandler(HttpContext context,
            string requestType, String url, String pathTranslated)
```

```
        {
            if(context.Request.RequestType.ToLower() == "get")
                return (IHttpHandler) new MyGetHandler();
            else if(context.Request.RequestType.ToLower() == "post")
                return (IHttpHandler) new MyPostHandler();
            return null;
        }

        public void ReleaseHandler(IHttpHandler handler)
        {
            // nothing to do
        }
    }
}
```

When you use an HTTP handler factory, it's the factory, not the handler, that needs to be registered with the ASP.NET configuration file. If you register the handler, it will always be used to serve requests. If you opt for a factory, you have a chance to decide dynamically and based on runtime conditions which handler is more appropriate for a certain request.

Asynchronous Handlers

An asynchronous HTTP handler is a class that implements the *IHttpAsyncHandler* interface. The system initiates the call by invoking the *BeginProcessRequest* method. Next, when the method ends, a callback function is automatically invoked to terminate the call. In the .NET Framework, the sole *HttpApplication* class implements the asynchronous interface. The members of *IHttpAsyncHandler* interface are shown in Table 23-5.

Table 23-5 Members of the *IHttpAsyncHandler* Interface

Method	Description
BeginProcessRequest	Initiates an asynchronous call to the specified HTTP handler.
EndProcessRequest	Terminates the asynchronous call.

The signature of the *BeginProcessRequest* method is as follows:

```
IAsyncResult BeginProcessRequest(HttpContext context, AsyncCallback cb,
    object extraData);
```

The *context* argument provides references to intrinsic server objects used to service HTTP requests. The second parameter is the *AsyncCallback* object to invoke when the asynchronous method call is complete. The third parameter is a generic cargo variable that contains any data you might want to pass to the handler.

> **Note** An *AsyncCallback* object is a delegate that defines the logic needed to finish processing the asynchronous operation. A delegate is a class that holds a reference to a method. A delegate class has a fixed signature, and it can hold references only to methods that match that signature. A delegate is equivalent to a type-safe function pointer or a callback. As a result, an *AsyncCallback* object is just the code that executes when the asynchronous handler has completed its job.

The *AsyncCallback* delegate has the following signature:

```
public delegate void AsyncCallback(IAsyncResult ar);
```

It uses the *IAsyncResult* interface to obtain the status of the asynchronous operation. To illustrate the plumbing of asynchronous handlers, let's examine the pseudocode that the HTTP runtime employs when it deals with asynchronous handlers. The HTTP runtime invokes the *BeginProcessRequest* method as follows:

```
// Sets an internal member of the HttpContext class with the current
// instance of the asynchronous handler
context.AsyncAppHandler = asyncHandler;

// Invokes the BeginProcessRequest method on the asynchronous HTTP handler
asyncHandler.BeginProcessRequest(context, OnCompletionCallback, context);
```

The *context* argument is the current instance of the *HttpContext* class and represents the context of the request. A reference to the HTTP context is also passed as the custom data destined to the handler to process the request. The *extraData* parameter in the *BeginProcessRequest* signature is used to represent the status of the asynchronous operation. The *BeginProcessRequest* method returns an object of type *HttpAsyncResult*—a class that implements the *IAsyncResult* interface. The *IAsyncResult* interface contains a property named *AsyncState* that is set with the *extraData* value—in this case, the HTTP context.

The *OnCompletionCallback* method is an internal method. It gets automatically triggered when the asynchronous processing of the request terminates. The following listing illustrates the pseudocode of the *HttpRuntime* private method:

```
// The method must have the signature of an AsyncCallback delegate
private void OnHandlerCompletion(IAsyncResult ar)
{
    // The ar parameter is an instance of HttpAsyncResult
    HttpContext context = (HttpContext) ar.AsyncState;
```

```
    // Retrieves the instance of the asynchronous HTTP handler
    // and completes the request
    IHttpAsyncHandler asyncHandler = context.AsyncAppHandler;
    asyncHandler.EndProcessRequest(ar);

    // Finalizes the request as usual
    ⋮
}
```

The completion handler retrieves the HTTP context of the request through the *AsyncState* property of the *IAsyncResult* object it gets from the system. As mentioned, the actual object passed is an instance of the *HttpAsyncResult* class—in any case, it is the return value of the *BeginProcessRequest* method. The completion routine extracts the reference to the asynchronous handler from the context and issues a call to the *EndProcessRequest* method.

```
void EndProcessRequest(IAsyncResult result);
```

The *EndProcessRequest* method takes the *IAsyncResult* object returned by the call to *BeginProcessRequest*. As implemented in the *HttpApplication* class, the *EndProcessRequest* method does nothing special and is limited to throwing an exception if an error occurred.

Writing HTTP Modules

So we've learned that ASP.NET runs as an ISAPI extension within the IIS process. Any incoming requests for ASP.NET resources is handed over to the ASP.NET worker process for the actual processing within the context of the CLR. Both in IIS 5.0 and 6.0, the worker process is a distinct process from IIS, so if one ASP.NET application crashes, it doesn't bring down the whole server. (In IIS 6.0, the handing over between the Web server and the worker process is more direct and faster.) ASP.NET manages a pool of *HttpApplication* objects for each running application and picks up one of the pooled instances to serve a particular request. As discussed in Chapter 13, these objects are based on the class defined in your global.asax file or on the base *HttpApplication* class if global.asax is missing. The goal of the *HttpApplication* object in charge of the request is getting an HTTP handler.

On the way to the final HTTP handler, the *HttpApplication* object makes the request pass through a pipeline of HTTP modules. An HTTP module is a .NET Framework class that implements the *IHttpModule* interface. The HTTP modules that filter the raw data within the request are configured on a per-application basis within the web.config file. All ASP.NET applications, though, inherit a bunch of system HTTP modules configured in the machine.config file. In Chapter 13, we discussed and commented on the default modules that provide features such as authentication, authorization, and session-related services.

Generally speaking, an HTTP module can pre-process and post-process a request, and it intercepts and handles system events as well as events raised by other modules. The good news is that you can write and register your own HTTP modules and make them plug into the ASP.NET runtime pipeline, handle system events, and fire their own events.

The *IHttpModule* Interface

The *IHttpModule* interface defines only two methods—*Init* and *Dispose*. The *Init* method initializes a module and prepares it to handle requests. At this time, you subscribe to receive notifications for the events of interest. The *Dispose* method disposes of the resources (all but memory!) used by the module. Typical tasks you perform within the *Dispose* method are closing database connections or file handles.

The *IHttpModule* methods have the following signatures:

```
void Init(HttpApplication app);
void Dispose();
```

The *Init* method receives a reference to the *HttpApplication* object that is serving the request. You can use this reference to wire up to system events. (See Chapter 13 for the complete list of system events.) The *HttpApplication* object also features a property named *Context* that provides access to the intrinsic properties of the ASP.NET application. In this way, you gain access to *Response*, *Request*, *Session*, and the like.

A Custom HTTP Module

Let's come to grips with HTTP modules and write a custom module named *Marker* that adds a signature at the beginning and end of each page served by the application. The following code outlines the class we need to write:

```
using System;
using System.Web;

namespace ProAspNet.CS.Ch23
{
    public class MarkerModule : IHttpModule
    {
        public void Init(HttpApplication app)
        {
            // Register for pipeline events
        }

        public void Dispose()
        {
```

```
                // Nothing to do here
            }
        }
}
```

The *Init* method is invoked by the *HttpApplication* class to load the module. In the *Init* method, you normally don't need to do more than simply register your own event handlers. The *Dispose* method is, more often than not, empty. The heart of the HTTP module is really in the event handlers you define.

Wiring Up Events

The sample *Marker* module registers a couple of pipeline events—*BeginRequest* and *PreSendRequestContent*. *BeginRequest* is the first event that hits the HTTP application object when the request begins processing. *PreSendRequestContent* is the event that signals the next sending of the response, and it's your last chance to modify the contents for the browser. By handling these two events, you can write custom text to the output stream before and after the regular HTTP handler—the *Page*-derived class.

The following listing shows the implementation of the *Init* and *Dispose* methods for the sample module:

```
public void Init(HttpApplication app)
{
    // Register for pipeline events
    app.BeginRequest += new EventHandler(OnBeginRequest);
    app.PreSendRequestContent += new EventHandler(OnPreSendRequestContent);
}

public void Dispose()
{
}
```

The *BeginRequest* and *PreSendRequestContent* event handlers have a similar structure. They obtain a reference to the current *HttpApplication* object from the sender and get the HTTP context from there. Next, they work with the *Response* object to append text or a custom header.

```
public void OnBeginRequest(object sender, EventArgs e)
{
    HttpApplication app = (HttpApplication) sender;
    HttpContext ctx = app.Context;

        // More code here
        ⋮

    // Add custom header to the HTTP response
    ctx.Response.AppendHeader("Author", "DinoE");
```

```
        ctx.Response.Write(topText);
    }

    public void OnPreSendRequestContent(object sender, EventArgs e)
    {
        // Get access to the HTTP context
        HttpApplication app = (HttpApplication) sender;
        HttpContext ctx = app.Context;

            // More code here
            ⋮

        // Append some custom text
        ctx.Response.Write(bottomText);
    }
```

OnBeginRequest writes the page header and also adds a custom HTTP header. *OnPreSendRequestContent* simply appends the page footer. The effect of this HTTP module is visible in Figure 23-9.

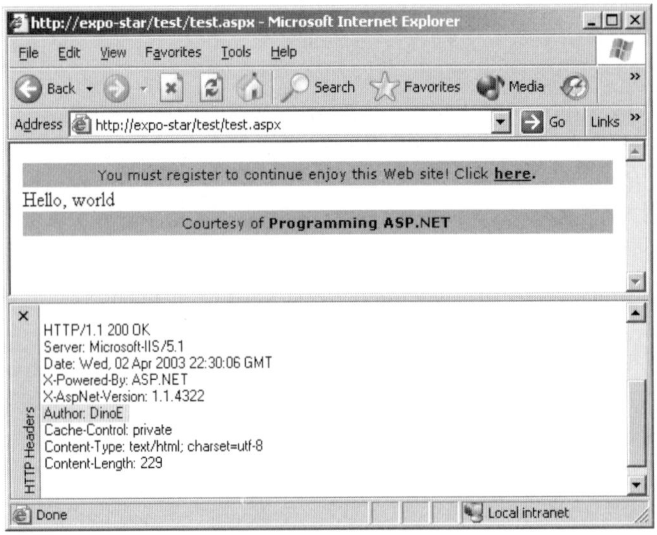

Figure 23-9 The *Marker* HTTP module adds a header and footer to each page within the application.

The dockable window at the bottom of Internet Explorer is a free tool that snoops for the HTTP header being sent and received by the browser. The custom header in the response text is clearly visible.

Note that technically speaking the work done in *BeginRequest* could also go in the *PreSendRequestHeaders* handler, which occurs at the last possible moment before ASP.NET sends the headers out.

> **Note** At this point, a good question to ask would be the following: why shouldn't we wire up the *EndRequest* event instead of *PreSendRequestContent*? As the names clearly suggest, the two events fire at very different moments. *EndRequest* indicates that the system is done with the request; *PreSendRequestContent* arrives when the system is going to flush the response buffer to the output stream. If your goal is simply to add a common footer to all responses a user gets out of a Web application, the two events are functionally equivalent. However, when *PreSendRequestContent* arrives, the buffer is still held by the *Response*'s output stream object and can be modified before being sent to the browser. So by writing a handler for *PreSendRequestContent*, you can not only append a custom markup string but also modify the markup the handler has generated.

Accessing Other HTTP Modules

The sample just discussed demonstrates how to wire up pipeline events—that is, events fired by the *HttpApplication* object. But what about events fired by other modules? The *HttpApplication* object provides a property named *Modules* that gets the collection of modules for the current application.

The *Modules* property is of type *HttpModuleCollection* and contains the names of the modules for the application. The collection class inherits from the abstract class *NameObjectCollectionBase*, which is a collection of pairs made of a string and an object. The string indicates the public name of the module; the object is the actual instance of the module. To access the module that handles the session state, you need code like this:

```
SessionStateModule sess = app.Modules["Session"];
sess.Start += new EventHandler(OnSessionStart);
```

You can also handle events raised by HTTP modules within the global.asax file and use the *ModuleName_OnEventName* convention to name the event handlers. The name of the module is just one of the settings you need to define when registering an HTTP module.

Registering with the Configuration File

You register a new HTTP module by adding an entry under the *<httpModules>* section of the configuration file. The overall syntax of the *<httpModules>* section closely resembles that of HTTP handlers. To add a new module, you use the *<add>* node and specify the *name* and *type* attributes. The *name* attribute contains the public name of the module. This name will be used to select the module within the *HttpApplication Modules* collection. If the module fires custom events, this name is also used as the prefix for building automatic event handlers in the global.asax file.

```
<configuration>
<system.web>
    <httpModules>
        <add name="Marker"
             type="ProAspNet.CS.Ch23.MarkerModule, Marker" />
    </httpModules>
</system.web>
</configuration>
```

The *type* attribute is the usual comma-separated string that contains the name of the class and the related assembly. The configuration settings can be entered into the application's configuration file as well as into the machine configuration file. In the former case, only pages within the application will be affected; in the latter case, all pages within all applications will be processed by the specified module.

The order in which modules are applied depends on the physical order of the modules in the configuration list. You can remove a system module and replace it with your own that provides a similar functionality. In this case, in the application's web.config file you use the *<remove>* node to drop the default module and then use *<add>* to insert your own. If you want to completely redefine the order of HTTP modules for your application, you could clear all the default modules by using the *<clear>* node and then re-register them all in a different order.

Conclusion

HTTP handlers and HTTP modules are the building blocks of the ASP.NET platform. ASP.NET includes several predefined handlers and HTTP modules, but developers can write handlers and modules of their own to perform a variety of tasks. HTTP handlers, in particular, are faster than ordinary Web pages and can be used in all circumstances in which you don't need state maintenance and postback events. To generate images dynamically on the server, for example, an HTTP handler is more efficient than a page.

Everything that occurs under the hood of the ASP.NET runtime environment occurs because of HTTP handlers. When you invoke a Web page or a Web service method, an appropriate HTTP handler gets into the game and serves your request. At the highest level of abstraction, the behavior of an HTTP handler closely resembles that of an ISAPI extension. While the similarity makes sense, a couple of key differences exist. First and foremost, HTTP handlers are managed and CLR-resident components. The CLR, in turn, is hosted by the ASP.NET worker process. An ISAPI extension, on the other hand, is a Win32 library that can live within the IIS process. In the ASP.NET process model, the aspnet_isapi component is a true ISAPI extension that collects requests and dispatches them to the worker process. ASP.NET internally implements an ISAPI-like extensibility model in which HTTP handlers play the role of ISAPI extensions in the IIS world.

The second big difference between HTTP handlers and ISAPI extensions is that HTTP handlers provide a much simpler programming model. If you consider that just the programming model—overly complex, error-prone, and C++ oriented—is commonly believed as a major drawback of ISAPI, you should immediately grasp the importance of this ASP.NET innovation.

HTTP modules are to ISAPI filters what HTTP handlers are to ISAPI extensions. HTTP modules are good at performing a number of low-level tasks where a tight interaction and integration with the request/response mechanism is a critical factor. Modules are sort of interceptors that you can place along an HTTP packet's path, from the Web server to the ASP.NET runtime and back. Modules have read and write capabilities and can filter and modify the contents of both inbound and outbound requests.

The next and final chapter of the book is about hosting ASP.NET in existing Win32 processes. As we repeatedly mentioned, ASP.NET consists of an instance of the CLR hosted by a Win32 worker process. The great news is that the hosting process can be any Win32 process, including your own process. The capability of processing .aspx pages, therefore, is not an exclusive feature of IIS. We'll demonstrate this technique and its various uses in the next chapter.

Resources

- Securely Implement Request Processing, Filtering, and Content Redirection with HTTP Pipelines in ASP.NET (*http://msdn.microsoft.com/msdnmag/issues/02/09/HTTPPipelines*)
- Extend ASP.NET With HTTP Modules (*http://www.aspnetpro.com/features/2003/02/asp200302bn_f/asp200302bn_f.asp*)

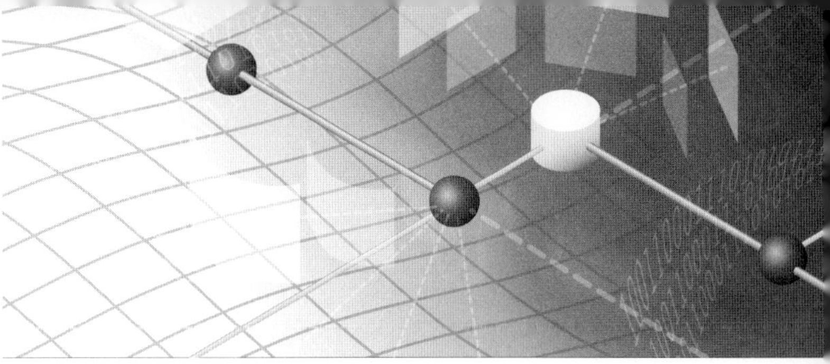

24

Hosting ASP.NET Outside IIS

There is nothing either good or bad, but thinking makes it so.
—William Shakespeare

A few years ago, when ASP was reigning and thriving, a client asked me to create a tool to make it possible for an ASP application to run without its native runtime environment. At first, I admit, it took me a while to make sense of that apparently weird request: "What is my client asking for, running ASP without the ASP engine? Is that even possible?" My brain promptly started a background thread to dig through the innermost recesses of my mind and retrieve any little piece of information that might be useful in outlining a solution. In the meantime, as the thread went to work, just like any software consultant on the face of the earth would have done, I promptly answered, "Sure, I can help you. Let's discuss the problem further." Admittedly, though, I hadn't the faintest idea of how to meet the request.

The client wanted to publish some content on CDs. The content to be published was subject to frequent updates and a number of runtime and security conditions. The client had the same content already published to an ASP-fueled Web site and hoped to deploy it to a variety of offline media, such as a CD or a DVD. "Where's the problem then?" I thought. "Just copy all the files on the storage medium, install it, and leverage the Personal Web server or the IIS Web server installed on the client machine. However, after conducting a survey with customers, my client realized that only a small percentage of potential users was actually running Personal Web server or IIS. Only a few of them declared themselves ready to upgrade the system to accommodate the new product. As a result, no assumption could be made about their installed software. The final user-requirements paper described the application as a piece of software capable of working like ASP but without any external support from a Web server. I had to devise a runtime engine capable of processing ASP files acting as a local Web server. Well, in ASP 3.0 this was much easier said than done.

One of the highest hurdles to overcome was the tight and rather inextricable connection between IIS, the COM+ environment, and the ISAPI extension running ASP—the asp.dll library. In short, the ASP environment is not designed to be hosted outside IIS and doesn't provide a well-known interface for interacting with a generic host application. I decided to work around the issue by constructing an ASP emulator and integrating it with a custom browser. My client was very happy, and I couldn't resist making my work public. (See the "Resources" section at the end of the chapter.)

Amazingly enough, I presented my work at a couple of conferences at the same time Microsoft presented the first beta of ASP.NET. I was very pleased to find out from the Microsoft speakers at those conferences that ASP.NET would provide a much simpler and built-in model for external hosting. In this chapter, we'll explore the techniques and tricks to host ASP.NET outside the natural habitat of IIS.

Hosting the ASP.NET Runtime

Although you'll mostly use ASP.NET in conjunction with IIS, keep in mind that IIS is just one possible host for the ASP.NET runtime engine. ASP.NET is designed in a very modular way and, as such, lends itself quite well to being hosted in external applications—IIS being just one of them. However, being capable of hosting ASP.NET in a custom application doesn't mean you have the off-the-shelf solution to build an offline Web browser to ship on a CD. Hosting the ASP.NET runtime engine in a custom application is only the first step for the delivery of dynamic content in an offline manner. Later in this chapter, we'll specifically tackle the problem of delivering your Web site on a CD.

An ASP.NET application doesn't require IIS as the host module. To some extent, ASP.NET doesn't even require a Web server to run. It exposes a well-known interface that any caller can use to connect to the internal HTTP pipeline and ask it to process a well-formed request. Two classes play a key role in the hosting of the ASP.NET engine—*HttpRuntime* and *ApplicationHost*.

As we know from Chapter 2, the *HttpRuntime* class is the entry point in the pipeline of objects that, much like an assembly line, transforms the original HTTP request for an .aspx resource into fresh HTML text. The *ApplicationHost* class makes it possible for a client application to host the ASP.NET engine. The class is also responsible for creating the AppDomain in the host process in which all the incoming requests for the new application will be handled.

The *HttpRuntime* class gets involved only when the application host (be it IIS or something else) has received and possibly preprocessed the request. The application host packs all the information about the request in a class derived from the *HttpWorkerRequest* abstract class or, more often, from its standard implementation class named *SimpleWorkerRequest*. After an instance of the request class is ready to use, the host hands the processing over to *HttpRuntime* by calling the *ProcessRequest* static method. The following code snippet illustrates the core code that fires the processing of an ASP.NET page:

```
// Prepare the request class
SimpleWorkerRequest req;

// Indicate the URL, the query string, and output stream
req = new SimpleWorkerRequest(aspxPage, null, Console.Out);

// Connect to the ASP.NET pipeline and have the request processed
HttpRuntime.ProcessRequest(req);
```

We repeatedly mentioned throughout this book that *HttpRuntime* is the entry point in the ASP.NET HTTP pipeline. The preceding code shows how a request for an ASP.NET resource is actually funneled into the pipeline to be processed. Figure 24-1 provides a graphical representation of it.

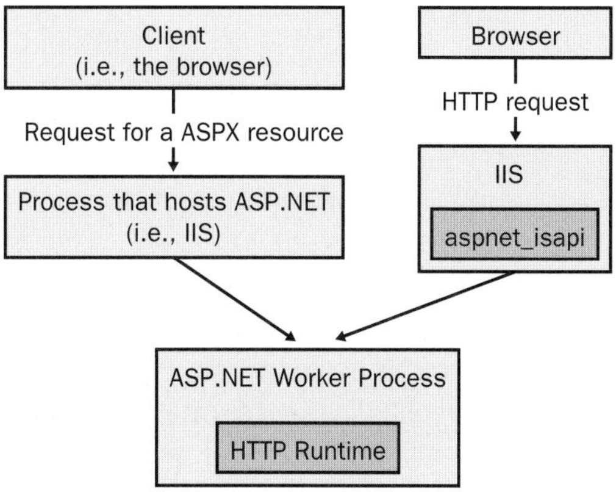

Figure 24-1 The general diagram that funnels an ASP.NET request into the HTTP pipeline. The diagram on the left represents the most general case; the diagram on the right illustrates the specific case of IIS.

The constructor of *SimpleWorkerRequest* takes the virtual path of the .aspx resource to process, an optional query string, and the text writer to use for the output. Instead of using the standard output console, one could use a stream writer object to save the HTML code to disk. The client makes a request for an ASP.NET resource—that is, for a resource that the ASP.NET runtime knows how to handle. The form and shape in which this request arrives at the ASP.NET host depends on the client and host involved. When browsers and IIS are involved, the request is an HTTP command. You should note that the request can take any form as long as it contains a URL and optionally a query string.

The *ApplicationHost* Class

The classes that govern the interaction between the host and the ASP.NET HTTP runtime are located under the *System.Web.Hosting* namespace. The namespace defines a couple of classes—*ApplicationHost* and *SimpleWorkerRequest*. The abstract class *HttpWorkerRequest*, which is the base class for *SimpleWorkerRequest*, is defined in the *System.Web* namespace. The *ApplicationHost* class enables the host process to create application domains for processing ASP.NET requests. The class is sealed—that is, not inheritable—doesn't implement any interface, and doesn't inherit from any base class other than *System.Object*.

```
public sealed class ApplicationHost
```

The class has a simple programming interface that consists of a single static method—the *CreateApplicationHost* method.

```
public static object CreateApplicationHost(
    Type hostType,
    string virtualDir,
    string physicalDir
);
```

The *virtualDir* argument represents the virtual directory for the application domain being created, whereas the *physicalDir* argument indicates the file system path behind that virtual path. The *physicalDir* argument specifies the disk folder from which requested .aspx files have to be loaded for that Web application. These pieces of information are associated with the domain and are consumed by the ASP.NET factory objects to create *HttpApplication* objects (global.asax) and page objects (*.aspx). However, the first argument, *hostType*, deserves more of our attention.

The *hostType* argument of *CreateApplicationHost* is a *Type* object that evaluates to the type of the application-defined host class. The *CreateApplicationHost* method just returns an instance of this user-supplied class. The instance is used to create a bridge between the default AppDomain of the host program and the newly created AppDomain, as shown in Figure 24-2.

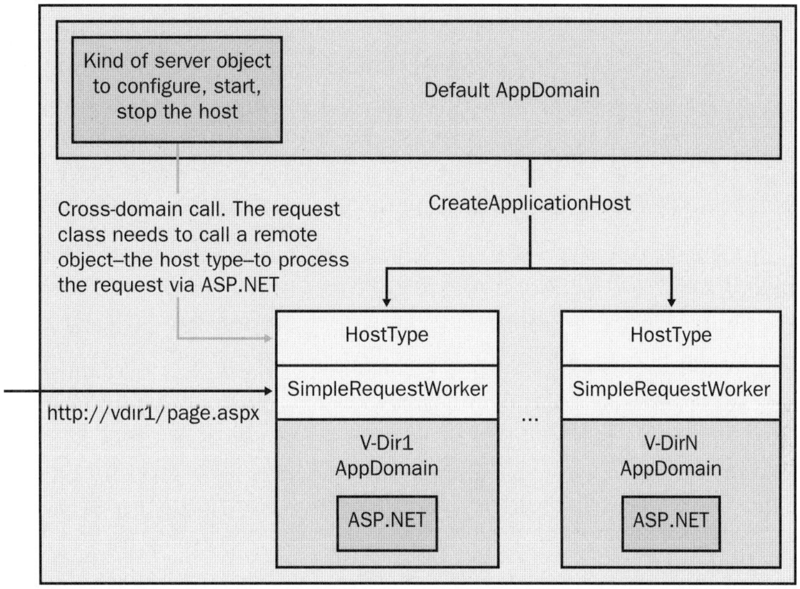

Figure 24-2 The host type is instantiated by the host application and creates an instance of the type that represents the request.

The Role of the Host Type

The programming interface of the host type is up to you. It normally provides methods through which a caller can issue requests of ASP.NET pages. If the host type has to emulate the behavior of IIS, and therefore act as a local Web server, it will provide methods to be started and stopped and will listen to port 80 (or whatever other port you decide to use). In this case, the host executable will implement a sort of controller object that starts and stops the listener.

The host type object is a sort of proxy between the core code of the host application and the ASP.NET HTTP runtime living in the target AppDomain that *CreateApplicationHost* had previously created. When a request arrives, it creates a *SimpleWorkerRequest* object and passes it to the ASP.NET pipeline. The request object is created in the same AppDomain that will actually service the request. *SimpleWorkerRequest* is a simple implementation of the base *HttpWorkerRequest* class and provides the ASP.NET runtime with minimal information, such as the requested URL and the query string. It also receives the ASP.NET output into a stream writer object.

The *SimpleWorkerRequest* Class

You should extend *SimpleWorkerRequest* and override the appropriate *HttpWorkerRequest* methods if you think you need more preprocessing functionality, such as parsing headers and posted data. The *SimpleWorkerRequest* class has two properties, which are listed in Table 24-1.

Table 24-1 Properties of the *SimpleWorkerRequest* Class

Property	Description
MachineConfigPath	Gets the full physical path to the machine.config file
MachineInstallDirectory	Gets the physical path to the directory where the ASP.NET binaries are installed

The list of *SimpleWorkerRequest* methods is longer. The details are provided in Table 24-2. Some of the methods (for example, *CloseConnection*) are simply blank overridable methods exposed to let you easily write custom code in derived classes. Other methods (for example, *GetHttpVersion* and *GetLocalPort*) return default values. If such default values aren't appropriate, you should override these methods too.

Table 24-2 Methods of the *SimpleWorkerRequest* Class

Method	Description
CloseConnection	When overridden in a derived class, terminates the connection with the client. In this class, it does nothing.
EndOfRequest	When overridden in a derived class, performs tasks needed when the current request is complete. In this class, it does nothing.
FlushResponse	When overridden in a derived class, performs tasks needed when sending all pending response data to the client. In this class, it does nothing.
GetAppPath	Returns the virtual path to the currently executing application.
GetAppPathTranslated	Returns the UNC-translated path to the currently executing application.
GetFilePath	Returns the physical path to the requested URI.
GetFilePathTranslated	Returns the physical path to the requested URI, and translates it from a virtual path.
GetHttpVerbName	When overridden in a derived class, returns the HTTP verb. In this class, returns "GET".
GetHttpVersion	When overridden in a derived class, returns the version of the HTTP protocol used by the request. In this class, returns "HTTP/1.0".
GetKnownRequestHeader	Returns the standard HTTP request header that corresponds to the specified index.
GetLocalAddress	When overridden in a derived class, returns the IP address returned in the request header. In this class, returns "127.0.0.1".

Table 24-2 Methods of the *SimpleWorkerRequest* Class *(continued)*

Method	Description
GetLocalPort	When overridden in a derived class, returns the server port number returned in the request header. In this class, returns 80.
GetPathInfo	Returns the additional path information that a URL might contain. For example, for the URL page.htm/tail, the return value is "/tail".
GetPreloadedEntityBody	Returns the portion of the HTTP request body that has already been read.
GetProtocol	Returns the HTTP or HTTPS, depending on the value returned by the *IsSecure* method.
GetQueryString	Returns the query string specified in the URL.
GetQueryStringRawBytes	Returns the response query string as an array of bytes.
GetRawUrl	Returns the URL path contained in the request header with the query string appended.
GetRemoteAddress	When overridden in a derived class, returns the client's IP address. In this class, returns "127.0.0.1".
GetRemoteName	When overridden in a derived class, returns the name of the client computer. In this class, returns "127.0.0.1".
GetRemotePort	When overridden in a derived class, returns the client's port number. In this class, returns 0.
GetServerName	When overridden in a derived class, returns the name of the local server. In this class, returns "127.0.0.1".
GetServerVariable	Returns a single server variable from a dictionary of server variables associated with the request.
GetUnknownRequestHeader	Returns a nonstandard HTTP request header value.
GetUnknownRequestHeaders	Returns all nonstandard HTTP header name/value pairs.
GetUriPath	Returns the virtual path to the requested URI.
GetUserToken	Returns the client's impersonation token.
HasEntityBody	Returns a value indicating whether the request contains body data.
HeadersSent	Returns a value indicating whether HTTP response headers have been sent to the client for the current request.
IsClientConnected	Returns a value indicating whether the client connection is still active.

(continued)

Table 24-2 Methods of the *SimpleWorkerRequest* Class *(continued)*

Method	Description
IsEntireEntityBodyIsPreloaded	Returns a value indicating whether all request data is available and no further reads from the client are required.
IsSecure	Returns a value indicating whether the connection is secure (using SSL). The default is false.
MapPath	Returns the physical path corresponding to the specified virtual path.
ReadEntityBody	Reads request data from the client (when not preloaded).
SendCalculatedContentLength	Adds a *Content-Length* HTTP header to the response.
SendKnownResponseHeader	Adds a standard HTTP header to the response.
SendResponseFromFile	Adds the contents of a file to the response.
SendResponseFromMemory	Adds the contents of a byte array to the response and specifies the number of bytes to send.
SendStatus	Specifies the HTTP status code and status description of the response; for example, *SendStatus(200, "Ok")*.
SendUnknownResponseHeader	Adds a nonstandard HTTP header to the response.
SetEndOfSendNotification	Registers for notification when all the response data is sent. The method requires a delegate that will be called back later.

The *HttpWorkerRequest* class contains several abstract methods. The *SimpleWorkerRequest* class represents a quite simple, but effective, implementation of a request class.

A Sample ASP.NET Host

So much for the underpinnings of ASP.NET hosting; now let's write some code to demonstrate how to host ASP.NET in a Windows Forms application. The idea is to use ASP.NET to generate HTML files starting from source .aspx files.

Compiling ASPX Pages to HTML

The following listing illustrates the source code of the host type. The only requirement is that the class is remotable—that is, inherits from *MarshalByRefObject*.

```
using System;
using System.Web;
using System.Web.Hosting;
using System.IO;
```

```
namespace ProAspNet.CS.Ch24
{
    public class WinAspNetHost : MarshalByRefObject
    {
        // Processes the ASPX file and creates the corresponding HTML file
        public void CreateHtmlPage(string aspx, string query, string html)
        {
            StreamWriter writer = new StreamWriter(html);
            SimpleWorkerRequest req = new SimpleWorkerRequest(
                aspx,       // ASPX file name
                query,      // Query string
                writer);    // Output stream (i.e., Console.Out)
            HttpRuntime.ProcessRequest(req);
            writer.Close();
        }
    }
}
```

The *WinAspNetHost* class has only one method, named *CreateHtmlPage*. As mentioned earlier, the number and the signature of the host class members are completely up to you. What really matters is that you come up with a programming interface that reflects what you are going to do. In this case, the ultimate goal is fairly simple—just take the .aspx file and translate it to HTML. A *SimpleWorkerRequest* object easily fits the bill and, in addition, the prototype of its constructor is exactly what we need.

```
public SimpleWorkerRequest(
    string pageURL,
    string queryString,
    TextWriter outputStream
);
```

The first argument is the name of the .aspx file to process. The second argument is an optional query string. Note that if you use a URL with command-line arguments, it will be mistaken for the real name of the file to open. (IIS in particular separates the URL from the query string while preprocessing the request.) The *SimpleWorkerRequest* class assumes it will receive the URL and query as distinct entities. Furthermore, note that the initial question mark (?) character of the query string must be removed. Finally, the third argument of the constructor is a stream writer object that will be used to bufferize the output text. Everything the .aspx page will send out through *Response* is accumulated in this text writer object. The text writer can work on top of a variety of streams, including the output console, strings, and files. In this example, we make the writer work on top of an HTML file. As a result, when we close the writer the HTML file is created.

The real host application is a sample Windows Forms application whose user interface is shown in Figure 24-3.

Figure 24-3 The user interface of the sample host application.

Upon loading, the form initializes the application host using the static *CreateApplicationHost* method.

```
void Form1_Load(object sender, System.EventArgs e)
{
    InitHost();
}

private void InitHost()
{
    m_host = (WinAspNetHost) ApplicationHost.CreateApplicationHost(
        typeof(WinAspNetHost),
        "",
        Directory.GetCurrentDirectory());
}
```

The virtual directory is unspecified (the empty string), and the physical path is the current directory. Note that the virtual directory parameter has to be something meaningful only to the host application. IIS requires it to match an entry in the metabase; other hosts might force it to be a physical disk folder or a database key. In this case, the host simply ignores that information.

The physical path—the third argument—must exist, otherwise a file-not-found exception will be thrown. The following code snippet shows what happens when the user clicks the Go button. The host application invokes a method on the host class, and the request gets processed by the ASP.NET runtime.

```
void buttonGo_Click(object sender, System.EventArgs e)
{
    string aspx = FilePath.Text;
    m_host.CreateHtmlPage(aspx, null,
        Path.ChangeExtension(aspx, ".htm"));

    MessageBox.Show("Done");
}
```

There is no limit to the ASP.NET features you can use. Feel free to use configuration files, ADO.NET adapters, view state, output caching, XML, HTTP modules, and whatever else involves ASP.NET and the .NET Framework. In addition, the application works regardless of the status of IIS. You can keep IIS running or even stop it—the ASP.NET runtime hosted by the sample application won't be affected. (Bear in mind that IIS is just another application host, although a particularly rich and complex one.)

Locating the Host Type

When you build an ordinary IIS-hosted ASP.NET application, you pay attention to deploying all required assemblies in the global assembly cache (GAC) or the Bin directory of the virtual directory. The locations where the ASP.NET runtime searches for assemblies are the same regardless of the characteristics of the host application. This means that even when hosted by a Windows Forms application, ASP.NET expects to load needed assemblies from the Bin subdirectory of the current physical path. As a result, you must ensure that the assembly that contains the host class is available in the same directory as the Windows Forms executable and also in the Bin subdirectory. For the preceding example to work, you must copy the assembly with the host type in a Bin subdirectory under the current directory of the host executable. I recommend that you code the application host class—the *WinAspNetHost* class in the previous example—in a separate assembly to make it easy to deploy the assembly in multiple paths.

The Cassini Personal Web Server

So, ASP.NET can be hosted in any managed application. More precisely, the ASP.NET runtime can also be hosted by an unmanaged application as long as it can host the common language runtime (CLR). Incidentally, this is exactly what happens with the ASP.NET worker process that IIS uses to serve .aspx requests—aspnet_wp.exe is a Win32 process, yet it hosts the CLR and subsequently ASP.NET.

ASP.NET has a modular design, and its interaction with the host environment is ruled by clear and well-known policies. As a result, any application—managed and unmanaged—that could guarantee such a habitat immediately becomes a good candidate for hosting ASP.NET.

Although this hosting feature is a quantum leap from Active Server Pages, what are the real-world scenarios in which it really gives you more programming power? Sure you can compile .aspx pages to HTML on the fly and without the involvement of a Web server; and you could perhaps set up an effective viewer for documents. But can you really believe that ASP.NET hosting alone lets you build serverless Web-like applications that run on a local machine without IIS?

If you're not convinced yet, think about what happens if the ASP.NET page contains interactive controls and posts back. Suppose that you compiled an .aspx page into an HTML page; and suppose also that the resultant HTML page is being viewed through Internet Explorer. Imagine the user clicks a link or push button. The browser's engine always processes the click event by packing input values into an HTTP *POST* command and forwarding it through port 80. What happens next?

Unlike IIS, the host application might not have a listener module active on port 80. As a result, a page-not-found error is returned. (This is exactly what happens with the sample Windows Forms host.) To work around this issue, you need to build a custom layer on top of the browser to intercept the postback and transform it into a local call to a specific component of the host application. In other words, with such a simple host, you can realistically exploit ASP.NET only to render static and read-only pages.

Generally, ASP.NET hosting alone is not sufficient to build a real-world serverless environment to consume Web sites offline. The good news is ASP.NET works without IIS and can be hosted in virtually any Win32 application. The bad news is that to obtain a reasonable functionality, you must write an IIS-like host application that behaves like a mini Web server and understands perfectly what the browser—any browser—does.

The Cassini personal Web server is the ideal tool for this kind of task.

Cassini in Person

The Cassini project (see *http://www.asp.net/Projects/Cassini/Download*) is just the revisited, ASP.NET-based version of the Personal Web Server we know from Windows 95. It is a compact, local Web server you can integrate and deploy with your solutions. Cassini employs the ASP.NET hosting API to create a simple managed Web server, and the *System.Net* API is used to handle socket connections. Cassini is available as a standalone download but is also integrated with Web Matrix. And the icing on the cake is that Cassini can be downloaded with full source code.

Figure 24-4 shows the typical architecture of an offline Web application based on Cassini. As you can see, the overall scheme is in no way different than that of a typical Internet-based Web application—only much simpler. It goes without saying that Cassini is neither a full replacement for IIS, nor the Microsoft version of an open-source Web server. Cassini is a local Web server designed for handling local calls directed at local folders.

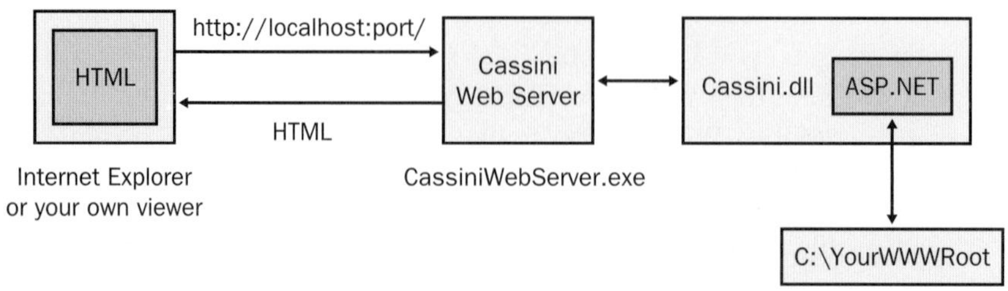

Figure 24-4 The architecture of an offline Web application using Cassini.

Let's first review the various pieces of technology that work together to set up the Cassini Web server and see how to deploy a Web site offline on a CD.

The Architecture of Cassini

The architecture of the Cassini Web server is shown in Figure 24-5. The Web server is a Windows Forms application named CassiniWebServer.exe.

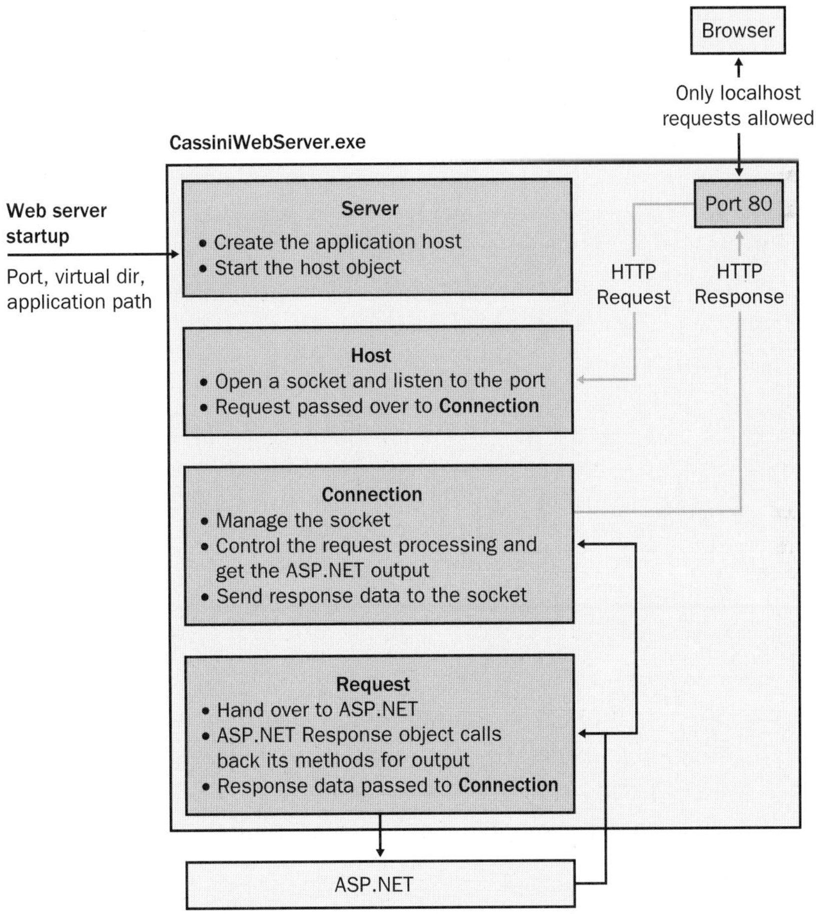

Figure 24-5 The architecture of Cassini.

You start the Web server by specifying the port number to listen to, the virtual directory to monitor, and the physical path behind that. As mentioned earlier, in this context the virtual directory name is just a unique name you use to address .aspx files in the specified physical path. Note that an IIS virtual directory is simply a name with a few related settings stored in the metabase; because you're not using IIS here, a virtual directory is simply a placeholder for a file system path. You start up Cassini through the form shown in Figure 24-6.

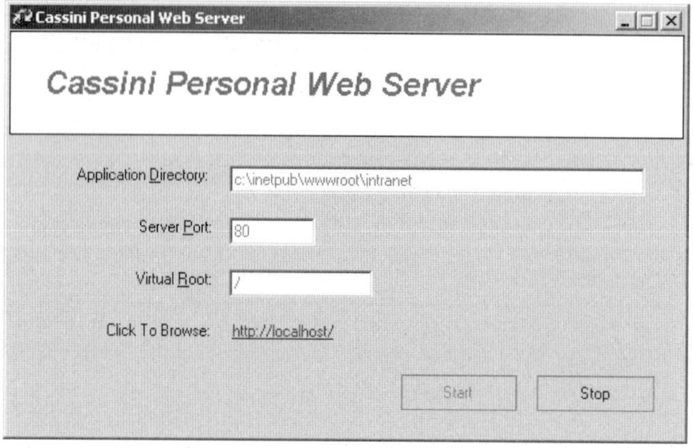

Figure 24-6 The startup form of Cassini.

You should note that Cassini can process only one virtual directory at a time and only accepts requests made through *localhost*. This is exactly what you need to deploy existing Web sites on offline media such as a CD or a DVD.

Cassini is a managed application whose executables take no more than 70 KB of memory. In addition to the program CassiniWebServer.exe, you also need to take into account the application host DLL—cassini.dll. The application host assembly must be stored in the GAC. To register an assembly with the GAC, you can use the following command-line instruction:

```
gacutil /i Cassini.dll
```

Table 24-3 lists all the public classes that make up the application host for the Cassini Web server. All classes are compiled in the cassini.dll assembly.

Table 24-3 Classes Used to Implement Cassini

Class Name	Description
Server	Provides the public API to start and stop the Web server, and creates the application host. Caches configuration information such as the port number and virtual directory.
Host	Remotable object (inherits from *MarshalByRefObject*), represents the Cassini bridgehead in the child AppDomain that hosts ASP.NET. The class is in charge of opening a socket on the port and accepts HTTP requests when they arrive.

Table 24-3 Classes Used to Implement Cassini

Class Name	Description
Connection	An instance of this class is created to process the request. It is passed the opened socket and asked to create and activate a new *Request* object to actually carry out the request. The *Request* object receives a reference to the *Connection* object and uses it to write response data to the socket.
Request	Inherits from *SimpleWorkerRequest*, and implements the logic necessary to process the HTTP request. Parses the HTTP payload, processes headers, prepares the response buffer, and finally hands the request over to the ASP.NET HTTP pipeline calling the *HttpRuntime.ProcessRequest* method. While processing the request and generating the response, ASP.NET calls back some methods of the *Request* class. The *Request*'s implementation of these methods funnels the calls into the parent *Connection* object to access the socket.

The *Server* class is the entry point in the host executable. Its constructor creates the application host, indicating the *Host* class as the host type.

```
void CreateHost() {
    m_host = (Host) ApplicationHost.CreateApplicationHost(
        typeof(Host), vdirPath, filesPath);
    m_host.Configure(this, port, vdirPath, filesPath, _aspnetPath);
}
```

Instances of the *Server* class are created in the Cassini AppDomain, whereas the *Host* object belongs to the new AppDomain just created for the processing of HTTP requests. The *Server* object also provides a sort of public API to start, stop, and configure the Web server. The Cassini Web server sees this object as its unique point of contact with the ASP.NET back end.

The *Host* class represents a remotable object and, as such, inherits from *MarshalByRefObject*. A remotable object is an object that can be called from within a different AppDomain. The *Host* class is responsible for opening a socket on the specified port and listens to incoming packets. When a request arrives and is accepted, the class creates a new *Connection* object to process the request.

```
Connection conn =  new Connection(this, (Socket) acceptedSocket);
conn.ProcessOneRequest();
```

The *Connection* class receives the socket and starts working on the HTTP packets. The *Connection* object is mostly an intermediary between the host and the actual worker request. The *Connection* first creates the request object and then asks it to process the payload.

```
Request req = new Request(host, this);
req.Process();
```

The *Request* object derives from *SimpleWorkerRequest*. It examines the HTTP packet, extracts and preprocesses the message headers, and prepares the response buffer. When done, it simply hands the request out to the *ProcessRequest* method of the *HttpRuntime* object. While carrying out the request, ASP.NET calls back several methods on the *Request* object. In particular, all the data sent out through the *Response* object results in a call being made to one of the public methods of the host's worker *Request* object. The actual implementation of Cassini entails that the *Request* object passes this response data to the methods of the *Connection* object which, in turn, will route that through the open socket and the port. For this reason, an instance of the *Connection* object is passed to the constructor of the *Request* class.

Cassini is the right tool for building serverless ASP.NET applications because it combines two key features: the ability to host the ASP.NET runtime to process .aspx requests and a simple, local-but-effective Web server infrastructure. With this structure, you don't need custom code running on top of the viewer to successfully process all page postbacks. Cassini is the missing link that now makes it possible to deliver entire Web sites on a CD and without the need of IIS.

Put Your Web Site on a CD

When I first examined Cassini, I created the following steps to test its overall effectiveness and make sure it was indeed a breakthrough in the building of offline Web applications. To begin, I stopped IIS and then launched the Cassini executable. (Note that to test Cassini, you must first stop IIS; otherwise, a conflict in accessing the port will occur.) Furthermore, Cassini processes only calls that go through *http://localhost*; you can't access the local pages by using the machine name (for example, http://contoso), nor can you access Web pages on a Cassini-equipped machine from a remote machine.

After that step, I opened Internet Explorer and typed *http://localhost*. To my great surprise, I was running my ASP.NET-based intranet without IIS! It goes without saying that if pages contain links to Internet Web sites, they will work as expected as long as an Internet connection is available.

Step-by-Step Operations

To successfully pack a Web site on a CD, however, a few preliminary checks must be performed. For one thing, make sure that all the links in the pages are either relative or explicitly rooted to localhost. Otherwise, you get an HTTP 403 error (forbidden).

To deploy the Web site offline, *xcopy* all the files to the storage medium along with the Cassini executables and the .NET Framework redistributable. Configure the setup to copy the Web site tree and to install the cassini.dll to the client machine's global assembly cache. In addition, you should start the Cassini Web server. A well-done setup, though, would also check for IIS and stop it if it's running. A Web site deployed over a CD can hardly work well with IIS unless the setup program is aware of IIS and configures its metabase accordingly. If you're using Cassini for your offline Web application, you're better off disabling IIS altogether. By the way, this is exactly what Web Matrix does when you try to build an ASP.NET page. Web Matrix includes Cassini, but it allows you to work with IIS if you can provide the page with a true IIS virtual directory. If you choose to use Cassini as the Web server, Web Matrix warns that it's going to stop IIS. From this point of view, Web Matrix behaves just like your ASP.NET host should.

The next listing demonstrates some code you can use in the setup to stop IIS, start Cassini, and open the root of the local host:

```
using System;
using System.Diagnostics;

public class OfflineWebSite
{
    public static void Main()
    {
        OfflineWebSite o = new OfflineWebSite();
        return;
    }

    public OfflineWebSite()
    {
        StartCassini();
        Console.WriteLine("Done.");
    }

    private void StartCassini()
    {
        // stop IIS
        Console.WriteLine("Stopping IIS...");

        Process p = new Process();
        p.StartInfo.FileName = "net.exe";
        p.StartInfo.Arguments = "stop iisadmin /Y";
        p.Start();
        p.WaitForExit();
        Console.WriteLine("IIS stopped.");
```

```
            // start Cassini (change the default URL)
            Console.WriteLine("Starting Cassini...");
            p.StartInfo.FileName = "cassiniwebserver.exe";
            p.StartInfo.Arguments = "c:\\inetpub\\wwwroot\\intranet 80 /";
            p.StartInfo.WindowStyle = ProcessWindowStyle.Minimized;
            p.Start();
            Console.WriteLine("Cassini started.");

            // open the the localhost
            Console.WriteLine("Opening the local host...");
            Process.Start("http://localhost");
        }
    }
```

Installing ASP.NET Without IIS

In many cases, ASP.NET is installed on a machine in which IIS is fully configured and running. You should note, though, that many aspects of the ASP.NET engine configuration are contingent upon IIS being installed on the system. If IIS is not present at the time of setup, the ASP.NET ISAPI extension is not installed. In addition, all necessary access-control changes on folders, the creation of the ASPNET account, and application mapping changes for side-by-side execution do not occur.

> **Note** Because multiple versions of the .NET Framework can be installed on the same computer, each installation contains an associated version of the ASP.NET ISAPI extension. An ASP.NET application uses aspnet_isapi to determine which version of the .NET Framework to use. Furthermore, an ASP.NET application can be configured to use any of the installed versions of the aspnet_isapi component. To specify the version of aspnet_isapi to use for an application, an application mapping is registered within IIS. An application mapping associates a file extension and HTTP verb with the appropriate ISAPI extension.

To make it easier for developers and administrators to properly configure the ASP.NET environment, an ad hoc tool is provided—aspnet_regiis.exe. The tool is located in the root folder of the .NET Framework installation path. A different aspnet_regiis.exe is included with each version of the .NET Framework.

The tool has various purposes, but here are two. First, it can be used to register a given application with a particular version of ASP.NET. Second, it can be used to register a particular version of ASP.NET on the machine to perform tasks such as registering the aspnet_isapi extension, setting up the worker process account, granting permission on folders, and so forth.

To register an application with a particular version of the .NET Framework, you use the following syntax, in which what follows the *–s* switch is the path of the application:

```
aspnet_regiis.exe -s W3SVC/1/ROOT/MyApp
```

The version of the .NET Framework is the version to which the utility belongs. To configure ASP.NET to work, you use the *–i* switch.

```
aspnet_regiis.exe -i
```

Using the *–i* switch is required when you install ASP.NET on a machine that lacks IIS. This means that ASP.NET won't work as expected after you install Cassini or any other host application. For ASP.NET to work, you must first run aspnet_regiis.exe with the *–i* switch to configure ASP.NET and update mappings.

Conclusion

Although it has been fully documented only with ASP.NET 1.1, the *System.Web.Hosting* namespace has been part of ASP.NET since the first beta. That ASP.NET can be hosted by any managed executable is definitely great news. Does this mean we can now solve an old problem and xcopy a Web site to a CD or a DVD? Well, not exactly.

Cassini is the other side of the coin and a crucial tool for getting ASP.NET applications to run offline and in lower-end, serverless scenarios. We need a tool like Cassini also because offline Web applications need a mini Web server that behaves like a real Web server and that listens to port 80 but accepts only calls that go through the local host. With Cassini—which, by the way, is a free download with source code included—you don't need to install IIS and you can still enjoy the power of a true ASP.NET application deployed locally.

A Web development environment that's completely independent from the Web server and capable of working within a non-Web server application is a kind of dream, especially if you've spent years working with ASP and IIS. Well, wake up because ASP.NET is pure reality!

Resources

- A Client-side Environment for ASP Pages—Part 1 (*http://msdn.microsoft.com/msdnmag/issues/0900/cutting/default.aspx*)
- A Client-side Environment for ASP Pages—Part 2 (*http://msdn.microsoft.com/msdnmag/issues/1000/cutting/default.aspx*)
- When IIS and ASP.NET Don't Get Along (*http://www.aspnetpro.com/features/2003/01/asp200301kd_f/asp200301kd_f.asp*)
- Web Matrix (*http://www.asp.net/webmatrix/download.aspx*)

Final Thoughts

Microsoft started working on what would eventually become ASP.NET soon after shipping the first version of ASP—which happened around the spring of 1997. People embraced ASP as a powerful tool to build Web applications without the need to invest too much time in untangling, and then learning, the intricacies of Web programming. ASP also allowed for the reuse of some existing COM and scripting skills. Although it wasn't quite the perfect tool, it was enough to bring Web programming to the masses. Over the years, one million developers have chosen ASP.

While successful and widely employed in thousands of real-world projects, ASP was only the first step along what was clearly a longer road. The more one used ASP, the more he or she realized that more was needed. ASP had the power of whetting the programmer's appetite, making him or her ask and wish for more. Coming up with a programming platform that was better than ASP proved to be difficult, however. But finally, there was ASP.NET.

This book attempted to cover all programming aspects of ASP.NET and to provide insight about its internal architecture. The ultimate goal of the book is to take less advanced people to a more advanced level of knowledge. Normally, advanced books skip over basic topics. A less-advanced book needs to cover all topics but focuses on the underlying infrastructure more than the high-level interface. This book is for users who want a resource that covers ASP.NET architecture, programming, and advanced stuff. I firmly believe that once you know the underlying API and infrastructure of ASP.NET, you can do whatever you want with ASP.NET, whenever and wherever you want to. I tried to explain the plumbing and the underpinnings of ASP.NET at various levels—including HTTP runtime, standard controls, configuration, security, intrinsics, and custom controls. I also tried to intersperse architectural tips with practical code and design principles. This book has many facets, and I really hope you'll find it useful and informative.

Writing the book has been a seven-month adventure. I haven't spent all this time hiding in a cave with the tapping of the keyboard as the only sign of life to the external world. I shared ideas, solutions, and code snippets with many of you through classes, seminars, conferences, and e-mail. Many of you loved the sneak preview and found even those small pieces of information useful. However, for the most part, this book is based on Microsoft public documentation that you can access via MSDN. Often, information you need can be found there, only a few clicks away—information that is public, clear, and concise. The information might not look as organic and personalized as a book could present it, but contentwise it is equivalent. Searching for information is an art, much like producing content.

My mom used to say, "Ask if you don't know." But I confess that I modified her advice to a more profitable, "Search for, and if you can't find it, just ask."

Index

Symbols

A

B

D

E

J

K

L

M

O

S

T

U

V

W

X

Y

Dino Esposito

Dino Esposito is one of Wintellect's ASP.NET and ADO.NET experts and a trainer and consultant based in Rome, Italy. He runs the Cutting Edge column for *MSDN Magazine*, is a regular contributor to ASP.NET DevCenter, and writes monthly columns for *asp.netPRO* and Windows::Developer. Dino also shares twice-a-month thoughts and tips about ASP.NET in the *ASP.NET2TheMax* newsletter. (You can sign up at *http://www.windevnet.com/newsletters*.)

Before becoming a full-time author, full-time consultant, and full-time trainer, Dino was a full-time employee and worked day and night for several top consulting companies. In particular, he pioneered DNA systems in Europe and in 1994 designed one of the first serious Web applications—an image data bank.

To meet Dino in person, just attend leading conferences such as DevConnections, WinSummit, or maybe Microsoft TechEd. If that doesn't work and you still want to meet in person, what about a geek meeting on some wild and uncontaminated beach in southern Italy?

Get a **Free**

e-mail newsletter, updates, special offers, links to related books, and more when you

register on line!

Register your Microsoft Press® title on our Web site and you'll get a FREE subscription to our e-mail newsletter, *Microsoft Press Book Connections.* You'll find out about newly released and upcoming books and learning tools, online events, software downloads, special offers and coupons for Microsoft Press customers, and information about major Microsoft® product releases. You can also read useful additional information about all the titles we publish, such as detailed book descriptions, tables of contents and indexes, sample chapters, links to related books and book series, author biographies, and reviews by other customers.

Registration is easy. Just visit this Web page and fill in your information:

http://www.microsoft.com/mspress/register

Microsoft®

Proof of Purchase

Use this page as proof of purchase if participating in a promotion or rebate offer on this title. Proof of purchase must be used in conjunction with other proof(s) of payment such as your dated sales receipt—see offer details.

Programming Microsoft® ASP.NET

0-7356-1903-4

CUSTOMER NAME

Microsoft Press, PO Box 97017, Redmond, WA 98073-9830